Maggie Craig is the acclaimed writer of the ground-breaking *Damn' Rebel Bitches: The Women of the '45* and its companion volume *Bare-Arsed Banditti: The Men of the '45*. She is also the author of six family saga novels set in her native Glasgow and Clydebank. She is a popular speaker in libraries and book festivals and has served two terms as a committee member of the Society of Authors in Scotland.

Also by Maggie Craig

Non-fiction

Historical novels

Glasgow and Clydebank novels

www.maggiecraig.co.uk

WHEN THE CLYDE RAN RED

A SOCIAL HISTORY OF RED CLYDESIDE

MAGGIE CRAIG

BIRLINN

This edition first published in 2018 by
Birlinn Limited
West Newington House
10 Newington Road
Edinburgh
EH9 1QS

Copyright © Maggie Craig 2011, 2018

First published in 2011 by Mainstream Publishing, Edinburgh

ISBN 978 178027 506 2

Designed and typeset by Initial Typesetting Services, Edinburgh
Printed and bound by MBM Print SCS Ltd, Glasgow

For my father,
Alexander Dewar Craig,
who first sang me the songs,
and first told me the tales of Red Clydeside;

and for the other exceptional human being who is his
beautiful grandchild and our brilliant younger child.

Contents

List of Illustrations

Room de Luxe, the Willow Tea Rooms, Glasgow

Mother and child in Glasgow, 1912

'A Cottage for £8 a Year' (J. Robins Millar)

'Left out!' The Tragedy of the Worker's Child'(J. Robins Millar)

Singer Sewing Machine factory, Clydebank, c.1908

Tom Johnston

Thomas Muir of Huntershill

Auld Scotch Street, Scottish Exhibition, 1911

Glasgow First World War female munitions worker

'Hallowe'en at the High Court' (*Glasgow News*, 1913)

Glasgow Rent Strike, 1915

Rent Strike poster

Willie Gallacher

John and Agnes Maclean and one of their daughters

Helen Crawfurd with children in Berlin, 1922

Mary Barbour in her bailie's robes

Davie Kirkwood

Acknowledgements

I should like to express my sincere thanks to the following people and institutions for the help they gave me with my research and in supplying illustrations for this book: Audrey Canning, librarian, Gallacher Memorial Library, with special thanks for pointing me in the direction of Helen Crawfurd and Margaret Irwin; Carole McCallum, archivist, Glasgow Caledonian University; all those who contributed to Glasgow Caledonian University's Red Clydeside website; the late Mr James Wotherspoon of Clydebank, still sharp as a tack at the age of 105; Pat Malcolm and her colleagues at Local Studies, Clydebank Library; Jo Sherington of West Dunbartonshire Libraries and Cultural Services; the librarians and all other staff at the Mitchell Library, Glasgow, with particular thanks to Nerys Tunnicliffe, Patricia Grant, and Martin O'Neill; Claire McKendrick, Special Collections, University of Glasgow Library; The Willow Tea Rooms, Sauchiehall Street, Glasgow; James Higgins and Christine Miller of Bishopbriggs Library; David Smith of East Dunbartonshire Leisure and Culture Trust; Marie Henderson of Glasgow Digital Library at the University of Strathclyde; Shona Gonnella and Anne Wade at the Scottish Screen Archive, National Library of Scotland; Kevin Turner of the *Herald* and *Evening Times* photo library; Neil Fraser of SCRAN; the Marx Memorial Library for permission to quote from Helen Crawfurd's unpublished memoirs; and, for permission to quote from his poem on the launch of the *Queen Mary*, The Society

of Authors as the Literary Representative of the Estate of John Masefield.

I should also like to express my appreciation of all the Bankies over the years who have shared with me their memories of the Clydebank Blitz, some of whom have now passed on. They have included Margaret Hamilton, Grace Peace, Grace Howie, Joen McFarlane, Jean Morrison, Andrew Hamilton and the late Maisie Nicoll, née Swan, with special thanks to Maisie for the pianos. My late parents, Alexander Dewar Craig and Molly Craig (née Walker), also told me of their experiences in Clydebank and Glasgow on those two terrifying nights in March 1941. For the first, hardback, edition of this book, thanks are due also to Kate McLelland for another great cover, and to everyone at Mainstream, most particularly Ailsa Bathgate and Eliza Wright.

For this new paperback edition, I'd like to thank Helen Bleck for her meticulous and sensitive copyediting. My thanks also go to Andrew Simmons, Tom Johnstone and all at Birlinn, and to James Hutcheson for the cover design.

I'd also like to thank the wonderful Will, Pim, Alexander and Ria for all their love and support, with special thanks to Ria for coming up with *le mot juste* in the nick of time.

Preface

This book is about Red Clydeside, those heady decades at the beginning of the twentieth century when passionate people and passionate politics swept like a whirlwind through Glasgow, Clydebank and the west of Scotland. It's also about the world in which those people lived. My aim has been to paint a vivid picture, telling the story by placing the people and their politics within the wider context of the place and the times.

These were years of great wealth and appalling poverty, when Glasgow was home to some of the most magnificent public buildings in Europe and some of its worst slums. This Glasgow welcomed the world to spectacular open-air exhibitions, chatted with its friends in elegant art nouveau tea rooms, fell in love with the movies in glittering art deco picture palaces and tangoed and foxtrotted the night away in the *palais-de-danse* which dotted the city.

This Glasgow also lost a thousand young adults each year to tuberculosis (TB). Overcrowded and insanitary tenements where a bed to yourself was an unheard-of luxury provided the perfect breeding ground for this terrible illness. Other spectres stalked the poor. Thousands of Glasgow's children were born to die. Thousands of women had a child every year until it killed them, dying worn-out before they were even 40 years old.

Outside the home, men and women worked exhaustingly long hours for low pay in filthy conditions where health and

safety had never even been thought of. Horrific workplace accidents were commonplace. Find yourself incapacitated by such an injury and the most you could hope for to help pay the rent and feed your family was a whip-round organised by your workmates.

National insurance was introduced only in 1911 and did not extend to workers' families or the unemployed. There was no social security or National Health Service. Other than the absolute last resort and shame of going on the parish, only the kindness of others caught you when you fell. Small wonder that one Red Clydesider described this Glasgow as 'Earth's nearest suburb to hell'.

Yet poverty, an unequal struggle and lack of opportunity do not always breed despair. Sometimes they breed a special kind of man or woman, one who uses their anger and apparent powerlessness to fuel a fight for justice and fair treatment for everyone. The Red Clydesiders belonged to this special breed. So did my father.

Growing up in Old Monkland in Coatbridge during the Depression of the 1930s, he and his family knew real hardship. Yet they knew how to laugh too, as they knew how to tell stories. A railwayman who worked his way up from shunter to stationmaster, my father travelled all over Scotland in his work and he knew the story behind every stone. A Buchan quine who loved her adopted Glasgow, my mother too had her stories to tell, as did our battalion of aunts and uncles. Two in particular whose experiences are included in this book are Alex McCulloch and his wife Elizabeth (née Craig), our family's beloved Aunt Elizabeth and Uncle Alex.

Growing up where I did, my earliest memories are of Clydebank and the Clyde and all the stories that went with them. Active in Labour politics and a life-long member of the National Union of Railwaymen, many of my father's stories were about the Red Clydesiders.

Rebels, reformers and revolutionaries, these radicals, socialists and communists were larger-than-life characters, yet

approachable to all. Far beyond their own family and social circles they were known by the affectionate diminutives of their first names. It was always Jimmy Maxton, Davie Kirkwood, Wee Willie Gallacher, Tom Johnston, Manny Shinwell.

It was during the turbulent years before, during and after the First World War that the Clyde earned the sobriquet of Red Clydeside. I've extended that period to include the General Strike of 1926, the Hungry Thirties, the Spanish Civil War of the late 1930s and the Clydebank Blitz of 1941. The great Clydebuilt ships belong in there too.

Meeting a debt of honour to my family and forbears, I wrote six novels set in Glasgow and Clydebank during the years when the Clyde ran red. This is the history that goes with them.

Enter, stage left, the Red Clydesiders.

1

Rebels, Reformers & Revolutionaries

'Distorted and destroyed by poverty.'

James Maxton was one of the great personalities of Red Clydeside. Known as Jimmy (or Jim) by friends and family, he was a man of great warmth, compassion and charisma. An inspiring public speaker, he could hold huge audiences in the palm of his hand, moving them to tears one moment and making them laugh out loud the next. His sense of humour was legendary, sometimes sardonic and cynical, but never cruel. Born in 1885, Maxton served for more than 20 years as a Labour MP at Westminster, where he also shone as an orator. Loved by his friends and respected by his political foes, he was described by Sir Winston Churchill as the greatest gentleman in the House of Commons. Former UK prime minister Gordon Brown wrote an engaging biography of him, entitled simply *Maxton*.

Maxton was born into a family which, while not wealthy, was quite comfortably off. Both his parents were teachers. His mother had to give up her career when she married, as female teachers of that time were obliged to do. Young Jimmy grew up as one of five children in a pleasant villa on a sunny ridge overlooking Barrhead near Paisley at the back of the Gleniffer Braes. He is remembered there today in the names of surrounding streets and the Maxton Memorial Garden.

Tragedy struck the Maxtons when Jimmy was 17 years old. After a swim during a family holiday at Millport on the

Isle of Cumbrae in the Firth of Clyde, his father had a heart attack and died. Left in strained circumstances though she was, Melvina Maxton was determined her two sons and three daughters were going to be educated as far as their brains would take them. Her determination paid off. All five became teachers.

His tongue firmly in his cheek, James Maxton was later to observe that his mother should really have sent him and his older siblings out to work. With typically cheerful sarcasm, he recalled that the family lived during those years after his father's death in 'the poverty that is sometimes called genteel'. It was a real struggle, although it helped that Maxton had won a scholarship at the age of 12 to the highly regarded Hutchesons' Grammar School, known more informally as 'Hutchie'. He did well, though he wore his learning and intelligence lightly, awarding himself some tongue-in-cheek distinctions. Honours in tomfoolery, first class honours for cheek, failure in intellectuality and honours advanced in winching. Unlike *wench*, this word could apply to both sexes, allowing grinning west of Scotland uncles to thoroughly embarrass both teenage nieces and nephews by asking, 'Are ye winchin' yet?'

Although nobody would have called James Maxton handsome, his dark and saturnine looks were undeniably striking. His tall frame and long, lantern-jawed face were framed by straight black hair which he wore much longer than was then fashionable or even acceptable. Curling onto his collar, it gave him a rather theatrical air. You could easily have taken him for an actor.

When he first went to Glasgow University his long hair was as far as any youthful rebellion went. He met Tom Johnston there. Later a highly respected Secretary of State for Scotland and prime mover behind the creation of the hydro-electric dams and power stations of the Highlands, Johnston was a young political firebrand from Kirkintilloch who took great delight in scaring the lieges through the pages of the *Forward*,

the weekly socialist newspaper he founded in 1906. When he first got to know James Maxton, Tom Johnston described him as a 'harum scarum' who just wanted to get his MA so he could make his living as a teacher. Maxton himself said the only activities in which he excelled at university were swimming, fencing and PE. He was a good runner too.

As his contemporary at Glasgow University, Johnston's first memory of him was indeed a theatrical one. A group of students had gone together to the Pavilion Theatre, where the evening grew lively with 'the throwing of light missiles to and fro among the unruly audience'. Young gentlemen and scholars indulging in some youthful high jinks. Throwing the well-educated hooligans out failed to dampen their enthusiasm. Maxton and his co-conspirators managed to get back in through the stage door and onto the stage, where they 'appeared from one of the wings, dancing with arms akimbo to the footlights'.

It wasn't long before the light-hearted young Mr Maxton began to think seriously about politics. Tom Johnston was an influence. So was John Maclean, the tragic icon of Scottish socialism. When Maxton was at Glasgow University in the early 1900s Maclean was four years older than him and had already got his MA degree. They often met by chance on the train, travelling into Glasgow from Pollokshaws, where they both then lived. A teacher by vocation as well as training, Maclean used these railway journeys to tell Maxton about Karl Marx.

Glasgow taught Maxton about life, especially when he began working as a teacher and saw the effects of poverty on his young pupils and their families. Later in life, in a 1935 BBC radio broadcast called *Our Children's Scotland*, he spoke about how his experiences had influenced his thinking: 'As a very young teacher, I discovered how individualism and their individualities were cramped, distorted and destroyed by poverty conditions before the child was able to react to its environment. That was the deciding factor in bringing me into the socialist and Labour movement.'

Maxton was 19 when he made the decision in 1904 to join the Independent Labour Party (ILP). Founded by Keir Hardie, Robert Cunninghame Graham and others who saw that the Liberal Party was not going to solve the problems of the poor, the ILP was particularly strong in Glasgow and the west of Scotland, one of the engines which powered Red Clydeside. Although later a component part of what is now the modern Labour Party, it was always a more radical group. As one of the ILP's most influential members, James Maxton devoted the rest of his life to politics, one of the band of Labour MPs which swept to power in the pivotal general election of 1922. Tom Johnston was also in that group.

Only once did a heckler get the better of James Maxton, as Tom Johnston recalled. Not long after he graduated from Glasgow University, Maxton returned to address a meeting at the Students' Union.

> That meeting remains in my memory for an interruption which, for once, left Maxton speechless and retortless. Maxton by that time had grown his long tradition-like actors' hair, and during his speeches he would continually and with dramatic effect weave a lock away from his brow. At this Students' Union gathering he was set agoing at his most impressive oratory ... '*Three* millions unemployed (pause). Three millions *unemployed* (pause). Three *millions* unemployed (pause).' Amid the tense silence came a voice from the back: 'Aye, Jimmy, and every second yin a barber!'

James Maxton's friend John Maclean comes across as a more sombre character. He was only eight when his father died, the catastrophe plunging his mother and her four surviving children into a poverty which was not at all genteel. Like Melvina Maxton, however, Anne Maclean was a woman determined that her children should be educated.

Both John Maclean and James Maxton lost their jobs as schoolteachers because of their political activities, which particularly aggravated their employers when they spoke out against the First World War and conscription. Maclean remained a teacher but outside the system, devoting himself to public speaking, writing articles, running the Scottish Labour College which he founded, and imparting the theory of Marxist economics in night and weekend classes. He advocated revolution rather than reform, his self-appointed mission being to convince the working classes the only solution to their ills was socialism, and that the only way to get that would be by seizing power. The ruling classes were never going to give it away.

Tom Johnston was a rebel rather than a revolutionary. Passionate, romantic and idealistic, he too could be cheerfully sarcastic, as when he described the decisions taken at the start-up of the *Forward*. 'We would have no alcoholic advertisements: no gambling news, and my own stipulation after a month's experience, no amateur poetry; every second reader at that time appearing to be bursting into *vers libre*.'

Johnston's sarcasm grew savage when he researched and wrote *The History of the Working Classes of Scotland* and *Our Scots Noble Families*. Often more simply referred to as *Our Noble Families*, this was published in 1909, when Johnston was 28 years old. One of his targets was the Sutherland family, notorious for the role they played in the Highland Clearances. He fired his first shot at one of their forebears.

> I began to be interested in this Hugo. He floats about in the dawn of the land history of Scotland, murdering, massacring, laying waste and settling the conquered lands on his offspring.
>
> Rooted in theft (for as every legal authority admits, the clan, or children of the soil, were the only proprietors), casting every canon of morality to the winds, this family has waxed fat on misery, and, finally, less than

100 years ago, perpetrated such abominable cruelties
on the tenantry as aroused the disgust and anger of
the whole civilised world.

The *Forward* soon attracted an impressive array of writers.
H.G. Wells allowed the paper to carry one of his novels as a
serial. Ramsay MacDonald wrote for it, as did suffragette
leader Mrs Pankhurst. James Connolly was also a contributor.
Born in Edinburgh of Irish parents, Connolly was a revolutionary socialist and Irish nationalist, shot by firing squad
after the 1916 Easter Rising in Dublin. The socialist newspaper also benefited from the skill of artist J. Robins Millar,
who drew many cartoons for it. A man of many talents, Millar
went on to become a playwright and the doyen of Glasgow's
theatre critics.

Trying to cover all bases, the young editor was sincere in
his views but very astute. Committed socialist and devout
Catholic John Wheatley attracted readers with the same deep
religious faith as himself, helping many of them realise it
was possible to be both a Catholic and a socialist. That had
taken some doing. When Wheatley first declared himself to
be a socialist his local priest and some members of the con-
gregation were so horrified they made an effigy of him and
burned it at his front gate. Wheatley opened the door of his
house, stood there with his wife and smiled at them. The next
Sunday morning he went to mass as he usually did and the
fuss soon died down.

The eldest of ten children, John Wheatley was born in
County Waterford in Ireland in 1869. Taking the path of many
with Irish roots who feature in the story of Red Clydeside, his
family came to Scotland when John was eight or nine years old.
The Wheatleys settled in Bargeddie, then known as Braehead,
at Coatbridge. At 14 John followed in his father's footsteps
and started working as a coal miner in a pit in Baillieston.

Wheatley was a miner for well over 20 years, during which
time he educated himself and became involved in politics,

another path many Red Clydesiders followed. In his late 30s Wheatley set up a printing firm and joined the ILP. Two years later he was elected a county councillor. He was in his early 50s when he too became one of the 1922 intake of Labour MPs, sitting for Shettleston.

Wheatley was much respected by his younger colleagues, especially James Maxton, who admired his intellect and organising ability. Ramsay MacDonald, Britain's first Labour prime minister, saw Wheatley's abilities too, appointing him Minister for Health in the first Labour government of 1924.

Another writer in the *Forward* stable was a coal miner from Baillieston who, under a pseudonym, specialised in laying into the coal owners and the vast profits they made at the expense of the miners who worked for them. Patrick Joseph Dollan later became Lord Provost of Glasgow.

The Red Clydesiders were always passionate about children, education, health and housing. Look at the Glasgow of the early 1900s and it is not hard to see why.

Yet this was a city which presented many different faces to the world.

2

The Tokio of Tea Rooms

'Very Kate Cranstonish.'

In the early years of the twentieth century Glasgow was the Second City of the Empire and the Workshop of the World. Scotland's largest city and its surrounding towns of Clydebank, Motherwell, Paisley and Greenock blazed with foundries and factories, locomotive works, shipyards, steel mills, textile mills, rope works and sugar refineries. This was the time when the North British Locomotive Works at Springburn produced railway engines which were exported to every continent on earth and shipbuilding on the Clyde was at its peak. The proud boast was that over half the world's merchant fleet was Clydebuilt.

In 1907 John Brown's at Clydebank launched the *Lusitania*, a Cunard liner destined for the North Atlantic run. The *Aquitania* was to follow in 1914. Before the Second World War came two of the most famous ocean liners of all, the *Queen Mary* and the *Queen Elizabeth*. The names of these Cunarders are redolent with the elegance of a bygone age.

Glasgow was elegant too. Talented architects such as Alexander 'Greek' Thomson and John Thomas Rochead, who also designed the Wallace Monument at Stirling, had fashioned a cityscape of infinite variety. The Mossmans, a family of sculptors, had adorned a huge number of Glasgow's buildings with beautiful life-size stone figures often inspired by the mythology of Ancient Greece and Rome. These included

the caryatids which decorate what is now the entrance to the Mitchell Theatre and Library in Granville Street, formerly the entrance to St Andrew's Halls. When they burned down in 1962, only the façade was saved. So many of the dramas of Red Clydeside were played out here, in what is now the Mitchell Library's café and computer hall.

In 1909 Charles Rennie Mackintosh finished the second phase of the project which gave the city and the world the Glasgow School of Art in Renfrew Street. Five years before that, he and his wife and artistic partner Margaret Macdonald Mackintosh created the Willow Tea Rooms in Sauchiehall Street for Mackintosh's patron, highly successful Glasgow businesswoman Miss Kate Cranston.

Along in the West End stood the extravagant red sandstone of the new Kelvingrove Museum and Art Gallery. Completed in 1901, it has been known and loved by generations of Glaswegians ever since simply as the Art Galleries, even if the young man about town who wrote it up in a guidebook called *Glasgow in 1901* had fun describing it as 'architecture looking worried in a hundred different ways'. In 1911 the builders were once again busy at Kelvingrove. Glasgow was looking forward to the third great exhibition to be held there. The Scottish Exhibition of National History, Art and Industry was scheduled to open at the beginning of May.

The gorgeously Italianate City Chambers dominated George Square, a physical manifestation of Glasgow's good conceit of itself. John Mossman created some of the figures which decorate it in his studio on the corner of North Frederick Street and Cathedral Street. On the other side of the square rose the dignified and rather more subtly ornamented Merchants' House. Designed by John Burnet senior, it had additions by his son and namesake. John Burnet junior crowned the highest point of the building with a model of the globe on top of which a sailing ship still rides the waves.

The *Bonny Nancy* belonged to Mr Glassford, one of Glasgow's powerful eighteenth-century Tobacco Lords. She's

a reminder that the city's fortunes were founded on trade and the enterprise of her traders. Those convivial gentlemen used to raise their glasses of Glasgow Punch – take about a dozen lemons, add sugar, Jamaica rum, ice-cold spring water and the juice of a few cut limes – in a confident and cheerful toast: 'The trade of Glasgow and the outward bound!'

Work had to be done on Glasgow's route to the sea before that trade could develop. People had first settled by the Clyde because the shallow river gave them fresh water and abundant fish, and was easy to ford. As ships grew larger the lack of depth became a problem. Goods had to be brought overland from Port Glasgow, causing delays and extra expense. Early civil engineering works such as the Lang Dyke off Langbank forced the Clyde into a narrower channel. Routine dredging also began, rendering the river navigable all the way up from Port Glasgow and the Tail of the Bank to the heart of Glasgow.

The 'cleanest and beautifullest and best built city in Britain, London excepted', which Daniel Defoe had so admired in the eighteenth century, could now grow into one of the world's busiest ports. The deepened river also made shipbuilding possible. The Clyde made Glasgow, and Glasgow made the Clyde.

The Anchor Line was one of many shipping companies operating out of Glasgow in the early 1900s. Its impressive headquarters in St Vincent Place, just west of George Square, was faced with white tiles from which the grime of an industrial city could more easily be cleaned off. And Glasgow was dirty. Soot-blackened. Buildings of honey-coloured sandstone took only a few years to become as black as the Earl of Hell's waistcoat. Anyone who lived in Glasgow or Clydebank before the Clean Air Act of the early 1960s will remember the choking yellow fogs of winter. They owed as much to what was streaming out of factory chimneys as they did to the damp climate of the west of Scotland.

There were few controls on pollution in the early 1900s. Factories, foundries and shipyards were risky places. The

people who worked in them took their chances, no other choice being available to them. In this city of nearly a million and a half souls, life for the majority was about economic survival. Over the course of the nineteenth century, people in search of work, and – just maybe, if the fates allowed – a better life for themselves and their families, flooded into Glasgow. Most came from the Highlands and from Ireland, some from farther afield. Traditionally a first settling point for new immigrants, the Gorbals became a predominantly Jewish area, many of those Jews fleeing persecution in Poland and Russia.

Meanwhile, as electric trams took over from horse-drawn ones and local rail links improved, comfortably off Glaswegians decamped to developing suburbs like Bearsden and Pollokshields. What they sought and found there were lawned gardens, woods, open spaces and plenty of fresh air. In suburbs north and south of the Clyde laid out with wide avenues and parks filled with trees, boating ponds, tennis courts and putting greens, families enjoyed life. The lucky few lived in spacious, high-ceilinged villas designed by some of those great Glasgow architects, others in solid tenement flats of warm red and honey sandstone. Out in the suburbs the stone had more chance of retaining its light colour.

Tradesmen who had worked their way up also moved out, taking their families to new houses built on old farmland which aimed to achieve a village-by-the-city feel. The dream of living in a country cottage where your children could play in a flower-filled garden with vegetables growing outside the kitchen door is an old and powerful one. It was shared by the socialists of Red Clydeside.

John Wheatley came up with the idea of the £8 cottage, so-called because that was what the yearly rent would be. A cartoon by J. Robins Millar in the *Forward* in 1911 shows a father coming home from his work to be greeted by his young son and daughter running eagerly towards him. His wife stands behind the low fence which surrounds the neat, well-tended

garden behind them, the baby in her arms. The first development in this style in Scotland was started before the First
World War and finished after it by a housing co-operative of
working-class families chaired by Sir John Stirling-Maxwell
of Pollok. Lying between the modern-day Switchback and
the Forth and Clyde Canal, the original name makes the
aspiration clear: Westerton Garden Suburb. It's now simply
Westerton but its residents continue to refer to it as 'the
Village'.

Westerton had a railway station, a school, a village hall,
a post office and shops. With its grocery and drapery,
Westerton Garden Suburb Co-operative Society was an
offshoot of the larger Clydebank Co-op. If you wanted the
bright lights of the city, they were on your doorstep, a short
journey away by train, tram or bus. Step off onto Sauchiehall
Street or Buchanan Street and you would find wonderfully
opulent shops like Treron's, Daly's, Copland & Lye's, Wylie
& Lochhead's, Pettigrew & Stephen's, the jewellers of the
Argyll Arcade, each offering all manner of delights: glittering gems, bracelets and necklaces, perfume, lace wraps and
handkerchiefs, kid gloves, fox furs and the latest fashions
from Paris.

The wives and daughters of Glasgow's industrialists,
shipowners and businessmen could wander freely through
this enchanted forest of gleaming wood and shining glass
counters. Department stores were a transatlantic import
which proved wildly popular in Glasgow. After the shopping
was done it would be up in the ornate brass lift to the restaurant to sip coffee while a pianist played discreetly in the
background. Or you could go to one of the city's fashionable
tea rooms. Glasgow made two indispensable contributions
to the popularity of the cup that cheers. Sir Thomas Lipton,
the man whose name is still synonymous with tea around the
world, was born in the Gorbals; and it invented the tea room.

It was not the famous Miss Cranston who originally came
up with the idea but her brother, Stuart. A tea merchant who

was an evangelist for the quality of what he sold, he offered his customers a tasting before they made a purchase. In 1875 he moved to new premises on the corner of Argyle Street and Queen Street, put out a few tables and chairs, offered some fancy baking to go with the tea, and started a trend.

Tea rooms were tailor-made for Glasgow's ladies of leisure. Their husbands and sons could go into pubs and chop-houses. In 1875 the department store hadn't quite arrived and there were few places where respectable women could go alone and unchaperoned. Tea rooms allowed them to meet up with their friends for a chat in safe and pleasant surroundings.

Kate Cranston raised the tea room to an art form. She owned and managed four in Glasgow, in Ingram Street, Argyle Street, Buchanan Street and, most famous of all, the Willow Tea Rooms in Sauchiehall Street. In her patronage of Charles Rennie Mackintosh, his artist wife Margaret Macdonald Mackintosh and their equally talented friends, Miss Cranston gave what became known as the Glasgow Style a stage on which it could flourish and grow. She was very much identified with this achingly fashionable and very modern look. Soon everything influenced by it, be that furniture, home décor or the crockery with which you set your table, was described not only as 'artistic' but also as 'very Kate Cranstonish'.

Oddly enough, although she was happy to give young designers such as Mackintosh and George Walton carte blanche to be as modern as they liked, she never updated her own personal style. Born in 1849, until she died in 1933 she always wore the long, full skirts and extravagant flounces of the Victorian era. Her only bizarre variation was to sport a cloak and sombrero.

Once the Cranstons had thought up the idea, tea rooms sprouted all over Glasgow and beyond. By 1921 the well-known City Bakeries had dozens of branches and ran a profit-sharing scheme with its bakers and waitresses. The 1930s saw the establishment of Wendy's tea rooms. They offered the

homely atmosphere of the country in the bustle and smoke of the big city: back to the rural idyll.

Reid's in Gordon Street gave men the chance to meet their friends over coffee and a smoke, in separate smoking rooms, of course. Miss Cranston provided those to her gentlemen customers at the Willow Tea Rooms in Sauchiehall Street, along with billiard rooms. Those were on the second floor, the Room de Luxe with the high-backed silver-painted chairs designed by Charles Rennie Mackintosh on the first.

In 1915 John Anderson's Royal Polytechnic in Argyle Street, advertising itself as it was always known to Glaswegians as the 'Poly', offered 'A Restful Den for Business Men' in its Byzantine Hall. The delights of 'Glasgow's Grandest Smoke Room' encompassed 'fragrant coffees, delicious teas, telephones, magazines and all the leading newspapers'.

In 1916 Stuart Cranston opened a new tea room in Renfield Street which included a cinema. This tea room became a popular gathering place for members of the ILP. During the First World War, Renfield Street itself became a focus for regular Sunday afternoon open-air meetings opposing the war.

Tea rooms appealed to men as well as women, particularly those who supported the temperance movement. The majority of the socialists of Red Clydeside did, having too often seen the damage alcohol could do. Willie Gallacher, a key figure in the story of Red Clydeside, grew up in poverty in Paisley in the 1880s and '90s, the son of an Irish father and a Highland mother. He was only 14 when he joined the temperance movement, having very personal reasons to hate alcohol. Gallacher's father was a good husband and an affectionate parent but his dependence on drink blighted family life. As Gallacher later wrote: 'I was still very young when my father died, but my eldest brother was already a young man. He was my mother's favourite child. She was fond of all of us, but how she adored the oldest boy! When he developed a weakness for alcohol it almost drove her crazy. Her suffering was so acute that I used to clench my boyish fists in rage every time I passed by a pub.'

Many men, particularly young ones living what could be a lonely life between work in a Glasgow office and lodgings, went to tea rooms to enjoy the company of the waitresses. The book which poked fun at the architecture of the Art Galleries waxed lyrical on the subject. *Glasgow in 1901* was written by three young men as a kind of guidebook, advising visitors who would be in the city for the exhibition of that year on local ways of going about things.

Describing Glasgow as 'a very Tokio for tea rooms', Archibald Charteris found it a great delight that tea-room waitresses were Glasgow girls who spoke with a warm Glasgow accent, 'the most accessible well of local English'. Describing what could happen after a young woman started working at a particular tea room, he was at pains to point out that she and her colleagues were highly respectable young ladies.

> Once installed, she may discover that a covey of young gentlemen wait daily for her ministrations, and will even have the loyalty to follow her should she change her employer. This is the only point in which she resembles a barmaid, from whom in all others she must be carefully distinguished.
>
> To other people she has a more human interest, and to a young man coming without friends and introductions from the country, she may be a little tender. For it is not impossible that, his landlady apart, she is the only petticoated being with whom he can converse without shame. So the smile which greets him (even if it is readily given to any other) is sweet to the lonely soul, and a friendly word from her seems a message from the blessed damosel.

Kate Cranston did not escape the censure of the Red Clydesiders. An article published in the *Forward* on Saturday, 15 July 1911, was headed 'How Miss Cranston Treats Her Workers', with a subtitle of 'The Limit of Tea Room

Generosity'. The piece was based on a set of typewritten 'Rules for Girls', so presumably one of those girls had made a copy of those rules and smuggled it out. Did Miss Cranston investigate afterwards to try to establish who the culprit was?

Hours were long. Six days a week, Miss Cranston's waitresses worked from seven in the morning till eight at night, five o'clock on Saturdays, except at the Willow Tea Room in Sauchiehall Street, which stayed open until eight o'clock on Saturdays too. Hours for girls under 18 were 'not to exceed 74 per week'. Unless you worked at the Willow, you were working 74 hours a week anyway. Maybe the breaks weren't counted, although these were not very generous. The *Forward* drew particular attention to the lunch break of only ten minutes, where each girl was provided with a cup of cocoa or a glass of hot milk and a biscuit.

In 1920 discontent among the waitresses who worked in Kerr's Cafés boiled over into a strike. Their boss was William Kerr, who advertised himself as 'the military caterer'. If his management style followed military lines, that may well have been part of the problem. A leaflet was printed to alert the people of Glasgow to the conditions under which the waitresses in Kerr's Cafés worked:

Sweated Workers in Glasgow
STRIKE OF WAITRESSES AT KERR'S CAFES

Citizens of Glasgow, your attention
is drawn to the conditions which prevail
at above establishments:
12/– per week for 12 hours per day

1/– deducted if girl breaks a plate
9d deducted if girl breaks a cup
6d deducted if girl breaks a saucer
2/– deducted if girl breaks a wineglass
3d deducted for being late in morning

The Girls decided to join the Union, with the result that the Shop Steward was dismissed, which is quite evidently an attempt to undermine the Girls' Union.

Previous to joining the Union, the minimum wage of restaurant workers was 10/– per week, and they had to purchase uniform from the firm.

We are asking the public to
SUPPORT THE GIRLS

Some of Kerr's Cafés stayed open for late suppers till quarter to eleven at night, so presumably being late for work the following morning was a not uncommon occurrence. The strike lasted less than a month and during it most of the waitresses at Kerr's voted with their feet and went looking for work elsewhere.

Harry McShane, Red Clydesider and Marxist, described the wages earned by the waitresses at Kerr's as pitiful. Yet away from the clinking of china cups, cake stands piled high with scones, shortbread and chocolate eclairs and the stylish décor of Miss Cranston's artistic tea rooms, there were plenty of Glaswegians who would have leapt at the chance to earn even those pitiful few shillings.

3

Earth's Nearest Suburb
to Hell

'A whole world of sacrifice and effort.'

Helen Jack, who became better known under her married
name of Helen Crawfurd, was born in 1877 in Glasgow's
Gorbals, where her father was a master baker. In her unpublished memoirs of her life and times she neatly summed up the
character of her birthplace as a Jewish working-class district.

Her father William had an open-minded attitude towards
his many Jewish neighbours not always usual among Gentiles
at this time, now and again attending services at his local syna-
gogue. He also had a highly developed social conscience in
respect of the poorer families among whom he and his more
well-off family lived. He and his wife brought their children
up to have a strong religious faith and this Christian family
practised what it preached.

When times were especially hard in the Gorbals during a
strike, William Jack set up a soup kitchen in his bakery for
those struggling to feed themselves and their families. As
Helen later remembered, even as a master and a man who
voted Conservative his sympathies were always with the
workers. As committed as he was to helping their fellow men
and women, Helen's mother and grandmother ran the soup
kitchen. See the problem, work out what you can do about it
and then do it. The example set was to form the pattern for
Helen Crawfurd's life.

Mrs Jack, also Helen, helped foster that social conscience in her children by what she read to them. *Uncle Tom's Cabin* was a favourite. Her daughter remembered that she and her brothers and sisters would call to their mother not to start reading until they had fetched their hankies, because they knew they would not be able to hold back the tears when they heard 'this tragic story of negro suffering'.

Helen junior saw suffering in Glasgow too, and with fresh eyes when the Jack family returned to the city after some years living in gentler surroundings near Ipswich in England. By now 16 years old, the maturing young woman was horrified by the Glasgow of the 1890s.

> I was appalled by the dirt, poverty and ugliness I saw all around in Glasgow. I felt that other women along with myself must feel the same resentment and indignation. I watched the faces of the workers in tramcars and buses. They were worn with worry. I do not think any city had more people with bad teeth. In my young days orthopaedic surgery was in its infancy, and a great many people in Glasgow had bandy or bow legs and were undersized. The women carried their children in shawls, and the soft bones became bent. It has been stated that Glasgow's water supply then lacked certain lime essential for bone building. To-day it is unusual to see these deformed people, but in my youth they were very common. The housing conditions and the death rate of infants were appalling.

One statistic in particular struck her. Occupied by large families though they were, 40,000 of Glasgow's tenement flats consisted of only one room and a kitchen. She wrote with feeling of how, when a member of the family died, the living had to share that one room with the body of their loved one till the day of the funeral. That loved one would too often have been a baby. Infant mortality in late

nineteenth-century Glasgow was indeed appalling and this grim statistic was to grow even worse. In the years immediately following the First World War, 40 per cent more babies died in infancy in Glasgow than in the rest of Britain as a whole. One in every seven children in the city did not reach their first birthdays.

The differences within Glasgow were also appalling, as statistics from 1911 show. That 29 babies in every 1,000 in middle-class Kelvinside died in infancy might shock and sadden us but down in the working-class Broomielaw the figure was even worse, standing at a horrific 234. In the Gorbals there were 145 infant deaths per 1,000 births, in Springburn 117. The most recent figures, for the whole of Glasgow in 2015, are of four infant deaths per 1,000 births.

The Red Clydesider who described Glasgow as 'Earth's nearest suburb to hell' was James Stewart, better known as Jimmy. Another of those Labour MPs who was to triumphantly enter Parliament in 1922, he knew what he was talking about. A hairdresser to trade, he kept the patients at Glasgow Royal Infirmary neat and tidy. Diphtheria, scarlet fever, pneumonia, all these diseases were rife. The great scourge, the captain of all the men of death, was tuberculosis, also known as consumption or phthisis. TB claimed 1,000 lives in Glasgow each year and its favoured victims were young adults. Spreading as it did where people lived on top of one another in overcrowded and unhygienic tenements, it was considered a disease of the poor and the feckless. There was shame attached to contracting TB.

The tenement is a distinctive form of architecture. It provided many Glaswegians with elegant, spacious and comfortable homes, others with less grand but no less substantial and respectable ones: and then there were the slums. As bare of comfort inside as they were rundown outside, many of these grimy grey tenements pressed hard against the city centre, well within walking distance of Glasgow's great public buildings and elegant shopping streets.

That so many well-off Glaswegians made their homes to the west of the city was no accident. That move had begun in Victorian times when the university, always known as the Old College, left its medieval home in the High Street in 1870. This was taking the students away from the beating heart of the old city but also from dingy closes packed tightly with slums which were breeding grounds for crime, violence and disease.

The Victorian city fathers commissioned photographer Thomas Annan to record the slums of Old Glasgow for posterity, the wynds and vennels crammed in behind the High Street and around the Briggait, south of Glasgow Cross. Staring back at the photographer, barefoot children and women in shawls stand under washing dangling from high poles sticking out across the narrow closes and alleyways of these shadowy spaces.

Up on Gilmorehill in the West End the students were able to breathe clean air. Like the well-off Glaswegians who were lucky enough to live in the gracious Edwardian townhouses of Park Circus, they could trust the prevailing westerly winds of the British Isles to blow any pollution or nasty smells back across to the East End. Over there the cholera and typhus which attacked Glaswegians in their thousands during the epidemics of the nineteenth century might have been swept away with the old slums. Plenty of diseases were left to incubate in the new slums which rose to take their place. Those who did not have to endure such awful living conditions could still manage to turn a blind eye to them.

There were others who found them impossible to ignore, people like James Maxton and Helen Crawfurd. Driven by the same passionate social conscience, another was Margaret Irwin. Among the many achievements of her long life, she was the driving force behind the establishment of the Scottish Trades Union Congress in 1897, a body which has always been completely independent of its English counterpart. Never a member of a trade union herself, Margaret Irwin was

the STUC's secretary for the first three years of its existence. Women might not yet have had the vote, but that didn't mean they couldn't play an active role in public life.

The daughter of a ship's captain, Margaret Hardinge Irwin was born in 1858 'somewhere in the China Seas' on board a ship called the *Lord Hardinge*. After this romantic start to her life, she grew up in Broughty Ferry near Dundee. Her father valued education and encouraged and supported his only child while she attended Dundee University College, part of St Andrew's University. In 1880 the university awarded her the Lady Literate in Arts (LLA) in German, French and English Literature. Run by St Andrew's, the LLA scheme operated for 50 years and allowed women and girls around the world the chance to study at university level in the days before female undergraduates were allowed to matriculate and study for the same degrees as men. Students could follow courses at home or take them at their own local colleges before sitting exams set by St Andrew's in places as far afield as Aberdeen, Brisbane, Cairo, London, Nairobi and New Zealand.

In her early 30s Margaret Irwin moved to Glasgow, where she took classes at Glasgow School of Art and in political economy at Queen Margaret College, newly established for female students within Glasgow University. From then on she dedicated her life to investigating and improving living and working conditions for poor women and their families. She became a recognised and respected authority on the subject. Coming as she did from Broughty Ferry, next door to Dundee and its jute mills, where an army of women toiled to 'keep the bairns o' Dundee fed', she already knew a lot about the living and working conditions of the poor. This may be where her interest in the difficulties facing the working classes started.

For 44 years she was secretary of the Scottish Council for Women's Trades. As an assistant commissioner to the Royal Commission on Labour, she compiled many reports on working conditions in laundries, shops, sweatshops and among

homeworkers. These housewives struggling to make ends meet had even less protection from unscrupulous employers than women in factories and earned ludicrously low wages.

Audrey Canning, librarian and custodian of the William Gallacher Memorial Library, describes Margaret Irwin as being like a modern-day investigative journalist, 'toiling alone up dilapidated tenement stairs to discover the slum housing conditions of women working for a pittance'. Her investigations and reports paint a vivid picture of just how bad those conditions could be.

Shortly before Christmas 1901 she gave a paper on 'The Problem of Home Work' at a Saturday conference in Paisley organised by the Renfrewshire Co-operative Association.

> Frequently one finds the home worker occupying an attic room at the top of a five-storeyed building, the ascent to which is by a dismal and dilapidated stair-case, infested by rats or haunted by that most pitiable of four-footed creatures, the slum cat. The landings are foul with all manner of stale débris; and the atmosphere is merely a congestion of evil odours. At every storey narrow, grimy passages stretch to right and left, on either side, close packed, is a row of 'ticketed houses' …
>
> On every landing there is a water tap and sink, both the common property of the tenants, and the latter usually emitting frightful effluvia. Probably the sink represents the entire sanitary system of the landing.
>
> Armed with a box of matches and a taper and battling with the almost solid smells of the place, one finally reaches the top, and on being admitted, finds, perhaps, a room almost destitute of furniture, the work lying in piles on the dirty floor or doing duty as bed clothes for a bed-ridden invalid and the members of the family generally.

Glasgow started ticketing houses in the 1860s in the hope of reducing overcrowding in the city's slums. Every house with fewer than three rooms was measured, and it was calculated that each occupant required 300 cubic feet of living and sleeping space. A metal ticket was then fixed to the front door, stating how many people could legally occupy the house. This was enforced by midnight visits from the sanitary inspectors.

By the 1880s, the city had over 23,000 ticketed homes. These housed three-quarters of Glasgow's population, probably rather more than that once the sanitary inspectors had done their rounds for the night. People were so desperate for a place to lay their heads that the ticketing rules were often flouted. Their unlikely landlords and landladies were in their turn so desperate to make a few extra pence or shillings they were prepared to squeeze in what Margaret Irwin called 'that unknown and highly elastic quantity, the lodger'. The number of ticketed houses in Glasgow just before the First World War was not much lower than in the 1880s, around 22,000.

While many Glaswegians have fond memories of the camaraderie and warmth of life in the old tenements and of mothers who kept their homes as neat and clean as a new pin and their children well-scrubbed and well-turned-out, there is no doubt that thousands who lived in the Second City of the Empire did so in poverty and squalor. The record is there, in photographs and written accounts.

There were always those who managed to rise above their circumstances. After describing the flat 'almost destitute of furniture', Margaret Irwin wrote, 'However, side by side with the worst of these one finds a little room exquisitely neat and clean and representing a whole world of sacrifice and effort.' It must have been heart-breaking, hard to witness, but this woman who could have enjoyed a comfortable middle-class life had set herself a task and she would not flinch from it. She was well aware that many of the haves saw no reason why they should worry about the have-nots. 'It is often said that

one half of the world does not know how the other half lives. It might be said, perhaps with equal truth, that one half does not care to know.'

As Audrey Canning emphasises, Margaret Irwin did care to know. Determined that everyone else should too, she was prepared to shout her findings from the rooftops. Her voice reached the legislators at Westminster, helping bring about reforms which made a difference to the lives of thousands. Speaking to the second reading of the Seats for Shop Assistants Bill in 1899 the Duke of Westminster quoted from a report Margaret Irwin had made on shop assistants in Glasgow. 'My attention has been directed by several medical men of standing and experience, and also by numerous grave complaints from the women assistants themselves, to two causes which, in addition to long hours and close confinement, operate against the health and comfort of women employed in shops. These are – want of seats, and the absence of, or defective, sanitary provisions.'

In other words, they wanted a few seats where they could sit down for a rest now and again, plus a proper toilet. Margaret Irwin recorded a pathetic plea. 'As has been more than once said to me, "If they would only allow us a ledge to rest upon for a minute or two we would be thankful even for that."'

Nor was there any entitlement to meal breaks, shop assistants having to snatch a bite to eat if and when they could. Hours were long, starting first thing in the morning and going on until nine or even ten o'clock at night. On average, shop assistants in Glasgow and Scotland's other cities at the turn of the twentieth century worked between 80 and 90 hours per week in return for wages of 10 shillings per week. So the waitresses at Kerr's Cafés working in excess of 70 hours for 12 shillings per week some 20 years later really were in a pitiful situation, one which had seen no real improvement.

Margaret Irwin was scathing, too, about how much less women were paid compared to men, firing off a few salvos in what might be described as a 100 years war.

Now, it seems reasonable to expect that when there are large discrepancies in the wages of the worker, a corresponding difference would be found in the prices charged to the public for the goods made by the respective sexes. So far as I am aware, however, the difference stops short at the pay-books of the worker, and the vest and cigarette made by the women has the same value put upon it when it goes into the market as that made by the man. If, however, any gentleman present can inform me of a reduction made in his tailor's or tobacconists' bill because of the goods being supplied being the product of women's labour, I shall be glad to note the fact for future reference.

How the shop assistants of the 1890s managed without a toilet is probably best left to the imagination. That Victorian shopkeepers, with that era's outward prudery and respectability, had to be forced by law into supplying this most basic of facilities to their predominantly young female workforce is a telling illustration of their lack of humanity and lack of respect towards the people who made their profits for them. The working classes were there to be worked and if that took them through humiliation to the brink of exhaustion, then so be it.

Working conditions in the many commercial laundries of the period were particularly brutal, employees having to work through the night in stifling temperatures. Margaret Irwin visited one girl of 18 whose health had broken down under the strain. She earned only six shillings for a working week of 90 hours. Small wonder that her mother described laundry work as 'murderous'.

It might seem ironic to us now that His Grace the Duke of Westminster spoke up for the shop assistants, describing their having to stand all day as 'long hours of enforced sentry duty which would provoke a mutiny if imposed upon soldiers of the Line'. However, there was disquiet at the time that what

was also described as the torture of young girls was causing them, when they became mothers, to produce weak and sickly children. There was philanthropy and real concern here, even, across the yawning class divide, an element of chivalry. Essentially though, this was about the future of the race, an obsession of the time.

This brings us uncomfortably close to eugenics, which sought to direct evolution towards a supposed improvement in the human stock. Very much in vogue in the early twentieth century, enthusiasts for eugenics included Marie Stopes, pioneer of birth control, economist John Maynard Keynes, US president Theodore Roosevelt, and Mr Kellogg of corn flakes fame. Eugenics was to be completely discredited after the Nazis took the removal from the human gene pool of what they deemed the degenerate, unfit and racially inferior to the nightmare extreme of the gas chambers. Before that Rubicon was reached, the idea of some intervention to improve humanity was supported by many socialists. The birth control movement was closely bound up with it.

Despite the lack of toilets for shop assistants, an associated preoccupation of the age was hygiene, both moral and physical. In July 1904 Glasgow's Chief Sanitary Inspector, Peter Fyfe, delivered a paper at the Congress of the Sanitary Institute at Glasgow University entitled 'What the People Sleep Upon'. His speech was also published by Glasgow Corporation's Committee on Health.

> It has been said that 'there are combinations of evil, against which no human energies can make a stand'. Combinations of evil, at all events in a sanitary sense, seem peculiarly attachable to a certain class of the people. It is this class I had in my mind when I put down the word 'people' in the title of the present paper. The major part of the people in this city are composed of those who nightly sleep in houses of one or two apartments. The most of them dwell in this

limited space because they cannot afford to pay for
more. Poverty compels them.

Peter Fyfe went on to list some of the medical complaints
which dogged the people who lived in these cramped houses:
dysentery, diarrhoea and other 'diseases the origin of which
we cannot trace'. Despite giving the city 'an irreproachable
water supply', the Victorian engineering marvel of running
clean water from Loch Katrine to Glasgow did not seem to
have helped. He believed that Glasgow had 'a reasonably
perfect sewage system'. Maybe not quite so perfect if people
suffering from diarrhoea and dysentery were sharing an outside toilet with every other family who lived up their close
and one tap and one sink with at least three other families on
their landing.

Peter Fyfe's diagnosis of what was wrong was that 78 per
cent of what he called the lower classes of Glasgow were
sleeping on mattresses made out of old rags, 'the offcast of
every class of the population, from the wealthy of the West-
end to the tramp and vagrant of the East'. Some of these rags
were filthy. None were cleaned or disinfected before being
processed into the flock with which mattresses were stuffed.
Fyfe got the Corporation chemist to carry out experiments
on that, comparing it to samples taken from Glasgow's crude
sewage. Full of dangerous bacteria, the mattresses were dirt-
ier than the effluent, leading Fyfe to conclude: 'It would be
manifestly safer to sleep on a bed filled with sewage than on
this material.'

Observing all this, those who wanted to change the lives of
the poor for the better took two different approaches. They
might meet one another in the middle, working together on
specific issues, but there was a profound difference between
their respective philosophies. There was philanthropy, and
there was politics.

Margaret Irwin spent her life working tirelessly to improve
the lot of women workers. Some see her as being very much

in the tradition of the middle-class philanthropist, helping the poor from the outside. In contrast, Helen Crawfurd believed in empowering the poor so they could improve their lot for themselves. Shocked though she was by Glasgow's slum housing and ill health, it took Helen Crawfurd a long time to see socialism as the answer to these ills. Socialism was a radical and a dangerous doctrine. She described her attitude to it when she was younger as being something she would run away from in the street.

Her politics gradually grew more radical, and it was becoming a suffragette that started her on the journey. Clear in her own mind that it was women who held the home and the family together, she came to the unshakeable belief that if only women had the vote and got themselves organised, they would do their utmost to improve these terrible living conditions.

As a young woman, Helen Crawfurd's religious faith was so strong it persuaded her to marry a man years older than herself because she thought this might be God's plan for her. Alexander Montgomerie Crawfurd was an evangelical minister in the Gorbals, a widower with a daughter and granddaughters. He was 58 when they married in 1898 shortly before Helen's twenty-first birthday. The marriage lasted for 16 years, until Alexander's death in 1914. They had no children.

Although there was affection between Helen and her husband, friction between them grew as she began to challenge what she read in the Bible, especially about the supposed inferior position of women. The command that women should keep silent in churches infuriated her. When she expressed her criticism of what she saw as the misogyny of the Bible aloud to Alexander Crawfurd, he would thunder his disapproval at his young and passionate wife: 'Woman, that is blasphemy.'

It was the hypocrisy of so many churchgoers which really got to her. As she saw it, religious people were too concerned

about the life hereafter and not enough about life on earth now, 'where God's creatures were living in slums, many of them owned by churches, amidst poverty and disease'.

Her views crystallised when controversy erupted over the proposed Sunday opening of the People's Palace. Established on Glasgow Green in 1898, this museum, with its beautiful winter gardens, had been designed as somewhere the working classes could go to enjoy their scant leisure time in pleasant and uplifting surroundings. A pity, then, that it didn't open on Sundays, the only full day in the week the working classes could count on having off.

A prominent figure in evangelical Christianity in Glasgow, Lord Overtoun was a vociferous defender of the sanctity of the Sabbath – but Lord Overtoun was a hypocrite. He was exposed by a pamphlet which supporters of the growing Labour movement began to sell on the streets of the city. This pointed out that the chemical works in Rutherglen which Lord Overtoun owned, just across the Clyde from Glasgow Green and the People's Palace, were open around the clock, seven days a week, including Sundays.

Helen Crawfurd described the pamphlet as showing pictures contrasting the slums in which his workers lived with the well-appointed stables where Lord Overtoun kept the horses which pulled his carriage. There were pictures, too, of the scabs and sores on the faces and arms of the people who toiled in his chemical works, as well as details of how badly they were paid. She found the pamphlet a powerful response to what she called the hypocrisy and cant of Glasgow's leading evangelists. The opponents of Sunday opening fell silent and the working people for whom the People's Palace had been built were free to visit it on their day off.

The influence of the pamphlet was greater than that. Helen Crawfurd believed the campaign for 'saner Sundays' and the exposure of Lord Overtoun's hypocrisy opened many people's eyes, including her own, to the idea that socialism might have more answers to what was wrong with

the world. She herself was to travel even further to the Left. In 1920, more than 20 years after the argument over the Sunday opening of the People's Palace, Helen Crawfurd became a founder member of the Communist Party of Great Britain.

The author of the pamphlet which so influenced her was Keir Hardie, the self-educated Lanarkshire miner, father of the Labour Party and an inspiration to generations of social-ists. In the early 1900s, he was joined by a new generation of fighters for fairness and justice.

One of the most bitter battles of Red Clydeside was fought in Clydebank in 1911.

4

Sewing Machines & Scientific Management

'It suddenly flashed on him how absurdly stupid it was to be spending his life like this.'

The Clyde made Clydebank too, arguably even more than it did Glasgow. Surrounded though it is by ancient settlements such as Old Kilpatrick, Dalmuir, Duntocher and Yoker, the town itself is a mere stripling, no more than 150 years old. The building of J. & G. Thomson's shipyard in 1871 called it into being.

In the most literal sense of the term, the forerunners of John Brown's chose a greenfield site. The area between the Forth and Clyde canal and the river was known as the Barns o' Clyde and it was farmland, dotted here and there with a few cottages. This made it an attractive proposition, too, for the Singer Manufacturing Company. Some ten years after Thomson's established their shipyard on the banks of the Clyde, the American company found the ideal spot on which to build the biggest sewing machine factory in Europe.

Set back a little from the river, Singer's 41 different departments soon spread themselves over a large expanse of ground bounded by the canal and Kilbowie Hill to the north and east, and Dalmuir to the south and west. The site is now occupied by Clydebank Business Park. Four strategically placed gates allowed workers to enter and leave the complex at the point closest to where they lived, or at the point closest

to the railway station. Although the factory has long since disappeared, the station is still called Singer.

Clydebank grew rapidly during the final decades of the nineteenth century and the first years of the twentieth. In 1881 the population was around 3,000. By 1913, it stood at over 43,000. John Brown's, Singer's and Beardmore's, whose yard lay downriver at Dalmuir, were big employers of labour. In the early 1900s their workforces numbered 5,000, 9,000 and 6,000 respectively.

There was a frenzy of housebuilding to accommodate these economic migrants moving down from Glasgow and over the river to what had so recently been the wide open spaces of the Barns o' Clyde. While many handsome tenements from this era still stand, some were flung up rather too hastily. These included the flat-roofed rows of the Holy City, which stood on the edge of Kilbowie Hill overlooking the sewing-machine factory and the river, and with fine views across the Clyde Valley and to the hills of Renfrewshire. You could almost have waved to James Maxton, over there on the hill above Barrhead.

Local tradition has it that the Holy City acquired its nickname when a sailor on a boat on the river remarked that the flat roofs reminded him of houses he had seen in Jerusalem. The story is picturesque, the reality of living in the Holy City less so. Within a year of the houses being built in 1904, tenants were refusing to pay their rent until the landlords carried out repairs needed because corners had been cut during construction.

Despite all the housebuilding, there still were not enough people in Clydebank to staff the sewing-machine factory. Thousands of workers had to be brought in every day by train from Bridgeton and other parts of Glasgow and from the Vale of Leven down at Dumbarton. This continued right up until the factory closed in the 1960s, 'Singer Specials' thundering through intervening stations to get the workers to and from Kilbowie.

At its peak, Singer employed around 14,000 people. In 1911, the workforce numbered well over 10,000, with 4,000 coming in each day on the special trains. A railway clerkess who worked at Singer station during the Second World War, my aunt, used to reminisce about the difficulties that could pose. Not being an octopus, it was well-nigh impossible to collect or check tickets when hundreds of people were piling out of each train and thrusting them towards her.

Singer's 41 different departments, known as 'flats', produced everything required to send a finished sewing machine out of the factory gates. The wood for the cabinets came into the company's own timber yard on the canal, transported there by Clyde puffers, the sturdy little seagoing workhorses of Scotland's west coast. The wrought iron for the beautifully curlicued legs which supported the sewing machines was forged in Singer's on-site foundry. The Kilbowie plant even had its own power station and railway line to move heavy materials about the complex.

After the opening by Howard Carter of Tutankhamun's tomb in the 1920s, the beautiful gold patterns on the shining black enamel of the sewing machines were often motifs inspired by Ancient Egypt. Those were applied in Singer's paintshop. The company's stationery was produced in the printshop, as was the famous 'Wee Green Book'. This neat little instruction manual was sized to fit comfortably into one of the long, narrow drawers of the cabinets which housed the sewing machines. The Wee Green Book was translated into several languages. Singer's exported from Clydebank to the world, one of Kilbowie's biggest markets being pre-revolutionary Russia.

Sadly, the style of Singer's management in 1911 was not to harness the pride all this engendered in those who worked in the town within a town. Like too many employers on Clydeside and elsewhere, they treated their workforce as a potentially volatile assembly of people who had to be kept rigorously under control.

If you were five minutes late for your work, you would find the gates shut against you, the gatekeeper under strict instructions not to allow you in until the midday break. Half a day's pay lost. If you made it in before the gates closed but arrived late at the flat where you worked after handing in your brass token or check at the nearest time office, you might be quartered, lose a quarter of an hour's pay. You couldn't argue you hadn't realised what time it was. High up on the tower which rose above the plant, the Singer's clock was a landmark for miles around. This fondly remembered timepiece survived the devastating Clydebank Blitz of the Second World War only to be demolished with the factory in the 1960s.

A large proportion of the workforce at Singer's was female, employed for the sake of their superior manual dexterity when carrying out fine work. In 1911 around 3,000 women and girls worked there. The standard working-class practice was for all pay packets to be handed over to the mother of the family at the end of the week. In return, she would give you back some pocket money. However, working outside the home brought more than financial benefits, especially for the girls.

They got out into the world, achieved the status of a wage-earner and had company of their own age during the day. Although they might have to put up with a strict foreman or supervisor, factories like Singer's bred girls and women who tended to be more self-confident than their sisters in domestic service. These girls, and most of them were only in their late teens or early 20s, were more likely to speak out if they perceived an injustice being done to themselves or their workmates. This was to be a significant driver in the trouble brewing at Singer through 1910 and 1911.

Much of the tension arose out of the practice of Scientific Management, for which the company's American bosses and senior managers were great enthusiasts. This broke work down into small steps, the assembly line concept. The principle could be more crudely expressed, and was. When the

inventor of Scientific Management backed up his theories
with the example of how to handle pig iron, he wrote: 'This
work is so crude and elementary in its nature that the writer
firmly believes that it would be possible to train an intelligent
gorilla so as to become a more efficient pig-iron handler than
any man can be.'

So trained gorillas were preferable to men and women
– less likely to ask for a pay rise, shorter hours or better
working conditions either. In this modern machine age of
the shiny new twentieth century, human intelligence, skill,
initiative and experience were not to be valued. Nor did the
enthusiasts for Scientific Management take into account the
unquantifiable benefits of allowing workers to carry out work
in which they could take a pride. In the drive to maximise
profits by getting as much work as possible out of people for
as little pay as possible, few allowances were made either for
the fact that human beings are not machines.

Scientific Management was popular with many companies on Clydeside at the time. Lord Weir of Weir Pumps in
Cathcart was another enthusiast. He and the Red Clydesiders
were to cross swords on many issues. The bible of the theory
was *The Principles of Scientific Management,* published in 1911.
Frederick Winslow Taylor was an American whose book was
based on a paper he had delivered some years previously
to ASME, the American Society of Mechanical Engineers.
Perhaps the first-ever management consultant, the man and
the theory became so mutually identified that Scientific
Management was often referred to as Taylorism. He was
scornful of the claims of 'labor agitators (many of whom are
misinformed and misguided)' about '"sweat-shop" work and
conditions'. In his view the real problem was that people were
intrinsically lazy, most workers naturally inclined, as he put it,
to loaf or soldier or '"ca' cannie," as it is called in Scotland'.
Although he cites no examples from Scotland in his paper, it
is intriguing to speculate how he became familiar with that
expression.

Taylor believed that bringing workers doing similar work together and paying them the same standard daily rate of pay only made this problem worse. 'Under this plan the better men gradually but surely slow down their gait to that of the poorest and least efficient. When a naturally energetic man works for a few days beside a lazy one, the logic of the situation is unanswerable. "Why should I work hard when that lazy fellow gets the same pay that I do and does only half as much work?"'

His solution was not to pay people by the day but by how much they produced each day, piecework. Ironically – or perhaps not, given that Taylorism did tend to view workers as no more than cogs in the machine – after the Russian Revolution of 1917 both Lenin and Stalin tried to introduce the ideas of Scientific Management into Soviet industry.

Taylor did suggest one concession to human biology. At a time when factory and office workers finished at noon on Saturday and thus had weekends which lasted only a day and a half, he advised: 'All young women should be given two consecutive days of rest (with pay) each month, to be taken whenever they may choose.'

Taylor argued that Scientific Management would benefit both bosses and workers, allowing the latter to earn higher wages without even having to think for themselves how to do the job. Their manager or supervisor would spell that out to them, each task broken down into the science of it. He was convinced only managers or supervisors would be capable of making such an analysis.

Knowledge is power. That is a clear undercurrent of Scientific Management. It is also clear that Taylor was reflecting bosses' fears of the intelligent and experienced worker. Knowing their jobs and trades inside out, they had bargaining power mere cogs in the machine could never have. A telling example of this provides an unintentionally comical vignette in *The Principles of Scientific Management*.

We have all been used to seeing bricklayers tap
each brick after it is placed on its bed of mortar several times with the end of the handle of the trowel
so as to secure the right thickness for the joint. Mr
Gilbreth found that by tempering the mortar just
right, the bricks could be readily bedded to the
proper depth by a downward pressure of the hand
with which they are laid. He insisted that his mortar
mixers should give special attention to tempering the
mortar, and so save the time consumed in tapping
the brick.

Whether any of us would have trusted Mr Gilbreth – 'who
had himself studied bricklaying in his youth' – to build a wall
which wouldn't have come down in the next high wind is
another matter entirely.

Scientific Management resulted in work which could be
both back-breakingly tiring and mind-numbingly boring.
Singer's at Clydebank was producing one million sewing
machines every year. Each of these went out with one needle
fitted plus a neat little packet of three spares. Spare needles
were also needed for the Singer shops found in high streets
all over Britain. So more than four million new needles were
required each year.

There were girls in Singer's who spent hours each and
every day tapping newly made needles with a light hammer to
correct any faults, straightening bends the machining process
could put into them. It was quite an art to know where to hit
and how strongly, a little harder than you might think so the
needle would bend briefly in the opposite direction before
coming back to rest perfectly straight. As soon as one batch
was finished, another box of needles would be delivered to
your workbench by a young message boy or girl – a job that
gave many people their start at Singer's – so you didn't waste
any time by going to fetch it. Nor, of course, did you get the
chance to stretch your legs or refocus your eyes.

Arthur McManus, who was to become a significant figure in the story of Red Clydeside, was just 21 years old in 1911 and working at Singer's. His job was to point the needles. Passionate, intelligent and well-read, one day he simply cracked. His friend and workmate Tom Bell told the story in his own autobiography, *Pioneering Days*:

> I remember Arthur McManus describing a job he was on, pointing needles. Every morning there were millions of these needles on the table. As fast as he reduced the mountain of needles a fresh load was dumped. Day in, day out, it never grew less. One morning he came in, and found the table empty. He couldn't understand it. He began telling everyone excitedly that there were no needles on the table. It suddenly flashed on him how absurdly stupid it was to be spending his life like this. Without taking his jacket off he turned on his heel and went out, to go for a ramble over the hills to Balloch.

McManus had to come back, of course. Like everyone else, he needed the job and he needed the money.

Later generations of Singer's workers were to have fond memories of their time there, when management encouraged and supported all manner of clubs, social activities and events. There was a Singer's theatre and an annual Singer's sports gala. One girl chosen from the factory would be crowned gala queen and celebrities were invited to officially launch the fun and games. In 1950, it was Hollywood star Dorothy Lamour who did the honours.

With the company filling all their working time and so much of their leisure time employees used to joke they had become 'Singerised'. It may be that the impetus to create this all-encompassing Singer culture had its origins in the troubles of 1911. Perhaps management realised it would be to their advantage to encourage loyalty rather than hostility from their employees.

In 1911 that radical thought hadn't yet struck. One man who worked there at that time described how the morning lasted from seven o'clock till noon and you weren't even allowed to break off for a cup of tea or a piece to keep you going. One foreman was notorious for checking on who was in the toilets. Anyone caught in there smoking and taking an unofficial break was sacked on the spot.

There was resentment too that, although British industry was beginning to emerge from the depression which had paralysed the economy between 1907 and 1910, pay had not risen with renewed profits. Wages were still being cut on the basis of timing and testing carried out by cordially detested imported American 'efficiency engineers'. Tom Johnston described the process in the *Forward*. A few months before, in October 1910, the sensational trial in London of the infamous Dr Crippen for the murder and dismemberment of his wife had been all over the newspapers, hence the reference here:

> In many of these departments foremen stand with watches in their hands timing the men and girls so that the maximum amount of labour can be exacted from the operatives in return for the minimum wage. In one department especially, a foreman has been nicknamed 'Crippen' because of his timing propensities. The watch is seldom out of this individual's hand. Wages are not reduced collectively. In Singer's the wages of two or three are broken today; a few others tomorrow and so on until all the workers have been reduced, and the game of SCIENTIFIC REDUCTION begins once more.

Singer's in 1911 was a powder keg waiting to explode – and explode it did.

5

An Injury to One Is an Injury to All:
The Singer Strike of 1911

*'We've struck work, son.
The whole factory's coming out.'*

One chilly March afternoon in 1911, ten-year-old James Wotherspoon was walking home from school in Clydebank. His route took him past Singer's, where his father worked. As he made his way up Kilbowie Road, the vast complex lay to the boy's left. To his right, where the Clydebank Shopping Centre now is, coiled the railway lines and sidings of the Singer Line. During the working day, the trains lay here which transported those 4,000 or so Singer employees who didn't live in the town to and from the factory.

As James continued his journey home, he saw a sight he was never to forget. Hours before the end of the working day, people began to stream out of the factory. This was unheard of. In the midst of the crowd he spotted his father, who hurried across to where his young son stood staring in amazement through the railings which surrounded the plant. Till the end of his long life, James Wotherspoon was to remember the exact words his father used that day: 'We've struck work, son. The whole factory's coming out.' What the schoolboy was witnessing was the start of a bitter industrial dispute which began with that mass walk-out, carried on with public meetings, rallies and much heady talk only to collapse in acrimony three weeks later.

The spark which ignited the strike was a dispute involving 12 young women who worked as polishers. Their task was to bring the cabinets which housed the sewing machines to a high sheen. When management transferred three polishers out of the department, the 12 remaining girls were asked to do their work as well as their own. A change in the way they were paid meant they would also have to accept a reduction of two shillings in their pay packet, a substantial loss when their total weekly wage amounted to around 14 shillings. Angry at being asked to do more work for less pay, the polishers downed tools and withdrew their labour.

Two thousand other girls immediately came out in sympathy. The men soon followed. By the middle of the following day, Tuesday, 22 March 1911, almost all of over 10,000 employees were on strike. Those who remained at their workbenches and desks were largely foremen, managers and skilled men. Pickets at the factory's gates on Second Avenue, Kilbowie Road and Dalmuir did their best to persuade them to come out too.

James Wotherspoon, the schoolboy who witnessed the start of the strike, died in 2005, a few months after his hundred and fifth birthday. He spent his own working life at Singer. Almost a century after the events of 1911 he retained a photographic memory of them. He vividly recalled seeing a group of 'girl strikers', as the *Glasgow Herald* quickly dubbed them, trying to get a foreman to join the stoppage. While one contemporary newspaper photograph shows female strikers in elegant large-brimmed hats, James Wotherspoon remembered that many of the younger girls wore brightly coloured berets – red, yellow, blue and green – pulled down over their hair and secured by a hat pin. He described the result as 'not very flattering'.

The attempt to persuade the foreman to join the strike was good-natured but noisy. The girls blew toy paper trumpets, linked hands and danced around the man. Keeping his cool, he repeatedly and politely tipped his bowler hat to them and walked on into the factory.

The initial dispute among the polishers set light to the bonfire of grievances which had been simmering inside the factory, the imposition of Scientific Management, the continual timing, testing and wage cuts. Union membership was another bone of contention. Singer's management was forced to tolerate those unions to which the relatively small number of time-served men, mainly engineers and printers, belonged. It refused to sanction any union activity in respect of the unskilled workers who made up most of the workforce.

Union activists had, however, been quietly recruiting inside Singer's for about a year before the 1911 strike. Tom Bell, author of *Pioneering Days,* was one of them. 'Factory gate meetings were held, literature was sold, and study classes begun. Soon contacts were extended inside and it was not long before every department had a small group.'

A group to which Bell already belonged changed its name to the Industrial Workers of Great Britain (IWGB), becoming part of the British branch of the US-based Industrial Workers of the World (IWW). The members of this magnificently named organisation, which still exists today, were more familiarly known as the 'Wobblies'.

One of the IWW's brightest lights was Joe Hill, the Swedish-American labour activist. Four years after the Singer's strike he was executed by firing squad in Utah for a murder people then and since don't think he committed, believing he was framed to get rid of a troublemaker. His life and his story inspired the ballad 'I Dreamed I Saw Joe Hill Last Night'. Most famously sung by Paul Robeson and later by Joan Baez at Woodstock, it's a song which continues to inspire rebels around the world. Novelist Stephen King and his wife Tabitha named one of their sons Joseph Hillstrom King in honour of Joe Hill.

The Wobblies gave the workers at Singer's a stirring slogan: 'An injury to one is an injury to all.' Tom Bell reported in *Pioneering Days* that it quickly caught on, helping to stiffen the resolve of the new union members.

The organisation of the Singer's strike was tight and highly effective. It was masterminded not only by the IWGB but also by the Socialist Labour Party (SLP). Small in membership, the SLP made up for that in dedication to their cause of socialist revolution and the creation of a workers' republic. They would have no truck with those who advocated reform instead. They come across as rather a dour bunch but they seized the opportunity the Singer's dispute presented to them with both hands. Strike headquarters were established at their committee rooms on Second Avenue, part of the Holy City. The flat-roofed houses where many Singer workers lived now belonged officially to the district of Clydebank known as Radnor Park. This geographically commanding location also had psychological significance, providing a lofty vantage point over Singer's. The Second Avenue gate, one of the factory's main entrances, was nearby. Once through it, a dizzyingly steep flight of stone stairs – still there 100 years later – plunged into the factory grounds.

A strike committee was quickly formed and strike districts established in Bridgeton, Govan, Dumbarton, the Vale of Leven and elsewhere to ensure the 4,000 workers who did not live in Clydebank were kept in the loop. Accurate information being deemed crucial to morale and the potential success of the strike, each district had a meeting place where the same trusted messenger gave them an update at half-past six every evening.

Much stress was laid on good behaviour. Workers at Singer's normally collected their pay packets or had them delivered to their workbenches when they finished work at midday on Saturday. On the first week of the strike, money still being owed to them, they marched en masse into the factory, lifted their pay packets and marched out again. Even the *Glasgow Herald* was impressed by how they did that. No friend to the strikers, the newspaper of Glasgow's establishment estimated that 10,000 people, not much short of the whole workforce, had taken part in the collection of the pay.

'Although extremely quiet and orderly there was something intensely dramatic about the whole scene.'

Mass meetings, parades and processions were held throughout the strike, in Clydebank and beyond, to gain publicity and support for the strikers' cause. On Thursday, 23 March, four days in, a demonstration estimated to include 8,000 people marched through Clydebank to John Brown's. A meeting was held with the shipyard's workers, requesting their solidarity and support. Headed by Duntocher Brass Band, those marchers must have been a sight to see.

Despite the biting March winds, commented on in contemporary newspaper reports, there's a sense of a carnival atmosphere at the beginning of it all. It must have been quite a novelty to be out and about in normally quiet but now bustling streets during working hours, away from the constant supervision and measuring and testing of the factory.

On Sunday, 26 March, another demonstration was organised on Glasgow Green, time-honoured place of protest. Again, strike leaders emphasised the good behaviour of the strikers. Who those strike leaders were is curiously hard to establish. The records aren't there, either for the strike committee or Singer's management. Other than the Singer managers, newspapers named no names either. This applies both for the socialist *Forward* and for what its readers called 'the capitalist press'. That the *Forward* was protecting those who might later be blacklisted by Singer's and other employers seems likely; that the capitalist press was doing the same, less so.

Perhaps some newspapers were choosing to diminish the leaders of the dispute by not naming them. After all, many of them were mere 'girl strikers'. Clearly these were females who did not know their place, neither the one allotted to them by class nor by gender. Or perhaps the newspapers were choosing not to give any of the strikers the oxygen of publicity.

The Singer Strike Clydebank, 1911 is an authoritative account of the strike published in 1989 by Clydebank District Library

and compiled by members of Glasgow Labour History Workshop. It names several names, making educated guesses as to these individuals' involvement in the strike. It seems highly likely that Arthur McManus, the 21 year old who had decided there had to be more to life than the processing of millions of sewing machine needles, was involved in the strike along with his friend Tom Bell. Bell was not only one of the prime movers behind the establishment of the IWGB union in Singer's, he was also for a time a member of the Socialist Labour Party. Both he and Arthur McManus later became yet more Scottish founder members of the Communist Party of Great Britain, McManus becoming its first chairman.

Neil Maclean, later to become long-standing Labour MP for Govan, may also have been involved, although there is no documentary evidence of this. However, he was doing his apprenticeship as an engineer at Singer's around the time of the strike.

Eighteen-year-old Frances Abbot, later Mrs McBeth, worked as a polisher in the department where the dispute began. Again, there is no documentary evidence of her involvement but her daughter described her as 'a fighter all her days ... right into "Red Clydeside"'. Fanny McBeth later came to know James Maxton and Davie Kirkwood, who became MP for the town, and remained throughout her life a dedicated member of the Labour Party.

Jane Rae was in her late 30s at the time of the strike. She worked in the needle flat and was sacked afterwards because of her involvement. She subsequently became a member of the ILP, a suffragette, local councillor, supporter of the temperance movement and a JP. In this role she earned a reputation for handing down the toughest penalties she could legally impose on men found guilty of domestic abuse.

It is curious that few references are made in the memoirs of the major figures of Red Clydeside to the Singer strike. John Maclean certainly wrote at the time about what he called 'this rather romantic effort' but he was not a member of the

SLP and there seem to be no accounts of him or his friend and fellow orator James Maxton addressing the strikers at their numerous meetings on Glasgow Green and elsewhere. Admittedly, Maxton was only 26 at the time and still serving his political apprenticeship.

Singer's management met the strike committee on several occasions but insisted there could be no discussion on any grievances until everyone went back to work. Management also emphatically refused to agree to factory-wide union recognition or the principle of collective bargaining, on which the strike had begun to focus.

One of the arguments advanced by strike leaders here was that any individual girl who took a complaint to management was likely to have it ignored. Outspoken and spirited the lassies at Singer's may have been, but nobody paid much attention to what girls had to say.

On Wednesday, 29 March, the *Glasgow News* reported the oddly quiet scene in Clydebank at noon, emphasising how unusual this was:

> It required only a cursory glance at the streets in the Radnor Park district today to discover that there was absolutely no change in the situation in connection with the strike of Singer's workers. There were the usual coteries of men who had come 'out', with numbers of girls who had also left their employment, and the factory itself, except for a few jets of steam issuing from different points, and a few curls of smoke from one of the chimneys, gave no indication of anything like its ordinary busy aspect.
>
> It is estimated that excepting the clerical staff and handymen generally, there are now little over a couple of hundred employees remaining at their posts.
>
> A view of the extensive works from the height of the 'Holy City' gives a picture of almost absolute **Desertion and Quietness.**

Fewer workers meant fewer trains. Instead of seven from Glasgow, only two had pulled into Singer railway station and only one from the Vale of Leven. All three were 'sparsely filled'. The next day, Thursday, 30 March, there was another demonstration on Glasgow Green. About 2,000 strikers listened to an unnamed speaker and 'thereafter assembled in military fashion, and headed by three bands, they paraded the principal streets of the city'.

Other than a handful of pickets haranguing 'the few workers who left the factory for dinner', things were much quieter down in Clydebank. Some of the pickets were angry, spitting out accusations of 'blackleg' and 'scab', but there was no violence, as throughout the strike. The *Evening News* told its readers that 'nothing noteworthy transpired'.

The papers were reporting other news too, of course. There was trouble in the Balkans, revolutionary groups seeking independence for Macedonia. The Athens correspondent of the *Manchester Guardian* took 'a grave view of the outlook'.

In sport, lots of people were getting excited about the Scotland versus England football international in Liverpool on April Fools' Day. The team travelled down by train on the morning of Friday, 31 March and special trains ran from St Enoch and Glasgow Central to take the fans down on Friday evening and Saturday morning, nine from St Enoch on Friday night alone. The *Glasgow News* promised its readers expert staff reporting from Goodison Park via telephone and telegraph, 'DESCRIPTION OF PLAY, NOTES ON THE GAME … FEARLESS AND IMPARTIAL CRITICISM, PHOTOS OF PLAYERS', and the Scottish fans were buoyant.

> The scenes at the stations last night were of a lively nature. One coterie of about thirty men were loaded with parcels apparently containing 'light' refreshments; while another group, also well loaded with packages, had six of their number as standard bearers of the Scottish flag.

> Many others were well provided with melodeons
> and mouth organs, yielding harmonic discords. Last,
> but not least, were a couple of pipers, whose skirling
> appealed to the patriotic heart.

Bless their hearts. Look away now if you don't want to know
the score. It was a draw, 1–1. In a busy day for sport, Oxford
beat Cambridge in the annual boat race.

Other Scots were embarking on rather more permanent
journeys in rather larger boats. Under a headline of 'To The
West To-Day: The Rush Continues', the *Evening News* reported
that a record 4,000 emigrants were leaving the Clyde that
Saturday to start new lives in Canada and the United States.
The Anchor Line was taking more than 1,100, chartering a
special train to Greenock, where the *California* was waiting to
carry them across the Atlantic to New York. 'Seldom has such
a boom in emigration been experienced as at present.'

Those emigrants were going to miss the Scottish National
Exhibition due to open at Kelvingrove in May. Preparations
were well in hand and lots of season tickets had already been
sold, although probably not to workers at Singer's. The union
had no funds to pay strike pay and money was getting very
tight. Half of all women in Clydebank who worked outside
the home did so at Singer's. In many households all the
wage-earners were employed there. That was how it worked.
You got a job in the factory because a relative or friend spoke
for you. If no money was coming in from Singer's, no money
was coming in from anywhere.

Singer's management had not been idle while the strikers
had been marching and protesting. As the strike entered
its third week Works Superintendent Hugh MacFarlane,
a Glaswegian, and F.A. Park, the American manager of the
Kilbowie plant, applied the tried-and-tested strategy of divide
and conquer. Questioning the right of the strike committee
to speak for all the strikers, they sent letters out to every
employee enclosing a pre-printed postcard which they asked

to be completed and returned as soon as possible. 'I wish to resume my work, and agree to do so on the day and hour which may be arranged by you, when you assure me that at least 6,000 persons have signed this agreement.'

After signing their agreement to this statement, employees were asked to fill in their names, addresses, check numbers and department numbers. Clerical and management staff at Singer's stayed up till one o'clock in the morning to get those 10,000 letters and postcards ready to send out.

The strike committee tried to persuade people to write 'Refer to Strike Committee' across the postcard and return it unsigned. Not many did. As ever, it came down to economic survival. If you didn't sign and return the postcard but 6,000 of your co-workers did, management could easily work out who those who hadn't signed were. That would be you out of a job at Singer's, and very probably blacklisted with other employers too. The *Forward* certainly alleged that blacklisting took place after the strike was over, calling for a boycott of Singer sewing machines in response. Singer management expressed their opinion on this via the pages of the *Glasgow Herald*: 'We cannot be expected to retain people in our employ who by word and deed plainly indicate that they are unfriendly to their employers.'

Whether the Singer plebiscite was fairly conducted is a moot point. The strike committee alleged that more than 1,000 postcards had gone to employees who no longer worked at Singer's, some of whom were dead. Singer management announced that 6,015 postcards had come back agreeing on a return to work. Several people at the time, on both sides of the dispute, observed that this was a very convenient number.

Three months later, a bitter reflection on the failure of the strike was issued by the Sewing Machine Group of the IWGB:

> We make our appeal not only to the Singer Workers, but to the whole working class. The lessons of the Kilbowie Strike are lessons for them too.

We are confronted by a determined and vindictive attack upon the whole principle of organisation ... The plot aims at reducing the workers to a mass of disorganised serfs, degraded and dehumanised instruments for producing wealth for others, incapable of helping each other or of offering the smallest resistance to the never-ending and ever-increasing robbery of the master class.

The workers might have lost the battle at Singer's but with rhetoric like that the war was still to be won. Some who had tasted the bitterness of defeat at Kilbowie moved on to other battlefields. They took their new and powerful slogan with them: 'An injury to one is an injury to all.' These words were to ring out through the story of Red Clydeside.

6

No Vote, No Census

'If I am intelligent enough to fill in this paper, I am intelligent enough to put a cross on a voting form.'

The suffragettes have an image problem. The popular perception is of well-off ladies with plenty of time on their hands for smashing windows, pouring acid into pillar boxes, tying themselves to railings and otherwise making mischief. That so many of them fully earned their place within the story of Red Clydeside can come as a surprise.

When asked what he had thought of the suffragettes, Mr James Wotherspoon, schoolboy witness of the start of the Singer Strike, looked a little nervously at his interviewer but stepped manfully up to the mark. He had thought them a bunch of silly middle-class women out to cause trouble.

In *The Hidden History of Glasgow's Women* social historian Elspeth King suggests we may not hear much about working-class suffragettes because their middle-class sisters-in-arms tried to protect them, believing the police would mete out rougher treatment to mere women than they would to ladies. Considering how brutally some middle-class women were treated in prison, this seems plausible. Descriptions of force-feeding of suffragettes on hunger strike make grim reading.

It is another curiosity that the depiction of suffragettes in popular culture seems always to show them doing what they did only in London. Although it was an important focal

point, suffragettes were active all over Britain, doing whatever they could think of to achieve their goal. The campaign was a long one.

In Scotland alone there had been women's suffrage committees for 30 years and more in all the major cities and towns, from Lerwick to Dumfries and Inveraray to Dingwall. A large number of Scottish town councils had also declared themselves in favour of extending the franchise to women. In 1870 school boards were created in Scotland, with both men and women eligible to stand for election to them. In 1882 some Scotswomen, essentially those who were householders in their own right, were given the right to vote in local elections. From then on, women not being permitted to vote in parliamentary elections struck many people as illogical as well as unjust.

By 1901, 17 per cent of people entitled to vote in local elections in Glasgow were women. They must all either have been single women, widowed or divorced, as it was almost always the husband who was the householder in any couple. In his unstinting support for women to get the parliamentary vote, Tom Johnston argued sarcastically that no evil results had followed from women being allowed to vote in local elections.

In 1892 the newly formed Scottish Co-operative Women's Guild (SCWG), a grouping of working-class women, sent a petition to the government calling for votes for women. There had been lots of petitions, literally millions of signatures gathered, but still the prize seemed no closer. Peaceful protests continued. One of the most colourful was held in Edinburgh in October 1909, when hundreds of suffragettes marched along Princes Street watched by thousands of interested onlookers. The female marchers were supported by a sizeable group from the Men's League for Women's Suffrage.

Again according to Elspeth King, this stalwart band had been formed by husbands, brothers and fiancés of suffragettes fed up with being seen as the poor henpecked yes-men of the women in their lives. One of their banners read 'Men's

League for Women's Suffrage. Scots wha hae votes – men. Scots wha haena – women.'

The Edinburgh march was also a pageant, with partici-pants portraying famous women from Scottish history: St Margaret, Mary, Queen of Scots, Jenny Geddes, the female Covenanting martyrs. The marchers' banners included the usual simple but effective demand of 'Votes For Women' and the confident claim that 'A Gude Cause Maks A Strong Arm'. The march was re-enacted a century after it happened, on 9 October 2009.

The Scottish suffragettes made a big deal of their Scottishness, as photographs and surviving banners show. It made for great publicity. What newspaper editor could re-sist a photograph of attractive young women in fashionable clothes well draped in tartan sashes or plaids? In 1908 Mary Phillips of Glasgow served three months in Holloway after being arrested at a demonstration in London. When she was released she was met by a group of her fellow suffragettes dressed exactly like that, Cairngorm plaid brooches and all. They were also carrying a banner with a slogan they had pinched from a long-standing advert for soap. 'Message To Mr Asquith, Ye Mauna Tramp on the Scotch Thistle, Laddie!'

The thistle was an emblem enthusiastically adopted by the suffragettes. Not only was its deep purple eye-catching – the votes for women movement had already chosen that as one of their colours – its 'wha daur meddle wi' me?' reputation struck a powerful chord. When someone advised Mary Phillips that women who wanted the vote might be more likely to get it if they were 'patient, gentle, womanly and flower-like', she told them she'd much rather be 'a great big prickly Scots thistle'.

Helen Crawfurd, the young wife of the minister, became a committed suffragette the year after the Gude Cause march. The first person she heard address the subject was Helen Fraser of Glasgow, speaking to an audience of holidaymakers

in Rothesay, where the suffragettes of the Women's Freedom League (WFL) had a summer base. Politics went doon the watter too. Listening attentively, Helen Crawfurd grew indignant at the heckling to which Helen Fraser was being subjected. With magnificent contempt, she described the hecklers as 'undersized bantams'. What they kept yelling at the young and attractive Helen Fraser was 'It's a man ye want!' You can just hear the shilpit wee nyaffs saying it, too.

In 1910, after a meeting in Rutherglen, Helen Crawfurd joined the Women's Social and Political Union (WSPU), which had been founded by Mrs Pankhurst and her daughter Christabel in 1903. The WSPU advocated a militant and increasingly violent approach. Seeking to belittle and diminish these dangerous women, the *Daily Mail* dubbed them suffra*gettes* instead of the correct suffra*gists*. The name the newspaper had come up with eventually stuck for all female supporters of votes for women.

One working-class Glasgow suffragette we do know about was very much in favour of the militant tactics advocated by the Pankhursts. She was Agnes Dollan, born Agnes Moir in Springburn, one of 11 children. She was only 11 years old when she had to leave school and go out to work. She was still a teenager when she began fighting for higher wages and better working conditions for women, and soon became involved in the suffragette movement. Her marriage to Patrick Dollan, miner, member of the ILP, *Forward* journalist and future Lord Provost of Glasgow, became a lifelong personal and political partnership.

Other women were disturbed by the violence perpetrated by the militant suffragettes and by Mrs Pankhurst's dictatorial leadership style. Helen Fraser, who had been heckled at Rothesay, was one of them, telling her, 'you don't use violence, you use *reason* to get the vote'. Many left the WSPU as a result, joining the WFL, which was particularly strong in Scotland.

Some socialists, including many on Clydeside, were ambivalent about extending the vote to women. One argument
was that men should come first. By no means did all of them
have the vote in parliamentary elections. The figure stood
at around 75 per cent, again essentially only householders.
During the First World War the telling point was made that
thousands of those killed or maimed had no say in the running of the country for which they were being called upon
to sacrifice their lives, health and youth. It was not until 1918
that the franchise was extended to all men over 21 and all
women over 30.

Ramsay MacDonald, who in 1924 was to become Britain's
first Labour prime minister, was a man said to be 'more at
ease with women than with men'. He fully supported female
suffrage but was dead set against violence being used to
achieve it:

> I have no objection to revolution, if it is necessary,
> but I have the very strongest objection to childishness
> masquerading as revolution, and all that one can say
> of these window-breaking expeditions is that they
> are simply silly and provocative. I wish the working
> women of the country who really care for the vote ...
> would come to London and tell these pettifogging
> middle-class damsels who are going out with little
> hammers in their muffs that if they do not go home
> they will get their heads broken.

Some socialists believed women would tend to vote cau-
tiously, favouring the political status quo and the established
parties. Believing them less likely to put their cross against
Labour Party candidates, they did not welcome the addition
of so many voters who might potentially increase the Liberal
or Conservative share of the vote. Yet many suffragettes were
themselves socialists. Mrs Pankhurst and her daughters were
members of the ILP and personal friends of Labour leader

Keir Hardie. He was always a supporter of votes for women. So was Tom Johnston, who gave a regular weekly column in the *Forward* to Glasgow's suffragettes.

Helen Crawfurd contributed many articles to *Suffrage Notes.* So did Janie Allan. The daughter of Alexander Allan, owner of the shipping company of the same name, she was a wealthy woman who was a committed socialist and member of the ILP. She was generous with her money and resources, on at least one occasion in 1911 loaning her car to fellow suffragettes campaigning during a by-election in North Ayrshire, allowing them to cover a lot more ground in this rural constituency.

Other contributors to *Suffrage Notes* were Frances and Margaret McPhun. These sisters with the great surname had a third sibling, Nessie, who was also a suffragette. Their father was Bailie McPhun, councillor for the East End of Glasgow, prime mover behind the creation of the People's Palace and proud parent to his three clever and politically engaged daughters.

Helen Crawfurd did a speaking tour of Lanarkshire with Frances and Margaret McPhun, on this occasion travelling by train. She was full of admiration for how Frances managed to read the complicated railway timetables and always get the three of them to their destination without any problems.

They always got a sympathetic hearing from the miners, who admired how the suffragettes were fighting to win the vote. Helen Crawfurd thought she probably went down well because her speeches were becoming ever more socialist in tone, peppered with quotes from the Bible so familiar to her and these Lanarkshire colliers. The miners would never take the fee they could have requested for the hire of their halls. They always took up a good collection, too. It was usual to do this at political meetings, the money going to the funds of the party or organisation the speakers represented. As far as the miners were concerned, class clearly didn't come into it. The suffragettes were fighting to right an injustice and they understood all about that.

The census of 1911 gave suffragettes throughout Britain another weapon with which to challenge the government and win publicity for their cause. 'If you're not going to give us the vote and consider us full citizens then you're not going to count us.' This was the message they wanted to send. The census was taken on the night of Sunday, 2 April. Presumably all the football supporters who had been down to Liverpool to see Scotland draw with England were home by then.

All over the country, thousands of women made sure they weren't at home or anywhere else they could be counted. Some wrote comments on the census form before they disappeared for the night in this mass act of civil disobedience. As one English suffragette put it: 'If I am intelligent enough to fill in this paper, I am intelligent enough to put a cross on a voting form.'

Refusing to be counted in the census was against the law, punishable by a fine of £5, but it was a peaceful and non-violent way of expressing strong feelings. So that the protest would have maximum impact, suffragettes made sure the press and the census enumerators knew well in advance what they intended to do. The enumerators were confident they could winkle them out, as the *Glasgow News* reported the day before the count was made:

> The services of the police will be requisitioned in the work. To-morrow night they will make search for the homeless. They will keep an eye on the
>
> **Nooks and Crannies**
>
> of the city, where the waifs and strays seek nightly shelter. They must also be accounted for in the Census.

The crews of ships on the Clyde would be counted by officers of HM Customs and the soldiers at Maryhill Barracks would be easy to count, as would visitors staying overnight at Glasgow's hotels. Then came the stern warning:

> It is just possible that some trouble may be occasioned
> by the
>
> ### More Militant Members
>
> of the suffragette movement in the way of withholding
> information. The officials, however, are prepared for
> any difficulty that may arise in this way, and arrange-
> ments made accordingly.

Bit of an unconvincing threat, that. What were these vague
'arrangements'? If you couldn't find 'em, you couldn't count
'em. How many women did take themselves off to some nook
or cranny where even those wily census enumerators wouldn't
find them, or concealed themselves at home, is not known.

The official census website for England and Wales estimates
that several thousand women may have boycotted the 1911
count. How many Scottish suffragettes might have done the
same is not clear. Although Helen Crawfurd makes no mention of the 1911 census in her memoirs, the Glasgow branch
of the Women's Freedom League certainly held a wee soirée
on the Saturday after the census where war stories were exchanged. 'A number of ladies gave their Census experiences,
which were of an amusing and entertaining character.' Then
they don't give any details of those amusing stories. Damn
their eyes.

The popular view in Glasgow in 1911 seems to have been
that many suffragettes had gone into hiding for the night.
A cartoon in the *Glasgow News* shows Mary Ann, a domestic
servant of mature years, entertaining a beaming policeman
friend in a cosy kitchen while a black cat with a jaunty bow
tied around its neck looks on. 'Ye needna hurry,' says Mary
Ann. 'The missis is yin o' them that's no fur fillin' in her census paper. She's below the bed up the stairs. She'll no come
oot as lang's ye're here.'

The point had been made, and in Glasgow attention
turned to the next big thing.

7

The Picturesque & Historic Past:
The Scottish Exhibition of 1911

*'Various Highland crafts will be engaged in by
native dwellers during their residence.'*

The bitter March strike at Singer's gave way to the summer
of the Scottish Exhibition. This was the third in a line of such
events held at Kelvingrove in Glasgow's West End. The first
was in 1888 and the second in 1901, when the beautiful red
sandstone building we know today as Kelvingrove Art Gallery
and Museum was opened, providing a grand new home for
Glasgow's civic art collection.

The full title of the 1911 extravaganza was the Scottish
Exhibition of National History, Art and Industry. As the *Daily
Record* wrote at the time, its purpose was 'to bind Scotland
more closely to the glories and victories of its past'. One of
the concrete aims of the exhibition was to raise money to
fund a Chair of Scottish History and Literature at nearby
Glasgow University, which it successfully did.

Rather unwisely for an Englishman in Scotland, the existing Professor of Modern History at the university up on
Gilmorehill overlooking Kelvingrove had given voice to his
opinion that there was no such thing as Scottish History.
Perhaps Dudley Medley – inevitably known by the nickname
of Deadley Mudley – was just trying to provoke debate. Or
perhaps, as eminent history professors have been known to

do, he set out to cause a stushie in the hope of getting his name in the papers.

The organisers of the 1911 exhibition set out to prove that Scotland had a very rich history indeed. Visiting the exhibition on the press preview day, Monday, 1 May 1911, the *Glasgow Herald*'s reporter had a bit of fun with that. As was usual at the time, there was no byline, so we don't know who he, or maybe she, was. There had been 'lady reporters' for quite some time by then. Allowed almost a full broadsheet page to record first impressions and describe the different exhibits, the reporter begins by quoting Huckleberry Finn, who 'has declared that the world has no need of dead persons'. Or, as Henry Ford, founder of the Ford Motor Company, father of the assembly line and big fan of Scientific Management, put it, 'History is bunk.'

Having repeated Huck Finn's uncompromising view on the importance of living in the present, shared by many in the excitingly new twentieth century, the reporter then has his or her cake and eats it. Full credit is given to the Scottish Exhibition (as it soon became known for short) for having balanced 'the priceless heritage of Scottish history and art with exhibits demonstrating the achievements of modern Scotland in industry, science and entertainment'.

Waxing lyrical about the exhibition's Palace of History, an interesting contradiction and a cautious rebuke surface. Although the Scotland of 1911 feels itself closer to the days of Bruce and Wallace than we, a mere century on, might have thought, perhaps, the reporter suggests, people don't care enough about those stirring times:

> The Scotch [*sic*] War of Independence is not yet remote enough to have become clustered with myth, and the fame of Wallace and Bruce has not yet suffered seriously from the attack of the historic iconoclast. Of the plain hero and the heroic king there

are many relics. Save among members of the Scottish Patriotic Association the tragedy of Wallace and the triumph of Bannockburn do not now arouse rage or joy, which perhaps is not as it ought to be. The records here should stimulate a large national memory.

On somewhat safer ground, the *Herald* reporter has absolutely no doubt that 'the romance of the Stuart dynasty retains its glamour', even if Bonnie Prince Charlie is dismissed as his father's 'futile son'. Was a fine line being trod here?

There's a sense at points in this long article of a tension between the political opinions of the journalist and those of the newspaper and its owners for which he or she wrote. Not an uncommon story then or now but even more of a dilemma back in the days when bosses were all-powerful and would have no compunction about blacklisting you to other potential employers if you stepped over onto the wrong side of that line.

Home Rule for Scotland was a hot topic in 1911, the idea gathering increasing support and momentum. Many of the socialists of Red Clydeside were passionately in favour. Other Scots of all political hues were opposed. Across the board, however, sentimental Scottishness of a type which tends to make modern Scots cringe seems to have been quite acceptable.

The crowds which flocked to Kelvingrove during the fine summer of 1911 loved the historical exhibits, and flock they did. More than nine million visits were made to where the exhibition spread itself lavishly out over the eastern end of Kelvingrove Park, the part which lies on the other side of Kelvin Way from the Art Galleries.

One of the most popular sections was the 'Auld Toun' with its 'Auld Scotch [*sic*] Street'. Although a few Home Rulers and patriotic Scots had been objecting for a generation and more to the use of the word *Scotch* rather than *Scots* other than for broth, shortbread and whisky, the word seems to

have raised few hackles in 1911. The *Glasgow Herald* reporter again:

> To step from thoroughfares lined with palaces and pleasure-haunts into the quaint courtyard of 'the Auld Toun' is like a piece of travel. There is, it is true, an admirable consonancy in the architecture of the entire Exhibition, but this quiet, old-world nook, with its towering turrets, its crow steps and its toppling chimneys, just so much awry as to accentuate the verisimilitude of it all, is a place apart, a spot to which one may retire from the din and ecstacy [*sic*] of the coming summer nights and recall the picturesque and historic past.

There were living exhibits, too. The Highland Clachan spread over three acres along the banks of the Kelvin stretching back to the Gibson Street entrance to the park: '… here and there are sprinkled the thatched cottages which are to be inhabited during the summer by native Highlanders. Various Highland arts and crafts will be engaged in by native dwellers during their residence, and all the attendants will be garbed in the "Earasaid", the ancient and becoming costume having been presented by the Marchioness of Bute.'

Well, at least the Clachan was being run on commercial lines and they were hoping to make a profit to be donated to *An Comunn Gàidhealach* and the Co-operative Council of Highland Home Industries. There was a village hall too, *Talla mhor a' Chlachain* in Gaelic, where audiences of up to 350 people could enjoy musical events and entertainments in both English and the language of the Garden of Eden.

If the attitude towards the 'native Highlanders' sounds just a wee touch patronising, they weren't the only people who spent the summer of 1911 being gawped at as quaint aborigines. Close by the Highland Village ('*An Clachan*') sat the Equatorial Colony, or West African Village. There were

about a hundred adults and children there, kindly requested to demonstrate their traditional way of life in a corner of a Glasgow park. They included musicians and dancers. Lest any visitors to the exhibition had any trepidation about that, reassurance was offered in advance that 'decency is maintained throughout'.

Not far from the West African village was the Arctic Camp, where a group of Laplanders, complete with reindeer, had been persuaded to spend several months for 'as much milk as they could drink', a statement which raises the art of patronising people of other cultures to a whole new level. Or lowers it to a whole new depth.

More sophisticated refreshment was available for the exhibition's visitors. As might be expected, the famous Miss Cranston ran two such establishments. One was the White Cockade, whose name fits in perfectly with the historic theme of the exhibition, referring as it does to the symbol adopted by Bonnie Prince Charlie's Jacobite army. Yet Miss Cranston's tea rooms at the Scottish Exhibition were bang up to date too, as she so much liked to be. She commissioned Charles Rennie Mackintosh to design the inside of the White Cockade, and Margaret Macdonald to create the menu cards. The Willow Tea Rooms on which they had worked together in 1904 was just a short tram ride away from Kelvingrove.

Examples of Margaret Macdonald Mackintosh's menu cards survive, very dramatic in white on black. Other than a glimpse of a spacious and airy balcony there are no known photographs of the interiors of the White Cockade or Miss Cranston's other tea room at the exhibition. She gave the commission for that to Frances Macdonald, Margaret's sister.

The blend of old and new was mirrored elsewhere. The Palace of History was the main building, designed to look like Falkland Palace in Fife. A modern concert hall could seat 3,000 people, and pageants and musical events were staged there, the inaugural concert given by Sir Henry Wood, knighted that same year, and his Queen's Hall Orchestra. A

pageant on the life of Robert Burns caused controversy by pulling no punches on the bard's fondness for a dram.

In the design of its exterior, the Palace of Industries followed the unifying historic style. Inside, as befitted Glasgow's proud boast to be both the Second City of the Empire and the Workshop of the World, it was crammed with displays on all types of industrial endeavour. It showcased examples from home and abroad, including what was being produced in Germany, Italy, Japan, Austria, Holland, Denmark and those countries then known as the Colonies.

The Palace of Industries had its own spacious quadrangle, with 'bandstand, tearooms, verandahs, and promenades – an exhibition in itself'. There was a 500-seat conference hall, plus the exhibition's offices, dedicated post office and telephone exchange.

In the lee of the beautiful Victorian and Edwardian houses up on Park Circus, the Garden Club provided exclusive accommodation for a thousand or so of the more well-heeled visitors to the exhibition. They paid a membership fee for the whole summer of two guineas apiece. The site as a whole being open to all, there had been some concern about the possibility of what was referred to as rowdyism. You never knew what might happen when the working classes set out to enjoy themselves.

Back in 1901, there had been hopes that the Kelvingrove exhibition of that year might leave behind it permanent improvements in both Glasgow and the lives of the working-class people who formed the bulk of the city's population. Bemoaning the fact that the Clyde and the Kelvin were polluted and that 'amid the blankness, uniformity and greyness, exasperated nerves find but one outlet – in drink', the hopeful young authors of *Glasgow in 1901* called for the city to solve the problem of 'how the lives of its workers may be made a little more gracious and tolerable and sweet. That the Exhibition will leave behind it a humanising influence we know. It will hasten the coming of our clean rivers, our

flowers and trees, and help to rend that intolerable blanket of smoke which, while it keeps out the sun, is not even proof against rain. We want some "niceness" in the condition of our citizens' lives, and justice done to our city's looks that we may love her in the sight of men as we have loved her shame-facedly and in secret ...'

Ten years on, all that was still only a hope. None of the buildings of the 1911 exhibition were permanent, all of them designed to be dismantled after the show was over, although everyone agreed they did look very solid. Given that this was supposed to be a celebration of Scotland's history, it seems a pity that the remains of the old Kelvingrove mansion around which the Palace of History had been built was completely demolished and swept away after the exhibition closed in November. Then again, as the old saying had it, the great-est vandals in Glasgow were always Glasgow Corporation. Off with the old, on with the new, that's always been the Glasgow way.

The aerial railway was absolutely part of the Modern Age. This thrilling form of transport allowed visitors to fly across the site, over the Highland Village and the Kelvin to the grounds of the university. An artist's impression and a surviving photograph show women in big hats, boys in sailor suits and girls in pinafores looking admiringly up at it and riding in a metal cage-style gondola suspended under a cigar-shaped machinery room running along elec-tric cables fixed to high pylons at either end of the aerial railway's track.

The Scottish Exhibition opened on 2 May 1911, six weeks before the coronation in London of King George V and Queen Mary. Another of the reasons for holding the exhi-bition had been in celebration of this royal event, London having its Festival of Empire in the same year. In the run-up to the coronation Borwick's Baking Powder took adverts in the Glasgow papers announcing a competition to win 20 free trips to London so their customers could be in the

cheering crowds when their majesties travelled by coach to Westminster Abbey:

Each Trip will consist of:

1. A return railway ticket to London from any part of Scotland.
2. First-rate hotel accommodation and board for 3 clear days.
3. A good seat to view the procession.

Full particulars of the Competitions and Coupons will be found in the 6d., 1s., and 2s.6d. tins of Borwick's Baking Powder sold in Scotland.

The Bonanza in Argyle Street, 'the largest millinery business in Scotland', was rewarding its customers with free admission tickets to the Scottish Exhibition 'with every pound's worth of goods bought for cash in one day's shopping'. You'd have had to buy at least two of 'The New American Sailors and Mushrooms' to be able to get one of those free tickets. Tragically for fashionistas, the advert shows no pictures of these creations.

Other than requesting its readers visiting Glasgow for the Scottish Exhibition to patronise its advertisers, the *Forward* took little interest in what was going on at Kelvingrove and declared the coronation to be 'neither here nor there'. They were more interested in the suffragettes' protest during the census and at what else was going on in the Scotland of 1911. Keir Hardie said it would be remembered as a year of strikes.

As well as the confrontation at Singer's, 1911 saw a UK-wide railway strike and stoppages in the Welsh coalfields. There were also strikes at the dye-works of the United Turkey Red Company in the Vale of Leven, on Glasgow's trams and among the carters, known in local parlance as *cairters*. Forerunners of today's 'White Van Man', this army of men

in old tweed suits and flat-cap bunnets worn at a rakish angle drove their horses and carts around Scotland's cities, transporting all manner of goods. Many of them were directly employed by town councils.

Socialists were clear as to why there were so many strikes. The cost of living was rising and wages weren't keeping pace. In its last edition of the year, Saturday, 30 December 1911, the *Forward*'s front page leading article was entitled 'The Struggle in Scotland during 1911 for a Living Wage'. Their round-up of the year's news included one shocking statistic they had published earlier in the year, that 17,000 women in Glasgow made their living by walking the streets as prostitutes. The socialist newspaper was scathing about how long it had taken the press and the Kirk to wake up to this.

Interestingly, Tom Johnston chose not to mention the National Insurance Act in his overview of 1911. Regarded now as the foundation stone of Britain's Welfare State, this initiative of the Liberal administration in which Asquith was prime minister and David Lloyd George the Minister for Pensions provided health and unemployment insurance for workers for the first time. Those who earned less than £160 per annum were to contribute fourpence a week, their employers threepence and the government twopence. Health insurance and the right to consult what became known as the panel doctor did not yet cover workers' families or the unemployed.

Germany had introduced compulsory national insurance as far back as 1884. Lloyd George used this in support of Britain's proposed scheme, arguing that we should be 'putting ourselves in this field on a level with Germany. We should not emulate them only in armaments.' Unfortunately, that race was already being hard run and no one seemed able to stop it, although some people did try.

On the same day as they previewed the Scottish Exhibition, the *Glasgow Herald* published an account of the inaugural meeting at the Mansion House in London of the Anglo-German Friendship Society. This appointed the Duke of

Argyll Honorary Secretary. Lord Aberdeen was also in
attendance. The aim of the new society was 'to encourage
cordiality and friendly feelings between the British and
German peoples'.

Lord Avebury asked, 'What in the world were we to go to
war about with Germany or Germany with us?' War, he said,
would be disastrous to both countries. 'If European monarchs
were to retain their thrones, if peace was to be maintained,
statesmen must devise some means of stopping this reckless
and ruinous expenditure on armaments, which pressed so
heavily on the springs of industry and aggravated so terribly
and so unnecessarily the unavoidable anxieties and troubles
of life. We were one race, we had a common religion and common interests, we were bound by ties of blood, by centuries of
peace, and a thousand years of immemorial friendship.'

Keir Hardie agreed with Lord Avebury on this one. In the
same edition in which he had written about the struggle to
make a living wage, Tom Johnston reported what Hardie had
written in *Vorwärts*, the German Socialists' counterpart of
the *Forward*. Invited by the editor of the German newspaper
to contribute, Hardie sent fraternal New Year's greetings in
advance of the forthcoming elections to the Reichstag on
12 January 1912:

> It so happens that the Social Democratic Party of
> Germany is universally admitted in this country to be
> wholehearted on the side of peace. If therefore the
> Social Democrats make substantial gains at the polls,
> every one here – anti-German and pro-German alike –
> will accept that as indisputable proof that the German
> people desire peace.
>
> It is for this reason that the result of the elections
> is being awaited with so much interest and why thou-
> sands of people who are not themselves Socialists
> are praying for the success of the German Social
> Democratic Party on 12th January.

A great Socialist triumph on that day would not only sweep the clouds of war from off the political horizon but would also make it easy for an understanding to be reached between Germany and Great Britain concerning future naval policy and thus the taxpayers of both countries would be relieved of the crushing burden which the present rivalry in Dreadnought building imposes.

Meanwhile, back at Kelvingrove, the fine summer of 1911 and the colourful exhibits, pageants and concerts of the Scottish Exhibition were fast becoming a fond memory. The event lives on in a few photographs, postcards and souvenirs. It had been hugely successful, surpassing all expectations.

It's only a pity that the corner of the park in which we're standing allows us to see the Angel of Death, lurking in the shadows under the rustling leaves of the autumn's trees as the lights of Kelvingrove's last great exhibition dimmed for the final time.

8

Radicals, Reformers & Martyrs: The Roots of Red Clydeside

*'George the Third and last, and
damnation to all crowned heads.'*

The Red Clydesiders had impressive forebears from whom
they drew strength and inspiration. Many were driven by
their Christian faith. They read their Bible, took its teachings to heart and saw Christ as the first socialist. Protestants
looked back to the Covenanters of the seventeenth century
and their fight to worship God in the way they thought He
wanted them to. Devout Catholics like John Wheatley found
their politics and their faith completely compatible. As an
advert in the *Forward* in December 1911 had it:

Are you a Socialist and a Christian?
Then for any Sake DO SOMETHING …
Get a copy of Brewster's Sermons (cost 6d., or 7d., per post), from the
Reformers' Bookstall. Read it and LEND it!
Brewster was the great Chartist minister of Paisley Abbey, and his Sermons
are the most eloquent Labour Appeals in the English Language.
MAKE MORE SOCIALISTS:
If you send 7d., we will post you a copy.
BUT DO SOMETHING!

In January 1926 the socialist newspaper carried an extract
from a sermon preached by the Reverend John Munro, who

was also Labour parliamentary candidate for East Renfrew.
He was in absolutely no doubt that 'the ideals of the Labour
Party are the ideals of the old Testament prophets, thousands
of years ago'. The italics which follow are his:

> We come to the founder of our Christian faith, the head
> of our Church, Jesus, the Carpenter of Nazareth. He
> fulfilled the sayings of these Old Testament prophets.
> He went further than any of them. 'Never man spake
> like this man,' the Bible says.
>
> He was a carpenter to trade, worked in the little
> Highland village of Nazareth, reading a great deal,
> and thinking a great deal.
>
> He set out to preach what we now call his gospel.
> He took with him as comrades a few labouring men,
> three or four fisherman, a farm labourer, and *one at
> least (Simon Zelotes) who had lost his job because of his vio-
> lent political opinions.*

Scotland's history also inspired the Red Clydesiders, although
many of them, like Communist Harry McShane, would have
no truck with a romanticised view of it, especially when it
came to kings and queens. In *The History of the Working Classes
in Scotland,* Tom Johnston took a similar and characteristically
robust view. He was particularly scathing about the hero of
Bannockburn. Since most ordinary Scots in the Middle Ages
lived as vassals to an overlord, for Johnston the battles fought
by Robert the Bruce were 'facetiously termed "The War of
Independence"'. He quoted Thomas Carlyle's comments on
Sir Walter Scott's *Tales of a Grandfather.* 'It is noteworthy that
the nobles of the country (Scotland) have maintained a quite
despicable behaviour since the days of Wallace downwards – a
selfish, ferocious, famishing, unprincipled set of hyenas, from
whom at no time, and in no way, has the country derived any
benefit whatsoever.'

Yet Johnston quotes Wallace too, using words attributed

to him when talking of the influence his uncle the Priest of
Dunipace had on him. By tradition, this was the man who
told his nephew, 'I have brought you to the ring – dance
according to your skill.'

> *Dico tibi verum; Libertas optima rerum,*
> *Nunquam servili sub nexu, vivito fili!*
>
> My son, I tell thee soothfastlie
> No gift is like to liberty.
> Then never live in slaverie!

All these words and more can be read on the dramatic, larger-
than-life statue of William Wallace which towers over Union
Terrace Gardens in Aberdeen.

Red Clydeside can be viewed as a class and economic
struggle, bosses and workers pitted against each other in a
never-ending battle. One of the slogans of the Wobblies, the
Industrial Workers of the World, neatly sums this up: 'The
interests of capital and labour can never be the same.' It may
then be somewhat ironic that Clydeside's innate radical bent
has roots in Glasgow's long history as a city of merchants
and traders. Such entrepreneurs had to be forward-looking,
always seeking opportunities, always willing to embrace
change. In the eighteenth century Glasgow and the Clyde
grew prosperous on the back of such business zeal, most
especially through the tobacco trade with America.

By the middle of the 1700s, the city was importing half of
all the tobacco produced in Virginia and North Carolina.
Although some of this was processed in Glasgow, much was
sold on, carried across the narrow waist of Scotland from where
it was re-exported to Holland and Belgium. It wasn't only the
Tobacco Lords who profited from this. Glasgow's factories
and mills geared up to send the tobacco ships back across the
Atlantic with the many different goods the American colonists
needed. The Workshop of the World was in business.

There was a trade in ideas too. Scots of the Age of Enlightenment watched with intense interest as Americans sought to free themselves from the British Crown and establish a new kind of government, one in which the people had a say, although sadly not the African slaves on whose unpaid labour the tobacco trade was so reliant. Scotland is only now beginning to face up to its extensive involvement in the slave trade.

That the people should even be thought of as being entitled to have their say was a profoundly radical idea. As far as most of Scotland's gentry and aristocracy were concerned, democracy was not something to be aspired to but something to be resisted at all costs. In the same way, reform was also a dirty word.

Decades before the American Revolution, in the Glasgow of the 1740s, merchants and traders were beginning to find the deference demanded by the gentry irksome. It got in the way of business, slowed everything down, put unnecessary checks on commercial and industrial progress. At Glasgow University at the same time, Francis Hutcheson was lecturing during Sunday evening extramural classes open to townsfolk as well as students on the need for religious tolerance and political liberty. The Ulster-born son of a Scottish father, he had been preaching this gospel for years before the Jacobite army under Bonnie Prince Charlie occupied Glasgow over Christmas and New Year 1745-6.

Charles Edward Stuart was never a noted fan of democracy. Many of those who rallied to his standard were seeing in him and the '45 the only focus for their discontent over Scotland's loss of independence a generation before and their desire for change and reform. Indeed, it can be argued that the Jacobites of 1745 forged a political movement ahead of its time. In the days before democracy, how else was change to be brought about other than by fighting for it?

One crucial principle Francis Hutcheson advocated was that people should see themselves as citizens and not subjects of the state. If you lived under a repressive government it

was not only to be expected that you would rebel, it was your duty to rebel. His ideas may well have influenced some of the Jacobites of 1745. Later in the century they certainly had an impact on the Americans who fought for and won the United States' independence from Britain.

Thomas Muir of Huntershill, whose home in Bishopbriggs still stands, was another man who believed tyranny should be challenged wherever it was encountered, a view which got him into trouble when he was a student at Glasgow University in the late eighteenth century. Originally destined for the ministry, he transferred to Edinburgh and studied law instead.

When he graduated and began to practise his trade, 'his rooms were the reform centre in Edinburgh'. Muir became a leading light of the *Friends of the People*, helping found branches throughout central Scotland. Tom Johnston wrote of him:

> Muir was a born rebel, and gathered about him everyone who had sympathies with the French Revolution, as a magnet attracts iron filings. It was he who organised a meeting of the middle classes in the Star Hotel, Glasgow, on the 30th day of October, 1792, for the purpose of forming a Friends of the People Society in the city which should co-operate with the London Society in demanding 'equal political representation and shorter parliaments'; it was he who conceived and organised the Convention of the Reform Societies for the December following in Edinburgh; it was he who framed the Convention's standing orders; it was he who denounced leaders, and congratulated the Convention upon paying little attention to leaders; it was he who insisted, despite the frantic pleadings of the milder conventionists, upon reading the treasonable address from the revolutionary society of United Irishmen ...

Nor did he confine himself to the middle classes. Thomas Muir of Huntershill believed democracy was for everyone:

> It was he who toured the weaving districts and addressed the mobs at Kirkintilloch, Kilmarnock, Paisley, Lennoxtown, and innumerable other places; it was he who, though, declaring himself meantime no Republican and setting his face steadily against riot and insurrection as being 'more likely than not to harm the people's cause,' inspired the three hundred delegates of the Edinburgh Convention to conclude the proceedings by standing, and holding up each his right hand, take a solemn oath to live free or die. Suddenly the Government swooped down upon the agitators.

In all this revolutionary fervour three Edinburgh printers drank a toast to 'George the Third and last, and damnation to all crowned heads'. They were sentenced to nine months' hard labour. An excuse to arrest Thomas Muir came when letters intended for him went instead to a different Mr Muir, who handed them over to the authorities.

These letters which so unluckily went astray contained information on the distribution of pamphlets written by Muir of Huntershill. One of the seditious statements he had made in these political tracts was to describe the House of Commons as 'a vile junta of aristocrats'. Those words alone were enough to get him arrested. It was 1793, and he was 28 years old. Released on bail, he travelled to France, where he tried in vain to persuade the revolutionary government not to guillotine Louis XVI and Marie Antoinette because this would damn the cause of reform in other countries. On his return to Scotland he was arrested when he stepped ashore at Stranraer and taken to Edinburgh for trial. He had the misfortune to come up before the deeply unpleasant Lord Braxfield, notorious as a hanging judge, but remained defiant when he spoke in his own defence:

> As for me, I am careless and indifferent to my fate. I
> can look danger and I can look death in the face, for I
> am shielded by the consciousness of my own rectitude.
> I may be condemned to languish in the recesses of
> a dungeon, I may be doomed to ascend the scaffold;
> nothing can deprive me of the recollection of the
> past – nothing can destroy my inward peace of mind
> arising from the remembrance of having discharged
> my duty.

Lord Braxfield responded with spluttering distaste for
the French and disbelief at the gall of those who dared to
demand democracy and universal suffrage. Braxfield spoke
the broadest of Scots, reportedly encouraging one of the
jury members to, 'Come awa', Maister Horner, come awa',
and help us to hang ane o' thae damned scoundrels!' His
response to Thomas Muir has come down to us translated
into Standard English.

> And what kind of folks were they? I never liked the
> French all the days of my life, and now I hate them
> … Multitudes of ignorant weavers … Mr Muir might
> have known that no attention could be paid to such
> a rabble. What right had they to representation? I
> could have told them that Parliament would never
> listen to their petition. How could they think of it?
> A Government in every country should be just like
> a corporation, and in this country it is made up of
> the landed interest which alone has a right to be
> represented.

Muir and his fellow defendants were found guilty and sentenced to 14 years of penal servitude in Australia. The French
tried unsuccessfully to rescue him on his way there.

Once he was in Botany Bay, Thomas Muir's social status
allowed him more freedom than other convicts. Three years

into his sentence he took advantage of this to make good his escape. After an extraordinary series of adventures which included a shipwreck and a violent clash at sea with a British frigate, he eventually made it back to Europe, where he found refuge in France.

Fighting in the naval skirmish had cost him an eye and a shattered cheekbone. His health never recovered from his injuries or the exertions of his journey halfway across the world. The Radical from Bishopbriggs died at Chantilly in France in 1799 at the age of 34. One hundred years later Tom Johnston pronounced an angry epitaph:

> He had given his life for political democracy in the land of his birth; perhaps had he known that the Scots people would value their franchises so lightly that they would hand them over regularly at election times to Braxfield's class – had he foreseen that, perhaps he had spared himself the sacrifice!

Muir was an inspiration to people in his own time, including Robert Burns. The poet might have had to keep his head down for the sake of his job as an exciseman and, more importantly, as he himself wrote, for the sake of 'having a wife and little ones', but his radicalism was never very far below the surface. It's believed Burns started writing *Scots Wha Hae* on the first day of Thomas Muir's trial and that the stirring words refer not only to Bruce and Wallace but also to Muir.

The harsh treatment meted out to the Radicals of the 1790s did not stop continuing political protest and agitation for reform. Twenty-one years after Muir of Huntershill died in France came the Radical Rising of 1820. The economic depression which followed the Napoleonic wars and the increasing pace of the Industrial Revolution helped fuel demands for reform throughout Britain.

More and more people had been attracted to Britain's

cities with the promise of work in mills and factories. The economic slump which follows all wars led to many of them losing their jobs. An infamous clash came at St Peter's Fields in Manchester in 1819, when a meeting calling for parliamentary reform and an extension of the right to vote was attacked by cavalry armed with swords. Eighteen people died in the Battle of Peterloo and 500 were wounded, including 100 women.

In the west of Scotland the same discontent came to a head in the spring of 1820. The government played the dirtiest of tricks, employing agents provocateurs to stir genuine radicals and reformers into actions which would lead to disaster. Spreading rumours that a revolution was planned throughout the British Isles, they chose a sadly appropriate date to post placards all over Glasgow and towns and villages in a wide area around it.

On April Fool's Day 1820, a Sunday, churchgoers found themselves confronted by an 'ADDRESS TO THE INHABITANTS OF GREAT BRITAIN AND IRELAND'. Purporting to be from the 'Committee of Organisation for forming a Provisional Government, Glasgow, April 1, 1820', it was a call to arms. 'Liberty or death is our motto, and we have sworn to *return home* in triumph or return no more!'

Disinformation spread by the government spies makes it hard to get at the truth of the Radical Rising but the discontent and the desire for change were real and profound. Having provoked the fight, the government readied itself to meet the revolution with lethal force. Tom Johnston again: 'Local eruptions were disregarded; the Government was in no hurry; the troops could bide their time until a Radical army of ill-armed, ill-disciplined rebel weavers had been gathered, and then, in one great carnage, would be taught a lesson that would serve to humiliate two or three generations of the discontented common folk.'

One of those rebel weavers was Andrew Hardie, a young Glasgow man. He and about 80 other men rendezvoused

on the hill which is now the Necropolis behind Glasgow Cathedral. There they were met by government spies masquerading as fellow Radicals and persuaded to march to the Carron Iron Works at Falkirk to seize cannons and meet up with a rebel army marching up from England. This army did not exist, an invention of the agents provocateurs.

The Radical army marched via Condorrat and Castlecary. At Condorrat Andrew Hardie met John Baird, the local smith, and the two men found themselves elected leaders of their small force. It grew smaller still as the government spies gradually peeled off. Fear also thinned the ranks, so that only about 50 men reached Bonnymuir, where the next bloody act of the drama was played out. As ever, Tom Johnston tells it beautifully, describing what happened when this ill-equipped army of weavers marched 'straight into the arms of the 10th Hussars':

> What followed is well-known. How the troops dashed upon them, and how they crouched behind a dyke and fought desperately until almost every man of them was wounded and some were killed, and how nineteen weary and wounded men that night lay prisoners of war in Stirling Castle. That was the great battle of Bonnymuir … the 'revolution' fell to pieces in a single night.

Blood was shed in Paisley and Greenock too, where six men died when the jail was stormed in a successful attempt to free Radical prisoners.

In Strathaven in Lanarkshire, James Wilson, a stocking-maker in his 60s, marched with another band which had been filled with false promises of a new dawn by the agents provocateurs. Wilson had carried a banner which read 'Scotland free or a desert! Strathaven Union'. They arrested him and hanged him in Jail Square in Glasgow at the end

of August 1820, afterwards giving him a pauper's burial 'as a last mean mark of contempt'. That night his daughter and niece disinterred his body and took him home to Strathaven. He had wanted to be buried 'in the dust of his fathers'.

John Baird and Andrew Hardie were hanged at Stirling just over a week later, on Friday, 8 September 1820. Eighteen other Radical leaders had been transported to Australia, but Prime Minister Viscount Castlereagh had called for a 'lesson on the scaffold'. Now in the National Library of Scotland, a contemporary broadside costing one penny gave a report of the execution:

> Yesterday, 8th September, 1820, the preparation for the execution of these unfortunate men having been completed, the previous night, this morning the scaffold appeared to the view of the inhabitants. On each side the scaffold was placed a coffin, at the head of which was a tub, filled with saw-dust, destined to receive the head. To the side of the tub was affixed a block.

The prisoners, it was noted, were 'respectably dressed in black'. Decency at executions was much prized. This was not bloody murder. This was justice. Well guarded by soldiers, they were marched out of Stirling Castle and down to the prison. The authorities were nervous, fearing trouble from the crowd. Although they had ensured it was smaller than it might have been, people did have to be there to witness the proceedings. How else would the lesson be taught?

When they reached the scaffold, 'Hardie looked up and smiled – Baird surveyed the dreadful apparatus with earnestness, but composure. Both prisoners, but especially Hardie, looked eagerly and keenly at their veiled companion, but did not address him.' Their veiled companion was the executioner.

Three ministers were also in attendance. Prayers were said and a few verses of the fifty-first psalm 'from the 7th verse, were sung by the prisoners and others present, Hardie giving out two lines at a time, in a clear and distinct voice, and sung the same without any tremulency'.

> Purge me with hyssop, and I shall be clean:
> Wash me, and I shall be whiter than snow.
> Make me to hear joy and gladness;
> That the bones which thou hast broken may rejoice.
> Hide thy face from my sins,
> And blot out all mine iniquities.
> Create in me a clean heart, O God;
> And renew a right spirit within me.

This was the same psalm James Wilson had asked the crowd who witnessed his execution to sing with him before he was hanged.

'Some refreshment being offered,' says the broadside of the Stirling executions, 'Hardie took a glass of sherry, and Baird a glass of port.' Both men then mounted the scaffold. It was now about half past two in the afternoon. John Baird addressed the crowd first, advising them to study their Bibles. Andrew Hardie told them, 'I die a martyr to the cause of truth and justice.' Instead of going to the pub to drink to him and Baird, people ought to go home and pray. At about ten to three, on a signal from Hardie, the men were hanged.

> After hanging half an hour, they were cut down and placed upon the coffins, with their heads upon a block; the headsman then came forward; he was a little man, apparently about 18 years of age; he wore a black crape over his face, a hairy cap, and a black gown. On his appearance there was a cry of murder. He struck the neck of Hardie thrice before it was severed; then

held it up with both hands, saying: 'This is the head of
a traitor.' He severed the head of Baird at two blows,
and held it up in the same manner, and used the same
words. The coffins were then removed, and the crowd
peaceably dispersed.

In *The King's Jaunt*, John Prebble says that this young heads-
man was a medical student. It was a long time since anyone
in Scotland had been hanged, drawn and quartered. The last
had been the Jacobites executed after the '45, and they were
all put to death at Carlisle, York and London. Perhaps Tam
Young, the hangman at Stirling, baulked at carrying out the
butchery.

The two men were buried in a single grave outside Stirling
Castle. Almost 30 years later a group of Glasgow Radicals ex-
humed them and took them back to Glasgow. They reburied
them in Sighthill Cemetery and raised a monument there to
the Radicals of 1820.

Only 12 years after Wilson, Baird and Hardie were so bar-
barically and publicly put to death came the Great Reform
Act of 1832, the measure which led the way to parliamentary
democracy in Britain. Andrew Hardie's mother put these
lines up on a card in her window.

> Britons, rejoice, Reform is won!
> But 'twas the cause
> Lost me my son.

In the 1840s the Chartists took up the fight. Seventy years on
from their struggles there remained plenty of work for the
Red Clydesiders to do, still a muddy and rough road to be
travelled until real democracy was achieved. Some might say
we're still on it.

Scotland's Radicals continue to inspire. They always have.
In 1938, the Camlachie Branch of the ILP produced a huge
banner in support of the people of Spain, fighting a civil war

against Fascism. It can be seen today in Glasgow's People's Palace. In large red letters, the legend reads:

THOMAS MUIR
BAIRD AND HARDIE
DIED
THAT YOU SHOULD BE FREE
TO CHOOSE YOUR GOVERNMENT.

WORKERS IN SPAIN
ARE DYING
BECAUSE THEY DARED TO
CHOOSE THEIR OWN
GOVERNMENT

UNITE FOR THE STRUGGLE!

9

Halloween at the High Court

*'It was afterwards found that the hard missiles
thrown at the Judge were apples.'*

In 1911 suffragettes' hopes were both raised and dashed. First
came the announcement that a parliamentary committee was
to draft a bill to give women the vote. Towards the end of the
year, Prime Minister Asquith announced the bill was to be
shelved for the time being.

As the frustration of many suffragettes boiled over
into anger, direct action and much smashing of windows,
one Glasgow glazier famously found a silver lining. James
Caldwell's advert in the *Forward* in 1912 advises potential customers that 'SUFFRAGETTES MAY BREAK WINDOWS, BUT
I AM THE WEE BOY [THAT] CAN PUT THEM IN.'

The destruction soon escalated way beyond the breaking of windows. In Scotland, militant suffragettes burned
down the railway station at Leuchars in Fife and the medieval church of Whitekirk in East Lothian, planted a bomb
at Glasgow's Botanic Gardens and tried to blow up Burns'
Cottage at Alloway. In June 1913, English suffragette Emily
Davison stepped out in front of the king's horse at the Derby
and sacrificed her life to the cause.

Many women were appalled by violent tactics and set their
faces completely against them. Others seem to have been
ready to carry out acts of terrorism without a qualm. Others
again had to do some real soul-searching before they could
contemplate less violent but still destructive acts. Helen

Crawfurd of Glasgow was one of those. Militant suffragettes were planning a window-smashing raid in London, to take place over three days in March 1912. When Scottish suffragettes started talking about heading south and joining in, she sought guidance in her husband's church.

Alexander Crawfurd was a powerful preacher, with a sonorous voice and a dramatic delivery. That Sunday he chose to weave his sermon around the story of Christ throwing the moneylenders out of the temple. All unknowing, he led his wife to her decision. If Christ could be militant, then so could she. She went to London, smashed a few windows, was arrested and tried and sentenced to one month in Holloway. It was another eye-opening experience for her and often a distressing one, giving her an insight into the lives of the poor London women who were her fellow inmates.

While all this breaking of glass might sound pointlessly destructive, the suffragettes did have a point to make. The law dealt very severely with crimes against property. In contrast, crimes against people, especially young girls who were raped or sexually abused, were often dealt with very leniently. In their destruction of property, the suffragettes were making a lot of noise to draw attention to their cause but also protesting against this injustice.

Helen Crawfurd was in Holloway with other suffragette friends from Glasgow, including Janie Allan and Frances and Margaret McPhun. When Janie Allan went on hunger strike, she was force-fed for a week. Ten thousand people in Glasgow signed a petition protesting against her imprisonment and ill-treatment.

The government which had not had time to discuss a bill bringing in female suffrage found time to pass a new law which became known as the Cat and Mouse Act. This allowed the authorities to release suffragettes on hunger strike on licence. Once they had spent time at home eating normally and regaining their health they were re-arrested and the whole cycle began again.

Ethel Moorhead was one of those who did time in Holloway after the window-smashing raid. Born to Irish parents, she lived for many years in Scotland, working as an artist at her studio in Dundee. She earned a fearsome reputation as one of Scotland's most militant suffragettes, as her entry in *The Biographical Dictionary of Scottish Women* relates: 'When her father died in 1911, Ethel Moorhead joined the WSPU. Using a string of aliases she smashed windows in London and a showcase at the Wallace Monument in Stirling; threw an egg at Churchill and pepper at the police: attacked a teacher with a dog whip; wrecked police cells and was involved in several arson attempts.'

It was attempted fire-raising which brought her to the dock at the High Court in Glasgow in October 1913, on trial with her co-accused, Dorothea Chalmers Smith. Helen Crawford was one of their many friends filling the public gallery.

Dorothea Chalmers Smith was a doctor, mother of six children and wife of the minister of Calton Parish Church in Glasgow's East End. She and Ethel Moorhead stood accused of having attempted to burn down a large empty house in Glasgow's West End. As the indictment read:

> ... the charge against you is that you did, on July 23, 1913, break into an unoccupied dwelling-house at No. 6 Park Gardens, Glasgow, and did convey or cause to be conveyed thereto, a quantity of firelighters, firewood, a number of pieces of candles, a quantity of paper, cotton wool, cloth, and a number of tins of paraffin oil and did place these, along with three venetian blinds, at or against a wooden door in a passage on the first floor of said house, and this you did with intent to set fire to said door and burn said house.

Dr Chalmers Smith and Ethel Moorhead refused to plead either guilty or not guilty. The judge told them he'd take that as a plea of not guilty and suggested they ought to have

got themselves a legal adviser. Ethel Moorhead's sharp retort drew laughter from their friends in the public gallery. 'We generally find that they make a muddle of it. We prefer to defend ourselves.'

The trial proceeded. One witness testified that he had been taken to Duke Street prison to see if he could identify the woman who had called at the solicitor's office where he worked asking to be shown around the big empty house in Park Gardens. He couldn't be sure. When he had visited the prison both of the accused had been in bed and had refused to get up. Not to be outdone by the troublesome females in the dock, the judge tried for a laugh. Now he saw her fully dressed, could the witness identify the woman who had called at his place of employment? The witness could. The two would-be arsonists were found guilty and sentenced to eight months' imprisonment. It was at this point that pandemonium broke out in the court.

The suffragettes in the public gallery had risen to their feet as soon as the judge had pronounced the sentence. Now they began shouting. 'Pitt Street! Pitt Street!' They yelled the name over and over again. They hurled projectiles down into the court. The *Glasgow Herald* was horrified by what it called this 'scene of indescribable disorder and confusion … creating a disturbance probably without parallel in a Glasgow Court of Justice'.

Some two weeks earlier, a much more lenient sentence had been handed down in a Glasgow court. A brothel at Pitt Street near Charing Cross had been raided and the rumour going the rounds was that several of Glasgow's prominent citizens had been found there enjoying what the house of ill repute had to offer. Yet they had suffered no censure and the husband and wife who ran the brothel had been sentenced to only two weeks in prison.

The *Glasgow Herald*'s sister paper, the *Evening Times*, gave a less formal account of the noisy protest at the court. 'Judge Pelted' read its headline. Under a subtitle of 'Pelting the

Bench', it described the uproar which broke out as soon as sentence was passed.

> A storm of protest from most of the women present was immediately raised. In chorus they shouted 'Shame, shame,' and, without further warning, a missile was hurled at the bench by someone near the front of the area. It struck the woodwork below the judge's seat with a resounding blow and fell to the floor.
>
> So sudden was the attack that Lord Salvesen involuntarily raised his arms as though to protect his face. The first missile was followed by a second which just missed the head of the clerk (Mr. Slight) and also struck the front woodwork of the bench.
>
> A scene of wild confusion followed.

Neither the *Glasgow Herald* nor the *Evening Times* reported that the women had shouted 'Pitt Street, Pitt Street!' as well as 'Shame, shame!' What the *Evening Times* did solemnly tell its readers was: 'It was afterwards found that the hard missiles thrown at the Judge were apples.'

So the suffragettes had gone prepared. Helen Crawfurd did note that the apples were small ones. Whether they chose these because the trial took place a fortnight before Halloween and there were plenty around or because small apples might hurt less – or perhaps more – she doesn't say. Glasgow, as it always does, saw the humour in the situation.

Like the other Glasgow newspapers, the *Glasgow News* carried a report on the trial the day after it took place and the day after that a cartoon depicting the scene in the court room. The story was obviously too good to let go. Whoever drew the cartoon must have witnessed the mayhem at first hand. The drawing perfectly depicts Mr Slight, the clerk of the court, ducking to avoid the flying apples. Some artistic licence allows both the wigged and gowned judge and prosecuting lawyer to get one in the eye while gripping a fork

between their teeth as though they were dooking for them at a Halloween party.

What happened after that was not so comical. In February 1914 Ethel Moorhead, who had been released and re-arrested under the Cat and Mouse Act, became the first woman in Scotland to be force-fed. This happened at Perth Prison. Many had believed Scotland would never resort to such horrific treatment of prisoners, especially when those prisoners were women. When in the summer of 1914 it emerged that two suffragette prisoners in Perth had been force-fed *per rectum*, the public recoiled in horror. A vigil was held outside the prison to protest and Helen Crawfurd was one of those who took part.

Freed by her husband's death in May 1914 to become more active in her political endeavours, she was now living in the West End of Glasgow with her brothers, William and John, and her sister, Jean. They had put their money together so as to be able to rent a flat in Hyndland and hire a housekeeper to look after them.

She was in Perth in July 1914 when the king visited the fair city as part of a Scottish tour. One placard displayed at a window extended a mock-invitation to the royal visitor: 'Visit Your Majesty's Torture Chamber in Perth Prison'. Then the news came through that two suffragettes had tried to blow up Robert Burns's Cottage in Alloway.

Force-feeding of suffragettes had garnered much public sympathy. The assault on Burns's Cottage threatened to swing the pendulum as far back in the other direction as it could possibly go. The *Glasgow Herald* described the attack as a 'dastardly outrage':

> Alloway Outrage
> Attempt to Blow up Burns's Cottage
> Suffragist in Custody
>
> A dastardly attempt was made in the early hours of yesterday morning by suffragists to fire and blow

up Burns's Cottage, Alloway, the birthplace of the
national poet, which is annually visited by thousands
of pilgrims from all parts of the world. The attempted
outrage was fortunately frustrated by the timely
appearance on the scene of the night watchman, but
the fact that an attempt was made to destroy a shrine
that Scotsmen in all parts of the world regard as sacred
has roused in the locality the most intense indignation.

There was further outrage when one of the two suffragists
responsible – *suffragette* had still not entirely caught on – was
found to be Frances Parker, niece of Lord Kitchener, the man
whose eyes were to follow people from the First World War
recruiting poster telling them that their country needed
them. Fanny Parker's accomplice at Alloway escaped by
bike, leaving behind two canisters, each containing 4lb of
gunpowder.

Engaged to address the crowd at Perth that evening after
the news had broken, fearing there might be people within
the throng feeling hostile towards all suffragettes as a result,
Helen Crawfurd summoned up her courage and the ghost
of Robert Burns. She started by telling her listeners it was his
words which had inspired her to be able to speak to them
after the shock of the attempted destruction of his childhood
home. In illustration, she quoted from 'Scots Wha' Hae'.

Wha' wad be a traitor knave,
Wha' wad fill a coward's grave
Wha' sae base as be a slave
Let him turn and flee

She explained that the two suffragettes who had tried to
destroy Burns's Cottage were not Scottish and simply could
not understand the high esteem in which all Scots, men and
women, held him. She finished by quoting Burns on the subject of the emancipation of women:

> While Europe's eye is fix'd on mighty things,
> The fate of Empires and the fall of Kings;
> While quacks of State must each produce his plan,
> And even children lisp the Rights of Man;
> Amid this mighty fuss just let me mention,
> The Rights of Woman merit some attention.

Giving Scotland's suffragettes the stalwart support he always did, Tom Johnston quoted Helen Crawfurd's speech to the crowd at Perth in full in the *Forward* of 18 July 1914.

Tried at Ayr Sheriff Court, Fanny Parker also quoted Burns, as the *Glasgow Herald* wearily put it, 'at some length'. She also declared: 'You Scotsmen used to be proud of Burns; now you have taken to torturing women.'

On 29 July 1914 Glasgow's *Daily Record* announced that the Austrians had declared war on Serbia. This dramatic news shared the front page with news much closer to home. The previous evening Mrs Pankhurst had visited Glasgow, where she spoke to a large audience in St Andrew's Halls. The *Daily Record*'s headlines were dramatic.

> WILD RIOT IN GLASGOW
> MRS PANKHURST ARRESTED
> REVOLVER SHOTS IN ST ANDREW'S HALLS
> Amid a scene of wild riot in St Andrew's Halls, Glasgow, last night, Mrs. Pankhurst, the suffragette leader, was arrested. The meeting, which was held under the auspices of the W.S.P.U., had an audience of about 5,000, the vast majority of whom were ladies.
>
> Mrs. Pankhurst, despite the vigilance of the police, entered the hall by one of the main entrances wearing a large picture hat with a yellow feather and trimmings, and a thick black veil.

You wonder how they could have missed her. Janie Allan was convinced the revolver shots were an indicator that

a government conspiracy was afoot to assassinate Mrs Pankhurst. In the event, the war between the government and the suffragettes was resolved by the conflict which was about to engulf Europe.

On 4 August 1914 Britain declared war on Germany. The suffragettes immediately called a truce with the British government.

Red Clydeside, however, was just about to initiate hostilities.

10

Not in My Name

'This murder business.'

As Red Clydesider Willie Gallacher wrote in his vivid auto-biography, *Revolt on the Clyde*:

> What terrible attraction a war can have! The wild excitement, the illusion of wonderful adventure and the actual break in the deadly monotony of working-class life! Thousands went flocking to the colours in the first days, not because of any 'love of country,' not because of any high feeling of 'patriotism,' but because of the new, strange and thrilling life that lay before them. Later the reality of the fearsome slaughterhouse, with all its long agony of filth and horror, turned them from buoyant youth to despair or madness.

Yet there were thousands who were passionately opposed to the war from the outset, many of them on Red Clydeside. On 15 August 1914, above a cartoon depicting a ferocious and wild-eyed female warrior headed 'Europe Goes Stark Mad', the *Forward* published a report on a peace demonstration held on Glasgow Green, estimating that 5,000 people were there. There's no way of corroborating those numbers as only the socialist newspaper covered the story, subtitling the piece 'Boycotted by Press'.

The peace demonstration was organised by the ILP and the Glasgow branch of the Peace Society. The *Forward* was at pains to assure its readers that the demonstrators had come from a broad social spectrum:

> The gathering was Cosmopolitan in character and included doctors and dock labourers and rebels of every possible brand from mild peace advocates to the wildest of revolutionaries. One thing was made obvious by the meeting: that the war is unpopular with people who think, while the rise in food prices is tempering the bellies of those who don't think.

One of the speakers was John Wheatley of the ILP, who had now been elected Councillor Wheatley. Another was his fellow ILP member Patrick Dollan. All of the speakers condemned the war, telling the crowd that 'the working people [of Britain and Germany] have no quarrel with each other'. This was reiterated by the chairman of the Peace Society, a Miss Adams. After she and her fellow members of the Society had spoken, resolutions were read out which had been agreed upon by: '... huge gatherings of workers in Austria, Germany and France against war. These workers did not want war, and yet, in spite of their friendship for each other, the shadow of Death overcast Europe. Few homes in Europe would escape scathless [*sic*] from the passage of that shadow.'

As we all now know, Miss Adams was proved horribly right in her prediction. At the time many other people really did believe it would all be over by Christmas. Harry McShane was one of them. In his autobiography *No Mean Fighter* he wrote that when the First World War broke out in 1914, 'everyone, including the socialists, thought it would be fought by professional armies and volunteers'.

Those volunteers continued to flock to the colours. Conscription had not yet been introduced, nor did there

seem any need for it. McShane too described the overheated atmosphere at the start of the war:

> A terrible war fever developed. Men rushed to join the army hoping that the war wouldn't be all over by the time they got to the front; they had to march in civilian clothes because there weren't enough uniforms to go round. Many young people, particularly those who were unemployed, were caught up in the adventure of the thing. On every hoarding there was a picture of Kitchener, the Secretary for War, pointing his finger, and saying 'Your Country Needs You'. There he was, and then along came daft middle-class women with white feathers trying to drive young men into the army.

As the cenotaph in Glasgow's George Square tells us, 200,000 went from Glasgow alone. Standing guard over the names of thousands more is Clydebank's beautiful art deco war memorial and, around the country, all the other impassive stone angels and sad soldiers, heads bowed over their rifles. Those who refused to be caught up in the war fever were swimming against a rushing tide. As many of them were to find out, on a personal level they were also treading a dangerous path.

The ILP was split over the war, although Keir Hardie knew exactly where he stood. He had always been against it. By 1915 he was failing fast, his ill health exacerbated by his efforts to prevent the slaughter having been in vain. In his biography of James Maxton, Gordon Brown offers a poignant vignette of Keir Hardie. 'It is said that latterly, because of his staunch opposition to the war, many of his old friends would ignore him or refuse to shake his hand.'

Willie Gallacher was another of those who spoke out against the war from the start. So did John Maclean, who called the fighting 'this murder business'. In her biography

of him, his daughter Nan Milton describes how he and other socialists and Marxists helped gather together those who were against the war.

From as early as the end of 1914, Maclean organised open-air Sunday evening meetings on the corner of Renfield Street and Bath Street. His friend and fellow socialist John MacDougall left a description of these, referring to himself at the end of this quote in the third person:

> From the very first the meeting attracted large numbers of Socialists. Sunday by Sunday it grew, as the seriousness of the War situation became plain to even the meanest intelligence, and after a number of weeks it had grown so large that the casual passers-by in Renfield Street were attracted. It is a broad street. It was packed from side to side so that a child could have walked on the heads of the people, and that condition extended a long distance down the street. Week after week there was to be seen a vast body of men and women, standing in tense silence, their attention riveted on the speakers for two or three hours on end, while a succession of speakers kept the meeting going. Maclean's principal assistants were MacDougall, George Pettigrew, Mrs Helen Crawfurd of the ILP and a famous suffragette, and William Gallacher.

The suffragettes might have declared a truce with Lloyd George and the government over votes for women. During the First World War Helen Crawfurd was one of many women who turned her energies to campaigning for peace. In June 1916 she, her friend Agnes Dollan and others established the Women's Peace Crusade, hanselling the new organisation with another mass meeting on Glasgow Green.

James Maxton was another Red Clydesider who was always bitterly opposed to the war. In August 1914 he wrote to his girlfriend Sissie McCallum: 'There's no chance of me

volunteering. I'm working for peace for all I'm worth.' Sissie
was also a teacher, she and Maxton having met while working
as colleagues at a school in Glasgow.

Like Maxton, John Maclean brought all his skills as a
speaker to the fight against the war. At the Bath Street
meetings, standing on a table in the middle of the crowd,
he told them what he and many socialists believed. War 'was
the continuation of the peace competition for trade and for
markets already carried on between the powers before hostilities broke out'. He told his audiences that capitalists and
employers were the real enemy and that they should not join
up to fight in a capitalist war.

> The men they were asked to shoot were their brothers,
> with the same difficulty on Saturdays to find a rent
> for their miserable dwellings, who had to suffer the
> same insults and impertinence from their gaffers and
> foremen. What did it matter if they looked a little dif-
> ferent? And spoke a different language? The Scottish
> miners when on strike had often received financial
> help from the German miners. The international
> solidarity of the working-class was not only the high-
> est moral sentiment that existed in the world, it had
> already found expression in many ways.

None of them was ever going to get away with any of this. As
John MacDougall put it when writing about John Maclean:
'His hearers knew that for these precious words of exhort-
ation and of hope the man would have to pay, and pay dearly.
Would he be shot? Would the traditions of British Liberalism
stand the strain of this unprecedented test when the British
Empire was standing with its back to the wall? Nobody knew.
Would he be drafted into the army like Karl Liebknecht?'

Liebknecht was a German Socialist, much admired by his
British counterparts. James Maxton had a dog called Karl,
named not after Marx but Liebknecht.

The Bath Street protests continued. Pushing it even farther, John Maclean raged against the 'British Junkers' who had introduced DORA, the Defence of the Realm Act. This imposed all kinds of wartime restrictions on freedom of speech and action. A new Munitions Act also enforced draconian rules and regulations.

For the duration of the hostilities strikes were made illegal. Ships and armaments manufactured on the Clyde being crucial to the war effort, nobody in what was now designated the Clyde Munitions Area was allowed to change their job without permission. This was enforced by having to secure a leaving certificate to show to a new employer. The Clyde's workers referred to this as a slave clause, depriving workers of their few hard-won liberties.

At the beginning of 1915 Willie Gallacher and fellow shop stewards including Davie Kirkwood and Arthur McManus formed themselves into the Clyde Workers' Committee. The CWC was soon to clash head-on with the Minister for Munitions, Mr David Lloyd George. For them, as for Maxton, Maclean and MacDougall, the fight against the war and for workers' rights was soon to become very personal indeed.

11

A Woman's Place

'My good lady, go home and sit still.'

Traditional ideas of what constituted women's work, acceptable female activities and behaviour took a hammering during the First World War. The men who marched off to war left huge gaps behind them. These were felt right across the social spectrum, the lack, of course, emotional as well as practical.

During the Glasgow Fair holidays of the summer of 1915, a poignant cartoon appeared in *The Bailie*, Glasgow's normally humorous weekly newspaper. Against the backdrop of a pier on the Firth of Clyde, a young woman sits on a bench under a tree, alone and thoughtful. The caption reads: 'THE "FAIR" WITHOUT THE BRAVE'. *The Bailie* also informed its readers that moonlit cruises doon the watter had been suspended for the duration.

The absence of men threw up some unexpected benefits. *The Bulletin* was a sister paper to the *Glasgow Herald* which specialised in bright and breezy articles accompanied by lots of photographs. Showing lots of smiling young Glasgow gels driving, cranking their open-topped cars into action and inflating their tyres, in August 1915 it reported on this new phenomenon. 'Since the chauffeur went away to the war the motoring girl has come by her own. Many ladies could drive cars in the old days, but the motoring girl may truly be said to be a product of the war. These types seem to enjoy all

the little troubles that afflict the chauffeur, and only refrain from burrowing beneath the car because nowadays that is unnecessary.'

This new ease of movement allowed middle-class women and girls a much greater social and personal freedom. Writing in the women's page of *The Bailie* in that same July of 1915, the unnamed journalist of a review of a book called *The Street of the Seven Stars* recognised this new development. Undoubtedly a lady reporter, she was still rather uncomfortable that a couple in the book were depicted as spending lots of time together '*sans chaperone*', which meant it 'wasn't quite the thing for a Sunday School prize book'. In the same column she made the interesting observation that the current shortage of men meant women were having more opportunity to socialise together and were finding that they enjoyed one another's company.

Language and the codes by which it indicated class was another preoccupation:

> Some years ago a London barrister referred for the first time to his charlady, and now the word he introduced in jest is allowed to describe a very useful section of the community. Within recent weeks we have seen 'lady' car-conductors, 'lady' lamplighters, and later, I suppose, 'lady' scavengers. Even the dignified newspaper just round the corner in Buchanan Street speaks of the 'ladies' appointed to such branches of public work. And why not?
>
> Meantime we have 'female' teachers and 'women' doctors and, instead of clerks 'clerkesses,' a word that offends me only a little less than 'chairman,' when it would not be in the least awkward to say 'chairwoman,' and would convey a sensible meaning without disturbing anybody's prejudices.

Some of us might agree with her on that last point, finding

it risible that the political correctness of our own days actually reinforces gender inequality by choosing the masculine form of a noun as the superior version (when it isn't turning human beings into pieces of furniture).

The Bailie's writer didn't believe the use of the word 'lady' could 'make two classes into one'. It wasn't that she was a snob. She believed completely that 'one woman is as good as another but that doesn't alter the fact that there are differences. As to the "lady" conductors, I like them; and they haven't yet begun to bully women as some of the gentlemen conductors certainly did when the women were elderly and of good social position. The car ladies are exceedingly pleasant, and now that they have left off wearing earrings and lace neckties they are good to look at too.'

A week later *The Bailie* reported again on the lady tram conductors, who don't yet seem to have become *conductresses*, the name by which future generations knew this fearsome form of Glasgow womanhood. The First World War variety were to be dressed in long skirts of Black Watch tartan, allowing *The Bailie* to go off on a flight of fancy that maybe they should also wear sporrans and carry skean dhus. A month later *The Bulletin* took a more serious look at the women working on the trams.

Allegations had been made that the new lady conductors were being overworked. *The Bulletin*'s lady reporter, again of course unnamed, was following up on a story which had appeared in a London newspaper. According to this interloper from south of the border, women working on Glasgow's trams were being asked to put in the same number of hours as the men they had replaced.

'The natural result' of this on one conductress was 'that after a few weeks she had to rest, because the strain was too great'. Even worse than that, when she took the time off to have that rest, she'd been sacked. With the distinct feeling that national pride was at stake here, *The Bulletin*'s intrepid lady reporter picked up her sword of truth. 'Manifestly it was

a matter to be investigated, and Mr James Dalrymple, manager of the Corporation Tramways, was the man to see. So I went up to the flag-bedecked building in Bath Street, and the recruiting sergeants standing at the door grinned as I passed in. I suppose they imagined I was one more applicant for the green and tartan uniform!'

Mr Dalrymple laughed off the story. So did the lady conductors to whom he gave the lady reporter full access: '"Of course we are treated as men in the matter of working hours," said one woman whose husband is in the trenches, "but we took up the work on that understanding, and – what is more important – we are treated as men in the matter of wages, too."'

The lady conductors worked six days a week, eight hours a day. At a total of 48 hours this was a lot less than the 74 hours and more waitresses in Glasgow's tea rooms were putting in. After interviewing a few more lady conductors, the lady reporter declared herself satisfied they did not feel they were being exploited and seemed to enjoy their work. One woman who had been in domestic service said working on the trams was infinitely preferable to doing housework all day long.

More traditional skills were still being valued. On the same page on which they carried the story about the new lady conductors on the trams, *The Bulletin* reported on the knitting achievements of an Ayrshire woman. Anticipating the arrival of winter and the consequent need for comforts for the troops, a smiling older lady is offered as a shining example for other women to follow. 'Mrs Ross, who resides at Darvel, is one of those whose industrious fingers have gone constantly since the first demand went forth. To date she has knitted 60 pairs of heavy sox [sic] for the boys at the front, and declares her willingness to knit more if need be.'

The Bulletin returned to the 'sox' and comforts issue three weeks later, making an appeal to patriotism with just a touch of advertorial in it, and another poignant observation: that there were more soldiers on the front line now so more

women needed to start knitting for them. With winter again approaching, the women's page tells its readers,

> ... we women must set to work again, and knit and sew as hard as we did last winter – and even harder still, because we have more men to knit and sew for than we had last year. It is obvious that a Tommy warmly clad and comfortable must be a more efficient fighting man than a Tommy who is cold and shivering and miserable. And that is just where we women come in. Nowadays, we never hear of the girl who used to announce boastfully that she 'couldn't knit a pair of socks to save her life.' The war has changed all that, and the girl who has reason to boast in these days of war is the one who can knit a 'record' number of socks or mittens or scarves for Tommy within a given time.

The Scotch Wool and Hosiery Stores were happy to give 'special discounts to work-parties buying large quantities of wool', and a free 100-page booklet of knitting patterns could be had from any of their branches. They had 260 of those all over Scotland, 14 in Glasgow alone. Or you could get the booklet by writing to their head office at the simple address of The Worsted Mills, Greenock.

The First World War freed many working-class women and girls from the drudgery of domestic service. Faced with the unthinkable prospect of having to make their own tea and put a few lumps of coal on their own fires, the middle classes whinged about that for the next 20 years, firing off irate letters to newspapers about the 'servant problem'.

Without an army of housekeepers, cooks and maids, a side effect of just not being able to get the staff these days was the encouragement it gave the inventors and manufacturers of labour-saving devices. These did not come cheap. Adverts which appeared in Glasgow newspapers during the First

World War offered electric vacuum cleaners for five guineas. One of those tea room waitresses working for Mr Kerr, the military caterer, would have had to hand over her entire pay for three months to be able to buy one.

Old attitudes continued to die hard, especially when women started working alongside men in industries which had previously been exclusively male preserves. Probably this is why Beardmore's provided a separate canteen for their 'girl munition workers'. They and their canteen gave *The Bulletin*'s lady reporter another subject to write up.

Beardmore's had converted a 'light, bright room' into a canteen for their 300 female workers. Since they worked in shifts around the clock, meals were served throughout the day and night. The food was substantial. On the day the lady reporter went, dinner at one o'clock consisted of lentil soup, meat and potatoes, with rice pudding for dessert.

Wearing 'neat holland overalls and frilled caps', the cooks and canteen staff were unpaid, doing their bit for the war effort. Glasgow College of Domestic Science, the 'Do School' for short, was one of the organisations which recruited and supplied the volunteers.

Given a glamorous makeover, the female munitions worker in her brown overall and unflattering matching hat became one of the war's poster girls throughout Britain, encouraging those other women to do their bit. This archetypal figure is remembered in a beautiful stained-glass window at what was the headquarters of the North British Locomotive Company and then Springburn College. This elegant building is now Flemington House, a centre for small businesses.

Other women from Glasgow, Clydebank and elsewhere in Scotland went off to war themselves, working as nurses, nursing auxiliaries and orderlies. Some joined the Red Cross, whose ambulance train toured Scotland before leaving for France. People queued for hours at Glasgow Central, Paisley Gilmour Street, Greenock, Stirling and elsewhere to view it and make a donation.

Voluntary Aid Detachment nurses served in both world wars. The VADs themselves liked to say that the letters stood for 'Virgins Almost Desperate'.

The Scottish Women's Hospitals grew out of the Scottish Federation of the NUWSS, the National Union of Women's Suffrage Societies. Their moving spirit was Elsie Inglis. She was an Edinburgh doctor and suffragist, one of those vehemently opposed to the use of violence to get the vote. When the war broke out, she immediately offered her services to the War Office.

The reply she got is almost magnificent in its breathtakingly dismissive sexism. 'My good lady, go home and sit still.' Elsie Inglis did the exact opposite. The Scottish Women's Hospitals were soon well-established at Royaumont in France, treating casualties from the Western Front, in Serbia and Russia. They appealed regularly for donations via adverts in the Scottish newspapers.

The Bulletin carried these frequently, as well as stories and pictures of the Scottish nurses and doctors, all women, in their field hospitals on the front line. They were looking for £100,000 to help them care for the wounded. By September 1915, one year into the war, they were able to tell the folks back home they had already cared for more than 1,250 injured soldiers, and they detailed what they needed so they could tend to more.

1. To MAINTAIN the HOSPITAL at ABBAYE DE ROYAUMONT, near Creil (200 beds), under the FRENCH RED CROSS SOCIETY.

2. To establish the new hospital at Troyes (200 beds) under the FRENCH MILITARY AUTHORITIES.

3. To SUPPORT TWO UNITS now at work in SERBIA under the SERBIAN RED CROSS AND MILITARY AUTHORITIES (600 beds).

4. To MAINTAIN an AMBULANCE FLOTTANTE

AT WORK between the Firing Line and the Two Hospitals in France.

5. To PROVIDE MOTOR AMBULANCES for these hospitals. It is hoped that the motorists of Scotland will assist in this appeal.

6. To SUPPLY COMFORTS, MEDICAL NECESSARIES, Etc., to the TROOPS in FRANCE AND SERBIA.

£50 WILL NAME A BED FOR A YEAR.

£350 WILL PROVIDE AND EQUIP A MOTOR AMBULANCE.

Donations could be sent to Mrs Laurie of Greenock or to Dr Elsie Inglis in Edinburgh. *The Bulletin* backed up the advert with photographs of Dr Robertson Butler and her husband, 'two Glasgow lady doctors', a group of Scottish nurses attached to Royaumont, and an approving editorial from its 'Paris correspondent': 'The Scottish Branch of the National Union of Women's Suffrage Societies, the non-militant section of the movement, has done splendid work in various directions since the war began, but in none more than in the equipping and staffing of military hospitals in France.'

Dr Butler had graduated with flying colours from Glasgow University in 1890, and had been working on a cancer research project in Austria when war broke out. Her husband worked as a chauffeur at Royaumont.

While the suffragettes were doing their bit for the war effort, the storm of war continued to rage and conflict began to brew on the Clyde. For a brief moment in 1915, however, the clocks stopped.

12

Death of a Hero:
The Funeral of Keir Hardie

'He got more Socialism from Burns than from Marx.'

On 26 September 1915 the ailing Keir Hardie died. Many believed the outbreak of the European war he had worked so hard to prevent was what really killed him. Tom Johnston was sure of it. His tribute on the front page of the *Forward* on 2 October 1915 spelled it out. Headlined 'The Passing of Keir Hardie', the sub-heading was unequivocal:

He Died of a Broken Heart.

By THE EDITOR

A Stroke. A Seizure. Pneumonia! Call it what you will, James Keir Hardie died of a broken heart. I know.

He died of a heartbreak at seeing his cherished dreams, his fondest hopes, his firmest faith shattered in an hour. He had given his all to the building of a Labour Party and to the making of that Labour Party a national wing in the International Army of Labour: he spent his energies and his health rushing feverishly on trains to forge the worker's weapon that would cease, for evermore, international murder: he organised, instigated, encouraged, and toiled for 'the Day' – 'the Day' when the masses of Europe would no longer be pawns in the great crime of war.

It was a heart-breaking end to the life of a man who had known much sorrow but had risen above it to devote his life to the fight against poverty and the achievement of a lasting peace among the nations of the world.

James Keir Hardie, founder of the Labour Party, was born into poverty at Legbrannock near Motherwell in Lanarkshire in 1856, the illegitimate son of a farm servant called Mary Keir. Before he was three his mother married David Hardie and the family moved up to Glasgow. David Hardie, a ship's carpenter to trade, found work in the Govan shipyards but was laid off five years later during a prolonged strike.

Young Keir, who had little formal schooling, had already started work. An accident in the shipyard had previously put his adoptive father out of commission. With no money coming in, his parents had no choice but to send their eldest child out to earn what little a boy could. He was only eight years old when he took on his first job as a message boy with the Anchor Line Shipping Company in central Glasgow. He moved on to heating rivets in the shipyard and there were hopes of him becoming an apprentice. However, his mother took fright when two other boys died in an accident in the yard, and pulled him out of this workplace. His next job was less dangerous but no less arduous, working full-time as a delivery boy for a local baker, starting at seven o'clock in the morning and finishing when the shop closed in the late afternoon or early evening. He earned four shillings and sixpence per week, his family's only income while his stepfather was still out of work.

In later life Keir Hardie was to recall what happened when he was late for work one morning. He had the saddest of excuses. Another of the Hardie children, nearest in age to him, was dying of what is described only as a fever. An exhausted Mary Hardie was pregnant with another child. Keir sat up during the night with his dying brother, allowing his mother to get some rest. Hardie's friend and first biographer,

William Stewart, allowed his subject to tell the story of what happened next:

> One winter morning I turned up late at the baker's shop where I was employed and was told I had to go upstairs to see the master. I was kept waiting outside the door of the dining-room while he said grace – he was noted for religious zeal – and, on being admitted, found the master and his family seated round a large table. He was serving out bacon and eggs while his wife was pouring coffee from a glass infuser which at once – shamefaced and terrified as I was – attracted my attention. I had never before seen such a beautiful room, nor such a table, loaded as it was with food and beautiful things. The master read me a lecture before the assembled family on the sin of slothfulness, and added that though he would forgive me for that once, if I sinned again by being late I should be instantly dismissed, and so sent me to begin work.

How awful it must have been for a ten-year-old boy who'd left the house with no breakfast that morning to be in the midst of all this plenty. He was filled with a burning sense of injustice at the baker's heartless treatment of him, made all the worse because there was no way he could express it. If you wanted to keep your job you didn't talk back to the master, especially not if you were a child.

Two days after this incident young Keir was once more late for his work. Once again he'd been doing his best to help his mother and comfort his dying brother. Whether the baker had any knowledge of the tragedy which was being played out in the Hardie home is not clear but he had issued a threat and he carried it out. The boy was dismissed on the spot. Not only that, the baker told him he was fining him his last fortnight's wages as a punishment. This was a disaster for the whole Hardie family, whose ability to buy food, fuel

and pay the rent rested solely on the small shoulders of one young boy.

Immediately aware of the crisis now facing his family, Keir Hardie began to cry, pleading with the woman who served in the shop to help change the baker's mind. Sympathetic to the child's plight, she spoke to the man from a speaking tube which linked the shop and the house.

> … presumably to the breakfast room I remembered so well, but he was obdurate, and finally she, out of the goodness of her heart, gave me a piece of bread and advised me to look for another place. For a time I wandered about the streets in the rain, ashamed to go home where there was neither food nor fire, and actually discussing whether the best thing was not to go and throw myself in the Clyde and be done with a life that had so little attractions.
>
> In the end I went to the shop and saw the master and explained why I had been late. But it was all in vain. The wages were never paid. But the master continued to be a pillar of the Church and a leading light in the religious life of the city!

How Mary Hardie reacted when Keir eventually went home is not recorded. Did she hug her tearful boy, tell him it wasn't his fault, that they would manage somehow, throw herself on the mercy of a kind neighbour?

The disaster of losing their sole source of income forced a prolonged separation on the family. Whether he had fully recovered from his accident or not, David Hardie went back to sea and Mary Hardie returned to stay near her mother in Lanarkshire. Keir, still only a boy of ten, went down the pit.

He did a boy's job below the ground, working as a trapper. They made sure the mine was well-ventilated by opening and closing a trapdoor, sending air flowing along the passages where men were hewing and digging out the coal. The job

was both lonely and cold, although on his first day, a 'kindly old miner ... wrapped his jacket round him to keep him warm. It was an eerie job, all alone for ten long hours, with the underground silence only disturbed by the sighing and whistling of the air as it sought to escape through the joints of the door. A child's mind is full of vision under ordinary surroundings, but with the dancing flame of the lamps giving life to the shadows, only a vivid imagination can conceive what the vision must have been to this lad.'

Thousands of working-class children in late nineteenth- and early twentieth-century Scotland had such heart-rending tales to tell. Thousands of us whose families lived through such hard times will have heard their stories and shed a tear for the sorrows and struggles of our forebears, been angry on their behalf over the injustices they endured. When Keir Hardie as a grown man spoke to and for those living lives blighted and narrowed by poverty, shared experience forged a powerful link. Education was the key. The belief that learn- ing and self-improvement would open the door to a better life was an article of faith among working-class Scots, who stretched themselves to the limit to get the education poverty had denied them, for themselves and for their children.

Keir Hardie worked down the pit for ten hours a day but still managed to attend night school at Holytown near Motherwell, where the pupils had to bring their own candles so as to be able to see during winter evenings. Even while he was in the pit, he taught himself Pitman's shorthand. Down in that Stygian gloom he used the wick from a miner's lamp to see by.

At home his mother sang him the old Scottish ballads, told him traditional stories of days gone by and encouraged him to read widely. *The Pilgrim's Progress* by John Bunyan was a great favourite in the Hardie household, as was Tom Paine's *Age of Reason* and, of course, the poems of Robert Burns. As his biographer William Stewart put it: 'He got more Socialism from Burns than from Marx: "The Twa Dugs," and "A Man's a

Man for a' that," were more prolific text books for his politics than "Das Kapital".'

Although she retained the strong religious faith of her childhood, the experience with the baker changed Mary Hardie's outlook on organised religion forever. From then on she would tolerate no religious hypocrisy, priding herself and her family on being free-thinkers. As William Stewart put it: 'All the members of the family grew up with the healthy habit of thinking for themselves and not along lines prescribed by custom.'

This was another characteristic of Red Clydeside at its best. Everything was open to question. Everyone had the right to ask why – and who and what and where and how. That society was arranged as it was, 'the rich man in his castle, the poor man at his gate', with the great mass of the population working long hours for little money and trudging wearily home to overcrowded houses and an inadequate diet was not only manifestly unfair, it could no longer be tolerated. That it might have 'aye been' like this was no justification for not trying with all your might to change it.

James Keir Hardie did more than most. After some time working with the pit ponies – his pocket watch apparently bore the teeth marks of his favourite cuddy – he spent a dozen years underground, becoming a skilled miner, a hewer of coal. At the same time he continued to educate himself, became a lay preacher, a temperance campaigner and an active trade unionist. Around the time of his marriage to Lillias Balfour Wilson he came up from the pit for the last time. Ironically, Lillie was the landlord's daughter, her father the owner of a pub in Hamilton.

Hardie started a small shop, a not uncommon way of trying to make a living in mining communities, and began writing articles for the newspapers. His union activism had been too much for the local pit manager, who sacked him out of hand when he found out about it. 'We'll hae nae damned Hardies in this pit.'

Over the next ten years he led the first strike of Lanarkshire miners, which saw bloody clashes with the police at Blantyre, founded a miners' newspaper and became ever more involved in wider politics. He had been a staunch Liberal, speaking from the platform at political meetings, but began to move further to the Left. He also began to travel, meeting other people with radical views, like R.B. Cunninghame Graham, the romantic and dashing 'Don Roberto'.

Through him, while on a visit to London, he met Friedrich Engels. Although Keir Hardie never became a Marxist, he did become a socialist and, with Cunninghame Graham, father of the Labour Party.

It's a quirk of history – and snobbery – that this Scotsman steeped in the history of his native country never sat in the House of Commons for a Scottish seat. The Liberals of Mid Lanark rejected him as a parliamentary candidate in favour of a wealthy London barrister who had been parachuted into the constituency.

Keir Hardie first entered Parliament in 1892 as MP for West Ham in London. He stood on an Independent Labour ticket and the following year helped form the Independent Labour Party. A few years later again, in 1899, he was one of those who helped found what grew into the modern Labour Party, of which he became the first leader.

After he lost the West Ham seat he stood in Merthyr Tydfil in Wales, where in 1900 he was elected as one of only two Labour MPs in Parliament. By 1906 there were 26 and by 1910, 40. Still the sitting MP for Merthyr in 1915, he came back to Scotland and to his home at New Cumnock to die. His younger brother David Hardie described how the end came:

That Keir was only 59 will come as a surprise to most people. He always looked more than his years, but the last 15 years of intense work and consequent strain gave him an aged appearance ... The outbreak of

war found him physically weak, and more rest was
ordered. He made every effort to rest, but rest by
effort is useless. The great crisis was ever present in
his mind. It hung over him like a dark cloud ... There
is nothing more certain than that the great slaughter
of his fellow-beings in the present European holo-
caust was the seat of his final trouble. The idea of a
world-wide peace and good will was not to him a mere
pious opinion, but a holy crusade, to which he had
dedicated his life's work.

Keir Hardie died peacefully, his wife and daughter at his
bedside. Thousands mourned his passing, although it rated
the merest nod of acknowledgement in most of Glasgow's
newspapers. The *Forward* offered a lyrical description of his
funeral and cremation at Maryhill in Glasgow. It's unsigned
but the words sound as though they flowed out of Tom
Johnston's typewriter:

A fitful sunshine on a late September day. A hearse
and carriages behind, filled with wreaths. Then comes
a long seemingly endless trail of cabs. Crowds line the
Maryhill tramway route. Thousands doff their hats
and caps as the black hearse passes: soldiers salute.
The cortege turns off to the Western Necropolis, and
behind the cabs fall in a long procession of Labour
and Socialist representatives, four deep. It is the
funeral of Keir Hardie.

Cunninghame Graham was one of the mourners. The service was led by Reverend Forson, a friend of Hardie. Once
it was over another friend stepped forward. He was Bruce
Glasier, who had succeeded Hardie as chairman of the
ILP. Tom Johnston noted how ill Glasier looked. He was
himself suffering from the cancer that would kill him five
years later.

Glasier put his hand on his friend's coffin and made an emotional appeal to the mourners to dedicate themselves afresh to the cause to which Keir Hardie had devoted his life. 'But he was pulled up suddenly as with a shock when the coffin began to be automatically lowered.' Fighting his grief, Hardie's brother George thanked everyone for coming. Outside on the steps of the chapel of the Western Necropolis a few more words were said to men and women reluctant to leave. 'And then the cabs refilled, and the crowd trekked home, and the tramway cars clanged again. Hardie had gone.'

On Sunday, 3 October 1915, a memorial service was held at St Andrew's Halls. Thousands gathered to listen to the three speakers. One was Mary Macarthur, trade unionist and dedicated member of the ILP. She'd married and become Mrs Anderson four years before but seems to have continued to use her maiden name in her political life. She told funny little stories about Keir Hardie, remembering that when he found that a 'capitalist newspaper' had said something complimentary about him he would go very quiet before asking what he had done wrong to be praised by the likes of them.

Another of the speakers was Bob Smillie, the leader of Scotland's miners who later became MP for Morpeth in Northumberland. Smillie spoke with great passion, 'in ringing tones'. He was scathing about the official 'we're all in this together' line currently being peddled about the war:

> 'They tell you,' he cried, 'that you and they are one, that after the war the Sutherlands, the Breadalbanes and the Durhams will be one with the wounded and torn working class, back from the trenches. O, do not believe them. Do not believe them. When the war is over our real fight with our real enemies will begin.' And every time he raised the slogan of Socialism and Peace the cheering, round after round of it, became more vociferous and more compelling.

Ramsay MacDonald also spoke. The audience in the packed hall gave him a standing ovation before he had even said a word. MacDonald threw away his notes and spoke from the heart:

> 'Here lies one,' he said, quoting Morton or John Knox, 'who never feared the face of man'. And MacDonald went on to describe the boy Hardie running errands in the rain, wandering about in sorrow because he had no wages for his mother; as a youth scraping short-hand characters on the smoke of a pit wall ...
>
> In him the spirit of the Covenanter lived again – Airds Moss tempered with the lyrics of Burns. From Hardie's mysticism: from the great invisible creative power in him came his persistency and his persever-ance, his power of seeing above and beyond.

In his written tribute too, MacDonald said that if Keir Hardie had ever written the story of the long struggle of the Labour movement, he would have begun with the Covenanters. He might have had their faults of obstinacy and dourness but he had also had 'the simple mind of a child' and an other-worldly mysticism.

With Hardie, wrote Ramsay MacDonald, you always got the feeling that he saw the world as ephemeral and 'that at any moment the vain show would melt into mist, and the spiritual substance of being resolve itself'. He went on: 'Such a man will offer his hand to every struggling and unpopular cause. But the personalities and powers cannot prevail against him. He will start great movements, he will reveal to men their own best qualities, he will be despised and rejected, but he will make more changes in the world than generations of others. Such a man was Keir Hardie.'

13

Mrs Barbour's Army:
The Rent Strike of 1915

'WE ARE NOT REMOVING.'

As the war progressed, British industry found itself working at full tilt to produce the ships, other hardware and munitions required to fight it. Many factories were turned over for the duration to the making of munitions, the Singer plant at Clydebank just one of them.

With the economy roaring up onto a war footing when so many men on Clydeside had already marched off to the trenches, an influx of labour was required to man – and woman – the munitions factories, shipyards and workshops. Concentration on the war effort had put an abrupt stop to the building of new houses. Accommodation in Glasgow was soon at a premium.

Realising demand now outstripped supply, many of Glasgow's private landlords saw an opportunity to increase their profits by raising rents. If the sitting tenant couldn't pay the increase, there were plenty of people queuing up to take over the tenancy. What the landlords hadn't reckoned with was the fighting spirit of Glasgow's housewives.

In 1914 they had already formed themselves into the Glasgow Women's Housing Association, whose aim was to improve the tenement homes in which they all lived. Their opposition to the rent rises the landlords tried to impose in 1915 was both practical and a matter of principle. So many

fathers and sons were away at the war and food prices had risen sharply. Household budgets were under strain and the improvements needed still hadn't been carried out.

Although the rhetoric of the time was that everyone had to pull together for the sake of the war effort, landlords and the factors who acted for them were ruthless about evicting tenants unable to come up with the extra rent. In March 1915 one case hit the headlines. Mrs McHugh of William Street in Shettleston had fallen into arrears. She owed less than one pound. She also had a husband wounded in the war, two sons serving in France, and five children at home.

When the factor arrived with the eviction order, he found himself dealing with not only one woman but also several hundred of her neighbours. Local councillor John Wheatley stood at the head of the crowd. The factor retreated and Wheatley addressed the angry people gathered in William Street.

Fired up, they headed off in pursuit of the would-be persecutor of defenceless women and children. By the time they caught up with him they had acquired an effigy which they burned in front of the windows of his office. Later they pursued him to his house and smashed some of its windows. As the *Forward* reported, John Wheatley gave them a gentle telling-off for that, pointing out:

> ... that they were not there to organise the wreck-ing of homes, but to prevent homes from being wrecked, and while they had been marching away to the Factor's residence, the Bailiffs might have ejected Mrs. McHugh. (Cries of 'We had enough left here to prevent that!') Anyway, he said, the burning of effigy business was wasted time and so were the demonstrations at the Factor's house. He knew, for if they remembered they had done it once to him. (Laughter, and cries of: 'Never mind! You're aye here yet!')

On the advice of the police, the eviction order on Mrs McHugh was not served. Her case became a cause célèbre. As the *Forward* told its readers, it even reached the 'English Sunday Press'. Other Glasgow newspapers picked up on it too. Landlords and factors scored a spectacular own goal every time they tried to turn a soldier's wife and children out into the street. Many of those threatened with eviction were also munitions workers, people whose labour was crucial to the war effort.

The ILP quickly offered support but it was the tenants themselves who led the fight. Willie Gallacher described the strategy adopted by women like Mary Barbour of Govan and Mrs Ferguson of Partick.

> In Govan, Mrs. Barbour, a typical working-class house-wife, became the leader of a movement such as had never been seen before, or since for that matter. Street meetings, back-court meetings, drums, bells, trumpets – every method was used to bring the women out and organize them for the struggle. Notices were printed by the thousand and put up in the windows: wherever you went you would see them. In street after street, scarcely a window without one: 'WE ARE NOT PAYING INCREASED RENT.'

Actually what the notices read were 'RENT STRIKES AGAINST INCREASES: WE ARE NOT REMOVING'. They cost one penny each and had a polite request printed on them. 'Please tack this to top of lower sash of window.' Thousands of people did. The rent strike was on.

People made up their own placards too. One was held aloft at a rent strike demonstration in Partick:

> Partick Tenants' Strike
> Our Husbands, Sons and
> Brothers are fighting the

Prussians of Germany.
We are fighting the Prussians of Partick.
Only alternative
MUNICIPAL HOUSING

Helen Crawfurd also wrote in some detail of the strategy women deployed in rent strike skirmishes to stop their neighbours from being evicted.

> One woman with a bell would sit in the close, or passage, watching while the other women living in the tenement went on with their household duties. Whenever the Bailiff's Officer appeared on the scene to evict a tenant, the woman in the passage immediately rang the bell, and the women came from all parts of the building. Some with flour, if baking, wet clothes, if washing, and other missiles. Usually the Bailiff made off for his life, chased by a mob of angry women.

The factors tried some strategies of their own. A favourite ploy was to convince individual housewives everyone else in the close had paid the increased rent until they had all been fooled into doing so. On one occasion when this was tried, Mary Barbour drafted in the men from Govan's shipyards. She led them to the factor's office and demanded the amount of the increase be returned.

'On the factor being shown the thousands of black-faced workers crowding the street,' wrote Helen Crawfurd, 'he handed it over.' Now a committed socialist, she addressed many meetings during the rent strike. She used her time on the platform to speak out against the war too, and argue the case for socialism.

It was by no means only socialists who supported the rent strikers. In September 1915 *The Bulletin,* sister paper to the *Glasgow Herald,* published an article very sympathetic in tone.

> The revolt against the increase of house rents in
> Glasgow threatens to become a very big problem. In
> three different districts strikes have been resorted to
> by tenants – first in Shettleston, then in Govan, and
> now in Partick. These movements have widespread
> sympathy and, given the slightest provocation, will
> assuredly spread.

The Bulletin made a suggestion that sounds very like a recommendation: since so many of the families involved were
munitions workers, maybe the government would intervene.
It wrote approvingly of the tenants in Partick who were
involved in the rent strike. There were around a hundred
of them and they lived in different closes in Hurlet Street,
Thornwood Avenue, Clyde Street, Rosevale Street and Exeter
Drive. 'The large majority of the tenants are of the respectable artisan type – steady workers employed in the local shipyards and engineering shops. In one of the closes, in which
there are 13 tenants, no fewer than nine of them are engaged
in war munition work.'

No long-haired and wild-eyed revolutionaries here, then.
The women who ran the rent strike were well aware of the
value of presenting a respectable face to the world. Look at
the photos of the protests and demonstrations and you'll see
neatly dressed women, men and children, all in their Sunday
best. Big hats at dawn.

On 16 October 1915, the rent-striking tenants living in
Thornwood Avenue and Clyde Street were due to be evicted.
The 'WE ARE NOT REMOVING' placards were up in the
windows, the tenants came out onto the street and 'the ranks
of the demonstrators were swelled by a contingent of women
from Govan'. Mrs Barbour and her army were on manoeuvres.
Probably they crossed the river on the Govan ferry, the wee
boat which used to come right up the steps of the landing stage.

Mary Barbour's counterpart on the north bank of the
Clyde was Mrs Ferguson, secretary of the Partick Rent Strike

Committee. She seems to be the same Mrs Ferguson involved with Helen Crawfurd and Agnes Dollan in the Women's Peace Crusade. She had gone right to the top, contacting Lloyd George. As Minister for Munitions, what was he going to do about these evictions of soldiers' wives and munitions workers? She really thought he should send a message about this to the tenants of Partick. Lloyd George's telegram in reply to Mrs Ferguson was read out to the assembled company. His response did not go down well. The Minister for Munitions advised that the Secretary of State for Scotland was setting up a committee to look into the matter.

Supporting the striking tenants, local councillor Mr Izett said angrily that 'he wished the soldiers could see and know that while they were defending the trenches abroad, the women folk were defending the trenches at home'.

Patrick Dollan declared that 'the law of humanity was higher than the law of the property owners' and that there was no way they were going to allow the threatened evictions to take place.

Mrs Ferguson got the best response when she told everyone that 'the men in the shipyards had asked that immediately there was any attempt to put the ejections into force word should be sent to the men, and they could come out on strike in a body'.

It was also decided that patrols be set up to guard the houses where the evictions had been threatened and that these should go on until confirmation was received that the eviction orders had been withdrawn.

What the landlords did then was go to law. They would circumvent people-power by not confronting it. Once again they had reckoned without the determination of Mrs Barbour, Mrs Ferguson and the Glasgow Women's Housing Association. The men in the shipyards made good on their promise too, swelling the ranks of Mrs Barbour's Army. It was Willie Gallacher who gave that name to the people who marched on Glasgow Sheriff Court on 17 November 1915 in support of the Partick rent strikers:

From early morning the women were marching to the
centre of the city where the sheriff's court is situated.
Mrs. Barbour's army was on the march. But even as they
marched, mighty reinforcements were coming from
the workshops and the yards. From far away Dalmuir in
the West, from Parkhead in the East, from Cathcart in
the South and Hydepark in the North, the dungareed
army of the proletariat invaded the centre of the city.

Like a latter-day Pied Piper, Mary Barbour led her troops
up and across the Clyde and into the centre of Glasgow,
calling first at Lorne Street School in Govan to pick up John
Maclean. He had just been sacked by Govan School Board
for his anti-war activities. The army was a noisy one, adding
to the pounding of its feet with tin whistles, hooters and a
dilapidated old drum. Following on behind, Willie Gallacher
describes how as they marched along Argyle Street near
to Central Station they passed a group of soldiers heading
for France. 'Some of the young chaps gave us a cheer as we
passed, but many others looked pathetically towards us as our
fellows shouted "Down tools, boys," and gave the impression
that very little persuasion would have brought them over into
our ranks.' But the young soldiers kept on going, filing into
the station to board the trains which would carry them to the
mud and blood of Flanders.

When they reached the city centre the marchers assembled in front of the City Chambers in George Square before
going the short distance along Ingram Street to the Sheriff
Court. It was then in its old home at the City and County
Buildings. Impressive even when its stone was still covered
in a layer of dense black soot caused by industrial pollution,
the large neo-classical building occupied a whole block
bounded by Ingram Street, Hutcheson Street, Wilson Street
and Brunswick Street. It still does.

Their approach not having been exactly stealthy, and
not meant to be, the police were waiting for the marchers

and would not let them into the court. Mrs Barbour's Army marched round the building before stopping in Hutcheson Street. According to *The Bulletin,* they were noisy but good-humoured. There were speeches from John Maclean, Willie Gallacher and Helen Crawfurd. Makeshift platforms were raised so they could be seen and heard above the heads of the crowd.

Reporting the next day on the 'Glasgow Rent Agitation', *The Scotsman* allowed that 'though the crowd was large there was nothing in the nature of disorder calling for the drastic interference of the police, who allowed the impromptu meetings to proceed for a time'. This and other contemporary newspaper reports back up Willie Gallacher's description of the scene. His account might contain a whiff of exaggeration and a little too much socialist bombast but it's still vivid and convincing:

> Into the streets around the Sheriff's Court the workers marched from all sides. All the streets were packed. Traffic was completely stopped. Right in front of the court, John Maclean was on a platform addressing the crowd as far as his voice could reach. In other streets near the court others of us were at it. Our platforms were unique. Long poster-boards had been picked from the front of newspaper shops. These were placed on the shoulders of half-a-dozen husky, well-matched workers and the speaker was lifted on to them. It was a great experience, speaking from a yielding platform and keeping a measure of balance while flaying the factors and the war-makers.

Dressed in that Sunday best, the tenants had posed for photographs outside the court. Their children held up placards. Smart in his Norfolk jacket and well-starched white shirt collar, a young boy carried one which read: 'My father is fighting in France. We are fighting the Huns at home.'

Inside the court, 18 tenants were about to begin the legal battle with their factor, Mr Nicholson. All parties had agreed there would be one test case and the sheriff's decision on it would apply to all 18.

The Bulletin reported the next day on what it headlined as:

THE RENT STRIKE
EXTRAORDINARY SCENES
MINISTERIAL INTERVENTION
A PACIFIC SHERIFF
Considerable excitement prevailed in Glasgow Small Debt Court yesterday when additional petitions for the ejectment of householders who refused to pay increases of rent were down for hearing. The court was crowded to overflowing by those chiefly interested and their sympathisers, and a number of policemen were called in to preserve order. The proceedings took an unusual course.

That unusual course began with Sheriff Lee trying to persuade Mr Nicholson the factor and his lawyer Mr Gardner to drop the legal action on 'patriotic grounds'. There was a war on, after all, and munitions workers were pivotal to winning it.

The packed court started sitting at 10 a.m. By noon, with the Sheriff still in his chambers trying to knock heads together, people were becoming restive. *The Bulletin* noted that those in the gallery 'evinced considerable impatience at the delay'. To loud cheers, Councillor Izett walked forward to the bar of the court and asked who was in charge. In the name of the workers present, he protested about the delay. 'The protest evoked a loud outburst of cheering, which brought the Sheriff from his chambers into court. He sternly rebuked the demonstrators, and threatened to have the court cleared if there was a renewal of the disturbance.'

One of the tenants came forward and asked his lordship if he would receive a deputation which might help resolve the

situation. Sheriff Lee was clearly a pragmatic man. Although he pointed out that 'his position was purely a legal one, and he had no authority to mix himself up with any political questions', these were exceptional times. He spoke privately with four of the tenants, after which the test case was heard. Mr Reid, whose first name was not given by *The Bulletin,* was secretary of the Tenants' Defence Committee.

Mr Reid stated that before the war had started his rent had been £1.18 shillings per month. It had subsequently risen to £1.19.2d. On 10 September he had been given notice that it would rise still further to £2 per month, making a total increase since the outbreak of hostilities of two shillings per month.

On 14 September a number of tenants including Mr Reid had stated they would not pay the increase. They were then given two weeks' notice to quit, required to leave their houses by 28 September. It was now more than three weeks later and Mr Reid and the other tenants were still in their houses and refusing to budge. The Commission of Inquiry was due to offer its opinion in another two weeks again, issuing its findings at the end of November.

Mr Gardner, the solicitor, chose that moment to inform the court that his client had received a direct request the day before from Mr Lloyd George asking him either to drop the legal action or at least suspend it till everyone heard what the Commission of Inquiry had to say. Sheriff Lee grew a little tetchy, understandably so if the solicitor had not told him during all that time in his chambers of this request from the Minister for Munitions. Besides which, the law was the law. Once set in motion it could not be started and stopped on a whim.

Seizing his opportunity, Mr Reid told the sheriff he and his co-defendants had decided they needed a decision today, whatever that decision was going to be. He weighed in with a pointed and patriotic observation: 'Munition workers were involved in 15 of the cases, and they did not wish to stay off

work to come there and discuss the question of rent. They had a bigger battle to fight in the workshops, and they wanted to fight loyally there.'

Those few words seem to have swung it as far as Sheriff Lee was concerned. He knew very well that munitions workers who stayed away from their work could be fined or even put in prison. The national interest surely required that the other side should drop the legal action. As this challenge hung in the charged air, it's easy to imagine every pair of eyes in the court swivelling round to Mr Gardner, the solicitor.

He agreed to drop the action, on one condition. The defendants had to agree to accept whatever the Commission of Inquiry said about rents. The Sheriff, who by this stage in the proceedings sounds as though he was completely on the side of the rent strikers, said that of course they would.

> The people affected by this rent dispute knew what was going on. They had observed that in many directions since the war began there was special legislation to meet particular cases of hardship or of difficulty due to the war, and they thought, rightly or wrongly, that the case of rent was one of those difficulties, and that there ought to be special legislation to deal with it.
>
> They [the rent strikers] thought their case called for special legislation, but he did not understand for a moment that if special legislation was passed they would dream of opposing it. They had appealed to the justice of their country, and when the country declared through Parliament their decision they would abide by it at once.

Mr Gardner, the lawyer, and Mr Nicholson, the factor, confirmed their agreement to drop the cases. As *The Bulletin* reported, 'The intimation was received with loud cheering.' The Sheriff told Mr Reid he hoped he would use his influence to see there would be no 'denunciations antagonistic to the

petitioner'. Presumably he meant no triumphalist taunting, variations on 'Yah boo, sucks to you, we just won and you just lost.'

The rent strikers were too dignified for that. Mr Reid assured the sheriff there would be no such trouble, 'and the proceedings ended by those in court giving a hearty cheer for the Sheriff'.

Final victory went to the tenants. The Commission of Inquiry recommended that rents be restricted for the duration of the war. Although there were rent strikes in other parts of Britain, it was the Glasgow rent strike which brought about this decision that made a difference to the lives of ordinary people throughout Britain. Even the *Glasgow Herald* was impressed by the stand taken by Mary Barbour, Mrs Ferguson and their supporters. 'Thanks to the fine stand made by the Glasgow women and the determined attitude of the Clyde munition workers, the Government has introduced a Bill to legalise pre-war rent during the war and for six months thereafter.'

Mary Barbour continued to make a difference, becoming a town councillor, Glasgow's first female bailie and helping to establish Glasgow's first family planning clinic. In 1921 she stood for election in Govan's Fairfield ward as a member of the ILP. Her fellow candidates were Manny Shinwell and Thomas Kerr and they issued a joint manifesto which stated their policies on housing, local rates, the cost of living and unemployment:

> As a Socialist, and the nominee of the Independent Labour Party, I have been selected to contest the Fairfield Ward as one of the Candidates of the Local Labour Party. I have been resident in Govan for over 20 years and during that time I have taken a keen interest in the public business of the town. My time and energies have all been spent in the working-class movements for the Social betterment of the whole community.

I do not wish to draw any distinction between men and women's questions, because essentially they are the same, but I am convinced and have always advocated that women should take their full share of public work.

Mrs. M. Barbour.

Above the names of all three candidates, the manifesto ends with these words: 'We have the honour to be your fellow citizens.'

14

Christmas Day Uproar: Red Clydeside Takes on the Government

'Mr Lloyd George visited the Clyde last weekend in search of adventure. He got it.'

The First World War was a voracious consumer of men and munitions alike. This led naturally to a shortage of skilled labour just when it was most needed and the introduction of unskilled labour to compensate. The process was known as dilution, short for dilution of skilled labour, and it gave rise to roars of protest on Clydeside. It was the engineers still working in the yards and workshops who were most vociferous in their opposition to dilution, loathing the very idea of unskilled workers coming in to do skilled jobs.

One of their biggest fears was that many of these unskilled workers, known by the unattractive name of *dilutees*, would be women, and that this would inevitably drive wages down across the board. They were right, of course. A woman might be doing exactly the same job as a man but everyone knew you didn't have to pay her the same wages. Margaret Irwin had pointed that out back in the 1890s.

It's a chilling statistic that twice as many British soldiers died in the First World War as in the Second. The demand for munitions so British troops could inflict the same slaughter on the Germans climbed with the terrible toll of death and horrendous wounds. For some reason this obscene idiocy made sense to the people in charge at the time.

David Lloyd George had been Chancellor of the Exchequer for seven years by 1915, serving first in the Liberal administration of Prime Minister Herbert Asquith and then in the wartime coalition government. In May 1915 he became Minister for Munitions, giving him a newly created portfolio and the task of persuading the skilled workers of Britain to accept dilution of labour. The wartime economy was going to grind to a halt without it.

Lloyd George was a wily operator but he came seriously unstuck in Glasgow, outwitted by the Clyde Workers' Committee. Arthur McManus, he of the millions of sewing machine needles, was one of the members of the CWC, as were Willie Gallacher and Davie Kirkwood. The shop stewards of the CWC were elected by their workmates at regular factory floor meetings. People had grown impatient with long-serving union officials. They were too cautious, unwilling to fight the workers' corner against the government.

For the duration of the war it was now illegal to strike, to try to persuade anyone else to strike or to change jobs without the permission of your existing employer. Any workers who did any of these things had not only broken civil law but also placed themselves under the jurisdiction of the military. They could therefore be tried by court martial, which had the power to sentence any man, soldier or civilian, to be shot by firing squad.

None of this was ever going to sit well with the men of the Clyde. Mentally and physically tough, intelligent, eloquent, full of cynical humour, angry, and raring to go, it's not surprising Lloyd George wasn't keen on having to confront too many of them in one room. This may be why he and his staff arranged the Local Trade Union Officials' Munitions Conference at which he would speak in St Andrew's Halls in Glasgow for the morning of Christmas Day. In 1915 that fell on a Saturday.

The Minister for Munitions and his officials may or may not have known that Christmas Day was not much celebrated

in Scotland at the time. After the Reformation, the Kirk had done its best to stamp out what had once been enthusiastic revelry at both Christmas and New Year, the time traditionally known as the Daft Days. Although some Scots in the early 1900s were beginning to reclaim the old traditions, other than children hanging up their stockings in the hope of some sweets or an orange it was considered a normal working day like any other. Lloyd George and his staff would certainly have known that Saturday mornings were part of the working week and taking one off meant forfeiting half a day's pay.

Lloyd George's team had another trick up their sleeves which might stop the minister from having to confront too many angry men. They would control the issue of tickets for delegates to the conference. Referring to the Byzantine manoeuvring which ensued, the *Forward* wrote: 'Not even Mr. Sexton Blake, the eminent detective, could unravel *that*!'

In *Revolt on the Clyde*, Willie Gallacher recounts the tale of how the Clyde Workers' Committee outfoxed Lloyd George. He tells the story of the run-up to the Christmas Day conference with a mixture of anger, humour and unholy glee. Two days before, on Thursday, 23 December 1915, the Clyde Workers' Committee called a meeting in Glasgow. An executive member of his union, which was also meeting that evening, Gallacher got there late. He found three of his fellow CWC members handing out tickets for the Christmas Day conference at St Andrew's Halls.

They explained to him how the tickets were to work: 'The Minister had agreed to pay each shop steward 7s 6d for expenses, so that they would have to be careful in distributing tickets, as each one represented that amount.' Hang on a wee minute, said Willie Gallacher, seeing at once that the business with the expenses and the careful handing out of the tickets was a way of reducing how many people would be at the conference. Besides which, the CWC hadn't decided yet whether it was even going to attend.

Harry Hill came angrily back at him. 'By Christ, I never met your equal for making trouble!' A furious Hill then threw the tickets down on the table and stomped off. His method of departure was so outrageously dramatic everybody laughed at it. Gallacher spoke up again. 'Have we no sense of responsibility to the organisations we represent? Are we to be at the beck and call of this avowed enemy of the trade union movement? To what are we being reduced when this man can send along tickets and instruct us to organise a meeting for him?'

Gallacher managed to convince them the Christmas Day meeting should be boycotted but as soon as it was clear the vote was likely to go that way, one of the other CWC members ran out into the corridor and phoned the Central Station Hotel, where, as Willie Gallacher put it, 'Lloyd George, with his tame trade union and Labour Party officials, had his headquarters.'

On the other end of the phone, Arthur Henderson was asking them to stay where they were. He wanted to come over and speak to them. Henderson was a member of the wartime coalition government, the first Labour MP to hold Cabinet office. Nicknamed 'Uncle Arthur', he had previously been a union leader. As far as Willie Gallacher was concerned, in both capacities Uncle Arthur definitely fell within the definition of a tame official.

Nevertheless, he jokingly suggested they should agree to wait if they could all get taxis home paid for after the meeting was over. The message relayed over the phone from Henderson was: 'He thanks you very much, and he has instructed his secretary to order a fleet of taxis.'

'Yes, sir,' wrote Willie Gallacher – whose vigorous turn of phrase often shows the evidence of the year he spent in the United States as a young man, visiting two of his sisters who had settled in Chicago, and learning how revolutionary syndicalist trade unions worked with the Wobblies – 'they had money to burn.'

Arthur Henderson arrived a few moments later and made 'a pathetic appeal to us to assist Lloyd George in the great fight he was making to win the war'. Willie Gallacher wiped the floor with him. 'Isn't it clear that Henderson isn't here as a free agent? He is permitted to come and speak to us as the servant of one of our worst enemies. How is it possible that a man can fall so low? Fellow members, let us send him back with a message to his master that the Clyde trade unionists are not the lackeys of the workers' enemies!'

The decision to boycott the Christmas Day meeting stood. Gallacher and the others rode home through the December night in the fleet of taxis waiting for them, laughing all the way back to Paisley.

The late night was followed by an early morning. On Christmas Eve Willie Gallacher rose at his usual time of half past four, the early start he needed to cross the Clyde to start work at six. When he arrived at the Albion Motor Works in Scotstoun where he worked as a fitter, he found the place buzzing with anticipation. Everyone was wondering if Lloyd George might come to the factory to plead the case for dilution directly to the workers and their increasingly influential leader. Willie Gallacher was beginning to get himself noticed. He rather liked that.

Sadly for the other employees, that excitement was not to be. Instead, the Albion's manager took a phone call which asked if Gallacher would go up to the Central Hotel to meet Lloyd George. He took the tram for this trip. When he arrived at the luxurious station hotel he found some fellow members of the CWC but as yet no sign of the Minister for Munitions. Tables had been arranged in a square and everyone sat down.

It was Lord Murray of Elibank who took the lead. A Liberal politician and a tactful man, he appealed to the CWC to support the national interest at this time of international crisis. Davie Kirkwood described him as having a face that would thaw an iceberg, one of those 'imperturbable gentlemen whom nothing can harrass'.

Britain needed men to serve at the front and Britain needed munitions. Dilution was necessary. Lloyd George sympathised with the workers, of course he did, but there was a war on. Surely the members of the CWC wanted to help their country win it? Once Lord Murray had finished speaking all eyes turned to Willie Gallacher. As usual, he called it as he saw it:

> None of us here is prepared to accept the statement that Lloyd George is, or ever was, a friend of the workers. If he's so keen on winning the war, let him tackle the employers, stop their profits. They're piling up profits at our expense. However, that's *our* war, the war against the employers. We don't mind him being with them. It's what we expect, but when he asks us to assist him in carrying through their plans, that's treating us cheap, to say the least of it. We stand for the workers we represent, and while there are employers reaping profits we'll carry on the war against them.

A Glasgow bailie leapt to his feet and declared that Gallacher was 'out for bloody revolution' and didn't care whether the war was won or lost. After some shouting, Lord Murray managed to call the meeting to order. It then emerged that Gallacher's own union had collected tickets for the Christmas Day conference and was ready to hand them out, which is when Lloyd George himself slid out of the woodwork. Dismissing everyone else, he asked Willie Gallacher to wait behind.

Lloyd George proceeded to treat the bloody revolutionary as though he were his new best friend. Could Mr Gallacher possibly arrange for him to meet representative members of the CWC that evening? No problem, said the wee man who lived in a tenement flat in Paisley to the mighty Minister for Munitions as they stood in one of Glasgow's most exclusive hotels, we'll see you here at seven o'clock tonight.

Lloyd George started the Christmas Eve meeting with the smaller CWC group by exercising his well-known charm, circulating a box of cigars. His own staff all took one. The workers of the CWC brought out their proletarian pipes. 'That's right, boys,' Lloyd George said, digging his own pipe out of his jacket pocket. 'Why should we be formal? If we are going to talk, let us be comfortable; and what's more comforting than a good pipe?' As Willie Gallacher observed, the Minister for Munitions was never one to miss a trick. Wreaths of cigar smoke and clouds of pipe tobacco. The air in that room must have been quite delightful. The two women who were present probably didn't smoke. Even if more ladylike cigarettes had been on offer, only fast women smoked in public.

Willie Gallacher tells us that the two women spoke but not what they said, a bit remiss for a man with such apparently accurate recall for dialogue. Socialists could be sexists too, and frequently were. It's an intriguing thought that one of those women might have been Jane Rae of the Singer's strike. She certainly attended the Christmas Day conference, keeping her ticket as a souvenir.

Through the tobacco smoke, Lloyd George launched into what Gallacher called a 'typical propaganda speech', explaining that:

> ... munitions were the key to victory. We were short of men to man the factories at present operating; new factories had to be built. Therefore thousands of workers were needed, and we had to find them. He looked to us for support. As he looked at us he could see that strong spirit of independence that would never tolerate the military domination of Germany. Yes, he knew that we were the very men to rely upon in a crisis.

Lloyd George had told the newspapers a few days before that he would have absolutely no truck with the Clyde Workers'

Committee. Now he was trying to schmooze them. They took their revenge via the eloquent words of one of their number, another shop steward from the Albion Motor Works called Johnny Muir. Willie Gallacher fair cries him up:

> Johnny was masterly in the handling of the subject. He dealt very briefly with the development of capitalism and with the fact that the one and only concern of the employers was profit; that in pursuit of profit every change in the method of production was used to cheapen the cost, and that this took the form of continually introducing new types of semi-skilled or unskilled labour at the lowest possible rate of wages. Thus he showed that dilution had always been a feature of capitalist development.

However, Muir continued, since it was obvious to everyone there currently was a shortage of labour, the CWC was prepared to accept dilution for the time being. On one condition. The government had to take the factories out of the hands of the employers and allow the workers to run them through factory committees.

It was an astonishing suggestion, yet this revolutionary idea did not immediately provoke a spluttering response from Lloyd George. Willie Gallacher described 'the pompous little peacock at the top of the room' as appearing not even to be listening to Johnny Muir. Instead, he was stroking his moustache and luxuriant hair, whispering to Arthur Henderson.

Gallacher exploded, demanding they should have the courtesy to listen to Muir. Lloyd George insisted that he was listening. After Johnny Muir had said his piece, Davie Kirkwood, Arthur McManus and the two female shop stewards spoke, all of them supporting Muir. As far as they were concerned 'this was a war for trade and territory, a war carried on for the purposes of imperialism', and they were completely opposed to it. The only question they were prepared to address was

who was going to administer dilution of labour and who was going to run the factories while the war continued to rage and cause the labour shortage.

Again according to Gallacher, Lloyd George praised Johnny Muir for his eloquence but told the CWC he could not agree to the demands that the workers should control dilution. That would be a revolution and they couldn't have a revolution in the middle of a war. As Willie Gallacher drily put it in *Revolt on the Clyde*, 'It was only a couple of years later, however, that Lenin and the Bolsheviks showed him just how that very thing could be done.'

Although many of the details in this story sound authentic, the tone of the interchange doesn't quite ring true. It seems unlikely that Lloyd George would sit for so long to be lectured on the iniquities of capitalism. Perhaps it wasn't quite so clear-cut as Willie Gallacher describes it. Be that as it may, the CWC did agree to attend the Munitions Conference at St Andrew's Halls the following day.

So, on the morning of Christmas Day 1915, shop stewards gathered where, as Gallacher put it, 'the modern St. George was going to slay the dragon of unrest and conquer the unruly Clyde'.

David Lloyd George was famously and proudly Welsh, speaking that language before he ever learned English, the son of a race which cherishes the dragon as one of its most revered symbols. Presumably Willie Gallacher was thinking of the government the Welshman represented, seeing that as English rather than British.

Although he does not mention the personal detail in his memoirs, Gallacher turned 34 on Christmas Day 1915. His birthday treat was coming right up. As the *Forward* put it: 'The best paid munitions worker in Britain, Mr. Lloyd George (almost £100 per week), visited the Clyde last weekend in search of adventure. He got it.'

Trouble clearly being expected, rows of policemen and barricades were lined up in front of the platform at

St Andrew's Halls. The delegates filing into the hall reacted by breaking into song, a rousing rendition of 'The Red Flag', keeping this up as the platform party arrived. According to Davie Kirkwood this started up in response to a choir singing 'See the Conquering Hero Comes' as the prime minister entered the hall. 'As Mr Lloyd George sat down, a lock of hair strayed over his brow. Shouts of "Get your hair cut!" came from all quarters.'

As soon as the singing finished, Arthur Henderson, on the platform with Lloyd George, rose to his feet. The crowd roared its disapproval at him, drowning out whatever he was trying to say. Henderson gave it up as a bad job and Lloyd George stood up. Willie Gallacher, a hostile witness to be sure, described the minister's attempts to get the audience to quieten down. 'He pranced up and down the platform; he waved his arms; he stretched them out in mute appeal.'

It was all to no purpose. The crowd continued to yell out its protest. Lloyd George tried to quell the tumult, shouting out: 'I appeal to you in the name of my old friend, the late Keir Hardie!' Daring to take that sacred name in vain only made the audience angrier. They started singing 'The Red Flag' again, refusing to allow Lloyd George to speak. Accounts of what happened after that vary.

There's the official report of Lloyd George's speech to the conference. Issued to the Press Association the day before, it says nothing about any trouble. It was published in most newspapers exactly as they received it, as they had been asked to do. 'Mr Lloyd George will address meetings at Glasgow, and it is particularly requested that no report other than the official version of his speech should be published.'

In this official version, the one which appeared in the newspapers on the Monday after Christmas, Lloyd George puts his arguments to the delegates. They all listen attentively, clap politely and then everyone goes home. *The Scotsman* did report that there were interruptions and 'some singing of the "Red Flag". The interrupters, however, were in a distinct minority,

and the meeting, was, on the whole, good-humoured.' As we might by now expect, that's not the way Willie Gallacher tells it.

He has Johnny Muir jumping up onto a chair and the whole hall immediately falling silent to listen as this supremely eloquent speaker begins to dicuss the issues around dilution. In this version Lloyd George, Arthur Henderson and the rest of the official party walk off the platform and the meeting continues without them.

Remarking that the audience was pitiless, Davie Kirkwood says that he called out from the body of the hall for Lloyd George to be given a hearing. The *Forward* confirms this, telling the story in some detail. They had a reporter there. Tom Hutchison took everything down, word for word, what the platform party said and what the audience hurled back at him in response.

Hutchison reported that Arthur Henderson did manage to make himself heard, although he was heckled throughout. His appeal to patriotism and how Britain had gone to war to save gallant little Belgium was given short shrift, with cries of 'That's enough! We don't want to hear that! Get to the Munitions Act! Come awa' wi' Davy!'

That last comment might imply some respect and even affection in the hall for David Lloyd George. Indeed, as Henderson told the audience the Minister for Munitions would shortly address them on the subject of dilution of labour, there was hissing and booing but also some cheering.

Arthur Henderson struggled manfully on with his introduction. 'The scheme of dilution that Mr Lloyd George will recommend to you did not come from any employer. It came from a Committee upon which there were seven Trade Unionists.'

Henderson's no doubt well-meaning but misguided assurance brought forth cries of 'Traitors!' and a demand that those trade unionists be named. He gave them the names, including that of Miss Macarthur, who 'certainly knows how to

deal with the women workers'. Cue a cry of 'Miss Macarthur's the best man o' the lot!'

This was the same Miss Macarthur who had spoken at Keir Hardie's memorial service some two months before. Same venue, very different kind of gathering. There was laughter but there was immense frustration too. Delegates felt they were being talked at, not allowed to express their own opinions on dilution. It didn't help when they were told any questions they had for the minister would have to be written ones, passed up to the platform.

When Lloyd George began to speak, the anger in the hall was too hot to allow him to do so unchallenged. In line with his approach to the CWC the night before, he appealed to patriotism and national unity at this time of crisis. 'Let me put this to you, friends: while we are comfortable at home on a Christmas Day,' he began, and was immediately interrupted by shouts of 'No sentiment! We're here for business!'

Lloyd George kept doggedly to his prepared speech, '… while we are comfortable at home on a Christmas Day there are hundreds and thousands of our fellow-countrymen, some of them our sons, some of them our brothers, in the trenches facing death'.

'You're here to talk about dilution of labour!' came another exasperated shout.

The Welshman tried to pacify his listeners by dropping another famous Scottish socialist name, that of Ramsay MacDonald, 'one of my greatest friends'. That got some cheers but not much else. This is when Davie Kirkwood intervened, asking the delegates to give Lloyd George a fair hearing, but the heckling and heated interruptions continued.

'The responsibility of a Minister of Munitions in a great war is not an enviable one,' Lloyd George told the hall. 'The money's good,' came the cynical response. Becoming ever more exasperated, the minister responded to the derisive laughter which greeted that sally with an eloquent few words about the war, telling the delegates what he thought it would

mean for everyone. 'There will be unheard-of changes in every country in Europe; changes that go to the root of our social system. You Socialists watch them. It is a convulsion of Nature; not merely a cyclone that sweeps away the ornamental plants of modern society and wrecks the flimsy trestle-bridges of modern civilisation. It is more. It is an earthquake that upheaves the very rocks of European life.'

In no mood to listen to this purple prose, the delegates continued to hiss and boo. Lloyd George announced that he would now begin answering the written questions. He might not get through them all, though, because he had an engagement at twelve o'clock. It was an astonishingly crass thing to say and may indicate just how badly this smooth operator had been rattled by the noisy and hostile reception he got at St Andrew's Halls.

According to Tom Hutchison of the *Forward*, this was when Johnny Muir jumped onto the chair and demanded to put the facts of dilution of labour as the Clyde Workers' Committee saw them. However, in this account an instantaneous and respectful silence does not fall. 'As it was impossible to hear either the Minister or Mr. Muir, the Chairman closed the proceedings, and the meeting broke up in disorder.'

Lots of sound and fury but nothing achieved for either side: and the mailed fist was just about to appear from beneath the velvet glove.

15

Dawn Raids, Midnight Arrests & a Zeppelin over Edinburgh: The Deportation of the Clyde Shop Stewards

'Banished to Edinburgh!'

Tom Johnston's newspaper was first in the firing line. Years later, long after the heat of battle had cooled, he took the same mischievous delight in telling the story as he did when he originally reported it. Make that as soon as he was *allowed* to report it.

In his *Memories,* he recalled one of the many interchanges of that faraway but well-remembered Christmas morning. Lloyd George had dolefully declared his burden as a minister of the Crown in wartime was a heavy one and had the reply thrown at him that the money was good.

'All this,' wrote Johnston, now himself a highly respected elder statesman, 'was too much for Mr. Lloyd George, who completely lost all sense of proportion and ordered a complete raid of all copies of the *Forward* in every newsagent's shop in Scotland; he even had the police search the homes of known purchasers.'

In the first few days of 1916 the military as well as the police were deployed to censor the upstart newspaper, raiding its offices in Howard Street, off St Enoch Square. This was carried out by 'high ranking police and military officers

Room de Luxe, the Willow Tea Rooms, Glasgow. Kate Cranston, doyenne of Glasgow's tea rooms, commissioned Charles Rennie Mackintosh and his wife and artistic partner Margaret Macdonald Mackintosh to design the original Willow Tea Rooms in Sauchiehall Street in Glasgow in the early 1900s. (The Willow Tea Rooms)

Mother and child in Glasgow, 1912. Infant mortality in the poorer and overcrowded districts of Glasgow in the early 20th century was shockingly high – between 100 and 200 infant deaths per 1,000 births. One in every seven children in the city did not reach his or her first birthday. (Glasgow City Archives)

A Cottage for £8 a Year.

Left Out! The Tragedy of the Worker's Child

'A Cottage for £8 a Year.' J. Robins Millar, *Forward*, 1913. Red Clydesider John Wheatley advocated the building of modest cottages around Glasgow where workers and their families could lead healthier lives. (The Mitchell Library, Glasgow City Council)

'Left out!' The Tragedy of the Worker's Child.' J. Robins Millar, *Forward*, 1913. The activists of Red Clydeside were driven by the need to create a better life for all, but especially for children. (The Mitchell Library, Glasgow City Council)

Singer Sewing Machine factory, Clydebank, c.1908. Of the 14,000-strong workforce at Singer's, around 3,000 were young women and girls. They were to play a pivotal role in the strike of 1911. (West Dunbartonshire Libraries & Cultural Services)

Tom Johnston. Political firebrand and editor of the Socialist newspaper *Forward*, Tom Johnston was a Labour MP for over 30 years, becoming Secretary of State for Scotland and the prime mover behind the country's hydro-electric schemes. (Herald and Evening Times)

Thomas Muir of Huntershill. Thomas Muir was a lawyer and political radical, a leading light of the late 18th-century Friends of the People. Sentenced to be transported to Australia, he escaped from there, dying in revolutionary France in 1799 at the age of only 34. (East Dunbartonshire Leisure & Culture Trust)

Auld Scotch Street, Scottish Exhibition, 1911. The Scottish Exhibition of National History, Art and Industry was held in Kelvingrove Park in Glasgow's West End over the summer of 1911. (Author's collection)

Glasgow First World War female munitions worker. Women worked outside the home in unprecedented numbers during the First World War. This led trade unionists to fear what they called dilution of skilled labour and consequent lowering of wages all round. (Glasgow Digital Library, University of Strathclyde)

Right. 'Hallowe'en at the High Court.' *Glasgow News,* 1913. Uproar in court as part of a protest organised by some of Glasgow's suffragettes. (The Mitchell Library, Glasgow City Council)

HALLOWE'EN AT THE HIGH COURT.

Glasgow Rent Strike, 1915. Glasgow's housewives banded together to stop the opportunistic raising of rents by landlords during the First World War. (Herald and Evening Times)

Glasgow Labour Party Housing Association

RENT STRIKE
AGAINST INCREASES
WE ARE
NOT REMOVING

Window notice used in the 1915 Rent Strike.
From an original in the People's Palace.

Left. Rent Strike poster. Supporters of the rent strikes tacked these posters to their windows. (Glasgow Museums)

Willie Gallacher A political activist and union shop steward, Willie Gallacher played an active role in many of the dramatic events of Red Clydeside. He was a founder member of the Communist Party of Great Britain and subsequently Communist MP for Fife. (Gallacher Memorial Library)

John and Agnes Maclean and one of their two daughters. John Maclean was the tragic icon of Scottish Socialism, a man dedicated to changing society and educating the young about politics and economics. A revolutionary Marxist, he went to prison for his anti-war activism during the First World War. (Herald and Evening Times)

Right. Helen Crawfurd with children in Berlin, 1922. Glaswegian Helen Crawfurd was a suffragette, a peace activist, co-founder of the Communist Party of Great Britain and an inter-nationalist. (Gallacher Memorial Library)

Below left. Mary Barbour in her bailie's robes. A Govan housewife, leader of the rent strikes of the First World War and co-founder of Glasgow's first birth control clinic, Mary Barbour later went into local government. (Gallacher Memorial Library)

Below right. Davie Kirkwood. An engineer, trade union activist and Labour MP, Kirkwood worked hard to bring about the resumption of the building of the *Queen Mary* at Clydebank, where work had stopped because of the Depression. (Author's collection)

Above. The *Queen Mary* Leaving the Clyde, 1936. 'She leaves a big gap in the landscape, and a hole in the hearts of thousands of Clydesiders.' (Scotland's Moving Image Archive, National Library of Scotland © NLS)

Left. James Maxton election postcard. Teacher and long-standing Labour MP James Maxton was one of the most popular personalities of Red Clydeside. (University of Glasgow Library, Department of Special Collections)

VOTE FOR MAXTON
AND SAVE THE CHILDREN.

Published by JOHN TAYLOR, Election Agent, 88 Canning St., Bridgeton.
Printed by JAMES HAMILTON, Ltd., 213 Buchanan Street, Glasgow.

Leaving Radnor Street, March 1941. Over the two nights of the Clydebank Blitz, on 13 and 14 March 1941, the Clydeside town was pounded by German bombers. Hundreds died and hundreds were made homeless. (West Dunbartonshire Libraries & Cultural Services)

Bloody Friday in George Square, 1919. Protests in favour of reducing the working week from 54 to 40 hours exploded into confrontation and running battles in George Square in Glasgow. The nearest Scotland ever came to revolution?

smelling through wastepaper baskets and old correspondence files in an endeavour somehow or other to find evidence
post facto for an amazing and petulant and wholly illegal act
of suppression'. The newspaper was banned from publishing
until further notice.

Questions were asked in the House of Commons about
this suppression of free speech. Tom Johnston was quite san-
guine about the whole affair, having just been handed some
brilliant free advertising. He played the game all the same,
making as much noise as he could and demanding compensation. Eventually, 'after five or six weeks of this hullaballo
Mr. Lloyd George bowed before the storm of ridicule'.

The young editor was invited to London to meet the
Minister for Munitions. He took his solicitor with him. He was
Rosslyn Mitchell, a dapper, charming and radical Glasgow
lawyer who later became Labour MP for Paisley.

Just as with Willie Gallacher, Lloyd George greeted Tom
Johnston effusively: 'as if I were a long lost brother, and shaking my hand like a pump handle'.

> 'My dear Johnston, you mustn't get me wrong. You
> really mustn't. I am the last man on God's earth to
> suppress a Socialist newspaper.'
>
> I laughed.
>
> 'My dear young man' (he was so ostensibly pained
> and distressed at my unseemly mirth). 'My dear young
> man, don't you believe my word? Why do you laugh?'
>
> 'Well, Mr. Minister, you say you are the last man on
> God's earth to suppress a Socialist newspaper. You are.
> You did it six weeks ago, and no one has done it since!'

They sat down to discuss the situation and at the end of their
chat Johnston 'walked out free to start again, and "it had all
been a mistake, and these happen in the best regulated families, Ha! Ha! And we must see more of each other and be
better friends in future."'

This avuncular approach did not extend to the other Clydeside socialists who had declared war on the Munitions Act. Perhaps some class distinction was operating. Or perhaps Lloyd George did not think Tom Johnston and the *Forward* were nearly so dangerous as the Clyde Workers' Committee.

Believing Tom Johnston disapproved of the CWC and wasn't giving them enough support in his newspaper, Willie Gallacher and Johnny Muir had started up their own. The first edition of *The Worker* appeared in the middle of January 1916, while the *Forward* was still officially forbidden to publish.

In a story he could only have got from Tom Johnston, Willie Gallacher maintained Lloyd George had shown the former a copy of the new paper during that visit to London. According to Gallacher, Lloyd George told Johnston he had thought the *Forward* was bad until he saw *The Worker.*

'Should the Workers Arm?' That was the article that did it. The piece actually said that the workers shouldn't but Gallacher and Muir were arrested anyway. John Wheatley and Davie Kirkwood visited them in prison, the latter telling them not to worry. He'd engaged a good lawyer to fight their case. Step forward once again Mr Rosslyn Mitchell. Willie Gallacher gives us one of his word pictures of him: 'He was a dapper little gentleman with a beaming, cultivated smile. Someone had told him that he resembled Lord Rosebery, and he tried to live up to the part, with winged collar, spats and all.'

Gallacher and Muir appeared in court the following morning to hear the charge against them: 'Having on or about January 29th at 50 Renfrew Street or elsewhere in Glasgow attempted to cause mutiny, sedition or disaffection among the civilian population, and to impede, delay and restrict the production of war material by producing, printing, publishing and circulating among workers in and around Glasgow engaged on war materials, a newspaper entitled *The Worker.*'

Rosslyn Mitchell got them released on bail but it was only a temporary reprieve. When their case came to trial Muir got a

year, Gallacher six months and the printer three. According to Davie Kirkwood, at least one innocent man was locked up. He told the story in *My Life of Revolt*, claiming that Johnny Muir was not the author of 'Should the Workers Arm?':

> John Muir was charged with having written the article. He did not write it nor did either of the other two arrested men. The man who wrote the article was married and had a family of five children. John Muir was unmarried. He accepted the responsibility. There were only three persons who knew the author – John Wheatley, Rosslyn Mitchell, and myself. It was suggested that Muir should reveal the secret. He refused, saying: 'Some one is going to jail for this because the Military has read it the wrong way. If ... goes, there will be seven sufferers. If I go, there is only one so I am going.'
>
> Many years later John Muir was elected to Parliament and became Under-Secretary to the Ministry of Pensions. To the day of his death he never by word or suggestion went back on his word, nor did the others who knew his secret.

The government's Dilution Commission had visited Glasgow at the beginning of 1916. They held meetings with employers and the Amalgamated Society of Enginers (ASE), the engineers' union, to hammer out the details of how dilution was to work but refused to meet with the Clyde Workers' Committee or allow shop stewards to approve new dilutees. Workers at Beardmore's, where Davie Kirkwood was a shop steward, promptly went on strike in protest.

Three other Glasgow munitions factories came out in sympathy, including Weir's of Cathcart, where Arthur McManus was one of the shop stewards. The government took swift and decisive action. On Friday, 24 March 1916, the shop stewards regarded as the main ringleaders were arrested and deported to Edinburgh.

Despite observing that the 'Minister for ad-Munitions' had given them the new motto of 'gang *Forward* warily', there was no sign of caution in the howl of outrage Tom Johnston splashed all over his front page on Saturday, 1 April 1916.

> BANISHED!
> Kirkwood and other Clyde Shop Stewards
> Expelled from West of Scotland.
> Taken from their Beds.

It was a dawn raid. Or as Davie Kirkwood put it in *My Life of Revolt,* 'During the night Lloyd George struck.'

> On March 25, 1916, at three o'clock in the morning, I was sleeping the sleep of the just. I was awakened by a violent rat-tat-tat at the door.
>
> My wife said: 'That's them for ye noo.'
>
> The same thought flashed through my mind. I went to the door and asked who was there. A voice answered: 'The police. Open the door.'
>
> 'I will do nothing of the kind,' I answered.
>
> 'You'd be better to open it. We have a warrant under the Defence of the Realm Act to take you to the Central Police Office. If you do not open the door, we shall batter it in.'
>
> I opened the door. There were four detectives with revolvers at their sides. I gave them the dressing-down of their lives.

None of the policemen involved having written their memoirs, we'll have to take Davie's word for it that he told them in no uncertain terms they had no right to arrest a man who had done nothing wrong. He was, he declared, neither a savage nor an anarchist. He'd read about these sort of things happening in Russia (where the Tsar still had a year left to rule) but never in his wildest dreams had he thought they could

happen in Scotland. How could Scotsmen stoop so low as to 'arrest another Scotsman who had done nothing, but simply was standing up for his rights and the rights of his fellows'?

Friendly but firm, the police told him to get dressed and come with them. They reiterated that they were acting under the authority of DORA, the Defence of the Realm Act, and on the instructions of the competent military authorities.

After a cold night sleeping on the floor of a prison cell without even a blanket Kirkwood discovered he had been court-martialled the day before in Edinburgh and sentenced to be deported. Understandably furious, he demanded to know how he could have been court-martialled without even having been there or knowing anything about it. He had never in his life been in trouble with the police. Where on earth was he supposed to go, anyway?

A Colonel Levita told him he could 'go to San Francisco or anywhere you like, so long as it is outside of the Clyde Munitions area'. Plucking his destination out of the air, Kirkwood said he would go to Edinburgh. After another night on his own in the cells he was collected by two detectives who took him home to Parkhead to collect some clothes.

Sparing no expense, they took him by tram. By the time they had walked from the stop to his home, a crowd of people were following him and the policemen. Perhaps fearing trouble on the streets, that evening the police used cabs to transfer the court-martialled shop stewards between the Central Police Station and Queen Street Railway Station. Police officers rode shotgun 'above and below' the cabs.

'In Queen Street Station,' wrote Kirkwood, 'I was handed a single ticket for Edinburgh and a 10-shilling note, and put inside the barrier. We were cast adrift.'

Bemused, their only instruction being to report to Edinburgh's Chief Constable immediately upon arrival in the capital, the six men on the train were stunned by the speed with which they had been wrenched away from their homes and families. One of those men was Arthur McManus.

Though worried about how his wife and six children were going to manage without him, Kirkwood was worried for himself too. On the journey through to Edinburgh he wondered if he might be destined to face a firing squad. Dublin's Easter Rising had happened only two weeks before and his friend James Connolly had been shot for his part in it. Meeting the same fate must have seemed a real possibility.

They came up out of Waverley Station into a blizzard. It had stopped the trams and the deportees stood for a while in the swirling snow, watching some men trying to reconnect one tramcar to the overhead electric cable. Kirkwood thought they could be in Russia: '… an antiquated method of engineering and transport, a blinding snowstorm, and my emotions outraged at being lifted in the middle of the night without any charge preferred against me'.

Things began to look up when they reached police headquarters. Captain Ross, the Chief Constable, was polite and kind, asking them where they were going to stay. They were permitted to live anywhere within a five-mile radius of the city centre.

None of them had much money. They did have friends in Edinburgh, though, and eventually they settled on John S. Clarke, later to become a Labour MP and subsequently a Glasgow town councillor. So it was that four of the dangerous revolutionaries of Red Clydeside deported under the draconian terms of the Defence of the Realm Act walked out through the snow to douce Morningside.

Known to his friends as 'John S.', Clarke was living in Edinburgh with his wife, son and mother. He came originally from Northumberland and was a member of a circus family. To describe him as a colourful character would be something of an understatement, as the title his biographer Raymond Challinor chose shows: *John S Clarke, Parliamentarian, Politician and Lion Tamer*. Davie Kirkwood thought Clarke's house was more like a museum than a home, full as it was of stuffed birds and animals.

John S. was not at home but his womenfolk were very hospitable, taking the refugees from Glasgow in until they could find work and seek out alternative lodgings. Finding work proving not so easy, the exiles had lots of time on their hands.

One day they walked out to take a look at Roslin (usually now spelled Rosslyn) Chapel and Castle. Reverend Morrison, the minister there, hated their politics but he and his wife gave afternoon tea to 'the wild men from the Clyde'. Sitting round the table in the manse, Davie Kirkwood said they were all 'as meek and gentle as schoolchildren at a Sunday School party'.

Banned from any political activity or attendance at public meetings though they were, one evening he just happened to be passing the Mound while Helen Crawfurd, 'well known as a militant suffragist, pacifist, and Communist', was addressing a meeting urging a negotiated peace to end the war. When a couple of Australian soldiers threatened to get violent with the speaker who followed her, Kirkwood intervened, defusing a potential riot.

Barely two weeks after he and his fellow shop stewards arrived in Edinburgh, the horror of war came to Edinburgh. Once again ignoring the ban on political activity, they were in the ILP hall in Edinburgh 'when the lights were gradually lowered'. This happened three times and on the third occasion the lights stayed out. 'The Edinburgh people knew what it meant,' wrote Kirkwood. 'They whispered: "Zeppelins!"'

There had been Zeppelin raids on London which had caused fatalities and injured hundreds, and there was a great fear the Germans might attempt a raid on Scotland. The warning drill had been well-rehearsed. 'Very silently we stole out into the pitch-dark streets. We walked to Morningside, a mile and a half, speaking in whispers, careful not to let our heels click too hard on the pavement. At last we reached the house where we were staying. Six of us entered. The only occupants were Mr Clarke's mother and her little grandson.'

Midnight came and went. Clarke's mother-in-law took herself and her grandson off to bed. And then it happened. 'Suddenly a terrifying explosion occurred. Windows rattled, the ground quivered, pictures swung. We all gasped. I ran to the window and saw Vesuvius in eruption.'

Everyone but Kirkwood ran out of the house to see what had happened, not even stopping to put their boots back on. Mrs Clarke reappeared in her dressing gown, concerned the noise of the explosion might waken the wee boy. Kirkwood smiled at her and told her that was probably it, and she went back to bed, but the Zeppelin raid was by no means over.

> I opened the window. A great flash greeted me from the Castle and then, above the roaring, I heard the most dreadful screeching and shouting. The inmates in the Morningside Asylum had started pandemonium. Another bomb exploded, but nearer Leith, then another, followed by a fire.
>
> When I was a young man I had read Dante's *Inferno*, which came out in parts at 4 ½d. each. Here it was in reality.
>
> And the old lady in bed and the little boy slept peacefully through it all!

The men who had rushed in their stocking soles out into the night gradually came back to the house, the last of them not until three o'clock in the morning. Kirkwood didn't like this man, describing him as a braggart who was now gabbling away, the shock of the raid making him talk nineteen to the dozen.

He told the other men he had not only seen the Zeppelin, but had heard the gunners being ordered to shoot him. Davie Kirkwood remarked drily that he must have learned German gey quick to be able to understand what was being said. He doesn't name this man but takes two more sideswipes at him: 'That fellow turned up at the forty hours' strike. While some

of us were being batoned, he cleared away, and, like Johnnie Cope, didn't stop running till he reached England. A few years later he put all Britain into a panic.'

Could Kirkwood be referring here to Arthur McManus and the notorious Zinoviev letter? Published by the *Daily Mail* in 1924, this purported to be orders from Soviet Russia to Britain's Communists and socialists urging them to work towards revolution. It was signed by the Russian Zinoviev and Arthur McManus, by then British representative on the Communist International. The resulting reds-under-the-bed panic helped bring about the defeat of the first Labour government in 1924.

The Zeppelin which bombed Edinburgh on Sunday, 2 April 1916 killed 11 people and injured many more. The bomb dropped at Leith hit a whisky bond, setting fire to the spirit and lighting up the night sky. Bombs were dropped on Marchmont and Causewayside, where a five-storey building was completely destroyed, although with no loss of life. In the Grassmarket, a bomb hit the pavement outside the White Hart Inn, killing one person and injuring three more. An engraving on the paving stones now marks the spot.

The raid was a shocking event, both physically and psychologically. It wasn't only that Scots had thought themselves too far away to be bombed. It was the reality of the Germans bringing death and destruction to Scottish soil. Anti-German sentiment intensified after the Zeppelin raid, feeding the flames of jingoism. This was bound to have an effect on how people regarded those, like Helen Crawfurd, John Maclean and James Maxton, who were speaking out against the war.

The deportation of the shop stewards had provoked an angry demonstration on Glasgow Green on Sunday, 26 March 1916, two days after they had been dispatched to Edinburgh. It was here that James Maxton, who was in enough trouble already, blithely got himself into some more.

It was midnight when they arrested him.

Prison Cells & Luxury Hotels

*'This is the vagabond, though he's mair like a
scarecrow nor a Russian revolutionary.'*

In December 1915 permission was refused for St Andrew's
Hall as a venue for a demonstration 'in support of free
speech and against conscription'. The meeting was switched
to George Square. When they were told they couldn't hold it
there, the speakers went up into North Hanover Street and
addressed a crowd of around 2,000 people from the traditional platform of the back of a lorry.

Those speakers were Manny Shinwell, John Maclean,
Willie Gallacher and James Maxton. They were arrested for
causing an obstruction, fined 20 shillings each and released.
The incident did not help Maxton's increasingly strained
relationship with the Glasgow School Board, which took a
dim view of his anti-war activities and the amount of time he
was spending outside the classroom in order to pursue them.

When he wanted even more time off to attend the Labour
Party Conference in Newcastle in April 1916, he offered John
Maclean as a substitute for himself. Since Maclean had already
been dismissed by the Glasgow School Board for his own
involvement in anti-war activity, it's hard not to see Maxton's
suggestion as deliberate provocation. The School Board reacted by transferring him from his school in Dennistoun to
one in Finnieston and put him on a final warning. Any more
trouble and he would be sacked.

When conscription came into force at the beginning of March 1916, Maxton was called up. He applied for exemption as a conscientious objector and appeared before a tribunal in Barrhead to state his case, launching into an eloquent argument as to why he should be allowed to claim this status. After he had finished speaking he was asked why his employers had not put in a good word on his behalf, as they had done for other teachers.

The answer was simple. The Glasgow School Board had made good on their threat. The troublesome Mr Maxton had received his letter of dismissal. The tribunal asked if he would consider joining the army as a medic. His retort was immediate and unequivocal. No, he would not consider that. 'It's all part of the game, and you know it.'

The tribunal said they would give their decision in a fortnight. By that time Maxton had got himself arrested over the deportation of the shop stewards to Edinburgh. At the angry demonstration on Glasgow Green on Sunday, 26 March 1916, he was one of those who addressed the crowd: 'It is now for the workers to take action and that action is to strike and down tools at once. Not a rivet should be struck on the Clyde until the deported engineers are restored to their families. In case there are any plainclothes detectives in the audience I shall repeat that statement for their benefit. The men should strike and down tools.'

Typical James Maxton. Passionate. Defiant. Challenging. Reckless.

Plainclothes policemen were indeed present, taking down every word. They waited a few days before they came for him at midnight on the following Thursday. Maxton had just got home after visiting his friend John Maclean, who himself was out on bail after having been arrested for the speeches he had been making against conscription.

James Maxton's dog Karl was ready to go for the policemen but his master restrained him and went quietly. Well, probably not at all quietly, but peacefully at least. After Maxton's

arrest, Karl the dog was stoned to death by thugs claiming to
be patriots objecting to his master's anti-war stance.

James MacDougall, with whom Maxton had shared a platform at Glasgow Green, was also arrested. Both men spent
the next four weeks in Glasgow's grim Duke Street Prison,
charged with 'attempting to cause mutiny, sedition and disaffection and with impeding, delaying and restricting the war
effort'.

Maxton was desperately worried about his girlfriend Sissie
and his mother Melvina, who now had two sons in prison.

John Maxton had also claimed exemption from military
service as a conscientious objector but was refused. After a
court martial, he had been sentenced to imprisonment in
Wormwood Scrubs.

Outwardly James Maxton put on a brave face. Unable after
all to attend the ILP conference in Newcastle in April 1916,
he sent his apologies. In the letter read out to the delegates
he explained he was unable to attend owing to the unfortunate circumstance of currently being confined to his room.
'People in the movement here have done everything they
could to make me as comfortable as possible. The prison
officials have been very decent and have shown every respect
and consideration. It is a valuable and instructive experience
and everyone should have at least ten days in prison annually
for the good both of their health and their immortal souls.'

While he was confined to his lonely cell he was thinking
deeply about life, his and Sissie McCallum's in particular. She
was allowed to visit him in Duke Street and it was in prison
that he proposed to her and was accepted. She must have
really loved him, for he certainly wasn't much of a catch,
out of work, in prison, facing a trial for sedition and an even
lengthier prison sentence. Understandably, Sissie's parents
were not exactly over the moon about their daughter's choice.

She had to buy her own ring, although her new fiancé did
arrange to get the money to her for that. He wrote movingly
to her on 4 May 1916:

My own dearest lass,

We've got our marching orders quicker than I expected so yesterday was our goodbye, I fancy for some time now. Whatever the time may be it will soon pass and then see how glad we'll be when we meet. Always look forward til then and things won't seem so bad. I'll make up to you for every sorrow you've suffered and every tear you've shed in every way I can.

I've only realised in the last four weeks what a woman's love means, and I'm sure that's one good thing prison has done. I never believed it possible in any other circumstances that any woman would do what you've done for me, or stick so loyally through thick and thin. I shall never forget it, and every power, every ability I have, and I'm afraid they're not many, will be used henceforward for your sake.

I haven't so much time as usual for this note so I'll cut off here. Keep cheery, enjoy yourself as much as possible, have as many friends as possible, and I'll be with you again soon.

Yours ever,

Jim

They were both thirty at the time of their engagement and it was another three years before they could be married. A major reason for the delay was that it was only Sissie who now had a regular income. The bar on female teachers being married meant she would be obliged to give up work as soon as they wed.

Maxton and MacDougall were tried at the High Court in Edinburgh, sitting in Parliament House off the Royal Mile. Their legal team on Thursday, 11 May 1916, included the indispensable Mr Rosslyn Mitchell and both defendants took the advice to plead guilty. The core of their defence was the strength of their feelings over the deportation of the shop

stewards of the CWC. They had felt this was a grave injustice and that was why they had spoken out so passionately against it. They realised now they should not have said what they had done.

The Lord Advocate, prosecuting, was having none of it. Maxton and MacDougall had incited the workers to strike while 'the flower of our British manhood' was fighting a war to save Britain from the Germans. Given the strong anti-German sentiment in Edinburgh after the death and destruction caused by the Zeppelin raid, the sentence imposed was considered lenient: one year's imprisonment.

The two men served their time in Calton Jail. Perched on the cliff which rises above the main railway line to London at Waverley Station, this occupied the site of today's St Andrew's House. There's not much left of the prison now apart from one of its fanciful Victorian towers, complete with battlements. Maxton joked about it being his ancestral home.

Conditions were pretty grim, with a monotonous diet of porridge and buttermilk, little comfort in terms of bedding and nothing to read except the Bible and a hymn book. The prisoners were isolated too, despite now having other friends occupying cells in the same building. Willie Gallacher and Johnny Muir were in Calton Jail at the same time. So, briefly, was John Maclean.

Maclean too had been tried and found guilty of sedition, sentenced to a harsh three years' penal servitude. He was soon transferred from Edinburgh to Peterhead, on the windswept Buchan coast north of Aberdeen. If the authorities hoped thus to put him out of sight and out of mind, they had badly misjudged the esteem in which thousands of people held him.

The prisoners in Edinburgh had friends outside the jail. Davie Kirkwood and the CWC shop stewards were still in Edinburgh.

> Another of our interests was to go to Calton Hill, over-
> looking the Jail, and wave to James Maxton, William

Gallacher, John W. Muir, Walter Bell, and James McDougall [*sic*] when they came into the yard for exercise.

Let it be said in honour of the good-nature of their jailers that, when it was discovered that we were sending greetings, the officers found something to attract their attention elsewhere for that one precious minute a day. It was an open secret that every one in Calton Jail learned to love James Maxton.

The warders certainly warmed to him. As Gordon Brown put it, he 'persuaded some of them to form a branch of the Police and Prison Warders' Trade Union and even inveigled a few into the ILP'.

Outside the prison walls, but with their internal exile enforced by having to report to the Edinburgh police three times a day, the CWC deportees spent varying amounts of time in the capital. The Amalgamated Society of Engineers, of which they were members, refused to give them any help, although some came from other quarters.

When rank and file members of the union elected a member to attend the Labour Party Conference in Manchester in January 1917, Davie Kirkwood won by a mile. After various shenanigans and the intervention of Colonel Levita, he was allowed to go. He told the colonel that when he was finished at Manchester he was going home to Glasgow. Levita dared him to do it. He did.

The Glasgow police called on him as soon as he got there, asking him to sign a document promising that in future he would interfere in no way with the production of munitions. He indignantly refused, on the grounds that he never had done. On the contrary, he had helped keep production going. Not quite sure what to do with him, the police asked him to give his word of honour that he would not leave home for the next 24 hours.

When they hadn't returned four days later, a bemused

Kirkwood consulted with John Wheatley and Tom Johnston. Seeing that he was under the weather physically, they advised a short rest and 'it finished up with me being packed off in my best clothes with bag and umbrella to Crieff Hydropathic'.

> It was a new experience for me. I had never before been in a hydropathic or any similar resort of the well-to-do. I was astonished to find that, as the old woman said, 'the place was fair polluted wi' meenisters'. It was like a ministers' guest-house. I was still more surprised in the evening to see the ministers and their lady friends dancing or sitting at a dozen tables, playing cards! So innocent was I of the fashionable world that I thought ministers looked upon card-playing as a sin and a folly. I could not play cards. I thought it strange to have dancing and card-playing during the War.

The police caught up with him the morning after his arrival. He had eaten a hearty breakfast, sung hymns at a morning service and was thinking good thoughts about everyone around him when the Chief Constable of Perthshire turned up and arrested him. The platoon of soldiers the Chief Constable had brought with him to the Hydro were to escort Kirkwood to Edinburgh Castle.

'All right,' said the dangerous revolutionary, 'but I'll need to go upstairs for my bag and my umbrella.' Although out-wardly he remained calm, seeing the soldiers had shaken him badly. 'They had come for me at last,' he wrote. Not only was this mere months after the Easter Rising, they were also in the middle of a war where terrified young men suffering from shell shock were shot at dawn. Facing that firing squad must once again have seemed a real possibility.

His senses clearly heightened, Kirkwood looked out of the window of his fifth floor room in Crieff Hydro and observed how beautiful the surrounding countryside was.

The Chief Constable looked, and said he had no idea that Crieff was such a beautiful place and that he had never seen it from such a height.

Then he turned to me and said: 'Kirkwood, you're a queer fish. I can't make you out at all. If I were you, I should have something more on my mind than looking at the ordinary things of Nature.'

They took me from the Hydro by a back door, lest I should give the place a bad name or disturb the peace of the ministers.

He had nothing but praise for the 'utmost kindness and good will' with which the Perthshire police treated him before he was sent off to Edinburgh. 'One of Britain's greatest achievements is the creation of a police force which performs its duty with efficiency and retains an attitude of detachment.'

When they offered him bread, butter and tea he told them he was a lot hungrier than that. What he wanted was 'steak, potatoes and a vegetable, and then a pudding'. The police burst out laughing, and obliged. 'These things were sent for, and a fine Scots lassie brought them in. I enjoyed my dinner. The train arrived. The Chief Constable shook hands and wished me good luck, and my soldier escort and I boarded the train. In little more than an hour I was in a dungeon in Edinburgh Castle, sitting on my bag, with my umbrella propped up in a corner!'

The two weeks he spent there were dark in more ways than one.

The Castle of Edinburgh is of great age. It was built at a time when oppression drove the people in rebellion and then cruelly crushed the rebellious.

My new habitation was a vault far below the ground, into which the only light entered from a small grated window high up near the roof. Above my vault were the guards' quarters, occupied by German and Austrian

officer-prisoners. They were a noisy crew, singing, shouting, and scrapping day and night. They seemed to want for nothing.

I thought it strange that I, who was innocent of any offence, should be in a dungeon while the captured enemy should be so cheerfully housed up above.

I was a done man. My mind refused to think. My body seemed incapable of exertion. I wondered what was to happen next.

Hours passed in utter loneliness.

On his third day a soldier flung open the cell door, slapped the revolver at his belt and threatened to dispatch him: '... I'd raither use it to shoot you nor a German. You're David Kirkwood o' the Clyde'. Kirkwood drew his own weapon in defence: words and reasoned argument. They soon got on to the Bible. 'I was grateful to Joseph – he occupied fully twenty minutes! Then we passed to Pharaoh and Moses, and the very pleasant story of the mother who made Pharaoh's daughter pay her for being a nursemaid to her own child. After that it was easy to tramp through the desert, though it took the Israelites forty days and forty nights. By the time we had reached the Land of Promise, in which I was more fortunate than Moses, I was becoming exhausted, but I was grateful to the minister whose Bible class I had attended in my youth!'

The soldier had long since stopped menacingly patting his revolver. Davie Kirkwood spent two hours talking to the man about the Bible and made a shrewd observation: 'He was more interested in the Bible than in shooting me, although he had come for that purpose. I have often noticed that people who are attracted by the blood stories of the Old Testament are inclined to look upon weapons of destruction as instruments confided to their care for carrying out what they believe to be the purposes of the Almighty. It is a kind of brain affection that has put a blight on religion through the ages.'

When the guard changed, Kirkwood told the soldier going off-duty that maybe one day he would see the light, that 'this was a capitalist war' and after it he might very probably find himself out of a job. Years later, Kirkwood met that soldier again. He came up to him at an open-air meeting, shook his hand and told him that he had indeed now seen the light. Kirkwood had converted him that day in Edinburgh Castle.

Unable to coerce him into signing any undertakings that he would cause no trouble in the future, an exasperated Colonel Levita released the stubborn Mr Kirkwood but reminded him that he was still under sentence of deportation and could not therefore return home to Glasgow. Kirkwood walked out of Edinburgh Castle into the fresh air of the outside world. He remembered to take his umbrella.

Once again he sought refuge with John S. Clarke. He told Kirkwood he should head south to Moffat Hydro. The Clyde Workers' Committee had already sent James Maxton, Willie Gallacher and James MacDougall there to get their strength back after their months in prison. The group stayed at Moffat for two weeks, the cost funded by a collection of the faithful taken up by John Wheatley, doing what he so often did and quietly making the necessary arrangements. Kirkwood's train was met by another chief constable. 'How had he known I was coming? He saluted and said: "Good afternoon, Mr Kirkwood." It was a most generous greeting. I raised my hat and said: "Good afternoon, Chief." It was like Stanley's meeting with Livingstone in Africa. The Chief Constable ought to have said: "Mr Kirkwood, I presume?" He turned away and I went on to the Hydropathic – the second time I had been in such a place.'

Davie Kirkwood once observed that James Maxton always looked so ill nobody noticed when he really was ill. That Maxton kept body and soul together on a diet which consisted mainly of cigarettes and tea probably didn't help. At Moffat, worried by his friend's persistent cough, Kirkwood insisted on taking him to see a local doctor. Dr Park was reassuring

about Maxton's health but damning of the wild men of the Clyde everyone was talking about:

> 'Traitor of the deepest dye,' he called Kirkwood, and said Maxton was a vagabond. It was a good thing they were both safe within the walls of Edinburgh Castle. We kept back our laughter with difficulty.
>
> As we were saying our good-byes, Jimmie said, pointing to me: 'This is the traitor of the deepest dye.'
>
> 'And this,' I said, 'is the vagabond, though he's mair like a scarecrow nor a Russian revolutionary.'

Dr Park's mouth fell open. Then he began to laugh, the traitor of the deepest dye and the vagabond joined in, and they all parted the best of friends. Davie Kirkwood made another astute observation. 'Like so many people who thought they hated us, he did not hate us. What he hated was his own idea of us.'

Relations with the many wounded officers staying at Moffat Hydro were not so cordial. 'It was tragic to see them, splendid men, hobbling about. Of course they knew who we were, but they paid no attention to us. They gave a good example of self-control, for I am sure that in their distress they must have hated us. In all the fortnight only two of them spoke to us.'

One of those who did was a Cameron Highlander who swayed up to their table one night when he was drunk and 'full of insulting remarks'. When the Red Clydesiders refused to rise to the bait, the soldier tried harder. 'Then he ruffled Maxton's hair, saying: "Look at his hair. He's more of a Frenchman than a Scot." That was too much for me. I rose up and said: "Look here, Captain, if you don't go over to your own table, I'll smash your jaw for you, and the whole British Army won't protect ye." He gave a silly wave of the hand and went away like a child. The other officers looked, but said nothing.'

Still a deportee, Kirkwood had to go back to Edinburgh when he left Moffat Hydro. Desperately worried about his

wife, who was expecting another baby, he had a crisis of conscience as to whether to sign the documents which would allow him to go home. When his son sent a telegram to say his mother had given birth to a baby girl, Kirkwood 'ran to the Scottish Command'.

Although Kirkwood still refused to sign the documents, Colonel Guest, the new commander, told him he was a married man himself and would do his best to get him home. Kirkwood went to Waverley, bought a single ticket to Glasgow and packed his bag. Once again he did not forget his umbrella.

Despite all sorts of complications, Colonel Guest was as good as his word, accompanying his prisoner through to Glasgow on a special late-night train. Kirkwood was horribly afraid the colonel's kindness meant his wife had died and that the military man was only waiting for the opportunity to break it to him gently.

At Queen Street, Glasgow, the station seemed to be full of soldiers, all drawn up in parade order. It was now one o'clock in the morning. Glasgow was silent and dark.

I was led to a motor-car in front of which were two soldiers. Colonel Guest sat beside me. We drove to my home. At the close-mouth he stopped and, in the gentlest way, said: 'I think you had better go upstairs by yourself. If I appear in these regimentals, it might give Mrs Kirkwood a shock. Go up and see how things are, and then come down and let me know.'

I ran up three steps at a time and chapped on the door in the way we both knew so well. Then I pushed open the letter-box and heard my wife say: 'There's Davie at the door.'

I think in all my life I have never heard anything so wonderful as that phrase.

When Kirkwood returned to the close-mouth where Colonel Guest was standing in the gloom of the night and told him mother and baby were both doing well, the soldier threw his arms about his prisoner and hugged him. 'I was speechless. We looked at each other. We clasped hands. He saluted, and moved away to his car in the darkness. I waved to him as he went.'

Impressed that he had not exaggerated how ill his wife was in the hope of gaining his own freedom, Guest gave it to him anyway, confirming that by letter at the end of May 1917.

All but one of the Red Clydesiders who had challenged the government were now free. A welcome-home social was held at St Mungo's Hall in June 1917. Everyone was still tremendously excited by the news of Russia's February Revolution and the overthrow of the Tsar.

Everyone also agreed that the priority now was to get John Maclean out of prison.

17

John Maclean

*'I am not here, then, as the accused:
I am here as the accuser of capitalism, dripping with
blood from head to foot.'*

John Maclean dedicated his life to teaching people about Marxist economics, the history of the working classes and the class struggle. For him, revolution was the only way to end poverty and injustice. The working classes must rise up and seize the power which, as the producers of society's wealth, was rightfully theirs.

Passionately opposed to the First World War, he spoke out against it at meeting after meeting and was arrested under the Defence of the Realm Act. His first prison sentence lasted less than a week but resulted in instant dismissal from his teaching post. This happened at the end of 1915. Mrs Barbour and her army collected him from the last school he taught in on their way to the Sheriff Court to protest during the rent strike.

Losing his job was a financial disaster for him and his family but freed him to carry on urging revolution, teaching outside the formal school system and protesting against the war and conscription. This got him arrested again in Feburary 1916 under DORA, when he was imprisoned briefly in Calton Jail with James Maxton, James MacDougall, Johnny Muir and Willie Gallacher, and then by himself in Peterhead.

When his wife was allowed to visit him there in the summer of 1916 they discussed the petition which was being mooted to

try to secure his release. Maclean was adamant that he would not beg for leniency. Any petition should focus on securing rights for him as a political prisoner. If countries like Germany, Russia and England recognised this category, why was Scotland insisting on treating him like a common criminal?

It wasn't much of a visit. Husband and wife were permitted to spend only 20 minutes together, had to talk under the supervision of two guards and were not even allowed to clasp each other's hands through the bars which separated them. Another visit would not be permitted until Maclean had served a year of his sentence.

Letters were also strictly limited. Agnes Maclean visited in July. She and her husband were not allowed to write to each other until the following November. He was allowed one book a week but no newspapers. Sentenced as he was to three years' penal servitude, he had to work out of doors in all weathers. The often harsh climate of the Buchan Coast was to take its toll on his health.

A campaign was mounted on his behalf: a demonstration on Glasgow Green, questions asked in Parliament, letters to the home secretary. Socialists in other countries asked their ambassadors in Britain to enquire into the case of John Maclean. Why had this man been dealt with more severely than others?

Sales of work were held and donations made to a fund to give financial support to Mrs Maclean and the couple's two daughters. Agnes Maclean wrote to her husband in November 1916: 'It would take pages to tell you of the people who are always asking about you and thinking of you.'

His continuing imprisonment had become a cause, one which fired up thousands. The burning sense of injustice found a focus at the end of June 1917, when Lloyd George, now prime minister, returned to Glasgow to be given the freedom of the city. That such an honour should be conferred on him was not a universally popular move on Red Clydeside.

Willie Gallacher remembered how Lloyd George was driven through Glasgow in an open carriage, surrounded by soldiers and policemen on foot and horseback, to St Andrew's Halls, where the ceremony was to take place. Was the venue coincidental or was the prime minister hoping to lay the embarrassing ghost of the Christmas Day Munitions Conference to rest? The Welsh Wizard was on top form, at his charming best:

> At the top window of a block of flats overlooking the west entrance to the hall used on this occasion, an old stalwart of the movement, Mrs. Reid, her white hair crowning a face alight with the flame of revolt against the mad slaughter of the war, was waving a great red flag.
>
> From the distant place to which we had been forced back Kirkwood was shouting encouragement to her at the top of his stentorian voice, while the crowd gave her cheer after cheer. Before entering the hall, Mr. Lloyd George, always acutely conscious of the mood of the crowd, stood up in the carriage which had drawn to a stop, looked up at our comrade bravely waving the scarlet banner, raised his hat and gave her one of his most gracious bows. Then he looked over the heads of the military and police, towards the mass of workers, nodding his head as though to say, 'You see, I'm a bit of a Red Flagger myself.'

Whether by chance or design, John Maclean was released from custody the morning after Lloyd George was given the freedom of Glasgow. Returned to the city the day before his release, he was freed from Duke Street Prison. He got his own welcome-home reception, chaired by Tom Johnston. When a telegram of congratulations was read out from the Petrograd Soviet, the cheering raised the roof.

It wasn't long before Maclean was back at the barricades. In October 1917, like so many on Red Clydeside, he drew

strength and inspiration from the second Russian Revolution. This saw the triumph of the Bolsheviks under Lenin and the establishment of a Communist state. Men like Maclean and Willie Gallacher and Arthur McManus longed to achieve the same in Scotland, with society run by workers' and soldiers' committees.

At the beginning of 1918 Lenin appointed John Maclean Soviet Consul for Scotland. It was a dubious honour. No country was as yet prepared to give official diplomatic recognition to the new Soviet workers' republic. Nothing daunted, Maclean opened a Russian consulate at Portland Street in Glasgow.

In April 1918 the police raided the premises and once again arrested him under DORA, charging him with sedition and attempting to spread disaffection among the civilian population. He was tried in Edinburgh on 9 May 1918 and the speech he gave from the dock that day has acquired legendary status. This ringing denunciation of capitalism took him more than an hour to deliver:

> It has been said that they cannot fathom my motive. For the full period of my active life I have been a teacher of economics to the working classes, and my contention has always been that capitalism is rotten to its foundation, and must give place to a new society. I had a lecture, the principal heading of which was 'Thou shalt not steal; thou shalt not kill', and I pointed out that as a consequence of the robbery that goes on in all civilised countries today, our respective countries have had to keep armies, and that inevitably our armies must clash together. I consider capitalism the most infamous, bloody and evil system that mankind has ever witnessed. My language is regarded as extravagant language, but the events of the past four years have proved my contention.

Looking at the blood and mud and carnage which had spilled over Europe in those past four years, you didn't necessarily have to be a revolutionary socialist to agree with him. 'I wish no harm to any human being, but I, as one man, am going to exercise my freedom of speech. No human being on the face of the earth, no government is going to take from me my right to speak, my right to protest against wrong, my right to do everything that is for the benefit of mankind. I am not here, then, as the accused: I am here as the accuser of capitalism, dripping with blood from head to foot.'

The jury did not retire but gave their verdict through their foreman: guilty on all charges. The Lord Justice General turned to Maclean and asked him if he had anything to say. 'No,' he said, 'I think I have said enough for one day.'

The judge told him he was not going to dwell on the gravity of his having been found guilty again of an offence under the Defence of the Realm Act: '... because you are obviously a highly educated and intelligent man, and realise the thorough seriousness of the offence you have committed'.

The Lord Justice General sentenced Maclean to five years' penal servitude, an even tougher sentence than the last time. In her biography, his daughter Nan Milton described what happened next. Maclean turned to friends in the court and told them to, 'Keep it going, boys, keep it going.' As he was being led out of the court, he turned and waved his hat to his wife and friends, who shouted back to him, 'Ta, ta, Johnnie! Good old Johnnie!' before standing up and belting out 'The Red Flag'.

Once again a campaign swung into action to demand his release. It gathered huge momentum, especially after the armistice which ended the First World War was signed on 11 November 1918. Lloyd George called an immediate election. The release of John Maclean was on the agenda at every political meeting in Glasgow and beyond.

Freed on 3 December, he had served only seven months of his five-year sentence but was not a well man, weakened

by going on hunger strike while in Peterhead and being force-fed. Bruised and exhausted, he wrote to Agnes Maclean saying she was the only person he wanted to meet him at Buchanan Street railway station, but word got out. Thousands were there to greet him when his train pulled in.

The welcoming party had hired a horse-drawn carriage so as many people as possible could see him. Someone handed him a red flag. The horse and the carriage driver picked a careful path through the sea of supporters thronging the city streets. Worn-out though he was, a defiant Maclean stood up and waved the red flag above his head. Now, there was a moment. 'Never in the history of Glasgow,' wrote Willie Gallacher, 'was there such a reception as John Maclean got that night.'

The joy so many people felt at John Maclean's triumphant return to the Clyde and the legendary position he continues to occupy in the history of Red Clydeside is reflected in two exuberant anthems written long after that December night in 1918: Hamish Henderson's 'John Maclean's March' and Matt McGinn's 'The Ballad of John Maclean (The Fighting Dominie)'.

When the Communist Party of Great Britain was founded in April 1920, Scotland's most famous Marxist did not join it. He wanted a Scottish communist party, not a British one, so he founded the Scottish Workers' Republican Party. One newspaper advert for it was cheerfully combative: 'Roll-up, Glasgow Reds, and join the new Revolutionary Party for a Scottish Workers' Parliament, allied to Russia, one big industrial union, Marxian education under the Scottish Labour College'.

Maclean served two more prison sentences, in 1921 and 1922. In both cases he was again charged with sedition, firstly for advocating that the miners of Airdrie should lead a workers' revolution and secondly for saying the post-war unemployed should steal food rather than starve. The first sentence lasted three months, the second a year.

When he was released from prison in 1922 he had little more than a year to live. Once a robust and healthy man, his prison terms, endless teaching and public speaking had seriously damaged his health. He spent the last months of his life working to build up his Scottish Workers' Republican Party.

He fought every local by-election he could, convinced as always that patching up capitalism was never going to be the answer. Only revolutionary socialism could sweep away poverty, injustice and war.

> I come before you at this election at the request of many members of your ward as a COMMUNIST or RED LABOUR candidate. Pink Labourism is of no use to the workers, never will be. Your poverty and misery are more intense today than ever before. Thirteen out of every hundred in Glasgow are getting Parish Council Relief, and the number is growing. World developments are bound to make things still worse, even if Britain is lucky enough to avoid another world war.

Maclean's manifesto goes on to damn unemployment as 'a weapon to cow the workers into accepting lower wages and a longer week'. His solution to the lack of jobs was a scheme to 'reclaim all the moorland lying round Glasgow, and establish a systerm of co-operative or collective farming on scientific lines'.

He called for a Scottish Parliament, one completely divorced from Westminster. Only a Scotland independent from England had any hope of becoming a country where the workers were in charge. England, he feared, would not be ready for Communism before the war Maclean believed was coming. 'I therefore consider that Scotland's wisest policy is to declare for a republic in Scotland, so that the youth of Scotland will not be forced out to die for England's markets.

The Social Revolution is possible sooner in Scotland than in England ... Scottish separation is part of the process of England's imperial disintegration and is a help towards the ultimate triumph of the workers of the world.'

The young members of the Scottish Workers' Republican Party loved John Maclean. In an age much more formal than our own, he insisted they call him by his first name. He encouraged them at every turn, building up their confidence so they could stand up and address a public meeting. 'In the winter all felt it their cardinal duty to attend the economics and industrial history classes,' wrote Nan Milton, adding that his students acquired the nickname of 'John Maclean's bright young things'.

Maclean remained a teacher to the end, giving his classes on economics and taking a close interest in the education of his elder daughter, Jean. At the beginning of 1922 she was coming up to her twelfth birthday. Her father's advice was that she should start reading the papers and finding out what was going on in the world.

> A good geography book and an atlas should always be at your side to enable you to know as much about the earth as possible. A general history of the world in all times should prove useful. Perhaps your aunt may be able to tell you about the great civilization of ancient Egypt, the mummies, and the tombs of the Pharoahs or emperors, and of the recent discoveries at Luxor on the Nile where the tomb of King Tutankhamen has just been found and is causing excitement all over the world.

He did not scruple to tell young Jean that people were already saying there could be another European war but he told her there was a way to stop war. 'The only way to end war and prevent all wars is for the wage workers of the whole world to unite and tell the wealthy that the workers themselves will

rule the world. For advocating that, your father was sent to gaol and may be sent again. But sooner or later the workers will do as your father wishes them to do.'

Sylvia Pankhurst was a friend and supporter of Maclean's. On a visit to Glasgow she went to his home in Pollokshaws, where he was living by himself and eating little more than porridge and dates. He had given what money he had to pay for food and a doctor for a sick child.

Some see John Maclean as a secular saint, the tragic martyr of Scottish socialism. Heart, head and soul, he was devoted to his cause. He saw those troubled years immediately following the national trauma of the First World War as opening a door to the revolution he so believed in. Believing that door would not stay open for long, he could not allow himself to rest until he had done everything in his power to make the revolution happen.

For that goal he sacrificed everything, including his own health and family life. Seeing how he was driving himself into the ground, Agnes Maclean had taken their two daughters and left him, telling him she would come back only if he stopped his political activities.

Maclean wrote to tell her that although he was on a short-list for the paid post of tutor at the Scottish Labour College, he couldn't pursue it, as the college was insisting the tutor should not be actively involved in politics. That restriction was something he simply could not contemplate. Agnes should also know his enemies were using her living apart from him as a stick to beat him with. She had to come home and be seen out and about with him.

> If you cannot come I'll be blackened worse than ever, and will be economically damned. If that is so, I have made up my mind for the worst – that we'll never come together again.
>
> If I go down, I must go down with my flag at the mast-top. Nothing on earth will shift me from that.

Now, there's the tragedy for you, as clearly and bluntly as I can put it.

If it's your duty to be here, as I maintain it now is, I contend it is your duty to stand shoulder to shoulder with me in the hardest and dirtiest battle of my life. If we have to go under we had better go under fighting together than fighting one another.

Realizing that this is the greatest crisis in our lives I cannot find words to say more.

If you come I'd prefer you to come at once and walk right in.

Whatever course we follow, remember that you are the only woman I love and can now love.

In June 1922 Maclean won a seat in the local elections for Glasgow's Kingston ward. His printed election address warns of the rise of the 'Fascisti' in Germany and Britain. He also warned voters off reforms which might seem to be to their benefit but in reality were only applying those patches to capitalism. Once again it all comes down to economics. 'The worker who votes for the upholders of the system of society that allows him to be robbed of the larger part of the wealth produced by him and his fellows, is clearly a simpleton.'

Right to the end, he kept faith with Marxism, as his final election address shows. 'For the wage-earning class there is but one alternative to a capitalist war for markets. The root of all the trouble in society at present is the inevitable robbery of the workers by the propertied class, simply because it is the propertied class. To end that robbery would be to end the social troubles of modern society.'

Elated by his success in the municipal election, he decided to contest the Gorbals as a Labour candidate at the upcoming general election. His decision plunged Agnes Maclean into despair. 'It is just throwing yourself away, and money that is needed to keep your family.'

Her own health was not too good at the time but she had

decided she would 'go in for nursing or something that will give me some independence and that will be a bit cheerier. We will need to arrange about the children in some way.' Angry and upset, she told him it was his duty to stand by her and leave politics alone for the moment. Perhaps hoping to persuade him, she agreed to go back to him.

She found him at a low ebb physically. It was November, month of freezing fogs, but he was still addressing meetings, many out of doors. He had loaned his only coat to a black friend from Barbados who was shivering in the cold of a Scottish winter.

Determined to work until his last breath to get his message across, John Maclean was on a platform at an open-air meeting when he collapsed and had to be carried home. He had double pneumonia. He died on St Andrew's Day, 30 November 1923, at the age of 44.

Tens of thousands of people turned out to see him make his final journey, his friend James Maxton one of the pall-bearers who carried the coffin out of the house to the horse-drawn hearse. Afterwards, money was collected which gave Agnes Maclean and her daughters a reasonable weekly income for quite a number of years. She died in 1953, 30 years after her husband.

The Soviet Union remembered John Maclean on the centenary of his birth. In 1979 they produced a postage stamp in his honour. In 1973 a cairn in Pollokshaws was erected to commemorate the fiftieth anniversary of his death. The inscription reads 'Famous pioneer of working-class education, he forged the Scottish link in the golden chain of world socialism.'

The revolution he called for never came. Yet there are those today who make the pilgrimage to that cairn and to his grave in Eastwood Cemetery, paying their respects and taking inspiration from John Maclean, the man whose dedication to his cause was absolute.

18

Bloody Friday, 1919:
The Battle of George Square

'Military Ready to Deal with Clyde Rioters . . .
We Didn't Regard the Forty Hours Strike as a Revolution.'

The year started with a tragedy. On Hogmanay 1918, HMS *Iolaire* put out from Kyle of Lochalsh heading for Stornoway on the Isle of Lewis. On board were almost 300 men, predominantly Royal Navy sailors, coming home from the war. In the early hours of New Year's Day 1919 the *Iolaire* struck notorious rocks a mile outside Stornoway Harbour. Valiant efforts saved many of the men on board but more than 200 drowned as the ship went down. It was a heart-breaking blow after four long years of war.

People were exhausted in 1919. The war was over but the peace had yet to be won. Promises had been made of a land fit for heroes but there were few signs this was about to arrive any time soon. After the strain and losses of the war, another blow was dealt when the influenza pandemic swept round the world.

Between May 1918 and the spring of 1919, Glasgow alone experienced three outbreaks which caused 4,000 deaths. Many of those were of children under five, who were particularly susceptible. Around the world, millions died of the 'Spanish Flu'. Yet it is almost a forgotten tragedy. After so many deaths during the previous four years, perhaps people simply could not absorb any more grief.

In politics, the Representation of the People Act of 1918 had given the vote to men over 21 and women over 30. Despite this hard-won and so long-awaited extension to the franchise, the post-war election disappointed many. There was a widespread view that the poll had been rushed and nothing much had changed.

As Davie Kirkwood put it: 'In that election the Socialists went down like ninepins. The country had only one hero, Lloyd George, and only one object: "Make the Germans pay."' The Welsh Wizard had now become the Man Who Won the War.

A new coalition government was formed. Although the Conservatives under Andrew Bonar Law had more seats, Lloyd George's popularity with so many voters meant that he remained prime minister. The Labour Party had returned 57 MPs to Westminster, the greatest number yet, but they had little power in this new Parliament.

Frustration mounted as the wartime economy slammed on the brakes. There was no longer the need to go hell for leather on munitions, and the Clyde's order books were beginning to look sparse. Thousands of demobbed servicemen were flooding into a labour market where there soon wasn't enough work to go round.

The STUC, Glasgow Trades and Labour Council and other trade unionists came up with an idea. Reducing industry's working week from 54 to 40 hours would allow what work there was to be shared out more fairly. Resistance to this idea from employers, the government and some unions led to calls for industrial action. The dispute became known as the 40 Hours Strike.

On Sunday, 26 January 1919, 10,000 people, some waving red flags, marched from St Andrew's Halls to the City Chambers. In their report the next day in which they gave their readers that information, the *Evening Times* quoted one of the speakers who addressed the marchers in George Square. Mr Cameron of the Discharged Soldiers' Federation

said his organisation was 'backing the workers this time and looked for the workers to back them. They had fought for their country and they now wanted to own it.' The next day St Andrew's Halls was again the focus. Three thousand people attended the meeting where the strike was officially called. Over the next few days the protest gathered momentum.

Workers at the Port Dundas and Pinkston power stations were among those who came out, cutting electricity supplies throughout Glasgow. They agreed to keep the lights on in the city's hospitals and streets and to keep Glasgow and their fellow strikers moving by keeping the trams running. By Friday, 31 January, 60,000 people had downed tools.

Putting the numbers of strikers at 40,000, the *Glasgow Herald* referred to them and their techniques as 'the methods of terrorism'. *The Scotsman* too referred to 'Terrorism on the Clyde'. *The Times* had sympathy for the exhaustion of working people after the strain of the war but no sympathy with the 'gangs of revolutionaries' it believed were exploiting them. 'The three firebrands named by the Lord Provost are notorious rebels against all social order.'

The three firebrands in question were Manny Shinwell, Davie Kirkwood and Neil Maclean. *The Times* noted that Manny Shinwell 'is described as a Polish Jew'. In fact, he was born to Jewish parents in the East End of London, moved to Glasgow with them and became an adopted Glaswegian. Formerly of Singer's, Neil Maclean was one of the 26 Scottish Labour MPs elected to Parliament in the previous month's poll. 'These are the men who have challenged the Government,' wrote *The Times* disapprovingly.

On Wednesday, 29 January, a committee of strikers asked Glasgow's Lord Provost to intervene on their behalf with the government. James Stewart said he would do what he could and asked the committee to come back to see him on the Friday. They brought a few friends with them. Davie Kirkwood described George Square as 'black with men'.

Notices requesting their presence had been placed in *The Strike Bulletin, Organ of the 40 Hours Movement*. The news-sheet was published daily over the course of the dispute and cost one penny, 'although admirers say it is worth Threepence'. On Thursday, 30 January, their notice 'TO ALL STRIKERS' told everyone to come to George Square the following day at 12.30 p.m. 'BE IN TIME AND BE THERE.'

Some say 60,000 people gathered in the centre of Glasgow that Friday. Other estimates put the number as high as 100,000. The famous photograph of the event which gives this book its cover is the classic image of Red Clydeside. The unknown press photographer who shot it certainly framed a surging mass of humanity, all crammed in together. Apart from the policeman turning to look at the photographer, all eyes are on the City Chambers. If Scotland ever really did come close to revolution, this is the favoured moment.

Some men shinned up the ornate lamp posts outside the City Chambers, Glasgow's seat of municipal power. Red flags were unfurled. Manny Shinwell, Willie Gallacher and Davie Kirkwood were to the fore. John Maclean was not in Glasgow, fulfilling speaking engagements and attending political meetings in Cumberland, Manchester and London. James Maxton was in Glasgow but did not come to the square. For once in his life he chose to avoid trouble.

Winston Churchill was now Secretary of State for War. The day before Bloody Friday, the *Evening Times* reported what he had to say about the 40 Hours Strike.

> The present situation in Glasgow had been brewing for a long time. The disaffected were in a minority, and, in his opinion, there would have to be a conflict to clear the air. We should be careful to have plenty of provocation before taking strong measures. By going gently at first we should get the support we wanted from the nation, and then troops could be used more effectively. The moment for their use had not yet

arrived. In the meantime the Defence of the Realm
Act was still in force, and some of the leaders of the
revolt should be seized.

At the same meeting of what was still called the War Cabinet,
the Secretary of State for Scotland said it was more clear than
ever that it was a misnomer to call the situation in Glasgow
a strike. This was a Bolshevist rising. Raising the hare and
the panic, perhaps seeking to justify those strong measures,
he stated there were no more than 10,000 malcontents and
he knew public opinion would 'support the Government in
quelling any disorder'.

The Deputy Chief of the Imperial General Staff advised
that six tanks and a hundred motor lorries with drivers were
going north by rail that night. The War Cabinet discussed
prosecuting the strike leaders under DORA but decided
that 'for the moment no further action was necessary by the
Government'.

It is no wonder the government was nervous of Glasgow's
strikers. Not only had Red Clydeside earned a powerful reputation for its readiness to confront authority, what was going
on in Europe must have sent a shiver down the spine. The
shock waves pulsing out from Russia's October Revolution
of not much more than a year before were still being felt.
Even socialists and Communists who had welcomed that with
such jubiliation had been astonished by how quickly and
completely the Tsar and the apparatus and institutions of
imperial Russia had been swept away.

The German Kaiser had abdicated at the end of the war
and Germany had just experienced its short-lived revolution.
That ended in spectacular failure and death for its leaders,
who included Karl Liebknecht and Rosa Luxemburg. On
15 January 1919, two weeks before the Battle of George
Square, they were taken from the Adlon Hotel in Berlin and
executed without trial. That the next European revolution
might erupt on Red Clydeside could not be ruled out.

Yet few of the strikers seemed to have thought that. Harry McShane said, 'We didn't regard the Forty Hours Strike as a revolution. We saw it more as the beginning of things.'

Neil Maclean, Shinwell, Kirkwood and Harry Hopkins of the Amalgamated Society of Engineers went into the City Chambers to meet the Lord Provost and hear from him what the government had said. Around noon, while they were still in there, the men and women who had made sure to arrive early in George Square began to get restive.

Nobody can quite agree on what happened next. What is undisputed is that, as Glasgow's *Evening News* put it: 'The police found it necessary to make a baton charge, and strikers and civilians – men, women and children – were felled in the melée that followed.'

The demonstrators responded with stones and bottles, taking these from a lorry which had got stuck in North Frederick Street. Sheriff Mackenzie came out of the City Chambers, saw what was going on, and decided to read the Riot Act, a copy of which he had conveniently brought with him, ordering the crowd to disperse. It was the first time in 50 years it had been read and the last time it ever was read:

> Our Sovereign Lord the King chargeth and commandeth all persons, being assembled, immediately to disperse themselves, and peaceably depart to their habitations, or to their lawful business, upon the pains contained in the Act made in the first year of King George the First, for preventing tumults and riotous assemblies. God save the King.

Sheriff Mackenzie wasn't very far into it before his copy of the Act was plucked from his hand by one of the strikers, but he managed to complete the words from memory.

Tramcars had become marooned in the ocean of people. One female driver was stopped by men jumping up onto her platform and making off with the reversing handle. Afraid

because of all the bottles that were flying about and because the windows of her car had been smashed, Mary Beattie left the tram.

She told her story at the trial of the strike leaders which took place at the High Court in Edinburgh in April 1919. One policeman giving evidence told the court: 'There was a dense crowd, and young men mounted the cars and were hanging on all over them like a Christmas tree.' This same policeman claimed to have heard Davie Kirkwood shout from a window in the City Chambers overlooking Cochrane Street, urging the crowd to rush the police. 'Never mind their batons. Get into them.' Glasgow's town clerk told a different story, saying Kirkwood was doing his best to calm the crowd, and had actually said: 'This is not the opportune time for us; our time will come.'

There's plenty of eye-witness evidence that Davie Kirkwood rushed out of the City Chambers and into George Square when he heard the noise of the disturbance and was almost immediately knocked unconscious by a police baton. A photograph taken at the time confirms this. Willie Gallacher was also injured and he, Kirkwood and Shinwell were arrested.

The fighting continued, spreading up into North Frederick Street, Cathedral Street and later developing into running battles down to the river at Clyde Street and along as far as Glasgow Green. Nobody died but both demonstrators and policemen were injured. Official figures put the wounded at 34 strikers and 19 policemen. Given the numbers in the square, this would seem to indicate most people in the huge crowd were not involved in the fighting. *The Scotsman* reported on some police officers who were.

WORSE THAN FRANCE

Sergeant John Caskie described how an inspector and himself were pinned up against the wall while the crowd threw missiles at them. Witness had his helmet bashed and received a severe blow with half a brick on

the shoulder. The inspector was hit by a number of stones. They dodged the heavy ones and submitted to the lighter ones. (Laughter.) The attack on the inspector and himself would last about five or ten minutes.

Constable Campbell Smart, who stated that he was hit on the head, hands, and feet, declared that while he had had some unpleasant experiences in France, where he had served in the Army up to the point of the Armistice, there was nothing worse than they had had in Cathedral Street.

Harry McShane agreed with that judgement of the situation up in Cathedral Street. 'Finally the police ran for it and the strikers went after them. There were a lot of closes in Cathedral Street and they rushed up these closes to try and get over the back wall. But there were men catching them by the legs and pulling them down. Some of them got a terrible hiding. I think the best fight was up in Cathedral Street.'

Glasgow's *Evening News* was first with the report on the day, carrying it that night.

STRIKE BATTLE

RIOT ACT READ

Police Charge the Mob

WILD GLASGOW SCENES

About 30 Persons Injured

LEADERS ARRESTED

In the tense hours and days which followed, those army tanks which had been dispatched north rolled through the streets of Glasgow in a show of strength designed to impress and subdue the troublesome natives. It's part of the romance of the story that the troops who marched in with them were young English conscripts, it being thought too risky to deploy the Scottish troops in Maryhill Barracks. The chances of their changing sides was too high.

This may well be true, although Harry McShane recalled going 'to explain things' to some soldiers arriving at
Buchanan Street, 'the main station for trains from the north'.
That doesn't necessarily mean they were Scottish, of course,
and McShane doesn't specify, more interested in them not
knowing very much about the labour movement. 'They were
quite prepared to use their weapons, about that there is no
doubt. I'll always remember one of them pointing at his rifle
and saying, "This is better than bottles." I tried to talk to them
on the road down to George Square, but the officers were
getting between us and the men. But those young soldiers
were aggressive too.'

The *Daily Record* did its best to diminish the demonstrators,
presenting them as rowdy youths, mindless neds and thugs.
Its report of the events of Bloody Friday refers to 'disgraceful scenes' and 'little groups of malcontents' who started
assembling in George Square from early morning onwards.
'Singing snatches of their favourite "Red Flag" as they swung
along, the demonstration presented a menacing and trucu-
lent appearance. For the most part the ranks were composed
of the prentice class, hefty young fellows upon whom a sense
of civic responsibility has not yet dawned.'

The *Glasgow Herald* was at least more honest about the fear
the Battle of George Square struck into the hearts of the city's
Establishment. John Wheatley might have stated quite clearly
in 1918 that the Independent Labour Party rejected revolution. 'The people of this country may have socialism when
they consider it worth their vote.' Not convinced, the *Glasgow
Herald* declared the people who had caused the trouble in the
square were Bolsheviks.

Bolsheviks, sometimes Bolshev*ists*, were entering popular
culture as the villains of the piece. *Glasgow 1919, The Story
of the 40 Hours Strike,* includes among its press cuttings and
Harry McShane's account of Bloody Friday and what led up
to it an episode of a serial which appeared in the *Glasgow
Herald* on 8 February 1919, one week later.

Banished from the World features 'Derek Clyde, the famous detective', a man who 'sauntered into the room in the cool, listless way that was habitual to him'. Naturally, the languid air is all a front. Our hero has already dealt with one of those cunning Russian revolutionaries: '… when Vladimir Tolstoi, one of the six Russian Bolshevists who had been sent to England and Scotland to spread their pernicious doctrine, had met with a tragic death. He had been blown to fragments at his lodgings in the Gorbals by the explosion of an infernal machine with which he had meant to destroy a vessel that was lying off the Broomielaw.'

The dramatic drawing which accompanies the serial shows an 'infuriated Bolshevist' pointing a gun at Derek Clyde, the famous detective. 'I mean to kill you! I shrink from nothing that is my duty. It will be no crime to destroy one who is the tool of tyrants and oppressors.' Adding to the mix that dash of casual anti-Semitism so common at the time, the story also includes 'a Jew named Finkelstein'.

By Sunday, 2 February, the *Times*'s special correspondent was reporting that the troops on guard in Glasgow seemed to be teaching the strikers a lesson, as there were 'signs of returning reason. The futility of violence in the face of machines guns and rifles has been realized.' Those machine guns were mounted on top of the buildings around George Square, with a howitzer in the City Chambers. Would Lord Provost James Stewart really have been prepared to sanction the mowing-down of thousands of Glaswegians, his fellow citizens?

The Bulletin showed two soldiers in tin helmets and with fixed bayonets at the power stations, describing them as 'this formidable guard – equal in strength to the guard at a bridge-end on the Rhine', although it has to be said that they and many of the soldiers in the photographs of the aftermath of Bloody Friday do look very young.

Despite the soldiers, the machine guns in George Square and the *Daily Record*'s headline of 'Military Ready to Deal with

Clyde Rioters', Harry McShane said, 'There was no open threat and we learned to live with them.'

On Monday, 10 February, the 40 Hours Strike was called off, with a recommendation that everyone should go back to work on Wednesday, 12 February. The *Glasgow Herald* was unable to resist a *de haut en bas* wagging finger, printing a 'WARNING TO REVOLUTIONARIES':

> The strike can hardly be said to have reached an official termination; it died a natural death because it had no moral or financial support, because so very few people wished it to live any longer, and because its continued existence was an obvious anachronism in a community which never took it seriously as a Labour movement, but which objected to it emphatically as a symptom of incipient revolutionary tendencies wholly foreign to the good sense and the political and social beliefs of the people.

Although James Maxton had not been in George Square on Bloody Friday he rallied to the support of those who had. A touching little vignette from Davie Kirkwood illustrates the characters of both men. 'When I was arrested after the Riot of the Forty Hours Strike, I was taken from the Central Police Station to Duke Street Jail in a Black Maria. Maxton was waiting outside the Central. As I passed he put something in my hand. It was a clean white handkerchief. He had remembered my great weakness for a clean hankey.'

The 12 men tried in Edinburgh in April 1919 were charged with 'forming part of a riotous mob to hold up the traffic in the Square and adjoining streets, to overawe and intimidate the police force on duty there, to forcibly take possession of the Municipal Buildings and the North British Station Hotel.' Five of the defendants, including Kirkwood, Gallacher, Shinwell and Harry Hopkins of the Amalgamated Society

of Engineers faced additional charges of inciting a mob 'of 20,000 or thereby riotous and evilly disposed persons'.

One of the witnesses for the defence was Rosslyn Mitchell. As a town councillor, he had been on a balcony in the City Chambers watching the crowd, with an excellent view of what was going on. He thought the police had initially drawn their batons to push the crowd back to clear the way for a tramcar to pass and it had escalated from there:

> ... some of the police poked the crowd. If the crowd had been determined to move forward with a vicious intent, the cars would have toppled over, and there would have been massacre. To his astonishment, the police charged the crowd at the double. In his view, there was no reason for that charge. After the charge the crowd took turf and daffodil bulbs from the plots in the square, and stones, and threw them. There was another baton charge, in which men were struck down indiscriminately, and a great many people were injured. It was some time after the second baton charge that the bottle-throwing began. After the first baton charge the attitude of the crowd was pretty ugly. There was no evidence of the crowd to do mischief that day.

King's Counsel Mr Constable also argued there had been no 'preconcerted design to do mischief on the part of the mob assembled in George Square' and that the trouble had largely been concentrated around the trams in one corner of it. Every time the police advanced 'the people ran before them like sheep. The conclusion was irresistible, that some at any rate of the baton charges were made without any excuse or provocation.' Another of the advocates concurred: 'The real cause of the trouble on 31st January was the hasty action of the police.'

Conducting his own defence, Willie Gallacher was dismissive of the idea that what is now the Millennium Hotel

on the north side of George Square was ever in any danger
of being stormed by the crowd: '... for good or ill he had
referred to the North British Station Hotel, but no one paid
any attention to it, and the authorities never thought there
was going to be any interference with that hotel. There had
never been such a ridiculous case put up against a body of
men, and whichever way the jury decided his conscience was
easy, and he would sleep as well in a prison cell as at home.'

In his final summing up, the Lord Justice Clerk told the
jury he was 'sure they were tired of the case, but he thought
it right to say that in his judgment the case had not occupied
any more time than it ought to have occupied'. Nor did his
lordship see much significance in the red flag having been
carried by the strikers on the Monday before Bloody Friday:
'... he was not sure he knew what the red flag meant. But
whatever it meant, it had the capacity, apparently, of exciting
paroxysms of indignation and derision in some quarters, and
exciting enthusiasm beyond bounds in others'. The crowd
which had gathered in George Square had done so perfectly
legitimately in order to hear from the Lord Provost what the
prime minister had said. Be that as it may, rioting or inciting
other people to riot was against the law.

Eight of the defendants were acquitted, including Davie
Kirkwood. That he had been struck by a police baton and
there was a photograph of him lying concussed on the
pavement had earned him a lot of sympathy. James Murray
and William McCartney were sentenced to three months
in prison, as was Willie Gallacher. This was despite the jury
recommending leniency in his case, as he had tried to get
people to disperse peacefully. Manny Shinwell was given a
sentence of five months.

The 40-hour week didn't come until the Second World
War, although after the strike hours were reduced from 54
to 47. The biggest difference that made was to start times,
meaning men and women no longer had to be at the yard
or factory gates for six o'clock. That had always been a killer.

On 1 February, *The Strike Bulletin* gave what happened in George Square the name by which it has been known ever since. 'Henceforth January 31, 1919, will be known to Glasgow as Bloody Friday, and, for the crime of attacking defenceless workers, the citizens will hold the authorities responsible. The police have once more been used as hirelings to bludgeon the workers. The workers will not forget.' The news-sheet also urged strikers to 'keep cheery'. It was a very Scottish affair, this revolution that never was.

19

The Red Clydesiders Sweep into Westminster

'We were the stuff of which reform is made.'

Another square in the centre of Glasgow, another massive crowd. As at George Square on Bloody Friday, estimates vary. Some say well over 100,000 men and women filled St Enoch Square and spilled over into Argyle Street and the other streets around it.

Those who had got there first stood in front of the two sweeping carriageways which curved up into the grand Victorian railway station. Extra lamps had been brought to light up the gloom of the November night and two large red flags fluttered over the entranceway.

There was music, of course, as there always was. The William Morris choir led the singing: 'The Red Flag', 'The Internationale', 'Jerusalem', 'Psalm 124'. The Covenanters knew this as 'Scotland's Hymn of Deliverance':

> If it had not been the LORD who was on our side, now may Israel say;
>
> If it had not been the LORD who was on our side, when men rose up against us:
>
> Then they had swallowed us up quick, when their wrath was kindled against us:
>
> Then the waters had overwhelmed us, the stream had gone over our soul;

> Then the proud waters had gone over our soul.
>
> Blessed be the LORD, who hath not given us as a prey to their teeth.
>
> Our soul is escaped as a bird out of the snare of the fowlers: the snare is broken, and we are escaped.
>
> Our help is in the name of the LORD, who made heaven and earth.

The men going off to London had been given a sacred trust, one they acknowledged in a printed declaration distributed to their supporters at services of dedication held earlier in the day: 'The Labour Members of Parliament for the City of Glasgow and the West of Scotland, inspired by zeal for the welfare of humanity and the prosperity of all peoples and strengthened by the trust reposed in them by their fellow-citizens, have resolved to dedicate themselves to the reconciliation and unity of the nations of the world and the development and happiness of the people of these islands.'

The election of 1922 might have returned a Conservative government to power but it also produced an earthquake which rocked the political landscape of Britain. For the first time ever, the Liberal Party was no longer the opposition: the Labour Party was. Its candidates and supporters had strained every sinew to win electoral success. This was an election fought with passion. Tom Johnston wrote in the *Forward* of the many female volunteers who helped him win his seat in West Stirlingshire: 'They hustled the indifferent to the booths; they lent shawls and held babies: they carried the sick and dying to the polls on mattresses – and they won. May black shame fall upon the individual or the party, who, having the trust of these women, ever betrays it.'

There were no Red revolutionaries or dangerous Bolsheviks here. This was all about using democracy and the parliamentary process to get into Westminster and start reforming the system from within.

James Maxton stood for Bridgeton in 1922, the constituency he was to represent at Westminster until his death in 1946. His election manifesto gives full details of where to vote and how to establish which ward you're in, providing the names of the relevant streets so you can work this out. Like other candidates, he spoke at numerous public meetings before the election to put his case. That was how elections were fought in those days.

Since he held two public meetings a night at different schools in the neighbourhood, all at 8 p.m., presumably he had a warm-up man or two, or quite possibly a warm-up woman. Under the details of the meetings is a polite encouragement to come along: 'All Electors cordially invited to attend. Ladies specially invited.'

Unemployment, housing and education were at the top of Maxton's list of issues. His experience as a teacher allowed him to strengthen the message:

> The welfare of children is of first importance to me. I have had experience of the children of Bridgeton, both as a teacher in the district and as a member of the Education Authority. I know that every year many clever and capable boys and girls lose the opportunity of developing their talents to the fullest through the poverty of their parents. It is the duty of the nation to see that opportunities of education are open to the children of the worker as to the children of the rich.

This was the first election to the Westminster government after the establishment of what was then known as the Irish Free State. Maxton's position on the Irish Question, of profound interest to all those Glaswegians of Irish extraction, was typically idealistic. He believed Britain should continue to give support to 'the Irish nation, both North and South. I look to the developing Irish Labour Party to put an end to the feuds that have rent Ireland asunder.' His manifesto

finishes with his stance on Scotland. 'Scotland's commercial and social progress would be considerably quickened by the establishment of a Scottish Parliament.' Crystal clear there too.

His deep appreciation of the women of West Stirlingshire notwithstanding, Tom Johnston later claimed he never actually wanted to be an MP, offering a tongue-in-cheek defence for having done so which basically amounted to 'Jimmy Maxton made me do it':

> ... it was not until James Maxton sent me a rather indignant letter saying he thought it most unfair that he should be landed for a contest in Bridgeton, while I should sit high and dry; in fact if fellows like myself were going to escape, he would jolly well get out too – not until then did I fall for the apparently 'hopeless' seat of West Stirlingshire. But I lived on the borders of the constituency: a hired car could bring me home every night: the constituency covered the field of Bannockburn, the Wallace Monument on the Abbey Craig, and parts of the bonny banks of Loch Lomond, and touched Loch Katrine; and above all there was not the remotest chance of winning.

They were in buoyant mood as they set off. One story attributed to Manny Shinwell has him telling the crowd the first thing they were going to do when they got to London was 'find the Prince of Wales and hang the bugger from the nearest lamp-post'. The Playboy Prince, briefly to become Edward VIII, did not lead the sort of life calculated to endear him to the working people of Red Clydeside.

The 1922 election returned 142 Labour MPs from constituencies throughout the United Kingdom, the highest number yet to sit in the Westminster Parliament. The change in the political landscape of Glasgow and the West of Scotland, where ILP candidates had won 18 seats, was especially

dramatic. In Glasgow alone, ten out of the city's 15 constituencies returned ILP candidates.

Above a cartoon of a bemused St Mungo wondering why a respectable person like himself was now casting a queer kind of a shadow, that of the sinister Russian Bolshevik who had so seized the popular imagination, *The Bailie* informed its readers that 'Glasgow is now two-thirds red. Politically and geologically Glasgow stands on shaky ground. It is said that there is a serious "fault" under our feet. Earthquakes are predicted.'

Like a victorious rebel army, blue bonnets crossing the border, ten of the new MPs were to travel down to London together on the night mail from St Enoch. In *My Life of Revolt* Davie Kirkwood offered a summing up of his comrades of 1922:

> What a troop we were! John Wheatley, cool and cal-
> culating and fearless; James Maxton, whose wooing
> speaking and utter selflessness made people regard
> him as a saint and martyr; wee Jimmie Stewart, so
> small, so sober, and yet so determined; Neil MacLean,
> full of fire without fury; Thomas Johnston, with a head
> as full of facts as an egg's full o' meat; George Hardie,
> engineer and chemist and brother of Keir Hardie;
> James Welsh, miner and poet from Coatbridge; John
> W. Muir, an heroic and gallant gentleman; and old
> Bob Smillie, returned for an English constituency
> though he was born in Ireland and reared in Scotland.

The Conservative prime minister, Sir Andrew Bonar Law, sat for a Glasgow constituency. It's probably a fair bet that the Right Honourable member for Glasgow Central chose to return to Westminster and Downing Street by a different train.

The Bailie was generous enough to observe that the 'ten wise men' deserved their electoral success: 'A new spirit is abroad in politics. In one respect we give credit to the Labour

Party. They take their politics seriously. Look at the send-off those Labour M.P.'s received on Sunday. Had the old parties shown the same enthusiasm the political complexion of Glasgow would have been very different to-day.'

Putting the number of people in St Enoch Square at 50,000, *The Bulletin* too gave remarkably generous coverage to the send-off of the 'elated labourists'. Perhaps the newspaper realised many of its readers had to be among the vast crowd.

SEND-OFF SCENES

Enthusiastic Crowds at the Station

At both the Metropole Theatre, where an I.L.P. rally was held to celebrate the Labour victory, and at St Enoch Station later in the evening when the new M.P.'s were leaving the city for the opening of parliament today there were scenes of remarkable enthusiasm, the crowds of well-wishers attending the departure being of such dimensions that they choked up all approaches to the railway station.

At the Metropole Theatre meeting the auditorium was packed in all parts. As the names of the victors were mentioned as speakers by the chairman, Bailie Dollan, there were outbursts of tremendous cheering, though, one of the most cordial receptions was given to Mr. E. Rosslyn Mitchell and others of the unsuccessful candidates.

The Bulletin reported Tom Johnston's mischievous observation, which 'raised a howl of laughter', that he was now the Duke of Montrose's representative in Parliament. He had given that gentleman a fairly comprehensive doing in *Our Noble Families*. There were more speeches and more laughter at St Enoch Square, where James Maxton, Patrick Dollan and Neil Maclean, re-elected as Labour MP for Govan, addressed the crowd.

They did so from the parapet of St Enoch's sweeping carriageway, up above the metal advert which for years extolled to travelling Glaswegians the benefits of the pens produced by an Edinburgh firm. 'They came as a boon and a blessing to men, the Pickwick, the Owl and the Waverley Pen.'

For James Maxton the euphoria of that send-off must have been bitter-sweet indeed. He and Sissie McCallum had married in the summer of 1919 and had a son two years later. Seriously ill through the first year of his life, the baby was nursed devotedly by his mother. The strain did not help her own health, which had never been robust. As young Jim returned to full health and strength his mother weakened. Sinking fast, she died at the end of August 1922, leaving a distraught husband behind her.

Maxton's mother stepped into the breach, taking over the care of her baby grandson. His brothers, sisters and friends rallied round, whisking him off to the continent on a journey which was half a holiday and half a research trip into how conditions for working people were in France, Germany, Austria and Czechoslovakia. Ramsay MacDonald, who had also been widowed young and left with a young family, advised Maxton that the only way to cope with his grief was to throw himself into his work.

Doing just that, he made the crowd in St Enoch Square laugh by poking fun at Bonar Law, promising the prime minister wasn't going to know what hit him when the Scottish MPs arrived at Westminster.

> Bonar, seek not yet repose
> Cast that dream of ease away,
> Thou art in the midst of foes,
> Watch and pray.

After the parody of the hymn came the warning – and the battle cry: 'When they went to the House of Commons, he said, they would make some of the genial old Tories from the

backwoods earn their £400 by the sweat of their brows. They could not work miracles, but they promised courage, hard work, genuine and strenuous service. They wanted to pass from the era of government by delusion to government by understanding.'

Davie Kirkwood remembered that when he and John Wheatley reached Westminster and walked together from the House of Commons to the House of Lords, he saw the physical manifestation of the world of privilege they all so hated. 'Turning to John Wheatley, I said aloud: "John, we'll soon change all this."' Looking back on it all, Kirkwood summed up the enthusiasm and the optimism:

> We were going to do big things. The people believed that. We believed that. At our onslaught, the grinding poverty which existed in the midst of plenty was to be wiped out. We were going to scare away the grim spectre of unemployment which stands grinning behind the chair of every artisan. We believed it could be done. We believed that this people, this British folk, could and were willing to make friends with all other peoples ... We were the stuff of which reform is made.

20

The Zinoviev Letter

'Another Guy Fawkes – a new gunpowder plot.'

The new Scottish Labour MPs were sometimes lonely in London at the weekends. It was too far to go home, and too expensive. In those days, MPs had to pay their own expenses, including railway fares between their constituencies and the House of Commons, out of their annual salary of £400.

They kept one another company, sometimes having a wander through the street market at Petticoat Lane. Speaking broad Scots, Davie Kirkwood was not always understood by the Londoners. He kept a guid Scots tongue in his heid in the House of Commons. Famously, in a debate on poverty in Clydebank, he was reprimanded by the Speaker for mentioning the king, reminded that the monarch must not be referred to in the House. Kirkwood thought for a moment and substituted 'the Prince o' Wales's faither'. The chamber erupted into laughter.

Sometimes on a Sunday a group of them went together to St Columba's, the Scots Kirk, and sometimes to an Anglican church in the East End where the 'parson … always put up a fervent word for strength and courage to the men from Scotland who had come down to Westminster to fight against needless poverty'. The opportunity to do so came sooner than they had expected.

Prime Minister Andrew Bonar Law resigned due to ill health only a year after that triumphant send-off in St Enoch

Square. Stanley Baldwin called another election, hoping to cement his new leadership of the Tory Party, but his confidence was misplaced. His party lost almost 90 seats, while Labour's share of the vote shot up to almost 200. Not considering his majority strong enough, Baldwin declined to become prime minister. King George V therefore asked Ramsay MacDonald to form a government.

Britain's first Labour government took office in early 1924. Its supporters had high hopes but these were swiftly to be dashed. MacDonald and other moderates within the Labour Party were anxious not to alarm middle-class voters by pursuing policies they might view as too radical. 'Alas,' Davie Kirkwood later wrote, 'that we were able to do so little!' One significant piece of legislation did come out of the first Labour government. John Wheatley's Housing Act started the building throughout the United Kindom of half a million local authority houses to be rented out to poorer families.

Manny Shinwell said hindsight showed the Labour Party in 1924 was not ready to govern. Being in a position to change things had been a dream for so long but the reality brought with it some unpleasant truths. He thought one of those was that the Conservatives had lost public confidence rather than the Labour Party winning it. Their coats were on a shoogly peg.

Ramsay MacDonald gave Shinwell responsibility for mines, which were administered by the Board of Trade. It was a poisoned chalice. Miners and coal owners loathed each other so much they could hardly bear to be in the same room with one another, let along sit down around a table and hold rational talks about wages and hours. In his memoirs, Manny Shinwell described how fierce the mutual hostility was. 'The miners were spoiling for a show-down with the owners. Both sides were frankly stubborn and suspicious, each regarding the other as enemies. For more than two years the miners had worked under a sense of grievance since being forced to take a wage cut after the cessation of work, as much a lock-out as a strike, in March 1921.'

The miners were now threatening to strike. Shinwell coerced the mine owners into agreeing a wage increase of 13 per cent and the strike was averted. For now.

Despite his desire to avoid controversy and be seen as a safe pair of hands, Ramsay MacDonald was convinced Britain needed to officially recognise Soviet Russia. This was simply facing up to reality. Unhappy that he might have to receive people who had shot and killed his cousin the Tsar and his family and thrown them down that mineshaft in Ekaterinburg, King George V was reassured by Ramsay MacDonald that this would never happen.

There was an economic argument for recognising the Soviet Union. If diplomatic relations between the two countries were resumed, Britain might be able to collect on the debts Russia had owed Britain since before the Revolution. The Russians said yes, fine, but we'd like a new loan to help get our industry and our agriculture moving. Britain's bankers and financiers were not the only people in whom this provoked a very sharp intake of breath. Although the king had been brought round to recognising the Russians, many in Britain were outraged by the very idea of it. The Soviet Union remained a bandit state, seen by many as a lawless country brimming with brigands and Bolsheviks.

Led by press baron Lord Rothermere, a campaign was mounted against Ramsay MacDonald and the Labour government. In other words, the *Daily Mail* struck again. They soon found two great big sticks with which to beat Ramsay MacDonald.

John Ross Campbell was a socialist from Paisley, a member of the Clyde Workers' Committee during the First World War and in 1920 yet another Scottish founder member of the Communist Party of Great Britain. By 1924 Campbell was in London, editing the party's *Workers' Weekly*. In July of that year he published an open letter to British servicemen, urging them to 'let it be known that, neither in the class war nor in a military war, will you turn your guns on your fellow workers'.

The Attorney General advised Ramsay MacDonald to prosecute Campbell under the Incitement to Mutiny Act of 1797. The senior law officer changed his advice when it emerged that John Ross Campbell had served with distinction during the First World War and been awarded the Military Medal. It wouldn't look good to prosecute a war hero. That argument didn't wash with Lord Rothermere and those so fundamentally and viscerally opposed to the Labour government.

In September of 1924 MI5 intercepted the infamous Zinoviev letter. This was apparently signed both by Gregory Zinoviev, chairman of Russia's Comintern, or Communist International, and Arthur McManus, formerly of Singer's and now the first chairman of the British Communist Party. The letter urged British Communists and socialists to work towards revolution in Britain. At the same time, Ramsay MacDonald was dealing with a motion of no confidence in the House of Commons because he had declined to bring a prosecution against John Ross Campbell.

The Conservatives and the Liberals alleged he was under the influence of the Communist Party of Great Britain, even that of Soviet Russia. MacDonald lost the motion of no confidence and resigned, precipitating yet another general election.

Someone then leaked the Zinoviev letter to *The Times* and the *Daily Mail.* Both newspapers published it four days before the election. The somewhat lengthy epistle was nicely summed up in the accompanying written protest from the British Foreign Office to the Soviet Chargé d'Affaires in London: 'The letter contains instructions to British subjects to work for the violent overthrow of existing institutions in this country, and for the subversion of His Majesty's armed forces as a means to an end. It is my duty to inform you that His Majesty's Government cannot allow this propaganda, and must regard it as a direct interference from outside in British domestic affairs.'

It was incendiary stuff. Ramsay MacDonald described it as, 'Another Guy Fawkes – a new gunpowder plot.' The resulting

panic among voters sealed the downfall of the first Labour government. After the election MacDonald returned to Parliament with 50 fewer seats, only 151 MPs as compared to the 412 now sitting on the Conservative benches.

Although Gregory Zinoviev always denied he had ever seen the letter which bears his name, and claimed he had nothing whatsoever to do with it, the Zinoviev letter remained controversial. When the late Robin Cook was Foreign Secretary in 1998, he ordered an investigation into it. While this stated it definitely was a forgery, the Zinoviev letter continues to exert a fascination over conspiracy theorists.

In August 1925, 12 members of the Communist Party of Great Britain were arrested under the Incitement to Mutiny Act on the basis of the allegedly seditious articles they had written and the Communist literature they had circulated. Willie Gallacher and Arthur McManus were among the defendants, sentenced to one year's and six months' imprisonment respectively. Arthur McManus died of a heart attack a year after he was released from prison. He was 38.

There's a conspiracy theory about these arrests too. Some believed they were a pre-emptive strike, an attempt to weaken the warriors of the Left. Another battle was brewing.

21

Nine Days' Wonder:
The General Strike of 1926

*'Law-abiding citizens should refrain from
congregating in the streets.'*

Everything stopped at midnight. Even the cross-border trains
between Scotland and London ground to a halt, stranding
their passengers wherever that happened to be. Maybe those
passengers should have had a little more foresight. The
General Strike of May 1926 had been well advertised.

It was called by the TUC, asking workers throughout
Britain to support Britain's miners. Mine owners wanted
them to take a cut in their wages and an increase in their
hours. The miners refused, going on strike on 30 April. Next
day, at the annual May Day celebrations, thousands marched
through Glasgow and on to Glasgow Green, where a rally was
held in support of the miners. Their leader, Arthur Cook,
had come up with a catchy slogan: 'Not a penny off the pay,
not a minute on the day.'

Workers in other industries – railwaymen, printers, engineers – saw the miners' struggle as their struggle too. If the
miners' pay was cut today, their pay would be cut tomorrow.
Britain's economy was in trouble and this was one solution
to fixing it. It was not the strategy favoured by the Left. John
Wheatley summed up what was wrong with it:

> In 1920, the millions of ex-Service men who had
> returned to industry gave us, with the aid of the

improved methods of production introduced during
the war, an enormous output. The standard of wages
did not enable the workers to buy up the goods as
rapidly as they were produced. The inevitable consequence was a glatted [*sic*] market, a collapse in selling
prices, industrial stagnation and growing unemployment. Competitive Capitalism's only remedy for this
was the paradoxical one of a reduction in wages when
the obvious need was more purchasing power.

The coal owners were, however, adamant. The miners of the
north of England, Wales and Scotland had to increase their
working hours and take a cut in pay. There was a feeling that
the men who worked below the ground had been singled
out to take the punishment first. Many working-class people
throughout Britain were already struggling to survive.

By the early 1920s, 5,000 people in Clydebank were unemployed. Others were on short time. When McAlpine's,
the factors of the Holy City tenements, decided to raise the
rents, a prolonged rent strike ensued. It was fought on the
tenants' side by the Clydebank Housing Association. Among
others, they were led by Andrew Leiper and David Cormack.
Support came also from the ILP, the Communist Party and
the National Unemployed Workers' Movement.

Women were once again to the fore, including Mrs
Hyslop and Mrs Pickles, female members of the ILP and the
Co-operative Women's Guild. Manny Shinwell and Patrick
Dollan were also involved, as was Davie Kirkwood, now
Labour MP for Clydebank. Telling the tenants to put the rent
money aside each week so they could pay when the dispute
was settled was not one of his smarter moves. None of them
could afford to put any money aside.

Quoted in Sean Damer's *Rent Strike! The Clydebank Rent
Struggles of the 1920s,* Mr Lambie of the Clydebank Housing
Association, whose first name is not given, recalled that there
were people on the verge of suicide because they'd lost their

jobs at Singer's. Those still employed in the sewing-machine factory were having their wages arrested by the company to pay the arrears of rent to McAlpine's the factors.

The Clydebank Rent Strike did not win the victory Mrs Barbour's Army did. The dispute dragged on and ended in defeat for the tenants. Many were evicted, six of them on Hogmanay 1925, the timing seen as deliberately vindictive. This renewed sense of class conflict was the atmosphere in which the General Strike took place.

The TUC first asked specific groups of workers to come out: transport workers and printers. On Clydeside as elsewhere the disruption to transport led to violent clashes on the roads and tramways and angry confrontations between strikers, non-strikers and the volunteers manning the trams and driving lorries and buses.

Those volunteers are often remembered as well-heeled university students having a bit of a lark. Glasgow Caledonian University's excellent Red Clydeside website points out that the Students' Representative Council of Glasgow University declared itself neutral during the strike and that fewer students were involved in strike-breaking in Glasgow than at Edinburgh or St Andrew's.

That some Glasgow students were involved is recalled on the same website by an oral testimony recorded in 1970 by Bill Cowe of Rutherglen. A member of the National Union of Railwaymen, Cowe was one of those who went on strike in 1926:

In Glasgow the Glasgow University students were arraigned by the working class as being the defenders of property and Toryism because the Glasgow students tried to break the General Strike.

The young students, they drove tramcars in Glasgow that led to battles in the Glasgow streets where these trams were wrecked and students were manhandled because every action was a mass action

and immediately a tramcar was surrounded by a mass of strikers, the police could do nothing. The students foolish enough to do this job really let themselves in for a lot of trouble.

To this day you'll get among good trade unionists an aversion to university students. Women in the street were encouraging their menfolk to really injure the students.

Class warfare was being waged here, and from both sides. Newspaper reports after the strike ended in failure exhibit an unmistakable sense of crowing that the middle classes had turned out and managed to do jobs the workers normally did, as a report in *The Scotsman* of 1926 illustrates:

> So far as the Clyde Trust was concerned, they got on with their work at Princes Dock, which they had selected as it was easily protected, central, and with many advantages. Their operations went on extremely well, and he asked the Trustees to concur with him in expressing their gratitude to Col. Wingate and the men of his organisation who came and did that work for them. (Applause.)
>
> It demonstrated that men who had never been accustomed to manual labour, but had their hearts in their work, and wanted to get it through, in the course of a very short apprenticeship, did about just as good work as the men who were employed from day to day. If that was not an object lesson in Trade Unionism he did not know what would be.

In Glasgow at least it feels like revenge was being taken for how scared the middle classes had been back on Bloody Friday in 1919. The *Forward* apart, the city's newspapers were either part of that middle-class establishment or highly deferential towards it. Three months after the end of the General

Strike, in August 1926, the Institute of Journalists met in Glasgow. Its chairman was Sir Robert Bruce, editor of the *Glasgow Herald.*

He won applause from the floor when he stated that his institute did not want to 'be dominated at a moment of crisis by a cabal of militant Trade Union leaders'. The Institute of Journalists also sent a loyal message to the king, by telegram to Balmoral Castle.

The printers who produced the newspapers were a horse of an entirely different colour, a group of men with a long tradition of political radicalism. One of the incidents which precipitated the General Strike was the refusal of those working on the *Daily Mail* to print an article calling the miners and those who proposed to strike in sympathy with them subversive revolutionaries.

With printers solid for the strike, Sir Robert Bruce and other newspaper owners and editors in Glasgow took a leaf out of Red Clydeside's book and got organised, producing the *Emergency Press,* which came out every day over the nine days of the strike. The papers which co-operated to get their side of the story out were the *Glasgow Herald,* the *Daily Record, The Bulletin,* the *Glasgow Evening News,* the *Evening Times* and *The Citizen.* The last-mentioned had both a daily and an evening edition.

On Wednesday, 5 May, the second day of the strike, the *Emergency Press* told its readers the country was quite calm, there were no scenes of disorder, government plans were working well and that in London thousands had walked to work. On Saturday, 8 May 1926, the fifth day of the stoppage, they reported there had been more rioting in Glasgow's East End, which they described as the city's 'Storm Centre'. They also got right up onto their high horses about a news-sheet the TUC was producing for the run of the strike called *The British Worker:* 'This paper announces that it is entirely worked by union men. It is thus clear that the strike in the printing trade is not a general strike, but only a strike against

those newspapers of whose political opinion the T.U.C. do not approve.'

The *Emergency Press* claimed that many in the printing trade had come out on strike 'with the deepest grief and reluctance'. They also carried a 'Notice to Citizens' from the Lord Provost of Glasgow and the Sheriff of Lanarkshire, issued on 7 May 1926: 'In the present emergency we earnestly recommend that law-abiding citizens should refrain from congregating in the streets, and should avoid the main thoroughfares as much as possible. This would not only conduce to their own safety, but materially assist the police in the exercise of their duty.'

There was a great sense of shared purpose among the strikers. Bill Cowe of Rutherglen found it inspiring. 'The strike was tremendously successful, the solidarity, the united determination of the working class. I've never seen it before or since, and as a young man it's always recorded in my memory as being the most outstanding example of how unity in action can bring a government to its knees.'

John Wheatley agreed, describing the response to the strike call as 'magnificent and electrical':

> Highly respectable, middle-class railway clerks who had never struck on their own behalf had stood shoulder to shoulder with the grimy miner. Railwaymen and dockers brought their wages agreements and placed them on the altar of sacrifice. General transport workers stood still. Compositors, printers, and builders, with two or three times the income of a miner, rallied to the call. Millionaire newspaper magnates discovered that a 'fifth estate' had appeared in the realm.
>
> Everywhere among the strikers there was order, determination and confidence. It was a wonderful, unforgettable spectacle which put fresh hope and courage into the hearts of men whose lives had been devoted to the cause of working-class unity and intelligence.

And then came the betrayal. That's how thousands on the Left saw the actions of the TUC, which capitulated on Wednesday, 12 May. The miners stayed out until November, when they had to go back to work and agree to longer hours and less pay. The General Strike had totally failed to achieve its aims.

Strikers and their supporters were stunned and confused, unable to understand why the TUC had conceded defeat while the strike was still rock solid. John Wheatley called them cowards.

> Some days must elapse before we learn accurately all the cause of the dreadful debacle. But I have no doubt that when everything is straightened out cowardice will occupy a prominent place. The qualities which distinguish men in a drawing-room, a palace, or a debating society are of little use in a vital struggle. Smart quips and polished manners play little part amidst grim realities. From the first moment of the struggle, and indeed before it, prominent Labour leaders were whining and grovelling. The day before the general strike was declared we were told by one of the men who were going out to lead us, that defeat was certain.

Tom Johnston said he'd had his doubts about the strike but once it had started, and with so many answering the call, the TUC should have had the courage to carry on 'until the Government had been compelled to throw the coalowners and their slave terms overboard'.

John S. Clarke dismissed the idea that what he called 'The Nine Days Wonder' had been a revolution in the making, a sinister plot to bring down capitalism. 'Because Mrs. McNab, good soul, lost her rag at Brigton and fired a bag of pease meal at a car conductor in spats, it hardly follows that attacks upon Woolwich Arsenal were contemplated in East Ham with a view to procuring howitzers and machine guns. Baton

charges by police are, in nine cases out of ten, the result of panic *in the police*. Many police, in Glasgow at any rate, were highly sympathetic to the strikers.'

Clarke quoted some lines from Karl Marx all the same:

EFFORT

Let us do and dare our utmost,
Never from the strife recede,
Never live in dull inertia,
So devoid of will and deed.
Anything but calm submission
To the yoke of toil and pain!
Come what may then, hope and longing,
Deed and daring still remain.

The *Forward* had of course not broken the strike. In its first edition after it, on Saturday, 22 May 1926, it launched a ferocious attack on 'the blackleg press', listing those newspapers by name and ownership. Those included all those Outram- and Hedderwick-owned papers in Glasgow which had joined together with others to publish the *Emergency Press*.

In Dundee, Tom Johnston's accusing finger was pointed at the Thomson Press, owners of the *Dundee Advertiser*, the *Dundee Courier*, the *Weekly News* and the *Sunday Post*. He lashed out at the *Sunday Post*, condemning its 'sheer fatuity' in its story of a religious revival in Kilmarnock – those were still happening – when young children had solemnly told their parents they did not want to go to the sinful cinema any more. 'No, papa: I will not look at Charles Chaplin. I sin no more! Slow music!'

Johnston's solution for how to deal with the blackleg press was not only to boycott the papers themselves but to write to the companies which advertised in them to say you would not buy their products if they continued to do so. The bitterness was intense. One letter to the editor suggested that while throughout history unsuccessful generals had been

court-martialled, he did not want the TUC General Council
to be treated in the same way. 'I think if they have any self-
respect left they will fold up their cloaks and disappear
silently into the night.'

Ramsay MacDonald tried to take some consolation from
the solidarity of the working classes:

> But we must not be blind to the wonderful demon-
> stration of working-class solidarity which we have seen.
> It has been a moving and heartening manifestation.
> It shows a single minded goodness and willingness to
> bear sacrifices which should put pride and thankful-
> ness into our hearts. If the nation could only under-
> stand it, it would be proud that it possessed the spirit
> which made the demonstration possible, whatever it
> may think of the action itself.
>
> The general strike of 1926 will be a glowing point in
> the history of British Labour.

John Wheatley saw the solidarity but was bitter about the
TUC. 'The workers have sustained a smashing reverse. It was
not inflicted by their bosses due to their own weakness. It is
a most astonishing result to a most magnificent effort. The
struggle will surely rank as the greatest and most bungled
strike in history.'

The strike was followed by prosecutions for assault, breach
of the peace and words and actions 'calculated to cause disaffection among the populace, contrary to the Emergency
Regulations'. Fines and prison sentences were imposed, the
latter with hard labour.

Many strikers had to apply to get their jobs back and give
an undertaking they were not in any trade union and would
not engage in any trade union activity. This happened at
Singer's in Clydebank and in many newspaper offices, including those papers owned by Outram's and Hedderwick's.
In its first edition after the strike on Saturday, 15 May 1926,

the *Glasgow Herald* spelled it out, listing rates of pay and conditions, which included two weeks' paid holiday each year, 'funeral and sickness allowances':

> Owing to the action of certain Trade Unions in breaking agreements with us, to which they were parties, we can have no confidence that any contracts which might be entered into in future would be observed. As continuity of publication is essential in the interests of newspaper readers and advertisers, we are compelled to protect them and ourselves against any repetition of what has taken place on this occasion.
>
> We quite recognise the difficult position in which so many of our former employees found themselves, and desire to say that we have no unfriendly feelings towards them individually.

Applications from former employees would be considered as along as they had been received by nine o'clock that Saturday morning. He who pays the piper calls the tune.

Defiant as ever, Johnston took some advertising space immediately after the end of the General Strike to promote his own newspaper and the cause of socialism.

SOCIALISM IS THE ONLY HOPE!

SOCIALISM—

WILL END POVERTY!

WILL ESTABLISH JUSTICE!

WILL ABOLISH WRONG!

WILL EXALT FREEDOM!

The way to get Socialism is to make Socialists.

The way to make Socialists is to the push the sale of '**FORWARD**'

Let your slogan be **FORWARD!**

22

Ten Cents a Dance

*'A low-class exotic from fourth-rate saloons
in the Argentine.'*

It was years before people came to terms in any way with the
shock, grief and sadness of the First World War. A generation of young women had lost their lovers. A generation of
men who survived the nightmare had gazed into the abyss,
seen how hideously far man's inhumanity to man could go.
Perhaps the burden was too heavy to keep on carrying it.

The shift in mood came around 1925. Women cut their
hair and their skirts short, dropped their waists and flattened
their chests. Fashionable young men took to wearing soft,
unstructured clothes, affecting a languid air to go with their
floppy shirts and flannel trousers. In some circles there was
a blurring of gender boundaries, as evidenced by the title
of one of the hit songs of the time: 'Masculine Women!
Feminine Men!'

It's not hard to see why some young men rejected the
traditional role. That kind of masculinity was lying dead and
broken in the green fields of France or, wounded in body
and soul, shuffling like a sad ghost around the edges of other
people's lives. Slamming the door on the nightmare, the
generation which followed declared that life was all about
having fun.

This was the Jazz Age, and the more its frantic gaiety horrified the older generation, the more the younger kicked up

its heels and enjoyed it. 'Jazz' was used as an adjective. Put it
in front of any noun and it meant modern, fashionable, just
the ticket, up-to-the-minute. Deploying a creative crescendo
of exclamation marks, an exasperated Helen Crawfurd had
a go at it in 1921. 'Today, we are living in the *jazz period*. We
have jazz music, jazz dancing, jazz frocks, jazz furniture, jazz
art, jazz politics, and Lloyd George the grand jazz master of
Britain, like the trickster on the fairground ... If it is something capable of fulfilment – then for God's sake stop jazzing
and get to work. Up Labour! Organise! organise!! organise!!!'

She was on a hiding to nothing there, especially when it
came to the dancing. Glasgow was famously dancing daft, as
the *Evening News* told its readers in 1927, informing them that
nowadays it had to be bright lights, swinging floors, palms
and buffets and that '*thé dansant* was French for dancing
interspersed with pastry. Now Sauchiehall Street blossoms
with dancing-palaces that vie in size with the greatest cinema-
houses; incorporate features – garages, tea-rooms, lounges
and club-rooms – out of the question for the theatres; and
it looks as if more and more young people (and not so very
young, either, some of them) are taking up evening dancing
as their life's career.'

Serious-minded socialists were not the only people who
disapproved of this shocking frivolity. Free Kirk ministers
and other puritans who had always nursed the suspicion that
dancing was the vertical expression of a horizontal desire
were absolutely appalled.

Fighting their corner, dancing teachers and owners of
ballrooms went to great efforts to present dancing as respectable. They'd had their work cut out when the tango arrived
in Glasgow in 1913. Fortunately, Mr James D. Macnaughton,
president of the British Association of Teachers of Dancing,
had a cunning plan. He staged a demonstration of tango
dancing in the eminently respectable surroundings of the
McLellan Galleries in Glasgow's Sauchiehall Street. As the
Glasgow Herald reported, during the evening he also delivered

a short talk which posed the provocative question: 'Is the Tango suitable for the ballroom?'

> ... the public, having formed their opinions of the Tango from exaggerated performances at variety entertainments, Tango teas, and through press pictures, had only become acquainted with the objectionable side of the dance, and therefore there was little wonder that the Tango as thus shown to them had been objected to, and he heartily agreed with those who thus objected. He believed that the Tango as commonly presented to the public was a low-class exotic from fourth-rate saloons in the Argentine. As such, it should be banned from the ballrooms.

Clever chap, Mr James D. Macnaughton. 'Fourth-rate saloons in the Argentine' was code for the brothels of Buenos Aires, where the tango began. Having met the major criticism head on – the tango was just too damn sexy – he reassured his audience that he and his fellow members of the British Association of Teachers of Dancing were working tirelessly to ensure good deportment and impeccable decorum in ballroom dancing.

Performed in the way these good people thought suitable, 'the tango rhythm was not only pleasing and fascinating but could be made as decorous and dignified as might be required'. After watching an exhibition of the dance, the *Glasgow Herald*'s reporter gave it cautious approval:

> It was certainly very different from some displays that have been witnessed in Glasgow and elsewhere. The dance gained much in gracefulness by the fact that the movements of all who took part in it were executed with uniformity to music of a strongly marked rhythm. And it did not appear to be difficult; quite suitable

indeed for the ballroom provided it were danced correctly.

A second *Herald* reporter, dispatched to the new Alhambra Tango Teas, was distinctly unimpressed, finding it all rather dull, even if there had been 'an exciting scramble for admission':

> As to the dance itself, it would be futile to attempt a description. So far as one could gather from a first impression a great deal of the Art of the Tango – if there is any art in it – consists in the endeavour of the lady and the gentleman to come as near as possible to treading on each other's toes without actually doing so. Stepping alternatively 'fore and aft,' posturing and swaying, and 'ducking' the right knee until it touches the floor, varied by cross-limbed movements and some of the convolutions of ragtime, seem to be the principal movements of the dance.

So there, with a great big disapproving Presbyterian sniff. Dancing Glasgow couldn't have cared less, embracing the new dances and the music which went with them. Ragtime was wildly popular, 'Alexander's Ragtime Band' the big hit of 1912. The foxtrot reached Scotland in 1914. In her definitive *Oh, How We Danced!,* Liz Casciani describes how well that went down:

> Of all the dances in the ballrooms, the Fox Trot seemed best suited to the times. The trotting movements and ragtime rhythm were new and different. Young men on leave from the War wanted to dance but had no time for formal instructions. Parents and girlfriends wanted to spend free time with them without the discipline of dancing lessons. The Fox Trot with its lack of

formal steps was easy for everyone to pick up and they
came along in droves to the ballrooms.

They danced on the ocean-going liners too. Glasgow's Louis
Freeman ran an agency to supply the orchestra and the sing-
ers and became musical director for both the Anchor Line
and the Donaldson Line. The musicians who worked on the
ships were known as Louis Freeman's Navy.

Tom Johnston did his bit for the formal teaching of dance
in 1911. Starting his political career by getting himself voted
onto Kirkintilloch School Board, he was put in charge of the
evening class committee. Many of Kirky's young adults were
not exactly bursting with enthusiasm to attend.

Hoping higher attendance would attract higher government grants, which would allow a more attractive syllabus
to be created, young Mr Johnston came up with the idea of
starting dancing classes. There would be free entry to these
for any students who regularly attended evening classes in
the less enticing subjects: maths, sewing, English, mining
and building construction. His idea proved hugely popular. They hired a band and a dancing instructor and the
students formed a committee to make sure everything was
conducted with that oh-so-important decorum. 'Indeed
the order maintained was draconian, any exuberant
being promptly and roughly conducted by a frog's march
to the open air; the students' Committee took its duties
very seriously. The experiment was a great success, and
we had to limit the first dancing class to one hundred
dancers.'

Attendance at classes in the other subjects shot up.
'Mothers sent letters of thanks in that they no longer feared
for their daughters dancing at disreputable howffs; the
ratepayers were saving money; further education was being
promoted; we felt as if we were on top of the world.'

Growing ever more ambitious, Johnston put on a boxing
class. He and his friends did some discreet social work there.

'Contestants on the first evening who disclosed holes in their socks or ragged undergarments only came so circumstanced once.' It was the boxing rather than the dancing which roused the ire of the local kirks:

> Elders held meetings and we were denounced from pulpits with bell, book and candle; foremen in public works interviewed young apprentices and strongly 'advised' against attendance; letters showered upon the local press condemning our wickedness in teaching violence and bloodshed, and asking sarcastically when we were going to start breeding whippets, and teaching faro and roulette; clerical deputations waited upon members of the School Board, some of whom got windy, and the poor boxing (or physical culture) instructor, unable to stick it out, packed up and went off in disgust.

The big dance of the 1920s was, of course, the Charleston. Those who thought the young and the lighthearted were having far too much fun warned them no good would come of this shocking and vulgar dance. They would damage their ankles. The jerky movements might even lead to permanent paralysis. The Black Bottom left the killjoys speechless.

People continued to dance the tango, loving the smouldering passion of it, especially when danced with a handsome young man paid not to complain even if you did tread on his feet. Enter the gigolo, the archetypal lounge lizard. Most paid dancing partners were perfectly respectable professionals. It was a sought-after job in the 1920s and 1930s, one way in which young working-class men and women with talent could dance their way out of poverty, although it was a hard slog. In Scotland it wasn't ten cents a dance but sixpence, of which the management of the dance hall or club kept fourpence.

In February 1927, Glasgow's *Evening News* reported on the boom in the dance trade, doubting it was going to be as short-lived as the enthusiasm for roller-skating, as some people thought. Some people had also thought the cinema was destined to be nothing more than a passing fad and look how wrong they had been.

> The teaching of dancing, and the provision of facilities for dancing have become a lively and profitable industry, giving occupation to far more men and women than are employed in all the theatres, music-halls, and picture-houses put together. It may be that the craze for dancing (and the term is not extravagant) may sooner or later fade away as quickly as it began, and that the case of the roller-skating rink was a true analogy, but as yet there is not the slightest sign of it in Glasgow.

There's not much evidence from Scotland of the humiliating dance marathons depicted in the film *They Shoot Horses, Don't They?* However, there was a dark side to the happy feet, elegant evening suits, glittering gold and silver shoes and fringed dresses. In a well-choreographed sequence of events reminiscent of Hogarth's *Harlot's Progress,* dancing partners could find themselves coerced into prostitution.

Take an attractive young woman or man with dancing talent, give them a job doing something they love and a place to stay, buy them some nice clothes. A month or so down the line demand to know how they're going to pay you back for all these nice things. You could go to the police and press charges against them, your word against theirs, or they could agree to be booked out for private dancing lessons. That was the euphemism. The manager of the dance hall took one pound, the dancing partner 10 shillings. It would take you an awful long time to earn that the respectable way.

The biggest dancing partner scandal of the 1930s in Scotland happened at Edinburgh's Kosmo Club on Lothian Road, and those were the sums involved there. At the trial in December 1933 one witness was asked, 'As a man of the world, what did you think that this fee was paid for?' This was the answer: 'If young ladies stay in lodgings, and gentlemen take them home, there is the probability that they would say good-night at the door, but if they were in flats the gentlemen might be invited in for coffee, and there is no knowing what might happen.'

Glasgow had acted to try to stop this covert prostitution in 1927, imposing a series of strict rules on the hiring of dancing partners, which included them having to give details of what they were doing on their day off and not being allowed to sit a dance out with a paying customer. The city fathers were mocked for this as 'grandmotherly Glasgow'. The entertainments licensing court at this time also banned smoking on stage at theatres and music halls unless it was necessary for the play. This seems less likely to have been a health measure than a precaution against a potential fire hazard. Cigarettes were still being advertised as good for your throat and your health, particularly recommended to people suffering from TB.

The *Glasgow Herald* defended the new rules for the hiring of dancing partners, albeit only very discreetly alluding to prostitution, not wanting to 'paint a lurid picture of the possibilities that are being guarded against'. The important thing was to make the 'dancing craze as happy, healthy, and enjoyably wholesome as may be'.

Using the pseudonymn of 'Open Turn', one dancing partner wrote an indignant letter to the newspaper, defending the professionalism and respectability of her profession. It was good that booking-out had been done away with but what on earth was wrong with sitting-out? 'The average gentleman who may visit a dance hall without a partner cannot, and does not want to, dance every dance, and he appreciates the fact

that he can have company between dances. To a stranger in the city the system is a perfect godsend. I talk from experience on this point, and there must be thousands of gentlemen who agree with me.'

And, with or without dancing partners, under the glitter balls of the fashionable *palais-de-danse*, the bright lights of public halls, the gloom of disreputable howffs or at home in the kitchen to the strains of a dance band on the wireless, Glasgow kept right on dancing.

23

Sex, Socialism & Glasgow's First Birth Control Clinic

'I never saw so many wives of comrades before.'

One of the allegations used to discredit socialists was that they all believed in free love. If the revolution they were doing their best to bring about ever happened, everything would be nationalised, including women. Take a look at the lives of the Red Clydesiders and this claim quickly becomes risible.

Willie Gallacher described himself and the rest of them as 'tee-totallers and puritans'. Davie Kirkwood agreed. 'We were all Puritans. We were all abstainers. Most of us did not smoke.' James Maxton made up for them there. There was always a cigarette between his fingertips.

When it came to love and family, almost all the key male figures of Red Clydeside were devoted husbands and fathers, who paid handsome tributes to their wives as friends and political comrades. Maxton remained a widower for 13 years after the death of his beloved Sissie. He was 50 when he married for the second time. Madeleine Glasier was a member of the ILP and worked with Maxton as a researcher. They had more than ten happy years together until his death in 1946.

Helen Crawfurd agreed with free love in its literal sense, asking what other kind there could be. She believed it was wrong to associate sex with sin, describing making love with someone you loved and creating a child out of that love as something beautiful, clean and holy. She responded to those

who accused socialists of believing in free love in the sense
of promiscuous sexual intercourse by quoting Lenin. Klara
Zetkin, one of the surviving leaders of Germany's Spartacist
Revolution of 1918, had told the Soviet leader many revolutionary socialists in Germany believed sex was nothing more
than an appetite to be satisfied. When you were thirsty, you
drank a glass of water. When you were sexually attracted to
someone, you had sex with them. No shame, no blame, no
guilt.

Helen Crawfurd disagreed, believing there was an issue of
gender equality here. Up until the sexual revolution of the
1960s and '70s, a woman could lose that most valuable of
attributes, her reputation, for what nowadays no longer even
raises an eyebrow. Living with a man to whom you weren't
married was shocking. Having a baby out of wedlock was a
disaster.

For men and women who had multiple sexual partners
there was also the threat of sexually transmitted diseases.
Lenin too spelled this out, making it clear that he disapproved
of the German revolutionary socialists' attitude towards sex:

> I think this glass of water theory has made our young
> people mad, quite mad ... I think this glass of water
> theory is completely unMarxist, and moreover, anti-
> social ... Of course, thirst must be satisfied. But will
> the normal man in normal circumstances lie down
> in the gutter and drink out of a puddle, or out of a
> glass with a rim greasy from many lips? Drinking water
> is of course an individual affair. But in love two lives
> are concerned, and a third, a new life, arises. It is that
> which gives it its social interest, which gives rise to a
> duty towards the community.
>
> This drink of water theory is a simplification of
> the problem. If you want a drink of water you want to
> drink out of a clean vessel. This is a question which
> affects two people, and may mean the life of a third

if a child is born. This drink of water theory must be combatted.

Birth control was a highly contentious issue. In July 1920 American Margaret Sanger visited Glasgow to speak on the subject. Scotland enchanted her: the countryside, the people and the Glasgow sense of humour:

> Guy Aldred, who was in Scotland, had planned my schedule there, and I had three weeks of a Scottish summer – bluebells so thick in spots that the ground was azure, long twilights when the lavender heather faded the hills into purple.
>
> When I had been in Glasgow before, I had encountered only officials, but on this occasion I met the people in their homes and found them quite opposite to the stingy, tight-fisted, middle-class stereotype. They were hospitable, generous, mentally alert, just as witty as the Irish and in much the same way, which rather surprised me.

She was struck by how interested Scots of both genders were in hearing what she had to say.

> Fourth of July, Sunday, we had a noon meeting on the Glasgow Green. Nearly two thousand shipyard workers in caps and baggy corduroys stood close together listening in utter, dead stillness without cough or whisper. That evening I spoke in a hall under Socialist auspices, Guy Aldred acting as chairman. One old-timer said he had been a party member for eleven years, attending Sunday night lectures regularly, but never before had he been able to induce his wife to come: tonight he could not keep her at home. 'Look!' he cried in amazement. 'The women have crowded the men out of this hall. I never saw so many wives of comrades before.'

Margaret Sanger is a controversial figure, accused by her critics of advocating some of the worst excesses of eugenics, but fiercely defended against those charges by her supporters. That her interest in birth control had a deeply personal and visceral basis cannot be doubted. She was the sixth of 11 children. Her mother gave birth to 18 babies, seven of whom did not survive childhood.

Sanger is credited with having come up with the term *birth control*, although initially she advanced her ideas under the name of *family limitation*. While she was touring Europe in 1920, her book (titled *Family Limitation*) was circulated by a fellow socialist and member of the Industrial Workers of the World, our old friends the Wobblies. That got her into trouble on her return to the States. It was illegal in both America and Britain to distribute literature advocating birth control.

Along with his partner Rose Witcop, Guy Aldred, who organised Margaret Sanger's speaking engagements in Glasgow, was prosecuted in 1922 for publishing *Family Limitation*, allegedly an obscene pamphlet. Aldred and Witcop are among the few characters in the story of Red Clydeside who advocated and practised free love.

Originally from London, Aldred was an anarchist who lived for many years in Glasgow. As an angry young man, he thought romantic love between men and women was incompatible with his political views and any hope for equality between the sexes. In 1907 he published a pamphlet titled *The Religion & Economics of Sex Oppression*. Although at this point he thought celibacy might be the only answer, he subsequently changed his mind.

Guy Aldred and Rose Witcop were married in front of a Glasgow sheriff in 1926 only to save her from being deported to her native Russia. By that time their relationship was over. As Aldred later wrote: 'We parted at the sheriff's chambers and each took a different way.'

There were some socialists who used free love to try to discredit birth control. Hiding behind a pseudonymn,

'Nestorius' launched his attack – and he does sound like a man – in an article in the *Forward* on 1 May 1926, just before the General Strike. He was responding to a letter to the editor from Dora Russell, wife of philosopher Bertrand Russell and one of Britain's most prominent campaigners for birth control.

'Nestorius' attacked Dora Russell for what she had written about free love. She was of course entitled to her views but if the Labour Party ever adopted these as party policy he thought the movement would be 'smashed to smithereens'. He was shocked by what she had written, that for younger women, the war had made sexual relations more free and easy: 'Sex, even without children and without marriage, is to them a thing of dignity, beauty, and delight.'

For her part, Dora Russell was furious with Clydeside's Labour MPs for not having supported moves to allow municipal child welfare clinics to give advice on birth control. Ernest Thurtle had brought a bill before Parliament in 1924 hoping to achieve this. First Labour Minister of Health in that first Labour government, John Wheatley told him in a debate in the House of Commons that he did not think public funds should be used to support such measures, 'which are the subject of controversy'.

Dorothy Jewson, a feminist and Labour MP who later married Red Clydesider Campbell Stephen, MP for Camlachie, did not mince her words when she responded to John Wheatley: 'Is the Minister aware that many working-class women attending these welfare centres are unfit to bear children and to bring up healthy children, and the doctors know they are unfit, and yet they are unable to give this information, which any upper or middle-class woman can obtain from a private doctor; and will he consider the bearing of this on the question of abortion, which is so terribly on the increase in this country?'

John Wheatley gave her a non-committal answer.

When Ernest Thurtle's bill was voted on, only one of the

Clydeside Labour MPs went through the lobbies. Rosslyn Mitchell, by then MP for Paisley, voted against allowing child welfare clinics to give out birth control equipment and advice. The others abstained: James Maxton, Tom Johnston and all. The *Forward* did carry regular adverts for birth control advice and supplies, to be bought by post from London.

The son-in-law of 1930s Labour leader George Lansbury, Ernest Thurtle also fought to abolish the death penalty in the British army for soldiers found guilty of cowardice or desertion. Supporters of this measure included T.E. Lawrence, Lawrence of Arabia. Thurtle's proposals, which stopped any more men from being shot at dawn, became law under a Labour government in 1930.

The continuing failure of Red Clydeside's Labour MPs to support birth control provoked Dora Russell's letter to the *Forward* in 1926. Describing birth control as 'the most burning women's question of the day', she berated them for what she called their stupidity:

> Not one of them voted for Mr. Thurtle's Bill, or seems to realise that one subject with which it dealt is more serious and urgent to the average mother than even the housing on which so much good Scottish eloquence is expended. Countless downtrodden women of Clydeside who seem indifferent to politics can be stirred to active responsibility by an intelligent propaganda on Birth Control and creative motherhood. The shadow of threatened religious opposition blinds many Scottish members and organisers to the reality of possible support – great in numbers and passionate in belief – from these awakening women.

It was the highly respectable Govan housewife Mary Barbour of the 1915 rent strike who helped set up the first birth control clinic in Glasgow. She was its chairman. She had aristocratic

support, from its 'patronesses', the Countess of Strathmore, Lady Geddes and Lady Colquhoun of Luss.

Both men and women served on the committee of the Glasgow Women's Welfare and Advisory Clinic. It had its offices at 123 Montrose Street in Glasgow, tucked in behind the City Chambers, and its clinic south of the Clyde, at 51 Old Govan Road. A questionnaire filled out by attending physician Dr Isobel Sloan in November 1927 offers some fascinating details, not least of the industries which surrounded the clinic in 1920s Govan. They included shipbuilding and engineering works, docks, ropeworks, the Scottish Wholesale Cooperative Society, factories, jam factories, biscuit and pickle factories.

Another question asks who had started up the clinic and who was now organising it. As with their support for the suffragettes, once again the mining communities of Lanarkshire show themselves to have been ready to embrace change. 'Interest was aroused by a birth control campaign carried out mainly among the miners and workers in Lanarkshire in the Spring of 1926 followed by the initiation of the Birth Control Clinic, by an enthusiastic group of women. These agreed to follow the lines of the Walworth Clinic, London under the Society for the Provision of Birth Control Clinics.'

The Govan Clinic opened in August 1927 in what had previously been a shop. It was well kitted out with three rooms and three cubicles, two gas fires and one radiator, various bits of medical paraphernalia 'and what Doctor requires'. Financial support came from a few trade unions, the Labour Party, the Independent Labour Party and women's guilds attached to the Co-operative Society, including Dumbarton, Clydebank and St Rollox.

A separate list of those who had made donations includes Janie Allan, suffragette and socialist. Other contributors preferred to remain anonymous, perhaps because birth control remained such a contentious issue.

Although there were no official links, moral support and

encouragement came from the child welfare clinics which had been set up in Glasgow. One of the doctors helping to run those was Dorothea Chalmers Smith, the suffragette who had been imprisoned in 1913 after the 'Halloween at the High Court' trial.

Dr Sloan noted that some probation officers were support-ing the new birth control clinic 'and one of those a Roman Catholic'. She and the nurse who worked with her offered two sessions a week, one in the afternoon and one in the evening. They dispensed advice and supplies of the birth control methods available at the time, essentially Dutch caps, spermicides and condoms.

Some of the women being advised, all of whom had to be married, were suffering from the great scourge of TB. Bearing another child would put their lives at risk. Others needed birth control for economic reasons, so they could have fewer children but look after them better. 'Unemployment, wages not equal to the maintenance of the family already there, also lack of housing accommodation and generally the depres-sion in industry specially felt in Glasgow and the Clyde area. With Birth Control Education, patients and mothers specially would be enabled to keep and raise the social condition of the family.'

The researchers who asked Dr Sloan to fill out the question-naire were keen to know if the clinic was 'getting information to the lower and less intelligent members of the working class as well as those of more foresight, initiative and intelligence', which would seem to bring us back to eugenics. One of the devices given out by the Govan birth control clinic was called the *Prorace* cap, a rather uncomfortable name when we now know where eugenics went next.

In a telling reply to another question, Dr Sloan wrote that she had never been taught anything about contraceptive methods during her medical training, nor while she was doing her hospital residency. By 1934, the Govan clinic was advising that they could offer training to 'lady doctors'.

In 1927 Glasgow's libraries were offered a free set of a journal called *Birth Control News*. This was published by Marie Stopes' Constructive Birth Control Society and Racial Progress, another uncomfortable name. John S. Clarke, socialist and lion-tamer, the man who had taken in the banished Clyde shop stewards in 1916, was now a Glasgow councillor. Serving on the libraries acquisitions committee, he and fellow councillor Kate Beaton, member with Helen Crawfurd and Agnes Dollan of the Women's Peace Crusade of the First World War, voted that the gift should be accepted. Two others voted against. One of them was Councillor Izett, who had been on the side of the angels during the rent strike of 1915.

The argument blew up into a controversy, the issue debated by a meeting of the entire Corporation. Twenty-three councillors voted in favour of Glasgow's libraries stocking *Birth Control News,* 62 against, and Marie Stopes' gift was rejected. While all those 23 councillors who voted in favour were Labour, other Labour members voted against. Others again, like the Clydeside MPs in Parliament, tried not to come down on one side or the other.

Attitudes were changing, even if too many men in the Labour Party did not have the courage of their convictions. As J.J. Smyth wrote in *Labour in Glasgow, 1896–1936,* by 1930 the second Labour government 'quietly allowed clinics to provide information on contraception on health grounds but, as these could be interpreted quite widely, this was close to the demand for free advice for married women'.

That year also saw the establishment of the National Birth Control Association, which a few years later became the Family Planning Association. When the Glasgow Women's Welfare and Advisory Clinic published its annual report for 1934–5, nine years after it had been established, it felt there was still a long way to go before birth control would be accepted simply as a branch of public health provision.

This report listed three women they had helped at the Govan clinic. As it says itself, the facts require no further comment:

Mrs. X. Aged 34. Husband (unemployed), carter. 11 pregnancies. 5 children alive now. 4 born dead. Mother anaemic.

Mrs Y. Aged 33. Husband (unemployed), miner. 10 pregnancies. 7 children alive. Mother anaemic.

Mrs Z. Aged 39. Husband five years younger. 17 pregnancies. 16 children alive now.

These examples speak for themselves.

24

The Flag in the Wind

*'No man was more generously international in his
outlook and spirit, and yet to the very core of his
being he was a Scotsman of Scotsmen.'*

Home Rule for Scotland was on the political agenda before
the ink had dried on the Treaty of Union. Universally unpopular, it is often argued that the Union of the Parliaments of
1707 which followed the Union of the Crowns of 1603 was only
contemplated because Scotland was bankrupt. This financial
disaster was caused by the catastrophic Darien Adventure, a
failed attempt to establish a Scottish colony in Panama.

Scotland's precarious economic situation gave England
the opportunity to finally neutralise the threat its troublesome northern neighbour had always posed. Bribes paid
by the English commissioners whose job it was to push the
Union through persuaded the Scottish nobility to vote their
own country out of existence. These were the people Robert
Burns branded 'a parcel of rogues'.

Ordinary Scots were devastated by this betrayal, dismayed
beyond measure that their country was now to be swallowed
up by England. When the Treaty of Union was ratified on
1 May 1707, the bells of St Giles' Cathedral in Edinburgh
played an old Scottish air which caught the despairing spirit
of the moment: 'Why am I so Sad on my Wedding Day?'

There were some honourable exceptions within the parcel
of rogues, most notably Andrew Fletcher of Saltoun. Other

members of Scotland's gentry and aristocracy who spoke out against the Union were Lockhart of Carnwath and Alexander Forbes, 4th Lord Pitsligo. Carnwath and Lord Pitsligo were also Jacobites, supporters of the exiled House of Stuart.

The longing to reclaim Scotland's lost nationhood was a powerful driver of the Jacobite risings of the first half of the eighteenth century. Some Jacobites wanted to restore the Stuarts to the throne because they believed they were the 'rightful kings', anointed by God. However, they were vastly outweighed by those whose support for the Stuarts had little to do with either religion or some mythic belief in that royal house's divine right to rule. What a restoration offered was a focus for discontent and the possibility of change in a country a century and a half away from anything faintly resembling parliamentary democracy.

When Radical leaders James Baird, Andrew Hardie and James Wilson died for this ideal, one of the rallying cries was 'Scotland Free or a Desert'. When the long march towards democracy and universal suffrage really got underway after the Great Reform Act of 1832, it always went hand in hand with the cry of Home Rule for Scotland.

During the nineteenth century the burning question of Home Rule for Ireland made many ask why this was desirable for one of the Celtic nations of the British Isles and not the others. One of those who advocated 'Home Rule All Round' was Liberal Prime Minister William Gladstone, the man who famously declared that his mission was to pacify Ireland.

The Gladstones were originally a Scottish family. The prime minister sat for 15 years for a Scottish seat. This may have had some impact on his position, although the pamphlet he published in 1886 put the case of Home Rule for Ireland, Scotland and Wales on the basis of logic. He argued that the Union should be replaced by a federal Britain.

The idea was clearly in the air. It was also in 1886 that the Scottish Home Rule Association was formed. Keir Hardie was a supporter from the start, one of the SHRA's early vice

presidents. As Ramsay MacDonald wrote in his foreword to William Stewart's biography: 'No man was more generously international in his outlook and spirit, and yet to the very core of his being he was a Scotsman of Scotsmen, and it is not all inappropriate that I came across him first of all at a meeting to demand Home Rule for Scotland.'

MacDonald himself was for some years secretary of the London branch of the SHRA. Scottish miners' leader Robert Smillie also served as vice-president, as did Robert Cunninghame Graham. Don Roberto was subsequently a founding father of both the Labour Party and the Scottish National Party.

Founded some years after the SHRA, the ILP and the STUC shared its commitment to Home Rule for Scotland. Not all Scottish nationalists were political radicals but almost all political radicals were Scottish nationalists. Momentum built up, culminating in a Home Rule bill being brought before the Westminster Parliament in 1913. It might well have gone through if the First World War had not intervened.

The war itself gave a boost to Scottish nationalism. As H.J. Hanham puts it in his *Scottish Nationalism*: '... complaints about the dead hand of the Whitehall bureaucracy were an important element in Clydeside discontent'. In 1917 the STUC passed a resolution in support of a Scottish Parliament: 'This Congress reaffirms its demand that the control of Scottish affairs should be placed in the hands of the Scottish people by the reinstitution of a Scots' Parliament, and regrets at this juncture the Scottish people should not be represented directly on the Imperial War Council.'

In the aftermath of the First World War, the Labour Party, of which the ILP was a more radical component, was also enthusiastic about Home Rule for Scotland:

> Now that the War is ended and an era of reconstruction
> begun, Scottish problems require the concentration
> of Scottish brains and machinery upon their solution.

> Your Committee is of the opinion that a deter-
> mined effort should be made to secure Home Rule
> for Scotland in the first Session of Parliament, and
> that the question should be taken out of the hands of
> place-hunting lawyers and vote-catching politicians by
> the political and industrial efforts of the Labour Party
> in Scotland which should co-ordinate all its forces to
> this end, using any legitimate means, political and
> industrial, to secure the establishment of a Scottish
> Parliament upon a completely democratic basis.

On the Left, it was only Communists like Willie Gallacher
who rejected Home Rule for Scotland, calling instead for
an international union of the working classes. John Maclean
believed in a Scottish Workers' Republic, independent of
England. Gallacher and Maclean's profound disagreement
on this point meant Maclean never joined the Communist
Party of Great Britain.

ILP members continued to advocate Home Rule, often
through the pages of the *Forward*. One of the paper's most
loyal backers was Roland Muirhead, long-standing chairman
of the Scottish Home Rule Association. Tom Johnston described him as the Grand Old Man of Scottish nationalism.
On several occasions Muirhead rode to the rescue of the socialist newspaper. 'Time and again it looked as if our ship was
heading for the bankruptcy rocks, but somehow we always
escaped ... A witty but rather cynical friend used to say he always knew when the *Forward* was in exceptionally deep water:
it would then come out with a specially strong Home Rule
issue: that would be preparatory to "touching" Mr. Muirhead
for a loan!'

The victorious Labour MPs who got such a resounding
send-off from St Enoch Station in 1922 were all committed
to Home Rule. Speaking at the service of dedication held in
St Andrew's Halls on the Sunday before they left on the night
mail for London, Govan MP Neil Maclean at first addressed

the still burning issue of rent. *The Bulletin* reported what he said next:

> When they went to London, Home Rule for Scotland would not be confined to the drawing-rooms of Brodick Castle. They would talk Home Rule in a way that several of these people did not realise. It did not mean a palace at one end of the glen and a ruined crofter's cottage at the other. It meant civilisation in Scotland, plenty and security for the Scottish people in the land of their birth.

Neil Maclean's 'drawing-rooms of Brodick Castle' is a reference to the Third Marquess of Bute, one of the aristocratic supporters of Home Rule. There were several of those. In *Scottish Nationalism*, Hanham described Bute as 'a Roman Catholic Tory philanthropist and antiquarian … outside the realm of ordinary party politics. He was one of the first to evolve something like a distinctive Catholic nationalist point of view.'

Yet the Marquess of Bute put Home Rule above his own traditionalist and Conservative views, expressing his point of view in a letter to Lord Rosebery way back in 1881: 'Allow me to say that I think there are many Tories like myself who would hail a more autonomous arrangement with deep pleasure. We would prefer the rule of our own countrymen, even if it were rather Radical, to the existing state of things.'

Another aristocratic Home Ruler was the Honourable Ruaraidh Stuart Erskine of Marr. His nationalism was rooted in the mysticism and mystery of Celtic Scotland and the Gaelic language. Despite having been born in Brighton and living for long periods of time in England and France as well as Scotland, he spoke Gaelic quite fluently.

As a Highlander, a Catholic, a royalist and a socialist stirred and excited by the Russian Revolution, Erskine of Marr's politics were something of a patchwork quilt. Communist Harry McShane described him as an old-fashioned Radical.

Robert Cunninghame Graham, one of the founding fathers of both the Labour Party and the Scottish National Party, also belonged to this group of aristocratic Radicals and Home Rulers. He was born into the Scottish gentry, and his maternal grandmother was a Spanish aristocrat. In the 1870s, when he was in his twenties, he went off to seek his fortune cattle-ranching in the Argentine. He spent much of his time there on horseback, living the life of a *gaucho*. The Argentinians called him 'Don Roberto', a name that stuck. So did the habit of riding around dressed as a *gaucho* on his return to his estate at Gartmore in Stirlingshire. He went into politics, his platform always a Radical one. He called for workers' rights, universal adult suffrage, the abolition of the House of Lords and Home Rule for Scotland, cheerfully stating he'd rather see his taxes being wasted in Edinburgh than in London.

The focus always came back to Scotland. At the time of John Maclean's 1918 sedition trial, Erskine of Marr was critical of Maclean for not having fought the charges brought against him under the Defence of the Realm Act as not being valid in a Scottish court. The Clydeside Labour MPs of the 1920s took the argument to Westminster. Speaking in a debate on Home Rule in 1924, Tom Johnston delivered a typically passionate and romantic speech:

> Our historical and cultural traditions are different; our racial characteristics are different. The Celt has long memories, the Englishman forgets quickly. There are members on these Benches and on those Benches too who fight their electoral battles upon, say, the Battle of the Boyne. We have members on these Benches who fight them on the Battle of Bannockburn. But the Englishman forgets quickly. We can never obliterate these national characteristics ...

Johnston went on to cite Robert Louis Stevenson, Robert Burns and William Wallace, allowing Englishman Rudyard

Kipling to sum up why you have to be a nationalist before you can be an internationalist.

> God gave all earth to men to love;
> But, because our hearts are small,
> Ordained for each, one spot should prove
> Beloved over all.

Despite having been known to say that the workers have no country, Davie Kirkwood said something very similar in the wake of the drama of the Zinoviev letter:

> I take no orders from Rome or Moscow.
> To the world I give my hand, but my heart
> I give to my native land.

On one occasion Kirkwood objected to an English MP being in the chair of the Scottish Grand Committee. Sir Richard Barnet told him with some indignation that he was a direct descendant of King Robert the Bruce. Kirkwood bowed and apologised, saying 'it would be a sin and a crime to torment a descendant of the victor at Bannockburn'.

In July 1924 Kirkwood brought forward a bill to return the Stone of Destiny from Westminster Abbey to Holyroodhouse in Edinburgh. The proposal went to a second reading, was co-sponsored by the Clydeside Labour MPs, and garnered considerable support.

Kirkwood gave a typically eloquent speech arguing the moral case for the repatriation of the Stone of Scone, calling it a symbol of Scottish nationhood. He quoted the Bible and eminent historians. He spoke of William Wallace and Robert the Bruce. Telling the House that he stood before his fellow Members of Parliament 'representing an unconquered race', he also talked of the 'great spiritual, historical and sentimental bonds that bring together a race. When we seek bread and shelter for our people, we also demand roses.'

John MacCormick, one of the founders of what was to become the Scottish National Party, first joined the ILP when he became a student at Glasgow University in 1923. In his memoir, *The Flag in the Wind*, from which this chapter has borrowed its title, he summed up the attitude of mind and spirit:

> Socialism in those days was not the doctrine of the State-planned economy which it has since become. The I.L.P. had inherited much of the old Radical tradition of Scotland and for the most part as a street-corner missionary I was expected not to expound the theories of Karl Marx but merely to give expression to the general sense of injustice and aspirations for a better way of life which were very natural feelings among the workers of Clydeside in the years between the wars.

'The general sense of injustice and aspirations for a better way of life': beautifully summed-up. MacCormick wrote of how much as a young speaker for the ILP he enjoyed 'the almost religious atmosphere of enthusiasm in which we all worked'.

Enthusiasm for Home Rule within the Labour Party began to lessen. There was a strong feeling that if Labour were to continue to make headway at Westminster it needed to do so as a British party, uniting Labour supporters from England, Wales and Scotland. The argument was again advanced that the workers have no country, as the STUC did when it officially withdrew its support for Home Rule in 1931. 'Workers should look upon themselves as workers, and not as Scotsmen or Englishmen. Let them be honest and get back to the ideals of international Socialism.'

Some kept the flame of self-determination burning. Two separate nationalist parties came together in 1934 to form the Scottish National Party. In 1948 John MacCormick and

the Scottish Convention launched the Scottish Covenant at a ceremony at the Church of Scotland Assembly Hall on the Mound in Edinburgh. Two million people signed this pledge 'within the framework of the United Kingdom, to do everything in our power to secure for Scotland a Parliament with adequate legislative authority in Scottish affairs'.

John MacCormick was by no means the only person to make the journey from the ILP to the SNP. Another was John L. Kinloch, a man who wore the kilt each and every day of his long life. Knowledgeable as he was about Scottish history and traditions, Kinloch was also a visionary. Like Tom Johnston, he was an early advocate of hydroelectricity and other developments which would bring work and people back to Scotland's deserted glens. Chief amongst these was a proposed new city and deep-water port at Loch Eriboll on Scotland's northern coast. The dolomite to be found in the surrounding rocks was to provide the abundant mineral wealth which would make this dream a reality.

In 1927, when Kinloch was a Labour Party candidate for Argyll, John MacCormick helped him campaign on Mull, 'addressing meetings in every clachan'. MacCormick noted that John L. was as keen on Home Rule as he was, as were their audiences. He also made a telling observation, which says as much about Labour and parliamentary politics as it does about John L. Kinloch, who had by then spent years putting the case for socialism and the Labour Party: 'But for his complete personal integrity and his ignorance of the art of wire-pulling he would by then have had a safe Labour seat in Parliament.'

There was a long road to be travelled for those who wanted Scotland once more to have control over her own affairs, with many disappointments and false starts along the way. On 11 September 1997, 60 per cent of Scotland's electorate voted in a referendum. By 75 per cent to 25 per cent, this demonstrated overwhelmingly that a Scottish Parliament in Edinburgh was 'the expressed will of the Scottish people'.

On 12 May 1999 veteran SNP MP and MSP Winnie Ewing opened the new Parliament at Holyrood in Edinburgh with these words: 'The Scottish Parliament, adjourned on the 25th day of March, seventeen hundred and seven, is hereby reconvened.'

In May 2011 the SNP under Alex Salmond swept to a stunning victory in the third election to the Scottish Parliament at Holyrood, securing an impressive overall majority of 69 seats out of a total of 129 and routing their political opponents. The Liberal Democrats won only five seats, Scottish Labour only 37. Tom Johnston might have had some advice for both those parties on the danger of betraying the electorate or taking their votes for granted. We might also hazard a guess that he and his contemporaries, internationalists as they all were, would have shared the pride taken in the cultural diversity of the Scottish Parliament of 2011.

Honouring their own family origins, the new and returning MSPs took their oaths in English, some also in Scots, Gaelic, Doric, Italian and Urdu. Glasgow Labour MSP Hanzala Malik offered a prayer in Arabic. Humza Yousaf, newly elected SNP member from Glasgow, wore an elegant traditional Pakistani sherwani, to which he had added a bright splash of colour. Pinned to his right shoulder by a handsome silver brooch was a red plaid in Partick Thistle tartan.

The sheer scale of the SNP landslide of 2011 took many commentators by surprise. Reaching for suitably dramatic metaphors, they told Scotland and the world that a seismic shift had taken place. We'd heard all this before. Back in 1922, when the first big group of Red Clydesiders was elected to the Westminster Parliament, *The Bailie* wrote that 'there is a serious "fault" under our feet. Earthquakes are predicted.'

Since 2011, the political tectonic plates have crashed ever more dramatically into one another. Despite the hard-fought Scottish independence referendum of 2014 resulting in a no vote, 55 per cent of voters rejecting independence and 45 per

cent being in favour, the SNP has gone on to even greater electoral success at both the Holyrood and Westminster parliaments and seen a huge increase in membership. It's clear that the issue of full Scottish independence, as opposed to devolution, has not gone away. Some Scots are profoundly dismayed by this. Others are passionately enthusiastic.

In the UK general election of May 2015, in an even more astounding landslide, the SNP won 56 of Scotland's 59 Westminster seats while Labour lost 40 of their 41 seats and were left with only one Scottish MP. What would the old Red Clydesiders have made of this previously unimaginable situation?

The snap UK election of June 2017, in the wake of the referendum vote in favour of Brexit, the UK's departure from the European Union, saw the SNP lose ground at Westminster, reduced from 56 to 35 seats. The election also saw a reduction in the Conservative majority south of the border but a modest revival in the fortunes of the Tories and Labour in Scotland. Under the leadership of Jeremy Corbyn, support for Labour across the UK, especially among younger voters, also saw an upturn. Some older voters too were drawn to what seemed to be a return to the traditional aims and values of old rather than new Labour.

The seismic shifts of both Corbyn's unexpected surge in popularity and the continuing support for Scottish independence have delivered one huge benefit to everyone who believes in democracy. People who were never previously interested in politics have become involved, daring to believe that their vote can make a difference and that their thoughts and opinions can influence others.

25

Socialism, Self-Improvement & Fun

'Love learning, which is the food of the mind.'

The ILP was always more than just a political party. Red Clydeside's socialists took an interest in all aspects of life, as *The Times* reported on 28 December 1922. In the wake of the Labour landslide in the November election, the newspaper had dispatched a correspondent north to find out how the political earthquake had happened. Unable to resist an amused curl of the lip at the fact that the ILPers were tee-totallers to a man, the reporter acknowledged the socialists had worked hard for their victory:

> I have been struck by the variety and extent of the propaganda. Even the stoniest ground has received its sowing. Socialist study circles, Socialist economic classes, Socialist musical festivals, Socialist athletic competitions, Socialist choirs, Socialist dramatic societies, Socialist plays – these are only a few of the devious ways in which they attempt to reach the unconverted. Then there are the Socialist Sunday Schools – a far more potent agency than the 'proletarian' Sunday Schools, with which they are not to be confused. Last, but not least, there are the Socialist newspapers, of which the *Forward* is the most important. From time to time free distribution of copies has taken place.

Socialist Sunday Schools were first established in London in the 1890s during a dockers' strike. Soup kitchens were set up to feed the strikers' children. Mary Gray came up with the idea of running classes for this captive audience, giving them the socialist analysis as to why they were poor, other people were not, and what might be done about that.

The idea caught on. By the beginning of the First World War there were 200 Socialist Sunday Schools throughout Britain. They had their own version of the Ten Commandments:

1. Love your school-fellows, who will be your fellow-workmen in life.

2. Love learning, which is the food of the mind; be as grateful to your teacher as to your parents.

3. Make every day holy by good and useful deeds and kindly actions.

4. Honour good men, be courteous to all men, bow down to none.

5. Do not hate or speak evil of anyone; do not be revengeful, but stand up for your rights, and resist oppression.

6. Do not be cowardly; be a friend to the weak, and love justice.

7. Remember that all the good things of the earth are produced by labour, whoever enjoys them without working for them is stealing the bread of the workers.

8. Observe and think in order to discover the truth; do not believe what is contrary to reason; and never deceive yourself or others.

9. Do not think that he who loves his own country must hate other nations, or wish for war, which is a remnant of barbarism.

10. Look forward to the day when all men will be free
    citizens of one fatherland, and live together as
    brothers in peace and righteousness.

ILP member and trade unionist Tom Anderson founded
the South Side Socialist Sunday School in Glasgow in 1897.
The children were taught about socialism, how to think for
themselves, and about working-class heroes and rebels. Songs
helped get the message across.

Anderson later joined the Socialist Labour Party, the revolutionary group which ran much of the Singer Strike of 1911.
The SLP set up proletarian schools and a proletarian college,
where they taught economics, history, sexual science, drama
and music. Anderson was principal of the college for 30 years,
assisted at times by John Maclean and John S. Clarke, who
wrote *The Young Worker's Book of Rebels*. Published in 1918 by
the Proletarian School at 550 Argyle Street, Glasgow, the first
rebel quoted was Spartacus.

Proletarian and Socialist Sunday Schools were anathema
to some, the issue raised several times over the years in the
House of Commons. In November 1920 the Conservative MP
for Nottingham demanded there should be 'supervision over
the Socialist Sunday schools of Glasgow and the industrial
districts of the Clyde, the teachings of which are of an un-
disguisedly revolutionary character'. He was told no control
could be exercised, as the Socialist Sunday Schools were outside the jurisdiction of the Scottish Education Department.

In the 1920s and '30s those who were appalled by the
very existence of Socialist Sunday Schools tried to legislate
against them. In 1927 a private member's bill got as far as a
second reading. In 1933 Sir Reginald Craddock, MP for the
Combined English Universities, tried again.

I have often heard quoted, from Lenin's article in the
publication called 'The Workers' Dreadnought,' these
two sentences: 'Give us the child for eight years, and it

will be a Bolshevik for ever.' 'Hundreds of thousands of teachers constitute an apparatus that must push our work forward.' It is no exaggeration to say that these two texts of Lenin are the inspiration of the anti-God campaigns which have, unfortunately, been introduced into this country. They are like the germs of some contagious disease, which may spread and destroy men's lives.

He based his information on the supposed iniquities of Socialist Sunday Schools on a lady of his acquaintance who had for years done charity work with disabled ex-servicemen. 'This work brings her into contact with working people, including some Communists. She keeps clear of all those things herself and is in no way a bigoted person.' Sounds like Sir Reginald himself didn't often come into contact with working people.

Exercising his cynical sense of humour, James Maxton told him the bill was never going to become law anyway:

When a new member of Parliament comes here and draws a place in the ballot, well down the list, he goes to his Whips and consults them, as a child does his parents. They look down a long list and say, 'How can we find something that will not do anyone much harm, will give the people who are foolish enough to come on that particular Friday a pleasant entertainment, while the members of the Government can go down to the country or to the seaside?'

Maxton told the Duchess of Atholl, Scotland's first female MP, that he was surprised to see her supporting the proposals, 'although I have some doubts about my own rights in opposing it, because I notice she has taken care to exclude her own native land from the provisions of the Bill'.

Another MP asked Maxton, 'Has my honourable friend forgotten that Scotland is still part of England?' Maxton

asked him, 'Has my honourable and learned friend, who has a distinguished career at the English bar, forgotten that as far as legal matters are concerned he is not allowed to practise in Scotland?'

Although the ayes had it, the Seditious and Blasphemous Teaching of Children Bill never did become law. North and south of the border, Socialist Sunday Schools kept on going right into the 1930s.

There were plenty of educational opportunities for adults too. Although short-lived as an independent body, in existence for only five years, the Scottish Labour College founded by John Maclean in 1916 taught and influenced thousands. Evening classes on Marxism, economics and history were held in Glasgow, Aberdeen, Dundee and Edinburgh. With the same belief as Maclean in the power of education, Helen Crawford worked with him within the Scottish Labour College.

Kinning Park Co-op put on Friday evening lectures on subjects which included geography and post-war literature. Govan ILP put on winter lectures at seven o'clock on Sunday evenings. Glasgow University held extramural classes in Glasgow, Pollokshaws and Paisley. Their ten-week courses cost only one shilling and threepence and were free to unemployed women and men. Astronomy was popular, as was 'English Composition; Writing and Speaking'.

In Glasgow, the ILP put on regular Sunday lectures in the Pavilion and Metropole theatres, the venues chosen suggesting large audiences, and Saturday afternoon classes on public speaking for women. In January 1926, a course of ten lessons cost two and six, half a crown. 'Come and prepare to spread the light when Summer days are fine.' The class books were Fred Henderson's *The Case for Socialism* and William Morris's *News from Nowhere.*

The same advert reminded ILPers of the carnival dance in the Central Halls in Bath Street. Socialists were allowed to have fun too. The *Forward* carried adverts for pianos, fur coats

and party frocks – bought at the Co-op, of course – engagement rings, bakers who would cater to 'picnics, excursions
and outings of all kinds', tea rooms and restaurants such as
the King's Café and Granny Black's, and Socialist holiday
camps.

One of those which regularly advertised was on the
Norfolk coast at Caister-on-Sea near Great Yarmouth, open
to both sexes from May to October. A week in a tent would
cost you one guinea, a week indoors one pound five shillings.
You could enjoy fine sea views, bracing air and lovely gardens.
'All surplus profits to the cause.'

Or you could go on excursions closer to home. One
'Catholic Socialist Notes' column advised: 'To all whom it
may concern notice is given that the following Sunday will
witness our annual descent on Gourock-on-the-sea. Pawn
something and come.'

The sense of humour which runs through the *Forward*
extended to its advertisers. In the first edition allowed to
publish after Lloyd George's censorship of the paper of
1916, 'Tom Lloyd, "Himself", British and Best Tailor for
Men, Argyle Street, Near Stockwell Street Corner', offered
'Uncensored News for Readers! The Greatest Tailoring Value
Ever Offered in Glasgow!'

John S. Clarke's take on 'The Folk-Music Craze' in an article
published in 1926 is funny but surprising. He didn't think
much of Marjorie Kennedy Fraser's newly published collection of Hebridean folk songs. 'It is simply marvellous, one
might almost write miraculous, that an old lady can wander
about the lone sheilings of the misty islands harvesting such a
crop of folk melodies.' Nor did he much care for 'the negro
singer, Paul Robeson', dismissing the music of the man who
was to be admired so much for his voice and the integrity of
his politics as 'Three moans and a few howls.'

For socialists and everyone else who could afford the
tickets, there was always plenty of entertainment on offer at
Glasgow's many theatres, the Pavilion, the Metropole, the

Empire, the Alhambra. In December 1915 at the King's Theatre, the D'Oyly Carte Opera were working hard to keep spirits up during the First World War. In one week, one night after another, lovers of light opera could see *The Yeomen of the Guard, Patience, The Pirates of Penzance, The Gondoliers, The Mikado* and *Iolanthe. The Bailie* was only a little sarcastic about Gilbert and Sullivan:

> If there was anything new to say we would say it, but there isn't. We welcome G. & S. as we do the song of the lark, the purr of the stream, and the laughter of girls. We grow young again under the influence of this essentially British opera, remembering first nights of their production away back in the 'eighties, and yet we do not envy those youngsters who are seeing these operas for the first time, for the reason that they grow better the oftener we see them.

More sombre entertainment was to be had on Monday, 13 December 1915 at St Andrew's Halls, when Mr Hilaire Belloc gave a talk with 'coloured lantern slides' on 'The New Development of the War'. Tickets went from five shillings down to one shilling. Those of an artistic turn of mind could view watercolours by an artist called W.B.E. Ranken. The proceeds of this show were being donated to 'Miss Fyfe's Belgian Relief Fund'.

The greater part of Belgium was occupied by the Germans during the First World War. Many Belgians fled before them, seeking refuge in the other countries of Europe. Britain alone gave shelter to 250,000. Dispersed throughout the country, an extensive relief effort helped support them. The vast majority went home once the war was over. One imaginary Belgian refugee stayed on to make his life in London: Hercule Poirot, Agatha Christie's great detective.

During the First World War, the Glasgow Corporation Belgian Workroom had premises in North Portland Street, off

George Street behind the City Chambers, and a central office in Bothwell Street. On behalf of the Belgian refugees, they gratefully received donations of clothes and shoes. Headed by the Lord Provost, the Corporation Belgian Committee was also 'pleased to receive offers to give Four or Five Days' Hospitality to Belgian Soldiers who are in the Trenches, and who, on getting leave of absence, are prevented from joining their Family Circle in the invaded parts of Belgium'.

One year-round and long-running attraction which cut across politics and social class was Hengler's Circus, a Glasgow institution which advertised in the *Forward* and every other Glasgow newspaper. In February 1920 they were promoting the last three weeks of *The Sioux*. Playing every evening at 7.30 and offering matinees at 2.30 on Tuesdays, Wednesday and Saturdays, this offered a 'Sensational Water Spectacle'.

Dramatic water effects were Hengler's speciality, along with real live horses and riders performing 'feats of daring horsemanship'. At times there were elephants in the show and another favourite act, 'Duncan's Scotch Collies, Wonderful Canine Intelligence'. All of this went on at the Charing Cross end of Sauchiehall Street, in the lee of Glasgow School of Art, on the site later occupied by the ABC Cinema and which is now a music venue.

For years the *Forward*'s masthead carried an advert couched as a challenging question: 'Are YOU eating the ALLINSON Wholemeal BREAD?' Like healthy eating, the great outdoors was always popular, the benefits of fresh air and exercise another of the enthusiasms of the age. Running was particularly popular with young working-class men, many of them members of clubs like Garscube Harriers.

The Clarion Scouts were active in Glasgow and Clydeside. This group, where Patrick and Agnes Dollan first met, combined spreading the word about socialism with cycle rides and country rambles, often camping overnight or staying in their own hostels. By the 1890s, they had 120 clubs across Britain and an estimated 7,000 members.

Guy Aldred originally came to Glasgow because the Clarion Scouts invited him to speak at the Pavilion Theatre in 1912. He went down a storm, also addressing open-air meetings, including a rally held at the well-known fountain at Charing Cross.

Davie Kirkwood recalled in his memoirs that for many years he and John Wheatley made a point on Sundays of going out together for a walk in the country. People didn't only want to get out into the natural world, they needed to. It was a necessary counterbalance to the harsh and unnatural surroundings of the industrial world in which they worked.

For many working-class Scots their upbringing was both urban and rural. Industrial development having occurred where the resources were and without any checks on its sprawling growth, the coal bings and forges and shipyards were often no distance from the bluebell woods, the sparkling burns, and the green and heather-clad hills. One woman who grew up as a girl in a tenement in Radnor Park in Clydebank remembered being sent up to what is now the Boulevard dual carriageway to buy eggs at a local farm. 'The countryside was at the end of the street.'

Hillwalking and hiking could take you further afield. That walking in the country for pleasure was still considered a somewhat eccentric thing to do is demonstrated by the inverted commas in a report in *The Scotsman* in October 1933:

An organised search for the Loch Ness monster by a party of Glasgow 'hikers' and ramblers took place yesterday, but it was unsuccessful. The monster was not seen. Wet, disagreeable weather prevailed, and the conditions were all against the possibility, a remote one at the best, of the monster making an appearance.

The monster hunt created mild amusement in the district of Loch Ness-side, where it was known that there was not the slightest chance of the Glasgow

party catching a glimpse of the monster. Local people exhibited no interest in the search, and wisely
remained indoors. The stricter Sabbatarians regarded
the Sunday search as an unwarranted intrustion.

So the 30 Glaswegians, all members of the Scottish Ramblers'
Federation, returned home without a sighting, and Nessie
remained undisturbed.

Founded in 1889 after correspondence in the *Glasgow
Herald*, the Scottish Mountaineering Club was considered
to be for those of a certain social status. Founded in 1930,
the Creagh Dhu Club was made up of shipyard workers from
Glasgow and Dundee. Their favourite stamping ground was
the Arrochar Alps at the head of Loch Long.

The right to roam the hills and climb the mountains
was hard won. This was even more the case in England
and Wales, where a law of tresspass applied and was often
invoked against hikers and ramblers. The argument had
been raging for 20 years and more when, in 1908, Scottish
Liberal MP John Bryce argued that 'the people should not
have this access to mountains on sufferance but as a right'.
The following year, Bryce brought forward his Access to
Mountains (Scotland) Bill. This aimed to 'secure to the
public the right of Access to Mountain and Moorland in
Scotland'. It got to a second reading. In 1927, with characteristic directness, Davie Kirkwood told his fellow MPs, 'We said
"Now" for the Access to Mountains Bill. Are we not going on
with it?'

Twelve years later, in 1939, Kirkwood's fellow Clydeside
Labour MP Campbell Stephen was still arguing for 'complete
access to the mountains of Scotland and the moorland of this
country'.

After decades of lobbying, confrontation and direct action
by the Ramblers' Association and others, the Countryside
and Rights of Way (CRoW) action of 2000 gave walkers in
England and Wales a legal and much greater right of access

to the countryside. What Scots often see as a time-honoured right to roam was finally enshrined in law in the Land Reform (Scotland) Act of 2003.

Everyone loved the Firth of Clyde, a sail doon the watter, from Craigendoran, Wemyss Bay or Largs to Kilcreggan, the Kyles of Butes, Millport or Brodick on Arran. Or you could glide along the Forth and Clyde Canal from Speirs Wharf at Port Dundas, heading for the little resort of Craigmarloch, just beyond Kirkintilloch.

Dominated by the massive cooling towers of Pinkston Power Station and the tall chimney of the whisky distillery, the embarkation point was in the heart of dirty, smoky Glasgow but the crew of the excursion boats cleaned the cobbles of the quay thoroughly before the passengers got there. The fondly remembered *Gypsy Queen* and the *Fairy Queen* were the pleasure craft which plied this run.

At Stockingfield Junction the Port Dundas spur of the canal joined in with the main part and the boats had to move slowly to negotiate the turn. In a poignant reminder of the poverty in which so many Glaswegians lived, boys there would dive for coins the passengers threw into the canal.

At Craigmarloch there was a tea house called the Bungalow, an 18-hole putting green and swings for the children. Cooked by students from the Do School during their summer vacation, the Bungalow's menu never varied: Scotch Broth, steak pie, pears and creamed rice, with ice creams to follow for those who had any room left.

The classes, lectures, clubs, hobbies and activities people with not very much time and little spare cash took part in continue to impress, the sheer volume and variety of them: cycling, hiking, dancing, photography, mending watches, sewing, knitting, playing in a band, putting on plays, stretching your body and your mind.

Men and women read widely. Many learned the poems of Burns, Byron, Shelley, Scott and others off by heart and, throughout their lives, delighted in reciting them aloud to

admiring younger relatives. Alex McCulloch, my uncle, was one of them.

In the 1930s he worked as a shunter at the College Goods Yard, off Glasgow's High Street and on the site of the Old College, the original University of Glasgow. The railwaymen there liked to joke that they were great scholars as they went off every day to the College. Some lived up to that, forming a reading group. Among the books Alex McCulloch and his workmates discussed during their meal breaks were *Das Kapital* and *War and Peace*.

Poverty denied so many Clydesiders an education. They went to enormous efforts to get one for themselves, express their creativity and simply have fun.

26

The Hungry '30s

'We don't just make ships here, we make men too.'

Despite the Wall Street Crash of 1929, the keel of a new Cunarder was laid at John Brown's in Clydebank just before Christmas 1930. The first rivet was driven home by the shipyard manager in front of a crowd of cheering workers. As was traditional, the new liner had as yet no name. For the time being she would be known by her job number and it was as the 534 that the ship which was to become the *Queen Mary* first became famous.

As the ship was built and began to grow, the skeleton of the 534 came to dominate Clydebank. Rising up like a spire over the tenement homes of the men who were building her, it made a pair with the Singer clock.

Disaster struck shortly before Christmas 1931. A year after the keel was laid, work on the 534 stopped. The slump which followed the Crash had begun to bite and Cunard could no longer afford to keep building. Looming as she did over Clydebank, the unfinished and rusting hulk of the 534 became a potent symbol of the Depression.

It was two years before work resumed, two years during which thousands in Clydebank and elsewhere had no other option but to go on the dole, two years during which masculine pride took a battering, and wives and mothers had an even tougher struggle than usual to make 10 shillings do the work of a pound. That the skeleton of the 534 was so visible

only added to the emotional as well as financial depression gripping the town.

One response to the mass unemployment of the 1930s was the hunger marches which took place throughout Britain. One of the Scottish organisers of these was Harry McShane, stalwart of the National Unemployed Workers' Movement (NUWM). The NUWM was established in 1921 and grew out of associations of demobbed sailors and soldiers. Those thrown out of work by the crash and the slump swelled its ranks.

The NUWM was dominated by members of the Communist Party, Harry McShane one of them. He took part in marches on London and in the summer of 1933, along with John McGovern, a Glasgow Labour MP, led the Scottish Hunger March to Edinburgh.

A huge amount of planning went into the Scottish Hunger March of June 1933. Field kitchens were set up along the routes of the marchers converging on Edinburgh, donations of food and money to stock them gathered from trade unions and co-operative societies along the way. Bo'ness Co-op donated 600 'twopenny pies'.

The marchers came from Glasgow and Clydeside, Fife, Lanarkshire, Ayrshire, with a handful from Aberdeen. They were required to fill out and sign a recruiting form. Putting their name to this committed them to accepting 'strict discipline, as I realise that unless discipline is observed the greatest danger will arise for the marchers'. They also had to state they fully accepted the aims of the march and the five demands which were to be made of the government. *The Scotsman* listed those on Monday, 12 June 1933, the day after the marchers had reached Edinburgh. That the first demand was for the abolition of the means test shows how detested this was. This method of establishing what people's financial circumstances were before they could be awarded any help was considered by many to be intrusive and humiliating.

1.   Abolition of the means test.

2.   An extra 1s. 6d. a week for each unemployed child and an extra 3s. 6d. a week for each adult unemployed and adult dependant.

3.   The reduction of rents by 25 per cent.

4.   The provision of relief work at Trade Union wages and under Trade Union conditions.

5.   The repudiation of social service schemes and voluntary labour connected with them.

The Glasgow marchers set off from George Square on Friday, 9 June. Mainly men, there were some women in the ranks. It was a Friday afternoon and they were given a great send-off, with music playing and flags flying. They marched up out of Glasgow to Bishopbriggs and then on to Kilsyth. *The Scotsman* put the numbers of the Glasgow contingent at 600.

According to Harry McShane, at Kilsyth the provost and the town councillors had found they had business elsewhere that Friday but the locals gave them a warm welcome, allowing them to spend the night in the local Salvation Army citadel. A meeting was held beforehand in the local park. Must have been quite an excitement on a long, light June evening in Kilsyth.

Along the route, people donated what money they could: 'Coppers, which could ill be spared, clinked into the boxes; women with tears in their eyes, wishing the men "good luck" and dropping their contributions into the collecting tins.' The next day was the longest of the march, 20 miles. McShane praised 'Comrade Heenan', '... whose feet were in a terrible condition and who wrenched his ankle six miles from Corstorphine, but who obstinately refused even to consider giving up, and kept tramping doggedly on. How can one tell of the humour, the healthy, salty humour, that refused even to consider downheartedness even when tramping

along at the end of a 20-mile march through two hours of pelting rain?'

The Glasgow marchers reached the arranged rendezvous at Corstorphine at four o'clock on the afternoon of Sunday, 11 June. Everybody cheered everyone else as they came in and there was a special cheer for the women. The field kitchens fed everyone and then they formed up behind their own bands and marched into Edinburgh. 'The Edinburgh workers sent out a strong contingent to meet us and march in with us. The streets were lined all the way into Edinburgh with sympathetic workers, tremendous enthusiasm prevailing.'

The Scotsman confirms Harry McShane's description of the arrival and assembly at Corstorphine, the subsequent entry of the marchers into Edinburgh and the enthusiasm:

> Fife and drum bands accompanied them, and, as they entered Corstorphine, the marchers sang 'The International' and 'The Marseillaise' and other tunes. With the Ayrshire section was a one-legged man, who marched upon crutches.
>
> Only the Ayrshire section complained of indifferent treatment on the way. They had marched from Hamilton, and had to sleep in a stable. Huts and halls had been found for the other sections.
>
> The marchers were met outside Corstorphine by the Edinburgh contingent, which, like the other sections, contained members of the Young Communist League. Cards with various slogans were particularly prominent among this section, which was headed by marchers in brown shirts and slouch hats, with red pompoms. When the two parties met cheers were raised, but a little further on these gave place to booing, as an armoured car containing soldiers passed the column.
>
> A collection was taken en route from the large crowd which had gathered at the Corstorphine tram

terminus and from sightseers and sympathisers who
lined the streets of the city. As the marchers reached
the city people were entering churches for the evening
service, and the collectors took up their stands in the
porches ...

While the marchers were still on the road officialdom had
agreed to meet a deputation on the Monday morning after
they arrived in Edinburgh. This meeting was to take place
at the offices of the Ministry of Labour, then located at
44 Drumsheugh Gardens. However, Sir Edward Collins,
Secretary of State for Scotland, had not responded to re-
quests that he should meet the marchers.

On the Sunday evening they headed for the Mound,
where an open-air meeting was held. Harry McShane says
20,000 were there. *The Scotsman* puts it at 'several thousand'.
Afterwards the marchers went on down to Leith, where they
were given a meal in the ILP Hall on Bonnington Road. After
a night in various hostels and halls they formed up again the
following morning and headed for Drumsheugh Gardens.

The deputation spent two hours in the Ministry of Labour
offices, the rest of the marchers waiting outside. Sir Edward
Collins had remained in London and made it clear he had no
intention of coming north to meet the marchers.

The deputation had some interesting demands. Although
such a huge number of people were unemployed, the middle
classes were still complaining about having to do their own
housework. The marchers insisted that young women who
were unemployed should not be forced into domestic service. Another suggestion was that new public works schemes
should be launched. These included the building of a road
bridge over the Forth 'and a new arterial road through
Glasgow'. The marchers also wanted more schools and
'better boots and books for the children of the unemployed'.
They also protested against the trade embargo currently in
force against the Soviet Union.

The Ministry of Labour officials told them all their points had been duly noted. Although the deputation didn't think much of that, its members withdrew and joined the rest of the marchers waiting outside in Drumsheugh Gardens. Their next move was to Parliament Square, where an impromptu outdoor cafeteria was set up, complete with those field kitchens and trestle tables. Harry McShane was very taken with the scene:

> The three camp-kitchens were soon belching forth large clouds of smoke. Gallons and gallons of tea were made, while boxes containing a large amount of food were unloaded. Some six or eight women assisted the Marchers' own cooks in preparing and serving the food.
>
> The unusual sight in this historical Square attracted large crowds of passers-by, and they seemed inclined to linger to watch the proceedings; but a large body of police arrived on the scene and kept them in motion.

The meal was simple: tea, a sausage roll and two slices of bread. Marchers sat down in Parliament Square to enjoy it in the bright June sunshine, on the steps outside the entrance to St Giles Cathedral and on the plinth around the monument to the Duke of Buccleuch. Harry McShane noted what a colourful lot they were 'with red flavours very much to the fore'. *The Scotsman* also commented on the profusion of red shirts and ribbons and one beret embroidered with a hammer and sickle.

Once they were fed and watered they marched down the Royal Mile, heading for Holyrood Park. The policeman at the gates of Holyroodhouse instructed them to wheel right. The marchers kept on going, taking a shortcut through the grounds of the palace. Harry McShane was beside himself with excitement, seeing huge political significance in this.

In his pamphlet he waxed lyrical about the 'proletariat in their ragged clothes' walking into 'the most sacred precincts in Scotland. The walls and grounds of the Royal Palace of Holyrood – that innermost sanctuary of all the Royal parasites in Scotland's history – echo the tramp of the first legions of the masses. The walls and grounds of Holyrood that heard the music of Rizzio, and Mary Queen of Scots, heard the song of that murdered Irish leader, "The Rebel Song", and then the thunderous battle cry of the world's workers, "The Internationale."'

On Monday night the hunger marchers spent the night sleeping on the pavement in Princes Street. The police kept an eye on them but stood back and let them get on with it. Contradicting the 'you'll have had your tea' slur, many Edinburgers stopped by during the evening and gave the marchers cigarettes.

> The police ... left the marchers to while the time away as they thought fit, contenting themselves with keeping the curious crowds on the move. This was not an easy task. The amazing spectacle was an unusual counter-attraction to the shops, and great patience and tact were demanded from the policemen to prevent serious congestion.
>
> From the police point of view matters were not improved when flute bands began to play and marchers took part in impromptu dances.
>
> One man was stretched out under a blanket, and had a white sheet laid across his forehead. A card on his chest informed passers-by that he was 'a victim of the means test'.
>
> The 'reveille' scene in the morning was remarkable. Men shaved with their mirrors supported on the railings of West Princes Street Gardens, and others washed and dried themselves at a fountain in the middle of the marchers' encampment.

> After a meal had been served in the middle of the day hundreds of banana skins were stuck onto the railing spikes, and remained there during the afternoon, forming a new decorative touch scarcely in harmony with the everyday dignity of the street.

Fortified by the bananas, the people, who surely must already have had enough blisters on their feet, spent Tuesday marching not once but twice through Edinburgh and the east coast haar which had come down after the golden sunshine of the previous day.

Now estimated by *The Scotsman* at 1,000-strong, it was midnight before they returned to Princes Street after a stravaig across North Bridge, South Bridge, Chambers Street, Candlemaker Row, the Grassmarket and through onto Lothian Road. Edinburgh came up trumps, having arranged for them all to spend the night in different halls around the city. 'It was stated that whether or not indoor accommodation had been found for the men last night, the women would have been accommodated indoors.'

On Wednesday morning breakfast was served on a piece of waste ground at Simon Square at the Pleasance. More bananas, in sandwiches this time, were washed down with tea. Meanwhile McGovern and McShane called at the City Chambers and asked for help to transport the marchers home. Fine, said the Lord Provost and the police, but there's one condition: You have to promise not to come back and do it all again.

McGovern and McShane refused to give that commitment and for a while the situation grew tense. Edinburgh blinked first. Nineteen free buses were laid on to take the marchers home to wherever they had come from in the first place: Fife, Central Scotland, Glasgow and the west. Separate arrangements were made for the five marchers from Aberdeen. Maybe they got a ride home on the train.

By half-past seven all the marchers had departed with the exception of one man from Glasgow, who for some reason or other refused to leave.

As the buses passed through the town and along Princes Street, with red banners sticking out from the windows, the departing demonstrators cheered, shouted, and sang songs lustily, their exodus attracting as much attention as their stay in the city had done.

MP and marchers' leader John McGovern 'warmly congratulated the Edinburgh police on the way they had behaved in a difficult situation'.

The marchers' demands might not have been met but they had made their point and gathered lots of publicity and sympathy for their plight, although not from all quarters. Kicking men while they were down, Greenock Corporation decided hunger marchers from their town would have three days' dole money deducted for the time they had been away. Motherwell showed more compassion, leaving the benefit payments as they were.

Lord Provost Swan of Glasgow heard representations from Harry McShane and John McGovern on hardship experienced by the Glasgow hunger marchers. People had lost between six and 16 shillings each when their unemployment benefit was docked. Significant sums of money for anyone in the 1930s, this was obviously a terrible financial blow for families surviving only on the dole.

The Lord Provost made up the full losses for the married men and asked McShane and McGovern to distribute money left over from this to the 'most deserving cases of single men. Mr McGovern thanked the Lord Provost for the interest he had taken in the matter, and for his generosity in meeting the situation so handsomely.'

Others among the unemployed tried different ways of improving their own situations. Smallholdings which came with a cottage and an acre of land where a man could grow

vegetables to feed his family were built around the country. There are surviving groups of them near Kirkintilloch and on the hill above Inverkeithing in Fife.

The Scottish Allotments Scheme for the Unemployed, operating a joint committee with the Quakers, the Society of Friends, was willing to help people who wanted to grow their own produce or keep chickens. One young man who found his way to their Glasgow office in the summer of 1935 was 22-year-old Alex Craig of Old Monkland, my father. As was usual in Scotland, his first name was abbreviated in writing to *Alex* but was always pronounced *Alick*.

He had initially written to the enquiry bureau of a magazine called *The Smallholder, Poultry-Keeper and Gardener*. They sent him back a sympathetic and helpful typed reply. 'We are afraid, however, that there is no society which would help you financially to start a poultry farm, but we think that were you to get into touch with Sir A. Rose, Commissioner of Distressed Areas, he might possibly be able to help you. We understand that funds are to be available for cases such as yours, and we think that an application from you would be very favourably considered.'

When he followed this up he was contacted by Scottish Allotments for the Unemployed and the West of Scotland Agricultural College in Blythswood Square in Glasgow. Robert Hislop of the college sent a postcard saying he would 'be very pleased to see you at Coatbridge on Monday 2nd Sept. I shall be at the Cuparhead Plots in the forenoon and at Whifflets Plots in the afternoon.'

Practical advice and small loans were on offer. You had to show willing by already having a plot no smaller than a quarter of an acre and be at least in your second year of working it. Loans were interest-free, with no repayment in the first year, half in the second, and the remaining half in the third.

The maximum amount of loan to each Plotholder will be £10. No cash advances will be made. Advances from

the loan will be made by the Committee by way of the purchase of goods, stock, plants, &c., as explained herein.

The Committee will be prepared to make advances to any approved Plotholder-borrower for the purchase of:-

Tools, Manures, Plants, Fruit Trees, Bushes, Poultry, Pigs, Bees, Goats, &c., and for the necessary equipment in connection with the management of these items.

Already keeping chickens and working a piece of ground near his home to help feed his widowed mother and brothers and sisters – he was one of six – Alex Craig received a two-page letter from the Scottish Allotments Schemes giving him detailed advice on how he should look after the hens. They could offer him financial help to buy henhouses or more birds. 'If you will first write out this in your own way mentioning any doubts or difficulties, it will assist me to do the best I can for you, as it is most pleasing to see a young man trying to do something for himself.'

Like the hunger marchers who wanted the government to start building a new road bridge over the Forth, Davie Kirkwood also believed the government ought to spend its way out of recession. As MP for Clydebank, he was doing his utmost to get work on the Cunarder restarted. 'For more than two years, 534 had been engraved on my heart. In the morning I woke wondering if something could be done that day to bring the skeleton to life again. During the day I made myself a nuisance to all and sundry. They said I had a bee in ma bonnet. In the evening I would try to plan something new for the morrow.'

Kirkwood's efforts did not go unnoticed. One evening in the lobby of the House of Commons, Conservative MP and society hostess Lady Astor came up to him and said the Prince of Wales was planning a visit to Scotland and wanted to speak

to him about conditions on the Clyde. Kirkwood at first refused, reluctant to have anything to do with the playboy prince.

Lady Astor persisted. When she sent him a formal invitation, he told her he had no evening clothes. She returned with the response that it was him the prince wanted to talk to, not his clothes. He could wear a serge suit if he liked. 'There was a Robert Burns ring about that, man to man, Prince of the Realm and Engineer of the Forge – and behind it the thought of the great silent Cunarder. So I said: "Then I'll go."'

Remembering the painting which shows the ploughman poet being lionised by Edinburgh society, Kirkwood thought of Burns again when he walked into an elegant first-floor dining room. He heard himself being announced and found Lady Astor and the Prince of Wales standing up and coming round the table to greet him. The Prince of Wales took him into the library of this grand house and asked him to give him the truth. What did the workers on the Clyde think about the current situation?

Kirkwood was an engineer to his fingertips and he had the soul of an engineer. He had been brought to meet the future Edward VIII in what he described as 'a beautiful motor-car, a masterpiece of the engineer's craft'. Now he told the prince they were all living in momentous times when 'Man's ingenuity applied to nature has brought the age of plenty. But instead of plenty, we have reduction.'

There was, Kirkwood told the attentive Prince, an atmosphere of fear and it was running right through society, 'so that those who are rich are curtailing expenditure'. There's a resonance with our own times in what he said next. 'It has become fashionable to be economical. It used to be fashionable to be lavish. Every one is afraid to spend, rich and poor. Those who have wages are afraid to spend them. They are banking their money instead of spending it.'

And, Kirkwood went on, it wasn't only manual workers who were suffering. There were 2,000 qualified school teachers in

Scotland who couldn't find work and the situation was similar in other professions. The Prince of Wales asked what was to be done. Kirkwood made his suggestion that the country should spend its way out of recession. Send the unemployed back to work and they would soon be able to start spending again, thus reviving the economy. 'Twenty minutes more passed in a friendly discussion. We were two British citizens talking about our land and our people. A man's a man for a' that. It was as if we were on a ship in a storm, when class and creed and caste are forgotten.'

Whether the Prince of Wales exerted any influence or not, the government did decide to bale Cunard out. Work on the 534 started up again on the Tuesday after Easter Monday in April 1934, with a projected launch date for the new Cunarder of that September. On the first day back, the workforce was led through the gates of John Brown's by two kilted pipers and the streets of Clydebank were decorated with bunting.

A foreman rebuked a returning worker because his tools were rusty. The quick-fire repartee came right back at him: 'You should see my frying-pan.'

27

Pride of the Clyde: The Launch of the *Queen Mary*

'Ten million rivets, sixty million hammer blows.'

The *Queen Mary* was launched from Clydebank on Wednesday, 26 September 1934. All Glasgow's newspapers produced special souvenir supplements for the occasion. The *Daily Record*'s entire front cover was given over to the now iconic photograph of the bow of the ship still known as the 534 stretching up towards the sky. By tradition, the name she would bear would only be revealed when it was pronounced by the Queen at the launch.

Queen Mary and King George V were joined there by their son, the Prince of Wales. He had flown home from Paris for the occasion, staying the night at his home at Fort Belvedere 'before entraining for Glasgow'.

Selected guests were presented to their majesties and the Prince of Wales at the launch: the directors of John Brown's and Cunard's White Star Line; local dignitaries; six shipyard workers with 50 years' service apiece at John Brown's; and Clydebank's MP and tireless campaigner to get work started again on the 534, Davie Kirkwood.

He contributed an article to the *Daily Record*'s souvenir supplement entitled 'WHAT TO-DAY MEANS TO ME'. His words were wrapped around a poem specially written for the occasion by Poet Laureate John Masefield:

For ages you were rock, far below light,
Crushed without shape, earth's unguarded bone.
Then Man in all the marvel of his might
Quarried you out and burned you from the stone.

Then, being pured to essence, you were nought
But weight and hardness, body without nerve;
The Man in all the marvel of his thought
Smithed you into form of leap and curve;

And took you, so, and bent you to his vast,
Intense great world of passionate design,
Curve after changing curving, braced and masst
To stand all tumult that can tumble brine.

Kirkwood's words were poetic too, and very personal. He recalled for the readers how he had cause to be grateful to John
Brown's. In his youth, seeking work, he had tramped the 12
long miles from his home at Parkhead in the east of Glasgow,
and Brown's had taken him on. He was fiercely proud of
the new liner, the largest ship that had ever been built, and
of all the hard work put in by the men who had built the
Cunarder.

As an engineer, I salute the architects and designers,
builders and platers, riveters, caulkers, blacksmiths,
joiners, carpenters, coppersmiths and plumbers. And
with them the labourers. 'Unskilled,' they call them.
None in a shipyard is unskilled and some of these labourers are as highly skilled as the craftsmen.

This is their Day, managers, draughtsmen, foremen, journeymen, apprentices and labourers, boiler-
makers, marine engineers, electricians and the rest.

It is everybody's Day. And how singularly British it
all is. The Day, not of War, but of Peace. The Day of
the Mercantile Marine.

The whole nation is built into this ship. Throne and
Parliament, Commerce and Industry, Arts and Crafts,
all feeling that they are moving onward as the 534
gangs doon the slip.

As the local MP, Kirkwood had a VIP ticket for the launch.
Thousands heading for the Clyde from all over Britain had
no ticket, and the touts were active. Anyone wanting to sell
one could get £25 for it, a substantial sum back in 1934.

Writing about the launch in the *Daily Record*, Sir John
Foster Fraser, 'the world-wide traveller – a journalist of unri-
valled experience and great descriptive ability', also reported
that the Queen was going to use a bottle of Empire wine to
launch the 534, which 'suggests Australian or South African
burgundy'.

Some locals thought a good Scottish bottle of whisky would
be more appropriate. One 'stiff-jawed engineer' told the
world-wide traveller he thought the ship ought to be named
David Kirkwood, although *Britannia* was the odds-on favourite.

Sir John Foster Fraser was indeed an excellent journalist,
describing a conversation he'd had with 'a genial fellow
primed with contrasts and bubbling with statistics'. He poked
a little gentle fun at this avalanche of facts and figures but
allowed his informant his pride in the Cunarder.

'Do you know,' he said, 'that if all the steel plates
were laid end to end they would provide a path from
London to Leicester?' No, I didn't know that.

'Or that there are ten million rivets, which means
that hammers have delivered six million blows to drive
them in?' I took his word for it.

'Has anybody told you that on one of the decks
you could have three football pitches and that in
the large lounge you could stack ten double-decked
omnibuses?' I confessed nobody had imparted the
information.

The local man told the celebrity journalist he should tell his English readers the Cunarder was taller than Nelson's Column in Trafalgar Square, with a promenade deck twice as long as the front of Buckingham Palace. That would 'make the Cockneys have respect for what we do on the Clyde'.

'Man, 94 years ago the Cunard people built their first ship here; the "Britannia" it was called, and it could be stuck end-on in one of the funnels of 534 and be lost. Why, when she slips into the water to-morrow, there will be 26 drag chains weighing over 2350 tons, so she won't bump on the other side of the Clyde and knock Renfrew out of shape.

'There are steel cables as thick as your wrist and four anchors each weighing sixteen tons. Four thousands miles of electric cables, think of that.'

I gasped that it was all very wonderful.

'Aye,' said he, 'nothing has been forgotten. You know, if anybody fell overboard the man on the bridge will just press a wee button and a whole bunch of lifebelts will be catapulted at him. But come over here and I'll tell you some more. It's thirsty work talking.'

It took almost two years to fit the *Queen Mary* out with her beautiful art deco interiors and her luxurious cabins, saloons and restaurants. She also had her own chapel, cinema, theatre, libraries and tennis courts. Huge amounts of Clydeside craftsmanship and huge amounts of Clydeside pride went into all of that.

Artists and craftworkers from all over Britain made their contributions, from the specially designed crockery and silverware to the large-scale original paintings commissioned for the public spaces of this great ocean liner. One of the most famous pictures was Kenneth Shoesmith's *Madonna of the Atlantic*.

The *Queen Mary* left the Clyde in March 1936. It's estimated that as many as a million people lined the banks of the river to watch her go. One of the best views to be had was from Erskine, on the southern shore. Amateur film-maker James Blair stationed himself there and shot some unique colour footage of the ship as she steamed past. This can be viewed online today in the Moving Image Archive at the National Library of Scotland.

The emotions of those who had come out to bid the *Queen Mary* farewell from the river of her birth ran high and deep. Another contemporary observer summed up the overwhelming mixture of enormous pride and real sadness: 'She leaves a big gap in the landscape, and a hole in the hearts of thousands of Clydesiders.'

28

The Spanish Civil War

'To fight by the side of the people of Spain.'

The Spanish Civil War began in July 1936 and ended, finally, on 1 April 1939. It started with a rebellion launched from Spanish Morocco by General Francisco Franco against the democratically elected Republican government of Spain. While Britain, France and the USA adopted a policy of non-intervention, Hitler's Germany and Mussolini's Italy weighed in on the side of the Fascists.

The Spanish Fascist forces styled themselves Nationalists, describing their rebellion as a crusade to save Spain from the Socialist Republic. Socialists, communists, anarchists and idealists in Europe, the United States and throughout the world found in this most vicious of civil wars a cause which set them alight. Thirty-five thousand people volunteered to defend Spain's democracy and the legitimate Republican government.

Those volunteers joined the *Brigadas Internacionales*, the International Brigades. Many were impelled to do so by the horror of the bombing of the small Basque town of Guernica in the spring of 1937. Nazi Germany and Fascist Italy were using Spain as a terrible training ground and dress rehearsal for the European war everyone feared was coming.

It was 26 April 1937 when the German Condor Legion bombed the market-place in Guernica, raining death out of the sky. Commissioned by the Republican government, Pablo

Picasso painted the masterpiece which forever remembers this event which so stunned the world. Wars were meant to be fought by soldiers on battlefields. In Guernica, innocent civilians – men, women and children – had been slaughtered while peacefully going about their daily business.

What made Guernica even more shocking was that death had been delivered by aircraft. The Zeppelins of the First World War notwithstanding, up until Guernica planes had been seen as a shining symbol of the modern age, a magnificent example of the progress of the human race. After Guernica it became chillingly clear that mankind could harness technological marvels to unspeakable evil, killing more people more effectively and with greater devastation than ever before.

Three thousand volunteers went from Britain to Spain to fight for the Republic, more than 500 of them from Scotland. Most of the Scottish volunteers were socialists and Communists who had seen plenty of action on the battlefield of politics. They went from Aberdeen, the coalfields of Fife, the shipyards of Glasgow, Dundee, Edinburgh and Inverness.

These people believed that if Fascism wasn't fought in Spain it would sweep across Europe, crushing everything in its path. One contemporary poster shows a child looking up at a sky full of planes. The caption reads: 'If you tolerate this, your children will be next.'

By January 1937 the *Glasgow Herald* was reporting that Nationalist forces were approaching Madrid. The Republican government had ordered civilians to leave the city and heavy fighting was raging around it. This is when Franco famously spoke about the fifth column he had within the city, covert supporters working in secret to bring about the Spanish capital's fall to the Fascist forces.

As Madrid was poised to fall, British volunteers, members of the ILP, were setting off from Victoria Station in London:

> Young men and girls sang the 'Internationale', and a
> grey-haired woman wept silently on the Continental

departure platform at Victoria Station, London, yesterday when 25 I.L.P. volunteers left on their way to
join the Spanish Government forces.

One voice of protest was heard above the farewells.

'It is suicide for all of you,' a young woman exclaimed. 'It is said that the volunteers have no de-
pendants,' she said to a press reporter, 'but some of
them have mothers who are pleading with them not
to go.'

James Maxton's friend Bob Edwards was the captain of the
ILP company, which numbered around 100 men in total.
Their service in Spain began shortly after that departure
from Victoria Station, when they served on Aragon front,
near Zaragoza. Edwards remembered the bravery of the
Spaniards with whom they fought. 'We spent much of our
time training members of the Spanish Militia how to take
cover and we were constantly trying to persuade them that to
walk upright and bravely into an offensive was not necessarily
the best method.'

Author George Orwell joined this ILP contingent. Later
he was to write about his experiences in Spain in *Homage to
Catalonia*. The Spanish Civil War attracted some famous volunteer combatants, writers and reporters: Orwell, Laurie Lee,
Ernest Hemingway, legendary journalist Martha Gellhorn.

Meanwhile, James Maxton and John McGovern, who had
led the Scottish Hunger March to Edinburgh in 1933, were
trying to win hearts and minds at home. Lifelong pacifist
though he had been, Maxton's standpoint on the Spanish
Civil War was clear. This was a conflict between Fascism and
freedom and it had to be fought.

In August 1936 he had dispatched John McNair to Spain
to see the situation on the ground. McNair and Maxton
were old friends and comrades from their early days in the
ILP. When McNair returned with the information, Maxton
initiated a fund-raising campaign for medical supplies

and ambulances. People all over Scotland raised money for Spain.

Quite disparate groups of people sent medical help. The Scottish Ambulance Unit wanted to render assistance to both sides. One of its volunteers was Roddy MacFarquhar of Inverness. He is quoted in Daniel Gray's *Homage to Caledonia* on the horror of seeing a Spanish mother and her three children running for cover. As the young man watched, one of the children was hit by shrapnel.

Newly arrived in Spain though he was, experiencing war for the first time, MacFarquhar knew the little girl wasn't going to make it. It was a baptism of fire, yet when the unit returned to Spain for a second time in January 1937, MacFarquhar went too, listed in the *Glasgow Herald*'s report of their departure from Glasgow:

> A crowd of several hundred persons gathered outside the Glasgow City Chambers on Saturday morning to see the reorganised Scottish ambulance unit leave to resume duties in Spain. The Lord Provost (Mr. John Stewart), in bidding the members of the unit farewell, said everyone knew the splendid work the unit had done previously. Taking on work of that kind in a country where civil war was being carried on was a heroic act, but notwithstanding the danger, the unit felt that their work had been so much appreciated that they must go back.

Now Communist MP for Fife, Willie Gallacher travelled to Spain during the civil war. Some of the British volunteers of the ILP Batallion he went to see may well have been his own constituents.

> Around Easter, 1937, I paid a visit to Spain to see the lads of the British Batallion of the International Brigade. Going up the hillside towards the trenches

with Fred Copeman, we could occasionally hear the dull boom of a trench mortar, but more often the eerie whistle of a rifle bullet overhead. Always I felt inclined to get my head down in my shoulders. 'I don't like that sound,' I said by way of apology.

'It's all right, Willie, as long as you can hear them … It's the ones you can't hear that do the damage.'

Afterwards Gallacher made a speech to the lads and when he had finished everyone sang 'The Internationale', as he wrote, 'with a spirit that all the murderous savagery of fascism can never kill'.

Back in his hotel in Madrid, Willie Gallacher met Ellen Wilkinson, Eleanor Rathbone and the Duchess of Atholl. All three women were MPs. Ellen Wilkinson sat for Middlesbrough and then Jarrow, helping to organise the most famous British hunger march of the 1930s. Eleanor Rathbone was an Independent MP who lobbied successfully for the introduction of family allowances paid directly to mothers.

Willie Gallacher shared some of the journey home with them, writing that 'those three women gave an example of courage and endurance that was beyond all praise'. It's a handsome tribute, especially from a committed Communist to the one woman in that group whose politics were the polar opposite of his.

Katharine Murray, Duchess of Atholl, was Scotland's first woman MP and the first woman to hold office in a Conservative government, spending five years as an under-secretary for education. One of those who saw that if Fascism triumphed in Spain it would march all over Europe, she clashed with her party over the issue. They nicknamed her the Red Duchess as a result.

Many women volunteered to go to Spain, a few to fight, some to work as nurses in the corps which became known as the Red Nightingales, others to fight the battle for hearts

and minds. The 'Bellshill Girl Anarchist' was one of those. Ethel McDonald was 25 years old when she went off to war with Jenny Patrick, who became the partner of Glasgow-based anarchist Guy Aldred after his relationship with Rose Witcop ended.

Although she joined the ILP in her teens, McDonald too became an anarchist and worked as Guy Aldred's secretary. In Spain she made broadcasts in English for the anarchist radio station in Barcelona, where she and her Scottish accent attracted attention. She stayed on in Spain alone after Jenny Patrick returned to Glasgow, as *The Biographical Dictionary of Scottish Women* relates: 'She visited anarchists in prison, helped others escape, and became known as the "Scots Scarlet Pimpernel" and the "Bellshill Girl Anarchist". Imprisoned for several days herself, she spent further weeks in hiding, unable to exit Spain legally. Consular intervention got her out and she was welcomed back to Glasgow, telling the press: "I went to Spain full of hopes and dreams ... I return full of sadness, dulled by the tragedy I have seen."'

Whatever their politics, people in Britain were gripped by Spain's agony. Glasgow's newspapers overflowed with stories from the war. Writing in the *Glasgow Herald*'s women's page, Ann Adair got a whole column out of an 'encounter in the gown department' of an upmarket shop in London's Regent Street, when she met Inez, 'a daughter of Spain', employed there as a model, trying on dresses to demonstrate them to potential buyers. Ann Adair was contemplating buying an elegant blue dress. 'It was a lovely shade. The girl who showed it was lovely, too, a tall brunette with the slender figure and swaying gait of her kind. The saleswoman asked her some trifling question. As she answered it, she looked directly towards us, and it was then I saw her eyes. They were dark with misery, the eyes of one who had lain sleepless all through the night.'

When the saleslady went off on some errand, the *Herald*'s correspondent started talking to the girl and found out that

she was Spanish. 'Spain! So that was the explanation of her tragic mien. On a sudden the professional mannequin was gone. In her place was the Spanish patriot. She told me things I dare not set down on paper. She told me her promised husband had been wounded outside Madrid, that her mother, her young sisters had been obliged to flee their home, that they were now refugees in Portugal.'

Both sides considered themselves to be Spanish patriots. There's no way of knowing which side the lady of Spain with the melancholic mien was on.

In late 1937 James Maxton went to Spain to see the situation for himself, an uncomfortable business for a man who was not in the best of health. He travelled by train from Paris to Toulouse and then by plane to Valencia, 'over the snowy peaks of the Pyrenees and I can't say I like the look of them from up above. The plane got oil and petrol and we got coffee ...'

Tearing themselves apart, riven by bitter political divisions, the Republicans in Barcelona had begun fighting each other instead of the Fascist enemy. Ideologically the ILP supported POUM, the anti-Stalinist Spanish Marxist Workers' Party against the pro-Stalinist Spanish Communist Party. The vitriolic war of words and internecine strife between people who might have been thought to be on the same side reminded many ILPers in Spain of Glasgow. Presumably without the guns.

Four POUM members and some International Brigade volunteers had been imprisoned as spies. Despite not speaking any Spanish, Maxton managed to secure their release. One ILP member who didn't make it home from Spain was Bob Smillie. The grandson of the miners' leader of the same name, Bob Smillie junior did not die in battle but in mysterious circumstances while a prisoner in Valencia.

The Spanish Civil War ended in defeat for the Republicans and ushered in decades of dictatorship and social repression. One million died during the war and the brutal peace which

followed. The psychological scars of the conflict sear Spain to this day.

When the volunteers from the International Brigades came home to Scotland, many found it hard to get a job. Roddy MacFarquhar was one of them. Having helped repatriate them, the Foreign Office wrote to all British members of the International Brigades asking them to kindly refund the £3.19.3d it had cost per head.

Many British and Scottish cities gave them a much warmer welcome. At railway stations and in city squares the 'Internationale' and the 'Red Flag' were sung. In December 1938, almost 100 Scottish members of the International Brigades came by bus from London to Glasgow and an official reception in the City Hall.

One of the speakers was SNP MP John McCormick, author of *The Flag in the Wind*. He welcomed home those who had taken up arms in 'the fight for freedom without which there is no civilisation'. Hugh Roberton, conductor of the fondly remembered Glasgow Orpheus Choir, was there too. He told them he was proud of them.

In Kirkcaldy, in a memorial garden on Forth Avenue North, a rugged granite stone and plaque commemorate the Scots who went from Fife to fight with the International Brigades. Their names are accompanied by these lines of verse:

> Not to a fanfare of trumpets,
> Nor even the skirl o' the pipes
> Not for the off'r of a shilling,
> Nor to see their names up in lights.
> Their call was a cry of anguish,
> From the hearts of the people of Spain,
> Some paid with their lives it is true:
> Their sacrifice was not in vain.

In Glasgow, the Scots who fought by the side of the people of

Spain are remembered by the dramatic statue on the banks of the Clyde of Dolores Ibárruri, '*La Pasionaria*', and her ringing words of defiance: 'Better to die on your feet than live forever on your knees.'

The battle for Spain was lost. The battle for Europe had yet to be fought.

29

On the Eve of War:
The Empire Exhibition of 1938

'Let the spirit of the exhibition live on!'

Visitors to the Scottish Exhibition of 1911 strolled around Kelvingrove Park in Glasgow's West End under sunshine and blue skies. Those who went to the Empire Exhibition at Bellahouston Park on the city's South Side in 1938 weren't so lucky. There were grey skies and end-of-the-world downpours throughout that summer. The 12 million visitors didn't let the weather stop them from enjoying themselves.

Read up on the Empire Exhibition and you immediately get the sense of a much more democratic affair than the 1911 event. Glasgow had changed over the intervening years. Now that the Depression was at last beginning to recede into the past, a new generation of working-class men and women had grown up not only to hope for more out of life but to expect it.

Clydesiders were still standing up for themselves. There was a strike at Bellahouston at the end of February when joiners building the place demanded higher wages. The plumbers on site came out in sympathy but the dispute was quickly resolved. Nobody wanted to hinder the birth of the exhibition. The world was coming to Glasgow.

What the millions of visitors saw was a celebration of all the British Empire had to offer, a showcase for Glasgow and Scotland and a celebration of the modern age. This was the

era of streamlining, of the Mallard steam engine designed by Sir Nigel Gresley, of the coronation-style Glasgow city tram.

Bellahouston's pavilions reflected this modernist aesthetic. One of them is still there today in the park. The Palace of Art was built to last, while the other pavilions were temporary structures, although no less impressive for that. Other than the two Scottish pavilions, rich blue to match the Saltire, the pavilions were painted in soft pastel shades. Also helping lighten the dull weather during the summer of the exhibition were the colourful paths which linked the pavilions. Those were made of red asphalt mixed with chips of white granite from Skye and pink granite from Banffshire.

There was one nod back to tradition. *An Clachan*, the Highland village, had been one of the most popular exhibits of 1911, fondly remembered by so many. It was re-created at Bellahouston, only bigger and better. It had traditional white-walled cottages from Skye and black houses from the Outer Isles and a burn with a bridge over it which flowed into a small replica of a sea loch.

Raise your eyes from the old stones of *An Clachan* and you saw a soaring and thrillingly tall tower. The Tower of Empire soon became Tait's Tower, named for the architect in overall charge of the design of the exhibition. One of the foremost architects of his generation and already famous as the architect of Sydney Harbour Bridge, people were proud to claim Paisley buddy Thomas S. Tait as one of their own.

Three hundred feet high, placed at the highest point of Bellahouston Park and visible for miles around by day and by night, Tait's Tower soon became the symbol of the exhibition: tall, futuristic, reaching for the skies and the years to come. Also reaching for the skies was the acrobat known as 'the Stratosphere Girl'. She turned and tumbled at the top of a 200-foot-high pole, accompanied by the gasps of those watching her from below.

At the South African Village people could taste passion fruit juice. More familiar refreshment was on offer at the

Empire Tea Pavilion. The colourful saris of the Indian women who served the tea were much admired. This being Clydeside, there had to be a Palace of Engineering. The Australian Pavilion featured a kangaroo on a lead. Scotland's major churches each had a pavilion.

The concert hall was off Bellahouston Drive, close to the junction with Paisley Road West. Gracie Fields sang there and returned to the exhibition on a few private visits. On one of those, Our Gracie stood in front of the exhibition's Atlantic Restaurant and wowed the crowds with 'Sally', one of her most famous numbers.

Paul Robeson, who at that time was living in Britain, gave two concerts at the Bellahouston Concert Hall. Shamefully, he was refused accommodation at one Glasgow hotel because of his colour. Thousands of Clydesiders loved him for his voice, his humanity and his politics. He donated his entire fee for his first concert at Bellahouston to the Spanish Civil War Relief Fund.

At his second concert he sang 'Ol' Man River', 'Swing Low, Sweet Chariot', 'Curly-Headed Baby' and a few Scottish songs, including one in Gaelic. He delighted the rebels and revolutionaries in his audience with 'The Ballad of Joe Hill', the tribute to the Swedish-American union leader shot by firing-squad for the murder he did not commit.

There was respite from the rain with a brief dry spell in August. The downpours began again in September, matching one of the year's biggest hit songs, 'September in the Rain'. While the crowds were enjoying themselves at Bellahouston, Britain was holding its collective breath. Look at one of the photographs of the picturesque ruined kirk of *An Clachan* and you'll see a man sitting on a stone bench with his gas mask in a carrying case slung over his shoulder.

In September 1938, while the Empire Exhibition continued to draw in the crowds, Britain's prime minister, Neville Chamberlain, was flying backwards and forwards to Germany to parley with Hitler. He made three separate visits there that month.

Hitler was determined to annex the Sudetenland, the area in the west of Czechoslovakia populated by ethnic Germans. Chamberlain called for talks. One country could not simply march into another and take over a part of it. Besides which, the Nazi leader wanted more *Lebensraum* for the German people. He wasn't going to stop at the Sudetenland. Not present at the talks, Czechoslovakia's fate was decided by Germany, France, Britain and Italy.

As tension mounted, Britain hoped for the best but prepared for the worst. Defensive trenches were dug in towns and cities, plans for evacuating children from the industrial areas were drawn up and gas masks were issued to all. Children had their own special small ones, known as Mickey Mouse masks. Their mothers were advised to play a game with them every day so they got used to them.

There were masks which fitted over babies' prams but no masks for cats and dogs. When war broke out a year later, some people made the heart-breaking decision to have their animals put to sleep rather than run the risk of them suffering in a gas attack.

Fear of air raids was high. Nobody could forget Guernica. In 1938 Spanish cities were still being bombed. Terror at the prospect of a gas attack went back to the trenches of the First World War. Everyone had seen the pitiful photographs of soldiers blinded by mustard gas, able to shuffle forward only because each had a hand laid on the shoulder of his comrade in front of him.

On the Clyde, the *Queen Elizabeth* was launched by the lady for whom she'd been named, the late Queen Mother. It was a low-key affair. This Cunarder was destined to spend her first years afloat painted in the drab colours of the Grey Funnel Line, the Royal Navy.

In Clydebank and Glasgow people tried to reassure themselves and one another that the Germans would never bomb the west of Scotland. It was too far away from Germany. Their planes couldn't carry sufficient fuel to make it. Pioneered by

Scotsman Sir Robert Watson-Watt, who is commemorated by a striking statue in his native Brechin, radar was still in its infancy. How would the Germans ever be able to find the Clyde among all the other rivers, lochs and inlets of the west coast?

There was a strange atmosphere, one of fear and gallows humour, a sense that the fight needed to come, that there had to be a showdown with Hitler. After his second meeting with the Nazi leader, Chamberlain made his famous speech. 'How horrible, fantastic, incredible it is that we should be digging trenches and trying on gas masks because of a quarrel in a faraway country between people of whom we know nothing.'

With the benefit of hindsight, the policy of appeasement has been much criticised. Yet it is all too easy to forget how desperately Chamberlain and so many other Britons wanted to avoid another European War. Memories remained vivid of the last one, in which Chamberlain himself lost a brother in the trenches. Despite Spain, despite the rise of Fascism, young people didn't want to believe there was going to be another world war. That horror was something which belonged to their parents' generation.

At Munich on 29 September 1938, Chamberlain, French leader Daladier and Italy's dictator Mussolini met Hitler. Together they decided the Sudetenland would be incorporated into Hitler's Germany within the space of the next two weeks. Neville Chamberlain flew home with his now infamous piece of paper and a promise of peace in our time.

The tension of the long wet summer exploded into acclaim for the prime minister. He was even nominated for the Nobel Peace Prize. When Chamberlain entered the House of Commons only four MPs did not rise to their feet and applaud him. James Maxton was one of them.

When Maxton did stand up to contribute to the debate he spoke of the ordinary people of Germany, allowed no voice under Nazi rule, and of his German socialist friends, some now in concentration camps, some now in exile. Maxton

reluctantly congratulated the prime minister on what he had achieved but told him and the House that this was only a breathing space. Not everyone had the courage to look so clearly into the future.

The celebrations for the last night of the Empire Exhibition at Bellahouston Park in October 1938 were euphoric. They danced the Lambeth Walk in the rain. They gazed open-mouthed at the sky as three aircraft staged a mock attack on Bellahouston Park. Caught in searchlights manned by the City of Glasgow Squadron of the RAF, the bandits were successfully driven off.

Then the lights went down and the vast crowd fell silent. Only Tait's Tower was lit up, standing out like a lighthouse in a dark ocean. The crowd sang 'God Save the King' and 'Auld Lang Syne'. The Union Jack on the tower was lowered and the lights began to fade. Once the darkness was complete, a voice rang out: 'Let the spirit of the Exhibition live on!'

It was over. The future beckoned. Whatever it might hold.

30

The Clydebank Blitz

'Make for where the fires are greatest!'

Some came from Beauvais in France, flying up the Irish Sea towards their target. Most travelled through the March night from Holland, northern Germany, Norway and Denmark. As they crossed over the Scottish coast near Edinburgh, people on the ground heard wave after wave of them pass above their heads. Every ten minutes there were more. In Dundee people watched as they flew up the moonlit River Tay, and knew they must be heading for Glasgow and Clydebank.

The drone of their engines could be heard as far south as Hull and as far north as Aberdeen. They were Heinkel 111s and Junker 88s. There were 236 of them and they were the German Luftwaffe, intent on dropping their deadly cargo on the shipyards, oil depots and munitions factories of Clydebank. The idea that the Germans would never be able to find the Clyde was proved horribly wrong on the devastating nights of 13 and 14 March 1941.

Clydesiders had watched the relentless bombing of London and other English cities over the winter of 1940 and shivered. The generation which lived through the Second World War came to have immense respect for the courage and resilience of Londoners, pounded by German bombers night after night for months on end.

The hideous whooping banshee wail of the air raid siren went off shortly after nine o'clock. It was a chilling sound but

there had been a lot of false alarms and for a moment everyone thought this was just another one. In Singer's, turned over for the duration to the making of munitions, there was a daily sweepstake as to when the alarm would go off each night. It soon became clear this one was for real.

Those whose job it was to watch for these things had been pretty sure Clydebank was going to be bombed that night, picking up the tell-tale sign of a German radio navigation beam. A decision was made not to alert the population. That might cause panic and a trek up into the Old Kilpatricks, the hills behind the town. Civil disorder might ensue. This was Red Clydeside.

One young woman whose father worked at John Brown's was already in bed and asleep in the family home close to the shipyard down on Dumbarton Road. Working long hours as a nurse, she was trying to catch up on her sleep. Wrenched from her much-needed rest, she demanded irritably that whoever was slamming those doors should kindly stop right now. Then she realised the banging doors were sticks of dropping bombs. The people who experienced the Clydebank Blitz use a distinctive word to describe the sound of death and destruction falling to earth. *Crump. Crump. Crump.* Like the footsteps of a malevolent giant, drawing nearer each time, the ground trembling with the impact.

Civilians headed for the shelters. Civil defence volunteers made for the control centre in the basement of Clydebank's public library on Dumbarton Road. They'd just come back from it after weekly training. One ARP warden who had already undressed reached for the trousers he'd laid over the back of a chair. There was a bomber's moon that night but inside a small house the darkness of the black-out was all-encompassing. The ARP warden slid both legs down the same trouser leg and promptly fell over. Not a man normally given to cursing, on this occasion he swore comprehensively and started again.

The main squadron of Luftwaffe bombers was preceded by

pathfinders. They dropped flares and hundreds of incendiaries to light the way, bathing the town in an eerie greenish glow. One young woman who saw the flares float down thought they looked pretty, like fairy lights. Only later did she realise what a risk she'd taken by standing there and watching them.

Clydebank was soon ablaze with light. The timber yard at Singer's was hit, creating a huge bonfire. The distillery at Yoker went up, setting fire to the whisky, the sweet smell drifting over the town.

Up in Glasgow's maternity hospital at Rottenrow, a junior nurse was told off for standing looking out of the windows. Criss-crossed though they were with brown parcel tape, an explosion some distance away could still shatter them into a thousand pieces. A nursing sister tried to reassure anxious mothers of newborn babies. 'Don't worry. It's Clydebank that's getting it.' One of the young mothers became distraught. She was from Clydebank.

Some bombs fell on the West End of Glasgow, one in Dudley Drive in Hyndland, others on Hillhead and Partick, another in Napiershall Street off Great Western Road. An expectant mother living in a flat there took shelter in the crypt of a church at the top of Byres Road, in what is now the Òran Mór bar and theatre.

That young woman's husband was working the night shift as a railway shunter in Rothesay Dock at Clydebank. He and a workmate took shelter under a wagon, from where they squinted up at the night sky. The colours lighting it up were beautiful. They later discovered the wagon under which they had taken cover contained explosives.

When the workmate returned the next morning to the Holy City, he found that his home no longer existed. The German bombers had devastated the flat-roofed houses which had reminded the sailor of Jerusalem. Hundreds died there. Only yards away, the nearby cinema, always called 'the La Scala', survived the onslaught. People in Clydebank have talked ever since about how strange that was.

While the bombs were still dropping a nurse went to Radnor Park Church Hall where casualties had been taken. ARP warden Mrs Hyslop was in charge there. Whether she was the same Mrs Hyslop of the Clydebank Rent Strikes is not clear. The young nurse appeared, saw there was no doctor, and took an injured baby in an ambulance she had commandeered up to the Western Infirmary in Glasgow. The Western's Accident and Emergency Department was busy dealing with the local casualties of the raid. Plenty of qualified doctors were on duty, to the frustration of a group of medical students who were desperate to help.

When the young nurse appeared, they made the decision to head for Clydebank. As they were all unqualified, although only nine days away from their finals, the Western's medical superintendent refused to give them any medical supplies. They approached a nursing sister, Isabella MacDonald.

In his definitive *The Clydebank Blitz*, I.M.M. MacPhail relates how Sister MacDonald immediately gave them what they needed, 'a comprehensive range of medical requisites, tied up in eight bedsheets like washerwoman's bundles'. The only thing she was not prepared to give them was morphine. The infirmary's senior medical officer had made it very clear that students could not be allowed to administer this.

Stopped by a policeman as they neared Clydebank because of the danger of unexploded bombs, they explained what they were about. 'Make for where the fires are greatest!' he told them. They made it Radnor Park Church Hall where a cry of relief ran round. 'The doctors have come! The doctors have come!'

They saved lives that night, tended to many of the wounded, although without the ability to use morphine to relieve terrible pain caused by terrible injuries. As a direct result of their experiences during the Clydebank Blitz, it was subsequently agreed that final year medics would be allowed to give the drug to those injured in air raids.

Only seven houses in Clydebank were left undamaged by

the Clydebank Blitz. How many people were killed or injured became a controversial issue. Although German bombing raids on British cities were reported during the war, those cities were often not named and the number of casualties tended to be played down for the sake of morale.

This could work the other way. Bombing raids on Liverpool, Clydebank and Greenock alike were sometimes reported only as having been 'on a northern port'. That could give people the sense that their own town's suffering had not been honoured. It was the same with the number of casualties. When told that 500 people had been killed in Clydebank, one member of the local Home Guard bitterly asked, 'Which street?'

More realistic estimates put the numbers who died in Glasgow and Clydebank during the blitz of March 1941 at 1,200, with 1,100 seriously injured. In 1954, the Commonwealth War Graves Commission compiled a list of as many names as they could establish. The list was placed in the Roll of Honour at Westminster Abbey.

On the eerily quiet morning after the first night of the Clydebank Blitz, a man through from Arbroath selling fish from a van eventually found a working public phone in Glasgow and reassured his family that he was safe. He kept repeating the same words. 'It was terrible. It was terrible. It was terrible.' Over and over again, that was all he could say.

Animals had suffered too. Only some had been put to sleep because of their owners' fears of how they might suffer in gas attacks. One of the most distressing sights in the aftermath of the Clydebank Blitz was that of dogs and cats running around wild and beginning to form themselves into packs. They were rounded up within the next few days and, sadly, humanely put down.

Many caged birds were luckier. As I.M.M. MacPhail put it in *The Clydebank Blitz*: 'On the Friday and Saturday mornings of the raids a not uncommon sight was that of a homeless family with one of them in charge of a canary or a budgeriar

in a cage, which remained with them wherever they went – to the Rest Centre in Clydebank, to the Rest Centre in the Vale of Leven or elsewhere.'

The workers were heroes now. As the *Glasgow Herald* put it, 'Clydebuilt has hitherto applied to its ships. All that it implies in rugged strength and reliability in times of stress has been won by its people this past week.'

For weeks afterwards, Maisie Nicoll, née Swan, the young woman who'd thought the flares were like fairy lights, couldn't hold a cup and saucer without the two of them rattling together. Years later, speaking of the compensation paid out after the raids, she said in her best deadpan tones, 'You would never have guessed there had been that many pianos in Clydebank.'

Always the humour. Running through all these stories even in the darkest of times, this quicksilver vein of wit is the birthright of the people of Clydeside.

Legacy

Much ink has been spilled in the debate over whether Red Clydeside ever brought Scotland close to revolution. After having researched and written this book, personally I don't think so, certainly not in the sense of the convulsion which seized Russia in 1917. Different country, different history, different kind of people. Or maybe it's because Scottish mothers bring us all up to be too well-mannered. You can't have a polite revolution. Or a cheery one.

I find it sad that some historians who have written about Red Clydeside view it only in these terms. Since the revolution never happened, they disdainfully declare the whole thing to have been a failure. In addition to so often rendering a thrilling and passionate period of history boring, I also believe they're missing the point. Nor do I think it's fair to judge the early Red Clydesiders by the subsequent history of the Labour Party.

Red Clydeside did bring about a revolution, a sea change in thought, attitudes and expectations. The legacy is all around us, so much part of our daily lives we often hardly notice it, take it completely for granted. In 1922 James Maxton said that he and his fellow Clydeside Labour MPs wanted to abolish poverty. Although they may not have entirely succeeded in that, they did improve the lives of hundreds of thousands of their fellow citizens. Life for the majority in the

Glasgow, Scotland and Britain of the twenty-first century is immeasurably better than it was 100 years ago: at home, in the workplace, in the health of men, women and children, in educational opportunity. Much of the credit for this must go to those who 'cared to know', rolled their sleeves up, got organised and worked for what they believed in.

Revising *When the Clyde Ran Red* for its paperback publication in 2018, it's more difficult to be confident that the future will be a better, brighter place. It can feel like we're living in a darkening world, one of food banks, a widening divide between the haves and the have-nots, erosion of hard-won rights, self-serving politicians who bend the truth to fit their own agendas and who seek power only for self-aggrandisment, terrorist attacks, continuing wars and armed conflicts around the world: attacks on the very notion of democracy.

None of this takes away from the achievements of the men and women who fill the pages of this book. And just as they chose to do something about the hardship they saw around them, so there are many in our modern world who also care to know. There are the people who set up and donate to food banks, those who give their all in our precious NHS and emergency services, those who welcome and support refugees, those who refuse to allow their communities to be polarised by terror attacks, honourable politicians like the late Jo Cox, people who work for and support charities at home and abroad, people like Raif Badawi in Saudi Arabia, standing up for free speech at huge personal cost, people who want the world to be fairer for everybody and for nobody to be left behind.

The Red Clydesiders inspired their fellow man and woman to expect more and demand more, for themselves, their children, their community and their country. They inspired them always to ask *why* and to speak out whenever they saw something which wasn't fair. It's a simple principle but one which in Scotland runs bone-deep. You might call it rebel spirit.

In 1971, under the leadership of shop stewards of whom the most well known became Jimmy Reid, Jimmy Airlie and Sammy Barr, the workers at the Clydebank shipyard which had been John Brown's fought to keep their jobs and to keep shipbuilding on the Clyde. The late Jimmy Reid made a famous speech at the Upper Clyde Shipbuilders' work-in. 'There will be no hooliganism, there will be no vandalism, there will be no bevying' – cue dramatic pause – 'because the world is watching us.'

Responding as people did to the UCS war cry of 'the right to work', support came from throughout the UK and from some unexpected quarters. During the dispute, a florist delivered a bouquet of red roses addressed to Jimmy Reid at the yard. Checking the gift card, one of the shop stewards told the others it had only one word on it: 'Lenin'.

'Lenin's deid!' someone protested.

'No' the one who spells his name Lennon,' came the laconic reply. John and Yoko Lennon sent a generous cheque towards the UCS fighting fund along with their blood-red roses. Davie Kirkwood would have approved. As he said back in the 1920s: 'When we seek bread and shelter for our people, we also demand roses.'

When Glasgow University's students chose Jimmy Reid to be their rector a few years later, he made another famous speech.

> The rat race is for rats. We're not rats. We're human beings. Reject the insidious pressures in society that would blunt your critical faculties to all that is happening around you, that would caution silence in the face of injustice lest you jeopardise your chances of promotion and self-advancement. That is how it starts, and before you know where you are, you're a fully paid up member of the rat-pack. The price is too high. It entails the loss of your dignity and human spirit. Or as Christ put it, 'What doth it profit a man if he gain the whole world and suffer the loss of his soul?'

Pure Red Clydeside. A passionate and instinctive sense of democracy, justice and fairness. The unshakeable belief that we all owe one another care and respect. Inspiring words well chosen to put the message across. The conviction that the pen is mightier than the sword. The familiarity with the powerful and beautiful language of the King James Bible. Jimmy Reid also quoted Robert Burns in this speech. Like a band at a demonstration, Burns always has to be there too.

Time and again while I was researching this book I came across these same bright threads which link each generation of Scotland's people to those who came before them. Whether it was Davie Kirkwood or James Maxton, one man born into poverty, the other into comparative financial comfort, there's always that love of language, love of poetry, love of Scotland and the firm conviction that Scotland is a country more than capable of running her own affairs.

James Maxton had something to say about revolution:

> The biggest mental revolution necessary is, I believe, the mental revolution which enables a man or woman to desire a social order in which no one will be better or worse off than himself or herself, a social order in which men and women do not get added prestige by the number of pounds they can show in their bank books, the numbers of superfluous rooms they have in their houses, or the number of spare suits of clothes they have.

Tom Johnston wrote an epitath for James Maxton which could equally apply to himself, Helen Crawfurd, Mary Barbour and so many more of the Red Clydesiders. 'He played a forever memorable part in changing a public opinion which was complacent and acquiescent in face of needless suffering in the midst of plenty, to one that was resolutely determined upon fairer shares for all.'

Warm and witty, kind-hearted and generous, interested in everything and everyone, the spirited men and women of Red Clydeside had one goal they set above all other things. It came before their own self-interest and self-advancement. Some sacrified their liberty for it, some their health, some even their lives. Their aim was this: to create a fair and just society, one in which the children of the poor had as much right as the children of the rich to good health, happiness, education and opportunity.

The world has changed. Politics has changed. We've all become deeply cynical about (most) politicians. Political earthquakes or not, we all recognise the truth in the old saying that we Scots don't need enemies, we have each other.

Yet one thing hasn't changed: the democratic spirit of the Scottish people, the belief that we're all Jock Tamson's bairns. Whatever our political views and the nuances within them, many of us still hold the ideals of the Red Clydesiders close to our hearts. It's what makes us who we are.

Select Bibliography

Bell, Thomas, *Pioneering Days,* Lawrence & Wishart, 1941

Brown, Gordon, *Maxton,* Mainstream Publishing, Edinburgh, 1986

Buchan, Alasdair, *The Right to Work: The Story of the Upper Clyde Confrontation,* Calder and Boyars, London, 1972

Casciani, Elizabeth, *Oh, How We Danced!,* Mercat Press, Edinburgh, 1994

Canning, Audrey, 'Margaret Irwin – S.T.U.C. 100 Years', *Scottish Marxist Voice,* Issue 6, 1997

Chalmers, A.K., *The Health of Glasgow 1818–1925,* Glasgow Corporation, Glasgow, 1930

Crawfurd, Helen, Unpublished Memoir, Marx Memorial Library, London (copy held by Gallacher Memorial Library)

Damer, Seán, *The Clydebank Rent Struggles of the 1920s,* Clybebank Library, Glasgow, 1982

Ewan, Innes and Reynolds (eds), *The Biographical Dictionary of Scottish Women,* Edinburgh University Press, 2007

Gallacher, William, *The Chosen Few,* Lawrence & Wishart Ltd, London, 1940

Gallacher, William, *Revolt on the Clyde: An Autobiography,* Lawrence & Wishart Ltd, London, 1980

Glasgow Labour History Workshop, *The Singer Strike: Clydebank, 1911,* Clydebank District Libraries, Glasgow, 1989

Gray, Daniel, *Homage to Caledonia*, Luath Press, Edinburgh, 2008

Hanham, H.J., *Scottish Nationalism*, Faber and Faber Ltd, London, 1969

Hood, John, *The History of Clydebank*, Parthenon Publishing/ Clydebank District Council, Carnforth, 1988

Johnston, Thomas, *Our Scots Noble Families*, Forward Publishing Co Ltd, Glasgow, 1909

Johnston, Thomas, *The History of the Working Classes in Scotland*, Forward Publishing Co Ltd, Glasgow, 1922

Johnston, Thomas, *Memories*, Collins, London, 1952

Kenna, Rudolph, *Old Glasgow Shops*, Glasgow City Libraries and Archives, Mitchell Library, Glasgow, 1996

Kinchin, Perilla, *Tea and Taste: The Glasgow Tea Rooms 1875– 1975*, White Cockade Publishing, Dorchester, 1991

Kinchin, Perilla, *Miss Cranston: Patron of Charles Rennie Mackintosh*, NMS Publishing, Edinburgh, 1999

King, Elspeth, *The Scottish Women's Suffrage Movement*, People's Palace Museum, Glasgow Green, 1978

King, Elspeth, *The Hidden History of Glasgow's Women*, Mainstream Publishing, Edinburgh, 1993

Kirkwood, David, *My Life of Revolt*, Harrap & Co., London, 1935

Leneman, Leah, *The Scottish Suffragettes*, NMS Publishing Ltd, Edinburgh, 2000

Lewenhak, Sheila, *Women and Trade Unions*, Ernest Benn Ltd, London, 1977

MacCormick, Neil, *The Flag in the Wind*, Birlinn, Edinburgh, 2008

Maclean, John, *Condemned from the Dock: John Maclean's speech from the dock 1918*, International Marxist Group, London, undated

McKean, Walker & Walker, *Central Glasgow: An Illustrated Architectural Guide (Limited Edition)*, The Rutland Press, Edinburgh, 1999

McKinlay, Alan, *Making Ships Making Men ... Working for John Brown's – Between the Wars*, Clydebank District Libraries, Glasgow, 1991

McLean, Iain, *The Legend of Red Clydeside*, John Donald, Edinburgh, 1983

McShane, Harry (Introduction), *Glasgow 1919: The Story of the 40 Hours Strike*, Molendinar Press, Kirkintilloch, undated

McShane, Harry, *Three Days That Shook Edinburgh*, AK Press, Oakland, California, 1994

Milton, Nan, *John Maclean*, Pluto Press, London, 1973

Muir, James Hamilton, *Glasgow in 1901*, White Cockade Publising, Dorchester, 2001

Rowbotham, Sheila, *A New World for Women: Stella Browne – Socialist Feminist*, Pluto Press, London, 1977

Sanger, Margaret, *The Autobiography of Margaret Sanger*, Dover Publications, USA, 2004

Smyth, J.J., *Labour in Glasgow, 1896–1936, Socialism, Suffrage, Sectarianism*, Tuckwell Press, East Linton, 2000

Stewart, William, *J. Keir Hardie: A Biography*, Cassell, London, 1921

Struthers, Sheila, *Old Clydebank*, Stenlake Publishing, Ayrshire, 2001

Young, James D, *The Very Bastards of Creation: Scottish International Radicalism 1707–1995: A Biographical Study*, Clydeside Press, Glasgow, 1996

Newspapers Consulted

The Bailie

The Bulletin

Daily Record

Evening News (Glasgow)

Evening Times

Forward

Glasgow Herald

The Scotsman

Online Resources

Glasgow Digital Library: www. gdl.cdlr.strath.ac.uk

Hansard Online: http://hansard.millbanksystems.com

National Library of Scotland: www.nls.uk

Oxford Dictionary of National Biography:
    www.oxforddnb.com

Scran: www.scran.ac.uk

Spartacus Educational: www.spartacus.schoolnet.co.uk

Index

KATHERINE FAULKNER is an award-winning journalist turned full-time writer. She wrote her debut novel, *Greenwich Park*, while on maternity leave with her first daughter and her follow-up, *The Other Mothers*, while juggling family life and work. She lives in London with her husband and two children.

THE OTHER MOTHERS

KATHERINE FAULKNER

R A V E N 🐦 B O O K S
LONDON · OXFORD · NEW YORK · NEW DELHI · SYDNEY

RAVEN BOOKS
Bloomsbury Publishing Plc
50 Bedford Square, London, WC1B 3DP, UK
29 Earlsfort Terrace, Dublin 2, Ireland

BLOOMSBURY, RAVEN BOOKS and the Raven Books logo
are trademarks of Bloomsbury Publishing Plc

First published in Great Britain 2023
This edition first published in 2024

A catalogue record for this book is available from the British Library

ISBN: HB: 978-1-5266-2652-3; TPB: 978-1-5266-2653-0; PB: 978-1-5266-2651-6;
eBook: 978-1-5266-2628-8; ePDF: 978-1-5266-6828-8

2 4 6 8 10 9 7 5 3 1

Typeset by Integra Software Services Pvt. Ltd.
Printed and bound in Great Britain by CPI Group (UK) Ltd, Croydon CR0 4YY

To find out more about our authors and books visit www.bloomsbury.com
and sign up for our newsletters.

For Emma and Maddie

TASH

North Cornwall police station
April 2019

We meet in a room with no windows in a town of pebble-dash houses, a high street pockmarked with boards and bookmakers' shops. They have taken me inland, to the nearest station, I assume. Here there is no crash of waves, no call of birds. No cheery stripe of blue peeping out from behind rooftops.

In the car on the drive down here, Tom and I had made a game of it for Finn. First one to spot the sea. I had seen it first, though I kept quiet to let Finn be the winner. Seeing that sapphire ribbon stretched across the horizon, my heart had lifted, despite everything. At the promise of a holiday. Days on the beach building forts and castles. Finn's feet making perfect prints in the wet sand of the bay.

I wondered if they might handcuff me, but they didn't. They seemed almost apologetic, the officers in the car. They kept asking if I was cold, if I would like a window open, a drink of water. I shook my head, tried to focus on the landscape outside the windows. I wanted to find a landmark, a place I knew. But I couldn't. And the further we got from the coast, the more unfamiliar it became.

They opened the door for me when we arrived, offered me a hand, but I stepped out on my own. Overhead, the cold sky, speckled with a swirling milk froth of stars, was so beautiful I'd actually caught my breath. We never see stars in London. I had a sudden sense that I was, only now, seeing things the way they really were. And that I, too, was finally being seen.

Now we are inside the room. It's just me and Detective Pascoe, a grey, wipe-clean rectangle of table between us. His colleague, Williams, said she would go and get some tea. She said it like tea was

1

the answer to my problems. When I look down, I see there is a dark smear of blood on the cuff of my jumper.

I find my voice is weak, like something far away.

'You are looking, aren't you? You need to look. On the cliffs. He fell, but maybe he's still …'

My mind forms the next few words, but I find my mouth cannot.

A loud buzz. The interview-room door opens. Williams is back, holding a mug for me and another for Pascoe.

'Careful,' she says as she sets them down. 'Very hot.'

There is nothing sensuous about Williams. She is slim as a Boy Scout, neat in her grey suit. She has a heart-shaped face, so pale you can almost see through it. Her hair is cut short, like a little child's. Like Finn's. I feel a twist in my gut. Finn.

Pascoe acknowledges the tea with a nod, then clears his throat into a balled fist, replaces his hands on the table in front of him.

'We're doing everything we can to locate him, Mrs Carpenter. Should I call you that, or do you prefer Natasha?'

'Please, call me Tash.' I am like you, I want to tell him. A professional person. I am a wife, a mother. I don't belong on this side of the table.

'Can we go over what happened tonight, Tash? On the cliffs?'

I try to focus on the details in the room. Count the polystyrene ceiling tiles, one by one. They don't know anything. They weren't there. They can't know.

'I went for a walk.'

We both know this is an opening offer. One Pascoe isn't likely to accept.

'Bit late for a stroll, isn't it? Especially on a night like this.'

When we'd got down to the water earlier, the storm had already started. The wind was plucking napkins from the tables on the seafront, sending them dancing up the cobbled lanes. The sea was beaten to a seething green foam. The man at the boat-trip kiosk had shaken his head, offered Tom the money back. I'd scooped Finn into my arms, promised him we would go tomorrow. I suppose we won't, now.

Of course, I scold myself. *Of course we won't. The holiday is over. Everything is over, now.*

'I take it you're not local?'

I shake my head. 'No. We're here on holiday.'

'Where are you staying? Rental? Second home?'

I listen out for an edge of hostility in Pascoe's voice. I used to holiday here with my family. Spoilt, middle-class teenager that I was, I couldn't understand why people would live in the grey towns we sped through on our way to the postcard-perfect coast. Why live in Cornwall, but here, rather than by the sea? As if it were simply a matter of choice, a kind of eccentricity on the part of the locals. Now I know the truth. What people like us were responsible for. A slow asphyxiation. Trimming away the prettiest parts for our Easters and Summers, leaving the rest to blank-faced decline. The ultimate selfishness.

If the hostility is there, though, I can't hear it. Pascoe's face is stone-like, impassive; the face of a man who sees the world as it is, and does not see much point lamenting it. Behind it is a logical mind, concerned with material things. Which sees patterns, and notices when they are disrupted. Like when a middle-class mother strays from a holiday home at night, and ends up bloodied on a cliff edge, someone screaming for the police.

'It's called Crugmeer House,' I explain. 'It belongs to a couple we know. We've been staying with them, a few other friends.' Friends. My tongue feels wrong as I say the word, my mouth emptied out of moisture.

'I see. Have you known them long, these friends?'

Less than a year. It doesn't sound like much, does it? But friendships are different when you are a mother. Your eyes meet those of another mother over the swings, the sandpit, the GP waiting room, and you just know. The lack of sleep, the exhaustion, the funny moments and the painful, the constant emotional wringer.

That was how it had been. Our lives had been so familiar to each other. I knew what they laughed about, what they cried about, what kept them up at night. At least, I thought I knew.

'How do you know each other?'

I open my eyes now, and force myself to meet Pascoe's gaze.

'We met …' It comes out as a croak. I clear my throat, start again. 'We met at the playgroup.'

The littleness, the innocence of the word almost makes me laugh out loud.

London Evening Post, 21 November 2017

WILD SWIMMING WARNING AFTER NANNY DEATH

by Natasha James

A warning about the dangers of open water swimming has been issued following the death of a young woman at a local nature reserve.

Sophie Blake, 21, went missing on the evening of 7 July 2017. Miss Blake, who worked as a nanny, had been reported missing by her employers. Her body was found several days later in the East Reservoir. She had suffered a large cut to her head.

A pathologist who carried out the post-mortem told the inquest it was possible Miss Blake could have sustained the head injury when she dived into the water.

The injury – combined with the water temperature, which had been cooler than usual for the time of year – could have left Miss Blake unconscious or dazed and unable to swim to the side, he said.

Miss Blake was known to enjoy open water swimming. The alcohol levels in her blood suggested 'a degree of intoxication', the inquest was told.

Coroner Victoria Carmichael said it was not possible to say for certain what had happened, but it was 'likely' Miss Blake had decided to go swimming after drinking alcohol and had got into trouble in the water.

She said her death should act as a warning to others amid the growing popularity of so-called 'wild swimming', which is not permitted in Woodberry Wetlands, a nature reserve comprising 11 hectares of reed-fringed ponds and dykes.

The reserve forms part of the Woodberry Down regeneration site, one of Europe's largest building projects which will see 4,600 new homes built.

Dave Holt, the manager responsible for the reservoirs on the site, admitted that wild swimming had become popular in the nature reserve which comprises the old East Reservoir.

'We have signs up to say that it is not safe,' he said. 'People just ignore them.'

Miss Blake's mother said her daughter was 'irreplaceable' and that her death was something from which her family would 'never recover'.

The coroner recorded an open verdict.

TASH

London, September 2018

The new flats are still being built, right against the reservoir. The two completed towers loom above like giant Lego, two glimmering rectangles of turquoise, their pale spines straight, their glass balconies mirroring the sun. As I stand on the wooden walkway, I can hear the faraway shouts of building workers, the clang of metal on metal. Red cranes sail back and forth, hauling metal pipes that glint in the light. A flock of geese, disturbed by the noise, takes flight over the surface of the water.

It was hard to avoid the feeling there was something uneasy about this place, even before the girl turned up dead. Most of the old social housing blocks are still here, sitting unrenovated just behind the new towers. They've been airbrushed out of all the promotional material, but if you walk round the back, onto the Seven Sisters Road, you see them. Big concrete balconies, damp stains creeping up the walls like hunched spectres. They'll knock them all down in the end. They started on one last week. It's still there now, standing half demolished against the sky, like a piece of paper torn in half.

I walk past the towers and into the nature reserve along the East Reservoir. Autumn has filled the branches of the trees, making them heavy with seed pods and crab apples, a rust starting to creep through their greenery. Underneath the slats of the walkway, wading birds huddle for safety. The little rounds of their nests are long abandoned, the shells of their eggs washed away.

I stand for a long time, looking over the reservoir. The sun disappears behind the clouds. It is eerily quiet. A pond skater disturbs the mirror flatness of the water. The reflection of the towers melts into ripples.

It's guilt, I suppose. The real reason I keep coming back here. I did a hopeless job on the day of the inquest, running out halfway through the evidence every time my phone went. I'd known deep down, when I dropped Finn off, that he wasn't right, and by the time I got to the coroner's court, I had three missed calls from the childminder. During the first witness, she'd called again, and I'd had to squeeze out, the others tutting as the door slammed behind me. Finn's temperature wouldn't come down, she said. I'd have to pick him up. I heard Finn wailing in the background, and her shushing him. I could see the clerk had started motioning from inside the room about me using my phone. A familiar heaviness had settled on my chest. Looking back, that day was probably the beginning of the end for me at the *Evening Post*.

Afterwards, I kept thinking there must have been something I missed. If I could just figure out where it was they found her, where she was supposed to have fallen. Where was Sophie supposed to have hit her head?

A flicker of movement on the far bank causes me to look up. There is a woman there, on the other side of the water, the nature reserve side. She looks middle-aged, maybe older. Oddly dressed for a walk around the wetlands – a long quilted coat, even though it's mild, an ill-fitting pleated skirt and leather loafers. Her hair is wild and unkempt, her mouth clamped in a straight line. There is something unsettling about her eyes. I feel as if her gaze is fixed on me.

Automatically, I raise a hand in greeting, but the woman makes no response. Just keeps staring at me, like she doesn't want me out of her sight.

My phone rings in my pocket, and I jump. That will be Tom, wanting to know if I'll be home for Finn's bath.

I silence his call, shove the phone back into my pocket. As I look up, the woman disappears into the bushes. I can't work out where she went. It is as if she evaporated.

I leave the walkway and start to head around the reservoir, the path pebbles crunching underfoot. It seems to take forever to get to the other side. Then, as I move closer, I see a path through the trees I haven't spotted before. That must have been where the woman went. Is it a bike track, perhaps? It seems to run along the side of a narrow waterway, off from the reservoir.

I follow the path. It quickly becomes muddy. Plants and weeds proliferate, a tangled canopy of branches blocking out the light. The stream on my right is clear and shallow, the bed a silty brown. Tadpoles dart over a collection of artefacts beneath the surface: a broken bike, a yogurt pot, a length of pipe, a coil of police tape. On the other side a chicken-wire fence is collapsing under the weight of ferns. Through its gaps, I catch glimpses of the reservoir plant and Portakabins. A hum of machinery drowns out the trickle of the water.

The canopy becomes thicker and darker, brambles and cow parsley growing across the path. I have to push them back to keep going. A sign tacked to the chicken wire reads: DANGER: NO ENTRY. Maybe this was a bad idea. I think about turning back when I hear the sound of rushing water ahead.

Around a bend is a metal bridge, a grid underneath. A sluice gate leading out of the reservoir, a muddy water bottle in its teeth. A willow tree is hunched overhead, its fronds trailing into the sluice, pale leaves sucked into the foaming pool beyond. The sound of water is now a roar.

There is no sign of the woman. I think again about turning back. But then I see it, tied to the opposite post of the bridge. A lone bunch of flowers. The petals are large and shrivelled, like wrinkled pillow-cases. The flowers have been tied with a long white ribbon, its fraying edge trailing into the water. But it is the photograph that holds my attention, enclosed in a cellophane wallet to keep off the rain.

When I turn the photograph over, I am startled to find the article with my byline on the other side. It has been scissored out of the paper, the print blurred on one side where water has leaked through.

Wild swimming. That's what the coroner had said, so I'd had to report it. But it had been so vague. The copy had been hard to write; I'd had to put caveats everywhere.

I feel the ribbon between my thumb and finger. So is this where her body was found? Not in the reeds of the reservoir, as I'd imagined, but up against a sluice gate, in a pool full of rubbish, the roar of water in her ears.

It didn't make sense. If Sophie had been swimming, how did her body get here?

TASH

When she knocks on my door a few days later, I don't remember her straight away. I just see a woman, around my mum's age. Maybe a bit older. It is drizzling softly. The woman's quilted coat has no hood. The rain is drawing a halo of grey-rooted frizz up around her temples.

'Hi.'

I wait for the woman to explain herself, but for a few moment she just stares back at me, as if it is me who should be doing the explaining.

'Are you Natasha James?'

'Yes.'

Actually, it is Natasha Carpenter now, officially, but the new name has never really stuck. It had suddenly felt important, when Finn was born, that the three of us would share the same surname, but then I'd found I couldn't shake my old one, or maybe I didn't want to, after all. So I'm still James, mostly. Mrs Carpenter festers in the wardrobe, like a new dress I can't get comfortable in.

'Great. I was hoping we could talk. Can I come in?'

I consider the woman. She looks like she's had a rough time of it, somehow. Briefly, I wonder if she might even be homeless. On second glance, I decide she is merely unkempt. Eccentric, perhaps, rather than destitute.

'I'm sorry,' I say, trying to keep my voice gentle. 'Have we met?'

The woman ignores my question. 'I only need a minute,' she says. 'I've come from Walthamstow.' Her jaw tightens. I detect a hint of menace. My hand tightens, automatically, on the lock.

9

'The thing is, it's actually not a great time,' I begin. 'My husband is trying to get some rest – he's a doctor, he's been working nights – so I'm on my own with –'

'Mummy!'

Somehow, I can hear in Finn's voice that he is standing in the high chair. Something about the manic pitch of it, or maybe I can hear he is higher up than he should be.

'I'm sorry, I really have to go and check on my son.' I throw her an apologetic smile and start to close the door.

'Wait. This is about Sophie Blake.'

I still my hand on the lock.

'I'm sorry?'

'I saw you,' she says, through the crack. 'At the wetlands. I know you wrote that story. I'm Jane. Sophie's mum. I want to talk to you.'

I get to the kitchen just in time to lift Finn out of the high chair, where he's poised like a diver ready to jump. Jane Blake stands awkwardly by the fridge and watches me lift him down, wipe his face, tell him off. He whines a little as I carry him into the next room and place him on the sofa. When I reach for the remote control, the whining stops.

'You can watch one *Bing*.' I wag the remote control at him, like a finger. 'Only one, OK?'

Finn's face breaks into a smile, his pale hair falling over his eyes, soft and fine as candyfloss. I reach out to push the silken strands behind his ears.

In the kitchen, Jane is still standing by the fridge.

'Have a seat.'

I motion to a chair, but she ignores me, fixes me with a cold stare.

'You don't remember me.'

The moment she says it, though, I do. 'The wetlands,' I murmur. 'The other day.'

'That's right.' She lifts her chin. 'I have seen you there before. Looking for the place where my daughter died. I want to talk to you. About all this – this rubbish you wrote.'

She tosses a printout of my article on Sophie's death onto my kitchen table. For a moment, neither of us moves.

'I see,' I say carefully.

Jane eventually sits, gingerly, on one of the kitchen chairs, ending up with her knees pushed up against a table leg. Our kitchen is so narrow we can only assemble one half-moon of the circular dining table we bought from IKEA when we moved in. The other half is folded down permanently next to the wall. I rummage in the cupboard for my notebook, a working pen, then sit down opposite Jane. She is unfolding the crumpled printout on the table, flattening it with her hands.

'Jane, legally, I had to report what the coroner found. Which was that Sophie's death was most likely an accident. That she had –'

'I know what the coroner said,' Jane spits. 'It didn't happen. My daughter was murdered, Natasha. Someone killed her.'

As I open my mouth to reply, Finn reappears.

'Mummay, Bing not working.' He starts fussing at my knees. There is a ghostly outline of milk around his mouth. I pluck a wet wipe from the packet on the table and bat at him with it.

'I'm really sorry,' I tell Jane, as Finn twists away in protest.

Once the TV is reanimated, I return to the kitchen. Jane shifts in her chair. Her eyes drift down to my leggings, where a glob of Finn's porridge has been deposited on my right thigh.

'I called your office.' Jane is still looking at the blob of porridge. 'They said you didn't work there no more.'

'Yes,' I say. 'I left. Quite soon after … after the inquest.' I start wiping the porridge off my leggings. I don't elaborate. I really don't feel like getting into the whole miserable story.

'So you don't actually have a job, then?'

'No, I mean … yes, I do, but I'm freelance now.'

'Oh.' The corners of Jane's mouth have turned down.

'It's a good thing,' I add, a bit too quickly and with a touch too much brightness. 'It means I can place stories anywhere.'

Jane can see that there is a degree of spin at work here, but she stays silent. She plucks a photograph from her handbag, sets it on the table. A peace offering of sorts, perhaps.

I haven't seen this picture of Sophie before. She looks younger than twenty-one. An elfin face. A smattering of summer freckles across her nose and cheeks.

'She was a lovely girl,' I say.

'She was.'

11

She was. And now, she is dead. There is a shameful part of me that wants to recoil from Jane, because of the terrible truth that she is proof of. This could happen to me. My child could die. Maybe that explains my feeling when I saw her on my front step. The tightening of my hand on the lock. You can smell it on a person, that sort of damage.

'You believe something else happened to Sophie, then.'

'Something else did happen.' Jane speaks slowly, as if to a child. 'Someone killed her. They killed her, and they put her into that water.'

I look up at Jane, place my pen down for a moment. Finn calls out in the other room. I ignore it.

'Do you have any idea who, Jane?'

Jane glowers at me.

'I wouldn't be here, if I knew that, would I?' She leans back in her chair. 'Anyway. That's your bit, isn't it?'

'I'm sorry,' I say, 'I don't follow.'

Jane's eyes narrow. 'I thought you said you were still a journalist.'

'I am, but …'

'Well, then,' she says, tapping a finger on the table. 'You need to investigate. You need to find out who killed her.'

12

SOPHIE

Fifteen months before

After I got out of the water, I sat on the banks a while. Usually the runner came around this time, but today there had been no sign of him. I kept missing him these days. I felt sure he'd be here today, but perhaps I had mistimed it. I'd been thinking about other things.

It was six years to the day, since Dad. I knew I should call Mum, that I was going to have to call her, at some point. But every time I pulled my phone out, I ended up not doing it. I couldn't think what I would say.

It was Dad who first got me into swimming like this. It wasn't called wild swimming then, didn't used to be something other people did. It was just our thing. He took me to so many places. You can swim anywhere, he told me. Don't let anyone tell you you can't.

Dad had showed me how under the water the cold can't hurt you. You can become the same as it. He taught me not to worry about reeds and plants, the wriggling creatures that live in mud. Sometimes you feel something against your foot, or you think you do, but it's no good looking for what. Eyes don't work down here. Their world, not ours. Only blindness and noise. You can't stay. Your air runs out, and you have to go back, into the light.

Then you come into the air and it's better and worse. Your lungs can fill; the sound of everything is clear and distinct in your ears. A plane overhead. The shuffle of the reeds at the banks. Far away, the sounds of traffic. Then you go under the water again, and it's a different noise, the noise of everything that's in it.

Afterwards, walking out, the banks always felt steep, my limbs heavy. You have to dress quickly or the afterdrop comes: a deep cold,

more frightening than the water, because it is a cold inside. You shake, faint sometimes. Dad had seen it happen.

Getting dressed was always the worst part with Dad, our hands awkward, eyes finding anything else but each other, until it was done. But then there would be blankets, and a flask of tea, just me and him and the good feeling. I missed it, the happy silence between us.

It wasn't the same any more. The ends of my hair were wet against my neck, my hands cold and clammy to the touch. The reeds moved around the water, like silk sheets.

I took my phone out again. My gold case was shiny in the light.

'Sophie.'

'Hi, Mum. Just thought I'd call.'

'Uh-huh.' We were quiet for a minute. I scratched the ground with my trainer. Somewhere there was a bird. I looked, but couldn't see it.

'Doesn't feel like six years, does it?' Mum offered.

I knew what she meant. And yet, sometimes I found it hard to remember the details of Dad. I was left with pieces. The soft, warm heft of his back. A soapy smell. The rough skin of his hands.

The bird, again. A soft, squeaking call. Dad would know the bird, beckon me to see. *C'mere, Soph. C'mere.*

The bird went silent. I listened to Mum's breathing on the line, the slight wheeze of it, like music.

'He'd be proud to see you now.'

This had all been said before. There was nothing else that either of us could say.

'How's things? You still taking your pictures?'

'Sometimes.'

My camera was next to me on the blanket. Last time there was a kingfisher here, a heron on the far bank. But today, there was nothing that made me want to lift the lens to my face.

'I saw the picture of the forest wall thing you made at the playgroup. Looked lovely.'

'Thanks.' It took me weeks to finish that. I came in early every day to cut out different leaf shapes, twisting the paper in my hands to make the wobbly edges of oak leaves. I showed the children how to fold paper butterflies in half, to cover both wings in paint. I cut all the shapes out before playgroup started, so they would look exactly right. I made other things too. Shiny cardboard stars and sequinned planets

14

to hang from the polystyrene tiles in the ceiling. A tissue-paper sea of silvery tinfoil fish, with ribbons of green seaweed.

'I'm glad it's working out there, for you.' The truth is Mum had wanted more for me, whatever that means. Couldn't see why it was what I needed, the simplicity of my sing-song days with the children, their duckling-soft hair, their sweet, fat little hands. Their love offered up so easily, without complications.

'Sophie,' Mum said. 'Will you come home and see me, soon, love?'

Silence on the line. Overhead, the tick, tick, tick of a helicopter in an empty sky.

Then, beyond the trees, I saw him. His T-shirt first, the orange one he always wore. He was in his shorts, his earphones in. I'd never got close enough to hear what sort of music he listened to. I smiled to myself. So I had timed it right, after all.

'I'll call you back, Mum.' Even as I said it, I pressed my thumb to end the call. I always liked this part, the moments before he saw me.

When he reached the gravel path snaking around the East Reservoir, our eyes met. His face was pink, the ends of his hair damp, his chest rising and falling as his lungs caught up with his heart. He raised a palm, and smiled, his face open, like a child's. I smiled back.

Then he brought his hand up to one ear, as if he was about to take an earphone out. For a moment, I thought this was going to be it, that he would speak to me. But something made him change his mind, a frown tugging at the side of his mouth. He looked away, picked up his pace, shook his head a little. And then all I could see was the back of him, the muscles under the skin of his calves.

TASH

I bag a table at the park cafe. Before we had Finn, Tom and I used to go for lavish brunches at a place called Ruby's, with big mango-wood tables, pendant lights with filament bulbs. These days, we're broke, and Finn is impossible in indoor cafes, so we trudge to Clissold Park most Saturdays, shiver at the same hard metal outside tables while Finn tears about on the grass.

Even though he is only two, Finn is terrifyingly fast on his balance bike. Tom runs behind him with the ludicrous, crouching gait of the anxious parent-of-one. I see my husband's mind scroll with a check-list of danger – dogs, climbing frames, low walls, electric scooters. No one tells you how much of loving a child is to fear his death. The dread of it flickers constantly at the edges of our existence, like a light we cannot look at directly.

Tom catches up with Finn, lifts him off the bike and slots him into the high chair.

'Did he have much breakfast?'

There is never any need to ask which 'he' Tom is asking about. Finn is our shared deity, the creature around whom our two lives orbit. Sometimes, parenting feels like being part of a two-man cult only Tom and I know the rituals of.

'Two Weetabix and a banana.'

'Nana?' Finn looks at me enquiringly. I sigh and lean to retrieve the emergency banana from the pushchair.

'Long week,' Tom yawns. 'I wish this one would learn to sleep in his own bed.'

'Tell me about it.' We both smile ruefully at our son, so beautiful and oblivious in his high chair, who has woken at four in the morning every day this week.

'You look knackered, Tash.'

'Oh, thanks,' I croak. I peel the banana and pass it to Finn. 'Say "Thank you, Mummy",' I remind him, pointlessly, as he mashes it into his face.

'Sorry,' Tom laughs. 'I just meant, you look like you need some sleep.'

I nod, let it drop, rubbing my eyelids with my fingers. I think about the crow's feet I noticed in the mirror yesterday, just starting to pinch at the corners of my eyes. The bags underneath seem to have become a permanent feature.

'Did you get any further with your gentrification thing yesterday?'

'The what?'

'Your article about the wetlands.'

'Oh, yeah. Fine. I mean, not great. It's just difficult, you know. Finn's still so unhappy going to playgroup in the mornings. I just … feel guilty about it. Can't focus.'

Tom reaches out to Finn, squeezes his chunky leg.

'You still don't like play group, mate?'

'Finn no like it paygroup,' Finn confirms, lowering his eyebrows. He starts twisting in the high chair, and I can see he is going to try and stand up again. He is too big for high chairs, anyway. I pull him out for a cuddle. His foot gets stuck and he cries in protest until Tom dislodges him.

'Oh, Finney.' Tom ruffles his hair, then turns to me. 'I thought you said most kids settle down within a few days?' Tom always talks as if I'm some sort of expert on these things.

'Well, not Finn, apparently,' I murmur, tucking Finn's head under my chin. 'He still screams the place down every morning.'

'But it's been weeks!'

'I know that, Tom!'

The playgroup drama is so frustrating. I can't work out where I'm going wrong. I thought Finn would love St Mark's. It reminded me of the local church playgroup of my own childhood: the cosy, primary-school smell of playdough and glue, battered picture

17

books, custard and floor cleaner. The walls of the inside rooms were covered in a sugar-paper forest of paint-splodge butterflies, cut-out ladybirds, parrots with yellow tissue-paper wings. Outside, there were raised vegetable beds, a weather station with twirling windmills, a rainwater gauge.

Everyone said we were lucky to get a place, that it was always oversubscribed. But Finn starts to cry as soon as the pram turns the corner and he sees the church building. Yesterday I had to force his hot fists open with my thumbnail to retrieve the strands of my hair he'd grabbed in a bid to hold on as I handed him over.

'Oh, Tash, it sounds like it's been so tough,' Tom says.

'It has.' Two breakfast plates and a smoothie are placed between us. Tom ignores them, reaches for my hand under the table and squeezes it. I squeeze back, attempt a smile, then pull my hand away to push Finn's hair out of his eyes, wipe a blob of banana from his cheek.

Tom picks the smoothie up and stirs it, thoughtfully, with the straw. 'Wasn't the woman in charge there … what's her name?'

'Elaine?'

'Wasn't she saying it might be a good idea to fix up some play dates, so he can get to know the other kids a bit?'

I reach over for a crust of toast, trying not to react to Tom's implication that 'play dates' are my domain. The pressure to befriend the other playgroup mums makes me feel on edge. They already seem to have dispersed into chatty little circles at the gates, even though term only started a few weeks ago, and every time I've struck up a conversation with anyone, I've had to abandon it to deal with Finn's campaign of resistance. We usually end up on the floor by the coat pegs, Finn wailing and me grinning and rolling my eyes to reassure everyone it is all under control, while other mothers file past, politely looking away.

I met one other mum in the first week who'd seemed nice. Her name was Christina. Her little strawberry-blonde girl, Eliza, was a bit clingy and reluctant, too, and we'd bonded over the shared settling struggle. When I'd asked Christina about a play date, though, she'd made a pained sort of face.

'Sorry – I'm a lawyer, and I work pretty full hours. You could ask Sal? She's my childminder. She picks Eliza up most days, and some of the other kids.' Christina had pointed me in the direction of a

harassed-looking woman in lumpy leggings, pushing a huge double buggy. I'd felt downgraded.

Since then, I'd noticed a clique of three mothers, who always seemed to leave together and disappear off somewhere. If there was a social hierarchy at the playgroup gates, I suspected these three were at the top: the willowy one with messy blonde hair and the stylishly vacant stare of an off-duty model, the one with a shiny black ponytail who carried a water bottle and always looked midway through a run, and the third, an English-rose type with chestnut hair and a wardrobe of stunning coats. I'd often watched them leave, wondered where they were going. Last time, I'd even walked the same way a bit, hoping I might catch up with them enough to say hello. But I'd been too far behind, and they had disappeared behind the shimmering leaves of the horse chestnut trees in Clissold Park, the sound of their laughter scattered after them.

'You're right,' I tell Tom. 'Finn would be happier if he knew some of the other children. I'll make an effort with that this week. Get to know the other mothers, try and find him some little mates.'

Tom smiles. 'I think that's a good plan. I'm sure it'll all settle down.'

'I hope so,' I say. 'It sort of has to, doesn't it? If I'm going to ramp up the freelancing work.'

I'd persuaded myself – and Tom – that having the playgroup for childcare would be a revelation in terms of me getting freelance work done. But so far, it's barely made any difference. By the time I've recovered from the trauma of dropping Finn off, got home, eaten, showered and tackled our mess of a flat and our mountain of laundry, it always seems to be time to pick him up again.

The egg in the bottom of my shakshuka has started to congeal. Finn rubs his eyelids with the backs of his hands. I glance down at Tom's feet. Despite the cool weather, he is wearing shorts and trainers. And he's only had a smoothie for breakfast.

'Are you going running, Tom?'

Tom has the grace to look a bit sheepish.

'I thought I might. Just while Finn's having his nap. Is that OK?'

I pick at the skin of my cuticles. I know Tom needs downtime too, but childcare is my domain all week. By the weekend, I'm desperate for a break from wiping the high chair down, washing scrambled-egg plates.

'Sure, OK.'

'I won't be long.'

Soon after, Tom jogs off, and I head home with Finn. By the time we are there, it has started to drizzle, and Finn's long eyelashes have already fluttered closed under the rain cover.

I transfer him to his cot, then message my friend Grace to see if she is free to come over. But she doesn't respond, and then I remember she will still be on her honeymoon. I've seen the pictures she has posted on Instagram. Her and Ben climbing zigzagged streets of multicoloured houses, eating ice creams. Gazing from a wrought-iron balcony over an azure sea criss-crossed with white speedboat trails.

I decide to use the free time to shower and wash my hair, instead. I brush my teeth, tiptoeing around the bathroom rug that is always unpleasantly moist, averting my eyes from the grubby sink tiles that need regrouting. I go to get dressed. The bedroom of our flat, as usual, is freezing cold. When I reach into my sock drawer, I find there are no clean pairs. As I fumble around for a pair of Tom's, I spot a piece of paper tucked down one side of his balled-up socks, next to his passport and driving licence. It's the photograph of Sophie. Jane must have left it on the table.

Why is it in Tom's drawer?

I feel cold again, all over. I snatch up some socks, and turn the photograph face down, and place it back where I found it. I keep my thumb to the edges, not wanting to mark her pretty face, then close the drawer, quietly, so as not to wake my sleeping son.

TASH

Halfway up the path to the playgroup entrance, it starts. Finn stops walking, his hand suddenly limp in mine.

'Finn no want to, Mummy.'

I had wanted to be on time so I could chat to some of the other mums, like I promised Tom. But as soon as I arrive I can see that we are really late. The chatty circles have dispersed, and the churchyard is silent.

Tom had seemed almost cross with me when I'd told him what I was planning on doing today.

'Sounds like a wasted morning to me,' he'd muttered, wiping porridge smears from the half-table. 'If a coroner has already ruled it was an accident, what more is there to say?'

Tom has a point. It's not likely that the coroner has got it wrong, but it's not impossible. It has to be worth a day's work at least – chasing the police and the coroner's office for any more information, going over the inquest witnesses, checking Sophie's social media for clues.

'The mother could be onto something, though, Tom,' I tell him. 'It's not obvious how Sophie could have hit her head around the reservoir. And there was no conclusive evidence she'd drowned. Look at all those true crime podcasts, where they go back over a cold case and find out what really happened. This could end up being like that.'

Tom snorts. 'This isn't Baltimore.'

'It could still be a case where something was missed,' I said stubbornly. 'Police are under pressure, coroners have had their funding cut ...'

21

Tom raised his eyebrows.

'What?'

'I just think you should be careful with this grief-stricken mother, that's all,' he says, holding up his hands. 'She'll be vulnerable. She might not be thinking clearly.'

'I know that. I'm just checking it out, that's all. I'm not exactly overwhelmed with other ideas at the moment.' I took a sip of my tea. 'By the way, I found the photo of Sophie Blake in your sock drawer.'

'What?' Tom picked my plate up too quickly, sending the knife clattering across the half-table.

'A photo of Sophie Blake,' I repeated. 'Jane Blake left it on the table the other day, when she came round. I found it in your sock drawer.'

Tom had turned away from me, stacking the plates on the sideboard.

'Did you?'

'Yep. Any idea how it got there?'

I saw Tom's shoulder blades rise and fall. 'Weird,' he said. 'No idea. Maybe Finn redistributed it.'

It was true that Finn had developed a habit of messing around with my work papers – tearing them or scribbling on them if I left them lying around in his reach. But the idea that he'd actually taken Sophie's photograph and hidden it in a drawer seemed unlikely to me. I had thought about pressing Tom more, but then I'd looked at the clock and seen that we were already late. It had buzzed at me all the way to playgroup drop-off, though, like a fly inside my brain.

Finn's lips are pursed in a way that means he is trying not to cry.

'Finn no want go in dere.'

'Oh, darling. Come on, let's see if they've got the police car out.' I scoop him up in my arms, trying to mimic the brisk confidence I have watched other mothers display at these moments. 'It'll be fine,' I tell him, pressing the intercom. 'Shall we have hot chocolate later, when I pick you up?'

Finn's eyes widen in horror. 'Mummy, no go away!'

Elaine, the playgroup leader, is at the door. I do the usual awkward smile through the glass window while she works the heavy lock on the other side.

'Hello, Finn,' she smiles. He writhes into my chest.

'Sorry,' I say. 'He's a bit …'

22

Elaine is used to this routine by now. She brings her face close to Finn's. 'Shall we find the police car?'

'Already tried that one.' I try to laugh, but it comes out as a choked sort of cough. Finn twists closer into me. His cheek, playdough-soft, is pressed against my neck. I feel the hot needles of anxiety along my arms as Elaine holds out her hands.

I force myself to say a cheery goodbye, and start to hand him over. The siren sound of his crying starts. He digs his fingers into the skin at the tops of my arms so tightly I gasp.

'No, Mummy! No go away, Mummy!'

The other children look up from the play tables and stare at Finn. The playgroup suddenly looks dreary and colourless, bare and institutional, compared to the soft cosiness of our messy flat. Why am I forcing him into this?

'No go away, Mummy!' His face is red now, streaked with tears and snot. Elaine is still holding her arms out. I hesitate. Finn has always been such a happy child. He is never like this. Surely you aren't expected to leave your child like this. He is only two.

'I know it's hard, but you should go. Really. He'll stop crying the moment you do.'

I turn to see who is speaking. The petite, chestnut-haired mother – the third of the glamorous-mum trio – is at my side. A smile of perfect teeth, pink lipstick, a pair of brown boots at the end of her extremely skinny jeans.

'Really?' I ask weakly.

'Definitely.' Her voice is smooth, treacly, like a late-night radio presenter. 'He'll be fine.' She reaches out to Finn's face and brushes his fringe out of his wet eyes. 'Hello, little one. I'm Laura. What's your name?'

I look from Laura to Finn. He squirms into me and away from her, the heel of his hand pressed clammily against a tear-filled eye.

'Oh dear. Poor little bean. That's my boy, Oscar, down there, by the way.' Laura gestures to a stocky little boy in a striped top, clutching a plastic digger in each hand. 'Oscar,' she says loudly, 'this is your new friend ...' She looks at me, one eyebrow raised.

'Finn,' I supply.

'Finn,' she repeats. Finn stops crying. The two children look blankly at each other.

'You have to just tell them they're friends,' Laura explains in a stage whisper, winking at me. 'They're simple creatures at this age, boys.' She returns her voice to its former pitch. 'Come on, Oscar. Give your friend Finn one of those diggers. You like diggers, don't you, Finn?'

Oscar hesitates, then selects his least favourite digger and reluctantly holds it out to Finn. Finn sticks out his bottom lip and shakes his head, but his eyes have drifted to the digger.

'I just think,' I begin, 'maybe if I stay for a –'

'Stay nearby,' Laura interrupts. 'There's a cafe over the road. I'll come with you – I could do with a coffee. Bye, Elaine!'

I open my mouth to protest, then close it again. Laura looks from Elaine to me and smiles, as if she has solved everything, then gives Elaine a nod. And before I know it, Elaine has taken a whimpering Finn from my arms, Laura's hand is at my back, and I have been ushered out, the heavy fire door shutting behind me, muting my son's howls as he is carried away.

TASH

At the cafe, two cappuccinos arrive in tall glasses, a little biscuit in a cellophane wrapper beside each.

'Feeling OK now?' Laura lays her coat over the back of the chair opposite me, followed by a sea-green pashmina which she pulls from her neck, tossing her hair free.

I swallow a lump in my throat. Laura looks at my face and laughs.

'He'll be fine, Tash! Stop worrying. What you need is caffeine.'

The heating in the cafe is on full blast, and the windows are thick with condensation. Steam rises from the umbrellas and pram covers slung over the radiator by the door. Through the window, I look over at St Mark's. Hunched under a metallic sky of thunderclouds, its walls darkened by the rain, it looks drab and cheerless, even eerie. Beyond the churchyard, the tarmac paths in the park are slick with rain. In the distance, two high-rise blocks of the new Woodberry estate loom like watchtowers. I itch to call Elaine to ask if Finn is all right.

Laura leans back into her chair and raises her coffee in the air, like a champagne flute.

'To freedom.'

'Freedom.' I force a smile back, let my shoulders drop a little. 'Thanks for making me do it, Laura. I have been on the edge of giving up.'

'I get it,' she says. 'I know it sounds awful, but you just have to dump and run.'

She is right, of course. Everyone says so. I'm being overprotective, need to relax.

'How old is Finn?' Laura asks.

'He was two in May. So two and four months. How about Oscar?'

'Oscar isn't two until January. He's just big for his age! He is one of the younger ones – he, Beau and Lissy were all born the same month. We all did NCT together.'

I nod, although I have no idea which children she is talking about. I start to take Laura in properly. She is wearing perfume and mascara, and a silk top with fluted sleeves. The top is pale and pearlescent, like the inside of a shell. She is looking at the large gold face of her watch.

'I can't stay long, annoyingly,' she says. 'My shift starts soon. In fact, that's what I meant to say – I think I know your husband, from the hospital where I work. Tom, right? Tom Carpenter? He's on rotation in A&E, at the Whittington?'

'That's him. Are you a doctor too?'

'I am. Tom and I are in the same department.' She pauses, tilts her head to one side. 'Did Tom never mention me?'

'He might have done – sorry, I can't remember.'

I think I detect a flicker, a little pilot light of annoyance behind Laura's eyes, but as soon as I notice it, it is gone. She picks up her coffee cup. Her nails are short and round, painted the colour of calamine lotion. Her wrist twinkles with a thin gold bracelet. I think I had imagined all the female doctors Tom worked with were like our friend Abi – brisk, practical, with hair permanently tied back and a face scrubbed free of make-up. I had never imagined Tom working alongside this sort of person.

'I've been there a few years now,' Laura says. 'It's a fab hospital.'

'Are you not rotating, then?'

Laura's forehead creases. I sense I have said the wrong thing.

'I'm just a bog-standard staff doctor.' She shakes a smile back onto her face. 'I did apply for the training post but ... this way has worked out better, actually. I can work slightly more regular shifts, so it fits in better with Oscar. Is Tom working today?'

'He's on nights this week.'

'Oh, bad luck. It's such a nightmare, isn't it? It's so lucky for us that Ed has a really flexible job. He usually does the pickups. Have you met him yet?'

I nod, realising I know which one Ed must be – he is one of the few dads who does regular pickups. He's always seemed very friendly, usually turning up slightly late, in his running gear, a discarded bike

26

or scooter over his shoulder, smiling apologies for having forgotten Oscar's hat or coat or water bottle. I hadn't known he was Laura's husband, and wouldn't have matched them. She seems so put-together, whereas Ed is quite scruffy and unshaven – although I suppose he's quite good-looking, in a used-to-be-in-a-band sort of way.

'He seems like a great dad,' I say truthfully. 'I wish Tom would do a few playgroup runs.'

Laura smiles, then changes her expression to something else, somewhere between a smile and a frown.

'Same hospital, same area, boys the same sort of age,' she says. 'How funny we've never bumped into each other before, Tash.'

I clear my throat. 'Well, Tom and I don't live around here, exactly.'

Our street is barely a mile north of here, but feels a world away from these neat, tree-lined avenues and pretty coffee shops. All the houses on our road have front gardens full of weeds and builders' rubble, bricks studded with satellite dishes and broken burglar alarms. The high street is all phone shops, money transfer places, kebab houses. Not pretty coffee shops like this.

Laura sets her cup down. 'What do you do?'

'I'm a journalist.'

'Really? Wow, interesting job.' She sits back in her chair. 'Working on anything at the moment?'

I hesitate. 'Not really. I've got a few ideas. Hopefully I'll be back in the swing of it when Finn's a bit more settled.'

Laura smiles sympathetically. 'Finn will settle, Tash, I promise. In a few weeks' time he'll be skipping there in the mornings, and you'll have your life back.' She checks her watch again. 'Yikes. I should go. But hey – let's get them together soon, shall we? Finn and Oscar? I bet Elaine's bent your ear about play dates – but she's right. They do help.'

I look up, pleased.

'Thank you, Laura – she has, actually – and I think it would really help Finn. I tried to arrange something with Christina, but, um …'

'Ah, Christina. Let me guess.' Laura grins, raising a groomed eyebrow. 'She was too busy with her top job to fit you in?'

I laugh. 'Well, she did say her childminder might be free …'

'What? Sal, you mean? She subcontracted you to her childminder?!' Laura shakes her head. 'Oh, Christina! I'm sorry, Tash. Never

mind. Let's get Finn and Oscar together for sure. When suits you? We could come over to your place, if you like?'

I open my mouth to reply, then close it again. I imagine Laura squeezed up against the chipped worktops in our galley kitchen, eyeing up the cheap, wonkily fitted cupboards, the broken extractor fan in the corner.

'If you'd rather come to ours,' Laura adds gently, glancing at me, 'we usually have a few kids over on Friday afternoons?'

'Thanks, Laura,' I say gratefully. 'That sounds perfect.'

TASH

Dave Holt's Portakabin smells of German shepherd and damp carpet. Outside, it has started to rain. Wind rattles the cabin, as if trying to work out who is inside. Dave makes us two mugs of tea and sets them on a melamine tray next to his old desktop computer.

Dave is the man who found Sophie's body. He was a witness at her inquest, but they hardly asked him any questions. I'm still not totally convinced that this Sophie Blake thing is going to amount to a story, but it's worth having Dave on tape, just in case. It is the sort of interview that provides good colour – the gritty reservoir bloke, describing how he stumbled across a corpse.

'Thanks for meeting me, Dave,' I say, checking the Dictaphone.

'No worries.' Dave presses the tea bag to the side of the mug. 'Makes a change from the people from the new flats forever coming round, moaning about the machinery noise.'

I am relieved I didn't mention the noise myself. It's awful, like a low whirr, a constant hum of dread.

'Are they nice, the new flats?'

Dave wrinkles his nose. 'Not my kind of thing. Don't like them floor-to-ceiling windows. Give me vertigo.'

'What do the old residents think about them?'

Dave shrugs. 'No one around left to ask.'

I had read that nearly all the old residents have been moved out now. 'Decanted', the developer's website calls it. Just a few still remain. The ones who aren't having it. The ones who are refusing to go.

I feel my phone vibrate in my pocket. I know, even without looking, it will be Jane again, asking for an update. I flick it onto silent.

Jane is so sure that Sophie was murdered. I find her conviction rubbing off on me whenever I speak to her. The trouble is, she has no proof, nor any idea who might have wanted to hurt Sophie, or why. I'm starting to sense that her knowledge of her daughter's life in the years before she died is hazy, that Sophie was keeping her at arm's length. She thinks it is possible Sophie had a boyfriend, or was seeing someone casually, but doesn't really seem to know who. She doesn't know who Sophie's friends were.

Dave leans over to pass me a chipped mug, sucking in his belly.

'So,' Dave says. 'You want to know about that girl I found last summer.' Dave gestures outside. 'I found her over there, by the sluice, face down. I called it in straight away. They sent a PC, just a kid really. Didn't even bring any waders.' Dave sighs. 'We got in, turned her over and ... well, it wasn't very nice.'

'Why ... what, in particular?'

Dave hesitates. One of his two German shepherds is fussing at his knees. He holds out a flat, pale hand, and the dog licks it.

'You ever seen a body that's been in water?'

I shake my head.

'You don't want to, believe me.' He starts rubbing the dog behind its ears. 'It's a shame. We do have the signs up about swimming. Not that people take any bloody notice. Ever since they started calling it a "nature reserve".' Dave makes the quotation marks in the air with two pairs of fat fingers, rolls his eyes at me.

I smile faintly. An accident, then. I glance down at the Dictaphone, disappointed.

'I told them it'd be trouble,' Dave continues. 'Especially now it's the trendy thing, all this open water swimming. They forget how cold it can be, even in summer. The surface water might seem still, OK for swimming. As you're getting in, where it's shallow, it doesn't feel so cold. But under that, the temperature drops fast. You get into the middle, suddenly you're in water only a couple of degrees. You get in trouble in no time at all.'

Dave carries on in this vein for a while, saying non-podcast-worthy things about the dangers of managed waterways. I glance down at the tea in my own mug, moon-pale, the bag still floating. I think of Sophie's bloated skin. I imagine her terror, unable to breathe, water filling her lungs.

30

'Were you not surprised, then, by the conclusion of the inquest?'

Dave pauses before replying. 'What d'you mean?'

'I mean, you didn't see anything – I don't know. Odd about it.'

Dave considers this. 'Well, the police looked at it, didn't they? They said it was an accident.'

There has been a shift in Dave. He is looking at me differently, and his words have slowed, like he is choosing them with more care.

'I just wondered what you thought, really.'

'Well … we do get it from time to time in the reservoirs,' Dave says. He gazes out into the darkness. 'I mean, it was a bit of a strange one.'

'Strange how?'

Dave screws his face up. His two dogs are at his knees, clamouring for him, their wet, panting mouths open. Dave hauls himself up, rattles biscuits into two bowls. The dogs rush to them, pushing past one another in a double helix, mirror images of each other.

'Usually,' Dave says, his back to me, 'we find the clothes before the body.'

'Clothes?'

'Every other time I've known about, we've found the clothes. A little pile by the water. Nine times out of ten, that's how we know. Body usually turns up later.'

'And you didn't? With Sophie?'

Dave shakes his head.

'She had all her clothes on. Somehow that didn't seem right to me. Who goes for a swim with all their clothes on?'

I frown, trying to remember if there was any mention of this at the inquest. I'm sure there wasn't. I'm sure I would have remembered.

'What about the head injury?'

Dave shifts slightly in his seat, glances to the side.

'They said she could have got it jumping or diving in,' I persist. 'I can't seem to work out how it might have happened.'

Dave is staring down at the dogs.

'I looked at that too,' he says quietly. 'I walked all round. If there was something, I wanted to have it made safe. But you're right. There's nothing she could have hit her head on.'

For a moment, there is silence. The dogs have settled at Dave's feet, their wet noses pressed against his steel-capped boots. Dave reaches down to stroke the ear of one, as if for comfort.

I hold my breath, glance down at the voice recorder between us, check it is on. I suddenly feel like maybe the podcast idea wasn't so far-fetched after all.

'Did the police interview you, Dave?' I ask. 'Did they seem to be investigating it?'

'They did. They seemed to be, for a bit. But then they said it was an accident. I figured they'd got some other evidence. By the time I found that phone, they told me they didn't need it for anything. They said now it was with the coroner, it was no longer a police matter.'

I look up. 'Sorry, Dave – did you say a phone?'

'Yeah. Hang on.'

Dave hauls himself up, pulls open a drawer and takes something out. 'We dredge that area occasionally,' he says. 'This was among the shopping trolleys and whatnot. Could be nothing to do with it. But I just thought the timing seemed to fit. And it looks like a girl's phone, you know?'

He passes it to me. I cradle it in both my hands, like a jewel.

'Might not have been hers, of course. I thought they'd want to check. But they told me no, the case had been passed to the coroner, so they didn't need it.'

I turn the phone over in my hands. The glass of the screen is cracked, the edges covered in a layer of silt. When I gently scratch the back of it with my fingernail, the dirt comes away. Underneath is a glinting case, shiny as a golden ticket.

TASH

'This? You want me to fix this phone?'

The Turkish man at the perspex counter picks the phone up between his thumb and forefinger and dangles it in front of his face.

'Careful with it, please.'

He raises his eyebrows, puffs out his cheeks with air. He rummages under the counter for a charger that fits and plugs the phone in. At first, nothing happens. Then after a few moments, the cracked screen illuminates, a perfect square of blue light. I place my fingers lightly on it, feeling the thrum of life inside. I feel as if I have witnessed a miracle.

'Yeah, I think so,' Jane had said when I asked her about the phone. 'She did have a gold case for a while, I think. She liked gold. Why?'

'Just checking a few details,' I'd told her, my pulse quickening. The phone had to be Sophie's, then. It had to.

Now, I have agreed to pay this man a hundred quid to remove the pass code security. He hasn't told me how he has done it, and when he emerges from his shop, I don't ask.

'Here you are.'

I almost snatch the phone, thumbing it greedily. I check the messages, WhatsApps, photo reel. But there is nothing. I flick miserably through the apps, but find just the basic stuff that came with the phone. It's all empty. No photos or videos, nothing in the calendar. There are no contacts in the address book, there's no call history. It looks like all the apps have been removed.

'I don't understand. There's nothing on it.'

The man folds his arms. 'I said I'd remove the security,' he says. 'I didn't do nothing else.'

'I'm not paying you a hundred quid – you've wiped the phone!' I grip the perspex counter until the skin around my nails goes white. The phone man narrows his eyes. I can tell this job is proving more trouble than it's worth to him.

'I told you, that wasn't me.'

'Are you saying this happened because of the water?'

He looks down at the phone. 'No, water won't do that, but –'

'So why is there nothing on here?'

'Swear on my life, babes, nothing I done will have wiped that phone. It must've been wiped before.'

'Before what?'

'Before you lost it in that river.'

'Reservoir.'

'Whatever.'

I pause.

'So you think someone deleted whatever was on here?'

He shrugs. I force myself to think.

'Can you recover stuff from a phone?' I ask. 'If it's been deleted, I mean.'

The man makes whistling noise, rubs the underside of his manicured beard with a flattened palm.

'Possible,' he says. 'Sometimes. I know a guy.' He gives me a hard look. 'But it's not cheap.'

'Tash! You made it!' Laura trills. 'Welcome to the madhouse. Can you fit the buggy in?'

Mine is the third or fourth that has been squeezed into the hallway – I have to yank it over to one side, adjust the handlebar to make it smaller. Laura's hallway is light and elegant, a huge cloud of flowers on the side table, a smell of pomegranates. I feel intensely aware of all the scuffs on the frame of my buggy, the stains on the seat fabric, the squashed rice cakes in the footwell.

I pick Finn up and follow Laura into her kitchen. I hear female voices in the living room next door. My underarms feel hot in my new top that keeps riding up, my black jeans still a little too tight, even all this time after he was born.

I put Finn down and look for something to distract him with. To my relief, he ambles off happily towards Oscar and starts to play alongside him with the cars.

'So,' Laura is saying. 'Tea? Coffee?'

'A cup of tea would be great.'

'Oh God! Isn't it time for wine yet?' I don't recognise the muffled voice that called from the other room.

'Sure,' Laura calls back, giggling. I join in with the laughter, try not to feel that it is directed at me.

Laura pulls at a long handle on the wall, revealing a fridge which opens via some hidden French doors. Laura plucks the wine out by the neck.

'Glass of white?'

'Oh, sure.'

'You can have tea if you like, it's fine.'

'No, no. White sounds great.'

Laura goes to locate three wine glasses. While her back is turned, I run my hand lightly over her grey-painted cabinets. On the shelves are a rainbow of cookbook spines, a neat line of glass jars filled with different pasta shapes. The smell of bolognese sauce bubbling on her stove makes my stomach contract with hunger.

'Oh,' I say, remembering my offering. 'I got you something, Laura.' I head back to the hallway to retrieve the small but outlandishly expensive box of chocolates from the shop on Highbury Barn. I reach under the buggy, my arm skimming the cool Victorian tiles of her hallway.

'Oh, wow, thank you,' says Laura. When I place it on the worktop, I notice the box has got slightly squashed. Laura sets down the wine glasses and picks up the box, then puts it down again, as if she is not sure what to do with it.

'No worries,' I say awkwardly. I instantly wish I'd just left the chocolates in the buggy.

Laura hands me a glass, holds up her own for me to clink. When I bring it to my lips, I realise I am longing for it, anticipating its taste and temperature, the softening of the muscles in my neck and jaw as I take my first mouthful.

In the living room are the two other mothers. The tall blonde one is on the sofa. The sporty dark-haired one is standing by the fireplace, a small baby in a carrier on her front. The children play at their feet on a wooden floor scattered with brightly coloured Lego bricks. As well

as Laura's boy, Oscar, there are two others – a dark-haired girl, and a pale child with shoulder-length strawberry-blonde hair, whose gender I've never been able to determine.

'Right, Tash,' says Laura. 'Do you know everyone? This is Nicole, mum of Lissy, who Finn might know …'

'Hey.' From her voice I identify Nicole as the requester of wine. She is bouncing in a slight squat, her thumbs hooked around the straps of the carrier like belt loops. Her baby has a strikingly full head of dark hair, like her. The dark-haired girl sitting with Oscar must be Lissy.

'Thanks,' Nicole says as I pass her the glass. She has an American accent. She stops bouncing, takes the glass and tips it straight into her mouth.

'… And this is Claire, who is mum of Beau. Claire, Nicole, this is Tash and Finn. Finn's new at playgroup. Tash's husband Tom works with me, at the hospital.'

'Lovely to meet you, Tash.' Claire throws me a full-beam smile, blinking away a thick, platinum-blonde fringe. She is tall and slim and sort of frail-looking, like a giraffe. She is wearing the stealthily expensive uniform of the thirty-something mother – white trainers, jeans cut off before the ankle. Her white linen T-shirt fits exactly right.

The strawberry-blonde child, who must be Beau, starts to fuss mildly at Claire's feet.

'Mummy, I want milk.' Claire plucks the child from the ground and lays it across her lap, brushing its fringe back from its eyes. Then, she yanks up her T-shirt and pulls a small, cream-coloured breast out of her black lace bra. Tucking the nipple between two fingers, she takes the child by the back of the head and pulls it onto her, inserting the nipple into its mouth. The child sucks contentedly, its left hand pressed against her other breast, its green eyes wide open. I become very aware of the muscles in my face.

'Are you all right, darling?'

I realise Laura's words are aimed not at one of the children, but at Claire. Laura's hand is resting lightly on Claire's temple as she feeds, tucking a hair behind her ear. There is something so intimate about the gesture that I look away, embarrassed.

'Just a glass of water, please,' Claire says quietly. 'Thanks, hon.'

I decide to sit down beside Nicole. The baby on her chest is asleep now, snoring slightly, its tiny nose pointed upwards.

36

'Congratulations.' I nod at the baby. 'Girl or boy?'

'Girl,' she murmurs. 'Charlotte. Thank God. I never wanted boys.' She glances at Finn. 'No offence,' she adds half-heartedly.

I laugh, unsure whether she is joking.

Nicole tells me she works for an investment bank, but is on maternity leave. She and her husband, John, live in Highbury, 'right by the fields'. The husband merits little comment, but on the subject of her friendship with Laura and Claire, Nicole proves to be an expansive talker. The three of them met at antenatal classes, she confirms. 'The three of us clicked right off the bat,' Nicole adds pointedly. 'We've been super close ever since.' I force a smile as she produces story after story signalling their shared history, her prior claim on Claire and Laura's friendship.

My focus drifts from what Nicole is saying. I find my eyes drawn to Claire, who is listening, with a bland smile, to some story that Laura is telling. She occasionally closes her eyes and purses her lips, as if trying to identify a sound she can hear from a long way away. She keeps Beau – a boy, it turns out – at her breast as Laura talks, stroking his hair without looking down at his face. Claire is one of those people who is so beautiful she is almost strange-looking. It is the sort of brittle, catwalk beauty that women admire more than men: her torso hard and boyish, her breasts so small her muscular toddler son is able to cup one fully in his hand as he suckles from the other.

The wine is dry and cool. I drink one glass, then another. When Laura begins spooning spaghetti and sauce into small plastic bowls and arranging toddler tables and chairs, my stomach starts to growl. Too embarrassed to ask for a bowl for myself – they don't seem like the sort of women who eat much – I sneak a couple of mouthfuls of Finn's when no one is looking.

When I carry his bowl to the sink, I find my head is swimming. I wash up the bowls, even though Laura calls at me not to bother. I wash out Finn's beaker and fill it with water, which I gulp down in one go.

I ask Laura where I can find the bathroom and she directs me upstairs. I think I've followed her instructions, but when I open the door, it is clear I've got the wrong room. Ed, wearing the workout gear I recognise from pick-ups, is sitting at a desk in a darkened study, a large screen glowing blue in front of him.

'Oh, hi, Ed.'

'Tash! I didn't know you were here.' Ed is smiling, but he looks flustered, guilty. His eyes flick from my face to his screen, his hand jerking forward to his mouse to click a browser window closed.

'Sorry to disturb.'

I feel my face flushing red. Was he watching a film?

'No, no, you're fine. Sorry. I was just in the middle of something.' He clears his throat. 'Is Finn downstairs?'

'Yep, yep, they're having a lovely time.'

'Oh, great, that's great.'

I wonder why this feels so awkward, why I feel as if I've wandered into something intimate – his bedroom, rather than his study. It certainly smells more like a teenage boy's bedroom. Ed's battered trainers have been kicked off under the desk. It is as if he's come straight from the gym or a run, and sat down at his desk without showering.

Ed clears his throat. 'If you're after the bathroom, it's the next door on the left.'

'Right,' I say. I stumble backwards. Ed watches me, the grin still fixed to his face, as I close the door.

TASH

When I get back to the living room, I feel disorientated. I notice the darkness at the windows, the orange glow of street lamps. I whip out my phone and am startled by the time. I have three missed calls from Tom.

Laura has put some music on in the living room. It feels slightly too loud to me. The wine is starting to give me a headache, pressure building behind my eyes.

'I should go,' I tell Laura. She smiles vaguely and I wonder whether I had been outstaying my welcome anyway. Laura appears to be sinking slowly into the sofa, her eyelids drooping. I have the distinct sense that a transition has occurred from day to evening without me realising, that I shouldn't be here any more.

'Would you like a lift?' Claire asks me mildly. 'Jez is picking me up in a minute.' I assume she is talking about her husband, although I do fleetingly consider the possibility she has some sort of driver.

'Thanks,' I say, raising my voice slightly over the music. 'But, uh, I don't have the car seat. For Finn. We'll be absolutely fine on the bus. Thanks, though.'

Finn looks up at me and rubs his eyes and I suddenly long to be cuddled up on the sofa at home with him.

'Come on,' I tell him. 'Let's get home.'

There is a knock on the door. Laura hauls herself up and heads towards the hallway. I notice a slight wobble as she navigates the corner. I hear the muffled sound of her greeting, a man's voice in reply, followed by a different laugh than the one I have heard her use before.

'It's Jez,' Laura calls through to the living room.

'Daddy!' Beau clambers to his feet and dashes into the hallway. Claire smiles after him. A few moments later, Jez walks into the room, carrying Beau upside down by his ankles. Jez is wearing a suit, no tie, his top button open. An air of work, energy and money has followed him into the room, like a breeze from an open window.

Beau is giggling uncontrollably. His T-shirt has slipped towards his face, leaving his pale tummy exposed. His strawberry-blond hair, caught in static, has fanned out at his father's knees, like a dandelion clock.

Once he has set Beau down on the floor, Jez pulls himself up to his full height, looks at the bottle of wine and grins, raising his eyebrows at Nicole, Laura and me in turn.

'Oh dear,' he says. Everybody laughs. The joke feels funnier than it really should be. 'Is Ed here?' he asks.

'He's working upstairs,' Laura says quickly. 'He's been flat out all day. Hey, Jez, this is Tash. She's a journalist.'

I flinch slightly at Laura's introduction. She sounds like she might have had too much wine. Jez's eyes move from Laura's face to mine.

'Hello, Tash the journalist.' Jez locks his gaze to mine and throws me an amused smile, flicking a quick glance at Laura in a way that implies he shares my suspicion about her and the wine. It is thrilling and shocking to me, the way Jez invites me immediately into this private confidence. And also, how willingly I participate in it, how readily I return his smile, at the expense of the friend who invited me here, to her home.

'Nice to meet you,' I manage, before I find myself forced to look away.

Finn presses his forehead against my leg. He is starting to flag now, his nerves with the other children fraying, the frequency of toy-snatching incidents increasing. We have stayed far too long. I ruffle his hair, start mentally locating my bag, Finn's shoes, his coat. Just as I'm about to stand up, Laura fetches Jez a beer and he sits down beside me, opposite his wife, rolling the neck of the bottle between his hands. I am tilted towards his body as his weight sinks into the cushions.

'I was just asking Tash,' Claire says vaguely, 'if she wanted a lift.'

'It's fine,' I say again. 'I don't have the car seat.' I have the strange sense no one can actually hear me.

Jez turns to me, the sofa sinking further. 'Where do you live?'

'Down at the bottom of the park. One of the roads before Manor House. Near ... do you know the new development? Woodberry Down?'

I think I see a muscle flicker in Jez's cheek, just for a second, before his genial expression returns.

'Know it well. Sure you don't want a lift? I can always come back for this lot.'

'It's fine,' I tell him firmly. I force myself to meet his gaze. His eyes are ice-cube pale.

I stand up, say my goodbyes. I haul the buggy outside and gulp in the cool evening air like a drink of water. I wait until we are out in the street to strap Finn in. I hand him my phone to play with, hoping it will keep him quiet on the way home, gambling that he won't drop it and smash the screen again.

Nicole passes us with her girls, headed for a shiny black car across the street. She has pulled on a black baseball cap, Puffa jacket and backpack. She smiles and winks at me.

'Good to meet you, Tash,' she calls over her shoulder, as she lifts her children into the darkness of her car. 'Nice to have you in the club.'

I smile back, with an effort. My head is pounding. My vision swims. I reach out for the top of the front-garden wall for support.

'You good?'

Jez is at my side. His tone is casual, but his voice is lowered, and as he says the words, I feel him slip his hand onto the small of my back, where my skin is exposed between my top and jeans.

'Fine,' I say breathlessly. 'I'm fine, thanks.'

His fingertips move over my skin, lightly, towards the bottom of my spine. The next moment, he is gone. Afterwards, I can't tell for sure whether the touch really happened, or whether I imagined it somehow.

SOPHIE'S IPHONE 5S

Deep retrieval [earlier data not present]

07.07.2017

MISSED CALL: 16.06
FROM: +44XXXXXXX422

MESSAGE RECEIVED: 16.16
FROM: +44XXXXXXX422
TEXT:
Hi Sophie, where are you? Was expecting you
here 20 mins ago.

MESSAGE RECEIVED: 18.34
FROM: +44XXXXXXX761
TEXT:
Hey Soph, just wanted to check you were ok
earlier? You didn't seem yourself. We've missed
you and T. Call me soon. L xxx

MESSAGE RECEIVED: 20.45
FROM: +44XXXXXXX669
TEXT:
Hey can u call?

MISSED CALL: 20.51
FROM: +44XXXXXXX669

```
MISSED CALL: 20.52
FROM: +44XXXXXXX669

MISSED CALL: 20.54
FROM: +44XXXXXXX669

MESSAGE RECEIVED: 21.06
FROM: +44XXXXXXX669
TEXT:
I don't think u shud use it Soph. U don't no
what they'll do.

MISSED CALL: 21.22
FROM: +44XXXXXXX669

MISSED CALL: 21.31
FROM: +44XXXXXXX669

MESSAGE RECEIVED: 21.36
FROM: +44XXXXXXX669
TEXT:
SOPHIE CALL ME PLEASE. No ur angry, but this isn't
the way. I shud of never given u that. Call me.

MESSAGE RECEIVED: 21.36
FROM: +44XXXXXXX669
TEXT:
SOPHIE CALL ME PLEASE

MESSAGE RECEIVED: 21.37
FROM: +44XXXXXXX669
TEXT:
I'm just worried about what they might do

23.59: FACTORY SETTINGS RESTORED [ALL DATA
DELETED]


REPORT ENDS
```

TASH

'Are you still there?'

I snatch the phone back up, Finn's coat and shoes in one hand.

'Yes, yes, I'm still here,' I tell the police press officer. 'As I said, if I could just speak to –'

'Remind me,' the press officer says. 'The investigation into the death of this person was discontinued.'

'Yes –'

'In September of last year.'

'Yes, but –'

'And the inquest concluded in November.'

'Yes …'

'And now you've found a phone.'

'Yes, and –'

'In a reservoir.'

'Yes, that's correct.' I try to stay calm, ignore the sarcasm in her voice.

The retrieval guy had only managed to get hold of a few messages – the last ones, all from the day that Sophie disappeared. But even these few seem intriguing to me. There is something really unsettling about them – not to mention the fact that they were deleted in the first place, along with all the other contents of her phone.

Surely there was at least a chance the police might look again at her case. And if they agreed to do that, then not only would Jane be satisfied, but I'd have an exclusive story to sell to the nationals. I just had to get this hopeless press officer to listen to me.

'The mother of the dead girl has identified the phone as hers,' I say.

'Perhaps it would be a good idea to give the phone back to her?'

'Yes, but you're not listening, there's stuff on the phone that I think –'

'Listen, Miss … Can you remind me of your name?'

'It's Natasha Carpenter.'

'And the news organisation you work for?'

I clear my throat. 'I'm freelance.'

'I see.' The temperature seems to drop several degrees. I glance at the clock; we should have left for playgroup six minutes ago.

'Look,' I say, 'can you please just arrange for me to have a two-minute conversation, at a time of his or her convenience, with the officer who …'

Finn has sensed that I am distracted. He has spotted the sugary fruit puree I mix into his porridge on the worktop and has grabbed it in both hands. I lunge to intercept it, but fail. He starts sucking the puree straight from the packet, grinning behind the plastic spout.

'The officer is not available to discuss this,' the press officer says. 'I can only suggest you –'

'Are you seriously telling me that the Metropolitan Police has no interest in a new piece of key physical evidence relating to the unexplained death of a young girl?'

There is a pause.

'Can you hold again, please?'

'Oh no, please don't –'

The hold music starts up again before I can even finish my sentence.

Christina arrives at the playgroup on her bike seconds after me, with a squeak of brakes, Eliza strapped into the child seat. I consider waiting for her, but she is still fumbling with her bike lock, so I bypass her and usher a reluctant Finn inside.

Christina catches up with me on my way out.

'Hey – how's it going, Tash?'

'Good, thanks.'

'Oh, I'm glad to hear it.' Christina is making no move to leave, but is fiddling with the clip of her helmet, her long dark hair tangled in the back of it. It is obvious there is something she wants to say.

'So Finn is settling in OK now?'

'A bit better.'

'That's great to hear.' Christina takes a breath. 'Look, I just wanted to say I'm really sorry about before, Tash – when I told you to talk to

Sal about a play date. I didn't mean to imply I was too busy to hang out with you … I didn't think about how it sounded.'

I smile, appreciative of the apology. 'Honestly, it's fine. Hanging out with me and my socially awkward two-year-old is not the most tempting prospect for anyone.'

She nods. 'Eliza struggles with shyness too. I know it can be difficult.'

There is something stiff in the way she says this that makes me wonder whether Eliza's shyness might be genetic.

'I wondered,' she continues tentatively. 'Are you free for a coffee by any chance? I'm on a rare day off and I haven't much planned. I thought I might go to Ruby's.'

'Sounds lovely,' I reply. 'I'm actually on my way there now – I'm meeting some of the others – Laura, Claire and Nicole. Why don't you join us?'

In a development that I find quietly thrilling, I seem to have been given a standing invitation to join the post-drop-off coffees at Ruby's. Claire, Laura and Nicole seem to think nothing of going there most days, despite the fact that even the croissants cost about a fiver.

As soon as I mention the others, though, the smile falls from Christina's face. Her shoulders tense.

'No thanks,' she says shortly. 'Another time maybe.' I open my mouth to ask why not, but Christina is already walking away, pulling the bike helmet a little too firmly back on her head.

Under the table at Ruby's, I tap out a message to Jane Blake, asking if we can push our meeting back by half an hour.

'Anything interesting?'

Nicole is staring at me over her black coffee. Claire and Laura look up too.

'Oh, sorry,' I mutter. 'Just a boring message about work.'

'I'm sure it's not boring!' Claire enthuses. 'Your job must be so fascinating.'

I smile awkwardly, but somehow I can't imagine bodies of dead girls, phones fished out of reservoirs and dodgy Turkish phone shops on Blackstock Road are the sort of thing they usually chat about over their morning coffees.

'It's just an invoice I need to chase,' I insist. 'Seriously. Very dull.'

'Were you chatting to Christina before?'

I look up at Nicole. Was she there when Christina and I were speaking?

'She wasn't trying to palm you off on the childminder again, was she?' Laura laughs and tells the others the story before I can protest.

'No!' Claire and Nicole look horrified. Laura rolls her eyes.

'It wasn't a big deal,' I insist. 'She seems nice.'

'If you say so.' Nicole raises her eyebrows.

'You ... don't get on with Christina?'

Nicole gives a little shrug. 'I barely see her. I just think it's a bit strange to go to all the trouble of ordering donor sperm on the internet to have a baby ...'

'Nicole, shush!' Laura admonishes, suppressing a chuckle.

'... to then barely ever pick her up from playgroup.' Nicole shrugs, brushing croissant crumbs from her fingers.

I clear my throat. 'Well, her job sounds pretty full on – isn't she a lawyer?'

'A public defender kind of lawyer,' Nicole says, flapping a hand dismissively. 'A lone working parent. It's her whole thing.'

'A lawyer and a single parent? That's impressive, no?'

I can instantly see I've said the wrong thing. Laura looks uncomfortable, and glances at Claire. Claire touches her hand lightly to her forehead. Laura nudges a glass of water in her direction and Claire smiles at her, weakly.

'I'd steer clear of the childminder, Sal, anyway, Tash,' Nicole says.

'Unfortunately, I agree,' Laura says, an exaggeratedly pained expression on her face. 'Sal's not good news, Tash.'

I want to ask what it is about Sal that is so objectionable, but the bill arrives on the table, and I am forced to suppress a wince. I still haven't even worked out how I'm going to tell Tom about the cost of that report I had done on Sophie's phone – let alone this new brunch habit I seem to have developed.

'Any plans for this week, anyone?' Claire asks brightly, changing the subject.

'I'm spending as little time at my house as possible,' Laura groans. 'We're having our kitchen redone.' This is baffling news. There is nothing wrong with Laura's kitchen. 'That reminds me – Claire, can you host a spag bol on Friday? Ours will be too much of a state.'

'Sure.' Claire nods, but she doesn't return Laura's eye contact.

The waiter asks us how we want to split the bill.

'Oh God,' Laura says, cupping her cheeks with her hands. 'I've forgotten my purse.'

'Again?' Claire exhales sharply. Laura looks wounded.

'I'll get your share,' Nicole purrs. 'It's no problem.'

'Thanks,' Laura murmurs, smiling gratefully at Nicole. 'I'll pay you back on Friday.'

'Can you make it, Tash?' Claire asks, her eyes fixed on me. 'Friday, at my place?'

'Love to,' I reply. I pick up my bag and tap my card for the waiter, silently praying that it won't be declined.

Jane is already there when I reach the park cafe on Highbury Fields, by the field full of grubby plastic toddler equipment and broken tricycles. Jane said it had to be somewhere outdoors, so she could smoke, but I am already regretting the choice of venue. It is windy, and the lids keep blowing off our takeaway cups.

Jane reads the phone data report, stirring her tea with one of the little wooden sticks. She has got a plastic laundry bag with her today – one of those red-and-blue-checked ones you sometimes see homeless people dragging around. I help her check the numbers one by one against her phone address book, me reading them out, Jane stabbing at her phone keys with a single yellowed finger.

'Nope,' Jane says eventually. 'Don't recognise any of these.'

'Are you sure?' I ask, disappointed. 'Do you want to check again?'

She shakes her head, pushes the report back over to my side of the table.

I take the report from her, deflated.

'Well, anyway, I'm hopeful the police might look at the case again in light of this,' I say. 'This last person sounds almost fearful for Sophie – don't you think?'

Jane's chin starts to wobble, and immediately I see that I misread the reason for her silence. Fat tears start to roll down her cheeks. She reaches a trembling hand into her battered handbag, takes a tissue from a small polythene packet and presses it against one eye, then the other. This whole routine is something she barely even notices she is doing any more, I realise. Managing her grief is now part of her muscle memory, like a smoker lighting up, a mother wiping her baby's face.

'Leave it to me,' I tell Jane, putting the report away in my backpack. 'I'll look into it, even if the police don't.'

Then Jane starts to talk, properly, for the first time. About what Sophie was like, as a child. How she loved drawing and painting and dressing up and animals and photographs and children.

'Did Sophie go straight into nannying?' I ask.

'No, she did a childcare course, then started as a nursery worker. She did her level 3 at St Mark's.'

I put down my coffee. 'Sorry – St Mark's?'

'The playgroup,' Jane says. 'It's very highly thought of.'

I swallow. 'That's – that's my son's playgroup.'

'Oh.' Jane looks at me and for a moment I am not sure what to say. 'When – when was Sophie there?'

'She left the summer before she died. June 2016.'

I count the months back on my fingers. We looked around the playgroup – yes, it must have been that June. Finn would have been a few weeks old. Could we have seen Sophie there, while she was still alive?

I try to think. There was a girl who worked there, who spoke to us, wasn't there? A blonde girl. She was talking to Tom. Tom had Finn on his front, in the carrier. I remember seeing the girl putting her finger in Finn's tiny palm. I only saw the back of her. Could it have been Sophie? I try to remember the playgroup worker's face, but my mind draws a blank.

'Are you all right?'

'Yes, sorry,' I mutter, recovering myself. 'So – she worked at St Mark's. And then … ?'

'A couple poached her from there. Hired her as a nanny.'

I feel suddenly exhilarated, then quickly remember it can't be any of the mothers I know. All our children started this term.

'Do you remember their names?' I ask Jane, opening my notebook. 'The couple she worked for?'

Jane frowns, then shakes her head. 'I don't,' she says. 'Sorry.'

'What did Sophie say about them? Were they good employers?'

'I don't know. Sophie said they had a beautiful house.'

'Anything else?'

Jane sighs. 'She didn't say much about them, really. It was the two boys Sophie always talked about.'

Two boys. I make a note. 'Did you ever visit Sophie at their house?'

49

'No.' Her face spasms with pain. 'It wasn't always easy, between me and Sophie. Especially after her dad died. Heart attack. Sophie was fifteen. We were … a bit lost, for a while. I drank. Too much.'

I didn't know Sophie lost her father, at the same age I did. Same as me. Out of a clear blue sky. Jane pulls out a cigarette and lights it.

'Do you think Sophie had a boyfriend?'

She blows a plume of smoke sideways from her lips.

'I think she was seeing someone at one point,' she says. 'But she never told me much.'

'Anything she might have said about him?'

'Only that she met him on … one of those app things.'

I lean forward. Nothing was said at the inquest about any boyfriend.

'Did she definitely never mention a name? How about where he lived? What he looked like? Where they met up?' I pause. 'Anything at all would help, Jane.'

Jane shakes her head. 'Like I said, Sophie was private. She didn't speak to me about it. She only mentioned it once, and then … I got the feeling it maybe fizzled out, anyway.'

'I see.' I put my pen down. Jane glances at me, seeing my disappointment.

'Look,' she says gruffly, pushing the laundry bag towards me. 'I brought you all this. I dunno if it might help. It's … Sophie's things. The stuff she left behind.'

I stare at the bag. My fingers itch to unzip it, but I resist when I see that Jane's eyes are reddening again.

As I try to think of the right thing to say to her, my attention snags on something in the background. There is someone standing on the path, on the other side of the railings from where we are sitting. A creak as they push the gate.

It is Sal, with the twins' battered double buggy. It looks like she is on her way through to the toddler plastic bit. But she has stopped, and is staring straight at Jane and me, her mouth a tight, pinched line, her heavy frame casting a pool of shadow.

I meet her gaze, and attempt a wave and smile. But Sal does not smile back. She looks from me to Jane, down to the laundry bag, then back to me. She glances at the table, where my hand is covering Jane's. When she meets my eye again, her expression is one of horror.

And then Sal closes the gate, hauls her squeaking buggy back onto the tarmac path and walks straight back the way she came.

TASH

'What in that big bag, Mummy?' Finn's hands, smeared with tomato sauce, are reaching for the zip of the laundry bag. I pull it to the other end of the table.

'Nothing, sweetheart. Eat your pasta, please.'

I push Finn back onto his booster seat, the smell of some other woman's perfume in his hair again from playgroup. It makes my heart lurch.

Finn chews thoughtfully, his cheeks smeared with red, still staring at the bag.

'It's a present for me, Mummy?'

'No, darling.'

'It's Paw Patrol?'

'It's not a present. It's not your birthday today, remember? No, Finn!'

I gasp as he lunges for it again. I lift it, with an effort, to the kitchen worktop, out of his reach.

'It's not for playing with, Finn, OK?'

Eager to get started on Sophie's things, I rush through Finn's bath and bedtime, caving immediately when he refuses to have his hair washed, pulling him into his favourite pyjamas wordlessly, limb by limb. Halfway through his story, Finn notices he is being short-changed.

'Do voices, Mummy!' He turns to examine my face, as if he is unsure whether I am really there.

'Sorry, sweetheart.' I brush his hair with my fingers and make myself slow down.

Here comes a dad, with a spade in his hand.

Stick Man, oh Stick Man, beware of the sand ...

Finn stops me, points a stubby finger at the picture of the beach, the family building sandcastles. 'Finn go dere, Mummy? In seaside?'

He asks the same question every time we get to this page. I'm dying to take him on a proper beach holiday. I think back to my last conversation with Tom about it. He'd said we should just go to Mum's in France for the holidays again, that it was a holiday as far as Finn was concerned, that he wouldn't know the difference.

'But I want to take Finn somewhere with a beach,' I'd told Tom. 'He never stops going on about it.'

There was no beach where Mum and Claude were – unless you counted their weird local lake that smelled of trout and chemicals and that Claude insisted people swam in. In any case, a summer holiday with my mother and her partner in middle-of-nowhere France was an absolute last resort, and Tom knew it. It was true that Finn liked it at Mum and Claude's – feeding the chickens, riding his trike around their big, messy garden. But it wasn't the same. Especially last year. We'd planned to spend our summer holiday there, but then Tom hadn't even been able to get the dates off work because his rotas had got messed up, so Finn and I had ended up going without him. It had been miserable.

'Look, I'll leave it up to you,' Tom had said in the end. 'But we need to start saving money at some point, Tash, if we're going to move to a bigger place, try for another baby. Isn't that more important than all the other stuff?'

Whenever Tom and I argued about money, the conversations always ended with this, the weight of the obvious solution to the problem hanging between us. We both knew what he was talking about – how we could get money for a holiday, or a deposit on a house, if we really wanted it.

When my dad died, his photographic works were held for me in a trust. Nearly two hundred of his best and rarest pictures, signed originals, sitting in storage at his agent's offices in Mayfair. Over the years, I'd sold the odd one to pay tuition fees, or for my journalism training, or when we needed the deposit on our flat. But I know he would have wanted me to keep them, and so the bulk of the collection is still there – all the stuff from the Gulf War, the one that won a prize; and his last shots from Iraq, which were found after his death.

Tom understands how I feel about the pictures, and he has never openly said he thinks I should sell them all. But I know that, if it were him, he would. And these images of mostly dead people, in places I have never been, weigh on us, lingering darkly in the background of our arguments, like shadows.

Finn looks up at me, searches my expression.

'Of course we can go to the seaside, darling,' I tell him.

'In sea?' His soft little face lights up.

'Yes, of course we can. We'll go in the summertime.'

When Finn is asleep, I head to the fridge and carve out a chunk of the lasagne I made for his dinners. The yellow square of the microwave light hums in the darkness. As I wait, I pull out the inquest documents Jane placed on the top of the bag to read as I eat.

The pathologist's report is like trying to read another language. I keep finding words I need to put into a search engine: haematoma, petechiae, hypoxia.

The section marked 'Cause of Death' states only: *1.a. Unascertained.* I skip to the end, to a handwritten section marked 'Commentary'.

Body has undergone some decomposition. Drowning cannot be ruled out as cause of death. No fluid present in lungs. Evidence of head injury, no skull fracture. No other positive sign of injury. Possible signs of minor petechial haemorrhage found under right eyelid. However, full examination of these features impeded by extensive lividity (body found in face-down position). One broken fingernail present. No foreign DNA present under fingernails. Examination for haematoma/subtle injury impeded by condition of the body at time of examination.

I pull out my laptop, open a browser window and type in 'petechial haemorrhage'. Images pop up of bloodshot eyes, speckled blood marks under eyelids. I click on the eyelid picture. The article is entitled 'Effects of Asphyxia'. *Asphyxia.* Could Sophie have got that from drowning? This article isn't about drowning. It is about cases of suffocation. Or strangling.

The chair is starting to hurt my back. I carry the bag over to the sofa in the front room, and start going through the rest of the contents. There is a pile of battered childcare textbooks – these must have been

from Sophie's college course. Most of the rest just looks like clothes, a battered washbag.

I pick up one of the textbooks. It is about child psychology. One dog-eared page falls open. It is a section about avoidant attachment, which doesn't mean much to me. In the margin, someone has written: *Jude?*

I make a note in my pad – *WHO IS JUDE??*

Before I can go through the rest of it properly, though, my phone vibrates loudly on the coffee table.

I snatch it up, not wanting it to wake Finn. I expect it is an update from Tom, who told me earlier he'd swapped his shift so he could go for a birthday drink with his friend Ravi. But the message is from an unknown number.

STOP DIGGING.

I startle, so much so I drop the phone, sending it clattering under the coffee table. I pick it up. Adrenaline pulses through me as I read the message again.

I stare at the images on my laptop, the pathology report by my side.

Then, a flash of light at the edge of my vision distracts me.

The security light outside our basement flat has flicked on.

SOPHIE

Fourteen months before

When he first started at playgroup, Jude never seemed to want to play with me. He never wanted to play with anyone. When he arrived in the morning, he sought out the toys he wanted, and lined them up on the table in front of him. He never, ever asked for help. I'd never met a two-year-old quite like him.

I found myself drawn to him, this little person, always in his own orbit. I started to sit down next to him, and talk about what he was doing.

After a while, he stopped ignoring me, started giving me sideways glances, to check if I was still there. Then he started to play near me, on the floor, occasionally showing me things. Then he started to watch me with my other children. After I'd given them some attention, he would go over to the child and knock over their tower of blocks, scribble on their picture.

Elaine just thought Jude was naughty. 'You need to spend time with your other key children, too,' she'd sniffed. I sensed there was something wrong, though. I spent my weekends reading up on it. I searched my textbooks, highlighted the passages that seemed to fit.

'Is that his mum, the woman who picks him up?' I asked Elaine one day. She was tall and pretty, dressed like a model, but always looked sort of lost, like she'd ended up at the playgroup by accident.

'Stepmum,' Elaine said. She gave me this look like we both knew what that meant.

I started keeping more of an eye on her, this stepmum. I noticed she didn't ask me much about what Jude had been doing. She always seemed stressed about him putting his coat on properly, making sure

he had all his things. Neither of them ever seemed very pleased to see each other.

'Thanks for that, Sophie,' she said to me once, after he'd refused to let her help put his shoes on. She looked knackered, and I suddenly felt a bit sorry for her. 'I'm sure you've noticed,' she added quietly. 'Jude is ...'

She seemed to be struggling to get to the point.

'Unusual?'

She pursed her lips. 'Oh. Is he? Unusual? I was just going to say he seems fond of you.'

I clamped my mouth shut, regretted saying anything, pretended to fiddle with the little backpack on Jude's peg.

'I suppose I don't really know what's, you know ... normal.' She put her head to one side. 'Is Jude not normal?'

I glanced at Jude. He didn't seem to be listening. I took my time, chose my words carefully.

'He is very independent, for his age,' I say slowly. 'Has he – has he always been like that? Resisting you helping with things?'

'I think so.' She nodded, scratching at a thumbnail. 'I just ... I find it hard to know what he wants.'

'That can be hard with toddlers anyway,' I said. She threw me a grateful smile.

I bit my lip, wondering why I didn't feel I could tell her the truth.

TASH

I sit perfectly still, frozen to the spot, wait for the sound of Tom's key in the lock. But it doesn't come.

The light flashes off, then on again.

The security light doesn't come on unless someone is really close to the house. I try to remember if this has happened before. Is the light broken?

Then I hear a sound outside. A shuffling noise, like footsteps, on the other side of the window glass.

I feel my stomach contract, a hot flood of dread. Someone is breaking in. Tom might not be home for hours. It is just me and Finn. The door of our basement flat is not even double-locked. Why do I never lock the door properly, like Tom always tells me to? I should have let him put that chain on it. We still haven't even got that bathroom window fixed.

The light flashes off, then on again.

I should just look outside the window, but I find I physically can't, that some deep and unfamiliar instinct has wrested the controls. My body has gone completely rigid, my legs locked to the floor, as if I can stop things happening if I stay as I am.

For a moment, there is nothing. Only the breeze, the low hum of traffic. Across the road, I can see the familiar constellation of red and green in the neighbours' shrub, Christmas lights they never seem to take down.

I ease myself from the sofa and creep into the hallway, pulling my hoody tighter around me. I edge up to the front door and slide the bolt across, muffling the sound with my hands. On the other side of

the glass, the safety light is still on. I can't see anyone. But the silence feels thick, as if someone is holding their breath.

I edge back from the door, feeling for my phone in my pocket. I can hear the throb of blood in my ears. I pass Finn's room in the hallway, and push the door open to check on him. He is there, sleeping and perfect, his hair falling over his face, his skinny wrists and ankles poking from the too-small digger pyjamas he refuses to abandon.

I step out into the hallway and look towards the front door. I feel a twist of terror as I hear something again. Something like a shuffle, or a scrape.

I'm sure this time. Someone is there, close to me. It is the rustle of human movement, of shoe leather against stone. The light flicks off, then immediately on again.

My hands shaking, I feel again for the hard edges of my phone in my pocket, like a talisman. Trembling, I pull it out and call Tom. It goes straight to answerphone.

The noise comes again, unmistakable this time. Footsteps. Not the soft footfalls you'd hear from the pavement. Sharp, distinct, close. Someone is on our basement steps. Then, there is a smash, loud as a shotgun.

I hear myself scream before I'm aware my mouth has opened. I leap back into Finn's room, slam the door shut behind me. I pull the nearest thing – his toy chest, overflowing with plastic cars – against it, but it's not heavy enough. I reach for more things, anything. Books, a lamp. A toddler table. Why does none of this stuff weigh anything?

Finn is awake now. He rubs his eyes and looks at me blearily.

'Mummy, Mummy? What, Mummy?'

I resist the urge to scoop him into my arms. I need to stay by the door. If I can keep the door shut, nothing can happen to him.

'It's all right, Finn,' I whisper, as calmly as I can. 'Go back to sleep.' I can feel tears pricking at my eyes as I pull my phone from my pocket and try to dial 999. The screen is unresponsive, my fingers refusing to work.

'This is 999, which service do you require?'

'Police. Please.'

It comes out as a whisper. I don't know if I'm trying not to scare Finn or trying not to scare myself. My heart feels like it might explode in my chest.

Finn is jolted awake at the word police. His eyes widen. 'Police mans coming, Mummy?'

I press a finger to my lips. I recite my address, my name, for the person on the phone.

'And what is the reason for your call?'

'Someone is ... at my house,' I stutter into the phone. 'I think maybe –'

The line cuts out. I stare at my phone in disbelief. My battery is dead.

My heart is pounding so fast my chest hurts.

'Mummy, what's happening?' Finn's mouth is turning down at the edges.

'Stay quiet, sweetheart,' I say, shushing him. 'It's going to be fine.'

'But what's happening, Mummy?'

'Shh, Finn. Please.'

I realise I haven't heard anything for a minute or so. The terror fades a little, my heart slows. I listen again. I can't hear anything. I put my ear to the bedroom door. It doesn't sound like anyone is inside.

'Mummy?'

I pull the duvet over Finn, kiss the soft skin behind his ear. 'Everything's OK,' I tell him. 'Mummy was just checking on you. Sleepytime.' It is the magic, sleep-training word. To my astonishment, his eyelids flutter shut, the pull of sleep thick on his little body. Within moments, he is snoring softly.

Carefully, I start pulling things away from the door. When I step into the hallway, the security light is off, the front door locked shut, the glass unbroken. There was no one there. But I heard glass smash. Could they be somewhere else?

I stand in the darkness and listen. But there is nothing. The safety light stays off.

When I am at the front door, I listen for a couple more moments. Then I slide back the bolt and open the door.

The air is cold on my face, the growl of the traffic on the main road thicker in my ears. I look around, and find nothing.

Then I take a step forward, and pain slices through my foot. The sensation is white hot, like lightning.

Gasping, I stagger back, lowering myself down just inside the front door, and take my foot in my hand. The red is everywhere. It doesn't

look real. A vivid scarlet line from the bottom of my big toe to the arch of my foot. I am only vaguely aware of a clipped police siren, a blue flashing light.

'Ms Carpenter? Are you all right?'

I look up to see two police officers on our basement steps. They are staring down at my feet, to the pool of blood, and our front step, which is covered in huge, jagged pieces of broken glass.

*Introduction to Child Psychology for Early Years
Professionals*, p. 162
[This edition first published June 2006]

Avoidant attachment: some key signs

– No distress caused by mother's absence
– Shows little interest when she returns
– Avoids eye contact
– Shuns physical touch
– Excessive independence
– Resists help to complete tasks

Avoidant attachment may be the result of abusive or neglectful
caregivers.

TASH

The two nice police officers have left by the time Tom comes home. He finds me in the front room, my leg propped up on cushions, blood still soaking through the bandage the officers helped me tie around my foot, bits of lasagne on a plate on the floor. As soon as I see him, I burst into tears.

'Tash! I came as soon as I saw your message. I saw the glass – are you OK?'

He pulls me into a hug. I swallow. 'It's fine, I think. Can you have a look?'

Tom pulls away and gently unwraps the bandage. I cry out.

'Sorry – Oh, Tash! You should have gone to hospital – this looks deep!'

'I couldn't go with Finn here, could I? Anyway, the police officer bandaged me up.'

'Not very well, they didn't.'

Tom is already going to find his kit. I can hear him rummaging in the top shelf of our wardrobe, washing his hands, pulling on latex gloves.

'You'll need stitches.' He produces a needle from the bag and starts filling it with a clear liquid. 'Lidocaine,' he says, seeing me looking. 'It's local anaesthetic. Sharp scratch, OK?'

I press my lips together. I feel the metal scratch of the needle, then the coldness of the liquid passing under my skin.

'Are you allowed to have this sort of stuff at home, Tom?'

'Of course. All doctors do.'

I gasp at the pain.

'Do you always make sure it's where Finn can't – Ouch! That really hurts.'

'Sorry. Hold still.' He is putting the stitches in now, black thread pinched between his teeth, his fingers red with my freshly shed blood.

'How did you manage this, then?'

I tell him the story. The light, the noises I heard outside. How sure I was someone was there.

'Jesus, Tash! Were you that worried? Did Finn wake up? What did the police say?'

As I recount my conversation with the police, I watch Tom's expression shift from sympathy to scepticism.

'Oh. So – the police thought it could have been a fox?'

'The police were hopeless. It wasn't a bloody fox, Tom. I heard footsteps. It was a person. How would a fox have covered our front step in broken glass?'

'I guess – could someone have chucked a bottle down the stairs? Maybe that's why you heard footsteps? Or maybe it was a drunk bloke, looking for somewhere to piss?'

'It really didn't feel like that to me.' I hesitate, then decide to tell him. 'And look. Just before it happened, I got this.'

I pull up the text, hand Tom the phone.

He reads it, then stares at me. 'What the fuck? Who sent that?'

'No idea. The number's not in my contacts.' When the police left, I also checked it against the numbers on the report on Sophie's phone. But nothing matched.

'Haven't you called the number?'

I shake my head.

Tom locks his jaw, then taps on the number to call it.

'Tom, wait …'

'What? Let's find out who this is.'

Tom holds the phone to his ear. He looks furious. I hear the muffled sound of an automated message. It says the number's out of service.

Tom takes a deep breath, then sets the phone down. I feel myself shiver. Tom picks up a blanket from the sofa and pulls it around my shoulders.

'It could just be a wrong number, I guess,' he says. 'Or a prank.'

'Bit of a weird prank.'

Tom frowns. 'The alternative being what?'

'That someone wants me to stop digging into the death of Sophie Blake.'

Tom is uncomprehending. 'What – the inquest case? The girl who died in the wetlands?'

I nod.

'Is that what you think?'

'I don't know what else that message could mean.' I shift position, wincing with pain. My foot is throbbing. 'I really do think that someone killed her, Tom.'

Since the police left, I have been turning it over and over in my mind. I keep coming to the same conclusion. Sophie's head injury that couldn't be accounted for; the fact that she was wearing clothes; the phone that had been wiped before it ended up in the reservoir; the deleted messages that suggested someone was worried about her on the night she died. And now, an anonymous message to me, telling me to stop digging. A person outside our home, broken glass that felt very much like a threat.

I hadn't told the police officers any of this, when they came around earlier. I couldn't see the point. I could see they didn't even really believe me that there'd been a real person there. They'd kept going on about foxes. But I know there was someone there. Someone trying to frighten me. The same person sending the messages. And the more I think about it, the more I can only think of one possible explanation. Someone killed Sophie Blake, and they got away with it. And now, that same person – or someone linked to them – is trying to frighten me off.

'But I don't understand,' Tom says slowly. 'How would anyone even know you were looking into her death?'

'I don't know,' I say more quietly. I try and remember who knows. Jane Blake. The reservoir guy from the wetlands. One police press officer. No one else. Unless there is someone else. Someone watching me.

Tom takes my hand, interlaces his fingers with mine. 'Don't you think a discarded bottle is a bit more likely, Tash? If you'd just got that message, it's understandable you'd be on edge about a noise outside, but –'

'Tom, I honestly heard someone, right outside. There was a smash ... it sounded controlled to me. Deliberate.'

Tom looks at me for a moment. 'OK,' he says. 'Well, in that case, maybe we get a stronger lock on the door. I've said before I think we need bars on the windows, too.'

I look away. I have always protested about the bars. But now, I'm not so sure.

'And maybe one of those doorbells. You know, where you can see who's at the door? Ravi's got one at his new place. You can see who's outside your house through an app on your phone.'

I laugh at this. 'Ravi's moved to the suburbs with his huge brood and turned into a nosy neighbour.'

'He loves a gadget.' I can see that Tom has had a nice evening with his friend, until this. His shoulders have dropped. He is smiling more.

'Thanks,' I say after a pause.

'What for?'

'For not telling me to stop doing my job.'

'Come here.' He pulls me into a hug. 'I'd never want you to do that,' he murmurs into my hair. 'I'm sorry I was out with Rav and you had a scary night. I feel bad I'm doing so many nights at the moment, too. It won't be forever.'

'I know. It's OK. Let's just go to bed.'

I lie awake for a long time, the weight of Tom's sleeping arm around my waist, my foot throbbing, adrenaline still fizzing underneath my skin. The fear I felt earlier hardens into outrage. Who is this person who wants me to frighten me, to make me feel my family is not safe? Who wants me to just shut up and disappear?

I've been a reporter long enough to know that when people start threatening you, it means there's something there. But the threats usually take the form of lawyers' letters. Not anonymous text messages. Not people trying to break into my flat late at night, while my son sleeps.

Stop digging? No chance, I think, shifting myself from under Tom's arm, curling onto my side. *I'm going to find out who you are, and what you did. I'm going to expose you.*

TASH

I feel different since the broken glass, my nerve endings heightened, as if I am missing a layer of skin. Every time my phone sounds, I snatch it up, heart pounding, in case it is another anonymous message. I have started jumping at slammed doors, motorbikes revving on the street.

My foot is still throbbing as I make my way to Claire's for the Friday play date. It's the first time I have been to her house. Everything about it is huge: the windows, the front steps, the stone lions either side. As I limp up to the front door with Finn, I have the sensation of us both having shrunk. Finn stares at the gold Victorian knocker shaped like a human face, with a crown of leaves in its hair and a heavy ring in its mouth. He looks worried.

'Mummy, what's that face?'

'It's a knocker, darling. Do you want to knock it?'

Finn shakes his head, so I do it instead.

Jez answers. 'Tash! Good to see you. Hi, Finn.' Jez is wearing a crisp white shirt and suit trousers, a red tie balled and stuffed in his trouser pocket, just the tip of its tongue protruding. On his neck, just underneath his ear, is a tiny razor cut.

We follow Jez through the front room and into the kitchen. I try not to limp. I'm sick of being asked what's wrong.

'What can I get you to drink?'

I forget to answer his question. Their house is unlike anything I have ever seen, except on the property finder app I'm borderline addicted to. The huge front room, with its marble fireplace and tall bay window, seamlessly turns into a kitchen, which gives way to an enormous dining space, contained in what looks like a floating glass

box. The house appears to have no wall at the back at all; the glass box is part of a huge double-storey extension, with a grid of slim Crittall windows and a black metal staircase. Beyond it is a wall of green, a jungle of mature trees and plants.

I put Finn down and immediately take his muddy shoes off, shoving them into a plastic bag in my backpack. I find his beaker of water and zip the bag back up. I wonder about leaving my backpack on the floor, but it looks wrong and messy against their furniture so I pick it up and put it back on. I imagine how I must look to Jez: a frumpy mother, bent over a backpack, clattering around with bits of toddler plastic.

Finn has already wandered into the front-room area and has his hands on a cream, vintage-style ride-on car.

'Finn, that's not yours.'

'He's fine.' Jez smiles over at Finn, who has frozen, legs already either side of the seat. 'Help yourself, mate.'

Finn grins at me triumphantly and plonks himself down on the seat. I glance nervously at the wood floors, the marble fireplace, the powder-painted ceiling roses. Please, I think, don't break anything.

'Can I get you a drink, Tash?'

'Oh, no thanks.' Truthfully, I'm not a huge fan of how much daytime drinking these play dates seem to involve. I keep returning home with a throbbing headache.

'A coffee, then?' Jez is at the kitchen island, next to a cherry-red expresso machine.

'I'm fine for coffee too, actually.'

'Oh, that's a relief.' He throws me a conspiratorial smile. 'I don't think I actually know how this works.' He touches one of the levers and it clatters onto the marble worktop. He feigns a look of terror, followed by a grin that reaches every contour of his face. I burst out laughing.

'I wouldn't mind a tea. Do you know how to make tea?'

'Tea I can do.'

He flicks the kettle on and starts to whistle something, a song I know, but can't place.

'Your house is beautiful.' I feel I can't not say it. I can't take my eyes off the glass at the back of the house, the garden beyond. It must be a hundred feet long or more. Banana trees arch overhead; wisteria

coils around a wooden pergola. Tucked at the far end, I spy another glass-fronted building, a garden room of some sort, painted a tasteful pale grey. A light is on inside it.

'Thanks. We like it. So, how's the world of journalism?'

'Oh, it's fine.' The words come out less convincingly than I'd hoped, with a sort of sigh.

'Oh God.' Jez laughs. 'That sounds bad.'

'Sorry.' I make a face. 'It's just – freelancing. I'm constantly chasing payments, basically begging for work. I do sometimes wonder if it's worth the effort, really.'

'Oh no. Don't give up, Tash. You must never give up.'

I hesitate, unsure how to respond. Before I can reply, Jez comes to stand very close, close enough for me to smell him. I can't work out what he is doing. I can actually feel his breath on the surface of my cheek. The memory of his hand on the small of my back. His wife is, presumably, here somewhere, likely to appear at any moment.

'I just need to get the milk,' he explains.

I jump back, as if I've been scalded. I am standing in front of the fridge. The cupboards all look the same, I can't tell. I step further away, further than I need to, a blush creeping up the side of my neck. When I look up, Jez hasn't opened the fridge. He is still looking straight at me.

'Here you both are. Hi, Finn!' Claire is in the kitchen, wearing a loose kimono jacket in patterned red silk over a white vest and jeans. I wheel round, smiling. I am sure she must see the colour on my neck.

'Hey,' I gabble. 'You look lovely, Claire.' She does look different – tanned, perhaps.

'Thanks, Tash.'

'Have you been away?'

'We had a few days in our Cornish place.' Claire rolls her eyes dreamily. 'We had amazing weather. It was quite hot for this time of year! We were so lucky.' She leans on the worktop, her silk sleeves settling about her arms like butterfly wings, smiles the smile of someone who is used to being lucky with the weather. 'Can you pop us another bottle of fizz, please, Jez sweetheart?' She winks at me behind his back. I wish I hadn't asked for tea. I seem to always get it the wrong way around.

68

'We'll go at Easter,' she adds. 'To Cornwall. With Nicole and Laura too.'

'Sounds wonderful,' I say honestly. 'Finn is desperate to go to the beach.' I think again of Finn's little fingers pointed at the picture of the beach in his favourite storybook.

'You should totally come, Tash!' Claire's eyes are wide. 'We'd love it!'

'Oh ... no!' I protest, 'I didn't mean –'

'You must! Bring Tom and Finn! The house is finished now, so there's loads of room. You can walk right onto a sandy beach. Imagine them all there playing together! Finn would love it!'

Jez pops a bottle of champagne from the fridge, starts to pour. I pause, try and work out whether Claire is serious. I have never known people who throw gifts around like these women do – play dates, brunches, spa days, holidays. I allow myself, briefly, to imagine us all in Cornwall together – those big open skies, sparkling blue coves, Finn running around with a bucket in the waves with his new friends, us drinking wine around a beach campfire, like models in the Boden catalogue.

Claire has already moved on, holding the stem of her glass delicately, the tiny bubbles sparkling behind her fingernails.

'How's Finn finding playgroup now?' she asks, as she takes a sip.

'So much better, thanks.' This is true. The play dates with Oscar, Beau and Lissy have really helped him. He's particularly keen on Oscar, who is very chatty for his age, and shares Finn's love of anything with wheels.

'That's such great news. I knew he'd be fine.' Claire beams. 'It's a really great place. Elaine always works wonders.'

I glance at her, wondering what she means by this. But Claire has turned away, gathering the champagne bottle and the flutes between her slim fingers.

'Right,' she says. 'Shall we go downstairs?'

The basement is full of stylish chairs and low tables, like the foyer of a Scandinavian hotel. Laura stands up to greet me; Nicole is bottle-feeding baby Charlotte in an armchair. She waggles her fingers with her free hand, but doesn't get up.

Claire pours the champagne, and the children play while we sit and chat. Later, I ask to go to the bathroom, desperate to have more of a look around their house. I feel as if I'm on the set of a film.

'Sure,' says Claire. 'We'll keep an eye on Finn.'

I'm sure there is a loo on the basement floor, but I want to see the rest of the house, so before Claire can protest, I take the staircase up from the front hallway. The stairs are painted a deep indigo, with a pale runner in the centre, a little brass rod holding it in place on each step. Off the first landing, I see what must be Beau's bedroom – except it seems a very grown-up bed for a not-quite-two-year-old. It has no pictures on the walls, or soft furnishings. Just a few toys thrown haphazardly in a basket. If it wasn't for the dinosaur quilt cover, you wouldn't even necessarily think it was a child's bedroom.

I make my way along the upstairs hallway. The floorboards are stained white, the walls papered with the palest pink ticking stripe. The brushed-gold light switch is cold to the touch. I am sure I hear a door closing, soft footsteps on the landing, but when I look round, there is no one there.

At the end of the long corridor, I spot what must be Jez and Claire's bedroom. The room is light-filled and magazine-bright, the bed plump with pillows and cushions and covered in patterned throws. Dark green walls, silk lampshades, a sheepskin on the floor. The air is cool, and there is a scent of fresh flowers.

I step into their en suite bathroom. My fingers feel for a switch, but instead, soft lights appear in the walls, sensing my presence. I place my hands under the tap and water appears, the temperature perfect. The hand wash in a glass pump-bottle smells of tangerine peel. I look around for a towel, but seeing nothing, I try the drawer under the sink.

There are no towels in there, though. Just bottles. Dark brown pill bottles with white plastic lids. Rows and rows of them, packed tight in the drawer, neat as an army. I stare at them, stunned. This is no normal family medicine cupboard, with half-full bottles of Calpol, cough mixture, plasters adorned with cartoon characters. This looks like the inside of a pharmacy.

I pick the bottles up one by one and hold them up to the light. They don't have prescription labels. Surely if they were prescribed, they would say for whom? The drug names don't mean anything to me, either. *Diazepam, temazepam, zopiclone.*

Behind the bottles, there is something else. A paper pill packet shoved right at the back of the drawer. I lever it out with my fingernail.

As I do, I can see that it is a packet of contraceptive pills. They are the ones I use myself. I recognise the purple stripe on the side of the box.

Unlike the bottles, though, this packet does have a pharmacy label, peeling at one edge. I turn the box over to read it.

When I see the name, I nearly drop the box. This can't be right.

It says these pills were prescribed to Sophie Blake.

SOPHIE

Thirteen months before

'I'll write my mobile number on here, and a few details,' she said, taking a piece of paper. 'This is the sort of salary we were thinking.'

I was finding it hard to concentrate on what she was saying. I was distracted by her house: the high ceilings, the shiny kitchen cupboards, the glass at the back, the black-and-white photographs on the walls in frames.

'You have a beautiful house, Mrs Henderson.'

She didn't seem to hear me right. 'Yes, the house. You'd be in the annexe.'

I looked at her blankly.

'It would be a live-in position. We think that would work best, for us. And Jude.'

She handed me the piece of paper. I forced my eyes away from the extension and looked at the number she had written down. I tried not to show how shocked I was. It was more than twice my nursery salary. Was this how much nannies were paid?

'Obviously we could negotiate,' she said quickly. 'If it's, you know, not what you were expecting.'

I look up from the paper.

'When you say, live-in,' I say, 'you mean ...'

'You would live here.'

'In this house?'

'There's an annexe,' she explained. 'You'd have your own space.'

I still didn't know what she was on about – annexe sounded like something out of Anne Frank – but then I thought of my shared flat above a kebab shop on the Archway Road junction. The extractor fan

72

that smelled of doner meat. The thump of the parties in the flat next door. The scream of sirens at night.

'I'm sorry my husband isn't here, Sophie. He very much wanted to meet you, but he had a meeting he couldn't get out of.'

I nodded, wishing she had said her husband's name. I couldn't remember it, couldn't remember him ever coming for pickup. The playgroup mothers were all distinct in my head – I knew them by their coats, the shades of their catalogue-perfect prams – but the husbands were so dull, so colourless. They tended to shape-shift in my mind, like ghosts. I could never be sure which one was which, which child to hand over to whom.

'What do you do for work?' I asked.

'I teach yoga, a bit. I have a studio, out in the garden.' She gestured vaguely to the back of the house. 'But I'm not really doing much at the moment, not with … well. You've probably noticed by now.'

She was smiling self-consciously, one hand on her belly. Her stomach was curved, just slightly, a little cantaloupe-sized bump. You'd never know unless you were looking for it.

'Congratulations.'

'So, you see, I'm afraid I'll definitely need some help.' She was looking down now, fiddling with a fold of her dress. She seemed to find this part shaming, the fact that she needed help, not because she had a career, like the other playgroup mothers, but because she just needed it.

'So.' She looked up, fixed me with her steely blue gaze. 'What do you think, Sophie?'

I paused. I already knew that I would take the job. There was no way I wasn't going to take the job. The money was double what I was paid at playgroup, plus I wouldn't have to pay rent. But something was preventing me from saying yes, and I wondered what it was. Not the house – so beautiful, so full of light, little toys tidied away at the edges of the rooms in wicker baskets. Was it her? She didn't seem so bad, the stepmum. She seemed quite sweet, really. She just wasn't used to things being hard, things taking time. I guessed that it wasn't her fault. But there was something here, nonetheless, something in the particles of the air between us. Something that was making me hesitate. Why hadn't she asked me any more questions? Didn't she want to know about my experience, my qualifications? Didn't she want to know who I was?

73

I rehearsed it in my head, the idea of handing my notice in. Elaine would be angry, but she'd get over it. One more disappointment to add to her life's little pile. Casey and Tara would have something to say. I was sure of that. *Good luck with that kid,* I imagined Casey saying. *I hope they're paying you enough.* Tara would be too nice to say anything, but she would think it was a bad idea. She'd told me once that you should never live in. *People take the piss,* she said. *Once you live in, it's like you're never off duty. You'll be babysitting every night. You won't be able to get away from them.* But what I would want to get away from, in this house?

'OK,' I said.

Her face broke into a hopeful smile. 'Really?'

'Yeah. I mean, I'll have a think about it. I'll let you know.'

She nodded vigorously. 'Of course, of course,' she said. 'You must take your time, Sophie. You just let us know.' She stood up.

'Thanks, Mrs Henderson.'

'Oh, honestly, Sophie.' She waved her hands, did a jangly little laugh. 'Please. Call me Claire.'

TASH

I slump onto the edge of the bath, the pill packet in my hand. My hand is trembling, my legs unsteady. Sophie Blake had been here. In this house. Had she been Claire's nanny? Or was there some other reason why they had her pills in their drawer?

I look at the drawer of pills, then back at my reflection in the glass, trying to work out what on earth is going on. But before I can make sense of what I am seeing, I hear Finn scream.

I know instantly in my gut that it is a real cry – something has happened to him. Even though I am two floors away, I can see his face exactly in my mind, crumpling like a crushed paper bag. I run down the stairs, through the kitchen and back down into the basement, his crying getting louder and louder.

Jez is kneeling at the bottom of the metal staircase. My screaming son is writhing in his arms. Laura is leaning over them both in doctor mode, her hands on Finn's cheeks, trying to look in his mouth. The other women are standing around, staring at him, like participants in some gruesome tableau. There is blood on the carpet. Finn's face is white. As soon as I appear, everybody, including Finn, fixes their eyes on me.

Jez passes Finn wordlessly to me. I hug my son tightly, then pull away to look at his face. The blood is coming from his mouth. I shush him, put my fingers inside to feel for his teeth. They are all still there. His bottom lip is split.

'Muh. Mee.' Finn is crying so much that he is gasping for breath.

'Put this on his mouth.'

75

I am vaguely aware of Jez's voice, of one of his hands on my shoulder, the other pressing a cloth, wrapped around something cold, against Finn's face.

'Shh, shh. All right, darling. All right.' I hug Finn into me, feeling his blood soaking through my top. I turn to Laura, Claire and Nicole. 'What happened?'

They all open their mouths, but Laura speaks first.

'He fell down the stairs. We didn't get there in time.' She takes a deep breath. I can't help glancing over at the table, the almost-empty bottle of champagne.

'I'm so sorry, Tash. We were talking and ... I'm so sorry.'

I try to steady myself. Finn is still sobbing, but the screaming has stopped. He feels puffed out, like a collapsed balloon.

'I had a look, it's not bad,' Laura soothes, coming close to me. She places her hand lightly on the back of Finn's head. 'It looks worse than it is. Lip injuries bleed a lot but heal quickly. I don't think it needs a stitch. He'll be fine.'

'OK. Thanks. I think I need to get him home.' I know it's not her fault, but I can't force myself to meet her eye.

I take Finn upstairs. He sobs softly as I zip him into his coat. 'Muh. Mee. Carr-ee.'

'You know I can't, Finney. It's too far for me to carry you and I need to push the pram.'

His face crumples again. 'No pram, Mummy.'

'Come on, please, darling.' The urgency in my voice makes him cry harder. I pull my phone out and try to hail a taxi. But the app produces nothing. The first ride cancels. The next says seventeen minutes. I hear footsteps on the stairs, a presence behind me.

'Tash? Let me drive you both home.'

I open my mouth to say no to Jez, but then the hopelessness of my situation dawns on me. It is rush hour. We might have to wait for two, maybe three buses before there is space for the pram. Finn is in pain, and tired. We have no car. I have a sudden pang of longing for our little car – the red Vauxhall Corsa that gave up the ghost a year or so ago. It broke down when Tom was driving it, and he said we didn't drive enough to justify a new one.

'OK,' I say. 'We'll take a lift. Please. Thanks.'

I pack Finn into the car seat in the back, fumbling with the unfamiliar straps. He is strangely calm now, distracted by the novelty of riding in a car. His swollen lip looks awful, upturned and fat, like a raw sausage. I try to smile so I don't alarm him.

'Are you comfy, sweetheart?'

He doesn't reply. I tuck my bag in next to him, zip open, so he can reach the snacks. There's another car seat beside where Finn is, so I get into the front. The seats of Jez's car are a soft leather, the colour of a milky coffee. Two iPads are strewn casually into the footwell. The passenger seat feels very high up, like a sort of throne.

As Jez pulls out of their drive I think again about what I found in the bathroom. Sophie Blake. Her pills were there, in that house. But why? Had she been there? Had she been in this car, in the passenger seat, where I am sat now?

'Thanks for this,' I tell Jez.

'Honestly, Tash. It's the least we can do.'

Jez is a careful driver. He doesn't lurch, like Tom does, at the speed bumps on their long road. He looks straight ahead, his hands firmly on the wheel. His forearms are tanned, the hairs sun-bleached. I turn to look at Finn. He looks like he is about to fall asleep, the shadows of the plane trees flickering over his cheek.

I rack my brain for a way to ask Jez about Sophie, about the pills. But before I can think of one, he speaks.

'So how did you become a journalist?'

At first, I mumble single-word answers, too rattled to think properly about Jez's questions. But somehow, as we drive on, I find myself relaxing. He is easy company, and I find myself telling him the whole story. The story I hardly ever tell, about why I'd really become a journalist. The story about my dad, and what happened in Iraq, just before I started my GCSEs. And how we found out after he'd died that he'd fixed up this work-experience placement for me at his paper. And it was as if he'd known exactly what I was made for.

'Hang on,' he interrupts. 'We're not talking about Dom James? The war photographer?'

I stare at Jez. 'You know my dad?'

Jez's eyes are wide. 'I've got all his books. He was an incredible photographer. Wow – you must be so proud!'

To my alarm, I feel a tightening in my throat.

'Oh God.' He looks at me, horrified. 'Sorry, Tash. I didn't mean to upset you.'

I shake my head, force myself to swallow. 'It's fine.' I exhale, recovering myself.

We sit in traffic for a while, the snake of cars edging forward painfully, the light starting to fall around us. Jez reaches across me to the glove compartment, opens it with one hand, extracts some gum.

'Would you like one?'

'Thanks.' As he replaces it, I spy a packet of cigarettes and a lighter. 'You smoke?'

Jez makes a face. 'Rarely. I mean, I was a social smoker. But Claire hates it, so I try not to.' He glances at me. 'You?'

I smile. 'Similar. Journalists are terrible for smoking. But yes, Tom doesn't like it, so I haven't for a long time.'

We inch forward. Buildings block the evening sun.

'Were you ever tempted to go to war zones and stuff?' Jez asks. 'Like your dad?'

I make a face. 'No,' I say. 'I mean, you have to be a top reporter, to get that sort of gig. I only ever made it to an evening paper, not a proper national.'

I think about the time a few years back, when I got a few weeks of shifts at a national. There was a top table of reporters there – a table that had its own coffee rounds, its own in-jokes, its own rules about who sat where, who talked to who. I'd sat on the periphery, at my temporary desk, and watched them. Blokes mostly, older than me. None of them worked as hard as I did. But that didn't matter. If a big story broke – a royal scandal, a terror attack, a Russian spy killing – I watched them open their little black books and call contacts they'd lunched and nurtured over decades of drinks and dinners, never worrying once about childcare.

'You might still get there,' Jez says.

I laugh. 'I won't.'

'I'm sure you're being modest.'

Jez's smile, his absolute self-confidence, irritates me, all of a sudden. 'You don't know anything about it, actually.'

The words spill out before I even know I've said them. I clamp my mouth shut. Jez fixes his eyes back on the road.

'I'm sorry,' I say quickly. 'That was rude and unnecessary.'

'Not at all,' he says gallantly. 'You're quite right. Sorry I said anything.'

We are nearly at the flat now. Jez brakes and indicates. I mentally grapple for something to say, a way to smooth things over.

'What about you?' I ask awkwardly. 'I haven't even asked about your job.'

'Oh, don't bother, really. It's nowhere near as interesting.' Jez slows down, gestures outside. 'Here we are – it's just here on the left, isn't it?'

I look out of the window. 'Oh, yes. Thanks.' I turn to face him. 'Jez, thank you. For the lift.'

'It's nothing.'

'I'm honestly – I'm very grateful. And I don't know why I reacted like that. Why I was so rude, I mean. When you asked about my work.'

'Really, Tash,' he says. 'You've had a horrible shock.' He glances in the rear-view mirror, at Finn. 'It's fine.'

It does not feel fine. I hesitate, not wanting to leave, wanting to explain, to redeem myself somehow.

'I think I just feel a bit lost at the moment,' I blurt.

I clamp my lips together, my tongue feeling suddenly thick in my mouth, my throat constricting. I have, I realise, never actually said this out loud. When I dare to look up at Jez, he is nodding, thoughtfully.

'I think,' he says, carefully, 'that everyone feels like that, from time to time.'

I take a deep breath. I should get out of the car. I should go home. But somehow my hand, which I have placed on the door handle, doesn't move. 'Tash,' Jez says, very softly. 'It's all right.'

Finn makes a noise in the back. Something in the atmosphere is broken. I start to feel around for my bags, Finn's coat. I pull at the door handle, but the child lock is on.

'Oh, sorry. Here.'

Jez releases the child lock, but then realise I still have my seat belt on.

'Sorry, I'm still strapped in.'

'Ah. Right.'

I move my hand to release the seat belt. In my haste, my fingers miss the clasp, and brush against Jez's.

Even though the contact only lasts a moment, it seems to linger on my skin. Long after I have opened the passenger door, hauled my sleeping son out of the car seat, carried him home and closed my front door safely behind me, it feels like it is still there. His touch, on my hand, like the brush of a stinging nettle.

SOPHIE

Twelve months before

The rain this morning had painted the paths with a mirror shine. Clissold Park smelled washed and clean and of itself. As I walked through the gates, Mum called.

'Oh.' She sounded surprised I'd answered. 'Is that Sophie?'

'Er, you called me, Mum.'

'I know, love, sorry. I'm just … pleased I caught you.'

I felt a stab of guilt. How many times had I ignored her calls this week?

'So how is it, love?'

'Fine.' I pinched the phone between my ear, changed hands on the bar of the pram. 'I'm just walking Jude. He's sleeping.'

'Oh. Does he still sleep in the day? I thought he was three?'

I bite my lip. Not you as well, Mum, I think.

'Sometimes.'

Mum pauses. 'They treating you well?'

'Of course.'

'What's your room like?'

'Nice.'

The annexe, as they called it, had turned out to be better than nice. It was more like a separate little house, stuck on one side of the main one. It had its own front door at the bottom of some basement steps, a little kitchen at the back looking out to the garden. It was my own little home.

'Isn't it a bit much?' Mum asked. 'Being there, all the time?'

'It's fine.' I had more of my own space now than I did in the house-share before. It was plenty of space for just me. It wasn't as if I had

anyone else to bring home. I thought briefly about the runner. The wet ends of his hair, his dark eyelashes.

'And she's a nice person?' Mum asked. 'The … wife?'

'Yeah.'

'And what's the husband like?'

'Nice as well,' I said evenly. 'Friendly.'

I wasn't used to being around a man like Jez, let alone living with one. When he got home, he scooped Jude up in his arms, cuddling and kissing him, calling him his 'best boy', joining in with his games, even if he was still wearing his suit. In the evenings, he tied an apron on over his shirt and cooked their evening meal from scratch. He had shelves and shelves of books, and he told me I could borrow any of them I wanted. I had a pile of them stacked by my bed, ready to start. I imagined myself dropping them into conversations with him, just casually. And him giving me that look he did sometimes, surprised and impressed, like he was still trying to figure me out.

It became very important to me that Jez thought I was doing a good job. I had decided to start making him espressos in the morning, so he didn't have to buy one on the way to work. I had been practising with the machine, when they were out. I got the grind amount just right, a perfect biscuit-coloured foam on top.

'Wow! No one never makes me coffee,' he had grinned, and Claire had pinched him, teasingly, at the bottom of his stomach.

'Well, why would I bother to learn to use the machine now, when Sophie does it so beautifully?' She'd turned, still touching him. Winked at me.

'It's fine,' I told Mum. 'It's all going well. Really well.'

'You know you can always come home. If you miss your home comforts.'

'I know.' Yeah, right, I thought. Beige food, nights on the sofa that smelled of fag smoke, watching her crap TV. No thanks.

'What do you do all day, then?'

Mum didn't believe good things like this just happened. She didn't believe in people like Claire and Jez. I could tell she didn't trust them.

'I told you all this, Mum. I get Jude his breakfast, take him to the playgroup –'

'But what about *while* he is in playgroup? What do they expect you to do then?'

82

In truth, I did find that part a bit weird. Not having anything to do all day. That morning I'd asked if there was anything I could do, while Jude was at playgroup. Anything that needed doing in the baby's room, maybe?

Claire had looked up, smiling at me. 'I'll do all that, hon.' She was lounging at the window seat, eating protein yogurt from the tub with a silver spoon, her bump cocooned in a stripy dress, like a mother from an advert. 'You just chill. Help yourself to anything in the fridge, if you're hungry.'

'But there must be so much –'

'Honestly.' Claire had shaken her head. 'You'll have more than enough to do when the baby's here.'

I guessed that Claire didn't think it was strange me not doing very much, because she didn't do much either. She was constantly in motion, flitting, moth-like, in her silk kimono sleeves and floaty skirts, dancing around to Blondie songs in the kitchen, not caring whether I was there looking. What she actually *did*, I couldn't quite put my finger on.

'There's not that much to do in the day,' I admitted. 'But they don't mind.'

'Hmph.' Mum exhaled, noisily, into the phone. I imagined the air battling through her tar-threaded lungs.

'What?'

'Well, I'd keep myself busy if I were you, Sophie. Can't you do their washing, or –'

'I didn't ask for advice, Mum.'

'You never do. More's the pity.'

I hung up, pressing harder than I needed to on the screen.

We walked through Clissold Park, past the cafe in the big grand house, along the shining tarmac paths by the water fountain, the straggly rose bushes. Down the hill, past the bottom of the park, you could see the strange old castle building that used to be a waterworks, and beyond it, the shimmering cranes on the Woodberry Estate.

By the time I left the park it was starting to rain again. The trees dripped, their branches meeting in an archway over the middle of the road, like interlinking fingers. I hurried up the stone steps and felt for the house keys in my pocket. It still seemed strange to me that I owned a key to a door like this, on a street like this. That I could just let myself inside it.

Claire was at the door. She helped me in, glancing at Jude's closed eyes. I whispered hello. Claire looked at her watch, then back at Jude, then at her watch again.

'I just find he's a bit happier in the afternoons, when he's had a nap,' I whispered, an attempt at explanation.

Claire hesitated. 'It's fine,' she said, after a few moments. 'You do whatever you think, Sophie.' She was smiling, but I was starting to suspect that what Claire said wasn't always what she meant.

I couldn't understand why she wouldn't want Jude to sleep. He got exhausted otherwise. But it was her call, I reminded myself. She was the stepmum. It wasn't my business.

I heard Claire closing the garden doors on her way out to the studio. I wondered if she was annoyed about the sleeping thing. It made me feel jangly all over. Maybe I should tidy the house, make it up to her.

I made my way from room to room, ending up in the new baby's nursery. It was twice as big as Jude's, and finished already, months ahead of time. Claire had had wallpaper shipped from Italy and got a man in to hang it properly, so all the pieces fitted perfectly together. It wasn't like normal paper – it felt soft to the touch, like cotton. The pattern had bamboo fronds and vines in the palest greens, monkeys and giraffes positioned at just the right height so that they seemed to be peeping over the cot.

I ran my fingers along the bars, pausing at the part where Claire had fastened pale grey bumpers, with ribbon ties. I had read that you weren't supposed to put newborns in a cot with bumpers, but I pulled my hand away. Claire's baby, I reminded myself. Not mine.

I gave the surfaces a quick clean, plumped the cushions on the pink armchair. Claire had left some baby things on the seat, still in paper bags from the little shops on Upper Street. Among the velvety sleepsuits, tiny soft towels with bear ears on the hoods, I spotted a patterned dress, a pink stuffed rabbit. They didn't know what they were having, and Claire insisted she didn't mind. It was obvious, though, that she was hoping for a girl. I'm not sure you can expect to keep secrets from someone. Not if they come and live inside your house.

TASH

Tom doesn't blame me for what happened to Finn's lip, or even really ask what happened. On the scale of disasters he has seen, a split lip barely even registers. He does think it needs skin glue, though, and seems annoyed with Laura for not doing anything with it.

'She should have erred on the side of caution.' He pulls his bag down from the high shelf in the bedroom wardrobe.

'I'm sure she meant well,' I say. 'Maybe she didn't have anything on her – not every doctor carries around a bag of all this hospital-grade gear.'

Tom tells Finn to close his eyes, then holds a needle to his lips. 'So how did this happen, Finney?' Tom asks.

We both look at Finn. His face starts to crumple again.

'All right, sweetheart,' I soothe. 'Maybe we shouldn't make him relive it, Tom.'

'OK. Sorry. Little scratch, buddy.' Finn screams.

'It's all right, sweetheart.' I breathe into the perfect swirl of Finn's ear, kissing the edge of it. Tom starts with the glue. His screams curdle into sobs.

'Nearly done,' Tom murmurs. I try to watch, but find myself forced to look away. 'Do you think he'll have a scar?'

'I don't think so. Try to hold still, Finn.'

'Daddy, stop!' Finn howls. I feel a sob rise in my chest as I clutch him to me.

'I'm sorry, kiddo,' Tom says gently. 'Not long now.'

'It was my fault,' I murmur. 'I should have been watching him.'

'Nonsense. You can't watch him all the time.' Tom looks away from the lip for a moment to lock eyes with me. When he sees my face, he reaches out, squeezes my hand. 'Hey – it's not your fault! You're the best mum, Tash. The best.'

I smile gratefully. Eventually, Tom finishes, packs his bag up.

'All done,' he tells Finn, ruffling his hair. 'Brave boy.' He gives my hand another squeeze. 'Now, do you want to have some TV and ice cream with Daddy?'

Tom has a shift first thing, so he goes to bed early. I pour myself a glass of wine and sit in the kitchen. It feels as if I have been holding my breath.

I type out a message to Jane.

Could Sophie's employers have been called Claire and Jeremy Henderson?

She doesn't reply. I suppose it is too late to call. I toss my phone onto the table in frustration. But then I remember about the report on Sophie's phone.

I look up Claire's mobile phone number, and go through the ones on the report. The first one is a match. It's Claire's mobile number.

Hi Sophie, where are you? Was expecting you here 20 mins ago.

Claire sent that message the day she disappeared.

I pull out the heavy bag of Sophie's belongings, to have another look through them all. I feel through the clothes properly, pulling out each item one by one.

The majority are cheap T-shirts, jeans and leggings. But some other things are quite different. A beautiful, long cashmere cardigan, impossibly soft to the touch. A jacket in fawn-coloured leather, smooth as butter. A sea-green clutch with a pearl-studded clasp. A belted trench jacket. A dark lace dress, cut low at the back.

My fingers slow. I check the necks, the insides. I find designer labels, the sort I've only ever heard about, never seen in real life, never touched with my own hands. I take my index finger and trace the silk folds of the clutch bag. Are these really Sophie's clothes?

When I move the bag closer to place the clothes back, I realise what is making it so heavy. The thing I thought was a washbag is actually a camera case, something heavy and angular nestling inside.

I open the zip and reach inside. The camera is an old-fashioned one, the metal casing cold to the touch, the weight of it so heavy I barely trust myself with it in my single hand. I lift it out, run my fingertips along the markings on the aperture ring, the metal shutter-speed dial. It reminds me of my dad's camera so much that for a moment I think it must be his. Even the battered leather strap looks the same.

A vintage Nikon. This is a proper camera. It would have cost thousands. Had Sophie really bought this?

I pull out the small metal lever to manually wind the film reel, then flick the door open. But there is no film inside.

A message arrives from Jane.

Yes I think that was there names.

I set the camera down, catch my breath. Sophie was Claire's nanny. She lived in their house.

Immediately, another message comes through.

She spoke more about the boys. There names were unusual I think there baby was Bo or something like that. The older 1 was Jude.

But I thought Claire only had one boy, not two. So where was this other boy? Where was Jude?

SOPHIE

Eleven months before

Claire had hauled a load of Waitrose bags into the hallway.

'It's just my old clothes,' she said, when she saw me looking.

'Can I help?'

'No, that's all of them.'

I peered inside one of the bags. A leather jacket. A lace dress, a silk clutch. The stuff looked brand new, maybe even designer. Some had obviously never been worn. They still had the tags attached.

'Do you think you could stuff them under the pram?' Claire was frowning at me. 'I guess you could do a couple of runs.'

'To where?'

'The charity shop.' She stretched her arms over her head, her fingers interlinked. 'Need to make space for my glamorous new maternity wardrobe.' She rolled her eyes at me to show she was joking.

I hesitated. Claire gave me a funny look.

'What?'

'Nothing, I just ... they look brand new, some of them. Have you thought about maybe putting these on Depop? You could make a fair bit of money.'

'Depop?' Claire pursed her lips. 'What's that?'

I looked at her. 'You must have heard of Depop.'

Claire burst out laughing. 'Wow,' she said, putting her hand on her hips. 'You make me feel very old sometimes, Sophie.'

I laughed. 'Sorry. It's an app. You buy and sell clothes. You just take pictures on your phone – it's super easy. I can show you?'

'Thanks, but honestly, I'm far too lazy.' Claire smiled. 'Just take anything you want, Sophie. Really.'

Later that night, in my bathroom, my hands searched greedily through the bags. I slipped the black lace dress on first. I had known it would suit me, but was startled by my reflection in the glass. I looked older, taller, more whole somehow. An adult.

I found my heels, rummaged in my make-up bag for a red lipstick, a dark eyeshadow. I held my phone up and snapped, pouting like I'd seen Casey and Tara do in their Instagram shots. I lay on my bed a while, fiddling with the filters, and by the end I looked like someone else entirely.

Lately, it really did feel like I was becoming someone else. It still took me a few seconds to remember where I was when I woke in the mornings. To recognise the swirls in the ceiling plaster, the dancing pale golden light on the walls, as belonging to a room of my own. My key ring suddenly had loads of keys – front and back and the fob for their Land Rover – just for getting the kids and their stuff in and out – I didn't know how to drive, although Jez had said he'd be happy to teach me. I had started to make my way through the little stack of books Jez had loaned me, too. At breakfast, I had started to eat the same things as Claire. It seemed to make her feel better about me cooking if I ate with her. At first I found the things she liked strange, but now I was used to them. Smoothies with kale and ginger, buckwheat porridge, sweet-potato pancakes, thick clots of Greek yogurt, fat, round blueberries.

I wasn't actually paid to start work until eight, but Jude would usually wake before six in the mornings, and there would be no sign of Jez or Claire. I didn't really mind. I was used to early starts, and Claire needed her sleep.

One morning, I decided to take him to play in the garden, so as not to disturb her. I wasn't dressed yet, but I guessed they wouldn't be up for ages. It wasn't really cold, but I grabbed a cardigan from the bag of Claire's clothes in my room and pulled it on over my pyjamas. It felt so soft in my fingers.

I held Jude's hands as he stepped into his red-and-navy wellies, then pulled the handle of the glass doors. The summer air was cool and wet with the smell of plants.

Jude ran outside, ahead of me, and I was surprised to see Jez was in the garden room, dressed and sitting at the desk. He smiled, raised a palm in hello. I pulled the cardigan tighter around myself, feeling suddenly self-conscious.

'Jude, maybe we should get you some breakfast,' I called to him. 'Shall I make you porridge, with honey?'

But Jude was running off, looking for his ball. He ran over to the solid door at the end of the garden office, the one I'd assumed was some sort of store. I followed him, but Jez got there first.

'Not in there, buddy,' he said, picking Jude up under his armpits. He turned to me. 'He can't go in there. It's a darkroom,' he explained.

'A darkroom, for photography?'

'That's right,' he said. 'You can't let the light in. I mean, you could, I guess, but I'd have to kill you.'

He smiled at me to show he was joking, and I found myself averting my eyes, like you would from a light that was on too bright. 'I can't believe you have a real darkroom. That's so cool.' I instantly cringed at my words. I sounded like such a baby.

Jez tilted his head. 'Are you interested in photography, Sophie?'

I cleared my throat. 'I used to be. I mean, I used to take pictures a lot. For art projects, when I was at sch— college.' I coughed. 'I've never been in a real darkroom, though.'

Jez's eyes were fixed on my face. I tried to picture what I must look like to him. My bare, unwashed skin, my hair pulled up in a ponytail. The grass was wet on my ankles, where the pyjama bottoms were too short.

'Sorry that I'm still in my … Jude came into my room again and woke me up.'

'Don't apologise.'

I thought Jez would look away then, but he didn't.

Jude started singing to himself, picking up stones from the gravel path, looking at each one in turn and putting them back again.

'He never used to sing like that,' Jez said, looking over at Jude. 'He's happier, Sophie.'

'I'm glad.'

'I mean it. The way he is with you, he is hardly like that with anyone. Just my mum, I guess. He loves his gan-gan. And you. That's it.'

I looked down, embarrassed. I noticed he hadn't said anything about Claire.

'So, you're a photographer,' he said. 'A multitalented nanny. Do you have a good camera?'

I nearly said yes, but then I realised it probably wasn't that good a camera after all, even though it had been the best my dad could get.

'My dad bought me one when I was thirteen. I – don't know if it's really a very good one.' I felt a twist of guilt in my gut as I said it. *Sorry, Dad.*

'What's the model?'

I told him.

'Oh. Not bad.' I thought about Dad, saving up to get it on special offer from a place on Tottenham Court Road. How he had edged it across the table to me on my birthday, the red-and-gold diagonal stripes of the naff paper he'd wrapped it in. How he couldn't look at me properly while I opened it because he wanted me to like it so much.

'If you want to try something different,' Jez said, 'you're welcome to borrow one of mine, Sophie.'

'Really?'

'Absolutely. Hang on.'

Jez jogged back to the house, ruffling Jude's hair on the way. I stood there for a while, watching Jude pile stones from the path around the raised beds into a plant pot. Jez returned, something metal in his hands and a leather strap coiled around his wrist. He held it out with one hand, as if it were a throwaway camera he'd picked up at the chemist.

'Here you go.'

I looked down. It was a vintage Nikon. It must have been worth thousands.

'Are you serious? I can use this?'

'Sure.'

'Don't you need it?'

'No, it's fine. I haven't had much time for it lately.'

'What do you take pictures of?'

'Buildings.' He grinned. 'I love buildings. Boring or what?'

Jez had told me about the glass towers they were building by the wetlands where I swam sometimes. He said they were part of some huge plan for a new community or something, but I'd found it difficult to focus on the details. He had kept saying words like urban regeneration, cultural ecosystem, social capital, splaying his fingers wide, drawing the estate for me in the air with his hands. It made me imagine him as an orchestra conductor, drawing the tall blue-green towers out of the earth, the muscles in his back flexing underneath his shirt.

'Are they your photos in the hallway?' I asked him. 'The black-and-white ones?'

'Afraid so.'

I wanted to say something about them, but I was worried I would sound really stupid or basic. I wouldn't use the right words. So I ended up saying nothing, except that was sort of worse, because I could see he was disappointed I hadn't even said I thought they were good, or anything like that.

'Keep the camera as long as you like,' Jez said eventually. 'Maybe you could take some pictures of Jude. I'll help you develop them in the darkroom if you want. Here, take it.'

He held up the camera again. This time, I took it in my hands. The cold weight of it caught me off guard, and Jez's hands closed around mine to stop me dropping it.'

'Sorry,' I mumbled.

'No worries. It's heavy! Oh, your hands are cold. Here.'

Jez hooked the leather strap over my shoulder, so I didn't need to hold it any more. Then he took my hands in his, cupped his own around them and brought them to his face. Jez blew gently, his breath warm against the skin of my hands.

I looked at him, surprised. He smiled. 'It's a hand house,' he said quietly. I suddenly I felt very aware of the space between our bodies.

'Fee! Come!'

It was Jude. 'Coming!' I called. I pulled my hands away, realising I had been holding my breath.

When I turned round to face the house, I saw Claire inside. She was standing at the kitchen window, her hair loose around her shoulders, her dressing gown undone. She was cradling her bump in one hand, a toy of Jude's in the other. She was looking straight at us.

TASH

Tom watches me from the barbecue. I'm at the table he wants to lay with food, cradling Sophie's camera in my hands, tracing the shape of it with my fingers. The inquest papers are spread out in front of me, my laptop humming between us.

Tom turns from lighting the kindling. 'Fancy a drink?'

I put the camera down and guiltily push the laptop shut.

'I'm fine, thanks. Sorry – let me move these.' I push the papers aside to make room for the food Tom has made. I promised him I'd do the salads, but I see he's given up and done them himself without complaint, basil already scattered over the panzanella I said I'd make. He has prepared elaborate marinades with garlic and lemon and sumac for the wet pink slithers of chicken he has neatly slid onto skewers.

Grace is coming over today, with Ben. I should be helping Tom, but I'm distracted by the breakthrough I had this morning. I have just found Sophie's profile on a dating app. It hasn't been deleted. Creepy that they don't get rid of these things when someone dies – but then, I suppose, who would have known to ask them to? Her profile picture is a selfie, taken in a bathroom with a long mirror. Sophie is wearing postbox-red lipstick, and what I'm sure is the black lace dress from the bag Jane gave me. She doesn't look much like a playgroup worker in this shot.

I need to find out who she met on this app. If she was killed, then, statistically, her killer is likely to have been someone close to her. Most likely of all – given the contraceptive pills – a boyfriend. Surely Claire would have known if she'd been dating someone. Maybe they even discussed the dating app. They were living in the same house, after all.

The thought of asking Claire directly about Sophie makes me feel uneasy, though. My friendship with her still feels too new and fragile – definitely too unsteady to weather the confession that I am looking into the death of her former employee. And anyway, it's not as if I seriously think she or Jez could have had anything to do with Sophie's death. The idea seems utterly ridiculous. The soft-spoken, camomile-tea-drinking mother who practises extended breastfeeding, and her thoughtful, charismatic husband? I couldn't see it. But if Claire found out I was looking into Sophie's death, she'd wonder why I hadn't told her that – or, worse still, she might assume it had been the reason I had become friends with her in the first place. I had endured enough comments over the years to know what most people thought journalists were like.

I decide that the best thing would be to try to talk to Laura first. I feel on safer ground with her, somehow. If Claire, Laura and Nicole had all been so close – as Nicole had been at pains to tell me the first time we met – then surely Laura would have come across Sophie. I could imagine Laura making an effort with someone like Sophie, a younger woman who might lack confidence or feel unwelcome. It wasn't impossible that Laura would remember Sophie mentioning dating, or a boyfriend. I was dying to ask Laura about Jude, too. Where was this secret son that Claire and Jez were hiding away?

'Ben says they'll be here in ten,' Tom says, looking at his phone. 'I'm just going to shower.' I see him glance at my laptop one final time, but he doesn't say anything.

I clear the table, wedge the back door open. I find the hammock at the bottom of the shed, dust it off and tie it up between the tree and the fence post. Our tiny back garden is still full of Finn's toys, but Tom has cut the grass, and with the sun shining it is not an entirely depressing scene. There won't be many more days like this, I think, flopping into the hammock. Already, the leaves on the tree next door are turning gold, scattering themselves over our grass.

Tom returns from his shower with two bottles of beer. He passes one to me, and brings the other to his lips.

'Cheers,' he says.

'Cheers,' I say. 'It's a shame Ravi and Abi couldn't make it.'

Tom shrugs. 'I guess it's a bit of a schlep for them now, with three kids.'

I'm secretly pleased they declined the invite. Ravi and his wife Abi – a child psychologist or psychiatrist, I can never remember the difference – have three children under five. It's quite hard work having them all over.

'How's the foot today?' Tom runs his hand along my elevated leg. His touch feels affectionate, rather than professional. He'd started kissing me in bed last night, sliding his hands under my clothes, but I just hadn't felt like it. I'd told him my foot was still really hurting and he'd made sympathetic noises, but I could tell he thought it was an excuse.

'Still really sore.'

'Ah well.' He gives my ankle a squeeze. 'I'm sure you'll be back in action and getting smashed with the Desperate Housewives again.'

I make a face. I haven't told Tom yet about what I found. The fact that Sophie was Claire's nanny. The mystery over the other son, Jude. I knew he'd say that I shouldn't be hanging around with them if I was investigating them at the same time. And to be honest, he would probably be right.

'They are not housewives,' I laugh, swinging in the hammock. 'Housewife isn't even a thing these days, Tom. Don't be sexist.'

'Why are they all free to sit around and drink Sauvignon Blanc all afternoon, then?'

'Well ... Nicole is on maternity leave and Laura works in shifts, as you know.'

'What about the other one? Claire?'

I'm still not actually sure whether Claire has a job. I can't see anything obvious online. It feels like an indelicate thing to ask. Along with a growing list of indelicate things I'd like to ask her. I change tack, look at Tom over the top of my shades.

'How come you never mentioned Laura before? She seems really nice.'

Laura has been brilliant this week. She has been meeting Finn and me on the way to St Mark's in the mornings, so that the two boys can walk in together. She somehow knew this was exactly what Finn needed. It is really helping. I don't actually have many other friends with children, and it's taken me by surprise, how much difference getting to know Laura has made.

'What?' Tom has his back to me now, the barbecue smoke floating away over his shoulder. I take my sunglasses off and shade my eyes with my hand, to get a better look at him.

'Laura always makes out you know each other quite well from the hospital. That you're friends.'

'We're colleagues, that's all.' Tom turns to the garden table and starts pulling open a packet of burger buns. He seems to be struggling with the cellophane.

Before I can ask what he means, the buzzer rings. Tom goes to answer it, and I stay in the hammock. I listen to him greeting Grace and Ben. Soon they appear in the garden, Grace wearing a lemon-yellow dress and sandals, her sunglasses pushed up into her curly hair, the tips of her cheeks just a little sunburnt. Ben is wearing a linen shirt and a straw hat, as if he's just strolled off the set of *The Talented Mr Ripley*.

I get up to kiss them both. 'You two look very tanned and happy.'

Grace gives a little half-twirl. 'Thanks. Hey, I love your new hair!'

'Oh, thanks.'

I feel a bit guilty about how much I'd ended up paying for my hair. I'd let myself be talked into honey-coloured highlights, as well as a cut and some sort of expensive Brazilian conditioning treatment Claire had told me about, which had made my hair so soft I couldn't stop touching it. I couldn't really afford it, obviously, but hanging around with the playgroup mothers had left me feeling drab and in need of a pick-me-up. I'd decided to make an effort to get my figure back, too. After all, I couldn't play the baby card for ever. The other mothers all had perfect arms and washboard stomachs, and it wasn't as if I'd just given birth – Finn was two and a half now. I couldn't keep sporting black leggings and a greasy ponytail for the rest of my life. I needed to get a grip.

'Good honeymoon?'

Grace smiles dreamily. 'Perfect. You have to go to Positano.'

I only met Tom because of Grace. She introduced us when I came to visit her in our first term at university. Homesick in my halls at Cardiff, I'd got the National Express to see her, secretly hoping she'd also be having a terrible time at Oxford, and that we could spend the weekend commiserating over wine and pizza, like we did in sixth form. But instead she'd been happy and glowing, and had led me excitedly into a wood-panelled bar, and introduced me to a new boyfriend, Ben, plus a string of posh new mates. They'd all nodded vaguely in my direction, then turned back to conversations Grace

didn't realise needed translating, and I was left cradling my cheap red wine and feeling like an impostor.

After a while, though, I noticed Tom, glancing at me across the table with a sort of shy interest, tilting the wine bottle in my direction enquiringly when it was his turn to take a glass. He had a northern accent and he had made me laugh. And he was quite good-looking, if you ignored his clothes. He told me he was studying medicine, and I'd rolled my eyes and laughed into my drink.

'What?'

'Sorry, I was just thinking about my mum. How ecstatic she would be if she knew I was being chatted up by a good-looking Oxford student who was planning to be a doctor.'

'I'm not chatting you up!' Tom had gone bright red, and I'd laughed even more.

'Oh. Aren't you?'

I had been drunk enough, by that point, to make a flirty mock-disappointed face, lowering my lashes, sticking out a glossy bottom lip. Tom had smiled and looked away.

Later, after a lot more alcohol, Tom had pulled me to him and kissed me as we danced, sweaty and drunk, on the sticky floors of some awful club. In the morning, I didn't remember much about it, but Grace had been delighted. 'He's such a nice guy,' she'd whispered into my ear as we hugged goodbye at the bus station the next day.

Tom and Ben start loading meat onto the barbecue. Grace comes to sit next to me. 'Where's that cute godson of mine?' she asks. 'I bought him this. I knew you'd hate it.' She hands me a stuffed neon-green crocodile with sunglasses on and a T-shirt that says 'I HEART CAPRI'.

'Thanks a lot,' I laugh. 'I'll wake him up in a bit.'

'Yes, please. You know I don't come here for *you* any more.'

'Of course.'

Tom serves up the kebabs he has made, the home-made lamb burgers with tomato and halloumi. There is a spell of quiet while everyone eats, chuckling and cupping hands to chins as the juices spill over.

'Well, when you said you were cooking, I was a bit worried,' Ben announces. 'But these burgers are almost as good as the Van of Death.'

Tom laughs. 'Cheers. Means a lot.'

I keep a polite silence. Even though I didn't go to Oxford, I know Ben and Tom are talking about the open-all-hours fast food truck

where they, Grace and the rest of their gang used to go for cheesy chips and burgers at the end of a night out. Sometimes I wonder whether they've actually forgotten I didn't go to university with them, or whether they just don't think that's enough of a reason not to talk about Oxford all the time.

'Obviously, Tash would have done a much better job than me,' Tom adds, with a supportive nod in my direction. 'But she's been otherwise engaged today.'

'Oh yeah?' Grace pivots towards me, puts her burger down.

'Just work,' I say, vaguely.

'How is it all going, then? Freelancing, I mean.'

Even though she's my best friend, I have found that lately I feel a tiny bit self-conscious talking about my work to Grace. She and the rest of the Oxford gang are all such high achievers. It didn't matter so much when I was doing well on my own terms. But since I left my job to go freelance, it has felt like more of a sore point.

To be honest, I have been privately stunned by how rapidly I have been downgraded since leaving my staff job at the *Post*. Within a few months, I seem to have gone from star reporter to a freelancer whose calls news desks can't be bothered to return. I have lost count of the precious playgroup hours I have spent on the phone this week, begging news desks to pay me for stories they'd used ages ago. The invoices are so modest it sometimes feels almost embarrassing to ask for the money.

This week's episode had particularly stung. I'd been really proud of the story, about women being refused pain relief in childbirth. When I'd first pitched it to the *Sunday Times*, the news editor had loved it. But last Sunday morning, when I rushed to look online, I couldn't find it. Thinking perhaps they'd held it for print, I had walked to the newsagent's and grabbed a paper, but it wasn't the splash story, as I'd hoped, or even any of the other, smaller stories on the front page. It had taken me ages to find my article. It had only made 400 words on page 19.

Still, I sent Louise, the news editor, a cheerful email first thing on Monday. I thanked her for using it, checking how much I should invoice for. Two days later, her secretary had got back to me. She suggested three hundred pounds, plus VAT. Would that be all right?

I called Louise, assuming there was some mistake. She had had the grace to sound embarrassed, at least. 'I'm sorry, Tash,' she'd said. 'We just can't pay more than that for a back-of-the-book page lead.'

'But I thought you said it had a shot at the front.'

'It did, it did. It's just, we had a minister resign on Saturday, and then …' On the line, I could hear the call for a news conference, then Louise saying she had to go. I'd kept the phone to my ear as the call had gone dead. I focused on the blinking cursor on my screen, trying to work out how many hours I had spent on my story. It probably wasn't even minimum wage.

The sun dips behind the clouds. Next door have started playing rap music inconsiderately loud, and Ben and Grace are pretending not to have noticed. I bet this doesn't happen in Laura's and Claire's back gardens. I notice a line of ants, trailing from the patio underneath the hammock to the garden shed. As soon as I see it, I am sure I can feel them on my skin.

'Another drink, anyone?' Tom asks.

'I'll get them.' I stand up, and immediately wince. I keep forgetting about the foot.

'Tash, let me,' Tom says.

'No,' I snap. 'I'm fine.'

I limp back into the house, pull the fridge open with more force than I need to, and stare at the contents. Beers have been angled in between bags of veg and leftover bowls of pasta for Finn. I miss the fridge we used to have before children, filled with expensive cheeses and pesto from the deli, seafood from the fishmonger, a bottle of gin chilling in the fridge door for spontaneous G and Ts. Now the gin is shoved in the cupboard to make way for milk and juice, and the shelves are full of the cling-filmed failures of meals Finn has refused to eat.

I should wake Finn up. It is definitely time. I know if I delay, he'll sleep badly tonight. But in this moment, I can't muster the energy. I consider more painkillers, then reach for the warm wine sitting on the worktop instead.

'Are you OK, Tash?'

Grace has followed me into the kitchen. She is leaning against the kitchen cupboards, her head tilted to one side.

'Fine,' I say.

'Really? You seem quiet.'

'Really,' I repeat, firmly. 'Want some of this?'

Grace looks away. 'I'm OK, thanks. I'm going to grab a Coke.'

She takes a can from a bag she and Ben brought over and faces me as she pulls the pin. I try to remember if I've ever seen Grace drinking Coke before.

'Hey – did you think any more about that copywriting work?'

Grace first suggested this a while ago. The bank where she works, Schooners, is looking for a copywriter to help with internal comms, or marketing, or some other dull-sounding thing. The first time she mentioned it, I thanked her but politely declined. If I was going to do copywriting, I was sure there would be more exciting firms to work for than Grace's bank.

But today, before I start on my thanks-but-no-thanks speech, I pause. I checked my overdraft this morning and actually winced. Even bearing in mind the payments I was overdue for stories, it didn't look good. At first, I couldn't work out what I'd been spending so much money on. Then I'd realised. It was the other mothers. It was relentless. Their version of coffee is more like extended brunch, with endless pastries ordered that mysteriously never got eaten, often moving seamlessly into the glasses of fizz or colourful cocktails which they seemed to feel were slightly more socially acceptable than daytime wine. I had tried just not drinking, but it made hardly any difference – the bill was always split. Claire has also invited me to a spa day at the Corinthia for Nicole's birthday, and Laura keeps talking about the four of us having dinner. I am so touched to be asked that I keep agreeing to it all. But it is costing a fortune keeping up with them. Then again, I love the idea of Finn being included, of him having his own little gang of friends.

'Oh please, think about taking the work,' Grace groans. 'The guy who's been doing our copywriting is *hopeless*. We'd pay you a good day rate, and you could work from home. You're such a brilliant writer – you could do it with your *eyes* closed.'

I have had the strong suspicion that Grace is not, in fact, desperate, but has worked out my freelance career is going nowhere, feels sorry for me, and is trying to do me a favour. Maybe this is what all my friends secretly think – that my post-baby professional life is a disaster zone.

'I'll think about it,' I say, forcing a smile.

Later, when I am washing up, I spot the ants again. They are inside now, making their way in a wobbly pencil line across the worktop towards the fridge. I feel faintly sick. What do you do about an ants' nest? My mind flicks through various possibilities, like a macabre brochure. Chemicals. Bleach. A boiling-hot kettle. *Move house*, my mother's annoying voice says inside my head.

I sweep my papers and Sophie's camera up away from the ants. As I put the clothes back, I feel something hard among the fabric. Something small, like a battery, or a lighter. It is inside the pocket of Sophie's buttery leather jacket.

I pull it out, unzip the pocket and reach inside. It is a camera film. One that is yet to be developed.

SOPHIE

Ten months before

The safety light was red on my hands, the smell of chemicals thick in my throat. I made an effort to concentrate, tipping my photograph paper in the tray like Jez had shown me.

'Like this?'

'That's it. You want to agitate it. Just a bit. But don't let it spill.'

I held my breath, tried to focus, but I still tipped the tray a little too steeply. Jez's hand was immediately on my wrist, steadying it.

'Here, not quite so much. That should be enough. Get it in your stop bath now. Next one along.'

I hesitated. I needed to step to the left, but I didn't want to rub up against his arm.

'Ah. Sorry.' He looked up, moved away. I quickly pulled the paper out and laid it face down into the next bath.

'I still can't believe you have a real darkroom,' I said.

'Yeah, it's fun. And it seemed like a good use of this – well, it's just a cupboard really.' I noticed they did this a lot. Tried to make out the things they had weren't that amazing. It was like they were trying to pretend they weren't rich.

'Do you always do portraits?' Jez asked me.

'I guess. Mainly.'

'Of your family, or … ?'

I paused, thinking about Jez's parents, Michael and Wendy, who had come to take Jude out for a day that week. They were like grandparents from a John Lewis advert. They had emerged from a taxi they'd taken from what they excitedly called the 'West End', Michael in chinos and a shirt, Wendy blow-dried in a linen dress and

jaunty scarf. When they'd seen Jude, Michael had made a silly face, and Wendy had dropped to a crouch and spread her arms and fingers wide for him, her face aglow with love, the shopping bags she was laden with clattering to the floor.

'My dad's dead,' I told Jez. 'And my mum's ... a bit of a screw-up. She drinks.'

Jez raised his eyebrows, blew a big breath out from his cheeks. 'Wow,' he said. 'I'm sorry.'

'It's all right.' I rubbed at an imaginary mark on my cardigan sleeve, trying to dismiss the guilty feeling. As soon as I had said the thing about Mum, I regretted it. I think I only said it because I wanted to be impressive, miraculous in some way, to him, to both of them.

'What about your boyfriend?'

I froze, feeling a blush creeping up my cheek. Had he really just asked me that?

'I – I'm not really seeing anyone at the moment,' I stuttered.

I decided to change the subject. 'Have you taken any good pictures recently?'

Jez shook his head, sending a lock of hair falling into his eyes. 'Nothing I'm proud of.'

'I really like the ones in the hallway.'

'Oh yeah?' Jez looked up, as if he was genuinely pleased to have my approval. I'd been studying the prints closely. Most were of glass towers, bridges, cityscapes I didn't recognise, from other parts of the world. One was a shot of Claire on a balcony somewhere, in side profile, a glass of wine in her hand. I had looked at that one a lot. It seemed like a strange sort of picture to have of your wife. She just looked like any beautiful woman. You couldn't really see her face.

The best one was a picture of Jude. He was being held upside down, his corkscrew hair fanned out, his dimpled grin. He looked about eighteen months old in the picture, chunkier than now, his features still soft and babyish. I couldn't help but wonder whether it was his mother holding him, in the picture, or whether it was taken after she died. Emily, her name had been. I had heard Jez say it, on the phone to his mum, when he thought no one was listening. If there were any pictures of Emily in the house, though, I hadn't found them.

103

On Fridays, Jude didn't go to playgroup. I had started taking him to a stay-and-play called Cuckoo Club, where lots of other nannies and childminders went. I was the only one of them who lived in. One of the childminders was Sal. I recognised her from playgroup pickups. Her own boy, Billy, went to the playgroup with Jude, and she had just started looking after a baby girl called Eliza, too.

'How are you getting on, living with Mr and Mrs La-di-da?' she asked me. Sal seemed fascinated by the idea that I lived with the family. She was deeply suspicious of all the middle-class mothers like Claire. When we went to Cuckoo Club, the local stay-and-play for toddlers, Sal spent most of the sessions eyeballing the ones she particularly disliked, laughing as their overpriced clothes got vomited on and the organic snacks they had packed got thrown straight on the floor.

'It's all right,' I told her. 'Claire's pretty nice.'

'I'm surprised. I always thought she was a bit stuck up.'

I hesitated. 'I mean, she is a *bit* la-di-da.'

Sal and I exchanged looks, then laughed. I looked down at my jeans. They were actually a pair of Claire's, from the bag she'd given me. I felt a little squeeze of disloyalty in the pit of my stomach.

'What about him?' Sal asked. 'Her feller, whatever his name is?'

I looked away, pretended to watch Jude. I could feel Sal's eyes on me, like cold air on the surface of my skin.

It had occurred to me, obviously, to wonder whether it was OK that Jez and I were spending so much time together. We were in the darkroom a few evenings a week, developing pictures of Jude.

I wondered why he kept coming. I didn't particularly need his help any more. He'd shown me how to do it. We didn't have very much to say to each other, really. There was just the buzz of the light, the chemical slosh of the water in the bath trays. We always went out of our way not to touch each other. I wasn't sure what it all amounted to, whether it amounted to anything at all.

'Jez?' I shrugged, trying to sound casual. 'He's not so bad.'

'Good-looking, isn't he?'

I averted my eyes. 'Is he?'

Sal gave me a hard stare.

'What?' I could feel my cheeks burning.

'Be careful there, Soph,' she said. Then she hauled herself up, went over to prise a snatched toy out of Billy's hand.

I think I was too young and stupid to really understand what she meant, to see the danger I was in. In my quiet moments, alone in the annexe, I sometimes thought about Jez, now, in the way I used to think of the runner. Dared to imagine there was more to him avoiding touching me than just being polite, or careful. Sometimes, touching myself at night, I would let my thoughts unravel to their logical conclusion. Imagine him touching me, at last. I knew these thoughts were shameful. But the mind can't be controlled like the body, can it? It goes to the places it shouldn't, even if you tell it not to.

TASH

The photo place opens at nine. I am their first customer. I pay over the odds for the one-hour service, and go to sit across the road in the chain coffee place, checking the time every few minutes. When they finally hand me the envelope, I walk back across the street to the coffee place and tear the packet open.

I spread Sophie's photographs out on the table. The pictures are all of the same curly-haired boy. Here he is with a tower of blocks, in a ball pit, on a climbing frame in Clissold Park. This boy must be Jude. And then, around five pictures in, I find Claire. Seated at her kitchen table, making glittery Christmas cards with the little boy by her side.

I examine the picture carefully, taking in all the details. They are wearing matching aprons, Claire's tied neatly over the bump that must be Beau. Jude has paint and glitter all over his hands, while Claire's are clean. The portrait is nicely shot, the colours Instagram-bright. But there is something strained about Claire's smile, the bags under her eyes deeper than I ever remember seeing. Jude is not smiling at all. He is looking intently into the lens, his mouth slightly open.

I couldn't understand why Claire had never mentioned Jude. Where was he? Why did she never bring him on play dates? I think about the page in Sophie's textbook. The passage on avoidant attachment, the suggestion that it could be caused by neglect. Surely Sophie had got it wrong. But then I think of that tiny, sparse box room I saw off their hallway, and I feel the hairs on the back of my neck stand up.

I move on to the next picture, of Jez and Jude, sitting in a cafe I recognise as Sunbeam on Blackstock Road. Finn loves Sunbeam, but

I am surprised to see the Hendersons in such a wipe-clean-menus, chips-with-everything sort of place.

In the picture, Jude looks happier. He is grinning, his face pressed against Jez's chest, a striped straw in his hands. Over their heads, the back of the cafe's awning is visible, with the word 'SUNBEAM', and a beam of light is pouring in next to them. It is a clever picture, playful with the light and the setting, and capturing a real moment between father and son. Sophie had talent, then.

The last photo in the pile just seems to be another picture of the same scene, in the cafe. This time, though, the image has been taken at an odd angle. All the other pictures are so carefully composed – and yet this one feels blurry, amateurish.

In this photo, a pregnant Claire is seated next to Jez and Jude at the table in the window. It looks to have been taken just a few moments after the last image; Jude still has the straw in his hand. Now, though, they don't look happy. Jez is staring blankly at Claire; she is looking down at her phone; Jude is rubbing his eye, as if he might be crying.

The three of them don't even seem to be the focus of the picture, this time. A whole load of random people in the cafe are in the shot, too. The composition is odd, with no obvious focus. It is almost as if the picture has been taken by accident.

I look at the image for a while. There is something unsettling about it, after all the others. I somehow can't imagine such a careful photographer taking this image by mistake.

SOPHIE

Nine months before

On the morning of Jude's fourth birthday, Claire asked if I knew anywhere we could take him for a birthday breakfast. I blinked at her. Had she and Jez really not arranged anything?

'Well,' I ventured, 'he likes a place called Sunbeam on Blackstock Road.'

Claire had made a face. 'Blackstock Road? Where's that?'

I could tell straight away that it had been a mistake to mention Sunbeam. Claire would hate it. 'It will probably be too busy anyway,' I said. 'How about I make us something?'

'No! Let's risk it,' Jez said cheerfully, half overhearing. He was steering a delighted Jude around the kitchen on the new scooter. 'If that's Jude's favourite, then Sunbeam it is.'

A week earlier, when I'd asked Claire what they were planning to get him for his birthday, she had thrown her head back in exhaustion, her icy-blonde ponytail flopping over the back of the sofa. She was looking more pregnant now, her bump round above her jeans, her breasts newly full of blue, marbly veins.

'Oh God, Sophie,' she'd said, rubbing her eyes, 'I haven't given it very much thought, to be honest. What do you think we should get him?'

It was pretty obvious, I thought. Jude needed a scooter. He must have been the only pre-school kid in north London who didn't have one. Whenever he saw a child on one, his little eyes followed it down the street, his lips pressed together. If it were up to me, I'd have got him one ages ago, a blue one, which was his favourite colour, one of the ones with light-up wheels, and a horn-cum-flashlight

that played different noises: police sirens, fire engine, rubbish truck backing up.

Claire had frowned. 'A scooter? Do you think? I bought him that bike, and he never rides it.'

It was true that Jude hated his balance bike, which Claire bought for him at great expense from Selfridges because, she told me, she had loved the look of the vintage cherry-red colour, the little woven basket on the front. But Jude didn't have the coordination to steady himself with his feet, nor the confidence he needed to push against the ground and trust himself not to fall. Also, he didn't like red. I could have told her that much.

I decided to order the scooter with the debit card Jez had given me for household shopping, complete with light and matching helmet. I was sure Claire would be grateful – she seemed stressed out about the whole birthday thing. Also, it was less than a hundred pounds which, I was learning, wasn't a lot to the Hendersons.

When it arrived, Claire was confused. 'Did you order this?'

I looked up at her. 'Is that OK? I thought … I thought you wanted me to help you find him something.'

'Oh, right,' she said, picking up the box.

'Sorry, did I get the wrong end of the stick? I thought you meant you wanted me to get him something.'

Claire put the box down, then smiled. 'It's fine. Thanks, Sophie.'

'Shall I wrap it for you? I bought some paper.'

Claire's smile faded just for a second, before reappearing. 'Nope, that's fine. I'll do it. Thanks, though.'

As I feared, Sunbeam was much busier on a Saturday. Jez had to raise his voice as he spoke into the waiter's ear to ask if they had space. To my relief, the family at the table by the front window were just leaving. The man at the door asked us to wait until they could clear it, but Claire sank down heavily into the booth seat, muttering that her feet were killing her. The waiter had to reach around her bump to clean up. She watched blankly as he squirted surface cleaner over the abandoned plate of chips in front of her, the smears of tomato ketchup. I could see she already hated it. The pressure of having made the recommendation felt like a hand on my throat.

I had enough items in my backpack to keep Jude occupied until the food arrived, if we ordered straight away – a packet of crayons, some action figures, games on my phone if things were really desperate. But Claire stared at the menu as if it was written in another language.

'Sorry,' she told the server eventually. 'Can you just give us a few more minutes?' Under the table, I dug my fingernails into the seat cushion.

I decided to let Jude play with Jez's camera, even though it put me on edge. Children always knew what was precious, I found. It was always those things they wanted to touch. It was as if they wanted to feel their power. Jude fiddled with the lenses so the focus went all wobbly. Click, click, clicked away, even though there was no film loaded.

'Easy, Jude,' Jez said. 'That's a nice bit of kit.'

Claire got up to go to the toilet. 'I'll have the salad bowl, please, darling,' she muttered to Jez as she left. I pulled Jude into my chest, moving my knees to one side to let her pass.

'So.' Jez brushed at some crumbs on the table. 'Why was it that you ditched the photography course, Soph?'

I shrugged. 'I guess I realised it was, you know, not an easy thing to get into. Someone basically told me you have to work for free for, like, years? And anyway, I didn't know anyone who would give me the … work experience or whatever.'

Jez looked at me, then away, rubbing his palm up and down his arm. 'I see.'

I prised the camera off Jude. 'Here you go, sit with Daddy.' I picked him up under his armpits and lifted him onto Jez's lap. I loaded a film inside and threaded the strap around the back of my neck. I positioned myself about two metres away, to the side of the cafe, and stood on tiptoe to get more height.

'You're standing on tiptoe,' Jez laughed.

'I want to shoot you from above and I'm five foot nothing.'

'That tall?'

'Be quiet.'

'You're the same height as Kylie Minogue.'

'Who?'

'Oh, don't tell me … All right, I get it. I'm completely past it.' Jez did an exaggeratedly pained expression. 'Are you going to take this picture or what?'

It thrilled me a little bit, the feeling of having him in my power. 'Ah, the light's all wrong,' I said. 'Hang on.'

I crossed the cafe, stood near the wall so I had a good shot of them both, with the light and the letters on the awning behind. Jude was getting bored now. He started to squirm. He took the red-and-white-striped straw from the juice on the table, bent it and stuck it up Jez's nose. Jez laughed. I pressed the shutter.

When Claire reappeared, Jez seemed to forget about the photograph. He stood up to let her into the comfortable seating of the booth, helped her to ease herself down.

I lifted the camera again, hid my face behind it. When Jez was sat down again, I trained the lens on his face, making sure I had the focus right. As I watched his face through the lens, though, I noticed his expression change. His features flattened, his easy gaze stiffened. I dropped the camera from my face, and followed his eyes across the cafe.

On the other side, near the serving hatch, was a woman. She was tall and dark, her long hair loose over one shoulder. She was staring straight back at Jez. Her cheeks were pink, as if with exertion.

Without thinking, I brought my camera to my face, and pressed the shutter again.

Later, after I had put Jude to bed, I came down to find Claire asleep under a blanket on the sofa. The dishwasher was humming, and Jez was doing the last bits of washing-up, his sleeves rolled up above the elbow. I went to help him. There was something soothing about the slosh of the water, the rhythm of our drying and stacking.

'Did you know that woman, in the cafe?'

I tried to make my question sound casual. I rubbed along the surface of the plate, being careful not to look directly at Jez. He didn't reply, but his arms had stilled in the washing-up water.

'What woman?'

'I thought there was a woman staring at you, in the cafe. Tall, with dark hair?'

Jez was looking away from me, so I couldn't see his face. He pulled the plug, and seemed to wait until the water had stopped gurgling before he spoke.

'Don't think so.'

He dried his hands on his jeans, headed to the fridge, pulled out a beer and strolled off to the garden room. I watched the reflection of the glass as he switched on the lamp, painting a little yellow square of light into the darkness of the garden. I wondered why he was lying. And also, why I felt so crushed by it, almost as if all the air had been stamped out of my lungs.

TASH

There is a crash of thunder as I leave the library. Outside the sky is darkening, the torrents soon dense and unstoppable, buses and cars throwing dirty water over the roads. I walk as close as I can to the walls, ducking under shop awnings, but by the time I reach the play-group, my expensive new leggings are splattered with mud.

Elaine's face tells me I am late again. She is standing with her coat already on, her face as thunderous as the sky. Rain is coursing down the church roof, bubbling down the drainpipe. I mumble my apologies, but Elaine is already looking away, turning the key in the lock from the inside.

Finn is in a hyper mood, laughing giddily, refusing to put his coat on or swap his trainers for wellies. He starts to splash in the little rivers of water running down from the church steps into the gutters on the road, his trainers getting soaked.

'Look, Mummy! Muddy puddles! Jump! Jump!'

'No, wait, Finn, you need to put your – Finn!'

Laughing, Finn barrels straight past me onto the grass where the gravestones are. I dash over and yank him up by the elbow, but it is too late. He has slipped into the puddle by the muddy verge, emerged with his trousers and the bottom of his jumper covered in mud. He is soaked through, his hands streaked with it, his trainers caked.

Through the pelting rain, I glance back at the church doors, but Elaine must have gone out the back way. All Finn's spare clothes are on his peg inside.

'I cold, Mummy.' Finn starts to shiver. I hear another crack of thunder, the clatter of rain picking up on the iron bike-shelter roof.

113

'Oh dear.'

I look up and see Sal. She is wearing grey tracksuit bottoms and a cheap-looking waterproof parka. Her hair is pulled back, her make-up-free face puffy and threaded with burst blood vessels.

'Yes, ahem. Bit of a disaster.' I have to shout over the rain. I feel flustered, caught out in my inept parenting. 'I think I'll just ... call a taxi.'

'A what?'

'A taxi. I'll get an Uber.'

Sal looks us up and down. 'An Uber won't let him in like that.'

'Flag a black cab, then.'

'Oh yeah? Where do you reckon we are, Piccadilly Circus?'

The wind picks up. All of Sal's charges are appropriately dressed. Eliza, Christina's daughter, is dressed in a neat yellow raincoat and boots, holding one side of the double buggy. A blond boy of about six on the other side is wearing a waterproof Spider-Man onesie and wellies.

'Bring him over to mine,' Sal says, looking at Finn. 'Don't want him getting cold. I'm only over the road.'

'Oh, it's fine, I, er ...'

Sal's hard gaze moves from Finn's face to mine. 'It's Tash, innit?' she says. 'I'm Sal. Come on. I need a word with you, anyway.'

I follow Sal to the housing estate at the side of the park. Hers is the last ground floor flat, an empty washing line swinging in the front. There is a gurgle of rainwater, a splash of overflowing drainpipes. A ginger cat is asleep on a plastic chair under the shelter by the front door.

Sal opens the door and shoves her buggy inside, and I follow with mine. There are toys all over the floor, clothes strewn over sofa arms and the backs of chairs. A plastic table is set out with poster paints in garish colours and pots of the sort of glitter I hate getting out at home in case Finn makes a mess.

'Sorry about all the crap everywhere.' Sal pulls her stretchy top down over her midriff, then reaches into her buggy and hands me a pack of baby wipes for Finn's hands. I take them, gratefully. She then pulls out a packet of chocolate buttons, takes a handful for Eliza and the blond boy in the Spider-Man get-up – 'This is my son Billy. Say hello, Billy' – then hands Finn the rest without asking me. Finn's eyes go wide. He tips them all into his mouth before I can object.

Sal unclips the twins from their buggy and sets them on the floor with a crate full of noisy plastic toys. The boy starts to mash the

buttons of one with his palms, and the girl takes a small tambourine and starts staggering around with it. Sal plucks a TV remote control from a faux-leather armchair and points it at a huge television on the far wall, and Eliza clambers onto a sofa on the far side in expectation, tucking her skinny legs underneath her, her face pointed at the TV. Billy sits in front of her on the floor, his legs crossed. They look tiny and slight beside the huge sofa, like little elves.

'I'll go and get some clothes for Finn,' Sal mutters in my direction. The twins' two sets of blue eyes follow Sal down the hallway, their necks craning to see where she has gone.

Sal returns with a colourful tracksuit, with cartoon characters on it. The fabrics are thick and soft. I lift Finn into the middle of the room and start to peel off his wet clothes. I feel dampness on my clothes too, my shoes, socks, the ends of my hair. Finn feels so little with only his pants on.

'Are you all warm now, sweetheart?'

I try to scoop him up for a cuddle but he is craning his neck around me to see the TV screen. I sit him next to Eliza, pulling a bobbled zebra-print blanket over his legs, trying to ignore the cat hairs, the smell of animal. I could do with a hot drink.

'Shall I make us some tea?'

'You can if you want.'

I head to Sal's kitchen and flick on the kettle. When I pull the fridge door open, the handle is sticky to the touch. The ginger cat appears on the worktop, rubbing his cheek against the edge of the fridge. I try not to look at the corners of his eyes, full of yellow gunk.

In the fridge are Peppa Pig yogurts, those plasticky cheese sticks. A tray of rice crispy cakes Sal has obviously made with the kids. A bag of carrot batons. A leftover Chinese takeaway, its orange noodles coiled like snakes. A pint of milk, a half-drunk bottle of white wine.

Sal comes into the kitchen, rummages in the freezer and pulls out a box of fish fingers, which she lines up one by one with surprising delicacy on a tray, then shoves it into the grill. She then takes the bottle of wine out of the fridge and pours herself a glass.

'Don't worry, I'm not having it now,' she mutters. 'I just like to have it out on the side. For motivation. Finn like fish fingers and chips?'

'That's so kind, but we'll be fine, thanks, Sal.'

'Did you say you wanted tea?'

'Only if you're making one.'

Sal raises her eyebrows, then reaches for mugs and a box of tea bags.

'Nice leggings.' Sal is staring at my legs.

'Oh. Yes. Thanks.'

'They're like those ones Nicole's always wearing.'

I feel a blush spread over my face. 'Oh, are they?' We both know they are.

The noise of the kettle rises, then lowers to a bubble. I glance at the Coca-Cola clock on her wall. It is barely four.

Sal perches on top of one of the kitchen stools.

'Saw you in that French place the other day. You, Nicole, Claire, Laura.'

'Yes, that's right.'

'You can get coffee for free at Cuckoo Club, you know. Three quid and there's tea, coffee, toast, the lot.'

'Oh, right.'

'I'm just saying. It's a lot cheaper.'

I know the place she is talking about. Cuckoo Club is a stay-and-play for pre-school children, run by volunteers in the community hall. The vibe is, in fact, quite similar to that of Sal's front room – a free-for-all of garish stuff I don't want in our flat. Walkers that play tinny nursery rhymes, huge plastic garages for toy cars, those bouncer things with flashing lights and jangling jungle animals, a neon-pink slide. Three pounds pays for unlimited slices of toasted white bread smeared with margarine, and tea that tastes like it has been made from a barely hot tap, served by grannies through a weird 1970s hatch.

Sal plucks a cloudy glass off the worktop and fills it from the tap.

'I saw you talking to Jane Blake,' she says.

I look up. My mind replays it again, how she'd frozen at the gate of the play area. The strange look she'd given us.

'You know, I'd watch it, if I were you, Tash.'

I stare at her. 'Sorry?'

'Talking to Jane. Hanging around with those other mums.'

'I'm sorry, hanging around with … ?'

'Laura, Claire, Nicole. I would just watch yourself, around them.'

I wonder if this is some sort of joke. But Sal is not smiling.

'Look, I ain't going to spell it out.' Her voice is low, now, barely audible. 'I am just telling you, I know what you're doing. And you really need to watch your back. OK?'

Sal takes a step towards me. She is tall and broad, meaty as a buffalo. She would be the wrong woman to pick a fight with in a club. I think about the anonymous message. *STOP DIGGING.*

'Haven't you asked yourself,' Sal asks, her voice lowered, 'why they suddenly seem so keen to have you in their little gang?'

It feels clammy in the kitchen. The windows over the sink are steaming up against the rain. I make a face, tried to feign nonchalance, but I feel my neck colouring.

'You've got no idea what you are getting into, Tash,' she says. 'Absolutely none.'

'Sal, I'm sorry,' I say. 'Is this – are you talking about Sophie Blake?'

At the mention of her name, Sal glowers.

'Sophie was a nanny, like you,' I say, working it out. 'She was a friend of yours, wasn't she?'

Before Sal can reply, there is a knock on the door. It is as if the sound breaks a spell that has been cast over the room. Sal gives me a final glare, then disappears to the front door.

I hear a muffled conversation, footsteps in the hallway. The rain outside, a drum roll, like a warning. The tea mugs sit forgotten beside the boiled kettle.

When I look up, Christina is in the kitchen. She has obviously come from work. In her smart black trousers, jacket, top and full make-up, she looks intimidating, which is perhaps the point of it all. I see her glance fleetingly down at my mud-splattered leggings, my baggy jumper.

'Hello again, Tash.'

'Oh, hi, Christina. How are you?'

'Fine, thank you. My court case was adjourned early today, so.'

She is being a bit stiff. I wonder again why she reacted the way she did when I suggested coffee with Laura and the others.

'Mummy!'

Sal has pushed the sliding door back, Eliza balanced on one hip. Christina's face softens and illuminates as she reaches for her daughter. 'Hello, sweetheart. Have you had a lovely day?'

'I'll just go and get her bits,' Sal tells Christina, and disappears down the hallway.

Finn bounds into the room. 'Mummy,' he asks breathlessly, 'can I have more sweets from dat lady?'

'No,' I tell him. 'We're going home now, Finn.'

'No, Mummy!'

Finn likes it here, I realise – the annoying, noisy toys, the TV-and-snacks routine.

'Finn, we need to get your wellies on now, please.'

I clip Finn into his buggy, taking longer than I need to to fit the rain cover. I want Christina to leave so I can continue my conversation with Sal. I want to ask her why she was so weird about Jane, and what she knows about Claire, Laura and Nicole. But Sal and Christina remain in the kitchen, so eventually, I leave, backing out of the hallway with the buggy, closing the door softly behind me.

When I glance back through the window, I can see Christina in the kitchen holding Eliza, chatting to her about her day, pushing stray strands of Eliza's pale hair out of her face. I wonder if I've seen Christina, in a different context. There is something familiar about her dark eyebrows, her strong jaw, her hair falling over one shoulder, dark as an oil slick.

Later that night, it comes to me.

I get up out of bed, and find the photographs again, the ones that Sophie took. I find the last one, the blurry one. The one I thought had no obvious focus.

I can see it now, the thing that Sophie was aiming for. At the back of the cafe, there is another woman, wearing an expression entirely distinct from those around her. She is staring straight at Claire and Jez. And she looks furious.

I looked at the picture closely. The eyebrows, the cheekbones, the hard set of her mouth. The small, quick, glinting eyes.

The woman in the picture is Christina.

118

SOPHIE

Eight months before

Sal and I sat on the playground bench together, watching Billy and Jude race each other up the climbing frame, baby Eliza tucked up asleep in a smart coffee-coloured pram. The air was frosty, but there was something pleasant about being out in the cold and the rowdy noise, away from Claire.

Eliza was making little, soft snoring noises. 'She's so cute,' I told Sal.

'I know,' said Sal. 'And she's so easy. I got a good gig there.'

'How did you get it?' I ask. 'The job, I mean. How did you meet her mum?'

Sal didn't reply. After a while, I saw she was looking over at Billy.

'I never told you about Billy's dad, did I?' she said eventually.

'I should have asked,' I replied. 'Billy ever see him?'

'He'd struggle,' she said, lowering her voice. 'He's in Pentonville.'

I winced, shook my head. 'Sorry,' I whispered. I wasn't sure what else to say.

'Don't be,' she muttered, brushing an imaginary crumb off her T-shirt. 'We're all better off, trust me.'

It had started out all right, she told me. Gifts, compliments, lifts to work. He was a builder, seemed honest. Put shelves up in the flat, redid the floors. Then once she was pregnant, things changed.

He made her stop seeing her friends, saying they were bitches, jealous of her, that they talked about her behind her back. 'And when they started telling me he was no good, he just said, there you go, there's the proof.'

He accused her of talking to other men. One time, when he saw her speaking to a neighbour in a shop, he waited till they got home, then

119

held a teaspoon in a boiling kettle, and pressed it against her neck until she screamed.

'Still got the mark. Just here.' Sal pulled up her earlobe. There was a coffee-coloured mark, the surface of her skin shrivelled like an over-ripe fruit.

'But … you were pregnant?'

'That was nothing. That was just the start.'

A clump of hair. A skull cracked against a fridge. Then the thing that happened at the end, a few months after Billy was born. The attack that made her hit him back. Then pack her baby into his pram, her hands shaking as she fastened the clasp, and run.

'He tried to do me for assault,' she said. 'They threw it out, though. Thanks to Christina. Eliza's mum.'

'That's how you met her?'

'She was assigned to my case,' Sal said. 'She was pregnant then, massive. Barely fit in the family courtroom.' Sal laughed, then looked sad. 'You don't get legal aid for the custody part. I didn't have anything to pay her, but she did it anyway.'

Eliza stirred, and Sal handed me her phone so she could rock the pram.

'But how did you end up looking after Eliza?'

'She suggested it.' Sal looked away. 'I think she realised, you know. That I needed money. She came round once and – well, they'd messed up my benefit. I had nothing in. Not even milk for a cuppa for her.'

Sal scratched a mark on her arm. I tried to imagine what that would be like. The anxiety, the shame. Then I thought about the boxes of expensive salads that Claire rarely finished, her smoothies that cost five pounds each.

'Christina said maybe she could help. She knew I'd worked in a nursery, like you, back in the day. I was qualified to be a childminder. She asked me if I fancied it. She helped me do my Ofsted and that. She told me I was doing her a favour, that she'd rather someone she knew. She was going back to work straight away after the baby – barristers don't get no maternity leave, apparently. And she's a single mum.'

'Really? No other half on the scene?'

'Not my business,' she said, in a way that told me she knew exactly what the story was, but that she wasn't going to tell it to me. 'So, yeah,

I started looking after this one.' Sal lifted a grizzling Eliza from the pram, sat her on her hip.

'Just like that.'

'Just like that.' Sal bounced Eliza on her hip and we made a song of it. Just like that, just like that. Eliza stopped crying, reached out and curled a finger around the gold hoop in Sal's ear.

'Sad for her that her dad didn't stick around,' I said.

Sal glanced at me. She knew I was being nosy. She looked away, untangling Eliza's finger and kissing her on the nose. 'Yeah, well. Christina's the cleverest person I know, but turns out she's about as thick as I am where blokes are concerned.'

TASH

That night, while Tom is watching TV, I stay in the kitchen, combing Sal's social media. I have to scroll nearly to the end of her posts before I find what I am looking for.

Like most of Sal's pictures, it is a selfie taken by her, blurry and poorly composed, but it is distinct enough to see that she is with Sophie. The two of them seem to be walking in Clissold Park, long shadows stretching in front of them. Sophie has a baby on her front. I can't make out her expression – the photo is too indistinct. I was right, though, I can see that much. Sal and Sophie were friends.

Later, Tom finds me in the hallway, double-locking the door. I feel his eyes on me as I pull the bolt across.

'I'll sort those bars out this week,' he says, sounding a bit guilty.

'OK.' I still don't love the idea of the bars on the windows of our flat, but since the broken glass, I haven't voiced any objections.

'I'm going to bed.' Tom is looking over at me, yawning. 'Will you turn the lights off?'

'In a bit.'

I return to the kitchen and sit back down at my laptop. Tom follows me, watches me as he pours a glass of water. 'Is it that Sophie Blake thing still?'

I nod, without looking up.

'You seem to be working so hard on all this, Tash.'

'So what?'

'So … are you sure there's going to be a story in it, at the end of it all?'

I shrug. 'It's too early to say.'

Tom folds his arms. 'I know you love a good mystery, Tash. But just bear in mind her mum might not be telling the full story.'

'I know what I'm doing, Tom. I have done this before, you know. This is what I do.'

'I'm just saying, you don't have all the facts.'

I roll my eyes. 'You never have all the facts, Tom. That's not how being a reporter is. You have to piece the story together, as best you can.'

Tom looks hard at me. 'Is that really what you're doing here, then? A story?'

'What do you mean?'

He runs a hand through his hair. 'I mean, is this journalism, or are you trying to solve a murder – a murder you don't even know was committed?'

I look up at Tom. I see now that he has built up to this speech, that he is choosing his words carefully.

'I can tell you think I'm being negative,' he says. 'But I just can't see how a newspaper could print an article speculating about this, Tash. It feels to me like you're putting a lot of energy into something that's very unlikely to come off. Do you think – I don't know. Maybe your judgement's a bit off, or something?'

I stare at Tom. 'Why? Because I've had a baby, and now I don't know what a story is any more?'

Tom makes a face. 'I wasn't saying that at all. Give me some credit.'

'Well, whatever you were saying, you're wrong. There is a story here. I know there is.'

Tom raises his eyebrows. 'OK. You know better than me. I would have thought from a legal point of view, you don't have enough.'

'Well, I guess I'd better keep digging then, hadn't I?'

It comes out harder than I mean it to.

'Let's get some sleep,' I say, in a stab at an apology. We don't argue much. Neither of us likes it.

'Let's.'

'I love you.'

'Love you, too.' Tom leans over and kisses me, but his mouth misses mine, lands between my upper lip and nose. He turns away and heads to the bedroom alone.

Back at the kitchen table, I pull up the photo on Sal's Facebook again, and look at it for a long time. It's the first picture I have seen

of Sophie with Beau. He is strapped on her front in a carrier, his face towards her chest. There is something about the way she is wearing him, so close to her body, one hand protectively over the back of his head. No one seeing her wearing a baby like that would think she was the nanny. She looks like the baby's mother.

I look at when the picture was taken. March 2017. Beau would have been tiny, just a couple of months old. Five months after this picture was taken, Sophie would be dead.

I look for Christina next. She doesn't seem to be on social media. She strikes me as that type. All I can find is her professional website, with details of her legal career. A black-and white headshot, a tight, cold smile for the camera. I save the links, decide to call it a day.

As I'm putting my laptop away, my phone vibrates, the lit-up screen announcing a message.

It is from an unknown number, a different one this time.

I WON'T WARN YOU AGAIN.

TASH

The next morning, it is blowing a gale, the stone path stained black with wet. The mothers at drop-off are hunched, harassed, avoiding eye contact.

'Ugh, isn't it horrible,' Laura complains when she sees me.

'Yep.' I am looking over Laura's shoulder. It's not her I am here to see. It is Sal, who has just arrived.

'No time for coffee today?'

'Afraid not.' Sal is by the entrance, unzipping Eliza's coat. Little tendrils of dark hair are plastered to her neck with rain, or sweat.

'Shame,' Laura says. 'You and Tom are still coming for dinner this Saturday, though?'

'Oh. Yes, lovely.' Laura had suggested this last week, but I hadn't been sure if it was a definite invitation. 'Sure. Thanks. Looking forward to it.'

When Laura is gone, I watch Sal return to her buggy under the bike shelter. She glances up at the darkening sky, then reaches into her coat pocket for her phone. As she does, I press call on the number that sent the latest anonymous message.

I feel a hot flood of adrenaline. What if I am right, and her phone rings? What is my plan then? But her phone stays silent, and she replaces it in her coat.

She could have used a different number, I tell myself. Doesn't mean it wasn't her.

Sal looks up and sees me staring. I walk over, pulling my hood over my fringe.

'All right, Tash? Off for coffee with the yummy mummies?'

'No,' I say. 'I'm not. I'm here to talk to you. Do we have some kind of problem, Sal?'

Sal looks at me, surprised and curious, rather than affronted.

'It wouldn't have been you sending me strange text messages in the middle of the night, would it?'

Sal screws up her face. 'You what? I don't even have your number.'

'Well, we're both on the WhatsApp group.'

Sal rolls her eyes. 'If I've got something to say, I'll say it.'

It is not obvious to me that she is lying. But I'm sure she is keeping something from me.

'What did you mean before, Sal? When you told me I needed to watch my back?'

'I meant what I said.' She works her chin defiantly. 'If you don't wanna take no notice, that's up to you.'

I consider Sal, her sweaty hair, her plasticky coat. Maybe she is one of those people who enjoys any sort of drama, who pretends they know more than they do.

'Is all this to do with Sophie?' I ask. 'Sophie Blake?'

Sal opens her mouth, then closes it again.

'I know you were friends,' I continue. 'Why wouldn't you want me to find out what happened to her? Why wouldn't you want me talking to Jane?'

Sal shakes her head slowly.

'Jane don't know anything,' she mutters eventually.

'You do, though, don't you?'

I take a step closer to Sal. Her eyes widen.

'You two talked. You'd have known who she was seeing. Who her boyfriend was.'

It's an educated guess, but it hits the mark, I can tell. Sal looks up, horrified. The rain is pelting down now in thick, icy rods, rattling the corrugated-iron roof of the bike shelter.

'Has he said something?' I ask her. 'Is he the reason you think I need to be careful? Is he the person who's been threatening me?'

Sal stares at the ground, saying nothing.

'And what about Christina?' I ask. 'Why was Sophie so interested in her?'

At the mention of Christina, Sal's head snaps up at me. 'Look, Tash. I don't know who's been sending you messages. I'm not threatening

you. I'm trying to do you a favour. If you've got any sense, you'll listen, OK?'

She flicks the brake of her pram up with her foot.

'Keep your nose out of it, Tash. Stay away from it.'

'From what?' I raise my voice over the rain, exasperated. But Sal is already heading away.

SOPHIE

Eight months before

I never really liked the women from Claire's antenatal classes. Whenever they came round, I was expected to act as a sort of waitress.

'Just in case people need anything,' Claire had said the first time. 'Drinks, or whatever.' She was in the hallway, plucking flowers from a long, slim cardboard box and arranging them in a vase. The flower boxes arrived every week – it was like a subscription. Claire had told me to leave them, that she liked to arrange them herself, but sometimes she forgot, and they wilted on the side for days before she noticed them.

'I'm really happy to help with anything, you know I am.' I shifted my weight from one foot to the other. 'It's just, I promised Jude we'd go to that music class he likes, with Billy and Sal, today.' It was the last class of the term, the Christmas special. Sal said they usually got the caretaker to dress up as Santa and hand out presents. I was excited to see Jude's face.

'Do you really think he'll remember?' Claire adjusted her hair in the mirror. She was wearing another new maternity dress, a soft white waterfall cardigan over the top. Her body lotion smelled like watermelons.

I didn't say anything. I knew Jude would remember.

When Claire turned round, she looked surprised that I was still there, that the conversation hadn't finished.

'Oh, Sophie. Look, I should have told you,' she was saying now. 'But don't worry, it won't be a lot of work. Plus, Laura and Nicole have said they'll come early, to help.'

Laura – one of the new NCT group friends – arrived early, beaming, her bump enormous under her dungarees. She seemed delighted to have been asked to help.

128

'Hey, Sophie,' Laura said brightly. 'Lovely to see you again!' She made a show of closing the door quickly so the cold air didn't get in, then rolling her sleeves up and asking where things were in the kitchen.

I couldn't honestly see what there was for her to help with. Jez had been tasked with putting up put up endless fairy lights and setting out sickly scented candles which said things like 'winter' and 'cinnamon' on the side. Claire had bought all the food in – cold dishes from the deli on Highbury Barn, where they measure the salads out to the gram, like uncut diamonds. Some overpriced mince pies and cupcakes had been delivered in large white boxes. The only thing Claire had made herself were some date-and-coconut flapjacks she claimed were healthy. I watched her bake them yesterday, staring at the screenshotted instructions from a food blog on her phone, mouthing them to herself and frowning. It took her the best part of a day to finish them. She had left all of the bowls for me to wash up.

Nicole, the other so-called helper, only arrived a few minutes before everyone else. By that time, everything had already been laid out.

'Hi, I'm Nicole,' she said, when she saw me. She shivered dramatically as she closed the door, then held out a heavy fur coat for me to take. I decided it was best not to mention that she'd met me a couple of times already.

Nicole glanced disapprovingly at the cupcakes – I wondered if, like Claire, she was one of these women who never ate sugar but constantly tried to push it on others – then turned to me.

'Can you fix me a drink, please?' she asked, stroking her bump. 'Just any kind of mocktail.'

'A what, sorry?'

Nicole blinked.

'A non. Alcoholic. Cocktail. If you don't mind.'

I made her a drink, silently. After I handed it over, I went over to the sink, and poured myself a glass of water. I finished it, then stood for a moment holding the cold glass against my cheeks.

Others started to arrive. Soon, a line of big-bellied women was gathered at the kitchen island, plucking the best bits out of the expensive salads and piling them greedily onto plates. Claire had set the flapjacks out on a plate at the front, but nobody was really eating them. Claire kept glancing over hopefully. I willed someone

to take one. Eventually I saw one of the women pick one up and bite into it, but she immediately spat it out into a napkin.

I felt a bit protective of Claire, but also irritated. I didn't see why she was trying so hard to impress these gossipy women who gaped at her extension when her back was turned and whispered about how much it might have cost.

When I went upstairs to check on Jude, he had fallen asleep on his bed, a Christmas film still playing on his iPad, his full lips parted, curly hair spread out on the pillow. I pulled his duvet over his chest and wished I could just stay with him.

Halfway back down the stairs, I heard Laura, Claire and Nicole in the front room. It took me a moment to realise that they were talking about me.

'I honestly don't know how you stand it,' Nicole was saying, in a stage whisper. 'I would absolutely loathe having someone in my house.'

Claire cleared her throat. 'I mean, look, it ... can be awkward, sometimes.'

I held my breath.

'I mean, is she around, like, all the time?' Laura was asking now. 'What about over Christmas?'

'Well, we haven't really worked out ...'

'Surely you have a rule that she stays in the annexe after, like, 7 p.m. or something?'

'Well, not exactly, but –'

'See?' Nicole interrupted, shaking her head. 'This is what I keep saying. You're *way* too nice, Claire, that's your problem. You need to set some boundaries. Firm boundaries. This is your home! She needs to do things your way.'

'Well, I don't know.' Claire was twisting a strand of hair in her fingers. She sounded uncomfortable. 'She does work hard. Jude likes having her around – he really loves her. So, you know. I guess we just have to put up with it.'

I don't know if it carried on after that. I couldn't listen to any more. I turned round and walked back the way I'd come. I found myself walking right up to the top of the house, where the nursery was.

I felt hot. I could feel my throat closing over, the sting of tears. A fizzing feeling under the surface of my skin. Something close to rage.

I looked for somewhere to sit, but the bloody baby clothes were still on the chair in shopping bags. They still had their tags on, the tiny hangers still in the shoulders. They had been there for weeks, now. They needed sorting out. New babies' clothes needed washing and drying before they were used, to avoid skin reactions. All my textbooks said so. Someone needed to do the right thing in this house.

I took them out of the bags, and started pulling the tags off, one by one. Then I gathered them all up, took them to the utility room on the first floor and stuck them on a boil wash. I threw the labels away in the bin, scrunched the pretty shopping bags into balls. Then I went back to the nursery and pulled at the ribbons of the cot bumpers, and tore them from the crib, leaving the bars of the baby's cot bare.

TASH

Laura has made a chicken dish with tomatoes and olives and feta cheese. She sets it down in the middle of the table beside a steaming bowl of new potatoes.

'Cheers.' Laura holds up a glass of red wine and smiles. Her lipstick is the same colour as the wine. It makes her smile look as if it has been drawn onto her face.

'Cheers.' Tom and I raise our glasses, to chink with her, Ed, Claire and Jez. 'Thanks so much for all this, Laura,' Tom adds.

I smile gratefully at Tom. He really hadn't wanted to come. He'd said that if we were going to the trouble of getting a babysitter, we should go out somewhere nice, just the two of us.

'It's been ages since we went into town,' he had pointed out. 'We could go to actual London! Soho, or somewhere. Have cocktails. Get drunk!'

'That sounds amazing,' I'd agreed, wrapping my arms around his waist. 'But can we do that another time? Laura really wants to hang out with us.'

'But I see Laura all the time at work as it is!'

'People are different outside work. And besides, we should make an effort with the playgroup gang. They've been nice to me, especially Laura, and they've helped Finn out, inviting him to play dates. He's enjoyed getting to know the other kids. It's made a big difference to him settling.'

Tom had pulled away from me, an eyebrow raised. 'I think you just like hanging out in their fancy houses and pretending we're rich like them.'

'That's not true!' But of course, Tom wasn't entirely wrong. I couldn't deny I found their company fascinating, even slightly thrilling. I had

always thought motherhood was a great leveller, but the more I saw of Claire, Laura and Nicole's lives, the more I could see how transformative money was for parenting. It had the power to magic the mothering experience into the very Instagram perfection I always thought was just a fantasy. Before I met the other mothers, I had known nothing of weekly flower subscriptions, macrobiotic recipe boxes, private family clubs, maternity nurses who would do all the night feeds for you. Housekeepers who morphed into nannies when needed, then faded into the background when you returned – changing sheets, tidying toys, keeping every surface gleaming. It made me realise what hard work my own life actually was. No wonder they all looked glowing, while I looked exhausted and haggard. I had been doing it all wrong.

'All right, all right,' Tom had relented eventually. 'We'll go. I'll even make small talk with that husband who judges me for never being at playgroup pickup.'

I looked at him, amused. 'Ed, you mean?'

'Yeah, Ed.' Tom chuckled, making a face. 'You always go on about how much of a hands-on dad he is.'

'That's not true. I mentioned once that he does a lot of Oscar's drop-offs! Once!'

'Hmm. Well, anyway, you did find him watching porn that time remember, so maybe he's not a hundred per cent perfect.'

I frown. 'Tom! I didn't say it was porn!'

Tom looked at my face and burst out laughing.

'Oh, Tash,' he said. 'From the way you described it, that was *one hundred per cent* porn he was watching.'

Jez is in a shirt and no tie, a new splash of designer stubble on his cheeks. 'Yes, this looks great, Laura,' he says. Laura smiles, waves her hand over the food.

'It was easy. I just went to Sainsbury's. It's all out of a packet.'

'I saw you buying it in the deli on Highbury Barn,' Claire mutters. 'Where everything costs a fortune.'

Heads snap up, eyes fix on Claire. She looks unusually severe in her black dress, her hair tied up.

'Sorry,' Claire mutters. 'It – it all looks lovely. Cheers, everyone. Nice to meet you, Tom.' When she leans forward to lift her glass, her dress slips from her bony shoulder.

'Yes, cheers, Tom,' Jez says. Both their eyes seem fixed on Tom for just a beat too long. I wonder why they seem so interested in him.

Ed has already started eating. He spears a potato with his fork and transfers it straight into his mouth without touching his plate. 'Cheers,' he says, looking up. 'Nice to have you all over.'

Laura starts to serve with a large silver spoon, but drops it onto a plate as she leans over. The clanging noise makes me jump and grab onto Tom, my pulse racing, fingers digging into the flesh of his leg.

Jez catches my eye over the table, lowers his voice. 'You OK, Tash?'

'Fine. Yes, fine. Sorry.'

Tom reaches for my hand under the table, and I take it.

I haven't actually told Tom about the latest threatening message yet, the one Sal denies that she sent. I wanted to let things settle a bit, after we argued the other night. In the meantime, I need to get a grip, stop jumping at everything.

'More wine, anyone?' Laura is asking, now. 'Tash and Tom brought this lovely … Oh, I'm not sure what that is.'

'It's a Cabernet Sauvignon,' I say, slightly defensively. It is a nice bottle. It cost us thirty pounds. I have also had my hair blow-dried, and my petrol-blue dress is new, although I told Tom I'd had it for ages.

'Of course. So, Tash, how's work?'

'Fine,' I say. 'Quite hard work, actually. I was complaining to Jez the other day.'

I say it without thinking, then immediately regret it, feeling the dreaded rise of colour underneath the skin on my neck. Tom doesn't look up, but I am sure I feel one or two curious glances in my direction. When I risk a glance up, Jez is smiling at me across the table.

'I was telling her she mustn't give it up,' he says.

Now, Tom looks up at me. I've never mentioned anything to him about giving up journalism. I shake my head slightly, tell him with my eyes that we'll discuss it later.

'What sort of journalism is it you do anyway, Tash? Magaziney stuff?' Ed asks his question through a napkin. He seems to be in a hurry to eat.

'No. I was a news reporter.'

He places the napkin down. 'Crikey. You're not doing an article on us, are you?' Ed laughs at his own joke.

134

'Tash works for the national press, mate,' Jez interjects. 'I'm really not sure your life is interesting enough for her.' He leans over to fill my glass, catching my gaze and rolling his eyes in Ed's direction. I find myself smiling back gratefully, tilting my glass in his direction.

'What about you, Ed?' I ask. 'I think Laura told me you worked in the City?'

According to Ed's last LinkedIn update – I have, of course, googled everyone here extensively – he works at the same investment bank as Grace, as a trader. I'm intrigued as to how he manages to work from home in such a high-powered job. Grace is always complaining about the bank's hours.

'Nah, I left there a while back. I work with Jez now, doing his financial stuff.'

I glance at Jez, hoping he'll elaborate, but he is staring into his wine, swirling it in the glass.

'Tom, can I get you some potatoes?' Laura is speaking more loudly than she needs to, like she wants us to change the subject, or stop looking at Ed, who looks like he might be a bit drunk. He is pushing a potato around his plate with his fork in his right hand, scowling as it keeps eluding him.

Laura gestures to Tom to hold up his plate, like a child.

'So, Tom.' Ed turns to him, speaking slightly too loudly. 'You're the one who took Laura's training post, is that right?'

I try and work out whether Ed has just made an honestly misjudged joke, or whether there is a vein of passive aggression beneath the remark. Tom looks intensely uncomfortable. Laura glares at Ed, the corners of her red-painted mouth downturned.

'Ed! It wasn't my training post. Obviously.'

Tom is smiling tightly. 'I was very fortunate to get it,' he says. 'Most doctors don't get one first time.'

'I bet you did, though, didn't you?' Ed persists. 'Oxbridge boy, I'm guessing?'

Tom blinks. When he speaks, his voice is glacial. 'I did go to Oxford, yes.'

After an awkward moment, Laura breaks the impasse. 'Oh, Ed!' she says. 'Stop being so silly! Tom's a complete superstar. We're bloody lucky to have him. He'll almost certainly get consultancy next year and he'll deserve it.' She gives a modest little smile. 'I was

disappointed not to get the post, but it worked out for the best – you know it did, Ed. We both needed more flexible hours, you see, with Oscar. I wouldn't have been able to commit to it as fully, not while he's little. There's always more time to, you know – "lean in", or whatever the phrase is!'

Laura forces a laugh, shoots a supportive smile at Tom, but I notice that Tom drops his gaze from hers at the earliest possible moment. I wonder why Tom never mentioned that he and Laura were in competition for his training post. Maybe that's why she always seems to make him feel so awkward.

'Tash, more wine?' Laura is tilting the neck of the bottle towards my glass, even though Jez just filled it up.

'No thanks.' Laura doesn't seem to hear me. She tilts the bottle so much that it glugs, filling my glass nearly all the way to the top.

After dinner we take our drinks into the front room. Laura has lit a fire. I find myself looking at the wedding picture on their mantelpiece. Laura looks beautiful, and I'm struck by how handsome the younger Ed looks in the photograph, too. In his dapper suit, he reminds me of a band member from the Britpop era.

'We met at a gig in our first term of uni,' Laura says, seeing me looking at the picture. 'I was a fresher, and he was playing the bass guitar. I was smitten. Tragic, isn't it? Think how much shagging around we both missed out on.'

I laugh. 'Tom and I met when we were students, too. Although not at the same uni. I wasn't at Oxford.' I don't know why I'm making such a point of it. I clamp my lips shut, and ease myself down onto Laura's red sofa.

'Whoops!' Laura wobbles down beside me. 'I feel a bit tipsy! It's that wine you brought. Too delicious!'

'I'm glad,' I say, even though she is clearly overcompensating on the wine front.

'I love your dress by the way. Is it new?'

'It might be,' I whisper. 'Don't tell Tom.'

'It's very hot.' She nods, approvingly. 'Don't worry. Your secret's safe with me.'

Claire is in Laura's kitchen, making coffee. Tom, Jez and Ed are standing around the vinyl player, chatting about some band I've never heard of. I glance nervously at Tom, but the awkwardness with Ed

seems to have passed. They look like they are getting on well enough now. After a moment, Jez sees me looking at them. He catches my eye with a smile. I quickly look away, annoyed with myself for making it look like I was looking at him.

'You look very serious, Tash,' Laura says, cradling her wine glass in her fingers. 'Is everything all right?'

'Of course,' I say. I pause, biting my lip. 'Laura, can I ask you about something?'

'Course.'

I take a breath. 'The thing is, I've been looking into something. A story. Well, I don't know if it's a story. Tom doesn't think it is. It might be nothing.' I shake my head. 'I'm not explaining it very well.'

'Go on. I'm intrigued!'

'OK, well … There was a girl who worked at the playgroup, a while ago. Sophie Blake. She was friends with Sal, I think, and then – I think she went to work for Claire, for a while? She died – she drowned. Did you … did you ever meet her, or anything like that?'

As soon as I say Sophie's name, Laura's face changes. The smile falls away, a line appears between her eyebrows. She glances at the kitchen, to where Claire is. She lowers her voice to a whisper.

'OK,' she mutters. She glances again at the men. 'Look, Tash – I can talk to you about it – but not here. And whatever you do, don't ever mention this to Claire, or any of the others.'

I blink. 'OK, but – why not?'

Laura clamps her hands around her wine glass.

'They … don't talk about her. They don't like me talking about her.'

'Why?'

Laura shifts in her seat, pulls herself up. 'To be honest, I don't really know. All I know is, we're not supposed to speak about it. About her.'

She smooths her skirt uncomfortably.

'Look, Tash, come over Monday, after drop-off. It'll be just us.' She stares down at the floor. She looks close to tears. 'I'd like to know what you've found out, Tash. I … I want to know.'

'You want to know what?'

Laura glances towards her kitchen, then back to me. She speaks in a whisper.

'I want to know what really happened to Sophie.'

SOPHIE

Seven months before

As her pregnancy crept on, Claire seemed more and more on edge. I felt as if I was always in her way – cooking for Jude when she wanted to make a smoothie at the kitchen island, in the family bathroom with him when she wanted to get in for a soak in their big claw-foot tub. She was enormous now, her bump reducing the space between us more each day, so that our kitchen interactions felt more and more claustrophobic. She seemed to want me out of the house as much as possible, Jude too.

I turned the conversation I had overheard between Claire, Laura and Nicole over and over in my mind, like a scab I couldn't stop picking at. In a way, I could understand how Claire felt. I felt it sometimes, too, how tricky it was to see the edges between her life and mine. Was it OK that Jude came through the connecting door to my annexe and crawled into my bed in the morning sometimes? Was it OK that I washed and dried Jez's underwear for him, and folded it away in his drawer? Was it OK that I had seen the soppy messages inside Claire and Jez's birthday and valentine's cards to each other, which had been left standing on bookshelves and mantelpieces for months?

It didn't occur to me that I needed to protect the edges of my own life, too. That if I didn't, I might be treading a path to disaster.

Sometimes, after being off with me for a few days, Claire would see me doing something for her, and I'd see her face soften. 'Thanks, Sophie,' she'd say. 'I don't know what we'd do without you.'

I didn't know what she would have done without me, either, to be honest. I seemed to be doing more and more for her and Jez, as well as looking after Jude. Washing the paint-spattered clothes and

urine-soaked pants that Elaine shoved under Jude's pram for me to deal with. The marital bedsheets, smeared with human fluids. Jez's sweat-soaked gym kit, decanted from his work bag. Claire's thongs and her comfortable pregnancy pants. In the family bathroom each morning, I wiped the thick tideline of skin cells around the bath, the black pattern of Jez's shavings in the sink, Jude's slivers of toothpaste and spit.

One night, there was a knock on the door. It was Laura, bundled up against the cold in a thick woolen maternity coat.

'Oh, Sophie, hi.'

I could see straight away that something was off-kilter with her. She was wearing more make-up than usual. Too much, I thought. It was making its way into cracks in her face that I hadn't noticed before. She had overdone the blusher, and her cheeks didn't quite match. Despite the concealer under her eyes, I could see they were purplish and tired. Her smile was too wide, the lipstick too dark for her face. I spotted a bottle of what looked like prosecco poking out of her bag, the edge of a squashed box of chocolates.

'Is Claire in?' Laura asked, glancing behind me. 'Or, um, Jeremy? I was hoping we could, er … have an early Christmas drink. Non-alcoholic,' she added quickly, cupping a hand to her bump. 'Elderflower. Although, I mean, the babies are so well cooked by now, a small glass can't hurt, in my medical opinion.' She coughed, looked down, then up at me again. 'Are they around?'

'I'm sorry. Claire is already in bed.'

'Oh, poor thing. I don't blame her.' Laura's face didn't match her words, though. She looked annoyed.

'And Jez is still at work, I'm afraid.'

This wasn't quite true, but he did say he needed to work, and I doubted he'd want to be disturbed by a friend of Claire's – whom he presumably barely knew – dropping over for a chat.

Laura didn't seem to be listening. She was looking past me, up the stairs, as if she thought I might be lying.

'When … do you know when Jez will be back?'

I tried to think if Jez had ever been around when Laura was here. What did she want Jez for?

I shook my head. 'Sorry.'

It seemed to me there was nothing more to say, and the air was cold, a breeze shifting in the bare branches of the plane trees overhead. I

wanted to close the door, but Laura showed no signs of moving. She was gripping the strap of her bag tightly with one hand. Her arm seemed to be trembling slightly, her teeth-gritted smile slipping. Were the edges of her eyelids pink? Had she been crying?

'I really need to see them,' she said. Her voice startled me. It came out as a sort of squeak.

'I'm sorry, Laura. I'll tell them you came. Could you come over tomorrow?'

'I'm on double shifts all week at the hospital.' Laura rubbed one eye. Her shoulders sagged. 'I need to see them tonight, Sophie.'

I paused, shifted on my feet.

'Maybe you … could try calling them?'

Laura paused a moment. Then I watched her pull herself up, straighten her spine, as an act of will.

'OK,' she said, brightly, forcing a smile. 'No problem! Bye, Sophie.'

I watched as she retreated down the road, the clack of her brown ankle boots sounding further and further away. After I had closed the door behind me, I kept wondering what it was she had wanted. What the question was that Laura thought they were the answer to.

TASH

When Grace walks into the pub, I spot it straight away, a tiny curve under her grey work dress. I gasp. She is grinning.

'I didn't know you and Ben were even trying!' I splutter.

Grace laughs. 'I thought you'd rumble me straight away when I wasn't drinking at your barbecue. Work still haven't noticed. I'm nearly fourteen weeks!'

I hug her to me, smelling her familiar perfume, her curly hair tickling my face. She sits down on the bar stool next to me. 'Do you want to sit somewhere comfier?'

'I'm fine.'

I ask all the usual questions about dates and scans and how they found out. She hands me her phone to show me the impenetrable black-and-blue pattern of her scan photograph.

'You'll have to tell me what the hell I do. And, ooh, I haven't told you – we finally bought a house.'

'You bought a house?'

'Yeah! I didn't want to say anything until it was all definitely happening. But it is! We've just exchanged! And it's really near you, in Highbury!'

Grace starts flicking through a gallery of pictures from an estate agent's site. It is a small Victorian terrace, three bedrooms – 'The third is just a box room really – but we could do the loft one day, I think.' There is a lovely bright window at the front, an apple tree in the over-grown garden. I push away a familiar stab of envy.

'It's perfect,' I tell her.

141

'We're so excited.' She grins, puts her phone away. 'Anyway, how are you? Is the copywriting going well?'

'It is, actually.'

I agreed to try it, in the end. To my surprise, I am actually quite enjoying it. It is nice to feel appreciated, to get paid on time, to feel I can do something so easily and well, even if it is a bit dull. And it's easy to fit it in alongside my Sophie Blake research.

'Oh, I'm so glad. I know it's not the dream, but you're really good, Tash. Everyone at work has been really impressed.'

'That's great.' I pause. 'Speaking of Schooners ... Have you ever heard of a guy called Ed Crawley?'

Guilty as it makes me feel, Ed is the real reason I've finally got around to arranging this long-overdue catch-up with Grace. It had nagged at me how weird Ed had been the other night, when I'd asked about his job at Laura's dinner. I checked again after I went home. As I thought, his LinkedIn profile claimed he still worked at Grace's investment bank, in the same division. But then, the day after the dinner party, the whole profile disappeared. Something about him didn't add up.

'Ed Crawley?' Grace looks a bit pale. 'Is that what you wanted to talk about?' She rolls her eyes. 'I could tell from your voice there was something, Tash. It's like being friends with a bloody detective.'

I grimace. 'Sorry, Grace.'

'Why do you ask about him?'

'He's my friend's husband. She ... mentioned he'd worked at your bank once.'

'Oh Christ.' She is glancing nervously over my shoulder as if he might be around here somewhere. 'You know his wife?'

'Yeah.'

'How well do you know her?'

I consider this. The truth is, I see more of Laura than I do of Grace these days. Or my mum, or any of my bridesmaids. I know where she keeps her mugs, her biscuits, her plasters and Calpol. I know which is the key for her back door, which of the new kitchen cupboards still sticks a bit.

'She's a pretty good friend.' I pause again. 'You know Ed?'

'Not personally,' Grace says. I can't read her expression. 'I mean, everyone at work sort of knows the name.'

'Why?'

Our drinks arrive. Grace takes her lemonade, brings the straw to her lips. 'There were ... stories about him,' she says.

I frown. 'What kind of stories?'

'About him and ... women.'

I stare at her. 'What? Really?'

Grace looks down at the floor. 'Sorry,' she says. 'I feel bad for your friend. I think the reason he left Schooners was ... something to do with all that.'

I think of the attentive Ed I see at the playgroup, high-fiving Oscar over the splodged artwork he waddles out with at pickup, slinging his tiny rucksack over his shoulder. But then another image comes into my head. Of Ed clicking the browser window closed in his office that time. Tom's words. *From the way you described it, that was one hundred per cent porn he was watching.*

'What happened?' I ask. 'Why did Ed leave the bank?'

'I don't know exactly. It was a couple of years ago. Nothing was ever said.' Grace sucks the glass empty. 'Lot of rumours, though.'

'Saying what?'

Grace pauses, rubs her temples. 'I honestly don't know, Tash.'

'But you said there were rumours ...'

'Which might not be true.'

Grace sits back, a hand floating to her little bump. She shifts on her sit bones, a gesture I remember from being pregnant with Finn. I remember that empty, jittery feeling of early pregnancy, wondering if things were OK all the time.

'All I know,' Grace says, 'is that it must have been something serious, because one day, he was just gone. His desk was cleared. No announcement, just an out-of-office reply to his email saying he'd left the firm.' She looks at me and rolls her eyes. 'Yes, all right, before you ask. I will try and find out.'

'Thank you.' I smile sweetly.

She smiles ruefully, raises an eyebrow. 'This isn't to do with that dead girl case you were looking into, is it?'

I avoid her gaze. 'It's just something I'm looking at.'

'You're looking at your friend's husband in connection with a girl's death?'

'Well, not –'

143

'You think Ed could have been involved?'

'No. I mean, not necessarily. It just ... might be relevant.'

Grace puffs her cheeks out. 'All right. I'll see what I can do. This is all very dramatic for a Tuesday night, Tash.'

'Sorry.'

Grace shakes her head at me, fondly. 'Don't worry.' Her eyes drift to the menu. 'Anyway. Can we order now, please? The baby wants chips.'

When I get home that night, I pull out my laptop, log into the dating app where I found Sophie's old profile, and run a search.

I had a feeling about it, but I still catch my breath when I see the picture come up. He is using a fake name, but it's definitely him. Ed Crawley, on Sophie's dating app. The app even tells me where he is. He is 1.4 miles away. When I look at his profile, it says he is looking for a girl, aged 18–30. Blonde, petite.

A girl, in other words, like Sophie.

SOPHIE

Seven months before

The internet dating had been Sal's idea.

'You need to get out of that house,' she told me. 'It's not normal, you spending so much time cooped up with Mrs Misery Guts.'

Sal was right. I needed to get out, even if it was freezing, Jude having to be bundled up in his puffer coat and woolly hat for the playground. Claire was close to her due date now, her frustration mounting, her moods erratic. Her belly seemed improbably huge and round at the end of her long, thin arms and legs. It made her look spiderish, unbalanced.

'Here,' Sal said. We were sitting on the playground bench, thick scarves knotted at our necks. Sal had a dating app open on her phone.

'You use this?'

Sal smirked. 'I have used it.'

'Meet anyone who wasn't a dickhead?'

'No, to be fair,' Sal sniffed. 'But that's me. I attract them. Anyway – stop changing the subject. There's a million blokes on that app. Must be one you like the look of.'

I had never told Sal about the runner. I hadn't told anyone about him. Not that there was anything to tell. But I felt like it would ruin it somehow, to have it as something me and Sal laughed about.

He'd spoken to me for the first time the other day. It had been cold and sunny, and I'd been hanging around in the cafe, killing time before Jude's pickup. He'd run right up to the cafe, and tapped his hand against one of the pillars outside, then hung his head, catching his breath. His cheeks were pink, his exhales forming little clouds of

steam. It made me laugh a bit, how he'd tapped the pillar like that, like he was playing a game against himself, like Jude would. First one to the cafe wins.

He'd bought a bottle of water and a coffee, then slumped into a chair on the table next to me. Then he'd turned and seen me, and smiled.

'Oh,' he'd said. 'Hello. You're the swimmer, right?'

Afterwards, I kept going over all the stupid things I'd said, all the funnier, cleverer things I should have thought of to reply. How I'd then let the silence get awkward, because I couldn't think of anything else. And then he'd said bye, lifted up his hand to wave, and I'd seen a ring on his finger. And felt sad in a way that didn't make any sense, not really.

Sal was still at it with the phone, hands clad in fingerless gloves, swiping through picture after picture of men on ski slopes, or with their T-shirts pulled up to show off their rippling abs, or holding a beer, as if that proved something.

'Do I have to do this? I'm not bothered about finding a boyfriend. And even if I was, look at the state of these. I read somewhere that, like, half the guys on dating apps are married.'

'You don't have to marry any of 'em,' Sal said distractedly. She snatched my phone, started flicking through, looking for a picture of me.

'Hey!' I objected. But she'd already found the selfie I'd taken, when I'd put on Claire's black lace dress.

'Too late!'

'What? You haven't!'

'Your phone is going to be on fire.'

'Sal!'

She was squinting up at Billy on the climbing frame. 'Oh, don't get the hump with me. You're only young, for Gawd's sake. You need some fun.'

I suspected there was more to Sal's internet dating campaign than concern over how much, or little, fun she believed me to be having. I think she sensed the danger I was in with Jez, and this was her way of trying to steer me away from the rocks. I didn't think she had any cause for concern. I wasn't stupid. I knew what the boundaries were. I wasn't a child. I knew that thinking and doing were two very different things.

146

That night, I lay on my bed in the annexe, flicking through the faces of unknown men on the app. Flick, flick, flick. No one.

Then, suddenly, I found him. I would have known him anywhere. The eyes, the dark lashes. He looked so different to the others. Hardly anything on his profile. None of the usual nonsense. It was the runner.

I looked at his location. Barely a mile away. It had to be him. But I'd seen him wearing a ring. Why was he on here? Was he separated, perhaps? Divorced?

I took a breath, and swiped right, left my phone on in case he replied. As I went to sleep, I imagined the whole thing. We'd go to the pub on Highbury Barn for our first date, or a walk on the Heath. I would casually mention his name in front of Jez, and then I would watch him be forced to think about me with another man. Touching him, kissing him, possibly fucking him, with the black lace dress hiked up to my waist. I wanted to see it on Jez's face. I wanted to light the match of it underneath him, and watch how brightly it burned.

TASH

Laura finally agrees to meet me the following week. I am relieved when she suggests her house. The terrible weather has continued, and going anywhere feels pointless. Plus, in a grim verdict on our finances, Tom says we have to stick to twelve pounds each per day for the rest of the month. My bank balance can't take many more unnecessary cappuccinos.

'Claire doesn't know you're talking to me, then,' I say gently.

Laura bites her lip. 'No,' she admits. 'She doesn't.'

'I see.' I need to tread carefully here, start with the easy parts.

'Did Claire hire Sophie when Beau was born?'

Laura shakes her head. 'They already had Sophie before Beau came along. Sophie was hired to look after Jude.'

'Jude?'

Laura stares at me. 'Yes, Jude, Claire's stepson. Jez's son from his first marriage. Sophie was hired to look after Jude, then help Claire with Beau when he was a new baby.'

Laura is talking as if I must know who Jude is. But he's never been around when I've visited. Not that I'm aware of, anyway.

'Did you know Jude's mother died?'

I frown.

'Jez's first wife,' Laura says. 'Her name was Emily. She was a lawyer, brilliant apparently. They found the cancer when Emily was pregnant with Jude – one of the blood tests picked it up. She insisted on holding off chemo to have him. She left it too late.'

I set my pen down. 'Oh God. That's terrible.' I pause. 'Laura – Claire doesn't seem to mention Jude much.' Ever, in fact, I think. 'How old

is he? Does he still live with them? I wondered if he was at boarding school or –'

'Oh, no,' Laura says, shaking her head as if this was a ridiculous idea. 'Jude wouldn't go to a ... he's six this month. He's at home.'

I take this in. 'OK. But I never see him. Claire doesn't bring him to play dates, or the park – and I've never met him, or heard her talk about him. Have you ever ... found that a bit odd?'

Laura looks away. 'I don't know. I guess he's at home less in the day, now that he goes to school. He goes to a private place, over in Barnsbury. I think he does after-school clubs, that sort of thing.'

I nod, but it doesn't feel like a whole explanation to me. I think again about Sophie's childcare textbook, her concerns about him. Laura's cleaner appears in the hallway and starts vacuuming the stairs, yanking the Hoover up behind her.

'So after Emily died ... ?'

'Jez met Claire. Claire moved into the house.'

'The house that was Jez and Emily's?'

Laura makes a face. 'Yeah, I know. They married within months. Claire adopted Jude. Jez had been getting his parents to look after Jude while he worked – they adore him, the grandparents – but Claire told Jez she didn't want their help. She wanted to do everything herself. She was madly in love, determined to make it all work, she told me.'

'And then?'

Laura looks down. 'And then it was hard, she said. Jude was difficult – probably grieving his mother on some level, although he was so little. Claire didn't know how to manage it, how to manage him. You remember what it's like before you've had your own. You don't know what to do with them.'

'That's why she got Sophie?'

'That's right. When Jude turned two, Claire and Jez started him at the playgroup. Sophie was his key person. She seemed to be able to relate to Jude like no one else could. Jez said that if Claire didn't want the grandparents around to help, then maybe she should ask this Sophie person Jude was always talking about whether she'd come and work for them, full-time, as a live-in nanny.'

'What was Sophie like?'

'She was really nice.' Laura sounds a little choked. 'She was lovely.'

The kettle boils and flicks off. Laura stares at it, as if she has forgotten what it is doing. She eventually stands and makes two instant coffees, slopping the milk in without much attention.

'Do you know what happened the night she died?' I ask. 'At her inquest, it said she was seen at a party in the Angel, and then she wasn't seen after that.'

Laura plays with her hands. 'It was Jez's fortieth,' she says quietly. 'They'd hired out an art gallery near the Angel. It was an amazing party.'

I stare at her. 'Hang on – it was Jez's party? You were there? You – and Ed?'

Laura blinks. 'Yes, we were. All Claire's friends were there. Sorry. I thought you'd have known that. We all had to talk to the police, afterwards.' There is a waver in Laura's voice. It has got under her skin, her family's brush with horror. I think again about what Grace said about Ed. I wonder how much Laura knows about it. Or whether there had been anything on Ed's record. Whether the police ever suspected him.

'Did you see Sophie that night?'

Laura shakes her head. 'Hardly. She only stayed a bit. Then she took the boys back to the house. Claire didn't stay late at the party either – I think she had one of her migraines.'

So Claire left early. Went back to the house. Sophie was there. They were there, alone, that night. Did the police think this was suspicious, that they'd been alone together in the house before Sophie disappeared?

'Claire told us that when she got in, Sophie seemed totally normal,' Laura says. 'Claire said goodnight to her, and went to bed. Then Jez came home later and went to sleep in the spare room, and didn't see either of them.'

I try not to betray my shock. Surely this means neither Claire nor Jez had a proper alibi for a good part of the night Sophie died. Only each other. Surely the police must have thought this worth investigating?

'The next morning,' Laura continues, 'Sophie was gone. And someone – someone found her in the wetlands a couple of days later. I mean, poor Claire and Jez. They were beside themselves.'

Laura is shaking her head a little, as if she still can't quite believe it. 'Such a terrible thing. And it was extra horrible for Claire and Jez because ... well, because of how things were left, at her inquest.'

'What do you mean?'

Laura hesitates. 'I mean, don't say that I said this,' she says. 'The coroner said she probably went swimming and drowned. Claire and Jez said it was a hobby of hers – the wild swimming thing. So I'm sure that's right, I'm not suggesting ...' Laura scratches at a patch of dry skin on her wrist. 'I just ... I think some people felt that the evidence made it seem like it wasn't clear whether ... whether it was really an accident or not.'

'What do you think?'

Laura starts fiddling with her cuff again. 'I don't know,' she admits.

'Did Sophie ever mention a boyfriend, or anything like that?'

Laura looks away, considers this. 'I think Claire thought she'd been seeing someone. The police asked us all a lot about that. But I never heard about him. And Claire had no idea who it was.'

There is no way around it, then. It sounds like the only person who really knew Sophie was Sal.

'Laura, when you told me a while ago to steer clear of Sal – what did you mean?'

Laura shifts in her chair. 'I shouldn't really say. But just between us – I think Sal has got some ... mental health issues. It's very sad.' Laura hesitates. 'Why do you ask about Sal, Tash?'

'I just wondered if she was worth talking to.' I pause. 'Look, Laura, I'm sorry. I had no idea when I started looking into this that you'd known her, that she was Claire's nanny.'

'It's OK,' Laura says uncomfortably. 'Like I said, I'm happy to talk about it – I just don't want Claire to know, it would be so awkward.' She makes a face. 'I know it sounds strange – but after the inquest, Claire told me and Nicole she didn't want to speak about Sophie any more. Not ever.'

'Why not?'

'She said she found it too upsetting. Someone mentioned Sophie's name once after that, and honestly, Tash – Claire had – I'd class it as a full panic attack.'

'Oh. That seems kind of extreme.' I wonder if there's a possibility Laura could be exaggerating.

Laura purses her lips. 'Look. Claire is quite sensitive. It's not my place to say but ... well, I'm sure you can see she is a ... fragile sort of person. After Beau was born she was ... well, I imagine she will share

151

that with you, when she is ready.' She pushes her hair behind one ear. 'I think the reason she is sensitive is that one of the police officers once insinuated something to Claire, that was the impression I got. Something that made her ... feel she was being accused of something.'

'Of having something to do with Sophie's death, you mean?'

Laura nods. 'It's ridiculous, obviously. But I guess they were always going to have some questions for her.' She holds the mug to her mouth, pauses before she takes a sip. 'I mean, she was the last one to see Sophie alive.'

SOPHIE

Six months before

It was a week or so before the baby finally arrived that I heard them talking about me.

It was a sodden day, the sky like a bruise. I was clearing up the remnants of one of Claire's failed activities for Jude, an overpriced Christmas craft kit. Claire seemed strangely fixated on this Christmas, as if it was some sort of test she needed to pass. She had ordered matching aprons for her and Jude, tubes of glitter that I knew would get absolutely everywhere, and set them out excitedly on the table.

'Come on, Jude. Let's make the reindeer!' Claire had sat down awkwardly, her belly pressed up against the edge of the table, fanning herself with her hand. Despite the cold weather, she kept complaining about how warm it was, removing layers of clothing and leaving them strewn around the house. Her pale cheeks were flushed with broken capillaries, like a piece of china blown too hot in the kiln.

'Let's start by cutting out the shapes.' She held up the little squares of coloured card, smiling like a *Blue Peter* presenter. She was trying, I could see she was. I took some sweet pictures of them, tried to encourage Jude, gently, to go along with it. But Jude just didn't like stuff like that. Within a few minutes, he'd poured all the green glitter onto his paper and started smearing it around in the paint and glue with his hands, and Claire was shouting.

'Oh, Jude, no, not the whole tube. Oh, it's everywhere. We just do a little bit – Jude, I said no!'

Jude looked up at me, trying to work out what he'd done wrong.

'Oh dear, Jude.' I wiped around him, trying to calm things down. 'Shall I just put a big mat on the floor and stick him in some messy clothes, Claire, and then he can use his hands if he wants to?'

Claire frowned. I could see this was not what she wanted. She wanted something to show from the activity: an Instagram picture of her and Jude getting just the right amount of messy, glittery decorations like the ones on the side of the craft kit packet, which she could cut out and then photograph hanging out to dry on the little string with wooden pegs she'd purchased.

She sighed. 'We're fine, thanks, hon.'

Before long, glue was dripping onto the floor, and Jude's sleeves and trouser legs covered in splodges of red and green paint. Claire kept trying to tidy up bits of his picture. I could feel the whole thing ebbing towards an inevitable meltdown, like the tick, tick of a stopwatch.

When Jude had calmed down, and the screaming had stopped, I gave him a cuddle and sat him on the sofa in front of the TV, his paint-stained thumb stuffed in his mouth. I could feel already that a bruise was forming on my cheekbone, another on the top of my forearm, from where he'd lashed out and I'd had to lift him, kicking and screaming, from a horrified Claire, who had recoiled from him, clutching her bump.

I rubbed at the table with a damp cloth to try and get the paint marks out. Then I went over to the sink and rinsed the paint pots, and started to tackle the dishes that were still there from breakfast. They could easily have been the same dishes I washed up yesterday, and the day before; the scrambled-egg pan, the small plate with smears of butter and toast crumbs.

After a few moments, I heard the sound of talking over Jude's cartoons. Jez and Claire were in the hallway.

'I'm sure she just thought she was being helpful,' Jez was saying. 'Please don't get so wound up about it.'

'But why does she always swoop in like that – always at the precise moment that I'm having a difficult time? Is this what she's going to be like with the baby?'

'Maybe she is trying to make things easier.'

'Make me feel useless, more like. She makes this face – I can't bear it. It's so obvious she thinks I'm doing the wrong thing all the time.'

I held my breath, my face stinging. Claire lowered her voice. I turned the tap off, so I could hear her better.

'She took them off while I was out and hid them somewhere! I'd just tied them all on, made the cot all ready and cosy for the baby. Why would she do that?'

'Well …'

'And the baby clothes, Jez! Who takes new clothes someone has bought for their baby, rips the tags out and sticks them on a boil wash? It's just a weird thing to do.'

'Maybe she was trying to save you a job, Claire. I think you are supposed to wash new baby clothes – I remember Emily doing that when –'

'Don't. Don't go on about Emily, not now. Please, Jez.'

'Claire, I need to go to work. Let's talk about this later, OK?'

As I dried my hands on a kitchen towel, I noticed they were shaking. I decided I couldn't be bothered to pretend I hadn't heard. I walked into the hallway to meet them. They froze, stared at me.

'The bumpers are in the bottom drawer in the baby's room, Claire,' I said quietly. 'I meant to talk to you about it. You are supposed to wait until babies are rolling. They can be a suffocation risk. I learned about it, at college. But I'll put them back if you like.'

I paused. Jez looked at me, then at Claire.

'I'm really sorry if you didn't want me to wash the clothes,' I went on. 'I just know you are advised to, and I thought it would be such a stress for you. You'd left them out for a while – I thought maybe you wanted me to do it. They are all like new, except for the tags. I'll ask next time. I didn't mean to upset you.'

Jez was still looking at Claire. Claire glared at him, then looked at me, then at the floor.

'I'm the one that should be apologising,' she mumbled eventually. 'I can see you were trying to help.'

'Look, it's a lot, having someone live in your house, when there's so much going on,' I said. I felt a lump in my throat, now. But I forced the words out anyway. 'If you need some time just the three of you. If would prefer me to move out. I would understand.'

Until I said it out loud, I don't think I had realised how precarious my life was now. What if they said yes? I'd be homeless, as well as jobless. Elaine wouldn't have me back – she pretty much ignored me

155

now, when I went to pick up Jude. I'd have to go back to renting, find a houseshare somewhere. Or back to Mum's. I couldn't go back there. I just couldn't.

So it was a relief to see it, I have to admit. The look of sheer panic on both of their faces.

'Absolutely not,' Jez said. 'We want you here, Soph. You are part of this family, now. Isn't she, Claire?'

'Of course,' Claire says. 'Of course.' But her eyes told a different story. And so did her hands, clamped firmly around her baby.

TASH

On the last day of term, the playgroup holds a nativity play. Claire has invited the playgroup parents for mulled wine and mince pies afterwards. She has extended the invite to the entire WhatsApp group in a message accompanied by a string of festive emojis, from tiny snowmen to trees to presents to candy canes. After its arrival, my phone had pinged all afternoon with enthusiastic replies. Even Christina is coming.

Laura has saved spaces in the church for Tom and me. I sit down awkwardly next to Ed, who grins at us. Claire is sitting just behind, wrapped in twinkling jewellery and Christmas-advert cashmere, beaming at the stage. Jez is beside her, his arm slung round the back of her bit of bench. Nicole and what must be her husband John, whom I have never seen, are on the other side, sitting apart from the others. Nicole is focused on the stage. John has not even removed his coat and scarf. He is jiggling one leg, stealing surreptitious glances at the phone in his lap.

Finn and Beau take to the stage, hand in hand, stuffed sheep under their arms and tea towels on their heads, looking deeply confused. Claire catches my eye and I try to ignore the hot sting of guilt about meeting Laura behind her back. Laura is beaming at Oscar, who is centre stage as Joseph, his arm around a terrified-looking Eliza, who is supposed to be Mary, and whose blue *Frozen* dress is slipping off her shoulder.

Christina looks smaller and softer out of her work clothes, in her jumper and jeans, her dark hair in a loose ponytail. I overheard her in the lobby telling someone she had booked the day off to watch the play. She is right at the front, glowing with pride as she watches Eliza.

I notice she keeps glancing over at us. I wonder if she feels excluded somehow, from our group. I think again about Sophie's photograph of Christina. How is she connected to all this? I watch her burst out laughing and realise Eliza has dropped the plastic Jesus. Seven minutes later, the whole thing is over.

Claire and Jez's tree shines out into the street like a glowing Christmas card to the world, all tasteful pale lights and Scandi-style wooden decorations. A huge wreath twisted with dried oranges, cinnamon sticks and holly is ribbon-tied to the gold knocker. The hum of music and chatter reverberates from inside.

'Looks like a nice party,' Tom says. 'Good of them to invite us.' I smile to myself. Tom hates parties, especially when he doesn't know many people. He is doing this for me, I know. I give his arm a squeeze.

We wait for Claire to answer the door. Finn is looking up with horror at the knocker. He turns away from the door, his hand tightening in mine.

'I don't want go in dat house, Mummy.'

It is an unusually articulate sentence for Finn, and he has said it with real feeling.

'Beau's house? Why not, darling?'

'Don't want to.'

It's odd that he should feel shy at Beau's house. We've been spending a lot of time with Beau and Claire lately. Tom scoops Finn up on his hip.

'It's all right, Finney.' He takes the tea towel off Finn's head, and his cardboard shepherd's crook. They look so little in Tom's hand. 'It's Beau's house, Finn. You love playing with Beau.'

But Finn presses his forehead into Tom's neck.

'I wonder if he remembers about the …' I trail off, gesturing at my lip to Tom.

'He's probably just tired,' Tom says. 'We'll just stay for one quick drink.'

Despite all the complicating factors, I am quietly excited about being invited to Claire's fancy Christmas party – even though it has necessitated another new dress I can't afford. I am almost sure that the food – and the company – will be better than at our actual Christmas, at Mum and Claude's in France. I am already bracing myself for their seasonal onslaught of heavy red wine and slimy pâté de canard, of the strange handmade presents Mum and Claude have picked up for Finn at some craft market that will inevitably disappoint.

I am also hopeful that, with Claire's house full of people, I might be able to slip away and poke around a bit. There must be stuff in the house, more clues about Sophie. If I can figure out where to look.

Claire and Jez are so kind, so hospitable. The more time I spend with them, the more inconceivable it is to me that either of them could have had anything to do with Sophie's death. But that doesn't mean there won't be clues here – especially if Claire was, as Laura said, the last person to see Sophie alive.

Claire answers the door. She has shed her cashmere and is now wearing a silk shirt, her cheeks flushed.

'Tash! Come in, come in! Finn, you superstar – you did so well!' She crouches down to give him a high five.

A little boy emerges from the front room, an iPad in one hand. He looks around six, a thick mop of curly hair. I can see instantly that this is the boy in Sophie's pictures, except he is taller and slimmer, as if the chunky toddler in the pictures has been stretched. He eyes us suspiciously.

Claire touches his hair, lightly. He flinches.

'Have you met my stepson, Jude, Tash?'

I shake my head, hoping I don't look too guilty. 'Hello, Jude.'

Jude doesn't respond.

'Jude, don't be rude. Say hello.'

Jude looks at Claire, then runs off, up the stairs. Claire's smile wilts, and she lets out a half-sigh. I want to smile at her to show it doesn't matter, but am forced to turn my attention to Finn, whose bottom lip is wobbling. When I try to take his coat off, he won't let me touch the zip.

'What is it, Finn?'

'I don't want to, Mummy.'

'Come on, Finney,' Tom says. 'Let's see if there's a biscuit for you.'

Tom carries Finn inside. Claire heads to the kitchen island, and dips a copper ladle into a pot of mulled wine. There are silver trays of miniature mince pies with a snowy dusting of powdered sugar. Ed is standing on his own, transferring crisps from a bowl wordlessly into his mouth, flicking through his phone in a way that can't help but make me think of the dating app.

I take a glass of mulled wine and join Laura by the open fire. The grate is stuffed with boughs of fir trees; the room smells like a burning forest.

'This is so nice,' I say.

'Isn't it?' Laura brings a hand to her mouth. 'Claire loves Christmas,' she adds, through a mouthful of mince pie. 'She's obsessive about it. Oh, Tash – your dress tag's hanging out. Let me get it for you.'

Before I can say anything, she yanks off the tag I'd deliberately left on the dress so I could return it. My stomach turns.

'Thanks,' I say weakly.

'No problem.' Laura looks pleasantly around the room. 'I can't believe Claire invited the whole WhatsApp group.'

'Kind of her to include everyone.'

'Yep.' Laura glances at Christina. 'Even the weird ones.'

Laura gestures to where Jez is standing by the Christmas tree with three or four playgroup mothers buzzing around him. They have swapped their usual leggings and trainers for blow-dries and make-up – two are even wearing heels. Christina is standing slightly apart from the group, staring into a glass of water, twisting her ponytail around her finger.

As I look over, Jez locks eyes with me. I give him a quick smile. As I look away, I'm sure I see his eyes glance down over my body. I hate myself for feeling slightly thrilled by the realisation that he is looking at me in my new dress, by the faint flicker of approval I register on his face.

'What are you guys doing for Christmas?' Laura asks.

'We're going to France, to stay with my mum and stepdad. You?'

'Working, sadly.' Laura gives me a rueful smile. I feel awkward. It does sound like she gets the short straw when it comes to shifts at the hospital, compared to Tom.

'Tash.' Laura lowers her voice. 'Did you ever get anywhere with the … thing you were looking into?'

Automatically, I glance over at Claire, who is chatting to Tom at the island.

'Not really.'

I am somewhat regretting letting Laura in on the fact I am looking into Sophie's death. She appears to be as keen as I am to ensure the others – Nicole and Claire – don't find out. But I don't want her clocking me sneaking upstairs at the party to scout for evidence.

'I've been really busy with other stuff,' I lie. 'And – I don't know. I guess I feel a bit uncomfortable about it all, given that she was Claire's nanny.' Not half as uncomfortable as you should feel, a voice in my head says.

Laura looks disappointed. 'I thought you said you wanted to try and find out the truth?'

I open my mouth to reply, but Nicole and Claire have come to join us by the open fire. Nicole is still talking about Lissy being passed over in favour of Eliza for the part of Mary.

'It's because Lissy's got an American accent, that's what it is.' She is glaring into the cup of mulled wine she has been handed by Claire. I watch her reach in with a red-varnished fingernail to pluck out a clove.

'I'm sure that's not true, Nicole,' Claire soothes. Beau is tugging at her top. She leans over to pick him up, and instantly he goes limp in her arms, his head on her shoulder, his eyelids at half-mast, like a much younger baby.

'How else can you explain it? Eliza couldn't even hold Jesus up straight!'

'Well, Eliza is a little bit older than our guys,' Laura says, gently.

'Hmph. I bet they only chose her because she's blonde.'

'It's more of a strawberry-blonde colouring, isn't it?' I say neutrally. 'Like Beau's.' Claire is ruffling Beau's gingery hair. She seems to be brushing it over a bruise on his head.

Jez appears between Claire and Nicole, collecting their glasses, even though they are still half full. 'Let's have some more mulled wine, shall we?' he is saying. 'And music. I'll put some music on.'

'Beau's nearly asleep, Jez,' Claire protests, in a stage whisper. She wanders off to the kitchen island. Jez doesn't seem to hear her. 'Alexa, play Christmas songs,' he commands the air. The room is filled with the sound of 'Jingle Bell Rock'.

I swallow the last of my mince pie and look around for Finn. Tom is at the kitchen island, saying something to Claire. When I walk over, Claire smiles and motions that she is taking Beau upstairs.

'Claire is so nice, isn't she?' Tom says, as she walks away. 'I was interested to hear about this free holiday in Cornwall we're going on, which you've failed to mention to me.'

I look up at him, but Tom looks amused, rather than cross.

'It sounds great! Why didn't you say anything?'

I clear my throat. 'I wasn't sure if Claire was serious about that.'

'Oh. Well, she says she is. Don't you want to go?'

'I …' I can't think of anything to say. 'Of course. I mean, I think Finn would love it.'

'Great! Let's do it then, as long as I can get the time off. It sounds like they have some huge place – she's invited quite a few people – but I guess we can always sneak off just the three of us sometimes, if it gets too much?'

I am not listening to him any more. I haven't seen Finn for ages.

'Tom, have you seen Finn?' Tom shrugs. 'I thought he was with you.'

I eventually find him in the hallway, sitting on the floor by the front door, his knees tucked under his chin.

'Finn! What are you doing here? Oscar and Lissy are in the front room. Don't you want to play with them?'

Finn looks at me, but doesn't respond.

'Can you go in that room with Daddy for a bit?'

Finn's head is down, bottom lip out. I can see he is upset about something.

'What is it, Finn?'

'I don't like it in this house.'

'Why not, sweetheart?'

Finn suppresses a sob, the sides of his mouth twitching. 'Don't want play in dis house. Don't want play with dat boy.'

'Which boy?'

'Dat boy.'

I follow Finn's pointed finger through the doors to the front room. In the far corner, away from all the other children, is Jude. He is playing on his iPad, headphones clamped around his ears. It is Jude that Finn is pointing at.

'Finn, darling,' I say into his ear, 'why don't you want to play with that boy?'

His lower lip is wobbling. 'No like dat boy,' he says. 'Dat boy hurted my face.'

'What do you mean, darling? When did he hurt your face?'

Finn is speaking quietly now. I can hardly hear him.

'Dat boy push me,' he whispers. 'On the stairs.'

SOPHIE

Six months before

The night Claire went into labour was the coldest of the year. They left in the middle of the night. The house was still and quiet with just me and Jude. I watched my phone, waited for news all Saturday, but there was nothing. I cancelled the first date I'd planned with the runner so I could eat pasta with Jude, snuggle up and watch a film with him under a blanket.

On the second night, I put Jude to bed, then settled on the sofa to watch TV. Neither of them messaged to ask after Jude, or to say how it was going. The house was so quiet. It had started to feel as if they were never coming back.

I tried to get into a film, but found I was distracted, scrolling through my phone, waiting for news. I could reschedule that meal with the runner, I thought. Yet something was making me hesitate. We'd still only spoken over the app, but I was finding it harder to push aside the feeling he wasn't telling me the whole truth. He said his marriage was over, but had admitted he was still living with her. 'It's complicated. We have a son. I need to find the right time.'

The next morning, I woke up to a message from Jez. They were coming home. I opened the shutters. The morning sky was mercilessly blue, the cold crushing. When I put the bins out, the steps were icy, and I nearly slipped. I imagined Claire falling, her arms clamped around the baby. I scattered salt on the stone, my breath coming out in little puffs of steam.

Jez came in first, beaming, gripping the handle of the car seat, the sleeping baby strapped inside. The baby was so limp and tiny, all slumped in on himself. Jude pressed his face into me. Jez bent down, cocked his head at Jude.

'Look at your baby brother,' he said. 'Just look at him. Isn't he great?'

Jude peered into the car seat, his curls flopping forward over his face. He looked huge, all of a sudden, compared to the baby.

'You're a big brother, mate. Isn't that great? How does it feel?'

Jude looked back to the baby.

'He is very little now,' I told Jude. 'And he'll sleep a lot at first. But when he's bigger, you can play together.'

Jude looked at me. 'Can you and me play now, Fee?'

'Of course.'

Jez watched Jude walk away. His brow creased a little. Then he went back to get Claire. It was obvious it had not been quite the moment he'd been hoping for.

When Claire walked in, I was shocked. She was walking like an old woman, pressing the tips of her fingers against the hallway wall. I hadn't known she would still look pregnant, only slightly deflated, like she had a slow puncture. Her skin looked blotchy and grey. I later found out she'd had an emergency Caesarean, that she had lost nearly three litres of blood.

'Claire, congratulations! He's so beautiful.'

She smiled, thinly. 'Thanks.'

I puffed the cushions on the sofa in preparation for her to sit.

'Can I get you anything?'

She shook her head and limped towards the sofa, wincing in pain. 'Where's the thing, Jez?' she muttered. Jez produced a dough-nut-shaped cushion from under his arm, and Claire sat down on it. Jez placed the baby down on the floor next to her in his car seat. Claire closed her eyes. I thought perhaps she'd want to see Jude, but when she didn't open her eyes, I ushered him into the kitchen.

I fed Jude his tea, got him bathed and ready for bed. It was starting to snow. Claire was with the baby, and Jez was at the shop, so I read him both his bedtime stories. I chose one of our favourites, *Stick Man*.

Stick Man is lonely, Stick Man is lost.

Stick Man is frozen and covered in frost …

Jude seemed to cling to me harder than usual. I told him we'd build a snowman together, if there was still snow in the morning. He was asleep before I even turned out the light.

Downstairs, Claire was sitting on the sofa, looking out at the snow. The baby was on a sleeping nest in front of her on the floor, curled and upturned like a little beetle. His fingernails were long. He was clawing at his own face.

The baby started to whimper, then to cry. His eyes were pinched shut, his mouth a little 'o' of need, searching for her breast. Claire was still staring out of the window into the darkness. When she finally looked down, she seemed surprised by the sight of her own child.

The baby's soft face was getting red now, from all the crying. Finally, Claire picked him up. I realised I had been twisting a tea towel in my hands. I was gripping it so tightly I could see the bones of my knuckles through the skin.

Claire held the baby to her and turned her face to the wall while she rocked him. But the crying didn't stop. I felt as if the crying was sucking the oxygen out of the room. I was finding it impossible to take a whole breath.

Claire put the baby to her breast to feed. Seconds later, she cried out, her face contorted. I rushed over.

'Are you OK?'

Claire looked up. There were tears in her eyes. 'Surely he can't have teeth?'

I looked at her, confused.

'He doesn't have teeth,' I said.

She looked down at the baby, doubtfully. Stuck a finger in his mouth to break the seal around her breast, and ran it along the inside of his mouth. The baby's eyes were open. They looked jet black.

'It feels like he has a mouth full of teeth,' Claire said again.

The baby was starting to cry again. I handed her a glass of water. 'Let me get you some paracetamol,' I said. 'And how about a camomile tea?' I brought it to her, sweetened with honey, a couple of biscuits on a side plate. Later, I found them sitting there, uneaten.

The next morning, when I carried Jude down in his pyjamas, Claire was already on the sofa, the baby at her chest. She looked exhausted, haunted. The baby squirmed on and off the breast, doing great gulping cries. Claire didn't seem to notice Jude come in.

'Jude,' I called, 'come and have your porridge.'

There was a sound of a key in the front door. Jez came in, a red scarf wrapped around his neck, sleet on the shoulders of his winter

coat. He was clutching a carrier bag of fancy pastries. I could hear two voices, and I realised he was with Wendy, his mum.

Jez came into the lounge, bouncing around in his trainers. 'Mum's here to see the baby, Claire,' he said.

Jude's eyes pricked up, and he ran to the hallway to see his granny. I heard the muffled sound of her picking him up and squeezing him, asking him about playgroup.

Jez walked over to Claire. 'Almond or plain? I wasn't sure. They had ham and cheese but … Anyway. I got you a coffee.'

He put croissants down in front of Claire. As he did so, he lingered, bent at the waist, to coo at the tiny face staring up from her lap. When Jez saw the baby, it was like a light coming on in his eyes.

'You take him,' Claire muttered to Jez.

Jez looked at her. 'I thought he was hungry?'

'I can't see your mum. I can't do all that right now. I need to sleep!' Claire almost shouted. Jez paused, silenced.

'Just running to the loo,' Jez's mum called from the hallway. Jude came in, racing up to me to show me a children's magazine she'd bought him.

'Oh, wow! Breakfast first, though,' I told him gently, lifting him onto a stool, ruffling his hair.

Jez scooped the baby up. 'Come here, son.' Held against Jez's shoulder, he looked so tiny, like a baby rabbit. I suddenly longed to hold the baby. I felt it like a physical ache in the centre of my body.

'Does he have a name yet?' I looked at Claire. Jez looked at her too.

'I'm not sure,' Jez said. 'Are we going to go with Beau, Claire?' Jez was bobbing at the knees. The baby seemed soothed. Its eyes were starting to close. 'Claire, darling? I thought Beau was your favourite for a boy?'

Claire exhaled heavily. 'I don't know,' she said finally.

'But I thought –'

'I don't *know*, Jez!' Claire was shouting now. Jude looked up, alarmed, from his porridge. 'I don't know what we should call it. I can't even decide about the croissant. I didn't think it would be a boy.'

In the days after, people came to the house. Midwives and health visitors. Never the same one. When the first one came, I played with Jude on the carpet while she talked to Claire and weighed Beau. Claire

166

undressed him and handed him over to the midwife without kissing him or anything. His hair was pale and fluffy, like a baby duckling. He was so vulnerable. He could not do anything. He could not even hold his head. When Claire picked him up, I couldn't help but think that she was not supporting his neck.

'He's lost,' the midwife said.

I looked up, not understanding what she meant. I saw Claire do the same.

'Three hundred and twenty grams,' the midwife said, pointing at the screen on her scales. 'We'll need to keep an eye on it. Are you feeding him, every two to three hours? Setting alarms at night?'

Claire stared at her. 'I feed him constantly,' she croaked. 'It feels like he never stops. When I lay him down afterwards, he screams. Why would I set alarms? Not one of us is ever asleep.'

The midwife packed away her scales. 'I'll be back in a few days to weigh him again.' She made it sound like a threat.

When she came back, Beau still hadn't gained weight. She asked Claire how she was finding breastfeeding.

'Agony,' Claire snapped. 'It's agony. It can't be normal. It just can't.'

The woman asked if Claire was sure she was doing it right. She told Claire all the things Claire knew already, all the stuff about nose to nipple, tummy to tummy. I could see that Claire was gritting her teeth.

'I take it you never breastfed your older son?' The midwife gestured at Jude, playing Lego on the floor with me.

'He's not my son,' Claire muttered.

Jude looked up, straight at her.

'Hey, Jude, let's build something together,' I said. I tried to distract him, show him how to put a long piece on top of two stacks of blocks to make a house. Anything to move on from the ugly words about him that hung in the air. But Jude didn't look upset. He didn't look anything. He just went back to stacking the blocks, one on top of the other.

TASH

Christmas at my mother's converted barn – 'semi-converted', as Tom muttered when he saw the state of our room – is a qualified success. Finn is intrigued by all its ramshackle nooks and crannies, and loves ambling about the cold, sunny courtyard, down the lane to where the neighbour keeps his pigs. Claude, who was hopeless with Finn as a baby, is marginally more interested now he can talk. He speaks to him as if he is an adult, gruffly ordering him to fetch chicken feed and help him brush the yard.

It is freezing, though. I dress Finn in layers, even to sleep. And we have to watch him on the stairs, which Claude made himself and which are a potential death trap.

I keep thinking about what he said at Claire's party, that Jude had pushed him on the stairs. Finn is a straightforward little boy, with little imagination. He doesn't lie much, and when he does, it is obvious. If Finn isn't lying to me, that means the others – Claire, Laura, Jez and Nicole – are.

Laura told me he had fallen, and none of the others had corrected her. There had been no mention of Jude, or a push. The uncomfortable thought occurs to me that perhaps I have been focusing too much on the things I have been keeping from Laura, Claire, Nicole and Jez.Maybe I should think more about the things they might be keeping from me.

'How's the free-writing going, Natasha?' Mum asks after dinner the first night.

'Freelancing, Mum.'

'I haven't seen your name anywhere lately. I wondered if you were still doing it.'

I grit my teeth. 'I email you the links to all my articles, Mum. You never reply.'

'Oh, darling, don't be so sensitive. I do click on them, but they are always behind those paywall thingies.'

'*Sunday Times*,' Claude bellows. 'Murdoch paper.' He encloses a log in his meaty fingers and throws it into the fireplace. Tom puts his hand on my knee. It's not clear to me whether he is applying support or restraint.

When Mum and I do the washing-up, she asks where Tom has gone.

'For a run,' I tell her.

'Now? In the dark?' Mum raises her eyebrows.

'What?'

'Well, is everything OK between you two?'

I look at her. 'Fine. Why do you ask?'

'Oh, I don't know,' she says. 'I suppose he seems a bit quiet.'

'Does he?'

Mum laughs. 'He's your husband. Haven't you noticed?'

Annoyingly, I realise she is right. Tom has been quiet lately. I struggle to think of a single conversation we've had since we left for France, outside of functional ones about Finn.

'He is always tired this time of year,' I tell her. 'Winter's tough in A&E, you know that.'

'Of course. Poor Tom,' Mum simpers. 'Such a hero.'

I hate that it winds me up so much, all this NHS hero stuff. I know Tom works hard, but after all, it is his career. He's not the one stuck in the house, cleaning splatters of food off the floor three times a day. A job for which I do not get paid.

Mum drifts away from the sink, dropping all pretence of helping me with the washing-up. She is off looking in the mirror now, checking how her hair is falling over her face.

'I take it you still won't sell your father's pictures? Try and buy yourselves somewhere a bit bigger?'

Ever since she married Claude, Mum has referred to Dad in this way, as if he is nothing to do with her any more. *Your father.*

'Your father wouldn't have wanted you to struggle, Natasha,' she goes on. 'He could never have dreamed that things would be so

difficult for you young people.' She comes closer, placing a hand on my jumper sleeve. 'If your father had known all that, I'm absolutely sure that he'd have wanted you to –'

'Enough,' I say quietly. 'Please. Let's not, Mum. I don't want to fall out.'

'No,' she mutters. 'All right.' I fix my eyes on the washing-up water as I hear her pouring another glass of wine and wandering off to watch TV.

The day after Boxing Day, Mum suggests Tom and I leave Finn with her and go for a walk to the local town. She says she needs bread, and that their dog Cassis – the Gordon setter that Tom adores – needs a walk.

It is quite nice walking Cassis over the ploughed fields, the frozen clumps of earth underfoot, the big, flat skies of central France clear and blue. When we reach the sleepy town square, the cafe is closed, the outside tables empty. But the boulangerie is open, a smell of dough and sugar rising from the vents in the pavement. In the window is a twee, twinkling snow scene display. Tom unclips Cassis so she can drink from the bowl of dog water by the door. 'I'll see if they'll do us a coffee to take away,' he says.

I sit down at one of the outside tables, zipping my coat up to my neck. The pot plants are festooned with coloured Christmas lights. Tom emerges with a paper bag of warm croissants and two hot chocolates in lidded cups. They are outrageously thick and sweet.

'These remind me of our skiing trips.' I smile at Tom.

He laughs. 'I'm surprised you even remember those.' Skiing trips with our friends belong to a life before Finn: drunken nights out in the resort, tales of bed-hopping at breakfast, pounding hangovers on the cheapest possible Ryanair flight home.

Tom passes his hot chocolate cup between his hands. His breath turns to steam in the air.

'How are you, husband?'

'I'm fine.'

'You seem a bit quiet.'

'Do I? Sorry.' He dusts croissant crumbs from the metal surface of the table. 'Work's been stressful lately.'

'More than usual?'

He looks away. 'Yeah. More than usual.' He rubs his beard. 'I was thinking I might not apply for the consultancy post.'

'What? Why?'

Tom scratches at a bit of melting snow with his trainer. 'Just the hospital. Some of the other doctors, the staff.'

I stare at him. 'You've never mentioned any of this.'

'It's not that big a deal.' He sniffs. 'I'm going to apply for other places, that's all. Keep my options open.'

'Hang on,' I protest. 'When you say you say the other doctors – you're not … you don't mean Laura, do you?'

Tom pauses. 'Not just her. But yes, I do find Laura a bit difficult.'

'Did you and her fall out over the training post?'

Tom is silent.

'Tom? Come on. I won't say anything.'

'It wasn't that – at least, I didn't think we'd fallen out over that. It was something else. I caught her doing something she shouldn't.'

'What sort of thing?'

'A breach of prescription protocols.'

'A minor thing?'

'Not really, Tash.' Tom runs a hand through his hair uncomfortably. 'These things are serious. I spoke to her first. She asked me not to report it.'

'And did you?'

'I had to, Tash. To protect myself.'

'Oh.'

I privately wonder if Tom really did have to report Laura. Tom does everything so by the book. He finds it hard to understand when other people have a more relaxed approach to rules; it doesn't always mean they are bad. I can imagine that if you didn't know Tom, he could come across as a bit abrupt about stuff like that.

'Laura didn't seem to see that I had no choice,' Tom continues. 'She was very cross with me, and she's just been really difficult and short with me ever since. And because she's been there longer, and she's so chummy with all the nurses – they all seem to think I'm the bad guy as well.'

He sets his cup down on the table, places his palms down either side of it.

'The weird thing is,' he says, 'whenever you're around, she goes out of her way to be nice. I don't know, Tash. I don't trust her, that's all.'

I shift on the metal chair. I trust Tom, of course I do. But I can't square any of this with the Laura I've got to know. I wonder if there is a possibility he is being oversensitive, or got the wrong end of the stick. Laura has been nothing but kind to us, as far as I can see. If it weren't for her, Finn would probably never have settled at the playgroup.

'I'm sorry,' I say. 'About the work thing. It sounds stressful.' I pause, unsure what else to say, so I try a joke. 'I thought it was just my mum driving you mad.'

We both laugh. 'No, she's all right,' Tom says. 'She winds you up more than me. I think she's pretty funny most of the time.'

Tom takes my fingers and presses them between his palms to warm them. The light is starting to seep away, and with it the small warmth of the watery winter sun. I pull my coat tighter around myself. For the first time, I feel sad that we are going home. Me and Tom need to get away more.

'We should head back.' Tom zips up his coat, pulling the neck right up to his chin against the cold. He whistles to Cassis.

'OK,' I say. 'Can you remind me to take my pill when we get home? I need to be better at remembering.'

'Sure.' I wonder if Tom might say anything about trying for another baby, but he doesn't. I try to work out whether I'm relieved or a tiny bit disappointed.

'Any other New Year's resolutions?'

Keep digging, I think to myself.

TASH

In the days after we get back from France, London feels silent, emptied out of people. All the cafes are closed, the roads clear. Finn and I cut lonely figures on the swings and climbing frame. The trees are bare and leafless overhead, the sky pale and featureless as an unpainted wall.

I was hoping to enjoy some time with Finn before playgroup starts again, but typically, after months of nothing, I have had a bite on one of my freelance pitches this week. To my surprise, one of the broadsheets wants the gentrification story I pitched ages ago, about the wetlands. With no playgroup until next week, I have no idea when I'm going to write it, but it's the first bit of freelance work I've had in a while, so I will just have to make it work.

'Yeah, it's dead, we've got a lot of space to fill over the New Year,' says the assistant news editor, who has obviously drawn the short straw over Christmas. I bite my tongue, try not to feel offended. 'Obviously, it would be great if you could dig into the money a bit,' he adds. 'And can you file by Thursday?'

'Sure,' I say brightly. 'No problem.'

At the weekend, while Tom looks after Finn, I make my way down to the wetlands to try and get some first-person accounts. It is bitingly cold, a white mist over the reservoir. I can't see the middle of the water. Geese emerge from the pale cloud like spectres, their black heads and necks just visible, their feathered bodies fading into white.

I manage a few quotes, but my heart's not really in it. An old lady in a poky ground-floor flat is desperate for company and invites me in, but after a few minutes, she starts repeating herself, getting confused,

so I politely make an excuse and move on. A few people glare at me, tell me to fuck off as soon as I say I'm a journalist.

Next, I head towards the new towers. The mist has lifted, but the light is starting to fade. Needle pricks of rain are starting over the reservoir. Across the water, the lights of the city glint like illuminations from a far-off planet.

As I pass the playground at the foot of the towers, I see Christina and Eliza. They are the only two figures there – hardly surprising, given the weather. Christina is pushing Eliza on a swing.

Christina arranges her features into a half-smile, gives me a curt nod. 'Hello, Tash.'

'Hi, Christina. How was your Christmas?'

'Fine, thanks. Yours?'

'Oh, you know. Exhausting.'

Christina is barely making eye contact. Her eyebrows are knitted together, her coat belted tightly. It feels like she is pushing the swing harder than she needs to.

'Do you live here?'

Christina looks at me warily, as if I have asked her something extremely personal.

'I only ask,' I say, 'because I'm writing this piece, and I was –'

'Look, Tash. I don't mean to sound rude, but I know what you're writing about. Everyone does.'

It takes me a moment to realise what she means. She thinks I'm here about Sophie.

'Sal told me what you were doing. I can't help you, OK? So please don't ask.'

There doesn't seem much point correcting her. 'OK,' I say. 'But, Christina – can I ask why you wouldn't want to talk about it? About Sophie?'

Christina ignores my question. She grabs the swing. 'Come on, Eliza,' she says. 'It's getting dark.'

'But, Mummy, you said –'

'I said no.' It comes out as a bark. Christina yanks Eliza out of the swing and grabs her hand.

'Christina, I –'

'Don't bother. Sorry, I'm just not talking to you about this, Tash. Not now, not ever.'

That night, I work late to finish the piece on time. The flat is dark except for the yellow puddle of light from the desk lamp I've dragged into the kitchen.

I use my credit card to pay for the access to Companies House records I'd always got for free as a staff reporter, and pull the records of Woodhill, the company leading the development. It's a privately owned company, but looking to go public in the near future. I try to work out how much money Woodhill have made on the wetlands development, but the structure behind the project is complicated. A lot of work has been subcontracted to other firms. I start sketching out the relationships between the companies on my pad, but I quickly run out of space.

One firm appears more frequently than others. Graphite Security Solutions. I start tracing all the transactions between the two. Graphite has been paid millions by Woodhill. And yet, there are transactions the other way, too – Graphite has bought up millions of pounds' worth of property in the development.

I do an internet search on Graphite Security Solutions. It seems it is a subsidiary of another company. I click on that company's website, and I realise I have been here before. I click the tab that says 'who we are', and am met with a list of directors, with their profile photographs and potted biographies. Five are listed.

The first is Jeremy Mark Henderson.

TASH

The woman at the Corinthia spa reception has the glassy expression of a doll. I lean over her marble slab of desk, her lit scented candle, trying to read her screen. I make an effort to keep the white heat of panic from my voice.

'I don't ... I don't think it's quite that much,' I stutter. 'I paid a deposit. And it is just a massage, a manicure and pedicure ...'

'That's right,' the woman says. 'Three treatments, a day pass for use of the facilities, and lunch also. Plus your friend advised us that the three of you would be splitting the cost of Ms DeSouza's food and treatments – as a birthday gift?' She pauses. 'Would you like to see the breakdown?'

I grip my card. The embossed numbers are sharp against the pads of my fingers.

'Can I just cancel my treatments?' I ask quietly.

'I'm afraid the cancellation cost is the cost of the treatment now. You'd need to give us twenty-four hours.'

I feel a plummeting sense of panic.

'You can pay when you leave, if you prefer.'

'No, now is fine – I just, um ...'

'Did you want to pay by card?'

I can feel there is someone else behind me, waiting. There is nothing I can do. I start to hold out the credit card, a slight tremble in my fingers. Then an arm appears over my shoulder, a flash of black plastic between outstretched fingers.

'I'll get this, Tash. It's on me.'

Jez looks like he has just come out of a shower. His hair is wet and he smells of shower gel. A sports bag is slung across his body. I feel

myself adjust to his presence, like you might to a change in altitude. I hold up my palm.

'Honestly, no. Jez, that's very kind, but it's far too much.'

Jez waves me away. 'My treat,' he says. 'For Nicole. I forgot about her birthday. I'd like to get it.'

I feel my face colouring. 'I can't let you pay for this, Jez,' I say, firmly. 'It's not appropriate.'

'Please don't worry. Claire and I are members. We get better rates.' He pauses. 'You can pay us back, if you really want.' He tilts his head to one side. 'You might as well take the discount, no?'

Jez shoots an authoritative nod at the woman in the blouse, who has been holding his credit card in the air. She smiles shyly at Jez and places his card in the machine. As I hear the payment go through, the tick of the receipt printing out, my panic is replaced by unease. The woman behind the desk hands me the receipt, and I shove it into the pocket of my dress.

'I'm sure Claire really appreciates you coming.'

'But, I …'

Jez drops the bravado, places a hand lightly on my arm and lowers his voice for a moment. 'Tash, please don't worry.'

His eyes meet mine, and we look at each other for a moment. I open my mouth to say something, but before I can think of anything, Claire and Laura appear.

'Great, you're here!' Claire smiles. 'Nicole's inside already. Let's go.'

As I make my way through the underground maze of the spa, there is something about the low lights, the hushed voices, the mirrors, that gives me a bad feeling, that tells me I should turn back. All the women look identical, disguised in white gowns, hair towel-wrapped, padding noiselessly in slippered feet.

After I change, I can't see Laura and Claire, so I head into the spa. Nicole is in the centre of a dark pool, floating on her back. Her eyes are closed, her black hair spread ink-like around her. The arch of the roof meets its reflection in the water below, like jaws. Nicole's body is motionless. Then, her eyes snap open, and she looks straight at me.

'Hello, darl,' she says. 'You look like you've seen a ghost.'

She flips over, a curl of water following her body under the surface. I watch her shimmering darkly at the bottom of the swimming pool,

gliding towards the side. Then she emerges, slick with water, strong and muscular as a lynx.

As I watch Nicole dry off, I shift in my dressing gown. My expensive new costume feels tight on my shoulders, the skin between my legs still sore from the wax I'd had to spend thirty-seven pounds – and a precious childcare hour – on.

I avert my eyes from Nicole's taut body and fix them on her face. 'Have you had a nice birthday so far?'

'Yes, thanks. I love it here. Everything OK? You want a frozen grape?' Nicole passes the tiny bowl to me.

'Thanks.' I pop the grape into my mouth. It bursts open, the frozen flesh on my teeth causing a cold, metallic pain behind my eyes.

'Are the others not here?'

'They went to the pods,' Nicole says, gesturing down a corridor at one side of the pool.

'Pods?'

'Sleep pods. You never tried them?' I shake my head. She explains what they are. I get the sense she is enjoying the fact I don't know. 'I don't like them, though,' she says, making a face. 'They remind me of coffins.'

She swings her dark wet hair over one shoulder to brush it. Then she interlaces her fingers and stretches them above her head, the muscles in her arms revealing themselves from underneath her coffee-coloured skin.

'So Laura tells me you've been asking questions,' she says. 'About Sophie Blake.'

I cough, nearly choking on my frozen grape.

'I'll tell you one thing. Well, three things, actually.'

I freeze, unsure what to say.

'One,' she begins. 'If you're thinking Sophie Blake was some kind of angel – you'd be wrong. Two – I really wouldn't ask Claire about it if I were you. She's been through enough, already.'

I chew the grape, my teeth stinging again. 'OK.'

'And three,' she continues, 'you and me never had this conversation. OK? Oh, look.' Nicole plucks her phone from her dressing-gown pocket. 'Nearly time for our massages. I need to shower first. See you on the other side.' She makes what I imagine is intended as a little excited smile. It sits uneasily on her face, like a badly hung painting.

178

I find it difficult to relax during my massage. The pressure feels uncomfortable, the Tibetan bowl music irritating, the padded circle around my face making my cheeks hot and clammy to the touch. It is difficult not to think about how much the experience is costing per second. My thoughts are still spinning with what Nicole has just said. What was the purpose of the conversation? Was she warning me off? And what did she mean about Sophie?

Next, we are led to a line of white leather recliners, like seats in a private plane. A woman in a mask hands me a key-ring thing with a string of fake fingernails in different colours attached to it. I'm relieved when I'm sat next to Claire, and not Nicole. I select the same dark red as Laura. Nicole chooses a molten aubergine purple, Claire a milky coffee colour. We lie back as the women slough off bits of our skin and rub orange-peel scrub into our foot arches.

'Is everything OK, Tash?' Claire asks.

'Fine,' I murmur. I find myself unable to look at her, unable to look at anything except the dots of coloured polish, swimming in front of me like inkblots.

'I'm really looking forward to Cornwall.' Claire flicks through the kaleidoscope of dismembered fingernails. 'It'll be so much fun having them all at the cottage.'

I keep telling myself that we can always pull out of this holiday if we need to – it's ages away still, and it's not like we are paying anything.

'Finn will love that,' I reply, uneasily. It's true – he would. 'I guess holidays with just the three of us must be a bit boring for him really.'

I pause.

'It must be nice for Beau,' I venture. 'Having a sibling to play with.'

Claire shrugs. 'I guess,' she says. Then she smiles, leans in. 'Between us, Jez is desperate for another.'

'Oh.' For some reason, I feel heat rising to my cheeks. 'And you're not … you're not keen?'

Claire's smile fades. 'Just a bit anxious, I suppose.' She looks down. For a moment, we sit in silence, watching as the masked women paint our nails in neat brushstrokes, left, middle and right, as gentle as butterfly wings.

'Did you … did you have a hard time with Beau?'

'I had postnatal depression. It was quite severe.'

179

I glance at her. 'Oh, Claire. I'm so sorry.'

'I didn't admit it, for a long time. I think the midwives knew, early on.' She pauses. 'One of them asked me outright, pretty much. She could see I was a terrible mother.'

'I'm sure you weren't.'

'I was. I didn't love him.'

I am silenced. There is a hardness in Claire's voice I haven't heard before. She glances at the nail technicians, straightens her back, then speaks more quietly.

'I mean, look. If he was on a sofa, or a bed, I'd make sure he didn't fall off. But that was it. He could have been anyone's baby. He didn't feel like mine.'

'And you never said anything?'

'I thought they'd take him away, and then Jez would be heartbroken.'

I exhale, put my hand on hers. 'I'm so sorry, Claire. I can't believe no one helped you.'

'I think on some level I was waiting for someone to ask the right question, whatever that might be. But whatever it was, no one asked it.' She has looked away, like she isn't talking to me any more. 'It was awful. I felt like nothing was normal. I felt full of absolute dread. Terrible thoughts got trapped in my mind, which I couldn't seem to shake.'

She is leaning forward, now. I look down and can see the hairs rising on my arms.

'I used to think, when he was a tiny newborn, his head still all wobbly – I used to think about what would happen if I just picked him up and his neck just snapped, backwards, like that, like a tree branch.'

I look up, shocked.

'I could imagine the whole thing in my mind,' she says, looking straight into my eyes. 'I could see it so vividly that I sometimes thought that this was actually going to happen. Or had happened already. Or that it was something I was going to do.' Claire bends her fingers towards her, blows on the drying polish. 'I mean, can you imagine what it was like, being inside my head? With thoughts like that?'

SOPHIE

Five months before

The crying went on all night. The noise made me grip the sheets on top of me, the surge of adrenaline that rose to greet each new scream shutting off my sleep. I listened to Claire and Jez upstairs, shuffling back and forth, shushing and hissing at each other, like noisy ghosts.

The house seemed to be in a constant state of crisis. Claire spent more and more time in her bedroom. Jez spent hours walking up and down the house with Beau on his chest, shushing him and rocking him while he cried. It was impossible to talk to either of them.

I was sure that Jez must see that something was wrong, that Claire was not behaving normally, that she wasn't doing any of the things she was supposed to be doing. I also wondered if he'd noticed Jude's indifference to the new baby, and whether that struck him as odd. I longed to talk to Jez about things, like I used to. But there never seemed to be a quiet moment.

The last midwife that came was called Fatima. She had a black headscarf and long fingernails painted dark red. They talked, the baby asleep between them in a Moses basket. I had made sure his temperature was right, his blanket tucked in at the sides. Fatima had her notes fanned out on her lap.

As she placed the band on Claire's arm to take her blood pressure, I saw Claire hold her breath.

'Try to relax,' Fatima said.

Claire exhaled. The machine beeped.

'It is a little high,' Fatima said.

'It's just because you're all here,' Claire muttered, looking at me.

'So,' Fatima said to Claire, 'how are you feeling emotionally?'

Claire didn't say anything. I watched her carefully. I wondered if I should say anything. And what that would be.

'Claire?' Fatima prompted her gently. 'I was asking how you were feeling emotionally.'

The weight of the silence was heavy and thick, like a dam about to burst. I willed Claire to say something. Anything, rather than nothing.

'It's normal to feel tearful, or overwhelmed,' Fatima told her, kindly. 'It's a lot. Especially your first time.'

Claire looked down, as if her throat was stuck.

'Do you feel like you've been able to bond with the baby?'

I looked at Beau. He was so tiny still, so curled up and squashed. His head was scaly with cradle cap, red spots on his cheeks. He did not look like a baby in a book or an advert. Claire was looking at him too. I could see in her eyes what the answer to the question was.

'We don't have to discharge you today,' Fatima said. 'We can put you on a longer term visiting plan, with extra support, regular mental health check-ins. If you think you'd benefit from that.'

Claire looked up from Beau, as if awoken from a dream. 'No,' she said firmly. 'I don't need anything like that.'

And so nothing happened. No one came, and it got worse, and worse. The days felt so long, with so little light. Jez was back at work. Laura and Nicole – both still pregnant – had called round, their hands full of presents and flowers, eager to meet the first of the new babies. But Claire made me send them away, make an excuse. She and I were on our own in the house. From four in the afternoon to seven in the morning the sky was dark, and Beau just cried and cried and cried.

TASH

After months of prevarication, the police press office have finally come back to me. The officer in charge of the original investigation into Sophie's death is willing to have a look at the phone. It feels like a breakthrough.

I arrive at my appointment at Tolpuddle Street. The officer on duty holds Sophie's phone daintily between her gloved thumb and forefinger before sealing it in a clear evidence bag.

'Thanks.' She smiles blandly, indicates that I can leave.

'But ... what happens now?'

'I was told to tell you to put any questions to the press office.'

'Can you just ask the officer whether he has a moment to speak to me? I think his name is DSI Hayden.'

'Did he say he wanted to speak to you?'

'No, he just asked me to leave this, but ...'

She sighs. 'Remind me of your interest in the case, sorry?'

I hesitate. 'I'm a journalist,' I admit finally.

Her face hardens, as instantly as if she'd pulled down the metal shutter.

'Can't help you, I'm afraid,' she says. 'All media enquiries are dealt with by the press office.'

I suspect the police press office are as sick of talking to me as I am of bothering them. They probably thought that if they finally agreed to take Sophie's phone into evidence, I would go away for a while.

'But can you just clarify whether this means you are reopening the case?' I'd asked.

183

'No,' the press officer had snapped firmly. 'The line is as I gave you last week. If there's any change in our position, I will be in touch.'

I press my fingertips down into the ledge in front of the glass door, until the flesh around my nails turns white.

'Please,' I say, leaning into the perspex hatch. 'Just give DSI Hayden this.' I slide the letter under the hole in the glass. The woman moves her fingers away from it, and wrinkles her nose.

'If you could move aside,' she says.

Defeated, I turn away, push the glass doors open. A blast of freezing air hits me in the face. As I head for the bus stop, I hear a male voice from behind me, a thick east London accent.

'Excuse me, love. I think you dropped this.'

I turn round. A tall man in a police uniform is holding out a folded piece of paper. I take it automatically, before pausing. I'm sure I didn't drop anything.

'Actually,' I say, 'I don't think that's mine.'

'Oh yes,' he says, meeting my eye. 'It is yours, Miss James.'

The tall man locks his eyes with mine, then turns on his heel. I notice his stab vest is slightly too short for his body.

By the time I unfold the paper, the uniformed man is already gone, disappeared back behind the glass doors of the police station. I stand in the street, staring at it, until my hands are cold.

TASH

'So a man claiming to be a police officer wants you to go alone to a pub on Woodberry Down and not tell anyone about it.'

I look at Tom in the mirror. His arms are folded.

'Yep.' I brush my eyelashes with mascara. When Tom doesn't reply, I turn to look at him properly. 'What? Finn's in bed. There's that curry in the fridge.'

'It's not that! It's unsafe, Tash! Do you even know his name?'

'Adam.'

Tom rolls his eyes. 'Adam what? How do you even know he's a real police officer?'

'I know he is a police officer,' I say. But privately, I wonder if I really do know that. He was there at the station, wearing what looked like a uniform. He could still be a mad stalker, for all I know.

'Look,' I tell Tom, 'that's how it is with sources. You don't want to push them for more details straight away. They might back out.'

'More details like a surname?!'

'Yes, like a surname! If you were going to whistle-blow to a journalist, would you want to give your surname?'

Tom is silent. It is a pointless question. Tom would never whistle-blow to a journalist. He does everything by the book.

'I just worry about all this, Tash. After you got those horrible text messages.' Tom is rubbing his nails over the back of his head.

'I know. But you know where I'm going. I'll message every twenty minutes or something.'

I stand on tiptoe to give him a kiss on the cheek. As I pull my coat on, he wanders into the kitchen, puts the steaks he has bought in the freezer. I blow him a kiss and he smiles sadly, then turns away.

The Happy Man pub in Woodberry Down has the air of somewhere long abandoned. The paper on the walls is peeling away, revealing an underside stained yellow by tobacco. The floor seems to be on a slope. Deep cracks spread over the ceiling, like tree branches.

The police officer I know only as Adam returns from the bar with a pint and a glass of wine. A purple-faced old man turns on his stool to heckle him.

'What's the weather like up there?' A ripple of laughter from the crowd around the fruit machine.

'I'm used to that,' Adam says cheerfully as he sits down.

'I bet. How tall are you?'

'Six six.'

Adam perches awkwardly on the stool. He glances doubtfully at my glass of wine as he hands it over.

'I hope that's all right. I'm not sure there's usually much call for wine in here.'

'I'm sure it's fine.'

As I set it down, the table wobbles. Adam puts out an arm to steady it. He inspects the legs to work out which is short, then starts to fold a beer mat between his hands.

'Nice choice of pub,' I mutter. 'Looks like it's been condemned.'

'It has, actually,' Adam replies, from under the table. 'It's being demolished. There's some kind of appeal, but they won't win.' He re-emerges and sits back on his stool. 'Making way for the next phase of the big development.'

'Jesus.' I should probably have known this, included it in the gentrification piece. I've got sloppy, I realise. Distracted by Sophie.

'I know. Bit of a dump, though, isn't it? To be fair.' Adam places his glass on the table, then repositions it slightly with his thumb and forefinger, so that it is exactly centralised.

'Are you going to tell me why we're here, Adam?'

Adam's expression clouds a little. 'Um, yes. Sorry. It's just — I know you've been asking questions about Sophie Blake. We had a message from the press office. DSI Hayden told us all not to talk to you. He won't help you, by the way. No chance.' He pauses. 'But the truth is, I'm sure he got it wrong. I'm sure something happened to that girl.'

SOPHIE

Four months before

It was boredom, in the end, I think, that made me agree to go on the date. That, and the thought of another night in the annexe alone with my phone.

The air in the house was becoming suffocating. Claire barely spoke to me. She seemed to barely speak to anyone. Our afternoons together were increasingly painful. I watched her spend nothing-filled hours with Beau, checking and rechecking her phone, while the rain flicked at the glass at the back of the house and the clock ticked out the minutes and hours of his babyhood, until it was time to collect Jude from playgroup.

I could see there was something wrong with her. Sometimes I caught her sitting in silence next to where Beau lay on the mat. His little legs were kicking, his eyes searching for her, left and right. But Claire's face would be fixed on her screen, checking and rechecking the time as if she was willing the hours to pass. I longed to scoop him up in my arms, read him a story, sing him a song. I couldn't understand how Claire didn't feel the way I did, caught between wonder and grief for every little stage of his that slipped by, watery and fast, impossible to stop or go back. Already, he was getting too big for the things I'd dressed him in at the beginning, the sleepsuits covered in jungle animals, the tiny hat with bear ears.

The air always changed when Jez walked in, like a window being opened. He strode in, laden with shopping bags, rolling up his shirt-sleeves, tipping Jude upside down, the energy of his world outside the house still on him, like whizzing, invisible particles. He'd take Beau from my arms and kiss his fluffy hair, then jog upstairs to put the

188

bath on, draw the curtains in the boys' rooms, find their pyjamas. He would come and see me too, ask quietly how I was. Occasionally, he put a hand on my shoulder, or my back, just briefly. It struck me as significant that he only did this if Claire wasn't looking.

Jez seemed determined to convince himself Claire was fine. 'I think the breastfeeding is really taking it out of her,' he said to me once, coming home to find Claire in bed, again. It felt to me like an excuse, though I wasn't sure what for.

Sometimes, if she was in bed, Jez would sit on a stool in the kitchen and talk to me while I cleaned up. It became my favourite part of the day. I made a point of having the kitchen spotlessly clean ahead of this moment, something fragrant in the oven. I liked to hear him exhale with the relief of it, the relief of having me there, the house perfect, the food done. He poured himself a glass of wine, and I told him about all the funny little things they'd done that day. Jez loved silliness. Claire didn't know how to be silly. I would flick through the photographs of the boys I'd taken on my phone. In the park, on the swings, at a music class. Jez would lean in to see better, the blue of my screen glowing on our cheeks, our lips. Close enough that I could feel the warmth of his chest through his work shirt. Close enough that I was sure he could smell the cocoa butter on my skin, the perfume on my neck.

The night of the date, I made sure that Jez saw me in my dress. I came out of the annexe and stood in the hallway, pretending I wanted to use the mirror to apply my mascara before leaving. I waited for his footsteps on the landing, then watched him do a double take, start to say something, then press his lips together, and formulate something else. Later, I played the moment over and over in my head.

'You off out tonight, Sophie?'

'Yep.'

'Anywhere nice?'

'A date. Dinner. In town.'

Jez's eyes locked with mine. Understanding. Accepting the challenge.

'Have fun,' he said.

I smiled.

'I will.'

189

TASH

'Look, what did I know?' Adam says. 'I'd only been on the force a few months. But I felt there were clear signs she'd been deliberately killed.'

'Like what?'

Adam hesitates. I sense we are moving into confirm-or-deny territory.

'Did you look at the people she met on the dating app?'

Adam takes an inhale. 'You found that, then. Yes. We pulled the records. She was in contact with a few people ...'

'Names?'

'I can't, you know I can't.' Adam is shaking his head. 'There was no evidence on her profile that she actually met anyone in real life. She could have deleted messages, of course. If it had been a murder inquiry, they'd have done a deep-dive on her communications, but ...'

'But they didn't. Because the pathologist couldn't find evidence of unlawful killing.'

He nods. 'Bodies in water can be particularly difficult. All pathologists say that.'

I pull the phone report from my backpack and hand it to Adam.

'I had this done on her phone,' I say.

He looks at it, then back to me. 'Who did this for you?'

'I'm not sure what his name was. A guy from Blackstock Road.' Adam raises an eyebrow, but makes no comment. He reads the messages, then looks up at me. 'Can I take this away, have a look at these numbers?'

'Sure.' I take a gulp of wine. I am not sure whether this is allowed, but I decide to leave Adam to worry about that. He folds the paper carefully once, then again, then puts it in his breast pocket.

'So you don't buy the coroner's assessment?' I ask him. 'That Sophie went swimming, got in trouble and drowned?'

Adam winces. 'No,' he says. 'I just don't see it. There'd have been CCTV of her closer to the wetlands, I'm sure there would. There's nothing.'

'Did you ask the estate for their CCTV?'

'We did. A lot of what should have been there was missing. Cameras in some of the key spots had been vandalised.'

'Cameras?' I immediately think of Jez's company. 'Didn't you think that was suspicious?'

'Of course. But Hayden didn't agree. Said it had always been a rough area, still was, even with the fancy facelift.'

'Wasn't Jez Henderson's firm responsible for the CCTV cameras? Graphite Security Solutions?'

Adam gives me a look. 'He insisted not. Said Graphite had been contracted to install the security system, but that they had subcontracted the ongoing running of them to another firm. Graphite build stuff all over London. They're a massive company – they turn over a hundred million a year. We couldn't find anything to contradict his account.'

'Hmm.'

'I know,' he says miserably. 'But Hayden said it all stacked up.'

'It seems a bit of a coincidence, doesn't it? Jez being her employer, one of the last people to see her alive, and he's been involved in the site where her body was dumped?'

'It does.' Adam gives me a slight smile. 'And I don't believe in coincidences. All of that rang alarm bells for me. If you're in a hurry to dump a body, you tend to choose somewhere you know pretty well, right? But Jez insisted he was barely ever at the wetlands himself, that his firm had projects all over London. Which, as I said, they do.'

I paused, considered this. 'Did you look at him? At him and his wife?'

'I looked at their movements, the movements of their car, for any evidence it went near the wetlands that night,' Adam says. 'I looked into every minute between Sophie's last sighting and her being found dead. But their car hadn't moved. And I couldn't place either of them anywhere near the wetlands. I even got the cadaver dogs to have a sniff around the boot of their Land Rover …'

'Wow. Really?' I can't imagine Claire was too happy about that.

'Yeah. The sarge told me off for that. Said it was heavy-handed.'

We exchange a look.

'And the dogs found nothing?'

Adam shakes his head. 'Not in the car, not anywhere in the house. So that scuppered my theory, you see. If there'd been a body kept in that house, or that car, they'd have smelled it.'

This makes sense to me. I have never really believed that Jez or Claire could have killed Sophie, dumped her body in the wetlands. But nor do I believe she went swimming. Something else happened that night.

'Look,' Adam says, leaning in to me. 'In the end, you've got a married couple who are each other's alibi – it wasn't ideal. But there was nothing else substantial to undermine them, either. Nice, wealthy couple. Nothing on their records. Totally cooperative, charming, consistent under questioning.'

'Which could just be because they are telling the truth, of course.'

'Of course,' Adam says. 'And that was Hayden's view.'

We sit in silence for a while. I take a gulp of wine. The pub is quiet now, the traffic noise from the road outside more distinct in my ears.

'What about other cars? They had friends at the party that night – did you look at their cars? Did you look at whether any of those went back and forth to the wetlands, after the party?'

'There were fifty-odd people at the party, Tash, all friends and family of the Hendersons. This was me on my own, not a murder investigation with a big team. Sophie went missing on the Friday and wasn't found until three days later – it's a huge time window in search terms. A search on a specific place is one thing, but going through all the movements of everyone at the party, for a whole weekend ... Do you know how many officers that would take?'

'But then how was your boss satisfied Sophie went to the wetlands of her own accord?'

Adam grimaces. 'How can I put this? DSI Hayden has a particular view of young women. And their alleged tendency to make daft decisions.'

'For God's sake.'

'I know, I know. I'm afraid ... that sort of sentiment – it's not uncommon among my, um, police colleagues.' He puts his pint down,

straightens it again. 'Look – he had a point in a way, Tash. We had no obvious dodgy boyfriend, the employers looked clean, no criminal associates, no drug habits. All we knew was Sophie had had a few drinks, it was a warm night and she liked wild swimming. Once the pathologist report came back saying cause of death was unascertained, but likely she'd fallen in and drowned, that was it. The way Hayden saw it, there was no investigation. He wanted it passed back to the coroner.'

A bell sounds for last orders. We both ignore it.

'I can't look into this any more, Tash,' Adam tells me. 'Hayden won't hear another word about it. But I think someone killed this girl. And that person is still out there.'

'I think they are too.'

Adam looks up. 'Why?'

'Because ever since I've been looking into Sophie Blake's death, I've been getting these.'

I hand him my phone and open the messages up. Adam looks at them in turn. He raises his eyebrows.

'You don't know these numbers, obviously?'

I shake my head. 'If you call them, they say out of service.'

Adam nods. He pulls his own phone out, saves the numbers in his notes. 'I'll see what I can do,' he says.

'Thanks.'

The pub is emptying out. I feel tired, and no further forward. I need to get home. I start to gather my things.

'Have you spoken to Jane?' I ask Adam.

'I did at the time.'

'She thinks Sophie had a boyfriend. One that she kept a bit quiet about, for some reason.' Plus I found her contraceptive pills when I was sneaking around my friend's house, I don't add.

'Interesting. I think she was seeing someone too,' Adam replies. 'This is what I came here to show you. I wondered if you might be able to shed any light on it.'

Adam pulls a laptop out of his bag and sets it on the table. 'This,' he says, 'is the last image we have of Sophie alive. She is at Jeremy Henderson's fortieth birthday party, at the Upper Space art gallery, the night she disappeared. It shows her leaving the venue, with the kids – the two boys. To me, it looks like there is a man with her when she leaves.'

I blink at him.

'Why was this picture never released?'

'Because it wasn't a murder inquiry.'

Adam still hasn't turned the laptop around. I can see in his face that he is crossing a line, showing me something he shouldn't. But I can also see that he wants to, that I'm not going to have to push very hard.

'This man,' he says, 'he looks like he's got an arm around her. But the odd thing is, this bloke isn't on the guest list for the party, and we were never able to eliminate him from our inquiries. Claire and Jeremy have always insisted they have no idea who this man was. They have no explanation for why he was there at their private party. None of the people at the party seemed to have any idea who he was either.'

'Is it a good enough image to ID someone?'

Adam nods. 'It's a bit grainy. But it's good enough.'

'Can I see it?'

Adam looks down.

'I can show it to you here,' he says quietly. 'I can't send it to you. I can't risk there being a record.'

He glances pointedly down at my phone, and I see what he is saying. I should take my own picture. He is going to look away.

'OK.'

Adam makes a few clicks, a little pool of blue light on his face. Then he turns the screen around. And there is Sophie, in her black lace party dress. And behind her, a man, with his arm around her shoulders.

I gasp, dropping my phone, clutching the table.

It doesn't make sense.

'Are you OK?' Adam leans into his bag, grabs me a bottle of water. I take it, gratefully, put it to my lips. I look again at the screen, wondering if I made some mistake. But there is no mistake. The walls seem to buckle.

'You don't know him, do you?'

I open my mouth, then close it again. I can't tell him.

The man with Sophie in the picture is my husband.

It is my Tom.

TASH

When Tom gets home, I am sitting at the table in the kitchen, still in my jeans and hoody. Tom doesn't seem to see me, or hear me when I say hello, ask how his day was. He doesn't seem to notice I have been crying. Or that I have got the photo of Sophie that I found in his sock drawer in my hands, and am turning it over and over.

'Tom, can you come and sit?' I say. 'I really need to ask you something.'

'Not now, Tash.'

'Tom?'

He turns away from me, shoves his hand into the bread bin, starts rooting around. I have been working up to this all day. I need to get it over with.

'Is something wrong?'

He shakes his head. 'It's total bollocks. I have no idea what's going on, Tash.'

'What is? What's bollocks?'

'Just work. Fucking hell.'

He shoves two slices of bread into the toaster, yanking the handle down so hard I wince. He stalks around the kitchen for a while, like a caged animal. Then he collapses into a chair, as if the energy of not telling me what's going on has defeated him.

'I've been suspended from work.'

I stare at him, unable, at first, to process what he is saying.

'What?'

The toast pops. We both ignore it, staring at each other.

'Someone's made a complaint. A woman. She says I ... I can't believe it. I'm actually shaking.' He holds his trembling hands out in front of him, stares at them as if they belong to someone else.

'Who? What kind of complaint?'

'I don't know, it's anonymous. A patient. They just said it's a woman and she's made a serious allegation. They won't tell me anything else.' He breathes out, brings his hands to his face and pulls them down his skin, like a child making a face.

'But what's their complaint? What are you supposed to have done?'

'I don't know. They won't say. But it's obviously bad.'

'They can't suspend you and not tell you why!'

'Apparently, they can. Christ, I need to eat something. I haven't eaten all evening.'

He works so hard. The fact that he still hasn't eaten anything for dinner at one in the morning breaks my heart.

He stands up, abruptly, and turns to the toaster. I watch the back of him, listen to the scrape of his knife against the bread. This is a bigger threat, I realise. An actual crisis, rather than one I am speculating might exist. This is our real life. Our home, our son. My income is nothing, barely enough to pay the playgroup, let alone live on. If Tom loses his job, it is not like he'll get another one. It's not like that for doctors. One complaint can ruin them.

I know I need to stay calm for Tom, but I am struggling, a juddering panic coursing through me. I can't imagine Tom as anything other than a doctor. He loves his work so much. This will destroy him. I will have to get a full-time job, copywriting or PR or something, anything to pay the bills. But what if it isn't enough? What if we can't pay the mortgage on our flat?

I swallow, try to organise my thoughts. 'What happens now?'

'I've got a meeting with HR in two weeks. They'll tell me more then.'

'And until then?'

'I'm on gardening leave.'

'So you're being paid?'

'For now.' I realise he is trying not to cry.

'Oh, Tom. Come here.'

I stand up and try to hug him. Tom hangs an arm limply around me, but he doesn't relax his torso into mine. After a few moments, I let go, and sit back down. I sense neither of us feels better.

Tom sits opposite me and takes a bite of his toast. I stare at the semicircle he has left in the neat, square slice.

'You said you wanted to talk to me about something.' He squints at my face through his glasses, as if he is looking at me properly for the first time. 'Tash, have you been crying? What's up?'

I think about the picture, the speech I rehearsed about it in my mind. Then I look at Tom's face. I put the photo face down on the table.

'It's nothing.'

SOPHIE

Four months before

The place he'd chosen was actually pretty fancy. There were white tablecloths held down with little silver clips, lots of different knives and spoons laid out, a big arched ceiling like a church.

The food looked incredible, but I found I couldn't eat much of it. After the third glass of wine – or maybe the fourth – I realised I was bored. It occurred to me that I didn't actually feel anything at all for this person. In fact, he was really starting to grate on me – complaining about his job, telling me how awful the mother of his child was, how she had been more bothered about her career than about him. I didn't care about him, about any of it. He was not the person I had built up in my head. All I kept thinking about was Jez. I kept wondering what he was doing at home, whether Beau was coughing, or Jude was having a nightmare. I couldn't remember why I was there.

I stood up, said I was leaving, but my legs felt unsteady. He tried to tell me to stay, but I wasn't listening. As I got up, I wobbled a little, so that I was glad of his hand. He took me to the lift, and pressed the button.

By the time I wondered why we were in a lift, remembered that there was no need to get in a lift because the restaurant doors opened onto the road, it was too late. We were in a corridor, and he was pulling me down it, his hand tight on my wrist.

'Let go, you're hurting me.' My voice was all slow and slurry, like a broken cassette.

He stopped at one of the doors, pulled a key card out of his jacket pocket. Started jamming it into the hole in the hotel-room door, again and again. The card wasn't working, the little light flashing red

198

instead of green. He jammed it again. The way he was breathing made me frightened.

'I want to go home,' I said.

'You're not well,' he was saying. 'I think you should lie down for a bit.' His voice was so calm, so clinical. I got that feeling then, the bad feeling, like when you miss a warning sign, and you're hurtling down the motorway in the wrong direction at a hundred miles an hour, and there is no way back.

His hand was still on my wrist. 'Let go,' I said again. But it was like he couldn't hear me. I said it louder. 'Let go!'

'Is everything all right here?'

Both of us looked up. There was silence suddenly, and calm. A lady had walked over to us, leaving her husband by the lifts. She had a lined face, bright blue eyes, a sparkling tunic top and matching necklace.

'We're fine,' he said. But she was not looking at him. She was looking straight down at my wrist, where he was holding on to it. I pulled myself free, and with the lady looking, he did not resist.

'I wasn't asking you.' The woman's voice was teacher-sharp. He cowered, and the woman turned to me.

'Why don't you walk with us, dear?' She held her palm out in the direction of the lift. Her husband was watching us.

'We can walk you to the Tube station, if you like? We're going that way.'

Before I knew it, the woman had placed a bony arm around my shoulders, and ushered me down the corridor. When I risked a glance backwards, I saw he was still standing there, staring after me, clutching his key card in one twitching hand.

Once I was on the Tube, on my own, I was glad of the way everyone averted their eyes, pretended not to notice anything. I sobbed and sobbed, unable to stop. No one sat down next to me. I saw my reflection in the darkness of the Tube windows opposite. I saw exactly what I looked like. A silly young girl in a too-short dress.

It was after midnight by the time I got home. I couldn't find my key to the annexe – maybe I'd dropped it somewhere. I climbed the steps to the main front door, turned my key quietly in the lock. The cold air had sobered me up a bit. When I started to slip my shoes off, I saw the kitchen light was still on.

Jez was in the hallway before I could do anything about the mascara streaks, the wine breath, the puffy eyes.

'Sophie?' He could see straight away that something had happened. 'Jesus. What have you done to your arm?'

I looked down at my wrist. My arm was unfamiliar, shocking: four thick welts and a bruise on the inside. It was hard to believe this was an arm that belonged to me. I looked away from him, ashamed of what had happened to me, of what he must be imagining.

'Come here.'

I didn't resist. It was such a relief, to be held, to feel the solid warmth of him. Jez's hand started to move up and down my back, in between my shoulder blades. We stood there together, for a long time. I felt so safe, at last. I willed it not to stop.

TASH

When Tom falls asleep, I turn the light back on to watch him. He is wearing his old university athletics shirt, his stubbly chin pointed upwards, the lines around his eyes and eyebrows puckered, as if he is trying to solve a problem in a dream. I watch his chest rise and fall, trace the edges of his fingers – long and slim, just like our son's, a band of silver matching mine on his left ring finger. Then I lean over him, unplug his phone from the charger on the bedside table and take it with me into the kitchen.

It can't have been Tom in the photograph, I decide. It just can't. I'll check our diaries for July 2017. We will have been together doing something dull that day, the day Sophie went missing. Taking Finn to the park. Ordering a takeaway and watching Netflix, like we do every Friday night.

I tap in Tom's pin, find his calendar and flick back to that week. There is nothing on the Friday at all. The only entry that week is for Thursday the 6th. 'Tash and F flight: 6.15 a.m.'

It takes me a moment to process. It was the week we went to my mum's in France, without Tom, because Tom had not been able to get the time off.

I take my own phone out then and check my calendar. The dates fit.

We'd argued about it, hadn't we? I had been upset that he hadn't got the time off, but more upset he didn't seem that bothered, that he was treating it like just one of those things. We had exchanged messages tersely all week, and when I got home he'd been distant. Both of us felt we'd been somehow wronged.

201

What had Tom told me about that week? Had I even asked what he'd been doing? I'm sure he said he'd just worked. Gone for drinks with Ravi.

I flick through to the photo I eventually took of Adam's CCTV image. Each time I look at it I think I'll see it differently, find something that proves it can't be Tom. But the more I look at it, the more sure I feel. The line of his jaw, the set of his shoulders. The tatty orange T-shirt I always beg him not to wear.

I send Ravi a message.

Hey, can you meet me tomorrow? Really need to speak to you about something. T

There seem to be so many stops to get to Ravi's. I knew vaguely that he and Abi had 'moved out', as Tom was always saying, in search of an affordable house, but I'm still surprised the postcode doesn't even seem to be London, though it is – just – on the Tube. 'No-brainer' had been Tom's verdict. 'They've got four bedrooms now, a massive garden.' I hadn't said anything.

I follow Ravi's directions across a huge park with a cafe in a mock-Tudor building in the middle, a queue round the corner of parents in sunglasses and Puffa jackets, clutching takeaway coffees. I am forced to grudgingly admit to myself that it has its charms. The play area is five times the size of our local one, with a zipwire and a huge tunnel slide. On the other side, the tennis courts are full, the staccato thump of bats and balls mingling with a smell of damp, raked leaves.

Ravi comes to the door straight away, enclosing me in a big hug. Then he leads me through a hallway covered in baby photos, and into the living space at the back of the house. I note the huge island, the skylight over the dining space. I greet his three sweet children with as much enthusiasm as I can muster, ruffling each head of shiny black hair in turn.

'Coffee?'

'Please.'

The children amble happily on walkers, Fisher-Price cars and tricycles, bifold doors opening out to a neat paved patio with a dining table and barbecue. Ravi starts making coffee.

'Your message sounded very serious,' he says, quietly. 'Everything OK with Finn?'

'He's fine. Sorry, I didn't mean it to sound so dramatic.'

'That's good.' Ravi sets a coffee down in front of me. 'Come on,' he says. 'What's all this about, Tash?'

I haven't thought properly about how to ask the question. 'I wanted to know if you remembered something. The summer before last, in 2017, Finn and I went to France without Tom, because he had to work, and while we were away you and him went out for some drinks. Do you remember that?'

Ravi thinks for a minute, then his face clears. 'Oh yeah – I remember. We ended up at that weird party. Did he tell you about that?'

'That's right.' I sidestep the issue of whether I have talked to Tom. 'Can you remember … how you ended up there?'

'Didn't Tom tell you this?'

'He … he said he couldn't remember.' I'm fully lying, now. There is no getting around it. But Ravi seems somewhat mollified. I know this isn't the first time he's been asked to relay the details of a night out to his friends. Ravi doesn't drink, so he's probably often the only reliable witness.

'Right,' he says. 'Well, it was a bit random. We started out in the pub. But then one of our mates from the hospital said there was this party with free drinks up in Angel, and that we could come if we wanted.'

'Do you remember who?'

'Girl called Laura – she's a staff grade medic in Tom's department, been working at the hospital a few years. She's sort of posh. It was a posh party.'

Even though I know it is the only thing that really makes sense, it still feels like a punch in the gut. He went to the party with Laura, the night Sophie died. Laura, who he claims to dislike, who he always acts weird around. And when Laura told me about that night, she completely failed to tell me that Tom had been there.

That can't have been accidental. She purposely omitted that information. Why? Was there something more to their relationship? My brain rejects the idea, but I force myself to confront it. Even if that's true, it certainly doesn't explain why Tom left with Sophie.

'Why did Laura want you and Tom to go to this party with her?'

Ravi laughs. 'I don't think she did. She was all dressed up, saying she was going to just have one, then head off to this party. She had

this great big gift with her and everything. But then someone pointed out that there was a Tube strike. She looked gutted. She started stressing out, trying to get an Uber, but everyone in London was trying to get one. In the end, I told her I'd just drive her. It was on the way, pretty much. And I'd already told Tom I'd give him a lift home, so he came too.'

'But if Tom wanted a lift home – how come he ended up going to the party?'

'We weren't going to,' he says. 'But when we got there, it looked amazing, a big flower arch thing over the door, like a wedding. It was a nice summer evening, really warm. Canapés, trays of champagne, people spilling out onto the pavement. Laura said, come in for a drink, I'm sure it's fine. I said to Tom, what do you think? He said, fine, let's just go for one.'

So it was a coincidence Tom was there. Could this really be true? Or could Ravi be lying to me, and covering for something Tom has done?

'Anyway,' he says. 'I left soon after that. Abi was at home, pregnant, with the kids – I didn't want to take the piss. I didn't know where Laura had gone by that point, she just seemed really distracted, and then Tom disappeared, so –'

'Hang on – Tom disappeared?'

Ravi hesitates. 'Well, I mean, just for a bit.'

'Who with? I thought you didn't know anyone else there?'

'I don't know, Tash.' Ravi looks down. 'Are you going to tell me what this is all about?'

I have made him feel awkward. I can feel my blood hot under the surface of my skin, but I know I can't push it. I need to keep Ravi onside.

'Tom knows you're here, yes? You have talked to him about all this?'

I avoid Ravi's gaze, look away from him into the glass doors. I catch sight of myself in the reflection. I look dreadful, the shadows under my eyes purplish, my eyelids raw, cheeks sallow, hair unwashed.

'Tash …'

'Oh, Ravi, OK. I promise I will talk to Tom.'

'Good,' he says, relieved. 'He's a mate.'

'I know.'

We sit in silence for a moment. I see Ravi glance over at the kids. They are starting to squabble over toys, rub at their eyes. I've taken up enough of Ravi's time.

'I'll get out of your hair. Thanks for the coffee.' I ease myself off my stool. 'Can I just ask you one more thing before I go?'

Ravi makes a face.

'Did you find Tom, in the end? Did he leave with you?'

'You need to talk to Tom, Tash.'

'I'm going to, I promise. But did he leave with you, Ravi?'

Ravi rubs at the back of his head.

'No, Tash,' he says. 'I don't think he did.'

TASH

I am halfway up the path from playgroup drop-off when I hear Laura's voice.

'Tash, wait! You left this!'

I turn to see her holding my laptop case. I feel a sick twist of horror at how careless I've been.

'God,' I mutter. 'Thank you.'

'Sal had it.'

'Sal?'

'She said you left it by the prams. I said I'd give it to you.'

'Thanks.' I take the bag, feeling the reassuring weight of my laptop inside. All my copywriting work is stored on there. It's due in tomorrow.

'Are you all right, Tash? You look exhausted.'

I force myself to look at Laura. As soon as I do, I can see she knows about Tom being suspended.

'How is Tom?' she asks gently.

'Not great.' I look at her accusingly. 'Do you know what it's all about, Laura?'

She looks down, fiddles with the little tassels on her pashmina. 'Only that it was a woman who complained.'

I close my eyes for a second before I face her. 'Is he supposed to have done something … inappropriate?'

Laura bites her lip, looks away. 'Look, Tash, we all know it's nonsense,' she says. 'Patients make things up. They almost always get found out.'

I can't reply. I feel like I am going to be sick. Almost always.

She reaches out and squeezes my arm, but I feel worse, not better. I feel irritated at being the recipient of her sympathy. Your husband's the creep, I feel like shouting. Not mine. My husband doesn't watch porn when there are kids playing downstairs, or look for young girls on dating apps.

'Do you want to go for a quick coffee?'

'No,' I say too quickly. 'No thanks.' I'm just not sure how much I can trust Laura. It feels like there is a growing list of things she hasn't told me the whole truth about. Finn being pushed down the stairs. That she'd fallen out with Tom at work. The fact that Tom was at Claire's party the night Sophie died.

'OK,' she says. 'Take care, Tash.' I watch as she walks away down the church path, her brown boots clacking against the cobbles.

I had intended to finish the latest lot of copywriting work when I got home. Instead, I sit at the kitchen table, staring out of the window. I try to make sense of what Ravi told me. I need to get everything straight in my head before I speak to Tom.

I decide to go through Sophie's social media again. You can still see a cached version of Sophie's old page, with a few images still available to view.

Of course there isn't going to be a picture on here of my husband that I've somehow missed. But there might be something else.

I search a long time. I don't find any pictures of Tom. But I do find something else. A person who I hadn't noticed before, who has liked a lot of Sophie's posts. Lydia Gracie. When I run the name through the electoral roll, I get lucky. Only one in the whole of north London. Aubert Park. A few minutes' walk from Claire's house. That can't be a coincidence.

I click on Lydia's own Instagram profile. She looks about my age. Lots of pictures of a toddler daughter, a small dog. I pick up my keys and pull on my coat.

Lydia's home is the best part of a tall, handsome Victorian house. I buzz the doorbell marked 'B', stand on the black-and-white tiles and watch as a figure moves behind the stained glass and slowly opens the door.

Lydia has a plain, round face, owlish glasses. Her hallway is littered with the toddler detritus I recognise from my own life: a scooter, a

doll's pram, a pair of abandoned leggings. Behind Lydia, a girl Finn's age is wearing a Disney princess costume over her T-shirt and playing on the scuffed stair carpet.

Lydia squints at me, impatiently. 'Hi,' she says. She glances down, as if she expects me to be holding an Amazon package, or a clipboard.

'I was wondering if you might have a moment to speak to me. It's about Sophie Blake?'

'What? How did you get this address?' Lydia's squint curdles into a frown. Her hand tightens on the latch. I am suddenly reminded of my own reaction when Jane Blake appeared at my door.

'I looked your address up on the electoral register. I'm a journalist.'

Lydia's mouth hangs open. She looks behind me, as if looking for the paparazzi.

'It's just me,' I say gently. 'I'm sorry – perhaps this is painful. Were you and Sophie friends?'

Lydia makes a sort of snort, her face incredulous. 'I already told the police. I know nothing about Sophie Blake. Absolutely nothing.'

'Do you mind me asking how you met her?'

Lydia snorts again. 'Good question,' she mutters. The girl on the stairs behind, tiring of the lack of attention, begins to whine something. 'One minute, Zelda,' Lydia says behind her. She speaks again, more sternly this time, her hand still on the door.

'Look,' she says, pushing her glasses up her nose, 'I don't know who you are and what this is about, but I don't want to be in any article.' Lydia looks close to tears. 'This whole thing – it's been horrible.' She waves her palms in front of her face, as if trying to waft me away. 'I'm sorry,' she splutters. 'I just don't want to hear about it any more. I don't want to hear her name. I'm going to go now.' She starts to close the door.

'I need to know if she had a boyfriend. Please.'

I blurt it out almost without thinking. Lydia's hand slows on the door.

'Why?' she asks. 'Why do you need to know?'

Because it might have been my husband, I think.

'Because she might have been murdered.'

Lydia's face creases. She shakes her head. 'No. No – I read the thing in the newspaper. They said it was an accident.'

'Lydia, please, just answer me this one question,' I beg. 'Did she have a boyfriend?'

Lydia folds her arms. 'She said she was with someone,' she says eventually.

'Did she give a name?'

'She might have done.'

I feel sick. Please, I think. Not Tom. Please.

'Can you remember the name, Lydia?'

Lydia glares at me. 'Listen,' she says. 'I seriously doubt any name I gave you would be helpful to you.'

'Why not?'

Lydia leans out of her door. She almost spits.

'Because every single word that Sophie ever told me was a complete fucking lie,' she hisses. 'All right? I have no idea who that girl was. If you ask me, she was a fucking psychopath.'

SOPHIE

Three months before

I decided to go and stay with Mum for a bit. I told Claire I was sick. I couldn't face being in the house with her, risk her asking questions about the bruises on my arm. I kept getting messages from the runner, saying he wanted to talk. I deleted them all. I thought about Jez, how he had held me when I'd got home that night, what it might have meant. A few times, I typed out a message to him, only to delete the characters one by one.

At dinner, I pushed my food around my plate. Mum had made toad-in-the-hole because I used to like it as a kid, but it looked so beige and colourless compared to the food I had got used to. I thought of the things I'd seen in Claire and Jez's fridge that week. Persian filo parcels. A slice of banoffee pie. Salads scattered with pink pomegranate seeds, like tiny jewels.

'You not hungry?' Mum asked.

'Sorry.' The sausage batter was tough and cloying in my mouth. The mixed veg, in Lego-bright shapes of yellow, green and orange, tasted of nothing.

Mum looked down, the sides of her mouth twitching, trying not to show she minded.

'How's that new baby, then?'

I look up, force a smile. 'He's cute.'

'What's his name again?'

'Beau.'

Mum wrinkles her nose. 'Honestly. Names these days. I blame celebrities. How's the mum getting on?'

I shrug. 'She just mopes around. Doesn't do anything with him.'

'What d'you mean?'

210

'She doesn't take him anywhere.'

Mum laughed. 'What do you want her to take him to, for crying out loud? He's a newborn, isn't he?'

I stab at my sausage, exasperated. 'You can do loads of sensory stuff, Mum. There's research. He needs exercise –'

'Exercise?!'

'Yes, Mum! Babies need time on their tummies from birth, to build their muscles. You don't know.' In my voice, I heard the sulky teenager I always felt like in front of Mum. She snorted and passed me the jug of Bisto.

'Anyway, it's not like you to stick up for her,' I said pointedly, taking the jug. She was usually sniffy about Claire and Jez, their fancy house, their fancy food, their waste-of-money takeaway coffees.

'Yeah, well, I feel for her,' Mum said gruffly. 'Having a baby's not easy, Sophie.'

'But she could at least have a shower, crack a smile. Wash up once in a while.'

Mum gave me a sharp look. 'Ain't you being paid to do that?'

'I'm not a maid.'

'Oh, Sophie ...' Mum made a noise like she was exasperated. 'Everyone's a perfect mum before they actually are one.'

I blink at her. 'What do you mean?'

'I just mean, I know you think you're the world expert these days. But you ain't never had one, have you? There's some things you only learn by going through it. Can't you just give her a break, take the baby round the block for fresh air? She needs rest, and the baby don't need anything else, whatever you heard at college.'

Claire didn't say anything when I returned. She didn't ask about my fake illness, whether I was feeling better. I suppose she had her own problems. The morning after I got back, I found her with the baby on her lap in the front room. She was holding her cracked, red nipple pinched between the knuckles of her middle and index fingers. Her teeth were gritted.

'Come on,' she was saying through her teeth. 'Come on.' Beau was turning his tiny face away.

'Claire, I don't need to get Jude until three. Shall I take Beau out in the pram so you can both get some sleep?'

Claire stared at me. Her hair looked like it had been painted onto her head, her skin grey and slick and sweaty.

'He won't feed.'

'But he's been up feeding through the night, hasn't he? I heard you getting up with him.'

Claire paused, then nodded.

'Do you think he might just be overtired?'

Claire covered her face with her hands. Her fingers were so slim, her skin so pale you could see every bone inside.

'I'm terrible at this,' she breathed through her fingers. 'I can't do it.'

'That's not true,' I said. 'You just need rest.'

Claire dropped her hands into her lap and looked at me. 'OK', she said weakly. 'Thanks.'

I went into the kitchen and made a formula bottle and a cup of camomile tea. Claire didn't know about my formula top-ups, but what she didn't know wouldn't hurt her.

Claire zipped Beau into his thick, padded snowsuit, and started clipping him into the pram. Beau was looking up at her, his tiny eyes searching for her face. But Claire wasn't looking at him. She was frowning at the clips, holding the parts together like pieces of a puzzle she couldn't fathom.

'I'll do that,' I said. 'You go to bed.'

Once Claire was upstairs, I took Beau out of the pram and put him in the sling on my front. I had worn him like this before when Claire wasn't around. I found it soothed him. As soon as I started walking, his pale eyelashes drooped, his tiny head lolling onto my chest.

I walked up to Highbury Barn, dodging the skeletons of discarded Christmas trees on the pavement. By the time I got there, Beau was snoring quietly, his miniature nose in the air. I looked down at him, the top of his head snug in the centre of my chest. His milk spots had cleared up now, and his scalp wasn't so scaly. His hair was kitten-soft.

The windows of the fancy deli were still filled with Christmas lights. There were benches set out inside, a smell of coffee and croissants. I felt for my expenses card in my pocket. I hadn't had any breakfast.

As I stepped inside, everyone smiled at me. I felt like I'd just walked into a surprise birthday party.

'Oh, congratulations! He's so sweet!' A woman sitting in the window blinked at me through an owlish pair of glasses. She was

212

wearing a baby too, a bit bigger than Beau. The tangle of white lights at the window shone around them both like a halo.

'How old is he?'

'Nine weeks.'

'Blimey! So small! You're doing well to be all dressed and out and about!'

I could have just told her he wasn't mine. Of course I could. But somehow, the gaps between her talking didn't seem quite big enough.

'This is Zelda.' She motioned to the baby strapped at her front. A flopping head of dark hair, two dangling legs in candy-striped tights, as soft and fat as sausages. 'And I'm Lydia. Do you want to sit? We can squeeze up.'

'Are you sure?'

'Of course! Come enjoy your coffee. I'm sure you need it. Nine weeks! Christ!'

As I bent to sit, Beau's sock fell off. A passing woman took a dive for it, and handed it to me with a smile, mouthing the word 'gorgeous'.

A man in an apron appeared. 'Can I get you a coffee? Decaf, I assume?' He was grinning at me. It took me a moment to realise he thought I was breastfeeding, that he was literally thinking about my breasts.

'Oh,' I stuttered. 'OK. Yes. Cappuccino. Thanks.'

Lydia scooted up on the wooden bench. 'Nice to meet you …'

'Sophie.'

'Sophie. Do you live around here?'

'Highbury New Park.'

'Oh, amazing! We're Aubert Park. Not far at all!' Lydia looked delighted. 'We're on our way to baby cinema. You should come! Zelda sleeps through the whole thing. They bring you tea and cake and you have a whole sofa. It's literally the most relaxing hour of my week!'

The man in the apron returned with my decaf cappuccino. Lydia looked at me.

'Do you fancy it?'

I looked up. 'Sorry?'

'Baby cinema. There's plenty of space. It starts soon.'

I hesitated, then smiled. 'OK,' I said. 'Sounds great.'

'Great.' She turned towards apron man. 'Sorry – can my friend get that to go? Thanks.'

We were friends, then. Just like that.

As she stood up, Lydia glanced at my stomach.

'Whoa,' she murmured, shaking her head. 'You look incredible. So slim! I could barely get dressed when this one was nine weeks old. You've got make-up on and everything!'

I could have, should have, said something. But I had agreed to the cinema, the decaf coffee. It felt like the moment had already passed.

'What did you say his name was?'

I paused. I privately agreed with Mum about Beau. I thought it a strange choice of name. What if Lydia asked me how I'd picked it? I wouldn't know what to say.

'Teddy,' I said eventually. 'His name's Teddy.'

That's what I would have called him, you see. If he was mine.

TASH

When I get home from seeing Lydia, Tom is pulling clothes out of the dryer.

'Tom! I thought you were going to call me after your meeting?'

'I did.'

'Oh.' I pick my phone out of my pocket and see the three missed calls. 'Sorry. How did it go?'

Tom stares grimly into the drum of the machine. 'I don't know really.'

'Did they tell you any more about what you are supposed to have done?'

Tom's shoulders slump like a puppet's, his hands tangled in a bedsheet.

'I don't even remember her,' he says quietly. 'It was just a routine exam. She declined a chaperone, and we were busy, so I just went ahead. So stupid ... and now she says ... She says I ...'

'She says you what?'

He takes his glasses off and rubs his eyes.

'She says I sexually assaulted her.'

'What?!'

I instantly regret my horrified tone. Tom recoils, if I have dealt him a physical blow. I sink down next to him on the floor and pull him into a hug.

'Oh, Tom, it'll be fine,' I say, even though I am not sure it will. 'You didn't do anything, so it will be fine. They will see through it. It'll be dismissed.'

'Will it?' Tom pulls away from me, his eyes wide with terror. 'How do you know? What if they believe her? Isn't the rule that you have to believe the woman, now? What if I lose my job, Tash?'

'You won't – you can't. It won't come to that. Anyway, I'll get more work,' I say, in as cheerful tone as I can muster. 'I just got paid for that wetlands piece I did at New Year, the one that was your idea.'

'Oh yeah?'

'Yeah.' The truth was, I'd made them pay me for the work, even though it hadn't made the paper.

'And this copywriting thing is good money.'

'Is it?'

'Really good. If I do a good job on this batch, they've said there's sure to be more. I could approach other firms, too. I could just do that full-time, if we needed – I think it would be a decent salary.'

Tom sniffs. 'OK. Thanks, Tash. Hopefully it won't come to that, anyway.'

'Of course it won't,' I tell him confidently. 'They'll see this is all nonsense. They'll have to.'

That night, Tom goes to bed early, the lamb chops I cooked to try and cheer him up left barely touched on his plate. I clear up, pour myself a glass of red and open my laptop. I'll send off the copywriting work tonight, I decide, a day early. I can invoice for it tomorrow, tell Tom the money is on its way. It will be one less thing for him to worry about.

Oddly, though, I can't find it. I can't locate the folder where I saved all the work. I try the search bar instead, type in the name of the folder, but that draws a blank, too. I go through all the likely places, but it isn't there. Annoyed, I log into the Cloud, where I keep all my backups.

There is nothing there either.

Amid the hot, heart-thumping terror, I force myself through the motions of checking, and checking, and checking again. I keep doing it long after it becomes obvious, to my rational mind at least, that it is gone. There is simply nothing there any more. Everything I have been working on, for weeks. Thousands of pounds' worth of work, that was going to save us, even if the worst happened. Work that is due in tomorrow.

It is all gone. The only thing left in my Cloud is a single Word file, named 'TASH'.

I click on the file, feeling a familiar sickness, and read it. It contains only two lines of text.

YOU WERE WARNED. BUT YOU DIDN'T STOP.
WHAT COMES NEXT IS ON YOU.

SOPHIE

Nine weeks before

'You can definitely afford to eat this,' Lydia said. 'Unlike me.' She looked sadly at the brownie that had been placed on the little sofa arm between us.

'Don't be silly. You look great.' I cut the brownie in half, pushing the larger piece towards her.

My trips to baby cinema with Lydia were now the highlight of my week. I loved the deep, red sofas of the premium seats, the little menu of cakes they came over with, the hot chocolates bobbing with miniature marshmallows.

'I don't look great. I look like I've just had a baby,' Lydia muttered. 'You, however, just look like some hot young nanny.'

I froze, my hand hovering over the brownie. Beau's eyes flicked open on my chest, sensing the tension in my body.

'W-what do you mean?' I stuttered. But when I dared to glance at her, she was chuckling away to herself. It had been a joke. She was joking. She was entirely oblivious to the fact I was holding my breath, that my hand had started to tremble.

Beau let out a half-hearted cry. I shushed him, patting his bottom through the sling.

'Little Teds,' Lydia cooed, leaning over to him. 'He is so adorable. Just wait until the others see how big he's got!'

Gradually, my heart rate slowed, and Beau settled again, snoring softly on my chest. The coloured lights from the screen flickered bright against his pale cheek.

It had been easier at first, all this. When it was just me and Lydia. I hadn't counted on her introducing me to her mates. There were loads

of different activities that the babies could do, it turned out. Not just the sensory classes, where a woman blew bubbles and shone lights at the babies to a tinny backing track on the floor of a dusty church hall. There were all sorts: music classes, baby Spanish, baby French, baby Mozart, baby yoga, baby massage, even. We followed Lydia to them all. I copied the way the other mothers rolled out muslins over the place mats before they laid their babies down, readied the wipes and bibs in case they vomited on their tambourines. I linked the app where you paid for the classes up to Jez and Claire's joint account. I was sure they never checked it.

After the morning activity, the babies would sleep in their prams, and Lydia and the other mothers would find a cafe to sit and drink coffee and eat cake. I tried to speak as little as possible about myself, but even so, the lies were piling up, and it was getting more difficult to keep track. But I found it was weirdly addictive, being part of their club. There was something comforting about the sugary dullness of it all, the easy camaraderie. I told myself I wasn't doing anything really bad by deceiving them all – Jenny, Margot, Lydia. I could just ghost them eventually, say that me and 'Teddy' had moved away.

'Didn't you and Teddy get on with breastfeeding, Sophie?'

Jenny, one of Lydia's NCT friends, was staring at my formula bottle. Her head was tilted to one side, her ponytail swinging behind her, her infant clawing at her exposed breast.

'I've never really had much milk,' I said, looking away. I mean, this was true.

'They're better off fed,' Lydia said supportively, rolling her eyes at me in Jenny's direction when she wasn't looking. I smiled. 'At least Sophie can get some help at night from … Was it James?'

'Jez.' I coughed. I wish I'd made up a fake name for him, too.

'Jez sounds like such a great dad,' Lydia simpers. 'I wish Olly would do that. I've expressed a bloody freezer full, but he never offers.'

'Does he get that unusual hair colour from Jez, Sophie?'

Ponytail Jenny was smiling sweetly, but there was an edge in her voice.

'Yep,' I said, stroking Beau's head. 'He looks so much like his dad.'

'Aren't genes funny?' Margot, another bobbing ponytail. 'I wonder if his eyes will go brown, like yours.'

Of course, I should have told Lydia the truth the first time that I met her, but it wasn't as if I could undo it now. Also, she'd never have

wanted to be friends if she knew I was just the nanny. Coffee invites were for mums only. Nannies were expected to seek out their own.

One day, when we stepped out of baby cinema, Lydia asked if I wanted to go to a playgroup with her. The sunlight was disorientating. It was a spring day, the warm air like an answered wish after months of cold. I glanced at my phone.

'Sure. I've got an hour or so,' I said.

'Oh, great. It's called Cuckoo Club. It's down near Highbury Barn. Apparently it's on every day. I'd never heard of it – have you?'

I froze. I couldn't go to Cuckoo Club. Sal might be there.

'Oh, do you know what, I've just realised I can't. I need to get back.'

'Oh, OK. No worries.' Lydia looked at Zelda sadly, rocking her to and fro in the pram. I got the sense she just didn't want to go home. She always seemed to be hoping for another coffee, another walk. She was forever scrolling her phone for more infant activities we could do, baby-friendly cafes we could visit. She never seemed to want to be home alone, with Zelda. I guessed that Lydia was a bit lost, and lonely, and bored. She reminded me of a friend I had at college who never wanted to go home at the end of a night out because she always wanted one more drink.

'Any plans this weekend?' Lydia asked.

'Um, not really. Might be heading out for dinner.'

'With your perfectly domesticated husband? Lucky you.' I averted my eyes to the floor. 'Oh, sorry, no, I've noticed before you don't wear a ring, do you?' Lydia gabbled. 'Sorry, there's no reason why you should be married.'

'Yeah, Jez and I just, um, never got round to it.'

Lydia was hungry for more detail, I could tell. The trouble was, I couldn't remember exactly how much I'd told her about Jez, or what, and it felt like dangerous ground.

For once, Lydia took the hint that I didn't want to talk.

'Oh well, enjoy your night out.' She sighed. 'Olly and I still haven't managed to go out for dinner since Zelda was born.'

This was the thing about Lydia – everything always became a conversation about her, in the end. Which had its uses, when your own life was something you had stolen from someone else.

TASH

I stay up most of the night, trying to cobble together as much as I can. But it isn't enough. In the end there's nothing I can do except send what I have, at four in the morning, along with a grovelling email.

I can't bear to tell Tom about it. I rush off early, strapping Finn into his buggy while he is still chewing his last mouthful of breakfast.

'The bloke is coming this afternoon to fit the bars on the windows,' Tom reminds me. 'He's throwing in the creepy doorbell half-price, too.'

'Great.'

I think about the pictures in the horrible security catalogue we'd chosen from. The bay window was the nicest thing about our flat. From now on, it was going to look like a cage. But then I think about the message I got last night, and I look at Finn, a piece of toast in his little palm, looking up at me from the pushchair.

'Have a good day.' I give Tom a quick hug. He clings to me for a second in a way that is not like him at all, before letting me go.

As soon as I'm outside, I call Grace's bank and ask for the woman who commissioned me to do the copywriting work.

'I'm literally just taking it in now to one of those laptop places that specialise in recovery,' I tell her. This isn't quite true, but it's very much what I intend to do, as soon I've dropped Finn. I am pushing the buggy with one hand, holding the phone with the other. 'Even if it's not retrievable – you know, um, worst-case scenario – I remember most of it. I can get the rest of it to you within 24 hours. I'm sure I can.'

I try not to sound like I'm panicking. I hear the woman's voice harden from courteous to glacial as she absorbs the horror of what I am telling

her. She tells me she will call me back, and I know from her voice that if I don't sort this today, there will be no more work. Not ever.

When she hangs up, I start calling around laptop repair places. I get a string of answerphones. Nothing opens until nine.

As I drop Finn off, I give him a tighter squeeze than normal, wishing I could just spend the day with him at home, feed the ducks in the park. But he squirms away and dashes inside, as he does now, without a second glance, and for once it's me with tears in my eyes, feeling abandoned.

As I turn away, I walk straight into Jez. He has just dropped off Beau.

'Hey, easy.' He steps backwards, his arms placed lightly on my shoulders. 'Are you all right, Tash?'

I nod, unable to speak. I try to catch my breath.

'Are you sure? You look really upset.'

I open my mouth to say I am fine, but find I have to look away, pinching my lips together.

Jez rubs the back of his head. 'Is there anything I can do?'

'No,' I tell him, forcing myself to swallow. 'Unless – do you know anywhere I can take a laptop? I need to recover some work I've lost. There must be places. I don't think anywhere is open yet. I've tried searching online …' I trail off. My voice has reached a panicked, squeaking pitch; to my horror, a sob escapes my throat.

'Hang on, hang on,' he says. 'Slow down. Why don't you come over? I know a bit about laptops – I can see if I can help?'

I hesitate.

'Come on,' he says. 'Got to be worth a try, right?'

I bite my lip. 'I should probably take it to a shop or something,' I mutter.

Jez stretches his arm out, revealing a glint of silver watch. 'Doubt anywhere will open before nine,' he says, cocking his head to one side. 'Come on. It's got to be worth a go.'

It is strange to be in Claire's house without her. Jez doesn't mention where she is, and I'm too choked up to ask. I sit at the kitchen island, the marble cold under my hands, and try to steady myself. I watch the wind moving in the trees at the end of their garden, where the wood-and-glass building is. Jude is playing outside, a woman I don't recognise crouched beside him.

While the laptop fires up, I distract myself by watching Jude for a bit. He is clutching a battered teddy, walking it up and down the garden steps, then throwing it. He seems a little old to be playing with a teddy like that.

'Jude not at school?'

'No.' Jez clears his throat. 'He sees someone on a Tuesday, at the house. A therapist.' He gestures outside. 'He hasn't been speaking much, since … well, for a while.'

I can see this conversation is painful for Jez, that maintaining his usual, genial tone of voice is an effort. I wonder if he's talking about Sophie's death. Whether that was when Jude stopped speaking.

'That must be a worry,' I say. 'I hope it works out.'

Jez gives me a pained smile, resets his voice to its normal, conversational pitch. 'Thank you. Now, what do you need? Coffee? Something stronger?'

'Coffee would actually be great, Jez. Thanks. If you've figured out the machine.'

'We'll soon find out.'

While his back is turned, I move my 'Sophie' folder onto a memory stick. I check twice that I've saved it there, then I delete it from the laptop and put the stick in my pocket. When he returns with two mugs, I turn the laptop to face him.

'Ok, let's have a look.' I watch Jez go into my settings. 'You should probably set up two-factor authentication on here. Could anyone else have used your laptop?'

'No. No one uses it except me. Occasionally Tom, but he has his own, so …'

'Finn couldn't have been mucking around with it?'

'I honestly don't think so.'

'OK. Let's see.'

I give Jez the filenames, and he starts tapping. 'I'll just run a standard file recovery program first. If it's on there, we should be able to find it.'

'Thank you.' I hesitate. 'Do you mind if I use your bathroom?'

'Not at all. Go ahead.'

Upstairs, in their bathroom, I decide to check the drawer again, the one with the bottles. But when I open it, all I can see in there are Claire's expensive face creams and serums, her teeth-whitening kit, a pair of exfoliating gloves. The pill bottles have all gone.

223

I head back down the hallway. At the end, I pause. There is a room with its door ajar. It looks like a study. There is a desk by a window, a pile of papers on top. I look down the hallway, then back at the papers, feeling the weight of my phone in my pocket. It takes all my self-control not to sneak into the study, flick through the pile of papers on the desk. But I decide I can't risk it.

When I get back to the kitchen, the light of the laptop is glowing on Jez's face.

'I'm sorry, Tash,' he says. 'I can't understand what's happened here. The files you want were deleted yesterday morning. Could have been accidental – although they've been deleted from the recycling bin as well.'

My stomach twists. And the Cloud. It can't have been an accident. This was done to me, by someone who wants to cause me harm. Laura said Sal had my laptop. Could Sal have done this?

'The thing is,' Jez says, 'my program's thrown them up – but it's telling me I can't recover them. It looks like they've been corrupted somehow.'

I walk round to his side of the island. I can see the files he's found are the ones I need. But they are in grey, the same error message popping up every time he tries to click on them. I feel sick.

'How did this happen?'

Jez shakes his head. 'It's not clear. Could be a virus, some kind of bug in your system. I can get one of my guys to take a proper look, if you like? It might take a day or two, but …'

I shake my head, unable to speak. I can't wait a day or two. I'll lose the contract. All of a sudden, it is too much. The threats, the lost work, Tom's suspension, the worries about money, the horrible new bars on our windows. Is a false accusation against Tom part of this, too? But what about the photo of him with Sophie?

I find myself overwhelmed by it all. Before I know it, I am consumed by sobs. I clap my hand to my mouth, as if I can somehow stop it, but my shoulders are shaking.

Jez's eyes are wide with horror. 'Oh my God, Tash, I'm sorry. Please don't cry.'

'I'm sorry.'

'I seem to have a talent for upsetting you.'

'It's not you.' I find I'm too choked to say anything else.

He scratches the back of his head. 'Do you want me to drive you home?'

'I don't – I don't know where is safe,' I say. 'I'm sorry –'

Jez frowns. 'Safe? What do you mean?'

'It's – someone has done this to me. This thing with the laptop. I know they have.'

Whoever it is, they are winning. Adam said he would look into the messages for me, but every time he's phoned, I've cancelled his call because I'm too scared he will ask me about the man in the picture. And I can't tell him the truth. I can't tell him it's Tom. Not until I can prove that Tom is nothing to do with this.

Jez stares at me. 'I wish there was something I could do.'

I shake my head, feeling the tears on my cheek. There is nothing anyone can do.

Jez doesn't touch me, for a long time. When he does reach out his hand, he stops it, mid-air, before it reaches my back. He doesn't look at me as he does it.

As he pulls me into him, it feels important to me that my hands are at my sides. I don't move them up or down, I don't move anything. I know that if I move, something is going to happen, and the realisation is both thrilling and horrifying.

This has not been in my head. The danger was real. We have been picking through a forest, tinder-dry. It will take only the smallest spark.

I feel the scrape of my cheek against his shirt as I tilt my chin upwards, towards his face. For a moment I am not sure whether it is already done, the line already crossed. I breathe in the air of him. He reaches out his hand, and pushes a strand of my hair behind my ear.

'Tash.' As he says the word, his mouth touches the edge of mine.

The contact, the sound of his voice, makes everything too real. My senses refocus. This is ridiculous. I am not this person.

I pull away, as if burned, and mumble that I have to go. I feel my feet take a step back. I snatch up my laptop, and back into the hallway.

Outside, a mizzling rain has started. My hands are shaking on my bag, my laptop. I haven't got a hood, or an umbrella. But it is a relief, when the door closes behind me, to gulp in the cold air, feel the rain on the hot skin of my face.

Only after I start down the stone steps do I realise that Jude is there. He has walked round the house and is sitting on the top step, clutching that ragged old teddy by the neck again.

I freeze. Should I knock, make sure Jez, or the therapist woman, knows he is here? There are big, locked gates, but surely Jude shouldn't be out here alone, in the rain.

'Hello, Jude. Does your dad know you're here?'

I hope I sound normal. I do not feel normal. I want to be away from here, as quickly as possible, but I don't feel I can just leave a six-year-old boy here, like this.

I walk to the bottom of the stairs. Jude watches me. Then, he starts to walk the bear along the stone banister. It should be sweet, but it isn't. It is the game of a much younger child. And Jude does not look like he is playing.

Then Jude throws the bear down the steps. The movement is sudden, deliberate. Violent. The bear falls to the bottom of the steps, into a filthy puddle. Its head is left at an odd angle, its arm over its head, one leg propped up. Jude looks fixedly down at it. His curls are darkening in the rain. In my mind's eye, I suddenly see Finn at the bottom of the basement staircase, blood streaming from his face. I open my mouth to speak, but can find nothing to say.

Jez opens the door. He looks from me to Jude, then down at the teddy. He doesn't ask what Jude is doing. He doesn't seem surprised. He just sighs deeply, his shoulders sagging.

'Come on, Jude,' he says. 'Stop that, now. Come out of the rain.'

I turn away from them, open the gate and pace down the street as quickly as I can. I move so fast I nearly trip over my feet, without fully knowing where I am going, except away, from him, from Jude, from that house. I find myself at the Clissold Park coffee kiosk. I mutter an order, then collapse into one of the metal chairs, my heart still racing. The place is empty except for me and a homeless man I see around here sometimes. He and I sit, clutching our coffee cups, watching the water drip from umbrellas overhead. Sheltering from the rain, with nowhere else to go.

SOPHIE

Six weeks before

I saw them in the queue for coffee at the cafe in Clissold Park. I'd taken Beau for a walk – he was wanting to be propped up in the pram now, craning his neck when I pushed him around, a little neckerchief tied under his chin for early teething dribbles, a milk bottle tucked in next to him. Claire seemed to have got the hang of breastfeeding now, and was still mostly feeding him that way, but Jez had started making him bottles occasionally. I'd heard him marvelling to Claire about how easily Beau had seemed to take to it. I had kept my mouth shut.

It was the first really nice spring day, and the cafe's outside tables were busy, the raised flower beds studded with snowdrops and nodding daffodils.

I heard Laura before I saw her. I gripped the push bar of the pram, ready to make my escape from the queue, then I hesitated a moment. She seemed to be having some sort of argument with the girl in the kiosk.

'There must be some mistake,' she was saying to the girl. 'There must be enough on that card. Can you just check?'

Nicole was with her. She was looking from Laura, to the girl on the till, and back again. I could see this wasn't the first time she had watched an interaction like this.

'Put it through again. That card should be fine.' Laura's voice had that squeaky, high-pitched quality I'd heard the night she came over with the non-alcoholic wine.

The girl in the kiosk tried again, then shook her head. Within a second, Nicole was reaching across Laura with her own card, settling the bill. Telling Laura it didn't matter. Laura was still muttering, shaking her head.

227

'It's – he's done this again, he always does this,' Laura was saying now to Nicole. She looked like she was about to cry.

'Don't worry about it,' Nicole was saying. 'You'll figure it out.'

I paused for a quick look into their prams, curious to see the babies their bumps had turned into. Nicole's pram contained a sleeping dark-haired girl, Laura's a chunky, dungaree-clad boy, bibbed and chewing on a strap, like Beau. I readied myself to leave, but had left it a beat too late. Nicole had turned round. She looked straight at me.

'Sophie! So good to see you!' Nicole moved towards me quickly, beckoning Laura to follow. 'Do you have a minute to sit?'

A couple stood up, deserting the table next to us, the lids of their coffees blowing off into the flower beds as they collected their plates. Nicole motioned me to take their spot. I sat down slowly, the metal seat hard and cold through my jeans.

'How's Claire doing, Sophie?'

She and Laura were staring straight at me, smiles pinned tightly to their faces.

'Um. You know. I think she's OK.'

I did not think this. Claire was much the same. She was looking thin, thinner than she had before the baby was born. Her jogging bottoms, which she wore constantly, hung off her hips. When she bent over, you could see the lines of her ribcage, the bumps of the vertebrae in her back.

'Have you guys not seen her for a while?'

'We've barely seen her since the baby was born,' Laura said.

'She's not returning our calls,' Nicole added. Her eyes narrowed, as if I might be in some way responsible.

'Oh.' I looked away, fiddled with Beau's blanket.

'Do you really think she's OK, Sophie?'

I was taken aback by how much Laura's question annoyed me. I was doing Claire's laundry, her cooking, her dishes, her shopping. I was caring for her baby, and her stepson, while she lay in bed most of the day. I was trying to put on a cheerful face for her husband, trying to cover up how crap she was being just so he wasn't too horrified when he got home. How was I to know if she was OK? No one ever asked if I was OK. I didn't want to be part of this conversation any more.

'You'd have to ask her,' I said. 'I'm sorry, I really need to go.'

I stood up, wiped my hands on my jeans. Nicole's gaze followed my hand.

'Is that Claire's jacket you're wearing, Sophie?'

I froze.

'Claire gave it to me.' I had said it too quickly. I sounded guilty, even though it was the truth.

'Sophie, wait,' Laura said. 'Can you just hang on a second?' I was already turning the pram round, flicking up the brake. She came to my side, placed her hand on my arm.

'We're really worried about Claire. I'm wondering if she might have postnatal depression.'

Hearing Laura say it out loud made me hesitate. She was right. The way Claire had been behaving since the baby wasn't normal.

'Maybe you should speak to Jez,' I said. 'Have you been in touch with him?'

Nicole and Laura glanced at each other. Laura withdrew her hand from my arm.

'We haven't spoken to Jeremy, no,' Laura said. I noticed the use of his real name. Was she telling me off, for referring to him so informally? I felt annoyed again, then. What did Laura know about what me and Jez had to deal with?

'I think maybe you should talk to him and Claire,' I said to Laura.

I started to move the pram away from the table. My heart was pounding, my palms slippery on the push bar.

'Hey! Sophie!'

I turned round. Nicole was right behind me. She had followed me. Laura was still at the table, out of earshot, but watching us both, stirring her coffee. Even from here, I could see the deep line between her brows.

'What's the big rush?'

Nicole's voice was chilly. She was pushing her pram back and forth in front of me in sharp, jagged motions.

'I'm meeting someone.'

'How lovely. Your day for the monkey music class at Clissold House, is it?'

Nicole's voice was light, but her gaze was not. She stared at me, twisting the end of her long ponytail around her finger. I felt the prickle of adrenaline.

'It's so strange. A friend of mine, Jenny, told me the other day that she'd met a Sophie at that class. A pretty young mum, with a little red-haired boy.'

I gripped the bar of the pram.

'I'm sure she was thinking of you. She was surprised when I told her you were just a nanny, though. She seemed to think you were his mum.'

I forced a laugh. 'That's funny,' I managed.

Nicole didn't smile. 'She said you had told everyone you were his mum. That Jez was your husband. And that the baby's name was Teddy.'

I told myself to breathe.

'She obviously just got the wrong end of the stick,' I said. 'I never said anything like that. I just said Jez was his dad. And Teddy's just a nickname. Like Teddy bear. Claire and I call him that all the time.'

Nicole stared at me. The silence was heavy. I badly wanted this conversation to be over.

'Teddy,' she repeated eventually. 'How cute. I must remember that. For when we see her.'

I swallowed, forcing a smile to my face.

'Well, I'm glad I ran into you. Good to clear it up.'

'Of course.'

'Thank God,' she grinned, zipping her jacket. 'For a moment I thought Claire had some kind of psycho nanny on her hands, trying to steal her life! Can you imagine!'

I held my breath.

'I'm sure I'll see you around,' Nicole called, as she walked off. 'Highbury is such a small world.'

I took a breath, and marched the pram out of the park. I needed to tread carefully from here, I saw that now. Very carefully.

'Stupid bitch,' I muttered, once we were at a safe distance. 'She doesn't know the half of it, does she, Teddy?'

TASH

As I wait for Abi in the restaurant, I find myself going over it again. Technically, of course, nothing happened. That's what I keep reminding myself. And yet, I have never done anything like that before. I have become fixated on it, replaying it over and over.

I find myself imagining it from different angles, trying to recall exact details. How much, I keep asking myself, had been him, and how much was me? It feels important to establish, somehow, the exact allocation of blame. Had I, in fact, made the first transgression, when I tilted my chin up, into him? Perhaps he had been reprimanding me, when he spoke my name. But no, because then he had touched my hair. Had it just been my hair? Or had he touched the skin of my face, or just my ear, or the back of my neck? The memory of it was hot under the surface of my skin.

Abi arrives, breaking my train of thought. She looks exactly the same as she did before kids, her skin just as smooth and clear. When I lean to kiss her cheek, she smells clean and soapy, medical rather than fragrant.

'Thanks for coming,' I say, feeling strangely stiff. I haven't seen Abi since Nisha was a newborn.

'Not at all,' she grins, sitting down. 'It's my first lunch out since I've been back at work. It's a treat.'

As she sits, Abi stills the ID card hanging from the blue NHS lanyard at her front. I notice it reads 'Paediatrics' where Tom's says 'Accident and Emergency', but doesn't refer to her being a Child Psychologist.

'I think I'll have the salmon.' She sets the menu down, folds her hands in her lap.

'No starter?'

'I'd better not.' Abi's eyes flick towards the time on her phone. 'So, how can I help?'

Abi has been too polite to remark on the fact that I've never suggested we go for lunch, or even a drink, before, despite the fact that our husbands are so close.

'I was hoping you could help me with something,' I admit. 'Something to do with your – professional knowledge.'

'Oh. You're not worried about Finn, I hope?'

'No, no. Nothing like that.'

I tell Abi about Jude. What I'd seen that day – him walking up and down the steps in the garden, throwing his bear down them. And what Finn had said, about being pushed.

'I hope this doesn't sound completely mad,' I say. 'But it just didn't look like normal playing to me. And after what Finn said about being pushed – on the stairs?'

Abi fiddles with her lanyard. At first, she doesn't say anything.

'Do you have any reason to believe he has experienced a trauma?'

I consider this. 'I mean, it's possible.' I pause. 'He lost his mother at an early age, and then his nanny died, who I think he was very close to.'

'Poor child.' Abi is shaking her head. 'Do you have any reason to believe the trauma involved the stairs? Someone falling, or being pushed?'

'I don't know.' I hesitate. 'Would his ... behaviour suggest he'd seen something like that?'

She looks thoughtful. 'Well, that sort of unresolved trauma would present differently in different children. One child might react by obsessively avoiding stairs. Another sort of child might – as you seem to describe – become obsessed with them.'

'What do you mean, obsessed?'

'The child might become fixated with walking on stairs, rolling down them. He might incorporate stairs into play – building a staircase from blocks, re-enacting toys falling or rolling down the stairs. He would be doing this to process what he has seen, and make sense of it.'

'And he might ... involve other children in those ... games?'

'Exactly. He might want to play at falling down stairs – either falling down himself, or throwing a doll or a teddy. Or – yes, it's not inconceivable he would want to throw, or push, another child.'

I hold my breath.

'It's easy to imagine that he might get so caught up in the game that he would fail to notice another child becoming scared, or starting to withdraw,' Abi says. 'These games might be repeated, and might become even more dangerous, or violent, with repetition.'

The food arrives. I ignore it, the thought of eating a bowl of pasta now unimaginable. I think of Finn's scream, his bloodied lip. I think of Sophie's head injury. Could Jude have seen Sophie pushed down the stairs? Could that have been what really killed her? And if so – who pushed her?

'Can I ask you something in return, Tash?'

I look up at Abi. She is hesitating, her knife and fork poised above her plate.

'Ravi says you came to see him the other day. Asking about some party?' She raises her eyebrows. 'Is everything OK with you and Tom?'

'Fine,' I say automatically.

Of course, everything is very much not fine with me and Tom. It's not just his suspension from work. Or the picture of him with Sophie, which I still haven't asked him about. The thought of what happened with Jez intrudes again, like a shadow blocking the sun.

'I'm glad,' Abi says. Her words seem pointed somehow. 'Tom is a good man, you know.'

Before I can reply, my phone rings. It's Adam. I grimace. I can't just keep ignoring him.

'Go ahead,' Abi says, taking a forkful of salmon.

I take the call outside.

'Hi,' I say. 'Look, Adam –'

'Just hear me out,' he says. 'I found out the name. The person your messages came from.'

SOPHIE

Four weeks before

He asked to meet me in the wetlands. I pointed out that I'd have the baby with me, that I was supposed to be working. But he'd insisted.

I got to the cafe early so I could put some make-up on while Beau slept in the pram. My stomach was swimming too much for coffee. It had been going on for a few months now, but I still felt like this, whenever I was seeing him. That's how I knew this was different, that what I was feeling was real.

I loved this side of the wetlands, with the cafe and the brand-new flats looking out over the water. The surface was sharp and glassy in the sunlight, it made me squint to look at it. There was a heron poised on the railings of the wooden walkway, its neck tucked in an elegant S shape into its grey feathers. As soon as I spotted it, it took off across the reservoir, its wings wide and beautiful.

Jez had told me about the flats loads of times, about all the high-tech features he'd worked on. It wasn't just security. Other stuff, too. The lights knew when to come on; you could talk to the music player and the TV. The internet of things, he called it, or something. He loved to talk about his work.

I wasn't really listening, a lot of the time. I preferred to think about what would happen when he left Claire, when we could finally be together. I had looked up how much their house was worth – I guessed he would have to give her half, and we'd have to share the boys, but even half was enough for a lovely place. We could even get one of the flats here, so that I could start doing my swimming again, like I used to before I got so busy with the boys. Three beds would

be best: the boys could share when they stayed, and we would have a baby of our own, in time – I was already fantasising about coming off the pill, surprising him with a positive test. Yes, I could see us in one of the nice ground-floor properties, the ones with sliding doors facing the water. It wouldn't have to be huge. It just had to be ours, mine and his.

The bell on the door jangled and he stepped in, raised a hand and both eyebrows at me. 'Sophie,' he said, smiling blandly. 'You OK for a coffee?'

I was confused by the way he was speaking to me, like we were here for a work meeting. Then I realised that that's probably just what he wanted everyone in the cafe to think.

He returned with his drink and sat opposite me, planting his feet apart. I started to speak, and he went at the same time. We both laughed.

'Sorry,' I said. 'You first.'

'All right.' He had stopped smiling. 'It's about us, Sophie. All this. I can't do it any more. I really can't.'

After the initial stab of panic, I told myself to keep calm. He'd had this before – attacks of guilt about Claire. It had never taken much to divert him, when it had happened at home, or in his office. I only had to slip my hand inside his trousers, or unbutton my dress a little, show him what I was wearing underneath. I loved watching him come, shuddering as he buried his head in my chest, crying out as if he were in pain. I imagined what he was used to with her – stretchy beige maternity bra, pyjamas and glasses. Sometimes I wondered whether it was this thought that thrilled me the most. The thought of getting one over on Claire, Laura, Nicole. Lydia. Margot. All those smug ponytail mothers.

'I'm serious, Sophie,' Jez was saying. 'It's over. We need to forget this. Move on.'

My mouth started to twitch at the corners.

'You don't mean that,' I soothed. 'Look, Jez, I know it's complicated, I know people will get hurt, but –'

'No, no.' He was speaking more firmly now. 'Nobody needs to get hurt.'

'But … but … I know you're not happy. With her.'

He leaned in towards me. When he spoke, his words were thick with danger.

'Sophie, listen to me,' he said. 'Claire is my wife. I would lose everything. My home. My boys ...'

'You wouldn't! We would –'

'Sophie ... this was just a mistake!'

I felt my jaw fall open. My expression must have shocked him into a different tack. He softened his tone. He took my hand under the table, started to move his finger up and down my wrist.

'It's my fault, all this,' he said. 'Everything is too complicated – You're just a child, I –'

'A child?' I pulled my hand away.

'Young. I just mean young. Keep your voice down, Sophie, please.'

'You know, I don't think I will.' I didn't care about the people in the cafe. I didn't care about them at all. 'Do you actually have any idea what I do all day?'

I stood up, took the handlebar of the pram and shoved it towards Jez, so hard that he gasped.

'Here's your son,' I tell him, pointing at Beau. 'Fast asleep at the appropriate time, in the soft, clean clothes I chose for him. There's his toy, tucked by his hand. There's the warmed bottles I made him this morning, underneath, for when he wakes. There's the home-made baby food, the weaning spoons, the nappies I topped up this morning, the spare blankets I washed and dried over the weekend.'

Jez clenched his jaw.

'I think you'll find I'm the adult in this scenario, Jez,' I hiss. 'And thank God for that! Somebody needs to be their fucking mother!'

I saw a muscle in Jez's cheek flicker, one I'd never noticed before. His mouth opened, then closed again. Then he stood up, and strode out of the cafe.

TASH

It is busy at Cuckoo Club, and at first I think perhaps Sal hasn't come. I pay my three pounds entry fee wordlessly. The gum-chewing girl at the trestle table at the front doesn't bother asking why I don't appear to have a child in tow. I make my way past the grubby carpet with roads printed on it, the fake kitchens and plastic food.

Sal is sitting at the back in a makeshift window seat with a chipped mug of coffee. The glass behind her is smeared with children's hand-prints. The twins are tottering around in front of her, mashing at buttons on plastic walkers.

Sal smirks. 'Fancied a go on the slide?'

'Very funny,' I mutter. 'I was looking for you, as it happens. I know it was you. I know about the messages.'

She looks blank. 'What?'

'And I know what you did to my laptop ...'

'Your laptop? Yeah. I found it. A thanks would be nice.'

I laugh. 'Oh, sure. So you didn't do anything to it? Put a virus on it? Delete my work, thousands of pounds' worth of work?'

'I literally don't know what you're talking about,' she says, in a bored voice.

'Right. Just like you don't know about the text messages.'

'Oh, that again! I told you, I never sent no messages.'

'Except I know you did. The police traced the numbers for me. They were registered in your name.'

At the mention of police, Sal's head snaps up.

'What? That's bullshit!'

237

I ignore her. My voice is shaking. 'I've been trying to work it out. Why would a supposed friend of Sophie's do all this, to someone who was just trying to find out the truth?'

Sal makes an outraged noise. 'You think I don't want to know who killed Sophie?' Her voice is different now. Thick with anger. 'Sophie was my friend, Tash. Not yours. You didn't even know her.'

The children playing nearest to us look up in surprise at the hostility of our conversation. We throw them matching bland smiles, then turn back to each other.

'Why did you send me those messages?'

'I told you,' she hisses. 'I didn't!'

Sal and I stare at each other. Behind her, the breeze picks up, scattering leaves across the church car park.

'What happened to Sophie?'

Sal gives me an incredulous look. 'Why? Why do you need to know?' She shakes her head, brushes some imaginary dust from her leopard-print leggings. 'I'm not interested in talking to you. None of us are. We all know you're a journalist, just after a story. And anyway, I don't know who—'

Sal glances at the toddlers, then lowers her voice to a whisper.

'I don't know who killed her.'

'But you know *someone* did,' I hiss back. 'What did they do? Was she pushed down the stairs? Is that what killed her?'

Sal opens her mouth, then closes it again. The twins have veered off towards the craft table. Sal stands up and follows them, busies herself rolling their sleeves up, handing out different-shaped sponges, little plastic bowls of paint. I follow her to the table.

'Tell me who the boyfriend was,' I demand. 'Was he there that night? At the party?'

Sal lifts the paintbrush for Aiden, starts mixing red into the blue. She won't meet my eye.

'I knew what was happening,' Sal says eventually. 'I knew she wasn't safe. I knew he was bad news. I should have done something. Stopped her.'

'Stopped her doing what?'

Sal keeps painting, furiously, daubing stroke after stroke of purple paint gloopily over the paper. In her fingers, the paintbrush is shaking.

238

'Sophie found something out. I told her. She was going to confront him. I think that's why she was killed. For what she knew.'

I lean towards Sal. 'What? What was it? Who was she going to confront? Please, talk to me.'

Sal shakes her head. 'You should leave this, Tash. You should leave it alone.'

'Why? Why should I? Who has told you not to talk about this?'

Sal carries on daubing marks on paper with the brush. She looks up, around the room, then towards the door, as if checking if she is being watched.

'What are you looking at?'

I try to follow her gaze, but I can't see anyone. I look back at her. She is still jabbing at the page with her brush, breathing heavily, her cheeks flushed, as if she is about to have a panic attack.

'What is it, Sal? Who are you so afraid of?'

Abruptly, Sal stands up and plucks one twin onto each hip. 'We're going,' she mutters. 'Don't forget your picture.' She thrusts the painting in front of me on the table, the paint still wet. I look down, confused. Then a jolt shoots through me as I see what she has daubed on the page.

'Wait – what? Sal, wait!'

Sal is already retreating through the double doors, the twins in the pram protesting that they want to stay. I try to push through to where she is, but am blocked by one pram, then another, before nearly tripping over a woman changing her baby on the floor.

'Do you mind?' she mutters. She glances, disapprovingly, at my heeled boots, my laptop case, my lack of child. 'This is a baby and toddler group, you know.'

When I finally get outside, Sal is already way down the street. I shout after her, but her eyes are glued to the pavement. She is refusing to look back.

Blood pounds in my eardrums. I turn away, towards the park. I take a moment, standing in the street, waiting for my senses to recalibrate.

It's then that I see the woman on the other side of the road. She is standing in the shadow of a doorway overhung with a thick bank of ivy. Dark leggings, dark glasses, despite the overcast sky. A shiny black Puffa jacket. Her hair is tied up, her cap pulled low.

She is hiding. Why else would anyone stand in a doorway like that? Then I look more closely, and realise who it is. It's Nicole.

I avert my eyes, pretending I haven't seen her. I walk off, turning down the nearest side street. Then, I double back round the next corner, and head down a different side street, so I can watch her unobserved.

Was she the person Sal was looking at? The person she was afraid of?

Nicole pulls her cap down over her face and sets off sharply in the direction of Highbury Barn. I follow at a safe distance, tracking her as she crosses over the road, walks along the parade of shops. But when I expect her to head over the park, towards her house, she instead steps into a coffee shop.

I pull my own hood over my head, and duck into the launderette opposite. I stand close to the window, pretending to fumble for coins for the machine in my bag. After a few moments, I risk a glance across the street.

They are all there. Claire, Laura and Nicole. Claire is talking an unusual amount, gesturing, Laura nodding back. Their faces are illuminated by a single pendant hanging over their circular table. They are leaning into the centre of it, their faces painted with the yellow light and, for a moment, they don't look like the women I know. They look like strangers.

SOPHIE

Three weeks before

Sal and I had taken the boys to the soft play, a huge wipe-clean maze of cargo ropes, ball pits and plastic slides, with a clown's face looming down from the entrance. Claire never took Jude or Beau to places like this. She said they were full of germs.

Jude knew I was upset about something. He'd kept close to me all week, snuggling up to me on the sofa and taking my face between his hands as if he was trying to work out why I was so quiet these days, why my eyes were always red.

While the older boys played, Sal and I sat and sipped our instant coffee from polystyrene cups and shared a chocolate muffin. Beau and Eliza napped silently in their prams.

The more I thought about what had happened between Jez and me, the more the soft edges wore off. I found myself remembering the embarrassing physicality of that first time, in the annexe, when I'd got home after that horrible night with the runner, my make-up all smudged. I thought how obvious my inexperience must have been. How I'd had to push my backpack and the Tupperware I used for sandwiches off the bed, how I couldn't undo my bra at the back. The squelching sound when he pulled out of me that neither of us acknowledged. How I felt him flinch slightly when I went down on him and my teeth accidentally made contact with his skin.

I obsessed about how I had looked, the last few times. His office. The darkroom. I thought endlessly about how recently I'd showered, whether there was any possibility I could have smelled.

More than anything, I thought about what I'd allowed myself to imagine, my childish fantasy of what I'd told myself would happen

next. A little place in the wetlands development, doors out to the front, a blue bedroom with bunk beds for the boys. He hadn't wanted any of that.

'You're very quiet today,' Sal said.

When I didn't reply, Sal took a bite of muffin, looked around the room.

'This place reminds me of a contact centre,' she muttered.

'Hey? A what?'

'Oh, don't worry about it.' Sal placed the muffin down, brushed the crumbs from her hands. 'Come on, spit it out. Whatever it is, it can't be as dumb as some of the shit I've done in my time.'

I tried to laugh, but I could feel my lip wobbling. 'It's nothing. I've just been a bit stupid, that's all.'

The tears started before I could do anything to stop them. I snatched the plasticky napkin from the sticky red table and held it against my face.

'Jez, is it?'

It wasn't in Sal's nature to comfort, but she didn't gloat either, even though she had tried to warn me. Just listened, and nodded, her face grim.

'I'm such an idiot. Such a stupid, stupid idiot.'

Sal shook her head. 'We all make mistakes. You're young. Put it down to experience.'

'I feel so stupid, though, Sal.'

And of course, that was a big part of the hurt. I wished more than anything that nothing had ever happened, that I had just kept him and me safe in my mind. Unreal, undamaged. Perfect.

'He's the one in the wrong. You do know that, don't you?' Sal sighed. 'It's just what he's like. Here, have one of these, your mascara's going.' I took the wipe from Sal's bag gratefully. I was crying unattractively now, my face wet, snot-filled, embarrassing. People were looking, but I couldn't seem to stop.

When I caught my breath, I asked her what she meant.

'Hmm?'

I sniffed. 'You said this was just what he was like. What did you mean?'

'Oh. Nothing,' she said quickly. 'I just meant – you know, I'm sure you're not the only one.'

242

I turned to face her. 'Who else? Who else is there?'

'Oh, I wasn't – I just meant that's what men are like. Men in general. Forget I said anything.'

The boys reappeared. Billy was sobbing, clutching his arm, wailing something about Jude hitting him. Jude was racing ahead to plead his innocence. Sal scooped Billy into her arms and shoved the remains of her half of the muffin into his hand.

'You should get out of that house, get away from them,' she said to me, over the boys' heads. 'I can't see it ending well, Soph. I really can't.'

I couldn't forget what Sal had said. I thought about it all that week. I thought about it when I watched Jez put his tie on in the morning, when I saw him checking his phone on the sofa. And when, one evening the following week, Jez announced he was going out, I thought about it again.

As soon as he was gone, I crept up the stairs. Jude was asleep, and soft, snoring sounds were coming from Claire's bedroom. The door was slightly ajar, and I could see her and Beau side by side in the bed, a makeshift circle of pillows around the outside.

The door to Jez's office was ajar. His desk was immaculately tidy. I opened one drawer, then another. Pens, paper clips, an old glasses case. Then I pulled the bottom one, and it jammed.

I studied the keyhole. Tiny and round. Nothing on his desk, or in the top drawer. So I pulled a grip out of my hair, and started on the lock.

TASH

The thunder bursts over my head as I reach the long brick balconies of Sal's estate. I pull my hood up and squint into the rain, trying to remember which is her door.

Eventually I recognise it, the one at the end, with the washing line outside, loaded with little boys' pyjamas and tracksuit bottoms. They are getting soaked, the colours deepening, droplets forming on the ends of the socks.

There is no answer when I bang on her door. The ginger cat leaps onto the back of the sofa just inside the window and scratches at the frame as if to get out.

The lights in Sal's front room aren't on, despite the darkening sky. I knock again. Still no answer. I glance at my phone. It is three minutes past seven. It was definitely a 7 she daubed on the paper.

I call Sal's phone, and I hear the faint sound of it ringing inside, just by the window. No one answers. I decide to clamber around the junk on her front patio to look into the window from the other side.

Sal is there. She is right next to her phone, curled into the back of the sofa. Is she asleep? I call the phone and its surface lights up, but Sal doesn't move. There is a taste of metal in my mouth. A shudder passes over my skin.

I don't notice my hood has fallen to my shoulders until I feel rain on my cheeks, my lips. I take a step back just as the roar and crack of thunder comes. Then I throw myself, shoulder first, against the door.

Incredibly, it works. The door is flimsy, the lock easily broken. I feel myself stumbling over her step, reeling from the impact, the pain

in the top of my arm. The ginger cat is around my legs immediately, purring and meowing. I push it away.

'Sal?'

As I call her name in the darkness, I am still hoping I have somehow got it wrong, that she is going to emerge from the front room, switching on the light and rubbing her eyes, asking me what the fuck I am doing breaking into her house.

But she doesn't.

A sound is coming from the door out to the patio outside; is someone in the backyard? Her kitchen door is definitely open; I can hear the sound of it banging against the fence in the wind, the howl of the storm at the windows.

On the sofa next to Sal, her phone is still buzzing, rotating slowly with each ring, my name, TASH, on the lit-up screen, the room's only source of light. The phone drops to the floor, and I jump.

'Sal?'

Her chin is tucked into her chest, her face right up against the back of the sofa. It looks wrong, but even then, as I place my hands softly on her body, I think that she might, perhaps, come to.

Instead I feel myself pulling her towards me, her limp body rolling heavily onto her back, her left arm swinging down beside her. I gasp, pull my hands away and jump back. Her eyes and mouth are open, her T-shirt wet with vomit. The smell hits me, sharp in my nostrils.

I fumble for my phone. Somehow my fingers can't find the edges of it. I dial 999, but when the voice comes through, asking for my location, I can't answer. My mind is white and cold, like a blank page.

The back door slams again. A sound is coming from outside, like something is clattering, or loose. The kitchen floor is wet. Clutching my phone to my ear, I step outside into the small, paved yard at the back of Sal's flat. I can't see anything, or anyone. Just a darkening sky, the twitch of lightning behind the clouds.

'Hello?'

I stammer a reply to the 999 responder, giving the name of the estate. 'I can't remember the flat number,' I hear myself say. 'It's Sal Cunningham – I think she needs an ambulance.' I hear myself say it even though I know no ambulance is going to help her now.

A low roll of thunder sounds. I step back into the kitchen. I hear the crackling voice from the phone I am still holding to my ear, asking again if the person is conscious, if the person is breathing.

Only then do I notice the empty wine glass on the worktop by the fridge, and next to it, a pile of brown, labelled bottles. White pills, scattered across the stone surface, like a handful of children's sweets.

TASH

There is a reception at the community centre on the estate after the funeral, but I can't face Sal's friends and family. People know I was the one who found her. I feel their eyes on me in the church, in the car park, as everyone files out at the end.

I know now that something is very wrong, that I am out of my depth. But Sal, my only real hope of finding out the truth, is gone. I have no idea which way to turn.

As I walk down the path, Christina catches up with me. 'Can you come for a drink?'

'I'm not going to the thing,' I tell her. 'Sorry. I can't.'

'Me neither. But I need a drink.'

There's no way I'll get anything else done today. I have nothing to lose.

We walk in silence through the park. It feels inexplicable that it is a sunny day, that life is carrying on as usual, when we have just buried Sal. Street sweepers are still sweeping, the white-van men still honking their horns on Green Lanes.

I follow Christina into a pub on the other side of the park. It is nearly empty, just a few committed day drinkers, one leaning on the bar, another staring up at the horse racing on the TV from a small corner table, a wrinkled betting slip in his hand. She asks for a bottle of white wine, even though it is barely midday, then carries it and two glasses wordlessly to our table.

Christina unbuttons her coat, and sets it over the back of the chair. 'So,' she says. 'You found Sal.'

It doesn't seem worth replying.

'What were you doing at her house that night, Tash?'

'What?'

'I wasn't aware you were friends with Sal.'

'I wasn't, exactly.'

'I'm just trying to understand what happened.'

We both know what the official explanation has been. Sal was depressed, and took an overdose of prescription drugs. The drugs had not been prescribed to Sal: the presumption is that she obtained them in street deals. There is still dealing on Sal's estate, despite the best efforts of police and residents to stamp it out with increased security. Enquiries continue.

I gaze into the glass of white wine Christina has poured for me. Clouds of condensation gather at the sides.

'I don't buy it,' Christina says.

'Don't buy what?'

'What the police are saying. Sal would never have killed herself. She'd never have done this to Billy. Never.'

At the mention of Billy's name, Christina's eyes redden. She cups a hand to her mouth. I close my eyes, and try not to think about the little boy in school trousers that pooled at his ankles, holding the hand of his nan, looking at the black oblong where his mummy should be.

Christina is looking past me, over to the bar.

'I have a spare set of keys to Sal's flat,' she says slowly. 'A few days before she died, they went missing.'

'Keys to Sal's flat?'

'Yes. Two at the front, one at the back.'

'Where'd they go missing from?'

'My bag. Someone took them.'

Christina sets her glass down between us, like a chess piece.

'Are you sure –'

'Of course I'm sure. I don't lose things.'

'Where had you been?'

'Normal places. Home. Work. Playgroup.'

I try to think who I'd seen at playgroup pickups and drop-offs last week. They'd all been there, all the mums. I think about Nicole outside Cuckoo Club, the way I'd seen them talking in that cafe. But surely they couldn't have been involved in something like this.

'Did you tell the police? About the keys going missing?'

She shoots me a look. 'Did you tell them what you were really doing at Sal's that night?' She tilts her head. 'How did you get in, anyway?'

'What? You think I stole your keys?' I almost laugh. 'Jesus, Christina. No. I saw her in there. I could see something was up. So I broke the lock.'

'It was locked from the inside?'

'Not double-locked. Clearly.'

We look testily at each other. I take a sip of my wine.

'You still haven't told me,' Christina presses, 'what you were doing there, in the first place.'

I take a large gulp of wine, and swallow it. 'I was asking her about Sophie Blake.'

Christina's eyes narrow. 'Why, Tash?'

'Because I'm a journalist,' I snap, exasperated. 'That's what I do. I ask questions. Even ones people don't want to be asked. In fact, especially those ones.'

Christina's eyes flick to the floor.

'I know someone killed Sophie,' I say. 'I think whoever did it wants to scare me into dropping it. I've been getting messages, threats –'

Christina looks back up at me. 'What kind of threats?'

I decide there is nothing to lose. I tell her about the text messages, the missing files on my laptop, the broken glass. I watch Christina's legal mind registering and weighing each item in turn.

'The numbers were registered in Sal's name, but when I confronted her, she insisted they were nothing to do with her.'

'When did you confront her?'

'The day she died. At Cuckoo Club.'

Christina stares at me blankly. 'What the fuck is Cuckoo Club?'

'It's a stay-and-play, in Highbury – oh, never mind. The point is, I went to find Sal there. I wanted to confront her about the messages. She said she hadn't sent them, but that she wanted to tell me something – that Sophie had known something, something she wasn't supposed to know. That she thinks that's why she was killed.'

Christina's head snaps up. 'Did she say what?'

I shake my head. 'No. But she was going to tell me. She painted a message on some paper – told me to come to her house that night, at seven. I went, like she asked. When I got there, she was dead.'

Christina opens her mouth, then closes it again.

'You know, don't you?' I say. 'You know what it is that Sal was going to tell me.'

Christina snatches her phone and keys up from the table, her ringless fingers rapping against the wood. Then she takes her coat and storms out of the pub, the door swinging behind her.

That night, I run searches on Christina. This time, I do a proper job. As I suspected, she is on the electoral roll at the wetlands development. She has lived there since Eliza was born. I pull the birth certificate for Eliza, using my old login for the genealogy site we always used at the *Post*, hoping no one notices. Eliza Imogen Sandwell was born in 2016, like Finn. No father is named.

From her LinkedIn profile, I find the name of Christina's chambers. I pull up its website again, and look through it more carefully this time. Christina's headshot is striking among a grid of mostly older, white men.

I click on a link to an award Christina was nominated for. I flick through the galleries of the awards ceremonies until I find 2011, the year Christina was nominated. I scroll through dozens of group shots. Finally, there she is, wearing a long green dress and standing with another female lawyer, being handed a prize by an old, grey-haired man in a tuxedo.

I scan the caption. Then I stop, and reread it.

Christina Sandwell at the Family Law awards 2011 with fellow barrister Emily Henderson, also of Eden Court Chambers, holding the Family Law Junior Barrister of the Year award.

I look closely at the picture. The curly hair, dark, intelligent eyes, porcelain skin. Emily Henderson.

The woman in the picture with Christina is Jude's mother. Jeremy's first wife.

SOPHIE

Nineteen days before

It was all Emily, all of it. The whole drawer was full of pictures of her. I picked one up that was near the top. She was small and pretty, curly-haired, dimple-cheeked, smiling. She looked clever and mischievous, like Jude. One of her hands was curled upwards to meet Jez's as it hung off her shoulder. The other rested on a swollen stomach.

The Jez in the pictures was younger. His skin was smoother, with no bags under his eyes, as if he'd been airbrushed. He was so handsome. I felt that everything would have been different, if I'd been older, if I'd met him sooner. But this younger Jez had his arm around someone else. Someone who didn't look like me, or Claire.

My hands shook as I sifted through photo after photo of Jez's first wife. Then I started to find other things. A will. Letters from a solicitor. A quote from a funeral director. Beneath them, a booklet of some kind. I picked it up, then immediately dropped it. It had a photograph of Emily on the front, and the words underneath said:

In memoriam
EMILY LOUISE HENDERSON
8.8.1980–2.12.2013

It was the order of service from her funeral. I felt sick. I shouldn't be touching these things. What was I doing?

I started to push the drawer closed, then froze. There was something else inside. A phone, an old one. It was switched on, with full signal.

I knew what it meant when a man had a second phone. It meant he was having an affair. Except I already knew that. He was having an affair with me. But we'd never needed phones. We lived in the same house. Besides, I was the nanny. Calls between us were hardly suspicious.

I picked the phone up, and tried the pin I'd seen Jez enter on his phone many times. It worked. But there was nothing. No numbers saved. No message history.

Who was he talking to on this phone?

TASH

Laura and I are standing at playgroup pickup. Laura is holding a coffee, but she isn't drinking it. She stirs the surface of it with her wooden stirrer, upsetting the perfect barista swirl of white and brown, until it is long past cold.

I suspect I know what she is thinking about. The same thought has been in all of our minds all week.

'I can't get over how awful it is,' she says eventually. 'Poor Billy. What he must be going through.'

The talk is that Billy is living with his nan, Sal's mum, for the foreseeable future. He hasn't yet been back at school, Claire says, but there has been a special assembly about it.

'It's the stuff of nightmares, isn't it?' I agree grimly. 'Leaving your child parentless.'

'It really is, isn't it?' Laura sounds choked with emotion. 'You'd do anything to spare your children that.'

Laura adjusts her scarf, as if to indicate that it is the scarf to blame for the choking noise in her voice, the tightness around her mouth. I reach over and squeeze her hand. It feels cold and slight in mine.

The doors open, and Oscar and Finn barrel towards us. Simultaneously, Laura and I reset our faces to happy, crouch down to kiss our boys, ask them how their day was, express our delight over the drawings they are clutching in their hands, straighten the jackets and backpack straps that flop down over their shoulders.

As we stand up, Laura glances at me.

'You got time for another coffee, Tash? In the park, maybe, so the boys can run around?'

I am about to say no. I'm still not sure I can trust Laura. I think again about the day Sal died, how I saw her and the others after Cuckoo Club. Behind Finn, I spot Christina, hurrying away with Eliza, almost dragging her by her arm.

I haven't spoken to Christina since the day of Sal's funeral, even though she is at playgroup pickup every day now for Eliza. When she arrives, all the other mothers fall silent. The squeak of her bike brakes feels deafening.

I feel sure that Christina is the key to this, now. She knows what Sophie knew, the secret Sal thought had led to her death. It must be significant that Christina had known Jude's mother, had worked with her in the same chambers, that Sophie had a photograph of Christina. But I can't work out why, and she won't talk to me. I'm still not getting any answers. Just more questions.

'Mummy, can we go and play with Oscar?'

Finn is tugging at my hand. I know he'll throw a fit if we say no. And anyway, maybe it wouldn't be a bad thing to have a coffee with Laura. Maybe it'll help me work out what the other day was all about. What she and the others were up to on the day that Sal died.

In the days since Sal's death, spring has burst into life along the park, the paths scattered with pink and white blossom, the beds dotted with the purple, yellow and white of municipal spring bulbs. Crocuses, snowdrops, daffodils. It is merciless, how the world moves on after the death of a person, how they can disappear without trace, like footprints in the melting snow.

Laura and I sit on the metal table by the grass where Oscar and Finn are playing.

'I find it hard to believe she did it,' I say after a while. 'Don't you?'

'What?'

'I just find it hard to believe Sal would have ... done something like that.'

Laura makes a face, squints over at the boys. 'I don't know. Depression is such a terrible thing. It really is an illness. Some people just can't beat it.'

'I suppose.'

Laura looks nervous. She is rolling a paper tube of sugar between my fingers. The paper comes away, surprising her in a scatter of grains across the metal surface of the table.

Laura turns towards me, her hand shielding her eyes from the sun. 'Are you guys still coming to Cornwall?'

I'd been so thrown by Sal's death, Tom's work crisis, that I'd been deliberately putting off thinking about Cornwall. It felt kind of un-imaginable to me now that we would spend a whole week under the same roof as Jez and Claire – not to mention Nicole, after I saw her following me, plus Laura's husband Ed, whom I had now mentally reclassified from supportive flexible-working father to possible weirdo. But when I'd told Tom I wasn't sure we should go, he had looked really disappointed.

'Oh. But I've booked surfing lessons for Finney and me.'

'Isn't he a bit young?' I protested. 'He can't even swim.'

'I'll hold him.' Tom grinned. 'He'll be body-boarding by the end of the week.'

I felt a sick roll of dread in the pit of my stomach. I could see the thought of time away was really lifting Tom's spirits, and I was relieved – I had been starting to worry that Tom was getting really down. I had told him only a brief outline of what was going on at the playgroup – he'd never met Sal, so while he was shocked by the news of her death, he hadn't asked many follow-up questions. He had been told, at his last meeting with bosses at the hospital, that they were still waiting for the complainant to come in for a formal statement, before deciding on 'the next steps'. I had started to tell myself that maybe a holiday, any holiday, was worth enduring, if it would take Tom's mind off it all.

'Oh please come,' Laura says. 'It would be really good to have you there, Tash. Plus, Ed can't come now, so I'll be solo parenting.' She rolls her eyes.

'Ed's not coming? Why not?'

'Some work thing.' Laura shakes her head. I hesitate. That's one less thing to worry about, I suppose.

'I ... I think we are coming,' I tell Laura uncertainly. 'It would ... certainly be nice. To get away.'

Laura smiles weakly. 'I'm glad, Tash. It's been such a strange few weeks. It'll be good to be somewhere else.'

I couldn't disagree with that.

That night, when Finn is in bed, I join Tom in the kitchen. I can smell soy sauce and sesame. There is a sizzle of frying onions, a pot on the

stove into which Tom is tipping a pack of noodles. A curl of smoke drifts in the air below the single working spotlight in the ceiling.

I open a window. The wood of the frame feels cold and damp, as if it might crumble away in my hand.

'Hey,' I say.

Tom throws a tea towel over his shoulder and leans back against the worktop, his fingers curled around the edge. When he looks at my face, he gives me a quizzical look.

'What is it?'

'Tom,' I say, 'I need to ask you about what happened when I went to France with Finn, the summer before last.'

SOPHIE

Thirteen days before

I watched them from the stairs. Claire was in the front room, watching TV, her back to Jez. He placed a hand on her shoulder.

'I've got to head back to the office.'

'OK,' I heard Claire say. 'Will you be late?'

'Might be. Sorry. But Sophie's here.'

I had to do this. I had to know who she was.

I used the annexe door when I left so I wouldn't be heard. It was raining, a soft, June rain, more like a cloudiness. I pulled my hoody over my hair and followed him.

By the time I turned the corner, Jez was halfway down St Augustine's path. I followed him, tacking close to the high walls of the church, fragrant with damp and moss, staying at the edges, in shadow.

Jez walked quickly. By the time we reached the alleyway between the New River and the wetlands, I felt out of breath. The gravel path was noisy underfoot, so I stuck to the grassy beds either side.

Jez crossed the boulders and the grasses, towards the newest, smartest part of the development. But when we reached the office, with the rushing silver fountain outside, he didn't go in there. Instead he pulled a key card from the breast pocket inside his suit jacket, waved it in front of a sensor outside a glass door opposite, and headed towards a lift.

I followed just close enough to shove my trainer in the gap between the glass door and the frame as he stepped into the lift. My heart was pounding as I watched the numbers rise steadily, then stop.

I went to the next lift, tried to call it. But nothing happened. The lifts were controlled by a key card. I couldn't get up.

I made my way out, hitting the exit button to open the glass door. The wind pulled my hair across my face. I rubbed it from my eyes and headed to the path.

From there, it was easy to see inside. The windows were floor to ceiling, the penthouse lit up like a theatre stage, a floating box of light.

I could see everything. The curving arch of the floor lamp, the glint of copper on the lights over the kitchen island. And I could see two figures. One fair-headed, and one tall and dark, her hair flowing out behind her as she reached up to him and he kissed her lips.

I couldn't see her face, but I knew it was her. The same person I'd seen that day in the cafe, watching Jez with Claire. This was Jez's other woman. And what did that make me? The words rustled in my ears like the sound of the wind. Nothing. Nothing. Nothing.

Looking up at them, I finally felt the full, sick sucker punch of it. It was as if all the blood had flooded to my face in one final hot, sick sting of humiliation. Of rage.

TASH

'Is this for real, Tash?'

I hold up my printout of the CCTV photograph.

'This is you,' I say. 'Leaving the party with Sophie Blake. Hours before she died. What were you doing with her, Tom?'

Tom takes the printout in his hands. He looks up at me; his voice is low. 'Tash,' he says, slowly. 'Have you completely lost your mind?'

I think in my head I expected some cataclysm. Instead, as the words come out, it does slightly feel as if the whole mad narrative that has grown up in the dark corners of my mind is collapsing in on itself in the light of our normal evening in the kitchen.

'Are we really having this conversation? Is this really you asking me if I had an affair with some girl we met once, and then ... what, murdered her? Because of this?'

He waves the paper at me. It's not printed properly at the edges, and the lines that make up Tom's hand have thinned slightly where the ink cartridge was running out, like a faded bar code.

'I'm just asking what happened. Why you never mentioned that – the week I was out of the country with Finn – you went to a big fancy party. A party hosted by Claire and Jez – who, at Christmas, you acted like you'd never met before.'

'But I hardly even –'

'And then I find out you went missing that night, abandoned Ravi –'

'Ravi?' Tom looks stunned. 'When did you talk to Ravi?'

'– and left the party with your arm around a very pretty girl –'

'My arm ... what the hell are you –'

259

'– a girl that we had met a few weeks earlier when we visited the playgroup. A girl who was then found dead, and whose picture I then found in your sock drawer!'

'I never had my arm around anyone!' Tom is staring at me. 'Where did this even come from? No – do you know what, Tash, don't even tell me. I don't care about your bloody investigation.'

'Tom, I'm just –'

Tom tosses the paper onto the worktop, and holds his palms up between us. 'We have been married five years – we have a child!' Even in his fury, he lowers his voice, is careful not to wake up Finn, and the fact of that twists at my heart. 'Do you actually believe there is a possibility I could have killed someone?'

'Of course not – I didn't say that!' This is true, I realise. I never really believed he could have killed anybody.

'Then what the hell is this?' Tom points at the crumpled photo, now lying face down by the sink, washing-up water soaking into the edges.

'I just want to know what happened that night,' I say, after a few moments. 'That's all. I'm not accusing you of anything. I just need to know.'

'Fine,' Tom said. 'I'll tell you exactly what happened.'

Tom tells me the same story I've heard already from Ravi. He went for a drink with some people from work, Ravi included. Laura asked Ravi if he would drive to 'some posey party'. He had promised Tom a lift, but Laura had 'wheedled away, said that we could both come along to some fabulous party instead if we drove her there, and get free champagne – even though no one – least of all Ravi – wanted free champagne'.

'The only reason Ravi said yes,' Tom says, 'is that he is too nice for his own good, and the only reason I was there was the lift – it was the Tube strike that week. You can look it up.'

'OK, OK,' I say. 'But why did you never mention any party to me? When we came back from France?'

Tom groans. 'Because you were already pissed off with me about the holiday, and I knew what it would sound like. Like I was living it up while you were hauling Finn to France and back on your own.' He rubbed his eyes with his hands. 'But honestly, Tash – it was just a posh, boring party. You know I hate that sort of stuff.'

'But Laura must have introduced you to Claire and Jez. It was their party!'

'I wasn't paying attention! I wasn't bothered about meeting Laura's posh friends ... you know what I'm like at parties!'

'And then what? What happened at the end of the evening?'

'I got bored of Laura prattling on, looking over her shoulder for – well, I don't know who, someone else she was clearly much more interested in talking to – I went off for a piss, and then I went home. That was it. This –' he plucks up the piece of paper – 'is a picture of me holding open a door for a girl who was leaving at the same time as me. I do remember it, actually. She had a baby in a pram – he looked about Finn's age. I might have asked about him. It made me miss Finney.' Tom's voice is cracking a bit. 'All I did,' he says, 'was help her get through.'

'You didn't recognise her? From our tour of the nursery?'

Tom shakes his head slowly. 'No, I didn't. And the photo thing – you know Finn hides stuff. Takes your work papers and puts them away.' Tom works his jaw, as if he's trying to contain his rage. 'You know, I have never actually said this out loud, because I knew how you'd react, but I am pretty sure he does that because he hates you working every single second of the evenings and weekends, when we're supposed to all be together.'

I gasp.

'That's not true.'

'Maybe, maybe not.'

Tom sighs. 'It's just a coincidence, Tash. Whatever happened to Sophie Blake – it was nothing to do with me. I'm not keeping anything secret from you.'

He pauses, looks away from me, out of the window with the horrible new bars.

'Can you say the same, Tash?' he asks quietly. 'Can you honestly say you're not keeping any secrets from me?'

I frown at Tom. 'What do you mean?'

'Anything you want to tell me about your secret credit card? About selling your dad's pictures?' He looks back at me, sadly. 'Or should we start with you and Jeremy Henderson?'

SOPHIE

Ten days before

When it became clear to me how stupid I'd been, how I had humiliated myself, even more anger started to seep into my sadness, like a
clean wound going bad. I found myself smiling less, not bothering
with please and thank you. I found it strange that I had ever bothered
to please people, to make their lives comfortable. I was ashamed of
myself for how obsessed I'd been with Jez and Claire's approval, how
hard I'd worked to help make their beautiful house more beautiful,
their easy lives easier. And now look. Look what they had done to me.

One day, Sal found me outside the playgroup, waiting in the bike
shelter for the rain to stop. The sound of it on the metal roof was
soothing, somehow. I rubbed at my eyes. They felt raw and red. When
Sal saw me, she shook her head.

'He shouldn't get away with it,' Sal said.

The rain dripped from the dips in the metal onto the tarmac path.
I kept imagining Jez in the penthouse with that woman, gazing out of
the big glass windows over the rainy city like a god. While down below,
me and Sal looked after these children, all day, filled their bellies, wiped
their bottoms, returned them at the end of the day, fed and clean and
happy. Their lives were kept clean and silent and perfect, because of us.

I saw what he and Claire had been doing now, for what it was.
Using me as whatever they wanted – a surrogate mother, a bit on
the side – then dismissing me when it suited them. I hated myself for
how grateful I'd been for the crumbs of their perfect life that they had
tossed me – the odd glass of white wine, their leftover granola, a used
cashmere jumper, an old clutch bag in a colour that no one wore any
more. They'd thought they could buy me. I hated them both.

262

'What do you want?'

I looked at Sal, at the two of us in our cheap Primark clothes, our cracked phone screens, our chipped fingernails.

'I want them punished,' I said. 'I want them to lose everything.'

Sal nodded. 'All right,' she said. 'What do you want me to do?'

TASH

Grace and I sit in the kitchen of her new house. Cardboard boxes are stacked in towers around us like building blocks. She has made us tea from a kettle plugged in on top of a chair. With her hair pulled back in a ponytail and her contacts abandoned in favour of glasses, she looks less like her adult self and more like the geeky girl I knew at school – except for the bulbous stomach.

'So,' Grace says, once Ben is out of earshot, 'has Tom forgiven you yet?'

I shake my head, cradling my mug. 'I don't think so.'

I don't know if I'd ever intended to tell him about any of it, if I could help it. Not the credit card debt I'd racked up. Not the picture of Dad's that I'd secretly sold, to try and pay a bit of it off. And definitely not about Jez. But Tom had found the receipt from the hotel spa – a bill in my name for more than a thousand pounds, paid for by a J. Henderson – and the whole thing had unravelled.

'How did you find the receipt?' I'd asked, miserably. Tom looked like he was nearly in tears.

'It was in your pocket. I was doing your laundry.'

I winced at that.

'Are you sleeping with him?'

'What? No! How can you even ask that, Tom?'

'Well, you just asked me if I killed someone, so I guess we're even.'

I had gasped at that. It wasn't like Tom to talk like this. None of this was like us.

'What am I supposed to think? You told me it was a spa day with the other mums – and then I find this!'

'Of course it was a spa day – the spa is inside the Corinthia hotel! You can ask them – ask Laura! Jez was just there using the gym, and –'

'And he paid a bill for you? Of more than a thousand pounds? Must have been some fucking spa day.'

I was silent, my cheeks burning. How could I explain to Tom my decision to go and spend this sort of money, so pointlessly, on myself? It had been awful, the whole day had been horrible. Why hadn't I just cancelled? What the hell was I thinking?

'Tom, I had no idea it was going to be that much,' I said eventually. 'Jez was just there, and I think he just ... he could see how horrified I was when the bill came. He felt responsible because Claire had organised it. They're rich – he knows we're not. He was just trying to help out. I tried to say no but, but ...'

Tom sighed. 'It's not just that that you've lied about, though? Is it?' He'd looked in my purse after he'd found the Corinthia receipt, found the credit card I'd kept secret from him. Then he'd looked through my emails, trying to find a statement for it, and instead found the emails between Dad's agent and me about the picture. I couldn't even blame him for snooping. I had looked at his phone. I'd done the same.

'I thought it was a complete no-go, selling the pictures,' Tom said. 'Otherwise, what the hell are we doing in this flat?'

I had been trying not to think too deeply about what I was really doing, about how I could be losing something that meant so much, for things that meant so little. I felt tears pricking my eyes.

'It was only one picture ...'

'It was worth two thousand pounds, Tash!'

'I know, and I'm sorry ...'

'I found your credit card statement – I looked it all up. Ruby's, Ottolenghi, Sweaty Betty, Petit Bateau. I'd never even heard of half these places! What does it all mean? Where the hell did two thousand pounds go? On what?'

And of course, I had nothing to say. Because the truth was that I had spent two thousand pounds on lattes and croissants, trinkets from the shops in Upper Street. Fancy new leggings. A cut-away designer swimsuit. Hot-yoga classes and manicures. A stupidly expensive coat for Finn. I had spent two thousand pounds on absolutely nothing. I was filled with a self-loathing so intense I started to shake.

Tom had slumped down into a chair. 'Tash, what is going on? I feel like I barely know you any more. You hardly speak to me, unless it's because you need me to look after Finn because you're going out on yet another investigative mission. Which I wouldn't mind, except it's all you ever want to do.' He hung his head. 'I thought we would try for another baby this year. I don't even know if we should, now.'

I had no answer for him. I felt tears in my eyes.

'I'll do whatever you want,' I said. 'Tell me how to fix it.'

Tom buried his head in his hands.

'I want you to stop it. All of it. All this crazy spending, this obsession with these rich women, and with digging around about Sophie Blake. You need to concentrate on us. For God's sake, Tash! I'm here, sick to death worrying about losing my job, about not being able to pay the mortgage. And meanwhile you're cashing in your family fortune without bothering to tell me, to fund spa trips and, what … yoga classes? I could understand overspending on Finn, or a holiday, or … I don't know. But this is just …'

I opened my mouth to try and explain. How keeping up with the playgroup mothers and looking into Sophie's death had become one and the same thing, without me noticing. I'd got in too deep, and didn't know how to get back. But as I started to say it, I realised I couldn't even make out how much of that was really true, and how much of it was a lie. Because there was a part of me that really did see them as my friends. And another part that had just become addicted to it. The coffees in their lovely houses, the trips to private members clubs in their flashy cars. The drama of trying to scratch beneath the surface of their perfect lives.

'I don't know who you are, Tash.' Tom was shaking his head. 'I don't understand you caring about this stuff. Can't you see how meaningless it all is?'

'Tom …'

'No, Tash. I can't even look at you, I'm so fucking angry.'

'You and Finn are everything to me – you know that!' But even as I said it, the words felt false. When was the last time I'd ever really thought about him, about us?

'Apparently not,' he muttered. 'Apparently we're not enough.'

It had, without a doubt, been the worst argument we'd ever had. I felt traumatised by it in a way that was almost physical, like whiplash. It

was as if Tom had discovered something hideous about me, an ugly underside to myself that even I had never fully acknowledged, but that now lay exposed. In the days afterwards, I found myself shrinking from people, as if they could see the ugliness in me too.

'I mean, I guess the pictures do belong to you, Tash,' Grace offers hopefully. 'It's up to you what you do with that money.'

But as we sit in her pretty new home, the dappled light from the window playing on the bare tiled floor, we both know this is just not true. I am supposed to be a partner, a wife, a mother. Part of a family.

Grace leans forward, wincing at the baby underneath her hips. She wraps a warm hand around mine.

'Hey,' she says. 'Don't give yourself such a hard time. He'll calm down.'

'He was so angry, Grace.'

'Oh, sure. But he loves you. You love each other.'

Is this true? I am starting to wonder. The way he looked at me, it was as if he was seeing someone else, someone he wasn't sure he even liked, let alone loved. The thought of not being loved by Tom is too frightening to contemplate.

I try to think about the last time I'd put any real energy into our relationship – the last time we'd done something nice together. I ended up thinking back to Christmas, sitting in that deserted square in France, with the Christmas lights festooned around us. We'd had a good couple of weeks after that, but we'd barely even touched each other lately. As I looked at Grace's belly now, I thought for the first time how nice it would be to share this with her. How lovely it would feel to look forward to holding a tiny new baby again.

'I thought you must have had a lot on your mind,' Grace said. 'Seeing as you hadn't harassed me about Ed Crawley since our drink.'

I realised this was true. I'd been so focused on what Tom had done, and what Christina was hiding, that I'd almost forgotten about Ed.

'Did you finally find out why he left?'

'I did, as it happens.' I see a flicker of pride cross Grace's face, then hesitation. 'None of this came from me though, OK, Tash? Everyone was told to keep quiet about it. I think the bank managed to hush it up. Even though, really, it should have gone to the police.'

As Grace tells me the story, I grimly realise I am listening to a tale so familiar that any woman could fill in the blanks. A senior man in

the office, people who turned a blind eye, even though everyone knew what he was like. Until the day it went too far. A younger trainee, a flirtation that had raised eyebrows, then work drinks that turned into a few too many for her. Ed had put her in a taxi, told her friend they were going the same way, he'd get her back safely.

'A few days later, it all came out,' Grace continues. 'She ended up in tears in the toilets, confessing to one of the senior women what had happened. She had passed out drunk, she said, and then she'd woken up to find him ...'

I think about Laura at the dinner party, her expression flickering with discomfort at her husband. Their relationship had always seemed odd. Now it was unfathomable.

'And then what?'

'The girl was adamant she didn't want the police involved,' Grace says. 'I think the firm were in a pretty difficult position. I know they took legal advice.'

'I bet they bloody did.'

Grace takes a deep breath. 'The next thing anyone knew, he was gone. The girl too – she wanted a fresh start. The rest of us have been sent on some kind of gender relations training, which you can imagine we're all thrilled about.'

I exhale, pressing the tips of my fingers against my eyebrows. 'My God, Grace,' I say. 'I know his wife, Laura. I know her really well.'

'She must know this happened,' Grace says, shaking her head. 'Surely, she must know.'

'Surely. But honestly, Grace – she's smart, educated, beautiful ... how could she stay with him?'

'Didn't you say they had a son?' Grace says quietly, raising an eyebrow.

'Yeah.'

She shrugs. 'There you go then. That's how.'

I tell myself Grace is wrong. But then I think about Tom, and wonder if I can really be so sure. Because my husband stands accused of molesting a female patient, and I have never even considered the possibility that this woman – whoever she is – is telling the truth.

SOPHIE

Six hours before

On the day of the party, Claire spent the morning at the venue, making sure everything was ready. In the afternoon, she messaged saying it was cold. Could I come and drop off her long cardigan?

It was a typically unreasonable request – it left me with less than an hour to get there and back before I'd need to collect Jude from the playgroup, and Beau was grizzly, unsettled. But obviously, I complied, strapping a confused Beau into the pram, his big blue eyes watching me, wondering where we were going. Halfway there, she sent me a message asking why I hadn't arrived yet.

When I got to the gallery, it was weirdly cold inside, my footsteps echoing around the empty space. Claire was arranging flowers in a huge vase, great spiky orange ones, their jaws open. They looked they might take your hand off.

'It's very chilly in here,' I said to Claire, as I handed her the cardigan.

'It's for the flowers. It'll warm up once everyone is here.' She gave a little shrug. 'I'm leaving now anyway. I need to go home and get ready.'

'I thought you said you needed this.'

'I didn't think you'd take so long.'

Claire and I looked at each other. I wondered how things between us had got like this.

We stepped outside the gallery. I was pulling the pram out backwards when I heard the voice.

'Sophie, hey!'

Lydia was trotting down Camden Passage, her pram laden with shopping bags, wheels bumping on the cobbles. Ludicrously, I tried to

duck down, pretending to get something out from the bottom of the pram. But it was too late. She had seen me.

By the time Claire had followed me out of the door, Lydia was crossing the road towards us, one hand on the push bar of her pram, the other waving.

'Oh my God, it's been ages since I've seen you, Sophie,' Lydia said. 'How are you guys doing?'

I can get away with this, I thought, breathing hard. I just need to control the situation.

'This is Claire,' I said, primarily to cut Lydia off before she could say anything else. 'Claire, this is Lydia.'

'Hi,' Claire said shortly, eyeing Zelda. 'Cute baby. How old?'

'She's nearly a year.'

'Ah, a bit older than Beau, then.'

A confused expression flitted across Lydia's face.

'It's so good to see you, Lydia,' I gabbled. 'We've got to get back, but let's catch up again soon, OK?' I flicked the brake off the pram.

'OK,' she said. 'Sounds good. Bye, Sophie.'

Claire was looking at her phone. She'd lost interest already. For a moment, I thought it was all going to be all right.

Then Lydia leaned into the pram, touching Beau on the cheek. Claire looked up at Lydia.

'Bye-bye, little baby Teddy,' Lydia said, in a sing-song voice. 'Me and your mummy will have to have another of our cinema dates soon, won't we, Sophie?' She grinned at me. 'Bye, guys!'

Lydia walked away. Claire and I stood frozen to the spot. The noise of the cars passing behind us felt loud.

'You've been telling people he's yours.'

It was a statement, not a question.

'It was … she just assumed,' I said. 'I just played along. I hardly know her.'

'She said you went to mother and baby cinema!' Claire's eyes narrowed as she took a step towards me, snatching the push bar of the pram out of my hands. I gasped with the violence of it. Then she brought her face close to mine.

'I knew there was something going on,' she hissed. 'But even when Nicole told me, I didn't believe it. It was too much. No one would do

that, I thought. No one would take my baby around, and pretend he belonged to them.'

'Claire, I –'

'Do you know the worst thing? Jez thought I was the crazy one!'

Claire started pushing Beau away, furiously. I chased after her, panic quickening the breath in my chest. I'd lost Jez, and now I was about to lose my job, my home. The boys. I was about to lose everything.

'Please, Claire,' I said. 'Let's talk about this. Claire!'

But she didn't turn back.

TASH

'No coffee today?' Claire is standing with Laura and Nicole at drop-off. She tilts her head to one side questioningly. 'You're always racing off these days.'

'Ah, I'm sorry, I really can't, Claire. I'm just slammed with work at the moment.'

Since the argument with Tom, I am avoiding all expensive coffee dates and lunches. I have been going straight to the library every day after drop-off, my head down and my Thermos flask in hand.

'Just a quick one maybe? We've hardly seen you.'

Laura sticks her bottom lip out in exaggerated dismay. Nicole tightens the belt on her coat, fixing her eyes on my face.

'I've just got a lot to finish before we go away. But see you soon!' I wave behind me, heading down the path before they can voice any more objections. Claire smiles weakly, Laura gives me a half-hearted thumbs up. Nicole is still unsmiling.

It's not true that I've got a lot of work to finish, of course. As of this week, Grace's firm are no longer returning my calls. I fear that the missing copywriting project has proven fatal to my chances of any more commissions. Without that stream of work, I know I need to redouble my efforts on getting freelance articles placed. But I feel bereft of inspiration, my focus clouded by Sophie.

Back home at the kitchen table, I try to fit the pieces together. Sophie had a secret – a secret Sal was planning to tell me about on the night she died – a secret she believes Sophie was killed to conceal. Whatever this was, it's obvious from the way Christina acted after the

funeral that she knows something about it, too. I know Christina is linked to Claire and Jez's past somehow, through his first wife, Emily. And I'm convinced Sophie sensed Christina was significant in some way, when she took that photograph of her.

Then there's Ed, who I now know has form for violence against women, and who was on the same dating app as Sophie, and who was actually there at the party, the night Sophie died. Could he and Sophie have been seeing each other? Or maybe he followed Sophie back to Jez and Claire's, and attacked her after she refused his advances? Pushed her down the stairs, in front of poor little Jude – leaving Jude traumatised, like Abi said?

But why would Claire and Jez cover for him, after coming home to discover something so awful? Did Ed have some sort of hold over them? Was the secret Christina and Sal knew about linked to that in some way?

In the end, I call Adam. He answers within two rings.

'Tash,' he says breathlessly. 'I didn't think I'd hear from you.'

I hear blood in my ears, throbbing, like a drumbeat.

'Did you confront this Sally Cunningham about the messages? Why did you take off like that in the pub? Do you know who the man in the picture is?'

'Sal's dead.'

'What?'

I clear my throat. 'Look, Adam – I just need to ask you one thing. Please.'

Adam makes an exasperated noise.

'All right,' he says eventually. 'I'm listening.'

'Ed Crawley. Did you ever look at him?'

There is a silence on the line. 'The name doesn't ring a bell. Who is that? Is that the man in the –'

'No,' I say. 'But I think he was at the party that night. And might have had form.' I take a breath. 'You might … look into whether a complaint was ever made against him, a few months before. By a girl who worked with him, at Schooners investment bank.' Grace said the girl at Schooners hadn't wanted to report it, but that was months ago. She could have changed her mind.

I hear the scratch of a pen.

'I'll check it out,' Adam says. 'But, Tash, wait –'

273

'I've got to go.' I hang up and immediately turn off my phone. I can't risk him knowing it's Tom in the picture, not yet. Not until I can prove to Adam that he's nothing to do with all this.

The thought of going on holiday with the others had already made me feel uneasy; now, it makes me feel physically sick. But Ed isn't coming. I tell myself that that's the main thing. And I can't cancel the holiday, the only thing Tom is feeling positive about. I'm hoping it might help us.

I'd never been seriously worried about me and Tom before. I've always thought we're just not the sort to get divorced – we didn't even used to argue. But now, communication between us is almost non-existent. I've spent the week exhausting myself trying to be perfect, getting through all the laundry, setting it out in neatly ironed piles, ready to pack. I resist the urge to buy anything new, resurrecting all our nicest things and making sure they are clean and ready. I fill Tom's drawers with freshly balled socks and folded T-shirts. In the evenings, a rotating menu of his favourite dinners, cooked cheaply with ingredients from the Turkish shops along Green Lanes, are ready on the stove.

'Tom,' I say, a couple of nights before we're due to go away. 'I know you're still angry with me. But I can't go on like this.'

I feel the tears prick at the sides of my eyes as I say it out loud. Tom looks at me and his face softens.

'Come here.'

He holds me so tight it is bordering on unpleasant. I have the uncomfortable thought that he is trying to physically hold our marriage together, like a building at risk of collapse.

'I really am sorry,' I tell him.

'I know.'

'It feels like you can't forgive me.'

Tom sighs. For a while he doesn't say anything.

'I do forgive you, Tash. But I also think things need to change.'

I nod. 'I'll do whatever you want.'

Tom pulls back to look at me. 'All right. I want us to try for another baby.'

I hold my breath. This wasn't what I expected.

'I really don't want Finn to be an only child, like we both were. We always said that. And we always said we wanted them close together – Finn's going to be three next month.'

274

'But, the flat …'

'That's the next thing,' he says. 'I want to sell the flat. I'm over it, Tash. I want to live somewhere where we can afford a real home.'

'But where –'

'I want us to move out of London, away from here. I don't care about London. I want a proper family house.'

'But what about your job, Tom?'

'I've been offered a post at John Radcliffe.'

'John Radcliffe? What's that?'

'John Radcliffe hospital. In Oxford.'

Tom pauses a moment, lets this sink in.

'When you said you might look at other jobs, other hospitals – I assumed you meant in London.'

Tom looks away. 'I honestly didn't think it was worth telling you about this one – I thought there was no way I'd get this job. But John Radcliffe is a really prestigious hospital. Obviously, they don't know about the complaint, but when – if – that's dropped, I want to take the post, Tash.'

'But … hang on! Oxford is *your* place, Tom. I don't know anything about Oxford.'

'I know. But we'd get to know it, together. It would be an adventure.'

I gape at him. 'But … what about our friends, our lives? What about Finn's playgroup?'

'I want to take Finn out of the playgroup.'

'But …'

'Ever since he started there, things have been different. Since you've been hanging around with those women.'

I hesitate. I know what he's talking about, but in some faraway place in my mind, an alarm bell sounds. Is Tom really telling me who I should and shouldn't see?

'They are my friends,' I say, sullenly. 'And you're the one who was so keen to go on holiday with them.'

'That was before all this!' Tom is pacing the room. 'And another thing, Tash. I need you to promise you'll leave this Sophie Blake thing alone, now. I could understand if it was for an article. But there's no story. Is there?'

I have no answer. I had been sure, for so long, that there was a story here. But Tom's right. This has become something else. Something bigger than that.

275

'I mean it. I've never seen you like this, Tash. You've become obsessed with it, and it is hurting us.'

'It might be a story,' I insist stubbornly. 'And I'm not obsessed. You're exaggerating.'

Tom explodes. 'You asked me if I'd had something to do with her death! Can you honestly not see how crazy that is? Of course you're obsessed with it!'

My phone rings.

'Who's that?'

'I don't know,' I say. 'Unknown number.' I glance at him. I know the conversation with Tom is more important; I should offer to cancel the call. But something makes me hesitate, my thumb hovering over the screen.

Tom stands up heavily. 'You might as well get it. I'm getting a beer.'

I answer the call.

'Is this Natasha Carpenter?' It is a male voice; businesslike, unfamiliar.

'It is.'

'I'm Richard Jeffries, the solicitor for the estate of Sally Cunningham. I have a document in my possession which she seems to have intended for you. It was in her living room when she was ... discovered. In an envelope with your name on it.'

TASH

When we arrive in Cornwall, we park the car and walk up the gravel path to Claire and Jez's imposing stone farmhouse, Tom carrying a sleepy Finn on his shoulders. There is no answer at the front door, no sign of anyone in the bay windows, so we trudge around the back.

Suddenly, the house looks completely different. It has been extended to create a huge open-plan space, with a farmhouse kitchen, island and large wooden dining table on one side, a log burner and sofas on the other, and full length windows facing the sea. Through the glass, I see Claire at the kitchen island with bunches of dried herbs hanging. She is rubbing oil and salt into the yellowish skin of a chicken carcass. Beau is on the stone floor, playing with trucks. Tom clears his throat, balls a fist and knocks gently on the glass. Both of them look up, delightedly, and Claire says something that can't be heard. I watch her walking over to open the door, like an actress in a silent film.

Claire throws a door open.

'You're here! Wonderful!' Her smile looks a bit strained, the creases around her eyes deeper than I remember noticing before. 'Come in, come in. Sorry, we don't use the front entrance, did it confuse you? You're the first here! You've done so well! Jez isn't coming until the weekend, but the others should be here tonight.' She doesn't mention Jude.

Finn is desperate to go straight down to the beach. 'Let's go then!' Claire washes her hands, throws a jacket on Beau. 'He'll want wellies. Here, don't unpack, have some of ours.'

A wooden gate at the bottom of their garden leads directly to the sandy coast path. It runs up the cliffs in one direction, and down to the

beach in the other. Higher up the cliffs, the path looks like it has been sealed off, a twist of black-and-yellow tape flickering in the wind.

Claire leads us down to the beach. Finn and Beau race ahead, whooping with delight. Green and purple heather shimmer on the path either side of us. The waves in the bay are huge and foaming. It doesn't look like a beach where a child would be safe to swim.

I hang back a bit, tapping out a text to Grace. She is staying in our flat – she and Ben are having their kitchen put in – and I have made her promise to call when the letter from the lawyer arrives. Infuriatingly, the lawyer has refused to discuss the contents of the envelope, insisting it had to be sent, recorded delivery, to my home address.

'Tash? Is everything OK?'

Tom is at my side. There is no disguising the edge in his question, the implication I shouldn't be on my phone.

'Fine. I was just trying to get some phone reception.'

'I don't think you can here. I asked Claire already. Their Wi-Fi isn't working, apparently. You have to walk up onto the cliff path to get a signal.'

'Really? The cliffs?'

'It doesn't matter, does it? We can put our phones away for a few days.'

I force a smile, shove my phone into my pocket. 'Sure,' I say. 'Of course.' The thought of having no phone signal is more alarming than I feel I can let on to Tom, though. I feel my stomach clench.

Claire has packed waterproof-backed blankets, a large flask of tea. We sit on the sand watching while the kids chase each other giddily around the windy expanse of beach. Finn shouts for Tom, pointing with a stubby finger at something in the wet sand close to the sea. Tom jogs ahead to join him.

'Be careful of the waves,' I call after him. The wind is up, the waves like huge walls of grey-green water smashing themselves against the sand. I have read too many news stories about things like this. It would only take a second.

Claire pulls herself up beside me. She is wearing expensive wellies and a big waterproof that must belong to Jez.

'This is stunning, Claire. Thanks so much for asking us.'

'Of course.' She squints at me.' Everything all right with you guys?' Claire has to raise her voice over the wind, pushing a stray lock of

hair behind her ear. I scuff the sand beyond the blanket with the tip of my trainer.

Tom is heading back over, and Claire turns to me, lowering her voice.

'Talk later? With wine?'

I force a smile. 'OK,' I say. 'Sounds good.'

I hear Laura and Nicole arriving as I am putting Finn to bed, their luggage clattering on the stone floors. I fear the noise will unsettle Finn, tucked in his little put-up bed. But he is exhausted, his eyes drooping shut before I have even turned off the light.

When I pad back downstairs, Tom is sitting on one of the sofas drinking a beer, and Ed is opposite him, kneeling on the floor and throwing a log into the burner.

I stop in my tracks. The shock must show on my face. Tom throws me a confused look. Ed smiles, stands up, dusts off his hands and sits down next to Tom.

'Hello, Tash,' he says.

'Hi,' I mutter. I don't feel I want to sit. 'I thought you weren't going to be able to make it.'

'Managed to swing it after all.'

I feel the hairs on my arms stand up, a prickle at the base of my head.

'Was just saying to your husband,' Ed smirks, 'natty little motor you've got there.'

Ed jerks his head in the direction of the window looking down towards the drive. Our hire car sticks out like a sore thumb among the other sleek vehicles, its branding plastered across the sides.

'What's wrong with it?' Tom says, smiling as if Ed's joke isn't at our expense. 'It's fine.'

'Bit of a pain for you both, isn't it? Not having your own car?'

'We did have one, a while back,' Tom says. 'But we got rid of it in the end. We decided we didn't use it enough to justify it.'

Claire walks in from the kitchen. 'Ah, Tash, Finn's down! Great! Laura's just putting Oscar down, and Beau is asleep too. They must all be knackered. Time for wine – what would you like?'

'Whatever you're having.' I glance at her glass. She looks like she is just drinking water. 'Or some red.' As I say it, it occurs to me we should have brought some.

'Is there anything I can get for tonight?' I ask Claire hurriedly. 'Some drinks, maybe? Is there a shop nearby?'

'A what?! At this hour?' Claire laughs. 'There's nothing for miles. This is the countryside, silly!'

I smile faintly, the feeling of queasiness returning to my stomach.

'No kidding,' moans Ed, swiping at his phone. 'No 4G signal, either.'

'Oh, come on, Londoners!' Claire winks at me. 'I'm sure we'll all survive the week!'

Dinner is served, and more wine poured. Through the windows, steamy with warmth and breath, I can still make out the lurid yellow branding of our hire car. It's been bugging me all evening.

'You OK?' Tom is leaning to fill up my water glass, giving me a squeeze on the knee.

'That wasn't what happened with our car,' I say to Tom, under my breath. 'What you said to Ed.'

He looks confused. 'What?'

'Our old Corsa,' I say. 'You said we'd decided it wasn't worth having it any more.'

'We did, didn't we?'

'No. You told me it had broken down when you were driving it. That you took it to the garage, and they said it needed scrapping. That it was going to cost more to replace it than it was worth.'

'Ye-es,' he says slowly, as if unsure what I'm asking. 'That's what I said. And then we decided it wasn't worth getting a new one. Isn't that the same thing?'

The truth is I can't remember now how we ended up getting rid of the Corsa, because I wasn't there when the car broke down. It's been bothering me ever since he said it. Why would Tom have been driving it without me?

'When did it happen?' I ask him.

'When did what happen?'

'The car breaking down, and having to be scrapped.' I pause. 'Was it … was it when I was in France with Finn?'

Even as I say the words, I know that I am right. It was that week. The week Sophie died. I came back from France, and Tom had got rid of the car. He said it had been knackered, and had had to go, and that was it. I never saw our car again.

'Not this again,' Tom mutters.

'But why were you using the car?' It didn't make sense to me. We only really used the car when we needed to take Finn on long journeys. 'Where were you driving?'

'I can't remember.'

I exhale, irritated. 'Can you try and remember?'

Tom shakes his head and stands up. 'I'm getting another beer.'

After dinner, everyone moves into the lounge. Tom is among the first to go, leaving me behind without a second glance. When I look into the lounge, I see that he is sitting with Ed again. I decide to stay in the kitchen with Claire, help her stack the dishwasher.

As I collect up the wine glasses, my stomach is swimming. I can't stop thinking about the car.

'Is this yours?' I ask Claire, seeing her wine glass looks unused. 'Are you not drinking?'

Claire hesitates. When I look up, her cheeks are flushed pink, a half-smile on her face.

'I might as well tell you – I can't exactly keep it a secret the whole holiday,' she says. 'I'm pregnant.'

It takes me a moment to process what she is saying. I force myself to recover, to grapple for the appropriate reaction. Even as, to my horror, I realise there is a tightening in my chest that feels very much like jealousy.

'Oh, Claire!' I reach out to hug her. 'Sorry – I didn't think – but that's amazing! I'm so pleased for you. How are you feeling?'

'Oh, you know.' She grimaces. 'Terrified.'

Claire sits down at the table, her fingertips brushing her belly. I see it now, a tiny rise under her clothes, barely noticeable.

'I'm sure it'll be easier this time,' I say gently.

'Well, I certainly hope it's nothing like the first time.'

I sit down next to her. 'You'll know what to look out for, won't you?'

'I guess.' We sit in silence for a while, listening to the low thrum of the dishwasher, the rise and fall of the conversation in the next room.

'When did you … when did you get help, in the end?'

Claire smiles sadly. 'Laura helped me. When I finally told her. But it had been months and months by then. I was such a mess, Tash. I'd have been a goner if it wasn't for her getting me…what I needed.'

I nod, slowly, as what she is saying sinks in. So this was what the pills were for, the ones Tom caught Laura stealing. The shock must

show on my face, because Claire looks down, as if I have admonished her.

'I know,' Claire says. 'I should have gone to the GP. I know it's silly, but I was so worried that they'd take Beau away – I didn't want anything on my medical record. Of course, that was crazy of me. But I wasn't thinking straight. I was having so many dark thoughts. About Beau, about Jude, about Jeremy … even about our nanny.'

'Your … nanny?'

'Yes. Her name was Sophie …'

I try to stop myself gaping. Claire is talking about Sophie, just like that. I have to say something. I can't miss my chance.

'I heard – that Sophie died.'

Claire looks straight at me. 'Yes,' she says. 'She died.'

'That – must have been awful.'

'Yes,' says Claire. The words seem automatic, somehow, as if she is reading from a script. 'It was a terrible tragedy. She was found in a reservoir. No one really knows what happened to her.'

Before I can say anything, Laura is in the room. When she speaks, I see her glass of red wine has stained her teeth.

'What are you two gossiping about?'

'I was just telling Tash our news,' Claire smiles, touching her belly.

'So exciting.' Laura grins at Claire and winks at me. She sits down in one of the dining chairs.

'Anyway, Tash,' Claire says. 'What's going on with you and Tom?'

Laura glances at me, surprised. I shift in my chair. I really don't want to talk about this with the two of them. Claire was one thing, but talking to Laura – who I know Tom doesn't trust – feels like more of a betrayal.

'Tom … thinks we should move to Oxford,' I say eventually. 'We've sort of been rowing about it.'

'What?' They both look at me, horrified.

'Oxford?' Claire gives her head a little shake. 'But why?'

'He's got a job offer there,' I say carefully. 'He thinks we need a fresh start.'

'Hang on, I thought you loved London, Tash,' Claire says. 'This is where you're from.'

'And I don't think you'll get much more for your money in Oxford, I'm sorry to say,' Laura chimes in. 'If that's what he's thinking. Not

if you want Summertown, or North Oxford. That's where all the schools are.'

I blink at her. I don't know anything about Oxford.

'What have you told Tom?' Laura asks.

'That I'll think about it.'

Actually, I had been starting to think Tom was right. Maybe we do need to move, have a fresh start. But the idea of leaving London, selling my dad's pictures – it feels like rubbing out a bit of myself. What would I do all day in Oxford? Who would I talk to? We wouldn't know anyone there. I wouldn't have anyone except Tom.

'Why does he think you need a fresh start?' Claire asks.

I hesitate. 'I think – well. He thinks I spend too much time on my work, for one thing. That I spend all my time on my job or Finn, and there's nothing left over for him, I suppose –'

'What?!' Laura makes an indignant noise at this. Even Claire, who always tries to be even-handed, looks shocked.

'That came out worse than it was when he said it,' I backtrack loyally. 'Tom just thinks that – I guess between seeing my friends a lot –'

'Does he mean us?' Laura asks, her eyes widening.

I shift in my chair. 'I think he just feels we should reset our priorities?'

'That sounds like he means *your* priorities.'

I search for a response. As I say it out loud, it does sound bad. I watch as Laura and Claire exchange a look.

'Sorry, Tash,' Laura says gently. 'You know how highly I think of Tom, but … it doesn't sound very fair, to me.'

'Didn't you say that Tom went to Oxford for uni, Tash?' Claire's brow is furrowed.

'So it's his place,' Laura says, folding her arms. 'Not yours. How can he ask to move so far away from your friends, your career, your network?'

The answer to that makes me feel uncomfortable, even in the confines of my own mind. Tom wants me to stop investigating the death of Sophie Blake. I think of the messages. *Stop digging.*

I stand up, take a clean glass from the cupboard and help myself to a drink. The window over the sink is dark, the scenery outside black and unknowable, the wind straining at the window locks.

When I get to bed that night, there is a single bar of signal, and a message from Adam.

Can't find any police log re: the allegation against E Crawley, he says.

Shit. So Grace was right. The girl never went to the police.

Something else I could look at?

Quickly, I tap out a reply.

Can we run car plates?

Adam replies straight away. *I can try.*

OK. Couple for you to check.

I take a breath. I note down the plate of the BMW X5 parked outside the window, illuminated by the outside lamps. The one that belongs to Ed. Then, my fingers shaking, I add a second number plate. One that I know by heart. The plate of our old red Vauxhall Corsa. I press send, pinching my eyes closed.

SOPHIE

Four hours before

As I got the boys dressed in their party outfits, I could feel Claire's eyes on me. Make-up didn't really suit Claire. It made her face mask-like, hard and unfamiliar.

Once they were dressed, I sat the two of them on the floor and read them stories while we waited for Jez and Claire to be ready. I scratched the raw skin on my hands and thought about the piece of paper in my rucksack, the one Sal gave me. It was there, in black and white. I'd held off until now. But I was starting to think that I had nothing to lose.

A message pinged through from Lydia. Was I OK, she wanted to know. I hadn't seemed myself. She wanted to meet up soon. I flicked it closed. I knew I would never see her again.

Beau was grizzling, refusing to settle on my lap. He'd barely touched his dinner, either. He was too ill to be going to a party. He had caught a summer cold, and had that pinkish, viral look around his eyes, a cough that made people wince at him at bus stops. Claire seemed almost cross with Jude for giving the cold to him.

'Maybe Sophie should stay here with the boys, if Beau's not well,' I heard Jeremy tell Claire in the hallway.

'No, I want him with me,' she replied, firmly.

Jez said nothing, but he was still looking at Beau, who was rubbing his eyes, slumped into my chest.

'We won't keep him there long,' Claire relented. 'We'll get him into bed early.'

By we, she meant me, as usual. But maybe this was the last time she'd let me put him to bed. She would get this party out of the way

and then I'd never be allowed near the boys again, I could feel it. The thought of it made me feel physically sick.

Jez didn't seem to notice Claire was being off with me. He didn't seem to notice me at all, in fact. I could hear him whistling upstairs, while he had a shave. The longer the whistling went on, the more furious it made me. When he finally emerged, he came down the stairs in the dance-like way he had, in his suit, the shirt unbuttoned, no tie. His shiny shoes tapped on the hallway tiles as he went back and forth fetching his wallet and his keys from the hook. I heard the music of the ice cubes in Claire's glass, the hushed whisper of her spraying the perfume she kept on the hallway table. The exclusive sounds of an exclusive life that I was no real part of.

'Wow. You look beautiful, Claire.'

'Thanks, darling. Can you do me up at the back?'

I was right by the door to the hallway, now. I heard the sound of the zip, and then the sound of lips parting. I imagined the feeling of his fingers on the skin of her back.

'Are the boys ready, Soph?'

I couldn't bear to hear him say my name. I worked Beau's spare jumper in my hands, the skin on my fingers chapped to bleeding between my forefinger and thumb.

Claire scooped Beau up and carried him out into the Land Rover. She left me to see to Jude, then climb into the back between their two car seats, like an older, unwanted child. The roads were jammed, a Tube strike clogging the arteries of the city. The weather looked ominous too, cloudy but warm, the sort of humidity that got under the material of your top. Claire hadn't said a word to me since we'd argued on the pavement.

I didn't understand what I was doing at the party, or why the boys had needed to come. Jez had said something about how the family wanted to see them. But apart from Michael and Wendy – who saw Jude and Beau all the time – none of the other guests showed much of an interest in them. Most took a cursory glance at Beau – 'oh, doesn't he look sweet in his outfit!' – then wandered off, eyes trained on the canapés.

I'd packed a mat and a bag of toys for them, but couldn't find anywhere to set them out. Jude ended up sitting under a table, eyes fixed on his iPad. The floor was too hard for Beau to play on – he was

crawling, but had still not taken his first steps – so I had to keep him strapped into the pram. He kept straining against the straps.

Claire and Jez seemed to be going to some lengths to avoid interaction with me. Jez ignored me when he came over to see Jude, who was by now sat on the floor next to me, looking miserable in his smart checked shirt and trousers, eating crisps from a cupped hand.

When no one was looking, I plucked a champagne flute from a passing silver tray then snuck off to the bar, away from Jez and Claire, and downed it in one, the bubbles cold in my throat. I assumed I wasn't supposed to be drinking, but I felt I needed to steady my nerves. It didn't work, though. I just felt dizzy and sick.

I turned round, intending to get back to the boys, then froze.

He was there. Standing between me and the entrance, his legs apart. He was talking to some other man, taking a canapé from a passing tray, shoving it into his mouth with a grin. Then his eyes met mine, and his face darkened.

TASH

The next day, after breakfast, Claire leads us on a walk over the fields – safer, she explains, than the cliffs. 'There have been some rock-falls up there lately. I think it's better not to risk it.'

We walk in single file along stony footpaths and tracks of down-trodden grass, our conversations shouted along the line, our shoulders wearing the legs of toddlers. Claire's skinny arms reach ahead for hawthorn branches and stray nettles.

Jez is arriving today, Claire says. He'll either catch us up on the walk or meet us back at the house. When I asked what was happening to Jude, Claire said he was with his grandparents. I noticed she didn't meet my eye.

We cross into a field studded with cabbages, the sky stretching in all directions, the distant shimmer of wind turbines on the hills inland. At last a bar of signal appears. I hang back, pull out my phone and text Grace.

All ok at home? Any news? X

After a few moments, the little blue dots appear to show she is typing, then a reply flashes up.

All fine here! No baby, no letters of note. Will message if that changes! G x

'Tash? What's going on?'

It's Tom. Finn is on his shoulders, waving a piece of grass in his hand.

'Nothing. I'm just sending a text.'

'We're supposed to be on a family holiday. You're on your phone the entire time.'

'I am not – this is the first time I've had signal!'

'Is it about Sophie Blake?'

I look at him.

'Well, is it?'

'I just texted Grace to ask her how things are.' I feel the eyes of the others glancing back at us and I hope desperately that they're too far ahead to hear that we're arguing. Tom doesn't reply.

'Tom, can we not do this now? Jesus!'

I turn round, aware of someone running up to us from behind.

'Hey, everything OK? Are you all right, Tash?'

I hadn't seen Jez arrive. He has jogged to catch us up. His face is flushed, his lips parted.

'We're fine,' I manage. 'Hello, by the way.'

He smiles faintly. 'Hello.' He glances at Tom, then back to me with a searching look. Tom looks furious.

'Hey, guys!' Claire shouts from a stile ahead. She is gesturing at a farm building at the end of a drystone wall. 'That's the farm shop, OK? Next field. Oh, hi, darling!'

She waves at Jez. I hold a thumbs-up in the air to acknowledge the location of the farm shop and she and the others carry on.

Tom looks from Jez, to me, then back to Jez. He pulls Finn more firmly onto his shoulders by the ankles, and turns away, leaving Jez and me alone.

Jez frowns at me. 'You OK?'

I nod, miserably. 'Fine.'

'You look a bit cold,' he says.

I rub my arms, feeling the goosebumps on them. I didn't think about the wind. Should have brought a jumper.

'Here.' Jez encloses his hands around my fingers, then blows gently on them. I glance up ahead. The others are too far ahead to see.

'A hand house.' He smiles. Despite myself, I smile back.

When we get back to the house, Claire shuffles all the kids into a cold utility room that smells of Barbour jackets and damp laundry. We strip off their mud-caked trousers and welly boots, before settling them in front of the TV. I feel shaken, jittery. The more I think about the way Tom spoke to me on the walk, the closer to tears I feel.

'Do you mind if I sneak off for a shower?' I ask Claire.

'Sure, although I think Tom just said the same,' she says. 'He'll be in the one in your room. Use our en suite if you like, at the top of the stairs. There's shampoo and stuff in there.'

The piping hot water on my cold skin is instantly soothing. I linger long after I've washed my hair, enjoying the feel of Claire's expensive coconut-smelling conditioner and the luxury of a few moments alone. When I shut the water off, I hear that the rain has stopped. From below come the muffled sounds of Nicole, Laura and Claire ordering the children outside. I hear Finn laughing as he chases Beau and Oscar. He is having a great time. I just need to get through the week. That's all. In the small bathroom window, I can just make out the bay through a maze of rooftops, puffs of white spray rising from the rocks each time a wave crashes, like little breaths.

I wrap Claire's towel around myself and gather up my clothes. I open the door and find Jez standing in the bedroom, his shirt undone and an open suitcase on the bed.

'Oh, fuck,' I say. We both say 'Sorry'. We both laugh. 'Claire said I could use the shower,' I blurt. I am extremely aware of my wet hair, my damp skin, my bare, scrubbed face.

'I assumed it was Claire in the shower.'

'I think she's outside.'

'Right.'

I shift, pulling the towel up as much as I can over my front. I need to leave, and I can't quite work out why I haven't done it yet.

'I'll just, um.'

Neither of us moves. From far away, I can hear the crash of the sea against the rocks, as the tide inches closer and closer to the beach.

TASH

When I wake up the next day, Finn has already abandoned his camp bed and gone to play outside. I get out of bed and walk over to the window. I can see him in the garden with Oscar. Claire is there with them. She has put a fleece I don't recognise over Finn's pyjamas to keep him warm. I feel a lurch of guilt as I creep back into bed.

Tom rolls towards me under the covers. 'God, this bed is comfortable,' he says.

'I know,' I say. 'Why don't we have a mattress like this?'

'I think we're probably due an upgrade. I'll treat you to one when we move to the burbs.'

I swat at him, somehow managing a laugh. I know that he will apologise, now that I have signalled I'm ready to forgive.

'I'm sorry about being an arse on the walk, about your phone,' he says. 'I just wanted to not think about all that stuff this holiday, that's all.'

'I know. Apology accepted.'

We both hear a shriek from the garden which is unmistakably our son's. We exchange a smile.

'Little scamp,' Tom says. 'He loves it here. Is Claire with them?'

'Yeah.' I hesitate. 'Tom, I have been thinking about Oxford.'

'Oh yeah?'

'Well, I suppose being here has shown what a difference it makes to Finn – a bigger house, a real garden. Space to play.'

Tom smiles. 'I think he'd love it.'

'I just ... I know what this sounds like, but – London is my whole world. I don't know anywhere else.'

291

Tom makes a face at me. 'You know Oxford. You visited me enough times.'

'I know, but our life was so different then. I only really remember the bars and that awful club, and the chip van, and your horrible college digs.'

Tom laughs.

'London is my home, and Finn's now,' I say. 'It's where I grew up, and apart from my miserable Cardiff years –' Tom smiles knowingly – 'it's the only place I've ever lived, and I …'

'Come here.' Tom pulls me onto his chest, laughing. 'It's not a complete cultural wasteland outside the M25, you know. Oxford has all the things you like. Coffee shops, and bookshops, cafes with pretentious breakfast food.'

'OK, OK,' I mumble. 'But, Tom, if we do move – if we do try for another baby – it would be a fresh start, wouldn't it? We could forget about the past. All the other stuff.' My throat feels thick, a lump rising that I can't swallow.

Tom pulls me closer into him. 'I really want that, Tash.' I can hear the emotion in his voice.

'OK,' I say. 'I'll think about it. Really. I promise.'

And then Tom is kissing me, and then his hands are moving down my body, our movements assuming a familiar rhythm. Afterwards, listening to his breathing, and the sound of the sea, I think that maybe I can do this, I can give this thing to Tom. I can make it what I want, too. And at the thought of that, I feel still somehow, and peaceful, in a way I haven't in a long time.

While Tom is in the shower, my phone rings. The signal must be back. I snatch it up from my bedside table before the signal goes. It is Grace. I answer, but as soon as I do, the signal cuts out.

'Fuck,' I say.

A few minutes later, one tiny bar of signal reappears, and a message pings through. It's from Grace.

Got your lawyer letter. Call when you can.

TASH

The signal doesn't return. That night, or the next day. We are confined to the house, rain hammering on the skylight windows, bubbling into the gutters. The wet beach shines like sealskin.

In the evening, Tom volunteers to put Finn to bed. While Nicole and Laura make dinner, I go and find Claire in the utility room, hanging the wet clothes out on hooks.

'Claire, have you had any signal at all? I know the Wi-Fi's bust, I just wondered if there were any good spots in the house I should try.'

Claire frowns. 'The Wi-Fi's not bust. Didn't Tom tell you? It's the BT one. The code is on the router behind the TV.'

I stare at her.

'He asked me about it the first day,' Claire says. 'Sorry – I assumed he'd tell you.'

I feel sick. I don't have time to think about why Tom has lied to me. I need the Wi-Fi signal; I need to speak to Grace. I find the router, type in the password and call Grace. I get her answerphone. 'Fuck,' I mutter. 'Grace, call me as soon as you get this.'

I head back to the kitchen. The children have all gone to bed. Claire pours drinks for Laura and Nicole as they emerge smiling from bedtime stories.

When Tom returns, Ed stands up. 'Shall we go to the pub for an hour or so, let the women have a gossip? Jez, Tom, you up for it?'

I flinch at 'the women', but Claire doesn't seem to react. 'Fine with me,' she says. 'We'll eat around eight thirty.'

'What's the local like?' Tom asks Ed.

'It's an acquired taste,' Jez grins.

'You can say that again,' Ed laughs. He slaps Tom on the back, squeezes his shoulder.

My phone buzzes. I pick it up. It is a text from Adam – sent hours ago, but only just coming through. Two missed calls from earlier, too. Fuck.

CALL ME. URGENT.

I step into the hallway, and try and use the Wi-Fi to call Adam. But his phone doesn't accept Wi-Fi calls. I need a proper phone signal. I need to get out.

When I return to the kitchen, Tom is standing with Ed, his jacket already half on. It looks as if they have just shared a joke. He catches my eye, grins and makes a 'what can you do?' gesture. He looks pleased at the prospect of male adult company, a trip to the pub.

I wait until Ed has moved away and speak into his ear. 'Please don't be long,' I say.

'Why not?'

I don't know why not. But I have a strange, jittery feeling tonight, an unfocused sense of panic.

'Why are you so pally with Ed all of a sudden?'

Tom looks at Ed, then back at me, confused.

'I'm not,' he says.

'Why did you tell me the Wi-Fi wasn't working?'

'Because Claire told me it wasn't working,' he says slowly. He pauses. 'What? What now? What's going on, Tash?'

I glance at Jez and Ed, waiting for Tom at the door. When I look at him, Jez averts his eyes, pretends to fiddle with his watch. Ed returns my gaze. I'm forced to look away.

'OK,' I whisper. Something makes me grab Tom's hand. 'Just please, don't be long, Tom.'

He frowns at me, confused, then glances over my shoulder at Jez and Ed. 'All right.' He gives me a quick kiss, and is gone.

I sit down next to Nicole on the sofa. She pours me a glass of wine. Laura emerges from the hallway.

'Let me guess, Ed's gone to the pub,' she says.

'They all have,' Claire says.

'Best place for them,' Nicole mutters.

Rain starts up again at the windows. There is something flimsy about the glass all around the kitchen extension. It doesn't feel like

294

enough of a match for the wind that is coming in off the sea, rattling at the windows, trying to get in.

'Oh dear. They'll be soaked,' Claire tuts. She is curled in a corner of one sofa, legs tucked up underneath her, drinking a camomile tea. She looks over at me, and smiles blandly.

'Serves them right for abandoning us!' Laura laughs. 'Can I do anything more for dinner?'

Claire shakes her head. 'It's all done.'

Behind us, in the kitchen, a pot of potatoes on the stove is bubbling, steam clouding the windows. The wind rattles them again. Claire brings a protective hand to her belly. I feel my stomach swim. One of them is lying. Her, or Tom.

There is a hiss from the stove. The potatoes have boiled over.

'I'll get them,' Laura is saying. She presses a hand on Claire's knee as she gets up.

I can't stand it any longer.

'I need to get some air,' I croak, standing up. Three sets of eyes look up at me. Then I see a glance pass between Nicole and Claire, just a flicker. I need to get out.

'Are you sure that's a good idea?' Nicole says, as I pull on my coat. 'It's pouring with rain.'

I avoid her gaze. 'I won't be long.'

As I leave, I look Laura in the eyes. 'Laura. You'll be here for Finn, won't you?'

'Yeah, sure,' she says, looking puzzled. 'But what –'

'Please, Laura. Promise. You'll look after him. Won't you?'

'Of course, but –'

Before she can say anything else, I've closed the door behind me.

At the bottom of the garden, I reach the path that goes both ways, down to the beach, and up to the cliffs. Down in the bay, I can see the boarded-up cafe, wave after wave of rain sweeping over its shuttered windows. The festoon lights shake. The chairs for the outside tables are stacked. Puddles gather at the feet of the open-air pizza oven.

I head up, on the path to the cliffs. There will be signal up there. I need to call Adam. I need to know what he has found out.

The cliff path is muddy, glassy rivulets of water running down each side, the way strewn with trailing brambles. One slices into my hand

as I hold out the torch on my phone. I realise I am relying on it for light, but the battery is low, and it is getting wet.

As soon as a bar of signal appears, I place the call.

'Hey, Adam? I got your message. What is it?' As I say it out loud, I feel the sobs start, heavy in my chest. 'Just tell me. I need to know.'

Adam doesn't say anything.

'Adam? Can you hear me?'

'Yeah, I hear you, but I'm confused. We spoke a few hours ago – remember?'

I think I've misheard him. 'No – we – you sent me a message saying I needed to call urgently.'

'And you did. This afternoon. Remember? I looked into the plates – I found something – I told you all this. We spoke.'

'No, no. We haven't spoken today, I …'

'But I … you answered … Tash? It … it sounded just like you.'

'When was this?'

'This afternoon – three, four hours ago, max?'

I had left my phone in the kitchen to charge. How long had I left it there? Half an hour? An hour? More? But now there's barely any battery. Someone obviously unplugged it. Who had been in the kitchen, then? It could have been any of them.

'Someone else must have answered my phone.'

'What?'

I feel choked by panic. 'Adam, what did you tell them?'

Adam is breathing heavily. 'I said I'd found something,' he says. 'Something about Ed Crawley.'

SOPHIE

Three hours before

For a moment, the party seemed to slow. No one else was in the room. It was just me and Ed.

I thought about all those times I had seen him, running in the wetlands. The nice things he'd written to me, at first. Then I thought about that hotel corridor, the crack of his hotel key as he tried to force it into that lock. How frightened I'd felt. Something had happened to me since then, though. I didn't feel fear any more. Just rage.

Before I could speak, Ed's head jerked to the entrance. I followed his gaze, tried to work out who he was looking at. And then I saw Laura. And as Laura walked up to him to brush something off his jacket, all the pieces fell into place.

'Ed, darling, come and talk to Jez,' I heard her say to him.

Ed pulled his gaze away from me to his wife. 'Sure,' he said. 'Just a moment.'

Laura looked annoyed. She glanced at me, smiled tightly, then walked back over to Jez and Claire, wobbling a little in her heels.

I moved towards Ed. I felt the champagne warming me, making me brave.

'Wow. You fucking liar.'

'Keep your voice down.' He looked over my shoulder, smiled at someone, as if to reassure them everything was fine. His face was flushed, his temples sweaty. In that moment, I couldn't work out how I'd ever found him attractive.

'On the blink of separating, are you? Funny. I've got a feeling that might come as news to Laura.' I did the maths, quickly, in my head.

We were messaging even before Beau was born. So Laura would probably have been pregnant.

Ed's eyes widen at my use of his wife's name.

'How do you … ?' He glances over at her, then back to me, straightens his tie. 'Look, we can talk about all this –'

'I don't want to talk to you about anything,' I hissed. 'I'd much rather talk to your wife. Maybe she'd like to see the messages you sent. Or the pictures? They didn't do a lot for me.'

The colour of Ed's face deepened.

'Hello, excuse me? Sophie?'

I hadn't heard Laura approach. She was standing beside Ed, looking from me to him, then back to me. Ed's eyes were wide, amphibian. Laura frowned at me.

'What's going on, Sophie?'

TASH

I reach, instinctively, for the crumbling drystone wall. It feels cool against my palm. I hear myself breathing.

'Nothing for the Corsa?'

'Nope,' Adam confirms. 'It wasn't anywhere near the wetlands that weekend. In any case, it was scrapped some time ago, that car.'

I breathe out, then in again, my heart pounding. Tom never lied to me. Tom was telling the truth.

'So what did you find, Adam?'

Adam makes an exasperated noise, like something catching in his throat.

'Adam?'

'I – it was the first plate you gave me,' he stutters. 'For the BMW X5, registered to Ed Crawley. It was caught on ANPR, late that night, near the Hendersons' address. Then later that weekend, it was driven to the wetlands and back. Parked right by where the CCTV cameras were so conveniently vandalised.' He pauses. 'I told you ... I thought it was you ... they sounded just like you, Tash.'

I take a breath. 'Are you sure? About the car?'

'I'm sure. Look, there's still work to do. But to me, this looks significant, Tash. Really significant.'

There is a crackle on the line. The signal is dropping. Adam pauses.

'Tash? Did you hear me? Tash?'

I felt a thump of terror. One of the women in the house had answered my phone. Had heard all this. One of them knew that I was looking into Ed. That I knew what he'd done.

'Adam, what did the person who answered the phone say, when you told them all this? Was it definitely a woman?'

'Of course it was a woman. Fucking hell, Tash.' I've never heard Adam swear, and it doesn't suit him. 'They said they'd call me back. Thinking about it, you did sound ... I just thought it was a bad line.' He exhales loudly. 'Who had access to your phone?'

'I don't know. All of them.'

'All of who?'

I am silent. They were all there. Claire, Laura, Nicole. It could have been any of them.

'So ... Was it was Ed?' I am speaking to myself as much as Adam, trying to unravel it all.

'Maybe, maybe not,' Adam is saying. 'But I think he was involved. I think his car moved the body.'

SOPHIE

One hour before

I wasn't sure how much she'd heard. I could have told her. Of course I could. But I realised that actually, I just didn't care enough. About either of them.

'I'm taking the boys home.' I walked away from Ed and Laura, ignoring the heat of their gaze on my back.

I found Jude on his own, still, under the table with his iPad. He looked up at me, his eyes tired.

'Are we going home now, Fee?'

I nodded, held out my hand and pulled him up. He was so tall now. He would be going to school in September. He wouldn't need me any more. Nobody would.

Beau was in Jez's arms, grizzling, his face puffy and red. I told Claire and Jez I thought I should take them home.

'Fine.' Claire pretended to busy herself packing their things. I held my hands out for Beau. Jez passed him over, awkwardly, avoiding my gaze. I realised he was trying not to touch me. The pain of it stabbed anew in my heart.

'Thanks,' he muttered. I forced Jez to catch my eye, just for a moment. He looked ashamed, embarrassed and actually, a tiny bit frightened. In that moment, I could see what was going to happen. They were going to let me go. Claire had wanted to for ages, and Jez wouldn't resist it now. I had become a wrinkle in their perfect lives, to be ironed out and erased.

Beau was so sleepy he didn't protest about the pram. As soon as I gave him his dummy, his eyelids drooped.

'Come on, buddy,' I said to Jude. 'Let's get home.' I took him by the hand. Suddenly I was holding a sob in my chest, my eyes blurry

with tears. I couldn't see how I was going to get through the next few hours, or what was going to happen after that.

'Are you OK?'

When I looked up, I saw it was one of the scruffy doctors that had arrived with Laura. He was wearing an orange T-shirt. He had a beard and glasses, and a kind face.

'Fine, thanks.' I rubbed at my eye, embarrassed.

'Bad party?'

I looked at him and half laughed, half sobbed. 'The worst.'

The doctor laughed. 'Not exactly my scene either,' he said. He was looking down at Beau with an expression I couldn't fathom. Then he looked back up at me, and squinted a bit.

'Sorry.' He shook his head. 'I thought I recognised you from somewhere – maybe not.' He sighed, reached behind me. 'Come on,' he said. 'Let me get the door for you.'

By the time our black cab arrived home, Beau was deeply asleep in the pram. I left him there in the hallway while I put Jude to bed. I read Jude his favourite story.

Stick Man is lonely, Stick Man is lost.
Stick Man is frozen and covered in frost …
He can't hear the bells, or the sweet-singing choir …
Or the voice saying 'Here's a good stick for the fire!'
Stick Man is lying asleep in the grate.
Can anyone wake him before it's too late?

I wanted Jude to have stayed awake long enough to hear the happy ending, but his eyes had closed. I imagined his dreams flitting over his eyes like shadows. I had a sudden sense that I didn't want to leave him in this cold, lonely house. A house full of secrets. Full of lies.

I went downstairs, lifted Beau from his pram, a warm rag doll. I carried him up to his beautiful bedroom, and onto the soft mattress of his cot. I brushed his pale hair away from his eyes, even though they were closed, and blew him a kiss in the darkness.

I went back to check on Jude, by now snoring softly. 'I love you,' I told him. The words snagged in my throat.

I'm glad he didn't know, when I pulled his dinosaur cover over his chest, that it would be the last time I did it. I'm glad he didn't know it when I kissed his hair, turned out the light.

I heard the key in the door, the shift in the air as it creaked open. The sound of footsteps on the tiles in the hallway, the brief music of keys hitting the bowl on the hallway table.

All night, Sal had been messaging me. Telling me not to do it, not to use it. *You don't know what they'll do.* But it was time for the truth. If not now, then when?

I took a deep breath, headed down the stairs, and finally opened my mouth.

'I need to talk to you.'

TASH

The storm is loud in my ears, the sea below the cliffs dark, seething, unstill. I hold my phone tightly to my ear, try to cover it with my hoody cuff.

'Was it Ed?' I find I am almost shouting at Adam, over the wind. 'Could he – have killed her? He was seeing Sophie? And then he got violent when she ended it?'

Adam pauses. 'Or there could be another explanation. I ran a financial search. Ed had some pretty severe money problems. Until Jeremy Henderson gave him a job at Graphite, soon after Sophie died.'

'You think ... that was some sort of payback?'

'It could have been.'

'So ... Jez could have been involved?'

'He could have. He could have got Ed to help him cover it up, in return for money.'

I swallow.

'I'm hoping I have enough now,' Adam is saying. 'To persuade the higher-ups to look into the case again. But, Tash ... you need to steer clear of these people, in the meantime, OK? All of them. Just in case we're right.'

'Oh God, Adam. I can't! I'm here with them in Cornwall. With Ed, and Jeremy. I'm in their house. Finn's here with me, and Tom.'

I look back at the house, alone on the cliffs, the little yellow squares of light in the windows illuminating the curtains of water washing wildly off the sea. My son is in there, with them.

Adam is incredulous. 'What? Why?! Can't you leave?'

I will call Tom now. I'll tell him to leave the pub, get home. He can make up some emergency. We can say Finn is sick, that we have to leave. Anything to get him out of there.

Adam is still on the line, but his voice is faint and tinny, the line distorted.

'Tash?' he is saying. 'How soon can you leave?'

'I don't know, I ...'

Before I can finish, I hear the line go dead.

My fingers cold and shaking, I close the call and ring Tom. It goes through to his voicemail. I feel like I want to scream.

'Tom, we need to leave. Call me back. I need you to get Finn, to meet me somewhere, with the car ...'

The signal cuts out before I can continue. I stare at the screen, willing a bar to appear, but there is nothing. The wind whips past again, nearly knocking me off my feet. I fumble for the torch again on my phone. As I do, I see that a message has come through from Grace, accompanied by some images.

Can't get through to you. Sending images of the letter. Hope it makes more sense to you than it does to me!

I have to zoom in on the images with my thumb and forefinger. At first, I can't make sense of the different columns, the lists of numbers, references to allele sizes, genetic markers. But other parts are clear.

Child: Eliza Imogen Sandwell.
Alleged father: Jeremy Mark Henderson.
Probability of paternity: 99.9999 per cent.

I think of Eliza, strapped onto the back of Christina's bike, eating crisps on the sofa with Billy, in her Elsa dress at the Christmas play. Her little pigtails, so fair, so pale and translucent. Hair that is nothing like her mother's. But that is just like Beau's.

Christina in the audience that time, craning her neck to look over to where we had been sitting. She hadn't been feeling left out of our group. She hadn't cared about that at all. She had been looking at the father of her child, watching their daughter, in her first nativity play.

This must have been it – the secret Sal and Christina knew. The secret Sal told Sophie – then decided she didn't want Sophie to use it, for fear of what might happen. *I don't think u shud use it Soph. U don't no what they'll do.*

Sophie must have gone ahead anyway. She must have confronted Jez over it, over his secret child.

What if Sophie had threatened to expose Jez's secret, and Jez had got angry? What if he killed her? Got Ed to help him cover it up – take the body – and in return, he made Ed's money troubles disappear.

This is the only thing that makes sense. And then I feel my hands, still clutching my phone, with the image on the screen, start to shake. Sophie was killed because of what she knew. And I know the secret now, too. Which means that I'm in the same danger she was.

I need to get through to Tom. I need signal. Maybe if I climb higher up the cliffs. I pull my hood up, squinting into the rain. I flick on my phone torch and hold it out in front of me to light the way.

And that's when I see, through the silvery rods of rain illuminated in front of me, a lone figure on the cliffs ahead. Waiting for me.

SOPHIE

Forty-nine minutes before

Claire stared at me. She looked as if she had just been woken from a dream she'd been in for the last year.

'What?'

'We've been sleeping together,' I tell her. 'At his office. And here, in this house.'

'You, and Jez?'

Claire's face was a mask of horror and disbelief, as if she'd just been bitten by a family dog she thought would never turn.

'No,' she said eventually. 'No. He would never.'

'He would. He did. Many times. But actually, it's not me you need to worry about.'

Claire was frightened. I could see it now. I was powerful, suddenly. All the stuff that she had, that I didn't. I was holding all of it in my hands. One move, and it all smashed to pieces.

'He's been having an affair with someone else. A woman called Christina Sandwell. It's been going on years. Way longer than me.'

Claire's eyes narrowed. 'You're way off the mark,' she spat. 'Christina is just an old friend of Jeremy's. She was best friends with Jeremy's first wife, Emily.' But I could see the doubt behind her eyes, hear the wobble of it in the pitch of her protest. Claire was not stupid. I could tell from the way she paused, waited for more. She had had her doubts about this woman before.

'Her baby –'

'She had that baby with a sperm donor.' Claire's voice was harder now, snapping like an animal.

'No,' I told her. 'Christina's daughter is Jez's. Eliza is Beau's half-sister.'

Claire froze for a moment, then actually laughed. 'What rubbish! You're making this up!'

'I'm not.'

I unfolded the piece of paper in my pocket, the copy of the one that Sal gave me. I placed it in front of Claire. She jumped up, backed away.

'You don't want to know the truth, do you?'

Claire looked up at me. She still hadn't looked at the paper.

'You,' she said. 'Ever since you came, nothing has been right. I haven't felt right –'

'But, Claire, I've tried to help, all the time, and you –'

'Liar! You don't want to help me.' She shook her head. 'You want to take the boys from me! And Jez, and this house ... I see it now. I see what you want!'

I held up the paper, but Claire turned her head, refusing to look at it, to read the names.

'You're wrong,' I told her. 'I don't want your life. Your life is a lie.'

'Get away from me. I don't want to hear anything you've got to say.'

'Because you don't want to hear the truth!'

'Get out. Get out of my house.'

'This is my house, too!'

My dad always said, you should never say you hate someone. If you hate someone, that means you want them dead. But the look she gave me then, Claire didn't have to say the word. I could see it, feel it all over my skin. But she didn't say it. Instead, she turned away, and started up the stairs.

TASH

'Tash, it's not what you think.'

Although I can see it is Laura, the voice doesn't sound like hers. It sounds like something from far away.

'I thought you were looking after Finn,' I stutter.

'Tom's back,' she says soothingly. 'I waited until they were back to come.'

I don't know whether I can believe her or not. I have no idea who to trust.

'You've got it all wrong, Tash,' she says. 'You think you know, but you don't.'

I take a breath. 'Did you answer my phone? Before?'

Laura looks at me, steadily.

'Why did you do that?'

Laura bites her lip. She says nothing.

'Answer me! I know you've been lying to me, Laura – you all have! About Sophie. And about how Finn got hurt, that day at Claire's. What's going on, Laura? What else have you lied about?'

Laura's voice is breaking, her face tortured, contorted.

'Tash, listen. Come this way – away from the house, away from the others. Trust me, Tash.'

I hesitate, but when I look at her face, I believe the pain etched on it; I can see that it is real. Haltingly, I follow Laura up the cliff. The rain floods the path, little rivulets down either side. I think of Finn. He's fine, I tell myself. Tom is there. He is tucked up in his bed. Tom wouldn't let anyone harm Finn.

Laura stops abruptly, then turns to me. 'You have to believe me, Tash. I didn't want any part of this.'

She moves closer and tries to take my arm. I pull away, as if scalded by her touch.

'Don't touch me.'

'I'm not a bad person, Tash.' Her lip is wobbling, like a child.

I feel myself shaking.

'Tell me the truth, Laura.'

'It was an accident,' Laura croaks. 'It was all an accident.'

SOPHIE

Thirty-three minutes before

For some reason, the way she turned her back on me made me angrier than anything else. I felt the cold grip of fury in my wrists, my jaw. I followed her, the paper grasped in my hand.

'Look! Look!'

I was screaming it now, pressing the paper into her face.

'Look at the paper!'

Claire was at the top of the stairs. Even as I followed her, I had the feeling that this was unreal, that this could not really be where we were, what we were doing. But the mist in front of me was thickening, and I could not stop. Even when I heard a key in the door, the voice of a man calling to us, asking us what the hell was going on. Even when I heard another door open on the landing, just a crack. A pair of dark eyes in a small, pale face.

Jude rubbed his eye, sleepily.

'Fee?'

'Go back to bed, Jude sweetheart,' I said. 'Go back.' But my voice seemed to wake him up even more. 'Jude, please,' I told him, but he took another step towards me.

I looked back to Claire. When she turned her face was pink and wet with tears.

'Claire, listen!' I cried. I tried to reach out to touch her arm.

'Get off me! I want you gone!'

It happened quickly, then. It was as if Claire hadn't seen Jude. Her eyes were fixed on me. She pushed me, hard, so hard that I was thrown against the wall. My head slammed against a corner of plaster. The

311

pain was white in front of my eyes. My hand, still clutching the paper, was too slow to reach out and stop my fall. And so fall is what I did, over and backwards, until I was at the bottom, my head slamming again, against the cold, hard tiles.

TASH

I look at my phone. A single bar of signal has reappeared.

'I'm calling the police,' I tell her. But as soon as I say it, Laura lunges at me, her eyes wild and glassy. She grabs my forearm and I gasp and shake her away. In doing so, I throw her off balance, and she drops to her knees in the mud, and sobs.

My instinct is to help her up, apologise. But all the rules have changed; everything has shifted. I can't reconcile the Laura who cooks spaghetti for Finn, sits him down with a spoon and fork, lends him spare clothes if he gets mucky, has him over to play in her garden, with the person in the mud front of me.

'Please listen, Tash,' she begs. 'I had no choice.'

'What do you mean, *you* had no choice?'

Laura staggers to her feet, holds her hands up in front of her, fingers splayed, as if I have a gun, and she is asking me not to shoot.

'What did you do, Laura?'

The tips of her fingers are shaking, the rain starting to darken the reddish colour of her hair. I tighten my hand on my phone.

'We were ruined, Tash.' Her voice is wavering. 'We were fucking ruined. There was this girl, at Ed's work. She said he had ... that he had ...' She shakes her head. 'It was nonsense – a lie, of course. Ed would never – But that didn't matter. They didn't believe him. He got sacked. You know what it's like now – men can't do anything ...'

She is shaking her head, her chin wobbling, eyeballs shot with red in the light of the torch on my phone. I wonder if she really thinks this. Perhaps she has told herself this lie so many times, she believes it to be true.

313

'He tried to get another job,' she goes on. 'But no other bank wanted to know. We had nothing. We needed Ed's income. We were mortgaged to the hilt. We couldn't live on just ... you know what doctors earn ...'

Her shoulders sag. Living on what a doctor earns. Like us, in other words. Was this the horror she was trying to prevent? The horror of not being rich?

'You don't understand,' she gabbles, seeing my expression harden. 'We were going to lose the house, Tash. Our whole life. Oscar was only a few months old – I was still breastfeeding – I couldn't go back to work, not yet. We were in real trouble. My cards had stopped working, I couldn't even buy a coffee – I had these letters piling up. Neither of our families could help. All I could think of was Claire and Jez.'

She hangs her head.

'I'd been trying to talk to them, to find the right moment,' she says. 'That's why I went over that night, after the party.'

'Hang on,' I say. 'It was you that drove the car over to theirs? Not Ed?'

She nods wordlessly, staring down at the ground.

'You drove the car,' I repeat, my voice shaking. 'You took her ... you took her body.' My vision swims. I feel sick.

Laura buries her face in her hands.

'Why, Laura? Why?'

'Please, let me explain,' she cries. 'It was all by accident. I had only gone over to try and talk to Jeremy, to ask him to help Ed. I'd wanted to find a moment to talk to him at the party, but it had been too difficult. I'd gone over that night to ask him – beg him, if I needed to – to help Ed.'

'And?'

'I got there. I knocked and knocked. They ignored me. But I could hear voices inside. I knew they were there. And then I remembered where Claire kept her spare key, under that bay tree pot. So I let myself in. And when I opened the door, they were both there, and ... and ...'

'And what?'

My voice is uneven. I realise I am cold now, to my bones.

Laura looks down. 'Sophie ... she ... she was on the floor. I checked for a pulse but it was no use. She was gone, Tash. It was over. There was nothing anyone could have done to change it.'

'You said it was an accident,' I spit, my teeth gritted. 'If it was an accident, you would have just called an ambulance.'

Laura drops her gaze.

'You knew it wasn't an accident. You knew she hadn't just fallen.'

Laura meets my eye. 'No, Tash. She didn't just fall. I could see she hadn't just fallen.'

I feel myself wobbling under the weight of it. I reach out automatically for a handrail, or a wall, but there is nothing to hold on to up here.

'How could you, Laura? How could you have helped them?'

Laura looks away, ashamed. 'Tash, you have to understand. If I'd called the police, what good would it have done?'

I want to tell her to stop. I can't bear to hear her rationalise it.

'All I could think was, we were all ruined,' Laura says quietly. 'Unless we helped each other. If I helped them, and they helped me. I'd have lost the life we'd built for our son. And those boys' lives would have been ruined too. Beau was still so little, not even a year old – he needed his mummy. And Jude, he'd already lost one parent, about to lose another.'

I inhale. 'So you told them you'd help them. What did they do for you in return? What was the price, Laura?'

'Tash, listen, I know it was wrong, but …'

'Well, now you can fix it,' I tell her. I still can't look her in the eye. 'You can come with me, to the police. We can tell them everything.' I lift my phone to my ear, my hand trembling. 'You need to do this. You owe it to Sophie's mum.'

Laura is close to me again, trying to take my phone.

'Tash – listen. Just wait. We can't do any of this now. They know you're on to them.'

'What?'

Laura glances down the cliff behind me. 'Claire. Your phone rang, when you were in the bathroom, and Claire answered it. And now I think they … I think they …'

I hear her gasp, her fingers clamp to her mouth, before I feel that my phone has been snatched from behind, and an arm clamped around my body, a hot palm putting pressure over my face. The light from my torch is gone, and from behind, I hear a voice in my ear, a voice I know all too well.

'I wouldn't do that, Tash, if I were you,' Jez says. And his arm tightens on my neck.

315

TASH

'I just need to talk to you, Tash,' Jez breathes. 'I just need to explain.'

Somehow, I break loose of him, and spin round.

'All right,' he says, holding his palms up. 'But please, let me explain.' But I am not looking at him. I am looking behind him.

Their faces are so smooth, impassive. They offer no explanation. They edge closer in unison, their eyes glinting like deer. Claire first. Then Nicole.

I take a step back.

'I'm sorry,' Claire breathes. 'None of us wanted it to come to this. Truly, Tash.'

My eyes cross from her to Nicole, then back to Claire, then to Jez.

'Tash,' Jez says, 'please, listen to me. I don't know what Laura has told you, but Sophie … it was a mistake …'

'You killed her.' I pause, stare at him. 'Was it because she found out about your little secret with Christina? Or had you been fucking Sophie, too?'

The anger is boiling over now, hot and throbbing on the surface of my skin, the insides of my ears. How could I have been so stupid? How could I not have seen what he really was?

'I would take it back if I could, Tash,' Jez murmurs. 'All of it.' Jez looks at Claire. He reaches out an arm to her, and she takes his hand. They both hang their heads. I feel like I might be about to vomit.

I turn to Laura. 'How? How could you help them?'

Laura sobs. 'I know, I know. I was so desperate …'

'You took her body!'

Laura sinks down into the grass, her body racked with sobs.

'She did the right thing.' Nicole is speaking now, in a bored voice, as if we'd already spent long enough on the topic. My head is spinning. So she knew about this, too?

'The nanny was dead,' Nicole shrugs. 'There was nothing anyone could have done. No rational person would have thought it worth ruining everyone's lives over a mistake. No rational person would see any point in raking it over. Unless of course, there was something in it for them.' Nicole steps towards me. 'When were you going to tell Claire, Tash? When were you going to mention the big article you were writing about us all? We've been waiting for it. The big reveal!'

Even in the freezing wind, my cheeks burn. A smirk rises to Nicole's face.

'No. Thought not. That's the thing isn't it, Tash? You've been lying to all of us. From day one.'

'That's not true,' I protest, but my voice sounds weak.

She gives a snort of laughter. 'Some investigative journalist. You really thought we just wanted the pleasure of your company? We knew your game. We needed to keep an eye on you, that was all.'

Nicole takes another step towards me and brings her face close to mine, so that I can smell the wine on her breath.

'You can tell yourself you were doing this for Sophie, out of solidarity for some lying little slut you never even knew,' she says. 'But I saw her for what she was. And I see you too, Tash. I've seen you from the start. This was always about you! It was supposed to be your big story, wasn't it? Your big break, finally, after years as a failed reporter?'

Claire pulls Nicole back. 'That's enough, Nicole,' she says. She turns to me. 'We are friends, Tash. We've all made terrible mistakes –'

Nicole shakes her off. 'Friends! What kind of friend is she to you, Claire? Snooping around in your house. Digging into your life behind your back. Cosying up to your husband.' She points a finger at Jez, then flicks it towards me. 'Don't think I haven't seen that, too.'

I back away from Nicole, from all of them. I can feel underfoot that I am leaving the path – the grass is thicker, mattress-like. I have no real sense of where the cliffs end, where they give way to the rocks beneath.

'I tried to warn you,' Nicole says, gesturing at me. 'I told you to leave it alone.'

I feel my jaw slacken with horror.

'You sent me those messages? You came to my flat?'

Nicole throws me one of her counterfeit smiles. 'You should have listened, shouldn't you? Think how much better it would have been. For everyone. Especially your stupid husband.'

The anger is hot now, under the surface of my skin. It was her. She made the complaint. She is the one ruining Tom's career.

'That's enough, Nicole.' Claire is speaking now. 'What's done is done.'

Laura sighs, mutters under her breath. 'We told you that you were taking it too far, Nicole.'

Nicole spins round to face Laura, her eyes illuminated with fury. 'Not far enough, clearly! Jesus – you're fucking deluded, all of you!' She jabs a pointed finger at me. 'Can't you see how out of hand she's gotten?'

Claire shakes her head. 'Nicole, please ...'

'Oh, cut it out, Claire. You've been too out of it on your dumb pills to see what's in front of your face for months.'

Claire shrinks from her, as if she's been scalded. Laura's eyes widen with concern. And in my mind, something starts to fall into place. The scattering of pills, like sweets, on Sal's counter. Pills that looked just like Claire's.

'Nicole,' Laura says, 'Claire's been through a lot ...'

'Oh yeah, so what's your excuse?' Nicole snaps at Laura. A polished nail jabs in my direction again. '*You* were supposed to be handling *her*!'

I look up at Jez. Even despite everything, I find myself looking to him, for a safe harbour.

'Where is Tom?'

'He's back home. With Finn.'

Jez sees my face soften. He takes a step forward.

'I swear to God, Tash,' Jez murmurs. 'It was all just a terrible mistake.'

It is unmistakable, the guilt in his eyes. It is hideous. I start to shake.

'What about Sal?'

Jez fixes his eyes on mine.

'I asked you a question. What about Sal, Jez? Was she just a mistake, too?'

'Sal?' Claire's face is confused. 'Sal killed herself.' Claire looks at me, then to Jez, then back to me again. 'Sal killed herself, Tash. That's nothing to do with any of this. Tell her, Jez.'

'Of course I didn't kill Sal,' Jez murmurs.

'Liar!' The rage is in front of my eyes now, hot and white. It had to be Jez, I saw that now. He would have known that Christina had confided in Sal about Eliza. He had the pills – Claire's pills. He had access to Christina's flat – her penthouse flat, that he put her up in.

'Did you go to Christina's house just for the keys, Jez?' I demand. 'Or are you still fucking her too?'

I stare at Jez, watch his expression flicker as he makes his calculations, plots his verbal escape. And finally, it is gone, the heady suck of attraction. I see this man, at last, for what he is. A liar.

'Oh my God.' There is a quiver in Laura's voice. 'Jez, tell me this isn't … tell me Tash is wrong.'

Jez comes to life, shakes his head.

'Right. This is bullshit. Laura, enough. Tash, I had nothing to do with Sal … I didn't even know her!' He is still holding my phone in his hand. As I glance at it, I feel pressure on my wrist. Laura has grabbed it, and is holding me, tightly.

'Tash. Please, believe me. I know I shouldn't have helped him, I –'

I push her away and lunge at Jez, managing to snatch my phone. I clutch it tightly to my chest.

'I'm calling the police right now, Laura,' I tell her, my voice wobbly with adrenaline. 'You can tell it to them.'

'Don't do that, Tash!' Jez is roaring now, following me, panting, edging closer to my face. He grabs at my phone and I swing away from him.

'Get off!' I scream.

'Please, let's just talk this through. You need to listen to me, not them. They are trying to manipulate you – it wasn't me –'

'You as good as admitted it was you!'

'It wasn't me, it was –'

'Stop lying!'

It comes quickly, like a struck match. The anger, the humiliation. Mine, and Sophie's together, a sudden flame that burns white hot. Jez lunges towards me, snatching at my phone again. Instinctively, I raise my hands to bat him away, and his hand misses the phone and

319

slams against my face. I feel the nauseous thud of injury, the wetness of blood on my nose, my chin. He looks shocked, and for a mad moment, I think he is going to apologise, clean me up. But instead, his face hardens, and he lunges again for my phone.

I grab at the lapels of his jacket in an effort to keep him at arm's length, twist my body in a bid to stay on my feet, to avoid the force of his movement knocking me over. As I twist, I feel the crumble of earth and rock underfoot, giving way. Instinctively, I release my grip on Jez, pushing him away, and leap, as if scalded, away from the cliff edge. just moments before the cliff edge disappears.

My strength was no match for his. But however I replay it in my mind, there is no escaping the fact that it was me that pushed him to his fall. It was me that pushed him over the disappearing cliff. Down the rockface, and into the darkness.

SOPHIE

Nineteen minutes before

After the fall, there was darkness, just for a few moments. Then something between darkness and light. A hot, wet place at the back of my head. My fingers and feet felt cold. I looked up to the top of the stairs and all I could see was Jude's little face.

I tried to call out to him, to tell him I was all right. But I couldn't.

'Fee!' Jude started to scream, and then there was the sound of a door closing. Behind the door, I heard him scream my name again and again. Fee. Fee.

And then another door opened and closed again.

A man's voice. It was him. Jez. I waited for him to save me, to pick me up, bring me back to life. But he didn't. He didn't touch me. He stood over me, terrified, looking at me as if I was something monstrous.

I heard them talking quietly, her sobbing, him pacing. His footsteps were loud in my ears. The two of them came close to me, and everything swam again. My eyes must have been open, but I could not focus on their faces now. Could not move, or speak. They moved away. More voices. More sobbing.

What are we going to do? Claire kept asking. *What are we going to do now?*

After a while, I thought I heard a third voice. An open door, the feel of the night air. A clanking, on the tiles. But I could not be sure. Things were slipping away – the house, the windows, the beautiful ceiling roses. The marble, the glass, the rainbow-coloured bookshelves.

Sometimes there was a beat of panic, and I tried to struggle, but more and more I let it lap at me, the warm water of it, and I let myself drift. Awake still, but no longer fearing sleep. Starting to want it, rather than fight.

TASH

Claire screams into the darkness beyond me. The sound is swallowed by the wind.

'Where did he go, Laura? Where is he? Jez!'

Claire is hysterical. Nicole holds her still, but even she looks at a loss.

'Where is he? Where is Jez?' I turn to Laura. My entire body is shaking. Laura doesn't answer me. Her eyes flit from me, to the cliff edge, then back again.

'What happened to him, Laura?'

She doesn't reply. But we all heard the scream. We all heard the crack of a body on the rocks. We all heard the splash.

'We need to get help,' Claire cries. 'Why are you all just standing here?'

'Just wait a minute,' Nicole hisses. 'Let's just think about this a minute.'

Laura puts her hand on my back. I shake it off. I don't want to be near any of them. Laura looks at my face, wounded.

'Tash, please. I'm sorry. I just wanted to protect Oscar. I didn't ... I didn't ...' She trails off, bringing a muddy sleeve to her eyes. 'Did Jez really kill Sal, Tash?'

There is a flash on the horizon. Two white cylinders of torchlight, edging closer. A crunch of gravel underfoot, raised voices.

'Hello? Police!'

The sound of the voice is like waking from a dream. I look down at my clothes, the mud-soaked path. The rain is still falling, the wind still howling. My leg is shaking. How long have I been here? How long has it been since the splash?

323

'Police. Is anyone there?'

Laura grips my wrist again. She pulls her face close to mine, forces me to meet her gaze.

'Listen, I think there was an accident, Tash,' she pants. 'Do you hear me?'

I stare at her.

'Jez fell.' Laura turns to Claire and Nicole. 'Right? Are you listening, Tash? He fell.'

TASH

The tea Williams brought me has gone cold. The storm outside is starting to quiet; the rain settling into a slow drumbeat. Pascoe leans forward on the wipe-clean rectangle of table, rests on his elbows.

'So,' Pascoe says. 'You didn't actually see him fall.'

The room feels so cold. I long for sleep. I gaze down at the flecks in the blue lino floor. I could curl up on this floor, just here, in the corner of this room. I could pull my hood over my head. If they would just let me shut my eyes.

I shake my head.

'For the tape?'

'Sorry. No. I didn't.'

'It's extraordinary,' he muses, tilting his head to one side. 'No one actually saw him fall. And yet, you all seem so sure that that's what happened.'

'Police!' The call had come closer. There had been a crack of thunder. Laura lowered her voice to a whisper.

'Tash came out to make a call and got lost on the cliffs,' she said. 'We all came looking for her. Jez lost his way. He fell.'

'He fell,' Nicole said. She glared at me, at Claire. Claire looked like she hardly knew where she was.

I looked at their faces, staring at me, waiting. I thought about the body at the bottom of the cliffs. And then I thought about Finn, about Tom. About the new life Tom wanted, far away from here. I saw the price that I would have to pay.

'Police!'

325

Laura had come closer to my face. I could feel the coolness of the rain, mingling with the blood coming from my nose.

'Are you hearing me, Tash? He fell.'

I had looked at Claire, and she had looked away, and howled into the wind.

I stare at the glass either side of the room. I want to know where Tom is. I long for him. I look at Pascoe, waiting. He has sat back in his chair, now, his arms folded. He passes me a tissue for my face. I told him it was just a nosebleed. He keeps looking at it, making it feel hot on my face.

'It's like I told you before,' I say. 'It was dark. I heard a rock fall, where he was standing. I heard a noise like someone falling, a cry. I recognised his voice. Then I heard someone falling into the water.'

The words are out, now. I have said my story, and the effort of it feels like a sucker punch.

'Please,' I say. 'Can I go home now?'

TASH

Four months later

'Mummy, there's Oscar!'

Finn does a little jig in excitement at the sight of his friend. He races off towards him and taps him on the shoulder. Soon they are giggling together, running off under a trestle table covered in home-made cakes in Tupperware. With an effort, I raise my gaze, from the red-painted toes and sandals at the foot of the table where they have disappeared, up to Laura's face.

Laura is looking at me, her smile tight in the scorching glare of the sun. She is wearing sunglasses, a new dress. She gives me a nodded hello. I do the same. I tell myself that this is the last time, the last thing.

The removals van arrived this morning. It's parked outside the flat, filling up with our furniture, including the last of Dad's pictures – we sold most of them, but some, the most special ones, are to be framed for our new place. I've left Tom to sort the endless baby junk I'd been tempted to give away or sell, but that we'll now soon need again.

Tom and I are leaving tomorrow, at first light. It all moved so fast once we got started – our flat sold over a single weekend. We will sleep in it for the last time, on roll-out mattresses, tonight. We'll order our favourite takeaway, from the Indian place on Church Street, one last time. We are leaving London, and Clissold Park, and Ruby's, and Highbury Fields, and the wetlands. The keys to our new home in Oxford – a real house, with a garden and, most unbelievably of all, four bedrooms – are hanging on the hook by the door. I get a little thrill every time I feel the keys, the cold metal of them, their edges rough in the palms of my hands.

I was nervous about coming here today, but the weather is due to break after today – a long, hot spell due to end in heavy thunderstorms – and Finn had been so excited about the summer fair. I thought he should see his friends one last time.

'Are you sure you don't mind finishing the packing?' I'd looked guiltily at all the toys, the books still on the shelves, the plates still stacked in the cupboards. But Tom had shaken his head. 'It'll be loads easier with him out of the house. Anyway, I'm hardly going to let you lift any heavy boxes, am I?'

Luckily there is no sign of Claire. I don't think I could bear seeing her again. I spotted her a few days ago, at the ice-cream van on Highbury Fields. She was queuing up, holding tightly to Beau's hand. In profile, her bump was like a perfect semicircle under her pale pink T-shirt. She was staring straight ahead, her lips pursed, as if she was still trying to work it all out.

Jeremy's parents were standing behind her with Jude. He was on his scooter, as usual, the blue one with the light-up wheels. I watched his grandfather hand him the ice cream, ruffle his curly hair. Jude is living with his grandparents in the countryside, now, one of the other mothers told me, coming down to see his half-brother every other weekend. Both boys are doing better than anyone dared to hope.

It had been enough to see them, to see the boys one last time. I had turned away and headed back up the Fields. I hadn't wanted her to see my face.

Then, at the top of the Fields, I had passed Nicole's house. The wooden shutters are closed over the windows now, like eyelids. There is no agent's sign outside, but I know it has been sold. Their move, too, all seems to have happened with breakneck efficiency: a private buyer, a property scout. The last photograph Nicole posted on Instagram was her with John and the girls on the steps of the house, the smart painted door behind them. Lissy was on her knee and John was holding the baby, bigger now, her fist in her mouth. *Bye-bye, London Town*, the caption read. Nicole and Lissy were waving with both their palms, a broad smile on Nicole's face. She was washing her hands of us.

As I go to lure Finn back from under the table, I brace myself for Laura.

'What do you recommend?' I ask, gesturing at the cakes.

'Definitely Bakewell tart.' She smiles. 'Although in this weather, most people just want the lollies.'

'I can imagine.'

'How are you all, Tash?'

'We're all right, I guess.'

'Heard you were moving out.'

'We are,' I tell her carefully. 'Tom took the Oxford job. And it seems we are in need of a bit more space.'

Laura smiles again, glancing at my belly. 'It seems so. Congratulations. I'm really happy for you both.'

With everything that happened after that night on the cliffs – the police investigation, the inquest, the endless, endless phone calls from reporters and news desks who'd ignored my invoices for months and now wanted to be my best friend – I'd barely noticed the nausea, the exhaustion, creeping up at me like a looming shadow. When I'd had to stop on the way back from playgroup drop-off to be sick behind a horse chestnut tree at the edge of the park, I had finally realised. I'd bought a test, one of the expensive ones. I wanted to know how many weeks. It said five to six.

Cornwall, then, I'd said to myself out loud. It was too soon. I didn't feel ready. But when I touched my belly, I was sure I felt her, even as early as that. A fluttering, no stronger than the beat of a butterfly wing. She was there, and there was no going back.

Laura takes a knife and cuts me a slice, revealing the deep red line inside. She has been true to her word, Claire and Nicole too. We all agreed the story, and we stuck to it. When Jez's body washed up a few days later, a mile or two down the coast, there was nothing really conclusive. Bodies in water can be particularly difficult.

The inquest heard there had been a gale-force storm that night. No moon, meaning it had been difficult to see the path. The coroner had recommended the erection of a safety fence, given the popularity of the route with holidaymakers, including children, and the growing evidence of rockfalls, coastal erosion. The police investigation had, eventually, been dropped.

I've kept my part of the bargain, too. There will be no new investigation into the death of Sophie Blake. No vindication for Jane, no award-winning podcast, no 4,000-word magazine piece in the *Sunday*

Times in which I lay out how I cracked a murder case on my own, in between my childcare commitments.

I feel my phone vibrate in my pocket. I ignore it. Somehow, I know who it will be. It's not the first time they have called today, and it won't be the last.

Laura holds the slice of tart inside a paper napkin, her fingers pinching either side. 'Best excuse for sugar ever, being pregnant. Make the most of it.'

I hand her a fiver and she waves it away.

'Don't worry.'

'It's for the playgroup.' I put the money in the Tupperware, weigh it down with some two-pound coins.

I find it difficult to meet Laura's eye. I am a journalist. I don't believe in secrets. But now, I've become part of one. Her secret, her lie. The lie that protects her and Claire, and keeps them safe inside their huge, beautiful houses. And I have no choice. Because now their lie protects me too.

In my quietest moments, alone with it, at night, I have told myself that Jez's death meant that justice was done for Sophie – some sort of justice, anyway. I tell myself again and again that Jez as good as admitted he killed Sophie. Maybe he got the ending he deserved.

But plenty of other questions remain, questions that my reporter's brain finds impossible to silence. Like exactly how much Claire did. She was home before Jeremy, after all – or so she said. Was she really just a bystander, crouched with horror over the body of the nanny Jez had hurled to her death? Or did she do more than that? Did I really know the Claire of then? Or had Sophie known a different Claire? A person gripped by dark thoughts and paranoia. A person who had been on the edge, and ready to snap.

And then there were other questions. How, exactly, had Ed – or Laura, or both of them – dumped her body in the wetlands? Had Jez fixed the CCTV, to ensure they wouldn't be seen – or told Ed where the cameras were, and let him get on with it? And what was the nature of the deal Laura brokered? How much did Jeremy have to pay Ed, to make all their problems go away?

Most perplexing of all was the question of Sal. Had I been right, on the cliffs that night? Had Jeremy really killed Sal, too?

I'd dared to ask Tom about it, weeks after, when things had settled a bit. We had been in the car on the way back from Oxford, one of

our house-hunting trips, a pile of brochures on my lap, my bump snug under the seat belt.

'No,' he'd said. 'It wouldn't be possible to trick someone into taking an overdose like that.'

'Are you sure?'

'Absolutely. Not that many pills. They'd taste it in a drink.'

He was adamant. But the picture still doesn't fit. And I'm not the only one who thinks so. My phone vibrates again. It's Christina. A text message this time.

You can't keep ignoring me. Come to mine, tonight. We really need to speak.

I delete the message, put the phone back. We'll be gone tomorrow. This will all be over.

Laura dusts the tart crumbs from her hands. I'm not sure whether there are any crumbs, really, or whether this is just a gesture of finality, of tidying the last threads. 'Good luck. In Oxford. In your new home. I hope you guys are happy.'

At last, I manage to look her in the eye.

'Thanks,' I say. 'You too, Laura.'

We force the boys to say goodbye. Laura mumbles something about letting her know if we're ever back in the area. I confect a non-committal reply. A sudden breeze lifts the tablecloth and Laura slams down a hand to steady it. I glance up at the sky to find that a swirl of dark clouds are gathering. The wind picks up, the bunting in the churchyard starting to flicker.

'Time to go,' I tell Finn, and I steer us towards the gate. I hear the familiar creak, one in a long list of last times. I take one last look over my shoulder towards the park, the pretty view of the church spire, the tall columns of Clissold House, the bright green lawn where Finn took his first steps. It twists in my heart, leaving the place where he has grown up. But like I keep reminding myself, we have no choice.

'Bye,' Laura calls. Oscar is in her arms now, and she makes him wave a floppy hand. The she puts him down and sets off back to her stall, her sandals slapping on the paving stones.

When I get home, Finn is tired. I put him down for a nap on a little futon among the boxes. As I bend down, I feel a wave of nausea. It's

been so much worse this time. I feel as if I'm at sea, on a boat, and I can't get off. The heat hasn't helped.

In the kitchen, Tom is wrapping mugs and kitchen knives in paper and packing them into boxes. I fill an unpacked mug with water and ease myself into a chair.

'How was it?'

'Fine.'

'Did you see Laura?'

'Yup.'

Tom leans back on the empty sideboard, raises his eyebrows. 'Rather you than me,' he mutters.

I wonder if Laura really thinks we believe her, if she really thinks we haven't worked out, by now, just how far she went to destroy our lives. Because although she might have sent a few weird text messages, Nicole couldn't have been the one who got Tom suspended from work.

I'd done some digging, after Tom was cleared. As I'd suspected, the hospital would never have taken the complaint so seriously if the name given hadn't been a genuine patient of Tom's. But it was – complete with NHS number, details of their treatment. Only someone with access to patient details could have made such a plausible false complaint. I knew it had to have been Laura.

That's when I knew it hadn't just been about frightening me, trying to keep me away from the Sophie Blake case. That wasn't enough. Laura hated us, anyway. She hated Tom for what he had done to her. And after a bit more digging, I found out why. She was still under investigation for the overprescribing Tom had reported her for, by the Medical Practitioners Tribunal Service. She could still lose her licence, though Claire is paying for a good lawyer. Tom might have ruined her career. Trying to ruin his was not just about scaring me. It was about payback.

I'd asked Tom which pills it was that he had seen Laura overprescribing, all those months ago.

'All sorts,' he'd said. 'Benzodiazepines, mostly. Very dangerous.'

I'd pressed. What would the drug names be? What would they look like?

'Zopiclone, I think. Maybe diazepam? They'd be in bottles, little brown ones. Why?'

332

It had finally made sense then – the rows and rows of pills, with no prescription labels. Laura had been giving them to Claire without prescription, for her postnatal depression. What was it Claire had told me? *Laura helped me … I'd have been a goner if it wasn't for her.*

Claire had been terrified about having postnatal depression on her medical record. Instead of encouraging her to see her doctor, Laura obviously offered her a way round it, promising to secretly get her some pills that would help her sleep, would help calm her anxiety. Most likely, without proper oversight, they'd have done the opposite, Tom thinks. They can be highly addictive. Claire would have become increasingly reliant on Laura for her supply. For everything. And I think that must have been what Laura wanted – otherwise, why risk her career to steal the pills? Perhaps that had been her plan A, to use Claire's addiction to extort money out of her and Jez. Of course, that was before she had the good fortune to find them with a dead body on their hands.

All of which had convinced me, in the end, that we had no choice. We needed to get away from Laura. I should have listened to Tom. I had no idea who she really was. I could not trust her. Tom and I needed her out of our lives.

Tom gestures to a pile of stuff on the table. It's all my research into Sophie's death.

'I wasn't sure if you wanted to pack all this,' he says. He picks up a document from the top of the pile. Sophie's post-mortem report.

I hesitate a moment. 'No. Let me sort it out, though. I'll have it all sent back to Jane.'

'OK.' Tom is still looking at the paper in his hand.

'What?' I ask him.

'Nothing. I just thought you always told me she'd had died of a head injury.'

'Well, the pathologist couldn't say definitively what Sophie died of,' I say, carefully. I don't tell him what Laura and the others admitted, on the cliffs. How I really know she died of a head injury.

'Look.' I point to the section of commentary on the pathology report, where it mentions the head injury. 'See? It talks about it here. It was the only wound on her body.'

Tom shakes his head. 'Sophie wouldn't have died of that head injury, Tash.'

I stare at him. 'What do you mean?'

He gestures at the report's conclusions. 'With a young person,' he says, 'you need a hard blow, sufficient to fracture the skull, to cause the death.'

'So?'

'So, it says here there was no skull fracture. That wound she had – it might have caused a period of unconsciousness, or concussion. But that wound didn't kill her. No chance.'

I suddenly feel cold all over.

'What – what could she have died of, then?'

Tom flicks through the pages of the report. 'It's not at all clear from this.' He pauses on the final page, mutters almost to himself. 'Strange – no fracture to her collarbone, was there?'

I shake my head. 'Why do you ask about that?'

Tom rubs his beard with his palm. 'Look, it's not my area. Don't listen to me. I did a pathology module years ago. I've forgotten most of it.'

'No, go on. What?'

'Well … it's just this part, where it talks about haemorrhages under her eyelid.' He tips his head to one side, looks away, as if remembering something. 'I'm pretty sure the only time I've ever seen that was on a case of strangulation.'

'But she wasn't strangled.'

'No,' Tom says thoughtfully, putting the report back. He stands up, wiping his moist brow with the back of his arm, then takes a stack of cardboard boxes for the bedroom. 'She could have been smothered, though.'

I sit for a while and sip the water, listening to Tom pack next door. I find my hand is trembling on the mug.

Maybe Jez still did it, I tell myself. He could have smothered her before he threw her down the stairs. Or after. Perhaps it doesn't matter exactly how it happened, in the end. Sophie is gone, and if it weren't for him, she would still be alive. It's all his fault. Isn't it?

But that is not the only thing that's bothering me. There is something else. The slapping sound I heard, when Laura walked away from me earlier today. It's a thing she has, I realise. A sound she makes, when she walks. Sort of heavy-footed. And I suddenly remember when I heard that sound before.

I walk into the bedroom. Tom looks up at me from the floor.

'Tash? What's wrong?'

Tom stands up, rubs his hands on his jeans. I can see this is painful for him, revisiting this. He had hoped this was over.

'Tash,' he says gently, placing his hands on my arms. 'I thought we said –'

'I know,' I murmur. 'I know.'

I rest my head against his chest for a moment. Then I pull away.

'But there's something I have to do.'

TASH

The slow boil of thunder follows me across the wetlands. The reeds are bowed in the wind, the geese huddled together, their heads tucked backwards into their feathers, their eyes closed. There is no rain yet, but I feel it is coming, the air close and stifling. I pass the playground, the fake Victorian lanterns. I head to the Heron Tower, the tallest, the showcase, right on the water. I press the buzzer for the penthouse.

Christina's apartment is huge, the views from the floor-to-ceiling windows spectacular. The lights of the city blink and shimmer to the south, the wetlands now just a dark pool at the tower's feet. Three copper lights cast a glow over the kitchen island in the centre, where Christina is standing, pouring red wine into three large tumblers.

'You came,' she says. 'I'm glad. You remember Adam, I presume.'

I hadn't even noticed Adam. He is standing on the other side of the apartment, his face half in shadow, his hands shoved in his pockets. I feel hot blood rising to my cheeks, an alarm bell sounding inside my brain.

'How do you two … ?'

'I found him,' Christina says. 'His name was on the inquest documents. He spoke to me. Told me you had been ignoring his calls, since what happened in Cornwall.'

I avert my eyes, unable to meet Adam's gaze.

'I can't stay long,' I say. 'I just wanted to –'

'This isn't going to go away, Tash.' She gestures to a stool at the island. 'Why don't you sit down?'

Clumsily, I take a stool. Christina passes me a glass of wine.

'I'm not drinking,' I say defensively.

336

'Oh yes, I see.' She glances down, her eyes lingering on my belly. 'How far along are you?'

I shift on the stool. 'About four months.'

Christina looks up. Her fingers twitch, as if she is counting down. 'April, then,' she says, smiling.

I return her gaze steadily. 'The baby's due in January.'

'That's what I meant,' she says, no longer smiling.

I feel a prickle on my arms. I don't want to be here. But I need to know how much she knows. And what she plans to do about it.

'Christina, what do you want?'

'To share some information with you. And I'm hoping you'll want to share some with me. Would you like to sit on the sofa?'

She gestures behind Adam to her lounge area. A large, apricot-coloured sofa, an armchair in a designer pattern, a curving floor lamp arched over a coffee table with a neat stack of art books. It must be four times the size of our flat. Eliza's toys are only just visible, tidied away in baskets.

'I'm fine here.'

'Great. Let's start with Nicole DeSouza.'

Christina starts pacing, holding her wine glass in her fingers. I have a sense that I am in her courtroom, though I'm still not sure what part I am supposed to be playing. Jury. Witness. Or accused.

'I'm sure you know by now that Nicole was behind the threats against your family,' Christina says. 'She took out the contracts for the burner phones fraudulently, in Sal's name – the evidence that Adam found, that he told you about. Easy enough to do.'

I look over at Adam, hunched over the marble top of Christina's kitchen island. He avoids my gaze.

'I'm sure you've also worked out that only Laura could have been behind the complaint against your husband.'

'How did you ... How did you know about that?'

Christina ignores my question. I glance at Adam, and he looks away.

'Did your husband mention why he'd raised the alarm about Laura?' Christina asks.

'It was to do with prescriptions.'

Adam clears his throat, speaks for the first time. 'Are you aware, Tash, that the medications Laura was illegally overprescribing are the same medications that killed Sal?'

337

I take a breath, clamp my mouth shut. I manage a nod, but I can't speak. I feel as if I will vomit if I open my mouth.

How could I have been so stupid? No, it wouldn't have been possible for an ordinary person to trick Sal into taking an overdose. But Laura was cleverer than that.

'Did Laura ever try to turn you against Sal?' Christina asks. 'Or undermine her, perhaps? Did she make any comments that would tend to suggest she was the sort of person that would kill herself?'

'Yes.' It comes out as a croak. I think back to that day in Laura's kitchen. *I think Sal has got some mental health issues. It's very sad.*

Christina raises her chin, triumphant. 'Laura and the others knew Sal had been close to Sophie, and they knew Sal was also close to me. They knew it was likely Sal knew things that Jez and Claire didn't want to be generally known. About Jez and me – and my daughter. And about Jez's – relationship with Sophie.' Christina gives me a hard look. 'They tried to stop you from listening to Sal, Tash. But when you were determined to listen, they had to make her disappear.'

Christina opens a rose-gold laptop on her marble kitchen top, and puts on a pair of thick-rimmed glasses. 'Adam,' she says, 'perhaps you could show Tash the images.'

Adam leans over Christina, makes a few clicks with the mouse. Christina moves out of his way, her hair falling over one shoulder. She looks beautiful, powerful. Terrifying. Behind Adam, the thunderous sky comes to life over the wetlands. Little seams of lightning twitch over the tall buildings of the city. The rain is suddenly loud against the glass.

Christina picks up the laptop and rotates it so I can see. It is a CCTV image, incredibly sharp. There is no mistaking who it shows.

'This is an image from the concealed camera situated at the alleyway behind Sal Cunningham's flat,' Christina says. 'The alleyway that adjoins the small patio at the back of her flat. The residents of her estate set up this camera to catch drug dealers, and I suppose, in a way, they have succeeded.'

A muscle in Christina's cheek twitches. Her voice is brimming with anger. She looks at me.

'This image was taken on the day that Sal was found dead.'

I look at the picture. A flash of green pashmina, hair the colour of an autumn leaf. It was her, the clack, clack I heard from the patio outside Sal's house, when I found her that day. Laura's brown boots, the heels she always wore. She was there that day. She was there when I came in. I missed her by a moment.

Laura knew I was going to Sal's that night. Because Nicole knew. Nicole was there that day, watching us at Cuckoo Club. She had seen the message Sal had written, and reported back to the others. Was that what they were deciding that day, when I saw them in that coffee shop, under the round pendant light? Deciding that Sal had to be got rid of?

'It could only have been Laura, Tash,' Christina was saying now. 'No ordinary person would have been able to talk Sal into taking an overdose. But an experienced A&E doctor? They could find a way.'

I close my eyes, force myself to swallow.

'Laura intubated her.'

Christina nods. 'It seems likely Laura slipped enough diazepam into Sal's wine glass to knock her out. She was able to intubate her once she was unconscious and get the pills into her that way. It was expertly done. Looked exactly like she had taken the pills herself.'

I shift on my stool, my heart beating fast. A sharp kick of heartburn forces me to move again. The baby feels huge. I already feel her pressing against my lungs, depriving me of space, of oxygen.

'So it wasn't … Jez was nothing to do with Sal.' I know it to be true, but somehow the thought of it is so difficult to bear. After what I've done. What I convinced myself I had to do.

'Jez?' Christina almost laughs. 'It certainly wasn't anything to do with him.' She spoke more quietly. 'Anyway, he was with me that night.'

I look at Christina. There is no trace of shame on her face. In her mind, Jeremy belonged to her. Her lover. The father of her child.

'You're shocked,' she says, refilling her wine. 'But it was me and Jez before everything. Before Sophie. Before Claire. Before Emily.' She gives me a hard look. 'Before anyone else.'

'Emily? You mean …'

'I introduced them,' she says, smiling sadly. 'I guess I came to regret that decision.'

My head is swimming. I find myself looking at Christina's wine and wishing I could take a long, deep drink.

'Look, Emily and I were friends,' Christina says throatily. 'I gave him up. Then she died. We grieved her together, and then ... well, I wanted my independence, back then. I kept ending it. And he kept coming back. But I mean, Claire? She was never ... She and Jez ... they weren't right. Anyone could see that. Jeremy and I would have ended up together.'

I feel unsteady as I step off the stool. I walk over to the edge of the room, the thunderous sky huge, the city spread out underneath. I stand close to the glass, close enough to feel the cold air on the other side of it.

I turn round, look back across the island to Adam, then to Christina, the wine bottle sat in the puddle of light under the eye-level copper lamps.

'The thing I can't understand,' I say quietly, 'is why she would agree to kill Sal. Just to cover up the fact that she and Ed helped hide Sophie's body.'

Christina looks at me. And I realise it does make sense, after all.

'She just ... wouldn't have done that ...' I say, 'Unless ...'

Adam and Christina exchange glances.

'Unless,' continues Christina, 'Laura had done something considerably worse than just hide a body.'

SOPHIE

One minute before

They were asking Laura if I was dead.

She was the woman who'd come in, her shoes making that noise on the hallway tiles.

Oh no, she said. *Oh no. What's happened? What have you done?*

The ceiling was swimming, closer then further away. My head hurt, where it was wet. It hadn't hurt before, the hurt was coming back. The light was fading and growing, as if someone had their hand on the dimmer switch. Then the light went black.

They were asking her if I was dead. They were saying it over and over.

Sounds now, but no pictures. Someone beside me, kneeling. Two fingertips at my throat, pressing. A silence.

I'm sorry, I heard her say. *She's gone.*

I was gone. I was dead. So why did the sounds keep going, the light coming on and off? The pain, still, louder and quieter at the back of my head. A thump of blood. My heart was beating, wasn't it? But it couldn't be. She said I was dead.

We should call the police. The ambulance. Should we, Jez? What do we do?

Think, for a moment, Jez was saying. *We think. Take a beat.*

Then Laura.

Look. I can help you. Ed and I will help. Here's what we do. You take the body, and you put it in our car.

I was the body. I was going in the car. I waited for someone to tell her no. But no one did.

Take all your clothes off, put them on a hot wash. In a few weeks, wear the same outfit, spill red wine on it, in front of witnesses. Get rid. Clean here. Only use products you already have. If you don't report her missing until Monday, no one will be looking for her.

No one would be looking for me.

A man's voice. Jez. And I hear the smallness in it, now. I didn't before.

Why are you doing all this?

A scratch, like a piece of paper. She was writing something.

This is the price.

Silence. Then Jez says something. I can't hear what. Then it's her, again. Saying something about no one would lose their house, or go to prison. *Our lives can stay the same,* she was saying. *Everything can stay the same.*

Pictures now, again. Blurred, as if underwater. Some muttered instruction, something about Claire. A shape that was Jez, walking away. Talking to Claire. Claire's crying louder, then quieter, a door closed behind.

She was kneeling beside me, now. Laura. I could see her green scarf thing. She was taking it off, winding it around one hand. She was going to see I was still here. She was going to help. She was going to stop the bleeding.

I felt sensations, then, the cold floor. I felt it against my back, my fingertips. The pain at the back of my head.

Her fingers at my throat again. She was checking again. This time she would realise I wasn't gone.

She put the scarf over my face, her hands over my mouth.

Softness, and a perfume smell. Then the pressure, and darkness. And terror.

No more words, then. No more pictures.

342

TASH

I wasn't aware that I'd been crying, but I find my cheeks are wet, my voice unsteady as I look at Adam.

'Sophie would have lived?'

'Yes,' Adam says. 'If it had just been the head injury, Sophie would have lived.'

'Laura could have helped her.' Christina's voice is harder than Adam's. 'Instead, she told Claire and Jez that Sophie was dead. She let them believe they were responsible for killing her. And then she smothered her.'

This can't be true. Surely, it can't. Setting Tom up was one thing, but this – first Sophie, then Sal – surely she couldn't have been capable of this.

'The forensic pathologist thinks Sophie would have been unconscious, or minimally conscious,' Adam explains. 'A scarf or a pillow would have been sufficient.'

I turn away, press my hand against the window. I feel like I'm going to throw up.

'Laura needed Claire and Jez to be so indebted to her that they would do anything she wanted,' Christina says. 'It was the only way they'd give her the kind of money she needed to keep her perfect life intact.'

'They couldn't exactly write her a cheque,' Adam continues. 'Too obvious. Even Hayden would have picked up on that, when we looked at the case.'

'But by giving Ed a job at Graphite, they could structure it as a bonus,' I finish. 'So it was able to go under the radar. Almost.' I look away from Christina, suddenly ashamed. How had I not seen these

people for what they were from the start? Not a friendship group, but a vile protection racket.

Christina studies my face. 'I want to be sure you understand this, Tash,' she says. 'Laura killed Sophie. She killed Sal. And if things had gone to her plan, that night on the cliffs, she'd have killed you, too. She had tried to warn you off, but it hadn't worked. You kept going. So she planned to get rid of you. I read all the documents at the inquest, Tash. I think Laura knew where the rockfalls were that night. I think she had led you to them.'

I breathe in and out. I feel as if I have stepped off a roundabout, the ground buckling under my feet. Adam's phone rings and he leaves the room, mumbling an excuse, closing the door behind him. Christina and I look at each other.

'What do you want from me?'

Christina plucks her wine glass from the kitchen island, and closes her laptop.

'I need you to tell the truth,' she says. 'About what happened on those cliffs.'

So here it is, then. I feel strangely numb. The realisation of my worst fear, of living my darkest nightmare. I thought I could make that night go away. But Christina knew what I did. She was going to make me pay.

'Why?' I whisper. 'Why do you need me to?'

'I know you are frightened,' she says. 'I understand why you are afraid of her. But, Tash – we've got her now. All I need is for you to tell the police the truth.' Christina comes closer to me. 'Tell them, Tash. Tell them how Laura pushed Jez.'

I look up. 'What?'

'It's OK,' Christina says. 'Nicole told me everything. She told me it was Laura who pushed him off the cliffs that night.'

My mouth hangs open.

Christina shrugs. 'I went to pay Nicole a little visit. We suspected she'd probably cooperate, when we told her we knew she'd taken out the burner phone contracts, and when we told her everything that Laura had done. We were right – she saw pretty quickly that she needed to play ball.'

'But why did she do it?' This was something that still didn't make sense to me. How had Nicole got involved, in the first place? Why would she have gone along with it?

'Nicole told me she'd found out by accident,' Christina said. 'She'd overheard Laura and Claire talking one day, and they'd realised, and then they'd been forced to tell her everything. She says they begged her to stay silent. Nicole told me she had agreed simply because they were her friends.' Christina pauses. 'She also said she sympathised with Claire because – her words – "she'd known that nanny was trouble from day one".'

Christina gives me a meaningful look. I shake my head, ball my fists in anger.

'I believed her, though,' Christina continues, 'when she said she had felt she was merely been protecting Claire from the consequences of one terrible mistake. I do believe that she didn't know the full extent of what Laura had done.'

I imagined the scene. Christina at the smart steps of Nicole's house on Highbury Fields. Nicole's pinched brow, her clever, racing mind, working out her best possible move. She could see what Christina wanted. She wanted a culprit. And Nicole had given her one. And in return, Nicole had been allowed to get her family on a plane to New York.

I think about our own escape. The removals van, parked outside our house. Tom, sat at home. He would be wondering where I'd got to with our last-night takeaway. The keys to our new home in Oxford, our new life, on a hook by the front door.

'I don't want to be involved in this.'

Christina laughs drily. 'That's exactly what Nicole said.' She folds her arms. 'Unfortunately, that is not negotiable at this point for you, Tash.'

'Please. You don't need me involved –'

'Oh no, I do,' she says. 'I made a deal with Nicole. This is the only way. It has to be you. And I think you will be involved, Tash. Unless you want me to recommend to Tom that he avail himself of the paternity testing services I used for Eliza. I'm sure the clinic will still have Jeremy's DNA sample on file.'

Instinctively, I cup my palm to my belly. Christina tips her head to one side.

'You can thank Nicole for that tip-off, I'm afraid,' Christina says. 'The walls in Crugmeer House are thinner than you think, apparently.'

345

I had almost convinced myself it hadn't even happened, not really. Jez's cool fingertips on my skin, picking the towel from my hands, and running them down my body. The feel of his wet mouth on my neck, between my legs. My soaking hair on the pillowcase. The sound of the waves, crashing on the rocks in the bay.

When I finally speak, my voice emerges as a croak. 'Why do I need to do this, Christina?'

'Because I had to make a deal with Nicole. The deal was that I'd leave her out of it, as long as she told me everything.'

'But I –'

'I want Laura punished, Tash!'

Christina slams her hand down on the kitchen worktop. The movement carries such force that I jump up. My head knocks the copper light, and sends it flying, its beam flashing alarmingly around the dark room. In the wild, flashing light, Christina's face goes from full beam, to dark, to full beam again.

'She killed Sophie. She killed Sal. And … and she killed Jeremy.'

With these last words, her steely voice crumbles, her chin starts to shake, like a rock edifice about to fall.

'Jeremy was not perfect, Tash,' she says, her voice thick with emotion. 'But I loved him, and he was the father of my child.' Then she glances down at my belly. 'I wouldn't be so impolite as to speculate as to whether he is also the father of yours.'

The copper light starts to still. I hear the sound of the rain outside. Tears prick at my eyes as I think about my kind husband, about our new house far away from here, with the pear tree in the back garden, the little window seat in the back bedroom I picked out for the new baby the first time we looked around the house. The baby who will be Finn's baby sister. Who I have told myself, in every sleepless night since that day, sobbing silently in the dark beside my husband, will belong to Tom and me. The baby will be ours. She will, she will. Whatever a test might say.

I think about what will happen if I tell the truth. And then, I think about what will happen if I do what Christina wants, and tell a lie she thinks is the truth.

I think about what I am, and who I want to be. Not a bad person, I do believe that, though I suppose everybody does. Not a victim, of course. Not really a journalist, probably, not any more. Just a person. A mother. A wife. An adulteress. And a killer.

346

I was, in that moment, at least. I think I knew, deep down, that the cliff was breaking behind me. I think I knew that if I moved out of Jez's way, if I let him go, then he wasn't coming back. I knew it, and I let it happen anyway. I never wanted to see him again. I didn't want the complication of him. It was better this way.

But of course, it's not the truth that matters, in the end. It's stories that matter. And whose is the most compelling. Hers, or mine.

ACKNOWLEDGEMENTS

I am so grateful to the many people who assisted me in research-ing and writing this novel, and who were so generous with their time.

In particular, the doctors, who – even amid the pressures of a pandemic – took the time to help me understand something of the life of a medic in the NHS. Thank you so much Ben Crooks, Deepak Chandrasekharan, Aravind Ramesh, Simeon Innocent, James Ray, and Juliet Raine, for answering my (many!) ques-tions so fully and thoughtfully. I am also grateful to Dr Melanie Smart for her invaluable advice on childhood trauma and attach-ment disorders, and also to the brilliant nurse Lara Willis, who patiently entertained morbid inquiries about how a medic might commit murder via intubation.

The original idea for *The Other Mothers* came from an inquest I attended many years ago in South London as a trainee news reporter. Thank you very much to the coroner and coroners' assistants who helped me research that case, and to Tom Stoate and Nicholas Rheinberg for helping me better understand the work of the coroner and the coronial system in England. I am also most grateful to Russell Delaney for a fascinating insight into the work of a forensic pathologist.

The beautiful wetlands at Woodberry Down in Hackney, East London, which provide the setting of this novel, were created thanks to London Wildlife Trust. I am very grateful to David Mooney, its Director of Development, for talking to me about the area's extraordinary transformation. I'm also grateful to Dr Meri Juntti of Middlesex University and Simon Donovan of the Manor House Development Trust for their very helpful insights, and to Chris at Thames Water, for a hugely enlightening discussion on the dangers of managed waterways!

I am so lucky to have my brilliant agent Madeleine Milburn in my corner. No writer could ask for a better champion, especially over the past couple of years, and I always feel a thousand times better about everything after we've spoken! Thanks so much to the whole MM team, and especially Liv Maidment, whose helpful and encouraging feedback on the draft manuscript came just at the point when it was most needed.

I had three incredible editors on *The Other Mothers*, and it was such a privilege to work with all of them. Thank you so much to the brilliant Alison Hennessey at Raven, Alison Callahan at Gallery and also Becky Hunter, whose input was so valuable. Thanks, too, to all those on the Raven and Gallery teams who have put so much work into the its publication. In particular, I would like to thank Katherine Fry, Emilie Chambeyron, Amy Donegan, Ben McClusky and Francisco Vilhena in the UK and Nita Pronovost, Jackie Cantor, Bianca Ducasse, Taylor Rondestvedt, and Lauren Truskowski in the US and Canada. Last but certainly not least, thank you so much Jen Bergstrom, for your huge support and passion. It is a privilege to be among your writers.

Writing this novel in lockdown – with a newborn and a toddler in tow – would have been impossible without practical and moral support from so many people: my wonderful agent, my editors and their publishing teams, but also my amazing family, and our wider support network. Thank you to all those who helped, when it was permitted, to look after our girls so I could find time to write – especially Mum, Jo, Kirsty, Sue, Brendan, Lara, Megellene, Andi and everyone at Coconut nursery. A special mention must go to Aimee Perry, too, for not freaking out when I told her I was writing a book about the murder of a nanny. Or not too much, anyway.

Thankfully, the real other mothers in my life are nothing like those in my novel. Thank you to all the remarkable women with whom I am lucky enough to share the experience in all its undignified, unfiltered glory. Without our gallows humour, the coffees, the shared school pick-ups and most crucially of all, the wine, I'm not sure how I would get through any of it. I appreciate you all.

Thank you to Pete, for being the best, most equal partner and the most patient, present and loving father. I am so lucky to have you by my side through all the tears, tantrums and broken sleep.

And finally, to Emma and Maddie, who are worth every single moment. This one is for you.

A NOTE ON THE TYPE

The text of this book is set in Linotype Sabon, a typeface named after the type founder, Jacques Sabon. It was designed by Jan Tschichold and jointly developed by Linotype, Monotype and Stempel in response to a need for a typeface to be available in identical form for mechanical hot metal composition and hand composition using foundry type.

Tschichold based his design for Sabon roman on a font engraved by Garamond, and Sabon italic on a font by Granjon. It was first used in 1966 and has proved an enduring modern classic.

'Next-level mum noir, *The Other Mothers* is a brilliant portrayal of the complexities of parenthood, work and – oh yes – murder. Smart, tense and gripping. Loved it!'
Ellery Lloyd

'Fans of *Motherland* will love the observations in this twisty, one-sitting read'
Woman & Home

'Wonderful sense of growing dread in the dark side of motherland'
Fiona Barton

'Glossy, privileged mummy posse – appalling humans, obviously – dead nanny, struggling, unglossy journalist trying to make sense of it all. I read this brilliantly plotted, brilliantly observed thriller in one sitting, and then thanked the Lord for no longer being the parent of a school-aged child. *So* good'
India Knight, *Sunday Times*, Style

'*The Other Mothers* is brilliant! Such a fast-paced, twisty story that takes you in completely unexpected directions. I read this in one sitting and adored every page. Katherine Faulkner's first novel was fantastic, but this is another step up. The characters are wonderfully vivid and Faulkner captures the worlds of both journalism and motherhood perfectly. She also nails the moment when they both start going wrong'
Holly Watt

'A wry and tightly plotted look at parent cliques, playgroup angst and when mum-life turns sour … *The Other Mothers* is *Big Little Lies* meets Silent Witness. I loved it!'
Harriet Walker

'Katherine Faulkner unpeels Fornasetti wallpaper and opens glass box extensions, revealing delectably dislikeable characters, secrets – and murder. This is *The Undoing* meets *Big Little Lies*. A fast-paced, decadent skewering of upper-middle-class motherhood'
Abigail Dean

'Once again, Katherine Faulkner so masterfully delivers a delicious combination of treacherous secrets and enviable lives, this time among a group of upper class moms whose perfection unravels after Tash, a new mom to the playgroup and struggling journalist, realizes things aren't quite what they seem. I couldn't part with this book until I'd finished—*The Other Mothers* is the elevated, devourable thriller you've been looking for'
Ashley Audrain

'An elegant and relentlessly twisty skewering of upper middle-class motherhood and a propulsive mystery, I was gripped by *The Other Mothers* and Katherine's immersive writing'
Sarah Vaughan

'Has all the skilfully handled red herrings you would expect from the creator of the deft final twist of Greenwich Park. But her real gift is for observing the currents beneath apparent surface perfection, and what the middle class is capable of when it can't have it all'
The Times

'Katherine's done it again! Anyone who enjoyed *Greenwich Park* will love this – maybe even more. Full of terrible people behaving terribly, it's such a compelling story. I read it in one sitting last night – extremely gripping'
Harriet Tyce

~

*Through the examples of current and past Quakers we are
helped to explore and question our way of life within the
Religious Society of Friends and our wider community.*
Participant, Northern Young Friends Summer Shindig 2015

~

Think it possible that you may be mistaken.
Advices & queries 17

~

*Quakers do not deny human weakness, but their tendency is
instead to give thanks for human strength. They believe in
the essential goodness of people, so they deny the notion that
we are by nature 'miserable sinners' and reject the habits and
customs that go with it... They do not want religious ritual,
symbol or costume to get in the way of their unmediated
communion with the divine. It is in that relationship that
they find their energy and spirit. They are not so much
staring into the darkness, as standing in the Light.*
Geoffrey Durham, *Being a Quaker.*

~

*Don't be ashamed of your religion; stand up for what
you believe in; don't be a victim of authority.*
Participant, Yorkshire Friends Holiday School 2015

~

~

I am a Quaker, completely, I don't think of it as a belief, it is just the way that I am... it's my identity, it is not about deciding you're a Quaker, it is about realising you're a Quaker... We are not Quakers because we are good, but because we are not.
Ben Pink Dandelion, *Celebrating the Quaker Way*

~

No one person can fully understand God or express His words or wishes fully. No matter how well intended rules are, if they are followed mindlessly they will lose their meaning and we will lose our touch with God and what God truly wants. Only through discussion and stillness can we try to learn.
Participant, Northern Young Friends Summer Shindig 2015

~

Meeting for worship

Gathered | *Listening*

Ministry | *Reflection*

Sharing | *Silence*

As a community, Quakers gather quietly for meeting for worship on most Sunday mornings. Meeting for worship starts as soon as the first person enters the room. Quakers will gather in silence; meeting is a silent waiting, listening for God's truth. At its best the silence is not just an absence of noise; it is a seeking for quietness of mind, of body and of spirit. In meeting we try to find the presence of God inside ourselves by listening and waiting. This is a shared occasion where the people in meeting all have the same aim; it is this sharing that makes the meeting a collective experience. The children of the meeting will likely have their own gathering but will probably join the main meeting for the first or last 15 minutes. The end of meeting for worship is indicated when two Quakers shake hands.

Meeting for worship can be entirely silent, but often someone will stand and speak. This 'ministry' will reflect their own personal search for the truth inside themselves. Any person may be moved to stand and speak during meeting, and people will be happy to hear ideas and truths presented by a variety of people in many different ways. We are asked to listen quietly and respectfully and with open minds – we don't have to be of the same mind; we are all

free to discern our own understanding of the Light. Spoken ministry may spring from many different sources. Each of us brings our own experiences, and Quakers will look for the underlying truth in what is spoken.

In the quietness of a Quaker meeting we may become aware of a powerful spirit of love and truth; we may feel that we have shared that of God that exists within each of us. Meeting for worship can be held anywhere or at any time. Many of us have experienced meeting on a hill, in a hotel lobby or under the stars; it is often on these occasions, with others, that the silence can surprise and the spirit can burn even more brightly.

～

We listened and heard the silence. We listened and felt the silence. We listened and tasted the silence. We closed our eyes and saw the great silence dwelling within.
Moses Shongo, a Seneca elder, 1800s

～

Lying upon a mound of rocks in a field somewhere near Yealand. Looking at the sky in total silence created an atmosphere of stillness and peace. It was the only meeting I have ever done outside and this made the silence seem so much more pure. The meeting halls of Bootham and Brigflatts may be beautiful but they were beaten by the beauty of having nothing. The darkness cast a spell over the meeting and closed the world in, making our togetherness feel absolute.
Felix Charteris, student, Bootham School, York

～

True worship may be experienced at any time, in any place – alone on the hills or in the busy daily life – we may find God... But this individual experience is not sufficient, and in a meeting held in the Spirit there is a giving and receiving between its members, one helping another with or without words.
Quaker faith & practice 2.11

～

~

For me the focused, expectant silence of the meeting was like
nothing I'd ever experienced. Birdsong or traffic noises would
mingle with the occasional cough, or creak of a seat, within the
room. And after perhaps ten minutes there would be a sense of
the silence deepening – like a coastal shelf falling away beneath
our feet. A profound, inner stillness would descend as fidgeting
diminished and superficial sounds receded into the background.
Tom Robinson (b. 1950)

~

I can find strength in stillness.
Participant, Junior Yearly Meeting 2016

~

The beauty of silence is that it allows us to engage where
we are. We are not dovetailed into someone else's sermon,
neither are our devotions determined by an outward liturgy.
Rather, our motions of faith can sit where they need to be,
close to us in their authenticity and sincerity, closer to God
in their directness and individuality.
Ben Pink Dandelion, *Celebrating the Quaker Way*

~

~

*Silence gives everyone the chance to be heard, which in
turn creates equality. In our busy world it is incredibly
important to stop and appreciate silence every once
in a while. Too much noise can be suffocating.*
Participant, Yorkshire Friends Holiday School 2015

~

Be still and know that I am God.
Psalms 46:10

~

*Don't feel restricted by the silence, it is there to set you free from
the pressures of life. No-one is judging your movements, your
thoughts... Freedom of expression is the freedom to worship God
on your own terms. Value the opportunity to think unguided
by the world. Learn what you feel you need to know, let other
information pass. No moment of silence is a waste of time.*
Rachel Needham, 1987; *Quaker faith & practice* 2.17

~

~

*Silence can be more than just nothing. It can
invade our senses and provoke our thoughts.*
Participant, Britain Yearly Meeting Young People's
Programme 2015

~

*Silence is more than just a lack of noise, but
is a feeling inside, 'dwelling within'.*
Participant, Yorkshire Friends Holiday School, 2015

~

*It's easy to be alone and think for yourself and gather your
own thoughts in silence, but it's even more powerful to be
together in the silence and to feel linked with others.*
Participant, Junior Yearly Meeting 2015

~

Are you open to new light, from whatever source it may come?
Advices & queries 7

~

Belief in action

Discernment | *Respect*

Responsibility | *Service*

Sharing | *Witness*

Quakers believe that there is that of God in every one. Thus we try to respond to need wherever it exists, in whomever it exists, not just among our friends but wherever we can. Working for others as service, the act of helping someone, is love made visible and helps both the giver and the receiver.

It is possible that some of us may have a blinding flash or revelation about what we are called to do. However, it is more likely that this awareness will arrive after a time of reflection, consideration, gathering information and comparing opinions, testing out in our mind and in our heart how we feel. The decision to take action can be quite simple and intuitive; in other situations the decision may be more complex and involved. It is likely that meeting for worship and our interactions with other Quakers will play a significant part in this process of discernment.

We are all moved to serve in different ways. Quakers have worked for the abolition of slavery, for prison reform, for the Friends Ambulance Unit, as hospice volunteers, for asylum seekers and refugees, for homeless people and in soup kitchens. Quakers have taken part in demonstrations, become politically involved, volunteered for work abroad,

'spoken truth to power' by writing letters privately and/or publicly. It may be right to be involved with the workings of your local meeting or with Quaker groups; and it is always possible that you will be called on to listen to a friend, to be with someone, to hold someone in the Light, to hold their hand, to give them a hug or just bake them a cake!

Our faith and our witness in the world are inseparable – each feeds the other. The Quaker testimonies to peace, integrity, equality and simplicity provide signposts to what we are led to do. Our actions can make the world a better place.

For online content go to
www.yqspace.org.uk/passages
www.yqspace.org.uk/playlists
www.yqspace.org.uk/bethechange

~

I expect to pass through this world but once. Any good
therefore that I can do, or any kindness that I can show
to any fellow creature, let me do it now. Let me not defer
or neglect it, for I shall not pass this way again.
Stephen Grellet (1773–1855)

~

Respect the laws of the state and consider your moral purposes.
If you have a strong conviction to break the law, search your
conscience deeply and seek the advice of others you trust.
Participant, Northern Young Friends Summer Shindig 2015

~

O brother man! Fold to thy heart thy brother;
Where pity dwells, the peace of God is there;
To worship rightly is to love each other,
Each smile a hymn, each kindly deed a prayer.
John Greenleaf Whittier (1807–1892)

~

Love your neighbour as you love yourself.
Matthew 19:19

~

~

*Live adventurously. When choices arise, do you take
the way that offers the fullest opportunity for the use of
your gifts in the service of God and the community?*
Advices & queries 27

~

*To work together we must have transparent conversations so we
can understand what everyone wants from working together.*
Participant, Junior Yearly Meeting 2017

~

*Let me light my lamp, says the star, and never
debate if it will help remove the darkness.*
Rabindranath Tagore (1861–1941)

~

Be the change you want to see in the world.
Mahatma Gandhi (1869–1948)

~

*You can change and inspire by saying what needs
to be said. You have more power than you know.*
Participant, Friends Summer School 2015

~

~

Past the seeker as he prayed came the cripple and the beggar and the beaten. And seeing them the Holy One went down into deep prayer and cried, "Great God, how is it that a loving creator can see such things and yet do nothing about them?" And out of the long silence, God said, "I did do something. I made you."
Sufi teaching

~

A young girl was walking along a beach where thousands of starfish had been washed up during a storm. When she came to each starfish, she would pick it up and throw it back into the ocean. She had been doing this for some time when a man approached her and said, "Why are you doing this? Look at all the starfish on the beach! You can't begin to make a difference!" The girl listened, paused and after a few moments bent down, picked up another starfish and hurled it as far as she could into the ocean, saying: "I made a difference to that one!"
Adapted from Loren C. Eiseley (1907–1977)

~

The Light is available yesterday, today and to eternity. What is thee doing about it?
Lucretia Mott (1793–1880)

~

There is hope. Lots of hope.
Participant, Britain Yearly Meeting Young People's Programme 2015

~

Truth and integrity

Honesty | Integrity

Respect | Sincerity

Trust | Truth

Quakers use 'Truth' to mean the universal values, principles and convictions of the life led by the spirit inside us. The concept is also seen as demanding honest, simple speech and a refusal to countenance the double standards of saying one thing and doing another. Truth is an integral part of the Quaker testimony to the Light within us all. We can only be true to our innermost self if we are faithful to the truth and honest in our dealings. Truth and integrity are fundamental guiding principles in our own lives and also in our community engagement. Early Quaker artisans and shopkeepers soon acquired a reputation for honesty and fair prices. Their integrity was a key factor in their great success in business and banking in the 18th and 19th centuries.

Quakers believe it is important to tell others about the truth as we see it. 'Speaking truth to power' means telling people with influence about your concerns and standing up for what you see is right when you think something is wrong.

The testimony to truth and integrity is essentially a call for consistency between what you think and say about yourself and what you actually do. To be the best you can, what you

think needs to come out in what you say and do. Quakers have always refused to swear oaths (in court or anywhere else), because promising "to tell the truth, the whole truth, and nothing but the truth" in court would imply that they did not promise to tell the truth everywhere else.

And how do we know what the truth is? When Quakers attend meeting for worship and listen to ministry, they may be searching for the truth. When we read and respond to *Advices and queries*, we are searching for the truth. This search will never end and we are likely to challenge ourselves time and again at different stages of our lives and in different circumstances. Answering honestly and with integrity is not a small matter. Then, when we have answered honestly, we can decide what to do, never forgetting that 'we are what we do'.

For online content go to
www.yqspace.org.uk/playlists

~

Dearly beloved Friends, these things we do not lay upon you as a rule or form to walk by; but that all, with a measure of the light, which is pure and holy, may be guided: and so in the light walking and abiding, these things may be fulfilled in the Spirit, not in the letter, for the letter killeth, but the Spirit giveth life.
Postscript to an epistle from the elders in Balby, 1656;
Introduction to *Advices & queries*

~

Take heed, dear Friends, to the promptings of love and truth in your hearts. Trust them as the leadings of God, whose light shows us our darkness and brings us new life.
Advices & queries 1

~

*Three things cannot hide for long:
the Moon, the Sun and the Truth.*
Gautama Buddha

~

We shouldn't forget the power of our obligation to speak the truth to those who lie, just as we must love those who hate us.
Who do we think we are? Young Friends General Meeting 1998

~

~

*Live your truth. Express your love. Share your
enthusiasm. Take action towards your dreams. Walk
your talk. Dance and sing to your music. Embrace
your blessings. Make today worth remembering.*
Steve Maraboli

~

*Truth is like the sun. You can shut it out
for a time, but it ain't going away.*
Elvis Presley (1935–1977)

~

*Live adventurously. When choices arise, do you take the way
that offers the fullest opportunity for the use of your gifts in
the service of God and the community? Let your life speak.*
Advices & queries 27

~

*This above all,
To thine own self be true,
And it must follow as the night the day,
Thou canst not then be false to any man.*
William Shakespeare, *Hamlet*

~

*Truth resides in every human heart, and one has to search for it
there, and to be guided by truth as one sees it. But no one has a
right to coerce others to act according to his own view of truth.*
Mahatma Gandhi (1869–1948)

~

~

*If pressure is brought upon you to lower your standard of
integrity, are you prepared to resist it? Our responsibilities
to God and our neighbour may involve us taking
unpopular stands. Do not let the desire to be sociable, or
the fear of being peculiar, determine your decision.*
Advices & queries 38

~

*Everyone's truth is different. It's how you
use the truth which counts.*
Participant, Friends Summer School 2015

~

Peace and conflict

Conflict resolution | Empathy

Nonviolence | Pacifism

Reconciliation | Seeds of war

Trust | Understanding

William Penn said, "We are too ready to retaliate, rather than forgive, or gain by love and information. And yet we could hurt no man that we believe loves us. Let us then try what Love will do: for if men did once see we love them, we should soon find they would not harm us" (William Penn, 1693; *Quaker faith & practice* 23:03). The act of love is at the centre of the Quaker peace testimony. We are asked to try what love will do in all parts of our lives and the world, not just by working on a national or global scale but by looking at our relationships and activities at all levels.

As Quakers we believe that our faith should be lived out practically in our actions. Working for peace can be a consequence of this wanting to live our beliefs. Handling conflict creatively can be a force for positive change and is more than just winning and losing. Many Quakers are pacifists as a matter of conscience, because we are asked to look for the love and truth in the hearts of others and ourselves. Violent actions contradict the search for the God in our lives.

The testimony to peace calls on us to strive for harmony among all people, nations and individuals. If we recognise that we all have a spark of God within, we try not to harm one another or to treat others aggressively. If we treat all people as if they have the same spirit within them that we have in ourselves, we practise equality. If we seek to eliminate conditions of inequality in the world, and to value people above possessions, we encourage simplicity.

From their beginning, Quakers have been known for taking a stand for peace and against military action. "During the world wars, Quakers took different paths. Some felt they had to join the armed forces, but many decided they could not" (Isabel Cartwright, 2014). Working for this kind of peace can be difficult. Those who served in the Friends Ambulance Unit (founded by Quakers in World War I) were brave indeed, as were those who were imprisoned in the world wars because they would not compromise on their beliefs and would not join up. Some Quakers may choose to join peaceful demonstrations, to work with the Alternatives to Violence Project, to take relief into areas recently ravaged by war or to give funds for peace education. Our inner voice will help tell us what course of action we are to pursue. We respond individually to what the spirit requires of us.

As Quakers we also try to live out our commitment to peace in every part of our lives. We may set up and support long-term individual and collective Quaker action as an expression of our peace testimony. We may develop and support alternative ways of resolving and engaging with conflicts, working for a reduction in armaments and a change to the conditions and circumstances that lead to war. Tackling the seeds of war is central to our testimony to peace. Simply 'bearing witness' to a different way – a way that affirms the value of all life rather than denies it through violence – is something we can all do. This too is an important part of our peace testimony. We all have a

role to play with our neighbours, in our school or college, among our friends and wider community, in our family, in our workplace and with our colleagues and peers. We each do what we can.

Conflict is inevitable at times in most human relationships and we can learn from interaction with those who disagree with our own view of the world. Empathetic understanding of another's viewpoint is vital when seeking to undo some of the hurt in the world and to build a better future. To be nonviolent is an active process in all our lives. As Penn said, "Let us then try what Love will do."

For online content go to
www.yqspace.org.uk/passages
www.yqspace.org.uk/playlists
www.yqspace.org.uk/bethechange

~

The peace testimony is about deeds not creeds;
not a form of words but a way of living.
Quaker faith & practice 24.11

~

You can choose whether you love and forgive or
stay angry forever. Choose forgiveness.
Participant, Friends Summer School 2015

~

Each time a person stands up for an ideal, or acts to
improve the lot of others, or strikes out against injustice,
he or she sends forth a ripple of hope. Crossing each
other from a million different centres of energy and
daring, those ripples build a current that can sweep down
the mightiest walls of oppression and resistance.
Robert F. Kennedy (1925–1968)

~

A grandfather was talking to his grandson about how he
felt about a tragedy. He said, "I feel as if I have two wolves
fighting in my heart. One wolf is the vengeful, angry, violent
one. The other wolf is the loving, compassionate one." The
grandson asked him, "Which wolf will win the fight in your
heart?" The grandfather answered, "The one I feed."
A Cherokee legend

~

~

Conflict happens, and will continue to happen, even in the most peaceful of worlds. And that's good – a world where we all agreed with one another would be incredibly boring. Our differences help us to learn.
Quaker faith & practice 20.71

~

A good end cannot sanctify evil means; nor must we ever do evil, that good may come of it.
William Penn, 1693; Quaker faith & practice 24.03

~

Peace is a journey and a way of life rather than something in the distance – it is more achievable than some think it is.
Participant, Junior Yearly Meeting 2015

~

Peace is not a distant goal that we seek, but the means by which we arrive at that goal.
Martin Luther King, Jr. (1929–1968)

~

The places to begin acquiring the skills and maturity and generosity to avoid or to resolve conflicts are in our own homes, our personal relationships, our schools, our workplaces.
Yearly Meeting of Aotearoa/New Zealand, 1987

~

~

All bloody principles and practices we do utterly deny,
with all outward wars, and strife, and fightings with
outward weapons, for any end, or under any pretence
whatsoever, and this is our testimony to the whole world.
Quaker Declaration to Charles II, 1660

~

When we engage with the brokenness of the world, one of our
tools can be our willingness to listen: to the vulnerable, to each
other, to those with whom we disagree, and to the leadings of
the Holy Spirit. This will enable us to work alongside others
powerfully, telling the truth of what is wrong in the world.
Sometimes listening will lead us to stillness, at other times
to practical action. In all things the Spirit will direct us.
From the Epistle of Yearly Meeting 2017

~

If we are angry we know how wars develop. It
does not matter who's wrong. What matters is
that we care enough to talk to each other.
Quaker faith & practice 20.68

~

The past two years have been some of the richest and most
transformative of my life. So often I have found myself wanting to
package and contain a moment, an interaction or an experience,
to somehow breathe it in and make it a permanent part of my
own organism... I have felt it when listening to Pastor Sebastian
who forgave the man who plotted to kill him during the war...
His story has sunk into my heart and has grown in me a desire
to continue coming alongside these kinds of effort.
Elin Henrysson, Quaker peaceworker in Burundi 2010–2012

~

Equality

Diversity | *Fairness*

Justice | *Love*

Respect | *Understanding*

Quakers recognise the equal worth and unique nature of every person. The belief in equality, sharing and community will often conflict with a world where self-importance and materialism can appear so central. If we stop supporting each other we risk despair, alienation and rejection, especially for those who find society a difficult place to be.

Early Quakers supported the equal spiritual authority of women and refused to use words, titles or actions that recognised or reinforced social inequalities. Using 'thee' or 'thou' and refusing to take off your hat may belong to the past, but today we address people by their first and second names only, rejecting titles (even the ordinary ones such as 'Mr', 'Mrs', 'Miss' or 'Ms'). Some Quakers may refuse to accept 'honours' of the kind given by the Queen, or, if they do accept them, certainly wouldn't use their titles in a Quaker setting.

Our concern for equality also involves looking at the way in which our own lifestyle and behaviour can potentially increase inequalities. We may be aware of issues concerning social inclusion, ethical investment, fair trade, the avoidance of exploitation and discrimination, work with

the homeless, asylum seekers, refugees and prisoners, and prison reform. Our concern for equality is a testimony of increasing relevance in today's complex and multicultural society, in which there is an acute need for racial justice and for empathy between all faiths.

In recent years our testimony to equality has led us as Quakers to change our marriage procedures. Before official new regulations were introduced (December 2011) in England, Wales and Scotland, Britain Yearly Meeting decided to seek to change the law to allow same-sex marriage in the same way as opposite-sex marriage in Quaker meetings. Quakers are clear that "the right joining in marriage is the work of the Lord only, and not the priests' or magistrates'" (George Fox, 1669).

The belief that there is that of God in everyone constantly challenges us in terms of equality. The questions that emerge from this belief are inescapable. We are led to go into our homes, workplaces, schools, shops, council chambers, country and world and seek equality for everyone. We are what we do.

For online content go to
www.yqspace.org.uk/playlists

~

*Quakers' commitment to equality is an essential
component of all their testimonies. You can't have
truth, simplicity or peace without it. And, as with those
testimonies, this one to equality is infused with love.*
Geoffrey Durham, *Being a Quaker*

~

*I have a dream that my four little children will one day
live in a nation where they will not be judged by the color
of their skin, but by the content of their character.*
Martin Luther King, Jr. (1929–1968)

~

*Refrain from making prejudiced judgements
about the life journeys of others.*
Advices & queries 22

~

*Do you respect that of God in everyone though it
may be expressed in unfamiliar ways or be difficult
to discern?... Listen patiently and seek the truth that
other people's opinions may contain for you.*
Advices & queries 17

~

*If we cannot now end our differences, at least we
can help make the world safe for diversity.*
John F. Kennedy (1917–1963)

~

~

*Gender equality is more than a goal in itself. It is a precondition
for meeting the challenge of reducing poverty, promoting
sustainable development and building good governance.*
Kofi Annan (b. 1938)

~

*Are you working to bring about a just and compassionate
society which allows everyone to develop their
capacities and fosters the desire to serve?*
Advices & queries 33

~

*As you grow up, always tell the truth, do no harm to others,
and don't think you are the most important being on earth.
Rich or poor, you then can look anyone in the eye and say, "I'm
probably no better than you, but I'm certainly your equal."*
Harper Lee (b. 1926), letter

~

*Are you alert to practices here and throughout the
world which discriminate against people on the basis
of who or what they are or because of their beliefs?
Bear witness to the humanity of all people, including
those who break society's conventions or its laws.*
Advices & queries 33

~

~

*Am I respectful of all persons regardless of race,
ethnicity, religion, culture, gender, income, age,
sexual orientation, physical or learning differences?*
Faith and Practice, Friends School of Baltimore

~

*There is inner light within us all, if we look and can find it.
This may be hard, so seek others' help. Whenever you can
feel your 'whole self', celebrate it: be happy and proud.*
Participant, Junior Yearly Meeting 2016

~

*We discovered that it is acceptable to have confused feelings, to
be different, to do things our own way. We should not feel guilty
when we are wrong, and appreciate that there must be room for
mistakes. There are people who want us to be exactly as we are.*
Epistle of Junior Yearly Meeting 1991;
Quaker faith & practice 21.06

~

Simplicity

Appreciation | *Balance*

Clearness | *Priority*

Reality | *Truth*

Many people are concerned about the excesses and unfairness of the 'consumer society' and the unsustainable use of our world's natural resources. Many try to live simply and to allow space for those things in our lives that really matter: the people around us, the environment and our spiritual experiences. Quakers believe that it is hard to concentrate on what really matters if our lives are dominated by worldly distractions: acquiring wealth and possessions, gambling, spending on alcohol and drugs, worrying too much about fashion and appearances, or taking too much pride in accomplishments.

Seeking simplicity involves trying to allow the divine to infuse our lives. This may lead us to question the way we live and recognise what our true needs are. We should be aware of how our own standard of living is sometimes achieved at the expense of others. Many of us are part of a privileged group of people, and we have a great deal to give to each other and to the world around us.

The Quaker form of worship reflects our striving for simplicity. We do not have clergy, icons or idols, a set creed or prayers, or altars or hymns. "One of the things that first drew me to the Quaker way was that uncluttered freedom we call simplicity. It's there in the way we worship, with its stillness and openness and its few spare words. It's there in

the way we do business and the shape of our communities. It's also there in the way we try to live, both in our everyday lives and in the wider world. Our values, our relationships and the choices and decisions we make are all formed by it. It is part of a way of life shaped and inspired by a clarity of purpose, heart and vision. It's a willingness to seek and find the best in others – a belief in that divine spark in every person" (Alistair Fuller, Head of Ministry & Outreach for Quakers in Britain). Meeting for worship also allows us time away from the busyness of a crowded world.

Living simply and finding opportunities to devote our time and resources to what really matters doesn't mean we live boring, unexciting lives. We are advised to 'live adventurously', to search for the ways we might make a difference to ourselves and others. If we find ways to be fulfilled, we can be much more effective for others and the world around us. The testimony to simplicity can be exciting and challenging. Sharing time with our friends and relatives and colleagues, informing ourselves, and finding out what we should be doing next... all these are part of our testimony to simplicity. Finding out who we are and who we might grow to be, can enable us to discern what we don't want and what we don't need. In this way we can discover what really matters.

For online content go to
www.yqspace.org.uk/passages
www.yqspace.org.uk/playlists

~

Unnecessary possessions are unnecessary burdens. If you have them, you have to take care of them! There is great freedom in simplicity of living. It is those who have enough but not too much who are the happiest.
Peace Pilgrim

~

Drop thy still dews of quietness,
Till all our strivings cease;
Take from our souls the strain and stress,
And let our ordered lives confess
The beauty of thy peace.
John Greenleaf Whittier (1807–1892)

~

Simplicity is not just simple clothes and a simple lifestyle. It's an organization of the mind that enables you to sort out the unimportant details that often clutter your thoughts.
Student, Sidwell School, Washington, DC

~

In order to improve your life, you need to appreciate what you have already. Simple everyday things such as playing in the garden as a child are very special to me, even though they seemed ordinary at the time. I guess that causes me to reconsider my priorities sometimes.
Participant, Friends Southern Senior Conference 2015

~

~

A common man marvels at uncommon things.
A wise man marvels at the commonplace.
Confucius (551–479BC)

~

'Tis the gift to be simple, 'tis the gift to be free
'Tis the gift to come down where we ought to be,
And when we find ourselves in the place just right,
'Twill be in the valley of love and delight.
When true simplicity is gained,
To bow and to bend we shan't be ashamed,
To turn, turn will be our delight,
Till by turning, turning we come 'round right.
Joseph Brackett, Shaker elder, 1848

~

Try to live simply. A simple lifestyle freely chosen is a
source of strength. Do not be persuaded into buying
what you do not need or cannot afford. Do you keep
yourself informed about the effects your style of living
is having on the global economy and environment?
Advices & queries 41

~

~

I ask for daily bread, but not for wealth, lest I forget the poor. I ask for strength, but not for power, lest I despise the meek. I ask for wisdom, but not for learning, lest I scorn the simple. I ask for a clean name, but not for fame, lest I condemn the lowly. I ask for peace of mind, but not for idle hours, lest I fail to hearken to the call of duty.
Inazō Nitobe, 1909; *Quaker faith & practice* 20.01

~

Silence, to me, allows us to become more aware of how complex our lives and minds are. Maybe there are different types of simplicity, one within us and one without us.
Participant, Friends Southern Senior Conference 2015

~

You can change and inspire by saying what needs to be said. You have more power than you know.
Participant, Friends Summer School 2015

~

Simplicity isn't just your outside appearance but what you think on the inside. It's not how other people see you but how you see yourself and know yourself to be like.
Participant, Yorkshire Friends Holiday School 2015

~

Young Quakers created the following guidelines for simplicity at Friends Southern Senior Conference 2015. These are simple versions of Richard Foster's ten principles for the expression of simplicity (*Celebration of discipline: the path to spiritual growth*);

* Take the time to realise that our mind's clutter can be just as obstructive as physical and material clutter.

* Appreciate the positive stuff in your life.

* Be generous towards others.

* Question the usefulness and pleasure that you will gain from an item when considering its purchase.

* Take moderately what you need and want, but know your limits.

* Make use of your material possessions.

* Understand the connection between you and the things you consume and where they come from.

* Be independently minded; think critically about the way you consume, and how that is influenced by society.

* Silence can help you develop as a person; embrace it as an alternative to life's constant stimulation.

* Find what simplicity means to you and act upon it.

* Both hoarding and minimalism are too focused on the material – true simplicity is in the mind and is spiritual.

* Simplicity is living adventurously.

Sustainability

Environment | *Equality*

Justice | *Peace*

Responsibility | *Simplicity*

Quakers believe we have a responsibility for protecting the environment and working towards a sustainable world. "The produce of the earth is a gift from our gracious creator to the inhabitants, and to impoverish the earth now to support outward greatness appears to be an injury to the succeeding age" (*Quaker faith & practice* 25.01). These words of John Woolman mean as much to us today as they meant in 1772. This belief is rooted in our testimonies to equality and peace. Sustainability is important to Quakers because we work to see 'that of God' in everyone and in everything.

In Britain many have a comfortable material lifestyle that uses more than our fair share of the world's resources. Quakers regard working against this inequality and seeking justice as a key part in our witness as Quakers. The material greed that can dominate our lives is also challenged by the Quaker testimony to simplicity.

We have long been aware that our behaviour impoverishes the earth, and it is our responsibility both to conserve the earth's resources and to share them more equitably. In 1989, Britain Yearly Meeting minuted that this concern "grows from our faith, and cannot be separated from it. It challenges us to look again at our lifestyles and reassess our

priorities, and makes us realise the truth of Ghandi's words: 'Those who say religion has nothing to do with politics do not know what religion is'" (London Yearly Meeting 1989; *Quaker faith & practice* 25.10).

We all need to take responsibility to act on whatever changes we are called to make. At the same time we need to pledge ourselves to act together as communities. "The environmental crisis is enmeshed in global economic injustice and we must face our responsibility, as one of the nations which has unfairly benefited at others' expense, to redress inequalities which, in William Penn's words, are 'wretched and blasphemous'" (Minute 36 of Yearly Meeting, 2011, 'Our Canterbury Commitment').

British Quakers tackle their concern for sustainability on many different levels, thinking nationally about how we as Quakers commit to sustainability and also looking at how we might seek to comment on public policy. Alongside this, we consider how we can campaign and speak out against those things that take us further away from a sustainable society and economy. Local and area Quaker meetings are encouraged to work in their own localities to encourage positive attitudes to sustainability. Individual Quakers are called to consider the effect of their lives on the world's limited resources and in particular on their carbon footprint.

The world is a wonderful resource for our material and spiritual needs. We should treasure it and preserve its capacity to sustain and inspire. That, in turn, calls for a creative responsibility towards the earth we have inherited and for proper sharing of its riches. It means seeing 'that of God' in the world around us and being moved by considerations other than personal gain. Habitats, species and the needs of others are too easily sacrificed to the immediate desires of the present. It cannot be right to leave the world poorer than we found it.

~

Treat the earth well: it was not given to you by your parents;
it was loaned to you by your children.
Kikuyu Proverb

~

All we possess are the gifts of God to us. Now in
distributing it to others, we act as his steward.
John Woolman; *Quaker faith & practice* 20.55

~

Our world is borrowed; some day we must give it
back. We are part of a system, not the controllers.
Participant, Yorkshire Friends Holiday School 2015

~

Everyone has the right to a standard of living adequate for the
health and well-being of himself and his family, including food,
clothing, housing and medical care and necessary social services.
Article 25.1, Universal Declaration of Human Rights, 1948

~

We do not own the world, and its riches are not ours to
dispose of at will. Show a loving consideration for all
creatures and seek to maintain the beauty and variety
of the world. Work to ensure increasing power over
nature is used responsibly, with reverence for life.
Advices & queries 42

~

~

Four in five of us are, to some extent, members of faith communities. If just a fraction of this huge body of believers were to connect their faith to sustainable development and act accordingly, with the support of their institutions, the gains could be world-changing.
Ian Christie, University of Surrey, writing in *Green futures*

~

Where we see crisis we also see opportunity to remake society as a communion of people living sustainably as part of the world.
Meeting for Sufferings, Britain Yearly Meeting, June 2009

~

You can never have an impact on society if you have not changed yourself.
Nelson Mandela (1918–2013)

~

In a few decades, the relationship between the environment, resources and conflict may seem almost as obvious as the connection we see today between human rights, democracy and peace.
Wangari Maathai (1940–2011)

~

There is a duty not only to do no harm but also to make positive change.
Participant, Junior Yearly Meeting 2015

~

~

We are here to live with the land, not to take control of the land.
Participant, Britain Yearly Meeting Young People's
Programme 2015

~

*This planet came with a set of instructions, but we seem
to have misplaced them. Important rules like don't poison
the water, soil, or air, don't let the earth get overcrowded,
and don't touch the thermostat have been broken.*
Paul Hawken, 2009

~

Membership

Celebration | *Community*

Convincement | *Discernment*

Meeting | *Truth*

In Britain, around 25,000 people attend Quaker meeting for worship. Around half of these are members of the Religious Society of Friends (Quakers); the others are visitors and people who attend our meetings and are not members (the name we use for them is 'attenders'). Membership links the individual to the community and the organisation. It enables us to have a public voice, to relate to other organisations and to support members and meetings.

Wanting to become a member starts with a Quaker deciding this is something they want to explore. Some people have attended a Quaker meeting for many years without applying for membership. Attenders may be intimately involved in the Society, helping to support the work of the meeting and Quakers more widely, being on rotas, providing financial support and occasionally being involved in committee work and decision making. Some may never seek membership; others, sooner or later, feel moved to do so.

'Convincement' is the word used to describe how people become Quakers. That 'convincement' could be just a slow realisation that this is the right thing to do. Membership is a way of saying that you accept, at least, the fundamental elements of Quakerism. There is no list of what these elements are but it is likely that you know Quakerism well enough to feel you want to be part of a group of like-minded

people, part of this community. Perhaps you and the meeting may recognise that you are still searching for the truth, but here and now you are searching along these lines and that, for the present, Quakers are your spiritual home. Membership is never based on 'being worthy' or attaining a certain 'standard of goodness'!

There is a simple procedure for applying to be a member of an area meeting (and therefore of Britain Yearly Meeting). Most often an applicant will have gone through a time of convincement and discernment that this is the right thing for them to do. Each area meeting can develop its own procedures. Often the applicant will write a letter to the area meeting clerk expressing a wish to become a member. Two Quakers will then be appointed (one local and well known to the applicant and one from a different part of the area meeting) to visit the applicant. There will be no set, expected questions or answers, but all three will probably explore and recount stories and ideas about their own spiritual journeys. One of the visiting Quakers will then write a report of the visit, which will be considered and agreed by all three who were at the meeting (including the applicant). This report does not make a recommendation about membership. The report is then considered by the area meeting and a decision is made on membership.

Membership can be seen as an outward expression of what is already there. It is always a cause for quiet celebration! Whether you choose to become a member or remain as an attender, it is important to remember that Quakers have long affirmed the priesthood of all believers. Everyone who is committed to Quakers has a responsibility for the health and maintenance of the meeting community. We are asked to contribute, in whatever ways are most suitable, to the life of the organisation we are part of. We benefit, have fun and hopefully find joy and spiritual fulfilment in working with others.

For online content go to
www.yqspace.org.uk/passages
www.yqspace.org.uk/playlists

~

Friends are together on a pilgrimage of hope. We continue to follow our inward teacher, sometimes falteringly, sometimes confidently, but always in the company of those who have travelled this way before us and those who are journeying with us now.
Epistle from Britain Yearly Meeting 2013

~

I scribbled a one-line letter to the membership clerk as if I had suddenly learnt the art of automatic writing. "Dear Sheila," it said, "I would like to apply for membership of the Religious Society of Friends." Nothing else. I signed it, stamped it and sighed with relief. It wasn't my problem any more. The Quakers could sort it out now. The ways in which they sorted it out I found to be gentle and beguiling.
Geoffrey Durham, *Being a Quaker.*

~

Membership does not require great moral or spiritual achievement, but it does require a sincerity of purpose and a commitment to Quaker values and practices.
Quaker faith & practice 11.01

~

~

For some young people, membership can be a meaningful personal formalisation of their faith. Others felt that Quakerism is defined more by its spirit of community and one's own sense of belonging. It is our shared goals, some of which may be embodied in the Quaker testimonies that bind us together as a religious group.
Minute 1, Junior Yearly Meeting, 2014

~

The Kingdom of Heaven did gather us and catch us all, as in a net, and his heavenly power at one time drew many hundreds to land. We came to know a place to stand in and what to wait in.
Francis Howgill, 1663

~

Decision making

Discernment | Respect

Responsibility | Truth

Upholding | Worship

Quakers make many of their decisions in a Quaker business meeting. This is essentially a meeting for worship, except that it has a pre-arranged agenda; this is why it is known as a 'meeting for worship for business'. Quakers gather in silence and seek the guidance of the Light in the matters before them.

The clerk opens the meeting. Clerks are a cross between a secretary and a chair. They carry a great deal of responsibility for the meeting for business; they will prepare the agenda, undertake the necessary administration and guide the meeting through the business. Often an assistant clerk will sit next to the clerk to help with the tasks and running of the meeting.

Often someone in the meeting will present an item of business and will be asked to answer questions of clarification. Then the meeting will try to discern what is required, in an atmosphere of worship. Spoken contributions are offered as ministry. There will be much use of silence to help consideration of the matter. Silence provides a space to reflect on what people have said, enabling our consideration to move beyond our initial response.

Everyone is welcome and encouraged to be at business meetings. There may be information available beforehand and it is suggested that we come 'with hearts and minds prepared', though open to new leadings. The outcome reflects the feeling of the meeting as a whole. In the meeting it is customary to stand and wait to be called by the clerk if you feel prompted to speak. The point of contributions should be not to win an argument but to uphold the workings of the community. We all strive together to find the way forward, to find what God is calling us to do.

The role of the clerk is to try to discern the outcome of each item, the 'sense of the meeting'. No vote is taken. Eventually a decision will be made that reflects the feeling of the meeting. If Quakers are not comfortable in allowing a decision to be made, the clerk may suggest the business is returned to at a later date, if that is possible. This way of making decisions can be very liberating; it ensures that minority views are not dismissed or ignored. Once a decision is reached the clerk will present a draft minute to the meeting; this will be written while the meeting waits quietly in support of the clerk doing this work.

If a Quaker feels that the draft minute doesn't reflect the sense of the meeting, now is the time to stand, wait to be called and then say so. Amendments may be suggested. It is important to have waited in the Light and eventually reached the right decision. The minute will be re-drafted and read again. The clerk will ask if the minute is acceptable to the meeting, and, if it is, people will respond 'I hope so'. A sensitive clerk will have helped the meeting to find a way forward by encouraging those at the meeting to be silent, to wait and to remember that the group is worshipping together.

Decision making in this way is not an easy process. It takes time, care and love. But it is worth the struggle; when the

process works the reward is a powerful sense of rightness and unity. The result can be enlightening, surprising and invigorating.

~

*The unity we seek depends on the willingness of us
all to seek the truth in each other's utterances; on our
being open to persuasion; and in the last resort on a
willingness to recognise and accept the sense of the
meeting as recorded in the minute, knowing that our
dissenting views have been heard and considered.*
Quaker faith & practice 3.06

~

*The job of the participants is to abandon any
preconceived notions and to listen not just to each
other, but crucially to the promptings of love and
truth, to the leadings of God, in their hearts.*
Geoffrey Durham, *Being a Quaker*

~

*Therefore, dear Friends, wait in the Light, that the
word of the Lord may dwell plentifully in you.*
William Dewsbury, 1675; Quaker faith & practice 20.19

~

*Are you prepared to let your insights and personal wishes
take their place alongside those of others or to be set
aside as the meeting seeks the right way forward?*
Advices & queries 15

~

~

*We are not to know where we may be led and we may
come to see that our hopes were for things way beyond our
imagination... What is important is being faithful to the next
step and knowing we take it not in our power but in God's.*
Ben Pink Dandelion, *Living the Quaker Way*

~

*Are your meetings for church affairs held in a spirit of worship
and in dependence on the guidance of God? Remember that
we do not seek a majority decision nor even consensus. As
we wait patiently for divine guidance our experience is that
the right way will open and we shall be led into unity.*
Advices & queries 14

~

*Listen patiently and seek the truth which other people's opinions
may contain for you. Avoid hurtful criticism and provocative
language. Do not allow the strength of your convictions to
betray you into making statements or allegations that are
unfair or untrue. Think it possible that you may be mistaken.*
Advices & queries 17

~

*Keep your meetings in the power of God... And when
Friends have finished their business, sit down and wait
quietly and wait upon the Lord to feel him. And go not
beyond the Power, but keep in the Power by which God
almighty may be felt among you... For the power of
the Lord will work through all, if... you follow it.*
George Fox, 1658; *Quaker faith & practice* 3.30

~

Life journeys

Community | Death

Education | Friendship

Marriage | Ourselves

Our lives are all a journey, or perhaps a series of journeys. Maybe the journey is more important than the destination. We learn things along the way and become changed by what we experience. Our lives are shaped by things that happen to us. Our journey is influenced and made richer by what we encounter along the way. This in turn shapes and, hopefully, motivates us to make life better for our fellow travellers.

Community

~

The more we listen carefully to one another the closer we come to an intimate connection with the greater whole. We are challenged to become beacons for change in the world and to have the courage to 'hope beyond imagination'.
Epistle of Britain Yearly Meeting 2014

~

~

We cannot seek achievement for ourselves and forget about progress and prosperity for our community... Our ambitions must be broad enough to include the aspirations and needs of others, for their sakes and for our own.
César Chávez, American workers' and civil rights activist
(1927–1993)

~

No man is an island, entire of itself; every man is a piece of the continent, a part of the main. If a clod be washed away by the sea, Europe is the less, as well as if a promontory were, as well as if a manor of thy friend's or of thine own were: any man's death diminishes me, because I am involved in mankind, and therefore never send to know for whom the bells tolls; it tolls for thee.
John Donne (1572–1631)

~

A person is only a person because of other people.
Ubuntu philosophy

~

Our Quaker identity and community supports us when we are in the world and countering its assumptions, and it informs and changes our lives. It helps me in the stands I want to make and it helps me see others I should be making.
Ben Pink Dandelion, *Celebrating the Quaker Way*

~

Death

~

*Saturday morning, making chocolate clusters, and you with
chocolate all smeared around your rosy mouth, looking very
comical, turned to me and said, "Will your body come back
again, Grannie, after you are dead?" "No, not this body," I reply,
putting a cluster neatly shaped upon the baking tin between us.*

*"But I'll be around all right, hovering somewhere,
laughing with you, feeling quite near as Grandpa
does with me." Your thoughts had very nearly moved
elsewhere but, satisfied, "That's OK" you said.*
Ruth Fawell, 1976; *Quaker faith & practice* 21.53

~

*But Death is but crossing the world, as friends do the seas; they
live in one another still. For they must needs be present, that
love and live in that which is omnipresent. In this divine glass,
they see face to face; and their converse is free, as well as pure.*
William Penn, 1693

~

Education

~

*Watching a million stars shine, feeling the waves break
on a volcanic beach, being moved by reading the next
line, being shocked by painting that colour... discovering
that living adventurously can free the spirit. We all
need to experience education, not just receive it.*
Graham Ralph, *Faith and Practice at a Quaker School.*

~

*Educating the mind without educating
the heart is no education at all.*
Aristotle (384–322BC)

~

Friendship

~

*Do you cherish your friendships, so that they grow in
depth and understanding and mutual respect? In close
relationships we may risk pain as well as finding joy.
When experiencing great happiness or great hurt we
may be more open to the working of the spirit.*
Advices & queries 21

~

~

That best portion of a good man's life,
His little, nameless, unremembered acts
Of kindness and of love.
William Wordsworth, 'Tintern Abbey'

~

Marriage

~

Friends, I take this my friend _____ to be my spouse,
promising, through God's help, to be unto him/her a loving
and faithful spouse, so long as we both on earth shall live.
Quaker faith & practice 16.42

~

Quaker marriage is not an alternative form of marriage
available to the general public, but is for members and
those who, whilst not being in formal membership,
are in unity with its religious nature and witness.
Quaker faith & practice 16.04

~

For the right joining in marriage is the work of the Lord
only, and not the priests' or the magistrates'; for it is God's
ordinance and not man's; and therefore Friends cannot
consent that they should join them together: for we marry
none; it is the Lord's work, and we are but witnesses.
George Fox, 1669; *Quaker faith & practice* 16.01

~

Ourselves

~

Through our discussions we recognised our anxieties and fears. We realised that we are individuals and that we are alone but, as part of a loving community, to be alone does not necessarily mean to be lonely. We discovered that it is acceptable to have confused feelings, to be different, to do things our own way. We should not feel guilty when we are wrong, and appreciate that there must be room for mistakes. There are people who want us to be exactly as we are.
Epistle of Junior Yearly Meeting 1991

~

We work for a more just and peaceful world, one with less discrimination and greater equality, a more sustainable approach to the economy and to the planet, and a greater degree of integrity amongst those entrusted with power and responsibility. We feel these certainties deeply, beyond conscious choice. These values are who we are. They affect what we buy and where we shop, how or if we travel, how we are in the workplace. We try not to be dissuaded from doing the right thing just because it is unpopular. We are active in all kinds of organisations to try to achieve these ends, not in our own power, but based on the holy imperatives given us in worship. We care passionately.
Ben Pink Dandelion, *Living the Quaker Way*

~

~

True Godliness don't turn men out of the world,
but enables them to live better in it, and excites their
endeavours to mend it: not to hide their candle under
a bushel, but set it upon a table in a candlestick.
William Penn, 1682; *Quaker faith & practice* 23.02

~

Things that are wrong and that we have learned to accept
should not be accepted. Only some people notice the
problems; be one of them. If not the wrongs will
grow until they are a threat to everyday life.
Participant, Young Quakers Participation Day 2017

~

Throughout our lives, we continue to ask the questions 'who are
we?' and 'where do we come from?', and we watch the answers
grow. Everyone forms their own identity in terms of what
they are committed to and what they belong to. It is through
commitment and belonging that a person becomes 'me'.
Who do we think we are? Young Friends General Meeting 1998

~

In my exam year my motto became 'we'll get there
in the end', and you do. The support of others
helps too; friends are there for you.
Participant, Young Quakers Participation Day 2017

~

For online content go to
www.yqspace.org.uk/passages
www.yqspace.org.uk/playlists

Advices and queries as compiled by young Quakers

The 42 *Advices & queries* of the Religious Society of Friends are a series of reflections and promptings that are reminders of the insights of the Society. Quakers use the *Advices & queries* as a source of challenge and inspiration in their personal lives and in their life as a community.

Young Quakers created the advices and queries given below at Junior Yearly Meeting in 2015. They are simple versions of each of the full advices and queries. They aim to be accessible while still containing insights into how to live faithfully.

1. Be true to yourself.

2. Try to be spiritual in all aspects of life.

3. Enjoy silence.

4. Remember our Christian heritage.

5. Use religious literature if it's helpful.

6. Multifaith communities are a source of richness.

7. Notice unexpected moments of spirituality in all parts of your life.

8. Value worship, by yourself or with others.

9. Consider your whole self – good and bad – in worship.

10. Come to meeting regardless of your mood; it'll make you feel better.

11. Be honest with yourself.

12. Try to stay focused in meeting.

13. When you feel moved to speak, speak.

14. You're not always right; listen to others.

15. Take some responsibility in your meeting.

16. Be open to different ways of doing Quakerism.

17. Everyone thinks of God differently; don't be judgemental.

18. Be welcoming to everyone. We've all got stuff going on, don't judge a book by its cover.

19. Children and young people are great; look after them and learn from them.

20. Talk about your beliefs and put them into action.

21. Enjoy time with friends, but also take time to challenge each other.

22. Don't be disrespectful or judgemental. Embrace diversity.

23. Marriage isn't just a legal contract, it's a religious pairing.

24. Sometimes it's difficult to work with children, but it's worth it.

25. Relationships take time and effort. Talk!

26. Appreciate your family.

27. Live adventurously.

28. Life is full of learning. Change always happens.

29. Don't worry about getting old.

30. We all die; accept it and support each other.

31. War is bad. No long-term good ever comes from it.

32. Be aware of prejudices and try to work past them.

33. Try to understand the causes of injustice and change them.

34. Don't just live in your own little bubble; there's a big world out there.

35. Sometimes breaking the law is necessary. But think about it and get some advice first.

36. People worry about different things – help them make positive change even if it's not your worry.

37. Be honest, truthful and open.

38. Don't give in to peer pressure.

39. Question the pressures of mainstream culture.

40. Be careful with drugs and alcohol.

41. Try to live simply.

42. Look after the world for the future. Reduce, reuse and recycle.

Organisation of Quakerism

Meeting for worship

Central to the practice and organisation of Quakers is the meeting for worship. As well as being our way of worship, it underpins how we make decisions in meeting for worship for business at every level of the Society. For more information see chapters 'Meeting for worship' and 'Decision making' (pp. 11 and 65).

Quaker structures

The following explanations draw on 'Quakers in Britain: A short guide to our structures' (Quakers in Britain 2014).

The individual Quaker

Because Quaker meetings for worship are open to everyone, the body of worshippers in Quakerism is made up of those who are members of the Society and those who are not members but regularly attend a particular local meeting ('attenders'). An attender can become a member through a simple process (see the chapter on 'Membership', p. XX). Most local meetings have both attenders and members.

Local meeting

The local meeting is made up of Quakers who worship together. In addition to being responsible for holding

weekly meetings for worship, the local meeting will have business meetings to deal with local matters. There is also a responsibility to nurture the spiritual life of the meeting and to ensure pastoral care of the members and attenders. Local meetings prepare for area business meetings and send representatives to them as well as reporting as appropriate.

Area meeting

An area meeting is a group of local meetings. When you become a member, your membership is with your area meeting, not your local meeting or Britain Yearly Meeting. The area meeting is the main body for 'church' affairs. Its role is to develop and maintain a community of Quakers, a family of local meetings who gather for worship and spiritual enrichment. The area meeting is also the body that has legal responsibility for property (e.g. meeting houses), employment matters (e.g. meeting house wardens), pastoral care, membership and marriage arrangements, and recording the deaths of members in the area. Area meetings hold regular business meetings.

National bodies

In addition to area meetings, Scotland and Wales have national bodies with particular responsibilities for Quakers in those countries. These are the General Meeting for Scotland and the Meeting of Friends in Wales (Cyfarfod y Cyfeillion yng Nghymru).

Meeting for Sufferings

Meeting for Sufferings is the standing representative body entrusted with the general care of matters affecting Britain Yearly Meeting. In the intervals between yearly meetings, it makes decisions and issues statements in the name of Britain Yearly Meeting. Meeting for Sufferings was

originally set up to establish and record the persecution of
Quakers and to seek help on their behalf. Today Meeting
for Sufferings is concerned with major policy decisions. It is
made up of representatives from each area meeting.

The Young People's Participation Day is an annual national
event that happens at the same time and in the same place
as Meeting for Sufferings. It is an opportunity for young
Quakers to be involved in decisions that affect them and
the organisation they are a part of. The day offers the
chance for participants to consider items on the Meeting for
Sufferings agenda that are of relevance to young people, and
to identify issues that might be of relevance to Meeting for
Sufferings.

Britain Yearly Meeting: The gathering

In England, Scotland, Wales, the Channel Islands and the
Isle of Man, Britain Yearly Meeting is the body to which all
Quakers belong. It is also the name of the annual gathering,
often referred to simply as 'Yearly Meeting', in which
Quakers from all over Britain come together for worship,
business, support, sharing of concerns and friendship.
Yearly Meeting has programmes for children and young
people, including Junior Yearly Meeting and the Young
People's Programme.

Junior Yearly Meeting (JYM) is an event for young Quakers
in Britain. Participants represent area meetings, Quaker
schools or overseas yearly meetings and other religious
groups; 'open' places are also available, for which any young
Quaker can apply. As a youth event JYM is planned and
facilitated by its own arrangements committee (with the
support of adults). The committee is a group of young
people appointed by their peers who agree the theme and
create a programme for the event, which links to issues
being considered at Britain Yearly Meeting (BYM). As well

as writing an 'epistle', JYM may write a minute reflecting discernment on the issues considered by BYM. The clerks of JYM will read the JYM epistle in Yearly Meeting.

The *BYM Young People's Programme* is a national residential event that happens at the same time as BYM and is planned by young people (appointed by their peers at the previous year's event) with the support of adults. The Young People's Programme is a chance to engage with the themes of Yearly Meeting through a variety of creative activities. It provides an opportunity to consider our Quaker faith and think about how we live as Quakers in the world today. As with the JYM epistle, at the end of Yearly Meeting the minute of the Young People's Programme, which is written by and agreed by the participants of the event, is received by the adult Yearly Meeting.

Britain Yearly Meeting: The organisation

Britain Yearly Meeting of the Religious Society of Friends (Quakers) is the national body of British Quakers. It is a registered charity and has trustees, appointed by Yearly Meeting. Much of the centrally managed work is based at Friends House in London. The organisation employs about 150 staff who undertake work on behalf of the Yearly Meeting. The staff are overseen by Yearly Meeting Trustees. They work within five departments, reporting to the Recording Clerk, who is the senior member of staff.

The four major committees for centrally managed work are: Quaker Life Central Committee, Quaker Peace and Social Witness Central Committee, Quaker Committee for Christian and Interfaith Relations and Quaker World Relations Committee.

Roles in Quakerism

Nominations committees

A nominations committee is an appointed group of Quakers entrusted with trying to find people willing and able to serve a meeting in various ways (e.g. to be clerks, elders, overseers). Having discerned as best they can the gifts and talents of those available, they 'bring their names' or 'nominate' them to the meeting concerned. For details on some of the various roles, see below.

Clerk

The Quaker responsible for the conduct of a meeting for business. The clerk will try to discern the 'sense of the meeting' (see below under 'Quaker terms') and help Quakers agree written minutes of any decisions. Clerks are usually appointed for a three-year term of service.

Elders

A Group of Quakers who have a particular responsibility for the spiritual life of the local meeting. They will make sure that meetings for worship are rightly held (they will shake hands to end the meeting), they may arrange study groups and they will organise funerals and memorial meetings. Elders are usually appointed for a three-year term of service.

Overseers

Group of Quakers from a local meeting who have a particular responsibility for the pastoral care of the members and attenders of the meeting. They advise individuals on applications for membership and befriend in order to help when personal difficulties arise. Overseers are usually appointed for a three-year term of service.

Registering officer

Each area meeting appoints a suitable Quaker as registering officer. The officer's role is to oversee marriage procedures and to register all marriages solemnised according to the custom of the Society within that area meeting.

Recording Clerk

The senior member of staff, who leads the Britain Yearly Meeting staff team. The Recording Clerk is appointed by Britain Yearly Meeting Trustees, is responsible for interpreting Quaker church government and acts as secretary to various Quaker bodies including Yearly Meeting, Meeting for Sufferings and Britain Yearly Meeting Trustees.

Words used by Quakers

Advices & queries
A reminder to Quakers of the insights of the Society. This series of 42 reflections and promptings is used by Quakers for challenge and inspiration in our personal lives and our lives in the world. (See the chapter 'Advices and queries as compiled by young Quakers', p. 79).

Clearness
The state of having reached clarity about the way forward, after searching for a response to a concern or dilemma. This is often achieved by having a 'meeting for clearness'.

Concern
A deep leading from the spirit prompting action on a particular matter that is subject to testing within the Quaker community.

Conflict resolution
Also known as reconciliation, conflict resolution is the process of facilitating the finding of a peaceful solution to a disagreement among two or more parties.

Convincement
As in 'Quaker by convincement': one who has become convinced of the truth of the Quaker way.

Discernment
The process by which Quakers try to sense what is truly from God.

Friend

A term used within Quakerism for a member of the
Religious Society of Friends. It can be used interchangeably
with 'Quaker' (a name that more people are familiar with).

Friends Ambulance Unit

An organisation set up in World War I that enabled Quakers
(and other conscientious objectors) to serve the injured in
war zones without bearing arms.

Gathered

The term used by Quakers to describe a meeting for
worship where there is a tangible sense of togetherness with
one another and with that something outside ourselves that
we may call God.

'I hope so'

Positive response to a question of Quaker business. For
example, after the clerk of a meeting reads out a drafted
minute of a decision, he or she will ask, 'Is this minute
acceptable to Friends?' If it is, Quakers will usually respond,
'I hope so.' This is because each Quaker can only answer for
his or her own discernment, not anyone else's, and hopes to
have correctly discerned the will of God.

Light

The presence of God in our hearts and lives, which shows us
the truth and gives us strength to act. 'Truth' is often used
in a similar way.

Ministry

Often this term refers to spoken ministry, which means
standing in a meeting for worship and expressing out loud
the leadings of the Spirit. You may have little firm idea of
what words are going to come out but suddenly, sometimes
shaking, you will find yourself on your feet talking.
However, 'ministry' also has the broader sense of everything

we give to others – how we 'minister' to them – as we live out our lives.

Minute

The record of a business meeting decision, capturing the 'sense of the meeting' (see below). The minute is written in the meeting and read aloud by the clerk, and is agreed – sometimes after alteration – by the assembled members.

Quaker faith & practice

An anthology of Quakers' testimonies, beliefs, reflections and practices. The book provides spiritual guidance and also details the structure and procedures of the Religious Society of Friends (Quakers). This is where all the information on procedures for membership, marriage, business, the structure of the Society and the spiritual experience that underpins them will be found.

Religious Society of Friends

The formal name for Quakers. Quakers use the term 'Religious Society of Friends' to reflect that they are a faith community with worship at its heart.

Sense of the meeting

In reaching decisions in business meetings, Quakers do not vote. After full consideration of a matter and allowing for new insights to develop, the collective decision of the Meeting is gathered and expressed by the clerk, in a minute, for the approval of the meeting. This is not a consensus; individuals are asked to accept the sense of the meeting, which may not be their own personal view.

Testimonies

Convictions based on the experience of Quakers that have given direction to their lives. They attempt to put faith into practice. The testimonies do not exist in any rigid, written form, nor are they imposed. All Quakers have to search for

the ways in which testimonies can become true for them. There are testimonies for truth and integrity, equality, peace and simplicity and a developing testimony around sustainability.

That of God in everyone
This is the core Quaker belief that the divine can be experienced in everyone. This is reflected in the following expression by George Fox "... walk cheerfully [courageously] over the world, answering that of God in every one."

Unprogrammed meeting
The style of meeting for worship in use in Britain and Europe, following the tradition established by George Fox and the early Quakers. These meetings are held in silence and ministry springs from that silence; they do not use a pre-determined programme.

Upholding *or* holding in the light
To silently hold in one's thoughts and heart someone who is experiencing joy or sorrow, or who is making a decision. Upholding may also be used in the context of a business meeting, for example upholding the clerk during the writing of a minute.

Some dates in Quaker history

1647	George Fox recognises God's light is within everyone
1652	Birth of Quakerism in the north of England
1655	Margaret Fell shapes national Quaker organisation
1660	Restoration of the monarchy – systematic persecution of Quakers
1661	Quakers present their peace testimony to Charles II
1681	William Penn establishes the Quaker state of Pennsylvania
1689	Act of Toleration allows Quakers to worship legally
1755	Quaker marriage becomes legal
1758	Quakers begin campaigning to abolish slavery
1796	Quakers pioneer humane mental care at The Retreat, York
1813	Elizabeth Fry starts her prison reform work at Newgate Prison
1825	Quaker firms open first steam railway, 'Stockton & Darlington'
1870s	Growth of Quaker chocolate makers Cadbury and Rowntree

1890s	Fair-trading Quaker banks Barclays and Lloyds thrive
1920	First conference of Quakers worldwide
1927	Friends House opens as the home of Quakers in Britain
1938	Quakers evacuate children from Nazi Germany on the Kindertransport
1947	Quakers awarded Nobel Peace Prize for their war relief work
1997	Quakers work at the United Nations to bring about the Mine Ban Treaty
2009	Quakers in Britain campaign for same-sex marriage
2014	Quakers in Britain disinvest from fossil fuels

Links, events and more information

A website for young Quakers:
www.yqspace.org.uk

Information about events for young Quakers:
www.yqspace.org.uk/events

Links to supportive organisations offering advice,
information or support:
www.yqspace.org.uk/advice

Links to the Children and Young People team at Friends
House, and to a selection of Quaker and non-Quaker
organisations:
www.yqspace.org.uk/contacts

Faith and Practice at a Quaker school:
www.aquakereducation.co.uk/home/pdf_download

Britain Yearly Meeting (the organisation):
Friends House, 173 Euston Road, London NW1 2BJ
(tel. 020 7663 1000).
www.quaker.org.uk

Quaker faith & practice online:
http://qfp.quaker.org.uk/

Information about Quaker work for peace and justice:
www.quaker.org.uk/working-peace

'Be the change', a resource to help young Quakers to take action on issues of Quaker concern: www.yqspace.org.uk/bethechange

Events

Summer events for young Quakers
Residential weeks of new experiences, spiritual growth, friendship and fun. For information go to www.yqspace.org.uk/find-event.

The Friends Summer School
Ages 11 to 17 from northwest and central England, mid-Wales and Borders, north Wales and Derbyshire, but young people from other areas are also welcome.

FSSE Junior Gathering
Ages 11 to 14 from the south of England and Wales. www.fsse.org.uk

Friends Southern Senior Conference
Ages 15 to 18 from the south of England and Wales. www.fsse.org.uk

Northern Young Friends Summer Shindig
Ages 11 to 16 from Scotland, Northumbria, Cumbria, the rest of the UK and beyond!

Yorkshire Friends Holiday School
Ages 13 to 18 from Yorkshire (open to applications from elsewhere).
www.yfhs.org.uk

Link groups and area meeting events for young Quakers

Day events, social gatherings and residential weekends for young Quakers to come together from across an area to have fun, build friendships and explore Quakerism. For information go to www.yqspace.org.uk/find-event.

More information

Young Friends General Meeting is the national organisation for young adult Quakers aged 18–30.
www.yfgm.quaker.org.uk

Quaker chaplains work in a wide variety of colleges and universities around the country. They offer pastoral support and provide a visible Quaker presence within an organisation. They also serve as a point of contact and support for young Quakers going away to college or university. They are available to students who have just heard about Quakerism and would like to know more.
www.quaker.org.uk/university-chaplains

The Woodbrooke Quaker Study Centre offers many opportunities for young adult Quakers aged 18–30, running a number of courses specifically for young Friends and a Young Adult Leadership Programme as a part of their education programme.
www.woodbrooke.org.uk/pages/young-adults.html

Quaker organisations

The Leaveners is a Quaker performing-arts project. Its members run workshops for meetings and residential theatre, music, singing and creative arts events.
www.leaveners.org
www.facebook.com/Leaveners

Quaker Action on Alcohol and Drugs (QAAD) works to meet the need for support and information in relation to alcohol, other drugs and gambling.
www.qaad.org

QAAD occasionally runs events for young people and has produced a DVD, 'Too much too young', exploring the health and social effects of alcohol on young people today.
www.qaad.org

Other resources

Resources for working with young people:
www.quaker.org.uk/working-with-12-to-18-years

Cafod Youth Topics: monthly activities on world issues.
www.cafod.org.uk/education

Christian Aid: resource for young people.
http://learn.christianaid.org.uk/

The British Youth Council is a youth-led charity that represents the views of young people to the government, decision makers and the media.
www.byc.org.uk

Bibliography

Christie, Ian (2011). 'Faith: The largest source of social capital'. Accessed online at www.forumforthefuture.org/greenfutures/articles/faith-largest-source-social-capital. London: Forum for the Future.

Durham, Geoffrey (2011). *Being a Quaker: A guide for newcomers*. London: Quaker Quest.

Foster, Richard (with Kathryn A. Helmers) (2008). *Celebration of discipline: The path to spiritual growth* (Study Guide Edition). London: Hodder & Stoughton.

Friends School of Baltimore (2003). *Faith and Practice*. Baltimore: Friends School of Baltimore.

Hawken, Paul (2009). Commencement Address to the Class of 2009, University of Portland, 3 May. Accessed online at www.up.edu/commencement/default.aspx?cid=9456.

Henrysson, Elin (2012). Journal letter of the Britain Yearly Meeting peaceworker scheme.

Maraboli, Steve (2013). *Unapologetically You: Reflections on Life and the Human Experience*. Logan, Utah: A Better Today Publishing.

Penn, William (2001). *Fruits of Solitude* Vol. I, Part 3. The Harvard Classics. New York: P.F. Collier & Son.

Pink Dandelion, Ben (2010). *Celebrating the Quaker way*. London: Quaker Books.

Quaker faith & practice: The book of Christian discipline of the Yearly Meeting of the Religious Society of Friends (Quakers) in Britain (5th ed., 2013). London: Britain Yearly Meeting.

Ralph, Graham (2013). *Faith and Practice at a Quaker School.* York: Quacks Books.

Tagore, Rabindranath (2007). *The English Writings of Rabindranath Tagore (volume two: poems).* New Delhi: Atlantic Publishers and Distributors.

Young Friends General Meeting (1998). *Who do we think we are?: Young Friends' commitment and belonging* (Swarthmore Lecture). London: Quaker Home Service.

INTRODUCTION

Oisive jeunesse
à tout asservie, Par délicatesse
j'ai perdu ma vie – Rimbaud,
'Chanson de la plus haut tour'

Isabelle Eberhardt, since her death at the age of twenty-eight in that startling flash flood at Aïn Sefra, has come to be seen as a highly romantic figure, touched with the dark hues of *fin du siècle* decadence. The eccentric and contradictory details of her life, viewed as they were in retrospect, only added to the mystique: a woman disguised as a man, an aristocrat living the life of a beggar, a sensualist haunted by the soul, and a transgressor in the best Byronic tradition.

But she was a modern figure, not a romantic one. Her ailments and obsessions were prematurely those of the 1960s, and hardly related at all to the sensibilities of her own era.

She must have suffered from our contemporary complaint, anorexia – which most often plagues young women – since a great many of its symptoms are remarkable in her physical and psychological constitution. She was painfully thin, completely flat-chested, with decayed teeth, an abundance of bodily hair, and no periods (these particular physiological characteristics, which many anorexics develop, made it easier for her to pass as a man). She was constantly depressed, often suicidal, and suffered from recurring bouts of mental debility and from an overriding and self-destructive promiscuity.

The drugs she began taking in late adolescence (following the example of her two half-brothers, Nicolas and Augustin, who no doubt initiated her in their abuse) could not have done much to help her already unstable nerves.

For the rest of her life, Isabelle would remain severely dependent on narcotics and on alchohol; in North Africa, she would function for days without sustenance, as long as she had enough *kif* and *arak* to stun herself with. Every last borrowed franc was spent on these habits, for she had the makings of a hardened addict – the loss of all will power, of all sense of reality and self-respect.

The voyage East for Isabelle was primarily a gateway to sex, as it had been and would be for countless other Europeans. It provided a way of attaining experiences more varied than those she could have expected in suburban Geneva. It satisfied her craving for adventure, her delight in disguise, as well as her sexual curiosity. Like the majority of Europeans who made this voyage of self-discovery, she carried with her a great deal of mental baggage, especially that stereotypical notion of the East as a coffer of erotic delights and unlimited freedoms.

Like Flaubert, who was finally able to shake off the moral restrictions of Rouen when he engaged Cairene prostitutes; like André Gide or T.E. Lawrence, who only managed to come out of their respective closets when they solicited the services of Arab boys; or like those endless droves of Western hippies who landed in India in the sixties and seventies, a paperback copy of *The Karma Sutra* in hand to elucidate the mysteries of 'Eastern' sex, and to assist them in 'letting it all hang out' (much to the embarrassment, the hilarity or the anger of the local people), Isabelle Eberhardt's North African voyage was a sexual trip in the contemporary sense of the word. It was a trip that offered erotic as well as narcotic highs; so much so that the place itself became slightly irrelevant to her purposes – she could just as well have been in Kashmir or Katmandu.

And like those hippies who left affluent middle-class homes to rough it in the East, arriving quite destitute and throwing themselves on the mercy of such impoverished communities as were unsuspecting enough to take them in, Isabelle went slumming when she went to North Africa. On her second trip there she landed with practically no money at all, having been irresponsible and impatient enough to quit Geneva without first sorting out her inheri-

tance. This, had it been handled properly, would have assured her a private income for life. Instead, she fled to Algeria with a few books and a change of clothes, leaving a financial transaction of such magnitude and of such importance to her future prospects in the most untrustworthy hands imaginable.

Once in North Africa, she began sinking into a penury from which, given her impractical and somewhat hysterical nature, she was incapable of ever again emerging. She slept wrapped in her dirty burnous in public gardens or in the houses of acquaintances; she arranged her social calls to coincide with meal-times, knowing that she would certainly be asked, in accordance with the custom of Arab hospitality, to remain and share food. She fell into debt with the local shopkeepers, was unable to pay her servant, and eventually took to begging, a few francs at a time, to buy more drink and drugs.

Unadapted to practical life, she nevertheless had a manic desire for financial security (even though she had neglectfully destroyed her chances of ever actually achieving it). Despising toil, she settled for the most menial labour, since she could not rouse herself enough to seek employment more in keeping with her true abilities. Unable to learn from experience, she repeated the same mistakes over and over again till they became the determining pattern of her entire existence. Her natural despondency could only have been aggravated by her incapacity to help herself.

She was a vagabond, a wanderer, not only because of frenzied boredom and innate restlessness, but because she actually had no real roots anywhere, and therefore belonged nowhere. The product of an eccentric, exiled family which had settled somewhat haphazardly on the outskirts of Geneva, while remaining completely isolated from the neighbouring community, Isabelle grew up believing herself to be the daughter of a deceased Russian nobleman, not imagining for a moment that her actual father was that very Trophimovsky whom she called 'Vava' (or Great-Uncle), whose advances she might well have suffered, and whose lunatic domination crushed them all.

Like Rimbaud, whose life and whose inner conflicts seem to parallel her own, Isabelle suffered from a profound

sense of *dépaysement*. 'I have given up the hope of ever having a corner on earth to call my own; a home, a family, peace or prosperity,' she wrote in her journal, almost echoing the poet's own poignant cry, when, prematurely aged, ill, his leg amputated and his mind tortured by endless financial worries, he felt life closing in on him: 'Adieu mariage, adieu famille, adieu avenir! Ma vie est passée. Je ne suis plus qu' un tronçon immobile.'

And like Rimbaud, whose only deliverance from the stifling atmosphere of the bourgeois home in Charleville which he so vehemently hated came when he buried himself in Africa, gun-running for the Abyssinians, Isabelle fled from her 'season in hell' at the Villa Neuve into a physical and moral desert from which there was no turning back.

Both she and Rimbaud represented existential breakdown; they were a metaphor depicting the moral collapse of the European in the East. Even though they both affected to despise the priveted world of the *colons* which rejected them anyway, and set up house with local spouses, they still functioned within and ultimately served the designs of colonialism.

Rimbaud profited from his trade in the goods of empire, in skins, ivory, gold, guns and slaves, becoming part and parcel of the imperial transaction; while Eberhardt, who had penetrated into the North African religious confraternities in her capacity as a Muslim convert, was happy to share her insider's information when it was found that it could help the French colonial authorities expand their sphere of influence and crush nationalist unrest.

Always an apologist for French rule, even when she suffered expulsion from French territories, Isabelle could not perceive a North Africa free from European domination. When pressed to write about incidents of nationalist uprising, such as the case of the Marguerite rebels, she demurred, perhaps not wishing to offend the French or align herself too closely with Arab aspirations.

The resistance movement (the *maquis*, as it was called) had long been underway, and its great nationalist hero, 'Abd al-Kader al-Jazairi, was the son of the Sheikh of the Kadrya confraternity to which Isabelle had been admitted; indeed, his message had been spread through the instantly

available religious network which bore him allegiance. After his exile and death, the struggle continued. But Isabelle's journals reveal nothing of this political ferment; she either chose to ignore it, or she was actually not fully aware of it, having had dealings only with those Algerians who collaborated with or were in the employ of the French. She lived in that grey area where two distinct worlds – that of the coloniser and that of the colonised – coincided uneasily.

Because Isabelle Eberhardt willed herself to adopt a male persona – she gave herself a man's name ('Si Mahmoud'), dressed in a man's garb, frequented a man's world – she deliberately put a distance between herself and other women. Her perceptions were affected by this; she became a mouthpiece for patriarchy, voicing traditional male views on sex, culture, religion and politics. Perhaps this position gave her a sense of power; after all, many woman travellers adopted a similar stance, thereby hoping to win acceptance as token men. Even though powerless and dispossessed in their own countries, these women often felt, when crossing into other cultures, that the codes and laws that restricted local women (often identical to the codes and laws that they had been restricted by at home) were not applicable to and did not limit them.

In Isabelle Eberhardt's case, the situation was slightly more complicated. Her dressing as an Arab man (a two-fold masquerade, since she was posing both a *man* and as an *Arab*) exiled her completely from the society of Arab women, who were socially sequestered from male company. Although no one for a moment supposed that she was either male or Arab, courtesy nevertheless required that this pretence of hers be respected. She, in turn, was aware that the formal codes of etiquette implicit in this segregation of the sexes were to be upheld. This would have suited her perfectly, since she hadn't the slightest desire to associate with women, for whom she felt only dislike and hostility.

Her disguise endeared her to no one. Arab women must have thought her a pitiful and uncouth creature for mixing in male circles which were better left alone; Arab men must have found her ambivalent persona rather trying and her

sexual presumptions perverse. French women would have been contemptuous of her for having de-classed and de-sexed and de-raced herself. She was untouchable as far as they were concerned. French men would have shared the view of their women, while also perceiving her as a dangerous symbol of female rebellion; her taking Arab lovers would have galled them too, for in a colonial society, miscegenation – if it occurred between a white woman and a non-white man (rather than vice-versa) – was considered a deadly sin. One French military man, Captain Cauvet, was scandalised when, informed that a lady wished to see him, he had encountered a slender young Arab whom he had taken for the servant of the lady in question, but who had turned out to be Isabelle herself. Ambiguity of this kind was dangerous enough in itself, and constituted a political liability.

Could Isabelle Eberhardt, given the limitations of her personality and of her political awareness, have judged the colonial climate any differently, have foreseen its consequences any better? Only five decades after her death the whole of Algeria would be knee-deep in bloodshed; the French *colons* she had so heartily defended would become the fiercest of torturers, whose kindliest cliché was 'Pas d'humanité pour les Arabes.' And those shadowy local women she had despised and ignored would produce daughters whose bravery would astonish the world; heroines such as Djamila Boupacha who was deflowered with a bottle by her French captors and subjected to countless other outrages; or Djamila Bouhired who was disfigured by the tortures she endured but who inspired a whole generation of resistance fighters to hide their guns beneath their veils, transforming the harem world into headquarters for guerrilla activity.

Perhaps farsightedness of this sort was historically impossible, especially for one who saw North Africa through a haze of literary clichés. Isabelle, like countless other Europeans, had come to the Orient on the flying-carpet of Orientalism; her notions of the place had already been determined by her early readings of the works of Gautier, Baudelaire, and Loti.

In any case her odyssey was an inward, not an outward

one. She explored the state of her psyche rather than that of the country. The reader becomes familiar, perhaps overly familiar, with her moods and fears, but hardly learns anything about the domestic or social or political dimension of her life. She may have been too depressed or too drugged or too *distraite* to offer such a portrait, but from the rare snatches in her diary where she describes things or persons outside of herself (as, for example, in her description of impoverished workers in Marseilles), one cannot help feeling a tremendous sense of waste, as one would have liked many more such acute observations to have come to us from her pen.

The real tragedy of Isabelle Eberhardt was that she was so consumed by her passions and her moods, so very much the victim of her own mishandling of her talent, that she never arrived at her true potential as a writer. Perhaps if she had lived longer, if she had survived the ravaging years of her second decade, she could have mustered the emotional strength to harmonise between her many warring selves.

Although her death was an accidental one, it somehow takes on the poignancy of a suicide. One can just picture her lying under the fatal timbers, the way the rescue workers must have found her, weighted down by her full clothes like a travesty of an Ophelia, 'the hoar leaves' of the tattered notebooks of her diary swollen by water as their entries had been swollen by tears.

In editing these diaries, I have found it best to delete such passages as seemed unjustifiably repetitious, as well as most of the poems or the bits of prose that Isabelle copied out from books in order to re-read later without having actually to carry weighty volumes around with her. Although the great bulk of the diaries was written in French, the entries she made in Russian are preceded by a cross (✝), while those made in Arabic are preceded by a crescent (☾). References to people or places or incidents that appear opaque have been explained in the notes at the end, which are folllowed by a glossary of Arabic terms.

In introducing these diaries, I have been inspired by Cecily Mackworth's biography, *The Destiny of Isabelle Eberhardt* (London; Quartet Books, 1977), and by Henry

Miller's study of Rimbaud, *The Time of the Assassins* (London; Quartet, 1984). I have also benefited from illuminating conversations with Annette Kobak, Isabelle's most recent and most thorough biographer, and with Khaled Kaak, of the Tunisian Embassy in London, who offered invaluable assistance with words in the North African dialects.

Rana Kabbani
London 1987

JOURNAL ONE

Isabelle records her thoughts during her visit to her newly married brother Augustin in Sardinia.

Cagliari, 1 January 1900

I sit here all by myself, looking at the grey expanse of murmuring sea ... I am utterly *alone* on earth, and always will be in this Universe so full of lures and disappointments ... *alone*, turning my back on a world of dead hopes and memories.

The torments and confusion of the last six months have tempered my soul for good, and I can now face the worst of time, even death or destruction, without turning a hair. The knowledge I have acquired of the human heart is now so keen that I know the two months ahead will only bring me more sorrow, for I simply pay no attention to anything other than the dreams that make up my *true* personality. I seem to wear a mask that bespeaks someone cynical, dissipated ... No one so far has ever managed to see through it and catch a glimpse of the sensitive soul which lives behind it.

No one has ever understood that even though I may seem to be driven by the senses alone, my heart is in fact a pure one filled with love and tenderness, and with boundless compassion for all who suffer injustice, all who are weak and oppressed ... a heart both proud and unswerving in its commitment to Islam, a cause for which I long to give my life some day.

I shall dig in my heels and go on acting the lunatic in the intoxicating expanse of desert as I did last summer, or go on galloping through olive groves in the Tunisian Sahel, as I did in the autumn.

1

Those silent nights again, those lazy rides on horse-back through the salty plains of the Oued Righ's and the Oued Souf's white sands! That feeling, sad and bliss-ful at once, that would fill my pariah's heart every time I struck camp surrounded by friends, among Spahis and nomads, none of whom ever considered me the despic-able outcast I had so miserably become at the hands of fate.

Right now, I long for one thing only: to lead that life again in Africa ... to sleep in the chilly silence of the night below stars that drop from great heights, with the sky's infinite expanse for a roof and the warm earth for a bed, in the knowledge that no one pines for me *anywhere on earth*, that there is no place where I am being missed or expected. To know that is to be free and unencumbered, a nomad in the great desert of life where I shall never be anything but an outsider. Such is the only form of bliss, however bitter, the Mektoub will ever grant me, but then happiness of the sort coveted by all of frantic humanity, will never be mine.

The light went out of my life when, two years ago, my white dove lay down to sleep in Bône's Cimetière des Croyants.[1]

Now that Vava has returned to dust as well, and nothing is left of all that once seemed so solid and so permanent, now that all is gone, vanished, for all time and eternity! ... and now that fate has so curiously, so mysteriously driven a wedge between myself and the only being who ever came close enough to my true nature to catch however pale a glimpse of it, Augustin ... [2]

And now that ... Enough! I must put all those recent events to rest once and for all.

I am here out of friendship for the man Fate put across my path,[3] just as I was in the midst of a crisis – ☽ *please Allah*, may it be the last one.

My feeling of friendship is all the stronger for it.

As a nomad who has no country besides Islam and neither family nor close friends, I shall wend my way through life until it is time for that everlasting sleep inside the grave ...

MAHMOUD ESSADI

Cagliari, 7 January 1900
Impressions in a park,
around 5 p.m.

A savage landscape, the jagged outlines of deeply gutted hills either reddish or grey in colour, cavalcades of maritime pines and Barbary fig trees. Greenery so lush it is almost out of place in the heart of winter. Salt lagoons with surfaces the colour of lead, dead and immobile like desert shotts.

And up there at the very top the town's silhouette straddles the steep hillside. Ancient ramparts and a square old tower, different levels of roofs, all cast in a pink hue against a sky of indigo.

Near the very top, barracks identical to the ones in Algeria, long and low in shape with red-tiled roofs and flaky, peeling walls. Dark old churches full of statues and mosaics, objects of great luxury in a country where poverty is the rule. Vaulted passageways that make for resounding footsteps and booming echoes. A maze of alleyways going up and going down, and intersected here and there by steps of grey stone; and because there is no traffic in a town located at this height, the tiny pointed paving stones are all covered with spindly grass of a yellowish-green hue.

Doors that lead to vast cellars below street level where whole poverty-stricken families live in age-old dankness.

Shops with small, coloured window displays; Oriental boutiques, narrow and full of smoke where one can hear the drawl of nasal voices ...

Here and there a young man leans against a wall and makes signs to a girl bending over the railing of her balcony ...

Peasants wearing headdresses that hang all the way down their black jackets pleated over their white calico trousers. Tanned and bearded figures with deep-set eyes, heavy eyebrows and fierce, wary faces, a strange mixture of Greek mountain-dwellers and of tribesmen.

There is an Arab beauty about the women. The expression in their large languorous and melancholy jet-black eyes is resigned and sad like that of wary animals.

Beggars whine obsequiously in their incessant pursuit of

3

the stranger everywhere he goes ... Songs that sound infinitely sad, refrains that are curiously gripping, just like those heard in Africa, a place one cannot help but long for.

Cagliari, Thursday 18 January, 5.30 p.m.

Ever since I have been here, memories of *La Villa Neuve*[4] haunt me more and more ... good ones and bad ones alike ... I say good ones, for now that all is dead and buried, I must not harbour any grudges against my poor hovel ... I must not forget that it did shelter Mummy and her sweet kind heart, Vava[5] and all his good intentions, none of which he ever carried out. Ever since I walked out of it, I have lived as if in a swift and dazzling reverie, moving through varied scenery under different names and guises.

I realise that the fairly restful winter I am spending here is but a breathing spell from the life that will be mine until the very end.

In a few days' time my aimless wanderings will take over again. Where? How? Only God can tell. I must not even speculate on that subject any longer, for just as I was about to stay on in Paris for months on end, I ended up in Cagliari of all places, an out-of-the-way spot if ever there was one.

Yet there is one thing to cheer me: the farther behind I leave the past, the closer I am to forging my own character. I am developing the most unflinching and invincible will, to say nothing of integrity, two traits I value more than any others and, alas, ones that are so hard to find in women.

That and the likely prospect of spending four months in the desert next spring make me feel confident of making a name for myself and, what's more, sooner or later fulfilling my life's goal.

I have given up the hope of ever having a corner on earth to call my own, a home, a family, peace or prosperity. I have donned the cloak of the rootless wanderer, one that can be a burden too at times. I have written off the thought of ever coming home to a happy family for rest and safety.

For the moment I have found a soothing enough temporary home here in Cagliari, and have the illusion of truly loving someone whose presence seems to have become a

4

must[6] ... Yet that dream too will be short-lived, for I shall need to be alone again and do without the tranquil indolence of a shared existence once the moment will have come again for rough and risky travel.

That is what must be, and so it shall be. And in the gloom of that future existence I shall at least have one consolation, the thought that upon my return a friend, a living being may be happy to see me again. What is so terrible though, is the length of time spent apart to make for such reunions ... And who knows, someone else may have taken my place by then. That is more than likely, given his ideas about women and marriage. It would be very strange indeed if he were never to meet a woman with whom to share those ideas which are so at odds with mine. I know that no such partner will appear while he is a vagabond outcast, unless he is prepared to make do with a wife somewhere who will quiver at the thought of him in danger, but only from a safe and comfortable distance.

But then he too, like Augustin, will yield to the lure of home and comfort once the present period of transition is behind him.

When that happens I will have no choice but to resume my journey, sad but certain of having nothing to look forward to but the empty hotel rooms, gourbis and tents that are the nomad's temporary shelter. ☽ Mektoub!

The only thing to do is take things as they come and enjoy this heady interlude, for it will soon be over.

Cagliari, 29 January 1900

My brief interlude in this ancient Sardinian town has now come to an end.

Tomorrow at this time I shall be quite far from these Cagliari cliffs, on that leaden, grumbling, turbulent sea.

Last night Cagliari was booming with the echo of its rolling thunder ... Today, the sea looks its most ominous; it has a dull shimmer.

I am full of the sorrow that goes with changes in surroundings, those successive stages of annihilation that slowly lead to the great and final void.

Isabelle travels to Paris and to Geneva in an attempt to sort out her inheritance.

Geneva, 27 May 1900, 9.30 p.m. [Sunday]

Back to this gloomy diary of mine in this evil city where I have suffered so much and have come close to perishing.

I have hardly been here a week and once again I feel as morbid and oppressed as I used to in the old days. All I want to do is get out for good.

I went to have a look at our poor house, with the sky low and sunless; the place was boarded up and mute, lost among the weeds.

I saw the road, white as ever, white like a silvery river heading for the Jura's great mountaintops between those tall velvet trees.

I saw the two graves in that faithless cemetery,[7] set in a land of exile so very far away from that other sacred place devoted to eternal repose and everlasting silence[8] ...

I feel that I have now become a total stranger on this soil which I shall leave tomorrow and hope never to visit again.

(Recorded later)
Paris, April 1900

In the misty light of stars and streetlamps one night I saw the Montparnasse cemetery's white crosses outlined like so many ghosts against the velvety black of big trees, and it occurred to me that the powerful rumble of Paris could not disturb the slumber of all the strangers lying there ...

6

JOURNAL TWO

In the name of God, the Merciful, the Compassionate!

Epitaph found on a grave in the little Vernier cemetery on 4 June 1899, the day I left Geneva and made a last pilgrimage to Vava's grave:
   Peace to your ashes, to those that lie buried
   in that far-off foreign country, and to you who
   rest upon that sacred mound above the Mediterranean's
   eternal blue waves ...

                                        Geneva, 8 June 1900
                    Upon my return from the Vernier cemetery. Feeling
                                        infinitely sad.

So much travelling will put the mind to sleep; one gets used to anything, whether to the most outstandingly exotic places or the most remarkable faces. Yet there are times when one suddenly wakes up and takes stock, only to be suddenly struck by the strangeness of one's surroundings.[9]

Over there in Africa, above the great blue gulf of unforgettable Annéba, stands the graveyard on the hill under the blazing sky. The white marble tombs, and those made of glazed, multi-coloured tiles must look like bright flowers among the tall black cypresses and geraniums the colour of blood or pale flesh, and fig trees from the Barbary Coast ...
   As I sat in the low grass of the Vernier graveyard facing the two grey tombs set among the weeds of spring, I thought of the grave of the † *White Spirit*[10] ... And in the

midst of all that indestructible Nature, my thoughts turned once again to the mystery of the end of people's lives ...

How useless and funereal are these notes of mine, and how despairingly monotonous, without even the slightest hint of gaiety or of hope.

The only consolation they contain is their growing sense of Islamic *resignation*. I would like it if Archivir[11] were to smile at me as only he can and if I were to hear him tell me in that tone of voice of his, the way he did the day I came so close to baring my soul: 'Go, Mahmoud, and do great, magnificent deeds ... Be a hero ...'

It is true that of all the men I have come across, this one, whose beloved picture I have in front of me, is the most spellbinding of all, and that his charm is of the most lofty and noble sort: he speaks to the soul rather than to the senses, he exalts whatever is sublime and stifles the low and contemptible. No one has ever had such a truly beneficial effect upon my soul. No one has ever understood and bolstered those blessed things that, since the † *White Spirit*'s death, have slowly but surely begun to take root in my heart: faith, repentance, the desire for moral perfection, the longing for a reputation based on noble *merit*, and a thirst for great and magnificent deeds.

I judge and love him for what I have seen of him so far. Time will tell whether I have been clairvoyant, whether I have seen him as he really is, or whether I have made another mistake.

That will be the end of it once and for all, for if what I hold to be purity itself turns out to have a hidden blemish, if what looks to me like beauty masks the usual horror, if the light I take to be a beacon in life's black maze is a trick meant to lead wayfarers astray, what can I expect after that?

Yet once again, nothing, absolutely nothing has so far suggested there might be anything in such an unthinkable thought ... If he is the way I think he is, he may well put me through terrible paces, but in a magnificent way ... he may well turn out to be responsible for sending me off to die, but spare me the worst of grievances, namely disillusionment.

8

Thus said the Lord, Stand ye in the ways, and see, and ask for the old paths, where is the good way, and walk therein, and ye shall find rest for your souls. [JEREMIAH 6:16]

I shall always cherish the memory of these past few days spent in greater *happiness* and less *gloom*, for they are moments stolen from life's hopelessness, hours snatched from the void.

People who interest me are those who are subject to that lofty, fertile form of suffering known as dissatisfaction with oneself; the thirst for an 'Ideal', something mystical and eminently desirable that fires their souls ... Self-satisfaction because of some accomplishment will never be for me, and as I see it, truly superior people are those preoccupied with the quest for better selves.

Not for me are those who feel smug, happy with themselves and their lot, content with the state of their heart.

Not for me those solid citizens who are *deaf, dumb and blind and never admit a mistake.*

I must learn to *think*. That may be painful and take time.

I cannot describe the contempt and loathing I have for my own inadequacy, my obsessive need to see people however banal, to prostitute my soul and go into sickening explanations.

Instead of looking into myself for what my soul requires, why do I look in others, where I know it cannot be found?

Why can't I react against this impulse that continues to encumber my life? Except with very rare people, there is no such thing as communication on an intellectual plane, so why insist on courting disappointment?

LITERARY IDEAS

I think that, as a beginner, I must first of all develop the artistic side of my work, that is to say my *style*.

A symbol of what my life is now all about, and probably always will be, is that sign saying '*Room for rent*' by the window of the seedy room I am living in, with a camp bed in it, some papers and my handful of books.

9

Following a night of suffering, a strange morning ...

I realise that I cannot write right now.

I shall confine myself to describing the situation: a purely cerebral wish to improve my conduct and get to work ... no enthusiasm, though, for either.

I am suddenly aware of my growing resolve to set off for Ouargla at any cost, and try once more to isolate myself for months on end in the total silence of the Desert and get used to that slow dreamy life out there.[12]

Nothing is standing in my way, come to think of it.

However limited my means, I will still be able to afford to live there as well as it is wise to live.

Oddly enough, I have not forgotten all that I went through down there, the unbelievable hardships, my illness...

They must have been due to unfortunate circumstances though, and the whole idea now appeals to me a lot.

This time around, life in the Desert will be a bit less exhausting as I will not have to stay up all night, but it will complete my education as a man of action, the Spartan education I need.

What bitter ecstasies await me: first the farewell to that strange man Archivir who has given me such a remarkable time, sweet and bitter all at once.

Next, there will be the solemn occasion of my boarding ship at Marseilles and saying goodbye to the brother who is the apple of my eye ...

Then there will be the sad but soothing moment of my pilgrimage to Annéba, to her grave on that hallowed hillside.

Then on to Batna, where I left behind so many nostalgic memories ...

Torrid Biskra, where I used to spend such charming evenings in front of the Moorish cafés ...

And that steep and blistering road to arid Oued Rir ...

And what about sad Tuggurt sleeping underneath its shroud of salt as it overlooks its hidden shott ...

And finally Ouargla, the very gateway to that mysterious

10

void known as the great Sahara, which so appeals to my imagination ...

I would like to go to Ouargla, settle there and *make a home, something I miss more and more*. A little mud house close to some date palms, a place to cultivate the odd vegetable in the oasis, a servant and companion, a few small animals to warm my lonely heart, a horse perhaps, and books as well.

Lead two lives, one that is full of adventure and belongs to the Desert, and one, calm and restful, devoted to thought and far from all that might interfere with it.

I should also want to travel now and then, to visit Augustin, and go to Paris, only to return to my solitary, silent retreat.

Fashion a soul for myself out there, an awareness, an intelligence and a will.

I have no doubt that my attraction to the Islamic faith would blossom magnificently over there.

Should anyone happen to take the trouble to read this diary one day, it would be a faithful mirror of the fast pace of my life which, for all I know, may already be in its final stages.

After two days of dreadful boredom, I am trying to get back to work.

I feel more and more disgusted with my second self, that no-good oaf who rears his head from time to time, usually, if not always, under the influence of physical factors. Better health, in other words, would clearly result in an improvement in the intellectual and spiritual side of my life.

Night before last I had a long discussion with Archivir about that perennial subject of ours, namely pleasure. I still hold on to my theory, which says that one should limit one's needs as much as one can to avoid disillusionment, as well as to avoid any dulling of the senses owing to unpleasant sensations.

11

Archivir, on the other hand, maintains that needs must be developed, and that one must use one's last ounce of energy to satisfy them.

It occurs to me this instant to write a dissertation on the subject, to be published perhaps in *L'Athénée*.

Once again, I feel that I am going through a period of intellectual incubation which I think will be the most fertile of my whole life so far.

Reading the *Journal des Goncourts* does me a great deal of good. I shall have to use my stay in Marseilles to read the other volumes and make notes.

I have so far opted for reading matter which focuses on feelings and on the imagination. As a result, my sense of poetry has been overdeveloped at the expense of rigorous thought.

The *Journal des Goncourts* is a work that forces one to think, and *deeply* so. I must look for other, similar books and use them for discussion and debate, while I am still surrounded by people.

I am clearly aware that certain things I do are absolutely *futile, stupid* and *actually bad* for my future; is my will not strong enough to stand up to my ego and prevent these things?

A matter to be studied, so that I can find out how to do better.

'*We now have only one main interest in life: the gratification that comes from observing reality. Without that, life is boring and empty*'.[13]

Written 30 June, 8 o'clock in the evening

The more I write and develop my story, the more I feel curiously *bored* with it, hence those nagging doubts about what possible interest it may have for the reader.

It is therefore no exaggeration to say that I can no longer make up my mind whether *Rakhil*[14] is or is not a sickening pile of badly written police reports.

That is why I need to read it out loud to someone. Needless to say, if the book makes the same impression on readers as it does on me, then no one will read beyond the second page after the foreword.

Everything seems so tranquil this evening, despite the noise coming from the boulevards that teem with people. Everything is in a soft grey fog, just like my mood: I am not feeling overly emotional, but feel no enthusiasm either. All I want to do is work in peace and develop what intelligence I have.

Such apparent egocentricity to be found on every page of this diary should not be taken for megalomania ... Oh, no ... To begin with, loners are given to constant introspection; and I do need to compile a record that will give me, later on, a true image of my soul as it is today. That is the only way I shall be able to judge my present life and to see whether my character has progressed or not.

Written at Geneva, 3 July, 1900, 11.30 at night

I am thinking of writing a short story, to go with *La Voie*,[15] but with very different characters: Semenov, Andreyev, Sacha in Paris.

The same night, at 2 in the morning

I am not asleep. I don't feel like it in the least. Downstairs I can hear the piercing screams of a Russian woman in labour. What an ominous way of entering into the world, on such a rainy night, ominous and *symbolic* as well.

The first thing we do in life is weep ... And how much our entrance resembles our exit, except that our exit is less sad than our entrance, with all the woes that it entails!

Weep ye not for the dead, neither bemoan him; but weep sore for him that goeth away: for he shall return no more nor see his native country. (JEREMIAH, 22:10)

Isabelle leaves Geneva for Marseilles, where Augustin and his wife have now set up their meagre household.

Departure from Geneva, 14 July 1900, 7.30 p.m.
The weather is grey and stormy and dark. Where am I going? ... ☾ *Where Destiny is taking me!*

Arrival in Marseilles. Fatigue. Superb sunrise over the Crau.

A sense of Africa. My voyage has gone well.

15 July 1900, 9.30 p.m., Marseilles

An idea occurs to me as I come upon the following phrase in the *Journal des Goncourts*: 'finished *Manette Salomon* today.' No work of literature is ever finished in the sense that it cannot bear improvement. To finish something is to feel satisfied with it.

Despite the chaos and my disgust those last few days in Geneva, that month of living the Russian way – for the last time in my life no doubt – will always be one of my most cherished memories.

My brief romance with Archivir also had its considerable charm, yet I have said goodbye to him for ever, without hard feelings of any sort.

The phenomenon of malice in the domain of love, whether such malice is physical or mental, is a sure sign that civilisation is on the wane.[16]

Marseilles, 16 July 1900

I would still like to make a stab at happiness, in the form of a solitary nest for myself in some far-off place where I can be independent.

That is the kind of nest I am going to try to build for myself in the middle of the Desert, far away from people. I want to be alone for months on end, without any human contact whatsoever. I must avoid sharing anyone's lot from now on, whether in embarrassing love affairs or in friendships.[17]

That will at least spare me a good deal of suffering.

I must also try to create for myself an inner world of thoughts and feelings, to compensate for my solitude and poverty.[18]

However difficult, I must live out my theory of limiting one's needs.

14

That will not be hard to do, as long as my health holds out.

Out there, I shall be able to have a hygienic sort of life if I lead a reasonably settled existence. That way I shall be able to avoid the roots of ill health.

As for my state of mind, it has now become more than urgent that I get down to work.

That would not only ensure me a chance to earn a living now that my feeble means have been wiped out but would also safeguard me against my usual despondency.

I must learn to live in the *present moment* and not in the future only. While to live in the past and think of what was good and beautiful about it amounts to a sort of *seasoning* of the present, the perennial wait for tomorrow is bound to result in chronic discontent that poisons one's entire outlook.

I must learn to feel *more deeply*, to see *better*, and above all, to *think*.

18 July 1900, 9 p.m.

It does look as though things have been decided at last, as though I am actually off to Africa on Saturday, after an absence of nine months. My God, if only upon reaching Ouargla I could muster the courage to set up the nest I need so much, and stay there for at least six months, I could do some *work*.

Tonight I will re-read the whole of my novel *Rakhil*. In order to discover what I think of it, I need the one thing I have not had – an overall view. All it now needs to stand as a story is the scene with the Jewish women going for a stroll, which would amount to a half hour's work. Before I do anything else, however, I must finish reading and annotating the *Journal des Goncourts* while I am still here.

Next, I must take note of the odd passage from other writers: Baudelaire, Zola, Loti.

While travelling, I must carefully write down not only *factual information*, but also my *impressions*. I must come up with an interesting and picturesque description of my crossing of the Mediterranean and my journey through the

15

ancient sites of Algeria and the Oued Rir. That will be the first thing to put down on paper there.

I must also write down everything I see in the oasis; a detailed summary with as much information as possible. After that, I shall start a *literary diary* about my life out there. Meanwhile, I must try to turn my book *Rakhil* into what it has got to be above all else – a true work of art.

I must also, for publication in Russian, write a description of my journey through the Sahel last autumn, plus a few ✝ short stories.

A gruelling workload, but it is my only road to salvation. Then, once I have *La Villa Neuve* out of the way, I shall go to Paris, if I can afford it, to lead an altogether different life than I did before. I shall do everything within my power to make a success of the material I bring along.[19]

That is the only sensible plan I can make for the moment.

If by autumn there is a move toward Morocco, I will of course go along and take detailed notes at all times.

Yesterday, 17 July, at four in the afternoon, I took the omnibus down the Cours Devilliers to the Quai de la Fraternité. I thought Marseilles looked very colourful, true to form.

I went for a long walk with Augustin, and we first stopped at the Fort Saint-Nicolas bridge. We watched the exertion necessary to turn the bridge around and let through a Greek sailboat named *Eleni*. At the bow stood a man with a coarse face, in shirtsleeves and a felt hat, who kept shouting: *Vira, vira, vira!* to the crew trying to steer the vessel.

Silhouettes of young bathers in their bathing trunks, who looked happy to be wet and naked in the sun and kept striking poses.

We crossed the old harbour by ferry below Fort Saint-Jean and paid a visit to the Quai de la Joliette, across from the Africa-bound ships.

Huge black heaps, black dust and black-looking men in rags and covered with soot; the whites of their eyes looked dirty, their mouths looked like wounds and any patch of real skin that showed through might as well have been the hideous mark of leprosy. Equally black tavern, where a sunburnt man with the face of a crook was having an

16

argument with a frightened coaldocker. Back to the jetty. The horizon looked a greenish aquamarine and the sea was slightly choppy. Watched a net being pulled in between two heaving boats.

Quai du Lazaret. Back in the coal tavern, a man had asked me for a light and, already very drunk, had kept singing and making a lot of noise. We saw him again on the quay, sitting on top of his cart, waving, holding forth and laughing in the midst of a crowd, under the gaze and indulgent smiles of the police who were probably biding their time to arrest him ... something about the drunkard having crushed a soldier's leg.

We came home at eight o'clock. Fatigue, intense headache and nausea.

Friday 20 July 10 p.m.
in Marseilles

Everything is finished, packed and closed ... The only thing left here is my camp bed, which must wait till morning.

At one in the afternoon tomorrow I leave for Algiers.

The fact is that I did not really quite believe I would actually be leaving for Ouargla. So many things had stood in the way of my carrying out my daring plan.

My chances of success are good, for I leave well equipped. As for my mood, I feel great sadness, as I now do every time I leave this house, even though I am no more than a passing stranger in it.

Yet I also feel a glimmer of hope. I know my present mood will pass as soon as I am with my friend Eugène[20] in Algiers, when there will be new impressions for me to take in.

In any event I must work, and write, over there ... My God, if I could only muster the energy to buckle down and finish part at least of all I have got to do! Would it not be a better idea to start my description of my trip through Algeria with Bône rather than Algiers? If I came across any impressions that warrant recording, I could present them as recollections from another period. That would give me the opportunity to produce some splendidly melancholy pages, in the vein of African perspectives.

17

That trip will give me the material for a book, a good one I can write quickly and that can perhaps be published before *Rakhil*.

I sometimes feel so pessimistic I look at the future with a feeling of irrational terror, as if it can only be bad and terrifying, even though many of those dark clouds have in fact gone from my horizon.

Isabelle quits Marseilles and returns to North Africa, arriving in Algiers on 22 July.

Algiers, 22 July 1900, 11 p.m.

It was hot yesterday afternoon when I boarded the same ship I took last September.[21] I kept staring at Augustin's silhouette till it disappeared from view when the ship tacked. I then studied the view. The harbour was full of the powerful red and black shapes of transatlantic steamers.

Then came the city ... to begin with, when the ship was in the middle of the harbour, Marseilles looked like a delicate palette of grisailles: the grey of the smoky sky, the blue tones of the mountains, the pinkish-grey ones of the rooftops ... the lilac hues of the sea, while the hardy vegetation growing among the rocks provided so many dots of a greenish-brown ... The green foliage of the plane trees, the cathedral's gilded cupolas and statue of the Virgin Mary were the only things to stand out in sharp and lively contrast.

Yet once the ship was at some distance, everything looked quite different: it was all a monochrome gold, so intense one could hardly believe one's eyes.

Spent a peaceful night on the sternside bench. Felt truly well; woke up by about 2.45 a.m.

Saw the sun come up while sailors were putting up the canvas. First there was a rosy dawn, then a crimson disc appeared, clear-cut in outline. Slightly above it were the lacy shapes of pink clouds outlined in gold.

All night long I had the feeling of mysterious well-being I always get when peacefully asleep with the ship's lights shining over my head.

I will continue this report tomorrow.

18

Oh, the sense of bliss I had this evening, knowing that I am *back* inside solemn mosques and in the ancient hustle and bustle of the Arab quarter in the Rue Jénina!

Oh that extraordinary feeling of intoxication I had to-night, in the peaceful shadows of the great al-Jadid Mosque during the icha prayer!

I feel I am coming back to life again ... ☽ *Lead us along the straight path, the one taken by those to whom you have been generous!*

For a long, long time all you could see of the Algerian coast was Matifou steeped in vapours ...

Next one could see the Algiers triangle, with the old part of town looking like an avalanche of snow ... this was followed by a splendid view of the entire panorama in full daylight.

After a very brief moment spent in my room with Eugène, he left and I went exploring by myself. My hat bothered me, though, for it set me apart from Muslims.

I went back to don my fez, and went out again with Ahmed, the manservant, to go to the al-Kabir Mosque. It was so cool and peaceful there underneath those white arcades. Went to greet the mosque's wakil, a venerable old man who sat in a side niche writing on his knee.

Nothing surprises him any longer. No undue curiosity, no indiscretion. I then went to that charming blue-tinted zawyia of Sidi-Abd-al-Rahman.

Stood for a while in the cool shade facing the mihrab upon those thick rugs. Drank some jasmine-flavoured water from the earthenware pitcher on the windowsill.

The zawyia is one of great beauty, and I will certainly go back there before I leave Algiers.

Dashes of an unvarnished bluish-white among the green-ery in the Jardin Marengo.

Smelled a sweet and heady fragrance I could not place as I walked through it, of flowers I could not identify.

Had supper at Al-Haj-Muhammad, on the corner of the Rue Jénina. Felt *intensely* happy to be here again, on this African soil to which I feel tied not only by memories but

also by that strange appeal it has always had for me, even before I had ever seen it, when I was still living in that boring *Villa* of ours.

I felt so happy sitting at that table, a feeling impossible to describe, one I have never felt anywhere but in Africa.

How much Arabs resemble each other!

At Haj-Muhammad's yesterday I saw men come in whom I thought I had known in earlier days, in Bône, Batna, or in the South ... but not in Tunisia, where they look very different.

After dinner this evening, went to say the icha prayer in the al-Jadid Mosque which is less beautiful than the two others, but the soaring sense of Islam was superb.

The place was cool and dark as I went in, and a handful of oil-lamps were the only source of light.

A feeling of ancient Islam, tranquil and mysterious.

Stood for a long time near the mihrab. Somewhere far behind us a clear, high voice went up, a dreamlike voice that took turns with that of the elderly Imam standing in the mihrab where he recited the *fatiha*.

Standing next to each other, we all prayed as we listened to the exhilarating yet solemn exchange between those two voices. The one in front of us sounded old and hoarse, but gradually grew louder and louder till it was strong and powerful, while the other one seemed to come from somewhere high up in the mosque's dark reaches as it sang triumphantly in regular intervals of its unshakable, radiant faith in Allah and His Prophet ... I was in ecstasy as my heart soared up towards the celestial sphere from whence the second voice poured forth in sweet and confident bliss.

Oh, to lie upon the rugs of some silent mosque, far from the noise of wanton city life, and, eyes closed, gaze turned heavenwards, listen to Islam's song for ever!

I remember the time I wandered around till daybreak one night last year. I ended up by the Morkad ruins at the foot of the minaret, where the windows were all lit up. In the dead silence of the night I heard the muezzin's voice, which sounded infinitely mysterious as it sang ☽ *Prayer is better than sleep!* Those rhythmical notes still echo in my ears.

20

After the icha prayer, which is a lovely moment of the day, I went out for an aimless stroll.

Upon my return around ten o'clock, I spent some time in front of a small shop in a narrow street. The place was lit by an oil lamp. A guitar, pipestems and decoration in the form of paper cutouts.

The shopkeeper was stretched out on an oval mat in front, a dark, handsome indifferent-looking man whose gestures were very slow, as though his mind were else-where. Might that have been due to kif?

Bought a small pipe and some kif.

That more or less sums up what I did yesterday.

The day of my arrival has turned out to be an incom-parably happy one.

Isabelle now begins her journey southward to the Souf region, where she sets up house in El Oued.

El-Merayer, 30 July 1900

Left Algiers on 27 July, eight o'clock in the morning.

Frame of mind fairly good, but spoiled by the presence of Lieutenant Lagrange's mistress, a horrible revolting creature.

At Sidi-Amram, I lay down near some burning dried djerid, next to a French soldier who had turned up out of the blue; drank some coffee, felt weak, slightly feverish. The fire's flames cast a strange red light upon the mud walls, underneath the stars.

Tuggurt, 31 July 1900, Tuesday noon

I am sitting in the obscurity of the dining room, to get away from the innumerable flies in my own room.

I am pleased to see the desert's torrid heat does not bother me too much, even though I am not feeling alto-gether normal because I am worn out by my journey and recent late nights. I can work and think. In fact, it is only today that I am beginning to recover. I will not really feel well, though, until the day I have settled in El Oued and all is quiet around me.

I am also beginning to find out about thrift and the willpower it takes to avoid squandering the little money I have left.

I must also remember that I have come to the desert, not to indulge in last year's dolce far niente, but to work, and that this journey of mine can either mean disaster for the rest of my life, or prove a prelude to salvation for both body and soul, depending on how well I manage.

I have an altogether charming memory of Algiers, from the first night to the last in particular.

The last evening I went with Mokhtar and Abd-el-Kaim Oulid-Issa to a tobacconist's on the Plateau Saulières. We had a rather lively conversation, and then went for a melancholy stroll along the quays. Ben Elimaur, Mokhtar and Zarrouk, the medical student, softly sang wistful Algerian songs.

I had several moments of great and altogether Oriental intensity at Algiers.

The long journey I made in third class, alone with someone as young as Mokhtar, also had its charm.

I have said farewell to the big Blue Sea, perhaps for a long time to come.

I travelled through wild Kabyle territory and a landscape of jagged rocks. Then, after the hills of the Portes de Fer, came the desolate plateaux gilded by fields cultivated by Arabs — long dots of a tawny-silvery hue upon the landscape's oranges and ochres.

The plains at Borj-bou-Arérij offer a desperately sad and dreary spectacle.

Saint Arnaud is a large village lost among the high plateaux of Cheonïya country. Yet Saint Arnaud, *Elelma* in Arabic, is a verdant spot. Its gardens are like those of the Randon column at Bône.

The Cadi is a noble and serene old man, who belongs to another age.

In ten, twenty years' time, will today's young Algerians resemble their fathers and be as steeped as they are in the solemn serenity of their Islamic faith? His son Si Ali seems at first sight to be sleepy and heavy. Yet he is an intelligent man who does care about the public interest. Si Ihsan, who is of Turkish origin, is a man whose charm lies in his candour.

Had an intense and ever so pleasant sense of old Africa and Bedouin country the first night at Elelma: there was the distant sound of dogs barking all night long, and the crowing of the rooster.

Crossed the Ourlana oasis around two in the morning last night: vast gardens enclosed by walls made of clay, segniyas reeking of saltpetre, humidity and fever.

The houses built of ochre-coloured mud all seemed to be in a state of slumber.

At Sidi Amram I stretched out on the ground by a fire that was burning dried djerids. The sand felt warm and the sky was ablaze with countless stars.[22]

Oh Sahara, Sahara so full of perils, you hide your soul in bleak inhospitable solitudes!

I love this country of sand and stone, inhabited by camels and primitive men, and dotted with treacherous shotts and sebhkas.

Between Mraïer and El Berd last night I saw bizarre, fetishistic forms garbed in red and white rags, at the exact spot where a Muslim was assassinated a few years ago. It is a forlorn monument put up in memory of the man who lies buried at Tuggurt.

Borj Terjen, 1 August, 7 a.m.

Set off from Taïbet at 4.45 yesterday afternoon on N'Tardjallah's mule with Muhammad al-Haj. Reached Mguetla by nine o'clock.

In spite of slight fatigue, had excellent impression of first encampment.

A wind that was almost cold during the night, and in the dunes a murmur like that of the sea. A feeling of desolation, for no reason at all.

Magnificent sunrise. Arose at 4 a.m. A pristine sky, cool and rather strong north-easterly wind.

Set off at five o'clock. Struck camp and made coffee in the dunes. The mailcoach caught up with us. Rode a camel till Terjen. Arrived at eight.

Excellent frame of mind. State of health, *ditto*.

How wise I have been to leave Europe and decide to make my home in El Oued, which is what I did yesterday.

Provided my health holds up, I must stay at El Oued as long as I can.

Above all, I hope this is not a waste of time, especially vis à vis my intellectual and spiritual development and my literary endeavours. ☽ *Please Allah!*

El Oued, 4 August 1900, 7 a.m.

As I finished writing in my diary at Terjen, I sat down on my bed, facing the door.

Had an indescribable sense of well-being and profound bliss at being there ... Siesta interrupted by children and goats.

Left with the mailcoach around 2.30 p.m. Intense heat. Did not feel well. Mounted the camel once more. Reached Mouïet-el-Caïd by maghreb [6 p.m.].

By 4 a.m. off to Ourmes, where we arrived by half-past seven. Crossed the biggest dune and came upon several dead camels, one of which was a recent casualty.

Ourmes. Siesta in the park. An enchanted sight. Did not sleep well because of inevitable flies and hot burnous. Was at El Oued around maghreb.

Went to see a house that belongs to a Caïd, on the town square opposite the Borj. Rented it. Have started moving in.

The evening of my arrival, beautiful ride on mules. A night that looked transparent on the white sand. A deep garden, fast asleep in darkness. Nothing but things cool and mellow all around.

Have now reached my goal at long last; now I must get to work with all the energy I can muster. As soon as I receive the money from Eugène, I must pay the rent, Habib, and buy basic necessities.

My luggage is to arrive today. As soon as I am living in less of a makeshift situation, I shall have to start writing the book about my journey, the first chapter of which will deal with Marseilles.

I am far from society, far from civilisation. I am by myself, on Muslim soil, out in the desert, free and in the best of circumstances, except for my health and even that is not too bad. The outcome of my undertaking is therefore up to me ...

I am beginning to feel bored, for my luggage has not turned up and I cannot get on with my house and life ...

Habib's house. A square building of unbleached toub, in one of the winding streets paved with fine sand, not far from the dune.

Off in a corner is a small dark goat with an amulet around its neck. Habib's many brothers come and go. The old man's wife, tall and slim, dressed in long white veils, a veritable mountain on top of her head: braids of black hair, braids and tassels made of red wool, and in her ears heavy iron rings held up by cords tied to the hairdo. To go out, she throws a blue veil over it all. A strange, ageless figure with a sunburnt skin and doleful black eyes.

Temperatures will soon start going down. There is already a little gust of wind from time to time.

To sum things up, I have not yet embarked upon my new way of life. Too much of it is still unsettled.

El Oued, Thursday 9 August 7.30 p.m.

For the time being there is nothing durable about this Arab lifestyle of mine, which is indolent but in no way dangerous for I know it will not last. My little household is beginning to look like one. I am still short of money though.

I must avoid borrowing any from the bach-adel, for he is clearly no altruist.

A few days from now I expect to change my lifestyle altogether.

Every evening we go to Bir Arby. We go across the snow-white sands translucent in the moonlight. We pass the gloomy-looking silhouettes of the Christian cemetery: high grey walls with a black cross on top ... The impression is a lugubrious one. From there we go up a low hill, and in a deep and narrow valley we see the garden, which is no different from any other Souafa garden. At the bottom stand the highest palm trees, the smaller ones grow near the wells.

In the bluish-green light of the moon they look diaphan-

ous, like delicate feathery plumes. Between their handsome chiselled trunks lies the odd verdant stretch of melons, water-melons and fragrant basil.

The water is clear and cool. The well's primitive iron frame made a squeaking noise and the goatskin fell in and made lapping noises in the well's dark interior before surfacing again, dripping wet. I threw my chechiya down on the sand, soaked my head in the oumara and took a few greedy gulps of water. It was refreshing and cool, and gave me the sort of shiver that a drink of water always does down here. After that we stretched out on the sand for a moment.

Slowly and laboriously, we headed back for the sleeping town and that white house that is now my home, God knows for how long ...

Isabelle meets Slimène Ehnni, and begins to frequent the Kadrya confraternity to which he belongs.

A few nights ago I spent a night in a large garden that belongs to the Hacheich Caidat, west of El Oued, together with Slimène.[23]

Not a soul was breathing in the palm trees' shadows. We sat down near a well where I had unsuccessfully tried to draw water with a torn oumara. We both felt sad, in my case because of the trouble owing to local indiscretions which loomed large in my mind.

My soul has aged, alas. It has ceased to delude itself and I can only smile at Slimène's dreams. He does not believe in eternity but thinks that earthly love goes on for ever. He also wonders what will happen in a year's, in seven years' time.[24]

Yet what would be the use of telling him, of making him sad and hurting him. That will happen soon enough, the day we go our separate ways.

After an hour spent talking, with tears in our eyes, about the truly awful possibilities ahead, we went to sleep under the palm trees on top of our burnous, using a thickness of sand for a pillow.

Slept till about 2.30 a.m. In the rising pre-dawn chill, we laboriously retraced our steps up the path through the dunes. A maze of tiny alleyways reeking heavily of salt-

petre, rather like the Oued Rir oases. Crossed the market-place which was deserted except for a few camels and their drivers, asleep by the great well's iron frame.

Rode the bad white horse last night, taking the road to Kouïnine through El Oued's tiny suburbs, where black and white goats graze on top of the roofs of zéribas made of djérid.

To the west, in the direction of Kouïnine and Tuggurt, the sun was a ball of blood sinking in a blaze of gold and crimson. The slopes of the dunes seemed to be on fire below the ridges, in hues that deepened from one moment to the next.

This morning the sky looked dark and cloudy, a most unexpected sight in this land of implacably blue skies and perennial sunshine.

The fact is that at the moment my time is not being put to good use. The siesta hour has a lot to do with that.

I would like to start working. That would mean getting up for reveille, at the very least, and not going back to bed after Slimène has left ... I do, alas, from sheer boredom and from the fact that I have nothing else to do.

I must go out right after reveille, for the occasional morning ride, on whatever horse happens to be available.

Spent a quarter of an hour taking measures against the swarms of flies in my two rooms. The day will come when I will cherish the memory of such tiny chores in this very simple lifestyle of mine.

Oh, if my present way of life could last, if Slimène could continue to be the good friend and brother he is right now. And if only I could share more in the local side of life and get to work as soon as the weather starts to cool!

When a girl gets married over here she is taken to her husband on a man's back. To see his wife, the husband must hide for seven nights, come after the maghreb and leave before the morning.

Obviously a vestige of the abductions of earlier days.

18 August 1900, 3.30 p.m.

Went riding by myself last night, through the little town-ships all along the road to Tuggurt. Went through Teksebet.

27

A melancholy, derelict-looking place, virtually deserted, where ruins crumble with every step.

Headed back for El Oued by sundown. Watched the sand pour down the greyish dunes in a constant stream.

Getting in the saddle yesterday I heard nearby wails, the Arab way of broadcasting someone's death. The daughter of Salah the Spahi, young Abd-el-Kader's sister, had died.

The little girl was buried in the hot sand yesterday at maghreb ... she was swallowed up for all time by eternal night, like one of those meteors one sees flashing through this land's infinite sky.

Isabelle travels around the area on her horse 'Souf', named after the region.

Monday 9 October 1900, 9 a.m.

Shortly after the maghreb last night, rode Souf by the back of the café through the white sandy streets along houses that are half in ruin.

A few moments earlier, just as the sun had been about to set and El Oued had been ablaze in gold, I had spotted the silhouettes of two Arabs garbed in white standing on top of the little dune where the lime kiln is; they looked as if set against a heavenly light. The impression was a biblical one, and I suddenly felt as if transported back to the ancient days of primitive humanity, when the great light-giving bodies in the sky had been the object of veneration ...

At that frontier between town and desert, I was reminded of those autumn and winter sunsets in the land of exile, when the great snow-capped Jura mountains seemed to come closer in an expanse of pale bluish hues.

It is chilly in the morning now. The light has changed colour. We no longer have the flat glare of stifling summer days. The sky is now a violent shade of blue, pure and invigorating.

Everything has come to life again, and so has my soul. Yet, as always, I feel a boundless sadness, an inarticulate longing for something I cannot describe, a nostalgia for a *place* for which I have no name.

For several days now, intellectual endeavour has seemed

28

less repellent to me than it did this summer, and I think I shall go on writing. The wellspring does not seem to have run dry.

For the moment I do not feel up to taking off and parting from Slimène for ever, even if I could afford to do so. And why should I?

I feel a tranquil heart is mine at last; the same cannot be said for any peace of mind, alas!

Isabelle gets to know the two sons of the Grand Sheikh of the Kadrya, Sidi-el-Hussein and Si Lachmi.

El Oued, *27 October 1900, 9 p.m.*

Went to Amiche on the 17th, to look for Sidi-el-Hussein.[25]

It was chilly when we left around six that morning. Arrived in no time at all at Sheikh Blanc's great zawyia, which seemed quite deserted, near those vast and gloomy cemeteries. Set off again with two menservants, and passed houses and gardens which looked quite picturesque.

Found Sidi-el-Hussein at long last at the far end of Ras-el-Amiche, facing the infinite stretches of sand that lead to the distant Sudan.

Spent the siesta hour with the sheikh in a narrow primitive room with no windows. It was vaulted and had sand on the floor, and it constituted the whole interior of the house, which stands all by itself.[26]

A strange figure showed up, an almost black Southerner with burning eyes who suffers from a form of epilepsy that makes him strike at anyone who touches or frightens him ... Yet he is also very congenial. Left at about three o'clock with the sheikh for the Chaambas colony. Set off again by myself around 3.15. Reached the cemeteries located to the right of Amiche by sundown. At the maghreb hour, stopped on the dune that overlooks the Ouled-Touati.

On my left the plains looked pink, and in the village I saw a few women in blue rags and an oddly shaped red dromedary. Utter peace and silence all around ... Came back home around 5.15 p.m.

I have now reached a state of destitution foreseen for some time. Yet, in bringing me to El Oued, Providence

29

seems to have wanted to spare me worse suffering in other places.

Who knows, it may be that all these strokes of bad luck will merely serve to forge my character and pull me out of the indolent *indifference* that often comes over me when the future is at stake.

May God help me succeed! So far I have always survived even the worst and most perilous of pitfalls unscathed. Fate will not quite forsake me just yet, perhaps. ✝ *The ways of the Lord are inscrutable*.

4 *November 1900*

Took Souf this morning to go into the dunes and gardens that lie between the road to Tuggurt and the one that goes to Debila. Steep paths leading to the dunetops overlooking deep gardens down below.

It rained last night; the sand was wet and yellowish in colour, and gave off a nice and cool, slightly salty smell.

On the monotonous-looking hillsides grows the odd succulent, a light green and spindly sort of sedum. In the gardens the carrots and peppers look like bright green carpets.

My life remains the same, monotonous and devoid of real changes. It has even become very sheltered, for I spend part of my time inside my house (which I consider as no more than temporary quarters as we are about to move) and part in Mansour's place. Often I go to the house of Abd-el-Kader, of whom I am growing truly fond. If I could come up with the odd book in his place, I would feel very gratified indeed.

As for Slimène, nothing has changed, and I grow more attached to him by the day, for he is truly turning into a member of my family, or rather *all the family I have got* ... May that last for ever, even over here among these perennially grey sands ...!

I occasionally stand still and marvel at my astounding destiny ...

In an oasis somewhere in the desert, after all those grandiose dreams of mine!

And how will it all end?

This December bears a curious resemblance to that of the disastrous year 1897. Same weather, same violent gusts of wind lashing against my face. In those days, I had the Mediterranean for a horizon, and I was still so young; even though recently bereaved I still had a full measure of *joie-de-vivre*.

I could never be content with the genteel pleasures of city life in Europe. The idea I had of heading for the desert to satisfy my strange need for both adventure and peace did require courage, but it was feasible and, as it turns out, inspired. As for domestic bliss, I have found it, and it seems to grow stronger day by day.

The only thing to threaten it is politics ... but alas! ☾ *Allah knows what is hidden in the heavens and on earth!* and no one can foretell the future.

Barely two weeks ago tonight I went to meet my *beloved* as far as the area south of Kouïnine.

I rode Souf in a darkness so grey it made my head spin.

Lost my way several times. Had strange impressions down in those plains, where the horizon seems to rise in the shape of dunes, and villages look like hedges made of djérid.

Was thinking about the passage in *Aziyadé* about Istanbul graves lit by dim and solitary lights, when I suddenly spotted the gate to the Teksebet cemetery's dome.

Poignant memories of the end of the ✝ *White Spirit*'s life have come to haunt me these last few days.

I am going to have a hard time getting through the winter without heat or money, for I am not at all able to leave this place.

I sat in the courtyard of the Elakbab Zawyia the other day, and marvelled at the strange scene I saw there: unusual-looking heads, those of sunburnt Chaambas from Troud in the South, half-covered in grey veils: the expres-

sion on their almost black faces was so spirited they looked ferocious ... in the dilapidated courtyard of the zawyia they all gravitated around that huge red-haired sheikh with his soft blue eyes[27] ...

My best memory of the South will no doubt be of that memorable day, the 3rd of December, when I had the good fortune to witness a breathtaking sight, the return of the great marabout Si Mahmoud Lachmi, a fascinating figure impossible to describe, whose strange personality had attracted me in Tuggurt. Si Lachmi is meant to have a strange hold over adventurous souls. On that winter morning, it was a heady experience to be engulfed by gunpowder, wild strains of music coming from the nefsaoua des bendar, frenetic shouts from the crowd welcoming one of the Prophet's descendants, and the frantic horses in the midst of all that smoke and uproar ...

24 December 1900 [Ramadan]

I have been feeling ill and weak, have had to cope with the side-effects of fasting, to say nothing of the far more serious matter of my financial problems, yet these Ramadan nights and mornings have quite unexpectedly brought me moments of a quiet and pleasurable serenity that borders on joy.

I see clearly now that the only way to lead a quiet life – which is not to say a happy one, for illness, misery and death exist – is to turn one's back on mankind with the exception of a tiny handful of chosen ones, still making sure one does not depend on them in any way.

Arab society as one finds it in the big cities, unhinged and vitiated as it is by its contact with a foreign world, does not exist down here. As for French civilisation ... from what I have been able to glean from the Infantry Lieutenant and especially the doctor, it has certainly gone downhill here.

Slimène is transferred to Batna; they must try to meet their debts.

28 January 1901, 8 a.m.

Once again, all has been shattered and destroyed: my indolent way of life has come to an abrupt end! No

32

more of the blissful serenity we had both begun to take for granted.

On the evening of the 23rd we found out by chance that Slimène was about to be relieved of his duties and sent back to Batna. It was a moment of unspeakable anguish and of near-despair ...

Nor was that all. To add to our sorrow at the thought of imminent departure and the hardships of life in Batna was our distress over our financial situation, and the hundred francs' worth of debts, which we could not even begin to pay.

A gloomy, sleepless night, spent drinking and smoking kif.

The next morning, a quick and worried visit to Sidi Lachmi. Found him surrounded by pilgrims about to leave for the sheikh of Nefta's great Ziara. Spent over an hour making small talk, while my mind was elsewhere and I had a lump in my throat. In the end I took the sheikh aside and agreed to come back with Slimène after the maghreb hour. I felt limp with exhaustion as I went home full trot, standing in the stirrups.

Found Slimène in a half-demented state, looking haggard and no longer aware of what he was doing. Went out on Souf that night shortly before maghreb.

We had a sinister ride by the uncertain light of a waxing moon. Very much afraid that Slimène might fall off his horse, anxious to know what the sheikh would do for us. We arrived at last, responded with impatience to the repeated greetings of Guezzoun and the other servants, and found ourselves seated all alone before the sheikh in that vast room with sand on the floor and low, powerful arches. A candle lit the great red carpet we were sitting on, which left the corners of the room in blurry shadows.

There was a ponderous silence. I could tell that my poor Rouh' could not speak and I myself felt as if I were being strangled.

I saw that Rouh' was crying and felt like bursting into tears myself.

Upset as I was, I tried for a long time to tell the sheikh about our predicament. He said nothing, looking overcome, as if his mind were elsewhere.

In the end the sheikh and I exchanged a glance. I tried to make mine as meaningful as possible in drawing his attention to Rouh', who was burning with fever and about to faint. The sheikh stood up and went into his house ... none too soon, for a glaze had come over Rouh's eyes by then.

A moment later the sheikh came back and put 170 francs in front of Rouh', saying: 'God will pay the rest.'

Without saying a word, without even taking the banknotes, Rouh' stared at them and began to laugh, a crazy laugh that frightened both the sheikh and myself.

I wondered whether he might be losing his mind altogether.

I stepped out for some air. From the rocky sand in front of me rose the eerie outlines of the little graveyard for the sheikh's children. Many an innocent creature lies asleep there; barely do these young souls come to life than they are whisked off again into the netherworld's dark, mysterious reaches. No sooner do their earthly eyes take in the sterile dunes along this vast horizon than they are dimmed at once.

I stopped among the piles of sand heaped up against the thick and heavily buttressed wall, and in that utter silence I saw a nocturnal animal I could not identify – perhaps a little desert fox – shoot by quite close to me. I raised my eyes to heaven and, on impulse, recited the fatiha under my breath.

I went back indoors. We left, feeling lighter of heart but wistful all the same ...

We were afraid we might lose our way among those vast stretches of cemetery and wan-looking dunes.

We did make our way home, though, via the village that lies to the east of the Ouled-Touati. As we came through the narrow path that overlooks the Hama Ayechi garden, the sight we saw was a curious one: the palm trees below us were all asleep in the shadows, yet there was the odd ray of silvery, occasionally vaguely pink light shining through their trunks.

It was nearly ten o'clock, and there was not a sound to break the silence in all that solitude and desolation.

The moon was setting as we entered the Ouled-Ahmed graveyard, and for an instant the only things visible by the

34

great dune's ridge were the crescent's two red points, a strange and disquieting sight; then they were gone and there was nothing but night and darkness.

We hardly made any headway for fear of stumbling and falling, for that road is littered with graves. When we had set off after the maghreb, there had been lamps burning all through the cemetery in those tiny grey necropolises, wan little flames in the falling dusk: it was a Friday night.

Everything was in shadow again by now, the lights were out and all those graves were slumbering in darkness. Oh, the thought of leaving that place and perhaps never seeing it again!

These days so full of sorrow and uncertainty have made me realise just how much I love this part of the world; the loss of this land of sun, sand, lush gardens and winds will be a bitter one.

Studied those curious cemeteries, in particular the one south of Tarzout: its tombs like pointed belljars, tiny koubbas in the shape of fortified towers, and all that picturesque profusion of necropolises that surrounds the twin cities of Tarzout and Guémar.

Had no trouble finding Sidi-el-Hussein's dilapidated zawyia. Had a depressing conversation, in that shabby-looking room giving onto a vast courtyard littered with stones in all sorts of odd shapes.

By the time I went into the outer courtyard, I spotted Rouh's red silhouette taking off along the road toward the market, and sent Ali after him.

Hearing our tales of woe and looking at Rouh's deathly pale face, the good sheikh wept at the thought that we would soon be parted.

Many a memory has created a bond between him and us. The times I rode to Amiche and Ourmès with him, the long talks we had and the mystery of our joint efforts ...

We left shortly before 'asr. We said goodbye in the dunes near Kouinine. Together with Ali I took the westward road for El Oued, skirting Kouinine on my left. A handful of women in blue veils were on their way home, bending under the weight of their guerbas loaded to the brim.

No sooner had we passed Kouinine than I turned around

and took off at a gallop by myself, in hopes of catching up with Slimène.

It was too late and I came home by sundown via the deserted road along the Sidi Abdallah cemetery.

Isabelle describes the arrest of the man who made an attempt on her life, an event she will detail in full in Journal Three.

9 February 1901

Around five o'clock this afternoon, Abdallah Muhammad[28] was put in a prison cell.

I saw him arrive and studied him while he was being searched by soldiers ... I had a poignant feeling of profound pity for the man, for he is but the blind instrument of a destiny he does not understand. And at the sight of his grey silhouette standing there head bowed between those blue uniforms, I had a sense of *mystery* that may well have been the strangest and most profound I have ever experienced.

Try as I may to feel any, I cannot find hatred for this man in my heart.

What I do feel for him is curious: whenever I stop to think about it, I have the feeling that I am in the presence of a mystery which may well *hold the key to the entire meaning of my life*. As long as I do not fathom that enigma – and will I ever! God alone can tell – I shall not know *who* I am, nor the *reason* for my curious life.

If my strange way of life were merely a *pose*, one could indeed say: 'She has asked for it ...' But that is not the case! No one has ever lived as haphazardly as I do, and it is the inexorable chain of events that accounts for my being where I am, events that are not of my making.

Perhaps the strange side of my nature can be summed up in a single trait: the need to keep searching, come what may, for new events, and flee inertia and stagnation.

JOURNAL THREE

Isabelle starts her third journal in the French Military Hospital where she is recovering from the attempt on her life. She is physically weak and morally dejected. Slimène is in Batna, where she joins him when she is recovered. She does not keep a chronological journal but goes back and forth in time, describing the murder attempt later than her convalescence.

'In the name of God, the all powerful,
the merciful!'

El Oued (February 1901)

The long and sleepless winter night seems endless in this deadly silence. It is dark and stifling here in this tiny, narrow hospital ward. The night light on the wall near the window throws a feeble light on the seedy decor: humid walls with a yellow base, two white army beds, a small black table and boards to hold books and bottles. An army blanket hides the window. Not a sound in the barracks' vast courtyard.

From time to time my sensitive invalid's ear picks up long and far-off barking and all is silent once again. Then comes the sound of soldiers marching, a clicking of rifle butts, a brief, impersonal command, while more footsteps go off in the direction of the infantry barracks. There has been a changing of the guard at the gate.

I lie here and languish all by myself. My injured, shattered head is burning and as for my badly wounded arm, it is giving me a lot of discomfort, and feels terribly heavy. I keep moving it around with my good right arm as best I can, but I am in pain no matter what I do with it, a nauseating sort of pain.

The details of that fatal day all suddenly come back to me. There I was, having received a blow on the head. The murderer stood in front of me, his arms raised high up. I could not tell what it was he had in his hands. I then began to moan and I was overcome with pain and nausea. My thoughts became muddled and suddenly everything grew dim.

Through the window over the door I can see wan moonlight shine on the building opposite where the autopsy ward is located, with its metal table and boxes full of disinfectants. I may well soon be lying on that hideous table myself. Not that I am afraid of death. What I do dread is suffering, long and absurd stretches of it, and also something vague, dark and sinister that hovers near me, something invisible that only I can see . . .

And should it be written, should it be my destiny to die right here in this timeless desert, no brotherly hand would come to close my eyes . . . In that last moment on earth, no brotherly lips would utter words of love and consolation.

21 February 1901, noon

Yesterday I went to Guemar for a visit to Sheikh Sidi-el-Hussein.

The wind had thrown a shroud of grey dust over all the palm trees and once again played havoc with the dunes between Kouïnine and Tarzout. Those sad little towns, Gara, Teksebet, Kouïnine, all seem so much more desolate and deserted when the great winds of winter do their blowing.

The Souf now looks wan under the pallid sky, and the dunes are at their most lacklustre. In the evening I sometimes hear magic sounds coming from the Messaaba, the poignant music of a tiny Bedouin flute.

In a mere few days' time I shall no longer hear those distant sounds.

The sound of the toubib's humming this morning suddenly brought me back to my stay in Tunisia – however dead all that is now and deeply buried under so many layers of grey ash, just like my life in the Sahara soon will be too.

38

I remember that September night two years ago, when Ali and I were leaning on our elbows by the little window at La Goulette; on one side I could hear the soft murmur of the placid sea, and on the other the clear and innocent voice of Sidi Béyène's little Noucha singing that sad Andalusian song:

☾ *My mind is gone, my mind is gone!*

Ali's warm and passionate, sonorous voice then took over the wistful refrain, as if in a dream, and all I did was listen ...

There are moments when I am suddenly reminded of the recent past like that, a period I rarely think of nowadays. Memories of Tunis in particular come to haunt me. Meaningless, forgotten street names come to mind for no good reason.

I went to my house today, and had an awful feeling of emptiness.

Going through the door I felt an inward shudder and thought: 'Rouh will never come in here again ...'

Never will we lie in each other's arms again in that tiny white vaulted room of ours, and sleep in close embrace as if we somehow knew that dark and hostile forces were trying to come between us. Never again will sensual ecstasy unite the two of us under that roof we have both held so dear.

Yes, the end has come.

In four days' time I too will head north, a place I would have been too happy never to see again.

The last of my wistful childish whims is to ask for burial right here in these white sands gilded at dawn and dusk by the scarlet sun ...

This part of the journal was written down in Marseilles, six months after the events it describes.

Marseilles, 8 July 1901, 9 p.m.

Departure from El Oued on Monday 25 February 1901 at 1.30 p.m.

26th – Reached Bir-bou-Chama by maghreb.

Black sky, grey night, a strong and icy north wind.

Caravan: Bach-hamar Sasi. Deïras: Naser and Lakhdar.

Infantryman: Rezki, Embarek, Salem and El Hadj Mohammed, from Guémar. Two mental patients accompanied by a young man (from Algiers). Hennia, Spahi Zouazouë's mother and her son Abdallah.

27th – Left on the 27th around 7 a.m. Reached Sif-el-Ménédi by five in the afternoon. Road: trees, plains consisting of mica and of talc, scrubs; a handful of shotts in the vicinity of the borj.

Sif-el-Ménédi: a borj set on a very low cliff, scrubby horizon. Well-tended garden, salt-water ponds near by. Excellent impression, similar to that of the Oued Rir's salt oases. Lakhdar's dromedary took off in the evening, and the deïra went to look for it. I felt exhausted, headache (walked one third of the way). Sat on my bed and thought how nice it would be to live in that borj for a while, with the vast maquis for a horizon. Children singing in the garden.

Isabelle is making her way to Batna to join Slimène.

Chagga, Friday 3 March 1901, 9 p.m.

Spent the night at Stah-el-Hamraïa. Spent the evening in the borj's main hall, listening to Lakhdar and the camel-drivers sing.

Bedded down with Khelifa and infantryman Rezki.

Set out on horseback. Terrain that varied between the salty and rocky kind. Shrubs of broom with white flowers, Sahara trees, little shrubs with blue flowers. A few shotts, salty soil and yellow sand. Dismounted by the first guemira.

A little before the guemira, in the maquis on the left, is a wonderfully cool wellspring. Bought some hares from hunters. Set off again on foot. Encountered several caravans. Spotted the tent of a captain in the Engineer Corps at the bottom of a hillside on the left.

Once again we caught sight of shott Meriri, a sea without a horizon, a milky expanse dotted with white islets.

1 March, Chagga.

Bedded down in the little room to the left, Khelifa, Rezki and myself. In the large room next door are Hennia and

40

her son. In the other one are the mental patients, their guide and the outcasts. The deïras sleep outdoors, with the camel-drivers, near the fountain.

In the nearby garden flooded with salt water, toads are croaking their melancholy song in the desert's silence.

All along the way this afternoon there was languorous bird song. Torrid heat all day.

Thought lovingly of the way the Sahara has bewitched me for life, and what bliss it will be to come back. Felt I was being bold in the face of destiny, and full of irrepressible energy.

Another thought has come to haunt me, and there is no sleep for my weary mind: there are ecstasies in store for me in Batna, and this is keeping me on tenterhooks of voluptuous expectation.

Day after tomorrow, that is to say in two days' time, I can give in to these physical cravings and spend whole nights in wild sensuality, the way we used to do in El Oued ... hold my master in my arms, hold him tight against the breast now suffering too much love and no gratification.

It has occurred to me tonight that I am still quite young, that life is not so black and dreary as all that and that I still have grounds for hope.

As long as the Sahara is there with its magnificent expanse, I will always have a refuge where my tormented soul can go for relief from the triviality of modern life.

Take Rouh' along to distant places, off into the desert, for the pursuit of bold adventures, and heady interludes.

Batna, 20 March, 11 p.m.

Reached Batna on the 18th at 8.30 p.m.

I do not mind the poverty, which has now become a fact, nor the cloistered existence among Arab women. I might even think it is a blessing to be so totally dependent on Rouh from now on. What torments me, though, and makes life almost unbearable is the sad and bitter fact that we are apart, and that I can only see him for a fleeting moment now and then. What do I care about the rest, when simply holding him in my arms as I did yesterday and looking into his eyes brings me back to life?

41

Without my being aware of it, the great love of my life, the one I did not think would ever appear, has actually come!

Batna, Tuesday 26 March, 1 p.m.

Took Souf for a ride today to the foot of the mountain, let the horse roam freely about the meadow, and stretched out underneath a pine tree.

I daydreamed with my gaze upon the great valley, the blue mountains opposite and Batna in its slum-like setting. A sensuous delight at being out of doors in the sun, far from the grey walls of my dreary prison. Everything is turning green again, the trees are in bloom, the sky is blue and countless birds are singing.

Where is that long-past autumn day when, eyes closed and with a peaceful heart (so much for human nature's utter blindness!) I listened to the strong wind rustle through the tough djerids of Debila's palm trees! Where is that Oued Souf of ours, with its white dunes and gardens, and Salah ben Taliba's peaceful house, a stone's throw from the dunes of Sidi-Mestour and the silent necropolis that is the Ouled-Ahmed's final resting place! Where is the land of holy zawyias and marabouts' graves, the harsh, magnificent land that feeds the flames of faith and where we found such bliss? Where is all that, and will I ever see it again?

Over here, my poverty is total ... No food, no money and no heat. Nothing!

The days all come and go, and blend into the past's black void; each new dawn brings us closer to the day of our deliverance, set for 20 February 1902, when real life will truly *begin* for the two of us at last.

Everything is in the hands of God, and nothing happens ☽ *against His will.*

Batna, Friday 12 April 1901, 5 p.m.

These days I go out every morning with my faithful Souf to spend a few hours of quiet in the open fields.

There I dismount and sit down by the edge of the road,

near a field of colza, at the foot of the dark Ouled-Abdi, for a smoke and time to dream; I hold on to Souf's bridle while he greedily grazes on the green blades of grass he carefully picks out among the flowers.

In the distance to the north, the outlines of the dreary city full of barracks and administrative buildings. My back is turned toward it and my gaze is on the countryside in bloom.

I have already come to know this place quite well, and it gives me moments of serenity and bliss.

The other night I was lying next to Slimène on Khelifa's mat. Through the window I could see the blue sky, a few clouds gilded by the setting sun, and the tops of trees that are suddenly green again: all of a sudden, I was reminded of the past, in a flash so keen it left me in tears. The overall landscape is so similar here that memories of *La Villa Neuve* keep haunting me.

Batna, 26 April 11 p.m.

I am feeling depressed tonight in a way I cannot define. I feel lonely without Ouïha, and cannot stand the boredom. Yesterday's storm has left Batna inundated, dark and freezing, and it is full of mud and filthy gutters. My poor Souf is very ill, so that I cannot even go for my strolls along the open road, or up to that desolate graveyard where damaged tombs, terrifying windows upon the spectacle of human dust, lie scattered among the fragrant tufts of grey chih near a green meadow full of purple flax, white anemones and scarlet poppies in full bloom.

The other day I wandered around among a crowd of Muslims brandishing the flags of ancient religious ceremonial occasions; to the accompaniment of tambours and flutes they prayed for rain, for an extension of their fleeting Algerian spring which already, in its haste to move on, is blending summer flowers with those of spring.

After six long days of only seeing Rouh' for brief and furtive moments by the gate of the hated barracks where he is quartered, he came to see me yesterday ... I held him in my arms and after the first wild, almost savage embrace, tears ran down our cheeks, and each of us felt a very

43

mysterious fear, even though neither of us had said a word or knew why.

I realised yesterday once again how honest and beautiful is my Slimène's soul, because of his joy that Augustin[30] was making up with me and was doing justice to us both. In spite of my past, present and future misfortunes I bless God and my destiny for having brought me to this desert and given me to this man, who is my *only solace*, my only reason for happiness in this whole world.

I have often been hard on him and unfair, I have been impatient for no good reason, so insane as to hit him, although secretly ashamed because he did not strike back but merely smiled at my blind rage. Afterwards I always feel truly miserable and disgusted with myself for the injustice I might have committed.

This afternoon I went to see the police official who is without a doubt an enemy spy in charge of keeping an eye on me. *He* was the first to come out with the theory that P[31] was the one who had wanted me killed, and that the murderer was bound to go scotfree. If so, that means I am doomed to die anywhere I go in the South, which is the only place where we can live.

If the crime committed at Behima is only slightly punished or not at all, that will amount to a clear signal to the Tidjanyas[32]: 'Go ahead and kill Si Mahmoud, you have nothing to fear.'

Yet God did stay the assassin's hand once, and Abdallah's sabre was deflected. If God wants me to die a martyr, God's will is bound to find me wherever I am. If not, the plots of all those who conspire against me will be their undoing.

I am not afraid of death, but would not want to die in some obscure or pointless way. Having seen death close up, and having felt the brush of its black and icy wings, I know that its proximity means instant renunciation of the things of this world. I also know that my nerves and willpower will hold out in times of great personal ordeals, and that I will never give my enemies the satisfaction of seeing me run in cowardice or fear.

Yet, as I think of the future, there is one thing that does frighten me: misfortunes that might befall Slimène or

44

Augustin. Faced with those, I would have no strength whatsoever. It would be hard to imagine worse poverty than the kind I am up against right now: yet the only reason it worries me is that our debts stand to spell disaster for Slimène.

Fortunately, my enemies think I am rich. I was right to spend money the way I did two years ago, here and in Biskra, for a reputation of wealth is just as useful for our defence as actual wealth would have been. Oh, if those rascals were to know that I am utterly destitute and that the slightest humiliation could be my undoing, they would not hesitate for a moment!

It is obvious that they are afraid. Otherwise they would arrest me as a spy, or expel me.

I was right to account for the wretched way I live down here as mere eccentricity: that way, it is not too obvious that I am in fact destitute.

I have begun to make a point of going to people's houses to *eat*, for the sole purpose of keeping fit, something that would have been *anathema* in the old days, like the other thing I have been doing lately, namely going to see marabouts, just to beg them for money.

I must have an iron constitution, for my health is holding up contrary to all expectation: those frightening last days in El Oued, the injury, the shock to the nervous system and the haemorrhage in Behima, the hospital, the journey, half of which I made on foot, my poverty here, the cold and the poor diet, which mostly consists of bread, none of that has got me down. How long will I be able to hold out?

How can one explain the fact that at home, where I had warm clothes, an outstandingly healthy diet, and Mummy's idolatrous care, the slightest chill I caught would degenerate into bronchitis; whereas here, having suffered freezing temperatures at El Oued, and at the hospital as well, having travelled in all kinds of weather, while literally always getting wet feet, going around in thin clothes and torn shoes, I don't even catch a cold?

The human body is nothing, the human soul is all.

Why do I adore Rouh's eyes so? Not for their shape or colour, but for the sweet and guileless radiance in their expression, which is what makes them beautiful.

The way I see it, there is no greater spiritual beauty than fanaticism, of a sort so sincere it can only end in martyrdom.

Isabelle was expelled from French North Africa after the trial of her would-be assassin.

Friday 3 May 1901, 9.45 a.m.

Found out last night that I am to be expelled again.

Everything has once again been shattered and destroyed.

I shall muster the courage needed to fight the injustice done to me, and hope to win with God's help.

Yet how can I go off, for God knows how long, and leave Rouh' with whom I am so close? How can I do without him?

Twice more shall we sleep in each other's arms. Twice more shall I see his beloved silhouette in the doorway of the shabby room we have come to cherish.

I will have the bliss of seeing Augustin again, but how can I survive without the presence of my sweet Zizou? His love and kindness have brought sunshine to this year's darkest hours; without him, all will be utterly gloomy.

After her expulsion, Isabelle makes her way once more to her brother's house in Marseilles.

6 May 1901

Left Batna and arrived at Bône at three in the afternoon. Spent the night of the 6th, the day and night of the 7th and 8th at Khoudja's house.

Written at Bône, 8 May 6 p.m.

No doubt about it, life without Slimène *will not do*. Everything is bleak and dreary, and time keeps dragging on. Poor Ouïha Kahla! Poor Zizou! When will I ever see him again?

Marseilles, 22 May 1901, 9 p.m.
Wednesday, departure

Sailed from Bône on Thursday 9th May on the *Berry*, of the Compagnie Générale des Transports Maritimes. Travelled fourth class under the name of Pierre Mouchet, deckhand.[33] Reached Marseilles on Saturday 12th, at 3 p.m. Disembarked at Le Môle. Took the tramway to the Rue d'Oran.

Tomorrow, when I will have recovered a bit from all the fatigue of these last two days, I shall write down a detailed description of my impressions of Bône, the crossing and the first few days in Marseilles. Tonight I only want to go into the *psychological* aspect of my recent experiences, for having started out in tears and apprehension, things have now suddenly taken a pleasant, *useful* turn and brought me strokes of good luck as, for instance, my amazing encounter with my old friend Sousse Abd-el-Aziz-Agreby, an encounter that may well bring a considerable improvement in Ouiha's predicament and my own; perhaps he will wangle some concession from Algiers; perhaps he will find someone to take Slimène's place in Tunisia? He will quite probably start reimbursing me for part of what he owes me, little by little.

There has been no decree expelling me from the country. That means I can go back and join Slimène again as soon as I can find the means to travel, and the Military Court will provide me with those before June 18th. In the meantime I must sit down and do my Russian work and finish it, for which I have now got the time.

The horizon has cleared up a good deal all around. After my strange encounter with Abd-el-Aziz, I felt *true friendship* for him. A feeling of great happiness and real emotion.

Perhaps he was sent by God to help me through this difficult period in my life!

I think of Slimène, and this may well be the *first* time I do so in *reasonable* terms.

Yes, once I am back with him again, I must start behaving differently towards him right away, so that our happiness as a couple is not jeopardised, since marriage must not be based only on love. No matter how deep and

47

strong, love alone is not a solid enough foundation. I must go out of my way to show him how devoted I am to him, and must let my kindness outweigh his bitter hardships.

I must learn to hold my temper and restrain my selfishness and violence in order not to tax his patience. I must learn the very thing that is hardest for someone of my temperament, namely obedience (which of course has its limits and must on no account turn into servility), thus making life so much easier for the two of us. To put it in a nutshell, I must change my ways and become easier to live with, which will not be too hard to do, what with Slimène's easy good nature and his patience.

Isabelle retrospectively describes her journey to Marseilles, starting from her departure from Batna.

I left the house on 6th of May at dawn; quiet in the streets. Went as far as the entrance to the railway station with Slimène, Labbadi and Khelifa. Sat briefly on a bench in Avenue de la Gare. I turned back one last time for another look at that beloved red silhouette as it already lost its contours in the shadows.

We parted without too much anguish, because we both had the feeling we would soon see each other again.

How I now miss Batna, city of sorrow, love and exile, where my poor good-hearted friend has stayed behind ... the same goes for Souf, my valiant and loyal horse, my mute companion on those unforgettable rides through the beloved dunes.

Bône's magic charm seems to have evaporated and I would not set foot in the place if it were not for † *The White Spirit*'s grave!

Once on the *Berry* I sat up front, disguised as Pierre Mouchet in my wretched sailor's outfit, and felt as sad as an emigrant being banished from his native soil. I was suddenly unable to fight back my tears, and had no place to go and hide them. The other passengers all seemed surprised, but did not smile. Felt profound distress at the view of that lively, colourful quay, reddish ramparts, and sacred green hill with its black cypresses. Felt a sharp twinge of pain at the thought that there, in the early dusk, was Africa vanish-

48

ing from sight, the ardently beloved soil that harbours both the glorious Sahara and Slimène.

My stay in Bône was so brief and fleeting, and above all so agitated and tormented, it might as well have been a nightmare.

Sitting on my bundle by the windlass, I mulled over the hopeless poverty I have come to, the utter destitution that will now be mine. Thought also of the settings I grew up in, the days long past when I was well off and would indulge my taste for dressing as a sailor, of all things.

Made my bed on the spot because it offered a bit of warmth, and dozed off.

Was awakened by a violent storm. Took my rags under the bridge, near the lamp depot. Was told to scram, and wandered around in the torrential rain.

Found shelter near the bow at last, thanks to a kind-hearted sailor, together with two Neapolitans and an old man on his way back from Japan, dressed in a black Arab kachébia.

Set off in search of some water. Drank from the reservoir! Had a fairly good night, lying on the floor. Slept all of the next day (10 May) till four in the afternoon. We were about to hit bad weather; the elderly Neapolitan was feeling seasick. A heavy swell drove me behind the anchor windlass. The ill-tempered ship's boy put me on top of a pile of ropes, on the starboard side.

Violent storm all night long, much heavy tossing and pitching, huge amounts of water taken in by the bow and constantly crashing down on deck with a thunderous roar. An awful night; kept getting splashed, the wind kept wailing and howling, huge waves kept roaring and rumbling.

Of all the *desperately* lucid thoughts I had that night so full of fever and delirium, I remember one in particular:

'This is the voice of Death bellowing[34] and lashing out against the *Berry*, a poor little hull shaken and tossed about like a mere feather on these hostile waters.'

All the passengers from the upper deck went down to third class during the night. Was left all by myself, cut off by the constant cataracts thunderously heaving above my head and hitting the deck, which made it impossible for me to pass without running the risk of being crushed.

It was clear and sunny when we docked that afternoon. Quietly took the tramway and dragged my bags all the way on foot.

Stunned at the lack of news from Slimène. Awoke with a sudden start in the middle of the night, in such a state of anguish I almost went to wake Augustin.

Not a moment's peace all morning, till Slimène's telegram arrived. It gave me the courage needed to bear the latest of my ordeals, the hardest of them all: the fact that we are apart.

A sense of contentment over here, in finding, if not affluence, at least the security of a certain comfort that, compared to my own degree of poverty, feels like wealth.

Old lively memories have come back to me, of the time I spent here in November 1899. Listening to the Marseilles church bells just now took me back to those days when Popowa and I would wander around the city, a place I love dearly but would not want to live in.

Who will give me back my Souf, though, with its white zawyias, its tranquil homes and grey cupolas, its boundless sandy stretches? And who will give me back Slimène, the friend and lover who is all the family I have on earth?

(*Copied and completed on 25th May.*)

Marseilles, 3 June 1901, 9 p.m.

I want to leave as soon as I can, go and join Slimène and never leave him again; do all I can to keep him, for I now know that he is all I have left in this world and that life is not worth living without him. Augustin, to be sure, does all he can for me, but that marriage of his has put a permanent wedge between us, and I can no longer rely on him the way I used to feel I could. And then there is the *thoughtlessness* of that wife of his, which is to be expected from someone as vulgar as that, which rules out any life in common with them for me.

The only person with whom I have been able to live in harmony is Slimène. I look forward to the moment of our reunion as to a time of *deliverance*.

As it would in no way affect the impending trial, if the money from El Agreby comes in Wednesday's mail, I might leave for Philippeville on Saturday to be with Slimène a week earlier and cut short the state of anguish I have been in since leaving Batna a whole month ago.

I will have to try and organise my life there in such a way as to make it bearable, especially if we are to stay in Batna for a certain length of time. When I go back after the trial we will only have eight more months of misery ahead of us, at the end of which lies our marriage and freedom. God has always had mercy on us so far and has never let us down even when things were at their worst.

I find that I have been through a period of *incubation*, and the odd result is beginning to show: I have a better understanding of people and of things, and my life's out-look is less bleak, although still infinitely sad.

Life is not just a constant struggle against circumstances, but rather *against ourselves*. That's an age-old adage, but most people simply ignore it: hence all the discontent, evil and despair.

The mind has vast power over itself, and actually exer-cising that power enhances it further.

Suffering is often the very thing it takes to release that power. Suffering is a positive thing, for it sublimates the emotions and produces great courage or devotion; it creates the capacity for strong feelings and all-encompassing ideas.

I now see that there is one thing I have never understood and never will: *Augustin's character and the kind of life he leads.* Has he become like this, or has he always been this way? He is getting more and more set in his ways and stuck in his present situation, which leaves no room for any intellectual development and strikes me as being alien and unpalatable.

What, then, lies in store for his child who looks so like me and, I am sure, although I cannot say why, will have a character very similar to mine ... Poor little Helen, I feel both *touched* and *frightened* by the resemblance! No doubt you will never get to know me, for I shall not be a presence in the house where you will grow up.

What became of the *affinity* that existed between

51

Augustin's temperament and my own? The closer I look, alas, the less I can find it!

O Slimène, Slimène, stay the way you were for ten whole months; you are all I have left!

Marseilles, Tuesday 4 June, noon

Had a terrible night doubting everything, especially Rouh'; felt so tormented I thought I might lose my mind.

I blew out my lamp at two o'clock and dozed for a while. Woke up with a start at three o'clock feeling inexplicably frightened, a prelude to the hideous state of despair that lasted until broad daylight.

Irritability, anguish, frayed nerves and a grief so sharp I felt I might go mad; all the rewards of this latest visit here. And my heart yearns for Slimène more and more every day. There, too, I will know hardship, poverty, boredom and chronic deprivation ... But I will also have the vast solace of knowing he is there, seeing him and hearing him speak to me, of having someone in whom to confide all my troubles and thoughts, who understands me almost completely.

I have a glimmer of hope that there may be some Russian assignment for me, which would improve things considerably.

Oh! If Atabek were to send me 20 francs and Agreby 30, I could leave on Friday, go to Batna and put an end to this intolerable state of affairs.

Anything, my God, anything to see him again, even for the odd glimpse by the barracks gate, as when he was on duty during the week!

Marseilles, Friday 7 June 1901

May 6th, publication of my letter concerning the Behima episode in the *Dépêche Algérienne*.

Sent letter of rectification on the 7th.

TEXT OF BOTH LETTERS

Sir,

On June 18th next, a native by the name of Abdallah ben Si Mohammed ben Lakhdar, from the village of Behima

near El Oued (district of Tuggurt) will appear before the Military Court at Constantine for trial. He stands accused of murder, or rather of attempted murder, and his guilt is an established fact.

I myself was the victim of his deed, which almost cost me my life.

I have been quite surprised to find no mention of the affair in the Algerian press, despite the fact that it is one of the strangest and most mysterious cases ever to have been tried in an Algerian court. I can only suppose that the press has been left in the dark about the facts. I believe that for the sake of justice and truth the public ought to learn a number of details before it comes to trial. I would be most obliged if you would be so kind as to publish this letter under my name. The responsibility for its contents is entirely mine.

I should like to preface my story with a few facts, in order to clarify the tale that follows.

The investigating magistrates have repeatedly expressed their surprise at hearing me describe myself as a Muslim and an initiate of the Kadriya brotherhood at that; they also have not known what to make of my going about dressed as an Arab, sometimes as a man, and at other times as a woman, depending on the occasion, and on the requirements of my essentially nomadic life.

In order to avoid giving the impression that I am merely following in the footsteps of Dr Grenier[35] or that in donning a costume and adopting some religious label I might be inspired by some ulterior motive, I wish to state unequivocally that I have not been baptised and have never been a Christian; although a Russian citizen, I have been a Muslim for a very long time in fact. My mother, a Russian aristocrat, died in Bône in 1897 after having become a Muslim and now lies buried in the Arab cemetery there.

Consequently I have never had reason either to have to become a Muslim or to falsely pretend that I am one. My Algerian fellow Muslims are so well aware of this fact that Sheikh Muhammad-el-Houssein, brother of the naib of the Ouargla brotherhood, Si Muhammad Taïeb, has had no misgivings about initiating me himself once I had been given a preliminary initiation by one of his mokkadem.

53

The reason for my explaining all this is to nip in the bud any suggestion that the motive for Abdallah's attempt on my life lies in a fanatical hatred of anything Christian, for I am not a Christian and the Souafas, including Abdallah, all know it!

What follows is a description of the attempt made on my life, at three in the afternoon on 29th January. It took place in the house of a certain Si Ibrahim ben Larbi, a landlord in the village of Behima, 14 kilometres to the north of El Oued along the road to the Tunisian Djerid.

I had visited El Oued at the time of my first journey into the Constantine part of the Sahara, in the summer of 1899, and had a vivid memory of the area's immaculate white dunes, lush gardens and shady palm groves. In August 1900 I went to live there for an indefinite period of time. That was where I was initiated into the Kadrya brotherhood, and became a regular visitor to the three zawyias located near El Oued, having won the friendship of the three sheikhs, sons of Sidi Ibrahim and brothers of the late naïb of Ouargla. In January I accompanied one of them, Si Lachmi, to the village of Behima. He was on his way to Nefta in Tunisia with a group of khouans for a ziara at the grave of his father, Sidi Ibrahim. For reasons of my own I could not go as far as Nefta, but accompanied the sheikh to Behima where the pilgrims were to spend the night. I expected to return to El Oued that same evening with my manservant, a Sufi who had followed me on foot. We entered the house of the man named ben Larbi, and the marabout withdrew to another room for the afternoon prayer. I myself stayed in a large hall giving on to an antechamber that led into the public square, where there was a dense crowd and where my servant was looking after my horse. There were five or six Arab figures of note, both from the village and the surrounding area, most of them Bhamania khouans.

I was sitting between two of them, the owner of the house and a young tradesman from Guemar, Ahmed ben Belkassem. The latter had asked me to translate three commercial telegrams, one of which was badly written and gave me a great deal of trouble. My head was bent in concentration, and the hood of my burnous covered my

54

*turban, so that I could not see what was going on in front
of me. I suddenly felt a violent blow to my head, followed
by two more to my left arm. I looked up and saw a poorly-
dressed man who was not a member of the group. He was
waving a weapon above my head that I took to be a
truncheon. I leapt to my feet and rushed to the opposite
wall for Si Lachmi's sabre. The first blow had landed on
the top of my head, however, and so had left me dazed. I
sank onto a travelling trunk, with a sharp pain in my left
arm.*

*A young Kadrya mokaddem named Si Mohammed ben
Bou Bekr and a servant of Sidi Lachmi's named Saad
disarmed the assassin, but he managed to free himself.
When I saw him coming toward me, I stood up and tried to
grab the sabre again, but could not because my head was
spinning and the pain in my arm was too sharp. The man
ran out into the crowd, shouting: 'I am going to get a gun
and finish her off.' Saad then showed me a sword whose
blade was dripping with blood, and said: 'That's what that
dog used to attack you with!'*

*Alerted by the commotion, the marabout came running
in, and he was immediately given the name of the assassin
by the people who had recognised him. He sent for Behima's
independent sheikh who, like the assassin, belongs to the
Tidjanya brotherhood.[36] It is common knowledge that the
latter are the Kadryas' staunchest adversaries in the desert.
The sheikh in question stubbornly resisted the marabout's
request with various ploys, telling him that the murderer was
a sherif[37], etc. etc. The marabout publicly threatened to tax
him with complicity in the eyes of the Arab Bureau, and
insisted that the assassin be arrested on the spot and taken
away. The sheikh finally did so, but with very bad grace.*

*The culprit was taken into the same room where I had
been put down on a mattress. He first pretended to be mad,
but was caught out by his own fellow citizens who knew
him to be a sane and sensible figure. He then said God had
sent him to kill me. I was fully conscious and knew that I
had no idea who the man was. I began to interrogate him
myself and he said he did not know me either, had never set
eyes on me but had come to kill me nevertheless. He said
that if he were set free, he would attempt it again. When I*

55

asked him what he had against me, he replied: 'Nothing whatsoever, you have done me no wrong, I don't know you, but I must kill you.' When the marabout asked him whether he knew that I was a Muslim he said he did.

His father, when summoned, said they were Tidjanyas. The marabout forced the local sheikh to inform the Arab Bureau, and asked for an officer to come and fetch the culprit and start an investigation, and for a medical officer for me.

The investigating officer, a lieutenant from the Arab Bureau, and the doctor showed up by eleven o'clock. The doctor found my head wound and the injury to my left wrist to be superficial; I owed my life to sheer luck: a laundry-line just above my head had cushioned the first blow, which would otherwise have been certainly fatal. My left elbow, however, had been cut to the outside bone; both the muscle and the bone had been severely slashed. I had lost so much blood in the six hours that I was so weak I had to be kept in Behima for the night.

The next day I was taken by stretcher to the military hospital at El Oued, where I remained till February 26th. Despite Dr Taste's efforts, I left the hospital a cripple for life, unable to use my left arm for anything at all strenuous.[38]

At the time of my first journey I had run into difficulties with the Arab Bureau at Tuggurt, which oversees the one at El Oued, difficulties that were due solely to the suspicious attitude of the Tuggurt Bureau. The head of the Arab Bureau at El Oued, its officers, those at the garrison and the army doctor have all been extremely good to me and I should like to express my thanks to them publicly.

The investigation showed that for five days before committing his crime, Abdallah had tried to buy firearms, but had been unable to find any. The day we arrived in Behima, he had transferred his family – the poor devil has young children – and his belongings to the house of his father, where he had not lived for six years. Although both father and son were prominent Tidjanyas, they had both suddenly withdrawn from their brotherhood; the father told me he was a Kadrya, and the son told the investigating magistrate he was a member of the Mouley-Taïeb brotherhood. The police officer, Lieutenant Guillot, established that Abdallah was telling a lie.

*A few days before I left El Oued there was a rumour
among the native population that shortly before the crime
Abdallah, who had been riddled with debts, had gone to
Guemar (the Tidjanya centre) and that upon his return he
had settled his debts and even bought a palm grove.*

*Abdallah's father went to Sidi Lachmi's zawyia, and said
in the presence of witnesses that his son had been bribed to
attack me, but that as he did not know the identity of the
instigators, he was seeking permission to speak to his son
in the presence of an official to urge him to tell all. The
marabout advised him to go to the Arab Bureau. The old
man also asked one of my servants if he could speak to me,
and told me: 'This crime was not our doing'; he also said
he was anxious to see his son and persuade him to come
clean. Those are the facts.*

*Now it is clear that Abdallah was not motivated by any
hatred of Christians, but that he was acting with premedi-
tation and on behalf of other people. I told the investigating
authorities that in my view the attempted murder can best
be explained by the hatred the Tidjanyas feel for the
Kadryas,[39] and that the reason for the Tidjanya kabal or
khouans wanting to do away with me was that they knew
their enemies loved me – witness the khouans' grief at
hearing about the crime. As I passed through the villages
around El Oued on a stretcher on my way to the hospital,
the inhabitants, men and women alike, all came to the road
to shout and wail the way they do for funerals.*

*I trust the Military Court at Constantine will not merely
try Abdallah ben Mohammed and let it go at that, but will
also attempt to clear up the mystery surrounding the affair.*

*It seems to me that Abdallah acted at someone else's
behest, and I would not see much point in having him
solely take the blame, nor would anyone else who cares
about justice and truth.*

*It is not Abdallah who should be standing trial but
rather those who were behind him, the true culprits, whoever they may be.*

*I trust, Sir, that you will not refuse to publish this letter
in your worthy newspaper, for I believe it to be of some
interest. From the political, if not the social point of view,
the Algerian Tell is not all that different from the other*

French provinces; however, the same cannot be said of the Sahara, where life is very different indeed, to a degree that people in France can hardly begin to imagine.

ISABELLE EBERHARDT

Marseilles, 7 June 1901

Sir,

I should like to thank you most sincerely for having published my long letter dated May 29th. I should add that I could hardly have expected less from a newspaper with your reputation for impartiality: the Dépêche Algérienne has always shown considerable moderation, compared with the excesses that have unfortunately become standard policy for other Algerian publications. It seems to me, however, that as the question of foreigners residing in Algeria is such a burning topic at the moment, I ought to expand upon my earlier letter for those who have taken the trouble to read it.

You have credited me with an honour I do not deserve in the least – that is, your assertion that I have a certain degree of religious influence on the native population in the district of Tuggurt. In actual fact I have never had, nor tried to have, any political or religious role, for I feel I have neither the right nor the requisite competence to meddle with anything as serious and complex as matters of religion in areas of that nature.

At the time I set off for Tuggurt in 1899, I felt it was my duty to go and see Lieutenant-Colonel Tridel, who was in charge of the district of Biskra, and inform him of my departure. This officer gave me a most cordial reception and, with military forthrightness, asked me point-blank whether I was an English Methodist by any chance. I showed him my papers, which are all in order and which leave no doubt about the fact that I am Russian and have permission from the imperial authorities to live abroad. I also gave Lt. Col. Tridel my opinions on the subject of English missions in Algeria, and told him that I have no use for proselytising of any sort and certainly not for that brand of hypocrisy that is so characteristic of the English and holds even less appeal for Russians than it does for the French.

58

The officer I found to be in charge of the Arab Bureau in Tuggurt in the absence of the commanding officer was a captain by the name of De Susbielle, a strange and, if I may say so, awkward figure. Once again I had to establish that I was no English miss in Arab disguise, but a Russian writer. One would think that if there is one country where a Russian ought to be able to live without being suspected of dubious intentions, that country should be France!

The officer in charge of the El Oued Bureau, Captain Couvet, saw for himself over a six-month period that there was nothing to be held against me, apart from my eccentricity and a lifestyle that is perhaps a bit unexpected for a young girl like myself, but quite innocuous just the same. It did not occur to him that my preferring a burnous to a skirt, and dunes to the homestead could present any danger to the public welfare in the district annex.

As I have stated in my earlier letter, both the Souafas belonging to Sidi Abd-el-Kader's brotherhood and those of other ones friendly to it have all let me know how sorry they were to hear there had been an attempt on my life. The reason these good people all had a certain affection for me is that I had helped them as best I could and had used what little medical knowledge I had to treat the ophthalmia, conjunctivitis and other complaints that are endemic to the area. I had attempted to be of some help in my vicinity, and that was the extent of my role in El Oued.

Hardly anyone in the world is without a passion or mania of some sort. To take as an example my own gender, there are women who will do anything for beautiful clothes, while there are others who grow old and grey poring over books to earn degrees and status. As for myself, all I want is a good horse as a mute and loyal companion, a handful of servants hardly more complex than my mount,[40] and a life as far away as possible from the hustle and bustle I happen to find so sterile in the civilised world where I feel so deeply out of place.

I am not involved in politics, nor am I an agent for any particular party, for as I see it, they are all mistaken in their exertions. I am just a dreamy eccentric anxious to lead a free, nomadic life, which I hope to try and describe in writing some day. The intrigues, stratagems and betrayals

*that characterise Le Roux's Sonia are as alien to me as is
her character as a whole. Nor do I bear the faintest resemblance to the English Methodist I was taken for.*

*It is of course true that in the summer of 1899 it was
unusually hot in the Sahara, and that mirages will distort
many a perspective and account for many an error!*

I.E.

At long last I am almost certain of being able to leave on
Friday. That means being here for only another seven days.
I am sure that Augustin will do all he can to procure me the
money I need.

Poor Augustin! However enigmatic he may seem, he is
good to me and nothing in the world will ever succeed in
killing the deep and everlasting affection I feel for him. Oh!
what a pity that marriage of his makes it impossible for
him to come and join Slimène and myself for a truly wonderful life!

It is best, though, for everyone concerned that I leave,
and at the end of this week I shall have the inexpressible
joy of seeing Slimène again, of holding him in my arms and
☾ if Allah is willing, never leaving him again.

Spent the better part of last night feeling abominably ill;
dizziness and awful headache.

Once in Batna, I will have to do my best to save every
penny I can, be reimbursed as much money as possible and
above all, work in Russian: that way lies the only chance I
have of earning an income fairly soon. That will not be too
trying, providing my health holds out after the frightful
shocks it has had. To work so that I can stay with Ouïha,
that is my duty. He will some day find a way to make it up
to me for the hard work I shall do.

This evening I wrote a letter for Ahmed Cherif and as I
was doing so, I remembered the Autumn of 1899.

What became of the life of mystery and adventure I led
then in the Sahel's vast olive groves?[41]

How very strange the names I knew so well now sound
to me: Monastir, Sousse, Moknine, Esshyada, Ksasr, Ibellal,
Sidi N'eidja, Beni-Hassane, Anura, Chrahel, Melloul, Grat-
Zuizoura, Hadjedj ... What became of that incomparable
country, an African version of Palestine with its lush green

meadows and little white villages lying reflected in the blue water of its tranquil bays?

What became of Sousse, with its Moorish white ramparts and revolving beacon, and of Monastir, where waves never cease to roar and break upon the reefs?

Isabelle returns to Constantine to attend her aggressor's trial. She describes her arrival in Constantine, her meeting with Slimène, the arrival of Si Lachmi and his Khouans, and the trial.

Arrived in Constantine on Saturday 15th at ten past nine. Went to the Café Zouaouï. Set out with Hamou the porter to look for Ben-Chakar. Located him around noon. In the evening, Café Sidi Ksouma. Sunday 16th, six o'clock train, met Ouiha. Night at Hôtel Metropole, rue Basse Damremont. Monday 17th, arrival of Sidi Lachmi.

The 18th, 6 a.m. – Trial. Came out at eleven. Thursday 20th, left for Philippeville at 6.30. Arrived there at 9.35. Night at Hôtel Louvre.[42]

Before leaving, she made the following statement concerning her expulsion:

ISABELLE'S STATEMENT

As I have already pointed out, both to the investigating authorities and in my two letters to the Dépêche Algérienne, *I have always thought, and will continue to think that Abdallah ben Si Mohammed ben Lakhdar was a mere tool in the hands of others who felt it was in their interest, real or imaginary, to get rid of me. It is obvious that if he was indeed bribed to kill me, which is what he told his father at the time of his arrest, he could not expect to reap any benefits from his deed, for he committed it in a house full of people whom he knew to be on friendly terms with me. He knew he would be arrested, in other words. It is therefore clear that Abdallah is mentally unbalanced and a lunatic. He has said he is sorry and even asked me for forgiveness during the trial. I therefore feel that today's*

61

verdict is out of all proportion, and wish to state that I deplore its severity. Abdallah has a wife and children. I am a woman and can only feel bottomless pity for the widow and orphans. As for Abdallah himself, I feel deeply sorry for him.

At the end of this morning's trial I have had the painful surprise of learning that the Governor-General has issued a decree expelling me from the country. According to the terms of the decree, I am being banned from all Algerian territory, whether under civilian or military control. I can only wonder about the rationale for this measure. I am a Russian citizen and can in all good conscience say that I have done nothing to deserve it. I have never participated in or had any knowledge of any anti-French activities either in the Sahara or in the Tell. On the contrary, I have gone out of my way to defend the late naïb of Ouargla, Sidi Mohammed Taïeb, who died a hero's death fighting alongside the French, against the accusations made by a handful of Muslims who have argued that the naïb had betrayed Islam by installing the French at In-Salah. Wherever I have been, I have always spoken favourably of France to the natives, for I consider it my adoptive country. That being so, why am I being expelled? Not only does this measure offend my Russian sensibilities, it also puts me in a particularly painful situation as it will separate me from my fiancé for months to come; he is a non-commissioned officer at the Batna garrison, and is therefore not free to leave. I could perhaps have understood my being banned from territories under military control, in order to avoid my falling victim to revenge from Abdallah's tribe. I have no intention of returning to the South, however. All I ask is to be allowed to live in Batna and marry the man who was at my side during my ordeal and is my only source of moral support. That is all ...

Thursday 4 July 1901, noon

Zouïzou has left on the *Touareg*. Day of gloom, utter boredom, anguish and despair. When will we see each other again?

Isabelle now returns to a description of her previous arrival in Algeria.

Marseilles, 5 July 1901

I had that feeling of well-being, of *rejuvenation* I always get when reaching the blessed coast of my African fatherland, a feeling so at odds with the way I react every time I reach Marseilles. My arrivals here are as depressing as the ones over there are cheerful!

Mountains, fertile slopes and plains until Constantine's magnificent rocks appeared on the horizon at last.

We disembarked at the station. I went into the Café Zouanouï at last, feeling embarrassed with my roumi's cap on. Stayed for quite a while and talked with the owner, an inveterate smoker of kif. I then set out with hamel Hantou to look for Mohammed ben Chakar. Steep and narrow winding streets, squares on a slope, intricate cross-roads, silent, shady corners, the immaculate, ornately carved porchways of old mosques, covered bazaars, it all went to my head the way ancient Arab decors always do.

We wandered around and asked ... At long last we found Ben Chakar's abode: way at the top of an alleyway's steps, a cul-de-sac with a floor made of wooden beams above it at barely six feet above the ground, the floor of a dark sort of den where one had to walk bent over for four or five yards. Suddenly we came upon a Moorish interior, bluish-white in colour just like the ones at Bône.

Mohammed ben Chakar's brother smokes chira as well as kif; he sometimes works as a porter, sometimes as a café-owner or a fritter-vendor, very congenial. Nice too was his wife, bright and mannish.

In the afternoon Ben Chakar and I set off for the Gorges du Rhummel, vertiginous chasms with frail-looking bridges hung across them, often in the shadows, subterranean stairways and endless labyrinths.

Met a few Constantinian craftsmen. Went to the Jewish baths, had great fun splashing about like overgrown children. Came back by the road above the abyss, along the shore opposite the city.

Went to Sidi Ksouma's café in the evening, and had the

distinct feeling that *Zouïzou was in Constantine*. Sat in a corner in my Arab garb, which made me feel at ease, and listened to the singing and beating of the tambourine until quite late. Feast of Beldia, pale, distinguished faces, empty of expression, eyes half-closed ...

Had a bad night, due to anxiety and *fleas* ...

Sunday, 16 June – Went to the station in vain.

By evening, still no news from Zouïzou; in desperation went to the station with Elhadj at 6.35 p.m. to meet the train from Philippeville. In discouragement we sat down on a stone and waited. Elhadj spotted Ouïha at last, in native civilian garb. Went for supper at Ben Chakar's, dressed as a Moorish woman and after that went to the Hotel Metropole, far away in the Rue Basse-Damrémont.

A night of bliss, tenderness and peace.

Early next morning, Monday 17th, went to the station to meet Sidi Lachmi. Spotted the tall figures of the Souafa witnesses in front of the station: Hama Nine, Muhamad ben Bou Bekr and Ibrahim ben Larbi.

Felt terribly moved at the sight of those *countrymen* of mine, who spoke with their local accent and all embraced me with tears in their eyes.

Went out onto the platform with the group of Souafas to welcome our beloved Grand Sheikh,[43] who smiled when he saw me.

Went on an endless search for a hotel with Hama Nine. Hostile refusals everywhere. Found temporary accommodations at the Metropole at last. Felt very comforted in being reunited with the sheikh, Bechir and all the others. Problems at the hotel. Transfer of the Nomads' *Zawyia* to the Hotel Ben Chimou, on the Marché du Chameau, near the theatre.

Spent the night in some Jewish furnished room, 6 Rue Sidi-Lakhdar, on the second floor.

On Tuesday the 18th, we arrived at the courthouse at 6.30 a.m. The guard brought me a cup of coffee in the witnesses' waiting room where I was by myself, an object of curiosity for the growing crowd of passers-by, officers, and ladies.

I saw Abdallah, in handcuffs, flanked by an escort of Zouaves.

Captain Martin, the Government Commissioner, came to shake my hand, as did his sister. At seven o'clock, the bailiff came to fetch me. The courtroom was packed. I did not feel too intimidated, and sat down next to Sidi Lachmi. Our two chairs faced the double row of witnesses on their benches. Not exactly run of the mill, those witnesses in their box: tanned, expressive faces, garbed in clothes either white or dark, with a single contrasting burnous the colour of blood, one worn by that traitor Mohammed ben Abdel-rahman, sheikh of Behima. Sidi Lachmi was dressed in green and white.

The court: a group of uniforms, medal-bedecked torsos, stiff and impassive in their attitude. Arms were presented; the presiding judge timidly opened the trial with a frail and quavering voice. The court clerk read the charges and called out the witnesses' names, starting with myself. We then were made to file out of the room one by one.

In the witnesses' room, Captain Gabrielli and the young lieutenant who is his secretary came to shake my hand. We talked for quite a while. Someone came to fetch me.

The judge was about to call the witnesses. The bailiff told me to stand in front of the presiding judge, and I was made to repeat the oath.

Still shy, the judge kept stammering as he questioned me on the basis of his notes. It did not take long. The interpreter called Abdallah and asked him: 'Have you anything to say to so-and-so?' 'No', was Abdallah's firm and simple reply despite everything that had been said, 'all I have to say is that I ask her to forgive me.'

I returned to my seat. Sidi Lachmi came in and testified in a simple and unruffled way. After that came the sheikh, who was followed by Ben Bou Bekr, Ibrahim ben Larbi, and then the assassin's father, simpering as usual.

After a five-minute recess we heard Captain Martin's speech for the prosecution which, although based on a theory that must be erroneous, was a vibrant plea in favour of the Kadryas and myself. The lawyer for the defence, whom I could not bear, spoke next. Reply from Captain Martin, and further words from the lawyer. The court withdrew. The room was buzzing with voices.

Isabelle begins to experience feelings of mysticism during this period.

I am going through a period of composure, both physical and emotional, of intellectual awakening and hope *without frenzy*, and time is going by fairly fast, which is the main thing just now.

Since that notorious trial in Constantine, I have felt a strong literary urge coming to the fore. My gift for writing is really reviving these days. I used to have to wait, sometimes for months on end, to be in the mood to write. Now I can almost sit down and write any time I want. I think, in fact, that I have reached a point where the potential I had been aware of all along has now begun to blossom.

As for my religious feelings, my faith is now truly genuine, and I no longer need to make the slightest effort. Before I go to sleep at night, I look deep down into my conscience, and never fail to find the blissful peace there that comes from the mysterious knowledge that will henceforth be my strength.

Two things are holding my attention at the moment: first my need for progress in the intellectual domain.

I must read certain books, in the vein of *Essais de psychologie contemporaine* by Bourget. As soon as I am settled in, I must register with a good library and re-read the *Journal des Goncourts*, which had such a good effect on me last year, as well as other works likely to improve my intellect.

The other question on my mind is of a very different order, one I would not dare come out with, except when talking to Slimène, for he will be the *only one to understand* and go along with it; and that is the question of becoming a *maraboute*,[44] a thought that came to me out of the blue the day Abdallah was taken from the civilian prison and put into his cell ... And Slimène had suspected it, by intuition, no doubt because we are so very close!

It seems to me that if I apply a great deal of willpower, I will have no trouble reaching a spiritual goal like that; it would give me infinite satisfaction and would open up

66

unforeseen possibilities. ☽ *Lead us along the straight path*, and I believe that for me the straight path lies in that direction.

God planted a fertile seed in my soul: utter indifference to the things of this world, faith, and a boundless love and pity for suffering of any sort. The way I forgive evil is an expression of my unlimited devotion to the cause of Islam, which is the most magnificent of all because it is that of Truth.

Oh, the long hours I spent in those woods so full of mystery and shadows, the sleepless nights gazing at a cosmos full of stars. I must have been headed for religious mysticism already at the time!

A different choice in life companion would certainly have thwarted the necessary progress toward a future of that sort. Slimène will follow me wherever I go, and of all the men I have known, he is the *only true* Muslim, for he *loves* Islam with all his heart and is not content with paying it mere lip service.

A scientist, psychologist or writer reading these lines would be sure to say: 'She is out of her mind!' Yet the fact remains that if ever there was a time when my intelligence was burning like a flame, that time is now, and what is more, I know that I am only on the threshold of a new life.

Maître de Laffont unwittingly hit upon a truth when he said that I ought to be grateful to Abdallah. That I am, yes, and what is more, I *sincerely love Abdallah*, for he *was* the heavenly emissary he said he was.

It is likely that others were behind his deed, people who are the true culprits; he himself, however, must have been sent by God, for ever since that fateful day in Behima I have felt my soul move into a whole new phase in its earthly existence. In some mysterious way, Abdallah's lifelong suffering will no doubt pay for the redemption of another's life.

What he has wrought will one day emerge from the shadows where I keep it hidden. That is my secret, one I must not reveal or talk about, except with the one man who discovered it all by himself one day.

All those who in their blindness think they have eyes to see may shrug or smile in the presence of the couple that we

form. It is a union based on sentiments and aims that have nothing in common with those marriages of theirs, motivated as they are by base ambition or infantile lust. Ours is a love *beyond* their understanding.

Thursday 11 July 1901, 9 p.m.

I am not in the mood right now to go on with my description of the trial. For the moment other thoughts and other memories have come to haunt me.

Felt bored and ill at ease last night, just like the day before. Anxiety this morning and much physical tension in the absence of any letter from Ouïha.

Went down to the Cours du Chapitre around 9.30 this morning to post a letter to Zouïzou. In the afternoon I started on my Russian assignment without much conviction. Had a good letter at last by three o'clock. The question of Zouïzou's replacement has *definitely* been settled and his return is now only a matter of days; time will pass by very quickly, now that I *know* he is coming.

What a sigh of relief we will heave, my God, after our visit to city hall, which will bind us to each other at long last and mean that others are *obliged* to treat us as a couple. God treated us that way and gave us his blessing a long time ago, in the form of love. Now men will soon lose the right to part us!

Memories are haunting me ... Geneva, times of anguish and of joy in my Russian way of life out there; the moment of my sailing for the beloved, fateful land of Barbary whence I have now been banned, but where I shall soon be able to return with my head held high ☾ if it pleases Allah!, and white Algiers, where I used to lead a double life, an unorthodox and heady one among people who had respect and even admiration for me, even though they knew nothing about me, not even what my gender was! Strange, intoxicating rides with Mokhtar, kif-smoking sessions ... the way we sang sad Algerian songs on our strolls along the quays ... the white Zawyia of Sidi Abd el-Rahman ben Koubrine, miniature city of one's dreams basking in the sunset above the fragrant Jardin Marengo ... the ecstasy felt during the icha prayer hour in the Jadid

68

Mosque ... Tuggurt asleep in its desert of salt, with its mirror image in the sluggish waters of its shott ... and farther on, the goal of that long journey, the splendid outline of the one and only City, the city of my choice, predestined El Oued!

Monday 15 July 1901, 11 a.m.

Felt very odd last night, for no discernible reason: a memory of my arrival at Sousse, two years ago ... and the desire to travel by myself to some uncharted place in Africa, where no one knows me, the way no one did when I came to Algiers last year ... but with adequate means this time.

Generally speaking, I feel a desire for mental *isolation*, although not for long, for I still miss Slimène. I would like to have a month all to myself before his return, and the necessary funds for a leisurely voyage by myself ... I know I would come back with very valuable, pertinent observations.

Yet this is a period in which my outlook is lucid and level-headed, and above all it is a period of work. The hope that a better life is just around the corner has of course a good deal to do with my present frame of mind.

It will soon be six months since that fateful episode at Behima. Even though I did not realise it then, that day was the beginning of another period of incubation, of the sort I have experienced all my life, for quite clearly my intellectual development has always been achieved by *fits and starts*: periods of restlessness, discontent and uncertainty have always been followed by the emergence of a better version of myself. A subject to be analysed, and described perhaps in a short story or a novel.

During the six or seven months we will have to spend here we must come to a definite decision about our future, and I must also devote that time to literary work of every sort.

Since I left for Bône in 1897 – how long ago that seems, alas! – I have neglected an art I love, namely drawing and painting. I plan to take them up again and while here will try to take a few lessons and acquire some instruction in portraiture and genre painting.

69

Our life, our *real* life will not take off again till after 20th February 1902.

If the Moscow business is settled by then in the form of a pension,[45] the best thing would be to go and create a peaceful haven for ourselves somewhere in the Tunisian Sahel – if it is not, the only feasible thing would be a career as an interpreter for a few years, somewhere in the South, it does not matter where exactly – a few years of living in the Desert, which would be wonderful too.

The time has now come to face the fundamental question of what my life is all about ... All the things that have happened so far have been mere passing phases ... ☾ *And Allah knows all that is hidden in the heavens and on earth.*

Tuesday 23 July

Over here,[46] we have now reached the depths of poverty, which is all the more frightening as there is nothing I can do; had I been surrounded by people like myself, I could perhaps have managed on tiny sums to provide for tiny needs. But such is not the case, and they have got appearances to keep up. For Slimène and myself, though, the end of our woes is near. I still need to lend a helping hand here, though, and that will not be easy. With what Slimène will earn and my way of keeping house, the two of us can scrape by in peace without giving up what little we need ... How will it all work out, though?

There will be no way out if they do not accept to have their meals with us, for I will never have enough money to support two households. As soon as Zouïzou gets here, he and I will have to discuss it, unless the steps I must try and take *vis-à-vis* Reppmann turn out to be successful. In that case I will then let them have all of what Reppmann sends me, and they will then have at least the wherewithal to manage for a month, a month and a half, if Reppmann agrees to lend me 100 rubles, which is nearly 250 francs. That would save us all, for it would give the two of us a chance to set up our own little household, and buy the few things I need. Once I dress as a woman, I am bound to find a little odd job while waiting for something better.

70

With that in mind, I must make good use of the last few days of solitude I have left and progress with my literary work as much as I can, write a few articles and copy them out, so that if I get any favourable replies from any quarter, I will have something to show and will not have to do any writing at the outset of our life together; that way I will not miss any opportunities that might turn up with newspapers and magazines after the summer.

There was a violent wind as I went to post a letter to Slimène, which may or may not reach him. I have very little hope. I went to Arenc on foot, and walked home via the Bar d'Afrique.

I will see tomorrow whether I can't earn a few pennies here and there writing letters in Arabic. I rather think that I am not going to lose heart. The one I fear for is Augustin. I just pray he will not think of doing what Volodia[47] did when he was down and out! As long as I am in the house, a collective suicide is out of the question. But after that?

☾ *May it please Allah* that we have seen the last of sombre dramas.

A thought to consider, which I found in *Notebook* I:

Do as much good as you can today,

For tomorrow you may die.

(Inscription on the Calvaire de Tregastel, Trécor, Britanny) which is a paraphrase of the words of Epictetus:

Behave as if you were to die the very next moment.

Few people could survive my lot.

I have now reached the depths of poverty, and may well be going hungry soon. Yet I can honestly say that I have never, not even for a moment, entertained the notion of doing what so many hundreds of thousands of women do. That is *out of the question*, period.

To say ☾ *There is no God but God and Muhammad is his prophet* is not enough, nor even to be convinced of it. It takes more than that to be a Muslim. Whoever considers himself to be a Muslim must devote himself body and soul, to the point of martyrdom if need be, to Islam for all time; Islam must inhabit his soul, and govern every one of his acts and words. Otherwise, there is no point in mystical exercises of any sort.

God is Beauty. The word itself contains everything:

Virtue, Truth, Honesty, Mercy. Inspired by such faith, a man is strong ... His strength may even seem to be supernatural. He becomes what they call a Marabout. As the knowledgeable and inspired Sheikh Ecchafi'r put it: 'Whatever you do, wherever you go, say: "Bismillah al-Rahman al-Rahim".' What he meant though, was not merely to *say*: in the name of Allah, when one undertakes something, but to actually do things *only* in the name of God, to do only what is true and good.

Those are things I thought about for years, and after Behima, I have come to understand them; no doubt the uninitiated, in their mindless craving for hollow phrases with which to mouth empty formulas, will shrug them off as mystical. If, as I hope and *think I can forsee*, it is written that I will complete the blessed cycle, it will be through Suffering, a path to which I sing a hymn of gratitude beforehand. One thing is certain, though, and that is that my soul has at last emerged from the gloom where it dwelt for so long.

Thursday 25 July, around 11 p.m.

Isabelle's depression increases as her relations with her brother and sister-in-law deteriorate.

I am finding it more and more difficult to stay here, especially in the absence of Rouh . Neither Augustin nor Hélène[48] is capable of loving me, nor will they ever be, for *they will never understand me*. Augustin has become deaf and blind to all of the sublime things I have understood at last.

I feel *alone* here, more so than anywhere else. The end of the month is in sight, though, and it cannot be long now before Zouïzou comes to put an end to my torments.

Received the two issues of *Les Nouvelles* from Algiers, dated July 19th and 20th, which carry the text of *El-Magh'reb* and *Printemps au Désert*.[49] I feel comforted by that success, and it does open up some possibilities at least. It means that I must have patience all the way and persevere. Above all, however, I must make up my mind to be aloof and stop discussing my affairs and ideas with people who do not *understand* them and do not *want* to.

72

No doubt about it (appearances these last two years notwithstanding), it seems destined that of all the people who lived the abnormal existence at the *Villa Neuve*, I am the *only one* whose soul might be saved.

I am not asking God for very much: simply that Slimène comes back, that we be married, that there be an end to this state of affairs over here: let Augustin and his wife find a way out! May they have enough to live on, especially as I have no way of helping people so diametrically opposed to me in every conceivable way.

Friday 26th, 10 p.m.

To close this chronicle of the last six months of my life, which I began in sadness and uncertainty in hospital, I have nothing but dreary things to report, although my spiritual progress remains steadfast. Of course the reason for my depression of the last three or four days lies in my environment and its insoluble financial problems. At bottom my soul is serene.

The only thing I find really hard to bear is the delay in Slimène's return, and the enormous effort it costs me to be patient. Now more than ever I am in need of his beloved presence. My heart overflows with love and I feel irresistibly drawn toward him, for he is the last refuge I have left on earth.

Having switched places with someone else, Slimène was drafted into a regiment of Dragoons stationed in Marseilles, where he and Isabelle were officially married.

Saturday 29 October 1901, 4 p.m.

The terrors of three months ago are now mostly gone from our horizon.

On the 17th of this month we officially became man and wife, never to be parted again. I am no longer forbidden to enter Algeria and in any event my period of exile is almost over: we will be off to our beloved land across the sea a month from now.

73

The following entry was added by Isabelle seven months before her death.

Algiers, 8 April 1904, 9 p.m.

I have not recorded the thoughts I had in January 1902 ... What does it matter? Three years later, in a different place of exile, in the midst of poverty just as wretched, of solitude just as hopeless, I see what ravages time has wrought in me ...

Many other corners of the African continent still hold me in their spell. Soon, the solitary, woeful figure that I am will vanish from this earth, where I have always been a spectator, an *outsider* among men.

JOURNAL FOUR

Isabelle retraces the period she spent in Marseilles after being forced out of North Africa, while she awaited Slimène's transfer and their marriage.

'In the name of God, the all powerful, the merciful'
THOUGHTS AND IMPRESSIONS

Begun in Marseilles, 27 July 1901. Finished at Bou Saada on 31 January 1903.

In memory of † *the White Spirit*

Marseilles, 27 July 1901

After several days of anguish, I got up this morning feeling full of energy again, of patience, and of an eagerness to get down to work.

If the torture of waiting for Slimène could only come to an end, if I knew the *exact date* of his arrival, this could prove to be one of the best periods of my life from the spiritual point of view.

In the autumn there will probably be some funds, which means the end of many a problem, and above all the end of my feeling so powerless. Oh! to come into the money for that hapless *Villa Neuve* at long last and go to see Africa once again, who knows, perhaps even the unforgettable Souf at that! To be able to read again, write, draw and paint, enjoy the intellectual side of life and lay the ground-work for my literary career. Should I be reasonable and, instead of going to Algeria, go to Paris with a certain number of articles for sale?

Slimène, who suffered from tuberculosis, was hospitalised during this time.

1 August 1901, 11 a.m.

Had a letter from Slimène yesterday that has upset everything one more time. He has been in hospital since the 28th. How could I ignore those mysterious premonitions I have had all these years about the stages of my *via dolorosa*!

I am shaking from head to foot. Yet I must sit down and write, copy the text of *Amiria* and send it off to Brieux.

The same day, half-past midnight[50]

Slimène, Slimène! I do not think I have ever loved him as deeply and as *chastely* as I do now, and if God wants to take him from me, let His will be done. After that I will undertake to go where there is fighting in the south-west, and die there no matter what, proclaiming ☽ *that there is no God but Allah and Muhammad is his Prophet*. That is the only death worthy of me and of the man I love. Any attempt to make a new life for myself would be in vain, and criminal as well.

Slimène wishes he had known my mother, but perhaps he will soon be with her. He can then tell her our two hearts are *united for all time*, and how much they have suffered here below.

You who are up there, White Spirit, and you, Vava, no doubt you can both see the tears I am shedding in the silence of the night, and you can read deep down into my heart. You know that at his side I have purified my poor soul in suffering and persecution, that I have not surrendered and that my heart is pure! See for yourself, and as you have left us to fend for ourselves in this world so full of woe, call for God's mercy now on the two of us, mercy from that same God who put the White Spirit to rest among the faithful. Call for His punishment, too, on those who hound us with such venom.

Why did I not do as I had wanted and go off with Sidi Muhammad Tayeb, why did I not go and die with him at Timmimoun? Why did fate have to take that poor child

away from the peaceful existence that was his, to make him share the doom that will be mine and saddle him with so much suffering and, perhaps, an early death?[51] Why should I not go off by myself? Does he regret having loved me, regret having suffered this much on my account?

Who will ever guess how infinitely bitter are these hours I am going through, these nights I spend in solitude? If any help comes my way, everything will be all right. No matter how ill he is, if I am there to nurse him, he is bound to get well ... Otherwise, bereft and needy as he is, his frail health will deteriorate, and that hereditary disease of his will have the upper hand[52] ...

Tuesday 6th, 11 a.m.

Had a letter from Brieux: I realise that in the literary domain, I have a vast amount of work to do. Am determined to *do it, because I must.*

How strange: as I was writing the above, I felt a slight improvement in my outlook, no doubt because I think I might be able to do that short story for *L'Illustration.*

Thursday 8 August 1901, midnight

After reading Dostoyevsky as I do every day, I suddenly feel a great deal of affection for this tiny room of mine. It looks just like a prison cell and bears no resemblance to the rest of the house.

A room that has been lived in for a long time will absorb some of its occupant's essence, so to speak, and thoughts.

Thursday 15 August 1901, 8.30 p.m.

I have been longing for the desert again these last few days, with an intensity so keen it almost hurts. Just to go as far as old Biskra's last segnia, where Slimène and I stopped that night *six long months ago*!

Oh, to be free right now, the two of us, to be well off and leave for that country which is *ours*! Will I ever set eyes on those magnificent sands again?

To go away and be a tramp again, free and unencum-

bered as I used to be, even if it means all sorts of new ordeals! To run as fast as my legs will carry me along the Quai de La Joliette – the only part of this town that I love because it is the gate to Africa, and board ship – a humble, unknown figure – and flee, flee at last *for good*!

Oh, to turn my back on all this and go away for good, now that I am more of an outsider here than in any other place. They do not respect the sacred things I hold so dear, for they are blind and *bourgeois*, bourgeois to their very fingertips, and mired in the base obsessions of their greedy, brutish lives.

Yet they are *quite right* to push me to the limits of my endurance, for that way my heart lets go of them completely. These coarse and nasty scenes of theirs do not affect me any longer. I no longer care and only cling more passionately than ever to the beloved Ideal that is my salvation and my *raison d'être*, and also to Slimène. From his letters I can tell he too has begun to think, a development that is bound to steer him along the same luminous course I am pursuing.

All the pain I feel is due to my being on tenterhooks while waiting for Slimène.

I must stop sacrificing all for the sake of people over here, and start thinking of a home of my *own*.

Reppmann and Brieux[53] have no idea, especially Reppmann, that his largesse has not benefited me and that I did my begging for the sake of others, who simply took it all for granted!

Saturday 17 August

I feel a deep uncertainty about Slimène's transfer. And then there is something else as well. To judge by his last letter, he seems to be thinking of the same thing as I am, namely, the heady subject of physical love. The most delicious and unchaste dreams are visiting me these days. Of course I could not tell anyone about a secret like that, except Dr Taste,[54] a confidant who used to be as brutal as he was sensitive.

78

There is no doubt about it, I do love Taste ... physically the least attractive man I have ever known, at least where the senses are concerned. Not that I did not care for the man's eroticism, the way it would go from the rough and brutal to a form so subtle it would verge on the neurotic. I used to say things to him that no one else has ever heard me say ... D.[55] is too down-to-earth and there is something about him that reeks of a tolerance too sweeping and too coarse.

Now that those people are all gone from my present life, I look back with amazement at a figure like Toulat,[56] and wonder if there too there is not some age-old atavism at work: how can the Arab way of life, the *Arab soul* itself, have rubbed off on a Frenchman from Poitiers? Oh yes, Toulat is an Arab all right. He broods, and goes in for harsh and savage living in the desert; of all the French officers I ever knew, he is the only one who is not bored there. His very harshness and his violence are Arabic, in fact. There is something savage too about the way he loves, something un-French and un-modern, for love me he did without a doubt. His love was at its peak the day he wept such desperate tears when we came to Biskra. But he did not understand me and he was afraid of me. He thought the only thing to do was run.

All that does seem so long ago! All the more so as I feel no anger at the thought of any of *them*: the woman who used to think she loved those distant ghosts is now *dead*. The one who is alive today is so different she can no longer answer for past errors.

Sexual matters will continue to hold my attention, of course, from the intellectual point of view, and I would not give up my research in that domain for anything in the world. As far as I am concerned, though, I now have a focus for my sexuality, and the silly phrase: 'I am no longer my own master' is quite to the point. When it comes to the senses, Slimène is my one and only, undisputed master. He is the only one I feel attracted to, the only one to put me in the mood to forget the intellect and descend – is it a descent? I doubt it very much – to the proverbial realm of sexual exploits.

Our modern world is so distorted and so warped that in

marriage the husband is hardly ever the one to do the initiating into sensuality. Stupid and revolting as it is, young girls are hitched to a husband for life, and he is a ridiculous figure in the end. The woman's physical virginity is all his. She is then expected to spend the rest of her life with him, usually in disgust, and suffer what is known as her 'marital duty', until the day that someone comes along to teach her, in a web of lies, the existence of a whole universe of thrills, thoughts and sensations that will regenerate her from head to toe. That is where our marriage is so different from any other – and shocks so many solid citizens: Slimène means two things to me – he is both friend and lover.

Just what did that strange, compelling man, Colonel de R, who held so many first-rate women under his spell, mean when he said: 'You were much sought after in Algeria' ...? That was something I already knew too well, having found it out at my expense.

None of the men I have known, and that goes for the officers in particular, can understand what Slimène is doing in my life. Domercq had no choice but to accept it in the end. Taste *pretends* he does not understand, but he probably does. What does De R. think of it? I would certainly like to see that man again and get to know him better. He cannot have been an ordinary fellow.

So far I know nothing about Brieux's benevolent personality, except that he must be very kind ... Is he unaffected, like those brief letters of his, simple, open and straightforward, or is he the most complicated of men?

Among the local figures of note, there is that nice man Mohammed ben Aïssa, who must have left for Algiers by now, and has a very kind heart.

Smaïne ben Amma – a man who is rotten to the core. His alcohol intake will lead to either *delirium tremens* or general paralysis.

I could not find him more unpleasant, and there was no need for Zouïzou to put me on my guard against him.

If I had to choose between that 'aristocrat' and the porter who likes his kif, I would definitely choose the latter.

80

Marseilles, Thursday 22 August 1901, noon

My ordeal is not yet over. Yet if I try to *reason* instead of giving in to instincts, there has actually been a change for the better in my plight: Zouïzou has left that horrible Batna, he is on his way and what is more, he is now in Bône, the city where my mother's grave is. May she make him feel at home, inspire him and take him under her posthumous protection for the rest of his life.

No point in insisting. Augustin is hardly to blame, in fact – except where his weakness is concerned – and that is not all his fault.

He has made a fatal mistake in his marriage and there is nothing anyone can do about it now.

My God, what a relief it would be if Exempliarsky were prepared to lend Augustin enough money to spare us any further expense that might be disastrous!

We have so many debts and needs. Those 25 francs from the old lady would really come in handy. ☺ *May Allah lend a helping hand!*

I must make a huge effort to get through this week without giving in to depression and put the time to good use – which is the hardest part.

The writer I like best right now is Dostoyevsky – perhaps because his novels remind me so much of the diffuse and hazy, troubled outlook that has bedevilled me for so long.

I re-read my friend Eugène's letters last night. My God, how he has changed in the six years that we have been friends! What a difference there is between his first rather green letters and his last ones, after his return from the heart of the desert, from Toulat, a place whose very name is enough to make my imagination soar! What a pall has come over that soul of his! I have the feeling that the romance he had in Algiers had a lot to do with it. The affair in question must have been serious and genuine, to judge by his very despondent letter in which he wrote that he was off for the deep South, almost as if he were on the run.

Friday 23 August 1901, 11 a.m.

Had an awful day yesterday, because of yet another pin-prick from Augustin's wife.

81

Kept wandering through town from three to five in the afternoon, tottering on my feet, exhausted and worn out, looking for Smaïne. Did not find him. Went to Joliette, found my friend the porter. Borrowed 55 cents, sent cable to Zouïzou, and bought some tobacco. Went home. Great fatigue, felt ill, pain all over my body.

Saturday 24 August 1901, 10 p.m.

Allah has heard us at long last! After the bad news I had yesterday, the colonel came in person to tell me the transfer is official. Zouïzou will definitely be here in three days' time, and we have the colonel's protection.

Oh how enigmatic human destinies are! How unfathomable the paths where God leads his creatures!

Monday 26 August 11 a.m.

Having felt vaguely unwell these days, I had a curious fit yesterday ... I lay down in the afternoon because I had a bad colic and pain in my lower back. By four o'clock I had a headache that grew sharper by the minute, plus a high fever. I knew I was in a state of delirium, which wore me out.

They simply left me all alone in the house till 10 p.m., without any help whatsoever. When they did come home, they did not even bother to come in and see how I was. Thanks to Allah, though, I have only two more days to go in this horrible existence.

If I do not feel ill tonight, I ought to go and see the room at the hotel, for tomorrow I should go and look for the porter and for Smaïne.

Tuesday 27 August 1901, noon

It has been a long time since I have felt as calm as I do today. The mistral is blowing hard, and it is a lovely autumn day. The air is pure and clear. It is cool outside, the sun is shining and *tomorrow I shall leave this house*.

To put it in a nutshell, I forgive them for everything, and

82

let Him be the judge. I have done my human duty and will keep doing it for the sake of my dead mother.

Things have simmered down a bit, both in my outward circumstances and within my soul. There still are many questions to be settled, such as that of our marriage, which only raises a problem because we have no money. As we have the colonel's protection, I hope all will be well on that score too.

How many clouds are gone from our horizon! And most importantly, if God does not part us by death, the days of separation are now over *for good*.

27 August, in the evening

We have left Augustin's house.

At four o'clock to Quai de la Joliette. Zouïzou arrived on the *Ville d'Oran* on 28 August 1901 at 8.30 in the morning, lovely clear weather, strong wind ...

Isabelle takes up her journal again a few days before her marriage.

1 October 1901, 3 p.m.
67, rue Grignan

A month has gone by since I wrote those last lines. It is true that everything has changed. Zouïzou is with me here, and his health is not as bad as I had expected it to be. We are alone and in a *place of our own* – a wonderful feeling! We shall be married in a few days' time and the *Villa* has been sold.

Poor dear *Villa Neuve*, I know I will never set foot in it again.

Ever since I found out yesterday that *the house* was sold on 27 September I have been haunted by memories of it.

That means the end, for good this time, of the story of my life there, the first life I had on earth! Everything has been dispersed, it all lies buried or is gone. In a few days' time even the old furniture, inanimate witness of our past, will be auctioned off and scattered.

God has had mercy on me and granted me my prayer:

83

He has given me the ideal companion, the one I had longed for with such ardour. Without him, my life would always have remained all gloom and incoherence.

For the moment we are having a hard and penniless time, but then again, ☩ *he who suffers till the very end will be the only one to find salvation.*

God knows what He has in mind for us. That means we must resign ourselves and have courage in the face of adversity, in the firm conviction that life on earth is but a phase along the way to other, unknown destinies.

It has been a year already since that luminous, melancholy autumn in the Souf ... The palm trees over there are shaking their shroud of dust by now, the sky is clear and limpid above the splendid dunes.

Meanwhile we are here in this dreary city full of gloom and boredom!

Marseilles, 21 November 1901, 8 p.m.

For several days now, the two of us have been full of sadness, and I am getting a premonition that we are about to leave. ☽ *God knows!*

Memories of the Souf make for an obsession that is thrill and torment all at once. I only need to hear the sound of bugles for a thousand feelings to start stirring in my heart.

Those are the same thoughts I used to have about the netherworld, when I would stand by the window in my room and daydream in the silence of the night, looking at the vast sky above the Jura's jagged, often snow-clad outline, and the black and heavy mass of great trees.

In the springtime there were always countless nightingales in the lilac bushes full of dew. A mysterious sadness would come over me as I listened to them warble. Particularly in childhood, my mind always found strange associations in memories and feelings.

It all comes back to me now, in the insecurity and sheer monotony of my present life.

For the first time since my beloved parents died, I am beginning to *exteriorise* a bit; I now have a duty to fulfil *outside myself*. That alone enhances the days I spend here, for they would otherwise lack meaning; the same goes for

the five long months devoid of charm I have spent as an outcast in this city where I have no ties, where everything seems so alien and abhorrent.

How it rankles the common man to see anyone – and a woman at that – depart from the norm and be *herself*!

I am finding out these days that I have a talent I did not know I had for writing essays on such topics as history that are not without a certain depth.

Now more than ever do I realise that I shall never be content with a sedentary life, and that I shall always be haunted by thoughts of a sun-drenched *elsewhere*. The only place where I could end my days would be El Oued.

26 November 1901, 1 a.m.

Feeling calm and sad today, longing to leave, to flee this room, this city and everybody in it.

I feel more and more that these must be the last few days of our exile ... May God make it come true, for the nightmare of our Marseilles days has lasted long enough!

What makes me very happy is that Ouiha is now getting closer to the arcane world of thoughts and feelings, so that I am no longer on my own there.

It is clear that he is the companion I was always meant to have, and how unfathomable is the enigma that surrounds our lives on earth: we lived far apart from each other for ten, twenty, twenty-five years without either of us having the slightest inkling of the other's existence, yet we were both in search of the *one and only* partner, the one without whom there could be no happiness on earth.

The curious thing is that on 19 June, 1900, I had the first hint of the sort of life that I might lead. It happened in the grim and dirty room I had at Madame Pons's. I was writing a chapter of *Rakhil*, when the notion of *going to Ouargla* came to me out of the blue! That thought of mine was the beginning of it all!

Oh, if at every moment of our lives we could know the consequences of some of the utterings, thoughts and deeds that seem so trivial and unimportant at the time! And should we not conclude from such examples that there is no such thing in life as unimportant moments devoid of meaning for the future?

85

To change the subject altogether: As I go over the history of Carthage with Ouïha, I am struck by the resemblance of the callous Carthage of antiquity to present-day England: their greed, their contempt for anything foreign, their boundless, intransigent egotism ... Might those traits be characteristic of all great *maritime* powers?

To broaden my vision further, I would need to make a serious study of history. Grocery bills and tailor's invoices are taking up the precious time, alas, that I would like to devote to thought!

Saturday 30 November 1901, 3 p.m.

It is freezing cold and all we have to keep warm with is the wood M. gives us, but he has an *ulterior motive* ... ☾ *May Allah's curse come down on all those who do wrong*, as Slimène puts it.

What will be the outcome of our present mess?

If we manage to settle our worst debts and if my friend Eugène sends me another hundred francs, we will of course leave for Bône on the spot and stay there for an indefinite length of time. When will we be able to head for Algiers? God only knows!

Yet despite all the trouble, the physical and emotional strain, there is one thing that delights me: Zouïzou's soul is constantly growing closer to mine. I have found the partner of my dreams at last. May he live as long as my life on earth lasts!

A thick dark fog of conjecture and uncertainty is all around us. Yet there is one ray of hope, and that is that we may soon be on our way home to the country of our choice, probably to stay there for good.

Before we do, there will be one sad, quick and almost stealthy visit to Geneva.[57]

Isabelle and Slimène finally return to Algeria.

Bône, Tuesday 21 January 1902

Sailed from Marseilles on 14 January at 5 p.m. on the *Duc de Bragance*. Reached Bône on the 15th at eight o'clock in the evening.

Our dream of going home from exile has come true at last; we are back on the soil where the sun is always young, our beloved land facing the great blue murmuring sea whose vast empty stretches make one think of the Sahara's.

May this year mark the beginning of a turn in our lives, with the serenity we have yearned for and deserve as our reward!

Outdoor living and the simplicity of life down here are beginning to restore my strength. I had none left at the end of that long and painful period of exile in Marseilles. What is more, my brain is stirring too, and I think I may do some writing here.

Twenty-one days from now, Zouïzou will also be free of his obligations to the army, so that he will have far more freedom and will no longer need to be wary of indiscretions. We will then have to manage by ourselves in this vast, magnificent universe that has its lures and disappointments.

The brief span of time I must spend on earth does not frighten me; the only thing that does is the thought that I might lose my partner and be left all by myself.

As for my morale, *almost* total resignation and equanimity, which, as I have said before, all has a good deal to do with physical factors. I don't wish to have anything to do with the world at large and be a city-dweller once again: I am thrilled to be a hermit.

When the two of us went by ourselves the other night to meet Ali Bou Traïf on the Pont de la Casbah, we saw the full moon rise over the tranquil sea. We stopped at the turn in the road that goes to the cemetery.

The bridge looked like the mystical one of the Slavic legend, the one that is woven for nymphs out of moonbeams in the silence of the night. All golden, it trembled slightly against the waters' shifting background. A strip of grey cloud came between moon and water, so that its shadow could be seen there, the shape of a low dune with two promontories dividing the sea in two halves, one very blue, vast and bright, the other a dull misty grey melting

87

into the horizon. In that one there was a fishing boat with a Latin sail. There was no reflection of it on the waters' misty surface; it was not moving, but seemed like a phantom vessel that vanished slowly into the fog.

14 February 1902, 3 p.m.

A month has gone by since we left that inferno in Marseilles and everything has gone awry already over here because of the constant intrigues of these Moorish women.

Here, as elsewhere, I can see how volatile Slimène's character is, and what a bad influence his environment has on him. Will that change some day? I do not know, and in any case, a temperament such as his can do nothing to alleviate the poverty to which we are now reduced.

Far better to start another life of poverty over in Algiers – which would in any event be less dreadful than in Marseilles – than stay here, where hospitality takes the form of constant snubs and endless arguments.

My literary bent is stirring, and I shall try to make a name for myself in the Algerian press at least, while waiting for the opportunity to do the same in Paris.

To do all that I would have to have total peace and quiet for a while, almost to the point of seclusion. I would have to find someone in Algiers to teach Slimène all the things he does not know, which is a tall order, and that would take a lot of worries off my hands and leave me free to work. ☾ *Allah will see to it!*

I shall go and say one more goodbye to the white grave on its green hill basking in the exuberance of spring, and after that we will be on the road again and lead our lives according to the whims of fate.

Left for Algiers by a coach of the Messageries du Sud on 12 March 1902, at 6.15 in the morning. The weather was bright and clear. Mental outlook – good, peaceful. The journey up the slopes of the Sahel was long and laborious. Birmandreis, Birkadem, Birtouta. Boufarik, Beni-Mered. Reached Blida by half-past noon, went to the café on the Place d'Armes. Had lunch at the station, left again by the coach for Medeah. Sidi-Medani, the Gorges. Ruisseau des Singes, hotel, magnificent torrent, narrow gorge. All

along the road countless waterfalls that vanish under-ground. Thickets of viburnum in bloom and masses of ferns everywhere.

Reached Medeah by 8.30 p.m. Visit to Moorish café. Sent cable to Ouïha. Spent some time sitting on a bench in the square, and then in the café-restaurant at the station. Took the train coming from Maison-Carrée. Reached Algiers by 9.35 in the evening on Friday 14 March.

☾ *Allah does not put the majority of fools on the right course!*

Isabelle meets Victor Barrucand, the journalist and editor.

30 March 1902

Present situation: no money. We rely on Si Muhammad Sherif to come to our rescue and take care of us during these last few days. During the day, I work.

Last Thursday went to see Barrucand at the Villa Bellevue; had a pleasant impression.[58] A modern mind, subtle and perceptive, but biased by the notions of his time. Went to rue du Rempart Médée to Mme Ben-Aben's workshop. Enjoyed my conversation with intellectuals, something I had not experienced in a long time.

A generous man will record the harm done to him in pencil, the good in ink.

'*Behave in this world as if you were to live for ever, and act as if you were to die tomorrow!*' to be compared with Marcus Aurelius's thought on the subject [*Meditations*].

1 April 1902, 9 p.m.

We are still hard at work. We have so little time left – so little! – and so much studying to do to catch up that we cannot stand it. It all takes a huge effort these days. The trouble is, there are so many subjects. Well, ☾ *Allah will help!*

For the moment, I must continue to muster courage enough for two, and when things are really bad, cheer up Zouïzou and restore his optimism, for without that we have no hope at all.

I think it is impossible for human minds to think of Death as a final, irrevocable end to life. As for myself, I have a *conviction* that *eternity* does exist.

Yet ☾ *may Allah the Great forgive me*, if Death did really mean the end of everything, that would not be so bad. Does not, after all, three-quarters of all suffering lie in the memory we have of it, which is to say, in our *awareness* of it?

Algiers, 22 April 1902
17, rue du Soudan

For once, we do not have too much work tonight. I have a moment to myself and after doing some translating for dear, kind Mme Ben-Aben, I have been reading Nadson.

Along the distant shores of the Rhône at the foot of the snow-clad Jura mountains, spring must be about to stir. The trees are covered in a mist of foliage, and the first rock-plants are blooming at the *Villa Neuve* in the shadow of the great pine tree and by the two graves in the Vernier cemetery.

Things are no different this spring from any other year, and Nature is doing what it always does ... The difference is that I am no longer there to do my dreaming and my grieving ... Vava, Maman and Volod have departed for the great Unknown! ... Everything is gone, finished and destroyed.

Algiers, 4 May 1902, about 10 p.m.

Went to see a sorcerer today, who lives in a tiny place in a street in the upper town, via dark stairways in the Rue du Diable. I now have absolute proof that the mysterious science of Magic does actually exist. How vast are the perspectives such knowledge opens up for me, and also what a relief there is in the blow dealt to my doubts!

I am in a calm and wistful mood these days. Algiers is clearly one of those cities which fire my imagination, and certain parts of it in particular. I like the area we are living in, and our lodgings too, after that horrible dump in the rue de la Marine.

How can all those fools in social and literary circles say there is nothing Arab about Algiers?

There is for instance that lovely moment of the maghreb over the harbour and rooftops of the upper town. The place teems with merry Algerian women, all frolicking happily in their pink or green garb against the bluish-white of the rooftops. I see them from the little moucharabieh window at Mme Ben-Aben's.

Together with the one at Bône, the bay of Algiers is one of the prettiest and most captivating seascapes I have ever seen.

Despite the riff-raff French civilisation has brought over here, whore and whoremaster that it is, Algiers is still a place full of grace and charm.

The more I study the history of North Africa – very poorly and too fast – the more I see that I was right: the African soil devours and absorbs all that is hostile to it. It may well be the land where the light is destined to shine forth one day and regenerate the world!

An old man once turned up at the French encampment after the 1830 landing in Sidi-Ferruch. He had a pacific manner, and all he had to say was: 'There is no god but God and Muhammad is his Prophet!' With that he left and was never seen again.

No one understood what he meant by that. He had come to say that Islam and the mesmerising soil of Africa are one for all eternity!

8 June 1902, 11.30 p.m.

Life goes on, monotonous as ever, yet there is the hint of some future direction in the midst of all this dreadful emotional turmoil.

I am going through another slow period of gestation which can be quite painful at times.

The two people who have been helpful to us here, Barrucand and Mme Ben-Aben, are both kind and thought-ful and I am beginning to understand what makes them tick.

Barrucand is a dilettante in the domain of thought and even more so when it comes to feeling, a spiritual nihilist in

other words. From a practical standpoint, though, he is someone very positive who knows how to handle himself.

As for Mme Ben-Aben, after my mother, she is the only woman I have met who is both good and enamoured with an ideal, although quite ignorant of 'real life'. Even I, who am totally *inept* at handling myself, know better than they do.

Augustin is now gone from my life; as far as I am concerned the brother I used to love so much is dead. That shadow of him in Marseilles who is married to Jenny the work-horse does not exist for me, and I very rarely think of him.

Now that the torrid heat of summer has suddenly come again, the notion that I am back in Africa is slowly sinking in. Soon I will feel completely at home, especially if my plan to go to Bou-Saada comes off ... Oh, that journey! it will mean a brief return, not to the magnificent Sahara itself, but to a place nearby that has all the palm trees and sunshine one would want!

Remarks about Algiers

While the weather was cool, the shadows in the upper town's dark streets were grey and dark, to the point of gloominess. Now that there is a sudden sharp contrast between light and dark, it all looks African again, or Arab in any event.

No, the true African landscape is not to be found in any of the large cities, certainly not in those of the Tell. African perspectives are hazy with a distant horizon. Vast space and emptiness, a blinding light, are what makes a landscape African! The architecture of Algiers boasts none of those traits. Its houses are all piled on top of each other and huddle fearfully at the bottom of culs-de-sac, in a city accustomed to raids and sieges.

The mindless noise of the crowds, where the only Arabs are those awful Kabyles in European garb, makes certain parts of town look like places of ill repute where no one's life is safe.

The uninitiated European thinks those men in dirty burnouses over tattered European clothes, and those Moorish women are all part of the local colour. But that is precisely what is so un-Arabic about Algiers, for it is con-

trary to Arab custom. The truth is that Old Algiers is medieval, Turkish, Moorish, or what have you, but not Arabic and certainly not African![59]

In truly Arabic towns like the Ksours in the south, the magic of Africa and its poignant mystery are actually tangible. They lie in the wide open space, the small, low, tumbledown houses, either very white or in the same hue as their hazy environment, in all that light and bleakness.

The trouble with Algiers is its abject population. Any sort of contemplative streetlife, of the calm and fertile, gratifying sort I love so much, is out of the question there.

The savage hatred I feel for crowds is getting worse, natural enemies that they are of imagination and of thought. They make it impossible for me to feel *alive* here, the way I do in other places. Oh, how evil civilisation is! Why was it ever brought over here?

M'sila, 29 June 1902, 2 p.m.

I left Algiers yesterday, 28 June, at 7.50 in the morning. The weather looked ominous and cloudy ... There were almost no stops, and the journey went by in a flash, as in a dream.

I am in a tiny hotel room, where I am waiting for supper. The heat is stifling. There has been a sirocco ever since we passed the Portes-de-Fer, and the countryside looks like a steambath. The sky is misty in that incandescent way brought on by thunder.

The road from Bou-Arreridj to M'sila goes through solitary places; some of them are parched, others marshy. Here and there runs a winding valley, lined with oleanders in bloom, its smell an acrid one of humidity.

From Medjez to M'sila, slept any way I could on top of a crate. Reached our destination by three in the morning. Went to the Moorish café, and to the market with Fredj. Had lunch inside the mosque, where it was cool and dark and there were relatively few flies. After that I came here for the siesta.

As always, it all feels like a dream, this journey, and sudden separation from Ouïha ... Poor Ouïha, who is without a penny and has got to cope with the ever worsen-

ing tedium of Algiers! If I could at least bring him some relief with this journey of mine!

I shall now try to go back to sleep, so that I will not be worn out during the night.

Bou-Saada, 1 July 1902

After a morning spent on clarifications with the Sid-el-Hokkaïn, we spent the afternoon in a garden belonging to the zawyia.

M'sila is a town built of mud, and it is divided in two by a deep oued. The greyish-brown houses have the dilapidated look of the Ksour, an impression that is reinforced by the handful of palm trees.

It was the maghreb hour, and I went by myself to wait for Si Embarek near the mosque located by the oued's edge. The sun was setting in the sort of mist that always comes with the sirocco. On the other side of the oued stood the old part of town; its curiously shaped marabout shrines and its sombre gardens all gave it a decidedly Saharan air. Tahar Djadi's mare is an excellent horse and I could not resist the temptation to let her run a bit. I felt as if I were back in the old days, when I had peace and freedom. We reached the borj of the Tolbas after dark, a solitary edifice, square and sombre in its desert setting. Had a second supper outdoors by the wall.

Had a bad night inside the courtyard, where I was devoured by fleas. When I saw the moon in its last quarter come up, pale and drenched in mist, I woke up the talebs and we left. We took a number of Arab shortcuts, via Saïda and Baniou. All we saw of Saïda in the early morning darkness were the black outlines of houses built of mud, without so much as a tree or garden, a grim sight indeed in the midst of that desert.

Farther on, while the taleb were saying the fajr prayer, I stretched out on the ground at the westernmost point. Si Ali, the talba, then left us, astride the red mare whose graceful little bay foal trotted alongside.

We continued on our way by ourselves. Baniou, a borj built high up, and a handful of houses made of toub. An alleyway lined with poplar trees.

Had coffee thick with flies and a drink of muddy water, in the shadow of some tamarind trees growing in yellowish sand.

In the sebkha before Baniou I felt so exhausted by the grey mare I had taken in the borj of the Tolbas that I dismounted and went barefoot for quite some time.

After Banou, we stopped at Bir-el-Hali: dilapidated houses made of toub, a well with good water. It was getting hotter and I continued my journey by mule. Drank along the way from a camel-driver's guerba.

Caught sight of Bou-Saada among the bluish mountains, with its casbah set on top of a rock, and a handful of very low, small dunes that looked white in the distance.

Arrival in Bou-Saada. On one side of it are spacious gardens enclosed by walls of toub. In the river bed stand oleanders in full bloom. On the high ground on the other side stand the town's houses. It is a picturesque and hilly place intersected by lush ravines where, among the dark green of the fig trees and vineyards, the odd oleander strikes a bright pink note and the pomegranate trees in bloom, vivid scarlet ones.

The heat was torrid yesterday thanks to the sirocco, and culminated in a violent storm last night. It does give the place that beloved and familiar atmosphere. Bou-Saada is surrounded by tall and arid, reddish-looking hills that block the horizon from view.

We dismounted under the arcade of the sheikh's house, near the justice of the peace. Facing it lies a scrawny, walled-in French garden. To the left stands a munitions depot and an unkempt garden where frogs croak all night long. The population is obsequious toward the 'hakkam', and a good deal more coarse and harsh than people in the Sahara.

Despite yesterday's heavy rainfall, the ground is parched. There are beautiful, slender-limbed camels of a Saharan breed that come to kneel down in front of the sheikh's house.

This afternoon we will set off for El-Hamel ... When will I be going home? When will I be seeing Zouïzou? Those are questions to which I do not know the answers.

The official tree here is a very green sort of mulberry, as

well as a variety of acacia whose flowers are like tiny yellow balls.

In any event, the journey alone has made it worth my while to come and discover this place which is, after all, part of my beloved South. In my present circumstances, this fairly long journey has been a golden opportunity.

The women's costume is unbecoming, in particular the huge flat headgear. Unless the Southern women's costume is worn by graceful, tall, slim women, it is dreadful. The one worn in the Souf is prettier and has more style. I cannot say anything about the women's physique, for I have not seen any. The little girls are heavily tattooed and have pale and savage faces.

El-Hamel, 2 July 1902, during the siesta hour

After the Moorish bath last night, we heard that Lella Zainab[60] had returned to the zawyia, but the darkness of the night, the wind and rain all kept us from setting out. Slept underneath the arcade.

Woke up very early. Talked with Sidi Embarek[61] till daybreak, and set off together without any coffee, he by mule, I on a handsome young white horse.

Slimène, Isabelle's husband, was named Khoja, or secretary to the administration of Ténès.

Ténès, 7 July 1902

My journey to Bou-Saada went so fast it felt like a dream, and I came back feeling all the stronger for it and cured of the morbid indolence that had been plaguing me in Algiers ... my soul too has begun to stir again. A nomad I was even when I was very small and would stare at the road, that white spellbinding road headed straight for the unknown ... a nomad I will remain for life, in love with distant and uncharted places.

Orléansville, 17 July 1902, 9.15 p.m.

Here I am again, back on the road, headed for Algiers. Luckily I will only be there for a few days on business for

the zawyia and Mme Ben-Aben. After that I will go back to Ténès, for a long time to come.

I left Ténès at six in the morning, in lovely clear weather. I was feeling tired and sleepy. When I got to the Trois Palmiers, I found the local policeman and a good horse. Went to see the caïd, whose name is Ahmed. The house stands on top of a high hill where the view is very beautiful: the African landscape's arid slopes follow each other in a variety of colours all the way into the very luminous distance. Set off again on horseback. Reached Orléansville by about six o'clock. It clearly is one of the prettiest cities in the interior, especially because of its setting. On its northern side it has a very high view of the Cheliff, and is surrounded by lush gardens.

I have been having a severe bout of fever ever since I got here, and I more or less lost consciousness for a few moments ... I am finding it difficult to write. I pray that I will not fall ill in Algiers, so far from my poor beloved Zouïzou!

Ténès, 25 August, evening

I am sitting on an arid hill facing the valley and the chaotic mass of slopes and mountains drenched in mist. The tall mountains along the horizon stand out in grey against the reddish-orange of the setting sun. All is peaceful in this Bedouin country, even though there may be the odd vague sound, the barking of dogs and the shouts of men.

To the right, beyond the gorges, lies a hazy stretch of sea, to judge by the empty horizon. To the left, at the top of a pointed hill, a dense thicket of shrubs which hide a handful of blackish stones that constitute a shrine, the grave of a marabout. Night is falling and all sounds are dying.

Ténès, Thursday 18 September 1902, 9 a.m.

The autumn has come. There has been a strong wind on quite a few occasions, and the sky is overcast with grey clouds. Our life is as monotonous as always, which would not be so bad if it were not for the perennial money problems. Yet here we do at least have the security of being able to satisfy our basic needs.

The problem with Ténès is its herd of neurotic, orgiastic, mean and futile females. Needless to say, here as elsewhere, mediocre people cannot abide me. All their mud leaves me cold, however, except when it comes too close for comfort.[62]

I have visited many places here, the Maïn, the Baghdoura, Tarzout, Cape Kalax, the M'guen ... Up and down the countryside I have been, through peaceful Bedouin territory whose boundaries are still so vast.

As for my mental outlook, these last few days have been bleak, and strangely enough, as usually happens nowadays, Ouïha is feeling the same way too. I am worried about his health. It may be, of course, that with regular treatment he will get better once and for all. If he was named caïd and if we went away from all the idiocy in Ténès, to some place in the mountains where the air is pure, with lots of rest and healthy living, he would certainly be happy.

As far as my literary activities go, these last few days have been a total loss. Today I am beginning to feel better, and this evening I will no doubt leave for the big annual feast at Sidi Merouan. My report on those festivities can give me the material for my next article for the ungrateful *Nouvelles*. The location and subject are just right for it. These last few days my health has been letting me down again. Is it the effect of my body on my mind, or vice versa?

Maïn, 21 September 1902, 10 p.m.

Once again I am the butt of the Algerian administration's boundless stupidity: the Commissioner has had a letter from Algiers. What will they think of next? The fact is, that the little folk in Ténès have turned in a report.

I am here in Maïn, in a small, clean room. The only drawback is that outside the window the billy goat keeps bleating and leaping about with female goats. Perhaps he will go to sleep at last ...

I came here by myself, in clear, very windy weather.

What is so strange and, on the surface at least, in total contradiction with the natives' character, is that the educated ones will confide in a woman like myself at the drop of a hat and talk to her in a way they certainly would not

98

talk to any man; witness the conversation I had with Si Elbedrani by the side of the road in the clear blue light just before dawn ...

Maïn, 22 September, 2 p.m.

I am all alone, in this small room of mine; the weariness of the last few days has *suddenly* evaporated and given way to a fruitful melancholia.

I have re-read my earlier diaries. No doubt about it, my present life is sheer bliss compared to that of recent years, even the Geneva ones! And as for any comparison between now and the time I spent in Marseilles!

There is a silence here that feels eternal. I should like to come and live here [or some place like it] for months on end, to shield my eyes from the ugliness of European humanity, for I loathe it more and more.

The only person in Ténès I like to talk to is my friend Arnaud.[63] But then, he himself gets no respect from that bunch of pretentious Philistines who strut about sporting tight trousers and silly hats.

Whatever their unenlightened way of life, the lowliest of Bedouins are far superior to those idiotic Europeans making such a nuisance of themselves.

Where can one go to flee them, where can one go to live far away from those arrogant, prying, evil beings who fashion everything in their own dreadful image?

I shall write to Nablus and look into the possibility of settling in Palestine, once I come into the ✝ *White Spirit*'s money, which will no doubt be soon.

Flee Europe, even in its transplanted form, go to some Arab country, similar no doubt to the one I love, and start a whole new life there ... Perhaps that will still happen! ☽ *Allah knows the things that are hidden and the measure of people's sincerity.*

Ténès, 26 September 1902, 9 p.m.

The year has almost run its course, and so has this note-book. Where will we be a year from now, at the start of the rainy season when the countryside dons its pale shroud and

99

takes its yearly rest, when asphodels bloom by winding roads? Neither of us thinks we will be here for very long. What ultimate direction will our destinies take?

It is cold and rainy. I worry about Ouïha's health in such bad weather.

It will not be long before my journey to Bou-Saada. Another visit to the South, its date palms, sandy wastes and grey horizons.

Algiers, Wednesday 13 October 1902, 5 p.m.

I have been here for ten days now, far from those peaceful lodgings of mine and from my sweet companion ... I am feeling sad, in the way that always produces ideas. Curiously enough, I am beginning to get a better notion of this part of the country and savour its special splendour.

The great bay of Algiers is as smooth as a mirror. The opposite shore looks violet with its pink houses ... Here on Mustapha's hill all is peaceful.

I may have to go to France this winter to see about writing a piece in defence of the Marguerite rebels.[64] Oh! if I could only say everything I know, speak my mind and come out with the whole truth! What a good deed that would be! In due course it would have positive results and establish my reputation too! Brieux was certainly right about that: I must start my career by coming out openly in defence of my Algerian Muslim brethren.[65]

I must stay here for at least a week. After that I shall have a great deal of work, for I shall have to do the brochure, probably write an article a week for *La Dépêche*, and little by little collect enough short stories to make a book and have them ready for the day my name will mean something in Paris, after the Margueritte trial. I shall be taking a big step this winter toward peace and salvation, so that my Ouïha and I will feel more serene at last.

Oh, Mama! Oh, Vava! Look at your child, who has followed in your footsteps and honoured you beyond the grave! I am not forgetting you. I shall always remember you. When things were at their worst, it was to you I turned.

The weather was beautifully clear Friday morning when I set out for the boundary of Oran province. Until the Bou-Zraya marketplace I had Lakhdar ben Ziou for a companion, a sombre and most unrewarding individual. At one point the road goes by the foot of a hill that is overshadowed by a sharp cliff. The cliff's soil is a beautiful and warm reddish-brown. There is a brief glimpse of Fromentin in the distance in between two mountains, or rather two high hills. It is a recently built village full of eucalyptus trees, a place without character, like all those villages built on lands taken from poor peasants who now work there on the ruthless terms set by the French Khammesat. The peasants do complain, but they bear their lot with utmost patience. For how long though?

The caïd of the Beni-Merzoug lives on a low slope below a hill called Mekamat al-Murabtine, so named after the Murabtine, a clan whose women are almost all prostitutes about whom the strangest witchcraft stories are told.

We could not find the caïd; so his son and I went back to Fromentin, where I was given a guide who was an idiot by the name of Djellouli Bou Khaled. We started out and kept wandering aimlessly. He did not know his way around.

The next afternoon we went to see the Ouled-Belkassem clan, an hour and fifteen minutes away. They live in a borj and mechta surrounded by a thornbush hedge, in a magnificent site. The regal-looking Ouarsenis Mountains[66] towered above the entire expanse of the Shelif plain. To the left, Orléansville looked like an oasis full of black greenery. To the right, the first plains of the Oran region stretched out as far as the eye could see.

The reason for our going there was a sad one, and apart from the admirable panorama I saw, the memory I have of that lap of my journey is a grim one, for we went to see a little girl who had been burned alive in curious circumstances that will never be explained.

Everything is very peaceful in this remote part of the world, very far from any contact with Europeans, a place where it is still possible to find repose.

Have good memories of that long trip. I suddenly had

101

another brainstorm, and think it was a useful one. I was travelling slowly in the sunshine along the road between Baghdoura and Fromentin, munching on a deliciously crisp cake I had bought in the market and on some dried figs I had been given by my travelling companion. Write a novel, tell the unique story of a man – rather like myself – who is a Muslim and tries to sow the seeds of virtue everywhere he goes. I must still find the plot, which would have to be simple and striking.

Today was the beginning of Ramadan,[67] a very special time of year, rife with strange emotions and, in my case, with wistful recollections. This is the third since the destinies of Ouïha and myself were joined. For the moment our life is peaceful and free of any immediate worries. ☽ *'Praise to Allah for delivering us!'*

Algiers, 25 December 1902

My discontent with people grows by leaps and bounds ... dissatisfaction with myself as well, for I have not managed to find a suitable *modus vivendi*, and am beginning to fear that none is possible with my temperament.

There is only one thing that can help me get through the years I have on earth, and that is writing. It has the huge advantage of giving the will a free hand, without making us have to cope with the world out there. That in itself is vital, whatever else it may yield in the way of career or gain, especially as I am more and more convinced that life as such is hostile and a dead end.

As of now, I will probably go to Medeah and Bou-Saada once the last five days of Ramadan are over.

Once again my soul is caught in a period of transition, undergoing changes and, no doubt, growing darker still and more oppressed. If this foray of mine into the world of darkness does not stop, what will be its terrifying outcome?

Yet I do believe there is a remedy, but in all heartfelt humility ☽ *it lies in the realm of the Islamic religion.*

That is where I shall find peace at last, and solace for my heart. The impure and, so to speak, hybrid atmosphere I now live in does me no good. My soul is withering and turns inward for its distressing observations.

As agreed, I set off for the Dahra on the evening of Thursday 11 December by the light of the Ramadan moon.

The night was clear and cool. There was total silence all over that desert town, as rider Muhammad and I slipped through like shadows. That man is so much a Bedouin and so close to nature that he is my favourite companion, for he is in total harmony with the landscape and the people ... not to mention my own frame of mind. He is not aware of it, but he is as preoccupied as I am with the puzzle and enigma of the senses.

At Montenotte and Cavaignac we went to the Moorish cafés there. We crossed oueds, went up slopes and down ravines, past graveyards ...

In a desert full of diss and doum, above a grim-looking shelf rather like those in the Sahara with shrubs perched high up on mounds, we dismounted to eat and to get some rest. The place felt so unsafe we started at the slightest noise. I spotted a vague white silhouette against one of the shrubs down below. The horses snorted restlessly ... who was it? The shadow vanished, and when we went by that spot, the horses were uneasy.

Our path led through a narrow valley intersected by many oueds. Jackals howled near by. Farther down we came to the mechta of Kaddour-bel-Korchi, the caïd of the Talassa.

The caïd was not there and we had to go farther still, until we found him in the mechta of a certain Abd-el-Kader ben Aïssa, a pleasant, hospitable man. We had our meal there and once the moon had set, we went off for Baach by paths that were riddled with holes and full of mud and rolling stones. At dawn the borj of Baach, the most beautiful in the area, came into sight high up on a pointed hill, looking very similar to a borj in the Sahara ...

Algiers, 29 December 1902, 2.30 a.m.

How curious and dreamlike is my impression – is it a pleasant one? I can't tell! – of life in Algiers, with all the weariness that goes with the end of Ramadan!

Ramadan! We spent its first few days in Ténès, in the soothing climate of family life the way it is at that

time of year. What a curious family we are, made up of people who have drifted together by accident, Slimène and I, Bel-Hadj from Bou-Saada, and Muhammad, who has one foot in the unforgettable Souf and another on those poetic slopes overlooking the blue bay and road to Mostaganem ...

31 December 1902, midnight

Another year has slipped by ... One year less to live ... I love life, out of curiosity and for the pleasure of discovering its mysteries.

Even when I was tiny, I used to think with terror of the time when our beloved elders would have to die. It seemed to me impossible they would! Five years have now gone by since Mama was laid to rest in a graveyard on Islamic soil ... It will soon be four years ago that Vava was buried in Vernier over in the land of exile, next to Volodia whose death has never been explained. ...

And everything else is gone. That fateful, hapless house has passed into other hands ... Augustin has vanished from my horizon where he used to loom so large. I have been roaming in anguish by myself, my only companion the man I found in the Souf, long may he stay at my side and bring me solace, ☽ *please Allah*.

What will next year bring us? What new hopes and disappointments? Despite so many changes, it is good to have a loving heart to call one's own, and friendly arms in which to rest.

Algiers, Sunday 9 January 1903,
midnight

It would be nice to die in Algiers, facing the harmony of that vast bay with the jagged profile of the Kabyle mountains in the distance.

Who knows how long my stay in Algiers will last, who knows how it will end? Who knows where I shall be tomorrow? Another journey southwards, in the direction of the desert, land where the sun is fiery and the palm trees' shadows blue upon the soil.

104

What I would like right now is to live over in Ténès, lead a quiet life there free of shackles, and keep going off on horseback in pursuit of my dream, from tribe to tribe.

Isabelle, after a series of short restless trips, journeys to Bou-Saada to visit the maraboute Lella Zainab.

Bou-Saada, Wednesday 28 January 1903, half past noon

Left Algiers at six o'clock on Monday 26th in clear weather. Reached Bou-Saada at 7.30 in the evening, stayed at the Moorish bath. Never have I been so keenly aware here of the vaguely ominous weight that seems to hang over all the occupied territories; it is something one cannot put one's finger on, but there are so many ambiguities and innuendoes, so many mysteries ...

In spite of my fatigue, and lack of sleep and food, this has been a good journey. The Ziar are kind and simple people, who sang their saint's *medha* to the accompaniment of gasba, zorna and bendar, each in turn, while the train wended its way in the sunshine I was so happy to have found again.

Chellal is a dreary village built of toub, a handful of wretched cottages set in a hollow full of water. An acrid smell of iodine and saltpetre hangs in the air.

The native population is made up of Ouled-Madhi and of Hachem, who are not very congenial. The maghreb was superb, with the mountains standing out in bluish-black against the reddish-gold of the sky.

I visited the Arab Bureau this morning, and by about one o'clock I went for a stroll in the Arab part of town, and in the oued, where Arab washerwomen stood out in blue and red dots of an incredibly warm intensity.

Once I rest tomorrow night at El-Hamel, I will do a better job of writing down my observations. The physical fatigue and lack of food I suffered till tonight have worn me out. The ride to El-Hamel will be good training for the long journey to Sahari and Boghar.

It looks as if I am no longer being persecuted. They tell me there had been no advance word of my arrival, yet they have been most pleasant, even the commanding officer ... how shadowy and mysterious these people are!

There is a heavy silence all around, and the only sound to break it is the occasional noise coming from the village or the zawyia, the distant sound of dogs barking and the raucous growls of camels.

El-Hamel! How appropriate that name is for this corner of old Islam, so lost in these barren mountains and so veiled in unfathomable mystery.

The same evening, about 10 o'clock

I am sitting on my bed, near the fireplace in the vaulted main room. That cheerful-looking fire and my bed right on the floor make the room look so much more gay and cosy than it did earlier in the day.

The 'hotel', a large square edifice, boasts a deep and desolate-looking inner courtyard full of bricks and stones. It leads to the upper floor which is divided into two rooms, a small and a large one, both of them with semicircular vaults, like well-to-do houses in the Souf. One of the windows looks out over the cemeteries in a south-western direction, the three others give out on to the east. There are three French beds, an oval table, chairs, all set on very thick rugs. With a few more authentically Arab touches, the room would look truly grand. I wish I could arrange it myself and do it justice. On the western side stand the tall buildings made of toub where the maraboute lives. To the north is the new mosque with its great round cupola surrounded by smaller ones, and inside it stands the tomb of Sidi Muhammad Belkassem.

I am going to lie down and rest, for tomorrow I must rise early to go and see the maraboute. No doubt I will return to Bou-Saada tomorrow afternoon, and will try to be there by the maghreb. After that I will have a week for a good look and that is a time I must not waste.

Bou-Saada, Saturday 31 January, 1 p.m.

We arrived here from El-Hamel yesterday at three in the afternoon.

106

Every time I see Lella Zainab I feel rejuvenated, happy for no tangible reason and reassured. I saw her twice yesterday in the course of the morning. She was very good and very kind to me, and was happy to see me again.

Visited the tomb of Sidi Muhammad Belkassem, very small and simple in that large mosque, which will be very beautiful by the time it is finished. I then went to pray on the hillside facing the grave of El-Hamel's pilgrim founders.

I did some galloping along the road, together with Si Bel-Abbès, under the paternal gaze of Si Ahmed Mokrani. Some women from the brothel were on their way back from El-Hamel. Painted and bedecked, they were rather pretty, and came to have a cigarette with us. Did fantasias in their honour all along the way. Laughed a lot ...

The legend of El-Hamel's pilgrims appeals to my imagination. It must be one of Algeria's most biblical stories ...

I began this diary over in that hated land of exile, during one of the blackest and most painfully uncertain periods in my life, a time fraught with suffering of every sort. Today it is coming to an end.

Everything is radically different now, myself included.

I have now been back in blessed Africa for a whole year, and hope to never leave it again. However poor, I have been able to travel and explore uncharted places in my adopted land ... My Ouïha is alive, and materially speaking, we are relatively well off ...

This diary, begun a year and a half ago in horrible Marseilles, comes to an end today, while the weather is grey and transparent, soft and almost dreamy here in Bou-Saada, another Southern spot I used to yearn for over there!

I am getting used to this tiny room of mine at the Moorish bath; it is so much like me and the way I live. I will be living in it for a few more days before setting off on my journey to Boghar, through areas I have never seen: a poorly whitewashed rectangle, a tiny window giving out on the mountains and the street, two mats on the floor, a line on which to hang my laundry, and the small torn mattress I am sitting on as I write. In one corner lie straw baskets; in the opposite one is the fireplace; my papers lie scattered about ... And that is all. For me, that will do.

There is no more than a vague echo in these pages of all that has happened these last eighteen months; I have filled them at random, whenever I have felt the need to *articulate* ... For the uninitiated reader, these pages would hardly make much sense. For myself they are a vestige of my earlier cult of the past. The day may come perhaps when I will no longer record the odd thought and impression in order to make them last a while. For the moment, I sometimes find great solace in re-reading these words about days gone by.

I shall start another diary. What shall I record there, and where shall I be, the day in the distant future when I shall be closing it, the way I am closing this one today?

'Allah knows what is hidden and the measure of people's sincerity!'

Isabelle Eberhardt was killed in a flood at Aïn-Sefra on 21 October 1904, nine months after this last entry in her journal.

NOTES

1 Isabelle's mother, born Nathalie Eberhardt, illegitimate daughter of Nicolas Korff and Fraulein Eberhardt, whose name she was given. She married General Paul de Moerder, a Russian nobleman and officer in Tsar Alexander's Imperial Army, by whom she had two sons and a daughter – Nicolas, Nathalie and Vladimir – before running off with her children's tutor, Alexander Trophimovsky, with whom she settled in Geneva, and by whom she had a son and a daughter – Augustin and Isabelle (who was registered in her maiden name). Madame de Moerder inherited the General's wealth, with which she subsidised her Geneva household. She became a convert to Islam, and died in Bône in Algeria, where she had gone to live with Isabelle.

2 Isabelle's brother Augustin, with whom she was thought to have been in love. It is not altogether clear whether Augustin was the son of General de Moerder (who recognised him, giving him his name) or of Trophimovsky. In any event, both he and Isabelle grew up believing that they were the children of a deceased Russian nobleman, and were never informed that Trophimovsky was their actual father.

3 Eugène Letord, a French Lieutenant attached to the Arab Bureau in South Constantine, with whom Isabelle corresponded in response to a request advertised in a newspaper. He was the first to suggest to her that she might establish herself in North Africa. He remained a good friend to her throughout her life, and may have been, for a brief period at least, her lover as well.

4 The name of the house in Geneva where Isabelle was born, bought with Madame de Moerder's money which had been left her by the General.

5 Alexander Trophimovsky, Isabelle's father (although unknown to her as such; she and Augustin referred to him as 'Vava', or 'Great-Uncle'). He was of Armenian origin, an ex-pope of the Russian Orthodox Church, an anarchist, a gifted scholar and a linguist. Engaged by the General as a tutor

to his sons, Trophimovsky instead became a lover to his wife.

6 Rehid Bey, a young diplomat of Armenian origin, who was attached to the Turkish Consulate in Geneva when Isabelle was in her late teens. He was a cultured man and an enlightened Muslim, who instructed his willing pupil in religious matters, and made passionate love to her. She called him 'Archivir', and he was to figure in her emotional life for several years to come.

7 The graves of her father, Alexander Trophimovsky, and of her half-brother, Vladimir de Moerder, at Vernier in Switzerland.

8 The Muslim cemetery in Bône where Madame de Moerder was buried.

9 Quoted from Pierre Loti's, *Le Mariage de Loti*

10 Isabelle's mother.

11 Archivir had by now been transferred to a posting in Paris.

12 Isabelle later wrote in the margin: 'In memory of that fateful date, 16 June 1900. That is how my fate was sealed, either by some unconscious mechanism or by pure inspiration. From the recesses of my soul came all of a sudden a picture of the road to be followed, the very road that was to lead me to the Bir Arbi garden and to Slimène, to the khouans, Behima, and salvation.' Marseilles, 23 July 1901.

13 Quoted from the *Journal des Goncourts*, Vol II.

14 An unfinished novel which Isabelle wrote, found among her papers at the time of her death, but rendered almost illegible from the effects of the flood which took her life.

15 All that we have of this is a fragment.

16 Quoted from the *Journal des Goncourts*, Vol III.

17 Isabelle later wrote in the margin: 'A few days later, the Mektoub saw to it that my lot was tied to Slimène's for ever.'

18 Written in the margin in 1901: 'My faith comes first, my Art comes next, and that will do, for those are the productive forces that embrace all of the universe.'

19 In the margin: 'The only thing that makes sense is the written word.'

20 Eugène Letord.

21 Isabelle left Marseilles on 21 July 1900, on board the SS *Eugène Pereire*. She arrived in Algiers at 3 p.m. the next day.

22 Isabelle noted in the margin: 'There was a French soldier there who had turned up from nowhere.'

23 This is Isabelle's first mention of Slimène Ehnni, a quartermaster of the Spahis, whose acquaintance she made one evening in the cool garden at Bir Arbi, and who was to become

her husband. She refers to him as 'Rouh', 'Zouizou', and 'Ouïha Kahla'.

24 Isabelle noted in the margin: 'A year's span! A year has gone by, and my life is linked to his for ever!'

25 Sidi Hussein ben Brahim, mokkadem of the zawyia of Guemar, and one of the sons of the venerated marabout and grand sheikh of the Kadrya confraternity, the late Sidi Brahim. Isabelle received her initiation into the sect through Sidi Hussein, who was impressed with her devotion, but who also thought that she might prove useful to him with the French authorities, with whom he believed she was affiliated.

26 Isabelle noted in the margin on 22 December 1900: 'A few days later, the house where we had that siesta was ravaged by typhus, which killed five people.'

27 Sidi Mahmoud Lachmi, brother of Sidi Hussein, son of Sidi Brahim, sheikh of the Kadryas. Si Lachmi had managed to impose himself as Grand Master of the Order, despite the fact that many refused to consider him as a marabout since his reputation for double-dealing and for scandal detracted from his powers of spiritual leadership. Isabelle fell under his powerful spell, becoming his sometime mistress and secretary.

28 The man who tried to kill Isabelle at Behima.

29 The day that Slimène was to be discharged.

30 Augustin wrote to Isabelle, thus making a gesture of accepting her union with Slimène, of which he had disapproved initially.

31 A French police officer.

32 The Tidjanya was an Algerian confraternity thought to be an ally of the French; it was hostile to the Kadrya confraternity to which Isabelle belonged.

33 Women were not allowed into the promiscuity of the fourth-class compartment, and Isabelle, who could not afford to travel in better style, was forced to disguise herself as a deck-hand.

34 Perhaps Isabelle had a premonition of her future death by drowning.

35 Dr Grenier was a former member of the French Parliament for the Doubs province, who paraded in native dress, claiming to be a Muslim for political reasons.

36 There is strong disagreement on this point. Some observers believed that the assassin actually belonged to the Kadrya confraternity, and had been ordered by Si Lachmi himself to do away with Isabelle, since the latter had tired of the mistress who had proved an embarrassment to him, especially as she wielded no power whatsoever with the French, contrary to what he had been led to suppose. But the case remains

111

mysterious, especially as accounts of it were suppressed at the time in the French North African press.

37 A descendant of the Prophet Muhammad, and thus a highly regarded notable.

38 Isabelle did in fact recover full use of her arm.

39 This was one of the explanations offered then. The Tidjanyas were thought to be in the pocket of the French, who did not much care for Isabelle during this period (although they were to find her quite useful at a later stage).

40 Some of Isabelle's more patronising sentiments. She was a colonial at heart, and something of an apologist for French rule in North Africa, which she believed to be both beneficial and benign.

41 During Isabelle's first journey to North Africa, she made a number of excursions on horseback into the Tunisian Sahel.

42 No sooner had the verdict been announced [twenty years of hard labour for Isabelle's assailant] than she was expelled from the country.

43 Sidi Lachmi.

44 A female marabout, a holy woman. In this fantasy, Isabelle was presuming a great deal about her status in North Africa. It is very difficult to believe that her aspiration to become a spiritual leader – the aspiration of a promiscuous foreign woman masquerading as a boy, and a penniless and power-less one at that – could have ever been taken seriously by a hierarchical religious society such as that of the confra-ternities, where maraboutism was on the whole an inherited spiritual and political eminence.

45 Madam de Moerder's money in Russia, left to her by the General on condition it be applied for in person at regular in-tervals. The question of this inheritance was appallingly mis-handled, so that Isabelle never managed to benefit from it at all.

46 In her brother Augustin's impoverished household in Marseilles.

47 Her half-brother Vladimir, who committed suicide in the Villa Neuve in Geneva.

48 Augustin's little daughter, Hélène.

49 Two pieces that Isabelle wrote in the hopes of finding a publisher.

50 After her expulsion from Algeria, Slimène went back to his barracks where he fell seriously ill. The letters he wrote to Isabelle at that time were those of a desperate man.

51 Slimène.

52 In fact, Slimène managed to recover from this bout of tuberculosis.

112

53 Editors who found Isabelle some work in journalism.
54 French doctor who cared for Isabelle after she was wounded at Behima. He was something of an anarchist himself, and a sensualist, and at some point in their acquaintance he and Isabelle had an affair.
55 Another of Isabelle's lovers.
56 A French officer who became Isabelle's lover.
57 Isabelle travelled to Geneva for ten days on 21 December.
58 The first time she actually meets Victor Barrucand, who was to be a help to her for the remainder of her life, finding her work and defending her interests, as well as those of Slimène. He would also edit her work for publication after her death.
59 Reflective of Isabelle's rather contradictory reaction to place.
60 An influential holy woman, a maraboute.
61 Sidi Embarek, another of the influential figures of the Kadrya.
62 A comment reflective of Isabelle's dislike of women.
63 The French Orientalist and writer, better known by his pen-name of Robert Randau, who had taken up an official post in the French colonial administration. He and Isabelle became firm friends, and he later wrote his recollections of her.
64 A nationalist revolt against the French in which a group of North Africans attempted to destabilise colonial rule by attacking a French garrison.
65 Although Brieux encouraged Isabelle to write about this subject, she never did, perhaps not wishing to offend the French colonial authorities.
66 L'Oeil du monde, one of the most spectacular peaks in the Algerian Atlas Mountains.
67 The Muslim month of fasting.

GLOSSARY

asr	afternoon, and afternoon prayer
bach-adel	notary
bach-hamar	head of donkey- or camel-drivers
benadir	chants
bendar	drum
borj	outpost building
burnous	traditional North African cape with hood, worn by men
caïd	notable, leader
chaouch	policeman
chechiya	headdress
chih	fragrant plant
ch'ile	torch
chira	variety of marijuana
deïra	head of locality
dikr	short prayer
diss	herb
djérid	palm leaves
dolce far niente	sweet do-nothingness
doum	herb
drinn	shrub
fajr	dawn, also morning prayer
fatiha	opening verse of the Quran
fellah	peasant
gasba	flute
gourbi	shanty town
guerbas	waterskins
habous	concierge
hakkam	ruler (referring to the French *colon*)
hamel	porter
hendie	cactus
icha	evening, the evening prayer
jujube	shrub
kabal	tribe
kachébia	Arab cloak

kenoun	coal brazier
kepi	cap
keram	fig tree
khammesat	agricultural system, whereby the peasant receives only one-fifth of the produce of the land he has worked
khouans	initiates in a confraternity
kif	literally meaning 'high', in this case referring to whatever induces the state: marijuana or tobacco
koubba	dome
ksar	county
ksour	counties
maghreb	literally, 'where the sun sets', but also meaning the time of day it sets, twilight, and the maghreb prayer
maghreb eddan	twilight call to prayer
maquis	bush, scrub (but also the anti-French Resistance Movement)
marabout	holy man
mechta	area surrounding the gourbi shanty
medha	religious ceremony of praise
mektoub	literally, 'that which is written', i.e. fate or destiny
mihrab	altar
misbahs	lamps
mokkadem	local sheikh
moucharabieh	carved wooden shutters
naib	delegate of a sheikh in a confraternity
nefsaoua des bendar	dervishes with drums
oued	valley, stream, ravine or river bed
oumara	vessel
roumi	literally 'Roman', but also Christian, western, etc.
sebkha	salt lake
segniyas	place where arms are kept
seguia	drinking bottle or pitcher
sekakri	seller of sweetmeats
sherif	descendant of the Prophet, a notable

115

shott	salt lake
shurafa	plural of sherif; notables
sobh	morning
souafa	connected to holy or burial ground
taam	feast
talba	student, initiate
tarika	holy sect
thujas	fragrant flowering plant
tolbas	students or seekers
toub	mud
wakil	keeper of the mosque
zawyia	home of marabouts, also serving as a school of theology and law, as a haven where students rest and persecuted men find sanctuary
zeriba	a sty or stable where livestock is kept
ziara	pilgrimage
zorna	flutes

Published by Virago Press Limited 1987
41 William IV Street, London WC2N 4DB

English translation by Nina de Voogd © Nina de Voogd 1987
Introduction and notes copyright © Rana Kabbani 1987

British Library Cataloguing in Publication Data

Eberhardt, Isabelle
    The passionate nomad: the diary of
    Isabelle Eberhardt. —— (Virago travellers)
    1. Eberhardt, Isabelle   2. Algeria ——
    Biography
    I. Title
    910.4′092′4   DT294.7.E2

    ISBN 0–86068–769–4

Printed in Great Britain by Cox & Wyman Ltd
of Reading, Berkshire

ISABELLE EBERHARDT (1877–1904) was born near Geneva, the illegitimate daughter of Nathalie de Moerder, née Eberhardt, and Alexander Trophimovsky, an ex-pope of the Russian Orthodox Church. Nathalie had left her husband, a general in Tsar Alexander's army, to elope with Trophimovsky, the tutor of her children. Isabelle, along with her half-sister Natalie, half-brothers Nicolas and Vladimir and brother Augustin, endured an unsettled, eccentric upbringing under the nihilistic and tyrannical Trophimovsky. But he grounded her well in Latin, Greek, classical Arabic, French, Russian, German and Italian. In 1897 she left the family home, the Villa Neuve, and went with her mother to the North African sea-port of Bône, where both of them converted to the Muslim faith. Later that year her mother died, to be buried in the town's Muslim cemetery, and Isabelle began her desert wanderings. She donned male attire, naming herself 'Si Mahmoud', a student and man of letters, and gained admittance to one of the North African religious confraternities, the Kadrya. She had numerous lovers, but just as controversial were her political sympathies, for Isabelle believed in French rule in North Africa, and through her association with the powerful General Lyautey worked directly as an agent of the Deuxième Bureau. In 1901 a mysterious attempt was made on her life, after which she was expelled from Algeria, returning only after marriage to her long-time lover, Slimène Ehnni, gave her the right to remain there permanently. Throughout her years in North Africa, Isabelle travelled widely, and often aimlessly, becoming much ravaged by the combined effects of poverty, starvation, disease, and excesses of *kif* and alcohol. She died at the age of twenty-eight in a flash flood at Aïn Sefra, on the Algerian–Moroccan border.

The notebooks containing her journals were found amongst her few possessions and were first published in Paris as 'Dans l'Ombre Chaude d'Islam' (1905), 'Notes de Route' (1908) and 'Pages d'Islam' (1920) by Victor Barrucand, who also included some of Isabelle's dispatches and made his own additions and deletions. Further manuscripts were later discovered and published in 1923 and 1944.

Preface

This book tells the story, from the point of view of the British Expeditionary Force (BEF), of the campaign in France and Flanders in 1940 that led to the evacuation from Dunkirk. It does not quite end there, for the British Army also participated in the fighting south of the Somme, a campaign almost unknown to most British readers. This was followed by yet another evacuation of nearly 150,000 British soldiers of what was sometimes called the 'Second BEF'.

The story of the saving of the BEF at Dunkirk has been told often, perhaps too often in the context of 'the dithering of Hitler and the immortal exploits of the "little ships" – to quote Brian Bond, a distinguished historian of the period. Less well known is the narrative of continuous hard fighting experienced by the main body of the BEF in the three weeks between the German invasion of France on 10 May 1940 and the end of the evacuation from Dunkirk on 4 June. When I mentioned that I was writing a book about the campaign to a field marshal, a distinguished veteran of the Second World War (but not of Dunkirk), his reaction was that there was plenty to say about the actual evacuation. He added, 'But the trouble is that the BEF did so little fighting before the evacuation.' The implication was that there was little to say on the subject. It has been my purpose to show that not only did the BEF have to fight hard, it had to do so while carrying out that most difficult phase of war, a withdrawal while in contact with a ruthless enemy. Many armies in history have found retreat more than they can handle and have disintegrated before surrendering, or have been cut to pieces with huge loss. The former was the fate of both of Britain's allies in this campaign.

The BEF of 1940 was not the best-trained or best-equipped army that has left our shores to fight overseas. Years of political dithering had seen to that. It was certainly nothing like as well trained as the superb German Army, throughout the Second World War perhaps one of the finest fighting organizations the world has ever seen. Viewed overall the BEF in 1940 lacked that difficult-to-define flair that marks out brilliant soldiers from plain practitioners of the art. Or put another way they were not 'quick enough on the draw' tactically speaking. Of course there were exceptions – some individuals

and units showed this flair – but it did not run through the whole force like a common thread. This comes only with training and good leadership. The BEF did not have enough time to train. It was not the fault of the soldiers, and the reasons for it are made plain in this book.

But, despite that, the BEF gave the Germans a testing run for their money, and this is made clear in the German assessment of the British soldier as a 'fighter of high value', in the report quoted in my final chapter. How much more challenging it would have been for the Germans had the BEF been better equipped and trained. It is hard to fault much of the leadership of the BEF – some of it was outstanding, as the reader will discover. From the ashes of the 1940 campaign in France and Flanders emerged many of the successful senior commanders in the British Army in the Second World War, starting with the man who would be the Chief of the Imperial General Staff from 1941 to the end of the war, Field Marshal Sir Alan Brooke (later Viscount Alanbrooke). The others include, and the list is not exhaustive, future army commanders Montgomery, Alexander, McCreery and Dempsey; corps commanders Lumsden, Horrocks, Ritchie (who briefly commanded Eighth Army) and Crocker; and divisional commanders Adair, Rennie and Whistler. These officers proved themselves in moments of the utmost danger in 1940, which would have broken lesser men, and sometimes did.

The soldiers they led were indomitable and were no different from their predecessors, in the words of Field Marshal Wavell writing of an earlier war, 'whose humorous endurance of time and chance lasts always to the end'. Of course there were instances where discipline broke down, of cowardice and of failure, but in the main these were a tiny minority. The manner in which they fought earned the respect of their opponents, which could not be said of their French and Belgian allies. It cannot be said too often that the retreat was not caused by failure on the part of the BEF; it was the consequence of their allies on either flank losing the battle. But in the end for the BEF it was a retreat to victory like that at Corunna in Spain in 1809 or Burma in 1942. Throughout, the soldiers of the BEF thought of themselves as better than their opponents, and this bloody-minded conceit sustained them in the darkest moments.

This is their story.

1

TWENTY WASTED YEARS

History provides many examples of a British Army being asked to operate under appalling handicaps by the politicians responsible for British policy, but I doubted that the British Army had ever found itself in a graver position than that in which the governments of the last twenty years had placed it.

Major General Noel Mason-MacFarlane briefing the press, 15 May 1940[1]

At 1334 hours on 3 June 1940, Admiral Jean Abrial, the French commander of the Dunkirk area, was ordered by the French high command to leave and embark for England. The British evacuation, less some of the more seriously wounded in hospitals and dressing stations, was complete. In peacetime Dunkirk was a busy commercial port; now chaos reigned in the town. The beaches were under German artillery fire, while French soldiers, sailors and civilians looted the burning buildings. British destroyers waited until darkness before heading for the moles to take off the French rearguard. Vice Admiral Bertram Ramsay, the Flag Officer Dover, asked that 'in return for the British effort on behalf of the French Army' the maximum number of British wounded should be included in the evacuation.

At about 2200 hours, Abrial burned his codes and embarked but, reluctant to leave his command, remained off the port and beaches until 0200 hours the next morning, before his ship steamed for Dover. Meanwhile all night crowds of weary men boarded a miscellany of craft including tugs, pleasure craft, cross-Channel ferries, launches, motorboats and destroyers that came alongside the moles at Dunkirk. At first light, on the orders of General Barthélemy, commanding the Flanders fortified sector, the French 68th Infantry Division that had been holding ground to the south-west of Dunkirk disengaged and withdrew to the port. Few of the division got away: a flood of deserters from the First, Seventh and Ninth French Armies, who had hidden in the town, emerged and blocked the route of Barthélemy's rearguard to the last ships. In desperation, some officers sent their men to the dunes in the hope of eventually finding ships off the beaches.

That morning the Germans entered Dunkirk to find the moles and approaches packed with enemy soldiers. For miles along the beaches lay a trail of military impedimenta: steel helmets, guns, trucks, small arms of all descriptions, boots and clothing, gas masks, wireless sets – and the bodies of men caught in the open on the beaches, killed in the fighting to hold the perimeter, or washed in by the tide from ships and vessels bombed and machine-gunned by the Luftwaffe. Off the beaches the wreckage of all manner of vessels protruded above the surface of the sea, or lay like stranded whales at low tide, their hulls and decks littered with dead French and British soldiers.

Before the French commanders surrendered to the Germans at the Hôtel de Ville, they signalled General Weygand, the French Supreme Commander, that nothing more could be done, adding that 'Admiral Abrial considers the operation of the English [sic] this night magnificent'. Admiral Darlan, the French Chief of the Naval Staff, signalled his thanks to the British Admiralty and to Admiral Ramsay. Nearly half as many French troops as British had been evacuated, but thousands more were marched off to Germany as prisoners. Perhaps some of them overheard the remark made by an unknown German officer: 'Where are the Tommies? Tommies gone and you here. You crazy?' The recriminations that ensued among the Allies were bitter, stoked among others by the Anglophobes Darlan and Marshal Philippe Pétain, the latter soon to be the head of the French government.

The arguments last to this day, and can be traced back to a misalignment of French and British perceptions about the situation as the Battle of France unfolded in May 1940. The French government, believing that the war was lost, with their army totally defeated and heading for destruction, a successful military outcome was unimaginable. They wanted the British to fight long enough in northern France, and eventually at Dunkirk, to buy time for both France and Britain to obtain an acceptable peace for both nations. The French did not articulate this desire, they merely hinted at it, hoping that this was what the British would do. The British had no intention of falling in with this vague and probably fruitless concept; they had an escape route and would take it, to live to fight another day. Brigadier Swayne, head of the British Military Mission to General Georges, commander of the French North-East Front, remarked: 'We who live in a small island regard the sea as a high road. For the French it is the limit of their country. To take to the sea would be to abandon their country and would be disgraceful.' To the British the evacuation at Dunkirk was a 'miracle'; to the French it was desertion. How did it come about?

The words of General Mason-MacFarlane quoted at the head of this chapter provide part of the clue to the situation in which the British found themselves in May and June 1940. Although often forgotten now, it was not until February 1939, only seven months before the outbreak of the Second World War, that the British government decided to commit a small part of the army to the continent in the event of German aggression in the west. This field force was to consist of four regular infantry divisions, the first two to arrive in their assembly area in France thirty days after mobilization. It was smaller than the British Expeditionary Force (BEF) of 1914, less well trained and lacking much essential equipment.

Britain had ended the First World War twenty years earlier with the best-trained, best-equipped and best-commanded army in her history. In the space of three months in the autumn of 1918, this army had fought and won a series of battles, each bigger than any in which it was to engage in the Second World War. By November 1918, the British Army had soundly defeated the German Army, taking more prisoners and guns than the French and American armies put together. No other army was in the same league. This was to change as the years passed. With the 'war to end all wars' won, Britain rapidly disarmed, while others talked about it and did nothing, or – like Germany – having disarmed, secretly rearmed. Starting in 1918, successive British governments assumed that there would be no major war for ten years, and from 1928, as each year passed, the assumed decade of peace was moved forward with it. The armed services were reduced, and for thirteen years these small forces were kept starved of equipment. In March 1932, seeing that others had not followed this example, leaving Britain dangerously weak, the government abandoned the ten-year policy and a policy of rearmament was discussed, though little was actually done.

> One would have lingering wars with little cost;
> Another would fly swift, but wanteth wings;
> A third thinks, without expense at all,
> By guileful fair words peace may be obtain'd.[2]

In January 1933 Hitler became German chancellor. The following year the British finally decided on a measure of rearmament, but by 1936, when Hitler's troops reoccupied the Rhineland in breach of the 1925 Locarno Treaty, there was little to show for it. By then Italy and Germany had formed the Axis alliance and were beginning to build large armies, while Japan – which joined the Axis a year later – was spending 46 per cent of her national income on armaments. In April 1938 London concluded that in the event of war with Germany the British contribution

to the Allied response should be provided mainly by naval and air forces. A large army would not be sent to the continent of Europe; instead its role would be confined to defending the United Kingdom and her overseas territories. So priority in the way of equipment for the army was given to anti-aircraft guns and coastal batteries. The five divisions of the field force trained and were fitted out for imperial defence, not for continental warfare against a first-class enemy. The Territorial Army (TA) was to be supplied only with training equipment. This was the state to which successive governments had reduced the British Army.

This army had been the first to use the tank in battle, in September 1916. After the First World War two men, Captain Basil Liddell Hart and Major General J. F. C. Fuller, preached that the future lay in massed formations of fast tanks, supported by mobile self-propelled artillery and infantry carried in tracked armoured vehicles. Instead of hammering away at a wide sector of front, as in 1914–18, the armoured formations would exploit a weak spot in the enemy defences and pour through in what Liddell Hart and Fuller called an 'expanding torrent', to attack vital points in the enemy's rear and paralyse him. In 1926, the British Army set up an experimental mechanized force to practise and develop these theories of armoured warfare. But two years later the conservative element within the army disbanded the force. Mechanization was eventually carried out but far too late for the whole army to assimilate the changed tactics that might have brought success in the ensuing campaign in France and Flanders in 1940.

Once the British government woke up to the dangerous situation that faced the country thanks to the failure to rearm, the Royal Navy and the Royal Air Force were rapidly, if belatedly, re-equipped (not always with the happiest results, but that is outside the scope of this book). The tasks envisaged for the Royal Navy did not impinge on operations ashore in France and Flanders in 1940. The role assigned to the RAF most certainly did. The 1938 re-armament programme called for a greatly expanded RAF capable of defending Britain and mounting bombing offensives against Germany. There was no provision for support of land operations that would have meant sending a large, mobile air force overseas. Although a proportion of the RAF's bombers might be stationed forward in France to decrease the range to German targets, these were expressly not in support of ground operations. The RAF had stoutly defended its independent existence since its creation in April 1918, and preached a doctrine called the indivisibility of air power. In essence, the RAF would decide where and how air power would be exerted. Simply expressed, the RAF's thinking was 'We will win the war on our own, and certainly

will not waste our time supporting you brown jobs' – or, if addressing the Royal Navy, 'you blue jobs'.[3]

Rearmament in Britain was boosted by the aftermath of the Munich meeting in the autumn of 1938, when it became apparent that despite the appeasement of Hitler by the British Prime Minister, Neville Chamberlain, peace was not at hand. The snag with rapid rearmament is that putting it into effect is considerably more difficult and time-consuming than deciding to go ahead with it. This is especially true if, as was the case with Britain, the armaments industry had been allowed to run down. Factories have to be geared up for a hugely increased rate of production, while new workshops may have to be built to augment existing ones that could not cope with the expanded output required. Weapons and equipment that are still in the trial stage of development, or even just a gleam in the eye of the inventor, may need further trials before production in quantity can begin. Finally soldiers have to be trained to use and maintain the new equipment. But it does not end there. Introducing a new gun into service usually involves designing and manufacturing a new type of ammunition. So yet more plant is required, and a workforce trained to operate it. Equipment needs spares to ensure that it is kept serviceable. These have to be manufactured too, sometimes in vast quantities. Rearming on a large scale involved placing orders abroad to supplement British production, or even to manufacture every piece, from complete equipments to spares. As in 1914–18, the bulk of these orders went to the United States. The British government should have been well aware of all the hurdles that had to be overcome in the great rearmament catch-up effort. Britain had undergone exactly the same experience in the First World War only twenty years earlier. There were plenty of people around in senior government posts who could remember this, and there was no excuse for being caught out a second time.

In February 1939, in addition to committing the army to deploying in France, and therefore to a war for which it was not equipped or trained, the British government doubled the size of the TA to 340,000, creating twelve new infantry divisions with supporting arms – thus compounding the problem the country already faced in the race to rearm. If that was not enough, a limited form of conscription was introduced. The conscripts needed equipment on which to train too.

Events now speeded up. On 14 March 1939, German troops invaded what had been left of Czechoslovakia after the dismemberment of the country at Munich the previous year. On 29 March, six months before the outbreak of war, Anglo-French staff talks began. The French made clear that the defence of their own territory was their first priority in the

event of invasion by Germany. When this had been secured, they intended remaining on the defensive until they had built up sufficient resources for a counter-offensive, while at the same time maintaining an economic blockade of Germany. The British had no difficulty in agreeing this strategy; indeed, since their contribution was so small, they could hardly do otherwise. At this stage in the talks the British revealed that there would be a gap of eleven months between the arrival in France of the first two divisions and the advent of the second two. The build-up for the counter-offensive would, the Allies agreed, be a matter of years not months, given that there was so much ground to make up in terms of equipment and manpower. They had to assume that they could force a stalemate on the Germans and ensure a repetition of the static warfare on the Western Front of most of the years 1914–18. This assumption was made despite the advances in warfare and equipment since 1918, especially in tanks and aircraft. It was a strategy based on the hope that the enemy would do what suited the Allies.

As the weeks went by, the British were able to tell the French that their proposed contribution was a general headquarters and two corps, each of two regular divisions, and an air component of the RAF. When the French Commander-in-Chief, General Gamelin, visited London in June 1939, he was told that the first two divisions of the British field force would now be able to arrive nineteen days after mobilization, and the whole of the rest of the regular contingent of the BEF in thirty-four days. British follow-up forces would consist of one armoured division, which would be available in early 1940, followed by another much later. As the TA divisions became ready for overseas service between four and six months hence, they too would be made available.

The French would have eighty-four to eighty-six divisions, of which twelve would be needed to guard the Italian frontier. So seventy-two to seventy-four would be available to garrison the Maginot Line, and to stem the German offensive wherever this took place. Along with the four British divisions the Allies could muster at minimum seventy-six divisions. Germany would be able to field 116 divisions. It was assumed that the Germans would attack Poland first, and that it was unlikely that France would be attacked until Poland was defeated. The Germans, having the initiative, would be able to deploy their greater strength at their main point of effort, whereas the Allies would be forced to cover the whole 500 miles of front from Switzerland to the North Sea until the Germans showed their hand.

The Germans also outnumbered the Allies in the air. At this stage, with four months to go before war broke out, the Germans could muster a total of 3,700 aircraft of all types against the Allied total of 2,634. If

Italy came into the war she would bring another 1,400 aircraft into the battle.

Staff talks were not held with Belgium or Holland. Both countries hoped that their neutrality would protect them from invasion. The Belgians believed that any staff talks with France and Britain would give the Germans the excuse to attack them when the time came to invade France. The Belgians had failed to learn the lessons of history: neutrality in 1914 had not deterred the Germans from attacking them when it suited them to do so as part of their attempt to outflank the French Army. Holland, having managed to retain its neutrality in the First World War, imagined that it could do likewise in any subsequent conflict.

In the months before war broke out, in an atmosphere of growing menace, Britain introduced full conscription, and partially mobilized the Fleet and the Royal Air Force.

*

On 1 September 1939 Germany invaded Poland after bombing her airfields without warning. Britain ordered full mobilization and, honouring her undertaking to come to Poland's assistance if she were attacked, sent an ultimatum to Germany timed to expire on 3 September. The Germans did not respond and, at 11.00 that morning, the Second World War began.

The British government made two other important decisions that day. The first was to appoint General the Viscount Lord Gort as Commander-in-Chief of the BEF. Gort, who was then fifty-three years old, was a highly decorated Grenadier Guardsman who had served with distinction in the First World War, eventually commanding in turn the 4th and 1st Battalions of his regiment and briefly 3rd Guards Brigade. He had been wounded four times, mentioned in despatches on nine occasions and awarded the Military Cross, the Distinguished Service Order with two bars and the Victoria Cross. A man of great personal and moral courage, he was not suited to high command and had been promoted well above his ceiling. It would be hard to better the description of his character by that very great soldier, then Lieutenant General Alan Brooke, commanding II Corps in the BEF, whose diary entry for 21 November 1939 reads: 'Gort's brain has lately been compared to that of a glorified boy scout! Perhaps unkind but there is a great deal of truth in it.'[4] On 22 November 1939 his criticism is more measured:

> Gort is queer mixture [sic], perfectly charming, very definite personality, full of vitality, energy and joie de vivre, and gifted with great powers of leadership. But he just fails to see the big picture and is continually

returning to those trivial details that counted a lot when commanding a
battalion, but which should not be the concern of a Commander-in-Chief.[5]

The second decision was to determine how Gort should conduct British
operations in France. The British government placed him under the
orders of General Georges, commanding the French North-East Theatre
of Operations. Gort was told, 'You will carry out loyally any instructions
issued by him.' He had the right of appeal to his own government if
at any time an order given by Georges appeared to imperil the BEF.
Gort was also told that, if General Georges wished to detach part of
the BEF for operations elsewhere, such an arrangement should only be
temporary.

As the Second World War began less than twenty-one years after the
end of the First, there were plenty of officers in the British Army with a
wealth of fighting experience. Thanks to the slow pace of promotion in
peacetime, men who had fought the Germans in the previous contest
could be found down to the rank of major. The commanders of I and II
Corps were both older than Gort, and had been senior to him before his
sudden and unexpected elevation to C-in-C of the BEF. Lieutenant General
Sir John Dill of I Corps, who was five years older, had risen in the First
World War to be a Brigadier General Staff (BGS) under Haig, and had
been a key planner of Haig's final and highly successful offensives in the
autumn of 1918. Lieutenant General Alan Brooke of II Corps was three
years older than Gort, had a keen brain and was to prove the star corps
commander in the BEF.

One of the youngest divisional commanders, at forty-seven, was Major
General the Hon. Harold Alexander, commanding the 1st Division in I
Corps, lately of the Irish Guards, having commanded a battalion of that
regiment at the age of twenty-five in France in the First World War.
Always immaculately turned out, nothing ever seemed to worry him.
Major General Bernard Montgomery, commanding the 3rd Division in II
Corps, was nearly fifty-two years old, and had already crossed swords
with Gort when chief instructor at the Staff College at Quetta in what
was then India. Gort, director of training on the staff of C-in-C India, had
taken exception to Montgomery's self-assertive instructional style. Montgomery never left anyone, however senior, in any doubt about what he
thought of them. Brooke was one of the few people he was in awe of, and
if anything his admiration for him increased as the war progressed.
Brigadiers, colonels and lieutenant colonels with fine fighting records in
the First World War were plentiful in the 1939–40 BEF. Some would go
on to high command later in the war. Others would fade out of the
picture.

The transportation of the BEF to France by the Merchant Navy, escorted by the Royal Navy, took place without the loss of a single life. The main ports through which the BEF landed were Cherbourg, Nantes and Saint-Nazaire in western France, the Channel ports through which the 1914–18 BEF had disembarked being deemed too vulnerable to air attack. The two corps of the BEF were deployed hundreds of miles to the east near the Belgian border and took over French positions between Maulde and Armentières, with French First Army on the right and French Seventh Army on the left. This was only the start. As the months passed, the build-up of the BEF continued, until a third corps was operational. By early May 1940, the BEF had grown from four divisions in two corps to ten divisions in three corps. The corps commanders were: I Corps, Lieutenant General M. G. H. Barker, who had taken over from Lieutenant General Sir John Dill on his appointment as Vice Chief of the Imperial General Staff (VCIGS); II Corps, Lieutenant General A. F. Brooke; and III Corps, Lieutenant General Sir Ronald Adam Bt. Meanwhile everybody waited for Hitler to begin his assault in the west, having carved up Poland in less than a month with his new ally the Soviet Union.

The German Army had used the opportunity of sending 'volunteers' to fight on Franco's side in the Spanish Civil War of 1936–9 to practise some of its techniques and theories. But, much more important, the war in Poland provided an excellent live-firing rehearsal for what was to follow in France six months later. The Germans learned a number of useful lessons, and were able to hone their procedures for employing battle groups, infantry–tank co-operation tactics, and the use of aircraft to provide intimate support for ground formations, as well as the necessary liaison and communications to orchestrate the modern all-arms battle.

The British were more up to date than the Germans in just one aspect, that of mechanization or motorization. The BEF that went to France in 1939 was a totally mechanized army. Like the German and French armies it had tanks, but in addition every infantry battalion had ten small open-topped tracked vehicles called Bren-gun carriers designed to provide some mobile protected firepower for the troops. Specially designed motorized vehicles towed all the BEF's guns, and all its supplies were carried in trucks, as were some of the troops. Cars, small vans and motorcycles were provided for commanders, for liaison and for carrying messages. On the outbreak of war, many of these vehicles were requisitioned from civilian firms. Like most other British formations, Major General Montgomery's 3rd Division went to war with laundry and bakers' vans. None of these commandeered vehicles were really suitable for military use – they were often underpowered and because they did not

have four-wheel drive were almost useless across country – but they were better than nothing.

The German Army on the other hand had many horsed formations and units, and persevered with them until the end of the war in 1945. Indeed, the vast majority of formations were not mechanized. Infantry divisions marched on foot, and although each had some 942 motor vehicles, the bulk of their supplies was carried in horse-drawn wagons, 1,200 per division. In addition horse-drawn artillery hugely outnumbered motor-towed pieces. Slow-moving horse-drawn transport should be allocated dedicated roads to avoid blocking the route for its motorized counterpart, but this was not always possible, and the resulting traffic jams sometimes impeded the progress of the army as a whole. Horses consume bulky fodder – yet another unwelcome problem for the logisticians. This horse–motor mix created a quartermaster's nightmare and was to contribute to the failure of the German campaign in Russia that was launched in 1941. Tactically there were two German armies: one fast and mobile, the other slow and plodding. This Achilles heel in the mighty German war machine was to be amply demonstrated in 1940. Only operational and tactical ineptness, principally on the part of the French, prevented the Allies from exploiting this fundamental weakness in the German way of making war.

The French pinned their defence hopes on the Maginot Line, named after the War Minister from 1929 to 1932 who as Sergeant Maginot had been wounded at Verdun early in the First World War. A great deal of the fighting at Verdun in the eleven-month battle of 1916, in which Maginot did not participate, had taken place in and around forts and concrete strongpoints on vital ground defending the city. Paradoxically, before the First World War, the French had scorned the concept of fighting from fortresses, opting instead for aggressive tactics out in the open, attacking the enemy with infantry and light guns regardless of casualties. During the Verdun fighting of 1916, the nature of the terrain and the determination of the French not to cede an inch of ground brought home to them just how important the fortress system was. Loss of some of the key forts nearly cost them the battle. That experience and the terrible losses the French had incurred in the First World War, not only at Verdun but also in numerous engagements both before and after that bloodletting, persuaded them that fortresses and artillery were the answer in any future war. In effect they fell into the age-old trap of planning to fight the next war on the basis of the last one. In 1921, Marshal Pétain, then Supreme Commander, set the scene for the French Army's doctrine on the use of armour, saying, 'Tanks assist the advance of the infantry, by breaking static obstacles and active resistance put up

by the enemy.'⁶ This was not the last time that Pétain, the saviour of Verdun, was to have a baleful influence on his country.

Constructed between 1930 and 1935, and extending from Luxembourg in the north to the Swiss border in the south, the Maginot Line was not really a line, but a string of concrete forts built about three miles apart, interspersed by smaller casemates. Both types were well buried, with only observation cupolas and gun turrets visible, and even these in many cases could be lowered flush with the roof. Advanced warning posts, anti-tank obstacles, wire and mines screened the forts. The garrisons varied from twelve to thirty men in the casemates, and from 200 to 1,200 in the forts. The latter were like underground villages, with barracks, kitchens, generators, magazines and even electric railways to transport men and ammunition from barrack and magazine to the gun positions. Casemates contained machine guns and one 47mm anti-tank gun, with heavy artillery in the forts.

Belgium was still an ally of France while the Maginot Line was under construction and so extending the line to cover the 250 miles of the Franco-Belgian border was considered tactless, as it would send a signal of no confidence in Belgium's capability to resist invasion, and would isolate her on the 'wrong' side of the wall. An added disincentive to extending the line was the expense. The eighty-seven miles completed by 1935 had cost 4,000 million francs in excess of the 3,000 million allocated in the budget. Finally, an extension of the line would run through the heavily industrialized region of Lille–Valenciennes on the Belgian border, causing major disruption to French industry. Experience in the First World War had persuaded the French that, if they were to avoid losing this northern industrial region, they would have to stop the invader before he crossed the French frontier. So when Belgium elected for a policy of strict neutrality, the French realized that they would have to enter Belgian territory from the west the moment the Germans invaded it from the east. In this event, instead of fighting from behind the concrete and steel of the Maginot Line on which so much treasure had been spent, the French would be forced to engage in a mobile battle of encounter in open country, a contest for which they were neither mentally prepared nor organized.

The French aimed to fight a methodical battle under a system of rigid centralization and adherence to orders from the top. Unit and formation commanders were supposed to remain at their command posts – the theory being that here, at the centre of communications, they were best placed to receive information and orchestrate the battle. This of course begged the question what one should do if the communications did not work. It was a question that demanded an answer, but the French failed

to provide one, and it was a key ingredient in their defeat. For there were few radios in French units and formations, and communication was mainly by messengers or by telephone, using either the civilian system or lines laid by the military. Initiative in subordinate commanders at whatever level was frowned upon. No one was trained to react to the unexpected, and therefore how to work through the chaos. The French doctrine ignored the German commander Helmuth von Moltke's dictum that 'no plan of operations will ever extend, with any sort of certainty, beyond the first encounter with the hostile main force', and that success in battle was, and still is, gained by the commander's ability 'to recognize the changed situation, to order its foreseeable course and to execute this energetically'.

French planning envisaged that as soon as the enemy attacked he was to be stopped by concentrated artillery fire and static defence, rather than by counter-attack. Local reserves would be placed in front of enemy penetrations to slow him down and eventually stop him. Meanwhile local superiority of men and equipment would be assembled, and then, and only then, would counter-attacks be mounted. The armour would not be employed in mass, but in penny packets accompanying the infantry as mobile pillboxes. Even had the communications worked, this rigid, pedestrian operational concept was hardly the best way to fight a mobile enemy. Once the two-way flow of communications was slowed by enemy interdiction, or even brought to a complete standstill, commanders sitting in their command posts would be completely out of touch and unable to influence events.

The German system was totally the opposite, and stressed personal initiative and what modern soldiers call mission command. Subordinates were told what their superior's mission was, and were expected to adapt their plans and the execution of them to achieve it, and to exploit a changing situation to their advantage, while their superiors supported them with all the means at their disposal. Everybody was trained to command at least one if not two levels above their own, and therefore able to take over when superiors became casualties. The leaders of Nazi Germany knew that their country was not well placed economically to fight a long war, but instead had to win swiftly. Thus was born the principle of lightning war, Blitzkrieg, which, following Moltke's teachings, demanded flexibility and the will to win. The German Army was adept at combining mass and aggressive tactics, and in achieving this the commander's mental alertness and drive were essential factors, for the force of his personality affected the whole of his command.

The Germans often used a tactic that today we would call recce pull. Armoured battle groups preceded by reconnaissance would find, or lever

open, the weak spots in the enemy defence and, using radio communications, 'pull' the main force through behind them; if necessary the main force would switch its axis on to the new line. This is the opposite of everybody bashing forward in a setpiece attack supported by a mass of artillery, only to come up against a rock-like defence. The success of mission command and recce pull depended not only on commanders being well forward where they could 'read' the battle, but also on their being in a position to communicate the necessary orders to take account of the changing situation, either face to face with subordinates or by radio. The German system demanded good secure radio communications, and they had them. In addition, German commanders were able to call upon support from their air force, not least dive-bombers that they used in lieu of artillery, particularly if they had advanced beyond the range of their guns. In this way the Germans fought a true all-arms battle, with infantry, armour, artillery and air. Their armour and mechanized infantry were concentrated in elite armoured (panzer) formations, with tanks used in mass.

For the Germans had taken note of British writings and experimentation on armour. Above all, Captain Heinz Guderian, who in the First World War had been on the staff of the German Crown Prince at Verdun, had become convinced that any future war should be fought very differently. He studied the works of Liddell Hart and Fuller and saw the importance of armoured formations, with tanks taking the leading role, not just as adjuncts to infantry. By 1931 he was commanding a motorized battalion equipped with dummy tanks – all that Germany was allowed under the terms of the 1919 Treaty of Versailles. He kept abreast of experiments by Brigadier Hobart's British 1st Tank Brigade on Salisbury Plain in 1934 by employing a local tutor to translate the articles Liddell Hart wrote reporting these exercises. The following year Guderian published a book *Achtung – Panzer!*, which analysed the successes and failures of the Allied use of tanks during the First World War – the Germans having used tanks only fitfully during that war, and those mainly captured Allied ones. He concluded that what was needed was a fast-moving, medium 'breakthrough' tank, not a heavy infantry-support tank of the kind fielded by the French Army. Hitler's accession to power saw Guderian's theories turned into reality, and by 1935 he was commanding the 2nd Panzer Division. The first pamphlets issued to the new panzer divisions were based on British Army manuals on the use of armour, not on the French equivalent, because of the rigidity of the latter's doctrine on the relationship between armour and infantry. *Achtung – Panzer!* was never translated into French or English, nor was it studied at staff colleges or by the general staffs of either country, although it foretold

precisely how Guderian would carry out the breakthrough at Sedan in 1940.

At this point it might be helpful to lay to rest some of the myths about the relative strengths and types of armour on both sides. The ultimate German success has been ascribed to superiority in the numbers and types of equipment, especially tanks. The French possessed some 4,000 armoured fighting vehicles of all types. Of these around 2,000 were fit for modern warfare. A good proportion of these modern tanks were the S-35s (known as Somuas from the initials of the maker). This was one of the best tanks in service in the world, with a 47mm turret-mounted gun. The French also had some slower but more heavily armoured Char B1s, with a hull-mounted short-barrelled 75mm gun, and a 47mm in the turret. The Somuas were grouped in three light mechanized divisions (*divisions légères méchaniques* – DLMs), very like the German light divisions in that they comprised motorized infantry with a powerful tank element. The excellent Somua medium tank was more heavily armoured, as fast as any contemporary German tank and, except for the *Panzer Kampfwagon* Mk IV, had a heavier gun. The Char B1s were grouped in three armoured divisions (*divisions cuirassées*). These had only recently formed and had undergone little or no collective training. A DLM had 220 tanks compared with only 150 in a *division cuirassée*. The DLMs were allocated to separate armies, and the *divisions cuirassées* to the reserve: one to the general reserve and two to the reserves of the French First Army Group in the centre, and deployed piecemeal.

The Germans had 2,539 tanks at their disposal when they started their offensive in the west, but of these 1,478 were obsolete Mk Is and Mk IIs, whose main armament consisted only of machine guns or 20mm cannon. The only battleworthy tanks were 349 Mk IIIs with a 37mm gun main armament, 334 Czech tanks also with 37mm guns, and 278 Mk IVs, which in 1940 had a short-barrelled 75mm and were intended as a close-support tank for the Mk IIIs. The Mk IVs were not upgunned until later in the war. So the French outnumbered the Germans in battleworthy tanks.

The British fielded three types of tank: the light Mk VI with one .303in and one .55in machine gun; three Marks of cruiser tank each with a 2-pounder main armaments; and two Marks of infantry tank. The Mk I infantry tank had a .303in machine gun, and the far heavier Mk II or Matilda had a 2-pounder and a .303 machine gun. One of the legacies of the preaching by Liddell Hart and Fuller on the subject of armoured warfare was that the British went to war with these three types of tanks: light tanks for reconnaissance; with cruiser tanks grouped in armoured divisions, highly mobile but weak in firepower; and infantry tanks

suitable only for infantry support. The correct answer, which took the British most of the war to arrive at, was a medium or main battle tank, combining firepower, protection and mobility in one type of tank. For technical reasons this was a difficult balancing act, but it was one which the Germans achieved long before the British. The tanks produced by the British were undergunned and, except for the Matildas, lacked armoured protection. Wedded to the 2-pounder gun, the British built tanks with turret rings far too small to accept any bigger-calibre guns. The 2-pounder was too small calibre to produce an effective high-explosive (HE) round, and fired only solid shot, which was useless against infantry and bunkers. Dual-capability and larger-calibre tank guns did not feature in the British inventory until the American tanks arrived (Lee-Grants and Shermans).

One of Liddell Hart's notions of future warfare, propounded in the inter-war period, was of 'fleets' of fast tanks, like ships at sea, roaming the area behind the enemy lines causing so much mayhem, especially by destroying his communications and headquarters, that the enemy was unable to continue the contest. Hence the British term 'cruiser' tank, following Liddell Hart's nautical analogy. This happy state of affairs could, so Liddell Hart predicted, be achieved at a low cost in casualties, provided the correct tactical formulae were applied. Unfortunately, Liddell Hart's theories of the 'indirect approach' (not attacking the enemy at his strongest point but finding a way round, or attacking a vital point in the rear), and the vision he dreamed up of 'fleets' of tanks swanning about, begged a number of questions: how did one break through the enemy in order to burst out into the open country beyond without a tough fight, especially if there were no open flanks; and what if the enemy was equally agile and mobile but reacted correctly, that is with a force of all arms, artillery, anti-tank guns, infantry and air? The British were to learn that armour must be accompanied by infantry (to deal with the enemy infantry, especially if equipped with anti-tank weapons) and by artillery (to destroy anti-tank guns, or at least neutralize them by killing and wounding their crews or by forcing them to keep their heads down in the interests of survival).

The French Army either had not read Liddell Hart or, in typically Gallic fashion, deemed any idea, military or otherwise, that had not originated in France as unworthy of a second thought. Whatever the reason, as mentioned earlier, the French also arrived at a flawed concept for the use of armour.

Almost all tanks, British, French and German, were vulnerable to all the types of artillery employed by either side. The exceptions were the British infantry tanks and the Char B1, which were so heavily armoured they were proof against the German 37mm gun, although not against

heavier guns. As the Battle of France was to show, as were later encounters in North Africa, tanks could be destroyed by 2-pounders, 75mm and 18-pounder field artillery, 105mm howitzers, 3.7in mountain guns, 25-pounder guns, and of course the 88mm anti-aircraft guns, provided that all these guns were firing using direct laying (pointing directly at the tank, not being fired from a position out of sight, directed by a spotter).

No Second World War tank could withstand a direct hit by a medium artillery shell, a 155mm or 5.5in gun. Tanks caught in artillery concentrations that included medium shells, even if not hit directly, could be set on fire, have tracks blown off and turrets jammed by shell splinters. Artillery fire could severely punish infantry and towed artillery accompanying armoured attacks, blow off radio aerials from tanks, and force commanders to shut down inside their turrets, which restricted their vision. Most commanders liked to move and fight with their heads out of the top of the turret, and the more thrusting ones would sit on the rim of the hatch to get the best view possible. Well-sited and resolutely handled field artillery batteries could repel a tank attack – a technique that the British practised before the war. The British 25-pounder was provided with an anti-tank sight, and when in action with its wheels on the round metal platform with which it was eventually fitted could be trained round quickly to a flank. The French 75mm field gun had been specifically designed to fire direct, which reduced its capability as a field gun, but made it a first-class anti-tank gun. In short, tanks often achieved their effect by appearing to be all-powerful, but they could be stopped.

It is sometimes forgotten that Hitler was not averse to building fixed defences, but for a rather different reason from that favoured by France. In the Rhineland, he constructed a line of concrete forts opposite the Maginot Line, known as the West Wall or Siegfried Line. In 1936, Churchill predicted how the Germans would use this line, which because of its intrinsic strength could be held by fewer troops than defences consisting of trenches, to release sufficient troops to 'swing round through Belgium and Holland'. The Siegfried Line would deter France and Britain from rendering aid to their eastern allies, first Czechoslovakia and subsequently Poland. Hitler could dispose of his enemies in the east at his leisure, before turning on the French with his rear secure.

In November 1939 Allied planners, expecting the Germans to outflank the Maginot Line and attack through Belgium, came up with what was known as Plan D. This called for the French 1st Army Group under General Billotte and the BEF to rush into Belgium and create stop lines to slow down and eventually halt the Germans in accordance with current French tactical principles. This would, it was hoped, buy time to

build up reserves for a counter-attack. The stop lines were based on river courses, particularly the Escaut (Scheldt to the Belgians) and the Dyle. The Dyle, further east than the Escaut, was where the initial stop line would be established – hence Plan D for Dyle being preferred to Plan E for Escaut. The Belgians were fully aware of the plan but, clinging to their neutrality, would allow only a few British officers in plain clothes to carry out reconnaissance.

The command arrangements were entirely of French design, the French being senior partner in the forthcoming campaign in France and Flanders by virtue of their overwhelming superiority in numbers over their British allies. The Supreme Commander, the sixty-eight-year-old General Maurice Gamelin, had no radio contact with the commanders in the field. He gave orders by messenger from his headquarters in the Château de Vincennes outside Paris. It would be misleading to imagine Gamelin as an earlier version of Eisenhower, the Supreme Commander of the Allied Expeditionary Force that fought in north-west Europe in 1944–5. Unlike Eisenhower, Gamelin did not have a staff of Allied officers working together to produce a common and agreed strategy. Instead a military mission under Major General Sir Richard Howard-Vyse was appointed to Gamelin's headquarters to represent the British Chief of the Imperial General Staff (CIGS); this was known as the Howard-Vyse Mission. Furthermore there was no Anglo-French equivalent to the Anglo-American Combined Chiefs of Staff, introduced after America came into the war at the end of 1941, to which Eisenhower as Supreme Allied Commander reported. Gamelin reported to the French government, and the British Chiefs of Staff effectively had no influence whatever over his decisions, other than representations by the Howard-Vyse Mission or personal visits by CIGS.

The outline command structure is shown in Appendix A. In addition to his responsibilities for the defence of France against German attack, Gamelin also commanded French troops in the Alps (facing Italy), Syria and North Africa. His deputy General Georges commanded the North-East Front, stretching from Switzerland to the Channel. Georges had three army groups under him, of which Billotte's French 1st Army Group was earmarked for operations in Belgium. This army group consisted of three French armies and with it, but directly under command of Georges, would go the BEF. Also directly under Georges was the French Seventh Army, which had an independent role operating behind and to the left of the Belgians at Antwerp to cover their left flank and also, if possible, to link them to the Dutch. It was a complicated and muddled set-up, with the BEF and French Seventh Army out on Billotte's flank, and having to co-ordinate their activities with his, which given the French

paucity of communications was not going to be easy. A mission under Brigadier J. G. de R. Swayne (known as the Swayne Mission) was sent to Georges' headquarters to represent Gort.

At the outbreak of war, the German offensive was under way in the east, carving up Poland. Poland's allies France and Britain did almost nothing, despite Gamelin having assured the Poles in May 1939 that immediately war broke out the French Army would take the offensive against Germany, and that by the fifteenth day after mobilization it would throw in the majority of its forces. The so-called Saar Offensive that Gamelin authorized in September was a pathetic affair. The trumpeting in the British press of a major attack on the Siegfried Line, and stories of secret 70-ton French tanks crashing through German lines, turned out to be eyewash. No more than nine divisions took part in the Saar operation. They were ordered not to advance beyond the outposts of the Siegfried Line, and to avoid casualties at all costs. Apart from taking some abandoned villages, the French gains were negligible. Not one German formation was diverted from Poland. When Poland capitulated, Gamelin ordered a withdrawal to the Maginot Line. When the Germans obligingly allowed the French to retreat unscathed, Gamelin sighed with relief.

The Germans were amazed and relieved. They had expected a full-blooded assault. The Siegfried Line was nothing like as strong as the Maginot Line, and was anyway not complete. As the frontier from Aachen to Switzerland was held by only twenty-five reserve divisions, with not one tank, and with sufficient ammunition for only three days' fighting, many German generals assessed that the French would be on the Rhine within fourteen days, and might even have won the war by then. Neutral observers noted how low morale was in Berlin, 'facing war with something approaching abject terror', in the words of Joseph Hersch, Berlin editor of the *Christian Science Monitor*. They were convinced that Hitler's bluff was about to be called at last; but they were wrong again. So began a period known as the Phoney War. During the Saar Offensive the morale of French soldiers had been high, but it sagged when this was called off. Arthur Koestler was an intellectual who fled Germany and was temporarily interned by the French as a suspicious alien in October 1939. He witnessed the French attitude first-hand:

> We talked to many of the soldiers. They were sick of the war before it started ... they wanted to go home and did not care a bean for Dantzig and the Corridor ... They rather liked La France, but they did not actually love her; they rather disliked Hitler for all the unrest he created, but they did not actually hate him. The only thing they really hated was the idea of war.[7]

Danzig was created a free city on the Baltic by the Treaty of Versailles in 1919, the aim being to give the Poles access to the sea through the territory called the Polish corridor. The city's population was overwhelmingly German and this played an important part in Hitler's case for going to war with Poland.

As the months of the Phoney War passed with no German attack, some British formations were sent to help man the French sector in the area of the Maginot Line. When it came to the 4th Division's turn, Lieutenant James Hill, a platoon commander in the 2nd Battalion Royal Fusiliers, spent Christmas 1939 in the *ligne de contact* (contact line) forward of the Maginot Line. It was bitterly cold that winter, and the forward companies lived in trenches dug by the French. The ground was covered by snow and one could see almost as well by night as by day. The nearest Germans were about four miles away. In the event of a heavy attack, the troops in the contact line would withdraw to the Maginot Line. Hill remembers that British troops manning the contact line were taken round the Maginot Line and were very impressed by what they saw.

The Germans patrolled, as did the British, in section strength (eight soldiers led by a non-commissioned officer), in the hope of capturing a prisoner. Hill did not seize any prisoners, but another company in the 2nd Royal Fusiliers managed to bag a couple. The French were not as aggressive as their opponents or their allies – in Hill's opinion, they did not want to stir things up. Winston Churchill, then First Lord of the Admiralty, commented:

> The prevailing atmosphere of calm aloofness often struck visitors to the French front, by the seemingly poor quality of the work in hand, by the lack of visible activity of any kind. The emptiness of the roads behind the line was in great contrast to the continual coming and going which extended for miles behind the British sector.[8]

Frenchmen also noted that their troops were occupied growing roses to pretty up the Maginot Line and painting the steps white, and that they seemed to have plenty of time for football instead of training.

Second Lieutenant Peter Martin, serving in the 2nd Battalion the Cheshire Regiment, a machine-gun battalion in Barker's I Corps, also had a low opinion of the French soldiers he came across. Martin had joined his battalion just before war broke out, but to his chagrin was not allowed to accompany them to France. He was deemed too young, the lower age limit for deployment on war service being nineteen and a half in those days. Having completed a machine-gun course, and still desperate to get to France, he was ordered to the Regimental Depot. There he learned from the adjutant that anyone who made advances to the niece

of the depot commanding officer got sent out straight away. So he made advances, which was not a chore as she was pretty and charming. Within three weeks he was on his way, joining his battalion in the Lille area. A machine-gun battalion had forty-eight Vickers medium machine guns. Martin took over number 7 platoon, consisting of two sections, each of two guns. In his own words he 'was raw and useless. I had some wonderful sergeants who "carried" me. The Platoon Sergeant really took charge. The soldiers were wonderful – if they liked you they "carried" you, if they didn't, they ditched you.'

More senior British officers were also less than satisfied with what they saw of the French during the long months of the Phoney War. The commander of II Corps, Lieutenant General Alan Brooke, who had a fine First World War record, recorded in his diary a visit to the Maginot Line on 20 December 1939. It is important to remember that these were his opinions at the time and were not written with the wisdom of hindsight: 'It gave me but little feeling of security, and I consider that the French would have done better to invest the money in the shape of mobile defences such as more and better aircraft and more heavy armoured divisions than to sink all this money into the ground.'[9]

Subsequent trips to the line did nothing to alter Brooke's view that the money could have been better spent. After inspecting the forts in the line, he went to visit 12th Infantry Brigade, which included Hill's battalion:

> We first went to the Black Watch [6th Battalion] in the 'Ligne de Recueil' [literally Line of Collection, a French expression referring to the line to which the outposts retire when pushed back by an attack], some 3,000 yards in front of the Maginot Line. This line has no defence and a rotten anti-tank ditch. From there we went up to the PWV [Prince of Wales's Volunteers – 1st Battalion the South Lancashire Regiment] holding the outpost line some 6,000 yards further forward. A line with no power of resistance, a few isolated posts far apart and only lightly wired in. German patrols penetrate right in behind our posts at dusk and at night. A no-man's land of some 1,500 to 2,000 yards exists between ill-defined fronts. But practically no activity on either side, a certain amount of shelling was going on either side and an air battle in the afternoon, otherwise absolute peace. The defence does not inspire me with confidence.[10]

Nor did the French soldiers he saw impress Brooke: 'French slovenliness, dirtyness [sic] and inefficiency are I think worse than ever.'[11] After attending a service to commemorate the Armistice that ended the First World War, he stood alongside General Corap, commanding French Ninth Army, to take the salute:

I can still see those troops now. Seldom have I seen anything more slovenly and badly turned out. Men unshaven, horses ungroomed, clothes and saddlery that did not fit, vehicles dirty, and complete lack of pride in themselves or their units. What shook me most was the look on the men's faces, disgruntled and insubordinate looks, and although ordered to give 'eyes left', hardly a man bothered to do so.[12]

Brooke was no Francophobe. He had been born in France and had spent his early years there, loved the country, and spoke French before he learned to speak English. He had visited Verdun in 1916, during the time of France's greatest trial, and had come away deeply imbued with the lionhearted spirit of the French soldier and the people. What he saw now devastated him.

He was just as critical of the state of training of the BEF, although not of its spirit, writing in his diary on 1 November that his corps still needed months of training before it could be considered fit for war.[13] After visiting the 4th Battalion The Gordon Highlanders on 26 November, he observed, 'It is totally unfit for war in every respect and it will take at least 2 months to render it fit. It would be sheer massacre to commit it to action in its present state in addition to endangering the lives of others.'[14]

The lamentable state of training of the BEF was of course a direct result of the way the British Army had been starved of funds by successive governments for twenty years. For example it was commonplace on pre-war field exercises to find flags representing anti-tank guns and football rattles taking the place of machine guns. Restrictions on the use of land resulted in exercises that lacked realism. Therefore when Brooke's II Corps arrived in France, having been promised a much needed period of intensive training, only to be told by Gort to take over part of the French defensive positions south of Lille, he was extremely put out. In this as in other matters Gort was deficient as a commander. During the whole eight months of the Phoney War, he did nothing to prepare the BEF headquarters for war, not once conducting a signals, command-post or movement exercise. An army, like any other military unit or formation, is the creation of and reflects its commander. Gort failed to give the lead required to ensure that his army used the precious time available to put right all the many deficiencies in training that had piled up in the locust years of the 1920s and 1930s. Brooke was the only senior commander who did prepare for the time ahead; taking his cue from him, Major General Bernard Montgomery, commanding the 3rd Division, did so too. Montgomery wrote later that 'in September 1939, the British Army was totally unfit to fight a first class war on the Continent of

Europe'. The other division in II Corps, the 4th, was not so well trained, and curiously Brooke did not sack the divisional commander. Montgomery trained his division rigorously, practising it in moving by day and night over similar distances that it would encounter during the advance into Belgium when the balloon went up. His exercises were designed to shake down his division into a fighting team so that it would hold together under the shock of battle and the chaos it brings in its train. For a collection of soldiers, however well trained in individual skills, does not make a unit or formation – it is the articulation of the whole that counts.

Training was not helped by the French insistence on radio silence, which severely limited the scope of command-post exercises that are so important in achieving the cohesion without which an army cannot exert its full fighting power. This ridiculous ruling by the French was not such a hindrance to training at battalion level as it would be today; in the British Army at that stage in the war there were no radios from battalion headquarters to companies, and on down to platoons and sections. Communication forward of battalion was by telephone, motorcycle despatch rider or runner. Lack of radios was to prove a considerable disadvantage in the war of movement that would actually take place, as opposed to the slow pace of most operations in the previous war.

The British regular divisions had a foundation of discipline, skill at arms and tactical proficiency that could serve as a basis for improving standards of training, and they used the long months of the Phoney War to do just that. The territorial divisions, lacking this grounding, and having been sent to France much later than the regular formations, found it more difficult to improve and become battleworthy. The general level of toughness and training was patchy throughout the BEF. To remedy this would have taken a far higher standard of strong leadership from the very top, based on an up-to-date doctrine of tactics and operational-level skills promulgated BEF-wide, than Gort and some of his formation commanders provided.

One of the problems encountered by the BEF during this period was the rising incidence of VD. This is hardly surprising. Brothels flourished in all the major towns and larger villages. Most of these were an eye-opener to young British soldiers brought up in what by today's standards were somewhat straitlaced circumstances. Girls and pin-ups in the modest bathing costumes of the time were commonplace, but going topless in public wearing just a thong as today's girls often do was unknown. So the reactions of young men like Bombardier Harding on going into a brothel for the first time are not surprising. 'We'd never seen anything like it. Girls with long black hair down their backs,

wearing just G-strings and high-heeled shoes. The G-strings disappeared leaving just their bottoms showing. You couldn't help yourself really. You couldn't get up the stairs fast enough.'

Montgomery's solution was to demand that the troops be educated and to insist that the subject of sex and disease was not buried under a blanket of sanctimoniousness. He issued an order on the subject, requiring that condoms be on sale in the NAAFI canteen and that the men be taught the French for 'French letter', in case they wanted to buy one in a shop. Outraged, the senior chaplain at General Headquarters demanded that Gort take action. Gort was minded to sack Montgomery, but Brooke persuaded him against the idea.

Captain White, the adjutant of the 1st/6th East Surreys, a TA battalion in the 4th Division, also under Brooke, recorded that their newly arrived commanding officer got into trouble when he bought up all the condoms in town and distributed them to the battalion free of charge. The padres were incensed, believing that he was encouraging the men to sin. They seemed oblivious to the outcome of the CO's initiative: the 1st/6th East Surreys had virtually no cases of VD, in contrast to most other units in the 4th Division.

Although morale in the BEF never approached the depths reached by the French, many units and formations succumbed to the boredom of the Phoney War, with the result that their preparations were lackadaisical. This air of unreality also affected some of the top civilians too. The British Prime Minister, Neville Chamberlain, visited the 3rd Division just before Christmas 1939 and whispered to Montgomery, 'I don't think the Germans have any intention of attacking us do you?'[15] Montgomery replied that the Germans would attack when it suited them, probably when the weather improved.

On 10 January 1940 Major Helmuth Reinberger, serving on a German airborne planning staff, flew in a light aircraft to Cologne, carrying with him a briefcase containing top-secret documents. The pilot got disorientated in bad visibility, and then his engine cut out, obliging him to perform a forced landing. To his horror he found himself just inside Belgian territory. Reinberger tried to burn his maps and papers, but only partially succeeded before they were taken from him by a Belgian captain who, accompanied by troops, arrived hotfoot at the crash scene.

The papers were soon at Belgian GHQ and, although badly scorched, were sufficiently legible to reveal that the Germans intended to invade France via Belgium and Holland. The Dutch and French were duly informed. The French Army, in a state of high alert, closed up to the Belgian frontier in appalling weather. The Belgian frontier barriers were raised, and for a moment it looked as if the Belgians were going to invite

the Allies in. But King Leopold, whose naivety had led to Belgian neutrality in the first place, rescinded the order, dismissing his chief of staff. By 15 January the flap died down. Spurred on by sight of the German plans, Gamelin strengthened the force that would go into Belgium in the event of a German invasion. Now instead of ten French divisions and the BEF, thirty would go in, among them the best the French Army could offer: two out of France's three new armoured divisions, five out of seven motorized divisions, and all three DLMs.

On the extreme left flank was to be deployed General Giraud's Seventh Army of seven first-class divisions, including one DLM. Until Gamelin made these changes, the Seventh Army was to have constituted the major part of General Georges' operational reserve. Gamelin's decision to commit it in Belgium from the outset was to have dire consequences. On Giraud's right would be Gort's BEF, positioned on the Dyle from four miles north of Louvain to Wavre. South of the BEF would come Blanchard's First Army, tasked with holding the Gembloux Gap down to Namur on the Meuse. Corap's Ninth Army was to occupy the line of the Meuse in the Belgian Ardennes south of Namur. General Huntziger's Second Army would deploy from Sedan to Longwy and the start of the Maginot Line.

Thus the main striking power of the French Army was to be committed to operations in Belgium north of Namur. This, as we shall see, was exactly what Hitler wanted. For years after the Second World War the French believed that the forced landing by Reinberger had been a 'cunning German plan'. It was nothing of the kind.

2

INTO BELGIUM: FIRST SHOCKS

'Hitler has missed the bus,' claimed Chamberlain in a speech on 4 April 1940, at the Central Hall in Westminster. Five days later the Germans occupied Denmark and began the invasion of Norway. The story of the ill-starred Allied campaign in Norway in response to the German invasion has no place in this book, but its last act was still being played out, during and after the evacuation of Dunkirk, and so provided an unwelcome distraction for the British government at that time.

At first light on 10 May, the Luftwaffe attacked Allied airfields, rail centres and other key points in France in an attempt to disrupt communications while the German Army had already started moving west. The British Official History dismisses the attacks, and it certainly did nothing to affect the British plans or moves. The main weight of the Luftwaffe fell on Holland that day, and much of their fighter force was flying top cover over the long columns of tanks, guns and infantry as they streamed forward to the attack, crossing the frontiers of Belgium, Holland and Luxembourg. The BEF's move to its positions on the Dyle went without a hitch. There was a moment of farce, however, when a frontier guard demanded that the leading unit of Montgomery's 3rd Division show him a permit to enter Belgium. The British charged the barrier with a 15-hundredweight truck, and the advance of the division proceeded. The leading mechanized cavalry reached the Dyle that night. The movements that day and the next, although carried out in daylight, were not interrupted by the Luftwaffe, which was busy destroying the Belgian Air Force, most of which was caught on the ground, and supporting the airborne invasion of Holland. Even so, the Germans managed to destroy six of the Blenheim light bombers of the RAF's 114 Squadron at Condé Vraux and render unserviceable the remaining twelve, as well as setting fire to the fuel dump. There was another reason why the German air force did not want to hinder the move of the Allies into Belgium unduly: it suited their plan. Not even the wily Brooke seems to have suspected that the BEF and French Seventh Army were being led into a trap.

As the BEF motored through Belgium, the civilians turned out to

cheer. Lieutenant Dunn led his troop of guns of the 7th Field Regiment, part of Montgomery's 3rd Division, through Brussels at about 0800 hours. As the guns bumped and rattled over the cobbled streets, crowds threw flowers, fruit and sweets to the soldiers riding on the gun quads (motor towers). The soldiers waved and grinned. Dunn thought of Wellington's army moving out of the same city on the way to Waterloo.

Eventually Dunn's troop arrived at their designated harbour area in a small village in a valley. A harbour area for any kind of military unit, be it a battery of guns, squadron of tanks or battalion of infantry, is a place where sub-units or units gather while waiting to move forward or back. Replenishment, especially of armoured units, may take place in the harbour area. Sentries will be posted and other defensive measures taken, such as digging slit trenches and siting anti-aircraft guns. But a harbour area is not a position from which one aims to fight – so field artillery, for example, will not be sited for firing. The countryside was green, rolling and wooded, a pleasant change from the industrial region of France where the regiment had spent the winter. As they were camouflaging their guns and vehicles, a German reconnaissance aircraft flew low over the village. The Bren gunners and riflemen blazed away, their shining faces turned to the skies. A quarter of an hour later two aircraft appeared and each dropped a bomb on the village. As far as Dunn was concerned it was the best lesson they could have had. From that moment on, he never saw any of his men fire at an aircraft with a rifle or Bren gun, as both were ineffective except at low level. Thereafter they lay low and kept still, or took cover. Looking up at aircraft is a sure way to be spotted, something that not everybody in the BEF learned.

The BEF deployed with two corps up along seventeen miles of the Dyle. On the right Lieutenant General Barker's I Corps had 1st and 2nd Divisions in the front line, and 48th Division held back; and on the left Brooke's II Corps had the 3rd Division up, and the 4th Division in reserve. Two other divisions, 5th and 50th, were in general reserve (elements of these two had been sent to Norway before the German attack in the west). Two more divisions, 42nd and 44th, were deployed in depth some fifty miles back on the River Escaut under Adam's III Corps. It was a good defensive layout with plenty of depth. Four more divisions of the BEF would be involved in the battles ahead: 12th, 23rd and 46th, which had been sent out for pioneering work (unskilled labour on the lines of communication) and to complete their training. They had no artillery and lacked much other vital equipment. Lastly, the 51st (Highland) Division had been detached in April to the Saar front to gain experience in the Maginot Line under French command, and never rejoined the BEF.

By 11 May, the only confrontation in the BEF's sector involved the

3rd Division which, by agreement of the Allied command, had been ordered to defend Louvain. As the division approached the town at dawn on 11 May, Belgian infantry fired on its machine-gun battalion, 2nd Battalion the Middlesex Regiment. When Montgomery informed the commander of the 10th Belgian Division that Louvain was to be defended by the BEF, the Belgian general said that King Leopold had entrusted the defence of Louvain to him, and that he would never leave his post without orders from his King, despite the agreed deployment that allocated a sector *north* of Louvain to the Belgians. Gort's reaction to this nonsense, instead of immediately taking the matter to Leopold, was to back down and tell Brooke to 'double-bank' the Belgian division. 'Not a satisfactory solution,' Brooke wrote in his diary.[1] Brooke went to see Leopold the next day, addressing him in fluent French, but found him totally under the influence of his malignant ADC, Major General van Overstraeten, and was not able to persuade him to change the order. Overstraeten interposed himself twice between Brooke and Leopold, rudely interrupting him, so that eventually the King stepped to one side and looked out of the window.

> I could not very well force my presence a third time on the King, and I therefore discussed the matter with this individual who I assumed must be the Chief of Staff. I found that arguing with him was a sheer waste of time, he was not familiar with the dispositions of the BEF and seemed to care little about them. Most of his suggestions were fantastic. I finally withdrew.[2]

Brooke found that Montgomery had solved the problem by putting himself unreservedly under the Belgian divisional commander's orders, which thrilled that officer. When asked what he proposed to do when the Germans attacked, Montgomery replied that he would place the Belgian under arrest and take command. In the event Montgomery did not have to carry out his stated intention. As German pressure on Louvain built up, the commander of the Belgian 10th Division decided not to fight but to move out so that he could, in his own words, 'rest his tired troops'. Montgomery was delighted to be shot of them.

That same day, Gort's Chief of the General Staff, Lieutenant General Henry Pownall, also had an audience with King Leopold, who seemed dazed. Pownall found Overstraeten suave, glib and specious. There he also found Generals Georges and Billotte, whose main aim appeared to be to persuade the Belgians that Billotte should co-ordinate the operations of the BEF and the Belgian Army, as a representative of General Georges. Gort should have been told about this change of command relationship long before battle was joined. However, Pownall, speaking

for Gort agreed, as did King Leopold. Gamelin, having been unaware of what Georges had cooked up, told him that it was 'an abdication', but did nothing to correct his subordinate's decision.

Gort loyally supported the new command arrangement, and the next day sent his vice chief of the general staff, Major General Eastwood, to Billotte to tell him that he was not only willing to accept him as co-ordinator, but would be glad to receive orders from him. Yet no radio link was established with Billotte, although the BEF had one with the French First and Seventh Armies, with Georges' headquarters and with the British mission at Belgian GHQ near Antwerp. Comparing Appendix B with Appendix A may give the reader a clearer idea of the alteration in the chain of command. From now on Gort understood that he had to look to Billotte for orders, and could no longer expect to receive orders from Georges. In such a situation, the co-ordinator (in this case Billotte) must be able to translate the directives from above (Georges) into practical orders which those he is supposed to be co-ordinating (Gort) can carry out. Equally important, the commander whose actions are being co-ordinated (Gort) must have confidence in the co-ordinator's judgement and be willing to act on his orders. The British Official History's understated comment is: 'In this instance the arrangements worked but haltingly, for neither of these conditions was ever wholly fulfilled.'[3]

It was a muddled command arrangement and also one that was not in accordance with the British government's directive to Gort when he was appointed to command the BEF in September 1939. The change was the outcome of a unilateral decision made by General Georges without any discussion with the British government, and Gamelin's reaction is evidence that it was sprung on him unexpectedly. The Allies had had eight months in which to sort out the command set-up before 11 May, and the situation they found themselves in after moving into Belgium was no different from that envisaged by the plan. That Gort's status was now effectively lower down the chain of command could be lived with in the interests of Allied solidarity, but much more serious was the confusion and lack of co-ordination that ensued.

The French high command had assumed that the Belgians' defence of their frontier and the delaying action of the British and French mechanized cavalry screen would suffice to prevent the Germans reaching the main defence line, the Dyle, before the Allies' move forward was complete. As far as the French Ninth Army was concerned this assumption was at fault, because some units of this army were engaged before they were established on the Dyle Line.

General Blanchard's French First Army, heading for the Gembloux Gap to the right of the BEF, was in an even unhappier position than the Ninth

Army. As it advanced it met a flood of Belgian refugees heading for France from the Liège area, and the air was thick with rumours of treachery and of a fifth column.[4] General Prioux's Cavalry Corps (2nd and 3rd DLMs, each with 174 tanks), the first to arrive at Gembloux, was disconcerted to find how thinly the Belgians had fortified this area, an open plain and excellent tank country. Worse, news came in that Eben-Emael had fallen. This supposedly impregnable fortress, sited behind the twin obstacles of the River Meuse and the Albert Canal, south of Maastricht, was designed to cover by fire the Albert Canal bridges at Briedgen, Veldwezelt and Vroenhaven west of Maastricht. It was garrisoned by 700 men and was the lynchpin of the Belgian defences on the Dutch border east of Brussels and Antwerp. On 10 May, seventy-eight airborne engineers of the Luftwaffe Koch Assault Detachment landed on top of the fortifications in gliders and, using hollow charges, kept the garrison cowed, while German parachute and glider troops captured the bridges. The following day the German 223rd Infantry Division arrived and captured the remaining fortifications. The Koch Detachment lost six dead and twenty wounded. Not since the German capture of Douaumont at Verdun in February 1916 had a fort been taken with so little loss on the part of the attackers and such pathetically weak resistance by the defenders.

Prioux, in view of the feeble Belgian resistance, and assessing that his corps would not have time to establish good defensive positions before the Germans arrived in strength, suggested to his army commander, Blanchard, that they should now switch the defence to the Escaut, some forty-five miles further back. Blanchard agreed, and told Billotte, who was shocked and told him that revising the plan at this stage was out of the question. Prioux would have to hold on until 14 May, while First Army speeded up its move to support him.

Meanwhile in Holland the situation unravelled with lightning speed. A combination of airborne troops and the 9th Panzer Division prised open the Germans' route to Rotterdam. On 11 May, Giraud's French Seventh Army, heading, as planned by Gamelin, for a link-up with the Dutch at Breda, ran into 9th Panzer at Tilburg. Unnerved by this unexpected turn of events, Giraud fell back towards Antwerp, now being flayed from the air by the Luftwaffe. The link-up with the Dutch, upon which Gamelin had gambled his mobile reserve of seven divisions, including 1st DLM, had now evaporated.

At this stage the BEF did not suffer directly in the way that the French First, Seventh and Ninth Armies did. The main German effort was not directed at the BEF's front, even though the Belgian Army was forced back more quickly than expected. Moreover in the British sector the Dyle

position was fairly strong, although three divisions covering some 30,000 yards meant that the defences on the actual river line were quite thin, and in any case the so-called river is only a stream. Furthermore, the banks were wooded in places, which made infantry infiltration by the enemy easier. But the river and the railway, which for most of the sector followed the eastern bank, were together quite effective in slowing down armour, and some stretches of the Dyle valley were flooded, which offered more of an obstacle. A system of dykes in Belgium's low-lying country held water drained from the land. Sluices, or gates, in the dykes could be opened to allow water into the rivers or, as a defensive measure, to flood the terrain. Near Louvain the Belgians had built some pillboxes. All things considered, attacking the BEF between Louvain and Wavre would be no walkover, especially against the well-sited British artillery.

The BEF had three days to prepare their positions on the Dyle, instead of six as planned. The few scattered pillboxes and wire entanglements left by the Belgians were a poor exchange for the numerous concrete defences, well protected by belts of wire and mines, that the British had prepared on the Franco–Belgian border during the winter. But at least there was something of an obstacle in front, which to an army trained to fight a static defensive battle, preferably behind an obstacle, rather than relying on manoeuvre and speed, was some comfort. The BEF also had plenty of support in the form of one heavy and eight medium regiments of artillery and eight machine-gun battalions shared between the three front divisions. In addition each division had its own three field regiments (each of two twelve-gun batteries of 4.5-inch howitzers, or 18-or 25-pounders) and an anti-tank regiment in direct support. The two battalions of the 1st Army Tank Brigade arrived by train and, after unloading off the flat cars on 14 May, rumbled into the Forest of Soignes, between Brussels and the field of the 1815 Battle of Waterloo. Both its battalions, the 4th and the 7th Royal Tank Regiment (RTR), were allocated to I Corps. Each was equipped with the heavy infantry tank. The 4th RTR had fifty of the old Mk I, weighing eleven tons but armed only with one machine gun. The 7th RTR had twenty-seven Mk Is, and twenty-three Mk IIs, the Matilda, weighing twenty-six and a half tons, and armed with a 2-pounder as well as a machine gun. Although slow, with a maximum road speed of 8mph for the Mk I, and 15mph for the Mk II, the British infantry tank was more heavily armoured than every other German or French tank of the period, except the French Char B1.

The air was thick with rumours and uncertainty as the BEF dug in and reconnoitred gun positions. Lieutenant Dunn's harbour area was bombed, but there were no casualties. Several men were shaken, but morale remained high, as it does when one has escaped bombing or

shelling without a scratch. Shortly afterwards, a despatch rider appeared with an alarmist message saying that the Germans were seven miles from Louvain, and the battery was to be prepared to pull back to another harbour some five miles away. Dunn listened to the German news in English on his wireless as the battery waited to move; it sounded so sinister that his morale was lower than at any time during the ensuing campaign. It was not the news that the Germans had crossed the Albert Canal, it was not the demoralized Belgians, some of whom were beginning to trickle back through the BEF, that dismayed him so much as the feeling that those who controlled the battery's movements had lost their grip. The battery area had after all been changed at least twice in eight hours. Dunn had heard the expression order-counter-order-disorder, but had never encountered the reality of it before. He was to discover that, throughout the campaign, men would carry out orders provided they were clear. The orders might be unreasonable, they might even be suicidal, but men would simply assume that they were the best possible in the circumstances. However, if they were constantly changing, doubt, fear of the unknown and loss of confidence set in. Dunn went to bed that night exhausted and unhappy. It was his first experience of war and its effects. He was to see plenty more in France in the course of this campaign, and would encounter it subsequently in the desert and again in north-west Europe in 1944–5.

Good leadership was, and is, the key to success in situations such as faced the BEF in May 1940. No less important, it has to be said, is the hardening of the heart and inner toughness that experienced troops acquire so that they expect chaos and learn to work through it. These were early days, and too many of the BEF lacked the demanding, realistic and exhaustive training that is one of the ingredients in inuring soldiers to the unpleasant surprises and shocks of war.

Bringing the guns forward from the harbour into a position in the forward edge of some woods proved a difficult task for Dunn the next day. The roads were completely blocked with Belgian troops and civilians. Eventually, having brought the guns into action, he went to choose an observation post (OP) from which he could spot for the guns, communicating with them by radio. He eventually found it on a hill to the west of Louvain, in such a position that he could see the forward side of the town, the direction from which the enemy would come. Having satisfied himself that his OP was well concealed, he crossed the Dyle and drove through Louvain, to fix targets in what would shortly be German-occupied Belgium. Arriving back at his OP, he found that the hill was now occupied by the King's Company, 1st Grenadier Guards. They were full of rumours: the Americans had given Hitler forty-eight hours

to get out of Belgium; Mussolini had shot himself; the King of Italy had abdicated.

One of the rumours that was to plague the BEF throughout this campaign concerned the sudden arrival of enemy parachutists. The use of parachute troops was a new form of warfare, which the Germans had not been slow to exploit, and had done so successfully. Because it was so novel, and neither the British nor French had paratroops in their army, and knew very little about their strengths and limitations, this form of warfare was invested with a mystique far beyond what was feasible. In the event the Germans never used parachute troops against the BEF or the French. But this did not prevent numerous false alarms, such as experienced by Lieutenant Dunn, who had a disturbed night on 12/13 May when some of his young soldiers saw a parachutist behind every tree in the gun position, and fired at them. In the end he had to beat the wood with a lighted torch before they were convinced that no such enemy had descended out of the skies.

The next day refugees were still pouring by, and the scenes of desperation were enough to cause even the most hard-boiled of Dunn's soldiers to remark, 'It makes you want to fucking weep, sir.' That morning reports came in that the British armoured cavalry were in contact with the Germans about ten miles beyond Louvain. Belgian units were withdrawing in a steady stream, some batteries moving at a brisk trot. Presently, a message was passed to the British artillery batteries that the armoured cavalry were clear, and registration of targets could begin.

Soon after the British blew the bridges over the Dyle in the afternoon of 14 May, German motorcyclists from the divisional reconnaissance battalions of three German divisions (19th, 14th and 31st) appeared out in the open beyond the river. Careless about taking cover, having had an easy advance so far, they were assailed by numerous Brens, and 'malleted' soon after by British artillery. German horse-drawn artillery came into action, and shelled some British forward positions, giving the soldiers their first experience of the 'whoeeer' noise of incoming artillery fire, followed by the ringing crump of a shell exploding. The British artillery rapidly replied, which was good for their own side's morale. Lieutenant Dunn felt supremely confident, and enjoyed directing his battery's first shoot in anger. The guns were in a good position, which was being made stronger every hour. He slept dreamlessly and well.

The German infantry first came into action at Louvain, in the form of the 19th Infantry Division, precipitating the Belgian withdrawal that so pleased Montgomery. But the delays caused by the misunderstanding over who was responsible for the defence of Louvain had the effect of impeding the British preparation of defensive positions. However, the

Germans hard on the heels of the fleeing Belgians were given a warm reception by the 3rd Division's Vickers medium machine guns, Brens and rifles, an onslaught soon joined by the division's field artillery. The 2nd Royal Ulster Rifles of the 9th Infantry Brigade, Montgomery's right-hand forward brigade, saw off the German attack with ease. But the 1st Grenadiers of 7th Guards Brigade, the left forward brigade, had been drawn further forward than they wished by the need to conform to the Belgian defensive layout. During the night they withdrew from the railway line to the Dyle Canal, suffering a number of casualties. The Dyle Canal ran north from Louvain a few hundred yards west of the River Dyle and the railway. The enemy managed to infiltrate some warehouses by the canal in 1st Coldstream's sector (7th Guards Brigade), but when they attempted to launch a pontoon bridge it was reduced to matchwood by British 25-pounder high explosive, a cheering sight for the guardsmen.

Soon after dawn the next day, the Germans – having reconnoitred the 1st Royal Ulster's positions by the railway station, goods yards and signal boxes – brought down two hours of artillery fire on them. Then German infantry came skirmishing in supported by their MG 34 machine guns. At the station the fighting swayed back and forth from platform to platform, as shellfire brought the glass roof smashing down on the defenders. Second Lieutenant Garstin, one of the Ulster platoon commanders, used the subway system to bring a Bren into action on the flanks and behind the attackers, forcing the Germans back to their side of the line. One of the signal boxes became the scene of a hectic grenade battle, which held the Germans at bay. At one point the attackers managed to cross the railway line and holed up in a tangle of wrecked and undamaged railway trucks in a goods siding. A brisk counter-attack by the Ulsters and the 1st King's Own Scottish Borderers, supported by the guns of 7th Field Regiment, turfed out the intruders.

The 1st Coldstream also had to mount a counter-attack. Having withdrawn from the riverbank to maintain contact with the Grenadiers when they pulled back, the position had to be retaken. The reserve company was brought up, and following a fifteen-minute 'stonk' by field and medium guns, and supported by two troops of the 5th Royal Inniskilling Dragoon Guards in Mk VI light tanks, the Coldstreamers retook the position with no losses to themselves.

The southern end of the British line also came under attack on the morning of 15 May. The German 31st Infantry Division, having reached the river before dawn on the 14th, had twenty-four hours for reconnaissance, and time to select a good spot for the attack. It chose a bend in the river, just north of Wavre, in the sector held by the 6th Brigade of 2nd Division. As an assembly area the Germans used the cover afforded

by the village of Gastuche near the river. Following a brief firestorm bombardment, the enemy infantry charged in soon after dawn on to positions held by the 2nd Durham Light Infantry (DLI), 6th Brigade's right-hand battalion. Before anyone could spot the attack, the Germans overwhelmed a platoon of the centre company holding a château. The Durhams' left-hand company also lost some ground and men. But the left-hand platoon, commanded by Second Lieutenant Annand, held fast at a demolished bridge and frustrated all the German attempts to scramble across on girders and planks. Apparently unconcerned by the mortar bombs and bullets raining down on the position, he repulsed the Germans twice, the second time by himself, rushing forward hurling grenades.

As the DLI were on a forward slope, they found it difficult to move about during daylight without drawing fire. Although a counter-attack by the reserve company managed to seal up the breach in their positions, they were unable to drive all the German infantry back across the river. But the field artillery and the Vickers medium machine guns of the 2nd Manchesters kept the Germans at bay and subdued as the day advanced. A company of the 1st Royal Welch Fusiliers was frustrated in its attempt to eject the enemy by counter-attack on the forward slope, but blocked any further incursion. Meanwhile, as evening approached, Annand was fighting off fresh attempts by the Germans to cross the bridge, dashing in and hurling grenades, although himself wounded. His platoon sergeant remembered that he came to platoon headquarters and asked for another box of grenades, as he could hear the Germans trying to repair the bridge. 'Off he went and must have been having a lovely time, because he was soon back for more. Just like giving an elephant strawberries.' Eventually Annand was ordered to withdraw, and on bringing his men back to the rendezvous he discovered that his batman Private Joseph Hunter was missing. Back he went and, having found Hunter wounded, carried him off in a wheelbarrow. He was making good progress when his path was blocked by a fallen tree. Now weak from loss of blood, he was unable to lift Hunter over. Reluctantly, he left his batman in an empty trench and set off for help. Eventually he collapsed but was later taken to safety and evacuated. For his rescue attempt and his courageous actions, Annand was awarded the VC, the first won for the army in the Second World War. Hunter was captured by the Germans, but died in hospital a month later.

So far the Germans had not succeeded in penetrating the Dyle positions held by the British at any point. However, on the right in the French First Army sector a 5,000-yard breach had been made where there was no river protection. Gort offered the 48th Division from British I

Corps reserve to plug the gap, but Blanchard, the French First Army Commander, preferred to pull back to the line between Châtelet and Ottignies. This meant that the British I Corps had to conform, and swing back from Rhode-Sainte-Agathe along the line of the River Lasne, a tributary of the Dyle about four miles to the west, to link up with the French. Accordingly orders were given to the 2nd Division and right-hand brigade of the 1st to withdraw that night. Unfortunately the notice was short and the enemy were active, especially on the front of the 6th Brigade, all of whose battalions were fully engaged. A withdrawal in war is difficult enough, but hugely more so if one is in contact with the enemy. First-class discipline and control are needed if the operation is not to end up with the enemy following up like wolves tearing down a stricken prey and turning withdrawal into a headlong rout. A clean break covered by heavy fire is the recipe for success. In this case a bombardment by British artillery covered the noise of transport and troops moving to the rear, and kept the enemy distracted and their heads down.

The 1st Royal Berkshires had the most difficult time. Their CO, Lieutenant Colonel Furlong, arrived back from receiving orders at brigade headquarters at 2300 hours, and, finding that his telephone lines to his companies had been cut by shellfire, sent a subaltern on a motorcycle to pass on the orders for the withdrawal. About an hour later, he discovered that the young officer was in the regimental aid post (RAP) dying of wounds. So he himself set off, riding pillion behind a despatch rider. On the way a shell-burst knocked some of the spokes off the back wheel, but they carried on, and Furlong managed to communicate the orders. The Berkshires successfully broke contact, the noise of their transport and that of the other battalions covered by the guns in support. The guns' muzzle flashes lit up the dark night as they fired off stocks of ammunition so carefully built up over the preceding days, and which they would have neither the time nor the trucks to take away.

Although the Lasne was a poor substitute for the Dyle and did not offer any prospect of being held for long, the general situation on the BEF's front was encouraging. At Louvain, where the heaviest attacks had been made, the position was still being held, and everywhere the BEF gained immensely in confidence from these first encounters with the enemy. By now, the morning of 16 May, the Dutch had been out of the fight for two days.

Up until 12 May, Gamelin, along with most other senior commanders, British as well as French, had had their attention firmly fixed on the developments in Belgium and Holland. Gamelin's HQ, Grand Quartier Général (GQG), was convinced that the German main point of effort was between Maastricht and Liège. The London *Times* military correspondent

declared, 'This time there has been no strategic surprise,' an allusion to
the Schlieffen Plan of 1914 which had hoodwinked the British and
French. General Ironside, who was one of Britain's most experienced
battlefield soldiers but was probably past his best when appointed CIGS,
a job for which he was unsuited by temperament, wrote in his diary, 'We
shall have saved the Belgian Army. On the whole the advantage is with
us. A really hard fight this summer . . .' By the time these words were
written, strategic surprise was about to be unleashed upon the Allies. It
was called *Sichelschnitt* by the Germans, in English 'sickle-cut'. It was to
hack through the French, and almost took the British in its deadly swing.

Plan Yellow

The first version of the German plan to attack in the west, Plan Yellow,
was prepared by the Army General Staff and issued on 19 October 1939.
This version stated that the attack would be made on the western front
through Holland, Belgium and Luxembourg, with the aim of defeating as
much as possible of the Allied armies, to win as much as possible of
Holland, Belgium and northern France as a base for air and sea warfare
against 'England' and also to provide a wide protective area in front of
the Ruhr.[5] Having stated the general purpose of the plan, the order dealt
only with operations against Holland, Belgium and Luxembourg, taking
the invading forces up to the northern frontier of France; the scheme for
subsequent operations was not covered. Army Group B, consisting of
three armies, was to attack north and south of Brussels, before heading
for the coast between Ostend and Boulogne.

The plan was changed at the end of October 1939, and in this second
version the aim was changed to defeating as substantial a portion of the
Allied Armies in northern France and Belgium as possible in order to
create favourable conditions for the continuation of the war on land and
in the air.[6] The main emphasis was no longer on the axes north and
south of Brussels; the attack on Holland was omitted (although the
Maastricht appendix would be crossed in the advance on Belgium to the
north of Liège); and the axes of the attacking formations would fan out
from north of Brussels to Sedan. This was the plan the Allies believed
they would face when Hitler attacked, and on which all their plans were
based, including rushing into Belgium.

Colonel General von Rundstedt, on being appointed to command Army
Group A, concluded that Yellow version two was a bad plan. He had not
seen version one because he had only just returned from Poland. His
objection was that it did not cut off the Allies from the Somme but

merely pushed them back, which risked a replay of the stalemate of the First World War. Colonel General von Brauchitsch, the C-in-C of the German Army, did not agree. The argument continued until the end of December, whereupon there was some tinkering with the plan, and it was reissued as version three, but without changing its overall concept. Rundstedt and his brilliant chief of staff, Lieutenant General von Manstein, continually pestered Brauchitsch to strengthen the southern wing with more armour, and to concentrate the main point of effort here, but to no avail. All along, the driving force behind this concept was Manstein. The offensive was ordered for 17 January 1940. The forced landing of Major Reinberger's aircraft, described in Chapter 1, occurred on 10 January, and gave the Allies valuable information on Plan Yellow. But, although this caused much pother in the German camp, the plan was not changed. The offensive was cancelled because of the weather, *not* because the plan had been compromised. Indeed a fourth version of Plan Yellow was issued. Rundstedt, with Manstein supplying the vision, continued to badger Brauchitsch.

Two Army Group A war games were held in early February, a normal part of the German operational planning process.[7] In the course of the one carried out on 7 February, attended by Brauchitsch's chief of staff, General Halder, it seems that the latter began to warm to what Rundstedt wanted. On 17 February, Manstein was dining with Hitler on his way to take up a new job commanding XXXVIII Infantry Corps. After dinner, he took the opportunity to expound his and Rundstedt's views that the whole plan of campaign should be changed by placing the main striking power on the left wing. It is possible that this was the first time that Hitler had heard of this concept, because Brauchitsch had refused to report Rundstedt's views to him. The Führer was immediately taken by the idea. Whether Brauchitsch learned of what had transpired at the dinner is not clear, but the next day he and Halder briefed Hitler that they intended to strengthen the left wing, that is fall in with Rundstedt's wishes. Hitler approved, and in the end Rundstedt got far more armour than he had asked for. The whole weight of the attack was transferred to the left wing. Colonel General von Bock's Army Group B, consisting of twenty-six infantry and three panzer divisions, would still attack into Belgium, distracting the Allies' attention. But Rundstedt's Army Group A, of forty-four divisions, would attack through the thinly defended Ardennes, then turn north and cut off the French and British forces. The armoured sickle of Army Group A consisted of three panzer corps: Hoth's XV (5th and 7th Panzer Divisions); Reinhardt's XLI (6th and 8th Panzer Divisions); and Guderian's XIX Panzer Corps (1st, 2nd and 10th Panzer Divisions). Guderian had the largest corps with over 800 tanks, and was

supported by the crack GrossDeutschland Infantry Regiment. Guderian's and Reinhardt's corps were formed into a panzer group under General von Kleist, giving a total of 1,222 tanks, 41,140 vehicles and 134,370 men. Colonel General von Leeb's Army Group C remained behind the Siegfried Line, a threat to the Maginot Line.

Commanding the 7th Panzer Division in Hoth's XV Panzer Corps was the newly promoted Major General Rommel. After commanding Hitler's personal guard battalion, Rommel had been appointed to a panzer formation although he lacked previous experience of armour. He was to give a breathtaking performance in the campaign.

In both November and January, when the Germans had intended to mount Plan Yellow but had subsequently called it off, the Allies had received six days' notice that an attack was impending, mainly from intelligence about troop movement forward to the start positions. This gave rise to the assumption that when the attack finally came the Allies would have six days to prepare positions from the moment movement forward was detected. However, when the final version of Plan Yellow was approved, the Germans did not have to allow time for preliminary moves, because on the previous two occasions when formations had begun advancing, only to have the offensive cancelled, the troops had remained where they were. So, of the six days allowed for movement, three had already taken place. The Germans had also tightened up their security, which allowed them to close up to the frontier in great secrecy. When the order was given to start Yellow at midday on 9 May, the Germans were able to attack at daybreak on 10 May. The Allies reacted only *after* the attack had actually begun.

Guderian crossed into Luxembourg at 0435 hours on 10 May. The French had estimated that it would take an enemy force ten days to reach the Meuse through the Ardennes from the Luxembourg border. In the event 1st Panzer Division arrived at the river at 1400 hours on 12 May. The French detected armour in the Ardennes, but had their eye taken off the ball by Army Group B to the north. The Allies agreed that the Ardennes would not be the main effort. The French in the Ardennes were in such disarray that Sedan was occupied by the Germans along with the north bank of the Meuse by last light on 12 May. The French now expected a pause, as laid down in their manuals, to allow the enemy to concentrate before tackling such a major obstacle. But on 13 May Guderian, in modern soldiers' language, conducted a bounce crossing of the river with all three panzer divisions using massive air support. The Luftwaffe backed the crossing with 310 bombers, 200 Stuka dive-bombers and 200 fighters. A mere seven French aircraft appeared over Sedan, and were seen off. The German commanders were close up behind their

leading troops, while the French as required by their doctrine sat in their command posts; while Guderian was overlooking Sedan or on the banks of the river, the commander of French X Corps, General Grandsard, was more than twelve miles away.

It was the German infantry and assault engineers, with Luftwaffe support, who made the crossing and subsequent breakout possible – not the armour. None of Guderian's tanks went over on 13 May. The first to do so, from 1st Panzer Division, crossed the bridge constructed by the assault engineers at 0200 hours on 14 May. Reinhardt at Monthermé, in the centre between Hoth and Guderian, was having a harder time crossing in the face of regulars of the French 102nd Fortress Division, a tougher proposition than the B reservists positioned elsewhere on the Meuse. It was to take Reinhardt another two days to get his armour across. Further north, Hoth at Dinant also started pushing his armour over the Meuse during the night of 13/14 May, a crossing made possible by the drive and bravery of the infantry and assault engineers, and the support of the ubiquitous Luftwaffe. It was here and thereafter in the breakout that the Stuka (Ju 87) was used in lieu of artillery which, being mainly horse-drawn in the German Army, could not keep up with the armoured advance. This development shattered the confidence of the French; they simply could not believe the speed at which the enemy armour moved. Thinking in terms of the First World War, and in particular of the way both sides had used artillery in that war, they believed that the armour would have to wait for the guns to catch up at each phase of the battle.

Early on 14 May, General Georges flung himself into a chair and burst into tears. 'Our front has been broken at Sedan,' he announced. On 15 May, the German armour began its breakout from the Meuse bridgeheads. That day at nightfall Georges heard that Corap's Ninth Army had been routed along a fifty-mile front, and likewise Huntzinger's Second Army. Georges replaced Corap by Giraud; in addition, the remnants of Giraud's own Seventh Army were to come south, passing behind the BEF, in an attempt to plug the hole torn in the French defences. Huntzinger, whose army's defence had been no less ineffective than Corap's and his command style no less unsure, was left in charge.

Holland surrendered on 15 May, adding to the gloom. Her tiny army had been swept away, but it was the bombing of Rotterdam that had shattered Dutch spirit. The Dutch claimed that 30,000 people had perished in Rotterdam in seven and a half minutes. Post-war investigation revealed the true figure to have been 980. But the damage was substantial: a square mile of the centre of the city set alight, 20,000 buildings destroyed and 78,000 people made homeless. Rotterdam was the first city

in history whose bombing was the cause of national surrender; the next
two were Hiroshima and Nagasaki in 1945.

Also on 15 May, the French Premier, Paul Reynaud, telephoned Winston Churchill, the new British Prime Minister, and told him, 'We are
defeated – we have lost the battle.' Churchill decided to fly to Paris the
next day. Gort knew very little more about the disaster to his south other
than what he could glean from broadcasts over the radio. The supposed
co-ordinator on this front, General Billotte, whose duty it was to keep
Gort in the picture, was in the same state of despair as Georges. Major
Archdale, a liaison officer at Billotte's HQ, was horrified by the lack of
order and decision, and by the spectacle of weeping staff officers. Gort
knew that the Belgians on his left were on their last legs, and was aware
of the serious breach in the French Ninth and Second Armies. His most
immediate concern was the withdrawal of the French First Army on his
right, and its supine attitude towards mounting a counter-attack. By
nightfall he assessed that Louvain might be enveloped, so he sent off
Major General Eastwood early on 16 May to ascertain what Billotte
intended doing about the situation on the Allied front in Belgium.

Billotte had already moved his HQ once, to Caudry, about eighty miles
from Gort's forward command post. Caudry was uncomfortably close to
the battle, and actually lay in the direct path of the German armoured
thrust, so a further move, to Douai, was ordered. Eastwood arrived at
around 0600 hours and found Billotte amid the scurry of preparations
to relocate the HQ. He had nevertheless made a plan: his armies were to
fall back on the Escaut starting that night, 16/17 May. The withdrawal
was to be carried out in two stages, so that over three successive nights
the positions would be established as follows:

Night 16/17 May	Charleroi–Brussels–Willebroeck Canal (known to the BEF as the Line of the Senne)
Night 17/18 May	Maubeuge–Mons–Ath–River Dendre to Termonde, thence line of River Escaut to Antwerp and the sea (known to the BEF as the Dendre Line)
Night 18/19 May	The frontier defences to Maulde – the line of the River Escaut to Ghent and thence the canal to Terneuzen (known to the BEF as the Escaut Line)[8]

Gort issued a warning order to the BEF to pull back to the Senne Line
that night, 16 May, beginning at 2200 hours. He held a conference at
I Corps HQ to give orders for the plan of retirement. Major General
Needham, head of the British Military Mission at Belgian Army HQ,
attended, and on his way back to report to the Belgians was seriously

hurt in a car crash. Several hours elapsed before the Belgians knew of
the British withdrawal to comply with Billotte's orders.

When the order to retreat percolated down to the soldiers in the BEF,
they were astonished and aggrieved. Only six days before they had
advanced sixty miles to meet the enemy. They had encountered them on
the Dyle and had so far frustrated all their attempts to break their line.
Now they were to fall back. They were in tremendous spirit and the
fighting had increased rather than sapped their confidence. Second
Lieutenant Martin's men of 7 Platoon, the 2nd Cheshires were typical in
being 'staggered' to be told to withdraw. They had experienced some
good machine-gun practice shooting German snipers who had tied themselves to trees about 1,000 yards to their front, followed by shooting the
men who had been sent to cut them down – 'good fun without much
danger'.

In the early evening of 16 May, Lieutenant Dunn's battery was ordered
to continue firing until all the dumped ammunition, some 600 rounds
per gun, was expended. It appeared that the enemy had broken through
on the right of the 1st Division, and the battery was to withdraw to the
River Dendre. The regiment was moving at once, but Dunn's troop was
to remain in action until 2000 hours under command of the 8th Brigade,
the rearguard for the 3rd Division. Dunn was to report to the brigade
commander in the scout car at once. The guns were red hot by this time
and the gunners stripped to the waist. They could not understand why
they were being told to retreat: 'Why, sir? Why? Why don't we advance?
If they leave us here, nothing will ever get through this.' Dunn explained
that nothing would, but that it was elsewhere that things had gone
wrong, and that unless they moved they would be cut off.

Telling them that the French front miles away to the south had been
shattered did not seem to the soldiers sufficient reason to pull out. But
the pattern was set: now and for the next ten days the position on the
flanks of the BEF, rather than the actions of the enemy directly to their
front, would chiefly determine events. Gamelin's master plan lay in
ruins. On 16 May, Churchill learned just how much of a ruin when he
arrived at the Quai d'Orsay in Paris for a meeting with Reynaud and
Daladier, Minister of National Defence and War. Churchill had taken
over from Chamberlain as Prime Minister only five days before. Gamelin
told him that north and south of Sedan German armour had broken
through on a fifty- to sixty-mile front. The French Army in front of them
was scattered and destroyed and the Germans were advancing at speed
either towards the coast via Amiens and Arras or straight for Paris.
Behind the armour, eight or ten German divisions, all motorized, were
driving onwards, making flanks for themselves against the two separated

French armies on either side. Churchill asked, 'Où est la masse de manoeuvre?' (Where is your strategic reserve?). Gamelin shrugged and replied, 'Aucune' (There isn't one).[9] Churchill, looking out of the window of the Quai d'Orsay, saw clouds of smoke rising from huge bonfires where 'venerable officials' were burning large wheelbarrow-loads of archives. By his own admission, he had experienced one of the greatest surprises of his life: that any commander having to defend 500 miles of front would not have a strategic reserve had never occurred to him. That the British government or War Office had not known about it was inexcusable. Gamelin and the two ministers were convinced that all was lost. The general made some remarks about bringing in divisions from Africa and withdrawing some from the Maginot Line to mount a counter-attack on the flanks of the German penetration, or 'bulge' as he called it, during the next two or three weeks. His remarks carried no conviction. That was the last Churchill saw of Gamelin.

Meanwhile, unaware of events in Paris or of the true magnitude of the French disaster, the BEF withdrew from its positions on the Dyle and Lasne. The general plan for the withdrawal of the BEF was for the two front-line brigades of each division to thin out and finally retire through the reserve line held by the third brigade. This well-practised method of withdrawal by night would be replicated down the chain of command. So brigades would thin out their front-line battalions, which would finally retire through a line held by the rear battalion, and so on through companies and down to platoons and sections. Thinning out usually meant that about half a battalion, company, platoon and section would quietly move back to a rendezvous in rear, perhaps behind the rear reserve line. When joined by the balance of the battalion or company that had held the position until the time for the final withdrawal, everyone would set off for a pre-designated rendezvous at which the whole battalion or formation would assemble before moving off to the new defensive position either on foot, in transport or both.

All formations and units usually send back reconnaissance parties to lay out the new position in rear, and receive their units and sub-units and allocate them to the new locations immediately on arrival, thus saving time. These reconnaissance parties usually consist of the seconds-in-command at all levels from lance-corporals in rifle sections up to majors in battalions and senior staff officers in brigades and divisions, and hence sometimes known colloquially as 'the second eleven'. Reconnaissance parties move back in a body under control, and at a predetermined time probably laid down by divisional HQ. As discussed earlier, conducting a successful withdrawal when in contact with the enemy demands well-trained and disciplined troops, and tight control.

It is usually easier at night. In daytime, if the enemy is alert, well trained and in contact, the forward units and formations may not be able to thin out but may instead have to conduct a fighting withdrawal, with sub-units covering each other by fire as they withdraw in stages covered by fire from artillery and the reserve unit or sub-unit. A daytime withdrawal in contact is one of the most difficult phases of war to conduct successfully, and the ability to do so without losing cohesion in spite of casualties is the mark of a first-class outfit.

Lieutenant Dunn, having been told to support the 8th Brigade, drove up to find Brigadier Woolner and his staff having dinner, and they sent him to Lieutenant Colonel Bull, the CO of the 4th Royal Berkshires, whose battalion was covering the withdrawal of the brigade. Dunn arrived in the middle of the CO's conference, and he got the impression that the CO was a bit 'rattled'. He told Dunn to stay as long as possible, to fire an SOS defensive task at high rate at midnight, and then be in a position to cover the battalion on the eastern outskirts of Brussels at 0300 hours.

At last light units began thinning out, and two hours later forward units and sub-units pulled back through rearguards. Once all forward troops were through, these too pulled out, and except in one or two cases a clean break was achieved. This was a manoeuvre that most had practised, none more assiduously than Montgomery's 3rd Division. The 2nd Royal Ulster Rifles of Montgomery's 9th Brigade, after two days of fighting in Louvain, had no difficulty breaking contact; likewise the 1st Grenadiers of Montgomery's 7th Guards Brigade on their left. The 1st Coldstream, also of 7th Guards Brigade, on the extreme left of the BEF, had it less easy. The Belgians on their left started withdrawing prematurely, in the early afternoon, and the Germans following them up started to work round the Coldstream and engage their left flank and even their centre companies from the rear. Supporting fire from the divisional artillery and the machine-gunners of the 2nd Middlesex took their toll of the Germans, and held them. But any move out in the open by the Coldstream rifle companies drew fire. Here the carriers came into their own, bringing ammunition forward and taking wounded to the rear. At 2100 hours, as planned, the withdrawal began, timed to be complete by 2300 hours. As the first troops came back under cover from their own artillery, the Germans crossed the Dyle canal and entered the town of Herent, through which the withdrawal route lay. The rearguard of reserve and headquarters companies fought desperately to hold the road open, as the forward companies came back with bayonets fixed to turf out the enemy. Streams of tracer arced across the withdrawal route and mortar bombs crumped around the guardsmen. The Coldstream

casualties mounted to 120, mostly in the left and centre companies. But the rearguard held Herent, and checked that all the survivors of the forward companies were through, before pulling out itself. The 5th Inniskilling Dragoon Guards now assumed the rearguard, carrying some of the lightly wounded on their tanks.

Dunn's troop in support of the 4th Royal Berkshires, having fired ten rounds per gun at intense rate on each SOS target, limbered up and got away. As they passed the long columns of infantry on the road, the gunners were loudly cheered. At 0240 hours, Dunn's troop came into action in a suburb of Brussels, and he reported to Lieutenant Colonel Bull that he was ready to support him.

The 1st/6th East Surreys, from the 44th Division, were among those units covering the 3rd Division's withdrawal over the River Dendre. Captain White, the adjutant, watched some units of the 3rd Division withdrawing in good order. It was a great fillip to morale to see the soldiers with all their equipment and their immaculate discipline. It provided a strong contrast to the Belgians he had seen earlier retreating through the battalion's position, 'a rabble without rifles or tin hats'.

Some of the closest scrapes were experienced by the divisional cavalry regiments covering their divisions while they fell back. Often covering long sections of front, and spread thinly, they needed initiative and skill at all levels, and sometimes a degree of cunning, not to get cut off. The 4th/7th Royal Dragoon Guards covered the 2nd Division withdrawal from the Dyle in the sector north of Wavre. Just as A Squadron was about to move, having received orders from regimental headquarters to withdraw, it came under fire from about six anti-tank guns at 400 yards' range. As the squadron pulled out of position, they engaged the anti-tank guns, with uncertain results, except that by the end of the scrap only two enemy guns were still firing. 'Bad shooting by the Bosch,' recorded the squadron diary, 'only one carrier hit and overturned.' The crew, although badly shaken, got out and mounted other vehicles. A Squadron rallied at Wavre, and the bridge was 'kept open' and not demolished for an hour in the hope of getting Troop Sergeant Major Emmerton back, one of the troop leaders missing from earlier that day. Although Emmerton did not turn up, Lieutenant Owen did, having also been missing for a while. He had had to take avoiding action and work his way round the enemy by taking a cross-country route. Eventually the bridge had to be blown, as the Germans were getting too close. It was later learned that Emmerton and his crew, as well as a despatch rider, had been taken prisoner. Despatch riders were especially vulnerable in a withdrawal, because as they took messages from one part of the battlefield to another they

sometimes found that the sub-unit they were looking for had gone, and been replaced by the enemy, or that the route they were using was suddenly thick with enemy vehicles. That night, 14/15 May, was the first night since crossing into Belgium on 10 May that most of the 4th/7th managed to get some sleep.

Everywhere else in the BEF sector, the withdrawal proceeded without serious loss, although not without some hard marching in cases where the transport arrangements failed. The 6th Brigade of 2nd Division, which had been holding the Lasne position, marched forty miles in twenty-seven hours after being in close contact with the enemy for thirty-six hours. The attack on Herent by the Germans' 19th Infantry Division was the only attempt at frustrating the British withdrawal. All their other formations, as was their custom, closed down operations during the night for rest and reorganization. With a few exceptions, the Germans were to exhibit this reluctance to fight at night throughout the Second World War, in all theatres. As the war progressed, Allied troops who were aggressive and led by bold commanders would take advantage of this habit. On this occasion the Germans must have known something was up, because the British artillery kept up an almost continuous barrage until the withdrawal was complete. The medium guns of I Corps alone fired 12,150 rounds that night, around 150 per gun. The gunners had a demanding time moving their guns to cover one line after another, siting new positions, coming into action and getting out again, handicapped for much of the time by refugees fleeing west.

All through the morning of 17 May, British troops marched through the streets of Brussels on their way to the canalized line of the River Senne, part of which runs through the western half of the city. They were watched by a sullen population, which only six days before had welcomed them as heroes coming to their aid. British remorse was tinged with resentment of the Belgians for their foolishness in maintaining their neutral stance right up to the moment of invasion, and for the poor performance of their troops.

The airmen had also been busy in these first few days of fighting. Although the Luftwaffe was busier over other Allied formations than over the BEF, that is not to say it was not a threat, and the activities of the RAF were crucial to the successful daylight movement and fighting by the BEF. In defending the sky over the BEF, the RAF lost sixty-seven aircraft in the first six days. RAF bombers attacking German columns found them well protected by light anti-aircraft (AA) (20mm and 37mm) guns at low level and by fighters and heavy 88mm guns at high level. The RAF did not have enough fighters deployed in France to cover strikes

by their own bombers, so sorties were flown at low level, and the bombers were vulnerable to ground defence as they attacked the long columns of German armour and transport.

The British bombers interdicting German ground forces were the Fairey Battle and the Blenheim. The Fairey Battle, or Battle for short, was a disaster. A single-engine light bomber with a crew of three, it was under-powered and lacked both speed and defensive firepower. It was suspect even before it reached squadron service. The Blenheim was better; it too was a light bomber with a crew of three and was under-gunned, but it was twin-engine, and faster than the Battle. Within hours of the outbreak of war, the inadequacy of the British light bomber force was exposed. On 10 May, beginning at about midday, successive waves of Battles took off to attack German columns advancing through Luxembourg. These waves of four formations of eight bombers each were a puny force compared with the waves of hundreds of aircraft being sent over by the Luftwaffe. Out of thirty-two Battles, thirteen were shot down, and every one of the survivors was damaged. The Battles went in at 250 feet, and most of the losses were due to ground fire. The Battle pilots were greeted with intense fire from German vehicles on the roads, and static targets and key points such as bridges were ringed with AA guns. These missions were suicidal, yet the dedicated aircrews went on flying until the squadrons of Battles were wiped out. The Blenheims did no better. When six Blenheims of No. 600 Squadron attacked the captured Dutch airfield at Waalhaven, five were shot down by Me 110s, a loss rate of 83 per cent. Day after day brought bad news of the fate of Battles and Blenheims thrown in against staggering odds. For example, on 11 May, of eight Battles sent to attack enemy columns near Luxembourg, only one returned and it was badly damaged and beyond repair – a 100 per cent loss rate of airframes. The following day was a bad one for Blenheims: seven out of nine aircraft of No. 139 Squadron were brought down in an attack on German columns near Maastricht, followed directly by ten out of twenty-four Blenheims lost attacking Maastricht itself. But worst of all was No. 12 Squadron's attack on the bridges over the Albert Canal west of Maastricht. Attacks on these had already cost ten out of fifteen Battles of the Belgian Air Force; now volunteers were called for from No. 12 Battle Squadron RAF. The entire squadron stepped forward, and the first six on the duty roster were chosen. Only five aircraft took off, because one proved unserviceable, as was its replacement. One Battle returned to base, crash-landing on arrival. All other aircrew were killed or captured. Flying Officer Garland and his observer Sergeant Gray were both posthumously awarded the VC, the first for the RAF of the war. For some reason, the air gunner, Leading Aircraft-man Reynolds, received no award.

These losses are made the more poignant by the fact that the effort that led to them was misdirected. General d'Astier de la Vigerie, commanding the French Air Force, had already reported the mass of armour and other vehicles approaching the Meuse crossings, and said, 'One can assume a very serious enemy effort in the direction of the Meuse.' This was of course the 'sickle', the main body of the German Army. To Vigerie's disgust, the French high command refused to believe him. Billotte continued to allocate air priorities to the Maastricht sector, completely ignoring the threat on the Meuse.

When the penny dropped on 14 May, and the French high command realized the seriousness of the situation on the Meuse, they asked the RAF to provide a maximum effort against the German pontoon bridges and the German armour crossing them at Sedan. Between 1500 and 1600 hours on 14 May, seventy-one light bombers took off protected by around 250 Allied fighters. The Germans had three times that number of fighters protecting that sector, and the bridgeheads were ringed with flak. The result is shown below:

RAF bomber losses on the Meuse, 14 May 1940			
Wing No.	Squadron No.	Aircraft despatched	Losses
71	105	11 Battles	6
	150	4 Battles	4
	114	2 Blenheims	1
	139	6 Blenheims	4
15	88	10 Battles	1
	103	8 Battles	3 (possibly 7)
	218	11 Battles	10
76	12	5 Battles	4
	142	8 Battles	4
	226	6 Battles	3

Out of seventy-one sorties, forty (or forty-four) aircraft were lost, some 56 (or 62) per cent. In addition sixteen Hurricanes were lost that day. For the RAF the Meuse was a valley of death.[10]

The only encouraging news, for the British at least, during these days of air combat and bombing sorties was the overall success of the Hurricanes. At least the Hurricane was a modern fighter, the only one the Allies possessed in France (the Spitfires were not involved over France and Flanders at this stage). The performance of the Hurricane was a marvellous boost to morale of its pilots and ground crew. It was a success

that was, as so often, not so evident to the British soldiers on the ground. Because they could not see the Hurricanes above them, they imagined that the RAF was not playing its part; nothing could have been further from the truth.

On 17 May, as the BEF was trudging and motoring back to the Senne, Gort was aware that although Barker's British I Corps was in touch with the French First Army's III Corps on his right, and knew their position, further south the situation was far from clear. Gort knew that the French First Army was engaged in serious fighting with the northern prong of the German armoured advance, and as the Germans proceeded west they threatened the British right flank. To protect this flank, Gort ordered his director of military intelligence, Major General Mason-MacFarlane, to form a scratch force under his command. Macforce, as it was dubbed, consisted of: the 127th Infantry Brigade from the 42nd Division; two regiments of field artillery and an anti-tank battery; the Hopkinson Mission; engineers, signals and elements of the Royal Army Medical Corps (RAMC) and Royal Army Service Corps (RASC). The 1st Army Tank Brigade was to join later. The Hopkinson Mission, under Lieutenant Colonel Hopkinson, was a ground reconnaissance force mounted on armoured cars, trucks and motorcycles whose task was to gather information from corps, division and brigade headquarters and pass this to the RAF headquarters and to Gort's HQ. The mission was fully mobile and equipped with high-powered radios. It was the precursor of what became known later as the highly successful GHQ 'Phantom' Regiment. Macforce's task was to protect the right rear of the BEF. In particular it was to deny the crossings of the River Scarpe from Raches to Saint-Amand, some fifteen miles. Macforce was the first of a rash of ad-hoc forces that Gort formed as the campaign progressed – a habit that was to persist in the British Army after the 1940 campaign in France and Flanders, and right up to August 1942 in the Western Desert in Egypt. Montgomery stamped firmly on the practice when he arrived in the desert.

In retrospect, the formation of Macforce was unnecessary, and the French First Army never gave way. But Gort was not to know that. However, it would have been better to have used a complete division in this role, rather than weakening the 42nd Division. Far more serious, and ultimately detrimental to the command of the BEF, was sending to the force his head of intelligence as well as Lieutenant Colonel Templer, the GSO 1 intelligence. The lack of intelligence at Gort's command post was to be a grave handicap. It was exacerbated by the faulty organization of Gort's HQ staff, which affected other staff branches as well as intelligence. When Gort formed his command post and moved into Belgium, he took with him Mason-MacFarlane and two staff officers (including

Templer) from the intelligence branch at GHQ, which was left behind at Arras. Thereafter information received at Arras often failed to pass from the intelligence staff at the command post to formations forward in time for them to act on it, while much of the information sent in to the command post by divisions in contact was never passed back to the GHQ at Arras. Depleting the intelligence staff at the command post by removing Mason-MacFarlane and Templer aggravated the problem (which had already manifested itself) of co-ordinating information received there with that received by the intelligence staff at GHQ. Other branches of the staff experienced the same difficulty. The apportioning of responsibility between GHQ and the command post was not well planned, and the difficulties of maintaining communications between them were accentuated by the need for the command post to move frequently as the battle flowed westwards at speed.

As the growing threat to the British lines of communication and rear areas became apparent, two steps were taken. First, GHQ at Arras organized a garrison for the defence of the city under command of Lieutenant Colonel Copland-Griffiths, CO 1st Welsh Guards, consisting of his battalion, less one company detailed to guard Gort's command post. Some light tanks drawn from the ordnance depot, and manned by men from the 2nd Reconnaissance Brigade Headquarters (who called themselves Cooke's Light Tanks after their commander), and sappers and gunners provided support to the garrison.

It was decided to entrust control of part of the rear-defence organization to the General Officer commanding (GOC) 12th Division, Major General Petre. Leaving his divisional headquarters at Fressenville, south of Abbeville, and accompanied by his GSO 2, Major Haddock, Petre reached Arras at 1300 hours on 18 May, thinking he had just come for a conference, after which he would return to his division. He now learned that he was to remain there, as a sort of poor man's corps headquarters, taking command of the 23rd Division, his own 36th Brigade (but not the rest of his division) and the Arras garrison. For this purpose he was provided with a rear-link radio set, and the loan of the assistant military secretary from GHQ, Lieutenant Colonel Simpson, as his GSO 1. It was a pitifully small staff for a corps headquarters, even a miniature one. It was called Petreforce.

Second, the three territorial divisions, the 12th, 23rd and 46th, that had been working on the lines of communication were to redeploy, to Amiens, the Canal du Nord and Seclin respectively. At the same time, the chief engineer, Major General Pakenham-Walsh, was told to organize all the sappers employed on the lines of communication and at GHQ into battalions; and the provost (military police) marshal, Colonel Kennedy,

was to concentrate all available provost (military police) and concentrate them as a reserve too. All branches of GHQ that could be spared
were to be transferred to Boulogne, while GHQ itself was to pull back to
Hazebrouck on 19 May.

In short, the BEF was gearing itself up for the unpleasant prospect of
a German breakthrough, which looked increasingly likely. The seven
panzer divisions of Army Group A had poured through the fifty-mile
gap in the French defences, and with the bit between their teeth
brushed aside pockets of resistance, overtaking and disarming hordes
of demoralized, fugitive French soldiers. Only lack of fuel threatened to
stop them, but they seized ample supplies from the French. By the
evening of 19 May they were breasting up to the Canal du Nord, 110
miles as the crow flies from the Meuse, and 170 miles from their start
lines on 10 May.

3

BACK TO THE ESCAUT AND DISASTER
ON THE BEF'S SOUTHERN FLANK

By the time the rest of II Corps started footslogging back to the Senne on the 16 May, the 4th Division had already established a layback position there (a temporary defence-line), and was awaiting the arrival of the 3rd Division. The 11th Brigade was established on the canalized line of the Senne running through the western half of Brussels, and the 12th Brigade was five miles further north opposite Vilvorde. There were twenty-three bridges and one tunnel in the divisional sector, and all had to be blown. The time for demolition was set for 1400 hours, but one bridge had to be kept open longer to allow the 15th/19th Hussars to bring along some very tired infantrymen and locate a lost carrier of their own. There was no time to waste; the main bridge at Vilvorde was blown as German motorcyclists came roaring up to cross. German infantry were not far behind, and the 2nd Royal Fusiliers on the left of the 12th Brigade soon found themselves in the same circumstances as the 1st Coldstream of the 3rd Division the previous day – with their flank turned thanks to the early departure of the Belgians on their left fleeing ahead of the enemy. The Fusiliers held on until nightfall, making good use of their carriers to protect their flanks with fire from Brens and from their two 3-inch mortars. The latter kept up a high rate of fire for some hours before both were destroyed.

The 1st Division, in I Corps sector, took up position on the right of 4th Division. Its sector included Hal, where two brigades of the 5th Division were establishing themselves. This division had been part of the War Office reserve located at Amiens and released to Gort's command on 16 May. It had completed an exhausting journey, partly in transport and partly on foot against a stream of refugees, with many interruptions caused by Luftwaffe attacks on the road.

The other divisions kept marching back to the rear. The infantry of the 3rd Division found transport waiting for them in the western outskirts of Brussels, behind the layback positions established by the 4th Division. The infantry of the 48th Division had marched back and forth

to support the 'crumbling' right flank, only to find that it was not crumbling, at least in the sectors to which they had been directed. Now they slogged back to an intermediary line west of the Senne. Large parts of the 2nd Division also had to march, although it had been intended to transport them to the Dendre. Some were lifted by dint of dumping stores from trucks, while others, having waited, marched off muttering. The 6th Brigade, after marching forty miles from the Lasne as already related, staggered in at around 0300 hours, tumbling wearily into houses in the villages short of Grammont, their intended destination. They had made the first contact with the enemy on the night of 13/14 May, spent the whole of 15 May fighting, withdrew at very short notice that night, spent 16 May working on new positions under fire, and began their forty-mile march as soon as it was dark.

The 12th Lancers (an armoured car regiment, the only one in the BEF) had been moved to the right flank to cover the crossings over the River Haine, which runs from west to east towards the Dyle, on the boundary between the BEF and the French First Army. They blew the bridges in the early hours of 17 May, the enemy snapping at the heels of the long, plodding, horsed transport column of the French 2nd North African Division. The Lancers held the Germans at bay until 1030 hours, giving the 48th Division time to fall back through positions prepared by the 13th Brigade of 5th Division at Hal.

The fact that all was now well on this flank should have been known to I Corps HQ, because the Lancers had maintained touch meticulously by radio. But Barker, the corps commander, was showing early signs of cracking under the strain. This was very evident to his fellow corps commander, Brooke, who wrote, 'he is so overwrought with work and the present situation that he sees dangers where they don't exist and cannot make his mind up on any points'.[1] Barker issued a series of orders followed by counter-orders. For example, the 4th and 7th Royal Tanks, but not their brigade headquarters for some reason, were ordered to move at once to Hal to stem a breakthrough by German armour. At that moment they were attempting to load their tanks on to a train at Enghien in the middle of an air raid on the station. Having set off, and driven most of the nine miles to Hal, they encountered Brigadier Miles Dempsey, the newly appointed commander of the 13th Brigade. He told them he had not asked for any tanks and had no knowledge of any German armour in the vicinity. It was now too late to entrain the tanks before the next stage of the withdrawal, and in addition to the unnecessary eighteen miles they had just driven, they had a long drive ahead, bad enough for the drivers and crews, but an unwelcome strain on the tank tracks.

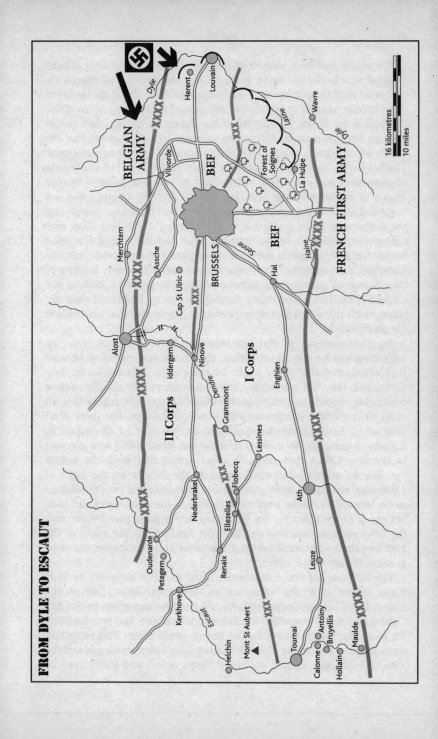

FROM DYLE TO ESCAUT

Louvain
Herent
Dyle
Wavre
Lasne
Forest of Soignes
La Hulpe
Vilvorde
BEF
BEF
Merchtem
Assche
Cap St Ulric
BRUSSELS
Senne
Haine
Hal
FRENCH FIRST ARMY
Dyle
Alost
Iddergem
Ninove
I Corps
Enghien
II Corps
Dendre
Grammont
Lessines
Flobecq
Ellezelles
Ath
Nederbrakel
Renaix
Oudenarde
Petegem
Kerkhove
Escaut
Helchin
Mont St Aubert
Leuze
Tournai
Calonne
Antoiny
Bruyellis
Hollain
Maulde

BELGIAN ARMY

16 kilometres
10 miles

The alarm had been caused by a report that the 2nd North African Division was in trouble again. In fact it had restored the position without assistance by putting in a counter-attack. But as far as Gort was concerned it was not to be trusted, any more than the rest of his allies. Disillusion set in on 17 May when the extent of the German breakthrough became clear, and Gort was worried, with good cause, that the enemy would cut in behind his right flank, across the Scarpe at Douai. This led to the formation of Macforce, mentioned earlier. The inadequate co-ordination and conflicting orders from Billotte and Georges were a source of exasperation to Gort. His lack of faith in Georges was not improved when a confusing message was received from him, postponing the withdrawal from the Senne to the night of 18/19 May. Gort sent Eastwood to Billotte's HQ to establish what was happening. Eastwood found that Billotte indeed intended to postpone the withdrawal, because Blanchard's French First Army was too exhausted to move. In spite of this, Eastwood managed to persuade Billotte to agree to stick to the original plan. Having previously pleaded for a delay, Blanchard suddenly changed his mind and had to be persuaded not to abandon his position too precipitately.

As a consequence of this late reversion to the original plan, the Belgians asked for protection of their right flank next morning, because they anticipated that there might be some delay in completing their move, and they did not want their flank left in the air. This was a reasonable request and the British Official History comments that an order to this effect was presumably issued to II Corps. But there is no note of its issue in the command-post records, nor of its receipt in II Corps documents. So a costly mistake was made. GHQ sent a report to the War Office that night in effect saying that both the British and Belgian armies were withdrawing to the Dendre on the night of 17/18 May, and that a flank guard would be maintained for the Belgians as far forward as Assche until eight o'clock in the morning of the 18th. But the II Corps order for the formation of the flank guard states that the Belgians were not retiring from the Senne until the night of the 18th and their open flank between the Senne and the Dendre was to be guarded *throughout* the 18th.[2]

The Belgians did retire during the night of 17/18 May, and by 0900 hours on the 18th they were back on the Dendre–Escaut line on the British left. The flank-guard task for the Belgians was given to the 2nd Light Armoured Reconnaissance Brigade, which also had responsibility for providing the rearguard for the British 4th Division. This reconnaissance brigade, consisting of the 5th Inniskilling Dragoon Guards and the 15th/19th Hussars, carried out the II Corps orders and maintained its

position instead of falling back at 0800 hours. Attached to it for the withdrawal were the 32nd Army Field Regiment and 14th Anti-Tank Regiment, Royal Artillery (RA); and the 4th Division's machine-gun battalion, the 4th Gordon Highlanders. The Reconnaissance Brigade failed to find the Belgians, which was not surprising as they were already behind them on the Dendre. Earlier that night patrols from the brigade north of Vilvorde encountered some Belgian stragglers, who expressed doubts that the Belgian 5th Division, to which they claimed to belong, existed any more.

The British 4th Division had some trouble making a clean break during the night of 17/18 May. The enemy started attacking at last light to secure crossings at Vilvorde and elsewhere in the Belgian sector. The 10th and 11th Brigades had to fight hard to hold off the Germans, and got away with difficulty in the early hours of the 18th. Soon after first light the whole division was on the move westwards, protected by the 2nd Light Armoured Reconnaissance Brigade, whose two armoured cavalry regiments were deployed across the western outskirts of Brussels waiting for the GOC 4th Division, Major General Johnson, to give them permission to withdraw to an intermediate line running north–south through Assche and Merchtem, the latter inside the Belgian area of responsibility. German light aircraft came over, and the Reconnaissance Brigade found its radios being jammed, forcing its commander, Brigadier Clifton, to relay messages to the 15th/19th through the 5th Inniskillings. Meanwhile on the right flank of the BEF the 13th/18th Hussars and 12th Lancers covered the withdrawal of the 1st and 5th Divisions.

At 0845 hours, Clifton received the order to pull back on the Assche line. At the same time he sent a liaison officer to find the Belgians, who, on his return, reported that they had gone. By now, Johnson was also aware of this and sent the information to Clifton by despatch rider, who never found him – a situation that was to become all too familiar as the days went by. The 4th Gordons, who, together with the 14th Anti-Tank Regiment and 32nd Army Field Regiment, were to come under Clifton's command as soon as the withdrawal started, had been posted on high ground around Assche. Clifton had not been consulted about the siting of these units, and in some cases never even saw them. During the withdrawal to Assche, the 15th/19th had two tentative contacts that revealed the proximity of the Germans. One involved the sound of firing from a distance, followed by loss of radio contact with a subaltern who had, it was discovered later, been killed. At 1100 hours it became clear just how far the Germans had penetrated, using the route allotted for the Belgian withdrawal running through Merchtem. As the 15th/19th approached the village, they saw soldiers, horse-drawn artillery and

tracked vehicles, and quickly realized these were not Belgians. Artillery fire was requested, but the gunners said the target was outside their arc – a specious answer, since any field gun can easily be swung round by lifting the trail and training it round.

Also at 1100 hours, the 5th Inniskillings saw that the 13th/18th on their right, covering the 1st Division, were withdrawing. The 13th/18th sent an officer over to the 5th Inniskillings to convey his colonel's apologies, but he had received strict orders to withdraw from his divisional commander, Alexander, under command of I Corps. Two corps pulling back from the same line would have problems synchronizing the movement of the line of rearguards to ensure that withdrawing one did not expose its neighbour to the danger of being outflanked. Lack of synchronization at army group level was also causing problems, and the staff at Gort's GHQ fumed at the failure of co-ordination by Billotte.

Soon afterwards the 5th Inniskillings were attacked, on their left rather than on the open right flank. German armoured cars, motorcyclists and a self-propelled anti-tank gun sped in between two of the Inniskilling tank troops and gained the road behind them, losing an armoured car in the process. The tanks charged the anti-tank gun, machine guns chattering, and all swept past, except the troop leader's tank, which crashed into a telegraph pole. The squadron regrouped in Capelle-Saint-Ulric, continuing to exchange fire with the German mobile troops. But there was now a wide gap between them and the 15th/19th on their left. A patrol from the reserve squadron of the 5th Inniskillings discovered that the Germans now held Assche in strength.

The 15th/19th were also having a hard time beset by infantry with anti-tank guns and armoured cars. The mechanized cavalrymen destroyed three armoured cars and a horde of motorcyclists, as well as some infantry who had dismounted from their trucks out in the open, well within range. But other German infantry, using the cover afforded by stream beds, took a steady toll of the 15th/19th with anti-tank guns and, by lobbing mortar bombs among the tanks, forced commanders to close down their hatches, thereby restricting their vision. But most serious were the Germans in Assche. One of the 15th/19th squadrons tried to barge through from the east and lost their squadron leader killed, the second-in-command and squadron sergeant major wounded, and four of their six troops wiped out. The town of Assche was soon a mass of 'brewed-up' tanks (i.e. in flames), with long oily columns of smoke marking the path of destruction.

Clifton decided to extricate his brigade, whether or not the 4th Division had got back across the Dendre. He motored over to the Inniskillings, and while talking to their CO he picked up a distorted

message from the 15th/19th that indicated that the enemy now held the routes to both bridges on the withdrawal route south of Alost. The Inniskillings accordingly raced for the bridge opposite Iddergem, further south, and secured a bridgehead there. The supporting gunners and the Gordons were told to get across quickly. The 32nd Field Regiment crossed complete. The 14th Anti-Tank Regiment was isolated, and had to leave seven guns behind. The 4th Gordons also got back, except for one company supporting the 15th/19th with their Vickers medium machine guns deployed between Assche and Merchtem; the machine-gunners resisted until overrun section by section.

Clifton searched for the 15th/19th, unable to contact them by radio. He found one squadron still in good order, although it had suffered some losses at the hands of the enemy, who had attempted to get across its intended withdrawal route. Clifton sent this squadron back over the bridge held by the Inniskillings, and it was clear by 1400 hours. Some time later, a message was heard on the radio from the regimental second-in-command saying that the squadron he was with was bogged down and surrounded as it tried to reach the river. The third squadron had been destroyed at Assche. Clifton, with a heavy heart, ordered the Inniskillings to pull back, and the bridge to be blown.

The second-in-command of the 15th/19th, Major 'Loony' Hinde, ordered his party to split up and break out in groups. Although wounded in the neck and arm, he himself evaded the enemy. As he swam the Dendre the British 3rd Division opened fire on him, but missed. Two other officers and several soldiers also reached the Dendre. The next day the Germans caught the CO, his intelligence officer and French liaison officer, who had set off from further away. The 15th/19th had lost seventeen officers, of whom seven were killed, one on a ship bombed at Ostend, which he had reached in civilian clothes. About 140 soldiers were lost, and only a weak squadron remained.

On the BEF's right flank, the 5th Division's 13th Brigade, around Hal, came under attack late in the afternoon of 17 May, and the 2nd Royal Inniskilling Fusiliers and 2nd Wiltshires had their first experience of action repelling the Germans. Two companies of the Inniskilling Fusiliers went astray and got caught up in the human flotsam of refugees for two days. The 12th Lancers had their work cut out covering the withdrawal, with enemy motorcyclists and armoured cars continually trying to out-flank them, while tanks could be discerned not far off. Lieutenant Colonel Lumsden, the CO, fought his regiment brilliantly, but was called upon to hold on far longer than planned, not crossing the Dendre until 2000 hours on 18 May.

Headquarters I Corps had considerable difficulty locating its two

divisions, despite sending out numerous despatch riders and liaison officers. One suspects poor staff work under the direction of a commander who was fast losing his grip. The GOCs of both 1st and 5th Divisions only learned of the planned withdrawal from the Senne to the Dendre by consulting each other. For lack of firm orders the 5th Division withdrew too far and its place on the right of I Corps between Ath and Lessines had to be filled by the 48th Division, earmarked as corps reserve. The 2nd and 1st Divisions were on their left. The II Corps line was held by Montgomery's 3rd Division, with the 25th Brigade of the 50th Division under command.

At 1000 hours on 18 May, Gort gave orders at headquarters I Corps for the final stage of the withdrawal. Barker of I Corps seemed obsessed by the memory of Lieutenant General Smith-Dorrien's stand at Le Cateau in 1914, and said his troops could not withdraw from the Dendre until the following night, 19/20 May. In harking back to Le Cateau, where Smith-Dorrien had stayed to fight because his troops were, in his opinion, too tired to continue marching, Barker was showing his lack of appreciation of how armour and mobile troops had changed the game for ever. Brooke was horrified, being all too aware of the need to secure the Escaut Line without delay. He succeeded in getting agreement that the Dendre should be held only until midday on 19 May, and in having the 1st Division, which alone had defended each successive line, transferred to his corps. Later he heard that Barker, on receiving a report of armour on his right flank, had decided to start his withdrawal at dawn after all. Alexander and Montgomery of 1st and 3rd Divisions were told to comply with this change of timing as best they could.

It turned out that the soldiers of the 2nd and 48th Divisions were perfectly capable of marching, and their last sub-units left their positions at first light. The infantry battalion Bren carriers and Vickers machine-gunners of the 4th Cheshires and 2nd Manchesters provided the rearguard along with the 4th/7th Dragoon Guards, the 12th Lancers and the newly committed 1st Armoured Reconnaissance Brigade. This last consisted of the 1st Fife and Forfar Yeomanry and the 1st East Riding Yeomanry. Although new to armoured warfare, and inadequately equipped with light tanks, they were posted on the right flank to guard against the tanks of XVI Panzer Corps that had so alarmed Barker.

The marching infantry of 2nd and 48th Divisions were delighted to find transport to lift them back over the Dendre. However, the Luftwaffe was about to cause havoc in the bright May sunshine. The 2nd Division, by using side roads, had greater choice of routes, but there were many confusing junctions and maps were in short supply, so wrong turnings were taken which caused delays. The 48th Division route passed through

Tournai, and every road was crammed with traffic, smart civilian cars and creaking wagons loaded with refugees, intermixed with armour, trucks and staff cars. The Luftwaffe hit Tournai, setting the town ablaze, before turning its attention to the traffic. Among the toiling refugees on the roads was a travelling circus, and the horrified troops were treated to the sight of elephants with gaping wounds in their sides going berserk, and four white horses bolting with the corpse of a girl caught in their traces.

The 48th Division's greatest moment of trial was at Leuze, ten miles east of Tournai. Here a sapper major took it upon himself to marshal the vehicles carrying the 145th Brigade and ordered them to close up. No sooner had this officious idiot departed than nine Heinkel bombers appeared overhead and unleashed their load on the cramped vehicles. The 2nd Gloucestershires lost 194 men, and the 2nd Oxford and Buckinghamshire Light Infantry 48, together with many vehicles. This was the worst blow struck from the air against British troops on the move in the whole campaign.

The I Corps rearguards kept the enemy back from the Dendre until midday. Although pressed hard, they inflicted a great deal of damage on the enemy. The 4th/7th in particular had a tough fight, ordered to hold a crossing over the Dendre at Ath until the 48th Division had got over. There were so many bridges across the river that all three squadrons had to be brought up into line, but gradually the bridges were blown and the 48th Division came back, very tired but in good order. There was some confusion about what the regiment was to do next; it was supposed to come under the command of the 50th Division, but nobody knew where this was. The colonel went to corps headquarters where he found an atmosphere of great tension, and was told to hold a 12,000-yard front on the River Dendre from midnight to noon the following day (19 May).

Two anti-tank batteries and a machine-gun battalion were to be placed under the regiment's command, but by dark none of these had turned up, and the three squadrons took up positions on their own. During the night some of the supporting troops arrived, and were in position by first light, except for one anti-tank battery that never materialized.

B Squadron on the right of the regiment learned at 0700 hours that enemy tanks and infantry had crossed the river further to its right. By 0900 hours the enemy were beginning to approach B Squadron from the other side of the river, and soon the Squadron was engaged along its complete frontage. Troop leaders had chosen their positions with skill, and the light tanks were camouflaged and dug in, making them difficult to locate. Furthermore the tanks were so sited that they were able to engage the enemy by crossfire, hitting them in the flank, rather than

directly across the river, and this made it more difficult for the enemy to locate the source of the fire. The Germans kept approaching the far bank of the river in parties of about twelve, and attempting to inflate and launch rubber pontoons. As the battle progressed, the 4th/7th held their fire until the pontoons were launched, and not one got across.

All troops were still heavily engaged some thirty-five minutes after the planned time for retirement, and eventually the order to pull back was given. Unfortunately the right-hand troop took a wrong turning and ran into a strong force of enemy who had crossed lower down, and the troop was never seen again. But B Squadron was well pleased with its work, and full of confidence.

Major Frink's A Squadron in the centre had a similar story to tell of inflicting heavy casualties on the enemy as they repeatedly tried to cross. The Germans were first seen at dawn on the far side of the Canal. The squadron diary recorded:

> We had an excellent field of fire – some excellent targets of which we took full advantage. One company of Cheshires MG [machine-gunners] had arrived to reinforce me, also a battery of anti-tank guns. Heavy casualties were inflicted on the enemy. Among targets were infantry, cavalry patrols, artillery, rubber boats. Had orders to hold on till midday. At 1000 hours things became very warm – all troops under artillery and mortar fire – moved headquarters three times. Still getting good targets and doing a lot of damage.

On the left of the regiment, C Squadron also had a good shoot, but the troop in Lessines had difficulties with Germans trying to enter the town by a bridge that was only partly blown and working round its left flank. The troop held the enemy, and destroyed an anti-tank gun. By 1045 hours it was being heavily shelled, and only four members of the troop were unwounded, but it held on until relieved by another troop. As the pressure on the regiment grew, the colonel sent a reconnaissance party back to see how far the infantry had got, and the party reported that all roads to the west were clear for at least twelve miles. Having been told by corps HQ over the radio, 'Infantry withdrawal most satisfactory', the colonel ordered all squadrons to pull back. Pulling out was tricky because the enemy had crossed in strength both above and below the regimental front, and some enemy had infiltrated between squadrons. With all three squadrons deployed the colonel had no reserve to provide a layback position through which the regiment could withdraw. But they skilfully made a clean break, and the regiment moved back some twenty miles, crossing the Scarpe at Antoing, just south of Tournai.

But the move of the 4th/7th was not made without loss. Major Frink's

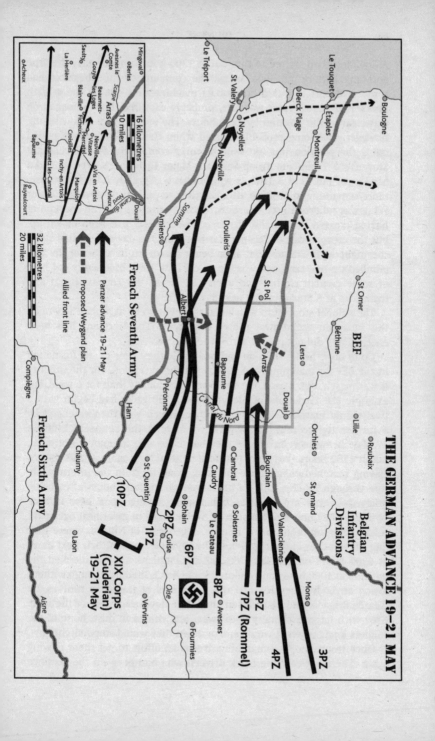

THE GERMAN ADVANCE 19–21 MAY

Belgian
Infantry
Divisions

BEF

French Seventh Army

French Sixth Army

16 kilometres
10 miles

32 kilometres
20 miles

Panzer advance 19–21 May

Proposed Weygand plan

Allied front line

10PZ
2PZ
1PZ
6PZ
8PZ
7PZ (Rommel)
5PZ
4PZ
3PZ

XIX Corps
(Guderian)
19–21 May

A Squadron had started to thin out at 1200 hours under heavy fire. The anti-tank battery got away safely; the company of the Cheshires had some transport captured but got its machine-guns out on the 4th/7th tanks. A despatch rider was lost, probably captured, but the squadron was clear of the position by 1245 hours. The enemy were following up, however, and some probably crossed when the first tank troop pulled out – the position was too wide to cover completely. Both Lieutenant Stevens's 3 Troop and Troop Sergeant Major Lashmore's 4 Troop had a 'sticky get out'. But 3 Troop's withdrawal was greatly assisted by Lashmore remaining in position after the time to pull out had passed. Major Frink was relieved to see the squadron through the squadron checkpoint having crossed the canal at Tournai. Two carriers had been blown up, but the crews escaped. Trooper Harrison, lost the day before, had spent the night with C Squadron; after being blown up in a carrier, he had climbed on to a tank and was blown off that. He subsequently got hold of some civilian clothes and a bicycle, swam the Tournai Canal and turned up at A Squadron the next day.

The colonel stopped to watch the regiment go by at a place where all the squadron withdrawal routes converged. The Germans had been checked and did not pursue across the Dendre.

Up to now the 1st Division had had the hardest time of any formation in the BEF for marching, and 19 May was no exception. For the infantry it was march, dig, march, dig and, very occasionally, halt for a meal. For example the 1st Loyals, of Alexander's 2nd Brigade, had begun with a twelve-mile march back from the Dyle, which was then extended by a further twelve miles to bring them beyond the Senne at 1400 on 17 May. Being in reserve here they had been able to enjoy a hot meal, but at 1700 hours they were told to start marching again at 2300 hours. Having marched eight miles, they dug in at dawn on the intermediate line through Assche, only to be moved on at 0800 hours after being relieved by the armoured reconnaissance taking up a new layback position. They now had a march of twelve miles in great heat over pavé roads, bringing them to the Dendre, south-west of Ninove, where they dug slit trenches in the cornfields. The Loyals learned of their next move at 0200 hours on 19 May. Detailed as rearguard, they abandoned the position at 1000 hours and endured some fierce shelling, though without losing anybody. They reached the main road at the same time as 1st Guards Brigade, and marched in single file down each side of the road. Grey with fatigue, clammy with sweat and coated in dust, none of the soldiers knew where it would end or when they would stop marching.

Once troops stopped marching, it was an effort to get them moving again. The troop-carrying truck drivers, who had been on the go since

10 May, were equally tired, and every time they stopped, even for a moment, they fell asleep. Sometimes the convoy would move on without them, and in the darkness especially it was easy for a convoy to split, with the part behind a dozing driver becoming lost or badly delayed.

After a march of some ten miles, the Loyals embussed in trucks at 1300 hours, but there was insufficient transport to lift all the marching personnel in the battalion. They had eighteen miles to go before reaching the bridge over the Escaut at Kerkhove; the last man was over at 2000 hours. Now they had to dig, and were somewhat sceptical at being told that this was where they were to stay. They had marched at least fifty-four miles, had prepared for battle four times over three days, and now were making ready again.

The experience of the 1st Loyals was typical, but that of the 3rd Brigade in 1st Division was even more exhausting. The speedy withdrawal of the I Corps screen threatened Alexander's right flank. So he ordered the 3rd Brigade to hold the high ground east of Renaix, using radio to pass his orders. Familiar as it may seem to us now, this was novel at the time. The 2nd Sherwood Foresters marched into Renaix to be met by the burgomaster in full regalia. He said he had come to offer them the town's surrender, and was mortified when he discovered they were not Germans. However, the battalion was able to reassure him that the Germans were not far behind. The carrier platoons of the three battalions in the 3rd Brigade made up the rearguard, for the 13th/18th Hussars had pulled back on 1 Corps orders when Barker initiated the precipitate withdrawal. Alexander managed to hijack four troops of their rear squadron as they were on their way back, and doubled the size of his carrier rearguard. The rearguard fought some brisk encounters on the high ground round Ellezelles, Flobecq and Ogy, buying time for the footsoldiers to meet their transport and drive to the Escaut at Kerkhove. As before, there were insufficient trucks, and some had to walk. For example, 300 Foresters under Major Temple fought their way back on foot, and on arrival found all the bridges blown, so had to be ferried across the river. Like other parties that had marched all the way, they had covered some seventy miles on their feet.

There were instances of bridges being blown before all troops were on the 'home' bank. The 2nd Division rearguard was cut off when an officer was sent from I Corps headquarters to order the bridge at Tournai demolished. The 1st East Lancashires holding the town disputed the need to be so precipitate, but to their surprise the bridge was blown at 1900 hours, leaving the 2nd Division's rearguard cut off. The rearguard burned its vehicles or ran them into the river, and managed to get across by swimming or finding boats to use. All succeeded except the gallant

Captain Lewis of the 1st Royal Welch Fusiliers, who on hearing, wrongly, that two battalions were cut off on the enemy bank, swam across and fixed a lifeline. On moving forward to make contact with the 'cut off' men, he was shot by the Germans.

The BEF was now behind the Escaut river line, and by midnight on 19/ 20 May the withdrawal was complete. At 1600 hours on 19 May, Germans quickly following up had got across the river, and the 1st Buckingham-shires had to counter-attack to drive them back over it. In the northern sector German artillery began to register the British positions. This and heavy bombing of Audenarde seemed to presage a serious attack in the near future. All three corps were up, and seven divisions held a thirty-mile front. On average each forward battalion held a mile of riverbank. Company and platoon positions were sited to give mutual support and all-round defence. It was impossible to keep every yard of river frontage under constant observation, so there were places where the enemy could cross and penetrate for a little distance, especially in darkness or morning mist.

The terrain also gave scope for some bold patrolling, if COs were so minded. The CO of the 1st/6th East Surrey personally led a patrol along the banks of the Escaut in broad daylight and captured a prisoner. This was where the battalion was first 'blooded', in the opinion of the adjutant Captain White, and the CO's action did a lot to enhance the battalion's morale. The battalion was enthusiastic but lacked expertise, and if the CO could lead a patrol and defeat the Boche, reasoned the soldiers, so could they. The CO had been a prisoner in the First World War, and, according to White, his one aim was to kill the Boche.

The Escaut is normally a sizeable obstacle, and in stretches it still was. However, thanks to a long period of dry weather and the closing of sluices in the local dykes, the water level had fallen considerably and so in places was fordable by infantry. Most of the ground on the enemy side overlooked the BEF's forward positions, granting a view well to the west, as far as the French frontier. The question in Gort's mind must have been how long he could stay here. For the strength or otherwise of the Escaut position was not the deciding factor in how long the BEF could hold on. What was happening to the south was going to determine that, and indeed possibly threaten the continuing existence of the BEF altogether.

In the early hours of 19 May, Billotte paid his first visit to Gort at his command post, which had just moved from Renaix to Wahagnies. In the car on the way he kept repeating to Major Archdale, the British liaison officer, 'Je creve de fatigue – et contre les panzers je ne peux rien faire' (I am bursting with fatigue, and against the panzers I can do nothing). That must have been encouraging for Archdale to hear. Billotte had some

reason to be gloomy: Giraud, who had been summoned to take over from Corap and bring his Seventh Army to prop up the crumbling Ninth, was missing. His headquarters had been overrun, and he was a fugitive, to be taken prisoner later that day.

Billotte showed Gort a map on which nine or ten German armoured divisions were marked. Their leading elements had approached Cambrai and reached Péronne that day, and there were no French troops between them and the sea. Gort, having at last heard the true situation from Billotte, realized that it was even worse than he had feared. In his despatch, he wrote that as he saw it there were now three courses of action open to the French. It is plain that he did not discuss them with Billotte. The first option was a counter-attack, and he had no idea what resources, if any, the French had to carry this out. The second was to pivot back on to the Somme, in order to preserve the lines of communication. The French lines of communication naturally ran back to France – as did the BEF's, to Le Havre, Cherbourg and Brittany. But whether pivoting back on a flank that had already been torn open was feasible is open to question. The third option was to fall back on the Channel ports as a precursor to evacuation. It was not an option that could be discussed with the French or Belgians, who would see it as British treachery. It is clear, however, that in Gort's mind evacuation was becoming the best, and indeed the only, option. In retrospect he was right. The GHQ staff immediately began to plan a withdrawal to Dunkirk. Brooke, when he heard of this, suggested that the BEF should swing back its right flank on to the River Lys, up the canal to Ypres, and thence by the Ypres canal to the sea. This was turned down for fear of what the Belgian reaction would be to hearing that the British planned a withdrawal, and Dunkirk offered better facilities. Major General Martel, the commander of the 50th Division, was ordered to act as a flank guard along the waterway between La Bassée and Béthune. This waterway flows past Aire into the canalized River Aa, which reaches the sea at Gravelines, between Calais and Dunkirk. A glance at the map on p. 66 shows that this is the one continuous water barrier flanking the route to Dunkirk, and was to become known as the 'canal line'. To cater for the extensive demolition of bridges and other key points that a further withdrawal would involve, the chief engineer, Major General Pakenham-Walsh, asked for 200 tons of explosive to be delivered from England immediately.

Pownall telephoned the War Office twice to discuss withdrawal, explaining the undertaking in guarded terms, but emphasizing that it was the failure of the French to repulse the armoured flood that had caused the trouble. Even at this stage, neither Gort nor Pownall had any faith in the French ability to mount a counter-attack sufficiently powerful

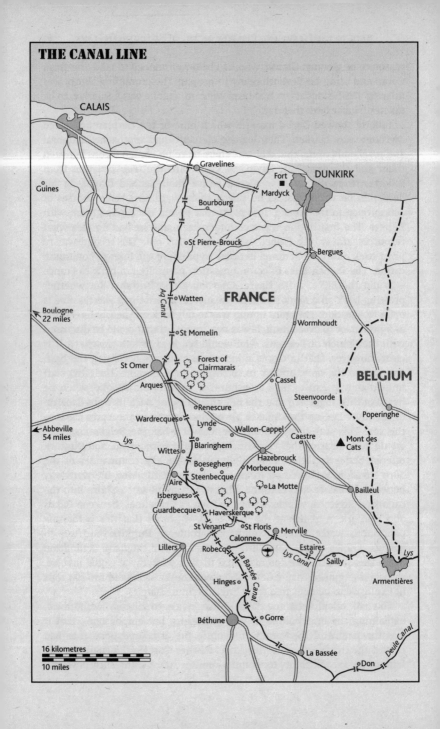

THE CANAL LINE

CALAIS

Guines

Gravelines

DUNKIRK

Fort Mardyck

Bourbourg

St Pierre-Brouck

Bergues

FRANCE

Aa Canal

Watten

Boulogne 22 miles

St Momelin

Wormhoudt

BELGIUM

St Omer

Forest of Clairmarais

Cassel

Steenvoorde

Poperinghe

Arques

Renescure

Wardrecques

Lynde

Wallon-Cappel

Caestre

Mont des Cats

Abbeville 54 miles

Lys

Blaringhem

Wittes

Boeseghem

Hazebrouck

Morbecque

Bailleul

Aire

Steenbecque

La Motte

Isbergues

Guardbecque

Haverskerque

St Venant

St Floris

Merville

Calonne

Estaires

Armentières

Lillers

Robecq

La Bassée Canal

Lys Canal

Sailly

Lys

Hinges

Béthune

Gorre

16 kilometres

10 miles

La Bassée

Don

Deule Canal

to stem the German armour, let alone defeat it completely. Pownall spoke with the director of operations, Major General Dewing, who seemed taken aback by this news to the point of obtuseness. General Ironside, the CIGS, was so appalled that he managed to have the War Cabinet assembled by the afternoon. He told them that it might be possible to supply the BEF for a limited time through a bridgehead based on the Channel ports, but that complete evacuation was impossible. His solution was for the BEF to move south-west, towards Amiens, to get back on its line of communication. In making this suggestion, which was the most amazing nonsense, he was showing that he was as out of touch with events as his French counterparts. However, Churchill agreed with his proposals and told him to go to Belgium and order Gort to comply with this plan.

Sunday 19 May was also an eventful day for Gamelin: he was sacked. He had played absolutely no part in restoring the situation, and his final contribution was to visit General Georges at his headquarters at La Ferté. Here he called for an offensive, which had it been mounted a week earlier and in strength might have succeeded. But it was far too late now. At this juncture, he received a message from his headquarters at Vincennes that General Weygand had been summoned from Syria, which signified the end of the road for Gamelin. A 'quick lunch' with Georges followed. It turned out to be a substantial repast, which Gamelin tucked into with evident pleasure, and perhaps with relief that the burden had been lifted from his shoulders. After lunch, General Dill, the Vice Chief of the Imperial General Staff (VCIGS), arrived from London bearing the tidings that the BEF would do everything possible to co-operate. Georges was called away to speak on the telephone to Billotte, who told him that Gort was contemplating withdrawing to Calais and Dunkirk. Apparently, Billotte had gleaned this news by tapping Pownall's conversation with the War Office. Gamelin, after reminding Georges of the reassurances Dill had brought from London, left.

Weygand arrived to take over early on 20 May, ending the career of Gamelin, perhaps one of the most ineffectual generals in the history of France. Weygand was seventy-three years old, small and dapper with a foxy face, and reminded one British officer of 'an aged jockey'. At the very beginning of the First World War, he had been selected by the French commander Marshal Foch as his chief of staff, apparently at random. Weygand remained with him until after the Armistice. He had never commanded troops in battle. As Major General Spears (British Liaison Officer at GQG) remarked of him, commanding troops in battle and being a chief of staff were 'as different as riding in the Grand National from taking photographs of its jumps'. Weygand was an

ambitious officer, who on arriving and being shown a map of the German advance exclaimed, 'If I had known the situation was so bad, I would not have come.' Spears commented, 'It meant he was thinking of his reputation.' Weygand learned all too soon how serious the situation was. Between 10 and 19 May the French had lost fifteen divisions. In the north a further forty-five were in danger of being cut off or hurled back into the sea. There were no reserves; the arsenals were empty. Between Valenciennes and Montmédy the gap measured nearly one hundred miles. The time for a counter-offensive had passed.

On that Monday, 20 May, Guderian's corps headed for Amiens and Abbeville. He told his soldiers that there were no Allied formations ahead of the armour and, having already crossed the Canal du Nord, there was no barrier between them and the coast. Gort's task was to hold the thirty-mile sector of the Escaut Line. Against Army Group B this was a big enough job in itself. The fate of the Belgian Army on his left and the French First Army on his right lay in his hands. But, given that the French First Army was bent back in a bow from Valenciennes to Douai, not only were his communications with his bases in distant Normandy threatened, but he was in danger of encirclement. He was not responsible for the threatened territory; it lay well beyond his boundary. The British 23rd Division had already been deployed on the Canal du Nord at Georges' request, to hold the sector from Douai to Péronne. Gort knew that this division could do little to stop the German armour. The British 12th Division had been ordered to cover Albert, Doullens, Amiens and Abbeville, all important traffic centres. The 12th and 23rd Divisions were, in the words of the British Official History, 'alone interspersed between the oncoming German armies and the sea'.[3]

An unequal struggle was about to be fought out on a thirty-mile-wide belt of country between the Scarpe, just north of Arras, and the Somme. The German spearhead consisted of seven armoured divisions – the armoured sickle of Army Group A. From north to south, they were 5th and 7th, of XV Panzer Corps (Hoth), 6th and 8th of XLI Panzer Corps (Reinhardt), and 1st, 2nd and 10th of XIX Panzer Corps (Guderian). In addition to their seventeen tank battalions, this force had fifteen battalions of motorized infantry, five motorcycle battalions and twelve batteries of field and medium guns, as well as anti-tank and anti-aircraft guns. Facing them were two British infantry divisions, both Territorial sent out for labour duties and to continue their training. The strength of each was little more than half a division. They had engineers but no divisional artillery. The 23rd Division had two brigades instead of the normal three. The 12th Division was provided with an improvised troop of four field guns manned by soldiers from a Royal Artillery school of

instruction. The 23rd Division was luckier, having eleven field guns and two 4.5-inch howitzers from the same school. But they had no artillery instruments; eleven of the guns could fire only over open sights, the others had no sights at all. Both divisions had one Bren per platoon, instead of three, one anti-tank rifle per company, two carriers, and one 3-inch mortar. About a quarter of the men had not completed their war course with the rifle, and less than half had fired the Bren. The panzer divisions had fought in Poland and had just inflicted a crushing defeat on the French. Neither of the British divisions had fired a shot in anger.

As the British divisions were deploying on 18 May, the 37th Brigade of the 23rd Division was caught sitting in trains at Amiens by a heavy bombing attack by the Luftwaffe. That evening the leading troops of the German 1st Panzer Division reached the Canal du Nord and occupied Péronne. On pushing out of town the other side, the Germans encountered the 7th Royal West Kents and the four field guns. The leading motorcyclist was shot. He was followed by three tanks, which engaged the British with machine guns and were peppered back with anti-tank rifle rounds, pepper being the right expression as it was discovered that the Royal West Kents had been issued with training ammunition with half-charges. The field guns firing over open sights set one of the tanks on fire. Fighting continued until dark, and the Germans, having made no headway, pulled back into Péronne. The Royal West Kents and their field guns were ordered to retire to Albert, and moved without interference. The German reluctance to fight at night, even against weaker opponents, proved a blessing.

The next day the Germans closed up to the Canal du Nord in force, having outflanked Péronne to the south in a sector that was supposed to have been held by the French but was not. Soon five panzer divisions were over the canal, with two more echeloned behind. The 23rd Division was ordered to fall back. The 69th Brigade was to withdraw to the River Scarpe to the east of Arras, and completed the move during the night without enemy interference. The 70th Brigade was to deploy west of Arras and cover the Arras–Doullens road as far south as Saulty. The only continuous obstacle, and not much of one at that, was the railway line running near the main road, and there were no anti-tank guns to cover the crossings. The 7th Royal West Kents arrived in Albert at 0600 hours on 20 May and were greeted by a Stuka raid. Two companies rushed to cover the approaches to the town. They soon heard the sound of engines and the clatter of tracks, and saw the enemy armour accompanied by motorcyclists and armoured personnel carriers converging on Albert on more roads than the battalion had troops to cover. These were the leading troops of the 1st Panzer Division. The Germans

encircled the town and burst in. As the two companies out on a limb started to embus, the armour caught them, massacring them in the trucks and by the roadside. Within a few minutes they were wiped out.

Lieutenant Brown, the acting adjutant of the battalion, determined to inform brigade headquarters of the disaster, stopped a civilian motorcyclist at pistol-point and made him take him on the pillion. As they turned a corner, they ran into Germans rounding up some troops of battalion headquarters. The civilian braked and gave himself up. Brown slid on to the driver's saddle and shot off, with bullets pinging around him. He ran out of petrol a mile further on. A gunner officer who escaped in a car eventually took the news of the fate of the 7th Royal West Kents to brigade headquarters. The Germans found the four guns still in the main square with a quantity of training ammunition.

The infantry of the 70th Brigade were tired after several days of marching, so their commander, Brigadier Kirkup, decided to ferry as many soldiers as possible in the transport the brigade had managed to rustle up over the preceding days. The brigade marched to Neuville-Vitasse during the night of 19/20 May and rested there until daybreak – possibly a mistake. A British fault, the counterpart to the German reluctance to fight at night, was a lack of ruthlessness that sometimes manifested itself when troops were tired, both in withdrawal and in attack. On occasions, throughout the war, lives would have been saved had commanders pushed their soldiers harder.

In the early hours the brigade headquarters and advance parties from battalions were transported to their new locations: the headquarters to Gouy and the remainder to Saulty and Beaumetz-les-Loges on the Arras – Doullens road. The transport began ferrying the battalions, picking up a load of men and taking them to the new position while the rest marched on; the trucks would then return to collect the next load. With daylight came the Luftwaffe, so the men marched in open formation at wide intervals. The first lift consisted of about half of the 11th Durham Light Infantry. The other half had halted when the armour of Rommel's 7th Panzer Division appeared and surrounded them, killing or capturing them all. The SS Totenkopf (Death's Head) Division came up on the left flank of Rommel's division and also hit the 70th Brigade.

The Tyneside Scottish (Black Watch) were resting at Neuville-Vitasse when reports of enemy approaching at about 0700 hours got them moving again. The leading company marched about five miles and ran into an ambush near Ficheux, and efforts to work round the ambush ran into tanks. The rear company was trapped in Neuville, and attempts to fight from the houses were stymied when the tanks set fire to them with

tracer and high-explosive rounds. At Mercatel, more Tynesiders and two companies of 10th DLI were surprised resting and cut to pieces.

Other Tynesiders were caught embussed in trucks along with a large body of Ordnance Corps soldiers and some pioneers, mostly unarmed, who had attached themselves to the brigade. As the trucks began their westward journey they ran into the leading elements of the 8th Panzer Division, while the tanks of the division attacked the marching troops. The panzer division had waited until daybreak to start. The marching infantry fought back, but against the armour, with light weapons, it was a hopeless task. A running fight took place over about five miles of road. The provost sergeant, Chambers of the Tynesiders, was last seen alive standing on a tank trying to lever open the commander's hatch with his bayonet. A few got away, and made for brigade headquarters. The enemy armour followed up and brigade headquarters was forced to flee to Houdain, on the road fifteen miles north-west of Arras. The remnants of the brigade joined them there, totalling some fourteen officers and 219 soldiers. The Tynesiders alone had lost over a hundred dead.

The 7th Panzer Division, under Rommel, spent an unsuccessful day attacking Arras, stoutly resisted by 1st Welsh Guards well established in their defences, and reinforced by the 9th West Yorks taken from airfield defence. Rommel went forward to see what the trouble was, and on his way back to rejoin his division, protected by one tank and an armoured car, encountered what his war diary describes as heavy tanks at Vis-en-Artois. They were probably French cavalry patrolling south of the Scarpe. They surrounded him and put his tank out of action. Regrettably they did not realize who they had netted, and he managed to get away. Had they taken him, much future trouble might have been avoided.

The 36th Brigade, less the 7th Royal West Kents, was able to take up its positions without interference. The 5th Buffs covered a frontage of six and a half miles from Pommera to La Herlière. They managed to scrape out some slit trenches forward of the railway line and set up flimsy roadblocks. On their right, the 6th Royal West Kents covered the approaches to Doullens, where Gort had intended to establish his headquarters when, as planned, his command expanded to an army group with the BEF split into two armies. In anticipation of this, it was well provided with a network of telephone lines, as well as containing the main map depot of the BEF. Unfortunately the maps had not been removed to a place of safety, which was to have serious consequences later. Brigadier Roupell warned the battalion commanders that if further withdrawal was necessary they should make for Frevent. At 0930 hours the gunner officer arrived bearing the news of the catastrophe at Albert.

A few truckloads of men escaped, but the Germans caught the quartermaster of the 6th Royal West Kents as he was distributing rations. A throng of French soldiers started coming back through the positions held by the 5th Buffs, ignoring suggestions to join in the defence. At La Herlière, on the left of the line, a woman enraged by this behaviour was seen to tear down a propaganda poster that read, 'Nous vaincrons parce que nous sommes les plus forts' (We will overcome because we are the strongest).

It was at La Herlière that Private Lungley of the 5th Buffs refused to surrender to overwhelming force, firing his Bren to the end and ignoring demands for surrender. A round from a tank gun killed him, and he was buried in the slit trench he had defended so stoutly. The villagers laid flowers on his grave each night, and when he was reburied in the village cemetery they attended in such numbers that the Germans stopped the ceremony. He was buried clandestinely at night.

One column of the 6th Panzer Division advanced rapidly on the 6th Royal West Kents, supported by artillery and machine guns, while the other column headed for the divisional objective, Le Boisle. By 1230 hours the whole of the brigade forward line was being engaged. Commanders at all levels could communicate only by runner, many of whom never got back, being cut off by infiltrating enemy infantry and armour. A despatch rider from the Buffs' left flank did, however, manage the ten-mile journey to Doullens, having two motorbikes shot from under him, experiencing several close shaves evading enemy tanks, and shooting two Germans with his pistol on the way. At 1300 hours the 5th Buffs were ordered to withdraw. None of the messages reached the forward companies. Afterwards it became clear that some of the Buffs had held out for up to two hours, and had knocked out at least two tanks with their Boyes anti-tank rifles, of which they had one to each two miles of front.

The 6th Royal West Kents were far less stretched out and so could put up a tougher resistance. The battalion kept the Germans out of Doullens until late in the afternoon, which allowed the administrative transport to get away, and a sapper officer to set fire to all the petrol in various dumps all over town. The Germans, having been denied access on the main road, came in from a flank and pumped shells into the houses, reducing them one by one. By 1700 hours about a hundred defenders were holed up in a building in the centre of town, and held out until 2000 hours. Black smoke curled up from destroyed petrol and devastated houses.

The headquarters and reserve company of the 5th Buffs joined brigade headquarters in Lucheux to find the only street through the village

blocked by a German armoured car disabled by a Boyes rifle. At dusk, Brigadier Roupell led this party north but at 0400 hours, with enemy all around him, he ordered them to disperse and make their escape in small parties. Cut off from brigade headquarters, the remnants of three companies of the 6th Royal West Kents did the same, after holding out until last light in the north of the town. Most of these parties made their way south heading for the Somme. Here there were fewer enemy, and some parties of Buffs and West Kents crossed the Somme and reached safety. Brigadier Roupell hid in a farm, where he remained trapped for two years, before escaping home through Spain. All three battalion commanders were taken prisoner. Vehicle parties of the 5th Buffs and 6th and 7th Royal West Kents, with the 262nd Field Company, Royal Engineers (RE), forced their way through the teeming refugees, dodged the German armour and reached Saint-Pol. From here they were directed to Boulogne to reinforce the garrison. This party consisted of some 300 men, of whom about half were sappers. Only one officer, a captain of the 262nd Field Company, was able to report to Petre, his divisional commander, in Arras on 23 May, having spent the intervening days dodging German armoured columns.

Other battalions of the 12th Division were also involved in the mayhem in the path of the panzer divisions. These battalions had started out by train from Rouen on the night of 17/18 May, heading for Abbeville. But GHQ decided that the 37th Brigade should go to Amiens, and two trains were diverted while en route by Movement Control. The first contained the 7th Royal Sussex and the 263rd Field Company RE, and the second the 6th Royal Sussex with the 264th Field Company. The headquarters of 37th Brigade remained with the trains heading for Abbeville, and the third battalion, the 2nd/6th East Surrey, was detached on duty elsewhere. The leading train arrived on the outskirts of Amiens on the afternoon of 18 May and was pulverized by a bombing raid. Lieutenant Colonel Gethen of the 7th Royal Sussex found he had a hundred casualties including eight officers. He took his battalion into the cover of a wood, while awaiting a new engine to continue his journey. He had been told, wrongly, that his destination had been changed to Béthune, some fifteen miles on the other side of Arras from Amiens. The train carrying the 6th Royal Sussex was stopped by attacking aircraft further down the line, and the troops took shelter in woods near Ailly-sur-Noye, ten miles south-east of Amiens. Both battalions were cut off from their brigade headquarters and each other.

Still without a train, Gethen found a French headquarters in Amiens, and there was assured by a facile staff officer that the German advance had been halted at Sedan. There was no defence plan as far as Gethen

could make out, and no sign of any other troops. The streams of refugees and continual appearances by the Luftwaffe made nonsense of the staff officer's assurances. Gethen decided to take up a defensive position on high ground south-west of Amiens, astride the road to Poix and Rouen.

The 1st Panzer Division arrived in the early afternoon of 20 May, and engaged the 7th Royal Sussex with its tank guns, sitting out of range of the forward companies. After drenching the positions with fire, the tanks clattered forward and overran the forward companies. The reserve companies held on, resisting until dark, long after battalion headquarters had been overrun. Gethen was captured, and his second-in-command shot for not putting up his hands speedily enough. One company commander, Lieutenant Jackson, wounded four times, was congratulated by his captor on the fight his men had put up, and was offered the German's car to convey him to hospital. Jackson preferred to remain with his soldiers.

A mere 200 of the 7th Royal Sussex survived, and the Royal Sussex, alone of all the regiments in the British Army, were awarded the battle honour 'Amiens 1940'.[4] Their sister battalion, the 6th Royal Sussex, commandeered an engine and train, and made a long journey via Rouen and Le Mans, back to Nantes, one of the British bases.

Headquarters 12th Division was at Fressenneville, well south of the Somme, eleven miles south-west of Abbeville. It was from here that the GOC Petre had left for Arras on 18 May, expecting to return, only to be detained to command Petreforce. Back at his own headquarters at Fressenneville, he spent Sunday 19 May in search of information, the whereabouts of the GOC and of missing units, and indeed any scrap of news that would throw some light on an increasingly obscure picture.

Because the 35th Brigade, the last brigade in Petre's 12th Division to be deployed, had been ordered to go to Abbeville, initially only the 2nd/5th Queen's reached the town. The other two battalions in the brigade (2nd/6th and 2nd/7th Queen's) were mistaken by Movement Control for the 46th Division and routed to Béthune. Eventually the 2nd/6th and 2nd/7th Queen's arrived at Abbeville station, after a hair-raising journey which had included a halt at Arras, where they were advised to try and return to Abbeville. The journey took thirteen hours, and, with only biscuits to eat, they were fed up with all this order and counter-order, and very hungry. They marched to billets in villages to the north and east of Abbeville: Drucat and Vauchelles. It was intended not that they should defend these localities, but that they should eventually deploy from them.

Earlier, Brigadier Wyatt of the 37th Brigade had had the 6th and 7th Royal Sussex arbitrarily, and in error, removed from him by Movement

Control, and the 2nd/6th East Surreys had been sent on lines-of-communication duty. Consequently, he had nothing to do until 20 May, when the GSO 1 of the division, the senior operations staff officer and de-facto chief of staff, decided that Petre's two-day absence might become permanent and that Wyatt should take command of the division, or what was left of it. At 1400 hours the Luftwaffe mounted several heavy raids on Abbeville, and there were spurious reports of paratroops landing. Headquarters 12th Division was still totally in the dark as to the situation. At this juncture Northern District at Rouen said that the division had been transferred to the direct command of GHQ and that the Germans were attacking Amiens. At 1700 hours a staff officer on return from a reconnaissance reported that the Germans had cut the road to Arras and reached the outskirts of Doullens at midday.

The 12th Division had been sent to Abbeville as a reserve, not to defend the town, and it was decided that the wisest course in view of the continued air attacks was to withdraw the three battalions of the Queen's in 35th Brigade back across the Somme rather than risk them being cut off. At 1715 hours Brigadier Cordova, standing in as brigade commander for Wyatt, sent a despatch rider to his battalions summoning the commanding officers and reconnaissance parties to implement the withdrawal. Abbeville was in a state of mayhem. Clouds of smoke and dust hung over the town; many roads were blocked with rubble and littered with corpses. Panic-stricken refugees crammed every passable road, fleeing hither and thither uncertain in which direction lay safety. Mixed with the civilians were equally agitated French soldiers in an assortment of army and civilian vehicles struggling to get over the Somme.

The Queen's battalions, being outside the town, survived the bombing without casualties. But the withdrawal message reached only the battalion nearest the river, the 2nd/5th. The tanks of 2nd Panzer Division had already penetrated between the centre battalion, the 2nd/7th, and the left-hand and most northerly, the 2nd/6th. The battalions had only had time to construct a few rudimentary roadblocks and some emergency slit trenches for local defence near their billets; they had not expected to defend the location against a panzer division. The 2nd/7th Queen's covering the Doullens road were hit first. The tanks sat back and pumped shells and sprayed machine guns at the exposed positions. The battalion responded with the six rounds of anti-tank ammunition per Boyes rifle, which was all it had. The commanding officer now sent a despatch rider with a message to all his companies to withdraw behind the Somme. Although he had not received Cordova's message ordering withdrawal, he had been warned earlier that moving back across the river was an option if the situation demanded it – now it did. He saw his two forward

companies fall back and, thinking that his message had been received, he went to find the best crossing place. The order had in fact reached only one company; the others were withdrawing to the village of Vauchelles, in the belief that the buildings there would offer better cover than the meagre slits they had dug in the open. Vauchelles lies off the main road, and the Germans poured past, without spotting the 250 soldiers hiding in the houses. After a quiet night, however, they found themselves surrounded by German tanks and infantry, and were forced to surrender. An exfiltration in small parties by night might have proved their salvation, but possibly they lacked the necessary leadership, or they were not well trained enough to think of it, or to carry out such an operation. Their commanding officer managed to lead about a hundred of his men over the Somme crossing on the debris of a bombed railway bridge.

The 2nd/6th Queen's sat tight and unmolested in Drucat, north of Abbeville. Lieutenant Colonel Bolton, the CO, waited until nightfall, having put his transport out of action. Marching by compass in bright moonlight, he led his men westwards until he reached the bridge he was heading for, and found no Germans there. This battalion returned intact, except for the platoon covering the rear.

Brigadier Cordova planned that the 2nd/5th Queen's, sited astride the Amiens road and nearer the river than the other two, should form the layback position through which the other two battalions would withdraw. He had to dispense with this scheme when he saw that the other battalions were now in contact and had no hope of withdrawing to the south-east or even of getting his orders. An order was sent to the 2nd/5th to cross the bridge at Epagne, but it was too late. The Germans advancing down the road from Amiens had already pinned down all four companies of the 2nd/5th in Bellancourt, two miles north of the Somme. A corporal at great risk got through with the order to pull out. But only five parties, totalling around a hundred men, made it past the Germans around Bellancourt. The first, a platoon unwisely travelling in trucks, encountered tanks on a minor road to the bridge; they tried surrendering but were cut down. After this, more circuitous routes were attempted using the cover of darkness. Most who crossed the river did so by swimming, the CO among them. Some drowned in the attempt. A lifeline made of rifle slings broke and men were swept away by the strong current.

Unbeknown to the 35th Brigade they were not the only British troops in Abbeville. Two lines-of-communication battalions, the 4th Buffs and 2nd/6th East Surreys, as well as the 137th Brigade of the 46th Division, along with a battalion of the 138th Brigade, were caught up in the chaos caused by the great German breakthrough. The majority got

clear on foot or in trains, usually displaying considerable initiative and resourcefulness.

The Germans' stunning advance had cut the Allied armies in two with stupefying speed, completely severing the BEF's lines of communication to its bases in Normandy, Brittany and further south. They had almost wiped out nine British battalions, and had captured Amiens, Albert, Doullens and Abbeville before the Allies could put together a plan for their defence. The way to the Channel ports was open. The 12th and 23rd Divisions had ceased to exist. What did they achieve? The war diary of the German XXXXI Corps says of the 6th and 8th Panzer Divisions that 'from about 1300 hours onwards they were only able to gain ground slowly and with continual fighting against an enemy who defended himself stubbornly'. This is praise indeed of the fighting quality of the Territorial infantry who, though widely dispersed, fought armoured divisions far stronger numerically and incomparably better armed.[5] One of these battalions claimed afterwards that it had delayed the German advance for five hours. Whether or not this modest claim is an accurate assessment, it has to be borne in mind that a delay of even one hour was of huge benefit to the British forces in France. But one cannot resist the thought that these battalions might have been used better, instead of being sprayed out over the countryside, to confront armour out in the open or on the edges of villages. The British Army had simply not given enough thought to how infantry should fight armour. This had to wait until later when the invasion of Britain looked likely; and by then troops were taught to hold the rear half of built-up areas, entice the armour in and destroy it at close range. Even that tactic was susceptible to the village or town in question being bypassed by armour, while enemy infantry remained behind to mop up the defenders. But the trick would have been to pick key points which the enemy could not afford to bypass, at least for long, such as Amiens and Abbeville.

The fundamental problem was that neither the French nor the British could match their thinking and planning to the speed of the German armour's progress. In modern terminology the Germans frequently got inside the Allies' Observation Orientation Decision Action loop, or OODA for short. Too often by the time the Allies had *observed* the enemy, worked out what they were about to do (*orientation*), decided what to do, and taken *action*, including giving the necessary orders, the game had moved on, with the result that the action taken did not fit what was actually happening on the ground. If Allied commanders ignored what air reconnaissance was telling them, as happened at the Meuse crossings, the OODA process could not even begin.

The RAF played an insignificant part in these momentous days. On

20 May, reconnaissance Hurricanes had reported the German armour crossing the Canal du Nord, and produced other sighting reports. Unfortunately at that very moment plans were being made to withdraw the RAF Air Component back to England because the German advance threatened its airfields. At the same time the Advanced Air Striking Force, situated south of the German breakthrough, and intended not to collaborate with land forces but to bring the aircraft nearer to military targets in Germany, had difficulty communicating with the BEF on the other side of the gap torn in the Allied lines. Co-ordinating what were effectively three air forces, the Air Component with the BEF, the Advanced Air Striking Force, and the rest of the RAF in the United Kingdom, was becoming impossible for the Air Ministry. So all squadrons were in the process of pulling back to Britain.

Nevertheless two squadrons of bombers with fighter protection were ordered to attack the armoured columns on the Canal du Nord. By the time the bombers arrived the columns were no longer there, and the panzer divisions were moving rapidly, widely dispersed, across country between Arras and the Somme (the Germans had got inside the OODA loop, yet again). On the critical day when the Germans were in full cry, the air force took no effective part in the fighting. Although some 130 bombers of Bomber Command and the Advance Air Striking Force attacked a variety of targets in support of ground forces, or 'collaboration targets' in the jargon of the day, 'it is impossible to conclude that their action had any very significant effect on the course of the battle', to quote the British Official History.[6]

By 21 May the only British fighter squadrons still in France were Nos 1, 73 and 501, very much reduced in serviceable aircraft. Thereafter, all air support for the BEF and neighbouring Allied forces would have to come from England. As the Germans advanced and the Allies retreated towards the Channel, the air umbrella from south-east England became increasingly effective. But it was never totally sufficient. In just twelve days, starting on 10 May, the German advance had put the BEF in peril of its existence and at the same time had almost completely stripped it of its close air support. This close air support, moreover, was never as good as that which the Germans enjoyed, for a number of reasons, not least lack of organization and the means to communicate with the supporting aircraft. In addition, it has to be said, at senior level in the air force there was a less than can-do attitude towards support for the army – an attitude, it must be emphasized, that was not to be found among the air crew.

Air Marshal Barratt, the commander of the Advanced Air Striking

Force, remarked, 'the RAF could not win the war if the French infantry [sic] lost it'. This was an interesting admission on the part of a senior RAF officer when one bears in mind that the British Air Staff policy before the war had in effect maintained that any future war would be decided by air strikes before ground operations became pressing. Barratt's eyes had been opened to the reality that air power alone does not win wars, a principle that holds good to this day. Whether any other RAF officer would have admitted this is quite another matter. There were some RAF senior commanders who would not see it almost to the end of the Second World War; and a handful of airmen who still do not perceive this fact over sixty years later. The RAF had spent the inter-war years planning to fight a very different war from that which it found itself fighting in May 1940. The blame does not lie entirely with the Air Staff, but must be shared with successive British governments who shied away from the continental commitment until too late. By that time the RAF's doctrine, operational concepts and force structure were unsuitable for this assignment in France and Belgium, sprung upon them almost at the last moment.

One bright spot in the gloom of Monday 20 May was that Arras still held out, although more than half encircled. In order to check the enemy at this important place, Gort ordered the 1st Army Tank Brigade and Major General Franklyn's 5th Division to join the 50th Division in the Vimy area, north of Arras, and to prepare for offensive action. The force was to be called Frankforce, after the GOC of the 5th Division.

Also on this day, General Ironside, the CIGS, descended on Gort's headquarters at 0800 hours. With him he bore an order from the War Cabinet resulting from his discussions with them the previous day, known as Order A. This read:

1. The Cabinet decided that the CIGS was to direct the C-in-C BEF to move southwards upon Amiens attacking all enemy forces encountered and to take station on the left of the French Army.
2. The CIGS will inform General Billotte and the Belgian Command making it clear to the Belgians that their best chance is to move tonight between the BEF and the coast.
3. The War Office will inform General Georges in this sense.[7]

This intervention by the War Cabinet was the result of the conversation Pownall had had with the War Office the previous day. Order A was based on an appreciation by the War Office of 19 May which in summary argued that:

1. Unless, therefore, the French are in a position to launch an organised counter-offensive on a large scale, the chances of preventing the German thrust reaching the sea are receding.
2. If a counter-offensive is considered impossible the only alternative would be to endeavour to hold the general line Ham–Péronne–Douai for sufficient time to enable the Allied left wing to withdraw to the line Péronne–Amiens–the sea.
3. The Germans cannot yet be in great strength and must be considerably disorganised by demolitions, the distance they have marched, and above all by air action. The present appears a favourable moment with the German mechanised forces tired and main bodies strung out.[8]

By the time Ironside arrived at Gort's headquarters, Condition 1 of the War Office appreciation had already been realized because the French were not in a position to launch a counter-offensive. The 'only alternative' outlined in Condition 2 was nonsense. By the evening of 19 May the Germans already held most of the line Ham–Péronne–Douai on the Canal du Nord, and by the evening of Ironside's visit the following day would hold Amiens, Abbeville, Le Boisle and Hesdin as well. Although the second sentence of Condition 3 was accurate, the first sentence was wishful thinking on a grand scale, especially the reference to the Germans being considerably disorganized by air action. The effect of air action on the Germans was negligible; the only significant damage was to the RAF.

What the War Office was seeking in Condition 3 would come to pass four and a half years hence. In December 1944, in a replay of the Ardennes offensive, as German armour with their tails up headed for the coast, the US Army's General Patton could pronounce with glee, 'they've stuck their heads in the meat grinder, and I've got my hand on the handle'. But in 1940 the Allies had neither air supremacy nor battle-practised armoured divisions; the French Army's performance in 1940 bore no resemblance to the dogged resistance by the Americans in 1944 that contained the thrust; they did not have a Patton, and in 1940 Montgomery was only a divisional commander.

Gort was perfectly well aware that everything the War Office proposed was impracticable. His right flank was already turned, and he had to do all he could to prevent his left flank from being turned as well. If the French could not close the gap, he would have to withdraw northwards. He had heard nothing from the man who was supposed to be commanding him, Billotte, or from Georges, under whose command the British government had placed him. He explained this to General Ironside and told him that he intended mounting a limited offensive south of Arras.

The last entry in the German Army Group A war diary for 20 May says: 'Now that we have reached the coast at Abbeville the first stage of the offensive has been achieved . . . The possibility of an encirclement of the Allied armies' northern group is beginning to take shape.'[9] Gort was right. Although Order A was a fantasy of *Alice in Wonderland* proportions, Pownall's conversation had one good outcome. It goaded the War Office into initiating discussions with the Admiralty that very day on the practicability of evacuation from Dunkirk.

Despite the outward signs of confidence evinced by the war diary entry above, the German command had become alarmed by the speed of their own advance. Hitler had an attack of nerves, as did Rundstedt, who had an over-inflated respect for Gamelin. This was based on Gamelin's performance as Commander in Chief General Joffre's operations officer, and especially his successful plan for the celebrated flank attack on the German Army on the Marne in September 1914, which had brought the whole scheme of manoeuvre of the German invasion of France in the First World War crashing down. Worried about his flanks, Rundstedt ordered a halt on 16 May. When Kleist came forward to order Guderian to comply, the latter threatened to resign, and kept moving. There was of course some activity by the Allies that understandably caused the odd wobble of confidence among German commanders – for example, the attack by Brigadier General de Gaulle's improvised 4th Armoured Division at Montcornet on 17 May in an attempt to cut Guderian's line of communication. More of an armoured raid than an attack, it fizzled out within twenty-four hours and did not achieve its objective. De Gaulle's next attack at Crécy-sur-Serre on 19 May was equally unsuccessful. However, despite the confidence displayed by press-on types like Guderian, anxiety within the German high command about exposed flanks and consequent differences of opinion over the right course to follow were to surface again. What Gort was cooking up at Arras was to feed some of these fears.

4

COUNTER-STROKE AT ARRAS

The limited offensive south of Arras that Gort had mentioned to Ironside, the CIGS, during his visit on 20 May was just that – limited. Gort's original intention as expressed in his orders to General Franklyn early on the 20th was to 'support the garrison in Arras and to block the roads south of Arras, thus cutting off the German communications [via Arras] from the east.' He was to 'occupy the line of the Scarpe east of Arras' and establish 'touch by patrols' with the French. Gort did not mention a counter-attack or any more ambitious aim, nor was there any suggestion that the French would take part.

Gort convinced Ironside that the gap had to be closed if disaster was to be averted, but the French would have to undertake this task. All the BEF divisions except two committed to Arras were fully engaged on the Escaut Line. Ironside, taking Pownall with him, went to see Billotte at his headquarters at Lens, and found him with Blanchard, the commander of the French First Army. Both gave Ironside the impression of being totally defeated, and with no idea what to do next. Ironside lost his temper. At six foot four, and like many large men in the British Army nicknamed 'Tiny', he towered over the two French generals. He shook Billotte by the button on his tunic, writing later in his diary, 'the man is completely beaten'. Ironside having bludgeoned him into attacking towards Amiens, Billotte snapped to attention and said that he would make an immediate plan to do so. It was agreed with Billotte and Blanchard that the BEF and the French First Army would both attack on 21 May with two divisions.

Ironside took the opportunity to telephone Weygand and tell him that there was neither resolution nor co-ordination at Billotte's headquarters, adding that Billotte should be sacked. It was plain that the French were only agreeing to attack under the pressure of Ironside's unnerving presence. When Ironside called at Gort's headquarters on his way back to England, Gort convinced him that the French would never attack. Ironside's visit had one positive outcome: it opened his eyes to the true state of affairs in France. The scale of the defeat of the French Army was now much clearer in his mind – as was, consequently, the desperate situation

1. *Left*. General Lord Gort, C-in-C of the BEF, left, with General Gamelin, Supreme Commander French Land Forces, right.
2. *Right*. General Maxime Weygand, left, after being appointed Supreme Commander French Land Forces in Gamelin's place. Centre, with briefcase, French Prime Minister Paul Reynaud, examining papers proffered by an official. Lurking in the background, Marshal Pétain.

3. Hitler at his headquarters at Bruly-de-Pêche in the Belgian Ardennes during the campaign in France and Flanders 1940. On Hitler's left, Field Marshal von Brauchitsch, Commander-in-Chief of the German Army, and on his right General Jodl, Chief of the Operations Staff of the German armed forces (Wehrmacht). Far right, Admiral of the Fleet Raeder, Commander-in-Chief of the German Navy.

4. A sergeant of the Royal Ulster Rifles in 1940s-style battle order (minus haversack), with First World War vintage steel helmet, .303in Lee Enfield bolt-action rifle slung, gas mask between his ammunition pouches, and eighteen-inch long bayonet slung on his left hip.

He is wearing battledress, only recently issued to the British Army, based on contemporary ski fashion, not a clever design for a fighting soldier. The blouse had insufficient pockets, provided no cover for the nether regions, and after a few minutes' crawling about often parted company with the trousers. The map pocket on the front of the trousers, instead of the side, made extracting maps difficult when lying down taking cover.

5. British soldiers in the ubiquitous 15 cwt truck. These soldiers are wearing the old-style 1914 tunic, and haversacks on their backs in place of the large pack.

6. Left to right:
Major General B. L. Montgomery
(GOC 3rd Division),
Lieutenant General A. F. Brooke
(GOC II Corps), and
Major General D. G. Johnson
(GOC 4th Division).

7. Major General the
Hon. Harold Alexander,
GOC 1st Division
in the BEF (left) with
Lieutenant General Sir John
Dill who commanded I Corps
in the BEF until April 1940
when he was appointed
Vice Chief of the Imperial
General Staff. Dill handed
command of I Corps to
Lieutenant General Barker.
Taken at an exercise at
Aldershot in May 1939.

8. General Heinz Guderian standing in his command vehicle. An Enigma for encrypting and decrypting radio messages is in the bottom left-hand corner of the picture.

9. 'Phoney War': The King's Company 1st Battalion Grenadier Guards practising 'going over the top' in 1914–1918 War style, 8 April 1940; one month before the German invasion of Holland, Belgium and France.

10. Light tanks of the 4th/7th Royal Dragoon Guards on exercise, winter 1939–1940.

11. Soldiers of the 4th Battalion Royal Northumberland Fusiliers on their motorcycle/side-car combinations. The British dispensed with these vehicles as a means of transporting infantry to battle after the 1940 France and Flanders campaign.

12. 'Phoney War': a Bren gunner and his number two in a 1914–1918 style trench in the winter of 1939–40.

13. Matilda Mk I tanks exercising with the 2nd Battalion North Staffs in January 1940.

14. (Left to right) General 'Tiny' Ironside, Chief of the British Imperial General Staff: General Georges, Commander-in-Chief of the French North-Eastern Front; Winston Churchill, then First Lord of the Admiralty; General Gamelin, Supreme Commander French Land Forces; General Lord Gort, Commander-in-Chief of the BEF; pictured in France in January 1940, before the German offensive in the West.

15. A British cruiser tank on a training exercise.

16. Bren-gun carriers on a training exercise in France before May 1940.

17. A French Char B tank on a training scheme.

18. A British Bren-gun carrier crossing the border into Belgium, 10 May 1940.

faced by the BEF. He began to wonder if it would ever be able to fight its way to the Channel coast. In his diary he wrote: 'God help the BEF, brought to this state by the incompetence of the French command.' Believing that only a minute portion of the BEF could escape, he was disturbed to find that Churchill 'persists in thinking the position no worse'.

Although Gort may have remained personally unconvinced that the French would attack to close the gap, the British Official History claims that Franklyn's operation was beginning to be seen at Gort's command post as part of a bigger push. Franklyn, however, was not told that his operation was now regarded as being part of a larger counter-attack in which the French would participate.[1] He visited General Prioux commanding the French (mechanized) Cavalry Corps, whose patrols were on the Scarpe. There he found Blanchard and Billotte. The French were discussing the possibility of an attack southwards towards Bapaume and Cambrai. They asked if Franklyn could co-operate by attacking towards Bapaume the next day, 21 May. Franklyn replied that he could not do more than the operation he had already been ordered to undertake. For this operation he suggested that Frankforce should 'occupy the line of the Scarpe on the east of Arras' and be responsible for its defence between Arras and Biache, and that the French mechanized cavalry, on being relieved, should move to the west of Arras and watch that flank. Prioux, one of the few French generals to maintain an offensive spirit, offered more; he would order part of a mechanized cavalry division (3rd DLM) to operate on the outer flank of the British force on 21 May. This promise would be fulfilled.

Billotte and Blanchard had tried to arrange for General René Altmayer's French V Corps to attack with two divisions east of Arras in the direction of Cambrai, as they had promised Ironside they would. Blanchard had sent a liaison officer to Altmayer to impress upon him the importance of this attack. The liaison officer reported back that Altmayer had wept silently on his bed, saying that his troops had 'buggered off' and refused to carry out the attack.

That evening Blanchard despatched a letter to Gort saying that, because of congestion on the roads, Altmayer could not mount his attack towards Cambrai before 22 May. Franklyn had already been told. He was in no way put out. As far as he was concerned his plans were not affected at all, and he would be able to carry out the limited tasks he had been given. In Gort's headquarters, where the notion had taken hold that the British and French operations were part of a major counter-attack, there was a feeling of being let down by the French.

What has been known ever since as the British 'counter-attack' at Arras was not intended as a counter-attack, but was designed as a large-scale

mopping-up operation to support the Arras garrison by blocking German communications from the east. This is why the major part of two divisions was used to bolster the defence of Arras on the River Scarpe, and a minor part, all that could be spared, was employed to clear the country to the south of the town. The two infantry divisions (5th and 50th) totalled only four brigades, instead of the usual six. The 13th Brigade from the 5th Division had been detached to relieve Prioux's cavalry on the Scarpe so that the latter could take part in the attack. Franklyn decided to keep the other brigade (the 17th) in reserve until the first phase of the operation was complete. One of the brigades of the 50th Division (the 150th) was sent to reinforce the Arras garrison and to hold the Scarpe to the immediate east of the town. Only the 151st Brigade of the 50th Division was to take part in the clearing-up action, and, of its three battalions, one was kept back in support of the attacking troops. Thus, although Ironside and Pownall had told Billotte when they visited his headquarters that the British were mounting an operation with two divisions, the assaulting infantry on 21 May were in fact two battalions. Most of the infantry in what were already under-strength divisions were going to be holding ground, not attacking.

The attacking force consisted of what we would now call two battle groups of infantry, armour and artillery. The 1st Army Tank Brigade provided the armour. This brigade had covered long distances by road, so tracks and engines were worn, and there had been little time for maintenance. Of a total of seventy-seven Mk I tanks and twenty-three Mk IIs, fifty-eight Mk I and sixteen Mk II tanks were still runners, and many of these were badly in need of a good overhaul.

Franklyn ordered that the Arras–Doullens road should be the start line for the operation: the line which the attacking force crosses at the designated time for the attack to begin, shaken out in formation. The road fulfilled most of the requirements of a start line – or, in modern parlance, a line of departure. It was easily identifiable, and it lay at approximately 90 degrees to the axis of attack. The most important requirement it did not meet was that a start line should be secure, that is not held by the enemy. Franklyn was aware that the 70th Brigade of the 23rd Division had been sent to secure the road on 19 May. Perhaps the news of the disaster that overcame this brigade while it was on its way to its positions (covered in the previous chapter) had not reached Franklyn. The 12th Lancers had reported enemy south and west of Arras, but possibly Franklyn did not realize that they were already far beyond the Doullens road.

Indeed the strength of the enemy in the area was grossly underestimated. Air reconnaissance from the RAF was not available as all the

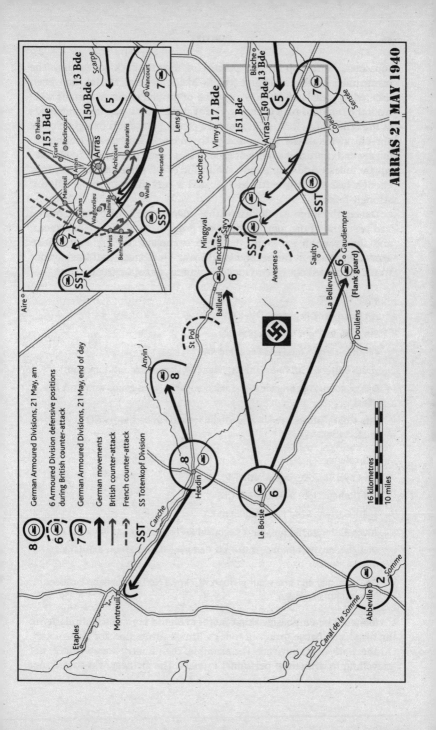

ARRAS 21 MAY 1940

13 Bde
150 Bde
151 Bde

Scarpe
Wancourt
Thélus
Roclincourt
Écurie
Arras
Anzin
Marœuil
Achicourt
Beaurains
Duisans
Wagnonlieu
Dainville
Warlus
Berneville
Wailly
Mercatel

SST

Blache
13 Bde
Sensée
Coleul
150 Bde

17 Bde
151 Bde

Lens
Vimy
Souchez

Arras
SST
SST

Mingoval
Tincques
Savy
Bailleul
Mingoval
Avesnes
Sauty
La Bellevue
Gaudiempré
(Flank guard)
Doullens
St Pol

Anvin
Hesdin
Le Boisle

Canche
Montreuil
Étaples

Abbeville
Canal de la Somme
Somme

German Armoured Divisions, 21 May, am
6 Armoured Division defensive positions during British counter-attack
German Armoured Divisions, 21 May, end of day
German movements
British counter-attack
French counter-attack
SS Totenkopf Division

8   6   7

SST

16 kilometres
10 miles

Aire

squadrons were still in the process of moving back to Britain. The commander of the attacking troops, Major General Martel, had been ordered to clear and capture a swathe of ground about five miles wide from the Doullens road to the Arras–Bapaume road. If one imagines Arras as the centre of a clock, this involved a piece of terrain from eight o'clock anti-clockwise all the way round to five o'clock. This meant clearing of enemy and capturing a piece of ground that covered an area of over forty square miles – fine if only light enemy forces were present, but still a big enough task for two battle groups, and a very different proposition if strongly held.

During the inter-war doldrums that affected the British Army, Martel had been one of the most enthusiastic proponents of the use of armour, and thus was an excellent choice to command the first-ever British armoured attack in the Second World War. He decided that the advance would be carried out by two mobile columns, or battle groups, thus:

Right column

7th Royal Tank Regiment (7th RTR)[2]

8th Durham Light Infantry (8th DLI)

360th Battery, 92nd Field Regiment RA

260th Battery, 65th Anti-Tank Regiment RA (2-pounder anti-tank guns)

One platoon, 151st Brigade Anti-Tank Company (Boyes 25mm anti-tank rifles)

One scout platoon, 4th Royal Northumberland Fusiliers (4th RNF) (motorcycle)

Left column

4th Royal Tank Regiment (4th RTR)

6th Durham Light Infantry (6th DLI)

368th Battery, 92nd Field Regiment RA

206th Battery, 52nd Anti-Tank Regiment RA (2-pounder anti-tank guns)

One platoon, 151st Brigade Anti-Tank Company (Boyes 25mm anti-tank rifles)

One company and one scout platoon, 4th Royal Northumberland Fusiliers (4th RNF) (motorcycle)

It should be emphasized that neither column bore much similarity to an armoured battle group in today's British Army, nor, for that matter, in the 1940 German Army. For example, the infantry were on foot, not travelling in armoured personnel carriers. The artillery was towed, not

self-propelled, and the anti-tank guns likewise. The only truly 'mobile' elements in each column were the tanks and the motorcycles.

Both columns were ordered to cross the start line (the Arras–Doullens Road) at 1400 hours. The infantry, having debussed from their trucks on the Vimy Ridge (the old First World War battlefield), had an eight-mile march to reach their forming-up positions, the place where an attacking force marries up with its support and shakes out into assault formation, before advancing to the start line. As the force approached the forming-up position, they crossed the roads radiating out northwards from Arras, jammed with refugees, so the troops were late arriving. The second-in-command of 8th DLI bringing up the rear of the battalion reported that enemy aircraft had appeared and attacked with machine guns only, possibly because they had already dropped their bombs. The air attack caused no casualties among the battalion, merely some punctured tyres or radiators among the vehicles moving with them. The infantry of the 50th Division were trained as 'lorried infantry'. In theory, and sometimes in practice, they would be taken close to, or even right up to, the forming-up position in trucks, or lorries as they were called at the time. They did not fight from the lorries, which being 'soft-skinned' vehicles were in no sense armoured fighting vehicles, such as the contemporary German half-track. But, having trained to carry out all their moves in transport, the 50th Division, a TA formation, had not spent much time marching, so the Geordies of the DLI were not march fit and now their feet were soft and badly blistered from a twenty-five-mile move three days earlier, carried out without benefit of transport.

For lack of time there was no reconnaissance, and orders were hurriedly passed down the chain of command. The process could have been speeded up, and some misconceptions ironed out, if Martel had given orders to the infantry and tank commanders all together at one orders group (O Group). Instead he adopted the more conventional method of briefing just the commanders of the tank brigade and the infantry brigade. These commanders then held their own O Groups independently of each other, at which they briefed their own commanding officers, who in turn briefed their company commanders, and so on down, ending with section commanders briefing each section of eight to ten men. The most serious misconception concerned the command relationship between armour and infantry. The infantry COs, commanding each column, thought the tanks were under their command, whereas the tank COs thought they were merely in support, and not bound to follow the column commander's orders. This was not a happy state of affairs.

The British Army still had a great deal to learn about infantry–tank co-operation, and the DLI battalions and the 4th and 7th RTR had not even

begun the process. Furthermore, the infantry had no means of communicating with the tanks other than by runner or motorcycle despatch rider. Nor, it must be borne in mind, did battalions have any wireless contact with their companies, a crippling disadvantage in a mobile battle, such as this was intended to be. The tank commanders also had communication problems caused by lack of time to tune and net in their wireless sets. In 1940 and throughout the Second World War, and for years afterwards on all but the smallest sets, this was a tedious procedure involving twiddling knobs to set pointers on dials, tuning the aerial, followed by laborious and often time-consuming netting-in calls to all stations on one's own net (all the radio stations on the same frequency belong to a net). Command tanks would be on at least two separate nets, thus increasing the complexity of the process.

Operating was probably the most difficult in the Mk I tank, which had a crew of only two, commander and driver. A section commander, like Lieutenant Hunt of C Company 4th RTR, had to navigate his tank, fire the gun and command the other two tanks of his section. There was no intercommunication (intercom) system between commander and driver, so directions from commander to driver were given by kicking him using an agreed set of signals (kick on left shoulder = go left, and so forth) or by shouting. The Mk II tanks with a crew of four were better, but had no intercom at this stage in the war.

By 1100 hours the infantry column commanders had sorted out who was supposed to be in their columns and were ready to set off for the start line. Unfortunately, the 8th DLI right-hand column had to move off without their motorcycle reconnaissance platoon and their field gun battery, which had both been held up on the gridlocked roads in rear. This was a pity, because this column was on the exposed right flank, and being on the outer edge of a wheeling manoeuvre had further to go. To assist co-operation the CO of 7th RTR left a liaison officer in a scout car with the CO of 8th DLI. But the RTR liaison officer lost wireless communication with his own CO early on, and 8th DLI had no contact with 7th RTR for the rest of the day.

For the first three miles there was no opposition. The tanks clattered off ahead, steadily drawing ahead of the infantry slogging through the dust churned up by the armour. The tanks of the left-hand column were preceded by a posse of 4th RNF motorcyclists, as well as ten of their own. Behind the infantry rode Martel in his staff car, followed by his reserve, the 9th DLI. In rear the artillery bumped along behind the gun towers. The tanks crossed the River Scarpe by the small road bridges, and as the right-hand column crossed the Arras–Saint-Pol road, the soldiers were cheered by the sight of the smouldering wreckage of a German mecha-

nized 150mm howitzer battery, caught and pulverized by the 12th Lancers. No one seems to have wondered what an enemy medium battery was doing so far north.

A few minutes later, 8th DLI came under fire from the village of Duisans to their right front. The tanks of 7th RTR and the French 3rd DLM, which as promised was on the right of the British advance, swiftly retaliated. For a moment there was a danger of them shooting each other up, but once identities were established the misunderstanding was quickly resolved. A and D Companies of 8th DLI pushed on through Duisans while B Company picked up prisoners in the grounds round the château. Major McLaren found that the Germans had no fight left in them. The commander of B Company took twelve prisoners single-handed in the village cemetery. But the Germans reoccupied the cemetery, and had to be cleared out by C Company supported by French tanks. In the process eighteen more prisoners were taken, all wounded, and according to McLaren the tanks killed about a hundred Germans.

At this juncture, the CO of 8th DLI, Lieutenant Colonel Beart, decided to leave B and C Companies at Duisans as a flank guard, under the command of McLaren, while A and D Companies, the carrier platoon, mortars and battalion headquarters went on to Warlus. The 8th DLI advance reached Warlus at about 1630 hours and were ordered to press on. The carrier platoon commander, Lieutenant English, and A Company could see the Arras–Doullens road ahead, but as soon as they left Berneville they came under heavy fire. This, as far as English could tell, was mainly from mortars from German positions in the vicinity of the road. It stopped the two DLI companies in their tracks. The solution now would have been to call down fire from their own artillery on the German mortars and guns, but the battery of field guns supporting 8th DLI was miles away still trying to get into position through roads jammed with refugees. The advance by 8th DLI ground to a halt.

Meanwhile, at Dainville, on the start line, Y Company, 4th RNF, put in the first and only attack ever mounted by a British motorcyclist unit. Major Clarke, the company commander, attacked with one platoon dismounted, supported by a section of 4th RTR.[3] A column of German half-tracks towing anti-tank guns had been seen motoring between the right flank of 4th RTR and the left flank of 7th RTR, the boundary between the two at that point being a railway line. Lieutenant Hunt of C Company, 4th RTR, took part in this action, ambushing the Germans in a section of sunken road, which led to an archway under the railway line. He sited one of his tanks so that even if it was damaged or destroyed it would plug the route under the railway line. Most of the German vehicles brewed up, some forty prisoners were taken, and Dainville was

secured. As a result of this successful little action, one of Hunt's tank commanders, Corporal Beetham, was awarded the MM. On completion, Hunt's section was ordered back on to the original axis.

The rest of 4th RTR swept on, crossing the start line on time at around 1400 hours. As they moved down into the valley, a few gouts of earth were thrown up around them by enemy shellfire. The tanks crossed the railway line, some gleefully barging through the closed level-crossing gates. Breasting the tree-lined Orinchon stream between Achicourt and Agny, 4th RTR saw streams of German lorried infantry trundling south across their front. This was almost too good to be true, and the machine guns on the Mk Is and Matildas ripped into the trucks, the tracer setting fire to the vehicles and cutting down the German soldiers as they jumped down and scuttled for cover. The German 37mm anti-tank guns speedily came into action, but to the horror of their gunners the solid, armour-piercing shot bounced off the armour of both the Mk I tanks and the Matildas. One of the latter with its 70mm of armour shrugged off no fewer than fourteen hits by German anti-tank guns. The tank crews were jubilant at the sight of the hitherto invincible enemy fleeing in disorder.

Continuing up the slope to Beaurains and beyond to Wancourt, still firing at enemy troops legging it, 4th RTR suddenly ran into trouble. German medium guns, firing direct, smashed into the tanks, brewing up at least twenty, including the CO's light tank. Lieutenant Colonel Fitzmaurice was killed. The adjutant, Captain Cracroft, seeing a battery at point-blank range, charged the guns, annihilating the crews. But more distant, concealed guns continued firing, wreaking havoc among 4th RTR. Cracroft ordered a speedy withdrawal, as black smoke poured from wrecked tanks, bodies hung half out of turrets and hatches, and wounded men dragged their torn bodies through the grass.

Plodding on behind 4th RTR, the 6th DLI had entered Achicourt and Agny, and mopped up large numbers of shaken Germans. The CO, Lieutenant Colonel Miller, sent two companies on to Beaurains, taking more prisoners to bring the battalion's total up to 400. The news that 4th RTR had run into trouble coincided with a message that the Germans were bringing tanks along the road from Cambrai.

Meanwhile the right-hand column had split, with 8th DLI advancing on Warlus, and 7th RTR, not realizing that Warlus was one of the objectives, swinging left towards Wailly. At that moment communications in 7th RTR broke down, and the CO, Lieutenant Colonel Heyland, was shot when he got out of his tank to re-form the regiment using hand signals. His adjutant, trying the same, was also cut down by machine-gun fire. Some tanks headed for Wailly, others on to Mercatel. Here two Matildas commanded by Major King and Sergeant Doyle knocked out

four tanks, overran two anti-tank batteries and crashed through a road-block. Their headlong advance was eventually brought to a stop by some 88mm anti-aircraft guns firing in the ground role, possibly the first recorded instance of their being employed in this capacity. These guns were to cause British, Russian and American tank crews much grief right up to the last day of the Second World War. On this occasion, King and Doyle knocked one out before King's tank caught fire, leaving Doyle to press on until hit by another 88 and brewed up.

During the attack on Wailly, a lone British tank caught another German infantry column on the move, and shot up a howitzer battery, putting it out of action by killing, wounding and putting to flight all the gun crews. General Rommel, who had been leading his tanks to the south and west of Arras through Warlus, was greeted by scenes of chaos when he returned to bring up his two infantry regiments. He found that they had been shot to pieces by the two British tank regiments. He personally redeployed a number of 88mm and 20mm anti-aircraft guns, as well as some anti-tank guns and howitzers of his divisional artillery in the Wailly area, and ordered them to open fire on British tanks deployed near by. Although the shells from the 20mms could not penetrate the British tanks' armour, their crews' habit of lashing their kits on the outside was to prove unwise. The incendiary rounds set these alight, and the fire spread to the engine. The howitzers were lethal, even against the Matildas, as were the 88s. This was the fire that brought 7th RTR's advance to a dead stop. As the surviving tanks withdrew, their final burst of fire killed Rommel's ADC.

Both 4th and 7th RTR, having rushed ahead of the infantry and out of range of their supporting artillery, were caught by guns and brought to a halt. It would take British armoured commanders plenty more such unpleasant shocks in the years to come, many at the hands of Rommel in the desert, before the penny dropped that tanks on their own charging well-sited anti-tank guns and 88s were dead meat. You needed your own artillery to deal with the enemy guns, and infantry working with the tanks to winkle out the anti-tank guns from their covered positions. Unfortunately, the teaching of Liddell Hart had affected British thinking on armoured warfare, and led to armoured commanders deluding them-selves that tanks could swan about the battlefield like ships at sea, and need take little or no account of what the infantry and artillery could do for them.

The crews of tanks out on their own, beset by enemies, often found the battlefield a lonely place. Sergeant Hepple was the commander of a light tank, 'Guinevere', five-and-a-half tons, with 14.4mm of armour, two machine guns in the turret, a .303 and a 5.5, a maximum road speed of

35mph, and a crew of three. His task was reconnaissance for the Mk I tanks of B Company, 7th RTR.[4] As he motored forward, having crossed the start line, his tank was hit three times by anti-tank fire, probably on the tracks, because the effect was like hitting a large stone at speed, and he could see the right-hand track a couple of yards in front of the tank. None of the crew was hurt. Two more shots followed, but missed. The guns that had fired on him were silenced either by him or by the Mk Is that went on past him without stopping. Hepple's tank was subjected to small-arms fire for some minutes, but this stopped in his opinion because the enemy thought the crew was dead. Whatever the reason, about fifty Germans appeared and stood around in groups in the road near by. Hepple opened fire on them and despatched those who did not run off or take cover immediately. The Germans tried to bring an abandoned anti-tank gun into action, but Hepple put a stop to them as well. His attempts to get in touch with B Company by wireless proved fruitless, as the aerial had been damaged by small-arms fire.

The appearance of a second wave of British Mk I and Mk II tanks, followed by infantry, persuaded Hepple that it was safe to dismount and inspect the damage. Although he and his crew, Troopers Tansley and Mackay, attempted to repair the damage to the tracks, and to the radiator, it became clear that the tank was beyond local repair. As they worked they were subjected to shellfire and air attacks. Hepple investigated a Mk II stopped near by, but its right track was off, and the commander, Sergeant Temple, and a crew member lay dead beside it.

By this time dusk was approaching. The infantry had withdrawn, and Hepple decided to abandon 'Guinevere'. He set fire to her, and she was soon burning fiercely. He also set fire to three German motorcycles abandoned in the vicinity. He found a map in one, which he later handed over to one of his officers. He then came upon an abandoned British Bren carrier, which he managed to start, and piling on to it all removable kit, including his two machine guns, he headed for Achicourt, where he found some of 4th RTR.

General Franklyn had spent much of the day in fruitless attempts to get the RAF to provide some support. But the only aircraft that appeared in the sky over the Arras area were German Stukas. At around 1800 hours, they hit 8th DLI on the ridge between Warlus and Berneville, and kept up the attacks for approximately ninety minutes, according to Major McLaren, the second-in-command, who tried to get in touch by motor-cycle with the half of the battalion that had gone forward with the CO. This proved impossible because of German tanks between him at Duisans and the rest of the battalion. The effect of the Stukas' screaming sirens,

the crash of bombs and streams of bullets directed at men lying in the open was shattering. Few were hit, but Lieutenant English had to kick dazed men to their feet.

When the noise of the last attack died away it was replaced by the sound of approaching enemy tanks. Fortunately there were three tanks from the 3rd DLM close by and, while these held off the Germans, 8th DLI withdrew to the cover of Warlus. The two companies took up positions of all-round defence in the village, which Lieutenant English found took some time because of the shock of the air attack. Despite the terrifying noise the total casualties inflicted on 8th DLI caught out in the open were ten men wounded and three trucks destroyed. It was a useful lesson, that troops well spread out in the open, rather than in a village or town, were hard to hit, and the air-to-ground weapons carried by the Stuka were nothing like as lethal as those borne by other aircraft later in the war and after it. On subsequent occasions when the battalion was dive-bombed, they took cover, and carried on as normal after it was over.

Back in Warlus, the two 8th DLI companies started taking casualties from German artillery. The CO was among those wounded, but carried on. The German attacks were not pressed home, which was fortunate as the front half of the battalion was out of touch with the rear half back at Duisans. The CO sent the mortar platoon commander back to brigade headquarters, and after giving him a situation report the brigade commander ordered the battalion to withdraw.

Meanwhile at Duisans, some soldiers of B Company, 8th DLI, came running back to McLaren saying they were under attack from enemy tanks. McLaren had to take the men forward to their positions himself, while an anti-tank gun destroyed enough of the enemy to persuade them to withdraw. But the anti-tank gun was damaged and two of the crew were wounded in this exchange. A Matilda coming back through Duisans went out and sat in front of the anti-tank gun to shield it from enemy fire, while a new crew dashed forward and moved the gun to a less exposed position. McLaren judged that B Company's nerve was 'bad', but C Company was steady.

The Stukas also dived on 6th DLI at Agny, Achicourt and Beaurains, causing far more casualties than 8th DLI suffered. With reports of German armour approaching from several directions, Franklyn authorized Martel to withdraw his columns back to the River Scarpe west of Arras. During the day the 150th Brigade had raided across the Scarpe and caused some mayhem among the enemy. The 13th Brigade had established a bridgehead further east in preparation for the second phase of the operation. But Franklyn realized that with the enemy continuing to

work round his right flank no further attacks could be made, and his main concern must be to stave off the threatened envelopment of his whole force.

The 6th DLI pulled back at last light on Achicourt, leaving Y Company, 4 RNF, and scout cars as a rearguard between Achicourt and Beaurains. A German tank approached from Beaurains as the last of 6th DLI were passing through the rearguard, and was knocked out by Y Company with an anti-tank gun. The Germans took some time to react, and the next attack by infantry with artillery support, which came in at dusk, was repulsed. German tanks followed and outflanked the Y Company position, setting fire to the houses with high explosive and flame throwers. Although surrounded, the Northumberland Fusiliers fought on, buying time for the rest of the column to get clear. The 5th Panzer Division, which had been responsible for the attacks on the rearguard, took the survivors prisoner.

Captain Cracroft, the adjutant of 4th RTR, stationed himself near Achicourt, assembling what was left of the regiment. When a tank approached, he waved his map in the driver's face as he peered out of the hatch, only for an unmistakeably German head to pop up out of the turret. Cracroft ran for his tank, chased by a burst of machine-gun fire. After an exchange of fire, both sides withdrew. The weary British were lucky that the Germans were not more aggressive in following up. The soldiers of 6th DLI were so bone-tired that they kept flopping down in the road at every halt, and had to be kicked to their feet by officers and NCOs.

Lieutenant Hunt of 4th RTR never reached the objective, but met the battalion coming back. One tank commanded by Sergeant Strickland was escorting about fifty Germans with their hands on top of their heads. Although the Germans did not know it, he had run out of ammunition, and did not even have one round 'up the spout'. During the withdrawal, Hunt's tank threw a track in soft ground, a fault to which the Mk I was prone. Unable to replace the damaged track, Hunt and his driver were rescued by the company second-in-command in a staff car, after first destroying the wireless set in the tank.

Sergeant Hepple of 7th RTR, having arrived at Achicourt after abandoning 'Guinevere', drove out in the carrier he had found, but this broke down. Trooper Nichol, also of 7th RTR, and an infantry straggler tagged themselves on to his party, which now numbered five. They managed to find two Bren guns and some water bottles, and set off across country, arriving at Arras the next morning. On reporting to the area headquarters, they were sent to join the remnants of their units at Vimy.

The rearguard for the Right Column was also found by the scout

platoon from 4th RNF. They were attacked by Rommel's 7th Panzer Division and all killed or taken prisoner. But the 2-pounders of the 260th Battery of the 65th Anti-Tank Regiment did good work covering the withdrawal of 8th DLI, as did the French tanks of the 3rd DLM. Three battalions of the 25th Panzer Regiment had to fight their way back to the rest of the division against what Rommel judged, incorrectly, to be a superior force. They made it after nightfall, with a loss of twenty tanks, but they claimed to have destroyed seven heavy tanks, French Somuas, and six anti-tank guns – difficult to substantiate in the chaos of a battle fought in the gloom of approaching night.

With the 7th Panzer Division on the Arras–Hesdin road, 8th DLI were cut off, with two companies in Duisans and the rest of the battalion in Warlus. After dark an officer from A Company turned up at Duisans and told McLaren that he with four others on a Northumberland Fusiliers' scout car were all that were left of A Company at Warlus. He was closely followed by four men of D Company, who told the same story about their company. At that juncture, another four men, including the orderly-room clerk, arrived in the CO's car, with a similar account concerning battalion headquarters. At around 2300 hours, McLaren sent an officer to their brigade headquarters in Maroeuil, north-west of Arras, to apprise it of the situation. The officer was not seen again until he turned up in England, having arrived there via Boulogne with other flotsam and jetsam from the Arras battle (see Chapter 6).

McLaren tried to contact the CO, but could not do so because burning vehicles on the road gave enough light for German tanks to shoot up anything that moved towards Warlus. C Company reported German tanks at the rear of Duisans, and this was confirmed by French cars arriving to pick up their wounded, with news of panzers between Duisans and Maroeuil, north of the Arras–Hesdin road. At midnight, McLaren sent back the battery commander from 92nd Field Regiment, who was with rear battalion headquarters, with a message to his battery asking for defensive fire on the north end of Duisans. Sending messages by runner, in this case an officer, was an indication of how poor wireless communications were in the BEF. The fire fell short, wounding soldiers in both B and C Companies.

At about 0100 hours, McLaren, having heard absolutely nothing from brigade headquarters, sent off Captain Potts to find out if there were any orders. By now everyone at Duisans was saying that they should withdraw, but McLaren refused to do so without orders. He was sitting in the château at about 0230 hours when he heard the sound of transport starting up, and discovered that the anti-tank gunners had gone, and B and C Companies were preparing to do so. The motor transport platoon

had also gone, leaving four vehicles without drivers. McLaren could not find anyone to drive them. In 1940, unlike today, few soldiers and not all officers and NCOs could drive. The wounded in the château were left behind because the doctor would not move them. McLaren decided that as the anti-tank gunners and motor transport had 'fled', the remainder might as well go too. Leaving the wounded in the care of the doctor, McLaren sent an officer to catch the motor transport in Maroeuil and hold them there, which he managed to do. McLaren then marched with the remainder, encountering French tanks but no Germans. He arrived in Maroeuil at about 0315 hours, finding most of 9th DLI in the village, and Captain Potts, who said that the brigade commander had instructed him to tell McLaren to withdraw. McLaren was 'much relieved' that the withdrawal had been authorized. Some accounts mention that an officer on a motorcycle from brigade headquarters managed to bring orders to the two companies at Duisans to withdraw. It may be that in the confusion whoever took the message failed to tell McLaren, hence the precipitate withdrawal without his knowledge.

The CO of 9th DLI told McLaren to defend the west side of the village. After McLaren had moved his men into the houses, they all fell asleep. At dawn, he was told to withdraw, and had a very hard time waking the exhausted soldiers and getting them on the move in transport to the battalion rendezvous, a road junction north of Maroeuil. The company sergeant major of HQ Company overshot the rendezvous and was never seen again. McLaren took the men from the road junction back to Vimy, where they lay up in woods on the north-east side.

At approximately 0600 hours, Lieutenant Colonel Beart with three officers, including Lieutenant English, and some thirty men joined McLaren in the woods; he had believed them all to be dead. They had abandoned Warlus, where they had been shelled, bombed by Stukas and obliged to fight off attacks. At around 0300 hours tanks had been heard approaching. They turned out to be six French tanks and two armoured troop carriers. Lieutenant Colonel Beart, who had himself been injured, got all his wounded loaded on to the French vehicles, and they set off to traverse some four miles of German-held territory. They were shot at but only sporadically. They found Duisans empty and pressed on to Vimy. Beart was sent to hospital with a flesh wound in the thigh, and McLaren took over command. So by 0600 hours what was left of 8th DLI was back at the point from which it had started twenty-four hours before, Vimy Ridge. Here McLaren deployed the battalion, using woods for cover where possible, as German aircraft were very numerous overhead, and (as he put it) 'by now no English [sic] aeroplanes were ever seen'. The next day, more survivors of A and D Company came in to rejoin the battalion.

Lieutenant England's carrier platoon was down to six carriers out of an original strength of thirteen. Everybody was very tired.

Although now temporarily out of contact with German ground forces, the units on Vimy Ridge came under frequent air attacks as McLaren's remark indicates. The 2nd Light Anti-Aircraft Battery with its 40mm Bofors was sited on the ridge in an effort to give some protection from the Luftwaffe. Second Lieutenant McSwiney's 2 Troop was in action pretty well throughout the Arras counter-attack and until the withdrawal from the ridge. Most of the enemy bombers cruised overhead just out of range of the Bofors and, because there were no heavy anti-aircraft guns on the ridge, were untouched. McSwiney moved his headquarters from a wood, which he felt was distinctly unhealthy after a visit by enemy reconnaissance aircraft, to a brick kiln. The reconnaissance aircraft had been fired on by French troops with every light automatic available, reminding McSwiney of the continental habit of shooting at anything that flies, including sparrows. His intuition was right – the wood was dive-bombed a few hours later and went up in flames. But he was not to escape the Luftwaffe's attentions. As he and his battery commander, Major du Vallon, arrived at one of his gun sites, the air sentry spotted three sections of dive-bombers starting on the circular flight that normally preceded an attack, and sure enough they were the target. Attacked from three angles at once and regrettably out of support range from the other guns, he and du Vallon took shelter in the shallow gun pit. One gunner lay outside with his back exposed, and had his right shoulder almost ripped off by a bomb splinter.

When the last aircraft made off, McSwiney jumped into the driving seat of a French ambulance, whose driver was still shivering with fright in a nearby ditch. Before setting off he opened the back and discovered five French corpses, which he and some of the gunners removed, before taking their own casualty to the nearest dressing station.

Early in the afternoon of the next day, three Dornier bombers crept very low up the valley between Souchez and Vimy Ridge, clearly with the object of eliminating McSwiney's guns. One of these was positioned behind a haystack. The leading aircraft dropped a stick of bombs as it approached this gun, four of which failed to explode, but the fifth landed just the other side of the haystack, lifting it completely off the ground and dumping it on top of the gun and its crew. Watching from a respectably safe distance, McSwiney could not help laughing first at the spectacle of the erupting haystack itself, and then at its aftermath as faces and bodies emerged from the hay. The last man to struggle clear was the Bren-gunner who had been firing until the last moment; he now ran yelling down the cart track. When McSwiney picked him up in his

truck, he explained that the strap of his steel helmet had been under his chin, and the blast had forced the hat upwards carrying him with it to a height of three or four feet, until the descending haystack brought him back to earth. Apart from stretching his neck and spine, he suffered no other ill effects. Two of the three Dorniers were destroyed by the battery. An hour later, the battery was ordered to withdraw

Thus ended the Arras 'counter-attack'. It was a foolhardy undertaking. Two regiments of tanks and two battalions of infantry formed into two weak battle groups, plus a battalion in reserve and part of a French DLM, had encroached on the territory of three panzer divisions. The spearhead of this attack thus comprised about 1,400 infantry and 74 tanks, against around 7,000 infantry and 740 tanks, not to mention the discrepancy in artillery, and the total lack of air support for the British.

The question remains why the attack was launched in the first place. When Billotte had warned Gort and Pownall that nine panzer divisions were racing west with nothing to stop them, someone at GHQ or Gort's command post should surely have worked out that some at least of these formations – in fact six – would be somewhere south of Arras. The factors contributing to this failure of comprehension were threefold. First, by now the British high command were thoroughly sceptical of anything the French told them in general, and of their ability to fight in particular. Consequently, by extension, it was assumed that the French must be exaggerating enemy strengths as a way of explaining their panic and defeat. So, one properly asks, what about intelligence? The answer lies in the second factor: the handling of intelligence was never particularly efficient at either GHQ or Gort's command post, and, as we have noted, sending Mason-MacFarlane, the chief of intelligence, to command Macforce had made the situation worse. When Pownall wrote in his diary, 'we haven't yet encountered the real German Army; this is only their armoured cavalry that is sending us reeling', there was no intelligence staff with sufficient authority and knowledge to correct this misconception. Third, the British, along with the French, failed to appreciate the fighting power and tempo in attack that panzer divisions supported by aircraft could generate.

The price of this venture was the loss of all but two Matilda Mk II tanks and twenty-six Mk Is, out of a total of seventy-four Mk Is and Mk IIs with which the two tank regiments had gone into battle. That was the bad news.

The good news was that the Arras counter-attack gave the Germans a very nasty fright. Why? To a German looking at a map, the panzer corridor was a tentacle about 30 miles wide and 200 miles long vulnerable to attack from either flank, and there were British and French

divisions well placed both north and south. Nor was this 'tentacle' uninterrupted, a solid obstacle. On the march in peacetime conditions, a panzer division occupied fifty miles of road. In operations there were traffic jams that caused a concertina effect in some places, while in others the columns were strung out, with long gaps between the armour, the infantry, the supply train and the artillery. The motor infantry, towed artillery and unarmoured supply vehicles stretched along the road were especially susceptible to air attack along the line of the road or to ground assault from a flank. Only French paralysis, a flawed operational concept and inept command-and-control arrangements (to the point of there being hardly any) precluded the mounting of a counter-attack that would have inflicted a massive defeat on the Germans.

In the event, the Arras action was the only Allied counter-stroke singled out for special mention in the German propaganda film *Sieg im West* (Victory in the West). This is a measure of the psychological effect that these two weak British battle groups had on the Germans. They had advanced up to ten miles at the furthest point and had captured more than 400 prisoners, more than in any other action against the Germans since 10 May. They and the 3rd DLM had destroyed a large number of tanks and trucks. The 7th Panzer Division war diary speaks of 'hundreds of enemy tanks and following infantry'. The situation map marked in Rommel's own hand shows arrows suggesting a counter-attack by five enemy divisions. It certainly cost Rommel's division more tanks than any other operation so far, and 89 killed (including seven officers), 116 wounded and 173 missing (mostly captured) – four times the number suffered during the breakthrough into France. The remainder of the prisoners bagged by the 50th Division were from the SS Totenkopf Panzer Division, of whom Guderian was to write they 'showed signs of panic' – a damning indictment of Hitler's SS elite.

Rommel's angst reverberated up the German chain of command. General von Kluge, commanding the German Fourth Army, wrote that 21 May was 'the first day on which the enemy had met with any real success'. He wanted to halt any further advance westward from Arras until the situation had been stabilized. In Kleist's Panzer Group, the 6th and 8th Panzer Divisions were ordered to swing back from Hesdin and Le Boisle to take up defensive positions on the flank of the supposed five enemy divisions. At the Nuremberg Tribunal after the war Rundstedt said:

A critical moment in the drive came just as my forces had reached the Channel. It was caused by a British counter-stroke southwards from Arras on 21 May. For a short time it was feared that our armoured divisions

would be cut off before the infantry divisions could come up to support them. None of the French counter-attacks carried any serious threat as this one did.[5]

General Halder, the chief of staff to Brauchitsch at Supreme Command of the German Army (Oberkommando des Heeres, or OKH), expressed concern in his diary, and the shock transmitted itself all the way to Hitler. It was to contribute to decisions he made later which were to be of immense importance to the BEF.

The action at Arras, or rather its failure, had another beneficial effect. It persuaded Gort to question very carefully the notion of trying to bulldoze a way south to join up with the French Army, as envisaged by Churchill. He was coming round to the view that the BEF might have to move in another direction.

5

FIGHTING ON TWO FRONTS

As the Arras 'counter-attack' began, General von Bock's Army Group B attacked the BEF on the Escaut. Gort's sector on the Escaut from north of Oudenarde to Maulde on the French frontier was about thirty-two miles long. He deployed seven divisions along it, having sent his other two as well as his tank brigade to the Arras sector in the attempt to plug the gap torn in the French Army. Every division had to take its place in the Escaut Line, and in some places there was very little depth to the defence. The complete river line had to be covered, for failing to do so would have been a tactical error; an obstacle is no bar to the enemy's progress unless it is covered by fire, a principle as old as warfare itself and drummed into every young officer and NCO at an early stage in his training.

On the extreme left of the British line was the 44th Division, abutting the Belgian Army. This junction point with the increasingly ineffective Belgians was a potential weak spot, and the Germans were all too aware of it. The 44th Division was deployed in greater depth than any other British division on the Escaut. But to achieve it the division was deployed with four battalions forward and five back, which meant that its fire-power in the 'shop window' was not perhaps as strong as it might have been had the GOC chosen a different defensive layout. The commander, Major General Osborne, was a former Royal Signals officer, the only non-infantry divisional commander in the BEF, which might explain his choice of deployment. A key piece of ground, the Anseghem–Knok ridge, lay in the 44th Division's sector. If the Germans seized it, they might well turn the whole Escaut position.

The other division in Adam's III Corps, the 4th, had five battalions forward on a frontage of five miles, somewhat shorter than that held by its left-hand neighbour, the 44th. The 1st East Surreys of 11th Brigade were responsible for the bridge at Kerkhove. While the BEF was still withdrawing to the Escaut, the battalion had two companies (C and D) on the east bank and two (A and B) on the west. When the order to blow the bridge was given, C and D Companies under Major Bousfield were withdrawn. 'Bouser', as he was known in the battalion, had served in the First World War, first as a private soldier, then as a lance-sergeant, and

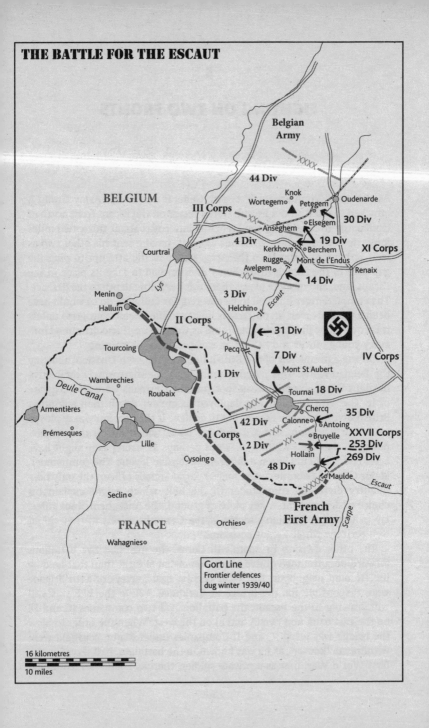

THE BATTLE FOR THE ESCAUT

Belgian Army

BELGIUM

44 Div

III Corps

Knok

Wortegem

Petegem

Oudenarde

30 Div

Elsegem

4 Div

Anseghem

19 Div

XI Corps

Kerkhove

Berchem

Courtrai

Rugge

Mont de l'Endus

Avelgem

Renaix

14 Div

3 Div

Menin

Helchin

Escaut

Halluin

II Corps

31 Div

Tourcoing

Pecq

7 Div

IV Corps

1 Div

Mont St Aubert

Deule Canal

Wambrechies

Roubaix

Tournai

18 Div

Armentières

Chercq

35 Div

Calonne

Antoing

XXVII Corps

Prémesques

42 Div

Bruyelle

253 Div

Lille

I Corps

2 Div

269 Div

Cysoing

Hollain

48 Div

Maulde

Escaut

Seclin

French First Army

Scarpe

Orchies

FRANCE

Wahagnies

Gort Line
Frontier defences
dug winter 1939/40

16 kilometres

10 miles

from 1915 as a commissioned officer. He was now forty-seven years old. When the 1st East Surreys first came out to France in 1939, in common with many other battalions every company commander had fought in the First World War, but by May 1940 some of these had been replaced.

Brooke's II Corps held the face of the shallow salient the river made into the British front. No major road entered this sector from the east, so it seemed the least likely to come under attack. It was however the worst-developed section of the BEF's area of responsibility, because Montgomery's 3rd Division, on the left, had not arrived until the afternoon of 19 May. Alexander's 1st Division had moved in even later, and was pretty exhausted for the reasons described in Chapter 3. The corps commander (Brooke) and the two divisional commanders (Alexander and Montgomery) in II Corps were the best in the BEF, and they deployed most of their firepower on the river line. Mont Saint-Aubert, to the east of the Escaut, overlooked much of the 1st Division's sector.

To the right of 1st Division, the 42nd Division, with one brigade short (it was still with Macforce), held the river line each side of Tournai. The 1st Battalion the East Lancashires covered demolition parties responsible for blowing the main bridge over the river that ran through the town. During the night the Germans could be heard approaching, and in broad daylight the next morning, 20 May, one of them approached the river and shouted in English, 'Heil Hitler, you democratic swine.' A Lancastrian soldier responded, 'You square-headed bastard,' and shot him dead. Some of the Germans approaching the Escaut were clearly full of confidence, or perhaps alcohol, because a party of six in a staff car and on a motorcycle drove up as bold as brass to another part of the riverbank and were wiped out.

The deployment of I Corps reflected the less than exemplary staff work that had characterized Barker's command since day one. Originally, the 6th Brigade of 2nd Division had been put in under command of the 42nd Division, with the 48th Division continuing the line right on down to Maulde. When Barker realized that the Escaut was supposed to be held for some time, the 2nd Division was shoehorned in between the 42nd and 48th Divisions, and some readjustments were planned for the night of 20/21 May. The 6th and 143rd Brigades were to be relieved by 4th and 5th Brigades respectively. But, before this could happen, the Germans struck.

During the late afternoon, the German artillery rained down shells, especially on the 1st/8th Royal Warwicks, the right forward battalion of the 143rd Brigade. Part of their front included the village of Calonne. Factories and cottages on the water's edge on the British bank prevented the rear companies from seeing the forward companies sited among, and

in some cases on the other side of, these buildings. The spires and turrets in buildings in Antoing, under a mile from Calonne, provided the Germans with excellent observation posts overlooking the riverbank. The Germans also infiltrated soldiers into a factory building on the Warwicks' side of the river, allegedly dressed in civilian clothes. However they got there, they caused considerable trouble to the inexperienced Warwicks. As the German bombardment intensified, it spread to the 1st/7th Royal Warwicks, the left forward battalion of the brigade. The British artillery fired back, but not as effectively as on the Dyle, because there had been less time to register targets, and there was less ammunition.

This activity disrupted the relief plan, so that eventually – despite a certain amount of order, counter-order, disorder – two battalions of the 4th Brigade (2nd Royal Norfolks and 8th Lancashire Fusiliers) took over from the 6th Brigade, while the third battalion in the brigade, the 1st Royal Scots, relieved the 1st/7th Royal Warwicks. The relief was completed just before first light on 21 May, amid bursting enemy shells, and some instances of 'friendly fire' in the confusion. The 1st Queen's Own Cameron Highlanders of the 5th Brigade assembled for a counter-attack, which was then cancelled. The 1st/8th Royal Warwicks waited for relief, while trying to keep the Germans out of Calonne.

Just after first light on 21 May, the Germans assaulted in strength, preceded by a heavy bombardment. But before this, in the 2nd Royal Norfolk's sector, Captain Barclay commanding A Company saw some Germans on the far bank, apparently totally oblivious of being under observation. Barclay told his company to hold their fire until he sounded his hunting horn. A German officer appeared, got out a map and seemed to be holding a briefing with his senior warrant officers. After this they withdrew into a plantation, followed by sounds of chopping, and young trees falling. Eventually they emerged from the plantation carrying a number of long hurdles constructed from the trunks of saplings, and started to lay these across the rubble and concrete blocks that were all that remained of a bridge across the canal in the A Company sector. It was clear that the Germans had no idea that the British were so close and watching with interest. As they started to cross, Barclay decided to wait until there were enough to make a good target on the home bank, but not so many that they could not be disposed of quickly. When about twenty-five had crossed and were milling about, he blew a blast on his horn and his company cut down all on the home bank and most on the other side too.

The outcome was a storm of artillery and mortar fire. The battalion headquarters of the 2nd Royal Norfolks was hit, wounding the CO, adjutant and intelligence officer. Major Ryder took command of the

battalion. Captain Barclay was wounded in the stomach, back and arm, and had a field dressing put on each wound. As by then the company had suffered several casualties, there were no more stretchers. But his batman, with great presence of mind, ripped a door off its hinges, and in spite of Barclay's orders to the contrary tied him to it. Barclay then told his batman to carry him round the position so he could visit his men. The door was so heavy that it took four men to carry him.

At this moment, the Germans opened fire on A Company from the home side of the canal. Barclay sent his sergeant major, Gristock, in charge of a small force of about ten men from company headquarters, including a wireless operator, to deal with this new menace. Barclay told Gristock not only to hold the company's right flank, but to eliminate a German machine-gun post that had set up just off to the right of the company. Gristock sent some of the party to attack the post, and they succeeded in wiping it out. While this was in progress, another group of Germans opened up on the company. Gristock, spotting where they were, ordered two men to give him covering fire while he went forward to deal with this new threat, which consisted of a group of men behind a pile of stones on the canal bank. He got to within about twenty yards of them without being spotted when a machine gun opened up on him from the far bank, smashing both his knees. In spite of this he dragged himself until he was within grenade-throwing range of the pile of stones, lobbed a grenade over the top and finished off the survivors with his rifle.

The fighting went on. Private Leggett of A Company was manning a Bren on the upstairs verandah of a cottage and 'killed a lot of Germans'. Although they reached the far bank of the canal several times, they were unable to cross, but retaliated with mortar and artillery fire. Leggett was hit; first his left leg went numb, then his back from the waist down. He had multiple minor wounds, but more seriously a shard of shrapnel about three inches long had ripped through his left buttock and exited via his groin, tearing a huge hole out of which blood was pouring. His comrades took all the field dressings they could find, plugged the entry and exit wounds, bound on two more to hold these in place and used a piece of rope to tie a tourniquet. They carried him downstairs, dragged him outside and returned to their posts as they had to, leaving Leggett to crawl to company headquarters. They had taken his trousers off and in his underpants and battledress top he inched forward, showered with earth from exploding mortar bombs and shells. He had some hundred yards to cover, and his hands bled as he dragged himself along. He was almost at his last gasp when a mortar bomb exploded very close, knocking him unconscious and showering him with earth. When he

came to he found himself being tugged along by his arms, and looked up into the faces of two bandsmen carrying out the duties of stretcher bearers. He heard them say, 'Bloody hell, he's had it.' He, Gristock and Barclay were evacuated with severe wounds. Gristock died of his wounds in England before he knew that he had been awarded the Victoria Cross.

The 1st Royal Scots were still sorting themselves out after relieving the 1st/7th Royal Warwicks when the Germans came surging up the banks of the river. The Royal Scots went for them with bayonets fixed and, supported by their carriers, drove them back some 300 yards to the outskirts of Calonne. At that moment they were hit by a great weight of shellfire. The 'Jocks' went to ground, and eight of their ten carriers were smashed. Nearby, the forward companies of 1st/8th Royal Warwicks were in serious trouble, cut off in a small area on the edge of the village. Their CO, Lieutenant Colonel Baker, tried to break through to assist them with a platoon and a couple of carriers. The party was cut to pieces by heavy fire on an open slope. One survivor came back after dark bearing the news that the CO and the officers with him, all members of battalion headquarters, were dead. The second-in-command was killed by a mortar bomb within half an hour of assuming command of the battalion.

The 1st Cameron Highlanders, having spent a fruitless night marching to mount a counter-attack and marching back again, set off once more at mid-morning to launch an attack at Calonne, through positions held by the 5th Gloucestershires at Bruyelles. At 1300 hours they attacked, gaining a ridge from which they could see Antoing, but short of the riverbank. At last light they put in another attack in an attempt to clear the bank. The right-hand company succeeded for a few moments, but the left-hand company could make little progress against machine-gun fire from enemy firmly established in Calonne. The Camerons had to be content with forming blocking positions to check further gains by the enemy. Their presence eased the pressure on the Royal Scots and allowed survivors of 1st/8th Royal Warwicks to pull back in the night. The 2nd Dorsets provided a back-stop while this was in progress.

During the day's fighting Gort sent out a message, referring to the Arras counter-attack: 'News from the south reassuring. We stand and fight. Tell your men.' His aim was probably to tell them that there would be no more retreating – laudable enough, but perhaps a bit premature in view of the situation unfolding to the south. It is unlikely that many of the BEF, some engaged in fighting for the first time and others dog-tired, actually received the message.

To the south of Calonne, the 144th Brigade fought off repeated attacks by the German 253rd Infantry Division throughout the afternoon of 20 May, but by daybreak on the 21st the enemy had gained the wood

north of Hollain, driving a wedge between the 2nd Warwicks and 5th Gloucesters.

Major General 'Bulgy' Thorne, GOC of 48th Division, summoned the reserve battalion of the 143rd Brigade, the 1st Oxfordshire and Buckinghamshire Light Infantry, or 43rd Light Infantry as they preferred to be called, to regain the wood. The battalion had spent most of the night marching hither and thither in response to orders to counter-attack that were subsequently cancelled. The CO of the 43rd was both shocked and irritated to be told by Thorne to remember Nonneboschen. In the same way that General Barker had earlier likened the Dendre Line to Le Cateau, Thorne was harking back to the First World War, but rather tactlessly. The charge at Nonneboschen during the First Battle of Ypres in 1914 had been carried out by the 2nd Battalion the Oxfordshire and Buckinghamshire Light Infantry, or 52nd Light Infantry for short. There was little love lost between the 43rd and 52nd.[1] The 43rd were desperately tired after marching for twenty-four hours, following a week with less than two hours' sleep in any twenty-four. But they set to and attacked the wood, driving the Germans out of this foothold that threatened the whole of the sector. The Germans also threatened the I Corps left flank north of Tournai, but a series of brisk counter-attacks ejected the infantry groups that had infiltrated across the canal.

The 1st Division had no German attacks to contend with during the whole of 20 May, and the exhausted soldiers were able to catch a modicum of sleep. But the next day, after a heavy bombardment, German infantry under the cover of morning mist crossed the river and secured a foothold between the two forward battalions of the 1st Guards Brigade, 3rd Grenadiers on the right and 2nd Coldstream on the left. Following speedy reinforcement by rubber boat, the Germans swung to their left and overran the Grenadiers' left-hand company, killing the company commander and his one officer. The attack threatened the flank of the whole battalion. The Grenadiers quickly mounted a counter-attack, which was thrown back with the loss of three more officers. The Germans had now penetrated so far that they threatened the 2nd North Staffs on the Grenadiers' right, who in turn quickly sent a reserve company to counter-attack. But this too failed.

The Grenadiers now put in a more deliberate counter-attack using their reserve company, supported by the carrier platoon and two 3-inch mortars. The attack began well, but soon communications problems with the poor wireless sets issued to the British Army made it so difficult to direct the mortar fire that they stopped firing. Passing through waist-high corn as they advanced towards their objective some 300 yards away, the right-hand group of Grenadiers were lashed by machine-gun fire,

killing three more officers, including Lieutenant the Duke of Northumberland and the carrier platoon commander, Lieutenant Reynall-Pack,
who had attempted to use his carriers as tanks. At close range, machine-
gun bullets ripped through the thin armour. The group went to ground,
and any attempt to rise drew a hail of bullets.

All now depended on the left-hand platoon. Lance-Corporal Nicholls,
the regimental heavyweight boxing champion, was commanding a section. At the start of the counter-attack he was wounded in the arm by
shrapnel, but continued to lead his section. As the platoon moved over a
small ridge, they came under heavy machine-gun fire. Nicholls grabbed
the Bren, and followed by Guardsman Nash carrying spare magazines,
charged forward and killed the crew of one machine gun, followed by
two others. Although hit by a splinter in the head, he crawled up on to a
slight ridge with Nash and continued to engage the German trenches
near the river. He was hit for a third and fourth time, but continued
firing until he ran out of ammunition. He was seen to collapse at his gun.
The Germans rallied and gained the ridge from which Nicholls had so
gallantly engaged them, and despite every effort the Grenadiers were
unable to turf them out. With help from the 2nd Hampshires, the third
battalion in their brigade, the battalion did, however, seize back most of
the ground lost.

At dusk a Grenadier patrol approached the ridge and found it abandoned except for thirty German corpses below it and on the riverbank.
Guardsmen taken prisoner had buried other bodies. The enemy had
relinquished the position, thanks mainly to the efforts of Nicholls. He
was awarded the Victoria Cross, at first posthumously, until it was
learned some four months later that he was recovering in a German
hospital.

In the 3rd Division sector, it was another battalion of the 1st Regiment
of Foot Guards that bore the brunt of the first attack, this time the 2nd
Grenadiers at Helchin. The enemy approached with an engineer bridging
'train', waving maps and shouting. This party was soon despatched. More
serious was a party of German snipers who infiltrated into Helchin in
civilian clothes. The Grenadiers, who had had quite enough of being
sniped at from behind both on the Dyle and the Dendre, rounded up
seventeen of this crew and executed them on the spot. As an aside, one
wonders what the outcome would be to this entirely understandable
piece of summary justice in today's politically correct society.

The Germans put in another attack on the 3rd Division, in the 8th
Brigade sector, but Montgomery had the waterline well covered and it
was repulsed. By first light on 22 May the II Corps front was still intact.

In the III Corps defensive zone, the 4th Division rebuffed all German

attempts to cross the river. Especially good work was done by the 2nd Royal Northumberland Fusiliers, whose well-sited Vickers medium machine guns, firing along the length of the river, carved up no fewer than seven attempts to cross by boat. German shelling inevitably caused a number of casualties; for instance in the 1st East Surrey sector, the cottage containing the RAP took a direct hit, killing several wounded men, the drum major and the NCO in charge of the stretcher bearers. The medical officer (MO) Captain Bird was lucky not to be hit. Battalion headquarters near by also suffered, with signallers killed and the signal officer and sergeant both wounded. The second-in-command was hit by shrapnel in the same part of his body as he had been in 1917. During this very unpleasant time the CO, Lieutenant Colonel Boxshall, sitting in a shallow trench behind battalion headquarters, with splinters and clods of earth flying, saw Regimental Serjeant Major (RSM) Adams standing up calmly shaving, which was 'very good for everybody's morale'. The dead were buried, the wounded evacuated and the battalion waited for the enemy to attack.

The situation on the left flank of III Corps, held by the 44th Division, was more serious. The attacks started at 1530 hours on 20 May against the 1st/6th Queen's of the 131st Brigade, astride the village of Elsegem. The brigade commander Utterson-Kelso, a four-times-wounded and highly decorated officer in the previous war, reacted robustly. The Germans were hurled back by means of carriers and the use of the brigade's reserves, the 1st/5th Queen's and a company of 1st/6th, but at some cost including the life of the company commander. In order to bolster this flank Utterson-Kelso took the reserve company of the 2nd Buffs, his left-hand battalion, to take over from the 1st/6th Queen's company. The 2nd Buffs had joined the division in the first week of May, having been employed on pioneer duties for the previous eight months with only a short period of training – a curious way to use a regular battalion. They had not had the opportunity to shake down and learn the skills necessary to face a ruthless and well-trained opponent. Second Lieutenant Blaxland, a recently commissioned platoon commander, described his company commander as 'having no views on how his company should be deployed in battle', and the company second-in-command, 'a veteran of the First World War, [had] little notion of subsequent developments'.

The 2nd Buffs were deployed in an area where the river took a right-angled bend, which exposed the battalion to an attack from two directions. Just before dusk the enemy hit them, having crossed where woods grew right down to the riverbank. They overran a platoon and came in behind the Buffs' centre company, now left unprotected by the brigade commander's removal of the reserve company. Before he could stop

them, the company commander, Major Bruce, saw two platoons of the centre company begin to edge away to the flank in the face of this unexpected attack from the rear.

The brigade commander sent the Buffs' reserve company back as well as the 1st/5th Queen's carrier platoon with orders to restore the situation. A confused night followed. At first no artillery support was used by the Buffs, for fear of hitting their own men. Repeated attacks followed, all without artillery support, although it had been promised after the first abortive attack. Meanwhile Major Bruce tried to get the remnants of his own company forward by resorting to short rushes and hurling grenades. After being wounded for the third time, he passed out, to wake at dawn on a stretcher with Germans all around him. At that moment a salvo of shells whistled in – the promised artillery support at last. The Germans ran off, leaving Bruce behind. The Buffs were shaken and not in the best position to receive the next attack, which came in the morning. The Germans penetrated the centre of the battalion position and levered open a passage between their two flank companies. Counter-attacks failed to eject the Germans. This infiltration alarmed the divisional commander, Major General Osborne, to the extent of persuading him to issue the order that the artillery was not to withdraw but should stay and fight it out over open sights if necessary.

The battle swayed back and forth, as each counter-attack was followed by further German attacks. The German penetration of the 44th Division's sector reached Petegem, two miles south-west of Audenarde and a mile from the river. Eventually the town was retaken and cleared of the enemy, but the Germans still retained a bridgehead on the western bank as a result of the long day's fighting on 21 May.

The experience of Second Lieutenant Blaxland and his platoon of the 2nd Buffs, during the fighting on the BEF's left flank in the 44th Division sector, gives a flavour of the chaos of war, especially to men in battle for the first time, and after inadequate preparation. Blaxland's company were thinly spread, as was the rest of the battalion. He was a long way from company headquarters and the other platoons, and for much of the time he had not the slightest idea what was happening. Without wireless sets within battalions, the only way to pass and receive information was by runner or by visits of the company commander. The first attack by a Stuka in the vicinity of Blaxland's platoon position found the Bren that had been mounted for anti-aircraft protection standing alone and unattended. Blaxland felt he could hardly arrest the soldier who should have manned it and who had instead precipitately taken cover, when he, the man's platoon commander, had dived into his slit trench with equal speed. Despite being told that Stukas were designed to spread fear rather

than destruction, it was hard to remember this advice the first time one was subjected to a dive-bombing attack, the shriek of the aircraft's sirens mounting to a frenzy as they plunged vertically to attack.

The second evening after their arrival on the Escaut, the right-hand part of the battalion position came under heavy attack. Blaxland could hear bursts of heavy fire and streams of tracer. The latter was especially significant to him because it proved that the Germans were in breach of the Geneva Convention, which forbade the use of tracer – a rule which the British quixotically observed at this stage in the war, to the extent of allowing tracer to be loaded in Bren magazines at a rate of only one round to every eight of ball, but only if engaging enemy aircraft.[2] The discovery that the Germans were prepared to flout international conventions with such ruthlessness merely increased Blaxland's awe of the enemy.

A flurry of Verey lights (flares) during this battle on their flanks led to an altercation between Blaxland and one of his section commanders, Corporal Pilling, who claimed that a red Verey light followed by a green signified withdrawal, as stated in standing orders at Aldershot. Although Blaxland said it did not apply here – the meanings of the colour combinations changed frequently to avoid the enemy using the flares to cause confusion – doubt had been sowed in his mind. He wished he could discuss it with his company commander, sited a long way off. He found that his platoon sergeant, Skippings, was not being as supportive as platoon sergeants should be and had become silent and withdrawn, offering no help or advice.

During the night, one of the section commanders hurled a grenade into the darkness, followed by a long burst from one of his Brens and a spatter of rifle fire from the rest of the section. Blaxland could see nothing. Two words were heard from the gloom: 'Fookin' 'ell.' Clearly these were not Germans, and on being questioned the strangers turned out to be from a South Staffordshire pioneer battalion. 'Pass, friend, hope no one was hit,' called out Blaxland, at which an officer and sergeant stepped forward, both equally elderly. 'You weren't good enough to hit any of us,' observed the sergeant drily. They were on their way to reinforce Petegem, which to Blaxland seemed ominous.

Blaxland sensed from firing and other activity that a counter-attack had been mounted by members of his own battalion somewhere in his vicinity, but had not the slightest idea where or with what purpose. Their first sight of enemy was an attempt at infiltrating the position by some infantry, who took up a position in a nearby cottage and fired on the platoon. A burst of Bren fired by Blaxland seemed to quieten them down. Some wounded men passed through the position, including C Company's

cook, bringing bad tidings that A Company, which had indeed been counter-attacking, had been wiped out, and C Company on Blaxland's left had had an entire platoon captured by German soldiers disguised as Belgians.

By now well over twenty-four hours had passed since Blaxland had been visited by his company commander, and there were prolonged sounds of fighting from where he thought the other two platoons in his company were located. He began to think that perhaps a withdrawal was now called for. Some time later a platoon of C Company appeared, marching to the rear. The platoon sergeant major knelt by Blaxland's trench and told him that C Company had been badly mauled and that he was taking his platoon to the rear to regroup before returning to the battle, adding that they were all that was left.

At this point, Blaxland, who lacked the experience to challenge the unlikely assertion by the platoon sergeant major that he was going to return to the battle, having apparently pulled out with no authority, decided to withdraw his own platoon too. Doubt assailed him after he had retreated about 400 yards, but sheeplike he followed the retreating backs of the C Company platoon. Utterly ashamed, he continued, eventually to stumble upon a barn held by a company of Royal West Kents. Here he and his platoon were given tea and sympathetically treated by the Royal West Kents, who had heard that the Buffs had been roughly handled.

After spending the best part of a day with the Royal West Kents, and being sent off to hold part of their perimeter, Blaxland was astonished to see a carrier coming up the road containing the adjutant of the 2nd Buffs. Having felt the rough edge of the adjutant's tongue on more than one occasion, Blaxland was surprised to be greeted warmly. He told his story of being abandoned without orders during the battalion's withdrawal and extricating his platoon without loss, thus in his words 'enrolling himself into an army of sole survivors who are to be found roaming every battlefield'. He was taken aback when the adjutant said this was the first he had heard of withdrawal and that the Buffs had not fallen back on Courtrai as Blaxland appeared to imagine. The battalion was still defending Petegem, was having a hard fight and would be glad of Blaxland's help. He could join them by marching his platoon back up the road and turning left at the first T-junction. His little party was comprehensively shelled as it advanced up what was clearly a main axis road and therefore likely to be a prime target. Their heads splitting with concussion from the shelling, but with no other form of damage, his platoon encountered some soldiers obviously retreating, not Buffs but 1st/5th Queen's, being harangued by a brigadier whom he did not

recognize shouting, 'We can't let this beastly Hitler fellow win the war – we've got to stop him somewhere, why not here?' The retreating soldiers ignored him. Blaxland pressed on, reaching the T-junction with the adjutant's words ringing in his ears: 'Turn left for the battle being fought by the Buffs.' At that point Blaxland collapsed and was taken to the RAP of the reserve battalion of his brigade, where he was diagnosed as suffering from battle exhaustion. Here he met his company commander with a badly wounded leg. In the ambulance some lines of Latin learned at his preparatory school ran through his head: 'Alii pungent, alii fugunt' (Some fought, others fled). He passed out.

In the 4th Division sector, the enemy succeeded in forcing a crossing of the Escaut in a number of places. In some cases inexperience led to overreaction. The first intimation of trouble in 1st East Surreys' position was a breathless sergeant waving a revolver as he arrived at Captain Ricketts's C Company, saying that A Company was surrounded and needed the reserve company to help. Ricketts had been the RSM of the battalion on arrival in France in 1939, and had subsequently been commissioned. Normally he would have been appointed quartermaster, but he asked for a combatant commission instead. He took the sergeant to battalion headquarters, where he repeated the story to Major Bousfield – the CO was out visiting the companies at the time. Bousfield told Ricketts to go in with his company, drive the enemy back across the river and extricate A Company.

Ricketts advanced to A Company's assistance, two platoons up and one back. The only enemy they encountered was a small party in a house. These were quickly despatched by Ricketts with a Bren and Platoon Sergeant Major Gibson bowling a couple of grenades. On arrival at A Company's headquarters, it appeared that the situation was not as bad as the sergeant had painted, although in the words of the company commander, 'the company was taking a belting and could do with some help'. Ricketts left his riflemen with A Company, but took his Brens back. On his return he encountered a small group of Germans and, in the exchange of fire, both he and his only officer were wounded. It was an unnecessary sortie, sparked off by a sergeant in a panic, but Bousfield – based on what he had learned from this NCO – was probably right to order a counter-attack. In fact the CO had only recently been with A Company and had assessed that there was no cause for concern.

The main threat to the battalion was actually from its left flank, which was in danger of being turned as a result of penetration of the 44th Division's front. Captain Buchanan of B Company maintained contact with the 5th Northamptons, the left forward battalion of their own brigade, and had seen several groups of Queen's coming back through

them and into his own position. It was when he went to visit the Northamptons, found them gone and Germans there instead that he realized that the East Surreys' flank had been turned.

High-Level Decisions

While his soldiers were fighting hard on two fronts, some sixty-five air miles apart, Gort held a corps commanders' conference at Brooke's headquarters. After remarking that the picture looked gloomy, Brooke commented in his diary, 'Decided that we should have to come back to the line of the frontier defences tomorrow evening [22/23 May]. Namely to occupy the defences we spent the winter preparing. Unfortunately we are too thin on the ground and forced to hold too wide a front.'[3] Gort undertook to get the agreement of his Belgian and French allies to the withdrawal. He was bitter about the 'complete lack of effort by Billotte and Blanchard', and described sending his only reserves to Arras as a 'desperate remedy to put heart into the French'. From Brooke's corps headquarters at Wambrechies, Gort moved to the new location of his command post, which had just opened at 1800 hours at Prémesques, between Lille and Armentières.

While Gort had been conferring with his corps commanders a great deal had been happening at Ypres, much of it epitomizing the chaos that was descending on the French and Belgian armies. General Weygand, the new French Army C-in-C who, whatever his manifold faults, did not lack personal courage, had eventually arrived at Ypres at 1500 hours, after a nightmare flight from Paris during which his escorting fighters successfully beat off attacking Messerschmitts. He had stopped at his planned destination, Norrent-Fontes, north-west of Béthune, where he had hoped to meet Billotte, the purpose of the trip. Here there was no transport to meet him, the driver having gone to Abbeville, only to find the town in flames and narrowly escaping being put in the bag (taken prisoner) by the 2nd Panzer Division. Eventually by flying on to Calais Weygand learned that King Leopold, who was C-in-C of the Belgian Army, was at Ypres town hall, waiting for him and Billotte. When he arrived Billotte was not there. Three separate meetings took place. The accounts of what happened are confused and vary greatly. What follows is merely a summary.

At the first meeting attended by Weygand, Leopold and his malevolent ADC, General van Overstraeten, Weygand said that the Belgian Army should now withdraw as soon as possible from the Escaut to the line of the Yser. This would shorten the left flank and allow the BEF to strike

south at full strength. Overstraeten said that the Belgian Army was disintegrating. Leopold said he would think about it, but gave Weygand the strong impression that the position was hopeless and that he was expecting defeat.

At this juncture Billotte arrived. But two key commanders were still missing: Gort, who had been invited (of which more later), and Blanchard, whose opinions on the matters being discussed were equally important, but who had *not* been invited. Billotte was not able to record his impressions of what occurred at this meeting, and opinions of its outcome differ. Weygand outlined his plan, involving a simultaneous offensive, south from Cambrai and north from the Somme, meeting near Bapaume. Although Billotte did say that the French First Army was very tired, he did not make it clear that Weygand's plan was in the realms of cloud-cuckoo land. He failed to tell Weygand that Blanchard had said that he was unable to launch a two-division attack until 22 or 23 May, nor did he reveal that Gort's 'counter-attack' consisted of a mere two battle groups, with some additional elements. If Gort and Blanchard had been present, they might have been able to disabuse Weygand of the supposed virtues of his plan, which he was to present to Churchill and Reynaud in Paris the next day.

Weygand waited for Gort until 1900 hours, and was contemplating remaining at Ypres until he could be found, when Admiral Abrial, French commander of the Naval Forces of the North, told him that flying back to Paris was now out of the question thanks to the air situation. He offered a passage in the French torpedo-boat the *Flore*, then alongside at Dunkirk. Weygand accepted and departed. After another action-packed journey, which included being bombed as he left Dunkirk, and calling at Dover to top up with fuel, Weygand disembarked at Cherbourg after first light on 22 May. He reached Paris at 1000 hours showing no signs of wear and tear. One has to admire the man's stamina, if nothing else.

Gort arrived at Ypres about an hour after Weygand had left. Very reasonably both Overstraeten and Leopold had urged that he be brought to Ypres, because without him much of the discussion would be academic. Eventually Overstraeten, with Admiral Sir Roger Keyes, Churchill's representative at Leopold's HQ, unearthed Gort in his new command post, having first driven to the old location at Wahagnies. All Gort knew about Weygand's visit was a message from Churchill to Keyes, copied to him, saying, 'Weygand is coming up your way tomorrow to concert action of all forces.' The message from the British Mission at French GQG warning Gort that Weygand would land at Norrent-Fontes was never received either at BEF GHQ or at Gort's command post. Not using the laid-down

procedure for ensuring that important messages get through was bad staff work on the sender's part. In short, one should finish the signal with the word 'acknowledge'; then if the addressee does not acknowledge receipt, there is a chance it has not arrived, in which case it should be transmitted again or sent by other means. Gort had spent the whole day wondering where Weygand was, without, it must be said, doing very much about finding out. Until Overstraeten went on his personal hunt for Gort, neither Billotte nor Weygand thought of sending people out looking for him.

From then on Weygand believed that Gort had deliberately played truant in order to avoid falling in with his attack plans. To this day, the Anglo-haters in France believe that Gort's absence is proof that all along he intended pulling out the BEF (which he did not *begin* contemplating until 22 May when the Arras operation failed). To be fair, many French historians have criticized Weygand for not waiting for Gort.

At the third Ypres meeting, the Belgians were persuaded to withdraw to the Lys, to release British formations for the counter-stroke offensive. This was nothing like as satisfactory as pulling back to the Yser; as a glance at the map on p. 119 shows, it actually makes the Belgian line longer and the Allied position more dangerous. The British and Belgian lines would be at right angles. The Germans would attack the hinge and drive the Belgians back to the north, thus separating them from the Allies and leaving them no option but surrender. In saying that the Belgian Army could not withdraw to the Yser, Leopold and Overstraeten were in effect accepting defeat.

It was agreed that the BEF should withdraw to its old position on the French frontier between Maulde and Halluin, and in order to free British divisions the Belgian Army would relieve one and the French two. Neither could do this until the night of 23/24 May, and the relieved divisions would not be ready to attack until 26 May at the earliest. Gort reported that the progress of the Arras operation was not very encouraging and that he had committed all his reserves. He, and the French commanders present, believed that sooner or later, and preferably sooner, the Belgians would have to swing back to the Yser. But, when the matter was raised, all Leopold would agree was that if forced to withdraw from the Lys no alternative to the Yser existed. Beyond this he would not commit himself. It was a depressing meeting.

The failure of Gort and Weygand to meet on 21 May had disastrous consequences. Weygand returned to Paris mistrusting Gort, but determined to carry out a plan that Gort could have told him had not the remotest chance of success – as indeed Billotte could have confirmed had he had the guts to do so.

Soon after leaving the conference, Billotte, on his way to brief Blanchard, was mortally injured when his car rammed the back of a refugee truck. He died without regaining consciousness. Some writers have suggested that Billotte was the most outstanding of all the French commanders; if so, based on his performance so far, the standard was pretty low. The contention by General d'Astier that Billotte was the only one who could have staved off disaster is also questionable, given his condition as early as 18 May, especially the incident related in Chapter 3 ('I am bursting with fatigue . . . and against these panzers I cannot do anything'), which was hardly the conduct one would look for in the potential saviour of the French Army.[4]

What is beyond doubt is that because the French command dithered while Billotte lay in a coma, instead of appointing his successor straight away, three days passed without a guiding hand to co-ordinate the French, British and Belgian Armies to execute the Weygand Plan, if indeed the plan as envisaged was achievable. The successor appointed was Blanchard, already a broken reed. Brooke visited him on 24 May before he was to step into Billotte's shoes. In an afternote in his diary Brooke wrote:

> He [Blanchard] was standing studying the map as I looked at him carefully and I soon gathered the impression that he might as well have been staring at a blank wall for all the benefit he gained out of it! He gave me the impression of a man whose brain had ceased to function, he was merely existing and hardly aware of what was going on around him. The blows that had fallen on us in quick succession had left him 'punch drunk' and unable to register events. I was badly shaken and felt that if he was to take the tiller in the current storm it would not be long before we were on the rocks![5]

At his headquarters at Vincennes on the outskirts of Paris, on 22 May, Weygand briefed Churchill and Reynaud on the plan, which he said he had thoroughly explained to Leopold and Billotte the day before, giving the impression that everybody who would have to implement it had been present and concurred. But he had not seen Gort, and Billotte was dying. Churchill was immensely impressed by Weygand, as was Reynaud. The latter made much of the fact that Weygand had been Foch's right-hand man, responsible for restoring the situation when the Germans threatened to break through in 1918. Having received approval for the plan, Weygand drafted his General Operation Order No. 1, which can be summarized as follows:

(I) The group of forces being co-ordinated by the General Commanding the First Group of Armies (the Belgian Army, the BEF, and the French First

Army) has the imperative task of preventing the German attack from making its way to the sea, in order to maintain contact between the armies, to restore contact with the main body of French forces, and to regain control of the British lines of communication through Amiens.

(II)   The only way to hold, and beat, the Germans is by counter-attacks.

(III)   The forces necessary for these counter-attacks already exist in the group, which is moreover much too thick on the ground, namely:

certain infantry divisions of the First Army;

the cavalry corps;

the BEF, which could with advantage be moved in its entirety to right of the disposition by accentuating the movements already begun, and by extending the Belgian Army's front.

These counter-attacks will be supported by the entire strength of the British air forces based in Britain.

(IV)   This offensive movement in a southerly direction should be protected on the east by the Belgian forces retiring in successive bounds on to the line of the Yser.

The German Panzer Divisions must be hemmed in within the area to which they have so rashly advanced.

(V)   Enemy mobile detachments which, supported by bombing of aero-dromes and ports, are trying to spread confusion and panic in our rear between the frontier and the Somme have taken a chance and should be wiped out locally.[6]

This order was fantasy and bore little relation to the reality on the ground. The Germans had already reached the sea two days earlier. There was no sector where the Allies were 'too thick on the ground'. What would Bock be doing with Army Group B while all this redeployment was taking place on his doorstep? Certainly not passively leaving the Allies unmolested. The BEF was having enough difficulty holding off the Germans on the Escaut, and certainly could not mount an offensive off to the south. The Belgians had *not* agreed to withdraw to the Yser, and even if they changed their minds, they would have their hands full enough retiring in good order and staving off a headlong rout, and so could not even contemplate extending their line and covering the BEF's movement to the south. To dismiss seven panzer divisions as 'enemy mobile detachments' indicates that Weygand was, to put it unkindly, away with the fairies. Finally, until a successor to Billotte was appointed, there was no one to plan and co-ordinate this crackpot scheme.

Churchill followed with a message to Gort that was if anything even more fantastic than Weygand's order. Having told Gort that he had met with Reynaud and Weygand, he said that it was agreed:

ALTERNATIVE DEFENCE LINES

Scheldt

HOLLAND

Ostend
Bruges
Nieuport

BELGIUM

Dixmude

Yser

Roulers

Ghent

Lys

Ypres
Menin Halluin

Audenarde

Escaut

Hazebrouck

Roubaix

Lille

Tournai

Bethune

FRANCE

Maulde

Lens

Douai

Valenciennes

16 kilometres
10 miles

	Belgian Army	B.E.F.	French First Army
ESCAUT LINE (Line held on 21 May)			
LYS – FRONTIER LINE (Line to which immediate withdrawal was agreed)			
YSER – FRONTIER LINE (Line proposed for subsequent Belgian withdrawal)			

1. That the Belgian Army should withdraw to the line of the Yser and stand there, the sluices being opened [to flood the terrain, as the Belgians had done in 1914].
2. That the British Army and French First Army should attack south-west towards Bapaume and Cambrai at the earliest moment – certainly tomorrow with about eight divisions – and with the Belgian Cavalry Corps to the right of the British.
3. That as this battle is vital to both Armies and the British communications depend upon freeing Amiens, the British Air Force should give the utmost help both by day and by night while it is going on.
4. That the new French Army Group which is advancing upon Amiens and forming a line along the Somme should strike northwards and join hands with the British divisions who are attacking southwards in the general direction of Bapaume.[7]

Churchill repeats the mistaken belief that the Belgians had agreed to withdraw to the Yser. Perhaps he was unconsciously harking back to what the Belgians had done in the First World War, as possibly was Weygand. Next, there was absolutely no chance that eight divisions, some 100,000 men, facing east and locked in battle with the enemy, could turn their backs on them and march away to attack south-westwards at such short notice. Weygand several times made much of his association with Foch, the implication being that the great man's mantle had descended on his shoulders. Foch, however, had always known the strength and fighting power of forces he could commit to battle. Weygand clearly did not. He had gone north the day before to meet Billotte having already fixed in his mind that a counter-attack from the north would sort out the mess, and seemed to be in a state which psychologists call perseveration: an inclination to allow judgements made in the early stages of a developing situation to affect later assessments, without revising them in the light of new evidence. Or in the vernacular, 'Don't confuse me with the facts, my mind is already made up.' It did not of course help that Billotte never told him the facts, and that he did not meet Gort, who one assumes would have put him in the picture.

There was no new French army group advancing upon Amiens, and Weygand must, or should, have known this. South of the Somme in a ninety-mile swathe of country between the coast and the Crozat Canal were five divisions in General Frère's newly cobbled-together Seventh Army. In addition the 2nd and 5th Light Cavalry Divisions (DLC), which had been savaged in the Ardennes battle, and the newly arrived British 1st Armoured Division were deployed to the left of Frère, under command of General Robert Altmayer.[8]

Finally, the big gap behind the advancing panzer divisions, and the many spaces between them, into which a properly co-ordinated counter-attack in sufficient force would have been so devastating, would be filled by German infantry divisions by 23 May, which would steadily advance to cover the southern flank of the 'panzer corridor' and reinforce the bridgeheads over the Somme at Abbeville, Amiens and Péronne.

Reality

By the evening of the conference at Vincennes, the Allied position was considerably worse. It was to be the last day on the Escaut. The southern and central sectors were comparatively quiet, mainly because German preparations for attacks here were broken up by artillery fire, and attempts at crossing were beaten off. That night, 22/23 May, the withdrawal to the old Gort line was carried out, the carrier platoons and machine-gun battalions doing sterling work as rearguards.

It was a different story in the north of the BEF sector on the Escaut. Here Bock's attempts to break through were renewed, and at 0700 hours the 44th Division was under severe pressure, which by the afternoon extended to the 4th Division on its right. The enemy pushed out from the small foothold they had acquired the previous day and overran many positions. The fighting was bitter and confused, and, uncharacteristically for the Germans, continued unabated into the night. Withdrawal for the 4th and 44th Divisions while in contact and fighting was a hazardous and difficult business.

When orders for the withdrawal reached the 1st East Surreys, it was still daylight. The CO sent his written orders to the companies by runners. Line communication had been repeatedly cut by shellfire, and there was, of course, no wireless below battalion level. Because of the intensity of enemy shelling and mortaring and the possibility of some or all of the runners being knocked out before they could deliver their messages, the CO decided to send his adjutant, Captain Bruce, in a carrier to D and B Companies, and Lieutenant Lindsay, his anti-tank platoon commander, on foot to C and A Companies. Captain Bruce reached D Company, but on his way to B Company his carrier was hit by shellfire and overturned in a ditch. Captain Bruce crawled out and resumed his journey on foot. He had not gone far when another salvo of shells fell all around him, wounding him and knocking him unconscious. He came round to see a German soldier standing over him with a sub-machine gun. He spent the next five years as a prisoner of war.

Lieutenant Lindsay got close enough to B Company headquarters to

shout the message about withdrawal to the company commander, Captain Buchanan, but could not get through to A Company. After seeing B, C and D Companies on the move, the CO set out in a carrier towards A Company, which was still, as far as he knew, in position. The carrier was first hit by an armour-piercing round, the shock of which gave the CO a bruised backside, and was then assailed by shells falling so close that the steering failed. The CO, now at the tail of the withdrawing battalion, dismounted and followed his three companies up the slope as they moved well spread out away from the river. In addition to enemy machine-gun, mortar and artillery fire, low-flying German aircraft now appeared bombing and machine-gunning and causing further mayhem and casualties.

The CO had left a small rearguard consisting of the RSM and the intelligence section under Lieutenant Bocquet to cover the withdrawal of battalion headquarters. The enemy followed up so closely that Lieutenant Bocquet flung his empty pistol at them as they overran his position. He was lucky to get away, and was later awarded the MC.

Meanwhile, Captain Finch-White's A Company on the right of the battalion position still had not received the order to withdraw. One platoon under Lieutenant Faulkner was in touch with the 2nd Lancashire Fusiliers on A Company's right, the left-hand platoon was on the riverbank, and the reserve platoon with company headquarters was in a village. The village was being subjected to heavy artillery bombardment and low-level bombing, which caused several casualties. During the afternoon, the company quartermaster sergeant, Clarke, pointed out to Finch-White that the Germans were advancing unopposed across positions previously held by the Lancashire Fusiliers and would soon be behind A Company. Finch-White went to the riverbank and withdrew his left-hand platoon. By then the Germans had crossed the river on both flanks. Finch-White withdrew the company, less Faulkner's platoon, to a crossroads in rear of the village, and headed for battalion headquarters to report the situation. He had only gone a short way when he was fired on from what had been the position occupied by battalion headquarters, and he decided to get his company out quickly. By this time the Germans were in between the main body of the company and Lieutenant Faulkner's platoon, and most of the platoon were taken prisoner, except for one section that managed to get away and join the main body. For a while, A Company withdrew with Germans advancing parallel to it on either flank. Either they mistook A Company for friends or were too preoccupied to fire on them. Whatever the reason, the company next came under fire from its own brigade rearguard, not its own battalion, as Finch-White was subsequently swift to point out. The

company went to ground, and after a time it was recognized and allowed through. The soldiers were able to get a lift in some transport and rejoin the battalion.

Thus the battalion, withdrawing under fire, succeeded in breaking off the engagement and, marching through the night, crossed the French frontier near Halluin, where it had been stationed during the Phoney War. Everyone was now completely exhausted, and on one occasion when giving out orders at battalion headquarters the CO himself fell asleep. The French, with memories of the previous war, were not pleased to see them: the enemy were at the gates, and the British had failed to defend them. There were the familiar rumours and reports of fifth columnists and collaborators engaging in spying, signalling the enemy and other clandestine activity, and the intelligence officer of the 1st East Surreys, Lieutenant Bocquet, was present when one suspect was summarily shot in the garden at brigade headquarters.

Other units also had to fight their way out. A company of the 1st Royal West Kents in the 44th Division had to mount a hasty counter-attack at 2200 hours to allow the rest of its battalion to disengage. Only good discipline and steady troops can carry out such a disengagement without it unravelling and becoming a debacle. Casualties were heavy. For example, the 1st/6th Queen's in Utterson-Kelso's brigade suffered 400 casualties in two days, mostly in the four rifle companies, which were down to platoon strength. The field guns of the 44th Division had been told by Osborne to stay and fight it out, and when the order arrived for them to withdraw, the enemy were almost upon them. The gun towers were some way back, the road was choked by refugees, and in the confusion thirty-four field guns were lost or destroyed, over half the divisional artillery of seventy-two guns. But Bock did not break through. His army group situation report states that 'the enemy is offering stubborn resistance, supported by strong artillery'.

During the night the withdrawal was completed, and by 23 May the BEF was back where it had started on 10 May. Brooke wrote in his diary on 23 May:

> Nothing but a miracle can save the BEF now and the end cannot be very far off!
>
> We carried out our withdrawal successfully last night back to the old frontier defences, and by this evening were established in the defences we spent the winter preparing. But the danger lies on our right rear; the German armoured divisions have penetrated to the coast, Abbeville, Boulogne and Calais have been rendered useless. We are therefore cut off from our sea communications, beginning to be short of ammunition,

supplies still all right for 3 days but after that scanty. This evening the
Germans are reported to be pushing onto Béthune and on from St-Omer
namely right in our rear. If only we now had the armoured division, and at
least two of them, to clear our rear![9]

In contrast to Weygand, Gort, Brooke and indeed all the British corps
commanders were absolutely clear what the Allied situation was north
of the Somme. To the right rear of the BEF on the Maulde–Halluin line,
the Arras garrison still held off the enemy, as they had been doing for
four days. To the west of Arras, the Germans were beginning to press the
British back from the line of the River Scarpe. But the Allied forces north
of the Somme were now threatened from three sides. The Belgians, the
BEF and French First Army were engaged with German Army Group B on
the east. Arras still held, and from there a meagre line of defence was
spread along the line of canals towards Gravelines and the sea. Boulogne
and Calais were still held, and between these ports and the BEF were the
advancing Germans.

The Belgian and French armies had been fighting and withdrawing,
and had suffered heavy casualties. Until 20 May, the main weight of the
enemy armour had fallen on the French. For the British, who also had
been fighting hard and marching long distances, and were back where
they had started, on the frontier, things were different in that they had
not been leaving large parts of their own country, along with most of its
population, in enemy hands. But they were in danger of being cut off
from escape, and their lines of communication and supply had already
been severed. On 23 May the BEF was put on half-rations. The airfields
from which air support should have come were in enemy hands, and all
but one flight of Lysanders of the Air Component were back in England.
Without fighter protection, this flight was unable to perform reconnaissance and liaison duties for the BEF. On 22 May, the RAF sent 198 fighter
sorties from England, mainly over Boulogne and Calais, where, as will be
related later, there was to be much fighting. There was little RAF activity
over the main battlefront, and the Luftwaffe was able to carry out
reconnaissance and interdiction on the BEF unhindered.

Bad as the situation was for the BEF, it would have been worse had
not Gort, foreseeing the possibility that the French might not be able to
close the hole torn in their line by the panzer divisions, made provision
to protect his southern flank by some of the measures already described
– such as setting up Macforce, and then creating Polforce to extend the
line along the canals from Saint-Omer to La Bassée via Béthune, the
Canal Line. Polforce was commanded by Major General Curtis, the commander of the 46th Division, and so named because St Pol was the

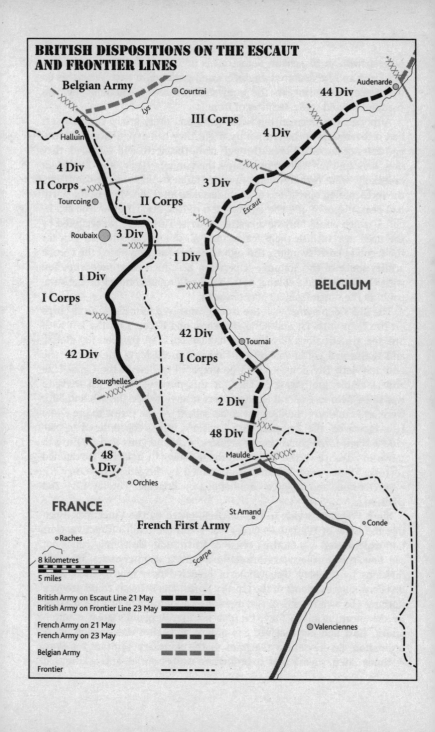

BRITISH DISPOSITIONS ON THE ESCAUT AND FRONTIER LINES

Belgian Army

Courtrai

Lys

Halluin

44 Div

Audenarde

III Corps

4 Div

4 Div

II Corps

Tourcoing

3 Div

II Corps

Escaut

Roubaix

3 Div

1 Div

1 Div

I Corps

BELGIUM

42 Div

42 Div

I Corps

Tournai

Bourghelles

2 Div

48 Div

48 Div

Maulde

Orchies

FRANCE

St Amand

Conde

French First Army

Raches

Scarpe

8 kilometres

5 miles

Valenciennes

British Army on Escaut Line 21 May
British Army on Frontier Line 23 May

French Army on 21 May
French Army on 23 May

Belgian Army

Frontier

biggest town in his sector. Some of his units had already been sent to Macforce and he acquired engineers and gunners in lieu. With this ad hoc force amounting to the equivalent of seven battalions he was required to hold some 48 miles of front.

Although the German high command and army group commanders had recovered from the temporary fright they had experienced at Arras, and fears of an Allied breakthrough from the north had subsided, they now had another matter to occupy their minds. They, and Rundstedt especially, were turning their minds to the next phase in the campaign, the forthcoming operations to be undertaken after the Allies in the north had been disposed of – the culmination of Operation Yellow (the sickle-cut) – which could only be a matter of days. They were preoccupied by the need to refurbish their armour and all the myriad preparations for the second phase, swinging through 90 degrees and smashing the French armies south of the Somme – Operation Red. Increasing preoccupation with Operation Red explains much of the German conduct of the campaign in the north from 23 May onwards.

The BEF's deployment on the frontier involved four divisions: I Corps on the right with 1st and 42nd Divisions, and II Corps on the left with 3rd and 4th Divisions (Brooke had handed back 1st Division to I Corps, and reassumed command of 4th Division on 23 May). Meanwhile the 2nd and 48th Divisions were to be prepared to defend the Canal Line and assemble south-west of Lille for this purpose. The 44th Division was to be held in General Headquarters reserve, while the 5th and 50th were, as Frankforce, holding the Arras salient. As the threat to the Canal Line increased, the 2nd and 48th Divisions were each ordered to provide a small force consisting of artillery, machine guns and infantry to move in advance of the divisional main bodies to hold the threatened sectors. These were X Force commanded by Brigadier Lawson CRA 48th Division, and Y Force commanded by Brigadier Findlay CRA 2nd Division.

Since Weygand's visit to the north, followed by the Vincennes meeting, the issue of Weygand's Order No. 1 and Churchill's directive, Gort had experienced a mounting sense of frustration. He simply could not see how the northern armies could mount a counter-attack by eight divisions by 23 May. The whole of French First Army totalled eight divisions, plus elements of the Cavalry Corps. The Belgians could produce nothing. His own reserve of two divisions was fighting hard around Arras. By the morning of 23 May, the day set for Weygand's great counter-attack, Gort had not received any orders, and there was no sign of co-ordination. So he sent a telegram to the Secretary of State for War, Anthony Eden, saying that co-ordination was essential, and asking that

General Dill, the VCIGS, be sent out to assess the situation on the ground. He added, 'my view is that any advance by us will be in the nature of a sortie and relief must come from the south as we have not, repeat not, ammunition for a serious attack'.

Blanchard turned up at Gort's HQ that morning and agreed with this judgement. But Gort, without knowing what the plans were for the attack from the south, suggested that the northern attack should be by two British divisions (where these were to come from at the time he said it is a mystery), plus one French division and what remained of the French Cavalry Corps, and that it should be mounted on 26 May. This was the earliest possible date given of moves and reliefs currently being carried out by formations of the BEF.

Churchill's reaction to Gort's telegram to Eden was to demand that Reynaud issue orders to French commanders in the north and south and to the Belgians to carry out the counter-stroke immediately; time was vital and supplies were short. Although not responding in full to Gort's request, Churchill was beginning to have his doubts about Weygand's grandiose schemes in particular, and about the French ability in general to pull off any sort of counter-blow. By the evening of 23 May, as no orders had been received by Gort, Churchill fired off another telegram to Reynaud, in effect asking him to lean on Weygand to produce some action, and repeating Gort's view that the main effort had to come from the south, because the BEF had insufficient ammunition for a major attack. He added that Gort was still obliged to implement the agreed plan.

Far more encouraging was the telegram Gort received from Eden, also on 23 May:

Should, however, situation on your [line of] communications make this [Weygand Plan] at any time impossible you should inform us so we can inform the French and make naval and air arrangements to assist you should you have to withdraw on the northern coast.

It was a welcome indication that the British government was at last beginning to realize how desperate the situation was, and was coming to terms with reality. This, as Gort saw it, gave him the opportunity to act on his own initiative. He was absolutely clear that the Weygand Plan would never come off, that the French would never attack, and that if he was to save the BEF he would have to fall back on Dunkirk without delay. It was fortunate that he came to these conclusions, for Weygand's signals and orders over the next two days displayed an increasing descent into a world of fantasy. Weygand persisted in the view that the French First Army could attack southwards with five or six divisions. The orders

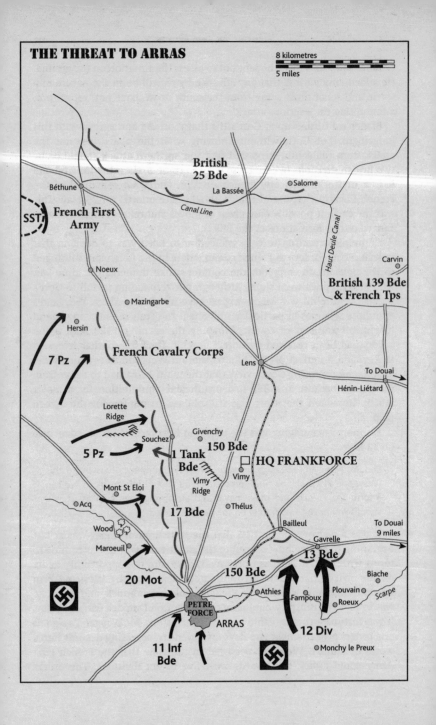

THE THREAT TO ARRAS

8 kilometres

5 miles

British 25 Bde

Salome

Béthune

La Bassée

Canal Line

SST

French First Army

Noeux

Carvin

British 139 Bde & French Tps

Mazingarbe

Hersin

7 Pz

French Cavalry Corps

Lens

To Douai

Hénin-Liétard

Lorette Ridge

Souchez

Givenchy

150 Bde

5 Pz

1 Tank Bde

HQ FRANKFORCE

Vimy

Mont St Eloi

Acq

Vimy Ridge

17 Bde

Thélus

Wood

Bailleul

To Douai 9 miles

Maroeuil

Gavrelle

13 Bde

20 Mot

150 Bde

Biache

Athies

Fampoux

Plouvain

Roeux

Scarpe

PETRE FORCE

ARRAS

12 Div

11 Inf Bde

Monchy le Preux

issued by General Georges, C-in-C North-East Front, were equally fanciful. Weygand deluded himself that the manoeuvre to join up the First and Third Army Groups and close the gap was in 'good shape', as he believed that the French Seventh Army, south of the Somme, had already recaptured Péronne, Albert and Amiens. In fact it had not even reached the Somme, where the Germans were strongly established with numerous bridgeheads held by infantry divisions.

While this high-level discussion was in progress, the situation in Arras was becoming increasingly dangerous. With three German panzer divisions (SS Totenkopf, 5th and 7th) and 20th Motorized Division pressing in from the south-west and within striking distance of the road on the line Arras–Béthune, the German 11th Infantry Brigade investing the town from the south, and 12th Infantry Division advancing on Bailleul northwards from the Scarpe, Frankforce and the Arras garrison were in danger of being cut off at the end of a long sack. The bottom of the sack was about 40 miles wide and some 70 miles inland from the coast. The neck of the sack was very much wider than the bottom, and stretched some 90 miles from Gravelines to the Belgian positions on the left of the BEF. Boulogne and Calais were still in Allied hands but not for much longer.

The Canal Line was also under attack. As matters stood on the evening of 23 May, it looked highly likely that the sack would eventually be bounded along its whole south-western side by nine panzer divisions and on the eastern side by Army Group B, and not only the Arras garrison but the whole BEF and French First Army would be in the bag.

The night of the Arras 'counter-attack', Franklyn decided he would have to commit his reserve, the 17th Brigade, to prolong the defences of Arras along the Scarpe to the north-west. The leading troops of the brigade did not arrive until 1300 hours on 22 May. Half a mile to the right rear of the right-hand battalion, the 2nd Northamptonshires, the remains of the abbey of Saint-Eloi stood on the summit of the sharp little hill of that name. As a key piece of ground it attracted the attention of Rommel, who proceeded to attack it, driving off troops of the 1st DLM, who regained it with a swift counter-attack. Although the Northamptons were not directly involved in this part of the battle, the woods in which they had hastily dug shell-scrapes were comprehensively shelled. The rounds bursting in the trees acted like airbursts, spraying shrapnel down on the soldiers, whose first experience of battle this was. Their morale was not helped by the sight of a company commander breaking down and having to be relieved of command.

Petreforce, garrisoning Arras, consisted of the 1st Welsh Guards holding the south and eastern sectors (their CO, Lieutenant Colonel Copland-Griffiths, was the garrison commander); the 5th Green Howards

(detached from 150th Brigade) holding the Citadel and western sector; the 8th Royal Fusiliers (from the 23rd Division) on the northern side of the town; a company of 25mm guns and a battery of 25-pounders; Cooke's Light Tanks; the 61st Chemical Warfare Company RE; detachments of the 9th West Yorkshires (originally on airfield defence), some Military Police and Pioneer Corps troops; a collection of unattached troops known as the Station Rifles; and a veteran French officer and nine Zouaves who had refused to leave when other French troops had pulled out.

In an atmosphere of increasing chaos, the Luftwaffe subjected the town to Stuka raids, their sirens screaming. The BBC added to the mayhem by broadcasting on 21 May that the town had been captured by the Germans, only to announce that it had been recaptured by the French. The two remaining battalions of the 150th Brigade, the 4th East Yorkshires and 4th Green Howards, posted along the Scarpe to the east of Arras, were having a quiet time until an order arrived telling them to withdraw that night (22 May). This order, whose origins were never established, was also passed to Petreforce. The battalions' transport came forward in daylight to remove ammunition and equipment that could not be carried on the men, and this movement attracted heavy shellfire. On the heels of the bombardment, the Germans began crossing the river in the Green Howards' sector. Luckily the battalion was still in its defensive positions, so was not caught withdrawing. The Germans pulled back across the river, at which point the battalion learned that the withdrawal had been cancelled.

The 13th Brigade held some four miles of river line on the Scarpe between Biache and Fampoux, placed there to relieve the French Cavalry Corps to enable it to participate in the Arras attack on 21 May. In contrast to the rearward movement being planned by the 150th Brigade on its right, the 13th Brigade was planning an advance that night (22/23 May). Whether this was on the orders of Franklyn or Brigadier Dempsey is not clear. The 2nd Wiltshires, holding the deserted villages of Roeux and Fampoux, covered a frontage of about two miles which meant that all four rifle companies were in forward positions. On arrival the battalion had been cheered to see that there were numerous French tanks in their area, but no sooner had the Wiltshires started to dig in than the tanks moved off, never to be seen again. The enemy occupied the high ground on the other side of the river, giving them good observation over the British positions and restricting movement by day in forward localities. About twenty-four hours after occupying the position, the Wiltshires along with other battalions of the 13th Brigade could hear the sounds of

battle to their west, where the Arras 'counter-attack' was going in, before eventually being driven back to its start point.

As a prelude to the move forward on the night of 22/23 May, the 2nd Wiltshires sent a company across just before first light on a pontoon bridge to establish a bridgehead opposite Roeux, from where the 2nd Cameronians were to push on to Monchy-le-Preux. The Germans had been waiting in carefully prepared positions, and at daybreak the Wiltshire company came under heavy mortar and machine-gun fire from either flank, causing casualties and mayhem. With no wireless, and thanks to heavy German fire unable to use the pontoon bridge, one of the platoon commanders, Second Lieutenant Chivers, swam the river and, having been given permission to withdraw, swam back. Only Chivers, his company commander and thirty soldiers made it back to the home bank.

On the evening of 22 May, Franklyn was warned by the 12th Lancers that two columns of enemy armour were moving round his right flank. By first light the next day it became clear that the greatest threat was on this flank. The battle ebbed to and fro, ending in the Germans seizing Mont Saint-Eloi and endangering the vital ground of Vimy Ridge to the north of Arras. Franklyn was not allowed to move the 25th Brigade from the Canal Line, some sixteen miles to the north, and so had to resort to stripping the 13th Brigade of its anti-tank battery and the 2nd Cameronians to reinforce the battered and under-strength 151st Brigade on the ridge whence it had withdrawn after the counter-stroke two days earlier. With the 2nd Northamptons in dire straits and the whole of his 17th Brigade in imminent danger of being cut off by the 5th Panzer Division and under attack by 20th Motorized Division, Brigadier Stopford was allowed to fall back to the line of the Arras–Béthune road. The battalions succeeded in bringing off that most difficult of movements, a daylight withdrawal in contact. But the Stukas dived in, sirens howling, as the soldiers occupied their new positions. The most casualties following this attack were suffered by the 6th Seaforth Highlanders. The battle cost the Northamptons 352 casualties, including the CO, Lieutenant Colonel Hinchcliffe, his second-in-command, adjutant and RSM. As darkness fell, the exhausted soldiers dug in on the rolling chalk down, without the cover they and their fellow formations had enjoyed on the river line, where copses, villages and tree lines had provided some camouflage and cover from view from the Luftwaffe.

The withdrawal of the 17th Brigade had been greatly assisted by the 7th Royal Tank Regiment. Making good use of ground, the few Matildas remaining from the battle on the 21st caught the German armour in the

flank as they rolled down the forward slopes towards Souchez, threatening to cut the Arras–Béthune road. All the while the bombing and shelling of Arras continued unabated. At 1600 hours, preceded by a two-hour bombardment, the German 12th Infantry Division began to put in an attack in strength on the Scarpe line east of Arras, now held by only four battalions. As the German infantry and engineers moved forward with their assault boats down the open slopes from Monchy-le-Preux in front of the 13th Brigade, they were comprehensively malleted by the 25-pounders of the 91st Field Regiment and the Vickers of the 9th Manchesters, and the attack ground to a halt. The enemy shelling continued, and at 2000 hours an attack in greater strength came in on the 4th Green Howards, the left-hand battalion of the 150th Brigade, east of Athies. The attack curled round and cut off the right-hand Green Howard company. The characteristic, slow 'bagga-bagga-bagga' sound of the Brens, easily distinguishable from the higher-pitched, faster chatter of the German MG 34s, died away as the company was overrun. The remainder of the battalion, after vainly trying to break through to the cut-off company, pulled back to high ground astride the Arras–Gavrelle road.

The 2nd Wiltshires, the right-hand battalion of the 13th Brigade, took the brunt of the German attacks crossing the river west of Roeux, and one company was overrun. The battalion was ordered to withdraw. The experiences of Sergeant Giblett of the Wiltshires provide a vivid example of the hazards of a night withdrawal in contact, especially if the enemy has the initiative. By the time the withdrawal began it was almost dark, but being early summer the darkness was not intense, except where buildings, high hedgerows or trees cast deep shadows. All the battalion transport was well back, the exception being that each company's 15-hundredweight truck had been sent to a pick-up point some way in rear of the position, to collect digging tools, spare ammunition and other bulky company stores. Wearing greatcoats and battle order, carrying gas masks, rifles or Brens, and encumbered with picks and shovels, spare ammunition and grenades, the men of Giblett's company started trudging back to the rendezvous.

The sections withdrew one at a time, formed into their platoons at the platoon rendezvous and moved off towards company headquarters, before setting out again, making for the rendezvous, where they would pick up the rear platoons and head for the rear. The company moved as quietly as heavily encumbered men could, with a section acting as rearguard in the expectation of trouble from that direction. The route was planned to take them through Roeux to a crossroads where the

company 15-hundredweight truck would relieve them of much of their impedimenta.

As they neared the crossroads and were emerging from the village, a burst of sub-machine-gun fire rattled out ahead and from a flank; several men fell to the ground. For a second there was utter confusion, followed by everyone dropping their loads of spare kit and diving for cover. The German fire came from several directions and was accompanied by a shower of stick grenades. Some men were hit as they dived through gateways or over low walls. Giblett, having hurled himself over a garden wall, lay panting, straining eyes and ears to try to locate the enemy. The sound of heavier machine-gun fire joined the clatter of the sub-machine guns as the fighting spread along the area where the company had gone to ground. The company fired back. But the Wiltshires were scattered, making control impossible, and uncertain of the location of the enemy, so only a spatter of fire was returned, mostly from bolt-action rifles, which could not compete with the streams of automatic fire from sub-machine guns at close range, let alone the MG 34s. The enemy in concealed positions knew where their fellows were, whereas the Wiltshires found it difficult to distinguish friend from foe, so that any movement was likely to draw fire from comrades as well as enemies. After a while many Wiltshires lay still, not wishing to draw attention to themselves, as the Germans continued to douse the road with fire.

Giblett, having lain low briefly, rolled over a low garden wall and joined two other soldiers. They wondered what, if anything, would be done to gather the company together and restore the situation. As time passed and nothing seemed to be happening, Giblett crawled out from cover. Hearing the sound of movement almost at once, he froze in the shadow of a wall, and saw Germans with British prisoners walking along the road about forty yards away. Clearly the enemy were rounding up prisoners, and getting away was preferable to joining them. He crawled back to the other two men, who were still so shaken that initially they were reluctant to move. He proposed withdrawing through the gardens behind the houses and back through the village to see if they could link up with what remained of the company. Unknown to Giblett at the time, some of the company had been extracted, but the majority being so scattered could not be gathered up.

Giblett and his two companions crept through one of the gardens and were just approaching a wall when a burst of sub-machine-gun fire and bullets striking the ground near them showed that they had been spotted. Shouting 'Come on!' Giblett dashed to the wall, rolled over and landed in a shallow ditch. He paused, waiting for his companions, but

they did not materialize. Hearing Germans shouting in the garden behind him, he ran crouching along the ditch, over another garden wall, through gardens and eventually into a field, where he paused for breath by a convenient haystack. There was no sign of the other two, and he conjectured that perhaps the enemy had been too preoccupied with taking them prisoner to follow him up. He could hear considerable activity in the village, and to avoid being scooped up by enemy clearing the area he worked his way round the village, through the fields, using shadow as much as possible, until he struck a road leading in a direction which he hoped would take him back to British troops.

Pausing in the ditch alongside the road to get his bearings, he heard the sound of a vehicle coming from the direction of the village and therefore likely to be German. Peering carefully over the rim of the ditch, he saw as the vehicle passed that it was a British 15-hundredweight; from the troops packed in the back he heard the unmistakable sound of English voices, and he made out the outline of British steel helmets. Jumping to his feet, he shouted and waved his arms, breaking into a run as the truck accelerated away. He raced up the road after it, whereupon it slowed and stopped. On reaching it he found himself covered by several rifles bristling from the back. 'You're lucky,' the soldiers told him. 'We nearly shot you thinking you were German – they're everywhere. Jump on.' With the back of the truck crammed full, and three men in the front as well as the driver, Giblett perched on the front mudguard, grasping a bracket in one hand and his rifle in the other. They set off.

There was no one at the battalion rendezvous designated in the orders they had all received, so they pushed on, until after a mile or so they heard the sound of a tracked vehicle. The two vehicles stopped about fifty yards from each other, while the men in the 15-hundredweight debussed and crouched behind it, straining their eyes to see who the occupants of the tracked vehicle were. It looked like a British carrier, but they could not be too sure. Slowly the tracked vehicle edged towards them, and a faint British challenge was called out. Giblett and his companions were quick to answer it, before standing up and walking towards what transpired to be a carrier from their own battalion, whose crew they recognized. They were part of a group of carriers sent forward to establish a patrol line while the battalion regrouped further back.

Giblett and his companions were directed back to battalion headquarters and from there sent to rejoin their company. They were to find that, not counting their own party, a mere thirty had escaped from the village, more than half the company being dead or prisoners of war. Most

of those who got away did so thanks to the usual German reluctance to attack or follow up in strength at night.

The German 12th Infantry Division fanned out, having crossed the Scarpe, and initially forced the Wiltshires back to a position of all-round defence with brigade headquarters at Gavrelle. The 2nd Royal Inniskilling Fusiliers were also in danger of being outflanked, and only got away by charging with their carriers and wheeled transport over a ploughed field and over any Germans who happened to be in the way. Eventually the whole of 13th Brigade was repositioned on the line of the Biache–Gavrelle road, with a dangerous salient forced by the German 12th Division between them and the neighbouring 150th Brigade.

Franklyn's first request, at 1800 hours, to evacuate Arras, now in danger of being completely surrounded by the following morning, was refused by Gort. At 2200 hours Franklyn telephoned again to warn Gort's command post that if he did not get out that night it would be too late by morning. To his surprise he was told that the order to withdraw had been given an hour previously, and the instruction was being brought by a liaison officer. It seems strange that it was not passed over the telephone. It later transpired that the decision had been made by Gort at 1900 hours based on a report that the Germans were attacking near Béthune and had destroyed many Somua tanks. Gort took this to mean that the Cavalry Corps was shattered. Since Frankforce's line of communication depended wholly on the Cavalry Corps, it is highly likely that this news persuaded him that he had to pull the force out without delay. In fact his deduction was incorrect, and in the morning the French Cavalry Corps found to their consternation that the British had gone.

Franklyn's orders took some time to reach the formations under his command – two hours in the case of the 13th Brigade. The orders to General Petre in Arras nearly failed to get through. The officer carrying them in a car found the road to Arras blocked by a German tank. He continued on foot, but the British soldiers guarding the perimeter would not let him in and greeted any attempts to approach with a fusillade of bullets. Eventually the order was passed by wireless, reaching Petre in cipher at 0130 hours on 24 May. By the time it had been decoded, time was running so short that it was passed to the Welsh Guards as 'wake up, get up, pack up'.

The designated withdrawal route was the Douai road via Bailleul and Hénin-Liétard, and most of the transport used this. Fortunately the French railway engineers had blown the bridge over the railway on the Gavrelle road, the most direct way for some units to take to get

to the Douai road, so most of the transport avoided running into German forces that had penetrated as far as Gavrelle. The 5th Green Howards and 8th Royal Northumberland Fusiliers were not so lucky. The Green Howards forced their way through, but the Northumberlands had 125 all ranks taken prisoner, including their CO.

The main body of the Welsh Guards made a wide sweep to the north out of Arras and, apart from being shelled, avoided contact with the enemy. For some reason the transport of the Welsh Guards and Cooke's Light Tanks took the 'scenic' route through Athies, where they ran into the enemy. Forty soft-skinned vehicles under the command of the quartermaster were jammed nose to tail in a narrow lane. The carrier platoon commander, Lieutenant the Hon. Christopher Furness of the Welsh Guards, said he would occupy the Germans while the vehicles were turned round. He set off with three carriers, supported by Major Cooke and six light tanks. The Germans were well established in a heavily wired strongpoint with machine guns and anti-tank guns. Although they attacked with great gusto, all six light tanks were soon brewed up. The carriers, by virtue of being smaller and by keeping moving and racing around the position, survived for longer. But in the end all three were hit and stopped. Furness, with his driver and Bren-gunner dead beside him, carried on fighting from the wrecked carrier, until he too was killed. All the surviving British witnesses were wounded and captured, so Furness was not awarded a posthumous Victoria Cross until after the war.

The quartermaster managed to turn all his vehicles round and get back on the correct route, before heading for Carvin eighteen miles from Arras where the 139th Brigade was holding the Canal Line. On the morning of 24 May, General Franklyn sat by the roadside as the men and vehicles of the two divisions of Frankforce marched, staggered or drove up the road. Lieutenant General Adam of III Corps found him there, and told him that he was taking the 5th and 50th Divisions under command to mount a counter-attack on Cambrai in conjunction with the French V Corps, whose commander General René Altmayer would be in overall command. This was the attack that Gort had discussed with Blanchard in response to Weygand's Operation Order No. 1, that the BEF and French First Army should attack south-west with eight divisions. It would never take place, and indeed the 5th Division, within an hour of reaching its concentration area, was ordered to defensive positions along the Deule Canal. The Arras salient, with the enemy pressing in from two sides, was no place from which to mount a counter-attack.

To keep his force intact, Gort very properly ordered the withdrawal from Arras before it was too late. His action, however, gave the French,

humiliated by an unrelieved succession of thrashings, the perfect excuse to shift the blame for their ultimate defeat on to Gort. The recriminations started immediately with a telegram on 24 May from Reynaud to Churchill which, having reminded him that he had ordered Gort to take part in Weygand's plan, included this passage:

> General Weygand however informs me, according to a telegram from General Blanchard, and contrary to formal orders confirmed this morning by General Weygand, that the British Army had carried out, on its own initiative, a withdrawal forty kilometres towards the ports at a time when our forces from the south are gaining ground towards the north, to join up with the Allied Armies of the North. This withdrawal has naturally obliged General Weygand to modify his plan. He is now compelled to give up his attempt to close the breach and establish a continuous front.[10]

Reynaud's assertion that the unilateral action by the British had scuppered Weygand's plan and forced him to give up any idea of closing the gap and restoring a continuous front was complete nonsense and indicative of the cockeyed world inhabited by Weygand; but Reynaud depended upon the French commanders to give him the true picture, and cannot be blamed if almost everything they told him was eyewash.

The southern forces were not 'gaining ground towards the north'. The BEF had not 'carried out a withdrawal forty kilometres towards the ports'. Only two divisions had been withdrawn from the Arras salient to the Canal Line some twenty-five miles away. The withdrawal was not 'contrary to formal orders', for Gort had never been ordered to hold at Arras. By early on 25 May, Weygand knew from Blanchard's liaison officer the true state of the French First Army, and that the attack from the south was a dead duck (although he had not told Gort yet). General Besson, assigned to command the southern attack, had leaped on the Arras withdrawal as a perfect excuse for his inability to deploy the requisite forces. He lied to Weygand, telling him that the First Group of Armies had had to withdraw to the north, and that the enemy in front of him had been reinforced, adding that the offensive could not now proceed. The First Group of Armies had not withdrawn. The French front between Douai and Valenciennes had not moved. The distance between the Allied forces north and south of the Somme had not changed. Only Frankforce had withdrawn from Arras, and its two divisions were now preparing to attack to the south on 26 May.

But, as Major General Spears, the British liaison officer at GQG, observed, 'Gort's inevitable withdrawal is being seized upon as an excuse for the fact that no French forces have advanced from the south.' As early as 23 May it was actually too late for a counter-attack from the north; any

attempt by the Allies to break out from that direction would itself have
come under attack on both flanks by more mobile forces. The Weygand
Plan was on its last legs, although it lingered on for two more days.

During 24 May, the tempo of the German advance slackened, albeit
temporarily. German Army Group B, following up the withdrawal from
the Escaut, had made contact with the four divisions of BEF on the old
frontier line facing east, but was not yet in sufficient strength to put in a
full-blooded attack on the British. Four German divisions attacked the
Belgian line on the Lys, forcing the Belgians back and beginning the
process of opening a gap between them and the BEF. This came as no
surprise to the British, who saw this as the inevitable outcome of the
Belgians' refusal to withdraw to the Yser. The British reaction was to
strengthen the left flank by moving up a machine-gun battalion and an
anti-tank battery. The second front, the Canal Line facing south-west, was
coming under increasing pressure. Calais was besieged and Boulogne
was about to fall (the story will be told in the next chapter). A series of
engagements took place, fought in many cases by scratch mixed forces.
At Gravelines, the 6th Green Howards and detachments of the 3rd
Searchlight Regiment guarded all the bridges for three miles to the south
of the town and resisted all attempts by the 1st Panzer Division to take
the bridges. During the day they were relieved by French troops. At Saint-
Pierre-Brouck, a detachment of the 1st Super-Heavy Regiment fought as
infantry, and held off elements of 1st Panzer Division for several hours
until forced back. Similarly some of the 3rd Super-Heavy Regiment held
the crossing at Watten against a German panzer reconnaissance battalion
until relieved by the French. The 52nd Heavy Regiment fought as infantry
at Saint-Momelin, until French troops relieved them on the night of
25 May. The most dangerous development occurred between Saint-Omer
and south of the River Aire. Here elements of two panzer divisions and
an SS motorized division gained a foothold on the east bank of the canal.
Counter-attacks by the 5th Inniskilling Dragoon Guards, and defence of
the area by the 4th/7th Dragoon Guards, a squadron of the 13th/18th
Hussars and miscellaneous infantry from a reinforcement camp, as well
as machine guns of the 9th Royal Northumberland Fusiliers, managed to
contain the enemy penetration but not drive it back. The enemy now
held key ground between the Forêt de Clairmarais and the Forêt de
Nieppe. South of this elements of the SS Verfügungs Division had also
crossed the canal, and been contained by the 2nd/5th West Yorkshires.
From here south through Béthune to La Bassée and as far as the junction
with the French First Army at Raches, all enemy attempts to cross the
canal were repulsed.

Why was there no large-scale attempt by the Germans to break

through the Canal Line? It is clear from the German war diaries that on 23 May Rundstedt believed that there was a possibility of concerted action by the Allied forces north and south of the Somme. In addition there was a need to close up their mobile formations and consolidate the German northern flank. The British and French attacks at Arras and Cambrai had underlined the importance of this. Because the German XIX Corps had so far failed to take Boulogne and Calais, and because the defence of the Somme flank was not yet secure, the advanced units of the Kleist and Hoth Groups were instructed to deny the Canal Line to the enemy but not cross it. Orders to the two groups to this effect were given on the evening of 23 May: 'in the main Hoth Group will halt tomorrow; Kleist Group will also halt, thereby clarifying the situation and closing up'. At this stage the corps grouped under General von Kleist and General Hoth were as follows:

XIX Corps, General Guderian: 1st, 2nd and 10th Panzer Divisions, and smaller motorized units

XLI Corps, Lieutenant General Reinhardt: 6th and 8th Panzer Divisions, and the Motorized SS Verfügungs Division

XVI Corps, General Hoepner: 3rd and 4th Panzer Divisions, and the Motorized SS Totenkopf Division

XXXIX Corps, General Schmidt: 5th and 7th Panzer Divisions, and the 20th Motorized Division

The 9th Panzer Division was in reserve at this time.

Eighteen hours after the issue of this order, Hitler visited Rundstedt at his headquarters, at around 1130 hours on 24 May. The Führer agreed completely with the view that east of Arras the attack must be made with infantry, while mobile forces could be halted on the line Lens–Béthune–Air–Saint-Omer–Gravelines in order to intercept the enemy under pressure from Army Group B. He insisted that it was necessary to conserve the armoured forces for future operations, and that any compression of the ring encircling the enemy would have the undesirable effect of restricting the activities of the Luftwaffe.[10] It is clear from these extracts from the German war diaries that the decision to halt the armour on the Canal Line was taken by Rundstedt and subsequently endorsed by Hitler. But, after Hitler had left, Rundstedt issued a directive which stated, 'By the Führer's orders . . . the general line Lens–Béthune–Air–Saint-Omer–Gravelines (Canal Line) will not be passed'. The panzer divisions were to close up to the canal and use this day for repairs and maintenance. After the war, the German commanders were to quote this interference by Hitler as the reason why the British were able to escape

at Dunkirk. The inference was that, if the upstart ex-corporal Hitler had not stuck his oar in on this and other occasions, the brilliant German generals would have won the war instead of losing it. Although his decisions on many occasions contributed to that eventual outcome, this was not one of them.

Gort took advantage of the comparative lack of activity on 24 May to make a number of adjustments in the deployment of the BEF. From 0300 hours on 25 May, Frankforce, Petreforce, Polforce and Macforce were abolished. The British sector of the frontier line facing east would continue to be held by I and II Corps. The defence of the Canal Line would be the responsibility of III Corps. Almost immediately the instruction was modified: III Corps (5th and 50th Divisions, and 1st Army Tank Brigade) was relieved of responsibility for the Canal Line and ordered to prepare for the Anglo-French counter-attack planned for 26 May. The defence of the Canal Line was now assigned to the 2nd, 44th and 46th Divisions under Major General Eastwood, vice chief of general staff at GHQ BEF. The 48th Division, less one brigade, was ordered to the Dunkirk area. Other tidying-up moves were also made, including the allotment of artillery and armoured cavalry units.

The long sack containing the BEF and French First Army stretching from the coast was now seventy miles long and twenty-five miles wide, narrowing to thirteen. To the north-east, in an appendix to the sack some thirty-one miles by twenty, stood the Belgian Army. The roads were jammed with refugees trying to escape the German armies pressing in on three sides of the sack. Mixed with the hordes of refugees were men separated from their units in the chaos of fighting, and trying to find their new location. The lines of communication to the BEF and French First Army were totally disrupted by the panzer corridor, and the supply situation was dire. Amazingly in the light of the actual situation, planning for the counter-attack on the objectives Plouvain–Marquion–Cambrai was still grinding on and was to be completed by early on 25 May. According to this plan, the following day General Adam with three divisions (two British and one French) was to advance east of the Canal du Nord, and General Altmayer with two divisions was to advance to the west of the Canal du Nord, his right covered by the French Cavalry Corps. No one can accuse Gort of not loyally doing everything possible to fall in with Weygand's plan.

At 0700 hours on 25 May General Dill arrived at Gort's headquarters from England. They were joined by Blanchard, and together they discussed the plans for the Franco-British attack to the south. Blanchard confirmed that two or three French divisions with some 200 tanks would co-operate with Adam's two divisions. He did not regard the withdrawal

THE SACK

Ostend

Bruges

BELGIUM

Dunkirk

Gravelines

Bergues

Thielt

St Pierre
Brouch

**Misc
French
Troops**

Roulers

Documents
captured here

**Belgian
Army**

Wormhoudt

**French
Troops**

Ypres

48

Courtrai

Watten

Cassel

Wytschaete

Menin

Hallun

St Omer

Warnaton

Comines

Hazebrouck

44

Armentières

Roubaix

Lille

Aire

**Rusty
Force**

143
Bde

GHQ

Prémesques

Gort Line

Tournai

Robecq

2

La Bassée

50 5

Béthune

23

Cysoing

42

Sealin

Attiches

Carvin

**French
First Army**

Maulde

46 &

French V

**French
III**

FRANCE

Deule Canal

French V

French IV

Douai

Valenciennes

Arras

Sensée

Cambrai

32 kilometres

20 miles

from Arras as rendering the operation impossible, nor the difficulties he had reported to Weygand as insurmountable. However, he made it clear that the attack from the south was the principal offensive. He evidently had not been told that Weygand had given up the idea of the attack *the day before*.

All that day, 25 May, Brooke, commanding British II Corps, urged that his left flank, and that of the BEF, be strengthened, for the Belgians were being pushed back and the gap between the Belgian right and British left was now some eight miles wide, screened only by armoured cars of the 12th Lancers. Early that morning the Germans began probing west from Menin along the north bank of the Lys, which raised fears that Army Group B was about to attack across the rear of the BEF and link up with the panzer corridor, cutting the British off from the sea. Prisoners taken by the 1st/6th East Surreys at around this time were very 'cocky', in the opinion of Captain White, the adjutant. Their attitude was that 'this isn't going to last for long. We'll soon be back with our units.'

Brooke ordered the 4th Division to extend its left flank to cover his own left flank, while sending two machine-gun battalions (1st/7th Middlesex and 6th Black Watch) with a battery of 20th Anti-Tank Regiment to cover the southern bank of the Lys from Menin to Comines. Machine-gun battalions with their carriers and Vickers were again proving invaluable as mobile firepower with a modicum of protection. At 0200 hours on 25 May, Brooke persuaded Gort over the telephone to send the 143rd Brigade, the BEF's last reserve, to cover the gap between Ypres and Comines. He had already sent another machine-gun battalion, the 4th Gordon Highlanders, there.

The liaison officer from the 4th Division sent to make contact with the Belgians found their soldiers drinking in cafés, unconcerned about who, if anybody, was holding their front a bare mile away. The British liaison officer with the Belgian III Corps, despite the lies he was being told, gained the strong impression that, far from withdrawing to the Yser, the Belgian Army was swinging back to Bruges. These and other reports built up the picture in Gort's HQ of a Belgian Army falling apart in disarray, and exposing the BEF to an attack on its rear.

Perhaps the most compelling evidence of the impending threat to the BEF came in later that day. Sergeant Burford of the 1st/7th Middlesex, transferred that morning from the 3rd to the 4th Division, was told to patrol across the Lys from the battalion reconnaissance line on the southern bank. He took his section in a collapsible boat to a village between Comines and Menin, where he learned from an English-speaking Belgian woman that Germans had been seen. A few moments later, his Bren group covering him came under fire and suffered two casualties, one

dead. Almost immediately, to his astonishment, a large blue staff car with two German officers came up the village street. Burford had only a .38-in revolver, but he emptied it at the car, killing the driver, and it crashed into a house. The surviving officer leaped out and scuttled off, leaving a briefcase behind. Grabbing it, Burford gathered his patrol, and carrying his wounded man evaded the Germans, eventually reporting back to his battalion. The briefcase was sent to the 3rd Division head-quarters, because until earlier that morning the Middlesex had been attached to it. Here Brooke, visiting the division, found the staff poring over the contents, and ordered that they be sent to GHQ without delay.

The escaped passenger was Lieutenant Colonel Kinzel, a liaison officer with Colonel General von Reichenau's German Sixth Army. In the brief-case there were two documents. One, of which only four had been issued for taking forward, was of the very highest security classification. It contained a detailed picture of the whole German order of battle, right down to divisional commanders and their chiefs of staff. It gave the British the first true picture of the German Army, and was the stepping-stone for all assessments thereafter. However, the other document was even more important for the information it provided about the immedi-ate future, as it gave the German Sixth Army's orders for the attack that had begun that morning. It showed that the German XI Corps was to attack towards Ypres, and the VI Corps towards the Wytschaete or Messines ridge, round the BEF's left flank. The IX Corps was to assault Thielt, north of Courtrai, pushing the Belgians even further away from the BEF.

Gort was now faced with a dreadful dilemma: keep his promise to attack south, and face the prospect of the destruction of the BEF; or save the BEF by breaking faith with his Allies and heading for the coast. Lieutenant Colonel Templer, on his way to brief Pownall, had to pass through Gort's office in his temporary headquarters at Prémesques. Gort was standing gazing at a map of northern France, and Templer sensed that he was deeply troubled, although he did not know why. Rather than disturb him on his way out, Templer left Pownall's office by the window. Gort unburdened himself to Major Archdale, his liaison officer with the French First Army. He castigated the Belgians for letting him down, and for retreating to the Scheldt instead of keeping in line with the BEF.

At 1730 hours, Adam telephoned to say that despite Blanchard's promise, made that very day, of three divisions and 200 tanks, he could provide only one division for the attack the next day. At 1800 hours, Gort decided that he would extract the BEF. It was a brave judgement and the right one. By now he had totally lost faith in the ability of the senior French commanders to keep abreast of the swiftly changing situation

and arrive at the correct decision; they were always trailing well behind events, with the result that their orders bore little relevance to what was actually happening.

Gort ordered the 5th and 50th Divisions to abandon preparations for the attack southwards and to move immediately to close the dangerous gap between the BEF and the Belgians. He made the decision in the nick of time, for had these two divisions arrived a few hours later the BEF would have been surrounded. He then told French First Army of his intentions.

6

BOULOGNE AND CALAIS

To tell the stories of Boulogne and Calais, we must rewind to 20 May, and the German Army Group A war diary entry on that date, quoted in Chapter 3, which began, 'Now that we have reached the coast at Abbeville'. The German advance cut off the BEF from its main line of supply, which fed forward from various ports south of the Somme at Abbeville: Dieppe, Fécamp, Le Havre, Cherbourg, Saint-Malo, Brest and Saint-Nazaire. This system had been deliberately designed in an attempt to keep the flow of stores and equipment as free as possible from the attentions of the Luftwaffe while the BEF engaged the enemy in Belgium. Although Dunkirk, Boulogne and Calais were the nearest to the BEF's intended area of operation, and also played a part in the supply chain, they were by no means the major ports in the system. Now, however, Boulogne and Calais were the *only* ports, other than Dunkirk, available to supply the BEF. Gort had no troops to spare for their defence. So the War Office ordered the 20th Guards Brigade to Boulogne, and for the defence of Calais they sent the 30th Brigade and the 3rd Royal Tank Regiment. The 30th Brigade and 3rd RTR were actually part of the 1st Armoured Division, which itself was about to leave England for Cherbourg. As these units and formations left England, the Germans began to swing their armour north from the Somme.

Although the fighting at Boulogne and Calais was carried out at the same time, there was no tie-in between them, so it will be convenient to tell each story separately.

Boulogne

The Germans had bombed Boulogne on the night of 19/20 May, causing some damage and inflicting a few casualties, some of them officers and soldiers of Rear GHQ located in the Imperial Hotel. So Gort's adjutant general, Lieutenant General Sir Douglas Brownrigg, ordered Rear GHQ to move to Wimereux, some three miles north of Boulogne. He had already evacuated many of the 'useless mouths' from Boulogne, Calais and

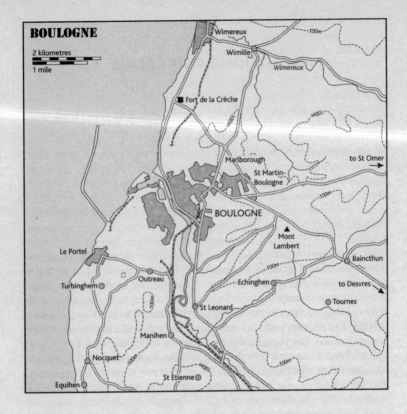

Dunkirk, including patients and convalescents from the various medical units that acted as satellites for the main casualty reception area around Dieppe. Although the news received by Rear GHQ of the German armoured advance was sketchy, it soon became apparent to Brownrigg that something was amiss, as hordes of terrified refugees poured in, full of stories of panzers supported by swarms of aircraft. Boulogne lay open for the taking.

There was no British garrison at Boulogne. The only British contribution to its defence, hurriedly provided on 20 May, consisted of eight 3.7-inch guns of the 2nd Heavy Anti-Aircraft Regiment, eight Bofors 40mm guns of the 58th Light Anti-Aircraft Regiment and one battery of the 2nd Searchlight Regiment. The French had two ancient 75mm guns two 25mm anti-tank guns and two tanks, one of which was broken down and immobile. There was an assortment of Allied troops at Boulogne.

These included French and Belgian recruits who had not completed their training and were totally unfit to fight. The largest British contingent consisted of 1,500 men of No. 5 Group Auxiliary Pioneer Corps. Some of their veteran officers and NCOs had experienced military service, but the vast majority of the soldiers were either elderly men who had volunteered for employment after years on the dole during the depression, or low-category conscripts (graded unfit for any other military employment being mentally or physically inadequate, sometimes both).

Since their arrival in France, No. 5 Group had been engaged on labour duties to the detriment of any training, which would have been difficult in any case since only a quarter of them had been issued with rifles, and of these only a handful had actually fired them. The youngest officer in the group was the CO, Lieutenant Colonel Dean, who had won the VC fighting with the 8th Royal West Kents in the First World War. The group had been working in the Doullens area, and on being ordered to evacuate in the face of the advancing German armour, Dean had extracted them by bribing the stationmaster and requisitioning a train at Saint-Pol. Here they had a brisk engagement with the first Germans to arrive, before reaching Wimereux early on 21 May. Leaving most of the group there, a large, unarmed party was sent to Boulogne as dock labourers (one of the roles of the Auxiliary Pioneer Corps). Other British troops also turned up, mainly the survivors of units and sub-units bundled out of their deployment locations by the advancing enemy or cast aside in the backwash of *Blitzkrieg*. These included most of 262nd Field Company, seventy of the 7th Royal West Kents (the survivors of the encounter at Albert with 1st Panzer Division – see Chapter 3) and fifty of the 5th Buffs, as well as some soldiers of the Durham Light Infantry separated from their battalions during the fighting at Arras.

The 20th Guards Brigade comprised the 2nd Irish Guards and 2nd Welsh Guards (the 2nd Loyals, the third battalion of the brigade, still in the process of training, was left behind in England), although, in the opinion of the brigade commander, Brigadier Fox-Pitt, the two Guards battalions still lacked much training. Support for the brigade was provided by the Brigade Anti-Tank Company and the 275th Battery of the 69th Anti-Tank Regiment (less one troop). The brigade had been recalled from a night exercise and embarked at Dover, arriving at Boulogne early on 22 May. The Guards battalions had been transported in two cross-Channel ferries which could embark carriers and motorcycles but no trucks. One Irish Guards company had to be left behind to follow on in the *Mona's Isle*, a small ferry converted to an armed boarding vessel. Before leaving England, Brigadier Fox-Pitt spoke by telephone to General Dill at the War Office and was just told to defend Boulogne while Rear

GHQ was evacuated. Fox-Pitt's staff consisted merely of the brigade major, as the staff captain and the intelligence officer had crossed to France in the destroyer *Whitshed*. When he reported to General Brownrigg at Wimereux, Fox-Pitt discovered that no one at Rear GHQ knew very much about the situation, other than that enemy transport had been seen at Etaples, sixteen miles south-east of Boulogne, and that armour had been reported in the Forest of Crécy. He was also told that General Lanquetot's French 21st Division was arriving by train to hold a line Samer–Desvres about ten miles east of Boulogne; three of its battalions were already in position. Brownrigg reiterated that Fox-Pitt's task was to hold Boulogne, and that he would be reinforced by 3rd RTR and the 1st Queen Victoria's Rifles (one of the battalions of the 30th Brigade), who would arrive from Calais the following day. With the promise of these additions to his brigade, Fox-Pitt set off in requisitioned or, as Fox-Pitt put it, 'pinched' cars and motorcycles to carry out his reconnaissance and make his dispositions. The two battalions also 'pinched' cars for their reconnaissances. (See the map on p. 146.)

Boulogne lies at the mouth of the River Liane, which flows to the sea through high, rounded hills. There is a small built-up area of level ground round the harbour. From here the town climbs the steep hill to the old walled town known as the Haute Ville or Citadel. The river and harbour cut the lower town in half. The Irish Guards held the sector between the river west of Saint-Léonard and the coast north of Le Portel. The Welsh Guards were allocated the ground north-east of the river, from the reverse slopes of Mont Lambert and the high ground through to Saint Martin-Boulogne, a sector about three miles long. Fox-Pitt intended that the area on the Welsh Guards's left, Saint Martin-Boulogne/Marlborough/ the coast, should be occupied by 3rd RTR and the 1st Queen Victoria's Rifles from Calais. The Welsh Guards in particular were thinly spread to hold what was the vital ground, as Mont Lambert dominates the town and the harbour. The rolling country lent itself to armoured action, and there were plenty of covered approaches. There was very little depth to any of the positions held by the brigade, and Fox-Pitt had no troops to spare for a reserve. The deployment of his battalions was not made any easier by the lack of maps. When Lieutenant Colonel Sir Alexander Stanier Bt, CO 2nd Welsh Guards, and Lieutenant Colonel Charles Haydon, CO 2nd Irish Guards, reported for orders, the maps issued before leaving England were unrolled. Except for five 1-inch maps of the Boulogne area which had to suffice for the whole brigade, all the maps were of England not of France, although on one set Boulogne was shown in one corner. There were two of these particular maps in the brigade, one per battalion.

General Lanquetot of the French 21st Division dropped in to see Fox-Pitt, and had a few words with him, most of which Fox-Pitt found difficult to understand. But Lanquetot finished by saying that his, Lanquetot's, troops were *pliés*, 'folded up', which Fox-Pitt understood as the equivalent of the English slang they had 'had it'. This was hardly encouraging. Lanquetot left abruptly, without saying where he was going. It transpired that he was off to command a miscellany of French troops in the Haute Ville.

There were some lighter moments. Stanier put his headquarters in the office of the local water board. After a while the adjutant came to Stanier to say that the head of the water board wanted to see him. When Stanier appeared, the official said, 'I won't have your soldiers walking across my flower beds.' At that moment there was a huge explosion.

> I thought it was a shell. Actually it was a primus stove cooking my supper, which had blown up. My quartermaster with great presence of mind threw a French mattress stuffed with feathers on the stove, it made a most awful stench, so we put on our gas masks. I was delighted that the head of the water board did not have one and had to leave immediately.

Lieutenant Colonel Dean of the Auxiliary Pioneer Corps brought Fox-Pitt the first firm news of the enemy. He had been sent on a somewhat bullish task to hold the River Canche some seventeen miles to the south with a company of men. On his way there he had run into enemy motorcyclists, but had returned with little loss.

The panzer divisions, whose advance had been slowed by the British 'counter-attack' at Arras on 21 May, had by now begun to resume their advance northwards. The war diary of Guderian's XIX Corps (1st, 2nd and 10th Panzer Divisions) has two entries on 22 May relevant to the forthcoming battle in Boulogne. The first, timed 1240: '2nd Panzer Division will advance direct to Boulogne via the line Bainethun–Samer; 1st Panzer Division via Desvres to Marquise in order to protect on this line 2nd Panzer Division's flank against attack from Calais.' At the end of the day's entries it was recorded that, recognizing the need for quick action, 'the corps commander sent 2nd Panzer Division towards Boulogne at noon without waiting for orders from [Kleist] Group. In consequence the division succeeded in penetrating to the town.'[1]

This division had difficulty overcoming French resistance at Samer, but reached the outskirts of Boulogne, making first contact with the Irish Guards in mid-afternoon on 22 May. No. 1 Company of the Irish Guards, arriving last on the *Mona's Isle*, had been put in to hold the left of the battalion sector to cover the Etaples road near Outreau, and had just begun to dig in when the Germans started to shell them. The 'Micks' dug faster.

A German Mk II tank came up the Etaples road accompanied by infantry. The Irish Guards knocked out the tank with seven rounds from a 25mm Hotchkiss anti-tank gun. This was an almost useless weapon, but somehow worked on this occasion. The infantry were beaten off. Another attack was similarly dealt with, followed by a third, on each occasion accompanied by armour. The third attack was more successful, overrunning most of a platoon and two anti-tank guns. The Irish Guards blocked the road with their carriers, while the battalion's despatch riders tried to find brigade headquarters to alert them of this dangerous situation. It is difficult to know what the brigade commander could have done about it since he had no reserve. With the onset of darkness, the German attacks died away and they failed to exploit the penetration they had achieved so far on this flank.

Meanwhile the Welsh Guards had also been under attack, but on each occasion the enemy were driven off. The German armour was starting to curl round and envelop Boulogne from the north-east, threatening Wimereux in the process. This persuaded Brownrigg that Rear GHQ should leave that night, which it did, Brownrigg departing in the destroyer *Vimy* at 0300 hours on 23 May.

With the departure of Brownrigg, Fox-Pitt was now the senior British officer left in the area. The only communications he had with England after Rear GHQ left were through whichever destroyer happened to be in Boulogne harbour. The message would be signalled by wireless-telegraphy (using a morse key, not radio-telegraphy, that is voice) to Dover, transmitted to the War Office via the Admiralty, and the reply would come back down to Fox-Pitt by the same convoluted route. Within the 20th Guards Brigade, there were no radios at all, even between brigade headquarters and battalions. Communication was by liaison officers on bicycles or motorcycles, all 'borrowed', or field telephone, which was useless once the battle began.

During the night Major General Lloyd, temporarily employed in Rear GHQ having been sacked as GOC of the 2nd Division, visited Fox-Pitt on his way to embark for England. He told Fox-Pitt that the 1st Queen Victoria's Rifles and 3rd RTR would arrive from Calais that morning. Unfortunately this was nonsense, as we shall see. Elements of the French 21st Division did manage to delay the 1st Panzer Division at Desvres throughout 22 May and well into the next day. But the Germans caught the bulk of the French 21st Division sitting in the trains in which it had arrived. The division was scattered to the four winds, and unable to form a stop line south of Boulogne as originally envisaged.

Fox-Pitt would have to defend Boulogne with the two battalions of the 20th Guards Brigade, the assorted French troops and what else he could

scrape together. The appearance of German armour to the north of the town with the coming of daylight on 23 May was a sign that no reinforcements would be arriving from Calais. Fox-Pitt decided to plug the three-mile gap between the Welsh Guards and the coast with the Auxiliary Pioneers. About 800 of these, mostly elderly, warriors established roadblocks in the built-up areas of north Boulogne. They had all been equipped with rifles by stripping weapons off soldiers about to embark. A further 150 armed Pioneers were sent to reinforce the Welsh Guards along with the 262nd Field Company RE.

The Germans completed the encirclement of Boulogne an hour after first light by seizing Fort de la Crèche and its French garrison. A troop of the 2nd Heavy Anti-Aircraft Regiment was overrun, but managed to knock out two tanks with their 3.7-inch AA guns first. As an aside it was a pity that the British did not see fit to employ these guns in this role more often, and failed to do so throughout the war – unlike the Germans, whose use of their equivalent, the 88mm AA gun, as an anti-tank gun has already been noted.

The Germans mounted a two-pronged attack on the defences of Boulogne, starting with an assault on the Welsh Guards' positions, followed shortly afterwards by an attack on the Irish Guards. Two Guards battalions with no artillery support and no radio communications faced a full-blooded attack by the experienced 2nd Panzer Division with numerous armoured fighting vehicles supported by artillery and the Luftwaffe. The open slopes around the town soon became untenable, and the two battalions fell back among the houses. The Welsh Guards had one platoon cut off, but still fighting, and the 'Micks' left a platoon in Outreau. Around noon, the two battalions pulled in to tight defensive positions, the Welsh Guards being allocated defence of the two bridges connecting the town with the harbour. The French still held the Haute Ville.

Throughout the fighting on the outskirts of town, Royal Navy destroyers provided support and continued evacuating troops. Lieutenant Lumsden was the navigator of the *Keith*, which with the *Vimy* was ordered into Boulogne. Both were alongside the quay and had begun to embark a mass of waiting troops into the two ships, who were blocking gangways and ladders on board, when at this critical moment the town and harbour were attacked by a wave of enemy aircraft. Thirty Stukas in a single line wheeled to a point about 2,000 feet above the harbour and poured down to attack the crowded quay and the two destroyers. The only opposition was some scattered rifle fire and light machine-gun fire, mostly from soldiers ashore, and from the single-barrelled 2-pounder pom-poms in each destroyer.

The captain of the *Keith* ordered the crews of the 4.7-inch guns below because they were useless against aircraft. He also ordered the bridge cleared. The bridge was just above quay level and was exposed to splinters from bombs bursting there. Lumsden stood back to allow his captain down the ladder to the wheelhouse, as seniority and courtesy demanded, but was invited to precede him; no captain likes to leave his bridge while under attack. Lumsden had taken only a couple of steps down when the captain fell on top of him, shot in the chest. The doctor arrived and pronounced him dead. The first lieutenant, now in command, was shot in the leg. He ordered everyone in the bridge structure to lie down, because German small-arms fire and splinters from mortar bombs fired from weapons sited in houses overlooking the destroyer's berth were piercing the sides of the wheelhouse and hitting frightened men struggling to get down the steep ship's ladders to the mess decks below.

It seemed a miracle that neither *Keith* nor *Vimy* suffered a direct hit by any bombs. But both ships, lying alongside one another, were open to further air attack and their bridges and upper decks were swept by small-arms fire from positions thought to be occupied by British troops but plainly already held by the enemy. Able Seaman Harris on the *Vimy*'s bridge noticed the captain, Lieutenant Commander Donald, train his binoculars on a hotel diagonally opposite but quite close to the ship. Another burst of fire from the hotel struck the captain down. He was choking on his own blood, so Harris moved him on to his side. His final order was 'get the first lieutenant to the bridge urgently'. As Harris rose to his feet, more shots from the hotel swept the bridge, and the ship's sub-lieutenant fell at his feet with four bullet holes across his chest.

The *Vimy*'s first lieutenant took her out to sea followed by *Keith*, also under command of her first lieutenant. Lumsden navigated the *Keith* out of Boulogne harbour stern first, conning the ship from the chart house looking out of a small porthole. No communication was possible with men on the upper deck to slip the wires, so after ringing on main engines Lumsden shouted orders to the signal officer and chief yeoman who were manning the engine telegraphs to make the ship surge ahead and part the wires. This achieved, it was not too difficult to swing her stern off the quay and start her moving astern. He rushed up to the bridge more than once to increase his view astern, but soon clattered down again when bullets whistled past as he showed his head. Keeping as close as he dared to the stone pier on the northern side of the channel, he was mightily grateful to round the corner successfully. Knowing that the rudder would be more effective at higher speed, he increased shaft revolutions to give 14 knots, still going astern. Outside the harbours, the

bridge was manned and the ship's company sorted out the load of disorderly refugees. Captain Simson and some dozen others were quietly buried at sea as the crew scanned the skies for enemy aircraft. The *Keith* returned to Dover to land evacuees and wounded.

Meanwhile other destroyers in the harbour and offshore from Boulogne shelled enemy gun positions and machine-gun nests, which gave much encouragement to the British troops still fighting in the town. At about 1500 hours Fox-Pitt decided to pull back his brigade to new positions, and moved his headquarters to a location by the quay to make communication to London via the destroyers easier. When the Irish Guards received the message by despatch rider it was to evacuate, rather than withdraw further back. The battalion pulled back to the docks area where they barricaded the approaches with vehicles and barrels, taking cover in warehouses. The order was premature as embarkation was still in progress, and the enemy were doing all they could to make it as difficult as possible by machine-gun fire. The Irish Guards were given close support by the destroyer *Whitshed* firing at point-blank range with a 4.7-inch gun, on one occasion stopping an enemy penetration almost in the middle of the battalion position.

Fox-Pitt sent the message to London, 'Situation grave'. With messages being transmitted to Dover and passed on to the War Office via the Admiralty, and back again, as already described, the response took a while to get through. Eventually the order to evacuate immediately was received by a destroyer at 1730 hours, by which time she had left the harbour loaded with wounded. An hour elapsed before the message reached Fox-Pitt. At this point some fifty German aircraft bombed the harbour. The attack had been asked for by the German commander on the spot, concerned at the lack of progress being made by 2nd Panzer Division. The German bombers ran into a mass of anti-aircraft fire both from the ships and from the guns ashore. They also encountered RAF fighters, who accounted for eight bombers, for the loss of three fighters.

It was now time to withdraw the 20th Guards Brigade, which had held off the enemy all day. The Royal Engineers demolished the bridges, while naval parties covered by Royal Marines sent in for the purpose destroyed dock installations. The whole harbour was under enemy fire, *Whitshed* and *Vimeira* were loaded with brigade headquarters and the Welsh Guards, and the Irish Guards stood by to board the next two, *Wild Swan* and *Venomous*. A third destroyer, the *Venetia*, was ordered in, although the tide was low. As she slipped in through the entrance, German gunners engaged her from positions north of the town, and were joined by tanks shooting at her from just across the harbour. She was hit hard and

seemed to be about to block the harbour entrance. But she went hard astern, clearing the harbour behind a great cloud of smoke generated by fires on deck and escaping back out to sea.

The Germans now switched their attentions to the destroyers berthed alongside, but as the tide was low the dock walls masked them and rendered them hard to hit. The Irish Guards and rearguards of the Welsh Guards embarked, and these last two destroyers engaged enemy armour at point-blank range with their 4.7-inch guns – absolutely devastating against even the heaviest tank of the period (the equivalent of a 120mm and far bigger than any tank gun of the Second World War). One German tank was seen to be blown into the air and somersault. Soon after 2100 hours the last Bren teams scrambled on to the decks of the two destroyers, and they slipped their moorings and steamed out of the harbour.

The Irish Guards came back some 600 strong out of the 700 who had arrived at Boulogne. The Welsh Guards were somewhat weaker – almost three companies were left behind. This was thanks to the complete lack of radio communication and the chaos of the withdrawal, including blowing the bridges connecting the harbour with the town while the Welsh Guards companies in question were still on the wrong side of the river. By the time some managed to cross on the wreckage, the ships had gone.

The Pioneers were also left behind, after fierce fighting at their roadblocks, where they notched up at least one successful tank kill by setting light to the petrol tank of an overturned truck while a tank was grinding its way over the top of it. Lieutenant Colonel Stanier had passed the order to Lietenant Colonel Dean to withdraw to the docks, but Dean was away from his headquarters, and before pulling out had first to extricate two of his posts surrounded by enemy. Taking his reserve company with him, he went to the relief of his men. The fighting was savage but brief, some of the Glaswegians in the reserve company resorting to what was then a favourite Glasgow gang weapon, cut-throat razors, in preference to rifles, with which they were less well acquainted. Four other posts were withdrawn, the remaining two having already been overrun. Dean and his men reached the harbour with some sappers of 262nd Field Company just after the Guards completed their embarkation.

At about 2230 hours the destroyer *Windsor* arrived and took off 600 men, including most Pioneers and demolition parties. The last ship to arrive was the *Vimeira*, making her second trip, at about 0140 hours on 24 May, entering the harbour in eerie silence. She stayed for over an hour, embarking 1,400 men, and in a dangerously overloaded condition made England safely. The *Wessex* had also been ordered to Boulogne, and had she arrived she might have taken off the 300 or so remaining Welsh

Guards. But she was diverted to Calais, and no further ships were sent to Boulogne.

All that now remained were the wounded, looked after by a doctor and the padre of the Pioneers, who had volunteered to stay, and three companies of Welsh Guards, plus a few Pioneers and some sappers. Two of the Welsh Guards companies set off in groups to try to make their way to an unoccupied part of the coast. No. 3 Company under Major Windsor Lewis withdrew to the harbour at daybreak just after *Vimeira* had gone. Windsor Lewis took about a hundred French soldiers, some sappers and unarmed Pioneers under his command. He began by defending some sheds, until German fire made this location too hot. So under the cover of parked railway wagons, he moved his party to the burned-out railway station, the Gare Maritime, which had some underground shelter for the refugees who had joined him. Here he held out until 1300 hours the following day, blasted by tank shells, pounded by artillery and mortars, and running short of food and ammunition. At last he decided to surrender. Just before this General Lanquetot surrendered at the Haute Ville under German threat to destroy the town if he continued to resist. By early afternoon on 25 May, the Germans could report that Boulogne had fallen.

General Lanquetot was bitter about the British withdrawal, and blamed them for the fall of Boulogne. The British Official History comments, 'it shows how easily misunderstandings may arise between allies in such a confused situation'.[2] The point is that the 20th Guards Brigade, in Fox-Pitt's words a half-trained brigade with no communications, was ordered to Boulogne at short notice by the British government for purely national reasons to defend a port through which the BEF was supplied. When it became apparent that two battalions could not hold the town they were, reasonably enough, ordered out, again by the British government. When Fox-Pitt was ordered to evacuate his brigade, he was unable to communicate with Lanquetot as the Germans were between him and the Haute Ville. So the latter was totally unaware that the British had gone. For his part, he had been ordered to hold Boulogne with his 21st Division. Arriving ahead of his division, and subsequently learning that most of them were cut off and could not join him, he deployed what French troops he had, taking into account the 20th Guards Brigade dispositions. Having done this he seems to have made no effort to find out what was happening to Fox-Pitt's brigade. Rather than visiting his subordinates, as the British were accustomed to do, Lanquetot sat in his command post in accordance with French practice, totally out of touch and unable to communicate with anybody. When he discovered on the morning of 24 May that the British had left for England without telling

him, it is easy to see why he might have been somewhat annoyed; but in view of his passive command style, one does not feel all that sympathetic. As the French in the Haute Ville held out for a further twenty-four hours, and of the British only Windsor Lewis's party remained to do likewise, it seems rational in French eyes to regard the defence of Boulogne as primarily a French effort. In truth, French *and* British action was responsible for holding up the 2nd Panzer Division at Boulogne for three days.

Calais

At 2000 hours on 21 May, a group of sergeants of 3rd RTR drinking in a pub at Fordingbridge, Hampshire, were told to report back to camp immediately – their regiment was moving in two hours. It came as no surprise because a few days earlier all the battalion's tanks had been taken by rail to Southampton and loaded on the cross-Channel steamer the *City of Christchurch*. The twenty-seven 14-ton cruisers and twenty-one 6-ton Mk VI light tanks had been stowed in the hold, with the battalion's wheeled transport on the deck and hatches. The battalion was under orders to join the 1st Armoured Division south of the Somme, and now it seemed the call had come.

After boarding a train at Fordingbridge, the battalion expected a swift journey to Southampton and were puzzled by an all-night trundle through Sussex and Kent, before arriving at Dover the next morning. There was no sign of the *City of Christchurch* with all their tanks. The CO, Lieutenant Colonel Keller, was summoned for orders and reappeared looking distinctly gloomy and clutching a letter. Meanwhile the battalion embarked on the *Maid of Orleans*. About halfway across the Channel the battalion was paraded by squadrons and told that the destination was Calais.[3] This order followed swiftly by counter-order was a foretaste of what 3rd RTR, and indeed everyone else involved with the action at Calais, were to experience repeatedly. It is a fairly common feature of all wars, but Calais was to provide an extreme version. The British Official History of the campaign, after commenting on the devotion to duty of all units that fought at Calais, remarks, 'Unfortunately the conditions under which they were required to fight show some of the failings which have been matched too often in the conduct of our military excursions.'[4]

Calais is an ancient port, and much fought over in its long history. It lies in flat country seamed with drainage ditches and canals. These confine any approach by vehicle to the roads, except in the south-west and west where high ground stretches across northern France to the sea between Calais and Boulogne. Here the high ground is only three miles

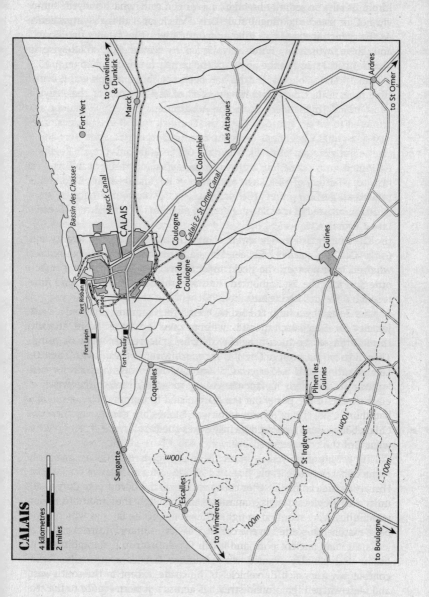

from Calais, providing observation over the town and hence the opportunity of good shooting by artillery. Much of Vauban's seventeenth-century fortifications still surrounded the town. The Citadel shielded the old town, which is almost surrounded by water. Eight of the eleven bastions still stood in the angles of the ramparts (see the map on p. 157).

On 19 May, Colonel Holland had been appointed to command British troops in Calais, which then consisted of one platoon of the Argyll & Sutherland Highlanders and some AA gunners. The Argyll platoon was ordered to set up a roadblock on the Dunkirk road. Two batteries of the 1st Searchlight Regiment were deployed in Forts Risban and Vert and in some outposts out of town. A battery of the 2nd Anti-Aircraft Regiment (3.7-inch guns) sited four guns near Sangatte and three near Fort Vert. Part of a battery of 58th Light Anti-Aircraft Regiment (40mm Bofors) sited their two guns to protect the lock gates in the harbour. French troops in Calais consisted of coastal gunners and elements of units driven ahead of the German advance.

The first British troops sent to reinforce Calais arrived in the personnel ship *City of Canterbury* on 22 May, as the 2nd Panzer Division was approaching Boulogne and 1st Panzer Division was motoring north from the Somme. The leading British unit was the 1st Queen Victoria's Rifles (QVR), a TA motorcycle battalion, but without their 142 motorcycles (99 with side-cars), without trucks, without 3-inch mortars, with only smoke bombs for their 2-inch mortars, without their forty-three Brens, and with two-thirds of the men armed with rifles, the remainder with pistols. When they had been ordered to move to Dover by train to embark, the embarkation staff told the battalion that there was no space for their transport, although in fact there was room for their motorcycles. At Dover, one of the porters at the station said to Corporal Day, a signaller with 1st QVR, 'I don't know what you blokes are going over there for. Everybody else is coming back.' This was the first anyone in 1st QVR had heard of the retreat.

They were deployed to block the main roads into Calais, guard the undersea telephone cable terminal at Sangatte, and patrol the beaches on either side of the harbour. Without any form of transport they took a while to deploy, carrying as much as they could of their stores and ammunition.

Next on the scene were 3rd RTR. The CO, Lieutenant Colonel Keller, was the only one to go ashore at this stage, because there had not been time to issue BEF identity cards to 3rd RTR. Reacting to the usual overblown fears of fifth columnists, a feature of this campaign, an order had been issued that anyone without identity papers would be shot. The CO, however, was determined to find out what 3rd RTR was supposed

to do. He accosted a British colonel on the dockside who had not the slightest idea what was going on and was bent on obeying his own orders to return to England. Keller requisitioned the British colonel's staff car, dumping the kit with which it was loaded on the dockside, and drove off to the Hôtel de Ville (the town hall). Here the gendarmes did not shoot him for being without a BEF identity card, but told him he could not enter without it and directed him to the Boulevard Léon Gambetta, where the British headquarters might be found. Here Keller found the addressee of the letter he had been given at Dover, Colonel Holland, an ex-gunner and, like most of his generation, a veteran of the First World War.

Holland told Keller that he would receive his orders from GHQ at Hazebrouck, forty miles away. He added that, as the Germans had already bombed Calais and were likely to do so again, the sooner he unloaded his tanks the better. Keller replied that the ship carrying the tanks had not arrived and, until it did, his battalion had only pistols with which to engage the enemy. On returning to the docks, he found that his battalion had disembarked without being shot for lack of identity cards, so he deployed them among the dunes to the side of the harbour entrance.

At around 1600 hours the *City of Christchurch* docked and 3rd RTR were astonished to see her decks covered with wooden crates. These turned out to be full of four-gallon petrol cans. The tanks were in the holds below. The French dockers were already exhausted, and were chary of being cremated alive if a bomb hit the ship or even landed close by. Every time a siren sounded they bolted into shelters. The ship' crew were equally nervous and an armed guard had to be posted to stop them leaving in a body. The electricity supply to the cranes was frequently cut, and the ship's derricks had to be used instead. Fortunately some sappers had travelled out with 3rd RTR and thanks to them the unloading continued, albeit very slowly.

With the deck cargo removed, the tank crews could descend to the gloom of the holds to locate their vehicles. The lighting in the holds was feeble, and it did not help that the internal lights in some of the cruiser tanks were not working, despite being fresh from the factory. Before loading, the tanks had all been prepared for the sea voyage in accordance with the manuals. This involved the liberal application of mineral jelly to gun barrels, breech blocks and other metal working parts to protect them from the salt-laden air. The heaviest tanks, the cruisers, were at the bottom of the hold, light tanks on the level above and scout cars on the top level. The ammunition, spares and radio accessories had been distributed around the holds to a stowage plan that suited the ship's first mate, and without regard for ease of access. There was an acute shortage of

cotton waste to clean off the mineral jelly, which consequently took hours.

To cap it all the .5-inch ammunition for the light tanks had been packed loose. Machine-gun ammunition has to be tightly held in the loops in the belt, otherwise the rounds fall out as the belt snakes up into the gun, causing stoppages. Loading is normally done by machine, forcing each round in, but there was no belt-loading machine on the ship. Loading belts by hand is a laborious process, very much second best, and the result is inevitably a rash of stoppages – inconvenient in action.

At 1700 hours that afternoon the adjutant general at GHQ, Lieutenant General Brownrigg, passing through Calais en route to Dover from Wimereux, ordered 3rd RTR to proceed *south-westwards* as soon as unloading was completed to join the 20th Guards Brigade in the defence of Boulogne. Six hours later a liaison officer brought orders from GHQ; 3rd RTR was to motor as soon as possible *south-eastwards* to Saint-Omer and Hazebrouck, and make contact with GHQ. During the night, Keller had received a signal from Brownrigg, sent from Dover, repeating the order for 3rd RTR to go to Boulogne. Keller debated with Holland which way he should take his battalion, and opted to obey the orders of the adjutant general, but send three light tanks off to Saint-Omer to see if the road was clear, while the rest of 3rd RTR headed for Coquelles, from where they could drive either to Boulogne or to Saint-Omer via Guines and Ardres.

Unloading the vehicles began in the early hours of 23 May. Each tank had to be hoisted out from the hold through the hatch and swung ashore. The ten Dingo armoured cars of the Reconnaissance Troop commanded by Lieutenant Morgan were out first. Sergeant Close was troop sergeant, and described the Dingo as 'one of the few vehicles I encountered (on our side) during the war which was ideal for the job it had to do'.[5] It is a biting comment on the poor design of British tanks and armoured vehicles throughout the Second World War, only put right with the advent of the Comet in late 1944. And Close was in a position to know. As the war progressed – he fought in France, the western desert, Greece and north-west Europe, from May 1940 right to the end in May 1945 – he had to bale out of eleven tanks destroyed by the enemy. The Dingo, less than five feet high and with a crew of two (driver and commander), open-topped, weighed 2.8 tons, could motor at 55mph forwards or backwards, and was armed with a Bren light machine gun.

The Reconnaissance Troop was the first away, in two groups of five Dingos each; one led by Lieutenant Morgan drove towards Gravelines up the coast, while Sergeant Close's group headed in a south-westerly direction to reconnoitre the area around Guines. As they left the bat-

talion, 'men were sitting in the dunes painfully forcing rounds into ammunition belts, blistering their hands and breaking their nails'.[6]

After motoring for about five miles, Close spotted vehicles parked under some poplar trees. Scanning them with his binoculars, he saw a line of trucks and soldiers cooking over small fires. A few seconds later a couple of high-velocity shells screeched over his head from anti-tank guns sited to cover the troops at breakfast: the vehicles were German. Close told his driver to 'get out of it quick'. His driver backed, swung the Dingo off the road, expertly crossed the ditch at right-angles and bounced away over a field of half-grown crops. Two other Dingos, either hit or by bad driving, tipped over and ended upside down in the ditch with their wheels spinning; no one got out. Of the other Dingos there was no sign. Close's Dingo raced off pursued by streams of machine-gun bullets, until he encountered a shallow valley, which led in the right direction back the way he had come and offered cover from view and direct fire. With no radio, he drove back and reported to the CO at Coquelles that the light forces he had been sent to locate were far from light.

The CO was not best pleased at losing two, possibly four, of his Reconnaissance Troop, and told Close to follow his tank when the battalion moved off. By now the light tanks sent to reconnoitre the Saint-Omer road had returned without incident, so Keller sent the GHQ liaison officer back to Saint-Omer escorted by three light tanks. The liaison officer returned, his staff car riddled with bullet holes, having driven into a mass of German motorcyclists from which he was lucky to escape with a light wound. Of the light tanks there was no sign.

The nearest enemy, as far as Keller knew, were somewhere in the vicinity of Guines and Saint-Omer, and it was there that he decided to take his battalion. At about midday, led by the light tanks of B Squadron in lieu of the missing Dingos of the Reconnaissance Troop, 3rd RTR set off to engage the enemy. The battalion was deployed with C Squadron on the left of the road, B Squadron on the right and headquarters on the centre line down the road. In the scramble to unload its vehicles and get them battle-ready, the battalion had not netted in its wirelesses properly.

Between Coquelles and Guines, Sergeant Cornwell of B Squadron spotted vehicle movement ahead. The road was clogged with refugees fleeing north, and it was difficult to make out whether the vehicles were enemy or refugees. He tried to pass a message back that he was investigating a possible enemy contact, but failed to get through. Annoyed at his slow progress, and unaware of the reason, Keller sent his adjutant forward in his cruiser tank to ginger up the reconnaissance. Muzzle flashes pricked the hedgerows and the adjutant's tank brewed up. Cornwell looked round and saw the battalion withdrawing to better fire

positions. From here it engaged the enemy to good effect. The cruisers with 2-pounder high-velocity guns were getting the better of the Germans, who were armed mainly with low-velocity guns firing HE, which had little effect on the cruisers' armour. Before long the Germans brought up anti-tank guns and artillery, and the boot was on the other foot. 3rd RTR learned for the first time a lesson British formations were to learn on many occasions, that, as already noted, armour on its own is unlikely to prevail against a combination of tanks, anti-tank guns and artillery such as the 1st Panzer Division was able to deploy. As Close moved his Dingo behind the CO's tank for shelter, a shell exploded on the turret jamming the gun, although the tank was still a runner. More of 3rd RTR's tanks were hit and reduced to flaming hulks, with ammunition cooking off inside. The intelligence officer of 3rd RTR, Lieutentant Ironside, moving with the headquarters, reported columns of German tanks as far as the eye could see. Keller withdrew his battalion by bounds to a spur of high ground south of Coquilles.

In the late afternoon a British staff car appeared in the wood where Keller had sited his tank. Out stepped an officer who introduced himself as Brigadier Nicholson. He had tried to contact Keller by wireless but had been told, 'Get off the air, I'm trying to fight a bloody battle.'[7] Nicholson said he commanded the 30th Brigade and had been sent from England to take command at Calais. He had with him the 2nd King's Royal Rifle Corps (KRRC) and 1st Rifle Brigade (RB), and was taking 3rd RTR and 1st QVR under command.[8] He ordered Keller to withdraw to Calais after dark, replenish with fuel and ammunition and concentrate in the Parc Saint-Pierre near the Hôtel de Ville. Sergeant Close was told to follow Nicholson back to town in his Dingo for the brigadier's use as an armoured battle taxi. There was room for only two people in the Dingo, so Close dropped his driver at the battalion concentration area, and after filling up with petrol and collecting ammunition for the Bren drove to brigade HQ in the Boulevard Léon Gambetta, which Colonel Holland had used as his headquarters.

Through no fault of its own, the 30th Brigade arrived without many of its weapons, and without much of its ammunition and equipment. The two infantry battalions were motor battalions intended to operate with the 1st Armoured Division, and their COs were exceptional officers with considerable battle experience. At 1800 hours on 21 May they had received orders to move, and by 2300 hours were loaded and motoring from Suffolk to Southampton. They had no idea where they were bound. As the battalions arrived, most of the maps were taken away from them and over-excited staff officers took charge of the vehicles. The COs were not allowed to arrange anything. Weapons and equipment

19. German parachute troops dropping on The Hague, Holland.

20. General von Rundstedt.

21. A German assault gun driving through Belgium on 29 May 1940. Equipped with a 75mm gun, it is an armoured self-propelled artillery piece designed to support infantry in a panzer division, not a tank.

22. German armour, including Mk III tanks, entering Sedan.

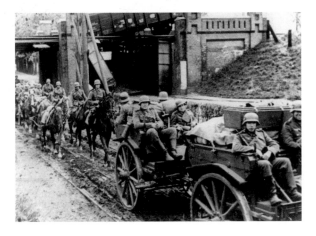

23. German horse-drawn artillery in Holland.

24. German troops and horse-drawn transport crossing a pontoon bridge over a Belgian river on 11 May 1940.

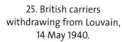

25. British carriers withdrawing from Louvain, 14 May 1940.

26. German panzer-grenadiers assaulting a farmhouse having dismounted from their half-tracks. This is very likely to be a posed propaganda photograph.

27. A British sapper takes cover round the side of a building while blowing a bridge in Louvain before retreating.

28. A rubber boat camouflaged with a bush lands infantrymen after crossing a river in Belgium. The horse has waded across with them. The German Army used vast numbers of horses throughout the Second World War.

29. Two German Mk IV tanks with short-barrelled 75mm guns wading a river in Belgium.

30. *Above*. Contrasting styles of transport in the German Army: a mounted German officer, possibly artillery or infantry, watches German armour moving up a road in Belgium.

31. *Above, right*. German troops and transport crossing a pontoon bridge over a canal near Nieuport in Belgium. German formations were well equipped with these bridges, and their engineers were adept at throwing them across water obstacles quickly.

32. *Right*. A battery of French 75mm guns of pre-1914 vintage with solid wheels deployed under token efforts to camouflage them.

33. A German half-track towing an 88mm gun. Originally designed as an anti-aircraft gun, the 88 first demonstrated its devastating effect on armour in 1940; a reputation which endured for the whole of the Second World War.

34. Major General Rommel, in cap with map board on his knees, and his staff of the 7th Panzer Division plotting the next move during the armoured advance through northern France.

needed by men on the personnel ships were loaded on the vehicle ships, and everything was loaded in a muddle. The confusion caused by offi- cious embarkation staff was to lead to difficulties the following day when the battalions disembarked at Calais with the enemy about three miles away. Eventually with vehicles loaded in the *Kohistan* and *City of Canter- bury*, and men, including brigade headquarters, in the *Royal Daffodil* and *Archangel*, the ships sailed in convoy from Southampton to Dover. Here they joined up with *Autocarrier* carrying the 229th Anti-Tank Battery and sailed for Calais. The *Autocarrier* was also loaded with six wireless trucks intended for another unit, so the anti-tank battery had to leave four of its twelve guns on the dockside; they never arrived at Calais. There was no field or medium artillery with the brigade.

By the time the 30th Brigade convoy docked at Calais on the afternoon of 23 May, the 1st Panzer Division was closing in on the town. Leading elements had reached but not yet taken Le Colombier, and had driven 3rd RTR almost back to Coquelles. Unbeknown to Nicholson, the 1st Panzer Division was ordered not to push on towards Calais, but to bypass it and head for Dunkirk, leaving the 10th Panzer Division to take Calais. The 10th Panzer Division had actually been pulled out of Guderian's XIX Panzer Corps to refit, leaving him with two divisions: the 1st Panzer Division which, in Guderian's opinion, should make short work of such a lightly defended town as Calais before heading off for Dunkirk; and the 2nd Panzer Division already attacking at Boulogne. But when the British unexpectedly reinforced Calais, the 10th Panzer Division was hastily hauled back from refitting to deal with this new threat, while the 1st Panzer Division was told to make straight for Gravelines and Dunkirk.

But, although Nicholson was not privy to this reasoning at high level in the German camp, he was absolutely clear that there was no question of moving to Boulogne or to Saint-Omer. His most urgent task was to defend Calais. He ordered the 1st RB to hold the outer ramparts on the east side of town, and the 2nd KRRC to do the same on the west side. Advanced posts of the Queen Victoria's Rifles and anti-aircraft units were deployed forward of the ramparts. Having just given his orders, Nichol- son was instructed by the War Office to take some 350,000 rations for the BEF to Dunkirk, and was told that this task was to be treated as 'over-riding all other considerations'.[9] Calais contained one of the biggest ration dumps in France, and these orders came direct from General Ironside, the CIGS. Although, as related in Chapter 5, Gort did not made his decision to withdraw through Ypres to Dunkirk until 25 May (two days hence), Ironside on assessing the situation had come to the con- clusion that the BEF might have to resort to retreating in this direction. If the ration convoy was to get through it had to go as soon as possible

with tanks and carriers to clear the way before the 1st Panzer Division
blocked the Calais–Dunkirk road at Marck.

Nicholson took some infantry from the perimeter defence and sent
them to picket the first part of the road to Dunkirk twenty miles away,
while the convoy was being formed. A patrol of one cruiser and three
light tanks of B Squadron, 3rd RTR, under Major Reeves was sent ahead
of the infantry. The 10th Panzer Division had by now come up from the
south, occupied the high ground overlooking Calais and started shelling
the town.

It took hours to load the rations into ten 10-ton trucks. As this was
being done, the ships that had transported the 30th Brigade vehicles
were being unloaded. This also took a very long time. Whenever shelling
started up, the stevedores, who were already exhausted after working
non-stop for thirty-six hours, took cover.

Meanwhile since midnight on 23/24 May, a composite company of the
Rifle Brigade under Major Hamilton-Russell had sat in its trucks waiting
for news of Major Reeves's reconnaissance. By 0400 hours Reeves had not
returned, and the convoy moved off. Reeves's patrol had an amazing
adventure. Not far out of Calais they lost wireless contact with Keller
and the tanks that were to follow up. They continued through three
unguarded roadblocks set up by the 1st Panzer Division and through
numerous other positions lightly held by Germans, who thought they
were their own tanks. The patrol reached Gravelines without a scratch.
They fought in the town the next morning, knocking out five German
tanks and two troop carriers.

Hamilton-Russell's force, which was accompanied by Nicholson, a
curious decision, moved with five tanks leading, followed by three
carriers, three platoons in trucks, the ration trucks and two platoons
bringing up the rear. About three miles east of Calais, between Le Beau
Marais and Marck, the column ran into a strong German roadblock with
anti-tank guns sited among the houses. The British tanks were forced to
stop, and although the platoons of the Rifle Brigade managed to outflank
the Germans it was clear by daybreak that the convoy and escorts would
be cut off if they did not pull back. Hamilton-Russell reluctantly ordered
a withdrawal, leaving two dead and taking several wounded with him.
3rd RTR was reduced to nine cruisers and twelve light tanks.

By now Calais was under heavy shellfire, for at dawn on 24 May the
artillery and mortar preparation for the 10th Panzer Division's attack on
Calais from the west started. Guderian had told Major General Schaal,
commanding the 10th, to advance carefully, so as to avoid excessive
casualties. He had ordered heavy artillery units up from Boulogne in
support. It should be borne in mind that only three days had elapsed

since the British counter-stroke at Arras that had caused such dispropor-
tionate dismay within the German high command. Kleist's staff were still
talking about 'the crisis at Arras' late on 23 May.

In Calais docks the *Kohistan* (brigade headquarters and KRRC vehicles
and stores) had been unloaded by 0400 hours on 24 May, but the *City of
Canterbury* (1st RB vehicles and stores) took much longer. At 0730 hours,
a sea transport officer, claiming that he had Nicholson's permission, gave
orders that the latter's holds were to be closed, although the ship was
still full of vehicles and ammunition. Wounded were unloaded from a
hospital train in the docks and placed in their stretchers on top of the
hatches, under which still sat most of the Rifle Brigade's vehicles and
ammunition. The *City of Canterbury* and other ships then sailed, taking
the stevedores and other non-fighting troops back to England.

It is possible that Nicholson had given permission for unloading to
stop, for early that morning, 24 May, he had been told by the War
Office that evacuation had been agreed 'in principle'. Although fighting
personnel had to stay to cover the final evacuation, non-fighting personnel had to begin embarking at once. It therefore made sense not to
unload equipment that would subsequently have to be restowed or more
probably abandoned. But, as the Official History comments, 'it was
unfortunate that the fighting troops were thus deprived of weapons and
equipment which they sorely needed'.[10]

During the afternoon of 24 May, the Germans attacked Calais on three
sides, using all of 10th Panzer Division's rifle battalions and a battalion
of tanks supported by 150mm guns. The French garrison of Fort Nieulay
west of Calais surrendered, along with a small detachment of the Queen
Victoria's Rifles which had taken refuge in the fort. The French Marines
in Fort Lapin disabled their coastal guns and escaped. By now the
surviving Queen Victoria's Rifles had been distributed between the two
regular battalions and the QVR ceased to function as a separate battalion.
In the south, the Germans made some gains in the town and could not
be dislodged. Ammunition on the ramparts was running short, and all
but two of the 229th Battery's anti-tank guns had been put out of action.
But the Germans were by no means having it all their own way, and the
entry in the 10th Panzer Division war diary for 1600 hours on 24 May
reflects this: 'Enemy resistance from scarcely perceptible positions was
however so strong that it was only possible to achieve quite local success.'
And three hours later XIX Panzer Corps headquarters was told that a
third of the German equipment, vehicles and personnel and a 'good half
of the tanks' were casualties; the troops were 'tired out'.[11]

Brigadier Nicholson was clear that he could not hold the outer perimeter for much longer, for he had no reserve with which to plug gaps

or to counter penetration. He received another message from the War Office confirming the decision to evacuate, but saying that final pull-out of the fighting troops was not to take place until 0700 hours the next day, 25 May. Responding to this order, Nicholson withdrew his infantry to the line of the Boulevard Léon Gambetta and Marck Canal. After more fighting, he ordered a further withdrawal, to take place at 2100 hours, to the old town and the area to the east enclosed by the outer ramparts. The weak points in this defence line were the bridges. The French had not prepared them for demolition, and the British had no explosives with them. Only two out of the eight anti-tank guns remained.

With the onset of darkness, the German assault petered out – the usual form. But as the British troops were withdrawing Brigadier Nicholson received a message from the CIGS in Whitehall telling him that the French commander in the north 'forbids evacuation'. By moving his headquarters from the Boulevard Léon Gambetta to underneath the Gare Maritime, Nicholson lost the use of the telephone cable to London. He was visited in his new headquarters at 2323 hours by Vice Admiral Sir James Somerville, who had just landed from the destroyer *Wolfhound*. Somerville had been commanding a destroyer force engaging enemy batteries all day, as well as battling with the Luftwaffe. He handed Nicholson a message which read: 'In spite of policy of evacuation given you this morning, fact that British forces in your area now under Fagalde who has ordered no, repeat no, evacuation, means that you must comply for sake of Allied solidarity.' Nicholson's role, he was told, was to hold on, and as the harbour 'was now of no importance to the BEF' he was to select a position in which to fight to the end. Ammunition was being sent, but no reinforcements. He was also told that a brigade of the 48th Division was marching to his assistance that morning. This information was nonsense: the 48th Division was never told to send a brigade to Calais, as it was fully engaged elsewhere.[12] Had it attempted to break through the panzer divisions between the main body of the BEF and Calais it would have been destroyed. The War Office order forbidding evacuation and talking nonsense about a brigade marching to Nicholson's relief reveals a state of unreality in Whitehall about the actual situation almost on a par with that pervading Paris. According to Somerville, Nicholson took the news in good heart and, although he appeared to be tired, was 'in no way windy'.

The appointment of General Fagalde to command troops in the three Channel ports is covered in Chapter 9. He had forbidden evacuation from Calais, as well as placing the French commander there under British command. The French commander in question had complained about the British intention to leave. Since the British risked losing more troops

of far greater value than the French stationed in Calais, it is questionable that Fagalde's order would have been heeded had Churchill not been feeling aggrieved by Reynaud's complaint about the British withdrawing from Arras. Believing that British honour was at stake, Churchill supported the stay-and-fight order. This is hard to justify in the light of hindsight, given that the mess the BEF found itself in was entirely of French making. But at the time it made complete sense to Churchill: almost anything that would buttress the sagging morale of the French would have seemed absolutely crucial and had to be seized upon if they were not to throw in the towel and abandon the war. However, the phrase 'for sake of Allied solidarity' he thought 'very lukewarm', saying 'this is no way to encourage men to fight to the end'.

One unfortunate outcome of the earlier instruction to evacuate the British was the loss of more of 3rd RTR's tanks. Orders had been passed to the battalion that nothing of value was to fall into enemy hands. It started burning its tanks and ammunition near the Gare Maritime, to the accompaniment of black pillars of smoke and loud explosions. By the time it was ordered to stop, five more cruiser tanks had gone up in smoke, leaving only nine.

Faced with the stark stay-and-fight order, it is arguable that Nicholson should have concentrated immediately behind the water barrier of canals and basins that surrounded the old town. But he decided to make the enemy pay for every inch of ground, and it is easy to be critical six decades later when one is not weighed down by responsibility and fatigue. Noting that the Germans, as usual, had not followed up his withdrawal during the night, he sent mobile patrols into the town, and finding it clear he ordered some of his troops forward. But at daylight on 25 May the 10th Panzer Division resumed the assault with its customary ferocity, and by 0800 hours the swastika was flying over the town hall. A little later the mayor walked forward under escort to discuss surrender terms. Nicholson detained him and sent the escort back.

In the Rifle Brigade's sector the Germans had penetrated at several points. Counter-attacks by platoons, all that could be spared, failed with heavy losses. The brigade lost five officers and two platoon sergeant majors killed in one hour.[13] The CO, Lieutenant Colonel Hoskyns, was mortally wounded.

The KRRC found that the town hall afforded the Germans excellent observation over their sector and they took advantage of it to shell the approaches to the forward houses held by the battalion. The KRRC sector included three bridges into the old town from the new, and guarding these took three companies. Their task was not made easier by the hordes of refugees, including 1,000 or more unarmed French and Belgian

soldiers. These added to the chaos by spreading rumours of fifth columnists. Although there were undoubtedly some fifth columnists in Calais (as elsewhere), they, like snipers, were not so pervasive as so often reported. As Lieutenant Davies Scourfield, a platoon commander in B Company, 2nd KRRC, discovered, the 'snipers' were more often than not single riflemen who had infiltrated into forward positions and climbed up on to the roofs of tall buildings. It is common in war for the so-called 'sniper' to be just a lone rifleman, not a specialist equipped with a high-performance rifle fitted with sophisticated optics.

The KRRC's fourth company was sited forward of the Citadel, itself garrisoned by around 200 French soldiers, two 75mm guns and a detachment of Royal Marines. Here the commander of French troops in Calais, Commandant (Major) Le Tellier, had his headquarters. Nicholson moved his forward brigade headquarters into the Citadel to enable him to keep in touch with Le Tellier. The Citadel was an immensely strong fort built by Vauban in 1680, and despite its age was able to withstand considerable battering even from the modern medium guns of 1940.

Sergeant Close benefited from the move to the Citadel. Nicholson told him that he had no further use for the Dingo, nor did Lieutenant Colonel Keller, so he could now return to England. Close knew nothing of the 'fight on' message, a good indication that few heard it, or subsequent such messages, because as the brigade commander's driver he would have been one of the first to learn about it, if only by overhearing conversations. He drove to the Gare Maritime, and before leaving the Dingo took a grenade from the box of six on the vehicle, pulled the pin and slipped it under the bonnet where it exploded. Arriving at the docks he saw a small naval vessel about to leave, and rushed down the gangplank just before it was pulled inboard. To the end of his life, Close never knew the name of the vessel or what she was doing there. But she might have been carrying a message for the naval detachment at the Gare Maritime. Once she was clear of the smoke in the harbour, Close could see the flashes of German batteries on the ridge above Coquelles shelling Calais. Offshore destroyers were engaging the enemy batteries, and zigzagging to avoid the Stukas. Ships would be engulfed in spray and columns of water and would emerge with pom-poms blazing at the enemy aircraft. Arriving at Dover, he was shoved on to a train for Aldershot, still wearing the revolver he had never drawn.

At about 1400 hours on 25 May Nicholson received a wireless message from the Secretary of State for War in London, Anthony Eden, who had served in the KRRC in the First World War. It had been generated by Churchill, who had been so unimpressed by the term 'Allied solidarity' in the earlier message. This one read:

Defence of Calais to the utmost is of the highest importance to our country as symbolising our continuing cooperation with France. The eyes of the Empire are upon the defence of Calais, and HM Government are confident you and your gallant regiments will perform an exploit worthy of the British name.[14]

The message was copied to unit headquarters, but it is doubtful that it was sent further forward. Indeed it may not even have got to some unit headquarters. Lieutenant Ironside, intelligence officer at 3rd RTR headquarters, did not know of it at the time. Even if it had been distributed down the chain of command, the impact on the fighting troops would have been minimal. In battle such exhortations usually have a derisory effect; soldiers fight for each other, their 'mates', not for some higher cause, however worthy.

An hour later, the German shelling stopped, and an officer approached with a flag of truce, accompanied by a French captain and a Belgian soldier. The German officer was taken to Nicholson and belligerently demanded surrender, threatening that the garrison would be given a pounding if it did not immediately lay down its arms. Nicholson's reply was entered in the war diary of the 10th Panzer Division, where it was recorded in English:

1. The answer is no as it is the British Army's duty to fight as well as it is the German's.
2. The French captain and the Belgian soldier having not been blindfolded cannot be sent back. The Allied Commander gives his word that they will be put under guard and will not be allowed to fight against the Germans.[15]

Just before sending in the flag of truce, the Germans dropped leaflets giving the garrison one hour to surrender. Along with many others, Lieutenant Davies Scourfield's platoon used this hour to bring up food and ammunition. The attack was not renewed until 1830 hours, starting with a massive artillery programme thickened up by mortar fire. The bridges were attacked at 1900 hours. At two of them the leading German tanks were knocked out on the bridges themselves, blocking access; at the third a tank got across, but was forced back by a vigorous counter-attack by the KRRC. At dusk the German assaults died away, because, according to the 10th Panzer Division war diary, 'the Infantry Brigade Commander considers further attacks pointless, as the enemy resistance is not yet crushed and there is not enough time before the fall of darkness'.[16]

During the night the Royal Navy brought in more ammunition and evacuated some of the wounded. Food was not a problem, as there was a

huge stock of undelivered rations. Also during that night a boat brought in a message from the War Office:

> Every hour you continue to exist is of greatest help to the BEF. Government has therefore decided you must continue to fight. Have great admiration for your splendid stand.[17]

Few of the defenders would have seen this message. The KRRC and Rifle Brigade fought on because they were the best-trained battalions in the British Army. As the first of the motor battalions they had been treated as 'experimental' since 1937, had been given every opportunity to train and were supplied with the means to do so – unlike the rest of the BEF. With the cohesion that follows good training, these well-led battalions did not need pronouncements from on high to persuade them to do their duty. The only people who mattered, other than their families, were those around them. This sustained them in the darkest moments.

The men of 3rd RTR also gave the enemy a bloody nose during the battle. They claimed six enemy tanks knocked out, and their light tanks had been invaluable in supporting the Rifle Brigade. With very little scope for further fighting, Keller decided to break out of Calais. He ordered his three surviving cruisers to make their way along the beach to Gravelines, and followed in a light tank. He and one of his squadron commanders, Major Simpson, were the only ones to reach their destination. Along the way the 3rd RTR tanks were engaged by the Germans, who had spotted them from the road running parallel to the beach, and others ran out of fuel. Keller's tank broke down. He completed the journey on foot, collecting a crew that had baled out of another tank. On reaching the Aa river at Gravelines, the party found the Germans holding the port, and although Keller and Simpson managed to swim the wide, fast-flowing river, the others refused to do so. On the morning of 26 May, Keller and Simpson walked into Petit Fort Philippe held by the French, were sent to Dunkirk and thence taken to Dover in a trawler. As they passed Calais they could see the cruiser *Galatea* firing into the town.

At 0700 hours the attacks on Calais resumed, and, assisted by a mass Stuka attack at 0930 hours, the Germans broke through on the west and isolated the Citadel. Lieutenant Colonel Miller reorganized his battalion into a tighter perimeter in the dock area. Around 1600 hours the Germans burst into the Citadel and ran into Nicholson, who had come up from the cellar. He was surrounded and had to surrender. It was a bitter moment. He was to die in prison camp, tortured by totally unjustified feelings that he could have done better.

The Rifle Brigade was driven back to the area of the Gare Maritime, fighting on until it ran out of ammunition, with many dead and even

more wounded. Lieutenant Davies Scourfield, having temporarily taken command of his company during his commander's absence at battalion headquarters, walked back to where his platoon was sited to find the whole place a shambles with bodies lying everywhere. As he moved around, he 'walked straight into a German machine gun'. He was hit in the arm and then in the ribs, and finally knocked senseless by a grazing round on the side of his helmet. He came round lying in a gutter, hearing Germans driving up and down the street shouting, 'Come out, Tommies! It's all finished.' But it seemed it was not over, as he heard shots being fired at the Germans. He passed out again to find a German standing over him with a knife in his hand, who proceeded to cut away Davies Scourfield's clothing and applied both the Briton's field dressing and his own.

The last organized resistance was by a company of the Queen Victoria's Rifles, cornered by tanks and infantry. It surrendered at 1700 hours.

Lieutenant Colonel Miller of the KRRC ordered his men to split up, go into hiding and escape after dark. Nearly all were rounded up, and the only ones to escape were some wounded and unwounded men who got away in the Royal Navy yacht *Conidaw*. She had come in with ammunition and had been lying grounded on the mud by the low tide most of the afternoon. While attempts were being made to refloat her, two bombs dropped near by and the blast wave floated her off. Sergeant Mitchell of the Royal Marines and a small party of Marines and soldiers who had been cut off from their units, a total of 165 in all, waded out to her and were taken off. Sergeant East RM, who had similarly been cut off, joined up with a party of others evading capture and hid from the Germans under the jetty. As a small motor yacht, the *Gulvar*, passed close inshore that night looking for survivors, East signalled with a torch. The *Gulvar*'s captain, concerned about German guns on the ‚etty, shouted through his loud hailer that he could not stop but would make one close pass and the men would have to swim for it. Four officers and forty-seven Marines and soldiers, including East, made it to the yacht.

Lieutenant Ironside, along with Captain Moss the adjutant and some of 3rd RTR headquarters, tried making their way on foot to Dunkirk along the beach. Their mental alertness was dulled by exhaustion. At daybreak, instead of finding somewhere to lie up for the day, they kept going and walked straight into a German armoured car. Ironside and Moss stood looking across at the white cliffs of Dover lit up by the early-morning sun. The armoured-car commander, who had been to Oxford and spoke perfect English, said, 'I wonder when you'll see those again.' Ironside replied, 'I suppose you'll have a go at getting over there next.' 'Oh no, our next task is Russia.' In retrospect that was an extraordinary

remark to make, bearing in mind that another year was to pass before Hitler invaded the Soviet Union.

Most of the Calais garrison spent the rest of the war, another five years, in prison camps. Some were to escape later. Captain Williams, the adjutant of the KRRC, and three staff officers from brigade headquarters slipped away from the prisoner column as it marched through France, as did several others. Only Williams, a fluent French-speaker, and the staff officers made it back to England. Airey Neave, who fought at Calais as a second lieutenant in the 2nd Searchlight Battery, escaped from Colditz Castle in January 1942, arriving in England four months later.

It was Churchill who had decided to order the garrison to fight on to the end. It is clear from his own account that the option to evacuate was still open for discussion in Whitehall until 2100 hours on the evening of 26 May, some five hours after Nicholson's surrender, which was unknown to Churchill at the time. In the belief that the garrison was still resisting, a sortie was made by the RAF on the morning of 27 May to drop water and ammunition, all of it into German hands, for the loss of three aircraft out of twenty-one. Having made the decision, Churchill wrote later, 'I could not help feeling physically sick as we afterwards sat silent at the table.'[18]

Opinions are at variance over whether the epic stand at Calais contributed to the escape of the BEF at Dunkirk. Churchill certainly thought so, writing after the war:

> Calais was the crux. Many other causes might have prevented the deliverance of Dunkirk, but it is certain that the three days gained by the defence of Calais enabled the Gravelines waterline to be held, and that without this, even in spite of Hitler's vacillations and Rundstedt's orders, all would have been cut off and lost.[19]

Those who fought at Calais and spent five years as prisoners of war drew much solace from this. Yet Guderian, again writing after the war, says that the defence of Calais made no difference to the effort he put into the attack on Dunkirk. That is an exaggeration. For what is beyond question is that the 30th Brigade at Calais tied up the 10th Panzer Division for three days, inflicted large casualties on the division's infantry and diverted all Guderian's heavy artillery from his main effort, which was to cut off the BEF heading for Dunkirk. If that is not 'making a difference', one has to ask what is. When added to the delay imposed on the 2nd Panzer Division at Boulogne, one has to concede that the holding up of two panzer divisions, two-thirds of Guderian's XIX Panzer Corps, by two under-strength brigades (one without any armour and one with only one battalion of armour) was no mean feat.

But did the 30th Brigade have to fight to the bitter end to achieve this aim, if indeed that was the aim seen for them at the time? They could have been evacuated on the night of 25/26 May, as the 20th Guards Brigade had been from Boulogne earlier, and the ultimate effect on the 10th Panzer Division would have been little different. Given the customary German supineness at night, many, if not most, of the brigade could have been got away. Was the purpose of sending the 30th Brigade to Calais as clear cut in minds in Whitehall as Churchill implied – that is, to slow down the German armour advancing on Dunkirk? The rain of contradictory orders that descended on Nicholson's head before and after his arrival at Calais suggests not; and that the reason for despatching the brigade had not been properly thought through (understandable in the chaos of the moment). It leads one to suspect that Churchill is justifying the decision he took. One could argue that writing after the war (the second volume of his war memoirs was published in 1949) Churchill realized that the 'Allied solidarity' argument would not wash. By then his British readers would have been well aware that the 'allies' in question had been almost entirely responsible for the plight in which the BEF found itself in May and June 1940, and they would also have been familiar with the subsequent woeful performance by the French that led to their capitulation. In the vernacular of the time, the French had made a horlicks of it, and although there was sympathy for the French people, there was none for their leaders, who had mismanaged the campaign and signed an armistice with the Germans. If this was Churchill's reasoning, the only line left to him to take was that the defence of Calais had delayed the German armour advancing on Dunkirk. It certainly had, but, for the reasons given above, the 30th Brigade could have done that *and* been evacuated. One is left with the view that maintaining Allied solidarity was the reason that the brigade was abandoned to its fate – a decision which may have seemed right at the time, but which would not appear so in the light of subsequent events.

7

THE WITHDRAWAL:

II CORPS ON THE EASTERN FLANK

Having told the story of Boulogne and Calais, and thereby gone ahead of the narrative of the main body of the BEF, it is time to turn the clock back to the evening of 25 May. Gort's instructions to his corps commanders that evening included orders to Adam to relinquish command of III Corps and prepare a defensive perimeter around Dunkirk; and to Brooke to build up a defensive line along the line of the Ypres–Comines Canal, extending it northwards along the Yser Canal to the River Yser. With this as a shield, the BEF would withdraw to Dunkirk, starting with I Corps. For this task, Brooke was allocated the 5th and 50th Divisions in addition to his own 3rd and 4th Divisions, and as the fighting withdrawal progressed he would take other formations under command as required.

The 5th Division was ordered to move to the Ypres–Comines line that evening. Franklyn's division was only two brigades strong, one being detached in Norway, so Brooke told him to take under command the 143rd Brigade that had already been sent to the Ypres–Comines Line. By midday on 26 May the 5th Division started digging in. The 50th Division had to disengage its 151st Brigade from the Canal Line first, and this, followed by problems with traffic congestion, resulted in the division arriving at Ypres on 27 May to extend the line to the north. Until its arrival, the section of front was held by the French 2nd DLM, which remained under II Corps command for the time being.

Brooke's task would demand some complex manoeuvring. First he had to form his eastwards-facing shield and protect the BEF against the assaults of two or more enemy corps. All the while, as the BEF withdrew, he had to sidestep his formations progressively northwards. North-west of his 'shield', in succession he had to create three south-facing defensive layback positions, through which formations could withdraw as they peeled away from the right flank of the defence. The first layback line would be along the north bank of the Lys. The second was planned to be along the line Poperinghe–Ypres, although this might be changed if circumstances demanded. The third would be the Yser river, and Brooke's

II Corps would withdraw through this layback to the Dunkirk perimeter, having shielded the BEF from Bock's Army Group B throughout.

Although Montgomery and others subsequently criticized the performance of the 1940 BEF, citing its lack of training for modern war and other inadequacies in both skill and equipment, most of the blame for these deficiencies can be laid at the door of the politicians, as is neatly summed up in the quotation at the head of Chapter 1. In his memoirs, Montgomery wrote: 'the campaign in France and Flanders in 1940 was lost in Whitehall in the years before it ever began, and this cannot be stated too clearly or too often. One might add after Whitehall the words "and in Paris".'[1] What one cannot belittle is the steadfastness of the soldiers of the BEF, their discipline and morale under the most testing circumstances – of retreat, uncertainty and the ever present scourge of the Luftwaffe. Of course there were cases of ill discipline, of men losing their nerve, and indeed of cowardice, but these were the exception. The BEF was fortunate in many of its senior commanders. They had been tempered in the fires and shocks of the First World War, and most, especially Brooke, Alexander, Montgomery and the much maligned Gort, remained calm in the face of the utmost danger, and their skilful handling of the withdrawal is testimony to their professionalism. Their performance shines forth compared with that of their allies, many of whose commanders were prone to breaking down in tears at stressful moments.

Second Lieutenant Martin's platoon of Cheshires were amazed when they were told that they were going to Dunkirk to be evacuated, as they thought they were 'doing all right' and could not see the reason for it. The performance of the BEF also says much about the leadership at junior level. In any army, the kind of discipline required is different from that required in the navy, where, as Captain White of the 1st/6th East Surreys wrote, 'they are all in the same ship, and when father says turn, they all turn. In the army on a dark and dreary night, they can hide behind boulders, or take Private Bloggins to the Regimental Aid Post and disappear.'

High morale and discipline is needed to withstand the shocks and surprises of war, including last-minute changes of orders and unpredictability. Lieutenant Robin Dunn of the 7th Field Regiment spent most of 26 May in the OP, and at 1900 hours handed over to another officer, his mind dwelling on thoughts of dinner and bed on return to his troop in their gun position. As he arrived he was told to report to regimental headquarters for the commanding officer's conference. Here he found all the troop commanders of the regiment with all battery commanders. The CO walked in with a 1/250,000 map of France, put it up against the wall, turned to the assembled officers and said; 'Gentlemen, the

Commander-in-Chief has decided that the BEF's position is untenable. We are to move to the coast and re-embark for England. Personnel only can be moved. All equipment is to be rendered useless and left.' There was more in the same vein. The officers listened in horror. It was impossible to believe that what the CO had said could be true. He continued, 'The Belgians have bolted on our left. The French counter-attack to close the gap has failed.' Looking round at faces he knew so well, Dunn saw that they all had the same air of bewildered depression. He thought of all their high hopes, their training, their confidence in their men.

The CO continued addressing them: 'Robin, you will take your troop back at once to beyond Wambrechies and will remain in action there to cover the withdrawal. John, you will stay in action here under command 8th Infantry Brigade. You will all remain in action until the last possible moment, when you will disable your guns and get away as best you can. On your way back you will shoot anyone on sight who tries to stop you.' Dunn drove back to his troop, his mind in a turmoil. After warning his troop to expect a move, he ate dinner. When the troop was ready, he told them what was to happen and why. There was dead silence for about a minute, before a gunner stepped forward and asked, 'It's not our fault, sir, is it?' Dunn reassured him that it was not their fault, but as he thought it over, he concluded that that made it worse. It was not their fault, but they had to go.

Just as he was about to give the order 'cease firing', which would bring the guns out of action, an order came down the telephone, 'Stand fast. No move until further orders.' The men slept in the vehicles, Dunn by the telephone.

The next day, Dunn was summoned again to regimental headquarters. He learned that the retreat was to be an orderly rearguard action, not a race to the sea as they had originally been told. A bridgehead was to be formed round Dunkirk, at first of substantial size but becoming progressively smaller. The 3rd Division was to hold the northern part of the Ypres Canal, to the north of Ypres. A mobile force consisting of some anti-tank guns, machine guns and two gunner troops was to go back to this line. The rest of the division was to move that night. In half an hour the two troops were limbered up and away.

Dunn's troop moved north through Messines and along the Messines Ridge. Everywhere there were war cemeteries and memorials to the 'war to end all wars'. And there they were doing the same thing against the same people over the same ground, only twenty-five years later. As he drove along the ridge, Dunn thought of the refugees, the desolate homes, the ruined towns and the wounded, and wondered how to make sure that twenty-five years hence his son would not drive along the Messines

Ridge leading his troop into action in the same area against the same enemy.

His daydreaming was cut short by shelling as they drove through Wytschaete. British batteries were firing on the left of the road, which was full of infantry all looking east. They all seemed very tired and were caked with dust and sweat. They waved as the guns drove by.

Dunn had been ordered to go via Messines, Wytschaete and Saint-Eloi. Approaching Saint-Eloi, he found some infantry, so he halted and spoke to an officer. The infantry was from the 1st Division, which was holding the canal south of Ypres. The Belgians had retreated more quickly than expected, and contact had been made with the enemy, who were in Ypres and over the canal at Hazebrouck, although only in small numbers. Dunn told the officer where he wanted to go, and the officer laughed, saying that they had just sent a patrol there, and there's the answer: he pointed at a tall German smoking a cigarette. Apparently this soldier had been part of a machine-gun detachment. He looked very like a guardsman, tall, slim, holding himself well. He seemed tired but fit, burned a good colour by the sun.

Dunn looked at his map to find a detour. At that moment two traffic-control policemen arrived to mark the route for the main body of the 3rd Division. He told them what the position was, and offered to take them with him. Telling the guns to swing round in a conveniently wide area formed by a crossroads, he set off to retrace his steps. As the last of his ammunition trucks pulled clear, four shells fell on the crossroads, followed by four more.

He stopped in Wytschaete, went into the headquarters of a medium regiment in action there and sent a message to headquarters 3rd Division via I and II Corps to say that their route via Saint-Eloi was blocked, and suggested an alternative. He asked if anyone knew what was happening north of Ypres, as he did not want to drive into the front line again. No one seemed to know, but the impression was that the Germans were some way beyond the canal, so he drove on through Dickebusch back on to the original route. There were some new shell holes all round, but his troop got through without a round falling on them, and finally arrived in their allotted area. There, they encountered some RASC men, due to embark that night, who gave them 500,000 cigarettes they could not carry.

When the 5th Division arrived on the Ypres–Comines Line (taking under command 143rd, and with its own 13th and 17th Brigades), it found that the eight-mile-long canal was disused, dry except for some mud, and in most places a poor obstacle, although better than nothing at all in this flat landscape. A railway line ran east of the canal, for most

of the way on a low embankment, giving the enemy a covered approach. There were numerous houses in the vicinity of the canal, some grouped into small hamlets, all packed with refugees who refused to budge. Three miles west of the canal lay the Messines Ridge, for which so much blood had been expended in the First World War. The ridge was the vital ground in this sector.

The 5th Division had enjoyed less than twenty-four hours of rest after their withdrawal from Arras, and, dog-tired though the soldiers were, there was not much sleep to be had sitting crammed in the jolting trucks that transported them to the position. Arriving from about 1000 hours onwards, the division deployed with the 17th Brigade on the left, in an area of low hills and woods, forward of the canal and behind the railway line which here ran about a mile to the east of the canal. The 2nd Royal Scots held Hill 60, that feature of ill fame in the First World War. The 6th Seaforths were posted behind the Zillebeke Lake a mile south of Ypres, and with an open flank within sight of the town. In the centre, the 13th Brigade held a front of two miles from inclusive Hollebeke to exclusive Houthem, with on the left the 2nd Cameronians and on the right 2nd Royal Inniskilling Fusiliers. The 143rd Brigade, originally responsible for the whole sector, concertinaed into its right to hold slightly less than three miles of the canal, with all three battalions forward – from left to right the 1st/7th Royal Warwicks, 8th Royal Warwicks, and 1st Oxfordshire and Buckinghamshire Light Infantry. Facing these three British brigades were three German infantry divisions – from north to south the 18th, 31st and 61st.

While Lieutenant Colonel Lumsden's 12th Lancers screened Ypres until the 50th Division arrived to take up its positions to the north of the town, what became known as the Battle of Wytschaete roared into life. Beginning on 25 May and continuing until the 28th, it was the toughest engagement Brooke faced in his shielding of the BEF's withdrawal. As the battle progressed, Brooke reinforced the 5th Division with the 13th/ 18th Hussars and three battalions from the 1st Division (3rd Grenadier Guards, 2nd North Staffordshires and 2nd Sherwood Foresters – one from each of Alexander's brigades, and with his happy co-operation). Alexander had sent them back to the Lys to form a layback for his own division's withdrawal. When Brooke asked for them, Barker transferred them to II Corps.

Brooke took the two machine-gun battalions covering the south bank of the Lys (1st/7th Middlesex and 6th Black Watch) and moved them to reinforce the 9th Manchesters, the 5th Division's own machine-gun battalion. The 5th Division was well served by artillery, having its own three field regiments, as well as one field regiment from the 48th

Division, and one from I Corps. In addition the guns of I and II Corps' four medium regiments were particularly effective in breaking up German attacks. In thirty-six hours these medium regiments fired 5,000 rounds, a rate of fire not to be overtaken by British artillery until the Battle of Alamein two and a half years later.

During 26 May, enemy probing patrols became more aggressive across the whole Ypres–Comines Line (see map pp. 180–1). But Brooke's main worry was that the Germans would attack Ypres and outflank the 5th Division. The 12th Lancers reported that there were no Allied troops in the area except for a party of about twenty Belgian sappers, who had failed to prepare the bridges for demolition. The 150th Brigade, the leading formation of the 50th Division headed for Ypres, had a difficult time forcing its way through the rubble in the streets of Armentières, which had been comprehensively bombed by the Luftwaffe. In the turmoil, many of the inmates had escaped from the nearby lunatic asylum, and stood by the road grinning at the British troops as they passed by, adding a grotesque touch to the proceedings.

At first light on 27 May, the enemy mounted a series of attacks by three divisions south of Ypres. First to be hit was the 143rd Brigade. Observation in this sector was difficult; there were no prominent features, but visibility was severely restricted by orchards, hedges, copses and houses. Given that there were no wirelesses within battalions at this stage of the war, once telephone lines were cut the CO, if he could not see much, had great difficulty in keeping abreast of the battle. The terrain lent itself to infiltration, a tactic the Germans were rarely slow to adopt wherever they could. In the confused fighting, the enemy worked steadily round the flanks of the battalions. Forward companies were cut off, and the 143rd Brigade held on as best it could, but – with no reserve in rear – of necessity had to concede ground. Some of the temporary stop positions held further back were actually easier to defend among the houses and copses than the more open ground just west of the canal.

The attack on the 13th Brigade in the centre of the line took longer to wind up and did less damage. But German penetration between the two forward battalions, the Cameronians and the Inniskillings, was especially worrying because the forcing back of 143rd Brigade endangered its right flank. Brigadier Dempsey, faced with the prospect of having his brigade split in half and outflanked, ordered a withdrawal to slightly higher ground in rear, but still forward of the Messines Ridge. Orders for this move reached battalions before 1600 hours, but transmitting it to companies and platoons was, for lack of wireless, undertaken by officers or runners, who had to find the company and avoid being captured or killed by parties of enemy milling around in the area. Unfortunately some of

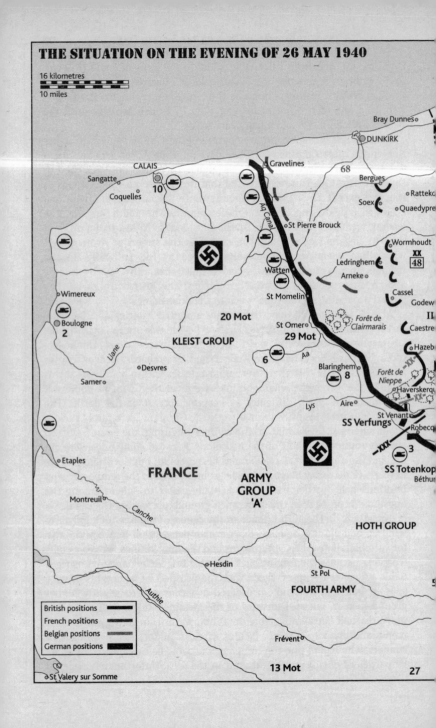

THE SITUATION ON THE EVENING OF 26 MAY 1940

16 kilometres

10 miles

Bray Dunnes
DUNKIRK
CALAIS   Gravelines
Sangatte   10   68   Bergues
Coquelles   Rattekc
Soex   Quaedypre
St Pierre Brouck
1
Wormhoudt
XX
48
Ledringhem
Watten
Arneke
St Momelin
Cassel
Wimereux   Godew
20 Mot   St Omer   Forêt de Clairmarais   II
Boulogne   29 Mot   Caestre
2   KLEIST GROUP   Hazeb
6   Aa
Desvres   Blaringhem   Forêt de Nieppe
Samer   8
Haverskerq
Lys   Aire
SS Verfungs   St Venant
Robecq
3
Etaples   SS Totenkop
Béthur
FRANCE   ARMY GROUP 'A'
Montreuil   Canche
HOTH GROUP

Hesdin
St Pol
FOURTH ARMY

British positions	——
French positions	——
Belgian positions	——
German positions	——

Frévent

St Valery sur Somme   13 Mot   27

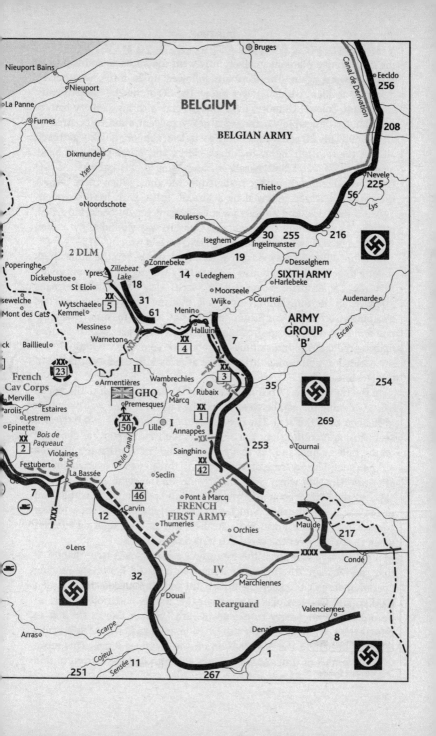

the Cameronian platoons inadvertently went too far back, and had to be taken forward again. The Germans followed up in force, whether by design or accident we shall never know. The CO of the 2nd Cameronians, Lieutenant Colonel Gilmore, took charge, and with his artillery battery commander (BC) rapidly arranged a heavy concentration to be fired by all the guns his BC could raise on the wireless. Gilmore quickly gathered all the men within sight, including clerks and other battalion head-quarters 'cooks and bottlewashers', and some of his carriers. As the Germans came on, they were malleted by the guns. When these ceased, the carriers charged followed by a line of 'Jocks' with fixed bayonets. This did the trick, and although some Germans fought back, most fled, pursued by screaming Cameronians. Gilmore was wounded by a shell splinter, but was awarded a bar to the DSO he had won in 1918.

The Inniskillings delayed their withdrawal, partly because orders took so long to get to them, but also because they were under the impression that the Cameronians were still in place. As a result the Germans followed up the Inniskillings so closely that the battalion headquarters became cut off in the confusion, and the CO, second-in-command, adjutant and RSM were all captured after a stiff but forlorn resistance. Further fighting reduced the Inniskillings to about one company strength. Dempsey decided to pull back a little further after dark to the forward edge of the Messines Ridge.

In the right of the 17th Brigade's sector the canal bent off to the north-west, widening the gap between it and the railway line to over two miles in the centre of the area. The two forward battalions (on the left the 6th Seaforths, and on the right the 2nd Royal Scots Fusiliers) were deployed on the railway line, and the rear battalion, the 2nd Northamptons, back on the canal. The pressure on the left flank threatened to overwhelm the 6th Seaforths, and when the 13th Brigade, on the right, pulled back, it exposed the 17th Brigade to envelopment on both flanks. A withdrawal to the canal was ordered, which was successfully carried out while in contact, but the 2nd Royal Scots Fusiliers lost all their fighting vehicles when the bridge over the canal was blown prematurely.

Brooke was aware from the captured German papers (see Chapter 5) that the German 7th Division's attack south of the Lys was a holding operation designed to keep the British 3rd and 4th Divisions fixed in that locality, and was less of a threat than the attacks north of the Lys. So he ordered Montgomery to extend his 3rd Division line to the left to release the 10th Brigade of the 4th Division, followed by its 11th Brigade, to come in behind the 5th Division on the Messines Ridge. This move was in the nick of time. At 2300 hours, the 10th Brigade arrived to find

that the enemy had almost reached the gun positions of the 91st Field Regiment east of Wytschaete. During the second half of the night the guns were withdrawn to Kemmel Hill, two miles further back. By 0900 hours on 28 May, the 10th and 11th Brigades were firmly established east of Wytschaete, but had not covered the gap to the north of the 17th Brigade. In the south of the 5th Division line, the Germans pushed forward to within mortar range of the bridge over the River Deule at Warneton by the evening of 27 May. The Messines Ridge was now threatened by a pincer movement from the north and south.

Fortunately, Franklyn was not content merely to shore up the line and wait passively to be attacked, but reacted vigorously. He decided to use the two battalions on loan from the 1st Division, the 3rd Grenadier Guards and 2nd North Staffordshires, to attack in the 143rd Brigade's sector with the canal as their objective. If successful it would restore the situation in the most threatened part of the division's line. He was asking much of two battalions that had marched all night, had a further eight miles to march to reach the start line for the attack, and had not eaten all day. As a precursor to this attack, he arranged for the 6th Black Watch with one of its own companies, the 7th and 59th Field Companies RE, plus a few tanks and a dismounted squadron of the 13th/18th Hussars, to attack along the banks of the Lys river up to Comines. These troops actually belonged to the 4th Division and had been sent to the Lys as a flank guard for this division's withdrawal. But Franklyn reasoned that by counter-attacking in the manner desired by him they would be fulfilling that task admirably; if the road north through Warneton fell to the enemy, the 4th Division's withdrawal route would be jeopardized. This preliminary attack was launched at 1900 hours, at which time Franklyn was able to brief the COs of the 3rd Grenadiers (Major Adair) and 2nd North Staffords (Lieutenant Colonel Butterworth) and tell them he wanted them to attack at 2000 hours. He was acutely aware that he was asking them to attack over ground that neither of them had seen and was giving them very little notice to prepare and issue orders to their companies, let alone to co-ordinate their attacks.

The North Staffords crossed their start line at 2012 hours, and the Grenadiers at 2032 hours, pretty good going given the circumstances. The North Staffords, on the left, advanced with two companies up, one each side of the Messines–Kortekeer road. At first they encountered only small groups of Germans, the backwash of earlier infiltration attacks. These were soon disposed of. After a mile or so, they came under heavy mortar and artillery fire, and increasing small-arms fire in the lengthening dusk. By midnight the leading companies had reached the Kortekeer

river, just under a mile from the canal, so Butterworth decided to consolidate and dig in. Both commanders of the leading companies were mortally wounded.

The Grenadiers also advanced two companies up, using the railway line on their right as an aid to maintaining direction. At the start line, the battalion intelligence officer gave the two leading company commanders the axis of the attack. Neither had had time to work out a compass bearing and as Captain Brinckman, commanding the right-hand company, recalled, 'the whole attack was taking place over ground which we had never seen in our lives'. After advancing for about half an hour against patchy resistance and in gathering darkness, they topped a low rise to see a farm building blazing to their right front, and British soldiers charging in with bayonets fixed. It was the Black Watch group rounding off their successful advance well supported by the 13th/18th Hussars' light tanks that had set the building alight with their tracer rounds. Encouraged by this spectacle, the Grenadiers pressed on against stiffening opposition, the darkness lit by bursting shells and mortar bombs, Verey lights arcing up into the sky and tracer rounds. Casualties mounted in the two leading companies, and all the officers, except the company commanders, were killed or wounded. Captain Brinckman was wounded by a shell or mortar-bomb splinter, followed by a round through the right shoulder and another through his left arm. He crawled forward in the darkness, trying to contact the platoon commander of his right forward platoon but could not find him. While lying there puzzling what to do, he saw other Grenadiers advancing near him and heard the voice of No. 1 Company commander. Brinckman hobbled across and told him that they must charge together. On the way back to his own company he was hit again. He shouted 'Charge!' to the men nearest to him, and they got up and followed him. The Germans in front immediately threw up their arms. One surrendered to Brinckman and then shot his runner in the back. Brinckman killed him with his revolver, then snatching up a rifle he bayoneted two more. This did the trick, and enemy fire ceased.

The Grenadiers were now on the canal, their objective. Captain Brinckman noticed a small cottage near by, which appeared to be full of Germans. Taking cover behind a hedge, he saw that with him he had only Sergeant Ryder and two guardsmen, and that of the four of them only one was unwounded. Brinckman sent the unwounded guardsman back to tell the CO that they were on the position but needed more men if they were to hold it. Brinckman then tossed a grenade through the cottage window, which seemed to quieten the enemy inhabitants, at which point a German fired at them point-blank through the hedge. Ryder despatched him. More enemy ran across the canal bridge, and

Brinckman threw another grenade at them. With difficulty he pulled the pin out of a third grenade, but realizing he was getting weaker and his right arm was becoming paralysed so that he would not be able to throw it, he asked Ryder to help, but the sergeant was wounded in the thigh and could not do so either. Brinckmann transferred the grenade to his left hand, still holding down the lever, and everything went quiet. The remaining guardsman was now dead, so telling Ryder that there was no point in staying, Brinckman started crawling back. By now the moon was up. They had gone about fifty yards when a bullet was fired from the cottage, wounding the captain in the leg, followed by another that hit Ryder. Brinckman threw the grenade he had been clutching, his last, underhand towards the flash of the weapon, and dragged himself on to where he thought some of his men might be hiding. But the pain was too bad and he was weak with loss of blood. Everything seemed quiet except for the sound of groaning men. He passed out and came round lying on a bed in the cottage, surrounded by dead Germans, and with a live one standing at the foot of his bed. His sergeant was next door in great pain.

The Grenadiers had found it impossible to hold the Canal Line, and Adair, with the other company commander killed, pulled back a little to the rear. But the efforts of the Grenadiers, the North Staffords and the Black Watch group had knocked the enemy off balance and, with the support of the artillery, positions east of the Saint-Eloi–Warneton road, some three miles east of Wytschaete were firmly held. All the next day, 28 May, the German attacks continued supported by mortars, guns and Stukas. But the British medium guns broke up the attacks, and the British line held. Had this section, Ypres–Comines, caved in under German attacks, the whole of Brooke's shield would have been outflanked and the BEF in all probability cut off.

The 2nd Light Anti-Aircraft Battery, in which Second Lieutenant Mc-Swiney commanded 2 Troop, was allocated to AA duty on the roads leading north towards Dunkirk. Each troop was to take up position at key points along these routes, and wait until the main bodies of Allied units had gone through. Nothing was said about how long they were to wait before moving themselves – the timing was left to troop commanders. The battery moved with gun layers (aimers) in the seats of the Bofors guns as they were being towed along, and opened up while still on the move at any aircraft attempting to attack. This tactic worked because usually enemy aircraft sheered off when fired on by the Bofors, and went off to look for easier meat. McSwiney's troop managed to bring down a Messerschmitt 110 on 27 May, and the lieutenant was feeling pleased at this coup when he was called to a battery conference in the vicinity of

Poperinghe. He got trapped in an air raid on the town, which lasted for the best part of two hours. About 80 per cent of the vehicles caught in the ensuing vast traffic jam were destroyed or temporarily immobilized. It was the worst experience of bombing and strafing he had experienced, and he arrived at battery headquarters seven hours late. Having been allocated new tasks he had to retrace his steps to collect his troop. Had there been a system of wireless communications from battery to troop, the task would have been simple, but it took him the rest of the night to work his way back against the stream of retreating vehicles, tanks and guns. Eventually outside Poperinghe the road suddenly became clear, and remained so for the last four miles. He imagined himself running into the advancing Germans at any moment. The troop sergeant-major had given up hope of seeing him again after an absence of about eighteen hours with no news. They got the troop on the road in double-quick time and made their way to their next position using side roads wherever possible. At one point they came across a French truck parked right in the centre of the road. The driver was asleep, and was so annoyed at being woken that he refused to budge. McSwiney drew his revolver and told him he would have no alternative but to shoot him unless he removed his vehicle forthwith. Neither the Belgians nor the French had any road discipline, but later when McSwiney's troop ran into a mêlée of prancing Belgian horses trying to drag some ancient howitzers out of a ditch, the situation proved more difficult to deal with.

By the early morning of 28 May, Brooke had completed the first of his major steps sideways, by pulling out formations south of the River Lys and extending beyond Ypres northwards along the Yser Canal to Noordschote. This involved the 3rd Division leaving its positions south of the Lys and coming in on the left of the 50th. This was the move in which Lieutenant Robin Dunn had carried out the preliminaries when he moved his troop north and discovered that the enemy were in Saint-Eloi. The 2nd DLM came into reserve to the left rear of the 3rd Division, and the 12th Lancers, now under Montgomery's command, covered the eighteen-mile gap to the left of the 3rd Division, opened by the Belgian retreat to the north-west. This all sounds so simple. In reality it was difficult, and fraught with potentially dangerous consequences. In essence the 3rd Division had to break contact with the enemy in such a way that they did not immediately follow up, motor in darkness to the east of Armentières, cross the Deule and Lys rivers, then drive twenty miles on minor roads, in front of the British gun positions, and a mere 4,000 yards behind where the 50th Division was engaged with the enemy, to occupy unprepared positions in full view of the enemy in daylight along the Yser Canal.

Fortunately Montgomery had spent the months of the Phoney War training his division for night moves in transport, including fitting his vehicles with shaded tail lights that shone forward on to rear axles painted white. When Brooke visited him the evening before he found him full of confidence and treating the whole affair as if it was a 'glorious picnic'. The manoeuvre unfolded like clockwork. Montgomery decided to disable and abandon the medium guns, to reduce the weight of traffic. He sent reconnaissance parties to the new positions, expertly thinned out his positions on the old line, and led the division himself, barging his way through traffic jams. His system of guides, and route-marking drills so painstakingly practised in peace, paid dividends, as did traffic direction by the Royal Military Police, when put to the test in war over a route that consisted mainly of country lanes, in the dark and pouring rain. Brooke described it in his diary:

> There was little possibility of sleep that night, as the 3rd Division was moving past [his HQ] and I repeatedly went out to see how they were progressing. The whole movement seemed so unbearably slow, the hours of darkness were slipping by; should daylight arrive with the road crammed with vehicles the casualties from bombing might well have been disastrous. Our own guns were firing from the vicinity of Mont Kemmel, the German artillery were answering back, and the Division was literally trundling slowly along in the darkness down a pergola of artillery fire, and within 4,000 yards of a battle front which had been fluctuating all day, somewhat to our disadvantage. It was an eerie sight which I shall never forget. Before dawn came, the last vehicles had disappeared northwards into the darkness.[2]

Even so, the 3rd Division arrived at 0700 hours on 28 May to find that the 12th Lancers and 2nd DLM had been fending off enemy attacks for three hours. The Belgians had thrown in the towel while the 3rd Division was still driving through the night. To give them their due, they held out for a day longer than predicted by Brooke, and enabled him to gain the line of the Yser Canal. But from now on the security of the eastern flank of the BEF's withdrawal was completely in the hands of II Corps.

That morning the Germans dropped some leaflets, which caused much amusement, not only among the British troops but also the French of the 2nd DLM, who impressed Lieutenant Dunn by their optimism and sangfroid. The leaflets included a map with the caption:

British soldiers!
Here is your true situation!
You are completely surrounded!
Lay down your arms!

On 27 May, Gort had been warned in a message from Admiral Keyes (Churchill's representative at King Leopold's headquarters) that the Belgians were about to fold. Gort was in his new headquarters at Houtkerque. The German advance had forced the headquarters off the underground cable route, and, without the telephone, communications were restricted to wireless. In 1940, and for a long time afterwards, military wireless sets for anything other than very short-range communications were heavy, vehicle-mounted and often inefficient at night thanks to the troposphere, off which high-frequency waves are bounced, moving closer to the earth during the hours of darkness. They were not secure, so any messages containing information that one did not wish to share with the enemy had to be encrypted before transmission, and decrypted on receipt, adding unwelcome delays before the information was in the hands of those who needed it.

Having no telephone communication with Blanchard, commanding the French First Army Group, Gort went to Dunkirk, to Admiral Abrial's headquarters, in the hope of contacting him, to tie up the next stage of the withdrawal. Here Weygand's representative, General Koeltz, told Gort that the King of the Belgians was surrendering unconditionally at midnight (27/28 May). It was actually to become effective at 0400 hours on 28 May, but as the Germans had been approached on the subject of surrender at 1930 hours on 27 May they had been given plenty of time to exploit the situation and get moves under way to take advantage of Belgian reluctance to continue fighting right up to the last moment.

On return to his headquarters, Gort received a message: 'General Weygand makes a person appeal to General Gort. The British Army must participate strongly in the necessary joint counter-attacks. Situation demands hard hitting.' There were no joint counter-attacks envisaged, nor was there any prospect of any such attacks succeeding even if they had been planned. This message indicated once again how far removed from reality Weygand was. Blanchard arrived at Gort's headquarters at 2300 hours, and Gort read to him Eden's telegram ordering him to move to the coast and evacuate the BEF. Blanchard tried to dissuade him from withdrawing, but Gort was unmoved: the situation on the south-west front (see next chapter) was as dangerous as it was on the Belgian flank. He emphasized how important it was for Blanchard to conform to the BEF's withdrawal. Blanchard was adamant that he would not allow French troops to be evacuated, and seemed to take comfort in doing nothing on the grounds that it was preferable to withdrawal and that honour was thereby satisfied.

The Yser Canal, a sizeable commercial waterway north of Ypres, was a far more substantial obstacle than the Ypres–Comines Canal. Throughout

27 May the defence of the Yser Canal had been the responsibility of the 12th Lancers, later reinforced by a machine-gun company from the 2nd Middlesex, which was 3rd Division's machine-gun battalion and part of the divisional advance party. As the 50th Division starting taking up its positions in Ypres and on each side of the town during the morning of 27 May, enemy probing attacks started. But the German attacks on the Yser Canal and Ypres took longer to develop than those against the 5th Division. The German XI Corps had been drawn northwards following up the Belgians, so was unable to support the German IV Corps to its south. The IV Corps had, therefore, to extend to its right to engage the 50th Division, while also fighting the 5th Division. Only on 28 May, following the Belgian surrender, did the four divisions of XI Corps start attacking the Yser Canal, as well as mounting attacks on both sides of Ypres starting early on that day. The Germans penetrated between the 17th and 150th Brigades north of the Zillebeke Lake. The 11th Brigade had just arrived and was not in a position to counter-attack. The 150th Brigade attacked with an adhoc force of motorcycle infantry from the 4th Royal Northumberland Fusiliers, and with sappers, gunners and lancers fighting as infantry. The 8th DLI was put in to beef up the counter-attack, but contact with the 17th Brigade was still not restored. The 150th Brigade refused (that is, turned) its right flank along the line of the Dickebusch road joining up with the 10th Brigade east of Wytschaete,[3] although the left of the 17th Brigade was open and it fought hard to avoid being encircled and cut off. As the German XI Corps came into the battle, the attacks on the front of the 151st Brigade intensified. Enemy attempts to cross the Yser Canal in rubber boats and by pontoon bridge were thwarted. In the afternoon, the Germans succeeded in establishing a small toehold on the western bank, but were wiped out by the Vickers guns of the 2nd Middlesex and tanks of 2nd DLM. The fighting north of Ypres never reached the intensity it did on the Ypres–Comines Line, mainly because the latter was not much of an obstacle.

Brooke visited Montgomery on 28 May to confirm the orders for operations on the night of the 28th/29th May. The 3rd and 50th Divisions were to swing like a gate with the hinge at Lizerne on the Yser Canal back to Poperinghe. This would be the second layback position through which the 4th and 5th Divisions would withdraw to form the third layback position on the Yser river. Back at corps headquarters Brooke was greeted by reports from the 12th Lancers that the collapse of the Belgians had allowed the Germans to threaten Nieuport, the anchor point of the eastern end of the planned Dunkirk perimeter. Only light forces held the town and the bridges were not prepared for demolition. Soon afterwards, the 12th Lancers reported that the Germans were

appearing in strength at Dixmude on the River Yser, Brooke's intended eastern anchor point for his third layback position. The imminent prospect of a Belgian collapse had persuaded Gort to withdraw to Dunkirk. Now his plans looked like being brought to naught by the surrender of the Belgian Army at 0400 hours on 28 May, and the swift moves by the Germans in anticipation of this event.

The 12th Lancers had been screening the eighteen-mile gap between the BEF and the Belgians, and destroying all the bridges over the River Yser north of Noordschote, selected by Brooke as the obstacle to protect his left flank. Before the main bridge at Dixmude could be demolished, a patrol of the 12th Lancers consisting of two armoured cars commanded by Second Lieutenant Mann saw a German staff car with a white flag and four German officers race across and drive up the road to Nieuport. Another Lancer patrol reported seeing an officer in the car engaged in an excited conversation with some French and Belgian officers. The car returned to Dixmude and was shot up by Mann's patrol, but it escaped. A French major came up to Mann and said that he was taking over the bridge garrison and ordered him to withdraw. When the rest of his patrol joined Mann, the French major disappeared. At this point, Lieutenant Smith of the Monmouthshire Engineers arrived, having demolished some minor bridges and barges. He discovered that the main bridge had been prepared for demolition by a party of Belgian sappers. Smith persuaded the Belgians at pistol-point to explain how the charges were set up, and blew the bridge. Ten minutes later a column of German motorcyclists roared up and skidded to a halt by the shattered bridge. Behind them appeared trucks carrying at least 250 soldiers, and several towed artillery pieces. The Lancers hosed them with machine-gun fire, driving them back to take cover among the houses. For the rest of the day, Mann frustrated all German attempts to cross the Yser, reinforced by another two armoured cars – which was all that could be spared from the thinly held 12th Lancer patrol line. His gallant efforts were recognized by the award of the DSO.

Montgomery, when apprised of the situation, sent the 59th Field Company Royal Engineers to augment the defences of Dixmude, but refused to commit his reserve brigade. He ordered the 2nd DLM to screen the Loo Canal in preparation for his own withdrawal that night, and this became the water obstacle on II Corps' left flank, in place of the eastern end of the Yser river. Soon after midnight on 29 May, the 50th Division and all but the 8th Brigade of the 3rd Division swung back to form the layback position on the Poperinghe–Lizerne–Noordschote Line. The 150th Brigade withdrew from the Yser Canal, covered by its remaining carriers and a squadron of the 4th/7th Dragoon Guards. The survivors of

the 4th/7th Dragoon Guards, enough for one squadron (henceforth called the Combined Squadron), had been formed into a composite regiment with the 5th Inniskillings. The 150th Brigade was digging in east of Poperinghe by 0800 hours. The 151st Brigade, having withdrawn from the Yser Canal at 0400 hours, came in on the left of the 150th. The line from east of Poperinghe to Proven was supposed to have been the responsibility of I Corps, but was left unoccupied. So Brooke ordered the flank held by machine-gunners of the 4th Royal Northumberland Fusiliers and the 13th/18th Royal Hussars.

During the night of 28/29 May, beginning at last light, the 5th Division, the 143rd Brigade and the 10th and 11th Brigades of the 4th Division broke contact on the Ypres–Comines Line. They destroyed their heavy and medium artillery, the ammunition on the gun position being exhausted, and pulled back through the Poperinghe–Lizerne–Noordschote layback line. The 4th Division got back mostly unscathed. But the 5th Division had a much harder time disengaging. During the 28th the Germans had enveloped the left flank of the 17th Brigade, and cut off its battalions one by one. The 2nd Royal Scots Fusiliers were encircled; the CO, Lieutenant Colonel Tod, and his remaining three officers and around forty men surrendered at about 1100 hours on 28 May. Only part of one company of the 2nd Northamptons got clear, the rest, including battalion headquarters, being overrun after fighting for four hours. A small group of the 6th Seaforths escaped capture thanks to a counter-attack by carriers of the 2nd Duke of Cornwall's Light Infantry from the 10th Brigade. The 17th Brigade now consisted of 441 all ranks. Also thanks to the 10th Brigade's efforts, the 13th Brigade came away with fewer casualties than the 17th, as did the 143rd. But the overall brigade strengths do not reveal entirely how the battle on the Ypres–Comines Canal, like most battles, had taken its toll on the infantry battalions and rifle companies especially – for example the 3rd Grenadiers were left with nine officers and 270 soldiers, and the 8th Royal Warwicks were down to four officers and fifty-four men. The 4th and 5th Divisions now, as planned by Brooke, headed for the Yser river line.

The journey was far from pleasant. A major choke-point was Poperinghe, on which the main roads in the area converged. The Luftwaffe had been busy as vehicles drove nose to tail. Marching men, mainly from the 1st Division, could bypass the town across country, but the weary drivers, dismounting to take what cover they could each time enemy aircraft came over, had no option but to join the queues of transport. All along the road edges, abandoned vehicles and guns restricted movement. Here and there broken-down ambulances laden with unattended wounded were scattered among other wrecks. The Luftwaffe continued

the attacks on Poperinghe by night, using flares to illuminate the target already lit by blazing fires. Most of the 5th Division was clear of the northern outskirts of the town by first light. Once out of Poperinghe, troops on the road were left untouched by enemy aircraft – the Luftwaffe was too busy bombing Dunkirk to spend much time interdicting the roads.

Now that II Corps line along the Ypres–Comines Line no longer existed, Bock's Army Group B was able to link up with the panzer divisions coming in from the south-west. The story of how these divisions had fared up to this point will be told in the next chapter. When Bock launched an attack in an attempt to outflank the right of the 50th Division at Poperinghe and against the 8th Brigade of 3rd Division, the panzer divisions were reluctant to participate. The first to be hit by Bock was the 8th Brigade of 3rd Division, which was still on the Yser Canal. Its right-hand brigade, the 9th, had swung back on to the new line; the Germans crossed the canal south of Lizerne and hit the right-flank battalion of the 8th Brigade, the 4th Royal Berkshires. The battalion was forced back, losing three company commanders and nearly being over-run in the process. The 1st Suffolks on the left of the brigade were also pushed back, but regained the ground in time to stop German sappers trying to build a pontoon bridge across the canal. By now the 7th Guards Brigade was marching back to Furnes, on the Loo Canal, as the first step in the 3rd Division's withdrawal.

At Nieuport, at 1100 hours on 28 May, an enemy motorcycle column moving unseen with a crowd of refugees had seized an intact bridge. A patrol of the 12th Lancers engaged the column, but, although they were reinforced by two tanks of the 15th/19th Royal Hussars and some hundred gunners fighting as infantry, as well as by four 18-pounders of the 76th Field Regiment, all efforts to regain or destroy the bridge were unsuccessful. The enemy lodgement grew steadily stronger. However, it is an ill wind that blows nobody any good. The Belgian collapse that led to the decision to rest the left flank of the final layback on the Loo Canal meant that the 4th Division, which originally was to hold the eastern section of the Yser, was now free to be sent to bolster the defence of Nieuport.

By 0700 hours on 29 May the 5th Division occupied the shortened Yser Line, where it linked up with the 42nd Division to its right. The Yser Line consisted of a number of positions covering the likely crossing points; there was no time to construct a fully interlocking defensive layout. The 2nd DLM held ground to the west of the Loo Canal. The division had done quite well, but it had lost all its tanks, and according to Brooke, who spoke to its commander, the DLM:

Now consisted of a column of buses and workshops, with a certain number of men with rifles. The whole outfit was more of an encumbrance than anything else, its fighting value was practically nil, whilst its power of blocking roads with its huge vehicles was unlimited.[4]

The DLM did more than block roads. Montgomery's brilliant GSO 1 (de facto chief of staff), Lieutenant Colonel 'Marino' Brown RM, was on his way to II Corps on the night of 28/29 May when he encountered DLM vehicles blocking the road. He got out of his car and, being a man who did not suffer fools gladly, gave the French a tongue-lashing. He was shot dead.

As troops moved north there was less choice of good areas in which to deploy guns and even essential vehicles. The 7th Field Regiment's new position just north of Oostverleteren, which it occupied on 28 May, was the worst the regiment had seen tactically. Open fields and hedge-rows offered little opportunity for camouflage. Lieutenant Dunn's troop wagon lines (the gunners still used this expression to describe the vehicle park), command post and administrative echelon were all crammed into a farmyard. Fortunately the enemy did not take advantage of such a tempt-ing target for aircraft and artillery.

The following day, Lieutenant Dunn's men found a large number of abandoned Belgian rifles and ammunition in the cellar of the farm and, as soldiers will, every man acquired a souvenir. All through the morning an almost continuous stream of traffic passed Dunn's troop heading along the main Ypres–Furnes road towards the coast. At about 0800 hours Poperinghe was comprehensively bombed. Just before mid-day, the enemy shelled Oostverleteren, which was a prime target as it contained headquarters 3rd Division, regimental headquarters of Dunn's regiment and a medium artillery battery. The latter was not deterred from shooting back despite shells falling all around.

During the afternoon, the 7th Field Regiment received orders to move back at 1800 hours to the final bridgehead round Dunkirk. The CRA of the 3rd Division made it clear that this was not simply a 'dive for the sea', but that the division was to cover the embarkation of other divisions, and it might have to fight hard, possibly for several days.

Dunn was deeply impressed by the conduct of the infantry. The artillery had some respite and at least could drive from position to position – unlike the infantry, who more often than not walked. Yet their dogged cheerfulness and courage seemed inexhaustible. There were exceptions, and one of the officers from 7th Field Regiment witnessed a failure of resolve in a battalion they were supporting. The officer con-cerned shared a cellar with the headquarters of one of the infantry

platoons, and the enemy were shelling heavily. Suddenly a man ran down the steps shouting that the anti-tank guns had gone. The platoon commander shouted that they should all go too, and they did. The rot was started by another subaltern who was seen leading his company out of the line without orders. Dunn's only comment: 'Fortunately for him he was killed.'

The 7th Field Regiment moving back to its final position near Coxyde, two miles north of Furnes, witnessed the only case of disorder it encountered in the campaign. Stragglers in torn uniforms shouted for lifts, and soon the vehicles, guns and limbers were overflowing with men. The road presented a chaotic scene, with ditched vehicles lining the sides, shells bursting at most crossroads, and infantry filing down the sides of the road. At one point Dunn passed the 1st Grenadiers, a single line of men on each side of the road, their equipment complete, marching, all in step, back to their final position – a fine sight. As he approached Furnes, the number of abandoned vehicles increased, and progress slowed thanks to traffic jams. At Coxyde the regiment found the artillery of the 4th Division firing hard in an attempt to stop a German attack which was in progress along the coast between Nieuport and Nieuport les Bains – the enemy were trying to cut the BEF off from this sector.

Throughout 29 May and the morning of the next day, II Corps trudged or drove into the Dunkirk perimeter. The loss of roads east of the Loo Canal, and French horse-drawn artillery and trucks crossing the roads funnelling into the perimeter to reach their sector west of Dunkirk, created huge traffic jams. The 2nd DLM's commander felt the rough edge of Brooke's tongue via Blanchard's liaison officer. When Brooke learned that Blanchard had ordered the DLM to withdraw to La Panne and embark, Brooke informed the liaison officer that if he did so he would uncover II Corps' left flank and add to the chaotic traffic jams. 'Told Liaison Officer that if the General [commanding DLM] disobeyed my order I would have him shot.'[5]

The military police ruthlessly ordered all non-essential vehicles to be driven off the roads before they entered the perimeter, and immobilized or destroyed. Anti-tank guns, 25-pounders, machine-gun and Bren-gun carriers, ambulances, water bowsers, bridging equipment, wireless vehicles and some staff cars were admitted. Sergeant Green, a platoon sergeant in the 2nd Bedfordshire & Hertfordshires, was marched with the rest of the battalion into a field where, after a meal, they were told to unload their large packs from the company B Echelon transport, take out what they wanted and throw the packs away. Some of the transport was smashed there and then. One of his soldiers came up to Green and said, 'It's going to take fifty years to live the shame of this down. It's a

general scuttle.' The men then loaded into some of the transport and were driven off to the perimeter, where most of the remaining trucks were destroyed.

The 2nd Light Anti-Aircraft Battery was ordered to move to one of the transport-dumping grounds at Killem, south of the Bergues–Furnes Canal which was to form the southern boundary of the Dunkirk perimeter. Apart from guns and tractors, all stores were to be destroyed, and every personal item of kit except what the soldiers were wearing. McSwiney adapted the order to suit himself and kept his air bed, a change of underwear and his mackintosh. Tons of ammunition, stores and equipment and hundreds of vehicles were going up in smoke. It was a depressing spectacle, relieved temporarily as far as the soldiers were concerned by the 'help yourself' sign on the NAAFI food and cigarettes.

The next morning, 29 May, the battery's commander Major du Vallon rode with the guns as far as the Bergues Canal. The French had blocked the bridge which the battery hoped to use. Du Vallon, rather precipitately, and without trying to find another bridge, of which there were certainly some open still, ordered them to destroy the much needed anti-aircraft guns by throwing the barrels and breech blocks into the canal. McSwiney's troop was ordered by du Vallon to form up on the other side of the canal and march away under command of the sergeant major. McSwiney was about to accompany them when du Vallon called him back and pointed to a considerable number of wounded men abandoned in RAMC ambulances. McSwiney was told to have these casualties carried on stretchers over the canal. Volunteers for this task were hard to come by, but in the end by persuasion and coercion twelve men managed to complete the job in an hour and a half. The wounded having been taken charge of by RAMC personnel on the other side, and the rest of the battery having gone ahead, du Vallon and McSwiney marched the 'volunteers' the ten miles to La Panne. Du Vallon then left the party to seek orders. Meanwhile the beachmaster added to McSwiney's party another fifty waifs and strays who were without an officer. So McSwiney found himself responsible for a motley crew of men, who belonged to such a wide variety of units that according to him no embarkation officer 'would look at them'.

The 1st East Surreys of the 4th Division managed to evade the order to destroy all transport, which turned out to be fortunate because on 29 May the battalion was rushed forward to take up a temporary position on the Furnes–Ypres Loo Canal. This was in response to the threat posed by German formations approaching the gap between the left of the 5th Division on the River Yser and Furnes. The 1st East Surreys carried out

this move just in time, using their own transport and some lent by their brigade. The fighting at Furnes amounted only to a skirmish, and a patrol sent across the canal by B Company accounted for a German sniper. It was here that a tired senior officer of the 1st East Surreys was heard to remark that he would give anything for a bottle of champagne. One was produced. On the Escaut, a Belgian had given the carrier platoon some cases of champagne rather than let them fall into the hands of the enemy – at least that was the carrier platoon version. From the Furnes position, the 1st East Surreys moved to the coast and took up a position of all-round defence in the sand dunes. Along with other units, the East Surreys had already sent all who could be spared for evacuation. These mainly consisted of B Echelon[6] personnel, cooks, clerks, storemen, drivers without vehicles, and of course the wounded. By now the battalion consisted of a small headquarters and four rifle companies, the strongest of which could muster about seventy men.

Now that the Germans held Dixmude, the 4th Division was forced to march to Nieuport via Furnes. The division's passage, held up by the scrum of refugees and all manner of units and other impedimenta on the roads, was not completed – with all three of its brigades able to take over the defence of this key point in the perimeter – until early on 30 May.

The Germans did not bother to mount a co-ordinated assault on the Yser Line, but followed up the withdrawal snapping at the heels of the retiring brigades. The rearguards were subjected to mortar and artillery fire, while main bodies on the roads were strafed by the Luftwaffe, as well as being shelled. But by noon on 30 May the formations of II Corps were manning their positions within the Dunkirk perimeter. Although, as will be related, formations on the other side of the BEF sack had fought hard and their contribution to the BEF's survival was important, II Corps' performance had been truly remarkable. The Corps had fought a continuous and sometimes fluid withdrawal battle against superior forces for five days, in the process covering a distance of over forty miles. Its tenacious defence and skilful night moves had kept it inside Bock's OODA loop at all times, a refreshing change in this campaign, and one of only a few examples of the Allies being 'quicker on the draw' tactically speaking than their opponents.

On 29 May, Gort told Brooke that he was to hand over II Corps and 'proceed home so as to be available for the task of re-forming new armies'.[7] Brooke protested, but Gort told him it was an order that had to be obeyed. He did however allow Brooke to remain until 30 May to see his corps into the perimeter. That day, Brooke went round his divisions and found:

3rd Div at 13,000 strong

4th Div at 12,000 strong

very satisfactory considering what we had been through.

> 5th Div, only 2 brigades, 17th and 13th, both very weak, about 600 per brigade, 50th Div a little stronger with 2 brigades about 1200 each.

There is no doubt that the 5th Div in its fight on the Ypres–Comines Canal saved the II Corps and the BEF.

I can hardly believe that I have succeeded in pulling the 4 [four] divisions out of the mess we were in, with allies giving way on all flanks. Now remains the task of embarking which will be a difficult one.[8]

Before leaving his corps, Brooke arranged that Montgomery should take it over, while Anderson commanding the 11th Infantry Brigade took over the 3rd Division, and Horrocks moved up to command the 11th Brigade. Before we look at how the embarkation went, we must turn our attention to the fighting on the other flank of the BEF.

8

THE WITHDRAWAL: FIGHTING THE PANZERS
ON THE WESTERN FLANK

To tell the story of the fighting on the western flank, we must return to 25 May, and Gort's order (see Chapter 5) assigning the defence of the Canal Line to the 2nd, 44th and 46th Divisions. The 48th Division, originally deployed in that area, was ordered to Dunkirk, leaving one brigade behind. However, on arrival at Dunkirk, the French general in command of the local defences told Major General Thorne, the GOC 48th Division, that there were sufficient French troops in the port and its immediate surroundings to protect it.

So Thorne deployed his 144th Brigade between Cassel and Bergues, and especially in Wormhoudt, shown on a captured German map as an objective; and his 145th Brigade at Cassel and Hazebrouck (his 143rd Brigade was deployed on the east side of the BEF salient, under Brooke's command). To cover the eighteen miles of front, the 48th Division deployed in a string of strongpoints from Bergues–Wormhoudt–Cassel–Hazebrouck, with two brigades and Usherforce along the Aa Canal. The latter consisted of the 6th Green Howards holding Gravelines and two bridges on the Aa Canal to the south, the 1st Super-Heavy Battery at Saint-Pierre-Brouck, the 3rd Super-Heavy Battery at Watten, and the 52nd Heavy Regiment at Saint-Momelin. The force took its name from Colonel Usher, left behind to command the lines-of-communication sub-area when the BEF advanced into Belgium. He had spent most of the First World War in a German prison camp, and was determined to save as many British soldiers as possible from the same experience this time round. The French held the Canal Line from Gravelines to opposite Saint-Omer.

The 44th Division moved up on Thorne's left into the area of the Nieppe Forest, occupying a sector exclusive of both Hazebrouck on its right and Merville on its left. The division occupied the Nieppe Forest with the 132nd Royal West Kent Brigade (2nd Royal Sussex on loan from the 133rd Brigade, 1st, 4th and 5th Royal West Kents). The division's right flank, held by the 133rd Royal Sussex Brigade (4th and 5th Royal

Sussex), curved in a hook towards Hazebrouck. The 131st Brigade (5th and 6th Queen's, and 2nd Buffs) occupied the centre of the division's sector.

The 46th Division, less 137th and 138th Brigades, was deployed around Carvin, with its right flank on the Deule Canal, and the French First Army on its left. French armoured cavalry covered the four-mile gap between the Deule Canal and the British 2nd Division, whose left flank rested on La Bassée.

Lieutenant General Sir Ronald Adam, commander of III Corps, had been sent to organize the Dunkirk perimeter and the evacuation of the BEF, and his corps was taken over by Major General Wason, who until then had been the Major General Royal Artillery at Gort's headquarters. The Canal Line defence had originally been assigned to Major General Eastwood, while Adam with III Corps headquarters was busy preparing for the counter-attack under the Weygand Plan. Now that the plan was dead, III Corps headquarters, under Wason, was available to command the formations on the Canal Line and assumed this duty.

The next day, 26 May, found the German panzer and other divisions of Army Group A still strung out along the Canal Line from Douai north-west to Gravelines on the coast, in response to the 'Halt Order' on 24 May. As the order applied only to panzer divisions, the infantry had pressed on and in some places they had crossed the canals and held shallow bridgeheads on the eastern banks – notably the SS Verfügungs Division across the Aire Canal opposite Merville, and 12th and 32nd Infantry opposite Carvin. Before the 'Halt Order' came into effect on 23 and 24 May, the British 2nd Division's sector had come under a series of attacks and, although in places the Germans had pulled back, all three brigades in the division had already taken casualties and were tired before the German armour started moving forward again in a concerted attack all along the Canal Line.

The other two British divisions on the Canal Line, the 44th and 48th, were granted two days' respite from attack, 24 and 25 May, to prepare their positions. The 'Halt Order' was rescinded on the evening of 26 May, and by the evening of the next day the panzer, motorized and infantry divisions were across the Canal Line and pushing east to squeeze the BEF and First French Army against Army Group B advancing from the east. The Germans pushed back the advanced companies of the 48th Division and Usherforce. French troops in the Clairmarais Forest reported being overrun by tanks. Spearheads of the 1st and 8th Panzer and 29th Motorized Divisions crossed the Aa Canal, with 6th and 8th Panzer Divisions echeloned in behind them, and with just a screen of French troops opposing them.

By the evening of 26 May, Major General Osborne, GOC 44th Division, was reporting frequent dive-bombing attacks in his divisional sector at Merville, the Nieppe Forest, Estaires and Armentières. During the night the BGS (chief of staff) of III Corps arrived at Osborne's headquarters, and told him several things. First, the BEF would withdraw to Dunkirk, although Osborne was not informed of the timings for this move. Second, the 2nd and 44th Divisions were to continue to act as flank guard to the French First Army, which held the sides of a sack about twelve miles wide and over twenty miles long, stretching from the right flank of the BEF's II Corps facing east, to Maulde and Raches facing south-east and south, and right round to La Bassée facing south-west. Eventually it was intended that the two British divisions were to withdraw using routes west of and inclusive of Armentières and Poperinghe. Third, Osborne should keep in touch with the French Cavalry Corps, which would be on his right. Fourth, Lieutenant General Adam had been placed in charge of the Dunkirk defences, and Wason, the new III Corps commander, would visit him the next day, 27 May. Finally, if possible, Osborne was to 'make some advance on to the plain between Cassel and Hazebrouck to help keep back the German mechanized advance'. Much of what Osborne had been told about co-operating with the French made operational sense, but only if they responded in a way that enabled him to provide the necessary co-operation – a big 'if'. The vague instruction to advance on to the plain between Cassel and Hazebrouck with what elements could be spared from his defensive tasks (at most a couple of infantry battalions on their feet, and probably without armoured support) to head off two panzer and two motorized divisions was meaningless. Being told to advance on a place without specific objectives is open to a variety of interpretations, not least how far to advance and for how long. The instruction indicated a lack of grip at III Corps headquarters.

The British 2nd Division, holding some twenty miles of the La Bassée Canal, had been stripped of most of its anti-tank guns for the defence of Dunkirk. It came under attack by three panzer divisions (3rd, 4th and SS Totenkopf), as well as part of 5th Panzer and the right-hand formation of SS Verfügungs. The first assault by the SS Totenkopf and 4th Panzer ran into the 4th Brigade in the centre of 22nd Division's line, but spread to the 6th Brigade, on the 4th Brigade's right. Because the Germans had held a bridgehead at Robecq since 24 May, they were able to rush tanks across without any preliminary bridging operations. The 6th Brigade was deployed with the 2nd DLI in the centre, with 1st Royal Welch Fusiliers to their left and 1st Royal Berkshires on the right. The tanks attacked them first at around 0800 hours, preceded by artillery fire that was well directed on the few anti-tank guns the brigade had left. In the open

country there was little cover, and soon every anti-tank gun was out of action. The tanks emerged as the artillery lifted, and turned their machine guns on defended positions, shooting in their own infantry: that is, the tanks engaging the defenders, while the German infantry closed in. Within three hours the 1st Royal Welch had lost their two forward companies, and the 2nd DLI were within a whisker of being cut off. Too late, Brigadier Furlong ordered the two battalions to fall back to the Lys Canal, about a mile in rear, covered by the Royal Welch. Unfortunately by now the German armour could flay the DLI every time they rose from their slit trenches, and shoot up the battalion headquarters in a barn. Only the right-hand company of the DLI got away. Their battalion headquarters was overrun, despite a last-ditch defence with Brens, rifles and even the CO engaging the enemy with his revolver.

A few of the Royal Welch got back over the Lys Canal to some cottages that afforded a modicum of cover. The CO, Lieutenant Colonel Harrison, was last over the pontoon bridge, carrying a wounded officer. He shouted that the bridge should be blown, but there was no one to carry out the order. A German tank approached and lurched over this bridge – which had been erected by the British. The Germans had demolished the main bridge two days earlier after withdrawing from a foray across the canal. The pontoon bridge, designed to carry only a 15-hundredweight truck, should have collapsed under the tank but unfortunately held together. Harrison was killed trying to stop the tank.

The 1st Royal Berkshires were beset on both flanks – by tanks on their left and infantry of the SS Verfügungs on their right. The Berkshire's reserve company mounted a counter-attack that allowed the battalion to keep open a withdrawal route across a little bridge, over which they fell back when ordered. The Berkshires, supported by their three remaining carriers, one anti-tank gun and some 18-pounders of the 99th Field Regiment, held Haverskerque, while the remnants of the Royal Welch and DLI took cover in the Forest of Nieppe. But the brigade transport never made it, being destroyed in the mayhem. As the Berkshires headed for the forest, two Panzer Mk IVs started to follow up, harassing them but inflicting few casualties, and were not inclined to pursue them into the forest. They may have been deterred by the prospect of fighting in the thick stuff, and some light tanks of the 4th/7th Dragoon Guards lurking in the forest possibly provided an added disincentive to a follow-up.

Along with the 6th Brigade, the 4th had already taken heavy casualties by dawn on 27 May. The 2nd Royal Norfolks had amalgamated their two right-hand companies into one sixty strong. This represented a total loss of around 180 men from these two companies alone, the equivalent of

the loss of a rifle company and a half – a severe drain on the fighting strength of the battalion. The 1st Royal Scots suffered casualties mounting a successful counter-attack. The 1st/8th Lancashire Fusiliers opposite Béthune were overlooked by Germans established in slag heaps and buildings. At 0330 hours on 27 May, a series of heavy artillery concentrations fell on the 4th Brigade positions, followed by an attack on both flanks. Brigadier Warren found himself unable to do much to relieve the situation. He withdrew his headquarters to Lestrem, leaving a platoon of Lancashire Fusiliers and a machine-gun platoon of the 2nd Manchesters at Epinette to impose a delay on the enemy. These were the only fighting sub-units of the 4th Brigade that got away.

The enemy attacks on Merville intensified. The village was held by the 6th King's Own, a pioneer battalion mainly of older reservists, and although attacked on three sides it held out all day. In the course of the day, a company of machine-gunners from the 6th Argylls had rushed to reinforce the King's Own and been cut to pieces in an ambush.

Major General Irwin, the GOC of 2nd Division, was forced by these German gains to commit his reserve, the 25th Brigade (originally of the 50th Division). He sent the 2nd Essex and some guns to the north of Merville. The 1st Royal Irish Fusiliers with machine-gunners of the 2nd Manchesters, and supported by the 5th Inniskilling Dragoon Guards, were posted out as a flank guard facing west. The light tanks of the Inniskillings notched up a success when they caught some German tank crews who had dismounted for a quick smoke and, charging in, sent them flying. The third battalion of the 25th Brigade, the 1st/7th Queen's Royal Regiment, was warned for a counter-attack towards La Bassée, and so Irwin had nothing to spare to save the 4th Brigade from destruction by the 4th Panzer and SS Totenkopf divisions.

As early as 0750 hours the CO of the 1st/8th Lancashire Fusiliers reported that he was cut off from all but one of his rifle companies. At about 1430 hours, he sent a message to brigade headquarters saying that they were now surrounded, the building was on fire and they were holding on. Brigadier Warren despatched an officer with orders for the battalion to withdraw after dark, but he was never seen again, and nothing more was heard from the Lancashire Fusiliers.

The 2nd Royal Norfolks went down fighting, resisting until 1640 hours. As the German armour started to overwhelm what was left of the rifle companies, the headquarters signallers were sent out to defend the perimeter of Druries Farm, where battalion headquarters was sited, on the outskirts of Le Paradis village. Here the adjutant, Captain Lang, ordered Private Brown, who was manning the telephone switchboard, to hand over this duty to the wireless operator on the brigade net and go

to keep watch for the enemy. With a Regimental Police lance-corporal, he kept lookout from one of the farm buildings and spotted a German motorcycle combination with a machine gun mounted on it coming in behind the headquarters. He and the lance-corporal opened fire and stopped the motorcyclist, but it was obvious that the enemy were surrounding them. Brown and his companion dashed back to battalion headquarters and told them the bad news, before diving into a small brick outhouse, which they converted into a little strongpoint by bashing holes in the brick walls to fire through. Others had done the same in the remaining outhouses, to provide all-round defence of the farm.

By the afternoon, all except battalion headquarters had been overrun. The acting CO, Major Ryder, went round saying that there was no chance of getting away and, with ammunition running low, canvassed opinion on whether they should surrender. To begin with everybody was for fighting on, which they did for a while. But soon Ryder said that with ammunition almost exhausted they would have to cease firing. Anyone who wished to do so could attempt to get away to save himself. The men in the stables and outbuildings tried going out through the stable door to the field outside, but were fired on and turned back. After a short while they went out again, this time with a white towel on a rifle, and were allowed out to surrender.

These men, and a few others captured near by, were marched away from Druries Farm by No. 3 Company of the 1st Battalion, 2nd SS Totenkopf Rifle Regiment, under the command of Hauptsturmführer (Captain) Fritz Knoechlein. Their subsequent behaviour towards men who had fought well was a foretaste of what SS troops would do for the rest of the war; they even adapted a slang expression for it, a *Rabatz*, meaning to have fun killing everyone in sight.

About a hundred of the Royal Norfolks were marched off the road into a meadow beside some farm buildings. Private Pooley, a signaller with A Company, saw two machine guns inside the meadow, pointing towards the head of the column. He 'felt as though an icy hand gripped his stomach' as the guns began to fire. For a few seconds the cries and screams of stricken men drowned the chatter of the guns. Men fell like grass before a scythe, and then the stream of bullets hit Pooley. 'I felt a searing pain in my left leg and wrist and pitched forward. My scream of pain mingled with the cries of my mates, but as I fell into the heap of dead and dying men, the thought flashed through my brain, "If I ever get out of here, the swine who did this will pay for it."'

Ninety-seven men were cut down. As the SS soldiers moved among the sprawling bodies they shot or bayoneted anyone who seemed to be breathing. Pooley was shot twice more in the same leg, but by a supreme

act of will he kept still until the SS men left. One other man survived the massacre, Private O'Callaghan, who had lain with a shattered arm under a pile of his friends. O'Callaghan pulled Pooley out from under the dead bodies and they dragged themselves away to the safety of a farm where a farmer's wife tended their wounds. After recapture by ordinary German soldiers, Pooley was eventually repatriated because he was so severely wounded. No one would accept his story until he returned to Le Paradis after the war and found the farmer's wife. She supported his story, and this time he was believed. Both Pooley and O'Callaghan were prosecution witnesses at Knoechlein's trial at the British Military Court at Hamburg in October 1948. The former Hauptsturmführer was found guilty and hanged. Pooley had kept his promise.

Other soldiers also escaped, including Private Brown and two other privates, Hagen and Leven. When they saw the others surrender, they crept away in the opposite direction to a neighbouring ditch under cover of smoke from one of the burning outbuildings. Here they discovered the adjutant of the Norfolks, who was wounded, and the MO. But before they could put any distance between themselves and the farm buildings, they were discovered by the Germans. These were also SS, but, according to Brown, after knocking them about a bit, let them keep their wallets and otherwise treated them correctly.

There was no excuse for what the SS had done. It is true that the moment of surrender is often fraught with danger for both sides. The victor may be uncertain that the vanquished is genuine about surrendering, and the vanquished unsure that his surrender will be accepted. Leaving the moment of capitulation too late, for example to the moment when the attacker is on the lip of the trench or position, may end in the assailant taking one more pace and killing the soldier who has belatedly put his hands up. The attacker simply cannot afford to take the chance; it could be him or his adversary. Nine times out of ten a soldier who leaves it too late, especially if firing his weapon up to the last minute, ends up with a bayonet or bullet in his gizzard, or a grenade in his trench. This was not the case at Le Paradis; the killing was done in cold blood.

Of the 2nd Royal Norfolks, only the cooks, drivers and other specialists of B Echeleon survived. Under the quartermaster they headed north and joined the mass of refugees making in the direction of Dunkirk.

The 1st Royal Scots, on the right of the Norfolks, fought on with the same intensity, and inflicted severe delays on the enemy. They might have been treated likewise by the SS, but for a German staff officer passing in his car, who saw the survivors of one of their companies being lined up to be shot and ordered them to be released. Some of the

battalion gathered to make their final stand around battalion head-quarters at a farm in the vicinity of Le Paradis. The command of the battalion had devolved on to Major Watson. He had, unknown to himself, been awarded the Military Cross for his service on the Escaut position and a DSO for leading a counter-attack on 24 May. He did not live to receive them in person, being killed within minutes of taking command. With the farm on fire, the remnants of the battalion managed to withdraw, covered by the officers'-mess corporal wielding a Bren to good effect. They were rounded up a couple of days later.

The 5th Brigade held a long front, about seven miles, from Gorre on the right to La Bassée on the left of the sector. The brigade defensive layout was right 2nd Dorsets, centre 7th Worcestershires, and left 1st Cameron Highlanders astride the ruins of La Bassée. The 1st DLM had some of their tanks deployed in the 5th Brigade's area. Their opponent here was Rommel with his 7th Panzer Division, who started his attack on the evening of 26 May, overrunning one of the Worcestershires' companies. A counter-attack by the Cameron Highlanders failed to dislodge the enemy, and at dawn a further attack enlarged the bridgehead and overran another Worcestershire company. The counter-attack by one company of Camerons, accompanied by six French tanks, drove the enemy away from about 300 yards of their bridgehead on the canal bank. This counter-attack momentarily put the wind up Rommel, who may have mistaken the tanks, probably Somuas, for British heavy tanks, which had caused him so much angst at Arras. But he brought down a substantial artillery concentration on them, forcing them and the Cameron company to withdraw. Only six men of this company were left unwounded when they returned to their battalion.

Rommel pushed his armour into the bridgehead with the energy which was to become familiar to many British soldiers in the desert a year or so hence. With German air support, spotting aircraft and observation posts on the slag heaps, British artillery trying to bring down fire on the enemy lodgement received short shrift. His position fast becoming untenable, Brigadier Gartlan issued a warning order for a withdrawal, to be preceded by a 'stopping' blow by the 1st/7th Queen's of the 25th Brigade, and the 1st Army Tank Brigade who were expected to arrive at any moment. This time it was the Germans who got inside the British OODA loop, which sadly was often the case. At 1425 hours Rommel sent in his tanks and infantry in three groups, carving up the Camerons' position. By 1515 hours the enemy armour was almost at the battalion headquarters at Violaines, when the codeword for immediate withdrawal was received by wireless. Private Ross roared off on his motorbike to deliver the message to the companies. He managed to get through, but

all the company commanders decided to lie low and wait for the battle to die down. This was a big mistake, as in the event only one platoon got clear. The remainder of the battalion at Violaines had better fortune thanks to the carrier platoon, and the anti-tank platoon, which claimed twenty-one tanks knocked out – probably an exaggeration, but there is no doubt that it did good work enabling some men to get back. A few Worcestershires, including their headquarters, also made it out of the cauldron.

At this critical moment, the 1st Army Tank Brigade arrived, a much reduced formation after the Arras battle. All it could muster was two Mk IIs, and eight Mk Is of a composite 4th and 7th RTR. The 1st/7th Queen's were no longer available as the complete 25th Brigade was now needed for other tasks. But the ten tanks set off to try to relieve the Cameron Highlanders. Two returned.

The entire length of the 2nd Division front was overhung with clouds of smoke, stabbed by the occasional German signal flare proclaiming objectives successfully achieved. As dusk fell, Irwin sent out staff officers to muster what was left of his 4th and 5th Brigades. They found fifty of the former and twenty of the latter.

There were still pockets of the 2nd Division holding out, of which the most substantial was at Festubert, held by the 2nd Dorsets. Here they had been on the edges of attacks by two panzer divisions (7th and 4th) that had brushed past their right rear and left. They had discouraged direct attack by the German armour using their Boyes rifles and a few 25mm guns. An infantry attack was also seen off. After dark, the CO, Lieutenant Colonel Stephenson, with a gunman on either side, set off on a compass bearing, leading some 250 Dorsets and an assortment of Lancashire Fusiliers, Worcesters and Argylls. It was seven miles to the Lys Canal as the crow flies, and Stephenson kept to the fields as best he could, avoiding German soldiers and blazing farms, and expertly navigating through the maze of lanes, dykes and hamlets. He met a German NCO, whom he despatched with his revolver. The column had to lie up for what seemed like eternity while a long convoy of trucks with lights on crossed his route. Coming to a wide canal, he got his men over, except for a few who drowned. Perversely, his route took him to this waterway again as it bent round in a curve. After crossing it, Germans were encountered again, this time a patrol, which went on its way without spotting the long column of weary soldiers. At 0500 hours they crossed the bridge at Estaires, which French engineers were about to blow. The British had all gone ahead, and were now followed by the Dorsets, exhausted but triumphant, and, thanks to their CO, at 250 strong the biggest battalion left in the 2nd Division.

The question has to be asked why the 2nd Division did not withdraw to the Lys Canal earlier and in good order, as all the brigade commanders in the division had asked of Major General Irwin. There are a number of possible reasons, among them the fact that Wason, the new commander of III Corps, spent two days after he took over from Adam trying to co-ordinate plans for the withdrawal ordered by Gort with the French commander on his left, General René Altmayer, commanding the French V Corps. Thanks to breakdowns in communications, frequent moves of headquarters, and traffic congestion on the roads, Wason did not manage to gain contact with his own divisions until they reached the Dunkirk bridgehead shortly before they were evacuated. Thus the formations of III Corps on the western flank of the BEF lacked the firm hand on the helm that Brooke applied in the east. Next, Irwin, recently promoted from command of the 6th Brigade, was unaware of the decisions taken to withdraw to Dunkirk and, without a corps commander to consult, may have felt unable to order a withdrawal off his own bat, surmising that this might uncover the flanks of the divisions on his left and right. Whatever the reason, Irwin did not order a withdrawal on the night of 26/27 May. This was a pity because, had he done so, instead of suffering heavy losses, the 2nd Division would undoubtedly have been in a better position to hold off the Germans – certainly up to the morning of 28 May. But their stout defence of the La Bassée Canal assisted the French III Corps in withdrawing two of its three divisions, and probably saved the British 42nd Division, out on a limb on Brooke's right flank, until the evening of 28 May.

On 27 May the German attacks continued without let-up. Although by that evening the 48th Division strongpoints were still holding, as was the 44th Division, the 2nd Division's battering and withdrawal had left the 44th's left flank dangerously exposed. The 46th Division had by now been ordered back to the Dunkirk perimeter, which increased the danger to the 44th Division. As the crisis built up, a guiding hand from III Corps commander was sorely missed, but he was stuck at General Prioux's French First Army headquarters. Here he found Prioux in a defeatist state of mind, although he did order the 1st and 3rd DLM to co-operate with the British.

Osborne, GOC 44th Division, spent most of 27 May hanging around at his headquarters waiting for Wason, who never turned up. Osborne sent a liaison officer to make contact with the French V Corps as instructed, but he did not return. It transpired that V Corps was now cut off, the French right flank south of the British 2nd Division having given way. During the day various French officers, including the commanders of IV Corps and the Cavalry Corps, and the chief of staff of First Army, turned

up at Osborne's headquarters. They were apparently concerned that he, Osborne, was not aware that he was to hold the flank, the implication being that he was not doing what he had been instructed to do. As the area where the Germans had punched through with three panzer divisions and threatened to cut off large parts of French First Army was well south of Osborne's sector, there was nothing he could do about it – a fact that may have been lost on the French staffs, whose information was usually so out of date as to be useless. The chief of staff of French First Army rudely emphasized that Osborne was under command of First Army, which Osborne acknowledged with mental reservations.

All the while, the 44th Division was under attack but holding, although the 2nd Royal Sussex on the left of the 132nd Brigade were having a tough time. From the time the BGS of III Corps had left the previous night, Osborne had heard nothing from III Corps, except three messages, all of which had been so delayed as to be out of date by the time he received them. He spent some of the day attempting to mount a counter-attack as ordered. Eventually he decided, wisely, that without tank support from the French, which was not available, the operation was not possible. During the afternoon, Major General Irwin's headquarters moved into a field close to Osborne's. Irwin told Osborne that his division was fought out, and the remnants were coming back across the River Lys at Estaires. Osborne and Irwin agreed that the 2nd Division could do no more and should start north the next morning, having handed over rearguard duties to the French. Osborne gave orders that his own headquarters was to move north during the night to a position from where it could more readily control the forthcoming withdrawal.

It rained heavily on the night of 27/28 May, and, thanks to bad going, the German armour got off to a slow start the next morning. The German infantry, not so affected by terrain conditions, attacked the Nieppe Forest and Hazebrouck. The 1st Buckinghamshires (a TA battalion of the Oxfordshire and Buckinghamshire Light Infantry), part of the 145th Brigade of the 48th Division, had already been forced back into the convent at Hazebrouck by attacks the previous day. The first concentration of enemy mortar bombs hit an ammunition truck at about 0630 hours; the ensuing explosions lasted for two hours. Already short of ammunition, the Buckinghamshires were soon down to a few rounds per man as they engaged the attacking infantry that swarmed around the position. By around 1000 hours, unable to make headway against the Buckinghamshires, and after being joined by some tanks, the Germans brought up heavy guns and demolished the upper and middle floors of the convent, setting the building on fire. The remnants of the battalion, about a hundred men under Major Viney, ran out and took cover in an adjacent

building. Eventually, completely surrounded and out of ammunition, they were forced to surrender. The Germans were moved to refer to their gallant resistance in a subsequent wireless broadcast as 'truly worthy of the highest traditions of the British Army'.

The 44th Division was attacked on both flanks: by the 8th Panzer Division in the north and SS Verfügungs and 3rd Panzer in the south. The fighting in the Nieppe Forest was confused and bitter. The 2nd Royal Sussex had the heaviest casualties, with few men left by the end of 28 May; the handful of survivors were cut off and rounded up. The Germans broke in behind battalions and attacked the divisional B Echelon area in rear.

By 28 May half the French First Army were surrounded in a pocket round Lille, where they held out for a further four days. There is no doubt that their stubborn resistance contributed to the BEF's escape to Dunkirk. In recognition of the garrison's gallantry, the Germans allowed them to march out with the full honours of war. But, equally certain, the fall of Lille added to the wave of anti-British sentiment in the French Army. Blanchard bellyached to Weygand that Gort had decamped north with the BEF leaving the French First Army in the lurch. As related in the previous chapter, Gort had almost pleaded with Blanchard to conform to his northwards movement – in vain, as the Frenchman preferred to do nothing.

Major General Osborne, commanding the 44th Division, was conscious that the situation on both flanks of his sector was deteriorating as 28 May wore on. He was, however, unaware of events elsewhere even on the western flank of the BEF, and unquestionably did not have the complete picture. He had received no specific orders about withdrawing, and merely knew he was to act in conjunction with the French. He was told that the French were concerned about the move of his divisional headquarters, but, by going to explain the reason to the commander of the Cavalry Corps, he managed to provide reassurance. He asked for tanks to assist the 133rd Brigade, which was having a punishing time particularly on its right, where German tanks were working round behind it. While Osborne was with the 133rd Brigade, some French tanks appeared and their presence appeared to have the effect of instilling some caution into the Germans because the tempo of their attacks abated – but only for a while, because the French soon withdrew without fighting.

Osborne's return to his headquarters was bedevilled by the increasing chaos in rear of the now disintegrating Canal Line caused by German penetration at several points, as well as French units mixed in with the residue of the British 2nd Division streaming northwards. The journey

was made all the more hazardous by German aircraft machine-gunning the packed roads but not, surprisingly, dive-bombing, which was something to be thankful for. The move of Osborne's headquarters was thrown into disarray when the signals, provost and other sub-units of the divisional organization ran into German armour at the intended new location, Godewaerswelde, five miles south-west of Poperinghe. The provost company was ordered by its commander to head straight for Dunkirk, and most of two field ambulance companies were wiped out.[1] The divisional staff collected at Mont des Cats, some two miles further south, where some remained, while others came to join Osborne who was by now with the 131st Brigade. From here he headed to General Aisne's French IV Corps headquarters, arriving at about 1430 hours, to learn that the Belgians had given up the fight. Aisne said that this meant that the German divisions in the east would close in from Ypres, and that on the next day the French First Army, and by implication the British in the area, would all have to surrender. Osborne disagreed, saying that if led by the Cavalry Corps it was possible to go out to Dunkirk. Aisne concurred, but said that General Prioux and First Army would not hear of it.

Osborne's next visit was to Prioux's First Army headquarters, where he found him in conference with his staff and saying gloomily that there was nothing for it but surrender. Osborne said he preferred to fight, and contended that by doing so it was possible to escape encirclement. One or two of the staff showed by their expressions that they agreed with him. The argument continued for about twenty minutes, and Osborne's French became 'abnormally fluent'. Prioux argued that withdrawal and evacuation was not an operation of war, that it was impossible, and that if anyone got away it would be the British and they would abandon the French. Osborne riposted that a breakout would be acclaimed as a great feat of arms, that as General Adam was organizing the embarkation it would succeed, and that every Frenchman would have the same chance of evacuation as an Englishman. He urged Prioux to send a cipher message to General Blanchard at Dunkirk asking permission to march north. Eventually Prioux grudgingly assented. A 'wishy-washy' signal was drafted, which Prioux signed, shrugging and commenting, 'C'est inutile' (It is useless).

Osborne said he would stay with the Cavalry Corps (while thinking that it might have been better to have reserved freedom of action, but at the same time calculating that his division might not last long without armoured support and Prioux's DLMs would do very nicely). He left saying that he was on his way to 132nd Brigade headquarters, which was

very easy to find, getting Prioux's assurance that he would send Blanchard's answer to him there.

At the 132nd Brigade headquarters, he found Brigadier Steele very hard pressed. In a fit of gloom he and Steele tore up their wives' letters, not wanting them to fall into enemy hands. Osborne told Steele that when he could hold no longer he was to withdraw behind the 1st DLM which held a line in rear, and come into divisional reserve. From the 132nd Brigade Osborne went to the 131st in the centre, where his staff were still located. He knew that by withdrawing Steele's brigade he would be weakening the flank, and thought he had better inform General Aisne of IV Corps. On arrival, Aisne told him that the French had started pulling out, and added that Osborne should see Prioux. Osborne found Prioux at about 2100 hours alone and in a dark room lit by a single candle, and here he learned that Prioux had ordered the two DLMs and II Corps to withdraw via Bailleul and Poperinghe to Dunkirk, but that he himself was remaining with IV Corps to surrender. The withdrawal was to start at 1200 hours the next day, 29 May.

Osborne asked Prioux why he had not told him and what he was expecting him, Osborne, to do since he was in contact with the enemy all along the line in the west. All Prioux could say was 'Go and see General de la Laurencie,' commander of III Corps. Osborne, spotting a copy of Prioux's orders on the table, neither addressed to nor sent to him despite his being 'under command' of First Army, picked it up and took it with him. De la Laurencie brusquely informed him that he was not waiting until noon the next day to withdraw, but was going in an hour, at 2300 hours, through Bailleul, and that he, Osborne, could do what he liked. Osborne, riposting that he considered it the grossest treachery, walked out. One of Osborne's staff extracted details of the routes the French were to follow, and Osborne returned to his division along roads packed with French troops. Just before arriving at 131st Brigade headquarters, which was doubling as divisional headquarters, Osborne met Brigadier Steele at the head of some of his 132nd Brigade. He had heard that the 1st DLM was pulling out and decided to do likewise. Orders for the withdrawal reached most of the battalions at around last light. But withdrawal was easier said than done. On the fringe of the Nieppe Forest which they still held, the 4th Royal West Kents could break contact only by counter-attacking first, which cost them dear. The 2nd Royal Sussex were surrounded and never broke out. The 1st Royal West Kents lost their headquarters and much of their F Echelon transport in a traffic jam at a level crossing.

Despite these losses, Osborne was relieved that at least part of one of

his brigades had got away. At headquarters 131st Brigade, he held what he described as a 'weird conference'. By now it was too late to disengage and get back behind the screen of the French Cavalry Corps. Brigadier Utterson-Kelso wanted to wait until morning and 'form square and die fighting'. Osborne vetoed this suggestion. He ordered the two remaining brigades to disengage and make for Mont des Cats, there being a good chance of reaching the feature before daylight and it was tank proof. If they could stay there for a day, the division could go in small parties to Dunkirk the following night. The CO of the 6th Queen's asked to be allowed to go to Dunkirk direct. He did and Brigadier Utterson-Kelso went with him. They got through, but any body of troops larger than a battalion would not have made it by the direct route.

There was an officer at the conference from the 2nd Buffs, who was sent to the battalion, sited out on a limb on the left of the 131st Brigade, with orders to withdraw. He failed to get through to them, and a warrant officer whom Utterson-Kelso despatched later was also unsuccessful. The 2nd Buffs never received the orders and the battalion, less a couple of detachments, went into the bag the next day.

Osborne sent one of his staff off on a motorcycle to Dunkirk to tell headquarters III Corps what he was about to do. The officer was not seen again. Then, having destroyed some vehicles and as much of their kit as possible, Osborne and what remained of his division trudged north to Les Cats, unhindered by the Germans, who had settled down for the night.

Mont des Cats was dangerously isolated and potentially easy to cut off. The Germans had approached the feature the previous day, and tanks had shelled it but inexplicably retired. Had they seized the feature, they would have sat astride one of the main withdrawal routes to Dunkirk. The Germans also shelled and bombed Cassel on 28 May, but did not attack. Meanwhile the German panzer and motorized divisions were pressing in to the north of Cassel and between the town and Mont des Cats to its south. The 2nd Panzer Division had taken Soex, which stands on a feature overlooking Dunkirk, and Usherforce had been forced back to Bergues (now the headquarters of both Thorne and Usher). Both 2nd Panzer and 20 Motorized Divisions were in a good position to exploit the four-mile gap between Bergues and Wylder opened up by the loss of Soex. Thorne's only recourse was to take troops from Cassel to plug the gap. Accordingly Brigadier Norman of the 1st Reconnaissance Brigade was ordered to bring one of his yeomanry regiments and the 1st Welsh Guards. The East Riding Yeomanry were exhausted by their harrying of the Germans as they bypassed the town, so, led by the Fife & Forfar Yeomanry, the Welsh Guards in trucks motored north-east on minor

roads, the main road having been seized by the Germans. At one point along the narrow road slow-moving French horsedrawn limbers imposed an unwelcome delay. But an attempt to block the route by leading elements of the 2nd Panzer Division, who had just reached Quaedypre, was quickly quashed when the 1st Welsh Guards smartly booted them out of the village. Norman's blocking force was beefed up by adding the 6th Green Howards removed from the vicinity of the beaches at Dunkirk.

During 28 May, the town of Wormhoudt, between Bergues and Cassel, was taken by the 20th Motorized Division. The defenders consisted of the 2nd Royal Warwicks, minus a company, and the 8th Worcesters, minus two companies, and the 4th Cheshire and Worcestershire Yeomanry. By 1800 hours, the three companies of Warwicks, holding the north and west of the town, were badly reduced by casualties and almost surrounded. About seventy-four all ranks commanded by Major Hicks fought their way out. The rest surrendered to the Leibstandarte SS Adolf Hitler, the leading troops of the 20th Motorized Division, supported by armour of the 10th Panzer Division. The SS troops murdered more than eighty of their captive Warwickshire and Yeomanry soldiers with grenades, bayonets and bullets. A few British soldiers survived the war to report yet another atrocity by the infamous SS. One of these was Gunner Fahey, a Royal Artillery anti-tank gunner, cut off from his unit and lying wounded in a ditch with some other soldiers, after their truck had been attacked by a German aircraft. A party of British soldiers being marched into captivity came by, and were told to pick up the wounded from the ditch. They were all herded into a barn, which by now contained about a hundred men. A German officer ordered the British out in groups of five to be shot. Fahey remembered hearing someone counting in German, 'Ein, zwei, drei, vier, fünf.' Eventually his turn came, and helped by another man he staggered out. At the last moment he turned round and was shot in the back. He thought he was dead, except that he felt blood bubbling in his lung and pain in his leg where he had been shot earlier in the day. During a lull, when the Germans lost interest and moved away, he managed to crawl back into the barn where there were several dead and dying men among soldiers who had survived untouched so far. At some point the Germans had stopped taking men out of the barn, and instead went in and shot them at random with rifles and sub-machine guns. The Germans left, and the British soldiers, terrified and despairing, lay there for what seemed to Fahey like all the rest of the day. The following morning, some ordinary German soldiers arrived, dressed their wounds and cared for them, before they were taken into captivity. These soldiers told them that they had been captured by the Leibstandarte SS Adolf Hitler (LSSAH).[2] One of the LSSAH battalion commanders,

SS-Sturmbannführer (Major) Wilhelm Mohnke, was believed to have been responsible. When the time came to bring him to justice he was a prisoner of the Russians. Following his release, he was never charged, and lived the remainder of his life in Germany.

The order to the rest of the 144th Brigade to pull out of the Wormhoudt area was received in good time, and the Worcesters on the southern side of the town managed to make a clean break thanks to a combination of excellent shooting by a troop of the Worcester Yeomanry and a rainstorm. The 5th Gloucesters were still holding Ledringham, about two miles south-west of Wormhoudt, when two soldiers appeared bringing the order to withdraw, having spent four hours evading the German infantry who had invested the village. The Gloucesters had given a good account of themselves in the village, using the buildings to maximum advantage, to make the enemy come to them, and destroying tanks among the houses. But they had also paid dearly themselves, and a bare 200 men were fit to fight. It took four bayonet charges to hack their way out, an officer being killed in each one. This left 143 survivors, who taking their wounded with them on two carthorses and in wheelbarrows eventually staggered into Bambecque at 1830 hours. They brought three prisoners with them, a German officer and two soldiers, surprised while asleep.

Thorne decided he should now withdraw his 145th Brigade from Cassel. A sergeant despatch rider sent with the order to pull out was told by the 144th Brigade, which he encountered en route, that he would be unable to get through on a motorbike. He transferred to an armoured car, but this crashed into a ditch. Attempts at sending wireless messages were jammed all night by the Germans. At dawn the intrepid sergeant got through and delivered his message. Brigadier Somerset, the commander of the 145th Brigade, decided to wait for the onset of night before pulling out.

By dawn on Wednesday 29 May, Cassel, itself on high ground, and Mont des Cats with its large monastery were like islands standing out in the approaching tide of German armour and motorized infantry. These were to prove a fortuitous diversion to German formations heading for the right flank of the 50th Division astride Poperinghe.

At Mont des Cats, General Osborne, having arrived at the monastery, told his CRE and CRA to organize the defences, and as his people came in they were deployed. Eventually the remnants of the division collected there consisted of the 5th Queen's, the 4th and 5th Royal Sussex, the 65th Field Regiment with guns but no ammunition, and a battery of the 5th Royal Horse Artillery (RHA) with four guns and some ammunition. The yard was crammed with vehicles, and there were many others out

on the road stretching down the hill. Osborne did not expect any German attacks before about 1000 or 1100 hours – according to him, this was their usual starting hour. But at first light the 44th Division survivors could see motorized infantry and tanks coming over the plain and in a very short time the enemy were engaging Mont des Cats with mortars. The RHA battery shot up some of the trucks carrying infantry, but before long two guns were knocked out. Wounded started to be brought in to the monastery. At about 0630 hours what they had all expected to happen happened.

A mass of Stukas arrived overhead and peeling off screamed in on Mont des Cats, inflicting around a hundred casualties. Despite a brave effort, the soldiers of the 44th Division had had little time to prepare the position, and were in no state to fight off the ground attack that would surely follow this pounding by the Luftwaffe. Although Osborne, the divisional commander, had said that he would stay and fight, he was persuaded by one of the infantry battalion commanding officers to order a withdrawal. He ordered a move in two columns to Poperinghe, where the French were supposed to be halting for that day.

His soldiers did not hang around, but streamed off the Mont and trudged northwards across country. The 4th Royal Sussex were the last to go, at 1100 hours, and took a number of casualties from shelling. It seems that the enemy did not see them go, for they kept on shelling and mortaring the monastery for several hours, eventually setting it on fire. The tanks of the French Cavalry Corps did sterling work laying down covering fire, which may have discouraged the Germans from snapping at the 44th Division's heels.

Nearly all the 44th Division's vehicles were abandoned on the Mont or on the approaches to Poperinghe. The area was a scene of devastation – guns, vehicles and other equipment lay burning or broken and abandoned. Everywhere groups of soldiers plodded north, French and British. As they headed for the coast, in the distance they could see a faint streak of smoke, rising from the fires in Dunkirk still over the horizon. The rumours, or in some cases information, that there they would find ships to carry them away sustained the British soldiers. Officers and NCOs worked to keep cohesion in units, helped by the innate bloody-mindedness of the British soldier, the comradeship within units and sub-units, and the general unwillingness to let down one's mates. The late-twentieth-century soldier's expression, 'You can't crack me, I'm a rubber duck,' would have been strange to the men of 1940, but expresses precisely how they felt.

At the tail of the horde of men came the 44th Division. The eleven miles between Cassel and Poperinghe were not defended. Had the Germans

taken advantage of it, they could have gobbled up the 44th Division and swung in behind the 50th and 3rd Divisions, themselves under attack by five infantry divisions. Fortunately the enemy were diverted by Cassel and, having comprehensively bombed the town, settled down to invest it.

North of Cassel, the Germans kept up the pressure on the 48th Division. Around Vyfweg and West Cappel the 1st Welsh Guards put up a staunch resistance, but the Germans continued to advance on Rexpoede and Rattekot, where Brigadier Norman of the 1st Reconnaissance Brigade had his headquarters. Four large German tanks appeared and attacked the headquarters, but were eventually driven off by 18-pounders of the 5th RHA. Fortunately the Welsh Guards held off the accompanying infantry, or tanks and infantry together would have succeeded in overrunning the headquarters. This pressure on the right wing of the BEF coincided with attacks over on the left wing, and especially on the 3rd Division, recounted in the previous chapter.

As planned by Brigadier Somerset, the men of his 145th Brigade left Cassel an hour after dark, to find that by now some German formations were five miles to the north-east and between them and the main body of the BEF. The 4th Oxfordshire & Buckinghamshires scattered the first Germans they encountered at the point of the bayonet. But the next enemy units stood firm, and the battalion was soon surrounded by tanks and infantry and forced to surrender. Brigadier Somerset, who was with the battalion, was taken prisoner, the most senior officer from the main body of the BEF to fall into German hands in the campaign. The East Riding Yeomanry lost most of their remaining armoured fighting vehicles in a minefield. The 2nd Gloucesters tried to creep down the anti-tank ditch on the Franco–Belgian frontier, but ended up in a wood surrounded by enemy tanks. All were taken prisoner, except Second Lieutenant Fane and thirteen soldiers who evaded capture and arrived at Dunkirk on 2 June, just in time to be evacuated from the beach in a semi-waterlogged boat. The last of the Gloucesters to be captured consisted of half a platoon holding an isolated blockhouse three miles north of Cassel. They held off all German attempts to seize it, even though the enemy gained the roof. On 30 May, after three days, cut off from all other British units, they tried to break out but, failing to get clear, were taken prisoner. By then, most of the units of the BEF that were going to get there were inside the Dunkirk perimeter.

The action by Brooke's II Corps on the eastern and south-eastern flank, described in the previous chapter, is often known as the manoeuvre that saved the BEF, and has tended to overshadow the fighting on the western and south-western flank. Here six panzer and three motorized divisions attacked three British divisions, of which one was short of a brigade –

whereas on the south-eastern and eastern flank there was no German armour. One is entitled to ask why the Germans on the south-western flank failed to slice through to link up with their comrades pressing in from the east much earlier than they did, destroying the BEF in the process.

The first reason is that the German armour attacked all along the line, and did not concentrate in a sickle-like thrust, as they had done after crossing the Meuse at Sedan a few days earlier. Indeed at one stage the general direction of Hoth's Group on the south wing of the attack diverged from that of Kleist's Group on the northern wing. The second reason lay in General Reinhardt's worry about Cassel, and the consequent failure of his XLI Corps to exploit the gap between there and Hazebrouck. His concern seems to have been about his flanks, and it is possible that the British counter-stroke at Arras may have made him edgy. Instead of pressing on, his 6th Panzer Division blocked Cassel, while his 8th Panzer, the SS Verfügungs and a regiment of the 29th Motorized Division were kept busy clearing Hazebrouck and the Nieppe Forest, before his corps pressed on.

It is easy to be wise after the event, pontificating from the calm of a book-lined study. But one has to remember that in war the true state of the opposition's capability is often far from clear. Even the superbly trained and astute German officers could be misled by the aggressive defence of the BEF into thinking that they were capable of more than they actually were. The BEF was dogged in defence, and could mount local counter-attacks that sometimes gained them elbow-room for a clean break. The war diary of XLI Corps sums up the German view of the British defence:

> Fighting for individual houses and villages prevents the Corps from gaining ground to the east and north-east. Losses in men and equipment are grievous. The enemy fights with determination and stays in his positions until the last moment; if he is expelled from one point he appears a little later at some other and takes up the fight again.[3]

The British soldiers certainly earned the respect of their opponents by their guts and determination, but in reality the BEF did not have any formations with sufficient mobile firepower to generate counter-attacks with enough punch and tempo and on a scale that would seriously discommode a panzer corps in full cry for long. Such puny armoured fighting assets that the BEF had possessed, the 1st Army Tank Brigade, had virtually shot their bolt at Arras. For the reasons given above, Reinhardt may have been unaware of this of course, hence his caution.

That the 6th Panzer Division failed to cut off the British 44th Division

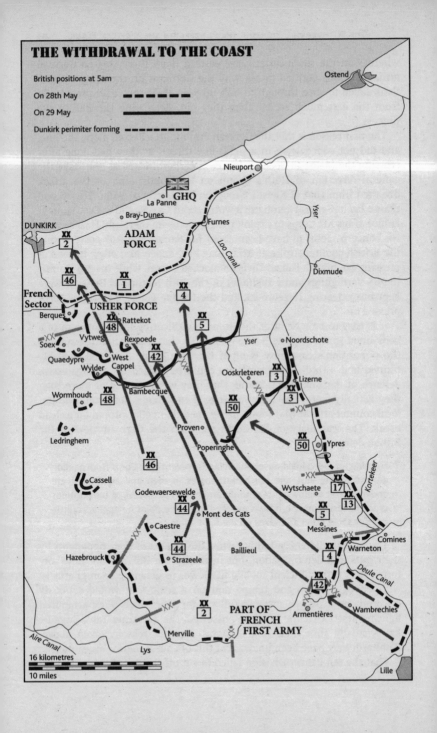

THE WITHDRAWAL TO THE COAST

British positions at 5am

On 28th May   — — — —

On 29 May   ————

Dunkirk perimiter forming   — — —

is astonishing, since by the evening of 28 May the armour was well north of the 44th, between the British and Dunkirk, and in a position to do so. The 29th Motorized Division in the Nieppe Forest clearly misread the situation, as its diary records that 'the enemy had abandoned so much equipment and vehicles that it was only possible to advance on foot'.[4] The lack of urgency on the part of the 29th Motorized also contributed to the British 44th Division getting clean away.

British anti-tank gunners also gave the Germans a nasty surprise. Well-sited anti-tank guns manned by resolute troops can cause heavy casualties to armoured formations, especially if the attacker has insufficient infantry and does not co-ordinate his artillery to best effect. The British were to learn this lesson again and again in the desert, and as late as July 1944 at the Battle of Goodwood in Normandy had still apparently not fully absorbed it.

On 28 May, the war diary of the XIX Panzer Corps commenting on the fighting around Wormhoudt included the passage: 'The Corps commander [Guderian] is not counting on any success from this attack and is of the opinion that further useless sacrifice must be avoided after the severe casualties which the 3rd Panzer Regiment has suffered during the counter-attack.'[5] The phrase 'useless sacrifice' appears in the XIX Panzer Corps war diary again after Guderian had returned from a tour of his formations, and the diary also states: 'in his [Guderian's] view the wise course is to hold positions reached and let 18 Army's attack from the east take effect'.[6] The German Eighteenth Army was part of Army Group B and had been engaged in Holland and against the Belgians. Guderian advised the chief of staff of Kleist Group as follows:

(1) After the Belgian capitulation continuation of operations here is not desirable as it is costing unnecessary sacrifices. The panzer divisions have only 50% of their strength left and their equipment is in urgent need of repair if the Corps is to be ready again in a short time for other operations.

(2) A tank attack is pointless in the marshy country, which has been completely soaked by rain. [It had rained heavily in the previous twenty-four hours.] The troops [German] are in possession of the high ground south of Dunkirk; they hold the important Cassel–Dunkirk road; and they have favourable artillery positions ... from which they can fire on Dunkirk.

Furthermore 18 Army [of Army Group B] is approaching [Kleist] Group from the east. The infantry forces of this army are more suitable than tanks for fighting in this kind of country, and the task of closing the gap on the coast can therefore be left to them.[7]

Kleist agreed, and General von Wietsheim's XIV Motorized Corps replaced Guderian's XIX Panzer Corps on 29 May. This change of com-

mand inevitably led to a reduction in tempo on the part of the Germans, just when the BEF was at its most vulnerable. In truth the German armoured commanders had lost interest in this battle. The infantry of Army Group B (Sixth and Eighteenth Armies) plus 9th Panzer Division reinforced and 20th Motorized Division could round up the BEF, while the bulk of the armour, eventually to consist of five panzer corps, concentrated on preparations to complete the defeat of the French.

9

COMINGS AND GOINGS AT DUNKIRK

Operation Dynamo is to commence.

Admiralty signal, 26 May 1940[1]

Dunkirk harbour in 1940 was the biggest on the Channel coast and the third largest in France. It had seven deep-water basins, four dry docks and five miles of quays. Surrounded by marshes that were easily flooded, it was the most defensible too, and although most of the fortifications around the town were old, they were capable of standing up to considerable shelling. Near the docks was the hugely strong Bastion 32, containing the headquarters of Admiral Abrial, the naval and military commander of the northern coastline, who took his orders only from Paris. The English-speaking General Fagalde, whose XVI Corps was transferred from the Belgian front, was ordered by Weygand to come under Abrial's command and take charge of the Boulogne–Calais–Dunkirk sector. So, in addition to his corps, Fagalde had three garrison battalions, two training units, three almost unarmed labour regiments, a couple of anti-tank batteries, five infantry battalions from the 21st Division and eleven batteries of artillery. By the time Fagalde arrived at Dunkirk, Boulogne and Calais were about to be invested by the Germans.

To follow the story of the forming of the bridgehead, we must wind the clock back and at times reiterate aspects of some events covered in earlier chapters. On the morning of Monday 20 May, Admiral Sir Bertram Ramsay, the Flag Officer Commanding Dover, held his first meeting at his headquarters to consider the possibility of large-scale evacuation if, 'as then seemed *unlikely*', the need should arise (emphasis in original).[2] The speed with which the situation in France and Belgium subsequently unravelled is brought home when one recalls that on the morning of Ramsay's 20 May meeting the BEF was on the Escaut Line, the Channel ports were still in Allied hands and the German panzer divisions had only just started crossing the Canal du Nord, south-east of Arras. By Sunday 26 May the whole of France north of the Somme was in German hands, except for the sack containing the BEF and the French First Army, and the Belgian 'appendix' – a sack which was being squeezed hard.

The evacuation of British troops from Dunkirk had actually started on 19 May when GHQ ordered that 'useless mouths' be sent back to England. There were plenty of these, as Dunkirk had been used as the port of entry for many non-combatant specialists. In addition there was an accumulation of wounded in casualty clearing stations in and around Bailleul, south of Poperinghe. From here the road and railway provided the safest evacuation route to Dunkirk, a route that became increasingly hazardous as the Germans closed in. Thanks to the attentions of the Luftwaffe, Dunkirk probably marked the most dangerous point in the journey. On 20 May the German bombing of the port had become so severe that all merchant ships were ordered out of port. Despite this, by midnight on 26 May 27,936 wounded and unwounded troops had been transported to England. The evacuation, codename Operation Dynamo, had begun.

There had been less than a week to plan, and furthermore no one could predict the scale of Operation Dynamo with any certainty. No one knew how many troops would reach the coast. Even if almost everyone made it, an evacuation of this magnitude was not just a matter of everyone slogging back to the coast and expecting it all to happen. To begin with, the planners in London estimated that the enemy could be held for a maximum of two days, and that around 45,000 soldiers might be brought off. Naval plans were made accordingly, and although not all the ships and craft that it was thought would be needed were yet assembled, the *Mona's Isle*, an armed boarding vessel, sailed for Dunkirk two hours after the Admiralty signal quoted at the head of this chapter was sent. She arrived in Dunkirk in the middle of an air raid, but embarked 1,420 troops. After leaving harbour to return to England, she was straddled by enemy guns on shore between Gravelines and Les Hemmes, and was then machine-gunned by enemy aircraft. Twenty-three men on board were killed and sixty wounded. She reached Dover at midday on Monday 27 May. Five transports that had sailed earlier that morning were so heavily shelled off the French coast that they could not reach Dunkirk, and turned back. A glance at the map on p. 222 shows how the fall of Calais on 26 May allowed the enemy to site guns on the coast and interdict the last leg of the most direct sea route from Dover to Dunkirk (Route Z). Accordingly an alternative route (Route Y) was swept of mines, but the diversion more than doubled the length of the passage. This longer route increased the danger of attack by surface craft, U-boats and the Luftwaffe, while doubling the turn-round time of vessels, thus halving the number of troops that could be brought off over a given period. Later, Ramsay brought Route X into operation. Against surface attack it was better protected by sandbanks and nearby British mine-

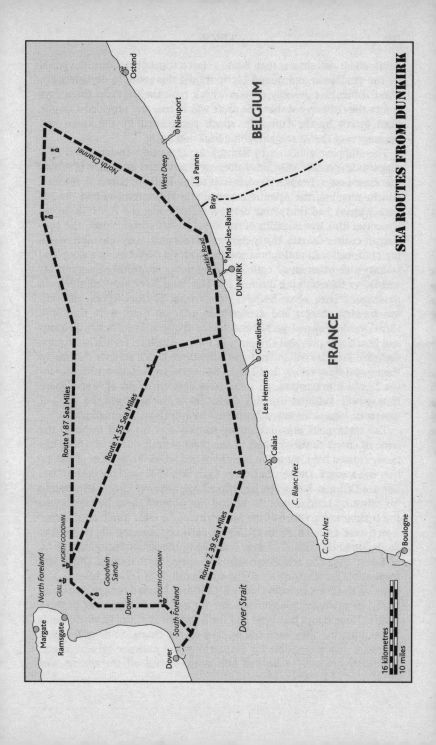

SEA ROUTES FROM DUNKIRK

fields, and it was shorter than Route Y. But navigational difficulties posed by the sandbanks and minefields restricted this route to daylight only. These difficulties possibly explain why it took the Germans three days before they discovered that this route was in use, and provided a respite from attack by the Luftwaffe, much appreciated by the crews and passengers of the vessels ploughing back and forth.

The shipping allocated to Ramsay for Operation Dynamo was of a magnitude inconceivable today after over sixty years of erosion of British maritime power. Despite the demands of the Battle of Narvik in Norway, still in progress, the Atlantic convoys, the Mediterranean and the Far East, Ramsay had thirty-nine destroyers, including the Polish destroyer *Błyskawica* (this was one-fifth of the Royal Navy's current total), the anti-aircraft cruiser *Calcutta*, thirty-eight minesweepers, sixty-one minesweeping craft, eighteen anti-submarine trawlers, six corvettes, one sloop and seventy-nine other small craft including motor torpedo boats, gunboats and Dover flare-burning drifters. The Merchant Navy provided thirty-six passenger ferries, seven hospital ships converted from ferries, and various trawlers, barges and dredgers. In addition there were the 'little ships', civilian-owned yachts and motor cruisers. The French, Belgians and Dutch also provided shipping, including nineteen French destroyers, sixty-five French civilian craft and forty-three Dutch schuyts ('scoots' to their Royal Navy crews). In all some 848 vessels served under Ramsay for the Dunkirk evacuation, an impressive demonstration of British maritime power. Without Britain's command of the seas and the array of vessels no large-scale evacuation could have even been contemplated.

The meticulous organization by Ramsay and his staff included the issue of charts to the skippers of the mass of craft, many of whom had never crossed the Channel in their lives and whose knowledge of navigation was meagre. Lieutenant George Grandage RNR, working in the Naval Control Office at Ramsgate, had three large boxes of charts delivered to his office by London taxi. As he had not ordered them he telephoned the Hydrographic Office of the Admiralty, to be told, 'You'll need them.' There were 1,500 charts in all, 500 in each set, covering the route from Ramsgate to Dunkirk. Grandage was told by the senior operations officer at Dover over the telephone that Ramsgate Naval Control Office was responsible for despatching all the small craft from Tilbury, London, and ports on the Essex coast to Dunkirk. Grandage worked out the route, and his typist produced 500 copies – one for each craft, plus a set of three charts. Three buoys had been laid from the north of the Goodwin sands to Dunkirk, but they were not marked on the charts. Some of the craft Grandage was responsible for despatching had navigational equipment, but many did not, so he and one assistant laid off the courses and

positions on about 1,000 of the charts. It took them all day and most of a night.

On Sunday 26 May, the day that Gort had been ordered to withdraw to the coast, and the Admiralty instructed to carry out Operation Dynamo, General Adam, having handed over command of III Corps, was sent to Dunkirk to organize its defence and the evacuation. He had to leave his corps staff to work for his successor, and took with him three staff officers from GHQ: the quartermaster general (QMG) Lieutenant General Lindsell; the chief engineer, Major General Pakenham-Walsh; and Lieutenant Colonel the Viscount Bridgeman, a GSO 1, who had earlier been sent to Dunkirk to start planning the perimeter defence.

The 27th of May was a crucial day in Operation Dynamo, and at 0600 hours another of the key players arrived at Dunkirk on board the destroyer *Wolfhound* – Admiral Ramsay's representative with the title Senior Naval Officer Ashore at Dunkirk, Captain W. G. Tennant RN. He brought with him a beach party of twelve officers and 150 ratings, later reinforced by another 200 officers and ratings. He found Dunkirk in the middle of an air raid, the latest in a series that had apparently been in progress for over twenty-four hours. Just before *Wolfhound* docked, Tennant saw a signal from Adam saying, 'Complete fighter protection now essential if serious disaster is to be avoided.' Tennant's reaction was to signal Ramsay at 0800 hours: 'Please send every available craft to beaches east of Dunkirk immediately. Evacuation tomorrow night problematical.'

The beaches to which Tennant had directed 'all available craft' stretched nearly twenty miles from Dunkirk to the mouth of the Yser. Behind the beaches the sand dunes dotted with clumps of grass provided good assembly areas for troops awaiting embarkation. The gently shelving sandy beaches each side of Dunkirk, one of the reasons for it being such a popular holiday resort, meant that even small craft could not get nearer than within about a hundred yards of the waterline, so soldiers had to wade out to them. There were no jetties, no little fishing harbours and no piers at the three resorts Malo-les-Bains, Bray-Dunes, and La Panne. The shoal water close in to shore meant that the larger vessels had to anchor well offshore, and the craft ferrying troops out to them had a long turn-round time. Tennant saw that the extensive inner docks at Dunkirk had been made unusable by German bombing. The outer basin was protected by two moles. The West Mole was connected to the oil terminal, which was on fire and blocking access to the mole itself. The 1,600-yard-long East Mole was connected to the beaches by a narrow causeway. Both moles were designed as breakwaters; neither was built for ships to berth alongside.

Early on the morning of 27 May, Adam met Fagalde in Cassel. Fagalde

had already discussed arrangements with Bridgeman the day before, and arriving ahead of the other French generals quickly came to an agreement with Adam on the plan drawn up by Bridgeman. A perimeter was to be established between Gravelines and Nieuport-Bains, past Bourbourg, Bergues and Furnes, thirty miles long and up to seven miles deep. The French would be responsible for the sector from Gravelines to Bergues, and the British from Bergues to Nieuport-Bains. At this stage the Belgians had not surrendered, but their intentions were too vague for any of their formations to be incorporated in the plan. The perimeter ran along a series of canals around Dunkirk; small waterways and ditches seamed the marshy terrain, the sea dykes had been opened and the ground was beginning to flood. It was not good country for armour.

Soon after the plan was agreed, Abrial, Blanchard (Commander of the French First Group of Armies) and General Koeltz, representing Weygand, joined Adam and Fagalde. The new arrivals did not question the plans, but it seemed to Adam that the French saw the bridgehead as a springboard for offensive action. Koeltz said that Weygand had proclaimed that the time had come to stop the retreat and attack the Germans everywhere. Clearly Weygand had still failed to come to terms with reality. Fagalde then rose and said he would return to his headquarters and give orders for an immediate attack on Calais, 'driving the Germans before him'. British jaws dropped, as the French applauded. Adam and his party withdrew as quickly as they could.

On their way to Bergues, Adam's party was machine-gunned by some Belgian biplanes wearing German markings. Pakenham-Walsh was wounded in the shoulder. Stopping at Bergues to see Thorne (GOC 48th Division), Adam found that he could not spare any troops to man the perimeter. Thorne did however lend him his CRA, Brigadier Frederick Lawson, to provide gunner advice on the establishment of the defences. Following a reconnaissance of the perimeter, Adam set up his headquarters in the town hall at La Panne. This seaside resort had a direct telephone line to England, installed by the Belgian King Albert to enable him to keep in contact with the London Stock Exchange while in his holiday villa.

Adam went on into the Bastion at Dunkirk, where he met Fagalde and Captain Tennant RN. Fagalde announced that, thanks to German pressure, he would have to pull back from the area west of Dunkirk. Adam, tongue in cheek, remarked that in view of his, Fagalde's, intervention earlier, he had expected to find him on his way to Calais. Fagalde replied that someone had to respond to Koeltz's moving speech, and he seemed to be the only one ready. Later that day, the French withdrew from Gravelines, to a new line Mardick–Spycker–Bergues.

The British sector was split into three corps areas. II Corps was to hold the eastern end and be evacuated from the La Panne beaches; I Corps would be in the centre and be taken off from Bray-Dunes, while III Corps would be on the western end and withdraw from Malo-les-Bains. Vehicles, except those essential for fighting, would be left outside the perimeter, and supply dumps were established in each corps area.

Meanwhile, Adam was already concerned that the small number of men being taken off the beaches would result in most of the BEF being left behind. He telephoned the War Office and pointed out in forthright language that the number of craft being provided, and the number of naval beach parties, was inadequate. (Naval beach parties were responsible for calling in boats for loading, controlling the embarkation of troops, ensuring that craft were not overloaded and despatching them when full.) Adam decided to send Captain Moulton Royal Marines, a GSO 3 on Gort's staff, to see Ramsay at Dover and tell him where the troops were concentrating.

Moulton had already been down to the beaches the previous night when three small sloops arrived, with no idea where the troops were. To take them off there was one motor boat and one 27-foot whaler per sloop (six boats in all). There was a strong current, and Moulton knew enough about seamanship to realize that the boats' crews would need assistance from the shore. So he waded out with some of the soldiers, and an RNR sub-lieutenant in the stern of one of the boats fired a revolver over his head, thinking perhaps he was about to be swamped by panic-stricken troops. Moulton calmed him down and eventually went off in the boat and saw the captain of one of the sloops. He got the ships moved towards one of the corps embarkation points. But the captain was worried about the shallow water and anchored off at some distance.

Moulton immediately returned to La Panne, with water dripping from his battledress. He called on Adam and said, 'This is not going to work.' He suggested he went over to Dover and see what he could do to sort it out. At first Adam was reluctant to let him go, suspecting that he was 'windy' and wanted to escape. But in the end he agreed. Moulton crossed in one of the Royal Navy sloops, and went first to the army headquarters at Dover, whose staff had absolutely no idea what was needed, and then made for Ramsay's underground headquarters, where he saw the admiral and showed him a map with the corps embarkation points marked on it. Having done this he caught a destroyer returning to Dunkirk, only for her to be ordered back before she reached France. Nothing loath, Moulton boarded another destroyer at Dover and eventually came ashore at Bray-Dunes. He then walked to La Panne. It must be emphasized that Moulton's only task was to tell Ramsay where the corps embarkation

points were. By his own admission, he had not thought of embarkation at Dunkirk, because of the risk of bombing. By this time the Luftwaffe had already bombed Dunkirk heavily, destroying part of the town and making the docks and harbour extremely dangerous.

Also starting on 27 May, the RAF began a supreme effort to keep the Luftwaffe away, an endeavour that lasted throughout the evacuation. Fighter Command provided sixteen squadrons to give continuous cover over the area from 0500 hours until nightfall, and on that first day flew 287 fighter sorties. Pilots flew two or even three sorties a day from airfields in England, nearly always being outnumbered by the enemy. Troops returning from Dunkirk claimed that the RAF was not in evidence over the beaches and town. Although the aircraft might not have been visible overhead for most of the time, the RAF's superb performance was critical in keeping the Luftwaffe from having a free run over the bridge-head, and without it only a fraction of the BEF would have been evacuated. But the troops were sceptical, and there were frequent shouts of 'Where is the RAF?' and 'We never saw a fighter.' Feelings were very bitter between the army and navy on one hand and the RAF on the other. Flight Lieutenant Deere, a Spitfire pilot of No. 54 Squadron, was shot down about fifteen miles from Dunkirk, and eventually made his way to the town. He joined a queue of soldiers on the mole and was about to board a destroyer when a major stopped him and said, 'For all the good you chaps seem to be doing, you might as well stay on the ground.' As he embarked, he was greeted with stony silence from a group of army officers, and when he asked what the RAF had done, one replied, 'That's just it, what have they done?' Altogether Coastal Command flew 171 sorties, Bomber Command 651 and Fighter Command 2,739, all directly in support of Operation Dynamo. The RAF lost 145 aircraft, of which ninety-nine were fighters, including forty-two Spitfires. The Germans lost 132 aircraft, all to Fighter Command, who were thus thirty-three 'kills' ahead by the end of the battle.

Life for the Luftwaffe over Dunkirk was made easier than it need have been thanks to a misunderstood order. The British 2nd Anti-Aircraft Brigade, consisting of the 60th Anti-Aircraft Regiment (3.7-inch heavy AA guns) and 51st and 58th Light Anti-Aircraft Regiments (40mm Bofors light AA guns), had been made responsible for the anti-aircraft protection of Dunkirk. On Monday 27 May, Lieutenant Colonel Bridgeman, the GSO 1 on Adam's staff, briefed the liaison officer of the Major General Anti-Aircraft Artillery at GHQ, Major General H. G. Martin, that all guns were to remain in action as long as possible, spare gunners were to fight as infantry, and any gunners incapable of fighting, because of wounds, lack of small arms and so on were to go to the beaches. This order

filtered down to the 2nd Anti-Aircraft Brigade as requiring that *all* gunners were to go to the beaches. Martin, reasoning that if all gunners were to go to the beaches the guns must first be put out of action, issued orders accordingly. In fact the 51st Light Anti-Aircraft Regiment did not spike its guns, but the protection afforded by the heavy anti-aircraft guns was to be sorely missed.

At midnight on 27/28 May only 7,669 men had arrived in England, and about two-thirds came on ships that had loaded in Dunkirk harbour before its use was suspended. By then Tennant, having already spotted that the embarkation from the beaches was painfully slow, ordered a destroyer to come alongside the East Mole. Early the next morning, six destroyers came alongside the mole and, under the cover of the RAF, quickly filled with soldiers. Tennant's gamble succeeded, and, thanks to the skill of the captains who came alongside the flimsy structure, this would become the principal means of evacuation. Late that afternoon, 28 May, the first of the 'little ships' appeared off the beaches.

That same day, mainly because of Tennant's bold decision the night before, and possibly because of what Moulton had told him, Ramsay shifted most of the effort from the beaches to the East Mole, mainly the larger ships and destroyers. Although not designed as troop carriers, the destroyers managed to squeeze in about 900 men each and sometimes more. Despite as many as possible being ordered below, the soldiers were reluctant to comply for fear of being trapped if the ship sank, with the result that the upper decks were so tightly crammed with men that the guns could not be fought, and the destroyers were so top-heavy they heeled disconcertingly as they zigzagged sharply to avoid air attack. On 28 May, 17,804 men were brought back to England. We should remind ourselves that by the end of that day the bulk of the BEF was still fighting to hold the sack, with divisions as far south as Armentières; only a minority had reached the perimeter. During that day the Belgians surrendered, and the dangerous gap along the Loo Canal had been opened up, as related in Chapter 7.

On 28 May Gort set up his headquarters at King Albert's holiday villa in La Panne. Adam's plan for the occupation of the bridgehead was: II Corps left, I Corps centre and III Corps right. As the BEF was in the process of withdrawing to the bridgehead there were some tense moments, mainly caused by the Belgian capitulation; some of these have already been covered in Chapter 7.

Because of the way its formations had been deployed, the headquarters of III Corps had never been able to keep as tight control over its divisions as the other two. On their way back to the bridgehead the troops of III Corps were intermixed with French troops of the First French Army.

Notices were erected at road junctions, 'Français à gauche, British to the right'. General de la Laurencie, commanding the French III Corps, who had defied orders from above to surrender and marched his 12th and 32nd Divisions back to Dunkirk, now ignored these notices, marching his men to the right. He headed for Gort's headquarters and asked that his divisions should be deployed with the British.

The experience of the 4th/7th Dragoon Guards was typical of the chaos of the final days. It will be remembered from Chapter 7 that the regiment had only enough tanks to equip one Combined Squadron to work with the surviving squadrons of the 5th Inniskilling Dragoon Guards ('Skins'). The remainder of the regiment formed a 'dismounted party'. At 1700 hours an order was received ordering the Combined Squadron, commanded by Major Frink, to remain in position until 2000 hours and then proceed independently to the area of Bergues, with the intention of getting to 'the boats at Dunkirk. Vehicles and guns will be destroyed.' The A Squadron diary comments acidly, 'Such an order would have led to chaos if it had been acted on. Some units did act on it, with the result that everyone [in those units] was extremely lucky to get away.'

Major Frink's diary continues:

Squadron came out a bit after 8 pm and proceeded via POPERINGHE–DUNKIRK road. Luckily the Boche, true to form, did not advance after dark. Four lines of traffic and absolute and complete chaos – everyone pointing revolvers at each other and shouting. Williams [OC C Squadron] continually at loggerheads with all in authority but won every round. Achieved one of my ambitions i.e. running down a large ASC [Army Service Corps] officer in large staff car making for first boat.

Our B Echelon had already been lost and all kit burned. Rather a blow as no one now had anything except what they stood up in. Drivers so tired that they went to sleep every time they pulled up which was every 50 yards.

The tracked light tanks could of course drive off-road.

Wednesday, May 29th. At dawn took to the fields as the only possible means of progress – quite a good line set by Williams – several vehicles packed up under the strain – arrived eventually on the Canal NE of Dunkirk – very tired and no rations. Found our old friends the Camerons holding the bridge, only 60 of them left. Luckily orders for destruction of vehicles had not been carried out as there were many jobs ahead of us. Found RHQ [Regimental Headquarters] and joined up with them. Parked in a potato field, excellent new potatoes were much enjoyed and practically our only rations. A lot of shelling and bombing, otherwise uneventful.

The Dismounted Party of the regiment also set out for Dunkirk on foot and, having put some abandoned trucks to good use, arrived at Dunkirk on the same day as the Combined Squadron. The Dismounted Party was eventually ordered by the 2nd Division to go down to the beach and get on board a boat as best it could. The beach was packed with troops, and there was no organization. Formed bodies took their place at the end of the queue, but individuals who emerged from streets that led to the beach usually tried to take a place anywhere, opposite where they hit the queue. Eventually an order was passed down the line that everyone was to form into parties of fifty. This was done after 'a certain amount of confusion'.

The queue in which the 4th/7th found themselves was about two miles long and advanced very slowly. From to time to time the Luftwaffe dive-bombed the area, but luckily concentrated on Dunkirk, especially the ships and the harbour. If the bombers had concentrated on the beaches, the slaughter would have been widespread. The space between the water's edge and the long causeway connecting the beach with the East Mole was 'black with troops'. Although some bombs did fall on the beaches, most fell on soft sand, penetrating some distance before exploding, and with most of the blast and splinters expended upwards, the resulting casualties were remarkably light.

A wrecked French destroyer about 200 yards offshore attracted some attention from the bombers, covering the queuing men with spray each time. Whenever the queue halted, each man would scrape a little depression in the sand as cover, unless he could occupy one dug by a predecessor who had now moved further up the queue. The onset of night brought relief from the dive-bombers, and some soldiers managed to sleep. During the night little progress was made, and most found themselves only a few yards nearer the head of the queue. By 30 May the organization, according to the 4th/7th short history, seems to have improved. 'Gate crashers' were being put back in their correct places. Low cloud resulted in reduced enemy air activity, and embarkation from the mole had speeded up; in the sector in which the 4th/7th found themselves beach embarkation had ceased for the time being. The Dismounted Party slowly filed up the mole and came under the 'efficient control of the Royal Navy', and a 'big Marine gave those who had receptacles a spoonful of hot stew. One officer had only a cocktail glass, which the Marine filled with hot gravy and added, "Can I put a cherry in it, Sir?"' Most of the Dismounted Party were evacuated during the morning of 30 May in the destroyer *Malcolm* and the passenger ferry *Royal Daffodil*.

The Combined Squadron, having been told it could go, 'elected to

finish the job with the "Skins" '.[3] The 4th/7th Combined Squadron took the opportunity to do some scrounging, and Lieutenant Verdin and Second Lieutenant Riley returned with two new Bedford trucks and one 8-hundredweight, twelve chickens, boxes of rations and some petrol.

Second Lieutenant Blaxland of the 2nd Buffs, who had been evacuated to hospital in the Dunkirk area from the Escaut, was discharged in time to join the remnants of his battalion, most of whom had become prisoners of war in the fighting on the western flank of the BEF's withdrawal to the sea (see Chapter 8). He found them waiting to be evacuated, and when their turn came he marched with them along the beach towards the mole. On approaching the causeway to the mole, Blaxland saw a lone Bofors 40mm AA gun lowering its barrel until it appeared to be pointing straight at him at the head of the column – it was clearly about to engage an enemy aircraft swooping low over the beach behind them. He threw himself down as with a series of deafening booms it engaged a target which he never saw, because his range of vision was restricted to the drainage ditch alongside the causeway. There were ten soldiers lying in it looking remarkably relaxed and unconcerned. Then he realized they were dead, evidently not at the hands of the Bofors, as they still had their heads. The Bofors stopped, and Blaxland saw the faces of the gunners relax. He led his party up the mole at a steady jog and was delighted to be greeted by the captain of a destroyer alongside, shouting at him to tell his men to hand over their rifles as they came on board and get below quickly. Officers were directed to the Wardroom. A steward asked him what he wanted to drink, and he asked for a whisky and ginger ale. He was in Dover by late evening that same day.

Thursday 30 May saw the final deployment within the perimeter, Adam having handed over to the three corps commanders on 29 May, his work done. The dispositions are shown on the map on pp. 246–7. This was to be the last stand by the BEF, in a campaign that had been a fight for survival from the outset. The BEF had retreated over 138 miles, with its flanks threatened throughout, and never more so than in the final stages. The Germans had nearly succeeded in breaking into the bridgehead in the gap between Nieuport and Dixmude on two occasions; the gap was held, but only just. The enemy had been held back by scratch British forces, and badly delayed by throngs of Belgian refugees on the roads. The Germans had lacked armour in this sector, and were plainly desperately tired. But the BEF could not relax, as the bridgehead could be held for a few days only. The canals along the perimeter were nothing like as formidable as those in the earlier defence lines. Flooding was widespread, though in many places only inches deep. But this was deep

enough to oblige the defenders to hold the houses and farms on the
bunds above the water level. This exposed them to observation and
fire from the more numerous houses and villages on the German side
of the canal. The British were bone weary. They had been tired enough
by 27 May, but few had managed a minute of sleep in the three days of
continuous movement and action that followed. Guns and ammunition
were desperately short. Out of sixteen medium and heavy regiments,
only the 59th Medium was operational. The remainder had abandoned
their guns on orders at stages on the way back. The field artillery
regiments mostly had their guns, but were short of ammunition, relying
on what was still carried in the divisional column, or by scrounging from
stocks discovered in the bridgehead.

On the morning of 30 May, Rear Admiral Frederic Wake-Walker arrived
at Dunkirk. The previous day he had returned to the Admiralty after
lunch away from his office, either in his club or in a restaurant, to be
told that the Vice Chief of Naval Staff, Rear Admiral Phillips, wished to
see him. Phillips asked Wake-Walker if he would like to go to Dunkirk
to try to get some organization into the embarkation there. Wake-Walker
replied that he would be delighted. Some discussion ensued about exactly
what he should be called, because it was not the intention that he should
supersede Captain Tennant who was already Senior Naval Officer Dunkirk. Eventually he was dubbed Rear Admiral Dover, and appointed to be
in charge offshore at Dunkirk. Wake-Walker would command from a
succession of ships offshore, feeding vessels into the beaches and Dunkirk harbour, and controlling the flow of shipping. Tennant would be
responsible for embarkation and the beach and dock parties ashore.
Wake-Walker and Tennant could communicate by wireless, and both had
a launch at their disposal and were thus able to make personal contact
with each other. This episode tells us much about the period. Now,
officers of the Navy Department, the modern successor to the Admiralty,
and indeed those from the other two services, however senior, and in
circumstances of considerably less peril for the nation, would probably
be found lunching at their desks thus projecting the politically correct
image of dedication and efficiency. But, when put to the test, they would
be no more effective than Wake-Walker.

On his arrival off the beaches Wake-Walker saw the long queues of
men from the back of the beach stretching into the sea as deep as a man
could wade. Behind each line was a large group, waiting patiently.
Destroyers and other vessels lay off the beaches while small craft ferried
the troops out to them. The light swell hampered the beach work, and
some craft had grounded and been caught by the falling tide, to remain
useless until the flood. There was plainly a need for many more small

boats. These were coming from Newhaven, Portsmouth and Sheerness, but had not arrived by the morning of 30 May. In addition six tugs were chugging across from Tilbury towing twenty-three motor and forty-six rowing lifeboats. Five were coming from Gravesend, towing barges. The assortment of craft heading for Dunkirk included car ferries, cockle-boats, speedboats, seaplane tenders, pleasure boats, private yachts and a Thames fire-float. By mid-morning with troops crowding to the water's edge there was a lull in the evacuation until, at last, the first twelve motor lifeboats, the most useful in terms of capacity and speed of turn-round, arrived. These, together with a miscellany of about thirty-two other craft, started ferrying troops out to the waiting ships.

That morning the engineers of 1st Division took advantage of the low tide to drive trucks as far as they could out into the sea to form a makeshift pier at Bray, which they decked with planks. As the tide came in it proved critical for speeding up the process of embarking men into the smaller craft. A similar pier was built at La Panne. From now on the evacuation began to gain momentum, although the 30th was the only day on which more men were lifted from the beaches (29,512) than from the harbour (24,311), and the day's total of 53,823 was the largest so far. Moreover shipping losses were the smallest, only two destroyers being damaged.

Mist and poor visibility had restricted the Luftwaffe all day. Naval officers had been frustrated by the slow progress of troops along the Dunkirk mole, resulting in what they perceived as a lost opportunity to take advantage of the lack of enemy air activity. Eventually a naval officer used a loudspeaker to address the troops slowly trudging along the mole: 'Remember your pals, boys – the quicker you get on board the more of them will be saved.' At that the soldiers broke into a double, keeping it up along the whole Eastern Mole for over two hours, during which time some 15,000 were embarked.

The enemy quickly followed up as the last of the BEF divisions entered the Dunkirk perimeter. All along the perimeter the Germans pressed in and shelled and mortared. Digging in was difficult for the defenders thanks to the flooded ground. The German reports state that 'the bridge-head is held by British troops who are fighting back very stubbornly'.

At 0100 hours Lieutenant Dunn's battery commander woke him and said that the 2nd Grenadiers were asking for artillery support. Their colonel and two other officers had been killed. Would he go and see what he could do? Dunn arrived in Furnes and found some of the weariest men he had ever seen. They were having trouble with snipers on the other side of the canal, and would he quieten them? As soon as it was light, he went up to their left forward company and was shown a

house from where he could see the target. It was on the canal bank, and there was still an old woman living there, almost out of her mind with terror.

Now began a most difficult task. The BEF was in an area in which no one had foreseen that it would have to operate, and consequently there were no maps. Dunn was faced with spotting for a close-in shoot with a Michelin road map. He added 500 yards for luck to his estimated range, and eventually saw one of his rounds fall, and was able to correct from that. Having hit the likely sniper positions hard, he returned to the Grenadier battalion headquarters for breakfast and a shave. To his fury he was told that the battery had now moved, and the registration would have to be done again. He returned to his house and registered two defensive-fire tasks in front of the Grenadiers. At this moment a dirty, unshaven captain of the 4th Berkshires walked in saying that they were holding the line to the left of the 2nd Grenadiers. When they were walking back from the last position, they came under heavy German shellfire and now had five officers and a hundred men left. They had no gunners allotted to them and could Dunn help? So Dunn crawled to the canal bank and registered three defensive-fire targets for them. These were to come in useful later. By this time the Germans had begun to shell the centre of Furnes with a battery of 5.9-inch guns.

Dunn had an excellent lunch with the left forward Grenadier company: pâté, bully-beef stew, hock, port and cigars in a cellar. After lunch he returned to battalion headquarters, which was being shelled hard. Uncannily, the Germans did not take long to find any headquarters and take action accordingly. The house had deep cellars and there Dunn and his OP party sat until 1800 hours. Eventually the house came down on top of them, but the rubble did not block their exit. Through it all a grandfather clock continued ticking. Dunn's admiration for the Guards, always high, became unbounded during that afternoon. They discussed everything under the sun except the war, and he thought the atmosphere of complete calm and self-control was marvellous.

At about 1800 hours the bombardment reached a climax. Major Colvin, who had taken over as CO of the 2nd Grenadiers after Lieutenant Colonel Lloyd was killed, returned from brigade headquarters saying that a smokescreen was being laid in front of the Berkshires, and an attack seemed imminent there. Dunn asked if he wanted defensive fire, to which the answer was yes. By now the telephone wires had been cut to bits, and Dunn's wireless had a splinter through it, so he got into his car and drove back to the battery. It was the most unpleasant drive he had experienced up to then. The exits from Furnes were being heavily shelled, but he got through. As soon as the SOS had been fired, he

returned to the town, enduring a repeat performance of his outward journey under heavy shellfire, and entered the battalion headquarters cellar. Here reports were coming in that the attack had been beaten off. The left-hand forward company sent back a message saying, 'Intense shelling, all positions held. All platoons in good heart.'

Major Colvin said although that attack had been beaten off he expected another that night, but on the front of the Berkshires. Would Dunn make the necessary arrangements? Dunn duly returned to the guns, and collected a wireless set. He had a couple of stiff drinks and ate some bully beef. The adjutant of 7th Field told him that they would have to stay for about five days – probably guesswork on his part. Dunn returned to Furnes convinced that they would never leave.

At about 2200 hours a message came in that bridging operations were in progress at the junction between the Grenadiers and the Berkshires. Dunn brought down defensive fire for about an hour, but without definite result. Defensive fire was called for again. It transpired that some Germans had got across. The under-strength Berkshires were forced to give ground, so the 1st Coldstream Guards from the 7th Guards Brigade were called in to put in a counter-attack. After confused fighting that cost all three company commanders killed, the Coldstreams regained enough ground to enable them to overlook a newly erected enemy pontoon bridge. They called down artillery fire and smashed it.

The position having been restored, Dunn was recalled to his battery, to be told that it would be withdrawing early the next day, but that a section with three officers would remain. A coin would be tossed to decide whose troop would find the section of two guns: heads Dunn's troop, tails Lieutenant Dill's. Dunn and the others sat trying to look unconcerned, while the battery commander flicked up a ten-franc piece. It spun on the floor for what seemed an eternity and finally dropped. Tails.

In the early hours of 31 May, the 7th Field Regiment abandoned its guns, except for one section per battery. Taking with them all their optical instruments including the gun sights and what kit they could carry, the gunners marched off towards the sea with heavy hearts. They arrived at the beach as dawn was breaking, and marched down to the shore line where boats were waiting. They had to wade up to their waists to get out to them, but quietly man after man climbed in and eventually they were taken out to the vessels that would take them back to England.

As dawn broke on 31 May, the enemy shelling increased. The prospects did not look healthy for the worn-out and greatly diminished battalions along the twenty-five-mile-long perimeter. Sergeant Green, along with everyone else in the 2nd Bedfordshire & Hertfordshires, was issued with

what turned out to be the last rations, one tin of bully beef and four biscuits between two men. For water they had to fend for themselves. The bridgehead was intact, but none of the officers and soldiers knew when, and indeed if, they could start withdrawing. Fortunately they also did not know that at last the Germans had got their act together and that a single commander, General von Küchler of Eighteenth Army, had been tasked with destroying the bridgehead, and had ten divisions with which to do it.

Until then there had been an uncharacteristic lack of grip within the German high command. There was no co-ordinated plan for the attack on Dunkirk, and much argument about whether Fourth or Sixth Army would undertake the task. Kleist had been told to get moving and attack on the south-western side of the perimeter, but replied that his formations were unsuitable since tanks could not be used among the canals and concrete fortifications. He was told that 'by higher orders an end must finally be made of the embarkation at Dunkirk', while the Fourth Army commander personally intervened to order all forces to the coast east of Dunkirk immediately. Kleist still dragged his feet, and reported that as the medium artillery had run out of ammunition attempts would be made to fire on Dunkirk with light artillery. It was at that point that Küchler was put in charge of operations against Dunkirk. His Eighteenth Army, which had been engaged against the Belgians, was now directed to destroy or capture all Allied troops in the bridgehead. Küchler had IX, X, XIV and XXVI Corps consisting of the 14th, 18th, 56th, 216th, 254th, 256th and 61st Infantry Divisions; two motorized brigades, the 9th and 11th, the motorized Regiment GrossDeutschland, plus the 20th Motorized Division, and the SS Adolf Hitler Regiment.

German Army Group A could now forget about attacking Dunkirk and concentrate on the next phase, attacking what Rundstedt believed was the major and undefeated portion of the French Army. He had already lost about 50 per cent of his armour, and did not want to lose more among the ditches and canals of the Dunkirk sector. To have done so would in his opinion have been bad judgement. The debate continues to this day about whether Rundstedt handled Army Group A as well as he might have done having ripped open the Allied front after crossing the Meuse. At one stage, while Gort had only the 5th and 50th Divisions in the Arras area and some scratch forces scattered thinly along the Canal Line, Rundstedt had seven armoured, six motorized and four infantry divisions in the rear of the BEF and no one to oppose him. With this potent force he contented himself with taking the lightly defended towns of Calais and Boulogne and harrying the BEF as it withdrew to Dunkirk. This was despite the fact that his Army Group alone was stronger than

the BEF, and in addition he had Army Group B engaging the attention of
the BEF on its other flank. What is absolutely irrefutable is that Rundstedt's 'sickle-cut' reduced the French high command to a state of
paralysis so severe that they never recovered their equilibrium.

There is no evidence that Hitler interfered with Rundstedt's operations, but he certainly contributed his pennyworth to Army Group B's
plan to attack Dunkirk, including suggestions for the use of artillery – an
early example of the Führer's inclination to become involved in minute
military detail. Hitler's helpful hints are revealed in a message from the
German Commander-in-Chief, Brauchitsch, containing personal suggestions for overpowering the Allies around Dunkirk. It makes nonsense of
the notion that Hitler wanted the BEF to escape.

Once in the Dunkirk bridgehead, Gort came under the command of
Admiral Abrial. Weygand was no longer talking in terms of the bridgehead being used as a springboard for a counter-attack, and ordered that
it should be used for evacuation, without laying down any policy for the
evacuation. Gort was uncertain whether he was to get the BEF out as fast
as possible or hang on with sufficient forces as long as Abrial wished him
to do so. If it was to be the former, Gort told the War Office on the
telephone, this should be made clear to the French. The British government response to Gort's question, received by him in the early afternoon
of 30 May, was dictated by Churchill. It read:

> Continue to defend the present perimeter to the utmost to cover maximum
> evacuation now proceeding well. Report every three hours through La Panne.
> If we can still communicate we shall send you an order to return to England
> with such officers as you may choose at the moment when we deem your
> command so reduced that it can be handed over to a Corps Commander.
> You should now nominate this Commander. If communications are broken
> you are to hand over and return as specified when your effective fighting
> force does not exceed the equivalent of three divisions. This is in accordance
> with correct military procedure and no personal discretion is left to you
> in the matter. On political grounds it would be a needless triumph to [sic]
> the enemy to capture you when only a small force remained under your
> orders. The Corps Commander chosen by you should be ordered to carry
> out the defence in conjunction with the French and evacuation whether
> from Dunkirk or the beaches, but when in his judgement no further organ-
> ised evacuation is possible and no further proportionate damage can be
> inflicted on the enemy he is authorised in consultation with the French
> Commander to capitulate formally to avoid useless slaughter.[4]

Gort's staff told the War Office by telephone that at this stage there
were about 60,000 British troops remaining. Assuming that the rearguard

would number about 15,000, and stay until early morning on 2 June, that left some 45,000 to lift on the nights of 30/31 May and 31 May/1 June. The position was complicated by the question of French evacuation. Large numbers of French troops were in the bridgehead, and the British government had laid down a policy of evacuation in equal numbers. But few French ships had arrived and, although Gort had allocated two ships to evacuate French troops, only a few thousand had got away so far. Churchill spoke to Gort at midnight on 30/31 May underlining the importance of evacuating French troops and requesting him to ensure that Generals Blanchard and Fagalde were evacuated.

Gort decided that II Corps, less the 50th Division, would withdraw for evacuation on the night of 31 May/1 June. At that stage, the part of the bridgehead that lay in Belgian territory would be abandoned, leaving the sector between Dunkirk and the French frontier to be defended. The 50th Division would withdraw behind the frontier and come under I Corps command. General Brooke, it will be recalled, had been told that he was to go back to England on the afternoon of 30 May, taking with him all of II Corps staff that could be spared. Montgomery was to command II Corps (his division being taken over by Brigadier Anderson).

Midnight on 30/31 May marked the fourth day of Operation Dynamo. By that time a total of 126,606 men had been shipped to England (77,412 from the harbour and 49,194 from the beaches). Gort asked permission to be the last to leave, but was told go once his command was down to the strength of one corps. On 31 May Gort issued his last operation order, extracts from which are reproduced below:

2. It is intended, after consultation with the French authorities at Dunkirk, that both Corps and Dunkirk base should continue the withdrawal of troops, maintaining the defence of Dunkirk in co-operation with our French allies, in accordance with orders already issued. It is further intended that the final withdrawal of II Corps shall be completed during the night 31st May/1st June. Shipping resources will be allotted accordingly, and action taken in the following para[graph]s. II Corps will not finally abandon the perimeter before 2300 hrs, 31 May.

3. I Corps will assume command of 5 and 50 Divs from 1800 hrs 31st May. I Corps will use those divisions to man the frontier defence and will issue orders, after consultation with II Corps, for their withdrawal to the frontier defences. 5 and 50 Div reps report HQ I Corps forthwith. An outpost line will be maintained to be selected by I Corps.

4. II Corps will be responsible for the evacuation of the beaches at La Panne.

5. When the withdrawal of II Corps is completed, GHQ will be withdrawn
   and command will pass to Command I Corps. In default of further
   instructions command will pass at 1800 hrs 31 May.[5]

The redeployment of 5th and 50th Divisions mentioned in Gort's
order was to ensure that the eastern flank of I Corps which lay along
the Franco–Belgian frontier would not be exposed by the withdrawal of
II Corps on the left. Despite Lieutenant General Barker's poor performance during the campaign, and evidence that he was on the verge of a
breakdown, Gort originally tasked him with command of the rearguard,
which would consist of I Corps. This is not mentioned in the British
Official History, which merely states that Gort appointed Major General Alexander as the commander of I Corps. Gort's original decision to
leave Barker in command is supported by Montgomery's diary entry for
30 May.

Montgomery, now commanding II Corps, had attended the meeting
of corps commanders at Gort's headquarters at 1800 hours on 30 May,
where, according to the former's diary,

C-in-C read out telegram from War Office ordering one Corps to be
surrendered to the enemy with the French at Dunkirk; Barker selected and
1 Corps, 2 Corps to be evacuated ... Barker (1st Corps) was excited and
rattled; his BGS was frightened and out of touch.... Brooke (who had
handed 2 Corps to me) was present for the first quarter hour & then left
for England; he was first class.[6]

Montgomery was even more forthright in a letter written in 1952 to
Gort's biographer J. R. Colville, in which he said that Barker was 'an
utterly useless commander, who had lost his nerve'.[7] Montgomery had
arrived early at Gort's headquarters, as his own corps headquarters was
close by in La Panne. It was obvious to him, as it would have been to any
competent soldier, that the withdrawal of the BEF would have to start by
rolling up from the left, with II Corps withdrawing through I Corps.
Gort's appearance and demeanour left a strong impression on Montgomery: 'He was incapable of grasping the military situation, and issuing
clear orders. He was incapable of instilling confidence or morale. He had
"had it" and I remember saying as much to Brooke.'

Montgomery remembered that Gort had a telegram in his hand, and
from what the C-in-C said next it is clear that this was the one dictated
by Churchill, quoted earlier. For, having outlined what he, Gort, had
been told to do, he finished by telling Barker that in his opinion I Corps
would not get away, and that Barker must stay with his corps and
surrender to the Germans. The effect on Barker, according to Mont-

gomery, was 'catastrophic'. After the conference broke up, Montgomery spoke to Gort alone and 'Told him that we could not yet say it was impossible to get 1 Corps away; but that it would never get away if Barker was in control, and that the only sound course was to get Barker out of it as soon as possible and give 1 Corps to Alexander. Gort agreed, and Barker was sent away.'[8]

It is evident from entries in the GHQ war diary that Gort believed that the rearguard would have to surrender; indeed at 0830 on 31 May Alexander, on visiting GHQ, was told to thin out his division, as it appeared probable that he would have to surrender the majority alongside the French. At this point he did not know that he was to command I Corps – indeed it took until 1300 hours that day for Gort to tell him. Alexander's reaction was to declare that it was his intention at all costs to extricate his command and not to surrender any part of it. No one at GHQ appears to have raised the matter of Gort's undertaking to Fagalde.

For General Fagalde had earlier been given the impression by Gort that the three divisions of I Corps were his to use as he thought fit, and had planned to integrate them with his own 60th and 68th Infantry Divisions, to hold the perimeter until capitulation was forced on them. Neither Abrial nor Fagalde was in favour of evacuation, even if it included French formations. Believing that the war was lost, Fagalde considered that the only honourable way out was to stand and not retreat. There was also an air of Micawberism in the French camp, a hope that something would turn up. This was based, correctly as it turned out, on their interpretation of the German deployment which indicated that the Wehrmacht aimed at driving south, rather than going straight on to invade the United Kingdom after Dunkirk fell. In that case it would be better to keep the armies intact in the hope that the enemy might make a mistake that would retrieve the situation rather than attempt an evacuation which in their view was doomed to failure amid losses so catastrophic they would be intolerable to the public. The German break-through at the Meuse had paralysed the French Army, reducing it to a state of doing nothing in the hope that the problem would go away. Little wonder that some days earlier General Dill, on hearing that Fagalde was threatening to use force against the BEF to prevent its embarkation, had suggested that he tell Weygand 'that through the failure of their Army we have lost the BEF'. Unpalatable though this was, and still is, to the French, it was nothing less than the truth. Although the BEF was not lost, this was due to the Royal Navy and the RAF, and to its own efforts, as well as to the gallant stand made by some French units. The BEF's survival owed nothing to the French high command. Indeed the sorry

242 DUNKIRK

tale leading to the predicament in which the BEF found itself was the product of inept command at senior level in the French Army.

While Gort and Alexander were conferring, the Supreme War Council was meeting in Paris. The British team, which had flown over that day, consisted of Churchill, the Deputy Prime Minister Attlee and Generals Dill, Ismay (Chief Staff Officer to Churchill) and Spears. During the discussion on the situation at Dunkirk it became apparent that the French seemed to have very little idea what was happening to the Northern Armies.[9] When the subject of evacuation came up, Churchill, overtaken by sentiment and much to Dill's alarm, said that the British would not embark first, but 'arm in arm' with the French. Dill intervened, and it was agreed that the British would remain as long as possible under Abrial's orders, and that British and French commanders on the spot would make the decisions. After the meeting, Churchill and his party flew back to London.

While the Supreme War Council was in session in Paris, Alexander went from Gort's headquarters to Bastion 32 at Dunkirk, taking Tennant with him. Here he found Abrial and Fagalde with their staffs, and General Altmayer, commanding French V Corps. Abrial said that Alexander would now come under Fagalde's orders. The latter outlined how he proposed deploying Alexander's units. Alexander, having listened without interrupting, laughed and said that Fagalde must be joking. His orders were to evacuate his troops, not defend part of the perimeter. Fagalde riposted by reading Gort's letter to him, and then asked if Alexander was in effect saying that the French Army alone would cover the embarkation of the British, while the British would not help the French to withdraw. Alexander replied that he would like to help, but that his orders were to evacuate. He intended pulling out his corps, consisting of 1st and 50th Divisions and a brigade of the 42nd Division, within twenty-four hours, and he added that they would all be taken prisoner if they stayed for longer. Abrial's chief of staff, Captain de Frégate de Lapérouse, interjected that if Gort knew this he had lied to Fagalde. If Gort had been telling the truth, Alexander must act as ordered by Fagalde. Alexander replied that all who could be saved would be saved. 'Except honour,' replied de Lapérouse. Alexander remained silent, and Altmayer asked him to obey Abrial.

Abrial suggested that, as there appeared to be some confusion about what Gort intended, they should go and see him, as he had not yet left the bridgehead. Alexander said that Gort had already gone. The French officers made it plain that they thought he was lying. Alexander went on to say that as he was now the senior British officer in France he was the C-in-C of the BEF, and answered only to the Secretary of State for War,

35. Vice Admiral Bertram Ramsay at his headquarters in Dover Castle.

36. British troops moving along the inner pier at Dunkirk.

37. British troops of the rearguard marching into Dunkirk town.

38. Lieutenant St Maur Sheil, London Irish Rifles, attached 2nd Ulster Rifles taking a nap in the bottom of his trench, outside Dunkirk.

39. 1 June 1940, soldiers of the Royal Ulster Rifles waiting to be evacuated from the beach at Dunkirk.

40. Soldiers of the BEF on the beaches near Dunkirk attempting to shoot down strafing German aircraft with their rifles.

41. British troops awaiting evacuation from the Dunkirk beaches.

42. *Opposite*. Fires at Dunkirk seen from a British destroyer during the evacuation.

43. HMS *Valorous* alongside the inner pier at Dunkirk, with a sunken trawler outboard. The destroyer *Imogen* is on the far side of the pier.

44. A destroyer arrives at Dover, her upper deck crammed with troops.

45. Bodies and wreckage at Dunkirk. Picture taken by the Germans.

46. The beach near La Panne at low tide after the evacuation.

47. A camouflaged A13 cruiser tank of the 2nd Armoured Brigade, British 1st Armoured Division at Fouacourt at the end of May 1940, during the division's operations south of the Somme.

48. Soldiers of the 7th Battalion Argyll & Sutherland Highlanders on the River Bresle, 6–8 June 1940, before the withdrawal of their division, 51st (Highland), to Saint-Valery.

Mr Anthony Eden. Fagalde said that disobeying Gort's instructions would bring shame on the British Army. Alexander agreed to consult Eden.

On his return to La Panne, Alexander telephoned Eden at 1915 hours, informing him that the French wished to hold for another three nights. He added that prolonging the evacuation would not enable more troops to get away; on the contrary the BEF would be 'wiped out'. He asked for a decision as soon as possible.

Meanwhile, Abrial had sent a signal to Weygand asking that Churchill be persuaded to order Alexander not to evacuate on the night of 1 June. Within an hour of receiving Alexander's call, Eden was back on the telephone saying: 'You should withdraw your forces as rapidly as possible on a 50–50 basis with the French Army, aiming at completion by the night of 1st/2nd June. You should inform the French of this definite instruction.'[10]

Alexander queried the '50–50 basis', which could be taken to mean that the British rate of evacuation should be slowed up until the French numbers reached parity with the British. He was told it meant equal numbers from then on. No one in the British Cabinet or War Office informed Weygand or the British liaison officer at GQG, Major General Howard-Vyse, that what Alexander had been ordered to do contradicted the arrangements agreed by the Supreme War Council in Paris.

Alexander returned to Bastion 32 at around 2300 hours and told Abrial that he would hold his sector until one minute to midnight on 1 June. By now the Supreme War Council decision had arrived at Abrial's head-quarters and was shown to Alexander. His reaction was to say that he did not serve under the Prime Minister's orders. Although this might strike one as somewhat cheeky, if not downright insubordinate, Alexander was correct. He had received instructions from Eden, who as Secretary of State for War was his political boss. The British Defence Operations Committee, acting in the absence of the Prime Minister, had approved these instructions. The decision had been taken based on considerably more up-to-date information about the true state of affairs in the Dunkirk bridgehead than was available in the fantasy world inhabited by Weygand and the French politicians. Abrial's reaction was to say that Alexander's decision dishonoured England.

The next day saw heated discussions between Paris and London. Churchill, having agreed to Abrial exercising overall command at Dunkirk, told Weygand in a telegram that

Situation cannot be fully judged by Admiral Abrial in the fortress, nor by you, nor by us here. We have therefore ordered General Alexander, commanding British sector of bridgehead, to judge in consultation with

Admiral Abrial, whether to try to stay over tomorrow or not. Trust you will agree."

It is possible that the attitude of the British War Cabinet, and of Churchill, had been hardened by Gort's accounts of the French perform-ance during the campaign. Gort had returned to London during the night of 31 May/1 June, and had lost no time giving ministers his opinions on, among others, Billotte, Abrial, Fagalde and the French Army's poor showing against the Germans.

The troops in the Dunkirk perimeter were unaware of the disagree-ments between the British and French at senior level, and it is time to return to the battle of the bridgehead.

10

THE END AT DUNKIRK

The problem facing any commander holding a bridgehead from which he wants to withdraw is maintaining a crust tough enough to resist enemy penetration, while thinning out troops to embark. From time to time he must reduce the length of the perimeter in order to release men to maintain the flow of troops back to the waiting ships and craft.

On 31 May, the day on which there was so much top-level discussion and dissension among the French and British, the Germans attacked at most points along the perimeter, but the heaviest assaults were on the eastern end. This suited the British because that sector, held by II Corps, was to be abandoned anyway that night. West of Dunkirk, the French were well protected by the maze of waterways round Mardick. The buildings of Bergues provided an easily defended anchor to the British right flank, held by I Corps.

Montgomery's plan for the evacuation of II Corps was that the Germans were to be strongly counter-attacked wherever they attempted to cross the Nieuport–Furnes Canal. After dark the 3rd and 4th Divisions were to thin out and head for the beaches of La Panne and Bray-Dunes. At 0900 hours on 31 May, Montgomery had summoned all the sappers in his corps and ordered them to construct piers at La Panne from vehicles run out into the sea. Squalls at sea brought evacuation from La Panne almost to a halt that morning, but this did not appear to worry Montgomery – he lunched with Brigadier Anderson, who had taken over the 3rd Division when Montgomery moved up to commanding the corps. At 14.30 hours, Montgomery gave his final orders for the withdrawal. He had moved corps headquarters to La Panne beach that morning where it would be in the best position to control the evacuation. He had also had reception areas set up in the dunes; soldiers were called from these down to the beach for embarkation when the beach commander summoned them. Fortunately the 3rd Division signallers had managed to bring enough telephone cable into the perimeter to link brigades with divisional headquarters and also to link reception areas with the beach commander. During the afternoon and early evening the embarkation of corps troops, administrative units and the rear-echelon elements of

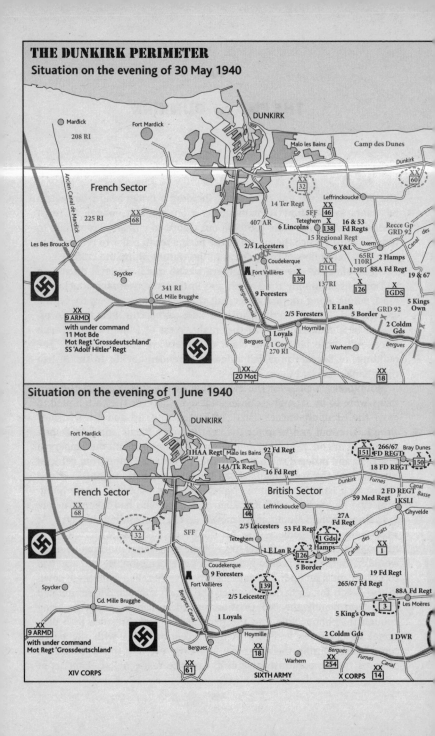

THE DUNKIRK PERIMETER

Situation on the evening of 30 May 1940

Mardick
Fort Mardick
208 RI

DUNKIRK
Malo les Bains
Camp des Dunes
Dunkirk
XX 60

French Sector
XX 32

225 RI
XX 68

Les Bes Broucks
Spycker
341 RI
Gd. Mille Brugghe

Ancien Canal de Mardick

14 Ter Regt
5FF
407 AR
6 Lincolns
Teteghem
15 Regional Regt
2/5 Leicesters
6 Y&L
Coudekerque
Fort Vallières
9 Foresters
2/5 Foresters

Leffrinckoucke
XX 46
X 138
16 & 53 Fd Regts
Recce Gp GRD 92
Uxem
65RI 110RI
2 Hamps
XX 21CI
X 139
129RI 88A Fd Regt
X 126
137RI
IGDS
1 E LanR
5 Border
GRD 92

19 & 67
X
5 Kings Own
2 Coldm Gds
Bergues

XX 9 ARMD
with under command
11 Mot Bde
Mot Regt 'Grossdeutschland'
SS 'Adolf Hitler' Regt

1 Loyals
Bergues
1 Coy
270 RI
Hoymille
Warhem

XX 20 Mot
XX 18

Situation on the evening of 1 June 1940

Fort Mardick
DUNKIRK
1HAA Regt
Malo les Bains
92 Fd Regt
14A/Tk Regt
16 Fd Regt

X 151
266/67 FD REGT
Bray Dunes
X 150
18 FD REGT
Dunkirk Furnes Canal Basse
2 FD REGT
59 Med Regt
1KSLI

French Sector
XX 68
XX 32
XX 46
Leffrinckoucke
SFF
2/5 Leicesters
53 Fd Regt
Teteghem
1 E Lan R
27A Fd Regt
X 1 Gds
X 126
2 Hamps
Uxem
5 Border
Canal des Chats
Ghyvelde
XX 1

Spycker
Gd. Mille Brugghe
Coudekerque
9 Foresters
Fort Vallières
X 139
2/5 Leicester
19 Fd Regt
265/67 Fd Regt
88A Fd Regt
X 3
Les Moëres

XX 9 ARMD
with under command
Mot Regt 'Grossdeutschland'
1 Loyals
Hoymille
5 King's Own
2 Coldm Gds
1 DWR

Bergues
XX 18
Warhem
Bergues Furnes Canal

XIV CORPS
XX 61
SIXTH ARMY
XX 254
X CORPS
XX 14

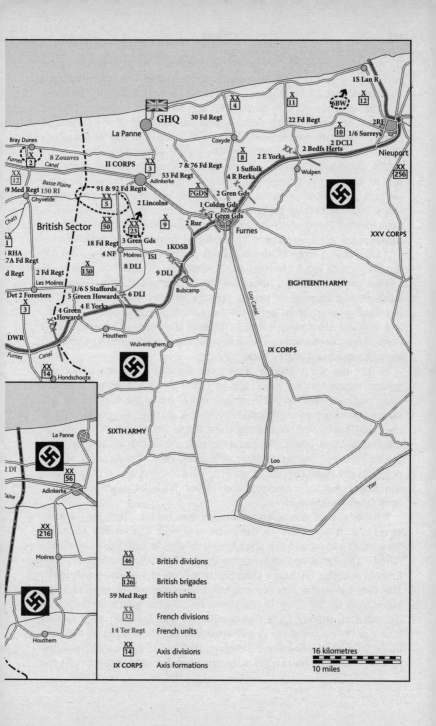

Bray Dunes

$\frac{X}{2}$ Furnes

8 Zouaves
Canal

La Panne

$\frac{XX}{12}$ 59 Med Regt 150 RI

Basse Plaine

Ghyvelde

Chats

$\frac{X}{1}$ RHA

7A Fd Regt

d Regt 2 Fd Regt

Les Moëres

Det 2 Foresters

$\frac{X}{3}$

DWR

Furnes Canal

$\frac{XX}{14}$ Hondschoote

GHQ

30 Fd Regt

II CORPS $\frac{XX}{3}$

Adinkerke

$\frac{X}{11}$

$\frac{XX}{4}$

Coxyde

$\frac{X}{8}$ 2 E Yorks

7 & 76 Fd Regt

53 Fd Regt

$\frac{X}{7GDS}$ 2 Gren Gds

2 Lincolns 1 Coldm Gds

$\frac{XX}{5}$

$\frac{X}{9}$ 2 Rur 1 Gren Gds

$\frac{XX}{50}$ $\frac{XX}{23}$

3 Gren Gds Furnes

18 Fd Regt

$\frac{X}{150}$ 4 NF Moëres ISI

8 DLI 1KOSB

9 DLI

1/6 S Staffords

5 Green Howards 6 DLI

4 E Yorks Bulscamp

4 Green
Howards

Houthem

Wulveringhem

1S Lan R.

$\frac{X}{12}$

$\frac{X}{10}$ 1/6 Surreys

22 Fd Regt 2 DCLI

2 Bedfs Herts Nieuport

Wulpen 2RF

$\frac{XX}{256}$

6BW

1 Suffolk
4 R Berks

XXV CORPS

EIGHTEENTH ARMY

Loo Canal

IX CORPS

SIXTH ARMY

La Panne

2 DI

$\frac{XX}{56}$

Adinkerke

laine

$\frac{XX}{216}$

Moëres

Loo

Yser

Houthem

$\frac{XX}{46}$ British divisions

$\frac{X}{126}$ British brigades

59 Med Regt British units

$\frac{XX}{32}$ French divisions

14 Ter Regt French units

$\frac{XX}{14}$ Axis divisions

IX CORPS Axis formations

16 kilometres

10 miles

II Corps went smoothly despite German shelling. At 2100 hours, as the pace of the evacuation accelerated, Montgomery and Alexander conferred and agreed that all was going to plan. Now that Gort had gone, these two had the situation well in hand. They agreed that if La Panne became unusable for any reason II Corps would use the beaches at Bray-Dunes, and if these could not be used, the port of Dunkirk would be closed to I Corps to allow II Corps to get away first – a providential decision.

The Combined Squadron of the 4th/7th Royal Dragoon Guards was sent to join the 150th Brigade in the area of Bray-Dunes. During the night German shelling blew in the windows and doors of the house where Major Frink had set up his headquarters, noting 'sixteen shells landed in field where 2 Troop and vehicles were – everyone well dug in – only one casualty, one pig – thus saving us trouble [of despatching it before eating it]'. The area in front of the squadron position was held by a French division, which Frink describes as 'excellent and efficient'.

That day on II Corps front, instead of concentrating, the Germans attacked at a number of places. German artillery observers located in Houthem brought down heavy fire on the 150th Brigade (4th East Yorks, and 4th and 5th Green Howards) holding the Furnes Canal line on II Corps' right flank. But any Germans who survived crossing the canal were eliminated or beaten back.

Within the 151st Brigade sector, the 8th DLI had been allocated a reserve location along the Ringsloot Canal about a mile north of the main perimeter line of the Bergues–Furnes Canal. The 9th DLI, the left forward battalion of the brigade, were slow getting into position up to the canal bank, and on arriving there found the Germans just on the other side. As a result the battalion suffered casualties as they were unable to dig in during the day, within full view of the enemy. If they stayed in the open they came under small-arms fire, and if they took to the houses they were mortared and shelled. With the onset of darkness, at last they could dig in.

Bulscamp provided a good covered forming-up place for German attacks, as it was close to the canal, and was also on the boundary between the 151st and 9th Brigades. From here, at first light, the enemy crossed the canal and drove a wedge between the 9th DLI of 151st Brigade and the 1st King's Own Scottish Borderers of the 9th Brigade. The two battalions counter-attacked and succeeded in regaining the home bank of the canal. In the afternoon, another attack on the left of the 9th DLI, driving back two companies, was followed by a further attack in the centre of the brigade position, and the 6th DLI on the right of the 9th had to give ground. However, the 8th DLI put in a stop position in rear, bolstered by the 3rd Grenadiers who managed to contain the

enemy, while the brigade commander patched up the gaps in the left and right of his sector using the 4th Royal Northumberland Fusiliers in their scout cars and motorcycles. The movement of all this transport gave rise to scares of German tanks. As evening approached, the shelling in the 151st Brigade sector became heavier, and the machine-gunners of the 4th Gordons and 2nd Royal Northumberland Fusiliers, sent forward during the day to dig in along the Ringsloot Canal, began to lay down a stream of defensive machine-gun fire in front of the 8th DLI. Under cover of this fire, the two flank battalions, the 6th and 9th DLI, came back and reoccupied their positions. The whole 151st Brigade front was by now a jumble of platoons of several battalions intermixed.

The château which had been the headquarters of all three battalions in the 151st Brigade, in various outbuildings, now became uninhabitable thanks to shellfire, so the three COs moved out to the woods behind. All day a joint RAP had been operating in the château, where the doctors assisted by Father Duggan, the brigade Roman Catholic priest, had been doing good work keeping the wounded calm, mainly 6th and 9th DLI caught by shellfire during their temporary retirement. At this stage the brigade commander divided the brigade front into two halves in an effort to restore a modicum of control over the patchwork of sub-units holding the sector. The CO of 9th DLI took over the left half, and McLaren, still commanding the 8th, the right, irrespective of which battalion the miscellany of soldiers belonged to. In the evening, the orders were given to the 151st Brigade to retire, not for evacuation but to hold positions in the vicinity of Bray-Dunes, which would become part of the new left flank of the BEF once II Corps had pulled out that night.

The 7th Guards Brigade (1st and 2nd Grenadiers, and 1st Coldstream) had some tough fighting among the ruins of Furnes. Brigade headquarters, dug into a dung heap in a farmyard, was treated to a heavy dose of artillery fire just as the battalion COs assembled to receive orders for the withdrawal that night. The Guards held on to enough of the town on their side of the canal to provide good observation posts for artillery and mortars, which had just sufficient ammunition for one day's shooting. The Guards had also kept some of their carriers and used these to good effect to counter-attack any attempts by the Germans to exploit their gains in the 4th Royal Berkshire sector the day before (see Chapter 9).

The main German effort along the perimeter was directed against the extreme left flank of the BEF at Nieuport. At dawn a heavy attack came in under the cover of smoke. But the brisk sea breeze dispersed the smoke and, shorn of its cover, the attackers were mown down in large numbers by Brens and Vickers machine guns. But a follow-up attack managed to penetrate south and north of Nieuport, threatening to cut

off the 2nd Royal Fusiliers. A company of the 1st South Lancashires, under Captain Butler, stopped the northern penetration.

Early that morning, the 1st East Surreys had received orders to embark, and moved along the coast to Coxyde-Bains. Here to their surprise some of the seaside hotels were still open and doing business. While waiting at this seaside resort, the embarkation order was suddenly cancelled and the battalion was turned about and sent to reinforce the 10th Brigade opposite Nieuport. A dangerous situation had developed on the open flank of the 1st/6th East Surreys, whose much depleted left-hand company was holding the brickworks. The 1st East Surreys moved in their own transport, which fortunately the CO had refused to destroy despite orders to do so. The CO and intelligence officer, Lieutenant Bocquet, went ahead to meet Brigadier Barker, the commander of 10th Brigade, and carry out a reconnaissance for the counter-attack. At this juncture, Bocquet was wounded, but managed to carry on. The counter-attack was launched with B Company leading and the remainder eche-loned back.

This counter-attack by 1st East Surreys stabilized the situation. At one stage, the two COs were seen firing a Bren gun together, fighting a private war of their own. In the late afternoon, the enemy could be seen forming up on the eastern side of the canal, clearly heading for another attack on the sector held by the two East Surrey battalions, when as if by a miracle eighteen Blenheim bombers and six naval Albacores flew over and bombed them. This was one of the very rare occasions when the RAF provided close air support to the BEF throughout the campaign; at this stage in the war the necessary procedures and communications did not exist, so describing this incident as a 'miracle' is not over-egging the pudding. The East Surreys certainly thought so as they stood cheering and waving in delight at seeing the Germans being treated to a dose of what they had endured at the hands of the Luftwaffe ever since 10 May. The two East Surrey battalions held the position until the 1st Battalion was ordered to withdraw at 0200 hours prior to embarkation.

This marked the fifth day of hard fighting and marching by the troops of 3rd Division, and these five days were themselves the culmination of some three weeks of marching, digging and fighting with little rest. Only when the orders for the withdrawal came through at last light did they know when their ordeal would end. As before, the task of pulling out was made easier by the German reluctance to fight at night, and the dark lines of British soldiers began to converge on the beaches. Here the evacuation was not going well, because between 2300 hours and 0300 hours the tide was too low for the makeshift piers to be used – something that the army beach staff had not foreseen, and perhaps the navy had

failed to alert them to this nautical fact. From 2300 hours the troops were told to march along the beach to Bray-Dunes. Here Montgomery directed them on to Dunkirk, a march of over fifteen miles for the battalions on the left flank. He described it in his diary:

It was clearly impossible to continue embarkation at the beaches and I ordered the troops to move on to Dunkirk and embark there; this they were loath to do as they saw the ships lying off and hoped that boats would come to the shore; but no boats came.[1]

The 1st East Surreys had been told to go to La Panne, and as the coast road was under shellfire the CO ordered the companies to disperse into small parties and march clear of the road wherever possible. The CO then drove in his car with Major Bousfield and Captain Hill, OC Headquarters Company and acting adjutant, to a bend in the road between Coxyde and La Panne, where they dismounted to see the battalion past. Unfortunately this part of the road was under intense and accurate artillery fire. The first casualty was the CO's driver, Private Dennis. The shelling continued and Major Bousfield cried that he was hit. The CO and Captain Hill hauled Bousfield into the car, and with the CO at the wheel drove into La Panne. Here Bousfield was taken into a field ambulance badly wounded. He was later killed when being taken by ambulance into Dunkirk.

At La Panne the CO assembled the 1st East Surreys in the sand dunes, disposing the battalion in defensive positions round an especially prominent dune, which he christened Surrey Hill. He was determined to get the battalion back to England in one body if it could be managed. Seeing an RNLI lifeboat high and dry on the beach, he decided to commandeer it as the battalion's private craft to ferry troops out to the shipping offshore. He ordered a cordon to be thrown round the vessel and the battalion fitters to get the engines going. Amid cries from the cordon of 'Anyone for the Skylark?', the two fitters descended into the engine room. They were unable to coax the diesel motors back into life, and emerged, the air blue with their opinions of marine engines and their designers. At this point, the divisional commander's ADC, or a member of his staff, appeared and said, 'The General's compliments and you are to take your battalion to Dunkirk for embarkation.'

Dunkirk was ten miles away along the sands. In the early-morning daylight, the 1st East Surreys could see the columns of black smoke rising from the town. In addition to the shelling and mortaring of the beaches, aircraft strafed the troops at low level with machine-gun fire and bombed the ships out to sea. The CO held his final O Group on Surrey Hill, stressing two points. The companies were to march well

dispersed in small groups, and every man was to carry a weapon. The beaches between La Panne and Dunkirk were black with troops and long queues waded into the water chest high waiting to be picked up by boats. There was a general move towards Dunkirk, which in spite of shelling and bombing seemed to offer better chances of embarkation. The battalion set off at intervals, marching close to the water's edge where the sand was firmer. They were soon caught up in an endless procession moving slowly along towards the harbour at Dunkirk, which never seemed to get any nearer. It was a laborious march along the sand, for the day got hotter and the men were exceedingly tired. The CO insisted that the soldiers picked up every serviceable-looking Bren he spotted. One young officer, marching along behind his CO, was ordered to pick these up and pass them back down the file, where most were dumped. The soldiers were already carrying their personal weapons and there was a limit to how much extra they could lug through the sand.

When the 1st East Surreys arrived at the outskirts of Dunkirk, the CO and adjutant went forward to arrange with the embarkation staff for the battalion to be embarked in one ship. There were several ships alongside the mole, and Lieutenant Colonel Boxshall was directed to HMS *Esk*, a Hunt-class destroyer. No sooner was he aboard and trying to arrange for the whole battalion to be accommodated than the ship, which was still quite empty as far as he could see, cast off. Boxshall, horrified at the prospect of leaving his battalion behind, dashed to the bridge demanding that the ship should wait. The captain was sympathetic but replied that a transport had been bombed in mid-Channel, and he had been ordered to pick up survivors. Boxshall would willingly have swum for shore, but the destroyer was moving out fast.

Travelling at full speed, the *Esk* soon reached the stricken ship, a two-funnelled transport, carrying the French 22nd Infantry Regiment. A bomb had gone down her after funnel, exploding in the engine room, and when the *Esk* arrived she was lying on her beam ends, with French soldiers around her, holding on to anything that would float. Several small craft had begun the task of picking up the soldiers, when German aircraft appeared and bombed the rescue operations. Some of the unfortunate soldiers were swept away by the strong tide, and their cries were pitiful to hear. But the majority were rescued. The *Esk* docked in Dover later that afternoon, with Boxshall frantic with anxiety about the battalion from which he had been so abruptly snatched.

Sergeant Green with his platoon of Bedfordshire & Herefordshires, having received the order to move to the road linking Nieuport and La Panne, thought that they would all march to the vehicle jetty and embark. His platoon got cut off and they found themselves mixed up

with A Company of the Duke of Cornwall's Light Infantry (DCLI). On arrival at La Panne they found the town on fire, shells dropping, vehicles and dead bodies all over the place, and men from all units trudging on towards the sea. Green led his platoon into the dunes and sat down for a rest.

By the time the 1st/6th East Surreys withdrew, there had been one case of desertion, an officer, found four miles in rear of the position. He was court-martialled on return to England, cashiered and sent to prison. No soldiers deserted. On arrival at La Panne, Captain White, the adjutant, was ordered to split up the battalion and tell them to make their way to beaches and embark where they could. White walked along the beach with Major General Johnson, the GOC of the 4th Division, who told him to take battalion headquarters towards the beach at La Panne, arriving early on 1 June. In White's opinion the embarkation was not chaotic. Although there were masses of people on the beaches and no one organized the evacuation, whenever a vessel approached, an officer or NCO would lead his group of men down to a lifeboat or small craft. There was, according to White, no panic. His party was picked up by a whaler from HMS *Speedwell*. Hanging on to the side of the boat as they could not all get in, they were rowed out to the ship. White went to a mess deck and fell asleep on the table, waking up several hours later in Dover. The remainder of his battalion embarked from the mole at Dunkirk, probably sent there by Montgomery. The problem, as White acknowledges, was the total lack of radios to companies within an infantry battalion at the time; once troops were on the move, the telephone was useless.

With the onset of darkness, McLaren had walked along the front of his half of the 151st Brigade sector. The machine-gunners of the Gordons and Northumberland Fusiliers, who had been firing almost continuously, had run out of ammunition at dusk and had pulled out. McLaren had some difficulty at first in persuading some of the DLI men not to follow, but after talking to them for a moment or two they steadied down. The German shelling of the château intensified, hitting an ammunition truck and setting it on fire, which after a huge explosion set the whole motor-transport park alight. During the night, McLaren walked up and down calming the soldiers. The Germans never came close, and the withdrawal began at 0200 hours so that all troops were clear of the position by 0230. Covered by the carriers, the 8th DLI marched north to the coast, and then along the coast to a position east of Bray-Dunes. McLaren lost his way thanks to a 'bad map' and fell into a ditch getting soaked. Eventually the battalion dug in among the dunes and had a meal.

As the last of the II Corps perimeter defences pulled out, it was vital that the complete corps should be within the sector held by I Corps by

first light. So Montgomery stayed at Bray-Dunes until 0330 hours person-ally directing the troops straight down the beach towards Dunkirk. While standing on the beach, his ADC, Charles Sweeney of the Ulster Rifles, was wounded in the head by a shell splinter. Montgomery cursed him soundly for not wearing a steel helmet, at which Sweeney pointed out that his general was not wearing one either. Sweeney remained with Montgomery through much of the war, being killed, much to Mont-gomery's distress, right at the end in Germany in 1945. Montgomery left Bray-Dunes and walked towards Dunkirk with Sweeney and his BGS, Ritchie. After about an hour, they struck inland and hitched a lift in a truck to Dunkirk. Here they embarked in the destroyer *Codrington*.

Sergeant Green became separated from his platoon among the crowds in the dunes and managed to hitch a lift on a carrier to Dunkirk, by which time it was daylight. Here he joined the crowd on the mole, which included French troops, some with suitcases and even bicycles but no weapons, in marked contrast to British troops who mostly had weapons. Before he reached the end of the mole, an RAMC orderly came up leading another man, about six foot six inches tall, wearing just boots, shirt and trousers. His eyes were opaque and he moved 'like a zombie'. At the end of the mole, Green spotted a naval party under a piece of canvas: with 'hell breaking loose all round them, they were all sound asleep'. Along-side the mole, there was a destroyer, beached and blown in half – 'you could see straight through her'. At the end of the mole destroyers came in with their guns pointing skywards firing at aircraft.

Green embarked on the forecastle of a destroyer by sliding down a table-top from the mole, and the vessel slipped at about 0800 hours. He was told to chuck his rifle down and go below. The destroyer went off at high speed, zigzagging. Every so often there was a near miss, and the ship lifted. After one particularly close one, Green asked a sailor if it would take more than one bomb to sink the ship, and received the reply, 'No. One will be enough. We've only light decks over the boilers in these ships.' One young soldier really 'went bonkers' for a minute or two, making a dive for the ladder to get up on deck. This was a relief because it gave the other soldiers something to do. Everyone piled on him, saying, 'Sit down, silly bugger.'

Brooke, on his arrival back at Dover the night before, had warned Ramsay that the greatest shipping effort would be required on the night of 31 May/1 June, and Ramsay had acted accordingly. As the exhausted II Corps soldiers arrived at Dunkirk, they found ships waiting for them. Some soldiers waited to join the queue at Bray-Dunes. Because there had never been a central organization for the embarkation, with communi-

cations between embarkation points, there was no mechanism for switching the effort from beaches where embarkation was slow or completely stopped to places where it was going better.

Frink's choice of location for the night of 31 May/1 June, between an artillery battery and the main road, was not so fortunate as both were shelled continually all night, but luckily this caused no casualties to the 4th/7th squadron. 'The whole countryside was lit up by burning vehicles and villages.' The soldiers' natural inclination to appropriate any kit left lying about had not been diminished by the death and destruction all round them, and Frink's troopers found a truckload of number 9 wireless sets (the ones used in armoured vehicles), some of which they fitted to their own tanks.

With the daylight came the Luftwaffe, in larger numbers than ever before. It sank two destroyers right away, one being the *Keith*, with Admiral Wake-Walker embarked. Lieutenant Lumsden, the navigator of the *Keith*, recalled that the first three Stukas from the attacking wave missed, but the explosions from their bombs were so close that the steering gear jammed. The ship was being steered by hand from the tiller compartment when another bomb exploded and holed the starboard side between the engine boiler rooms, inflicting heavy casualties and total loss of power. The ship listed heavily and stopped. The *Keith* was anchored, and Wake-Walker and his staff boarded a launch to continue their work. Another Stuka came in and bombed the stern, starting a fire and wounding more men.

The destroyer continued to list and settle in the water, so the captain ordered abandon ship, but asked Lumsden to stay with him with a skeleton crew, in case a tow back to Dover could be arranged. A Dutch coaster took the rest of the crew to Ramsgate. As the *Keith* sank deeper, the captain summoned an Admiralty tug alongside, and she embarked the wounded and everyone else alive. As the tug pulled away, another onslaught of bombers blew the *Keith* apart, sinking her instantly; she was gone before the bomb splashes subsided.

At this point the skies seemed clear of enemy bombers, except for a lone aircraft. In case he had any bombs left, the tug skipper made a circle to starboard, and as he did so the world seemed to stand on end. The tug split in half and the forepart sank in thirty seconds, trapping all those under the forecastle. Those lucky enough to be on the bridge, including Lumsden, struck out for the beach, about three-quarters of a mile away, a laborious process in full uniform and inflated lifebelt. Lumsden, reinforcing his will to swim on by 'picturing his wife's small but beautiful backside', aimed at a redbrick fort in the dunes at Bray. About a hundred

yards from the beach, he scrambled on to the deck of a wrecked yacht
for a breather. Finding that he was still wearing his heavy binoculars, he
hurled them into the sea.

Once he had completed the swim inshore, Lumsden was taken to the
fort by some French sailors. After a rest and a fortifying cognac, he set
off for Dunkirk dressed in a French sailor's uniform, complete with flat
hat and pom-pom, to replace his own soaked kit. Here he found Wake-
Walker in his launch alongside Dunkirk pier, who offered him a lift back
to Dover.

The onset of daylight found Major Colvin, the acting CO of the 2nd
Grenadiers, attempting to use the few small boats at La Panne to lift the
wounded out to the destroyers offshore. After an hour spent up to his
neck in water, under machine-gun and cannon attack by Messerschmitts,
he abandoned the task as hopeless. He joined the crowd heading for
Dunkirk, saddened by the sight of the wounded, who had to be abandoned where they had been cut down by the Messerschmitts, and who
would probably drown when the tide flooded. Incoming shellfire persuaded him that a ground attack was imminent, and he decided to try
another attempt at embarking from the beach as the tide was flooding
strongly. With some men he had gathered he waded out to a wrecked
steamer, hoping to attract the attention of a destroyer not far off. As they
scrambled aboard the wreck, they saw the destroyer sunk by Stukas, and
its crew being machine-gunned in the water.

Having waded back to the beach, he found an abandoned whaler, and
with fourteen soldiers, none of whom could row, headed for a naval
tender which was in the process of picking up sailors, many of whom
were covered in oil and in some cases badly wounded. No sooner had
Colvin and his party boarded the tender than three Heinkel bombers
screamed in, making several runs at the tender and eventually scoring a
hit with one bomb. The tender blew up, and Colvin found himself in the
water with a damaged leg and surrounded by drowning soldiers. The
survivors clung to pieces of wreckage and made desperate attempts to
attract the attention of a passing vessel. Men were now dying from shock
or drowning from cramp.

Colvin and a few others managed to swim to another wreck and drag
themselves up the dangling gangway, collapsing on deck with exhaustion. The Germans bombed the wreck but missed. A passing Thames
lighter spotted the survivors and coming alongside the wreck took them
off. The master of the lighter insisted on heading for the beach and
picking up some wounded. Fortune must have been smiling on him
because the Germans were very close by now, as the beach was in
Belgium. Having collected the wounded, the lighter picked up four

Belgian soldiers from a dinghy and two Grenadiers from another small boat, and returned to Dover. Colvin would almost certainly have had an easier time had he walked down the beach to Dunkirk.

There were several small parties of soldiers in the Dunkirk area who found that being separated from their unit was a disadvantage when it came to being allocated a boat or ship in which to get away. One such was Second Lieutenant McSwiney's group, which consisted of twelve gunners of his own sub-unit, 2nd Light Anti-Aircraft Battery, and about fifty 'odds and sods' added to them by a beachmaster at La Panne trying to wash his hands of them. At first McSwiney had tried marching them to Dunkirk. As they arrived there was a massive air attack, and both the town and the area near the mole were soon burning furiously. Deterred by this, he decided to return to La Panne, and on his way back tried joining several columns of troops that were embarking from small boats at the water's edge. But on each occasion that his party reached the head of the column, an officer asked what unit they were from. When he told the truth, the politest refusal he got was, 'Sorry we can't take odds and sods.' So he returned to the original beachmaster at La Panne.

After a brew of tea and a breakfast of bully beef and biscuit, they flopped down in the dunes, utterly exhausted, and slept until woken by shelling; the Germans had got the range of their section of the beach, and it created pandemonium. Men ran down to the water, tore off their clothes and started swimming to the destroyers and other craft, half a mile or more offshore; several were drowned. McSwiney managed to keep his party together with the help of a regimental sergeant major who had joined his group. When the shelling stopped, they returned to the water to try again, but the ships offshore seemed to be working with columns well to their right or nearer Dunkirk. The men were machine-gunned and bombed by aircraft at intervals. Their spirits were temporarily lifted when five of the party appeared with a quantity of tinned food, having raided a coastguard station, but the night passed slowly. It rained, and by morning they were cold and wet.

Early the next morning, McSwiney went to see the brigadier at the control centre near La Panne and told him his story. The brigadier's reply was to the effect that there were other groups like McSwiney's; he was very sorry, but they would have to fend for themselves. Either the RAF had established temporary superiority over the beaches or the Luftwaffe was busy elsewhere, for no German aircraft appeared over this section of the beach for a while. As the day wore on, McSwiney spotted what looked like three small ships' boats floating in on the tide assisted by a northerly breeze. They appeared to be empty, and he guessed that after being rowed out to one of the destroyers they had been abandoned. If his party

could grab them before they reached the men on the beach, they were theirs. Three men volunteered to swim out to take possession of the boats, and managed to pull them closer in to shore. While McSwiney and two others stood up to their armpits in water to stop the boats grounding, his men piled in, cramming twenty to a boat. At this point the Luftwaffe returned to this part of the beach, bombed the nearest destroyer and missed. But one bomb fell so close that McSwiney's boat capsized. It was a case of either swimming for the destroyer, which was about 200 yards away, or clinging to the upturned boat and drifting back to the beach. Fortunately he had ordered his party to take off their boots on the beach, in case they had to swim. Three non-swimmers paddled to the destroyer on McSwiney's air bed, which he had kept in defiance of his battery commander's orders. The remainder swam. Climbing up the scrambling net was the hardest part of all. At last they flopped on the deck gasping like beached whales. The party had arrived in the late afternoon, but the destroyer, HMS *Shikari*, remained offshore until the next morning, before heading for Dover.

During the daylight hours of 1 June, Frink's Combined Squadron of the 4th/7th Royal Dragoon Guards was kept busy patrolling the area of the British perimeter. The remaining four tanks were split into two patrols of two vehicles each and sent to locate the enemy if possible, while the rest of the squadron manned OPs on roads leading into the perimeter. As the roads were cratered behind them, the patrols and OPs were withdrawn. No enemy were encountered, but their shelling and bombing was all too pervasive. All likely targets such as roads and other key points were treated to comprehensive shelling. Frink, with his usual cavalry sangfroid, had time despite the mayhem all around him to go for what he called 'a country ramble' with Major General Martell, GOC of the 50th Division.

The men of the 50th Division among the dunes around Bray-Dunes were heartened at about midday when the RAF appeared and engaged the German aircraft in a series of dogfights. Little more was seen of the Luftwaffe overhead in that sector for the rest of the day. At around 1230 hours, the commander of the 151st Brigade reorganized the brigade into a force of mobile fighting units and marching units. McLaren found himself with about a hundred Grenadiers added to his battalion. He sent men down to the beach to gather any spare weapons lying about, and they came back with a quantity of Brens. He fully expected to have to fight his way to Dunkirk

Throughout 1 June the embarkation alongside the East Mole at Dunkirk went on under heavy attacks by the Luftwaffe, mainly in the gaps between RAF fighter sweeps, which had been reduced to eight per day in

order that each might be made in strength. That day the Luftwaffe sank thirty-one ships, including four destroyers. At 1800 hours, Captain Tennant decided that there would be no more daylight embarkations from Dunkirk or the remaining beaches still in Allied hands.

The 2nd Duke of Cornwall's Light Infantry arrived at Dunkirk at about midday, having walked all the way from the far end of the II Corps perimeter. While they were embarking, the DCLI were given the task of loading a hundred stretcher cases aboard the sloop HMS *Kingfisher* right at the end of the East Mole. The mole had almost been cut in half by bombing, and carrying stretchers over the narrow planking that bridged the gap was not made any easier by the attentions of the Luftwaffe. The mole was holed again while the long line of stretchers was being carried along through the debris and spray from several near misses. The ships' AA guns, as well as almost every rifle, Bren and even pistol in the battalion, added to the cacophony of noise. In a brief lull in the fire, the sloop's captain was heard shouting from the bridge, 'Get those bloody Pongos [soldiers] below, they are shooting away my aerials.' He was ignored: every man aboard was determined to do all he could to ensure that the Luftwaffe did not stop them getting away. The total number of troops evacuated during 31 May and 1 June was 132,443, of whom 40,290 were taken off the beaches and 92,153 from Dunkirk harbour. By now the accumulated total evacuated was 259,049. About 20,000 British troops remained, and a far larger number of French.

With II Corps embarked, all that remained operational of the BEF on the morning of 1 June was seven brigades under command of Alexander of I Corps. On the right were 139th Brigade (2nd/5th Leicesters, 2nd/5th and 9th Sherwood Foresters, plus 1st Loyals and C Company, 2nd Royal Warwicks), with 138th Brigade (6th Lincolns, 2nd/4th King's Own Yorkshire Light Infantry (KOYLI), and 6th York & Lancasters) in support, all under command of Major General Curtis of the 46th Division. On the left Brigadier Beckwith-Smith, the acting GOC of the 1st Division, had the 126th Brigade (1st East Lancashires, 5th King's Own and 5th Borders), 1st Guards Brigade (2nd Coldstream and 2nd Hampshires) and 3rd Brigade (1st Duke of Wellington's, 2nd Sherwood Foresters and 1st King's Shropshire Light Infantry). The 50th Division consisting of the 150th and 151st Brigades was located around Bray-Dunes behind the French 12th Infantry Division. The 5th Division had been withdrawn for evacuation. All battalions were short of men – for example, the 2nd/5th Leicesters were down to seventy all ranks. The composite regiment formed by the Combined Squadron of the 4th/7th Dragoon Guards and two squadrons of the 5th Inniskilling Dragoon Guards provided the only armoured support, having taken over all the available light tanks. The artillery

consisted of elements of one medium and six field regiments. All had some ammunition, but none was plentifully supplied.

The Germans deployed four divisions against the thinly held Canal Line, and a further two on the eastern flank. Here, although the ground was seamed with ditches, there was no serious obstacle. The German 14th and 18th Divisions had fought the BEF on the Dyle, the Escaut and on each side of Ypres. Preceded by a heavy bombardment, the 18th Division thrust towards Téteghem. In some cases the Germans swam the canal and gained a foothold on the British side. Despite taking heavy losses, the Germans drove back C Company, 2nd Royal Warwicks, from the Hoymille bridge. With no reserve other than the seventy men of the 2nd/5th Leicesters, Brigadier Chichester-Constable of the 139th Brigade ordered the 1st Loyals to abandon Bergues and mount a counter-attack to clear the north bank of the canal. Under heavy shellfire which caused many casualties (one shell alone killed nine Loyals and wounded seventeen), the Loyals left Bergues to the care of a French detachment. The counter-attack through knee-deep water fizzled out. However, backed by some Inniskilling light tanks, the Loyals were eventually able to prevent the Germans from gaining any more ground. The Germans in their turn were deterred by the prospect of attacking across the same sheets of water that had hindered the Loyals, and sat back to shell the British in their exposed positions.

In the confusion, so normal in war, the medical officer of the Loyals, Captain Doll, got left behind at Bergues. Told by one of his orderlies that the battalion seemed to be leaving, he sent a runner to ask the adjutant what was happening. The reply was not very helpful: he, Doll, must take what action he thought necessary. Doll went to battalion headquarters to find that all the troops had gone. He went to see the French detachment in an effort to learn what the situation was. As he approached he was met with a blast of heat from the burning ruins of the building they had occupied. Shells were still falling as he turned back to his own RAP. Here he gathered his orderlies and wounded around him and told them they could either remain and be taken prisoner, or try to get out in a 30-hundredweight truck that had been left behind by the battalion or in his Vauxhall car. Everyone opted to go. The able-bodied and walking wounded were loaded into the truck (Doll took the casualty tags off the men who could fire their weapons, remembering, even at this tense moment, that if they were to fight they could not, under the rules of the Geneva Convention, claim to be wounded). The badly wounded were crammed into the back of Doll's car, after he had administered a large dose of morphia. He also found a motorcycle, and this was allocated to one of his orderlies, a conscientious objector, who was appointed despatch rider.

With the despatch rider leading, Doll's party set out. They soon lost their way in the ruined streets of Bergues, and then had to turn back because the bridge they had hoped to cross had been demolished. After driving uncomfortably close to the enemy, they came upon a bridge that was still intact. Shells were falling quite close and the streets were heaped with rubble. By the bridge stood two trucks that had taken direct hits from shells, and a dozen or so bodies littered the road around them. But more encouraging, and to his relief, at this point Doll encountered Captain Lascelles commanding D Company, the 1st Loyals. Doll's party was back with the battalion at last – except for the despatch rider, whom he had been unable to stop taking a wrong turning just before they saw the bridge. He turned up later, after swimming the moat surrounding the town.

Lascelles, who was about to blow the bridge, was astonished to see Doll, convinced that he had got away long before. As they were talking, another despatch rider appeared with a message for Doll from the adjutant. It was a further answer to the MO's earlier query about what he should do and ordered him to rejoin the battalion, leaving his assistant to get the wounded away as best he could. Fortunately, as Doll remarked, 'the order was now out of date'. About a mile further down the road, Doll met Major Gibson, the second-in-command, and from him learned that the battalion was involved in a counter-attack. Having found a suitable barn near the advanced battalion headquarters, he established his RAP there. He sent the lorry with all the wounded into Dunkirk. That was the last he saw of it. Apparently the driver, upon reaching the harbour, was not allowed to return. All this activity was conducted under shellfire, most of it directed randomly at the roads and key points, while the Luftwaffe seemed to be overhead for much of the time. Occasionally these aircraft were greeted by volleys of small-arms fire from the British troops in the vicinity, though it had little effect. Most of the planes were heading for, or returning from, bombing Dunkirk or the beaches and as far as Captain Doll could see did not attack troops in his vicinity. Meanwhile he busied himself using his car to ferry wounded to his RAP. From here the wounded were taken to Dunkirk by ambulances, whose drivers earned Doll's admiration for returning immediately for the next load, and not succumbing to the temptation to go straight to the beach for evacuation as soon as they had delivered the wounded to the hospital.

Further east, the German attacks threatened the 1st East Lancashires. A hefty southern Irishman, Captain Ervine-Andrews, commanded B Company, which was holding about 1,000 yards of the canal line and was cut off by enemy attacks on both its flanks. His own battalion tried but failed to gain contact with him, although Second Lieutenant Griffin got through

with three carriers loaded with much-needed ammunition. Later in the day, Ervine-Andrews, learning that one of his platoons was about to be overrun, went forward and climbed on to the thatched roof of the barn which formed part of the platoon position. The Bren in this location had jammed, so he engaged the enemy with a rifle, killing at least seventeen. The Bren stoppage sorted out, it was passed up to him, and he accounted for more of the enemy, halting the attack. When the barn was set on fire, and he had run out of ammunition, he sent his wounded back in the one remaining carrier with Lieutenant Cetre to report to the CO. Cetre returned with more ammunition and orders to hold until the last round and then withdraw. With the last round fired and almost surrounded, Ervine-Andrews collected the survivors of his company and led them back. Wading through ditches, at times with water almost up to their chins, he brought them safely to another company position in rear. He was awarded the Victoria Cross. He learned about the award while dining in a restaurant in the West End of London some two months later, when the wireless was switched on for the nine o'clock news.

The German attack lapped up against the left flank of the East Lancashires and against the 5th Borders adjacent to them. Although they took their toll of the enemy, they were forced back to the Canal des Chats. This exposed the right flank of the 2nd Coldstreams, who like their sister battalion at Furnes had taken heavy losses in officers, including two company commanders. But with help from the 5th King's Own and the 2nd Hampshires they managed to cling to a foothold along the Bergues Canal, turning a cottage into a strongpoint and using the ditches to protect their flanks.

On the left flank of the Canal Line, the 1st Duke of Wellingtons had a frontage of 4,000 yards following the withdrawal of II Corps. After some bitter fighting, including a counter-attack by the 5th King's Own, the position was held. Fortunately the Dukes still had most of their carriers, and were supported by the medium machine guns of the 2nd Cheshires, as well as by some light tanks of the Inniskillings. The German attacks ground to a halt among the dykes and ditches, and their soldiers took cover on anything protruding above the flood water.

On the left flank of I Corps, the French 12th Infantry Division was able to use the existing frontier defences, dug in the previous winter. These soldiers gave such a good account of themselves that no British reserves were required to assist in the defence. Although the Germans had succeeded in penetrating the area where the BEF was making its last stand, they made no attempt to exploit their gains. With the onset of darkness came the moment for the British battalions to thin out and pull back. This was the sixth time that many of them had done this. Groggy

with fatigue, their aching legs clad in sodden battledress, the BEF infantry began to pull out and head for Bray-Dunes or Dunkirk. The gunners, having fired their remaining ammunition, removed breech blocks and sights before joining the throng trudging or, in the case of the lucky ones, riding north to the sea. Eventually the German booty included 1,016 field guns and 331 mediums and heavies.

The embarkation went well that night. Inevitably there were some incidents of indiscipline. Lieutenant Nettle RNVR was sent to the beaches for the last two days of the evacuation. After watching two ships' lifeboats drifting in on the tide capsized by soldiers overloading them, he saw a third boat appear, and the troops started wading out to it. Nettle went alongside the queue shouting to them to wait until it came into shallower water. They took no notice of the young RNVR officer, so he drew his revolver and fired into the water about three yards ahead of the leading man. They all stopped, and Nettle waded across to them waving his revolver, indicating that they should all return to shore. Ingrained discipline reasserted itself, and they accepted the order, moving slowly back. Nettle detailed two men to go out and tow the boat back to shallow water so that the others could embark. He asked for two men to volunteer to row the boat back once it had delivered its load, so that it could be used for another trip. He promised that the two would go out on the next trip. But no one volunteered, and he had to rely on getting the next lift out in boats drifting on the tide.

Earlier that day, Second Lieutenant Martin with his machine-gun platoon of the 2nd Cheshires, by now exhausted and out of touch with his parent battalion, found himself without orders. So he went into Dunkirk to discover what he was to do next. He met a French soldier with one eye hanging down on his cheek, screaming for help; but could find no one in authority. So he took the platoon to the water's edge and eventually got a lift out to the destroyers, just visible offshore in the darkness, in a boat manned by some sappers, his platoon of thirty men and a padre whom he had never seen before. When the boat was about a quarter of a mile from one of the destroyers, she weighed anchor and started to steam off. The padre leaped to his feet and shouted, 'Lord, why hast thou forsaken us?' The boat was so overloaded that water was already slopping in with every stroke of the oars, so when the padre jumped up the boat rocked and water started pouring in. Everyone yelled, 'Sit down!', so loudly that the destroyer must have heard, and headed back to pick them up.

At 1430 hours, the 8th DLI were ordered to march along the dunes to the mole at Dunkirk and there lie up to await ships to take them away. All gear was destroyed, except the remaining carriers, which were used

to transport wounded. The battalion set out carrying rifles, Brens and shovels to dig holes on arrival. They were machine-gunned from the air on the way, but on the whole saw little of the Luftwaffe, except for a raid on ships offshore. The beach was a scene of great confusion, a jumble of rifles, clothing, oil, bodies, all along the route. At sea the masts and funnels of sunken ships protruded above the surface, while smaller vessels and boats lay abandoned at all angles on the beach. As McLaren's battalion approached Dunkirk they were directed inland through Malo-les-Bains, which was a scene of almost total destruction at the hands of the Luftwaffe. Masses of abandoned transport cluttered the roads and spaces between the villas.

The 8th DLI arrived on the beach by the mole at about 1730 hours, and after digging holes the soldiers ate some cold food they had brought with them. There was nobody around to tell them where the battalion was to embark or when. Eventually, McLaren found the brigade major in Dunkirk and discovered what the arrangements were. On his return he found his battalion tightly packed in three ranks, heading for the mole. After dark, the battalion, in its turn, found itself on the mole edging forward with painful slowness, French on one side, British on the other, subjected to sporadic shelling. McLaren eventually boarded a minesweeper at about midnight, having felt very sick and wretched all evening. Once on board, he immediately fell asleep in an armchair, remaining there until the ship docked in Dover at around 0500 hours the next morning.

The Combined Squadron of the 4th/7th Royal Dragoon Guards was told to cover the infantry until 1900 hours, and then embark. These orders were subsequently altered because of a report of an enemy breakthrough. The squadron was sent to investigate. The 'breakthrough' turned out to be a section with a 50mm mortar, which was 'quickly disposed of'. Frink remarks dismissively in the diary, 'Reports due to a hysterical infantry subaltern who had drunk too much on an empty stomach.' By now Frink admitted to being so sleepy that he 'had to get Williams to work out the map references and orders for the withdrawal'. There were moments of humour when Lieutenant Verdin, the intelligence officer, appeared covered in black soot: he had been blown up with his carrier when a shell fell on a sapper stores dump, presumably containing much explosive.

The squadron handed over to the French on a demolished bridge and covered the last unit back at 2000 hours. By 2300 hours it had reached Dunkirk, destroyed its vehicles and guns, and joined the queue on the mole. 'Forgot to remove my gin bottle,' noted Frink. The mole was a 'seething mass of troops, mostly French'. But just before reaching the

point where they hoped to embark in a ship, Frink and his squadron were told there would be no more ships that day. This 'was rather depressing' news.

Just north of Hoymille on 1 June, Captain Doll, the MO of the 1st Loyals, had finished evacuating the wounded by about 2100 hours. The counter-attack was finished and the order was given to hold their positions for one hour before withdrawing to the beaches. Doll was driving his car to battalion headquarters when the shelling intensified, seeming to keep pace with him as he drove. On his arrival, shells started falling all round him, and he jumped into a waterlogged ditch by the road, to find fifty or so other men there. Miraculously no one was scratched. When the barrage lifted, they all withdrew approximately a hundred yards from the road, and waited another half-hour until 2200 hours and the battalion's final withdrawal.

Doll kept his car as it was now the only way of evacuating wounded – he already had one wounded man with him, and picked up a further two. He also had his orderly and the battalion regimental quartermaster sergeant (RQMS) with him. As they approached Dunkirk they thought the flashes and roar of gunfire ahead must come from ships offshore, and they were considerably heartened that they were now under the protection of the Royal Navy. It transpired that what they heard were guns of the Dunkirk fort. A four-mile journey found the battalion entering Dunkirk, and the CO sent Doll ahead to locate the beach. They had been told to aim for the mole at Saint-Malo-les-Bains. Doll headed for the largest pillars of flames, which he thought would mark some part of the harbour. He wished that he had seen the place by daylight. Eventually in the glare of fires he spotted the mole some way off, and columns of French soldiers making for it. He and Pennington, the RQMS, returned to where they had left the battalion, to find that they had all gone. After driving around searching for the battalion up likely roads for about ten minutes, the two men decided to find the evacuation point for themselves and returned to the beach, having immobilized the car as best they could. The mole, and the beach leading to it, seemed to Doll to be full of French troops, plodding slowly along in the darkness. Shells were falling at a slow but continuous rate. The French seemed to ignore them, but the only British troops he could see appeared to be separated from their units and jumped into the nearest hole in the sand at the first sound of a shell. The feeling of being cut off from their battalion made Doll and Pennington somewhat apprehensive, and soon they too made for holes, with which the sand seemed to be honeycombed. Most of them were already occupied by men who appeared to be waiting for someone to tell them what to do.

After about an hour, Doll decided that they must either push out along the mole or look for boats along the beach. He opted for the latter, and eventually he, Pennington and some soldiers who tagged along joined a queue of two or three hundred soldiers on the beach and in the water, and could see boats plying back and forth. He was delighted to see that it included two companies of Loyals and remnants of other units that had collected at Bergues, some of whom he recognized. Eventually, with water up to his chest, and up to the chins of the smaller soldiers, Doll's party reached the head of the queue and one by one were pulled over the gunwales of a boat. He was heartened to discover that in his boat was an officer from the Loyals who had been in the battalion rearguard; it was welcome proof that the battalion had got clear. Doll was rowed out to a paddle steamer and taken to the saloon, a smallish compartment containing some other officers. All seemed happy, except for an officer of the 2nd Coldstream Guards who had just seen his entire platoon killed or wounded when a shell exploded among them on one of the roads leading to the beach.

Doll soon discovered that his services were required. A sailor came to the saloon asking if there was a doctor present, and took him to a cabin where a naval medical assistant was working on some wounded soldiers on stretchers. Fortunately Doll still had plenty of morphia in his haversack, as the naval assistant had used all his. Some of the soldiers were very badly wounded, and he could not understand how they could possibly have got on board. One Coldstream guardsman, a survivor of the platoon whose officer was in the saloon, had six separate fractures in both legs; he died before the ship reached England. After seeing to the wounded in the cabin, Doll went round the ship attending to men who could not get into the cabin with the more badly wounded. He encountered one sergeant from the Loyals who at first glance seemed hardly to be hurt, until Doll cut his shirt away to reveal a shoulder almost blown off, the arm hanging by a small segment of muscle and skin.

When Doll finally came to register the time, it was 0500 hours the next day, 2 June, and the ship was well out to sea. The naval medical assistant found a bunk for him, and he fell into it, waking as the ship entered Ramsgate harbour. The other half of the 1st Loyals were not so lucky. They moved out along the mole and just missed the last ship of that night, so they had to spend another day on the beach before being taken off, but without suffering further casualties.

For at 0300 hours on 2 June, with daybreak imminent, on orders from Ramsay all the ships departed to avoid the massive losses of the previous days. The East Mole was packed with troops four abreast waiting quietly and in good order, British on the right, French on the left. The sudden

departure of the ships caused some confusion. Those at the front turned about, while those at the back pressed on. It presented a juicy target for the German gunners, but only the odd shell crashed down to blast a hole in the queue. The dead were pushed over the edge of the mole or of the causeway that linked mole to beach. Eventually everyone turned and walked back into town to take cover in the dunes or cellars of Malo-les-Bains and wait for the night.

It had become clear to Alexander that, with embarkation suspended during the daylight hours, he would not be able to complete evacuation on the night of 1/2 June as originally envisaged. He thought there were about 3,000 British troops left, although according to the embarkation returns it later turned out there were more. At this stage Admiral Wake-Walker was told there were about 5,000, with an unknown number of French. Alexander formed a tight perimeter round Malo-les-Bains, with twelve 2-pounder anti-tank guns that had been manhandled through the sand dunes, sited to take on any tanks that might break through. In addition there were three 3-inch anti-aircraft guns, and four 40mm Bofors to take on the Luftwaffe.

The Combined Squadron of the 4th/7th took cover not in cellars in Malo-les-Bains but in holes in the dunes. Some enterprising soldiers found, or 'borrowed', some deserted motorcycles and 'a certain amount of relaxation was provided by motor-cycle races on the sands between bombing raids, and lively betting as to which building would be the next to go up'.[2] Frink went to see Brigadier Haydon, commanding the 150th Brigade of the 50th Division, to find out if there were any orders for the next evening evacuation, but there was no news. A number of troops, not from the 4th/7th, took to small boats, but many did not make it. Everyone was very tired, hungry and thirsty, and under almost constant bombing and shelling. 'Most of the day spent examining sea life at very close angle from the bottom of a trench so deep that the water came in,' commented Frink on this day. The 4th/7th were heartened at one stage to find A Squadron of the 5th Inniskilling Dragoon Guards under their tanks on the beach. The 4th/7th had thought up to then that they were the only squadron to miss the boat. But morale in the squadron was 'excellent', and got even better when news came in by wireless at tea time that there would be sufficient transport for all that night. The remainder of the day was spent looking anxiously at the sky wondering whether the squadron would 'get away with it till dark'.

Thanks to devoted service by the French holding the Germans at bay, no British ground units were required to engage the enemy that day. Bergues fell as late as 1700 hours after the failure of a costly counter-attack by a French training battalion. On the west side of the perimeter,

the French 68th Division, firing their 75mm guns over open sights, saw off an armoured attack by the 9th Panzer Division; while the 32nd Infantry Division turfed the Germans out of Téteghem. The French 12th Infantry Division in their frontier positions repulsed all attempts to break in from the east. That the British took no part in this fighting was a breach of the promise that Churchill had made in Paris on 31 May. However, Alexander knew nothing of the pledge and was complying with the instructions given him by Eden, when he had spoken to him from La Panne on the evening of 31 May.

There were a large number of wounded in Dunkirk, and orders were that fit men would be given preference. Embarking wounded would have taken up too much time. But it was decided to try to get some wounded away in daylight in hospital ships, hoping the Germans would respect them. A hospital ship entered Dunkirk harbour in full daylight, bearing all the signs required by the Geneva Convention, and her arrival was broadcast in clear to the Germans. She was bombed and sunk. Another was so badly damaged she had to return without loading at Dunkirk. The wounded, other than those who could walk to the pier, had to be left behind. At the Casualty Clearing Station No. 12 at Château Rosendael, south of Malo-les-Bains, there were 230 stretcher cases left, with more coming in. To the surprise of the surgeons and staff, who had not expected to be evacuated, they received an order that one officer and ten orderlies would remain with the wounded and the rest would go. Three officers and thirty orderlies were chosen by ballot. Some patients made brave and sometimes poignant attempts to get to the evacuation points, knowing that only by their own exertions could they avoid capture.

At nightfall, the embarkation started, undisturbed by the Germans who had settled down for the night as was their wont. The soldiers filed quietly along the mole, by their demeanour greatly impressing Alexander. He wrote later: 'The men at no time showed fear or restlessness. They were patient, brave and obedient, and when finally ordered to embark they did so in perfectly disciplined groups, properly armed and equipped.' Throughout the day, Alexander's immaculate appearance and quiet good manners had raised the morale of all who saw him as he moved among the troops.

Frink's Combined Squadron 'formed up with the Skins [Inniskillings] Squadron and marched to the Mole at about 9 pm. Everything worked like clockwork – no shelling or bombing at what would have been a perfect target. Think largely due to the appearance of six Spitfires in the evening, about the only ones we had seen. All aboard by 1030 pm, and so to Folkestone; an unpleasant nightmare dispelled by a view of the white cliffs of Dover at dawn.'

The last of the BEF to leave were the 1st King's Shropshire Light Infantry, who had covered the withdrawal of the 1st Division the previous night. As they stood in the slowly moving queue on the mole, waiting for shells to fall on them, they were illuminated by the massive fires burning in the port and town behind them.

Just before midnight on 2/3 June, the Channel ferry *St Helier* slipped from the mole and made for England with the last of the BEF. Captain Tennant signalled Dover Command: 'BEF evacuated.' He and Alexander boarded a launch to tour the harbour and beaches in search of any remaining British troops. Alexander shouted through a megaphone, 'Is anyone there, is anyone there?' Having satisfied themselves that no one remained, they transferred to a destroyer, which was under machine-gun fire from the land.

Some 20,000 French troops were taken off in the night, and about 30,000 were left. Throughout 3 June they put up a magnificent fight. But by late afternoon the Germans were on the southern outskirts of Dunkirk, about two miles from the mole. Fagalde, however, retained a good grip on the situation, and the familiar German inertia at night allowed him to put into effect his plan for the final withdrawal. This necessitated holding an inner rearguard until 0200 hours on 4 June, and all went to plan, with no interference from the Germans other than some sporadic machine-gun fire.

It was thanks to the Royal Navy and Merchant Navy that a substantial number of French got away. It would have been unthinkable to have abandoned them, but Ramsay's sailors, both Royal and Merchant Navies, were almost at the end of their tether. There had been cases of civilian masters of merchant vessels refusing to take their ships to sea again. On 28 May, the master of the *Canterbury*, a large passenger ferry, had sailed for Dunkirk only after receiving a direct order, and with a naval officer and some ratings embarked to 'stiffen the crew'. On 29 May, after one round trip, the captain of the *St Seiriol* had refused to sail again. The ship finally sailed after the captain had been put under open arrest, and a Royal Navy party placed on board. She was hit and damaged on her way home – it was her last trip to Dunkirk. In the evening of that horrendous day, 1 June, the crew of the *Tynwald*, having completed three trips, also refused to sail. She sailed twenty-four hours later with a relief crew and a Royal Navy party, although with her chief officer as master, and five others of her ship's company. She ultimately completed five trips.[3] These were not the only examples of merchant crews refusing to sail. But those who did so were the minority.

The exhaustion of ships' companies was now the critical factor that Ramsay had to take into account when assessing how much longer

Operation Dynamo could be sustained now that most of those to be
evacuated were French. He wrote in his despatch with reference to 3
June:

> No assurance could be obtained that this coming night would terminate
> the operation and considerable anxiety was felt regarding the effect of the
> gradual exhaustion of the officers and men of the ships taking part in
> Dynamo. This exhaustion was particularly marked in the Destroyer force
> the remnants of which had been executing a series of round trips without
> intermission for several days under navigational conditions of extreme
> difficulty and in the face of unparalleled air attack.
>
> The Vice-Admiral [Ramsay] accordingly represented to the Admiralty
> that the continuance of the demands made by the evacuation would
> subject a number of officers and men to a test which might be beyond the
> limits of human endurance, and requesting that fresh forces should be
> used if execution had to be continued after the coming night, with the
> acceptance of any consequent delay.[4]

Despite this representation, Ramsay had already issued orders for
another night of operations involving all his destroyers and nine out of
ten of his ferries, with the usual mixture of supporting vessels and craft.
'We arrived off Dunkirk breakwater at 11.57 pm,' recorded Captain
Clarke of the passenger ferry *Princess Maud*. 'We entered the pier heads,
and looked for a berth. The narrow fairway was crammed to capacity . . .
Wrecks dotted the harbour here and there. The only light was that of
shells bursting, and the occasional glare of fires.' She sailed loaded with
French soldiers at about 0150 hours on 4 June. At 0255 hours the *Royal
Sovereign* sailed, the last of the passenger ferries to leave, having completed six trips and carried a total of 6,858 soldiers in the course of the
operation, one tenth of all those rescued by passenger ferries. The paddle
minesweeper *Medway Queen* completed her seventh trip. The elderly
destroyer *Sabre* completed her tenth sortie, having lifted a total of 5,000
men.[5]

The French Navy also played a part in the evacuation of French
soldiers. Some sixty-three vessels of all kinds were involved. The Allied
ships took off a further 26,175 soldiers in that final lift. The last ship to
leave Dunkirk, having already completed several trips, was the *Shikari*,
one of the Royal Navy's oldest destroyers dating back to 1919. At 0340
hours as the grey light of dawn began to lighten the sky through the
heavy pall of smoke that hung over Dunkirk, she cast off from the East
Mole with her decks crammed with French soldiers. The rattle of German
machine-guns close by marked where the French rearguard still gallantly
held off the Germans.

At 1423 hours on 4 June, the Admiralty made the signal ending Operation Dynamo. Originally it was thought that some 45,000 soldiers might be rescued. In the end a total of 338,226 were taken away, 308,888 in British vessels. If the troops evacuated in the week before Dynamo are included, the numbers transported to England rises to 366,162. But, as the historian Correlli Barnett has observed, the losses to the Royal and Merchant Navies were equivalent to those one might expect in a major sea battle. Of thirty-eight destroyers, six had been sunk, fourteen damaged by bombs and twelve by collision. Of forty-six personnel carriers (ferries and the like), nine had been sunk, and eleven damaged, eight so badly that they were withdrawn from service.[6]

The 1st East Surreys, whose CO had been so unceremoniously carted off to sea from the mole at Dunkirk in the destroyer *Esk*, were gathered at Axminster in Devon by 4 June. Everyone who arrived was questioned about those missing. Despite the CO's hopes, there had been no question of the battalion all embarking together, and they had been transported in a variety of ships. The medical officer stayed behind to look after the wounded, and was taken prisoner. One group of East Surreys had their ship sunk under them, but were rescued and brought safely home. One of the best athletes in the battalion, Lieutenant Hayfield, was mortally wounded in an air attack on his ship and died before reaching England.

The reception arrangements for troops returning to England were excellent. Captain White was greeted by the women of the WVS with buns and tea saying 'Well done,' which as far as he was concerned was nonsense: 'We were a defeated army.' Units were packed into trains at the port at which they disembarked and sent all over the country. The 2nd Bedfordshire & Hertfordshires whose regimental depot was in Bedford ended up at Brecon, the depot of the South Wales Borderers. It was Sunday 2 June and Sergeant Green had a big black beard. After a meal most flung themselves down on camp beds in the barracks gym, but after an hour everybody was up talking – they could not seem to relax. Second Lieutenant Martin's platoon disembarked at Margate and had their weapons removed; no reason was given. They were put on a train and found themselves in Wheaton Cavalry Barracks, between Birmingham and Stoke-on-Trent. Everybody was very ashamed of the ghastly rout, so he was surprised when everybody was assembled in the gym and told by the commandant that far from being ashamed they should all be proud of this wonderful achievement: 'We were all heroes, so we felt better.' He had broken a bone in his foot during the retreat, was sent to bed by the MO, and slept on and off for seven days. When he came to, his platoon had disappeared. Eventually he discovered that all machine-gun battalions were concentrated in Devon at Paignton, where he joined them.

Others also found their reception in England surprisingly welcoming. Lieutenant Robin Dunn with some of the 7th Field Regiment arrived in Dover on 31 May in a destroyer. After being bundled into trains, they were soon steaming through the countryside. At one station they were given hot tea, bread and marmalade, and at every stop a mass of women appeared with cigarettes, biscuits, lemonade and other food. One woman got into his carriage and insisted on feeding them and thanking them. It was astonishing to be treated thus – they had expected the population to turn their backs on them, a beaten army. Finally arriving at Shrivenham in Wiltshire, the officers were taken to a house converted into a mess and given razors, socks and underclothes. When he went into the mess for dinner, Dunn glanced at the clock – the time was 2055 hours: three weeks ago to the hour the leading gun of his troop had left the village in France in which they had been billeted, on their way to Belgium.

11

THE FINAL BATTLES

On 2 June 1940, Lieutenant General Alan Brooke just back from France, having handed command of II Corps to Montgomery, sat in the War Office in London talking to General Dill, now the CIGS. Brooke asked Dill what he wanted him to do. The CIGS replied that he wanted Brooke to return to France to form a new BEF. Brooke saw this as one of his blackest moments in the war, and there had been quite a few of those already, with many more to come. In an after-note in his diary he wrote:

> I knew only too well the state of affairs that would prevail in France from now onwards. I had seen my hope in the French army gradually shattered throughout those long winter months. I had witnessed the realization of my worst fears regarding its fighting value and morale, and now I had no false conceptions as to what its destiny must inevitably be. To be sent back into that cauldron with a new force to participate in the final stages of French disintegration was indeed a dark prospect.[1]

The force that Brooke would command consisted of the 51st (Highland) Division, the remnants of the 1st Armoured Division and an ad hoc force of lines-of-communication troops in three brigades commanded by Brigadier (later Major General) Beauman (incorrectly called Beaumont by Brooke in his diary), all of which were in France already, and corps troops consisting of artillery, engineers and machine-gun battalions in addition to those forming part of divisions. In addition he would be given the Canadian 1st Division, now based in England, and the 52nd Division (Major General Drew). Leading elements of the Canadian Division had arrived in France, and the 157th Brigade of the 52nd Division, which had already landed, had been put under command of the French Tenth Army. Under pressure, Dill agreed to give Brooke the 3rd Division, now back in England and under Montgomery's command again, when it had been refitted. On arrival in France, Brooke would take command of all British forces there, and come under the orders of General Weygand. He would take his old II Corps headquarters with him, as soon as they could be gathered together from the diverse locations they had been sent to in England after the Dunkirk evacuation.

On leaving Dill, Brooke was summoned to see Eden, the Secretary of State for War, who, after an affable greeting, asked if Brooke was satisfied with what was being done for him. Brooke astonished him by replying that he was far from satisfied, and that the mission on which he was being sent was of no value from a military point of view and would accomplish nothing. Having just escaped one disaster at Dunkirk, the British were now risking another. Brooke added that the move might have some political advantage but that was not for him to judge. It was up to Eden to decide whether the risks were justified in the hope of gaining any political advantage that might exist.

Brooke was correct in his surmise, and as the British Official History commented it was to be an unhappy story, 'relieved only by the loyalty of our intention to fight with all we had till larger forces could rejoin the battle'.[2] Demonstrating loyalty was the aim, and was to lead to more losses for no gain whatsoever.

It should be borne in mind that any action being described in this chapter that occurred before 4 June took place at the same times as, but separated geographically from, the dramatic events north of the Somme which culminated in the Dunkirk evacuation. While the BEF was fighting for its life in northern France and Belgium, there were over 140,000 British troops in France south of the Somme. As well as lines-of-communication troops in ports from Dieppe round to Saint-Nazaire, the 51st (Highland) Division, detached to the Saar front, had been cut off from the main body of the BEF by the German 'sickle-stroke' on 10 May. This division, commanded by Major General Victor Fortune, was stronger than a standard British infantry division. In addition to three full-strength brigades and the usual divisional troops (three field artillery regiments, an anti-tank regiment, three field companies and a field park company of engineers), it had been beefed up with an armoured cavalry regiment (1st Lothians and Border Yeomanry), three additional regiments of artillery, another company of sappers, two machine-gun battalions and two pioneer battalions. After 10 May the division was withdrawn, still under French command, from the Saar Line to the area of Metz.

The 1st Armoured Division, under Major General Evans, disembarked at Cherbourg between 15 and 19 May, to find the port full of troops from rear echelons saying that the war was over and trying to shove their way on board. The GSO 2 of the division, Major Charles Dunphie, a fluent French-speaker, had to push his way down the gangway to the dockside against the flow. The 1st Armoured Division was shorn of all its infantry and one of its tank battalions, diverted to Calais as described in Chapter 6. It now consisted of two armoured brigades, equipped with 143 cruisers and 114 light tanks, and a support group of anti-tank and anti-aircraft

guns. After his arrival in France, Evans was given a number of missions by the French, all totally unrealistic and no longer relevant by the time he received them, reflecting the chaos caused by the rapid German advance towards the coast. These included being ordered to attack across the Somme when the Germans already held bridgeheads on that river in strength – a situation that appeared to be news to the French. In this difficult period, no fewer than three generals tried to take charge of Evans (Gort, Georges and Altmayer). Both Gort and Georges could communicate with Evans via the British Swayne Mission at Georges' headquarters. General Robert Altmayer, commanding French Group A, was merely the closest geographically, and tried to hijack the 1st Armoured Division to cover the left flank of Seventh Army in an attack on Amiens. Eventually, responding to General Gort's orders, Evans sent the 2nd Armoured Brigade to attack the German bridgeheads between Picquigny, Ailly and Dreuil on the Somme north-west of Amiens on 24 May. At the time the remainder of the division was still moving forward, with some of the administrative tail still in England. The attack failed.

That night, 24/25 May, Evans now received orders that he would be required to co-operate with the French. Meanwhile the 51st Division would be transferred from the Saar front and sent to form a group with the 1st Armoured Division, whose task would be to take up a covering position from Longpré on the Somme to the coast. In the meantime Evans, according to instructions issued by General Georges, was to hold that line until the 51st Division arrived, and establish small bridgeheads and prepare all bridges for demolition. As the Germans already held the line of the Somme in strength and had pushed their bridgeheads south by several miles, this was yet another absurd order. On 25 May, with the approval of the War Office, Evans was put under the command of the French Seventh Army (which at that stage included Altmayer's Group A).

Evans went to see Altmayer and was told that his division would be split to support a French attack on the Abbeville bridgehead on the Somme. The following day, 26 May, the orders for the attack were issued. The British 2nd Armoured Brigade, commanded by Brigadier R. L. McCreery (the Queen's Bays, 9th Queen's Royal Lancers and 10th Royal Hussars), was to come under command of the French 2nd Light Cavalry Division (DLC), commanded by Colonel Berniquet, and with this French division was to capture the high ground south of the Somme from Bray to Les Planches south of Abbeville. The French were to supply artillery and infantry.

The 3rd Armoured Brigade, commanded by Brigadier J. G. Crocker (2nd and 5th Battalions, the Royal Tank Regiment), were to come under General Chenoine, commanding the French 5th DLC, whose objective

was the high ground from Rouvroy to Saint-Valery-sur-Somme. Again the infantry and artillery were to be supplied by the French. In vain, Evans tried to explain that his tanks were not heavies designed to make a breakthrough with infantry, but mainly cruisers developed to exploit a breach made by heavy armour. In short they were equivalent to a French light mechanized division, not a French armoured division. The decision by the French to break up the British armoured division in this way, and expect its brigades at little notice to co-operate successfully in its first battle with a collection of complete strangers, who did not even speak the same language, beggars belief, as do the objectives selected by the French. It illustrates the depths to which the French Army had sunk, and the unfitness for command of most, although by no means all, their senior officers. Both McCreery and Crocker were to rise to high command later in the war – unlike the French generals in the chain of command above them, who were to sink into oblivion.

The chain of command was also complicated. From division it stretched up through General Robert Altmayer's Group A (later Tenth Army) to General Frère's Seventh Army, Besson's 3rd Army Group, Georges' HQ North-East Front, finally to Weygand at the pinnacle. It was a chain of command incapable of reacting to events, and without adequate communications. It was, in a word, useless.

On 27 May the attack went in. The 2nd Armoured Brigade, told that the positions were lightly held by 'inferior troops' (how often has that phrase presaged disaster), ran into well-sited anti-tank guns covering open forward slopes. The two leading regiments, the Bays and 10th Hussars, got nowhere with heavy losses. McCreery had the good sense not to reinforce failure and did not commit his reserve, the 9th Lancers.

The 3rd Armoured Brigade made better progress, advancing about five miles and reaching the outskirts of Valery-sur-Somme and Moyenneville. The brigade lost eighteen tanks endeavouring to pin down the enemy, at which stage Crocker tried to arrange a co-ordinated attack with French infantry. But the French would not play, so Crocker pulled back.

In this battle the 1st Armoured Division lost sixty-five tanks and many crews. In addition, a further fifty-five tanks had broken down, overtaxed by the long and hasty move forward without transporters to relieve strain on tracks and drive mechanisms, and with insufficient time for maintenance – a loss of nearly 50 per cent of its armoured fighting vehicles. The 1st Armoured Division was now severely depleted after one fruitless action. The few remaining tanks of the Bays and 10th Hussars were formed into a Composite Regiment.

The French attacked on 28 May, but with markedly little success. General de Gaulle's 4th Armoured Division attacked on the next day, a

much stronger formation than the partially horsed DLCs, which were used on the first day and which the British had supported. De Gaulle learned the same lessons as the British: the use of armour to attack strongly held positions without infantry and artillery support was profitless. A fourth series of attacks was mounted, but by the end of 30 May the German bridgeheads on the Somme remained untaken, and the crossings were still the enemy's for future use.

While these ineffectual efforts were being made to regain the Somme crossings, the 51st Division arrived in the area of the River Bresle from the Saar front, coming under command of the French IX Corps along with the British 1st Armoured Division. Also in the area was the improvised Beauman Division. This had been configured into three brigades, lettered A, B and C, formed from battalions on the lines of communication, from men sent out as reinforcements and from pioneer units. They had almost as many Brens or the First World War Lewis guns, and rifles, as well as anti-tank rifles, as a battalion was supposed to have at full strength. They had three improvised anti-tank gun batteries, one battery of First World War-vintage 18-pounder field guns, and some sappers, but no signallers, which made command and control difficult. Originally formed into three forces – Beauforce, Vicforce and Digforce – in some ways it was a pity that it did not continue to be called Beauforce once all three were pulled together into one formation. It would have avoided much misunderstanding on the part of the French, who thought of it in terms of a standard infantry division, which it most certainly was not. In the First World War Beauman had commanded a brigade at the age of twenty-nine.

It was decided that the British 1st Armoured, the 51st and the Beauman Divisions would operate on the extreme left of the French under their command. But British interests would be preserved by a mission with right of direct appeal to London; this task being assigned to Lieutenant General Marshall-Cornwall. He was located with Altmayer's Group A, now redesignated Tenth Army. While these moves were in train south of the Somme, the BEF was being pulled into the bridgehead of Dunkirk and evacuated to England. The conversation between Dill and Brooke with which this chapter begins took place on 2 June, by which time the BEF had been evacuated from Dunkirk.

By now Weygand had given up any ideas of attacking north of the Somme, but he still regarded the retaking of the German bridgeheads south of the river as essential to the defence against the enemy breakout and advance on Paris, which was expected any day. The British were to be involved in the last attempt to seize those vital bridgeheads.

On the morning of 4 June, the 51st Division with the Composite

Regiment of the 2nd Armoured Brigade and the remnants of the Support Group of 1st Armoured readied itself for the attempt to recapture the Abbeville–Saint-Valery bridgehead. General Fortune, GOC of the 51st, had two French divisions under command – another example of thoroughly bad French command arrangements. A divisional headquarters is not constituted to command two other divisions in addition to its own brigades, effectively three divisions in all, having neither the staff nor, more importantly, the communications. It is a job for a corps head-quarters. The British 3rd Armoured Brigade was in the midst of having its tanks repaired and therefore not available to support this scheme.

Once again a hurried attack with poor preparation ended in failure. Some units of the two French divisions moved into the area only an hour and a half before the attack began. Reconnaissance the previous after-noon had been perfunctory. There were few air photographs available. Time for briefing the troops was short, and few of the enemy positions had been identified, this despite the fact that the Germans had been holding these positions for ten days. This was very largely thanks to the loss of air superiority by the Allies resulting in a lack of air reconnais-sance. The strength of the bridgeheads had been grossly underestimated, and behind them lurked the whole of Army Group B, waiting to unleash its attack on the French.

On the right, south of Abbeville, the 152nd Brigade had 563 casualties in four hours fighting against strongly held positions. According to Captain Lang, the adjutant of the 4th Cameron Highlanders, the battalion started the attack on Caubert some 600 strong and after three hours they were down to 250 all ranks. The battalion had run into a full-strength battalion of German infantry which was itself about to attack and fully alert. A desperate struggle ensued in which the Germans had the best of it. The Camerons fell back. After dark another 130 or so men infiltrated back to the battalion; was down to two companies, with three out of the four original company commanders killed.

French heavy and light armour in support ran on to well-concealed 88mm guns, which wrought havoc. The 1st Gordon Highlanders of the 153rd Brigade had the sole success of the day, tearing into the enemy in the thick Grand Bois wood, and with excellent artillery support took the position at a cost of forty casualties. But the French 31st Infantry Division failed to take the Rouvroy ride on the Gordons' right, and since it dominated the Grand Bois the Gordons were withdrawn, considerably vexed. The British line now stretched from Caumont, four miles south of Abbeville, to Salenelle near the coast.

At 0300 hours the next day, under cover of morning mist the German attack rolled in. The Germans had made good use of the six days since

the panzer divisions had been withdrawn from the battle against the BEF and French Sixth Army. They had reorganized their armour and motor infantry into five panzer corps, each made up of two panzer divisions and one motorized infantry division. Bock commanded three corps on the right of the German offensive, and Rundstedt two on the left. The two right-hand armoured formations were Rommel's 7th Panzer and Hartlieb's 5th Panzer Divisions under Hoth. From the sea to the River Meuse, the Germans deployed 104 divisions. Facing them on a front 225 miles long, the French had forty-three infantry divisions, three weakened armoured divisions and three under-strength light cavalry divisions. Twenty-five of the French divisions had been extracted from the Maginot Line, leaving another seventeen in position. The French armies in the north had either been evacuated at Dunkirk or been taken prisoner. The Germans could now concentrate their whole attention on the south.

Hitler had accurately assessed the French strength opposing his armies as sixty to sixty-five divisions. He was wrong when he declared that Weygand would 'withhold an operational assault group which is to be sought in the vicinity of Paris and eastwards. It is also to be expected that the enemy will settle down and prepare resistance further south.'[3] Weygand had actually given up all hope of defending the Somme as early as 28 May. He advised the French government that, once the defence here was breached, they should discuss the possibility of an armistice with the British government. He had mentally thrown in the towel before the final round began.

From the enemy point of view, in this chapter we are principally concerned with the actions of Bock's Army Group B, attacking across the Somme between Amiens and the sea. Kluge's German Fourth Army, consisting of two panzer divisions, six infantry divisions, one motorized division, one motorized brigade and one cavalry division, attacked from the Abbeville–Amiens area and advanced towards the lower Seine. In the sector held by the French IX Corps, which included the 51st Division, Kluge pushed four infantry divisions and a motor brigade across the lower reaches of the Somme between Abbeville and the sea, while the rest of his army, including two panzer divisions and two infantry divisions, crossed between Abbeville and Amiens. The effect was like a man smashing his opponent in the face with a shield held in his right hand, while thrusting into his side with a spear held in his left hand.

At 0400 hours on 5 June the Germans attacked along the whole of 51st Division's front. The 154th Brigade held a series of villages, too widely spaced to afford mutual support. By late afternoon the 7th Argylls had been cut off. The remnants of the battalion held out for another twenty-four hours, before being overcome. What was left of

the brigade pulled back to an intermediate line between Woincourt and Eu. The 153rd Brigade on their right had a hard fight but were driven back to a line Toeufles–Zoteux–Frières. The soldiers of the 51st Division had been attacking the previous day, suffering heavy casualties. They had enjoyed very little sleep before the Germans unleashed their attack on them, accompanied by heavy artillery fire and Stukas. It was mid-summer and very hot. While they held off attackers they could see other enemy units bypassing their positions and could do little about it. Casualties were again heavy. That first day the 7th Argylls lost twenty-three officers and nearly 500 NCOs and soldiers killed, wounded or missing. They were the worst case, but the whole division had been savagely battered. With the French 31st Division they held forty miles of front, well beyond the capability of two infantry divisions. Battalions had to hold wide frontages. For instance the 1st Black Watch of the 154th Brigade defended two and a half miles of broken terrain – far too much against a powerful enemy.

During the next day the German pressure seemed to slacken, and this provided the opportunity for the 51st Division to pull back behind the River Bresle, but not before the GOC, Major General Fortune, had written a strongly worded letter to General Marshall-Cornwall demanding that part of his front be taken over. All that Marshall-Cornwall could persuade Altmayer, commanding the French Tenth Army, to agree to was that the 51st should withdraw to the Bresle, but the position was to be 'held at all costs'. The French 31st Division was to take over the sector from Senarpont to Gamaches, and the 51st was to hold from there to the sea, a sector of some twelve and a half miles.

At this stage it was apparent that the German armour had broken through on the right flank of the French IX Corps, heading in the general direction of Rouen. It was clear to the British commanders on the spot and to the War Office that unless the 51st Division and the French formations alongside them were withdrawn, they would all end up cut off in the Havre peninsula, in a replay of Dunkirk. The British informed the French, through the Swayne Mission at Weygand's headquarters, that they intended that a new BEF would form in France. As proof of that purpose, General Brooke, commanding a corps, would arrive within a week, and brigade group of the 52nd Division was to sail for France the next day, 7 June. With these plans in mind, the War Office urged that a line of withdrawal be secured for the 51st Division, not into the sack of Havre, but towards the main French forces and the British bases south of the Seine. But Weygand was in a state of paralysis and the retirement order, when it came, was too late.

By now the 51st Division was so sorely reduced in strength that

A Brigade of the Beauman Division was sent to reinforce it. This brigade, consisting of the 4th Buffs, 1st/5th Foresters and the 4th Border Regiment, was only some 900 strong, only 150 more men than one full-strength infantry battalion. The Bresle was not much of an obstacle, except where flooding had been deliberately caused along the stretches downstream from Eu. Unfortunately the Germans had managed to cross at Eu and at Ponts-et-Marais about two miles upriver from there. All day on 7 June the 4th Borders and a company of the 1st/5th Foresters tried to eliminate the crossing at these points, without success. Meanwhile the situation south of the 51st Division deteriorated rapidly as the 5th and 7th Panzer Divisions outflanked the Bresle line south of Aumale.

The British 1st Armoured Division, less the Composite Regiment with the 51st Division, was now directly under the orders of General Altmayer. Evans and Altmayer agreed that the 1st British Armoured Division should move to Gournay and, from there, strike at the flank of the German advance. Evans had forty-one cruisers and thirty-one light tanks of the 3rd Armoured Brigade plus six light tanks from the 2nd Armoured Brigade, just back from being repaired in workshops. As these moves were under way, Weygand arrived at Altmayer's Tenth Army headquarters. Here he saw Marshall-Cornwall and Evans. Weygand was emotional and clearly stressed, saying that the Tenth Army battle was the decisive engagement of the war. Major Charles Dunphie was told to ask Weygand what troops were guarding the line of the Seine. The reply was 'Deux battalions des douaniers' (two battalions of customs officials) and as, according to Weygand, there were no other French reserves available, all now depended on the 1st Armoured Division.

The division was to hold the upper reaches of the Andelle river from Nolleval to Serqueux, while French formations would counter-attack from the south. That begs the question, what French formations? Weygand had already said there was no reserve. The divisions existed solely in Weygand's imagination. Evans protested, saying that he had already had all his infantry, artillery and anti-tank guns taken from him for use elsewhere, that his cruiser tanks were totally unsuitable for static defence, and in any case were already on their way to counter-attack the enemy flank. Weygand would not alter his decision, although he conceded that if Evans was forced to withdraw from the River Andelle he should pull back across the Seine where he would still be available for counter-attacks. Evans had to issue fresh orders and pull back his units moving to attack the German flank; some were already in contact with German reconnaissance five miles north-west of Gournay.

First light on 8 June saw the panzer divisions approaching Rouen and the French IX Corps, including the 51st Division, being cut off. It was

a relatively quiet day for the 51st Division, because the Germans were holding the 'shield' and not pushing too hard, while the 'spear' was hooking round the flank. It was in some ways a repeat of what had happened in northern France and Belgium in May. It would have been far better if the French Tenth Army had ordered IX Corps to fall back, using the numerous river lines as intermediate positions in order to keep contact with the French formations on their right and withdraw over the Seine. By staying put, IX Corps was in a trap.

To the south, the greatly reduced 1st Armoured Division stood on the Andelle. The division had suffered much vexation since its arrival in France. It had lost its infantry and one tank battalion to the Calais battle. It had never been allowed to fight as a division. Most of what remained of the 2nd Armoured Brigade was now reduced to a Composite Regiment which was fighting on the Bresle. All Evans had was the two tank battalions of the 3rd Armoured Brigade and some remnants of the 2nd Armoured Brigade.

The Beauman Division, less A Brigade with the 51st Division, was deployed between the River Béthune and the Andelle. On 6 June, it had been joined by more infantry. This consisted of Syme's Battalion made up of soldiers from the base reinforcement depot (commanded by Lieutenant Colonel A. G. Syme of the Royal Scots), and the 2nd/4th King's Own Yorkshire Light Infantry and 2nd/6th Duke of Wellington's, two battalions that had been involved in the fighting at Abbeville way back on 20 May. The three battalions were now deployed near Rouen: Syme's Battalion at Isneauville, the KOYLI on a bridge over the Seine, and the Dukes on the railway south of Boos. Beauman's widely scattered units hardly qualified for the name 'division'. They lacked wireless communication, artillery and other supporting arms. In some places they were intermixed with the 1st Armoured Division, and in others with French units of whose purpose and plans they had no knowledge. Beauman had no alternative but to issue orders that troops were to hold for as long as it seemed possible to do so, and commanders were given discretion to decide when to withdraw, which would be across the Seine.

The picture was further muddied by the command arrangements. The elements of Beauman's Division deployed on the Andelle Line with the 1st Armoured were under a different commander from 1st Armoured. For the three British formations were under three different commanders. The 51st Division was under the French IX Corps. The 1st Armoured Division was under Altmayer, but acting under the direct orders of Weygand. The Beauman Division was under the orders of Lieutenant General Karslake who, as commander of all British lines-of-communications troops, was

under General Georges, commanding the French Armies of the North-East.

On 8 June, the German formations swinging round IX Corps on the Bresle punched through to Rouen. They were preceded by streams of French refugees, making it difficult for Beauman's soldiers to close the roadblocks they had built. The refugees were closely followed by French tanks, which were allowed to go through, but these turned out to have been captured by the Germans, and were leading the main body of enemy armoured formations. Positions held by British infantry with no means of mobility were bypassed, cut off and eventually attacked from the rear, while the main enemy force motored on. The 1st Armoured at least had some mobility, but without anti-tank guns its machine guns and some 2-pounders were outgunned and it could not hold for long. Early that morning the Composite Regiment had been ordered to rejoin the 1st Armoured Division to assist with defending the left of the Andelle Line. On arriving at L'Epinay, in the afternoon, it ran straight into German tanks followed by motorized infantry hot-foot from Serqueux, twelve miles away. A confused roughhouse followed, in which some damage was done to the enemy, but a number of British tanks were put out of action. After three hours, with the Germans almost encircling it, the Composite Regiment, or what was left of it, broke off the engagement.

The 5th Panzer Division's leading elements ran into Syme's Battalion at Isneauville at around 1600 hours. Here the battalion, which had been in existence for only a week, put up a stout fight from behind roadblocks, wire and mines, delaying the 5th Panzer Division from entering Rouen that night.

That afternoon, and during the early part of the night of 8 June, the remnants of the 1st Armoured and Beauman Divisions pulled back over the Seine. Now, too late, Weygand ordered the French IX Corps, including the 51st Division, to pull back over the Seine. General Ihler, commanding IX Corps, received these orders direct from Weygand because Ihler's immediate boss, Altmayer of Tenth Army, had precipitately withdrawn his headquarters to the vicinity of Paris and was out of communication with his subordinate formations. After the meeting between Evans, Altmayer and Weygand the previous day, Altmayer had said that he would give orders the following morning. But when Dunphie went to collect the orders Altmayer had disappeared. Such was the state of French Army command-and-control arrangements. The British Official History is scathing, but still amazingly restrained given the consequences that were to flow from the dithering by the utterly incompetent Weygand and his equally inept fellow French commanders:

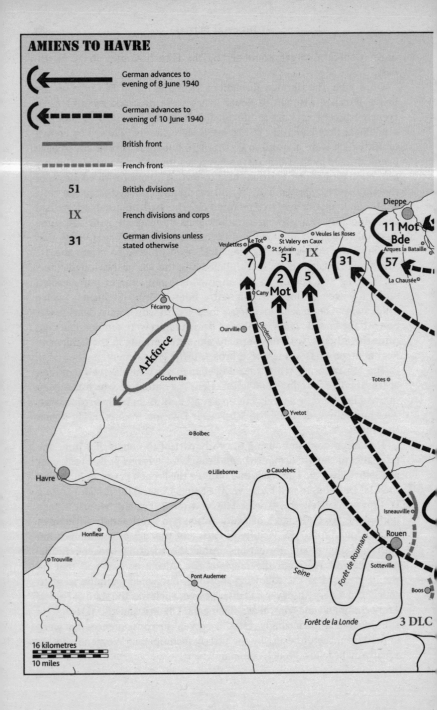

AMIENS TO HAVRE

German advances to
evening of 8 June 1940

German advances to
evening of 10 June 1940

British front

French front

51 British divisions

IX French divisions and corps

31 German divisions unless
stated otherwise

Dieppe

**11 Mot
Bde**

Veules les Roses

Veulettes o o Le Tot

St Valery en Caux

St Sylvain

IX

Arques la Bataille

7

51

31

57

Cany

2 Mot

5

La Chausée o

Fécamp

Ourville o

Durdent

Arkforce

Totes o

Goderville

Yvetot o

o Bolbec

o Lillebonne

o Caudebec

Havre

Isneauville o

Honfleur o

Rouen

o Trouville

Sotteville

Seine

Forêt de Roumare

Boos

Pont Audemer o

Forêt de la Londe

3 DLC

16 kilometres

10 miles

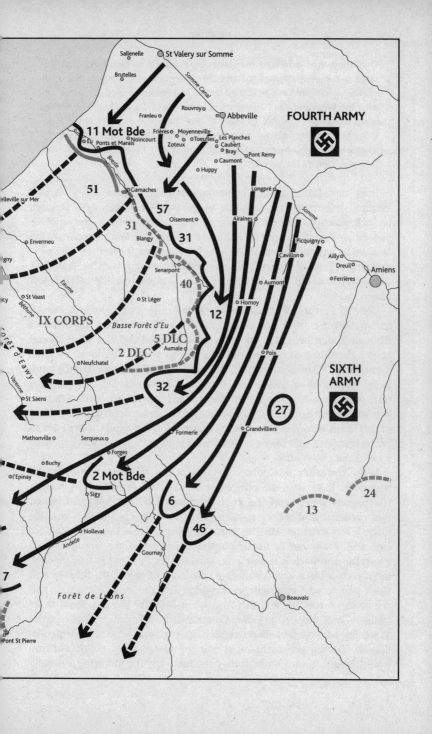

Thus there was exhibited the same initial refusal to face facts, and the same subsequent attempt to mask the consequences of delay by the issue of orders that could not be carried out, as had been displayed in connection with the Weygand Plan. The wisdom of early withdrawal from the Bresle, while it was still possible to retire behind the Seine, was not recognised: and when withdrawal could no longer be avoided the IX Corps was ordered to retire through an area which had been open to them earlier but was now occupied by the enemy.[4]

Ihler met his divisional commanders to give them his plan that evening. It envisaged a leisurely withdrawal over four days through layback positions, finally arriving at Rouen on day four. Yet another pedestrian French general had failed to grasp that enemy armour within four hours' motoring of Rouen was likely to get there first. The next morning, 9 June, the Germans entered Rouen unopposed. The French IX Corps was now cut off, as there were no bridges over the Seine below Rouen in 1940.

General Fortune had realized days before that the sluggish French command-and-control process might lead to the decision to withdraw through Rouen being left too late, but dismissed the idea of unilateral action. He addressed his brigade commanders on the afternoon of 5 June: 'Gentlemen, I know you would not wish us to desert our French comrades. We could be back in Le Havre in two bounds. But they have no transport. They have only their feet to carry them. We shall fight our way back with them step by step.' What his brigade commanders thought of this is not recorded. After their experience at the hands of the French, one conjectures that they would have been all too ready to leave them to stew in their own juice.

When the order to withdraw was finally, and belatedly, given, Fortune persuaded Ihler that the only place from which to withdraw was Le Havre, sixty miles away. He knew from naval officers who had visited him earlier that ships were waiting there, and it was the only suitable place for evacuation. He also persuaded Ihler, fresh from the Maginot Line and totally out of his depth, that a covering force would have to guard the approaches to Le Havre, between Fécamp and Bolbec. Accordingly such a force was constituted, made up of the 154th Brigade (4th Black Watch, who had switched brigades with the 1st Black Watch, and remnants of the 7th and 8th Argylls), A Brigade, the 6th Royal Scots Fusiliers, and supporting units. Commanded by Brigadier Clarke of the 154th Brigade, it was called Arkforce, having been formed at Arques-la-Bataille. During the night of 9 June the troops were pulled out and transported to Fécamp, which they reached early the following morning.

The main body of the 51st Division fell back to the Varenne during the night of 9/10 June.

Arkforce got out just in time, but not the 51st Division. At 1100 hours on 10 June, a wireless operator motoring to join Arkforce ran into the enemy at Cany on the River Durdent, and transmitted the news that he was about to be captured. In fact 7th Panzer Division, commanded by Rommel, had reached the sea at Veulettes. Fortune realized that his evacuation options had been reduced to Saint-Valery-en-Caux or Dieppe. It quickly became clear that the latter was about to fall into enemy hands, so Saint-Valery it would have to be. Saint-Valery had a tiny harbour which almost completely dried out at low water and was dominated by high cliffs on either side from which guns could fire on ships approaching the port.

The Commander-in-Chief Portsmouth, Admiral Sir William James, had arrived at Le Havre to supervise the evacuation and, realizing that the 51st Division and French IX Corps would not get there, sent a signal to the Admiralty and War Office telling them that he had made arrangements to evacuate the 51st Division from Saint-Valery, and had moved small-craft flotillas there already, adding, 'If General 51st Division will keep me informed of his intentions I will direct the evacuation forces to meet his requirements.'

The troops of the 51st Division were ordered to jettison all non-fighting equipment, such as blankets, in order to free as much transport as possible for troop-carrying so that all the men in the division could be carried on RASC trucks and in battalion transport. The move that night, 10/11 June, was a nightmare, as the allocation of roads between the 51st Division and the French units was not adhered to by the latter, and French transport, much of it horsed, kept breaking in from side roads, jamming the narrow ones. Fortunately the enemy were slow to follow up the withdrawal to begin with. This may have owed something to the efforts of D Company the 4th Border Regiment and A Company the 1st/5th Sherwood Foresters, who held two of the Bresle crossings. Orders to withdraw did not get through to them, and so, having heard nothing to the contrary, they stood fast. They denied the crossings to the enemy for six days, beating off all enemy attacks, even taking some prisoners. Only on 13 June, when the Germans brought up artillery, and when they learned that all other fighting north of the Seine had ceased, did they finally surrender.

By the morning of 11 June, Fortune had his division disposed in two parts, one facing east and the other facing west, about eleven miles apart, with a gap in the southern part which he hoped to fill with French troops, but they were in such disorder that he eventually filled it with

what he could scrape together of his own. At about 1400 hours the German armour began to close in. The German formations surrounding Saint-Valery consisted of two panzer divisions, 5th and 7th, 2nd Motor Division, 11th Motor Brigade, and two infantry divisions, 31st and 57th.

Rommel's 7th Panzer Division broke through at Le Tot and seized the cliff-tops overlooking Saint-Valery from the west. The 2nd Seaforths and 1st Gordons had valiantly fought against three German tank battalions, a total of a hundred tanks, and had been cut off though not overwhelmed by them, before Rommel achieved his objective. To the south of the 1st Gordons, the 4th Camerons were positioned facing west and south. The battalion had been reinforced by '150 Jocks and three officers, when we paused at Dieppe on our way back from the Bresle. Within three days they were in the bag,' remembered Captain Lang.

Meanwhile the battalions on the east side (2nd/7th Dukes, 4th Sea-forths and 5th Gordons) battled on against the German 31st Infantry Division and the 11th Motor Brigade, while the 1st Black Watch held Saint-Pierre against the 5th Panzer Division, where they too were cut off. Divisional headquarters, and IX Corps headquarters, had been with-drawn into the town, and from here Fortune tried to communicate with the ships offshore. He reckoned that the best, and indeed only, night for embarkation was that very night, 11/12 June. Shells from tanks and artillery crashed into the town.

The rain poured down as the 4th Camerons along with other battalions withdrew into Saint-Valery, the narrow lanes seething with disorganized French soldiers. The fires started by shelling and bombing became an inferno. There was no wireless communication between battalions or from battalions to brigade headquarters. Nor was there any from brigade headquarters to divisional headquarters. Fog crept in from the sea as men waited to be evacuated, but the ships did not come – the fog was too thick. The ships found the little fishing port of Veules-les-Roses, still within the perimeter, and from here took off 1,137 British troops, including three-quarters of the 2nd/7th Dukes, but not their CO, and some 1,184 French troops. At 0300 hours, with no craft in sight, Fortune gave orders for the perimeter to be manned again, in hopes of rescue the following night. The 4th Seaforths, originally on the east side, were given the job of driving the Germans back from the western cliff, while most others assumed their previous locations.

The rain fell more heavily, and the fog thickened. The evacuation from Veules-les-Roses went on, with the Germans held back by naval gunfire. The strength of the 51st Division was considerably reduced by now, one brigade having already been despatched to Le Havre with Arkforce. Three battalions, 2nd Seaforths, 1st Gordons and 1st Black Watch, were cut off

in positions they were still tenaciously defending on the perimeter and could not withdraw to Saint-Valery. As the 5th Gordons approached the cliffs east of Saint-Valery to take up their positions for the forthcoming day, German tanks moved in. French troops carrying white flags chose that moment to march between the Gordons and the enemy armour, masking the Gordon Highlanders' fire. The Germans closed in and it was all over in this vicinity. Similar situations occurred in the 1st Black Watch and 4th Cameron sector. At 0815 hours a white flag was hoisted on the steeple near the headquarters of the 51st Division. Fortune ordered it cut down and whoever hoisted it arrested. The offender was a French officer acting on Ihler's orders: the flag signalled that Ihler had surrendered. This was followed by a note from Ihler to Fortune, which being translated read, 'Fire ceases at 8 o'clock'. As if to rub salt in the wounds, Ihler then asked if Fortune could transmit the surrender telegram to French headquarters, as his IX Corps had no communications.

Fortune judged that there was no possibility of holding off the enemy until nightfall, and in addition, as he was serving under French command, reluctantly came to the conclusion that he might be forced to obey Ihler's orders. But he still would not give up, signalling the War Office at 1030 hours: 'I have informed corps commander that I cannot comply with his orders until I am satisfied that there is no possibility of evacuating any of my division later.' But all French troops had ceased fire and white flags seemed to be everywhere. So, before sending the message above, he added, 'I have now ordered cease fire.' Half an hour later, he received a signal from the Commander-in-Chief at Portsmouth, 'Regret fog prevented naval forces arriving earlier off St Valery last night. SNO [Senior Naval Officer] afloat will make every endeavour to get you off and additional ships are being sent to arrive tonight.' By the time this message had been received the ceasefire had been ordered. Some troops fought on, like the 1st Black Watch who had broken out to the south. They and the 2nd Seaforths and 1st Gordons did not surrender until 1700 hours.

It is impossible to say how many of the 51st Division would have succeeded in getting away if fog had not prevented ships from going inshore that night, 11/12 June. What is certain is that German artillery and machine guns on the cliffs overlooking the narrow estuary and entrance on each side would have sunk or damaged many ships with heavy losses, and wrought similar carnage among the soldiers in these vessels or awaiting embarkation. This is borne out by Lieutenant Hawkins, of the 7th Royal Norfolks (a pioneer battalion with the 51st Division). His company was attached to Fortune's headquarters, and he was sent to meet a naval officer at Saint-Valery to arrange the evacuation.

This officer told Hawkins that it was not possible to get enough large vessels into the port to take off the number of troops that needed evacuating. In addition, from the port area Hawkins could see German tanks on the cliffs overlooking the port.

One of Hawkins's platoons managed to make its way to Veules-les-Roses while the mist was still down and eventually steal out to the ships by rowing boat. The men got home safely, but were subsequently sent to the 18th Division, which was captured in its entirety at Singapore in February 1942 – and about half of that platoon never came home. The rest of Hawkins's company, after capture by the Germans, lost only one man, to pneumonia.

Captain Lang, the adjutant of the 4th Camerons, was another of those who headed for Veules-les-Roses. With some 'Jocks', he made his way along the beach, past bodies at the foot of the cliffs. As they crept along, a German machine gun on the heights above Saint-Valery fired on them but missed. On arrival at Veules-les-Roses they found two vessels, one British, which was aground, and one French offshore. Suddenly, the French vessel was hit and blew up. This left the British vessel, packed with soldiers waiting for the tide to float her off. Germans began to close in, and tanks fired from the cliff-tops, holing the grounded vessel so that even if she had floated off she would have sunk. Lang, who had climbed on board, was firing a Lewis gun with which the vessel was armed, and was wounded just before the Germans came out on to the beach and 'rolled us up'.

The Highlanders would return to Saint-Valery in 1944 to liberate the town. The reborn 51st (Highland) Division had to complete a long journey before that great moment – all the way from Alamein in North Africa, via Sicily and Normandy. By then they were commanded by Major General Thomas Rennie, who as a major and GSO 2 to Fortune had undertaken the unpleasant task of notifying the division of the order to surrender. He subsequently escaped from the prisoner column.

Others also escaped, including Captain Lang. With two others he too broke away at night from the prisoner column in the Pas-de-Calais area. After fourteen days they reached Le Touquet, to find every boat requisitioned by the Germans. While searching for a means to get away they were recaptured. Lang made a second break, this time when being transported through Belgium. He succeeded in getting clear this time, via Paris by train to the south of France, and eventually across the Mediterranean to Syria. From here he returned to Britain and eventually commanded the 5th Cameron Highlanders with distinction when they were part of the 152nd Brigade of the resurrected 51st Highland Division in north-west Europe.

After crossing the Seine, the 1st Armoured Division withdrew to a perimeter across the Carentan Peninsula. There were no British army maps of the area, and the division was reduced to using Michelin maps when they could be found. Evans was eventually made the scapegoat for what had befallen his division.

Arkforce made it to Le Havre, and by 1530 hours on 13 June the evacuation of this port was complete. Arkforce was shipped to Cherbourg, through which port it was intended that the British should send in reinforcements and continue the fight under the command of the recently knighted Lieutenant General Sir Alan Brooke. For, although the story of the BEF's travail in the campaign of 1940 was nearly over, it had a little time to run. By now, the Italians had joined forces with Hitler, declaring war on France and Britain on 10 June 1940.

Brooke arrived at Cherbourg early in the morning of 13 June. His first order was to continue with the evacuation of lines-of-communication troops not essential for the maintenance of the 'new BEF' of four divisions. He learned that one of those divisions, the 51st (Highland), had been cut off and forced to surrender. Next he drove to the British lines-of-communication headquarters at Le Mans and met Swayne, head of the mission to General Georges (still commander of the North-East Front). After discussions with Swayne and Howard-Vyse, head of the British mission at Weygand's headquarters, who happened to be visiting the headquarters, Brooke came to the conclusion that the French could not hold out for more than another few days. This impression was reinforced when he arrived with Howard-Vyse at Weygand's headquarters at Orléans the next day after a 170-mile drive. It was clear that Weygand had given up, and he told Brooke that the French Army had ceased to be able to offer organized resistance and was disintegrating into disconnected groups. The Germans would enter Paris that day, 14 June, and their divisions were scything through France.

As far as Weygand was concerned the only military recourse was to form a redoubt in Brittany by holding forward a line just east of Rennes, with one flank on the sea at Saint-Malo and the other on the mouth of the Loire, adding that this plan had been agreed by the Supreme War Council. Subsequently Weygand was to deny that he had given Brooke such a depressing portrayal of French disarray. It is hard to believe that Brooke did not hear him aright. He was a fluent French-speaker and described the meeting in his diary that night, giving his views on the Brittany plan, which he thought 'wild' and 'quite impossible'.[5]

Brooke and Weygand then drove to Georges' headquarters, which were sited near Weygand's. During the journey, Weygand turned to Brooke and said, 'This is a terrible predicament I am in.' Brooke was

about to answer that he could well understand the heavy responsibility of being entrusted with saving France in her agony when Weygand continued, 'Yes, I had finished my military career which had been a most successful one.' Brooke was astounded that all this man, on whom France had pinned her hopes, could think about was his military career. It would not have surprised General Spears, the British Liaison Officer at GQG who, as we have seen, received the same impression about Weygand when he met him on 20 May.

On arrival at Georges' headquarters, Brooke was shown a situation map, which clearly demonstrated that the French Army had lost all cohesion. He asked how Georges would find the troops to defend a front of 93 miles in Brittany, a minimum of fifteen divisions. The British were producing four. Where were the others to come from? The answer: there were none. Both Georges and Weygand considered the plan ridiculous, but as it had been agreed by the Inter-Allied Council it was an order. Brooke said he would participate in the scheme, but would report his views to the British government. Weygand did not reveal that he had already advised the French government to ask for an armistice.

Brooke sent a telegram back to London asking that the Brittany plan be reconsidered in view of Weygand's, Georges's and his opinion that it was absurd. Brooke despatched Howard-Vyse back to Britain to see General Dill, the CIGS, to tell him to stop despatching any more British troops and make preparations to evacuate those already in France. Having driven the 170 miles back to Le Mans, Brooke spoke to Dill on the telephone. He requested that the flow of British troops to France be stopped (the Canadians and corps troops). He added that there was only one course open, to re-embark the Expeditionary Force as quickly as possible. He then arranged for those troops in France not under the command of French Tenth Army, and still fighting, to be got out as quickly as possible. He sent for Marshall-Cornwall, still liaison officer with Tenth Army, and told him to discuss with the French the evacuation of British troops as soon as they could be released.

Brooke's recommendations were accepted by the War Office, as was his request that Weygand be told that the British Army would no longer remain under his command. Plans were made for the main body of the 'Second BEF' to embark at Cherbourg, while a covering force held the neck of the Cotentin Peninsula. Some lines-of-communication units would embark at the nearest convenient port, such as Saint-Malo, Brest and Saint-Nazaire.

At about 2000 hours, Brooke had another telephone conversation with Dill, who was at No. 10 Downing Street, and found himself talking to Churchill. Brooke had difficulty persuading the Prime Minister to agree

to the evacuation of the two brigades of the 52nd Division that had just arrived in France. Churchill suggested that they be used to close a thirty-mile gap between the French Tenth Army and the one on its right. Brooke talked him out of it. He was forthright and firm with Churchill, whom he had never met. It was a model of how a soldier should deal with a politician at moments of great crisis. A lesser man might have lacked moral courage and resorted to telling the Prime Minister what he wanted to hear. Brooke recorded this conversation in an afternote in his diary. Having been told by Churchill that he, Brooke, had been sent to France to make the French feel that the British were supporting them, Brooke replied 'that it was impossible to make a corpse feel, and that the French army was, to all intents and purposes, dead, and certainly incapable of registering what had been done for it'.[6]

During half an hour of talking, in which Churchill implied that Brooke was suffering from 'cold feet', Brooke managed to maintain his temper by looking out of the window at the GOC of the 52nd Division sitting on a garden bench talking to one of his brigadiers, and it reminded him 'of the human element of the 52nd Div and of the unwarranted decision to sacrifice them with no attainable object in view'. At last, when Brooke was exhausted, Churchill said, 'All right, I agree with you.'[7]

The next four days were critical, and Brooke's firmness kept the British both in France and back home in Whitehall on track, a track that for the remnants of the BEF led back to Britain. He was absolutely clear that the French were about to surrender, and was determined that as few British troops as possible should be caught up in the ensuing debacle. On 16 June, with embarkation in progress, Brooke moved his headquarters to Redon, north of Saint-Nazaire. Here he learned from Dill over the telephone that Weygand was complaining about Brooke's not honouring his undertaking to hold Brittany. Weygand appeared to have forgotten that two days earlier Dill himself had told him that British troops were no longer under his command and were therefore not available to take part in the Brittany redoubt scheme – a scheme which Weygand himself had described as fantasy. Dill had referred the matter to Churchill, who said there was no such agreement between the two governments.[8]

On 17 June, Brooke heard Marshal Pétain broadcast to the French armies to cease hostilities while he negotiated with the Germans. Neither Weygand nor any other French officer had seen fit to inform the British, who still had large numbers of troops and masses of equipment in France. Instead they were still carping about Brooke's refusal to partici-pate in the impossible Brittany redoubt plan. The French excused their failure to notify their allies by claiming that they would fight on if the terms of the armistice were not honourable. But nobody, least of all

Brooke, having seen the state to which the French Army had been reduced, could possibly be persuaded that Pétain broadcasting that the fighting had to stop could mean anything other than surrender. Fighting on did not figure on the French agenda.

Brooke left France on 18 June, via Saint-Nazaire. He had arrived at the port the day before to be told that the destroyer sent to pick him up was full of survivors from the liner *Lancastria* which had just been bombed with 6,000 troops on board, sinking in fifteen minutes with the loss of 3,000 lives. He was offered an armed trawler, the *Cambridgeshire*, that could just fit in his HQ staff and was sailing at once, or the *Ulster Sovereign* sailing the next day. Conscious that Pétain's negotiations with the Germans might include the internment of British troops in France, he decided not to wait, and boarded the trawler.

The evacuations went on until 25 June, the day the armistice terms signed between France and Germany came into effect. Between 16 and 25 June, the final evacuations took place from Cherbourg, Saint-Malo, Brest, La Pallice and Saint-Nazaire. During this period a total of 144,171 British, 18,246 French, 24,352 Polish, 1,939 Czech and 163 Belgian troops were transported to Britain. Some troops were even taken from Mediterranean ports until mid-August, by which time that region of France was Vichy territory and not under German occupation.

Brooke by his appreciation of the disaster about to overtake the French and by his refusal to carry out the British government's instructions, including standing firm against Churchill himself, saved three British divisions from the fate that befell the 51st (Highland) Division. These divisions along with lines-of-communication and other Allied troops, plus nearly 300 guns were taken to England to fight again another day.

12

RECKONING

> Personally, I feel happier now that we have no allies to be polite to and to pamper.
>
> King George VI writing to his mother after Dunkirk[1]

With the fall of France, British strategy for fighting the war against Germany lay in ruins. For years the government had shied away from committing Britain to fighting alongside the French on the continent of Europe. When they finally did so in February 1939 it was on the assumption that the next war would mirror the opening years of the last one: in the event of invasion, the French would contain the Germans. This would allow the British Army to build up sufficiently in both manpower and equipment to enable it to play its full part in what would be a replay of the previous war. It took nine months to build up the BEF from its original September 1939 strength of four divisions to the ten divisions that faced the Germans on 10 May 1940, plus another three that landed in France later in May. Many of these formations were neither equipped nor trained to face a first-class enemy. During those nine months leading up to the German offensive in the west, except for patrol skirmishes in the Maginot Line sector, the BEF had not been engaged in any fighting whatsoever. Despite being granted this intermission, neither foreseen nor catered for, the time vouchsafed thereby was still insufficient to manufacture the necessary equipment, and raise and train the units required to expand the 1940 BEF into the force comparable with the BEF of fifty-six divisions that eventually fought on the Western Front between 1916 and 1918. By May 1940 much more needed to be done to bring the BEF up to full fighting efficiency, let alone expand it. But thanks to the manner in which the Germans conducted their campaign, and the swift collapse of the French Army, time was not granted.

The evacuation of the BEF at Dunkirk was spoken about as a miracle at the time, and still is depicted in those terms to this day. The only miraculous element in the operation was the weather: gales and high

seas would have allowed far fewer troops to be taken off – probably none from the beaches, and drastically fewer from the seaward side of the East Mole. On the plus side, however, bad weather, especially if accompanied by bad visibility and low cloud, might have curtailed the activities of the Luftwaffe. The Dunkirk operation owed its success to the power and skill of the Royal Navy, not to any mystical intervention. The part played by the Royal Navy has been consistently underestimated; without it the considerable contribution by the RAF and the courage and skill of the BEF would have been to no avail. Ask anyone in the street what he or she knows about Dunkirk, and aside from the large number who will gaze at you blankly, most will say 'The little ships bringing the BEF home.' That the contribution of the 'little ships' to the successful evacuation from the Dunkirk beaches was significant is without doubt. But their role has become the enduring myth of the operation to the extent of obliterating the contribution of the Royal and Merchant Navies. This can be understood in the context of the time. To boost national morale and cohesion, the story of the 'little ships' was milked as hard as it could be. The facts are that more than two and a half times as many troops were taken from Dunkirk harbour as from the beaches, and of those taken off the beaches the majority were transported in destroyers or other ships, albeit in many cases ferried out to these larger vessels, either by 'little ships' or by ships' boats. The number of men taken directly from the beaches to England by the 'little ships' was small. The breakdown of figures is at Appendix C. One-third of all the troops evacuated were taken off in the fifty-six destroyers involved in the operation.

Without the Royal Navy the evacuations after Dunkirk would have been impossible too. These involved taking off some 140,000 British troops from formations and lines-of-communication units left south of the Somme after the German breakthrough. The only instance of the Royal Navy not fulfilling its obligation to the army occurred at Saint-Valery, and that was largely due to the weather and the proximity of German armour. But the Royal Navy did manage to evacuate 2,137 British and 1,184 French troops from Veules-les-Roses near Saint-Valery.

It is arguable that the defeat of the French Army in 1940, which led to the withdrawal of the British Army from the continent, was a blessing in disguise for the British – although not for the reason that King George VI gave in his letter to his mother, quoted at the head of this chapter; and it certainly would not have been seen as a godsend at the time. Indeed for reasons that will be covered later, the Fall of France was to make the British conduct of the war infinitely more difficult than envisaged by the Chiefs of Staff and politicians in 1939 and early 1940.

But there were bonuses as well. First, because there was no 1940

repeat of the events of 1914, that is an eventual halting of the German offensive in France and Flanders, there was no 1940s version of the 1914–18 Western Front, with all that would have flowed from that including massive casualties. Just over a year later, flushed with their victory in the west, the Germans invaded Russia. It was on the Eastern Front that the main body of the German Army was engaged from June 1941 until May 1945. It was here that the colossal casualties suffered by Britain and France fighting the Germans in the previous war were repeated, only on a vastly increased scale, and borne this time by the Russians. In the process the German Army was worn down, and unable to move sufficient divisions to the west to contain the British and Americans when they landed and liberated western Europe in 1944–5.

Thus Britain, because of the Fall of France, was granted some 'time out', respite from engaging the German Army. Indeed one could argue that Britain never again encountered the enemy's main effort on land for the rest of the war. There was tough fighting in several campaigns, yes, but not against the main body of the German Army; it was engaged in Russia.

The collapse of France, and the failure of the Luftwaffe to win the Battle of Britain, bought the time that Britain needed to absorb the lessons so dearly learned in France, to re-equip, and to retrain. In the process some of the dead wood among the middle-ranking and senior officers was cut out of the British Army. Generally, those who had done well were promoted, those who had failed were given administrative jobs or, if more senior, retired. On the whole, younger, fitter men commanded at all levels: most commanding officers were under thirty, some in their mid-twenties, rather than the over-forty-year-old veterans of the First World War that commanded units in 1940. Company commanders, and their equivalents, were correspondingly younger, mostly in their early twenties. These changes took time, but now there was time.

Time was also vouchsafed to get the Americans used to the idea that they might have to become involved in this war. The final catalyst was of course the Japanese bombing of Pearl Harbor in December 1941. The United States, whose army in 1939 ranked seventeenth in the world after Rumania, was, even as late as November 1942, in the words of Field Marshal Sir John Dill, 'more unready for war than it is possible to imagine'. It is therefore inconceivable that America could have played any part in stopping the expansion of the Axis had Britain given in when France fell, or made a separate peace with Hitler in 1941, as the late Alan Clark was fond of suggesting. Without Britain and her Empire and Commonwealth continuing to resist after the Fall of France, Hitler could have won the war.

Finally, still counting blessings, even the French may have benefited from their defeat in 1940 – bitter though the shame was at the time and even though the poison lingers still. But there was no equivalent to Verdun, or any of the other Western Front battles that in total cost France over six million casualties between 1914 and 1918.[2] Yes, there was the degradation of collaboration with a foul Nazi regime and all that went with it, including the labour camps and persecution of the Jews. But it is not for us to speculate on which was preferable: sparing France a second round of years of fighting on a 1940s Western Front (including the massive material damage), or the shame of defeat and all that followed. Only a Frenchman or woman can say what would have been right for France.

The debit side of the reckoning resulting from the defeat of France included a number of unpalatable realities. The French Army of ninety-four divisions was out of the equation, leaving a handful of badly equipped British, Commonwealth and Empire divisions to face some 160 German ones. Granted these would not immediately be encountered in Europe, and in Britain only if the Germans invaded. But, until Russia came into the war, as a result of German aggression (not, it must be emphasized, in order to assist the British), those German divisions were a potential threat to British interests in the Mediterranean and conceivably in the Middle East. Indeed, even when embroiled with Russia, the German Army could still spare sufficient formations to cause the British considerable grief in North Africa, Sicily, Italy, Greece and the Aegean over the ensuing years.

But more immediately menacing than the German Army were the Luftwaffe and the U-boats. With bases in France, Belgium and Holland the Luftwaffe could now reach every city in the United Kingdom and realize the nightmares with which British politicians had frightened themselves since the mid-1930s. These nightmares were to prove largely groundless until June 1940, for the simple reason that most German aircraft of that period, designed for tactical support of ground forces and not for strategic bombing, had a small radius of action, especially so in the case of their fighters.[3] To bomb London from even the nearest part of Germany would involve a 600-mile round trip. Flying from bases in Germany, the Luftwaffe simply did not have the capability to mount mass attacks on major cities and communication links in the United Kingdom. If attempted in daylight, without fighter escorts, the bombers would have been easy meat for the RAF. After the Fall of France it was very different.

From airfields in northern France to London the radius of action is 200 miles. Not only could the Luftwaffe attack the United Kingdom, it could

also attack shipping in coastal waters, especially in the Channel and North Sea. The Focke-Wulf Condors could range far out into the Atlantic, not only acting as eyes for the U-boat packs, but also able to attack shipping with bombs and machine guns. Between June and November 1940, Condors operating from Bordeaux had sunk 90,000 tons of Allied shipping, and for the next three years they were, in Churchill's words, 'the scourge of the Atlantic'.

In 1917, the U-boats had nearly brought the United Kingdom to her knees. Then they had only the short stretch of Belgian coast and Germany's North Sea coast from which to operate, and access to the Atlantic trade routes involved a long trip round the north of Scotland or through the Straits of Dover. Now, from occupied France's Biscay coast, the U-boats could sortie straight out to attack shipping in both the North and South Atlantic. The occupation of Norway also gave the Germans bases from which to send out Condors to spy on and attack convoys routed as far north as southern Greenland in an attempt to keep out of the clutches of the U-boats.

The Fall of France also drastically altered the strategic balance in other ways. The Royal Navy had counted on the well-equipped French Navy to cover the Mediterranean, while it protected trade routes and fulfilled Imperial commitments elsewhere. Now the French Navy was immobilized in French ports by the terms of the Armistice Treaty with Germany. At the same time Italy had come into the war on the German side, bringing with her a powerful battle fleet and large air force. Although the latter was equipped with obsolescent types of aircraft, with numerous land bases the Italian Air Force posed a major threat to shipping transiting the Mediterranean long after the threat posed by the Italian Navy had been severely reduced by the Royal Navy. As a result of the Italian threat, the main trade route through the Mediterranean was immediately abandoned by Britain, thereby lengthening the voyage from the United Kingdom to Suez and the supply of British forces in the Western Desert and Palestine from 3,000 to 13,000 miles round the Cape of Good Hope, and similarly to Bombay and British forces in India from 6,000 to 11,000 miles.

From June 1940 to June 1941, Britain and her Empire and Commonwealth were at war without an ally against two powerful enemies, Germany and Italy, with a third lurking ever more menacingly, Japan. This was the perilous strategic state to which the United Kingdom was reduced by the Fall of France.

The losses suffered by the Royal Navy during the evacuation have already been covered. During the campaign, the Royal Air Force lost 1,526 killed in action, died of wounds or injury, lost at sea, wounded or

taken prisoner. The vast majority of these were pilots and aircrew. Aircraft losses amounted to 931 failed to return, destroyed on the ground or damaged beyond repair.

British Army casualties were 68,111 killed in action, died of wounds, missing, wounded or prisoners of war. The material losses of the army were enormous, either in battle or destroyed, or left behind, as shown below.[4]

Material losses of British Army in France and Belgium, May to June 1940			
	Shipped to France	Consumed and expended in action or destroyed or left behind	Brought back to England
Guns	2,794	2,472	322
Vehicles	68,618	63,879	4,739
motorcycles	21,081	20,548	533
Ammunition (tons)	109,000	76,697	32,303
Supplies and stores (tons)	449,000	415,940	33,060
Petrol (tons)	166,000	164,929	1,071

Note: Of some 170 cruiser tanks, 175 light tanks and 100 infantry tanks, only thirteen light tanks and nine cruiser tanks were brought back to England.

Until the lost equipment could be replaced by British and American industry, the British Army faced the prospect of fighting an invading German Army armed mainly with rifles and light machine guns. The 4th/7th Royal Dragoon Guards were typical. In June 1940, the regiment was equipped with a vehicle called the Beaverette, named after Lord Beaverbrooke, the Minister of Aircraft Production and member of the War Cabinet, whose 'baby' it was. The Beaverette, officially known by the grandiose title the Ironside, was an ordinary Standard 14-horsepower family car fitted with a sheet of armour plate in front and on the sides, and open at the top.[5] Each squadron was organized into five troops of four Beaverettes each, and a bus troop, which provided a dismounted party that travelled to war in a luxury coach that had once carried happy holidaymakers to the seaside. Each squadron mustered about twenty-five Brens and six anti-tank rifles. These they would take to battle in a vehicle that did not keep out even an armour-piercing rifle bullet. The regiment was not re-equipped with tanks until April 1941, and what it got was the Covenanter, already obsolete by the time it was issued.[6]

Despite these losses, the morale of the British Army was undented. The BEF came back with an unswerving belief that given equal terms it could have defeated the German Army. Let the final word on this subject

be left to the enemy. In August 1940, German divisions training for the invasion of the United Kingdom were provided with a report prepared by the German IV Corps, which in Bock's Sixth Army had fought the BEF from the Dyle to the Channel coast. The report covers mainly technical detail of British fighting methods, but this is what it has to say about the British soldier (the italics are in the German original):

> *The English soldier* [sic] was in excellent physical condition.[7] He bore his own wounds with stoical calm. The losses of his own troops he discussed with complete equanimity. He did not complain of hardships. *In battle he was tough and dogged.* His conviction that England would conquer in the end was unshakeable...
>
> The English soldier has always shown himself to be a *fighter of high value.* Certainly the Territorial divisions are inferior to the Regular troops in training, but where morale is concerned they are their equal.
>
> In defence the Englishman *took any punishment that came his way.* During the fighting IV Corps took relatively fewer prisoners than in engagements with the French or Belgians. On the other hand casualties on both sides were high.[8]

Two other topics demand an airing in the reckoning: an assessment of Gort and an evaluation of the senior command of the French Army. Both will of necessity be short.

Gort's decision to evacuate his army at Dunkirk saved the BEF. He may not have been a brilliant army commander – his faults have been discussed already and need no repeating. But he was able to see with absolute clarity that the French high command were utterly bankrupt of realistic ideas and that consequently Allied plans would lead nowhere, and he had the moral courage and unwavering willpower to act in the face of censure and criticism, thus ensuring that the BEF was saved. There are few occasions when the actions of one man can be said to be instrumental in winning a war. This was one of those. Had the BEF been surrounded, cut off and forced to surrender, it is inconceivable that Britain could have continued to fight without an army. That is not to say that Britain would necessarily have been occupied, but a humiliating accommodation with Hitler would surely have followed. Without continuing British resistance, weak at first but daily growing stronger, Hitler would have won the war. For the reasons already given, the United States was incapable of intervening to limit Hitler's hold on Europe.

The French high command have been criticized in this book. Whatever excuses one might offer, in the end one has to ask how it was that the French Army, with better tanks and more of them than the Germans,

was so utterly defeated in so short a space of time. The deficiencies of
the French Army have been covered in the first chapter, and it is not
intended to repeat them in detail here. The French, having been on
the winning side in the First World War, were entirely content that the
lessons they drew from it were the right ones. They repeated the mistake
they had made after the Franco-Prussian War of 1870–1, when they
applied lessons they had learned in that war to the first half of the First
World War, suffering huge casualties and coming close to defeat in the
process. After the First World War, believing in the power of the defence
(a conclusion they had drawn from that war), they aimed to fight a static
war in the next contest. Conducting operations in this way would not
require good communications because the pace of events would, in
their estimation, be so slow that their inadequate arrangements for
radio and telephone links and rigid command-and-control organization
would be able to cope. There was no point in massing their armour,
they believed, because its principal role was to support the infantry in
defence and in local counter-attack. Events did not go as they had
foreseen, and the shock to an army whose morale was already flawed
was too much. The French Army met General James Gavin's definition:
'Organisations created to fight the last war better are not going to win
the next one.'

The German Army, having been defeated in the First World War, was
not above analysing the lessons at the tactical and operational level, and
drew the right conclusions. That their leaders, Hitler and his generals,
failed to learn the strategic lessons contributed to Germany's ultimate
defeat in the Second World War, as it had in the First.

Appendices

APPENDIX A

ALLIED LAND FORCE ORDER OF BATTLE AS AT 10 MAY 1940

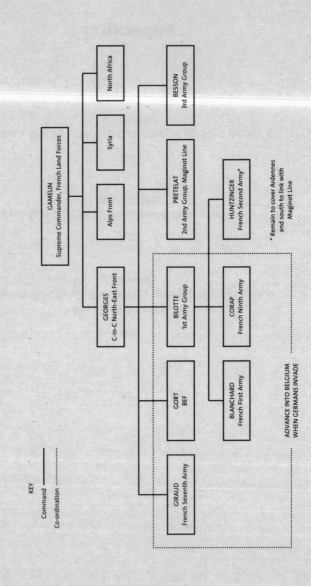

KEY

Command ———————

Co-ordination ·················

GAMELIN
Supreme Commander, French Land Forces

North Africa

Syria

Alps Front

GEORGES
C-in-C North-East Front

PRETELAT
2nd Army Group, Maginot Line

BESSON
3rd Army Group

HUNTZINGER
French Second Army*

GIRAUD
French Seventh Army

GORT
BEF

BILOTTE
1st Army Group

BLANCHARD
French First Army

CORAP
French Ninth Army

* Remain to cover Ardennes
and south to link with
Maginot Line

ADVANCE INTO BELGIUM
WHEN GERMANS INVADE

APPENDIX B

ALLIED LAND FORCE ORDER OF BATTLE AS AT 12 MAY 1940

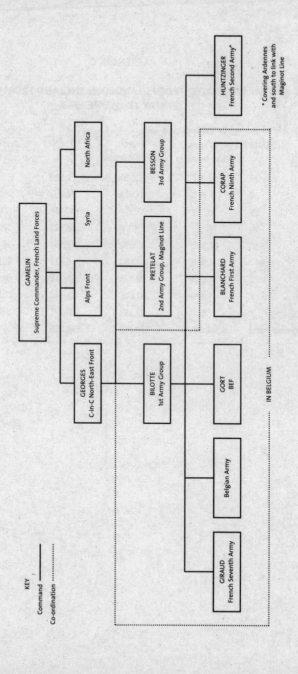

KEY

Command ——————
Co-ordination ·············

GAMELIN
Supreme Commander, French Land Forces

GEORGES
C-in-C North-East Front

Alps Front

Syria

North Africa

BILOTTE
1st Army Group

PRETELAT
2nd Army Group, Maginot Line

BESSON
3rd Army Group

GIRAUD
French Seventh Army

Belgian Army

GORT
BEF

BLANCHARD
French First Army

CORAP
French Ninth Army

HUNTZINGER
French Second Army*

IN BELGIUM

* Covering Ardennes
and south to link with
Maginot Line

APPENDIX C

BRITISH AND ALLIED TROOPS LANDED IN ENGLAND FROM DUNKIRK, 27 MAY TO 4 JUNE 1940

Date	From the beaches	From Dunkirk harbour	Total	Accumulated total
May 27	Nil	7,669	7,669	7,669
28	5,390	11,874	17,804	25,473
29	13,752	33,558	47,310	72,783
30	29,512	24,311	53,823	126,606
31	22,942	45,072	68,014	194,620
June 1	17,348	47,081	64,429	259,049
2	6,695	19,561	26,256	285,305
3	1,870	24,876	26,746	312,051
4	622	25,553	26,175	338,226
Grand total	98,671	239,555	338,226	

Glossary

AA – anti-aircraft.

Adjutant – the CO's personal staff officer in a battalion or regiment in the British Army. In the Second World War, and for several years thereafter, there was no operations officer at this level, so the adjutant was responsible for all the operational staff work as well as discipline and all other personnel matters. Not to be confused with adjutant in the French Army who was, and is, a warrant officer.

Artillery – the BEF in 1940 had the following types of artillery:

Field Regiments – each had headquarters and two twelve-gun batteries, further sub-divided into three four-gun troops. Their armament varied. The 18-pounder gun and 4.5-inch howitzer were to be superseded by the new 25-pounder, and until this was available 18-pounders were converted into 25-pounders. Field regiments were equipped either with 18-pounders, 4.5-inch howitzers, or converted 18/25-pounders.

Medium Regiments – each had headquarters and two batteries, each of eight 6-inch howitzers or eight 60-pounders. The new 4.5-inch/60-pounders were just coming in to production.

Heavy and Super-Heavy Regiments – each had headquarters and four batteries. Each regiment had four 6-inch guns, and either twelve 8-inch or twelve 9.2-inch howitzers. Super-heavy regiments were equipped with 9.2-inch or 12-inch howitzers.

Anti-Tank Regiment – each had headquarters and four batteries each of twelve 2-pounder anti-tank guns, or some 25mm guns.

Anti-Aircraft Regiment – each had headquarters and three or four batteries of eight 3.7-inch anti-aircraft guns.

Light Anti-Aircraft Regiment – each had headquarters and three or four batteries of twelve Bofors 40mm light anti-aircraft guns.

Battalion – the organization of a 1940 British infantry battalion is shown in the chart overleaf.

The organization of a German infantry battalion varied depending on whether it was part of the rifle regiment, or motorcycle battalion of a panzer division or

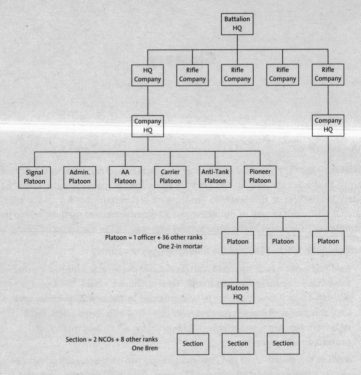

in an infantry division, but the table below shows the organization of a non-motorized German infantry battalion compared with a British infantry battalion. A German infantry battalion had three rifle companies each of three platoons of four sections, and one heavy weapons company of two platoons.

	BRITISH	GERMAN
Strength: officers and men	21 and 752	15 and 693
CO	Lt Col	Major
Sub-machine guns	none	about 30 (scale varied)
Light machine guns	50 with rifle companies, 10 with carrier platoon 4 with AA platoon	45 (36 with rifle companies)
Heavy or medium machine guns	none organic to battalion: could be allotted from divisional machine-gun battalion	12 (2 per rifle company, 6 in heavy weapons company)
Anti-tank rifles	22 (12 with rifle companies)	9
Light mortars	12 × 2 in (used mainly for smoke)	9 × 50 mm
Medium mortars	2 × 3 mm mortars	6 × 81 mm mortars

BC – Battery Commander.

BEF – British Expeditionary Force.

BGS – Brigadier General Staff.

Bofors – a 40mm quick-firing anti-aircraft gun of Swedish design.

Bren – the British light machine gun of the Second World War and until the late 1950s. Fired a standard .303 round from a thirty-round magazine (usually loaded with twenty-eight rounds).

Brewed up – a slang expression meaning a tank on fire after being hit. An allusion to lighting a fire to brew a cup of tea.

Brigade – in the British Army, a formation of three infantry battalions or armoured regiments commanded by a brigadier.

Brigade Major (BM) – the senior operations officer of a brigade, de-facto chief of staff.

Carrier – a lightly armoured tracked vehicle, in 1940 often called a Bren-gun carrier, although it was also used in machine-gun battalions to carry the Vickers medium machine gun.

C-in-C – Commander-in-Chief.

CIGS – Chief of the Imperial General Staff, the senior soldier in the British Army.

CO – Commanding Officer.

Corps – a formation of at least two divisions commanded by a lieutenant general. Also the generic term for arms and services except armour, artillery and infantry, hence the corps of Royal Engineers, Royal Signals, Royal Army Service Corps and so on.

CRA – Commander Royal Artillery. The senior gunner in a division, and responsible for commanding and co-ordinating the artillery support of the division.

CRE – Commander Royal Engineers, the senior engineer in a division and responsible for commanding and co-ordinating the engineer support of the division.

CSM – Company Sergeant Major.

DCLI – Duke of Cornwall's Light Infantry.

DCM – Distinguished Conduct Medal. Instituted in 1854 as the equivalent of the DSO for warrant officers, NCOs and soldiers of the British Army (and Royal Marines when under Army Command). Awarded for gallantry in action, a prestigious and rare award, second only to the VC. Now discontinued.

Defensive Fire (DF) – mortar, artillery, or machine-gun fire by troops in defensive positions against attacking troops or patrols. Usually pre-registered on a number of key places, and numbered, so a particular DF can be called down quickly by reference to its number. Guns and mortars will be laid on the DF SOS when not engaged on other tasks. As its name implies the DF SOS is the target deemed to be the most dangerous to the defenders.

Dingo – small, lightly armoured, turretless, four-wheel-drive scout car.

Direct Fire – weapons aimed directly at the target as opposed to indirect-fire weapons such as artillery and mortars. Vickers machine guns can also be fired in the indirect role.

Division – formation of two or more brigades commanded by a major general.

DLC – Division Légère de Cavalerie.

DLI – Durham Light Infantry.

DLM – Division Légère Méchanique.

DSO – Distinguished Service Order. Instituted in 1886. Until the awards system was changed in 1994, it was a dual-role decoration, recognizing gallantry at a level just below that qualifying for the VC by junior officers, and exceptional leadership in battle by senior officers. Officers of all three services were and are eligible. Since 1994 it has become less prestigious by virtue of a change in the rules for its award. It is now awarded for successful leadership and command in 'operational' circumstances. What constitutes 'operations' is open to question, since DSOs appear to 'come up with the rations' after so-called operations, such as Kosovo in 1999, when hardly a shot has been fired in anger, whereas DSOs for tough fighting in Iraq (from 2003) were too sparsely awarded, and deserving cases were palmed off with lesser awards or not decorated at all.

Forward Observation Officer (FOO) – an artillery officer who directs artillery fire. Normally one with each forward rifle company and provided by artillery battery supporting the infantry battalion.

GHQ – General Headquarters. In the context of this book, Gort's headquarters.

GOC – General Officer Commanding.

GQG – Grand Quartier Général. The headquarters of the Supreme Commander French Land Forces (Gamelin followed by Weygand), in the Château de Vincennes outside Paris.

GSO – General Staff Officer, a staff officer who dealt with General (G) Staff matters (operations, intelligence, planning and staff duties), as opposed to personnel (A, short for Adjutant General's Staff), or logistic matters (Q, short for Quartermaster

General's Staff). The grades were GSO 1 (lieutenant colonel), GSO 2 (major) and GSO 3 (captain).

HE – high explosive.

HMS – His Majesty's Ship.

Jocks – slang expression for private soldiers used in Scottish regiments.

KOYLI – King's Own Yorkshire Light Infantry.

KRRC – King's Royal Rifle Corps.

Layback Position – a temporary position established in rear of a withdrawing unit or formation to ensure that enemy following up is held off while the withdrawing troops get clear. They in their turn may establish another layback position further back through which the unit or formation protecting their backs withdraws in its turn – and so on.

Limber – wheeled (usually two wheels) trailer for carrying gun ammunition, originally towed by horses, with the gun hooked on behind in the case of field artillery. In the BEF of 1940 towed by a specially designed truck in which the crew rode.

LSSAH – Leibstandarte SS Adolf Hitler.

MC – Military Cross, instituted in 1914, it was awarded to army officers of the rank of major and below, and to warrant officers, for gallantry in action. Now all ranks are eligible.

Mk – mark.

MM – Military Medal. Instituted in 1916, it was awarded to army NCOs and soldiers for gallantry in action. Now discontinued; *see* MC.

MO – Medical Officer.

MTB – motor torpedo boat.

NCO – non-commissioned officer, from lance-corporal to colour or staff sergeant. See also Warrant Officer.

OC – Officer Commanding.

O Group – short for Orders Group, the group to which orders are given at any level of command from platoon to army. For example, at platoon level the platoon commander briefing his section commanders, and at brigade level, the brigade commander briefing his battalion and supporting arms COs, and other people who need to know the plan.

OODA – Observation Orientation Decision Action.

OP – observation post.

Pioneers – the Pioneer Corps was formed at the outbreak of the Second World War to undertake unskilled labour on the lines of communication in order to relieve trained infantry or engineers of the task. In the early days of the war some TA and regular infantry were temporarily employed on these duties.

Platoon Sergeant Major – *see* Warrant Officer.

Provost – military police.

QMG – Quartermaster General. Can refer to the appointment, or to the staff branch. The Quartermaster General's branch at all staff levels dealt with what we would now call logistics.

QVR –Queen Victoria's Rifles.

RA – Royal Artillery.

Radius of Action – the distance an aircraft or ship carrying out a sortie can cover from base to a target and back without stopping to refuel. *See* Range.

RAF – Royal Air Force.

Range – the distance to a target, or the total distance an aircraft can fly or a ship steam. *See* Radius of Action.

RAP – Regimental Aid Post, the place where the Medical Officer (MO) of a battalion or equivalent-sized unit set up his aid post. Usually the requirement here was to administer 'sophisticated first aid' to stabilize the casualty sufficiently to enable him to survive the next stage of evacuation.

RE – Royal Engineers.

Regiment – originally a regiment was of horse, dragoons (mounted infantry) or foot raised by command of King, and later Parliament, and named after its colonel, usually a royal appointee. The regiment has become the basic organization of the British Army for armour, artillery, engineers and signals units equivalent to battalions in those arms in other armies. In the case of the infantry, the British Army battalion belongs to a regiment, of which in the Second World War there could be several battalions. In 1923 many British cavalry regiments were amalgamated, retaining both their old numbers, hence the 4th/7th Royal Dragoon Guards was a combination of the 4th and 7th Royal Dragoon Guards, not the 4th Battalion of the 7th Royal Dragoon Guards. In typical idiosyncratic British fashion, this rule did not apply to infantry battalions, so that the 1st/6th East Surreys was the 1st Battalion of the 6th (TA) Battalion of the East Surrey Regiment, the 6th Battalion of the East Surreys having hived off several battalions. *See* Territorial Army.

Regimental Sergeant Major – *see* Warrant Officer. It is one of the idiosyncrasies of the British Army that infantry battalions and regiments (artillery and armoured) all have a Warrant Officer Class 1 called the Regimental Sergeant Major. He is the commanding officer's right-hand man and advisor on many aspects of the battalion/regiment daily life, especially matters involving the soldiers and NCOs. The CO and the RSM have very likely known each other since the former was a second lieutenant and the latter was a young private or equivalent.

RHA – Royal Horse Artillery. In the BEF of 1940 not horsed but towed by trucks. Later in the Second World War, and thereafter, RHA regiments were often equipped with self-propelled guns to enable them to keep pace with armoured formations. The title was a hangover from horsed days. The RHA was originally formed to accompany the cavalry, and consequently consider themselves a cut above the rest of the Royal Artillery.

RM – Royal Marines.

RN – Royal Navy.

RNF – Royal Northumberland Fusiliers.

RNLI – Royal National Lifeboat Institution.

RNR – Royal Naval Reserve, usually officers of the Merchant Navy who had volunteered to serve in the Royal Navy in wartime.

RNVR – Royal Naval Volunteer Reserve, usually civilians called up for service in the Royal Navy in wartime, often with no previous maritime experience.

Royal Army Service Corps (RASC) – the administrative corps responsible for transporting supplies.

RQMS – Regimental Quartermaster Sergeant. A warrant officer class II (*see* Warrant Officer) who was the assistant to the battalion or regimental quartermaster.

RSM – Regimental Sergeant Major.

RTR – Royal Tank Regiment.

Sapper – the equivalent of private in the Royal Engineers; also a name for all engineers.

Start Line – a line in the ground, usually a natural feature, stream, bank, ridge, or fence preferably at 90 degrees to the axis of advance, which marks the start line for an attack and is crossed at H-hour in attack formation. Can be marked by tape if there is no natural feature which lends itself to being used as a start line. Now called line of departure (LOD).

Skins – 5th Royal Inniskilling Dragoon Guards.

SOS – see Defensive fire.

SS – Schutzstaffel.

SS Verfügungs – a hangover from the early days of the formation of the SS when they were known as SS-Verfügungstruppe, and eventually became the Waffen-SS or military SS. The term disappeared as the war progressed.

Territorial Army (TA) – part-time soldiers who are mobilized in war. The pre-1939 TA was a large organization consisting of regiments and battalions of all arms: armour, artillery, engineers, signals, infantry, service corps and so on.

Vickers Medium Machine Gun – a First World War-vintage belt-fed, water-cooled machine gun, rate of fire 500 rounds per minute. Maximum range with Mk VIIIZ ammunition, 4,500 yards. Last fired in action in 1962.

VC – Victoria Cross, the highest British award for bravery in the face of the enemy. To date, in the 152 years since its inception by Queen Victoria for conspicuous bravery during the Crimean War of 1854–6, only 1,358 VCs have been awarded, including a handful of double VCs, five civilians under military command, and the one presented to the American Unknown Warrior at Arlington. This figure includes the many awarded to Imperial, Commonwealth and Dominion servicemen.

VCIGS – Vice Chief of the Imperial General Staff.

Warrant Officer – since 1913 there have been two classes of Warrant Officer (WO) in the British Army: WOII, typically a company/squadron sergeant major, and WOI, usually regimental sergeant major, of which there is only one in each battalion or regiment. Just before the Second World War a WOIII, or platoon sergeant major grade was created to command platoons or troops, but it was not a success and was allowed to lapse.

A WO has a warrant signed by a government minister or representative of the Army Council, unlike a commissioned officer (of the rank of second lieutenant and above), who has a King's or Queen's commission. Those junior in rank to WOIs and WOIIs address them as sir, and Mr (Surname); those superior to them formally refer to them as Mr (Surname), but often address them and refer to them as Sergeant Major or RSM. They are not saluted by those junior to them and live in the WOs' and Sergeants' Mess.

Wehrmacht – German armed forces.

WVS – Women's Voluntary Service (later WRVS, Women's Royal Voluntary Service).

Notes

1. Twenty Wasted Years

1 Ewan Butler, *Mason-Mac: The Life of Lieutenant General Sir Noël Mason-MacFarlan* (Macmillan, 1972) p. 116.
2 Shakespeare, *Henry VI, Part 1*, Act 1, Scene 1, lines 74–7.
3 See Stephen Budiansky, *Air Power: From Kitty Hawk to Gulf War II: A History of the People, Ideas and Machines that Transformed War in the Century of Flight* (Viking, 2003), pp. 97–9. The formation of the RAF was in Budiansky's words 'a radical, indeed almost a mad step', made in a mood of panic caused by the pin-prick raids on Britain by German bombers and Zeppelins during the First World War, whose total effort *throughout the war* caused fewer casualties than one would find on a typical 'quiet day' on the Western Front. The total property damage was less than half what the First World War cost the British each day.
4 *War Diaries 1939–1945: Field Marshal Lord Alanbrooke*, ed. Alex Danchev and Daniel Todman (Weidenfeld & Nicolson, 2001), p. 18.
5 Ibid.
6 Alistair Horne, *To Lose a Battle: France 1940* (Papermac, 1990), p. 79.
7 Arthur Koestler, *Scum of the Earth* (Macmillan, 1941), quoted in *To Lose A Battle*, p. 138.
8 Winston Churchill, *The Second World War*, vol. 1: *The Gathering Storm* (Cassell, 1948) p. 442.
9 *Alanbrooke Diaries*, p. 26.
10 Ibid., p. 27.
11 Ibid., p. 4
12 David Fraser, *Alanbrooke* (Hamlyn Paperbacks, 1983), p. 137.
13 *Alanbrooke Diaries*, p. 12.
14 Ibid., p. 20.
15 Nigel Hamilton, *Monty: The Making of a General 1887–1942* (Hamlyn Paperbacks, 1982), p. 344.

2. Into Belgium: First Shocks

1 *Alanbrooke Diaries*, p. 60.
2 Ibid., p. 61.
3 L. F. Ellis, *The War in France and Flanders: 1939–1940* (HMSO, 1953), p. 42.
4 The expression 'fifth column' owes its origin to the Spanish Civil War (1936–9), when the Nationalist leader General Franco told Republicans defending Madrid that, besides having four armed columns outside the city, he had a fifth inside waiting to rise and fight for him. German propaganda used rumour to intensify fears that fifth columnists owing allegiance to them were working inside countries that they wished to conquer. This engendered panic and suspicion, even though fifth columnists were mainly a myth.
5 Ellis, *The War in France and Flanders*, p. 335. The Germans, and the French, often used the term 'England' to refer both to that country itself in a geographical sense and to the whole of the UK. They used the word 'English' in the same way regardless of whether the people to whom they were referring were English, Scots, Welsh or Irish. The French found it difficult to rid themselves of the folk memory of the English as their oldest enemy since the early Middle Ages, the alliances of the First and Second World Wars being historical aberrations. There was plenty of Anglophobia among senior French commanders, and this attribute came to the fore only too readily when things started going badly.
6 Ibid., p. 336.
7 Mungo Melvin, 'The German View', in Brian Bond and Michael Taylor (eds), *The Battle for France and Flanders: Sixty Years On* (Leo Cooper, 2001), p. 212.
8 Ellis, *The War in France and Flanders*, p. 59.
9 Winston S. Churchill, *The Second World War*, vol. II: *Their Finest Hour* (Cassell, 1949), p. 42.
10 John Terraine, *The Right of the Line: The Royal Air Force in the European War 1939–1940* (Wordsworth, 1997), p. 134.

3. Back to the Escaut and Disaster on the BEF's Southern Flank

1 *Alanbrooke Diaries*, p. 64.
2 Ellis, *The War in France and Flanders*, pp. 66–7.
3 Ibid., p. 77.
4 Now borne by their lineal descendants, the Princess of Wales's Royal Regiment.
5 Ellis, *The War in France and Flanders*, p. 81. There is no record of a XXXXI Corps

anywhere other than in Ellis. Both 6th and 8th Panzer Divisions were in
Reinhardt's XLI Panzer Corps.

6 Ibid., p. 83. This is my summary of Ellis's much longer original.
7 Ibid.
8 General Robert Altmayer commanding Group A (later French Tenth Army)
   should not be confused with his brother General René Altmayer
   commanding French V Corps.
9 Ibid., p. 84.
10 Ibid., p. 85.

4. Counter-Strike at Arras

1 See Ellis, *The War in France and Flanders*, p. 87.
2 A regiment of armour in the British Army, whether tank, light mechanized
   cavalry or armoured car, is the equivalent of a battalion in most other
   armies. A regiment of artillery is the equivalent of an artillery battalion in
   most other armies, and is divided into gun batteries, of which in a field
   regiment there are three.
3 At that stage in the war, each RTR company (see note 4 below) was sub-
   divided into five sections, each of three tanks. An RTR squadron had five
   troops of three tanks each. Later in the war, a squadron had four troops of
   four tanks each.
4 Some battalions of the RTR were divided into companies at this stage of the
   war, not squadrons, as the armoured cavalry were – although eventually the
   RTR battalions would become regiments, and their companies squadrons.
5 Horne, *To Lose a Battle*, p. 582.

5. Fighting on Two Fronts

1 The officers of the 52nd are alleged to have counted as they cleaned their
   teeth, 1, 2, 3 and so on to 41, 42, then *spit*, 44.
2 The expression 'ball', a hangover from the days of muskets, was still applied
   to the solid, pointed, metal-jacketed bullet fired by all small arms. Hence
   'ball' ammunition as opposed to 'blank', or 'tracer'.
3 *Alanbrooke Diaries*, p. 67.
4 See Horne, *To Lose a Battle*, pp. 586 n. 19, and 589.
5 *Alanbrooke Diaries*, p. 68.
6 Ellis, *The War in France and Flanders*, p. 112.
7 Ibid., p. 111.
8 *Alanbrooke Diaries*, pp. 67–8.

9 Ellis, *The War in France and Flanders*, p. 142.
10 Ibid., pp. 138–9.

6. Boulogne and Calais

1 Ellis, *The War in France and Flanders*, p. 155.
2 Ibid., p. 159.
3 At this stage in the war, the RTR was in the process of reorganizing its companies into squadrons, and its battalions would shortly become regiments, bringing the RTR into line with the rest of the Armoured Corps. In May 1940, 3rd RTR, in common with the rest of the RTR, was still a battalion.
4 Ellis, *The War in France and Flanders*, pp. 159–60.
5 W. H. Close, *A View from the Turret: A History of the 3rd Royal Tank Regiment in the Second World War* (Dell & Breedon, 1998), p. 9.
6 Ibid., p. 11.
7 Airey Neave, *The Flames of Calais: A Soldier's Battle 1940* (Hodder & Stoughton, 1972), p. 53.
8 The 1st Rifle Brigade was not a brigade but the first battalion of an infantry regiment which in the idiosyncratic British fashion was called the Rifle Brigade. Both the KRRC and Rifle Brigade, having been amalgamated as the Royal Green Jackets in the 1960s, are now The Rifles.
9 Ellis, *The War in France and Flanders*, p. 163.
10 Ibid., p. 164.
11 Ibid., p. 165.
12 Ibid., pp. 165–6.
13 See Glossary for explanation of platoon sergeant major.
14 Ellis, *The War in France and Flanders*, p. 167.
15 Ibid.
16 Ibid.
17 Ibid.
18 Churchill, *Their Finest Hour*, p. 73.
19 Ibid.

7. The Withdrawal: II Corps on the Eastern Flank

1 Bernard Montgomery, *The Memoirs of Field Marshal the Viscount Montgomery of Alamein* (Collins, 1958), p. 65.
2 *Alanbrooke Diaries*, p. 71.
3 To 'refuse' a flank involves turning part of a unit or formation's front at

right angles to protect the threatened flank. In simple terms the deployment
becomes like the letter L, the horizontal part of the L being the 'refused'
flank.

4 *Alanbrooke Diaries*, p. 72.
5 Ibid., p. 73.
6 In the Second World War, and up to the present, a fighting unit in the British
Army (infantry battalion, armoured regiment, artillery regiment, sapper
squadron and so on) in war, as opposed to operations other than war (such as
Iraq after the 2003 invasion) was, and is, divided into three echelons. F Echelon
consists of the elements required to carry out the actual fighting, including
vehicles such as carriers, tanks, armoured cars, command vehicles, gun
towers and limbers, and immediate ammunition re-supply vehicles. A Echelon
consists of the vehicles and men usually held in the rear of unit locations for
short-notice logistic back-up, and often commanded by the unit motor
transport officer. B Echelon, usually commanded by the unit quartermaster,
contains the personnel (such as the armourer, vehicle mechanics and cooks)
and vehicles to provide longer-term logistic support on a daily basis, for
example cooking hot food (often brought up at night in special containers
called hayboxes) or the repair of weapons and vehicles. Frequently all Unit B
Echelons would be, and still are, centralized under brigade or divisional
control, with the aim of reducing the risk of chaos caused by each unit B
Echelon 'doing its own thing' at a time of its own choosing, especially on
restricted lines of communication. The detailed composition of the echelons
varied depending on the type of unit and the theatre of operations.
7 *Alanbrooke Diaries*, p. 72.
8 Ibid., p. 73

8. The Withdrawal: Fighting the Panzers on the Western Flank

1 A field ambulance company was capable of establishing an advanced
dressing station (ADS) to which casualties were taken from unit regimental
aid posts (RAPs). The field ambulance company had thirty-six stretcher
bearers and eight ambulances for this purpose.
2 Originally formed as Hitler's bodyguard of about a company strong and
designated Leibstandarte Adolf Hitler (LAH), it was the first of the Waffen
(armed or military) branch of the SS, to distinguish it from camp guards and
other SS security personnel. By 1940, with the letters SS added to their title
the LSSAH was a full-sized motorized regiment. In 1941 the LSSAH became a
panzer division, the 1st SS Panzer Division Leibstandarte Adolf Hitler.
3 Gregory Blaxland, *Destination Dunkirk: The Story of Gort's Army* (William Kimber,
London, 1973), p. 305.

4 Ibid.
5 Ellis, *The War in France and Flanders*, p. 206, quoting German documents captured after the war.
6 Ibid., p. 208, quoting German documents captured after the war.
7 Ibid.

9. Comings and Goings at Dunkirk

1 Ellis, *The War in France and Flanders*, p. 182.
2 Ibid., p. 183.
3 J. D. P. Stirling, *The First and the Last: The Story of the 4th/7th Royal Dragoon Guards 1939–1945* (Art & Educational Publishers, 1946), pp. 25–6.
4 Ellis, *The War in France and Flanders*, p. 230.
5 Ibid., pp. 233–4.
6 Hamilton, *Monty*, p. 387.
7 Ibid.
8 Montgomery Papers, letter of 25 August 1952, Imperial War Museum.
9 Churchill, *Their Finest Hour*, p. 97.
10 Ellis, *The War in France and Flanders*, p. 240.
11 Churchill, *Their Finest Hour*, p. 101.

10. The End at Dunkirk

1 Quoted in Hamilton, *Monty*, p. 392.
2 Stirling, *The First and the Last*, p. 26.
3 Correlli Barnett, *Engage the Enemy More Closely: The Royal Navy in the Second World War* (Hodder & Stoughton, 1991), pp. 159–60.
4 Ibid., p. 160.
5 Ibid., pp. 160–1.
6 Ibid., p. 161.

11. The Final Battles

1 *Alanbrooke Diaries*, p. 74.
2 Ellis, *The War in France and Flanders*, p. 249.
3 Ibid., p. 274.
4 Ibid., p. 282.
5 *Alanbrooke Diaries*, p. 80.
6 Ibid., p. 81.

7 Ibid.
8 Ibid., p. 84.

12. Reckoning

1 Brian Bond (ed.), *The Battle of France and Flanders 1940: Sixty Years On* (Leo Cooper, 2001), p. 49.
2 The figures for French casualties in the First World War, compared with those suffered by the British Empire and Germany, are:

Country	Killed (million)	Wounded (million)	Prisoners (million)	% of forces mobilized
France	1.3	4.3	0.50	76.3
British Empire	0.9	2.0	0.19	35.8
Germany	1.8	4.2	1.20	64.9

3 Statistics for some German aircraft in service by early 1940 are shown below:

Aircraft type	Bomb load (lb)	Radius of action (miles) with full bomb load
Messerschmitt Bf 109 fighter	n/a	365–460
Messerschmitt Bf 110 fighter	n/a	528
Dornier 17 bomber	2,205	721
Junkers 87 'Stuka'	1,500	373
Heinkel He 111	1,103	745
Focke-Wulf Condor*	4,626	2,206

* Used in anti-ship attack role only.

Comparable British aircraft statistics are:

Aircraft type	Bomb load (lb)	Radius of action (miles) with full bomb load
Hawker Hurricane	n/a	460
Spitfire	n/a	395
Fairey Battle	1,000	900
Blenheim	1,000	1,950
Whitley	7,000	470*
Wellington	5,000	2,200

* 1,650 miles with bomb load of 3,000lb.

Just for comparison, the Lancaster, a true strategic bomber, which did not come into service in the RAF until 1942, could carry a 14,000lb bomb load 1,660 miles.

4 Ellis, *The War in France and Flanders*, p. 327.
5 Standard was the brand name of a range of British saloon cars in the 1940s, such as Morris and Austin.
6 Stirling, *The First and the Last*, p. 27.
7 See Chapter 2, note 5, for the German use of the terms 'English' for British and 'England' for the United Kingdom.
8 Ellis, *The War in France and Flanders*, p. 326.

Select Bibliography

Many works were consulted during research for this book, but the following were particularly valuable.

Atkin, Ronald, *Pillar of Fire: Dunkirk 1940* (Sidgwick & Jackson, 1990)

Barnett, Correlli, *Engage the Enemy More Closely: The Royal Navy in the Second World War* (Hodder & Stoughton, 1991)

Bidwell, Shelford and Graham, Dominick, *Fire-Power: The British Army Weapons and Theories of War 1904–1945* (Pen & Sword Military Classics, 2004)

Blaxland, Gregory, *Destination Dunkirk: The Story of Gort's Army* (William Kimber, 1973)

Bond, Brian and Taylor, Michael (eds), *The Battle for France and Flanders: Sixty Years On* (Leo Cooper, 2001)

Budiansky, Stephen, *Air Power: From Kitty Hawk to Gulf War II: A History of the People, Ideas and Machines that Transformed War in the Century of Flight* (Viking, 2003)

Churchill, Winston, *The Second World War*, vol. II: *Their Finest Hour* (Cassell, 1949)

Close, Bill, *A View from the Turret: A History of the 3rd Royal Tank Regiment in the Second World War* (Dell & Bredon, 1998)

Danchev, Alex and Todman, Daniel (eds), *War Diaries 1939–1945: Field Marshal Lord Alanbrooke* (Weidenfeld & Nicolson, 2001)

Ellis, L. F., *The War in France and Flanders 1939–1940* (HMSO, 1953)

Forty, George, *British Army Handbook, 1939–1940* (Sutton Publishing, 1998).

Fraser, David, *And We Shall Shock Them: The British Army in the Second World War* (Sceptre, 1988)

——, *Alanbrooke* (Hamlyn Paperbacks, 1983)

Hamilton, Nigel, *Monty: The Making of a General 1887–1942* (Hamlyn Paperbacks, 1982)

Horne, Alistair, *To Lose a Battle: France 1940* (Papermac, 1990)

Montgomery, Bernard, *The Memoirs of Field Marshal the Viscount Montgomery of Alamein* (Collins, 1958)

Moore, William, *Panzer Bait: With the Third Royal Tank Regiment 1939–1945* (Leo Cooper, 1991)

Neave, Airey, *The Flames of Calais: A Soldier's Battle 1940* (Hodder & Stoughton, 1972)

Shepperd, Alan, *France 1940: Blitzkrieg in the West* (Osprey Publishing, 1990)

Stirling, J. D. P., *The First and the Last: The Story of the 4th/7th Royal Dragoon Guards 1939–1945* (Art & Educational Publishers, 1946)

Terraine, John, *The Right of the Line: The Royal Air Force in the European War 1939–1945* (Wordsworth, 1997)

Index

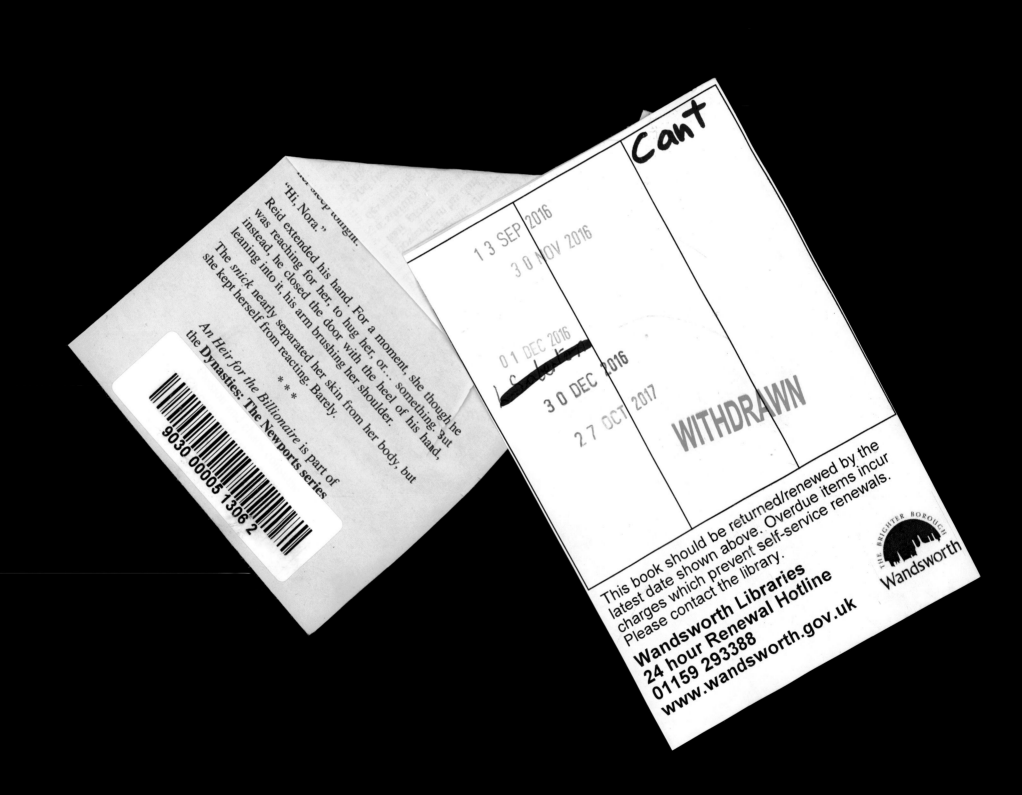

"Hi, Nora."

Reid extended his hand. For a moment, she thought he was reaching for her, to hug her, or... something. But instead, he closed the door with the heel of his hand, leaning into it, his arm brushing her shoulder.

The snick nearly separated her skin from her body, but she kept herself from reacting. Barely.

* * *

An Heir for the Billionaire is part of the **Dynasties: The Newports series**